THE ROUTLEDGE ENCYCLOPEDIA OF THE HISTORICAL JESUS

THE ROUTLEDGE ENCYCLOPEDIA OF THE HISTORICAL JESUS

Craig A. Evans
Editor

Routledge
Taylor & Francis Group

LONDON AND NEW YORK

First published as *Encyclopedia of the Historical Jesus* 2008 by Routledge
This paperback edition published as *The Routledge Encyclopedia of the Historical Jesus* 2010 by
Routledge
Taylor & Francis Group
2 Park Square
Milton Park, Abingdon
Oxon OX14 4RN

Simultaneously published in the UK
Routledge
Taylor & Francis Group
711 Third Avenue,
New York, NY 10017, USA

Routledge is an imprint of Taylor & Francis Group, an informa business

Typeset by Taylor & Francis Books

Library of Congress Cataloging-in-Publication Data
  Encyclopedia of the historical Jesus / [edited by Craig A. Evans].
    p. cm.
  1. Jesus Christ – Historicity – Encyclopedias. 2. Christianity – Encyclopedias. I. Evans, Craig A.
  BT303.2.E56 2008
  232.9'0803–dc22
                        2007029840

ISBN13: 978-0-415-88088-6 (pbk)
ISBN13: 978-0-415-97569-8 (hbk)

Contents

Introduction

Interest in the historical Jesus continues unabated. Scholarly and popular publications are more numerous than ever. Some of this work is quite eccentric and irresponsible, but much of it is competent and quite helpful, leading to new insights and, on the whole, advancing the discipline in significant ways.

Research into the life and world of Jesus has also become more complex as new discoveries are made and new approaches and methods are explored. Ongoing publication of primary materials, such as ancient manuscripts from the Middle East, and ongoing archaeological excavations in the land of Jesus and his followers have led to many new discoveries. The Jesus of history was never more interesting and challenging. And with these major advances comes the need for expert guidance. The *Encyclopedia of the Historical Jesus* offers this guidance through the entries written by the **110 international scholars** who have shared their expertise.

The *Encyclopedia of the Historical Jesus* is a reference work that assesses – in **227 entries** totaling nearly 500,000 words – the remarkable discoveries and developments of the last half century or so. For ease of access, the entries are arranged alphabetically. To further aid the reader, the front matter presents both an **A–Z entry list** and a **thematic entry list**. Each entry is thoroughly referenced with a **Further reading** section. A **thorough, analytical index** provides another entry point for the interested user.

These entries speak to all of the areas involved in the study of the historical Jesus. The *Encyclopedia* offers several entries treating the **major contributors and their works**, ranging from H. S. Reimarus of more than two centuries ago to N. T. Wright of today. All of the important **theoretical issues and concepts** are treated, including Christology, demons and exorcism, magic and sorcery, and Jesus tradition in Paul.

The *Encyclopedia* offers several entries addressing **methods and criteria**, such as the language of Jesus, the possibility of recovering the very words of Jesus, the criteria for determining authenticity, and critical assessment of the New Testament Gospels and the various writings outside the New Testament. The **New Testament Gospels** themselves are treated in separate and lengthy entries. Several entries assess the various **background literatures**, such as the Old Testament apocrypha and pseudepigrapha, the Dead Sea Scrolls, the Targums, and rabbinic literature. Inscriptions and papyri are taken into account, as well as the writings that make up the Old Testament itself.

The **teaching of Jesus** is treated under some three dozen headings. His views of evangelism, divorce and remarriage, faith, family, love, and suffering are only a few of the entries. Major entries treat Jesus' understanding of God, the Great Commandment, salvation, and the Sermon on the Mount. The **titles of Jesus** is another major category that is treated with a number of very important entries. These include Messiah/Christ, Lord, Master/rabbi, Servant of the Lord, Son of David, Son of God, and Son of Man. The entries in **teachings within the historical context of ethics** place the teaching of Jesus in the broader context of the philosophy and teaching of antiquity. Comparison is made with rabbinic thought, and even Buddhist thought.

The *Encyclopedia* offers several entries, many of them major, that treat the most **important events and related scholarship** in the life of Jesus and his disciples. These include his baptism, his exorcisms and healings, his entry into Jerusalem, his actions in the Temple precincts, his words at the Last Supper, his trial, his death and burial, and his resurrection and ascension. Several entries are devoted to important **figures in the life of Jesus**. These include Herod Antipas, who ruled Galilee, and Pontius Pilate, the Roman governor who administered Samaria and Judea. Readers will find entries that treat Annas and Caiaphas, the high priests, Pharisees, Sadducees, and several of the disciples and companions of Jesus, such as Simon Peter, James and John, sons of Zebedee, Mary Magdalene, and Mary, the mother of Jesus.

Several entries are devoted to various **biblical figures mentioned in the Gospels**, Old Testament figures who come into play in one way or another. These include Abraham, Adam, David, Daniel, Elijah, Moses, and Solomon, among others. **Places and regions** also receive generous treatment. Nazareth and Jerusalem, the Sea of Galilee, and Gethsemane on the Mount of Olives are just a few.

Important **institutions** are also covered. These include the Jerusalem Temple and its function in the life of the Jewish people, the circulation and use of Jewish and Roman coins, the practice of sacrifice, Jewish festivals and feasts, Jewish households, slavery, the Sanhedrin, and the synagogue, among others. There are also major entries devoted to the **history of the New Testament within the culture, politics, and law of the Roman Empire**, such as the geography and archaeology of Galilee and Judea, roads and commerce in Galilee and Judea, and the presence of Roman culture and authority in Israel.

Genres and historical styles includes entries on genealogies, prophecy, rewritten scripture, and allegory, among others. **Persons within the historical and rhetorical context of martyrdom and messianism** considers, among others, false prophets.

The *Encyclopedia of the Historical Jesus* will serve readers very well alongside its four-volume companion *The Historical Jesus: Critical Concepts in Religious Studies* (Routledge, 2004). This work assembles the most important statements (in English) treating the major topics covered in the *Encyclopedia*. It is highly recommended.

As editor of the *Encyclopedia of the Historical Jesus* I invite you to plunge into these pages, to discover the riches of the work that has been done, the discoveries that have been made, the remarkable theories that have been proposed, and the inspiration millions have derived from careful study of the teaching, life, and death of arguably the most influential person ever to walk the face of the earth. Your understanding of the historical Jesus will be greatly enriched through the reading of this encyclopedia.

Craig A. Evans, PhD
Payzant Distinguished Professor of New Testament
Acadia Divinity College
Wolfville, Nova Scotia, Canada

Contributors

Jostein Ådna
School of Mission and Theology

Dale C. Allison, Jr
Pittsburgh Theological Seminary

Paul N. Anderson
George Fox University

Rami Arav
University of Nebraska at Omaha

Andrew Arterbury
Baylor University

Richard S. Ascough
Queen's Theological College

Peter Balla
Károli Gáspár Reformed University

Michael F. Bird
Highland Theological College

C. Clifton Black
Princeton University

Barry L. Blackburn, Sr
Atlanta Christian College

Darrell L. Bock
Dallas Theological Seminary

Peter G. Bolt
Moore Theological College

Helen K. Bond
University of Edinburgh

Colin Brown
Fuller Theological Seminary

Gary M. Burge
Wheaton College

Richard A. Burridge
King's College, London

David B. Capes
Houston Baptist University

Warren Carter
Texas Christian University

Mark A. Chancey
Southern Methodist University

Bruce Chilton
Bard College

Carsten Claussen
University of Munich

I. A. H. Combes
Ashbourne

John M. Court
University of Kent, Canterbury

N. Clayton Croy
Trinity Lutheran Seminary

Peter H. Davids
St Stephen's University

Jacqueline C. R. de Roo
University of Sheffield

Stephen G. Dempster
Atlantic Baptist University

David A. deSilva
Ashland Theological Seminary

Jonathan A. Draper
University of KwaZulu-Natal

James D. G. Dunn
Durham University

CONTRIBUTORS

Neil Elliott
Metropolitan State University

Craig A. Evans
Acadia Divinity College

Roman Garrison
Independent scholar

Timothy J. Geddert
Mennonite Brethren Biblical Seminary

Jeffrey B. Gibson
Harry S. Truman College

Terry Giles
Gannon University

Mark Goodacre
Duke University

Lester L. Grabbe
University of Hull

Christian Grappe
Faculté de Théologie Protestante de Strasbourg

Joel B. Green
Fuller Theological Seminary

Leonard J. Greenspoon
Creighton University

Daniel M. Gurtner
Bethel College

Donald A. Hagner
Fuller Theological Seminary

Clay Alan Ham
Dallas Christian College

Mark Harding
Australian College of Theology

Thomas R. Hatina
Trinity Western University

Harold W. Hoehner
Dallas Theological Seminary

Tom Holmén
Abo Akademi

Jason B. Hood
Independent scholar

Morna D. Hooker
University of Cambridge

Jamal-Dominique Hopkins
Crichton College

Reidar Hvalvik
Norwegian Lutheran School of Theology

John S. Kloppenborg
University of Toronto

Michael P. Knowles
McMaster Divinity College

Scott A. Kohler
Acadia Divinity College

Veronica Koperski
Barry University

Hans Kvalbein
Norwegian Lutheran School of Theology

Michael Labahn
Martin Luther University

John R. Levison
Seattle Pacific University

Kenneth D. Litwak
Asbury Theological Seminary

Albert Lukaszewski
Logos Research Systems

Byron R. McCane
Wofford College

C. Thomas McCollough
Centre College

Lee Martin McDonald
Acadia Divinity College

Scot McKnight
North Park University

Bruce J. Malina
Creighton University

I. Howard Marshall
University of Aberdeen

Bruce Matthews
Acadia University

Joseph B. Modica
Eastern University

Michael S. Moore
Fuller Theological Seminary

Russell Morton
Ashland Theological Seminary

Dietmar Neufeld
University of British Columbia

Jacob Neusner
Bard College

John Nolland
Trinity College, Bristol

David Noy
University of Wales, Lampeter

Gerbern S. Oegema
McGill University

Terence Paige
Houghton College

John Painter
Charles Sturt University

Pheme Perkins
Boston College

Elaine A. Phillips
Gordon College

John C. Poirier
Kingswell School of Theology

Stanley E. Porter
McMaster Divinity College

Charles L. Quarles
Louisiana College

Brian M. Rapske
Association of Canadian Theological Schools

Marius Reiser
Johannes Gutenberg-Universität Mainz

Rainer Riesner
Universität Dortmund

Christopher Rowland
Queens College, Oxford

Karl Olav Sandnes
Norwegian Lutheran School of Theology

Ryan Schellenberg
Toronto School of Theology

Eckhard J. Schnabel
Trinity Evangelical Divinity School

Jeff Sears
Acadia Divinity College

Oskar Skarsaune
Norwegian Lutheran School of Theology

Barry D. Smith
Atlantic Baptist University

Dennis Stamps
Diocese of St Albans, England

Robert F. Stoops
Western Washington University

James F. Strange
University of South Florida

Chris Tilling
London School of Theology

Paul R. Trebilco
University of Otago

Allison A. Trites
Acadia Divinity College

Graham H. Twelftree
Regent University

Robert E. Van Voorst
Western Theological Seminary

B. T. Viviano
University of Fribourg

CONTRIBUTORS

Wesley H. Wachob
Candler School of Theology

Shelley Wachsmann
Texas A&M University

Matthew L. Walsh
Acadia Divinity College

Brandon C. Wason
Emory University

Duane F. Watson
Malone College

Jim West
Quartz Hill School of Theology

Edwin M. Yamauchi
Miami University, Ohio

Danny Zacharias
Acadia Divinity College

A–Z list of entries

Thematic list of entries

Background literatures
Apocrypha and Pseudepigrapha
Dead Sea Scrolls
Dead Sea Scrolls: Begotten Messiah text (1Q28a = 1QSa)
Dead Sea Scrolls: Jerusalem priesthood in the Scrolls
Dead Sea Scrolls: Messianic Apocalypse (4Q521 = 4QMessAp)
Dead Sea Scrolls: Self-Glorification Hymn (4Q491c)
Dead Sea Scrolls: Son of God text (4Q246 = 4QapocrDan ar)
Inscriptions and papyri
Old Testament Scriptures
Rabbinic literature
Scripture in teaching and activities of Jesus
Targums

Biblical figures mentioned in the Gospels
Abiathar
Abraham
Adam
Daniel
David
Elijah and Elisha
Isaiah
Jeremiah
Jonah
Moses
Solomon

Events and related scholarship
Ascension
Baptism of Jesus
Birth of Jesus
Death and burial of Jesus
Entry into Jerusalem
Exorcisms and healings
Last Supper, words of institution
Resurrection of Jesus
Temple action of Jesus
Temptation of Jesus
Tomb of Jesus?

Transfiguration of Jesus
Trial of Jesus

Figures in the life of Jesus
Annas and Caiaphas
Elders
Herod Antipas
James and John, sons of Zebedee
John the Baptist
Judas Iscariot
Mary Magdalene
Mary, mother of Jesus
Pharisees
Pontius Pilate
Ruling priests
Sadducees
Samaritans
Scribes
Simon, Peter
Sinners
Tax, tax collectors

Genres and rhetorical styles
Allegory
Apocalyptic
Biography
Chreia, apophthegm
Genealogies
Metaphor and simile
Midrash and rabbinic rules of interpretation
Miracle story
Parable and proverb
Prophecy
Rewritten Scripture
Rhetoric
Teacher, teaching forms, and styles
Typology

History of the New Testament within the culture, politics, and law of the Roman Empire
Archaeology of Galilee and Judea
Diaspora
Geography of Galilee and Judea
Greco-Roman culture in Israel

THEMATIC LIST OF ENTRIES

Roads and commerce in Galilee and Judea
Roman government in Israel

Institutions
Coinage, Jewish
Coinage, Roman
Festivals and feasts, Jewish
Households, Jewish
Praetorium
Roman rule in Palestine
Sacrifice, tithes, offerings
Sanhedrin
Slavery, servants
Synagogue
Temple

Major contributors and their works
Bornkamm, Günther
Bultmann, Rudolf
Cadbury, Henry J.
Conzelmann, Hans
Dahl, Nils Alstrup
Dibelius, Martin
Dodd, Charles Harold
Dunn, James D. G.
Fuchs, Ernst
Goguel, Maurice
Holtzmann, Heinrich Julius
Jeremias, Joachim
Jesus Seminar
Kähler, Martin
Käsemann, Ernst
Klausner, Joseph
Manson, Thomas Walter
Meyer, Ben F.
Quest of the Historical Jesus
Reimarus, Hermann Samuel
Robinson, James M.
Sanders, Ed Parish
Schillebeeckx, Edward
Schleiermacher, Friedrich
Schmidt, Karl Ludwig
Schweitzer, Albert
Strauss, David Friedrich
Taylor, Vincent
Theissen, Gerd
Vermes, Geza
Weiss, Johannes
Wilder, Amos N.
Wrede, William
Wright, N. T.

Methods and criteria
Aramaic and the *ipsissima verba Jesu*
Archaeology and Jesus

Authenticity criteria
Chronology
Form criticism
Gospels, extra-New Testament
Historical criticism
Interpretation of the Gospels
Language criticism
Literary criticism, new forms of
Redaction criticism
Social scientific criticism
Source criticism
Sources, extra-New Testamental
Textual criticism and oldest Gospel manuscripts
Tradition criticism

New Testament Gospels
Gospel as genre
Gospel of John
Gospel of Luke
Gospel of Mark
Gospel of Matthew
Q

Persons within the historical and rhetorical context of martyrdom and messianism
Jewish (false) Prophets in late antiquity
Martyrs and martyrdom in Jewish late antiquity
Messiah/Christ
Messianism and messianic figures in Second
    Temple Judaism

Places and regions
Bethany and Bethphage
Bethlehem
Bethsaida
Caesarea Maritima
Caesarea Philippi
Cana in Galilee
Capernaum
Chorazin
Decapolis
Gerasa
Gethsemane
Jericho
Jerusalem
Nazareth
Sea of Galilee

Teachings of Jesus
Apostleship, evangelism, witness
Beatitudes and blessing
Blasphemy
Compassion on the poor
Curses and woe
Divorce and remarriage

Eschatology
Eternal life
Ethics of Jesus
Faith
Family
Fasting
Fellowship, sharing
Gentiles
God
Great Commandment
Heaven and hell
Interpretation of Scripture
Jubilee, sin, and forgiveness
Judgement
kingdom of God
Law (Sabbath, purity, commandments)
Love
Oaths and swearing
Obduracy, hardness of heart
Passion predictions
Peace
Prayer
Ransom saying
Repentance
Righteousness, justice
Salvation
Sermon on the Mount
Suffering, martyrdom
Tithing and paying taxes
Tribes of Israel
Violence

Teachings within historical context of ethics
Buddhist thought and Jesus

Piety, Jewish
Rabbinic ethics
Stoicism and Cynicism
Wisdom

Theoretical issues and concepts
Angels
Anti-semitism
Child, children
Christology
Demons and exorcism
Demythologization
Disciples, discipleship
Disease, health, longevity
Divine man/*Theios Aner*
Food, hunger
Historiography
Holy Spirit
Jesus' self-understanding
Magic, sorcery
Messianic Secret
Parousia
Paul, Jesus tradition in
Visions

Titles of Jesus
Christ, Messiah
Lord
Master/rabbi
Servant of the Lord
Son of David
Son of God
Son of Man

ABIATHAR

Abiathar was the son of Ahimelech and (high) priest under David (1 Sam 22:22–23). He is mentioned by Jesus in a dispute with Pharisees over picking grain on the Sabbath (Mark 2:23–28). Mentioning Abiathar, rather than Ahimelech, as the "high priest" when David and his men were given sacred bread is problematic. According to 1 Sam 21:1–6 Ahimelech, not Abiathar, was priest when approached by David. This discrepancy has led some scholars to conclude that either Jesus himself was mistaken or that the Markan evangelist (or tradents before him) was mistaken.

The Markan evangelist reports Jesus as saying:

Have you never read what David did, when he was in need and was hungry, he and those who were with him: how he entered the house of God, when Abiathar was high priest, and ate the bread of the Presence, which it is not lawful for any but the priests to eat, and also gave it to those who were with him?

(Mark 2:25–26)

Sensing the difficulty, the Matthean evangelist abridges the saying:

Have you not read what David did, when he was hungry, and those who were with him: how he entered the house of God and ate the bread of the Presence, which it was not lawful for him to eat nor for those who were with him, but only for the priests?

(Matt 12:3–4)

The Lukan evangelist edits the saying in a similar fashion (Luke 6:3–4). Conspicuous is the omission of the phrase "when Abiathar was high priest."

Indeed, some manuscripts of Mark also omit the phrase (e.g. D W 1009 1546).

It would seem that the Matthean and Lukan evangelists, as well as several later copyists, sense the difficulty of the form of the saying in Mark. However, asserting that either Jesus or the Markan evangelist was mistaken does not adequately reckon with the complexities of this interesting problem.

In all probability, the solution to the problem lies in the recognition that there seem to have been two traditions with regard to the priestly figures Ahimelech and Abiathar. The major tradition narrates Abiathar as the son of Ahimelech. Accordingly, the latter is the priest who gave the bread to David and his men. This is the tradition of 1 Sam 21–22. But there is also a minor tradition, in which Ahimelech (or Abimelech in some manuscripts) is said to be the son of Abiathar, who survives and serves David alongside Zadok (2 Sam 8:17; 1 Chr 18:16; 24:3–31; contrast 1 Kgs 4:4, where it is Abiathar who serves alongside Zadok; see also 4Q245 frag. 1, col. i, line 7). The saying attributed to Jesus (whether uttered by Jesus or supplied by the Markan evangelist) apparently reflects the minor tradition (so Mulholland).

The diversity of the narrative traditions preserved in the Dead Sea Scrolls should caution against a reductionist approach. The Old Testament scriptures that have survived do not preserve the full range of tradition. Some of the variant traditions are hinted at here and there in the writings of Josephus, the Scrolls, and some of the writings lumped together as the Old Testament

1

ABRAHAM

Pseudepigrapha. But we only possess fragments of these diverse traditions.

Jesus' appeal to the action of Abiathar (or Ahimelech) touched on a very sensitive issue. According to Lev 24:5–9 the twelve loaves of the Presence were sacred and were to be eaten *only by the priests* (Lev 24:9 "for Aaron and his sons"). David's consumption of this sacred bread was potentially scandalous. Even in Jesus' day there was reluctance to acknowledge this part of the story. Although he provides an enriched paraphrase of the story, Josephus carefully sidesteps mention of the bread: "He requested to receive provisions ... once he had obtained these things" (*Ant.* 6.243–44). Josephus provides no hint that David and his men requested or ate sacred bread.

The author of *Biblical Antiquities* not only omits the part about David and his men receiving the sacred bread, it actually justifies the slaying of the priests, who "were profaning the holy things of the Lord and desecrating the first fruits of the people" (Ps-Philo, *Bib. Ant.* 63:1). Reference to "profaning the holy things of the Lord" may well have been prompted by David and his men eating the sacred bread.

Josephus and the author of *Biblical Antiquities* omitted the giving of the sacred bread to David and his men – probably out of religious embarrassment. This is the very point that Jesus wished to make: Special circumstances call for exceptional deeds. In view of the sensitive nature of this story, it is not difficult to see why Jesus appealed to it and why we have no indication that his critics were able to present a counter-argument.

CRAIG A. EVANS

Further reading

Evans, C. A. "Patristic Interpretation of Mark 2:26: 'When Abiathar was High Priest'," *VC* 40 (1986) 183–86.
Morgan, C. S. "When Abiathar was High Priest," *JBL* 98 (1979) 409–10.
Mulholland, M. R. "Abiathar," in Joel B. Green and Scot McKnight (eds) *Dictionary of Jesus and the Gospels*, Downers Grove, IL: InterVarsity Press, 1992, pp. 1–2.
Rogers, A. D. "Mark 2:26," *JTS* 2 (1951) 44–45.
Whitelam, K. W. "Abiathar," in David Noel Freedman (ed.) *The Anchor Bible Dictionary*, New York: Doubleday, 1992, Vol. 1, pp. 13–14.

ABRAHAM

The name "Abra(ha)m" is etymologically ambiguous. The book of Genesis preserves the popular etymology that God changes Abram's name to "Abraham" in order to represent more accurately his new status as "father of a multitude of nations"

(אַב הֲמוֹן גּוֹיִם). However, the Talmud, suggests that "Abram" changes to "Abraham" because "at first he became a father of Aram (אֲב אֲרָם), then later to the whole world" (*b. Ber.* 13a). At any rate, this name refers to one of the most revered characters in world history, a figure claimed by the adherents of all three monotheistic religions (Judaism, Christianity, Islam).

In the Hebrew Bible he enacts roles as "Chaldean nomad" (Gen 12:1–9; Neh 9:7), "wealthy sheikh" (13:1), "military general" (14:14), "covenant partner" (15:1–21), "father of Ishmael" (16:15), "priestly intercessor" (18:22–33), "father of Isaac" (20:3), "prophet" (20:7), "fearful husband" (20:10), "tested patriarch" (22:1–19), "servant" (Ps 105:6), and "beloved one" (Isa 41:8). Whereas the Abraham cycle in Genesis presents his life as a spiritual journey from "fear" to "faith" (Moore 35–48), the story of Abraham fits the type-scene format found elsewhere in the literary-historical context: (a) sonless patriarch suffers distress, (b) appeal to a deity for help, (c) deity responds favorably, and (d) male heir arrives (McAfee). Not only does this pattern shape the material in Genesis, it also helps shape the Canaanite myths of *Kirta* (*CAT* 1.14–16) and *Dnil* (*CAT* 1.17–18; see Hendel 37–59).

In the Second Temple period, the Abraham *tradition* widens considerably in response to a number of literary, political, and ideological pressures. Here Abraham assumes the roles of "seer/dreamer" (1QapGen 19:14), "prayer warrior" (20:10–29; *b. Ber.* 26b), "exorcist" (1QapGen 20.28–29; CD [A] 16:6), "religious enthusiast" (Josephus, *Ant.* 1.234), "wise man" (σοφός, Philo, *Cher.* 7), "model of wisdom" (*Somn.* 1.70), "faithful man" (*Post.* 373), "perfect man" (*Spec.* 3.203), "philosopher" (*Gig.* 62), "son" of God (*Spec.* 3.27), "God's beloved" (אֹהֲבִי, 4Q176 frgs 1–2 1:9; 4Q252 2:8; CD [A] 3:2), and "forefather" of the Arabs, Assyrians, and Africans (προπάτωρ, Josephus, *J.W.* 5.380; *Ant.* 1.214, 239–41). Among these varied roles two motifs predominate: (a) Abraham's renunciation of idolatry, and (b) his monotheistic faith (Calvert-Koyzis 49). Muslim *tafsīr* (commentary) tradition preserves these motifs in order to transform Abraham into a forerunner of Muhammad (Hauglid).

The NT focuses less on the *person* of Abraham than the exemplary character of his *faith* (Gal 3:6–18; Rom 4:1–17). Like Philo (*Mut.* 177), Paul gravitates to Abraham's faith-decision in Gen 15:6 ("he believed Yahweh and it was reckoned to him as righteousness," Rom 4:3). Yet where Philo draws from this passage the importance of distinguishing between "spoken faith" and "unspoken doubt," and the Talmud interprets it within the parameters of a legal system in which "righteousness" (צדקה) depends on human "merit" (זכות, *b. Ber.* 10b; Strack and Billerbeck 1.251), Paul cites the passage to point out that the God of Abraham reckons "righteousness" to his servant a full two chapters *before* he receives the mark of circumcision. Thus it cannot be the ritual of circumcision but faith itself which causes God to "reckon" Abraham as "righteous" (Levenson 272–77). For audiences used to setting Hellenized Jewish ritual within a pagan context in which the closest parallel is "ritual castration" this is a revolutionary interpretation (Elliott 233). For secularist (post)moderns, of course, this view of faith is absurd (Kierkegaard 51).

The Gospels mention Abraham several times, but two texts stand out. The first narrates the story of a poor man who dies and travels to "Abraham's bosom" after suffering a miserable life on earth (Luke 16:19–31). Interpreters noting the "netherworld tour" format shaping this text (Himmelfarb 45–67) find parallels in Egyptian (Gressmann, cited in Bauckham), Graeco-Roman (Hock), and Attic sources (Gilmour). The last of these probably shines brightest in Luke 16. In Book 11 of the *Odyssey*, for example, Odysseus goes down to the netherworld in order to (a) learn about the futility of worldly wealth, (b) learn about the reality of eternal torment, and (c) learn about the plight of loved ones failing to live up to these truths (*Od.* 24.1–204; Gilmour 24). Just as Homer has Odysseus learn his fate from the lips of a "wise ancestor" (the blind seer Teiresias), so Luke has the rich man learn his fate from "Father Abraham." By casting Abraham as the quintessential "wise ancestor" Luke thus underlines the lesson he wants to teach about the afterlife.

John 8:31–59 comes housed in a different format. In this text the Fourth Gospel preserves the highlights of an intense debate between Jesus and his adversaries over the validity of his claims to religious authority. Central to this debate stands a fundamental disagreement over the character of Abraham. Where his opponents claim Abraham as "our father," Jesus rejects this claim because (a) Abraham is not a murderer, (b) Abraham is not a liar, (c) their true father is "the devil" (John 8:44), and (c) "before Abraham was, I am" (8:58).

MICHAEL S. MOORE

Further reading

Bauckham, R. "The Rich Man and Lazarus: The Parable and the Parallels," *NTS* 37 (1991) 225–46.

Calvert-Koyzis, N. *Paul, Monotheism and the People of God: The Significance of Abraham Traditions for Early Judaism and Christianity*, JSNTSup 273, London: T. & T. Clark, 2005.

Elliott, S. *Cutting Too Close for Comfort: Paul's Letter to the Galatians in its Anatolian Cultic Context*, JSNTSup 248, Sheffield: Academic Press, 2004.

Evans, C. A. "Abraham in the Dead Sea Scrolls: A Man of Faith and Failure," in P. W. Flint (ed.) *The Bible at Qumran: Text, Shape, and Interpretation*, Studies in the Dead Sea Scrolls and Related Literature 5, Grand Rapids, MI: Eerdmans, 2001, pp. 149–58.

Gilmour, M. J. "Hints of Homer in Luke 16:19–31," *Didaskalia* 10 (1999) 23–33.

Gressmann, H. *Vom reichen Mann und armer Lazarus. Eine literargeschichtlich Studie*, Berlin: Akademie der Wissenschaft, 1918.

Hauglid, B. "On the Early Life of Abraham: Biblical and Quranic Intertextuality and the Anticipation of Muhammad," in J. C. Reeves (ed.) *Bible and Qur'an: Essays in Scriptural Intertextuality*, SBLSS 24, Atlanta, GA and Leiden: Society of Biblical Literature/Brill, 2003, pp. 87–105.

Hendel, R. S. *The Epic of the Patriarch: The Jacob Cycle and the Narrative Traditions of Canaan and Israel*, HSM 42, Atlanta, GA: Scholars Press, 1987.

Himmelfarb, M. *Tours of Hell: An Apocalyptic Form in Jewish and Christian Literature*, Philadelphia, PA: University of Pennsylvania Press, 1983.

Hock, R. S. "Lazarus and Micyllus: Greco-Roman Backgrounds to Luke 16:19–31," *JBL* 106 (1987) 447–63.

Kierkegaard, S. *Fear and Trembling*, trans. W. Lowrie, Princeton, NJ: Princeton University Press, 1968.

Levenson, J. "Abusing Abraham: Traditions, Religions, Histories, and Modern Misinterpretations," *Judaism* 47 (1998) 259–77.

McAfee, E. C. *The Patriarch's Longed-for Son: Biological and Social Reproduction in Ugaritic and Hebrew Epic*, PhD dissertation, Cambridge: Harvard, 1996.

Moore, M. S. "Abraham's Temptation," in *Reconciliation: A Study of Biblical Families in Conflict*, Joplin, MO: College Press, 1994, pp. 35–48.

Noth, M. *Die Israelitischen Personennamen im Rahmen der Gemeinsemitischen Namengebung*, Stuttgart: Kohlhammer, 1928.

Strack, H. L. and P. Billerbeck. *Kommentar zum Neuen Testament aus Talmud und Midrasch*, 6 vols, München: Beck, 1924–61.

ADAM

Adam appears first and most often in scripture in the opening chapters of Genesis (Gen 1–5). His name means "mankind" or "humanity," and a wordplay between *'adam* (Adam), *'adam* (humankind), and *'adama* "ground, earth," is found through the opening Genesis narratives. Adam was the first person created: God said, "Let us make man (*'adam*) in our image" (Gen 1:26). The Lord formed "the man" (*'adam*) from the dust of the ground (*'adama*)" (Gen 2:7). The man's (*'adam*) role was to till the ground (*'adama* 2:6). The man (*'adam*) was placed by God in the Garden of Eden to work it and care for it (Gen 2:15). Yet when the man, Adam ('adam), disobeys God, the ground ('adama) is cursed (3:17–19). This creates hardship for the man ('adam) in working the ground ('adama).

God made a woman from his rib, a "helper suitable for him" (Gen 2:18–25, RSV). Adam called his wife Eve, "because she was the mother of all living" (Gen 3:20, RSV). God made them clothing (3:20), and together they bore a son, Cain (4:1), who would slay their second son, Abel (4:8). Later Eve bore another son by Adam, Seth (4:25), when Adam was 130 years old (5:3). After Seth was born, Adam lived another 800 years (Gen 5:4) and died at the age of 930 (5:5). Adam is depicted as the father of the human race (1 Chr 1:1; cf. Deut 4:32; Job 31:33; Hos 6:7). Even a portion of the book of Genesis is called "the book of the generations of Adam" (5:1).

Ultimately Adam is banished from the Garden of Eden (Gen 3:23). From there, biblical witness is silent, but texts from the Second Temple period attempt to answer many questions raised by the brief but important biblical narratives. Foremost among these texts are the (Greek) *Apocalypse of Moses* and the (Latin) *Life of Adam and Eve*. The former narrates the story of Adam and Eve after their expulsion from the Garden, itself the result of their disobedience (8:2; 10:2; 23:4). Adam lies ill while Eve and Seth return to the Garden to acquire healing oil from the Tree of Life. Upon his death, Adam's spirit is taken to God where, by the petition of angels, he is forgiven and taken to the third heaven, where he looks forward to resurrection (28:4; 37:1–6; 41:3) and restoration of his former glory (39:1–3). Other Jewish texts likewise revered Adam's perfection (Philo, *Opif.* 47.136–41), honor (Sir 49:16), stature (*Gen. Rab.* 8:1 [on Gen 1:26–28]; 21:3; [on Gen 3:22] 24:2 [on Gen 5:1]) and wisdom (*Gen. Rab.* 24:2 [on Gen 5:1]). It is often unclear in Qumran documents whether the respective discussions pertain to Adam or generally "man," (both 'adam). In CD x.8, for example, the shortening of human lifespan is attributed to the sin of 'adam (mankind? Adam?). Some texts, however, particularly non-sectarian texts, clearly betray interest in Adam's rule over creation (4Q422; 4Q504; cf. 4Q423; Ps 8:7).

The only mention of Adam in the Gospels is found the genealogy according to Luke, which traces Jesus' lineage through "Adam, the son of God" (Luke 3:38). It seems that the inclusion of Adam in the genealogy, where he is excluded in the only other genealogy of Jesus (Matt 1:1–17), underscores the universal nature of Jesus' mission

and the humanity of his person depicted in Luke—Acts (cf. Acts 17:31; Nolland 1.173). Elsewhere in the NT, particularly in Pauline writings, Adam has a significant theological role in representing the fallen nature of humanity. Adam's life marked the beginning of an age when "death reigned" (Rom 5:14; see also Jude 14). The fallen nature introduced by Adam's sin is contrasted with the righteousness of Christ (Rom 5:12–21; 1 Cor 15:21–22; 45–49). Indeed, Adam was a "type" of Christ (Rom 5:14). All die in Adam, and all are made alive in Christ (1 Cor 15:22; cf. v. 45). Later, Adam and Eve are used as apparent exemplars for the roles of men and women, respectively, in the church to which 1 Timothy was written (1 Tim 2:13, 14).

DANIEL M. GURTNER

Further reading

Childs, B. S. *Introduction to the Old Testament as Scripture*, Philadelphia, PA: Fortress Press, 1979.

Harris, R. Laird, Gleason L. Archer, Jr, and Bruce K. Waltke. *Theological Wordbook of the Old Testament*, 2 vols, Chicago, IL: Moody Press, 1980.

Niditch, S. "The Cosmic Adam: Man as Mediator in Rabbinic Literature," *JJS* 34 (1983) 137–46.

Nolland, J. *Luke*, 2 vols, WBC 35A, B. Dallas, TX: Word, 1989, 1993.

Sharp, J. L. "Second Adam in the Apocalypse of Moses," *CBQ* 35 (1973) 35–46.

Wallace, H. N. *The Eden Narrative*, HSM 32, Atlanta, GA: Scholars Press, 1985.

Wenham, G. "Sanctuary Symbolism in the Garden of Eden Story," in *Proceedings of the Ninth World Congress of Jewish Studies*, Division A: *The Period of the Bible*, Jerusalem: World Union of Jewish Studies, 1986, pp. 19–24.

Wright, N. T. "Adam, Israel and the Messiah," in *The Climax of the Covenant*, Minneapolis, MN: Fortress Press, 1991, pp. 18–40.

ALLEGORY

Allegory requires a precise and historically contextual definition, in order that it might relate to other literary genres and rhetorical styles, and so contribute to a clearer understanding of what can be known about the historical Jesus.

The Greek root of the word 'allegory' suggests the idea of an 'alternative' meaning, a speech that is figurative: 'speaking one thing and signifying something other than what is said', as the philosopher Heraclitus observed about the way of interpreting the epic poetry of Homer. There may be practically no continuity between the appearance of the original words and the meaning that is extracted from them. So Augustine of Hippo offered a dramatic reinterpretation of the pastoral image in Song of Songs 4:2 ('Your teeth are like a flock of shorn ewes that have come up from the washing') in terms of the aggressive mission of the Church and Baptism. One obvious virtue of this allegorical method is that of problem-solving with a difficult text.

If this was an acceptable treatment to extract a palatable spin from such as Homer's account of the exploits of the Greek gods, then clearly it was a long-standing method of interpreting texts. Indeed, in the long history of Christian interpretation of the Bible, allegory was probably the method of choice for many among the Church Fathers and medieval theologians and subsequently, up until the preference for critical and scientific methods since the Enlightenment. Significantly, one aspect of the rise of new literary-critical approaches, and the study of symbolism, in recent decades has been a revival of interest in allegory.

But can the seductive freedom of such an uncontrolled, arbitrary and even unethical approach, applied to a Biblical text, have anything to contribute to the objective quest for the historical Jesus? The answer must be 'yes' simply because the allegorical method is known to have been a live option within the Jewish milieu in which Jesus lived and taught. It can be seen in the heady Hellenistic atmosphere of Philo Judaeus who saw the migration of Abraham, father of the Jews, to the promised land, as an allegory of the virtue-loving human soul wandering in search of the true God. Philo's near-contemporary Paul used the story of Hagar and Sarah, more as a type than an allegory, to present a mirror image of Jewish tradition in Galatians 4:21–31. And the ancient Jewish rabbis employed allegory, especially in interpreting the Song of Songs, not as a simple love lyric about a man and a girl, but as a dialogue between God (the Lover) and Israel (the beloved).

It is a widely accepted conclusion of modern criticism that the parables of Jesus found in the Gospels provide, at least in essence, reliable evidence about the nature of Jesus' teaching. As part of the search for the historical Jesus, the question can therefore be asked: to what extent does allegory appear in this teaching? Space precludes more than a comparative analysis of two examples: the parable of the Vineyard Tenants (as in Mark 12:1–12) and that of the Good Samaritan (in Luke 10:29–37).

First, the story of the Vineyard Tenants has been selected because it is the one parable attributed to Jesus in the Gospels which is presented explicitly as an allegory. The allegorical elements are identified as intrinsic to this story, and it seems to be directed to point prophetically to Jesus' own

death (in this way correlated with the key prophecies of Mark 8:31, 9:31 and 10:33). The owner of the vineyard is God himself, the beloved son is Jesus, the vineyard is Israel (just as in the Scriptural basis of the story in Isaiah 5), the tenants are the Jewish leaders, and the slaves are the Old Testament prophets. This is no simple story of agricultural malpractice; the conclusion with its proof-text makes the application clear, and confirms the correspondences which the hearers should (and do) recognise between the agricultural and the religious worlds. Other elements of the story, such as fence, pit, winepress and watchtower, do not appear to have allegorical equivalents. They form part of the story's realistic colouring; one might say that they are residual evidence of a natural story drawn from the countryside that has already evolved into a religious allegory.

By comparison, the second parable does appear to be a straightforward story, with the cutting-edge of controversy familiar from many of Jesus' parables. Of all people who could be chosen to illustrate neighbourliness, the Samaritan of Luke 10 would seem the most offensive to a Jewish audience, not least because they would assume that the unnamed victim of the story is a Jew. Several of the stories known only from Luke's Gospel sound like ethical examples, featuring the worst-case scenario (the unjust judge, the manipulative steward, the friend interrupted at midnight and the despised Samaritan); the ethical exhortation seems to be that you can do better than these.

The parable of the Good Samaritan is used in a homily by Severus of Antioch in the sixth century CE. In his reading the parable is clearly an allegory of all that has happened to humanity from Adam to Christ. The inn of the story stands for the Church which exists for all people (the Greek word used in 10:34 means literally 'all receiving'). The two coins are the talents which members of the Church must devote to others. The active Church is to be essentially useful, open and Christ-centred until such time as the Samaritan (who is indeed Christ himself) returns, as he promises he will (10:35).

Severus' homily may seem to present a rather extreme allegory. But perhaps the familiar ethical example from Luke's Gospel is also a mutation by the Church for teaching purposes. There is a case to be made that Jesus himself originally intended the story as a shock tactic, employing the allegory to identify himself as the Samaritan. There is some corroboration in John 8:48 ('Are we not right to say that you are a Samaritan and have a devil?'). Luke 10:33 employs the special word for showing 'pity/compassion' that the New Testament only uses with God or Christ as subject. If this, like other parables, exploits a pun, then, as Birger Gerhardsson suggested, the term 'Samaritan' can build a link to a Hebrew word for 'shepherd' (Hos 12:12) thus alluding to the Davidic shepherd/Messiah of Israel.

This comparison shows the potential significance of allegory within these parables. It is clear that the presence of signs of allegory in the text can no longer be taken as excluding the parable as inauthentic within the teaching of Jesus. But neither can allegory guarantee authenticity, however credible it may seem. One must keep an open mind and judge each case on its merits.

JOHN M. COURT

Further reading

Court, John M. *Reading the New Testament*, New Testament Readings, London and New York: Routledge, 1997, Chapter 8.
—— "Not (Just) the Plain Meaning: Origen and Allegorical Interpretation" in John M.Court (ed.) *Biblical Interpretation: The Meanings of Scripture – Past and Present*, London and New York: T. & T. Clark International (Continuum), 2003, pp. 10–21.
Birger, Gerhardsson. *The Good Samaritan – The Good Shepherd*, Lund, Copenhagen: Coniectanea Neotestamentica, 1958.
Longenecker, Richard N. *Biblical Exegesis in the Apostolic Period*, Grand Rapids, MI: William B. Eerdmans, 1975 [1883].
Porter, Stanley E. (ed.) *Reading the Gospels Today*, Grand Rapids, MI: William B. Eerdmans, 2004.
Simonetti, Manlio. *Biblical Interpretation in the Early Church: An Historical Introduction to Patristic Exegesis*, Edinburgh: T. & T. Clark, 2001 [1994].

ANGELS

Celestial, numinous, semi-corporeal (*2 En.* 1:5 [A]; but cf. *Jub.* 15:27 which describes angels as circumcised), powerful beings, anthropomorphic in form in earthly manifestation and often visually glorious (cf., e.g., *2 En.* 5; Luke 2:9; 9:26; Acts 12:7; 2 Pet 2:10; Jude 8; cf. Acts 6:15), who were regarded by all parties within first-century Judaism (the Sadducees, despite the apparent testimony of Acts 23:8, being no exception; cf. D. Daube (1990); B. T. Viviano and J. Taylor (1992)) as having been created by the God of Israel before or shortly after his establishment of the world (cf. Job 38:7; *Jub.* 2:2; *Bereshith Rabba* 3), and who, under the explicit direction or the permissive will of their creator, carry out a variety of functions, depending on their status as "heavenly" and "holy" or as "rebellious" and fallen."

The primary function of "heavenly" angels is to serve as divine "messengers" – envoys who speak in the name, and with the authority, of God himself. In this capacity they take on such tasks as announcing the births of important figures within the divine plan (cf. Gen 16:11–12; Gen 18:9–15; Judg 13:3–5; Matt 1:18–23; Luke 1:8–21, 26–38; 2:8–12), communicating "the word of the Lord" to prophets (Elijah, 2 Kgs 1:3, 15; 1 Kgs 13:18; 1 Kgs 22:19–22; Isa 6; Jer 23:18, 23), delivering the Torah (Acts 7:53; Gal 3:19), and relaying (and interpreting) divine injunctions and promises or revealing the future to those to whom they are sent (Zech 1:9; 4:5–6; Dan 8:16; 4QSerekh Shirot 'Olat ha-Shabbat, Matt 1:20–21; Luke 1:35; Rev 1:1).

But they also are commissioned as agents whose role is to give assurances to those in fear, to render service to those under trial, to protect those who travel (Dan 10:13, 20; 11: 1; 12: 1; 2 Macc 3:25–26; 3 Macc 6:18; Sus 45; Bel 34–39; *1 En.* 20:5; J 35:17; 1QH 5.21–22; 1QS 9,15; 1QM 9.16; *T. Jud.* 3:10), to bring the prayers and the petitions of the faithful before God (Tob 12:15; *2 Bar.* 11 G; 1QH 6.13), and to intervene at crucial moments of a person's life to change or guide that person's actions (Hagar, Gen 16:9; Abraham, Gen 22:11–12; Balaam, Num 22:31–35; the people of Israel, Judg 2:1–5; Joseph, betrothed of Mary, Matt 1:18–23; 2:19–23).

Notable, too, is that they are given the task of requiting disobedience to God in both the present (2 Kgs 19:35; 1 Macc 7:41; 2 Macc 15:22–23; Sir 48:2, Josephus, *J.W.* 5:388 Sus 55; LXX Job 33:23; Acts 12:23) and, especially, at the end of the age, when they will be witness to and an instrument of divine judgment and justice against apostates and all enemies of God's people (Dan 7:10; 1QM 17:5; 1QS 4:11–14; CD 5–7; *1 En.* 10:13; 90:24–26; 2 Thess 1:7; Rev 3:5; 14:14–20; 15:1; 16:1; 21:9).

They were envisaged as an army (*2 Bar.* 5:11, 70; *T. Levi* 3:3; Matt 26:53; Luke 2:13–14) which is drawn up in hierarchical orders and distinct ranks, headed by commanders called archangels (the number of these commanders varies: according to Tob 12:1 G; *1 En.* 81:5; 90:21–22; 2 Esd 5:20, there are seven; according to *1 En.* 40; 87:2–3; 88:1, four; according to *1 En.* 90:31, three), and were expected to participate in a final war against the wicked (Zech 14:13; 1QH 3.35–36; 10.34–35; 1 15.14).

And as T. H. Gaster has noted, the "holy ones" were also portrayed as the controlling spirits of such natural phenomena as celestial bodies and winds (*1 En.* 19:1; 40:4–5; 60: 12; 16–21; 61:10; 72:1; *Jub.* 2:2–3; 1QH 1.10–11~ 47.7–13) and of the seasons as well as of such abstractions as peace (*1 En.* 40:8;

52:5; *T. Dan* 6:5; *T. Ash.* 6:6; *T. Benj.* 6:1; cf. Isa 33:7), healing (Tob 33:17; *1 En.* 10:7; 40:9), and death (*2 Bar.* 21:23; cf. Prov 16:14).

"Fallen angels"

The primary function of "fallen angels," who, like their "heavenly" counterparts, are envisaged as ranked under the leadership of a prince (*śar*) – identified variously as Mastema (*Jub.* 10:8), Beelzebul, Satan (Matt 25:41; 2 Cor 12:7; 1 Pet 3:19 f.), the enemy, the evil one, the ruler of this world, the adversary, the devil, Beliar, and other names – is to separate Israel from God by ensnaring them in evil, inciting them to apostasy, and leading the elect astray. But they also, in conjunction with their primary function, and in conformity with their rebellious nature, serve to arouse and direct the "Nations," over whom they were originally set as guardians (cf. Dan 10:13, 20, 21; 12:1; *Jub.* 15:31–32; *1 En.* 89:59 among other texts), to dominate, if not to destroy, God's people in an attempt to frustrate or make impossible the implementation of God's purposes in and for the world.

Jesus and angels

The Evangelists record Jesus as speaking of both "heavenly" and "fallen" angels on a number of occasions. Accepting the authenticity of these dominical sayings, several things follow with respect to the question of Jesus's view of, and attitude towards, these creatures.

In concert with his co-religionists, Jesus:

1 had no doubts of their existence; he accepted without question, and proclaimed as an ontological given, both their reality and their division into categories of "heavenly" and "fallen" (Matt 25:41);
2 believed that angels were numerous, that they were arrayed in ranks and in hierarchies (Matt 26:53), and that "fallen" angels were led by, and were minions of, a "prince of demons" (Mark 3:23–26);
3 thought that in the present age angels were superior to human beings (though, like men, they were limited in knowledge of God's ultimate secrets (Mark 13:32//Matt 24:36); but in the world to come the righteous shall stand as their equals (Luke 20:36);
4 believed that the rebelliousness of the "fallen" angels and their work was doomed to defeat.

But if we allow an argument from silence and take as significant what is *absent* from Jesus's statements about angels vis-à-vis what Jewish sources attest their roles and activities to be, it appears that Jesus seems *not* to have shared all of his co-religionists' (or even the evangelists') beliefs about angelic functions. While he accepts the ideas that "heavenly" angels act as advocates of the pious (Matt 18:10; 26:53; cf. Luke 16:22) and that "fallen" angels, and especially their leader, strive to separate the faithful from God (Matt 6:13; Mark 8:33// Matt 16:23; Luke 22:31–32), we find no (recorded) emphasis placed by Jesus on their known roles as "messengers," "protectors," and intermediaries between God and men. Indeed, in contrast with the views of his co-religionists, it is only the "fallen" angels that he envisages as active among men. For Jesus, the work of "heavenly angels" is, rather, carried out in the realms above and at the dawning of the world to come.

Judging by the content of the bulk of the preserved dominical statements about angels, Jesus regarded their primary role to be that of divine agents who at the end of the age gather the elect and the wicked before the throne of God and act both as witnesses to the declarations of the Son of Man, as he testifies at a great assize against those who in Jesus's own age had been "ashamed" of Jesus and his words, and as the implementers of the Son of Man's judgments (Mark 8:38; Matt 16:27; 25:31, 41; Luke 9:26; 12:8; cf. Mark 13:26; Matt 13:39, 41, 49; 24:31).

Though it is beyond the scope of this entry to account for why it is that Jesus apparently held this comparatively circumscribed view of angelic functions, especially with respect to those of "heavenly" angels," the answer may lie somewhere along the lines of W. O. E. Oesterley's suggestion that it is due to a conviction on Jesus's part that he, along with the Holy Spirit, is the one who has been empowered with the roles of envoy, intermediary, and advocate that in Jewish tradition were thought to be angels' provenance.

JEFFREY B. GIBSON

Further reading

Bamberger, Bernard Jacob. *Fallen Angels*, Philadelphia, PA: Jewish Publication Society of America, 1952.

Daube, David. "On Acts 23: Sadducees and Angels," *JBL* 109 (1990) 493–97.

Davidson, Maxwell John. "Angel," in *The New Interpreter's Dictionary of the Bible*, Nashville, TN: Abingdon Press, 2006, Vol. 1, pp. 148–55.

Gaster, T. H. "Angel" in George A. Buttrick (ed.) *The Interpreter's Dictionary of the Bible*, Nashville, TN: Abingdon Press, 1962, Vol. 1, pp. 128–34.

Grundmann, W., Von Rad, G. and Kittel, G. "αγγελος, αρχάγγελος, ἰσάγγελος," in G. W. Bromiley (ed.)

Theological Dictionary of the New Testament, Grand Rapids, MI: Eerdmans, 1964, Vol. 1, pp. 74–87.

Meier, S. A. "Angel I," in Karel van der Toorn, Pieter Willem van der Horst, and Bob Becking (eds) *Dictionary of Demons and Deities in the Bible*, second edition, Grand Rapids, MI: Eerdmans, 1999, pp. 45–50.

Newson, Carol A. "Angels: Old Testament," in David Noel Freedman (ed.) *The Anchor Bible Dictionary*, New York: Doubleday, 1992, Vol. 1, pp. 248–53.

Oesterley, W. O. E. "Angels," in James Hastings (ed.) *Dictionary of the Bible*, one volume edition, New York: Charles Scribner's Sons, 1924, pp. 31–53.

Page, Sidney H. T. *Powers of Evil: A Biblical Study of Satan and Demons*, Grand Rapids, MI: Baker, 1995.

Russel, D. H. *The Method and Message of Jewish Apocalyptic*, Philadelphia, PA: Fortress Press, 1964, pp. 235–62.

van Henten, J. W. "Angel II," in Karel van der Toorn, Pieter Willem van der Horst, and Bob Becking (eds) *Dictionary of Demons and Deities in the Bible*, second edition, Grand Rapids, MI: Eerdmans, 1999, pp. 50–53.

Viviano, B. T. and Justin Taylor. "Sadducees, Angels, and Resurrection (Acts 23:8–9)," *JBL* 111 (1992) 496–98.

Watson, Duane F. "Angels: New Testament," in David Noel Freedman (ed.) *The Anchor Bible Dictionary*, New York: Doubleday, 1992, Vol. 1, pp. 253–55.

ANNAS AND CAIAPHAS

Annas was appointed high priest of the Temple in Jerusalem *c.* 6 CE by Quirinius and removed under Valerius Gratus in 15 CE (Josephus, *Ant.* 18:26–35). His removal scarcely reflects any official displeasure on the part of Rome's representatives, since five of Annas' sons – including the younger Annas (who saw to the execution of James, the brother of Jesus; *Ant.* 20:197–203) – all took high priestly office (*Ant.* 20:198). John 18:13 also says he was the father-in-law of Caiaphas, high priest at the time of Jesus' death.

Whether or not that was the case, Annas' continuing influence would explain the odd reference to the joint high priesthood of Annas and Caiaphas in Luke 3:2, and that also accounts for the reference to him alone as high priest in Acts 4:6. In John reference to Annas as high priest in connection with Jesus' death is even more persistent (John 18:13, 15, 16, 19, 22), becoming especially marked when Jesus is struck for answering the "high priest" disrespectfully (v. 22). The whole scene in John (vv. 12–24) uses Annas to cast the issues of high priestly enmity with Jesus in terms of his disciples and teaching (v. 19). In John, Caiaphas does not appear a conscious or willing agent of Jesus' execution, but he forecasts it prophetically (John 11:45–53; 18:14). Within the pattern in which Annas' status as high priest is dominant, calling Caiaphas "high priest that year" (John 11:49, cf. also 18:13) denies him the preeminence that his office normally entailed. Even when he is called

"high priest" without qualification in John 18:24, he seems only a place-holder of the office to which Annas had a greater claim. When Caiaphas is woven into the action, he is an incidental character (vv. 24–28).

By contrast, Matt (26:3, 57) is quite clear that the high priest at the time of Jesus' death was Caiaphas. This is supported by Josephus, who has Caiaphas appointed by Valerius Gratus around 18 CE and deposed by Vitellius in 37 CE (*Ant.* 18:35, 95). Additionally, an ossuary discovered in 1990 at Abu Tor, near the Temple, has Caiaphas' name carved in its back and side. The ossuary names him as "Joseph son of Caiaphas," agreeing with his name in Josephus, "Joseph Caiaphas" (*Ant.* 18:35, 95). On the narrow side of the ossuary, the name is written in Aramaic, "Joseph, son of Qepha"; on the longer, back side, in Hebrew, "Joseph, son of Qopha." A coin discovered in the cave is dated 42/43 CE (during the reign of Herod Agrippa I). If the ossuary were for Caiaphas the high priest, he would have been about sixty when he died (*c.* 46). Inside the ossuary marked with Caiaphas' name, the bones of a man aged around sixty years old were indeed found, along with the bones of an adult female, two infants, a small child and a young adult. Death apparently came to them all from natural causes. The ossuary's elegant carving distinguishes it from most ossuaries of that place and period. It is carved with a pattern of five floral designs, for the most part in spirals, arranged around a central, spiraling flower. The palm design that surrounds the circles on Caiaphas' ossuary picks up a motif in the Temple's decoration. Placed in the tunnel to the south of the cave, his ossuary was in fact oriented to face that Temple. His status, and his connection to the Temple, the preeminent sacred place in Judaism, is attested by this find.

In Matthew, the notice of a conspiratorial meeting of high priests and elders takes place in Caiaphas' courtyard (26:3–5; rather than Annas', cf. John 18:15), and the success of the conspiracy is marked when Jesus is brought to Caiaphas (26:57). Caiaphas' question and Jesus' response (26:62–65) brings Jesus condemnation for blasphemy (26:65, 66). Mark and Luke identify the high priest only by office in the passion narrative, although Luke 3:2 implicitly agrees with Josephus and Matthew on his identity as Caiaphas.

Cordial relations with Roman officials are implicit in Caiaphas' long tenure. Between Herod's appointments and the destruction of the Temple, Josephus counts twenty-eight high priests (*Ant.* 20:250–51), so that Caiaphas' longevity in office was exceptional. Removed by Vitellius with Pilate,

Caiaphas' exercise of office included the latter's tenure. Pilate was noted for his insults to the Temple, and Caiaphas does not feature in Josephus' description of Jewish objections (*Ant.* 18:55–62; *J.W.* 2:169–77). The same Vitellius who dismissed Pilate and Caiaphas also released the high priestly vestments from custody in the Antonia fortress (*Ant.* 18:90–95), a practice to which Caiaphas had evidently acceded.

The Temple was the center of Roman and high priestly cooperation. From the point of view of successive Roman administrations, the sacrificial cult in the Temple was valuable because sacrifices on the emperor's behalf, financed at imperial expense, were offered there (Philo, *Embassy* 157, 317; Josephus, *J.W.* 2:197, with *Ag. Ap.* 2:77 disagreeing with Philo over who shouldered the cost). Provided those offerings proceeded, Jewish refusal to sacrifice to the emperor's image could be overlooked. For just that reason, Rome dispatched legions in 66 CE when the authorities in the Temple refused offerings from Gentiles (*J.W.* 2:409–10).

Caiaphas oversaw the antithesis of that policy, collaborating with Roman officers. He also consolidated high priestly power. A Talmudic tradition has it that, forty years prior to the destruction of the Temple, the Sanhedrin was removed from the chamber of hewn stone in the Temple to Hanuth, the place of vendors on the Mount of Olives (*'Abodah Zarah* 8b; *Shabbat* 15a; *Sanhedrin* 41a). The Gospels as a whole show that Caiaphas had also arranged for the vendors and associated activities to be moved into the outer court of the Temple, a move that Jesus violently opposed (Matt 21:12–13; Mark 11:15–17; Luke 19:45–46; John 2:13–16).

Caiaphas, in pursuit of high priestly interests, engineered the installation of vendors in the Temple. Jesus' reaction was predicated on his insistence upon the traditional arrangement at Hanuth and the prophecy of Zechariah 14:21, that merchants had no role in God's eschatological Temple. Pilate, Caiaphas' collaborator, adjudicated the collision between the two.

BRUCE CHILTON

Further reading

Bond, Helen. *Caiaphas: Friend of Rome and Judge of Jesus?* Louisville, KY: Westminster John Knox Press, 2004.
Catchpole, David. *The Trial of Jesus*, StPB 18, Leiden: Brill, 1971.
Chilton, Bruce. *The Temple of Jesus. His Sacrificial Program within a Cultural History of Sacrifice*, University Park, PA: Pennsylvania State University Press, 1992.
Greenhut, Zvi. "Burial Cave of the Caiaphas Family," *BAR* 18:5 (1992) 29–36.

ANTI-SEMITISM

The study of anti-semitism is a relatively recent development in Historical Jesus studies. As such, it holds two social constructs in tension. It has little to do with the anti-semitism of modern parlance but is a matter of religious conflict involving Jews and non-Jews of the first century. As is to be expected, studies on the subject have tended to focus on the theological and socio-religious concepts and constructions of that time.

Terms and concepts

While not explicitly part of the current discussion on inter-Jewish polemic in the first century, there is an evolution of terminology about which one must be aware when approaching the present subject. In the time of the historical figure Jesus, the polemic represented a perspective, primarily religious, and not an ethnic lineage.

As it is commonly used, the term "anti-semitism" is used inappropriately as a reference to bigotry against Jews in particular and not Semitic people on the whole. Earlier studies tended to use the term to refer to the antagonism of the New Testament writers against other forms of Judaism. However, with respect to early Christianity, this term has been increasingly replaced by "anti-Judaism" or similar terms.

It is widely recognized that each of these terms have faults and reflect on the disposition of those who use them. The use of "anti-semitism" has been intended to emphasize an awareness of the problem in the modern, post-Holocaust period; however, use of the term has been faulted as anachronistic and as wrongly characterizing the nature of the ancient dispute. Similarly, use of the term "anti-Judaism" and its synonyms attempts to reflect the debate more accurately as non-ethnic but religious. While this latter term has gained in popularity, it does not account for the fact that Christianity was born of Judaism and was almost certainly a branch of Judaism at the time of the Gospel writers. The present topic thus pertains to all references to Jews and Judaism as being reflective of an inter-Jewish dialogue reflected in the Gospels.

Points of debate

Early twentieth-century studies tended to focus on the theological dynamics at play within Christianity and Judaism. As an example of the doctrinal approach, the Harnack school held the success of Christian mission as being dependent upon the success of earlier Jewish missionary efforts. Christianity then proved to be doctrinally more sound and thus won converts from Judaism.

This view obviously takes Jesus' commissioning of the disciples as normative (Matt 10:5; Mark 3:14; Luke 9:2; Matt 28:19–20). It also presumes upon the existence of Jewish mission in the first century, but no evidence exists for this. The view is now seen as outdated.

Harnack's view was eventually dispelled by what Miriam Taylor has called the "conflict theory", developed by Marcel Simon. Simon argues that Christian theology did not develop separately from its social environs. Rather, Judaism was also antagonistic towards Christianity. Anti-Jewishness within Christian writings is thus seen to be a result of both Christianity and Judaism vying for converts and subsequent status within the Roman Empire. Variations of this view continue to be prevalent.

Miriam Taylor has argued that this approach, intended to supplant the doctrinal views of the Harnack school, simply injects its own bias into the situation. She then argues for conflict based upon a theological perceptual view of history and existential truth: Jesus is the Messiah (Matt 16:16). However, as both Evans, Parkes and Herford have noted, the primary issue was the role of the Jewish Law, the Torah (Matt 22:35–40; Mark 12:28–31; Luke 10:25–28).

While the primary confession of the Christians is a radical statement, it also does not do justice to several historical realities outlined by Bruce Chilton. With regard to the separation which followed the conflict to which the New Testament writers attest, Chilton draws the more realistic situation:

> That separation did not come easily, or even willingly, in many cases: church by church, it was a matter of such factors as the social constitution of the community, the sort of evangelization (for example, Pauline, Petrine, or Jacobean) that had called the congregation into being, the view taken of the gospel by local Judaism, and the attitude of civic officials toward both the particular forms of Judaism and of the emergent Christianity that fell within their jurisdictions.
>
> (Chilton 41)

Major works

The vast majority of works prior to the Second World War painted Judaism in a negative light and frequently left unchallenged and unassessed positive statements about Judaism found in the Gospels. Notable exceptions to this trend may be found in the works of August F. Gförer, George F. Moore, Travers Herford and James Parkes.

Since 1945, several major works have been published on Jewish–Christian relations and anti-Jewish sentiment in greater antiquity (see Further reading). However, it was not until 1978 that a major treatment of anti-Jewishness in the New Testament writings was published: Samuel Sandmel's *Anti-Semitism in the New Testament?* Sandmel, a rabbi, concludes that, while Christians are frequently devoid of anti-semitism, the New Testament is full of it (160).

Up to 1987, the scholarly consensus held that the Fourth Gospel was the most anti-semitic of the four, lambasting the Jews for killing Jesus. Then Jack T. Sanders presented a comprehensive treatment of anti-Jewish sentiment in *The Jews in Luke–Acts*. Sanders evaluates every mention of Jews or Judaism and concludes that Luke maintains an anti-Jewish polemic which is focused on Jewish religious institutions and authority.

In 1993, Craig Evans and Donald Hagner edited *Anti-Semitism and Early Christianity: Issues of Polemic and Faith*, a series of essays which reconsiders the conclusions passed down in previous studies. While several studies have been published since, the arguments presented in this volume remain the most prevalent and best argued of recent years.

ALBERT LUKASZEWSKI

Further reading

Chilton, B. "Jesus and the Question of Anti-Semitism," C. A. Evans and D. A. Hagner (eds) *Anti-Semitism and Early Christianity: Issues of Polemic and Faith*, Minneapolis, MN: Fortress Press, 1993, pp. 39–54.

Cohen, S. J. D. *From the Maccabees to the Mishnah*, Philadelphia, PA: Westminster, 1987.

Crossan, John Dominic. *Who Killed Jesus?* New York: Harper San Francisco, 1996.

Evans, C. A. "Faith and Polemic: The New Testament and First-Century Judaism," in C. A. Evans and D. A. Hagner (eds) *Anti-Semitism and Early Christianity: Issues of Polemic and Faith*, Minneapolis, MN: Fortress Press, 1993, pp. 1–17.

Gförer, A. *Philo und die judisch-alexandrinische Theosophie*, Stuttgart: Schweizerbart Verlag, 1835.

Guelich, R. A. "Anti-Semitism and/or Anti-Judaism in Mark," in C. A. Evans and D. A. Hagner (eds) *Anti-Semitism and Early Christianity: Issues of Polemic and Faith*, Minneapolis, MN: Fortress Press, 1993, pp. 80–101.

Hagner, D. A. "Paul's Quarrel with Judaism," in C. A. Evans and D. A. Hagner (eds) *Anti-Semitism and Early Christianity: Issues of Polemic and Faith*, Minneapolis, MN: Fortress Press, 1993, pp. 128–50.

Harnack, Adolf von. *Mission and Expansion of Christianity in the First Three Centuries*, Vol. 1, trans. J. Moffat, Gloucester, MA: Peter Smith, 1972 [1908].

Herford, T. *Christianity in Talmud and Midrash*, London: Williams & Norgate, 1903.

—— *Pharisaism: Its Aim and Its Method*, London: Williams & Norgate, 1912.

—— *Judaism in the New Testament Period*, London: Lindsey Press, 1928.

—— *The Truth about the Pharisees*, New York: Intercollegiate Menorah Association, 1925.

McKnight, S. "A Loyal Critic: Matthew's Polemic with Judaism in Theological Perspective," in C. A. Evans and D. A. Hagner (eds) *Anti-Semitism and Early Christianity: Issues of Polemic and Faith*, Minneapolis, MN: Fortress Press, 1993, pp. 55–79.

Moore, G. F. *Judaism*, Cambridge, MA: Harvard University Press, 1924–1930.

Parkes, J. *The Conflict of the Church and the Synagogue: A Study in the Origins of Anti-Semitism*, London: Soncino Press, 1934.

Richardson, P. and D. Granskou (eds) *Anti-Judaism in Early Christianity*, Vol. 1, Studies in Christianity and Judaism No. 2, Waterloo, Ontario: Wilfrid Laurier University Press, 1986.

Ruether, R. *Faith and Fratricide: The Theological Roots of Anti-Semitism*, New York: Seabury, 1974.

Sanders, E. P. *Jesus and Judaism*, Philadelphia, PA: Fortress Press, 1985.

Sanders, J. T. *The Jews in Luke–Acts*, London: SCM Press, 1987.

Simon, M. *Jewish Sects at the Time of Jesus*, Philadelphia, PA: Fortress Press, 1967.

—— *Verus Israel*, Oxford: New York, 1986.

Taylor, M. S. *Anti-Judaism and Early Christian Identity: A Critique of the Scholarly Consensus*, StPB 46, Leiden: Brill, 1995.

Tyson, J. "Anti-Judaism in the Critical Study of the Gospels," in William R. Farmer (eds) *Anti-Judaism and the Gospels*, Harrisburg, PA: Trinity Press International, 1999, pp. 252–58.

APOCALYPTIC

The adjective "apocalyptic" derives from the Greek noun *apocalypses* (revelation). John, the writer of the New Testament's final book, called his work an apocalypse (Rev 1:1) – a revelation of transcendent mysteries – and the word has since become a label for the genre of revelatory literature of which his book is an exemplar. Though the English word is used in widely divergent ways, for the sake of clarity many scholars have adopted the three-fold distinction proposed by Paul Hanson (1992): "apocalypse" refers to a work of a certain literary genre; "apocalyptic eschatology" refers to a set of eschatological ideas commonly found in apocalypses; "apocalypticism" refers to millenarian social movements. Finally, interpreters of apocalyptic rhetoric use the phrase "apocalyptic discourse" to denote a particular range of rhetorical *topoi* used in early Jewish and Christian argumentation (Carey).

Apocalypse as literary genre

The word "apocalypse" refers to a literary genre that emerged in postexilic Judaism and was common in early Christianity. The Society of Biblical Literature Genres Project has provided the standard definition:

> "Apocalypse" is a genre of revelatory literature with a narrative framework, in which a revelation is mediated by an otherworldly being to a human recipient, disclosing a transcendent reality which is both temporal, insofar as it envisages eschatological salvation, and spatial insofar as it involves another, supernatural world, intended to interpret present, earthly circumstances in light of the supernatural world and of the future, and to influence both the understanding and the behavior of the audience by means of divine authority.
> (Collins 1979: 9; Yarbro Collins 7)

Apocalypse proper is quite rare in the canonical Scriptures: only the book of Revelation and the second half of Daniel (7–12) fully conform to the above definition. However, a number of passages in the postexilic Hebrew prophets manifest many of the characteristics of apocalypses. This "proto-apocalyptic" literature includes Isaiah 24–27, Third Isaiah (55–66), and Zechariah 9–14 (Hanson 1975). In the New Testament, Mark 13 and its Synoptic parallels contain many of the distinctive characteristics of apocalyptic literature.

Many more apocalypses were not canonized. The Ethiopic *Book of Enoch* (*1 En.*) contains five separate apocalypses, ranging in date from the third century BCE to (probably) the mid-first century CE. Other Jewish apocalypses include *4 Ezra, 2 and 3 Baruch*, the *Apocalypse of Abraham*, the *Testament of Abraham*, and *2 (Slavonic) Enoch*. The early Christians also composed apocalypses, including *Shepherd of Hermas*, the *Ascension of Isaiah* 6–11, the *Apocalypse of Peter*, and the *Apocalypse of Paul*.

Common features of apocalyptic literature include visions or otherworldly journeys, esoteric and abstruse symbolism, and pseudonymous attribution to a sacred hero. Other notable characteristics include *ex eventu* prophecy, fascination with primordial and eschatological events, cosmic and astrological speculation, and emphasis on resurrection or the afterlife. Almost all apocalypses portray the final destruction of evil, which often involves cosmic upheaval and renewal (Collins 1998; Koch).

Apocalyptic eschatology

The phrase "apocalyptic eschatology" is commonly used to describe the eschatological perspective presented in Jewish apocalypses, but is also found much more broadly in postexilic Judaism and early Christianity. Though the extant texts evince considerable diversity, most share a common repertoire of eschatological images.

Norman Perrin has characterized apocalyptic eschatology as "a child of hope and despair" (Hanson 1983: 121): When confronted with a historical situation that seemed to invalidate their trust in God, the Jews' tenacious belief in God's sovereignty generated considerable speculation concerning God's imminent transformation of history. Despair concerning the present state of affairs thus commingled with hope that the present aeon would soon end and a new era of salvation would ensue.

Apocalyptic eschatology is therefore characterized by pessimism concerning the ability of humans to redeem history: only the decisive activity of God can undo the tyranny of evil. God's judgment is often envisioned as a cosmic cataclysm out of which a new creation is reborn.

The resultant worldview is highly dualistic. Apocalyptic eschatology features dualism between the present age of darkness and the coming age of light. Cosmic dualism between divine and demonic forces is common, as is the division of humanity into two groups – the righteous and the wicked.

Probably the most vivid example of apocalypticism in early Judaism is preserved in the writings of the Qumran community. This desert community followed strict interpretations of holiness and purification laws and awaited God's imminent judgment, not only on Israel's enemies but also on the compromised Judaism administered by the "evil priests" in Jerusalem.

Apocalyptic discourse

The rise of rhetorical criticism has aroused considerable interest in the function of apocalyptic discourse within the communities that employ it (Watson; Carey). Significantly for the study of the historical Jesus, this emphasis facilitates the study of apocalyptic *topoi* outside the context of literary apocalypses.

Although the functions of apocalyptic discourse vary considerably, a few are characteristic. The claim of apocalyptic language to reveal divine mysteries endows a message with divine authority, often used to provide consolation or challenge. The dualistic worldview embedded in apocalyptic discourse typically functions to manage and reinforce a community's boundaries.

Closely related to questions of function are theories concerning the social location of apocalyptic discourse. Many have accepted Paul Hanson's thesis that disenfranchisement engendered the pessimistic eschatology of the early Jewish apocalypses; others have used sociological analysis to locate apocalypticism among groups that possessed significant social power (Cook).

Particularly significant for the study of the historical Jesus is the question whether apocalyptic discourse should be interpreted literally or metaphorically. Dale Allison insists that first-century apocalypticists intended their cataclysmic predictions to be understood literally and adduces considerable evidence of painstakingly literal exegesis undertaken by ancient readers (152–69). G. B. Caird, however, has argued that the ancients often used end-of-the-world language metaphorically to refer to events that they knew not to be the end of the world, thereby imbuing them with added theological import (243–71). A mediating proposal has been offered by N. T. Wright, who suggests that the metaphorical or literal quality of each incidence of apocalyptic discourse must be assessed individually (290–92) – a position that evidently leaves open the difficult question of how to distinguish between metaphorical and literal uses of apocalyptic discourse.

Jesus — interpretations

Whether or not Jesus shared the apocalyptic orientation of many of his contemporaries is perhaps the single most divisive question in the study of the historical Jesus. The issue has dominated Jesus research since the forceful proposal of Albert Schweitzer in 1906. According to Schweitzer, the attractive and relevant moralist described in the nineteenth-century "Lives of Jesus" was merely the projection of the scholars' own religious ideals. Following the work of Johannes Weiss, Schweitzer argued that the historical Jesus was instead possessed of an apocalyptic vision of the imminent arrival of God's kingdom. Jesus perceived himself as a messenger of this kingdom and set out to prepare Israel for the end-time upheaval. When God's decisive action was delayed, Jesus sought to force God's hand by bearing within himself the suffering that necessarily preceded the eschaton. For Schweitzer, Jesus' entire ministry must be interpreted through the framework of his "thoroughgoing eschatology": Jesus did not proclaim universal moral truths but rather an "interim ethic" for the days immediately preceding God's judgment.

Although few accept the details of Schweitzer's interpretation, his insistence that Jesus must be interpreted in light of contemporary apocalyptic eschatology remains influential. Bart Ehrman claims to articulate a scholarly consensus:

Jesus thought that the history of the world would come to a screeching halt, that God would intervene in the affairs of this planet, overthrow the forces of evil in a cosmic act of judgment, and establish his utopian Kingdom here on earth. And this was to happen within Jesus' own generation.

(3)

E. P. Sanders emphasizes the nationalistic dimensions of Jesus' apocalyptic vision. For Sanders, Jesus must be viewed within the context of "Jewish restoration eschatology" (1985). Like many of his contemporaries, Jesus looked forward to God's imminent restoration of Israel's fortunes. His disruptive action in the Temple was intended to prophetically symbolize the destruction and renewal of the temple – a common motif in Second Temple Jewish eschatology. His selection of twelve disciples similarly alludes to the widespread expectation that God would ultimately restore the lost tribes of Israel. In short, Jesus believed that imminent divine intervention rather than military power would bring an end to Israel's humiliation.

Whereas Sanders focuses on what was peculiarly Jewish in Jesus' eschatological expectation, Dale Allison has correlated the apocalypticism of Jesus with cross-cultural study of millenarian movements (1998). Like most millenarian figures, Jesus gained favor among the disenfranchised and proclaimed imminent reversal of the social and institutional status quo (Q 14:11; 17:13; Mark 10:31; cf. *Gos. Thom.* 4). Like many millenarian movements, Jesus' was simultaneously atavistic and profoundly innovative. Moreover, the cooling apocalyptic fervor and reinterpretation of eschatological expectations evidenced in early Christianity are typical characteristics of aging millenarian movements.

Other scholars challenge the assertion that apocalyptic eschatology is the framework within which Jesus' proclamation of the kingdom of God should be understood. Two distinct approaches can be identified: some believe that Jesus used apocalyptic discourse to refer metaphorically to a present reality; others deny that Jesus used apocalyptic language at all, arguing that the apocalypticism of the extant sources is best explained as an early Christian development of the tradition.

C. H. Dodd famously objected to Schweitzer's "thoroughgoing eschatology," proposing instead that Jesus proclaimed "realized eschatology"; that is, he used the apocalyptic imagery of the kingdom of God with reference to his own ministry (21–59). For Dodd, the eschaton had paradoxically become present in the person of Jesus.

N. T. Wright also emphasizes the metaphorical nature of Jesus' apocalyptic language. Insisting that apocalyptic discourse was used in the first century to refer metaphorically to concrete historical events, Wright argues that Jesus used apocalyptic language to interpret socio-political events in the life of Israel – not least his own role within the story of God's universal kingship (1996: 320–68; cf. Horsley 121–45).

Others assign the apocalyptic language of the extant sources to the early church. Marcus Borg follows Norman Perrin in attributing the "coming Son of man" sayings to later tradition, and argues that although some authentic sayings of Jesus admit eschatological interpretation, they do so only when an apocalyptic framework for Jesus' career is assumed. Borg advocates an alternative *Gestalt* wherein Jesus' "subversive wisdom" takes center stage (80–84). For Borg, then, the kingdom of God is not an apocalyptic concept; instead, it symbolizes the "present kingly power of God" (57; cf. Luke 17:20; *Gos. Thom.* 3, 113). In a similar vein, John Dominic Crossan has coined the term *permanent eschatology* to describe Jesus' proclamation of the kingdom of God: "the permanent presence of God as one who challenges world and shatters its complacency repeatedly" (1973: 26; cf. 1991: 282–92).

Amid these diverse views, a final option is to retain the basic contours of the Synoptic portrait. According to Mark's Gospel, Jesus espoused an "already/not yet" kingdom – one inaugurated within history but awaiting divine intervention for its consummation. The Markan Jesus' anticipation of his own resurrection provides a particularly lucid glimpse into this paradoxical "apocalyptic/non-apocalyptic" stance. Mark credibly attests that Jesus shared with many of his compatriots the conviction that God's eschatological victory would involve a general resurrection of the dead (12:18–27). But Mark's Jesus modifies this common belief by predicting that his imminent death would be followed by his own vindication by God in the form of a *personal* resurrection (8:31; 9:31; 10:32–34) – an apocalyptic event awaiting its fulfillment but already impinging on present reality. Whether or not one is inclined to accept the details of the Synoptic portrait as historically credible, it undeniably has the advantage of accounting for the attribution to Jesus of sayings that describe the eschatological coming of God's kingdom as well as sayings that emphasize its present availability.

Jesus — sources and issues

The question of the role of apocalyptic eschatology in Jesus' message is intimately related to the ongoing debate concerning the reliability of the various Gospel accounts. Apocalyptic portraits of Jesus continue to depend heavily on the Synoptic Gospels, which reveal elements of an apocalyptic orientation. Those who advocate non-apocalyptic interpretations of Jesus question the reliability of the Synoptic account, citing non-canonical sources – in particular the *Gospel of Thomas* – as evidence of early non-apocalyptic interpretations of Jesus' aphorisms. The significance of the hypothetical source Q is contested. The reconstructed document attributes a number of apocalyptic sayings to Jesus; however, John Kloppenborg has argued that the apparent apocalypticism of Q was absent in its earliest forms, arising only during the crises associated with the destruction of the temple in 70 CE (1987).

The nature of the relationship between Jesus and John the Baptist is also a subject of considerable debate. E. P. Sanders has thoroughly articulated the common argument that, since John the Baptist and the early church both manifested apocalyptic eschatology, it is reasonable to expect that Jesus also shared this perspective. After all, Jesus began his career as a follower of the Baptist (Sanders: 91–95). John Dominic Crossan disagrees, arguing that although Jesus initially shared John's apocalyptic expectation, he soon became convinced that God's kingdom was already present (Crossan 1991: 230–38; cf. Luke 7:28; Matt 11:11; *Gos. Thom.* 46).

Another question concerns the authenticity of the "Son of Man" sayings in the Synoptic Gospels. There are three clusters:

1 sayings concerning Jesus' earthly career, both his humility (e.g. Luke 9:58) and his authority (e.g. Mark 2:10, 28);
2 passion and resurrection predictions (e.g. Mark 8:31 par.);
3 sayings concerning the final vindication and future career of the Son of Man as apocalyptic savior and judge (e.g. Mark 13:26; 14:62; Luke 12:40).

Many have argued that Jesus used the expression "Son of Man" as no more than a circumlocution for himself as a human (e.g. Ezek 2:1), and that the early church, influenced by Daniel 7, supplemented sayings in the first two categories with the apocalyptic sayings of the third category. Others attribute sayings in this third category to Jesus, but maintain he was referring to someone else. Given scholarly diversity on all the related questions, it is no surprise that little consensus has been reached.

Notably, Mark's use of the phrase coheres with the "already/not yet" eschatology he attributes to Jesus: In Mark, Jesus himself combines the Isaianic theme of suffering servanthood with Daniel's portrait of "one like a Son of Man" (originally referring to Israel's faithful remnant), and then applies all this to himself, claiming earthly humility and authority, future suffering and vindication, and final participation in God's apocalyptic intervention to save and to judge (Hooker 88–93).

A final issue concerns the nature of the so-called "apocalyptic discourses" attributed to Jesus. Mark 13, for example, has frequently been called a "Little Apocalypse" and interpreters have sometimes assumed that its genesis was independent of any Jesus traditions, perhaps originating as an apocalyptic tract during Caligula's persecution of the Jews. The present form of Mark 13 and parallels in Matthew 24 and Luke 21 are frequently judged to be authentic or inauthentic based primarily on prior convictions about Jesus' basic stance – apocalyptic or non-apocalyptic. There are, however, plausible ways of interpreting these texts which emphasize, not apocalyptic speculation, but Jesus' call for discernment and vigilance, courageous testimony, faithful discipleship, and effective service – if necessary in the context of persecution and suffering (Geddert).

Though the influence of apocalyptic eschatology on the historical Jesus will surely continue to be debated, it is clear that so-called apocalyptic texts in the canonical Gospels do not promote sign-seeking, speculation about timing, nor pessimism about life – all typical features of apocalyptic literature. Rather they, like the Jesus they portray, call for faithful discipleship and confidence in the final victory of God, whenever and however that might be revealed.

RYAN SCHELLENBERG
TIMOTHY J. GEDDERT

Further reading

Allison, Dale C. *Jesus of Nazareth: Millenarian Prophet*, Minneapolis, MN: Fortress Press, 1998.
Borg, Marcus J. *Jesus in Contemporary Scholarship*, Valley Forge, PA: Trinity, 1994.
Caird, G. B. *The Language and Imagery of the Bible*, Philadelphia, PA: Westminster, 1980.
Carey, Greg. *Ultimate Things: An Introduction to Jewish and Christian Apocalyptic Literature*, St Louis, MO: Chalice, 2005.
Collins, John J. (ed.) *Apocalypse: The Morphology of a Genre*, Semeia 14, Missoula, MT: Scholars Press, 1979.
—— *The Apocalyptic Imagination: An Introduction to Jewish Apocalyptic Literature*, second edition. Grand Rapids, MI: Eerdmans, 1998.

Cook, Stephen L. *Prophecy and Apocalypticism: The Post-exilic Social Setting*, Minneapolis, MN: Fortress Press, 1995.

Crossan, John Dominic. *In Parables: The Challenge of the Historical Jesus*, San Francisco, CA: Harper and Row, 1973.

—— *The Historical Jesus: The Life of a Mediterranean Jewish Peasant*, San Francisco, CA: HarperCollins, 1991.

Dodd, C. H. *The Parables of the Kingdom*, revised edition, New York: Charles Scribner's Sons, 1961.

Ehrman, Bart D. *Jesus: Apocalyptic Prophet of the New Millennium*, Minneapolis, MN: Fortress Press, 1999.

Geddert, Timothy J. *Watchwords: Mark 13 in Markan Eschatology*, Sheffield: Sheffield Academic Press, 1989.

Hanson, Paul D. *The Dawn of Apocalyptic: The Historical and Sociological Roots of Jewish Apocalyptic Eschatology*, Philadelphia, PA: Fortress Press, 1975.

—— (ed.) *Visionaries and their Apocalypses*, IRT 2, Philadelphia, PA: Fortress Press, 1983.

—— "Apocalypses and Apocalpyticism," in David Noel Freedman (ed.) *The Anchor Bible Dictionary*, 6 vols, New York: Doubleday, 1992, Vol. 1, pp. 279–81.

Hooker, Morna. *The Gospel According to St Mark*, London: A. & C. Black, 1991.

Horsley, Richard A. *Jesus and the Spiral of Violence: Popular Jewish Resistance in Roman Palestine*, Minneapolis, MN: Fortress Press, 1993.

Kloppenborg, John S. *The Formation of Q: Trajectories in Ancient Wisdom Collections*, SAC, Philadelphia, PA: Fortress Press, 1987.

Koch, Klaus. *The Rediscovery of Apocalyptic*, trans. Margaret Kohl, StBT 2/22, London: SCM Press, 1972.

Miller, Robert J. (ed.) *The Apocalyptic Jesus: A Debate*, Santa Rosa, CA: Polebridge, 2001.

Plöger, Otto. *Theocracy and Eschatology*, translated by S. Rudman, Richmond, VA: John Knox, 1968.

Sanders, E. P. *Jesus and Judaism*, Philadelphia, PA: Fortress Press, 1985.

Schweitzer, Albert. *The Quest of the Historical Jesus: A Critical Study of Its Progress from Reimarus to Wrede*, New York: Macmillan, 1968 [1906].

Yarbro Collins, Adela (ed.) *Early Christian Apocalypticism: Genre and Social Setting*, Semeia 36, Decatur, GA: Scholars Press, 1986.

Watson, Duane F. (ed.) *The Intertexture of Apocalyptic Discourse in the New Testament*, SBLSymS 14, Atlanta, GA: Society of Biblical Literature, 2002.

Wright, N. T. *The New Testament and the People of God*, Christian Origins and the Question of God 1, Minneapolis, MN: Fortress Press, 1992.

—— *Jesus and the Victory of God*, Christian Origins and the Question of God 2, Minneapolis, MN: Fortress Press, 1996.

APOCRYPHA AND PSEUDEPIGRAPHA

"Apocrypha" is a term applied by Protestant Christians to a body of Jewish texts included in the Old Testament by Roman Catholic and Orthodox churches, but not included in the Jewish or Protestant canon. "Pseudepigrapha" denotes a larger collection of Jewish texts (often with much more fluid boundaries), for the most part sharing the literary device of being written under a pseudonym. Both collections constitute primary resources for understanding the history, theological reflection, piety, ethics, cultural values, social tensions and practices, and ideologies of the Jewish environment within which Jesus taught and the movement formed in his name took shape.

The Old Testament Apocrypha

The Apocrypha is a collection of Jewish texts composed between approximately 250 CE and 100 CE. Several of these were composed in Hebrew or Aramaic in Palestine or the Eastern Diaspora (e.g. Tobit, Ben Sira, Baruch, Ps 151), while others were composed in Greek in the Western Diaspora (2 Maccabees, which probably originates, however, from Palestine, Wisdom of Solomon, 3 and 4 Maccabees). Their existence as a collection is a result of the reading activity of early Christians, who found these texts to be important resources alongside the Jewish Scriptures, and of the ongoing discussions and disagreements within the Christian churches about their status as "canonical." The word *apocrypha* is Greek for "hidden things," and originates from Christian circles who preferred to exclude these books from the public reading of Scripture (hence, "hidden away"), although such terminology does not necessarily suggest a negative evaluation of their worth (see, for example, *4 Ezra* 14:44–47 on the *greater* esteem in which "hidden" books are held). All of the books included here as "Apocrypha" (save for 2 Esdras/*4 Ezra*) appear in one or more of the major fourth- and fifth-century codices of the Septuagint, attesting to their value in the Nicene and post-Nicene church; several were found among the Dead Sea Scrolls, attesting to the fact that they were prized and read in Jewish communities as well (these include Ben Sira, Tobit, and the Letter of Jeremiah, together with the important pseudepigrapha, *1 Enoch* and *Jubilees*). Ben Sira was widely used in rabbinic circles, though as the work of an esteemed colleague rather than as authoritative scripture.

Most of the books contained within the Apocrypha fall into genres familiar from the Hebrew Bible and show a high level of interaction with, and interpretation of, scriptural texts. First and Second Maccabees resemble the biblical "historical books," the former explicitly recalling the idiom and phraseology of 1–2 Samuel and 1–2 Kgs as it extends the "biblical" history into the period of the Hasmonean dynasty. These books tell of the radical attempts to refashion Jerusalem as a Greek city, the violent suppression of Torah observance, the martyrs who died rather than break faith with the covenant, and the successful revolution led by the family of Judas Maccabeus, restoring political independence and traditional Jewish observances. Second Maccabees is especially important as a witness to the development of the belief in the resurrection as the means by which God's promises to the righteous might be fulfilled when covenant loyalty led to being cut off from this-worldly blessings. The widespread observance of Hanukkah (the "Feast of Dedication," John 10:22) attests to the importance of the story of the Maccabees in early Judaism.

Several apocryphal books belong to the genre of wisdom literature. *The Wisdom of Ben Sira* preserves the collected teachings of a sage who kept a school, a "house of instruction," in Jerusalem in the first quarter of the second century BCE. During a time of rapid Hellenization, Ben Sira instructed the children of the Jerusalem aristocracy that nothing they did would ever increase their honor if it meant neglecting the practices of the very Jewish law (10:19, 22–24). The "fear of the Lord" is identified with observing Torah (19:20), which has in fact become the incarnation, as it were, of Wisdom herself (24:23). Far from being a burden or a manifestation of legalism, Torah was celebrated as God's special gift to Israel, an act of divine grace. Following Torah is the path both to personal honor and to national security, seen especially in the famous "Hymn to the Ancestors," praising Jewish heroes and censuring leaders who led Israel away from covenant loyalty. Ben Sira was not, however, altogether parochial. While he digested fully the Jewish Scriptures as he developed his teaching, he also incorporated Greek and Egyptian wisdom, particularly in regard to the advice they had to give on practical matters like friendship and enmity, judicious speech and weighing the speech of others, and successfully navigating political waters by means of appropriate caution. In addition to such practical advice, his work contains theological reflections (e.g. on providence and free will, prayer, temptation, forgiveness, and almsgiving) and windows into the social practices and values of his period (e.g. friendship, patronage, household management, etiquette at symposia, and the "ideal" woman, who exhibits modesty, silence, and submissiveness).

Wisdom of Solomon was composed in Egypt in Greek in the early first century CE, and devotes itself to developing a few principal themes: the trials of the righteous; their vindication after death in the presence of their persecutors; the divine figure of Wisdom and her role in creation and in mediating knowledge of God; God's care for God's people and punishment of their enemies; and a deconstruction of gentile religion, including the ruler cult, and its resulting moral chaos (the writings of Paul especially resonate with the sections dealing with this last topic). Two other texts bridge the span between wisdom literature and the thematic treatise. The Letter of Jeremiah (composed originally in Hebrew, perhaps as early as the fourth century BCE), seeks to insulate Jews from the religious pluralism of the Diaspora by stressing the artificial and manufactured character of the Gentiles' gods. Fourth Maccabees, written in the most artistic and rhetorically acute Greek in the collection, promotes strict Torah observance as the means by which to fulfill the Greek philosophical ideals of the perfect sage who has mastered the passions that hinder virtue.

Expansions and re-writings of Scripture constitute a third category. First Esdras presents an alternative telling of 2 Chronicles 35–36, Ezra, and parts of Nehemiah, giving prominence to Zerubbabel with the inclusion of an originally independent tale (the "contest of the three bodyguards") and the subsuming of Nehemiah's role into Zerubbabel's, perhaps to affirm that the Davidic line had, in some sense, been restored in Zerubbabel. Hebrew Esther was freely translated into Greek and expanded in stages to include six substantial additions, as well as minor additions throughout the text, explicitly introducing the theological dimension felt to be absent in the original version. Greek Esther explicitly affirms dietary regulations, purity concerns, and effective prayer, while providing additional windows into the motivations for ancient anti-Judaism. The cycle of stories in Daniel was expanded to include the story of Susanna, in which the young Daniel prevents a gross manipulation of the law courts by means of clever cross-examination, and Bel and the Dragon, in which the aged Daniel demonstrates to Darius the emptiness of Gentile idolatry and zoolatry (the worship of living animals).

The additions to Daniel cross into another genre, that of liturgical texts. The story of Azariah, Mishael, and Hananiah in Daniel 3 is expanded with a prayer for forgiveness and deliverance placed on the lips of Azariah and a psalm of thanksgiving sung by all three within the furnace. Similarly, the story of the repentance of Manasseh, the most wicked king in Judah, in 2 Chronicles 33:18–25 becomes an invitation to a pious Jewish poet to "recreate" the lost Prayer of Manasseh, an exquisite expression of the belief in the boundless mercy of God. These three texts have had a long history of use in Christian liturgy. Ps 151, a combination of two originally independent Hebrew psalms, commemorated God's choice of David and David's defeat of Goliath, reminding Israel of her own election even as she lives in the shadow of giant Gentile powers.

Baruch combines several genres, opening with the prescription of a liturgy of repentance for Jews in Judea and the Diaspora (resonating deeply with Daniel 9), moving to a poem about wisdom and Torah observance as the path to national restoration, then concluding with two poems in prophetic idiom – Jerusalem lamenting for her distant children and a reformulation of Isaiah's message of hope. This work has been criticized for its lack of originality, but it provides an effective summary of the Jewish scriptural tradition for Jews living under Gentile domination and looking for the path to experiencing God's promised blessings.

Tobit, Judith, and 3 Maccabees belong to the genre of "tale" or "romance." The story of Tobit, written in Aramaic in the late third century BCE, shares many of the values taught by Ben Sira, but gives voice to them by telling a story that both provides a narrative frame for several extended ethical instructions and provides a kind of narrative demonstration that those instructions really do lead to experiencing God's favor and timely deliverance. The plight of two pious Jewish families is resolved through prayer and the visitation of an angelic intermediary, who guides the main character, Tobit's son Tobias, through the hazards of his quest for success. The ethics of the book promotes the strengthening of the Jewish community – particularly the community of righteous Jews – through endogamy (marrying within one's people, and even within one's tribe if possible), charitable support of the righteous poor, duty toward one's parents and kin, and giving the dead a proper burial. The book also attests to the growth of angelology and demonology, bringing the world of pre-exilic Judaism and that of the first-century landscape, where angels are suddenly making regular appearances and demons are being everywhere exorcized from the individual humans they afflict.

Judith tells the story of God's deliverance of God's people "by the hand of a woman," the pious and courageous Judith who liberates her city by beguiling and beheading Nebuchadnezzar's general, Holofernes. At the same time that it celebrates a female heroine, the book reinforces chastity as an essential female virtue and the private sector as the "normal" sphere for women. The story also reinforces the observance of prayer, dietary regulations, and ritual purity. Third Maccabees gets its name from similarities in plot with 2 Maccabees, but concerns the forced apostasy of Jews in Ptolemaic Egypt. It affirms that God is as ready to hear and deliver God's people in Diaspora as God's people in Israel, and bears witness to the hostility and tensions between Torah-observant Jews, apostate Jews, and the dominant Gentile culture, as well as to the reality of "anti-Gentilism" as a correlate to "anti-Judaism."

Second Esdras, a composite work comprising a Jewish apocalypse composed at the end of the first century CE (2 Esdras 3–14 = *4 Ezra*) and two later Christian additions (2 Esdras 1–2 = *5 Ezra*; 2 Esdras 15–16 = *6 Ezra*), is now commonly printed as part of the Apocrypha, though it also quite properly belongs with the Pseudepigrapha (not being regarded as canonical by any Christian group). In the wake of Jerusalem's destruction, the author uses apocalypse as a medium within which to wrestle with questions about God's providence and justice, the possibility of keeping God's Law, and the value of the idea of "election." His Deuteronomic world view is only salvaged by means of visions of the fate of the righteous and the wicked beyond death, and the promise of God's eschatological intervention in the history of Israel and her gentile overlords.

The Old Testament Pseudepigrapha

Another vitally important collection of texts from the Second Temple Period (and into the first centuries of the Common Era) is the Pseudepigrapha. The term is a Greek word meaning "things bearing a false ascription," referring to the tendency of the real authors to assume, as it were, the identity of an illustrious figure from the sacred past. This is, for the most part, a consistent characteristic of this body of literature, though it is a characteristic by no means limited to this body of literature (see, for example, the Wisdom of Solomon, Baruch, Letter of Jeremiah, and Prayer of Manasseh among the Apocrypha or, according to a major scholarly consensus, the books of Daniel and Ecclesiastes among the Hebrew Scriptures and 1 Timothy and 2 Peter in the New Testament). The term "pseudepigrapha" carries distinctly negative connotations in many reference works, being heard as synonymous with "spurious," "forged," and "uninspired," but such claims need to be weighed against the evidence that several of these works (in particular, *Jubilees* and *1 Enoch*) were held to have the highest authority by Jewish groups such as the sect at Qumran and (in the case of *1 Enoch*) are even quoted by early Christian authors as authoritative pronouncements (see Jude 14–15).

The phenomenon of authors writing in the name of another is widespread in the ancient world, and attributable to many motives. Some of these motives were clearly considered base by their contemporaries, as in the use of pseudepigraphy to attribute damaging words to a rival, to claim undue authority for one's own thoughts, or to sell a "newly discovered" work of a venerated writer to a library. Some motives, however, were regarded as honorable, as in the attribution of one's writing to one's teacher as the true source of one's thoughts. Additionally, it is possible that some pseudepigraphic texts were recognized (and approved) as such when they first appeared, and only later were confused with "authentic" works of the ancient author. Something of this sort may have been the case with Daniel, which was counted among the "Writings" of the Hebrew Bible rather than the "Prophets," a sign, perhaps, that it was recognized as stemming from a post-prophetic author, whereas by the first century CE it began to be treated as an authentic product of the historical Daniel (see, e.g., Matt 24:15).

In *From the Maccabees to the Mishnah*, Shaye Cohen suggests that Jews in the Second Temple period, such as produced pseudepigrapha, understood themselves to be living in a postclassical age. With the emerging canon of early Judaism, and the sense that the prophetic spirit had passed from the scene, authors may have begun to seek a kind of secondary inspiration by attaching themselves to a figure from the sacred past, carrying on, as it were, the interpretation and reformulation of the Jewish tradition in his name, or simply patterning their messages after the "classical" forms and content of the venerated literature of their past. The process may be even more complex in the writing of pseudonymous apocalypses, texts that are highly suggestive of the blending of ecstatic experience with reflection on authoritative texts, with the real author identifying in some sense with the figure of the past and merging the horizons between the ancient sage and himself.

Published collections of Pseudepigrapha differ in content. The edition of Charles is the most limited, but preserves those that are of most interest to New Testament scholarship. The edition of Sparks is more inclusive, but still quite selective. The two-volume edition of Charlesworth is by far the most inclusive, providing translations of sixty-three texts (some of which, however, cannot be dated with certainty prior to the seventh to ninth centuries CE, though they are generally held to preserve earlier traditions).

Like the Apocrypha, many of the Pseudepigrapha fall into the literary genres found among the classic Hebrew Scriptures (e.g. apocalypses, wisdom texts, liturgical and poetic texts) or represent the rewriting and expansion of the traditions (e.g. "testaments" and expansive rewritings of the Pentateuchal narratives). Several, however, resemble genres current among Greek authors (such as biography, drama, and philosophical works).

The best-represented genre in Charlesworth's collection of pseudepigrapha is the apocalypse. Pride of place among the apocalypses goes to *1 Enoch*, a work that exercised profound influence on the literature and life of Qumran, the literature of the New Testament, and texts stemming from other Jewish circles, such as the *Testaments of the Twelve Patriarchs*. *1 Enoch* is a composite work that took shape between the early second century BCE and the first century CE. As a character who "walked with God" and had been taken up alive into heaven, Enoch became a natural focal point for Jews interested in revelations from the realm beyond ordinary experience. The earliest strata were written prior to the success of the Maccabean Revolt, and included the Apocalypse of Weeks (*1 En.* 91:12–17; 93:1–10), the Astronomical Book (chapters 72–82), and large parts of the Book of the Watchers (*1 En.* 1–36). The Astronomical Book lays out a solar calendar as the approved calendar for observing God's sabbaths and holy days, a calendar adopted by the Qumran community in opposition to the Jerusalem Temple, which followed a lunar calendar. The Book of the Watchers tells the story of the angels who left heaven to mate with human females, giving birth to the giants who wreak havoc on humankind, even as the angels introduce humanity to all the forbidden arts – the mining of metals for the production of weapons and currency, the arts of astrology and necromancy, and cosmetics and other charms for enticing the eyes – and God's judgments upon the angels, their hybrid offspring, and humanity. The latest stratum is the Parables of Enoch (*1 En.* 37–71), composed at some point during the first century CE. This section features the figure of the "Son of Man," also so prominent in the Gospels, and visions of judgment that bear remarkable similarities with those found in the Synoptic Gospels. Other apocalypses include *2 Baruch*, which, like *4 Ezra*, uses the genre of apocalypse to respond to the destruction of Jerusalem and promote Torah observance as the means by which to see God's forthcoming deliverance of Israel, *2 Enoch*, the *Sibylline Oracles*, the *Apocryphon of Ezekiel*, the *Apocalypse of Abraham* and the *Treatise of Shem*.

The "testament" is a genre based on Genesis 49, where Jacob speaks prophetically about each of his sons upon his deathbed. As the genre develops, it comes to include a lengthy reflection on the presumed speaker's life, usually as the basis for ethical exhortation and often some eschatological predictions. Because of the last element, and because several testaments include literary features such as otherworldly journeys and revelations, this genre is considered to be closely related to the genre of apocalypse. The *Testaments of the Twelve Patriarchs* is probably the most important example. These were most probably Jewish in origin, written during the first century BCE, but were expanded by Christian scribes. Each of Jacob's twelve sons, in turn, reviews major episodes of his life (some of which are not found in Genesis), draws moral lessons, and exhorts his children to virtuous living. Several include significant eschatological sections, bearing witness to the messianic expectations of their authors, who looked for a priestly messiah who would rule with, and above, a regal messiah (these are the sections that have been most heavily reworked by Christian scribes wishing to add more direct resonances with Jesus' story). Other important examples include the *Testament of Job*, which develops substantially the figure of Satan and bears witness to Jewish anti-idolatry polemic, and the *Testament of Moses*, an expansion of Deuteronomy 31–34 that develops Moses' role as prophet, mediator, and intercessor, that promotes a stance of non-violent resistance to unjust rule (in contrast to the more violent model of resistance promoted in 1 Maccabees and adopted by revolutionary movements in Palestine), and that anticipates a day of repentance prior to the coming of God's kingdom (cf. Mark 1:14–15).

Beyond what we find in testamentary literature, Second Temple Period Jews exhibited a great deal of interest in revisiting their sacred stories with an eye to answering unanswered questions, reinforcing core practices and values, and, to some extent, explaining the embarrassing. *Jubilees* is probably the most important example of "Rewritten Bible," since it was held to be an authoritative text in at least one major Jewish movement (the Qumran community and its extended network). Written in the second century BCE, *Jubilees* revises and expands the patriarchal story through the Exodus event, and is most notable for its introduction of the specific laws and practices of the Mosaic Law into the practice of the patriarchs, thereby asserting that the Torah was no innovation in God's dealings with the righteous, but was always the standard of conduct by which they lived – even Abraham. It recasts embarrassing facets of the story, like Rebekah's favoritism of Jacob and their deception of

Isaac, as actually in fact an act of obedience to Abraham's private revelation to Rebekah that God had chosen Jacob to be the recipient of the birthright. Other important examples of the rewriting and expansion of biblical narratives include *Joseph and Asenath*, a story of the courtship and conversion to Judaism of Joseph's wife, *The Life of Adam and Eve*, the *Martyrdom of Isaiah*, a work that has been heavily Christianized as a result of the New Testament usage of Isaiah, the *Lives of the Prophets*, which shares with *Martyrdom of Isaiah* an interest in the violent deaths of many of the prophets (cf. Matt 23:29–36; Acts 7:51–52), and the *Liber Antiquitatum Biblicarum*, a paraphrase of the biblical story from Adam to David.

Liturgical texts constitute another important group within the Pseudepigrapha. The eighteen *Psalms of Solomon* originate in first-century BCE Palestine. Several of these psalms reflect very clearly the circumstances of Pompey's invasion of Jerusalem (63 BCE) and death (48 BCE). These psalms, with their trenchant critique of the late Hasmoneans and their administration of the Temple, reflect the ongoing commitment to the Deuteronomic principle that transgression of God's law brings punishment, and the prophetic principle that the Gentile tools of chastisement will not go unpunished themselves. *Psalms of Solomon* 17 and 18 bear witness to a lively expectation of a messiah, a king from David's line, who would expel the gentile overlords and restore peace and justice to an independent Israel. Others are windows into a piety that lauds God's gracious provision for all creatures, criticizes all hypocrisy, and affirms the value of God's "discipline" (which at many points appears to be synonymous with living the "disciplined" life of Torah observance). Among this collection one will also find additional psalms attributed to David and the *Odes of Solomon* (a Christian collection of poems showing close affinities with the Gospel of John).

Among the remaining books included in the Pseudepigrapha are a number of wisdom texts showing engagement both with the scriptural heritage of Judaism and Greek proverbial wisdom, literary works (poetry and drama) modeled upon Greek forms, and with fragments of Jewish historians that tend to ascribe notable innovations in the history of civilization to the heroes of Jewish tradition.

Significance for the study of the historical Jesus

The Apocrypha and Pseudepigrapha are essential resources for investigating the cultural, traditional, and social setting of Jesus' ministry and the birth of the Palestinian Jesus movement. The discovery of several of the Pseudepigrapha in the nineteenth century gave rise to the recovery of apocalypticism as an important ideological strain within Judaism at the time of Jesus and led to the eschatological portraits of Jesus in the first quest (a tendency that persists in many authors of the third quest, such as one finds in Charlesworth's *Jesus within Judaism*). Study of these texts provides the broader contours of the various messianic models that were the focal point of Judean hopes for their future. First Maccabees and *Psalms of Solomon*, for example, give expression to the sharpening of the military messianism that surrounded the Jesus movement and that provided the framework within which the governing authorities and disciples alike interpreted his actions, and in contrast to which the early Christians formulated their understanding of a suffering and dying messiah whose death mediated divine favor (cf. 2 Maccabees 7:37–38; 8:5) and whose "coming in power" was deferred to a future visitation.

Perhaps one of the most important results of a thorough familiarization with this literature is a deeper appreciation of Jesus' continuity with, and embeddedness in, his Jewish environment than is commonly supposed when one limits one's resources to the Jewish/Protestant canon of the First Testament. When such a person finds Jesus and other leaders of the early Christian movement uttering teachings that he or she does not recognize from the Hebrew Bible or the Protestant Old Testament, he or she formulates a picture of a Jesus who stands against the Judaism of his day, who is introducing much more that is new rather than reaffirming the values and practices that he has learned within Judaism. When we devote ourselves to gaining familiarity with a broader sampling of Jewish literature than is contained in the Hebrew Scriptures, we find, on the contrary, that there is far greater continuity between Jesus and the Judaism of his time than we originally suspected. In turn, this contributes to a more nuanced understanding of how Jesus' contemporaries would have understood his message and his self-presentation.

For an example, we may consider the impact of Ben Sira on the teaching and self-understanding of Jesus. As a champion of traditional piety and head of a school of instruction in Jerusalem, Ben Sira was well poised to enter the mainstream of Jewish wisdom, and to have his teachings spread among and be transmitted by the generations of sages and rabbis that would follow. It should not be surprising, then, to find numerous correspondences between his teaching and the teaching of Jesus, a Jew raised in the synagogues of Nazareth and its environs and taught by rabbis who would themselves have learned Ben Sira's wisdom, at least in part, as part of their mastery of their own tradition. (Ben Sira's influence can also be seen throughout the Epistle of James, a text attributed to the half-brother of Jesus, whose ongoing work in Jerusalem expanded his opportunities to study or converse with other Jewish sages about the Jewish ethical tradition, and thus learn more about Ben Sira than he might have gleaned from his brother's preaching or his upbringing in Galilee.)

The sayings and instructions compiled by Matthew in the Sermon on the Mount (and parallels) contain numerous points of connection with Ben Sira. Like Ben Sira, Jesus expounds on the Law by extending the range of the commandments, particularly the prohibition of murder (Sir 34:25–27; Matt 5:21–22). Jesus' teachings on prayer incorporate several striking particulars found in Ben Sira as well (on prayer, fasting, and almsgiving as regular practices of the righteous, compare Tob. 12:8 with Matt 6:1–18). Both teachers warn against excessive speech in prayer (Sir 7:14; Matt 6:7), address God as "Father" in prayer (Sir 23:1, 4; cf. Matt 6:9; Luke 11:2), and insist that receiving forgiveness from God goes hand-in-hand with extending forgiveness to one's neighbor (Sir 28:1–4; Matt 6:12, 14–15; 18:23–35). Moreover, both caution against being presumptuous of God's forgiveness on the basis of any righteous works or pious practices one has performed (Sir 7:8–9; Luke 18:10–14).

Both mandate almsgiving (Sir 4:4–5; Matt 5:42; cf. also Tob 4:7), and promote care for the marginal as a manifestation of one's kinship with God (Sir 4:10; Matt 5:45). Jesus' emphasis on showing kindness even to one's enemies is a noteworthy extension of Ben Sira's teaching (but quite in keeping with, say, Seneca's exhortations to benefactors to give as the gods give), but the roots are otherwise clearly present in the older sage. The Torah itself, of course, already commanded almsgiving as an essential aspect of piety and covenant loyalty, but Jesus' teachings on almsgiving share more in common with the images and rationales offered in certain apocryphal texts. Ben Sira and Tobit specifically promoted the giving away of money to the needy, somewhat ironically, as "laying up a treasure" for oneself (Sir 29:9–12; Luke 12:33; 18:22; Matt 19:21; cf. also Tob 4:8–9), rather than allowing it to "rust" through hoarding (Sir 29:10; Matt 6:19–21; Luke 12:33). Showing charity now, rather than hoarding, is the way to avert future disaster (Sir 29:11b–13; Matt 25:31–46; Luke 16:19–31; cf. Tob 4:10; 12:9), the most noticeable difference being that Ben Sira sees this treasure as a source of help against future times of adversity in this life whereas Jesus applies the concept to post-mortem or eschatological consequences.

In light of such extensive points of contact, it becomes all the more significant now to note ways in which Jesus did *not* follow Ben Sira's teaching. Unlike the older sage, Jesus invites women into the male spaces where disciples gather and learn from Jesus, and values women as disciples and witnesses (Luke 8:1–3; 10:38–41). Similarly, Ben Sira fostered hostility against Samaritans (50:25–26), while Jesus, on the contrary, used the popular hostility against Samaritans to frame some of his most memorable teachings (e.g. Luke 10:29–37), and is remembered in Johannine circles to have included them fruitfully in his ministry (John 4).

Nevertheless, reading Ben Sira, we learn that many of the highest ideals of Jesus were formulated not *de novo*, nor in opposition to Jewish sages, but in keeping with their finest expression of the life that pleased God. Jesus is remembered to have invited people to be schooled by him in the way of life that pleases God and leads to success in words that very closely parallel the words used by Ben Sira two centuries before to invite students to his school (Matt 11:28–30; Sir 6:23–28; 51:23–27). Such an invitation, combined with Jesus' frequent use of maxims, sayings, and instructions in his own teaching, may suggest that one important category Jesus gave his contemporaries for understanding his ministry was that of a wisdom teacher or sage, one who showed the way to live well-pleasing to God and advantageously among people.

Similar discoveries await the reader of the Pseudepigrapha. In addition to some striking idiomatic resemblances ("into the fiery furnace," *1 En.* 98:3; cf. Matt 13:42, 50; "the chosen ... will inherit the earth," *1 En.* 5:7; cf. Matt 5:5), *1 Enoch* may also provide some missing clues to the logic of one of Jesus' controversies with the Sadducees, "who say there is no resurrection" (Luke 20:27–36). Jesus affirms two things that do not appear to be grounded in – or learned from – the Hebrew Scriptures, namely that, in the resurrection, people will be "like the angels" and that marriage will have no place in such a situation. Jesus may have learned these, however, from *1 Enoch* (see *1 En.* 15.4–7 on the inappropriateness of marriage and mating to the life of the angels and the later *1 En.* 51.1, 4 on the expectation that, in heaven, all will become like the angels, since immortality will render procreation superfluous). The Sadducees' "failure of logic" may result here from their reading only the canonical Scriptures!

Some of Jesus' most characteristic teachings resonate deeply with texts from his Jewish environment. For example, his redefinition of the "greatest" among his disciples as the one who becomes "the slave of all" (Mark 10:41–45), and his own posture among them as "one who serves," embodies the stance of Joseph, who "did not arrogantly exalt myself among them because of my worldly glory, but I was among them as one of the least" (*T. Jos.* 17:8). Similarly, the author of *T. Jos.* 18:2 had urged his reader to "treat well and pray for" anyone who tried to do them harm (cf. Matt 5:44–45//Luke 6:27–28). The author of *Pss. Sol.* 4:2–4 had already denounced the person who was severe in condemning the sinner, whose "hand is first upon him as if in zeal, while he is himself guilty of manifold sins and intemperance," whose "eyes are upon every woman without discrimination," showing that Jesus' sagacious response to the accusers of the woman caught in adultery would have been heard as a response from *within* the Jewish tradition (John 7:53–58:11).

A word needs to be said here in regard to the famous "criterion of dissimilarity." While none of the sayings of Jesus discussed above could be *affirmed* as authentic on the basis of this criterion, there being clear examples of parallels in earlier Jewish texts, historical Jesus research is healthfully moving beyond a "negative" application of this criterion at least where Jewish environment is concerned. The desire to construct a Jesus on the basis solely of what he did *not* share with Judaism was often predicated upon pejorative convictions concerning the nature of the Jewish faith. In their *Quest for the Plausible Jesus*, Gerd Theissen and Dagmar Winter suggest that "clearly Jewish elements" in the sayings materials "that cannot be explained as Jewish Christian reactions against the tendencies of Gentile Christianity" bring us "close to the historical Jesus." Such an approach opens up the way for a "historical Jesus" that is allowed fully to take on the flesh of his scriptural and extra-scriptural tradition, and to speak both within that tradition and to that tradition.

DAVID A. deSILVA

Further reading

Charles, R. H. *The Apocrypha and Pseudepigrapha of the Old Testament*, 2 vols, Oxford: Oxford University Press, 1913.

Charlesworth, J. H. *The Old Testament Pseudepigrapha*, 2 vols, New York: Doubleday, 1983, 1985.

—— *Jesus within Judaism*, New York: Doubleday, 1988.

Cohen, Shaye. *From the Maccabees to the Mishnah*, Philadelphia, PA: Westminster Press, 1987.

Collins, J. J. *Jewish Wisdom in the Hellenistic Age*, Louisville, KY: Westminster John Knox Press, 1997.

Delcor, M. "The Apocrypha and Pseudepigrapha of the Hellenistic Period," in W. D. Davies and L. Finkelstein (eds) *The Cambridge History of Judaism*, 4 vols, Cambridge: Cambridge University Press, 1989, Vol. 2, pp. 409–503.

deSilva, D. A. *Introducing the Apocrypha: Context, Message, and Significance*, Grand Rapids, MI: Baker Academic, 2002.

Evans, Craig A. *Ancient Texts for New Testament Studies: A Guide to the Background Literature*, Peabody, MA: Hendrickson, 2005.

Harrington, D. J. *Invitation to the Apocrypha*, Grand Rapids, MI: William B. Eerdmans, 1999.

Helyer, Larry. *Exploring Jewish Literature of the Second Temple Period: A Guide for New Testament Students*, Downers Grove, IL: InterVarsity Press, 2002.

Metzger, B. M. *An Introduction to the Apocrypha*, Oxford: Oxford University Press, 1957.

Nickelsburg, G. W. E. *Jewish Literature Between the Bible and the Mishnah*, second edition, Minneapolis, MN: Fortress Press, 2005.

Sparks, H. F. D. *The Apocryphal Old Testament*, Oxford: Clarendon Press, 1984.

Stone, M. E. (ed.) *Jewish Writings of the Second Temple Period*, Assen: Van Gorcum, and Philadelphia, PA: Fortress Press, 1984.

Theissen, Gerd and Dagmar Winter. *The Quest for the Plausible Jesus: The Question of Criteria*, Louisville, KY: Westminster John Knox Press, 2002.

APOSTLESHIP, EVANGELISM, WITNESS

Our sources indicate that at a very early stage in his ministry Jesus selected and trained an inner circle of disciples who participated with him in his ministry. The Synoptic Gospels and Acts designate these people "apostles." Scholarship has raised several questions about the origins of the apostles: the source of their title; what Jesus intended with them; whether their existence or number (twelve) are later creations; and how apostleship is defined differently by various New Testament (NT) authors.

Terms

"Apostle" translates the Greek *apostolos*, which is the noun form of the verb *apostellō*, "to send" (i.e. "a sent one"). Jesus could not have adopted this term from ordinary Greek, where it was used mostly for naval expeditions or colonists. In the Septuagint (LXX) – the Greek version of the Old Testament (OT) – the verb *apostellō* translates the Hebrew verb *šlḥ* ("to send"), and occurs in passages where an individual is authorized to perform a certain task on behalf of another. The noun *apostolos* occurs only once in the LXX (1 Kgs 14:6), describing the commission of a prophet.

Rengstorf attempted to show that the NT *apostolos* came from the Jewish institution of the *šaliah* (related to the verb *šlḥ*), a person who represents another: "A man's agent is like himself," said the rabbis (*m. Ber.* 5:5). This hypothesis has been criticized on the grounds that the *šaliah* is primarily a legal institution involving a short-term commission, and the evidence is from after the first century, whereas Jesus called to a permanent religious vocation, characterized by an eschatological urgency. Nevertheless, many hold a modified form of Rengstorf's view, linking Jesus' "sending" certain disciples with earlier Jewish terminology.

In the gospels, the term is rare except for the six instances in Luke (Luke 6:13; 9:10; 11:49; 17:5; 22:14; 24:10; Matt 10:2; Mark 6:30; as a variant in 3:14; John 13:16). Matthew, Mark, and Luke connect the name "apostle" to Jesus' sending a select group of disciples out on a preaching mission in Galilee (see later). As "sent ones," the designation ties in well with the generic meaning of *apostellō*. And because they are selected from a larger pool of disciples to represent Jesus, the term begins to take on connotations of authority.

Another way the gospels refer to this select group is as "the Twelve" (e.g. Matt 26:20; Mark 3:14; 14:17; Luke 9:1; 22:47; "twelve disciples" in Matt 10:1; 11:1; 20:17). In the synoptics, the story of the mission of the Twelve (Mark 6:6b–13, 30; Matt 10:2; Luke 6:13) identifies these with the apostles. Although some have argued that the two groups were originally separate, most see them as identical. "The Twelve" is used much more often in the gospels than "apostles," and has early attestation outside the gospels as well (e.g. 1 Cor 15:5). Even John, who never calls them apostles, uses the term "the Twelve" (John 6:67, 70–71; 20:24). Hence some scholars who doubt "apostle" could have been a title used during Jesus' lifetime prefer to speak of the Twelve, and this will be used in this article.

Historicity of the Twelve

Some have objected to the pre-Easter existence of apostles on historical and linguistic grounds. It is argued the term could not have referred to an office that early; and the definitions of an apostle in the post-Easter church do not align with the gospel descriptions (see later). A number of studies in the last century argued the term was invented in the early church to bolster its power, or coined by Paul to describe his ministry (J. Munck). Schmithals hypothesized that Gnostics invented the idea of apostleship, and Paul adopted it (not Jesus).

Some have questioned the number twelve: it is a symbol too rich not to have been invented by the early church to suggest the apostles as patriarchs of the twelve tribes of Israel. It is objected that the lists of apostles' names in the synoptics and Acts are inconsistent in order and content. Fatal to all theories that the church created these is that Paul refers to "apostles" or "the Twelve" who were in Jerusalem previous to his call (1 Cor 15:5, 7; Gal 1:17, 19), and most scholars would place Paul's conversion from two to five years after Jesus's death.

Others have argued for the historicity of an inner circle of twelve disciples of Jesus (Barrett, Kirk, Meier, Dunn, Schnabel). The evidence is summarized by Meier as fitting the criteria of: (a) multiple attestation in the sources; (b) embarrassment; and (c) the general historical trend of traditions about the Twelve in the New Testament. All four evangelists and Q contain references to an inner circle of twelve disciples (e.g. Matt 11:1; Mark 6:7; Luke 8:1; John 6:67; also Paul, 1 Cor 15:5). The inclusion of Judas the betrayer as one of the Twelve (Mark 14:10) is not a detail likely to be made up by those who later honored Jesus and glorified the apostles. And finally, if the idea of the Twelve were invented to retroject the authority of early church leaders back into the lifetime of Jesus, then we would expect that these twelve leaders would play a prominent part in the church's life and mission. Instead, the evidence suggests that their leadership role diminished as the church spread geographically and ethnically. New apostles come to prominence within and outside Jerusalem, such as James and Paul (Acts 14:4; Rom 16:7; Gal 1:9). The post-Easter developments cannot be the basis for the pre-Easter gospel accounts. In light of this, a number of scholars who doubt that Jesus used "apostle" as a title are willing to acknowledge he created "the Twelve" (e.g. Barrett, Meier).

The function of the Twelve during Jesus' ministry

The role of the Twelve during Jesus' lifetime has no exact parallel in previous Jewish institutions. We can, however, trace similarities to several facets of Palestinian Judaism which Jesus combines and modifies in a unique fashion. First, whatever else the Twelve are, they are *disciples of a teacher*. Like other Jewish disciples, they live with their master, hear his interpretation and application of scripture, and are expected to memorize it. They have no school building, but share whatever accommodations he has. This is the significance of Mark's telling us that Jesus called them "to be with him"

(Mark 3:14): both physical presence and learning. The idea that certain disciples are noted for passing on the teaching of their master is common to the traditions of rabbinic Judaism (*m. Eduyyot* 8.5; *'Aboth* 2.8; 3.9). It is unusual that Jesus chose the Twelve, for normally the students selected the teacher.

Second, the Twelve are *called by Jesus to a specific ministry*. In addition to learning, they are called to "follow" (Mark 1:16–18, 19–20 and pars.; Mark 8:34 and pars.; Matt 9:9; Luke 14:27) and eventually to proclaim the same message of the Kingdom that Jesus did, thus extending the sphere of his preaching to Israel (Mark 3:14–15; 6:6b–13 and pars.; see "mission" later). When sent out, the Twelve are charged with authority to represent Jesus. This is the aspect of their ministry similar to the *šaliah*.

Third, the Twelve's relationship to Jesus echoes that of *prophet and disciple* (note Josephus can call Elisha the "disciple" of Elijah, *Ant.* 6.5.4; 8.13.7; Meier). The designation of Jesus as a "prophet" by his own followers and by the crowds is well attested (Matt 21:11; Mark 6:4, 15; Luke 24:19). As prophet-disciples, the Twelve are given divine empowerment by Jesus to imitate his miracles of healing and exorcism as signs of the kingdom, bringing restoration to God's people (Mark 3:14–15 and pars.; Mark 6:7 and pars.; Matt 12:28). This function also includes the preaching noted above.

Fourth, the apostles *symbolize the restoration of the tribes of Israel*, in fulfillment of prophecy. That this is the intention of the number is confirmed by a tradition that linked the Twelve with an eschatological judging of Israel (Matt 19:28 par. Luke 22:29). Israel's prophets had looked forward to the day when the twelve tribes would be reconstituted by God's merciful intervention, gathered from out of the nations to which they had been exiled, returned to the land, and purified (Isa 49:6; Ezek 37:15–28; Mic 2:12). This eschatological hope continues in later Jewish literature from the second century BCE to the first century CE (Sir 36:10; 48:10; *Pss. Sol.* 11:2; *T. 12 Patr.*). At Qumran also there is emphasis on the number twelve in eschatological leadership (1QM 3:13–14; 1QS 8:1).

The Twelve and apostles after Easter

After Easter, the Twelve become witnesses of Jesus's resurrection (Acts 1:21–22; 1 Cor 9:1; Gal 1:12, 15–16). The title "apostle" becomes regularly attached to them, but other apostles arise also (Acts 14:14; Gal 1:19; 1 Cor 9:5–6; Rom 16:7). Their message changes to focus more on forgiveness offered through Jesus whom God sent, and his death and resurrection in fulfillment of scripture. Continuity with Jesus' ministry is seen in the themes of Kingdom, repentance and forgiveness, ethics, and coming judgment. Writers seem to differ as to whether an apostle must have been a disciple of the earthly Jesus (Acts 1:21–22) or not (Paul, Gal 1:1, 13–16; 1 Cor 15:8–10); or whether apostles travel and found churches (1 Cor 9:1–2; 2 Cor 3:1–3; Rom 15:18–21) or stay in Jerusalem (Acts 8:1). And there are "apostles" who are temporary church emissaries with special missions (2 Cor 8:23; Phil 2:25).

It is helpful to distinguish the role of the "Twelve" from that of "apostle." The Twelve have a historical role that cannot be repeated or passed on, and even finding a replacement for Judas post-Easter was a unique event (Acts 1:21–26). They are the principal rememberers and reciters of tradition, having the authority of Jesus who sent them out first during his ministry. But by the mid-first century some had died, some left Jerusalem on mission, and their role as a group declines. Yet the spreading church required more leadership – and church founders – who could be authoritative witnesses to the Jesus tradition. Hence new apostles are called into service by the risen Lord and recognized as such by the churches.

The mission(s) of the Twelve

Jesus is presented in the gospels as a man consumed by a mission from God to proclaim the kingdom of God to Israel. Matthew and Mark use the noun *euangelion* ("gospel" or "good news") to describe this, while Luke prefers the related verb *euangelizomai* ("to proclaim good news," "announce"; compare English "evangelize"), and John, using legal language, likes to talk about "bearing witness" (Greek *martureō*) or "testimony" (*marturia*).

In the synoptics, the Twelve are sent out on a mission to Israel in Galilee with Jesus' authority to preach and perform miracles (Mark 3:14–15 and pars.). His message is to be their message. In John, Jesus refers to God as "the one who sent me" (John 4:34; 5:24; 6:38, and *passim*), and he in turn sends the disciples (John 15:27; 20:21). Most likely the mission described in Mark and Matthew is representative of multiple sendings during Jesus' lifetime. Although a few critics have challenged the historicity of such a mission, the proclamation of the kingdom of God was so central to Jesus's teaching, and to his identity, that it is virtually unimaginable that he would have disciples without involving them in this task.

The OT prophets and later Jewish literature anticipated the restoration of Israel's twelve tribes in the end times, an event to be accompanied by an end of sinfulness and a renewed self in relation to God. This eschatological hope is evoked in the mission of the Twelve: the call to repentance, announcement of the coming Kingdom, and prophetic gestures of restoration (healing, exorcism, communal sharing, and the Twelve themselves). There is also a reminder of judgment associated with the Kingdom, making a response urgent.

Their mission may have been intended to reach a wider area than Jesus himself could, or to prepare for further visits by Jesus to those areas that were receptive (cf. Luke 10:1). The note of urgency in the mission is unmistakable: not even usual preparations such as a poor person would take for a journey are allowed (money, bread, or spare clothes), but the Twelve are sent out with almost nothing, dependent upon God and the hospitality of the villagers, to move quickly and with the least encumbrance possible. The severe restrictions on their provisions are understandable in a rural Galilean context. The landscape was dotted with small villages only a half-day's walk apart or closer. As fellow Galileans, the Twelve could expect to take advantage of family relationships or ethnic solidarity for hospitality. When the church moves beyond Palestine these restrictions are lifted, although the *Didache* still gives limits on support for traveling prophets (*Did.* 11:4–15; 12:1–8; around CE 95–105). That the disciples are adjured to go "only to the lost sheep of Israel" (Matt 10:6) – a saying hard to imagine the later church inventing – once again points to the historicity of this pre-Easter preaching. The Twelve were probably sent out in pairs (Mark 6:7, and the pairing of names in lists) to provide comfort and security, and also to fulfill legal requirements for witnesses (Deut 17.6; 19.15).

A mission by "seventy" (or seventy-two) is unique to Luke 10:1–20, though there are numerous parallels with Matthew 9:37–38; 10:7–16; 11:21–23. Some believe this is a "doublet" created by Luke (Fitzmyer), though it can be argued much of the material at least is from Q or other non-Lucan sources (Marshall, Nolland, Bock). The purpose and nature of the mission is virtually identical to that of the Twelve, and there is nothing in the text to suggest the audience is other than Israelites. The differences are (a) more emphasis on judgment on the unrepentant; and (b) the widening of the circle of those preaching, and a prayer that even more be included (Luke 10:1–2). This anticipates the post-Easter mission of the church, which will reach out to Gentiles.

Witness

The quasi-legal motif of giving "witness" in favor of Jesus and the gospel he proclaimed is found in all four gospels, though the terminology of testifying is most prominent in John, and outside the gospels in Acts. In Mark 13:9, in the apocalyptic discourse (also Luke 21:13; Matt 24:14; cf. Matt 10:17–20), the disciples are warned that their association with Jesus will prompt opposition, violence, and arrest; but this will mark another opportunity to further the "witness" they are entrusted with. Mark and Matthew have presented the warnings so that they point forward to a mission to the Gentiles, while Luke reserves an explicit mention of witness to the nations until the risen Jesus gives his charge to the remaining Eleven (Luke 24:48). Negatively, the Twelve sent on mission are instructed to shake off the dust from their feet "as a witness against" those who reject the gospel (Mark 6:11 and pars.), meaning the messengers have done their part to announce the coming Kingdom and are absolved of guilt in the judgment that will fall on the unrepentant.

For John, Jesus as the Son of God is the primary witness to God the Father via his words and deeds (John 3:11, 32; 5:36; 8:38; 14:7; 17:6–8; 18:37). God in turn witnesses to the Son (John 5:32, 37). Those who accept Jesus' testimony about the truth will be saved; and the disciples in turn are commanded to testify and bear witness to the truth, namely that Jesus is God's Son and that salvation is found in believing in him (John 15:26–27; cf. 20:21; this is the point of the gospel, 21:24). They will be assisted in this by the witness of the Spirit (John 15:26–27). When Jesus's integrity is questioned, he adduces witnesses: John the Baptist, the sign-miracles, God, and the scriptures (John 5:31–47). John echoes Isaiah's notion that Israel was meant to be a witness to the one God in whom alone salvation is found (e.g. Isa 43:10–13). Jesus has become the one true fulfillment of that goal. Though scholars debate to what extent Johannine speeches are shaped by the evangelist's editing, the occurrence of parallel ideas in Mark, Q, Matthew, and Acts clearly shows that there is a pre-Johannine historical tradition here.

The idea of the disciples witnessing is not restricted to the terms for witness, however, and such witness occurs in several ways in the synoptics. The disciples witness to Israelites about God's grace in offering repentance to sinners; they witness to the arrival of the hour of prophetic hope, the dawning of the kingdom of God in the coming of Jesus; about impending judgment in their warnings. And they bear witness to Israelites of their day about Jesus's prophetic authority and identity. These tasks of witness during Jesus's lifetime prepare them for the continuation of this ministry after Easter, with the added dimensions of Jesus' resurrection and open proclamation of him as Messiah.

TERENCE PAIGE

Further reading

General, apostleship and mission

Agnew, Francis H. "The Origin of the NT Apostle-Concept: A Review of Research," *JBL* 105 (1986) 75–96.

Barrett, C. K. *The Signs of an Apostle*, Philadelphia, PA: Fortress Press, 1972.

Dunn, James. *Christianity in the Making. Vol. 1: Jesus Remembered*, Grand Rapids, MI: Eerdmans, 2003.

Hengel, Martin. *The Charismatic Leader and his Followers*, New York: Crossroad, 1981.

Kirk, J. Andrew. "Apostleship since Rengstorf: Towards a Synthesis," *NTS* 21 (1974–75) 249–64.

Meier, John P. *A Marginal Jew: Rethinking the Historical Jesus. Vol. 3: Companions and Competitors*, New York: Doubleday, 2001.

Munck, J. *Paul and the Salvation of Mankind*, Richmond, VA: John Knox, Press, 1959.

Rengstorf, K. H. "ἀπόστολος," in G. Kittel (ed.) *Theological Dictionary of the New Testament*, trans. G. W. Bromiley, Grand Rapids, MI: Eerdmans, 1964, Vol. I, pp. 407–45.

Schmithals, Walter. *The Office of Apostle in the Early Church*, trans. John Steely, Nashville, TN: Abingdon, 1969.

Schnabel, Eckhard. *Early Christian Mission. Vol. 1: Jesus and the Twelve*, Downers Grove, IL: InterVarsity Press, 2004.

On the mission of the Seventy

Bock, Darrell L. *Luke 9:51 24:53*. Grand Rapids, MI: Baker, 1996.

Fitzmyer, Joseph A. *The Gospel According to Luke (X XXIV)*. New York: Doubleday, 1985.

Green, Joel. *The Gospel of Luke*. Grand Rapids, MI: Eerdmans, 1997.

Marshall, I. Howard. *Commentary on Luke*. London: Paternoster, 1978.

Nolland, John. *Luke 9:21 18:34*. Dallas, TX: Word, 1993.

On the gospel of John and witness

Beasley-Murray, George R. *John*, Waco, TX: Word, 1987.

Brown, Raymond. *The Gospel According to John*, 2 vols, New York: Doubleday, 1966–70.

Schnackenburg, Rudolf. *The Gospel According to St. John*, 3 vols, New York: Seabury, 1980–87.

Smalley, Stephen. *John: Evangelist and Interpreter*, London: Paternoster, 1978.

ARAMAIC AND THE *IPSISSIMA VERBA JESU*

In the interests of recovering historically reliable information about Jesus of Nazareth, it would be of immense significance to Historical Jesus Research if it were possible to recover some of the actual words of Jesus (*ipsissima verba Jesu*). Given the difficulty of this task, discussions have usually instead rested content with his authentic voice (*ipsissima vox*), that is, with sayings, which give the sense of what Jesus said, but not the exact linguistic form. Once the quest for his actual words is undertaken, the researcher is immediately confronted with the question of what language Jesus would have used in his teaching.

The Semitic language criterion of authenticity

The gospels, as indeed the entire New Testament, have only survived in Greek. Prior to their writing, the traditions about Jesus circulated orally. This simple observation immediately raises the question of authenticity: How do we establish which of the words that now appear in the gospels as those of Jesus, were, in fact, actually spoken by him – as opposed to words that may have been put into his mouth during the process of oral tradition, or by the gospel writers?

The conclusions drawn in regard to this question are greatly affected by the stance taken towards the gospels as a whole. At one extreme, the gospels can be regarded as products of the faith of the churches in the latter part of the first century, in which any genuine tradition about Jesus needs to be unravelled from the accretions and changes brought about under the influence of the churches and their needs. At the other extreme, the gospels are primitive accounts of the life and teaching of Jesus and there is no need to distrust them, unless there are demonstrable reasons for doing so.

In the endeavour to establish which of Jesus' sayings recorded in the gospels were 'authentic' to Jesus, various 'criteria of authenticity' have been formulated. These criteria, for the most part, arose within the context of form criticism, which tended to work from a more sceptical stance towards the gospels. It has always been recognised that a group of such criteria must be employed and that no one criteria stands alone. These criteria can be divided into negative criteria (those which rule out the genuineness of a saying), and positive criteria (those which demand genuineness).

One of the most important positive criteria has been the 'Semitic language criterion' – often also utilised in connection with the 'Palestinian context' criterion. In the face of the criticism that the well-known 'criterion of dissimilarity' does not adequately allow for Jesus' continuity with Judaism, the Semitic language criterion became all the more important. This criterion has usually been applied to individual sayings, or to a group of sayings which form one unit, such as a parable, although some have also applied the criterion to larger collections, such as the 'eucharistic words' of Jesus in Mark's Gospel, or the hypothetical document Q.

This criterion begins with the necessary assumptions that Jesus taught in Aramaic, and that this was the predominant language of Palestine in his day. If Aramaic was the predominant language spoken by Palestinian Jews, and Jesus was a Palestinian Jew, then it is a logical and historical inference that his primary language was Aramaic. Although the evidence shows that there were four languages operative to some degree in first-century Palestine (Aramaic, Greek, Hebrew and Latin), the majority of scholars (e.g. Wellhausen, Dalman, Joüon, Bardy, Black, Wilcox, Feldman, Torrey and Fitzmyer) have continued to support G. Dalman's conclusion, that though Jesus might have known Hebrew, and probably spoke Greek, he certainly taught in Aramaic.

If these assumptions are correct, then if a saying could be traced back to an underlying Aramaic original this would provide a strong presumption of authenticity.

Certainly there is evidence in the Gospels to indicate an Aramaic substratum. Despite surviving only in Greek, the Synoptic gospels (Matthew, Mark, Luke), especially, show many clear signs of an Aramaic influence that is not so clear elsewhere in the NT (apart from Acts). In addition, the survival of Semitic characteristics in Jesus' sayings, despite them being embedded in Greek Gospels, is evidence of restraint in the tradition, probably due to reverence towards the Lord. This is particularly noticeable in the case of Luke, 'in whose writing the more Semitic-type *logia* stand out strikingly from the smooth Greek of the framework in which they are set' (Jeremias).

Building on the work of Dalman, Joachim Jeremias was one of the leading proponents of this criterion. He noted that occasionally complete Aramaic clauses have survived in the sayings of Jesus, such as in his address to Jairus' daughter, *talitha koum*, 'little girl, arise' (Mark 5:41); possibly also in his statement about fulfilling the law (Matt 5:17b); and in his words on the cross, *eloi, eloi, lama sabachthani*, 'my God, my God, why have you forsaken me?' (Mark 15:34). Even if it is granted, as some would argue, that the latter saying is an expression of the early church's theology placed upon the lips of Jesus, this would show that the early church knew that Aramaic was Jesus' authentic tongue.

As well as these few sentences, after disregarding Aramaic place-names, personal names, designations of descent or of groups, Jeremias identified a list of twenty-six Aramaic words that have survived in Jesus' sayings. Many of these are well known from transliterations in the English translations, such as: *abba* (Mark 14:36); *bar* (Matt 16:17) and its plural combined with another Aramaic word *regis* in *Boanerges* (Mark 3:17); *satana* (Mark 3:23, 26; etc.); *mamona* (Matt 6:24); *rabbi* (Matt 23:7f); *sabbeta* (Mark 3:4). Others are familiar from common enough English usage of such terms as Gehenna (*gehinnam*, Mark 9:43, 45, 47; etc.); and Passover/Paschal (*pascha*, Mark 14:14). Still others are perhaps a little more subtle.

There are also many passages in which an underlying Aramaic wording can be disclosed, including Aramaisms, that is, expressions that are idiomatic, foreign to both Hebrew and Greek: ὀφείλημα for guilt, sin, not just for a money debt (Matt 6:12); the use of εἰς/ἐν before cardinal numbers (Mark 4:8). Scholars have also identified translation mistakes which show up on recourse to Aramaic: for example, Luke 7:45 εἰσῆλθον, 'I' makes no sense, but 'she' might be expected, both meanings of the one word in Galilean Aramaic. Different words used by Gospel parallels can also, at times, be explained by recourse to a single Aramaic word.

Alongside attention to Aramaic words and clauses, scholars have also detected Aramaic style in the sayings, such as Semitic rhythms, alliteration and assonance, and parallelism. In particular, antithetic parallelism is so much a feature of Jesus' sayings (Jeremias counts more than 100 instances) that C. F. Burney claimed that a saying with this feature brought us closer to the *ipsissima verba Jesu* than any other sentence.

Jeremias, however, was less confident about the possibility of recovering the actual words of Jesus than he was that this criterion revealed several indisputable characteristics of the *ipsissima vox Jesu*. He considered Jesus' parables, his riddles and his teaching about the kingdom of God to be without adequate parallel. In addition, Jesus introduced a new use of *amen* and of *abba*, which then left a trace in the prayer practices of the early church. Even if the *ipsissima verba Jesu* could not be established in every instance, the results of applying the Semitic criterion led Jeremias to conclude that it is the inauthenticity of the Synoptic tradition that needs to be proved, not its authenticity.

Matthew Black has been another major contributor to the Aramaic background to Jesus' sayings. His *Aramaic Approach to the Gospels*, which went through three editions and was recently reprinted, addressed questions of style, syntax, grammar and vocabulary, poetry, and issues of translation, including evidence from textual variants. Black's approach has generally been regarded as cautious and conservative, carefully arguing the case for an Aramaic substratum to the sayings of Jesus.

A modest Aramaic approach can be found in the work of B. Chilton and C. Evans, which continues to refine criteria for using the Targums for the interpretation of the New Testament – and modest because it is especially relevant for understanding Jesus' use of the Old Testament. These criteria include: dictional coherence (does Jesus' wording cohere with that of the Targums, as opposed to the Hebrew or Greek?); thematic coherence, which can be divided into thematic (proper) (such as Jesus' stress on the imminence of the kingdom of God, which has close affinity with Targum sayings); and exegetical coherence (where Jesus' exegetical practice appears to have been conditioned by the Aramaic paraphrase as it had come to expression in the synagogues).

It must be said, however, that the attempt of Joachim Jeremias and Matthew Black, and others after them, to modify the conclusion of sceptical form and redaction criticisms that only very few logia, parables and miracle stories can be attributed to Jesus himself, has had fairly limited success. Although the Semitic language criterion was most important for these scholars, others have not regarded it as highly, some even reducing its status to secondary or dubious.

The criterion under fire

The Semitic language criterion has not been without its critics. Although it is difficult to dispute the fact that our Greek Gospels contain Semitic features, what does this actually prove? Do these features find their origin in the original Aramaic sayings of Jesus, or are they just evidence of some other Aramaic phase through which the tradition has passed? Or do they simply show the influence of the Greek Old Testament on the Gospel writers?

Some of the staunchest proponents of an Aramaic substratum of the Gospels themselves argued that at least some of our Greek Gospels originated with Aramaic versions (e.g. Wellhausen, C. C. Torrey) or, in the case of Luke, at least with Aramaic sources. Others have understood the various

Aramaisms as evidence of a 'Jewish Greek', rather than of any original Aramaic source. If either of these scenarios are so, then how is the criterion helpful for establishing the words of Jesus?

The notion of 'Jewish Greek' introduces yet another debate associated with this question. What kind of Greek do we have in the New Testament? Rather than being a special 'Christian Greek', perhaps inspired by the Holy Spirit, with some older scholars (H. Cremer), or a special 'Jewish Greek' (N. Turner), the discovery of papyri written in the same Koine Greek of the New Testament now clearly shows that the New Testament needs to be situated within the context of the development of written Greek which stretches from Alexander the Great (356–323 BCE) to the first century CE. The early efforts of Deissmann and Moulton in this regard are still of enormous importance, and their work has been continued by many others. To complicate the picture a little further, recent studies have shown that some of the features previously regarded as 'Semitic' (although none of those raised previously) may actually be normal to the Koine (L. Rydbeck).

That the Gospels were published in Greek is an impressive fact in itself, especially given that they arose out of an aggressive missionary movement, which sought to use them in the service of persuading the world that the Jewish Messiah was for all. Three names in particular are associated with the view that the New Testament reflects the *lingua franca* of the day: Deissmann, Thumb and Moulton. Deissmann denied that there was any 'written Semitic Greek' and maintained that most Hellenistic Jews knew Greek as a first language. Continuing in the same direction as Deissmann's work, J. H. Moulton concluded that biblical Greek was the vernacular of daily life and very much a predominant language in the bilingual environment of Palestine. Deissmann argued that their Koine Greek was 'the language of the people', and there is no doubt much truth in that claim, even though scholars gradually became aware of how difficult it is to discover the language spoken by ordinary uneducated people at the time. According to M. Reiser, once Deissmann, Thumb and Moulton had died, the field was left open to those who focused upon the Aramaic basis of Jesus' sayings.

Without doubt, the historical and political background of Palestine adds complexity to its linguistic context. When the Jewish people returned from their exile in Babylon, they brought with them the Semitic language, Aramaic. Although it was once thought that Aramaic went into decline broadly around the time of Jesus (200 BCE to 200 CE), discoveries of the last sixty or so years have now established that Aramaic continued to be spoken in Palestinian across many centuries. This is established by evidence such as Aramaic among the biblical writings, as well as a large amount of inscriptional, epistolary, papyric and literary evidence, especially that discovered at Qumran.

Although Greek culture had already begun to spread its influence before his conquests, the aggressive achievements of Alexander ensured that Greek became the dominant language throughout his empire. It also speaks loudly for the deep penetration of Greek that its dominance continued even after the Romans had cast their mantle over much of this territory, also adding Latin to the linguistic cocktail. Palestine, too, was and remained deeply Hellenised, but despite Greek now being the *lingua franca* of the Roman world, the surviving evidence indicates that it never fully replaced Aramaic.

Given this multilingual historical background, it is not surprising that the surviving evidence shows a complex linguistic milieu for first-century Palestine, the exact shape of which cannot be ultimately decided. As a broad generalisation, it is certainly true to say that the archaeological, linguistic and sociological evidence seems to indicate that the region was multilingual, with the presence of Aramaic, Greek, Hebrew and Latin being demonstrable.

The complexities of the evidence, however, mean that such a broad-brush generalisation is not very helpful. Against the tendency to lump the evidence together both chronologically and geographically, the evidence that has survived requires a much more nuanced description, if theories about the linguistic milieu are to be well founded. So, for example, in the face of claims that first-century Galilee was strongly Hellenised, Chancey's work has questioned whether this can be supported by a careful description of the available evidence. Inscriptional evidence in particular is often utilised without recourse to the dating and provenance of the various inscriptions, and without asking what can and cannot be claimed from inscriptions when their function in ancient society is properly understood. Paying attention to such issues, Chancey argues that simply on the basis of the number of published Greek inscriptions, Jerusalem appears to have been more Hellenised than Galilee. This actually makes sense, since as a major urban centre, with governmental and administrative apparatus, and Diaspora Jews frequently in attendance for major festivals, it is more likely that Greek would have been spoken in Jerusalem.

The language of Jesus

If his environment was multilingual, what can be concluded about Jesus' linguistic ability? Perhaps it is true to speculate that this multilingual environment increases the likelihood that Jesus was also multilingual, but this makes a fairly minimal contribution to the establishment of the actual historical fact. The problem becomes obvious as soon as we ask whether the generalisation can be projected onto any individual living in Palestine in this period. The fact that multiple languages were spoken in a region does not argue for every (or any!) individual being multilingual. History, of course, must be content with probabilities of varying levels of certainty, but any conclusions to be drawn for any given individual must be carefully argued from the available positive evidence. Answers to historical questions should be firmly based upon the available evidence and assessed by means of good historical argument. When it comes to the question of the language spoken in Palestine and by Jesus, the researcher has to avoid the tendency to construct simplifying schemata, for the picture that emerges from the evidence is rather complex.

Given his environment, it is certainly possible that Jesus had some ability in Aramaic, Greek and Hebrew, and was able to use each in the appropriate setting. The first step to establishing whether this possibility was a reality is simply to ask with respect to each of these languages, whether the available evidence makes it probable (to whatever degree) that he spoke that tongue.

The Aramaic Jesus

Most scholars agree that the main language spoken by the Jews of first-century Palestine, and so by Jesus, was some form of Aramaic. This general presumption in favour of Aramaic being Jesus' main spoken language is reinforced by the positive evidence of Aramaic that has been identified in the Gospels, and especially in sayings attributed to him (see above). Since the Gospels have survived in Greek, these clear signs of Aramaic, even if not extensive, are certainly impressive.

The question of Jesus speaking Aramaic can be still more finely tuned. Which of the several dialects did he speak? This, of course, becomes significant for the kind of careful comparative work that is needed to establish the language that potentially lies behind the Greek of the Gospels' sayings.

Scholars have discussed which Aramaic sources are most likely to indicate the language of the first

century for some time. Before the Dead Sea discoveries, there was little evidence for Palestinian Aramaic between the final editing of Daniel (c. 135 BCE) to the *Megillat Ta'anith* (c. 135 CE). Because questions surrounded the origin of biblical Aramaic and the text of *Megillat Ta'anith*, the usefulness of these sources was also debated. To understand the language of Jesus, apart from some ossuary and tomb inscriptions, and some Aramaic words that were found in the New Testament and Josephus, scholars were therefore forced to rely upon Aramaic sources that were much earlier, or much later, than the first century. Since much of the earlier material was just coming to light at the turn of the twentieth century, discussion tended to centre upon the later sources.

In 1898 G. Dalman argued that *Targum Onqelos* – which he regarded as the most important source – best preserved the dialect of first-century Judea, and the Palestinian Talmud and the early midrashim reflected that of Galilee. For the distinction between the dialects in the first century, Dalman pointed to the incident in which Peter is recognised as Galilean by his accent (Matt 26:73), and to *b. Erub.* 53b, where the Galilean accent is mocked for not sufficiently distinguishing various words (חמר donkey; חמר wine; אימר ימר wool; אימר lamb). In his 1930 edition, after being criticised for the priority he gave to *Targum Onqelos* despite Jesus being a Galilean, Dalman esteemed the Palestinian Talmud and midrashim more highly, but he still regarded *Targum Onqelos* as the nearest representative of literary Aramaic to that used in first-century Palestine.

That same year, several fragments were published from the Cairo Geniza, dated to the seventh to ninth centuries CE, which were described as 'the Palestinian Targum'. Across the next thirty years, further texts were added to the 'Palestinian Targumim'. P. E. Kahle argued that the earliest Aramaic amongst these documents was to be found in the Geniza fragments and Codex *Neofiti I*. Although the reasoning behind his dating was later questioned, Kahle's position was soon accepted by a number of scholars (Macho, Grelot, Déaut, McNamara), who became known as the 'Kahle School' and who included Matthew Black. In the 1950s and 1960s representatives of this school debated with those who continued to champion the views of Dalman.

In fact, the basic shape of this debate was set firmly enough, that as the small but significant amount of Aramaic material amongst the finds at Qumran became known, the new evidence was used not for its relevance for the spoken Aramaic of the first century, but for evaluating previous views on the priority of either the Palestinian Targumim or *Targum Onqelos*. Matthew Black's *Aramaic Approach*, for example, argued that Christian Palestinian Aramaic, the Samaritan Targum and the Palestinian Targumim to the Pentateuch – texts from hundreds of years later – were more valuable for understanding first-century Aramaic, than the Qumran Aramaic material, which he regarded as exemplifying old, or classical, Aramaic similar to that found in Daniel–Ezra and the Persian period (Imperial).

From the late 1950s, debates between E. Y. Kutscher and Kahle began to refine questions of method and the appropriate use of Aramaic sources. How are late sources relevant for understanding the first century? Should later sources be given priority over those closer to the time, such as those found at Qumran? What is the relationship between written sources of a given period and the language spoken in that period? Kutscher's analysis of Qumran's *Genesis Apocryphon* showed that its language was different from biblical (and Imperial) Aramaic on the one hand, and later Aramaic on the other hand, and that Nabatean and Palmyrene inscriptions were neither Imperial Aramaic nor fully developed dialects. He concluded that the language of the *Genesis Apocryphon* was a way into understanding the locally spoken Aramaic.

Accepting Kutscher's methods for dating the language, Joseph Fitzmyer (1966) proposed a stage between Imperial Aramaic and the time when Eastern and Western dialects became clear, which he called 'Middle Aramaic' (200 BCE to 200 CE). The Qumran and other contemporary material were now located in a transitional period in which local dialects were beginning to break away from Imperial Aramaic. Fitzmyer's new understanding of the development of the language relegated later texts used previously to establish first-century Palestinian Aramaic to a confirmatory role and enabled him to make several trenchant criticisms of Black's *Aramaic Approach* (third edition) that were subsequently endorsed by others. He called for a radical break with previous methods and suggested that the evidence contemporary with the New Testament become the starting point in this new approach.

In the 1970s, Fitzmyer's position received critique from members of the Kahle school, who now proposed a 'synchronic understanding' of the development, which spoke of the interaction of two concurrent phenomena, the spoken Aramaic which was in progress, and the more rigid imitation of Imperial Aramaic. It also became clear that the same old methods were being used, now to justify the priority of the Palestinian Targumim over Qumran for establishing the spoken language of Jesus. In other words, the lines of the debate were still clearly drawn.

The publication of the Job Targum (11QtgJob) raised more questions by providing a further sample of Aramaic, now written in Herodian (first century CE) script. Was this Aramaic foreign to Qumran or native? And if native, does it reflect a different dialect to that of Galilee, and so of Jesus? Fitzmyer responded to this geographical focus on Qumran Aramaic by drawing in the other evidence for Aramaic in the Roman period (ossuaries, inscriptions, letters, business documents), which is closer to that of Qumran than it is to *Neofiti*, and probably preserves at least some spoken Aramaic. In the light of this evidence, and other considerations, the distinction between written and spoken forms of the language, which had been so strongly maintained in the past, was breaking down.

Even though methods of research and dating criteria have still not been fully worked out, in the 1980s Max Wilcox moved the discussion towards a synthesis by showing that, although Qumran should be the starting point, the later material should not be overlooked. Even if a word, form or phrase is *not* found in the middle period, if it is found in Imperial Aramaic and a western dialect of the later period, then Wilcox argued that it is not rash to suppose that it belonged to the language of Jesus and the earliest Christian communities in Palestine.

Did Jesus speak Hebrew?

Several scholars have maintained that a form of Hebrew was far more significant in Palestine than has been often granted. M. Segal argued that Mishnaic Hebrew was a prominent Jewish vernacular at all social levels from approximately 400 BCE to 150 CE. Segal was followed by T. W. Manson, J. A. Emerton, J. Barr, J. M. Grintz and C. Rabin.

T. W. Manson argued that Jesus was not only well able to speak the 'rabbinic Hebrew', which was used in the scribal schools, but that he actually used it in the polemical settings of the debates with the religious leaders. His extensive knowledge of the Old Testament, his recognition as a rabbi, his exposition in the synagogues (see especially Luke 4:16–20), and the probable eighteen-year-long continuation of the superior questioning he demonstrated when he was twelve, all provide a prima facie case that he knew and used the language of the schools. Positive evidence that he did in fact, comes from the accounts of his polemic with the scribes and Pharisees, as the dispute recorded in Mark 7:1–23 demonstrates nicely. Here Jesus speaks on the same topic (ritual purity) to three different audiences. When Jesus speaks in the Polemical setting (vv. 6–13), he uses three quotations from the Old Testament, numerous technical terms and one transliterated word, *qorban* – the exact term used by the Mishnah – and he then clearly (7:14) re-emerges to a more general setting. Manson argues that this evidence shows that the discussion was carried on in the language of the schools. Thus, just as Jesus clearly used the exegetical methods and the terminology of the rabbinical schools, he also used their 'rabbinic Hebrew'.

At a later date, with the benefits arising from discoveries of further Aramaic documents in the desert of Judea, we now know that Manson's 'rabbinic Hebrew' (that is, an earlier form of the Hebrew of the Mishnah) was probably a language actually spoken in various pockets of first-century Palestine, probably including the schools.

Thus, if the arguments such as those put forward by Manson hold, and Jesus used the Hebrew of the schools in the controversies with the scribes, presumably this would indicate that he had a fairly high level of proficiency to operate in the linguistic context of scholarly debate.

Did Jesus speak Greek?

Given the evidence that some (if not many) were using Greek in first-century Palestine, would Jesus have been among that number? There are several kinds of general arguments that have been used to suggest this likelihood: Greek being the *lingua franca* of the Roman world, and evidence for its presence in Palestine; Galilee was highly influenced by Greek culture; Nazareth was near Sepphoris and the Decapolis, where Hellenisation was strong; he was involved in a trade which brought him into contact with Greek speakers, as would his itinerant ministry; some of his disciples had Greek names and so could have been Greek speakers. Once again, these kinds of arguments are 'circumstantial' rather than probative, and, as Chancey has warned, several of them (such as the alleged Hellenisation of first-century Galilee) have too often been argued without due attention to dating and provenance of the various pieces of evidence.

As for positive evidence, Porter has developed several new criteria in an attempt to evaluate whether any of the sayings of Jesus were originally delivered in Greek. The three criteria give attention to the Greek language and sound linguistic methodology: the criterion of Greek language in its context; the criterion of Greek textual variance; the criterion of discourse features. As is usual with criteria of authenticity, these three criteria work as a group. Once the criterion of Greek language and context opens up the possibility that one of Jesus' sayings was originally spoken in Greek, then the other two can be applied in an attempt to establish an even greater probability.

When these criteria are applied, Porter concludes that there are at least five episodes in the Gospels which point to the conclusion that Jesus knew Greek. In three of these passages (Mark 7:24–30; John 12:20–28; Matt 8:5–13 = Luke 7:2–10), the criteria are not sufficient to demonstrate the actual wording of Jesus, but Porter is convinced that the scenarios and the linguistic characteristics suggest that on these occasions also Jesus spoke Greek. In the conversation at Caesarea Philippi, it is likely, if not probable, that Matt 16:13–20 records the Greek words of Jesus. Jesus' trial before Pilate provides the fifth and strongest case (Mark 15:2–5; Matt 27:11–14; Luke 23:2–5; John 18:29–38). Here, there is no indication of a translator being present, although it is unreasonable to think that Pilate spoke Aramaic, or that he and Jesus conducted a conversation in Latin, and when Porter applies his criteria he concludes that, although the exchange is not lengthy, it probably preserves the actual words (*ipsissima verba*) of Jesus.

If Jesus spoke Greek, then, of course, the likelihood increases that we have some of the actual words of Jesus recorded in the Gospels. The difficulty would be in the demonstration. What studies could help to differentiate between the Greek of Jesus' sayings and the Greek of the gospel writer? John Lee has contributed an interesting study in this regard, in which he argues that the Greek of Jesus' sayings is of a higher register at points than that of Mark (and Matthew)'s narrative itself. The fact that the features that he deals with are foreign to Aramaic (and Hebrew), and that their usage runs against that of the Evangelist, strongly indicates that they were already embedded in the sayings in the form received by the Evangelist. Although Lee agrees that it is difficult to know whether this phenomenon originated with Jesus, or whether it was incorporated into his sayings by someone who thought a higher formality to be appropriate to the Messiah, if the former then this would indicate that Jesus not only spoke Greek but spoke it well.

Conclusion

Thus, although our Gospels are preserved in Greek, and although the argumentation is necessarily 'finely tuned,' scholars have been reasonably happy to conclude that Jesus taught mostly in Aramaic. Although perhaps not accepted by all, the case has also been made that, on occasion, he also conducted himself in Hebrew, and also in Greek. It is probably fair to say that proponents of the various positions have generally been confident to use the traces of the three languages to point to the *ipsissima vox Jesu*, but they have generally been more cautious in using the language criteria to identify the *ipsissima verba Jesu*. The likelihood of his actual words being preserved increases to the degree that the Gospel writers were faithful servants of the Jesus tradition. With due care to good historical argument, attention to the languages of first-century Palestine in general and Jesus in particular still holds great potential for Historical Jesus Research and for the quest for the *ipsissima verba Jesu*.

PETER G. BOLT

Further reading

Black, M. *An Aramaic Approach to the Gospels and Acts*, Peabody, MA: Hendrickson, 1946, 1967³.

Calvert, D. G. A. "An Examination of the Criteria for Distinguishing the Authentic Words of Jesus," *NTS* 18 (1971) 209–18.

Chancey, M. A. *Greco-Roman Culture and the Galilee of Jesus*, SNTSMS 134, Cambridge: Cambridge University Press, 2005.

Dalman, G. *The Words of Jesus*, Edinburgh: T. & T. Clark, 1902.

Fitzmyer, J. A. *The Semitic Background of the New Testament. Combined Edition of Essays on the Semitic Background of the New Testament and A Wandering Aramean: Collected Aramaic Essays*, Grand Rapids, MI: Eerdmans, 1997 [1971 and 1979]).

Jeremias, J. *The Prayers of Jesus*, trans. J. Bowden and J. Reumann, SBT second series 6, London: SCM Press, 1967 [German, 1966].

—— *New Testament Theology*, trans. J. Bowden, London: SCM Press, 1971 [German, 1971]).

Lee, J. "Some Features of the Speech of Jesus in Mark's Gospel," *NovT* 27:1 (1985) 1–26.

Manson, T. W. *The Teaching of Jesus. Studies in its Form and Content*, Cambridge: Cambridge University Press, 1943.

Meier, J. P. *A Marginal Jew. Rethinking the Historical Jesus. Vol. 1: The Roots of the Problem and the Person*, ABRL, New York: Doubleday, 1991.

Porter, S. E. *The Criteria for Authenticity in Historical-Jesus Research. Previous Discussion and New Proposals*, JSNTSup 191, Sheffield: Sheffield Academic Press, 2000.

Rydbeck, L. "The Language of the New Testament," *TynB* 49:2 (1998) 361–68.

Stuckenbruck, L. T. "An Approach to the New Testament through Aramaic Sources: The Recent Methodological Debate," *JSP* 9 (1991) 3–29.

Torrey, C. C. "The Aramaic of the Gospels," in S. E. Porter (ed.) *The Language of the New Testament. Classic Essays*, JSNTSup 60, Sheffield: Sheffield Academic Press, 1991, pp. 98–111.

ARCHAEOLOGY AND JESUS

Discussion of Jesus in archaeological terms has traditionally been conducted in terms of artifacts that may be related to his life. Recent discoveries feature within that traditional consideration. Important as they are, however, they will only take up one part of this article. The second part deals with the profound influence that cultural archaeology has exerted on critical consideration of Jesus.

Recent discoveries

A first-century ossuary, discovered outside Jerusalem in 1968, contains the bones of a young man named Yochanan. An iron spike with an attached piece of wood is embedded in his right heel. The nail had been driven into a hard knot of olive wood, and could not be removed as the others evidently were. Properly tending to the dead was incumbent on Israelites, and any Roman official would court rebellion by deliberately flouting that imperative. The prefect of Jerusalem must have released Yochanan's broken body for burial: his ossuary indicates that the Romans honored Israelite concerns, even in cases involving crucifixion. Following ancient practice, those who received Yochanan's crucified corpse bathed and anointed it, wrapping the body in linen, and placing it in a funeral cave. According to usual burial practice, they deposited the bones in a limestone box after a year, and carved Yochanan's name on the ossuary's side.

This discovery contradicts the claim, fashionable among a minority of scholars since the suggestion of Alfred Loisy more than a century ago, that Jesus' body was tossed to the dogs or otherwise desecrated after his execution. Yet foundational texts of Judaism give precise instructions for dealing with corpses from crucifixion (see Deut 21:22–23; the document from the Dead Sea called 11Q64:11–13; Josephus, *Life* 421; *m. Sanhedrin* 6:5–6); a dead body that was exposed was a source of impurity and offended God. Yochanan's ossuary confirms that these concerns were honored even in cases of crucifixion.

Nonetheless, mourners in antiquity were not squeamish. Death's impurity had to be dealt with, and people accepted the temporary uncleanness of handling the corpse in order to assure the purity of the land and the community of Israel. The Babylonian Talmud (in an additional tractate, *Ebel Rabbati* 8:1) describes, not only practices of cleaning, anointing, and wrapping the dead, but also the custom of visiting the tomb each day for three days after a burial, to make certain that the deceased was truly dead, not simply unconscious. The story of the resuscitation of Lazarus in John 11:1–44 presupposes such a custom.

Another discovery of an ossuary has implications for the location of Jesus' burial. In 1990, a bulldozer took the top off a cave 1.5 miles south of Mt Zion, uncovering a mausoleum. An adult, even a short adult, could not have stood erect in the cave, but a pit had been dug near its entrance to allow mourners to stand while tending to their dead and praying. Corpses were laid out on a shelf, and after the flesh had decomposed, the bones were gathered and stored. Bone-storage for the anonymous poor was in a pit dug in the cave's floor, while the bones of wealthy, prominent people were kept in small limestone ossuaries which were placed in the shafts that ran outward from the central cave like spokes.

One such ossuary had the name of Caiaphas carved roughly into its sides. The name is carved roughly into the side and back of the ossuary, written in both Aramaic and Hebrew, and in the full form, "Joseph bar Cayapha," which Josephus attests was this high priest's whole name (see *Ant.* 18:35, 95). A coin discovered in the cave is dated 42/43 CE (during the reign of Herod Agrippa I). If – as seems overwhelmingly probable, given all the facts – the ossuary were for Caiaphas the high priest, he would have been about sixty when he died (*c*. 46). Inside the ossuary marked with Caiaphas' name, the bones of a man aged around sixty years old were indeed found, along with the bones of an adult female, two infants, a small child and a young adult. Death apparently came to them all from natural causes. The ossuary's elegant carving distinguishes it from most ossuaries of that place and period. It is carved with a pattern of five floral designs, for the most part in spirals, arranged around a central, spiraling flower. The palm design that surrounds the circles on Caiaphas' ossuary picks up a motif in the Temple's decoration. Placed in the tunnel to the south of the cave, his ossuary was in fact oriented to face that Temple. His status, and his connection to the Temple, the preeminent sacred place in Judaism, is attested by this find, and the ossuary is an eloquent witness of Judaism in the first century: a vibrant religion, centered on the Temple and passionately devoted to the worship of God through sacrifice in that holy place.

Joseph from Arimathea, a Sanhedrin rabbi, requested Jesus' body from Pilate and arranged for its burial (Mark 15:42–46; Matt 27:57–60; Luke 23:50–54). In John's Gospel, another rabbi, Nicodemus, lends a hand with the arrangements (John 19:38–42), and that seems plausible. Joseph's newly hewn cave was probably not far from the site of Caiaphas' family mausoleum on the hillside south of the Temple. Scores of burial caves from the first century of the kind that Joseph prepared for Jesus are visible there today. This probable location of Jesus' grave contradicts over fifteen hundred years of pious geography. During the fourth century the Church of the Holy Sepulcher was built, allegedly under the guidance of providential discoveries, just outside the walls of Byzantine Jerusalem (see Eusebius, *Vit. Const.* 3.25–40). Christians venerate the site to this day, and different denominations compete fiercely for control of the space inside, but there is no evidence of a first-century Jewish cemetery there. The site was likely within the walls of the city at the time Jesus died: exactly where a cemetery would contradict the Torah. Further, Jesus' burial must have taken place far enough away from the city to permit the initial visions at the tomb described by the Gospels to be as private as they are described. Abu Tor better meets these conditions than Constantine's Church of the Holy Sepulcher.

Archaeology opens new perspectives on Jesus' place of birth as well as on the place of his burial. The Hebrew Bible itself mentions a Bethlehem far to the north of Jerusalem, assigned to Zebulun (Josh 19:15), and in John 7:41–42 some apparently well-informed skeptics resist the idea that Jesus is messiah, on the grounds that he comes from Galilee and not from Davidic Bethlehem. In Hebrew the name means "house of bread," designating a settlement with mills capable of producing fine flour, rather than the coarse grade most people used for their daily needs. During the nineteenth century, this *Galilean* Bethlehem, also mentioned in the Talmud, attracted considerable attention, but the issue remained whether it could have been a Judaic settlement at the time of Jesus' birth. The Talmud was composed centuries after Jesus lived, so one cannot assume it accurately reflects ancient Galilee's geography. Now, however, archaeological excavations show that Bethlehem in Galilee is a first-century site just seven miles from Nazareth; what were once reasonable reservations can be laid to rest. There is good reason to surmise that the Bethlehem which Matthew and Luke remember, dimly and distantly (and through the lenses of scripture and legend) was actually in Galilee. With the evidence of excavation reports, an idea from the nineteenth century crosses the threshold of probability.

Matthew 1:18 provides us with a clue to why Jesus' parents were in Galilean Bethlehem in the first place. Had Joseph been domiciled there, that would explain both why Mary's pregnancy in Nazareth was a scandal, and why Joseph took her away from Nazareth to Bethlehem for Jesus' birth. (Such a change of site is, of course, much more plausible than having Joseph and Mary traveling to Judea for the birth, a journey of 100 miles which would have violated the custom of keeping a wife near her homeland, mentioned in Ketuboth 13:10 in the Mishnah.) The conditions of Jesus' conception as Matthew refers to them made him a *mamzer* in the eyes of Mary's neighbors in Nazareth – that is, an Israelite with an unknown father, because his parents were not residing together at the time of conception. Pressed into the caste apart which being a *mamzer* (or "silenced one," *shetuqi*, as the Mishnah later called such a person) made him, Jesus from the beginning of his life negotiated the treacherous terrain between belonging to Israel and the experience of ostracism within his own community. The aspirations of a restored Israel can only have been particularly poignant to those branded with the reputation of *mamzerut*.

Jewish Galilee

Well-researched work during the past twenty years has concluded that first-century Galilee accommodated a thriving Jewish rural culture as well as urban culture supported by the Roman occupation, that urbanization was influential but not ambient, and that the hypothesis of a "Cynic" Jesus, or an otherwise Hellenized portrait of him, is quite implausible.

Overall, Israelite settlement of Galilee shows a dip after the Assyrian conquest during the eighth century BCE, with some repopulation beginning in the Persian period. Hasmonean rule then brought substantial population growth with markers of Jewish identity such as stone vessels, *miqvaoth*, absence of pork bones, and secondary burial with ossuaries, so that by the early Roman period Judaism appears to have permeated rural Galilee.

Josephus' references to Galileans' militancy, including violence in the Temple, is explicable against this background and provides insight into Jesus' attitude toward, and actions in, Jerusalem. Many Galilean Jews evidently welcomed the Hasmoneans, and then resisted Herod the Great and Antipas. Within a largely illiterate society, genealogy and religion were primary tools for constructing social awareness, and reached their most vivid and public expression in sacrifice within the Temple, where the conduct of ritual therefore became a Galilean concern.

Urbanization was a key concept for the study of Jesus and Galilee during the 1980s, when Capernaum's population was estimated at 25,000, and a facile assumption equated urbanization with Hellenization. Sepphoris was indeed a consumer city in relation to Roman culture, because it was a garrison town, but there is no evidence it was a beacon of Greco-Roman philosophy, or drew Jewish teachers to mimic Hellenistic teachers. In any case, estimates of population should not be based upon ancient numbers or the size of public buildings (both of which were subject to notorious exaggeration), but by measuring the extent of habitation and assessing the density of residence.

Ostia and Pompeii are good indices of comparison, owing to their unusual extent of both preservation and excavation. The population of Ostia has been estimated at 30,000 and Pompeii's at between 8,000 and 12,000. Analogy with Pompeii would yield a population of 8,000–12,000 for Sepphoris during the first century, smaller and poorer than Caesarea Maritima and Scythopolis. Recent work has also cautioned against the tendency of attributing major urban status to settlements during the first century that only emerged as cities from the second century onward, as a result of changes in Roman policy and extensions of its road system after the Bar Kokhba revolt. Herodian Tiberias, founded in 18–19 CE, probably accommodated between 6,000 and 12,000 inhabitants. In contrast to philo-Roman enclaves, Capernaum's maximum population was a couple of thousand and Nazareth's a couple of hundred, more like a service town and a peasant hamlet respectively than cities.

Asking about the impact of Sepphoris on Galilee is within the purview of cultural archaeology, although some researchers have dismissed as "psychological" the question of whether Jesus had contact with the city. But the issue of what is psychological has become badly confused in the study of the New Testament. Psychology properly concerns individual factors that influence a person's emotional adjustments, and usually requires a case history. That is to be distinguished from self-consciousness, as in "the messianic consciousness of Jesus." The latter was a chimera of the last turn of the century, and has become conflated with psychology in scholarly jargon. Yet both psychology and self-consciousness are to be distinguished from development, which involves inferences from observable actions or contacts. In this case, if one could settle the issue of Jesus and Sepphoris, that would impinge on the issue of his development, quite aside from psychology or self-consciousness. But the issue is moot, because there is so little evidence. Still, it does seem clear that during his ministry Jesus avoided Sepphoris and Tiberias for a political reason: the enmity of Herod Antipas.

The indigenous fishing economies of towns such as Capernaum and Magdala, on the other hand, served Jesus well in providing a base for his activity much more consonant with the Israelite culture of rural Galilee than Roman settlements such as Sepphoris and Tiberias. Nonetheless, both Capernaum and Magdala had natural contacts with Itureans, Syro-Phoenicians, and the Decapolis, as well as with Tiberias after its foundation by Herod Antipas.

Once fishing and trade are seen as remunerative, certain other features of Capernaum become explicable. There is evidence of primitive locking mechanisms on doors, and remnants of decorated vessels and glass. Although a permanently deployed garrison in Capernaum is not attested, any increase of trade could well have brought greater contact with people such as the centurion (Matt 8:5–13; Luke 7:1–10) as compared to Nazareth. That same wealth that is also decried in "Q" (Luke 6:20, 24; Matt 5:3) probably came to Jesus' notice in Capernaum, where movable wealth was on display.

Disagreement among archaeologists is sometimes used as an excuse not to refer to them in exegetical, historical, and interpretative studies. But any discipline, by virtue of being critical, will involve differing judgments. If that is so, however, perhaps archaeologists would be well advised to tolerate disagreement among exegetes as they do among their colleagues. Dialog across the spectrum of relevant ancient texts with archaeological work should prove to continue being productive.

BRUCE CHILTON

Further reading

Arav, Rami and John J. Rousseau *Jesus and His World*, Minneapolis, MI: Fortress Press, 1995.
Chilton, Bruce. *Rabbi Jesus. An Intimate Biography*, New York: Doubleday, 2000.
Edwards, Douglas R. and C. Thomas McCollough (eds) *Archaeology and the Galilee. Texts and Contexts in the Graeco-Roman and Byzantine Periods*, South Florida Studies in the History of Judaism 143, Atlanta, GA: Scholars Press, 1997.

Evans, Craig. *Jesus and the Ossuaries*, Waco, TX: Baylor University Press, 2003.
Greenhut, Zvi. "Burial Cave of the Caiaphas Family," *BAR* 18:5 (1992) 29–26, 76.
Hanson, K. C. and Douglas E. Oakman. *Palestine in the Time of Jesus. Social Structures and Social Conflicts*, Minneapolis, MN: Fortress Press, 1998.
Horbury, William. "The 'Caiaphas' Ossuaries and Joseph Caiaphas," *PEQ* 126 (1994) 32–48.
Horsley, Richard A. *Archaeology, History and Society in Galilee. The Social Context of Jesus and the Rabbis*, Valley Forge, PA: Trinity Press International, 1995.
Oshri, Aviram. "Where was Jesus Born?" *Archaeology* 58:6 (2005) 42–45.
Reed, Jonathan L. *Archaeology and the Galilean Jesus. A Re-examination of the Evidence*, Harrisburg, PA: Trinity Press International, 2000.
Sawicki, Marianne. *Crossing Galilee. Architectures of Contact in the Occupied Land of Jesus*, Harrisburg, PA: Trinity Press International, 2000.

ARCHAEOLOGY OF GALILEE AND JUDEA

The territorial limits of Galilee

Galilee is the northern part of Israel that borders with ancient Tyre. It extends as far south as the Jezreel Valley, and in some historical periods it included the Jezreel, but not always. The Galilee of the Hasmoneans, particularly under Aristobulus from 104/3 BCE, seemed to have a northern border that extended northeast from the walled city of Acco and across the Jordan towards Paneas. This line is more or less established archaeologically by the distribution of Hasmonean coinage south of the line. North of the Sea of Galilee the line between Galilee and Lebanon and Iturea extended to the northwest from Keren Naphtali to Cadasa and on to Kh. ed-Duweir in modern Lebanon, all three of which feature pagan temples. The southern extent of Galilee was defined by the Great Plain, called the Jezreel Valley in the Bible. Thus Galilee followed the coast from Mt Carmel north to Acco. It extended east to the Sea of Galilee and the Jordan Valley. Thus Galilee was a small, thickly forested region of roughly 40 by 40 miles in the northern hill country of Hellenistic and Roman Judea.

Archaeological survey in the eastern part of Upper and Lower Galilee north of the Tiberias–Sepphoris road reveals that a large number of settlements appeared near the end of the second century BCE. There were suddenly large numbers of villages were none had existed before, both in the valleys and in the mountains. Even areas that were not so promising agriculturally were settled, which may imply that the villagers relied on other methods of income generation such as weaving, manufacturing, or trade. These villages were about twice the area of earlier settlements and were not fortified. Security was evidently not yet a problem.

With the advent of the Romans in 63 BCE the northwestern border of Galilee changed. The border shifted about 6 miles southeast, parallel to the old line. There is some archaeological evidence for Jewish abandonment of northern villages, perhaps from conflicts with non-Jewish neighbors. From 40 BCE Galilee formed part of Herod's kingdom. This was the Galilee of Jesus and the one ruled by Herod Antipas from 4 BCE to 39 CE. The capital of Galilee was Sepphoris until the founding of Tiberias in about 19 BCE. The other important towns were Arab (Gk. Gabara), Magdala (Gk. Taricheae), and Gush Halav (Gk. Gischala).

Population

In the late Hellenistic period most of Galilee was settled with small villages and only one city, namely Sepphoris. Some of these villages were occupied by transient populations. The westernmost parts of Galilee were settled by Phoenicians. The eastern part of Upper Galilee was settled by remnants of earlier populations and eventually Iturians, whom Jonathan Maccabaeus conquered in 105 BCE. Jonathan annexed part of their kingdom to his own and converted those under his rule to Judaism. The proper names on the *bullae* or seal impressions of the second century BCE unearthed at the administrative center of Cadasa in eastern Upper Galilee show that the local population had affinities with that of Tyre and Sidon.

The archaeology of Hellenistic Galilee shows use of a common pottery, called Galilean Coarse Ware, which is very similar everywhere it is found. It is virtually the hallmark of the indigenous, pre-Jewish population. Many stamped jar handles of foreign manufacture testify to an extensive trade with Mediterranean cities for their wines.

Nevertheless, the story told in 1 Macc 5:14–24 seems to imply that there was a small and weak population of Jews in western Lower Galilee around Arbatta. The neighbors to the Jews appear as "Ptolemais, Tyre, Sidon, and all the foreigners of Galilee" (1 Macc 5:15).

According to excavations in the burned and abandoned Hellenistic city of Beth Shean (Tell Iztaba), John Hyrcanus I attacked Beth Shean (and thus Galilee) as early as 108 BCE. Aristobulus is given the credit for adding Galilee to the Hasmonean kingdom in 105/4 BCE. The Hasmonean or

Maccabean conquest of Galilee resulted in migration of Jews from Judea and conversion of the local populations. Thus the population of the Galilee bloomed from the help and encouragement of the Hasmoneans. Many towns, villages, and hamlets were founded in the Hasmonean period (see above).

That the late Hellenistic population was indeed Jewish tends to be confirmed by the excavation of ritual baths within houses in Keren Naphtali, Tiberias, Sepphoris, Khirbet Shema', Jotapata, Gamla of the Golan Heights, and other sites. Further confirmation of the Jewish population is given by the find of hundreds of chalk stone vessels, which are not subject to impurity according to the Mishnah. These are also part of the material culture of Jewish homes. There was even a manufacturing center near ancient Abila of Galilee a few miles east of Sepphoris. These chalk stone vessels are to be found everywhere in the Galilee and the Golan Heights, following the Jewish population. There is also a surprisingly low (for some scholars) presence of pig bones in sites otherwise replete with ritual baths and stone vessels.

Pre-Maccabean religion

The diversity of local religion is revealed in the finds of various figurines from cultic worship. For example, at ancient Beersheba (north) at the east end of the Beth Ha-kerem Valley of Lower Galilee there were found figurines that reflected a mixture of imported deities: Aphrodite, Apis, and the infant Horus. The last two are Egyptian. A small pagan temple existed on the south slopes of Mt Meiron at the junction of Upper and Lower Galilee. Other figurines include the Egyptian deities of Isis and Osiris. A pagan altar of the period was unearthed at Bar' am in Upper Galilee. Hellenistic Galilean inscriptions name several deities: "the mighty God at Dan," Astarte in Upper Galilee near the border with Lebanon, Hamon and Astarte in northwestern Upper Galilee, and Tanit and Baal-Shamim at Cadasa (biblical Qedesh). Excavations at Cadasa show that the city was an important administrative and religious center, finally destroyed by Judah Maccabee in 145 BCE.

Columbaria for raising pigeons have been found in at least eight sites in the Galilee, including one at Khirbet Cana. These are usually interpreted as supporting the worship of Astarte or Aphrodite, whose names we have already encountered in inscriptions.

Hellenistic Galilee was encircled by large, Hellenized cities, namely the city-territory of Tyre to the northwest, Acco-Ptolemais to the west, Hippos-Susitha on the southeastern shores of the Sea of Galilee, and Beth Shean-Scythopolis further south in the Jordan Valley. Within Hellenistic Galilee fortified sites offered protection to the local population. At least ten of these fortifications have been identified so far.

Somewhere around the end of the second century BCE, glass-blowing was invented, some believe in western Galilee, which revolutionized the use of this material in households. The new, much cheaper glass vessels for oils, perfumes, medicines, make-up, and other personal needs spread throughout the Galilee in cities, towns, and villages.

The coming of Rome

When Pompey and his Roman legions entered Jerusalem in 63 BCE, a new era began in Judea, Samaria, and Galilee. Now Judea was a client kingdom next to the new Roman province of Syria. The presence of Roman culture is mainly visible architecturally in cities. Buildings modeled after Roman structures became pervasive from the time of Herod the Great, who was elected King of the Jews by the Roman Senate in 40 BCE. In fact, it was Herod who altered the architectural landscape in the Roman direction by building theaters, amphitheaters, palaces, baths, the city of Caesarea, its harbor Sebaste, temples to Augustus, the Second Temple in Jerusalem, and nine fortresses in the country, all of which were patterned more after Rome than on local Syrian or Nabatean models. None of these was built in Galilee, with the possible exception of Gabaa at the western end (the entrance) of the Plain of Jezreel and Herod's royal estates.

Synagogues dotted the landscape in Galilee, according to the gospels. We have archaeological evidence only for the Capernaum synagogue, where excavations have brought to light a black basalt first-century synagogue beneath the white limestone later synagogue. Across the Sea of Galilee in the Golan Heights at Gamla a second nearby synagogue has been excavated.

At the death of Herod the Great about 4 BCE, Galilee became one of the partitions of Herod's kingdom. It was assigned to Herod's son Antipas, who also ruled the trans-Jordanian territory of Peraea. At his death the Galilean city of Sepphoris revolted. It was destroyed in punishment by the Romans. Antipas had the razed site rebuilt as a showcase city, employing thousands of craftsmen in Galilee. Sepphoris had streets at right angles, municipal buildings, an aqueduct and reservoir, and a theater. Antipas founded and built the city

of Tiberias on the southwestern shores of the Sea of Galilee about 19 CE, again giving employment to thousands. Tiberias became his capital, until that title reverted to Sepphoris under Nero. Herod adorned Tiberias with public buildings, a stadium, a large synagogue, and a palace for himself (*Life* 65). Tiberias also had streets intersecting at right angles in Hippodamian plan.

Apparently the populations of Galilee lived prosperous lives. The wine and oil industries blossomed, as archaeological discoveries tend to confirm. In fact, wine presses are found in archaeological survey on most of the hilltops of the Galilee. Huge olive presses for the mass production of olive oil are found in ancient villages, sometimes in caves, a security measure. Villages and hamlets were to be found everywhere, though archaeologically they were founded with the Hasmonean occupation. Single farmsteads are also known. Excavations show us that some villages devoted most of their energies to manufacturing a single commodity. For example, at least three villages devoted their collective efforts to the manufacture of pottery vessels. At least one village produced glassware. Another village produced jewelry. Probably other villages were devoted to a single commodity, as the name of the village of Hittaya ("wheat") suggests.

These hamlets, villages, towns, and cities were enmeshed in a network of paths and roads that constituted a trade network. By the first century some of the roads with the heaviest traffic were paved with thick plaster, but not yet with stone. By the second century CE, Galilee was crossed from Acco to Sepphoris to Tiberias, from Acco to Capernaum, and from Caesarea to Sepphoris by Roman Imperial roads. In the first century the same network pertained, but it was not yet converted to Imperial dimensions. Much narrower roads and paths connected village to village, but all served the donkey caravans, as well as the single peddler with his donkeyload of goods. There were great marketplaces in Tiberias and Sepphoris, as yet not found. By this trade network the village of Kfar Hanania, for example, could distribute its pottery over all Galilee and into the Golan Heights. The citizens of Sepphoris used mostly pottery of Kfar Hanania. The local Galilean trade network was connected to the international trade network in the Mediterranean in the first century CE, as indicated by the excavation of trade goods from as far away as Italy and Egypt at the interior sites of Galilee.

Almost all the population of the Roman period was Jewish, as attested by the same evidence as from the late Hellenistic or Hasmonean period. Ritual baths have been found in many localities, as well as chalk stone vessels. When the Second Temple was destroyed in 70 CE, the twenty-four priestly courses fled northwards to twenty-four Jewish villages in Galilee, including Jotapata, Sepphoris, and Nazareth. These three localities yield archaeological evidence for Jewish occupation of the type mentioned above.

Valuable information about economic conditions and burial customs is found in the archaeology of tombs connected with villages and towns. Most Jews appear to have been buried in tombs with a few keepsakes, but without embalming, an Egyptian custom. Women were often buried wearing bronze jewelry, but not gold or silver, as found in non-Jewish tombs. Skeletal remains suggest that the Galileans were robust and healthy, but males often died in their forties of a simple infection or accident. Most commonly, women died of childbirth complications in their thirties or even earlier. Of course, a few lived to a ripe old age, as witness Anna daughter of Phanuel of the Tribe of Asher, whom Luke knew to be eighty-four (Luke 2:37).

Information about daily life abounds from archaeological excavations. For example, the find of spindle whorls and loom weights in many Galilean sites indicates that spinning, weaving, and the production of clothing was an ordinary part of daily life. Cisterns within houses show care at impounding water during the rainy season so as to have enough during the summer dry season. Cisterns also are found in the ancient fields. Many dwellings excavated at many sites attest to living that ranged from the simple and modest to the wealthy. Often, work rooms or storage rooms were cut in the soft stone beneath the floors of houses, as at ancient Sepphoris and Nazareth. Pottery kilns are known from ancient sites such as Jotapata, attesting to pottery manufacture in a site not known for pottery in the ancient literature. Daily pottery shows us that cooking took place on hot ashes in cooking pots.

Coins are found everywhere, demonstrating that the economy was not merely based on barter. Coins of the Late Hellenistic and Roman periods in Galilee begin with issues of the Hasmonean or Maccabean rulers and some Greek Seleucid rulers. The most common of these issues are of King Alexander Jannaeus (103–76 BCE), though coins of this diameter (about one inch) were minted also by the Roman Procurators after 6 CE. The Jewish coins stayed in circulation for many years and are often understood to be the "widow's mite" (the lepton) of Mark 12:41–44 and Luke 21:1–4.

Second are coins of Herod and his son Herod Antipas. The coins of Herod the Great (37–4 BCE) are of poor bronze. The dated coins are all from "year three." This is understood to be 37 BCE, since this coin was calculated from his election by the Roman Senate, not from his accession. The legends read "Of Herod the King" in Greek. The emblems on his coins were the tripod, the censer, caduceus, pomegranate, shield, helmet, *aphlaston* or stern of an ancient galley, the galley itself, palm branch, anchor, double and single cornucopia, and eagle. The eagle is the only emblem that contravenes a biblical commandment. The coins of Herod Antipas also served economic and political purposes. They are all issues of poor bronze and bear the Greek legend "Herod the Tetrarch." They show a wreath on one side and a palm branch on the other. The largest denomination is about 5/8 inch in diameter and was minted in Tiberias. They bear a year of issue, which is a number counting from the first year of his reign (4 BCE). The third type is city coins of Tiberias and other cities of the region, which are generally heavier and better struck than the previous examples. The earliest coin struck at Tiberias bears the date from the twenty-fourth year of the reign of Antipas, therefore 19/20 CE. The emblems on his coins are the reed, the palm branch, a bunch of dates, and a palm tree. There are no images of humans or animals. Three denominations can be distinguished. On the reverse one sees a wreath around the word "Tiberias" in Greek.

Excavations from many localities in Galilee have advanced our understanding of life in the Galilee of Jesus. These excavations are most notably at Sepphoris, Tiberias, Nazareth, Capernaum, Cadasa, Magdala, Cana, Kefar Kenna, Beth Shean-Scythopolis, Gush Halav (Gischala in Josephus), and other localities.

Unfortunately inscriptions are not common in Galilee so far, though we have the evidence of coins and two lead weights. The lead weight from Tiberias bears an inscription in Greek that identifies the ruler as "Herod the Tetrarch" and the market official (Agoranomos) as a certain Gaius Julius, a Latin name. The lead weight from Sepphoris identifies the Agoranomos and perhaps his assistant as "Simon son of Aionos and Justus." Simon and Aionos are Hebrew names and Justus is Latin.

Judea from Cyrus to Aristobulus – the territorial limits of Judea

The name Judea (sometimes spelled "Judaea") is derived from Hebrew "Yudah," the Old Testament tribe. Sometimes it appears to mean a political entity, but sometimes it appears simply to mean an area around Jerusalem.

After the conquest of Babylon in 539 BCE, Cyrus the Great, the Persian king, announced a new policy of allowing various ethnic populations deported by the Babylonians to return to their original homes. This story is told in Ezra and Nehemia. The name of the Jewish administrative unit belonging to the fifth Persian Satrapy was written as "Yehud" in Hebrew on Persian coins. Yehud was governed by a high priest and a Council of Elders (Ezra 6:7).

This province was quite small, judging from the archaeological evidence of storage jars with "Yehud" stamped on their handles and of "Yehud" coins. It included Jerusalem as its capital. Thus Yehud was confined to an area that extended from Ein Gedi on the west shores of the Dead Sea to Azekah west-southwest of Jerusalem and returning east to Jericho at the Jordan River. That is a space about 50 miles east–west and perhaps 30 miles north–south.

After the outbreak of the Maccabean Revolt in 165 BCE, control of Yehud passed into Jewish hands. As the Maccabee brothers pushed northward, they expanded their control to include Samaria and Galilee, but at first not the coastal cities. Yehud the political entity was still confined to an area around Jerusalem. Only under Simon, beginning about 142 BCE, did the coastal plain become Jewish again. The expansion of the territory of the Hasmonean kings is correlated with the distribution of their coins to the north, south, and west of Jerusalem.

The Hasmonean kings re-established the Temple Mount in Jerusalem with almost no alterations. It was a square, raised platform 861 feet on a side. The eastern side of this platform is today's eastern wall of the temple platform.

Judea expanded again with the conquests of John Hyrcanus I, who added Idumean territory to the south. He expanded Judea westward from 126 until his death in 104 BCE to include Jamnia, Joppa, and Apollonia and annexed Samaria and Galilee in the north. Thus by 63 BCE the kingdom included the regions of Idumea, Judea, Samaria, and Galilee, not to mention the trans-Jordan regions of Moabitis, Galaaditis, and Gaulana.

Population

From the ancient literary sources we can deduce that a Jewish population lived in and around Jerusalem in the pre-Maccabean period. For example,

from the Zenon Papyri, found in Egypt in 1915, we learn of a powerful Jewish family that ruled their own territory east of the Jordan in the third century BCE, the Tobiads. This name appears in a public, Hebrew inscription near Amman in Jordan and also in Ezra and Nehemia and on an ostracon from Lachish. There was a growing tension between the Greek religious practices of the Ptolemies of Egypt and the Seleucids of the East, on the one hand (both of whom claimed Judea at one time or another), and the Jews on the other. This tension grew to guerilla warfare at the outbreak of the Maccabean Revolt against Antiochus IV Epiphanes and the Seleucid Greeks in 165 BCE. Under the Maccabees, the Idumean or old Edomite populations south of Judea were converted to Judaism and annexed to Judea. Archaeological survey in the area south of Jerusalem shows that the number of Hasmonean Jewish villages increased about 35 percent over the previous period. This pattern of advancing numbers of Jewish villages continued in the first centuries BCE and CE under the Romans, when the number of villages increased another 16 percent over the populated area of the Hasmonean period.

From about 50 BCE. it is possible to detect the Jewish population from material culture, namely from the presence of chalk stone vessels in houses and public buildings. A manufacturing center has been found at Biblical Anathoth north of Jerusalem. Another such center stems from Jerusalem itself. About the same time, tomb architecture emerges in and around Jerusalem with floral decoration in low relief on the facade. A bit earlier one sees the construction of memorials on the surface above the tombs for leading families. The most famous are "Absalom's Pillar" and the "Tomb of Zachariah" in the Kidron Valley. A Hebrew inscription on "Absalom's Pillar" identifies the tomb as belonging to the "Sons of Hezir." Reburial in soft, chalk bone boxes or ossuaries is a Jewish practice in Judea especially from about the second half of the first century BCE to the middle of the second century CE.

Judea as Roman territory

In 65 BCE the Roman general Pompey sent his associate M. Scaurus to Syria with his legions, where Scaurus heard of a civil war in the independent Kingdom of Judea. The two royal claimants to Judea in this war were Aristobulus and John Hyrcanus II. They both appealed to Pompey, who eventually marched south to lay siege to Jerusalem. The Pharisees and most of the leading families of

Jerusalem supported Hyrcanus, and they opened the gates of the city to Pompey, who promptly laid siege to the Temple Mount where the Sadducees and Aristobulus had withdrawn. The Temple area fell to the Romans on "the fast day" (Yom Kippur?), and Pompey and his men entered the Sanctuary and the Holy of Holies. Rome was in Judea to stay.

The Romans reduced Jewish territory by annexing a series of cities to Syria, notably Scythopolis (Beth Shean) and Samaria inland and all the coastal cities from Dora south to Gaza. About 55 BCE the Roman Legate Gabinius divided the Jewish territory into three administrative districts: Judea, Samaria, and Galilee. Antipater, a Roman citizen and governor of Idumea to the south, was made procurator of all Judea. He installed his son Phasael as governor of Judea in the south and his son Herod as governor of Galilee in the north. Both were Roman citizens.

Herod the son of Antipater, also called Herod the Great, became a client king of the Romans in 40 BCE. The Romans called this territory the Kingdom of Judea (Greek "Ioudaia," Latin "Judaea"). His building projects changed the landscape of ancient Judea, making it even more like an integral part of the Roman Empire. He built huge palaces at Jericho about a mile from the ancient mound of Old Testament Jericho. He also built up Jerusalem significantly. He built an impressive fortress of Herodium and its town near Bethlehem, where he was finally buried. Another of his fortresses was Masada on the western shores of the Dead Sea. He strengthened other fortresses in the Judean wilderness, namely Alexandrian, Cypros, Dok, Hyrcania, and Machaerus across the Jordan, all of which have undergone excavation. He founded the city of Caesarea on the site of the Hellenistic town of Strato's Tower and named it for Caesar Augustus – today called Caesarea Maritima. The site has attracted archaeologists for more than a century. He built the largest port in the Roman Empire at Caesarea and named it Sebaste, Greek for Augustus. Underwater archaeology shows that the description in Josephus is largely correct. He built a temple to Augustus at Caesarea, the steps and platform of which have been found. His palace, theater, and hippodrome in Caesarea have been excavated. He expanded the Temple Mount in Jerusalem to its present size and completely rebuilt the Temple, decorating it with marble and gilt and colonnaded cloisters. He built his own palace in Jerusalem and provided it with three fortified towers named Hippicus, Phasael, and Mariamne. The bases of these towers are still

to be seen at Jaffa Gate in Jerusalem. In addition to founding Caesarea he founded or refounded the cities of Antipatris (biblical Aphek) and Phasael (northeast of Jericho) in Judea. He apparently built an enclosure at Mamré north of Hebron, the Herodian Machpelah. This is not mentioned in ancient literature, but easily detectable archaeologically.

There is no reason to think that synagogues were rare in Judea in the first century. Acts assumes one or more synagogues in Jerusalem, and the Theodotus inscription from Jerusalem speaks of another. First-century or earlier synagogues have been excavated at Jericho, Modi'in, Qiryat Sefer, and perhaps Shuafat. (The ancient names of the last two localities are not known.)

Surveys south of Jerusalem have established that many villages expanded their fields in the early part of the Roman occupation of Judea. New villages were not founded, but a prosperous population expanded steadily until the destruction of 70 CE. The villages formed trade networks and marketed wheat, barley, olives and olive oil, grapes and wine, figs, dates, and vegetables. Balsam was collected from a now-extinct plant in the Judean desert. One small vessel of this oil seems to have been recovered in archaeological excavation. Dates from the Judean desert formed a unique export, providing fruit, date honey, and perhaps other commodities.

Many inscriptions are known from the first century BCE and the first century CE in Judea. They are mainly Aramaic and Greek. A few are in Latin, and always in association with Roman legions. Thus the major languages are Aramaic on the part of the Jewish and Samaritan population with Greek the language of government, literature, international trade and diplomacy, and in certain Jewish literature. Hebrew inscriptions are known from the Temple Mount, such as the famous inscription referring to the place of trumpeting at the southwestern tower. On the other hand an inscription from the Temple Mount referring to a donation to the Second Temple was in Greek. Probably the most famous Latin inscription of the period is from Caesarea and reads, "[this] Tiberium Pontius Pilate, Prefect of Judea, has dedicated." Therefore Pontius Pilate, Procurator from 26 to 36 CE, is named as the patron of an edifice, perhaps a temple, to Tiberius Caesar, and his rank is given as "Prefect." Latin was the language of the Roman Procurators from 6 CE, though the most educated ones likely also spoke Greek. Of course, Hebrew was the main language of the Dead Sea Scrolls, which shows that it survived as a literary language. There are other scrolls in that collection which are in Aramaic.

Important information about Judea and its rulers comes from coins. Archaelaus, the eldest son of Herod the Great, ruled Judea from 4 BCE to 6 CE, when he was removed by the Romans for incompetence. Archaelaus' territory included the Mediterranean coast, so his coins often show images of a Roman war galley or an anchor. On the other hand they also show grape clusters, double cornucopias, or a caduceus. The Greek inscription on his coins reads "Herod the Ethnarch."

When Archelaus was deposed in 6 CE, the Romans sent governors or procurators to administer the new Roman province of Judea. Thirteen procurators governed Judea, ruling by the "right of the sword" (*jus gladi*), but only a few minted their own coins, namely Coponius (6 CE or 7-9 CE), Marcus Ambibulus (9–12 CE), Valerius Gratus (15–26 CE), Pontius Pilate (26–36 CE), and Antonius Felix (54–58 CE). These few procurators struck small bronze coins that showed a certain sensitivity toward the Jewish population and its abhorrence of images. These included uncontroversial images such as palms, palm branches, lilies, barley, wreaths and the double cornucopia. Only Pontius Pilate introduced designs on his coins calculated to offend the Jews: the *simpulum* (a vessel from the Roman cult in the form of a ladle with a long handle) and *lituus* (a short curving staff used in religious ceremonies). The inscriptions on his coins honor the Emperor, as in "of Tiberius Caesar" in Greek.

Agrippa I, the grandson of Herod the Great and a good friend of Emperor Claudius, reigned over Judea from 37 to 44 CE. Agrippa's coins minted in Jerusalem show a sun shade (umbrella) and barley heads. But his coins minted in Caesarea showed images of the Roman Emperor Claudius, Roman temples, and a royal chariot drawn by four horses or a *quadriga*. Furthermore, Agrippa I placed his own image on coins of Caesarea.

These images on coins in the Jewish areas of Judea and Galilee help explain why, during the First Jewish Revolt against Rome, Jewish coins bore symbols drawn from the older Jewish repertory: pomegranates, grapes, a chalice, an amphora, a grape-vine leaf and tendril, and palm trees. Until then the Tyre mint had produced the silver shekels used by the Jews as their temple tax. Now the Jews minted their own shekels until the destruction of Jerusalem and the Temple in 70 CE.

JAMES F. STRANGE

Further reading

Avi-Yonah, Michael. *The Jews under Roman and Byzantine Rule: A Political History of Palestine from the Bar Kokhba War to the Arab Conquest*, New York: Schocken Books; Jerusalem: Magnes, the Hebrew University, 1984.

Avigad, Nahman. *Discovering Jerusalem*, Nashville, TN: Thomas Nelson, 1983.

Broshi, Magen and Hanan Eshel. "Daily Life at Qumran," *Near Eastern Archaeology* 63:3 (2000) 136–37.

Edwards, Douglas E. and C. Thomas McCollough (eds) *Archaeology and the Galilee: Texts and Contexts in the Graeco-Roman and Byzantine Periods*, Atlanta, GA: Scholars Press, 1997.

Geva, Hillel. *Ancient Jerusalem Revealed*, revised edition, Jerusalem: Israel Exploration Society, 2000.

Hendin, David. *Guide to Biblical Coins*, fourth edition, Groton, CT: Amphora Press, 2001.

Horseley, Richard A. *Galilee: History, Politics, People*, Valley Forge, PA: Trinity Press International, 1995.

McRay, John. *Archaeology and the New Testament*, Grand Rapids, MI: Baker, 1991.

Murphy-O'Connor, Jerome. *The Holy Land*, fourth edition, Oxford: Oxford University Press, 1998.

Schürer, Emil. *The History of the Jewish People in the Age of Jesus Christ (175 BC–AD 135)*, trans. and rev. by Geza Vermes, Fergus Millar, Matthew Black, and Martin Goodman, 3 vols, Edinburgh: T. & T. Clark, 1973–87.

Strange, James F. and James R. Strange, "The Archaeology of Everyday Life at Qumran," in A. Avery-Peck, J. Neusner, and B. Chilton (eds) *Judaism at Qumran: A Systemic Reading of the Dead Sea Scrolls Theory of Israel*, Handbuch der Orientalistik 5/1, Leiden: Brill, 2001, pp. 45–73.

ASCENSION

Christian tradition owes the conceptualization of Jesus' 'ascension' almost entirely to Luke – particularly to the opening section of his Acts of the Apostles (Acts 1:9–11). There the climax of the forty days, during which Jesus appeared to his disciples following his resurrection, is 'the day when Jesus was taken up (into heaven)' (1:2, 11, 22): that is, the 'ascension'. This presentation, however, is unique within the New Testament (Davies).

(1) In the Gospels there is little or no chronological separation of resurrection and ascension. Matthew does not narrate an ascension as such and gives no weight to chronological considerations in his retelling of the final episodes of his Gospel (Matt 28:16–20). In his Gospel, Luke was evidently content to leave the impression that Christ 'was carried up into heaven' on the day of the resurrection itself (Luke 24:50–51). And John similarly talks of an ascension happening on the day of resurrection (John 20.17), though he also includes an appearance a week later (20:26–29); and the appendix includes a presumably

subsequent appearance of Jesus in Galilee (21:1–23), though both episodes tail off without indicating what happened next to Jesus himself.

(2) Elsewhere in the NT the somewhat different imagery used implies a single movement of resurrection-exaltation (Zwiep). For example, Peter's speech in Acts 2: 'this Jesus God raised up, and of that all of us are witnesses. Being therefore exalted at the right hand of God … ' (Acts 2:32–33); and the Philippian hymn: 'he became obedient to death, even death on a cross. Therefore God also highly exalted him … ' (Phil 2:8–9). The whole imagery of Hebrews is of an entry into the heavenly sanctuary as a priest bearing the sacrificial blood (his own): 'when he had made purification for sins, he sat down at the right hand of the Majesty on high' (Heb 1:3; etc.). And the theology of John's Gospel is of a single act of glorification, of ascension and of being lifted up which begins with the cross and climaxes in heaven.

So why is it only in Acts that we have such a clear distinction and separation (forty days) between resurrection and ascension? The simplest answer is that Luke wanted to mark a definite and indisputable end to the sequence of resurrection appearances. This is presumably the reason why he went out of his way to stress the visibility of Jesus' final departure before witnesses. No fewer than five times in the three verses, Luke emphasizes that the disciples *saw* what was happening. This also accords with what some have called Luke's 'absentee Christology', the ascension marking Jesus' departure and subsequent absence from earth, or the transition from physical presence to presence in and through his name (Acts 3–4) (Zwiep 2001).

For an historical inquiry all this raises further awkward questions. How did Luke conceive of Jesus' resurrected corporeality? Where did he think the risen Jesus was when he was not visible to the disciples? Acts 1:4, 'while he was staying/eating with them' (*synalizomenos*) could be taken to indicate lengthy periods of Jesus' visible sojourn, though the implication of the parallel episodes in Luke's Gospel is that appearances were of relatively short duration (Luke 24:31, 51). But if the risen body of Christ was no less physical than the crucified body of Christ (Luke 24:39), then what does that say about its alternate visibility and (presumably) invisibility during the forty-day period? Or was Jesus' state during the forty days conceived as some kind of transitional state, and did his ascension result in a yet further different state of being? Was he during the forty days located on earth, having not yet ascended to heaven, de-materialized or somehow 'in hiding'? Or again, if the ascension is intended to mark Christ's first going up to heaven – the appearances lasted 'until the day when he was taken up' (1.2, 22), that is, 'into heaven' (1.11) – presumably he was thought of as not yet in heaven (not yet ascended), or as not disappearing to heaven between resurrection appearances. Such questions may seem to be crude and even crass, but it is Luke's own account, with his insistence on 'convincing proofs' (Acts 1:3) which prompts them!

In all this we should recall that Luke could operate only within the conceptuality possible for him, in which heaven was conceived as literally 'up there', and departure into heaven could only be conceived in terms of 'being taken up', a literal ascension. It is not simply a matter of literary genre which Luke could choose to operate or dispense with. Rather the typical mind-set and world-view of the time *conditioned what was actually seen* and how the recording of such seeings were conceptualized (Dunn). Since there is little doubt that Jesus was seen by not a few after his death, however these seeings are interpreted, and since the sequence of seeings ceased at some point, as Paul agrees (1 Cor 15:8 – 'last of all'), we can easily envisage the last appearance ending with what was seen as a departure into heaven. Was, then, the ascension simply Jesus' 'farewell' appearance (Ramsey)?

We can make no further progress on such questions, and to focus solely on them is to miss the point which all talk of Jesus' ascension obviously counted as much the more important – hence the unconcern evinced over such questions in our sources. For the main point was the theological significance of what the ascension was asserting. It was evidently early on seen as of crucial importance that Jesus had not simply been raised from the dead, the beginning of or first to experience 'the resurrection of the dead', but also had been exalted to heaven. It is presumably because the first Christians found it necessary to claim these *two* things for the once-crucified Jesus (exalted to heaven, as well as raised from the dead) that Luke evidently thought it appropriate to retell the tradition of Jesus' resurrection appearances so as to state in a fresh and clear way the fact that *both* claims were important and that one should not be subsumed within the other.

JAMES D. G. DUNN

Further reading

Davies, J. G. *He Ascended into Heaven*, Bampton Lectures, London: Lutterworth, 1958.
Donne, B. *Christ Ascended: A Study in the Significance of the Ascension of Jesus Christ in the New Testament*, Exeter: Paternoster, 1983.
Dunn, James D. G. "The Ascension of Jesus: A Test Case for Hermeneutics," in F. Avemarie and H. Lichtenberger (eds) *Auferstehung – Resurrection*, WUNT 135, Tübingen: Mohr Siebeck, 2001.
Ramsey, A. M. "What was the Ascension?" *SNTSBull. II* (1951).
Zwiep, A. W. *The Ascension of the Messiah in Lukan Christology*, NovTSupp 87, Leiden: Brill, 1997.
—— "Assumptus est in caelum: Rapture and Heavenly Exaltation in Early Judaism and Luke–Acts," in F. Avemarie and H. Lichtenberger (eds) *Auferstehung - Resurrection*, WUNT 135, Tübingen: Mohr Siebeck, 2001.

AUTHENTICITY CRITERIA

The criteria of authenticity employed in current historical Jesus research display a great variety. In order to avoid a chaotic impression, this short discussion will concentrate on presenting one coherent and in itself fairly functional set of criteria. First, however, a quick glance at the research history is in order.

Overview of the criteria

The criteria of authenticity represent one of the latest developments in the scholarly endeavor to ascertain a historically genuine picture of Jesus. The gradual emergence of the criteria, their forming into a distinct branch of methodology, and the maturation of the discussion concerning them also importantly periodize the historical Jesus research in general.

Prior to the New Quest for the historical Jesus, the main methods used in the study of Jesus were the traditional New Testament source criticism and, since the 1920s, form criticism. However, already in 1901 P. W. Schmiedel had anticipated the criterion of dissimilarity to Christianity as well as the criterion of coherence ("Gospels"). In his classic *The History of the Synoptic Tradition* (second German edition from 1931), R. Bultmann also reflected these criteria when outlining the criterion of double dissimilarity (demanding dissimilarity to both Judaism and Christianity) and regarding eschatological consciousness as a hallmark of genuine Jesuanic teaching. Further, in the beginning decades of the twentieth century F. C. Burkitt (*The Gospel History and its Transmission*) and B. H. Streeter (*The Four Gospels*) had developed principles that formed the basis of the criterion of

multiple attestation. Even later in the New Quest and still at present, these three criteria, dissimilarity, coherence and multiple attestation, have kept appearing in discussion, scholars giving many diverging formulations of them (see shortly below N. Perrin's explications). The most controversial has been the criterion of dissimilarity which through the work of E. Käsemann and N. Perrin, among other New Quest scholars, was adopted in the double dissimilarity form.

Not until the commencement of the New Quest in the 1950s, however, did there emerge a more common awareness of the need for tools specifically designed for probing the authenticity of the Jesus tradition. A reason for the increase of the awareness at this point was that the revived interest in the historical figure of Jesus now had to face the skepticism about the historical reliability of the Gospels that mainly in the wake of form criticism had rather widely landed in scholarship. The usual methodological starting point, then, appropriate in view of the skepticism, was to place the burden of proof on showing authenticity: the analysis should seek to prove the historicity of a Jesus tradition; without any proofs to that end; however, the tradition would be assumed to be inauthentic. These decisions made at an early stage of development have caused the discussion about the criteria to traditional focused on finding tools that can provide arguments for authenticity, not against it or for inauthenticity.

Representative and one of the earliest examples of a distinct authenticating method consisting of various authenticity criteria is Perrin's discussion in his *Rediscovering the Teaching of Jesus* (1967). Perrin's list comprises the three pre-New Quest criteria of double dissimilarity, coherence, and multiple attestation:

- Criterion of double dissimilarity: "The earliest form of a saying we can reach may be regarded as authentic if it can be shown to be dissimilar to characteristic emphases both of ancient Judaism and of the early Church" (p. 39).
- Criterion of coherence: "Material from the earliest strata of the tradition may be accepted as authentic if it can be shown to cohere with material established as authentic by means of the criterion of dissimilarity" (p. 43).
- Criterion of multiple attestation: "This is a proposal to accept as authentic material which is attested in all, or most, of the sources which can be discerned behind the synoptic gospels" (p. 45). (Explication: the attestations,

which in practice are two or more in number, are to be found in mutually independent sources. This point was professed already by Burkitt and Streeter and is today upheld with emphasis.)

Perrin notably subjects the criterion of coherence to the criterion of double dissimilarity. That he at the same time is clearly doubtful about the criterion of multiple attestation further enhances the predominance of the double dissimilarity criterion in his methodology. Following the usual procedure of his time, Perrin demands that authenticity is proven. This demand made in the methodological discussion is, however, not consistently sustained in the concrete analysis, where Perrin is often forced to place the burden of proof on showing inauthenticity. These problems are indicative of an underlying methodological dilemma on which Perrin and his peers were soon challenged: overconfidence in the criteria of authenticity necessitated, in a way, by the lack of confidence in the sources.

The New Quest is usually seen to have wilted soon after the turn of the 1970s. In significant part, this was brought about by changes in methodological thinking, among the earliest signals of which were two critical articles of M. Hooker from 1970–1 and 1972 ("Christology and Methodology," "On Using the Wrong Tool;" the first builds on a paper read at a SNTS seminar chaired by Perrin). One of Hooker's main targets was the role given to the double dissimilarity criterion which virtually made everything depend on it. She convincingly argued that not even this criterion can with certainty assure a core of authentic sayings of Jesus. Instead, its crucial role will lead to unknowingly attributing genuine Jesuanic material to early Christianity, which is no less erroneous than attributing early Christian formulations to Jesus. Though sometimes labeled as pessimistic in nature, Hooker's observations and the plea to recognize the tentativeness of all results generated in the Third Quest a surge of new creativity, scholars being freed from trying to establish a "critically assured minimum" of authentic Jesus traditions as the necessary basis of discussion. This turning of tides would, however, not have been possible without a more trusting attitude towards the historical reliability of the sources also beginning to gain support.

The Third Quest, though more confident about the sources and less about the authenticating tools, has proven creative even in coining criteria of authenticity. Already in 1987, which according to the usual estimates belongs to the first years of the Third Quest, D. Polkow can in his important article

"Method and Criteria for Historical Jesus Research" enumerate no fewer than twenty-five suggested criteria (although some of them comes from New Quest scholars). Out of these, by dismissing invalid criteria and combining overlapping ones, he compiles a set consisting of dissimilarity, coherence, and multiple attestation as the primary criteria, and Palestinian context, style, and scholarly consensus as secondary ones. However, no arrangement of criteria has to date established itself as the definitive criteriology, but the almost chaotic expansion of Jesus research during the recent two decades has led to a situation where every more substantial study into the historical Jesus must carefully state and explicate its own approach. In order to give a taste of the available varieties, here are just a few important contributions to the recent discussion about the criteria:

E. P. Sanders and M. Davies, *Studying the Synoptic Gospels*, 1989. Suggested criteria: strongly against the grain, too much with the grain; uniqueness (= double dissimilarity); multiple attestation; view common to friend and foe.

J. P. Meier, *A Marginal Jew: Rethinking the Historical Jesus*, 1991. Primary criteria: embarrassment (special case of dissimilarity to Christianity); discontinuity (= double dissimilarity); multiple attestation; coherence; rejection and execution. Secondary (or dubious) criteria: traces of Aramaic; Palestinian environment (= Palestinian context; cf. Polkow); vividness of narration; tendencies of the developing Synoptic Tradition; historical presumption.

G. Theissen and D. Winter, *Quest for the Plausible Jesus*, 2002 (German original from 1997), suggest the criterion of historical plausibility which consists of the following sub-criteria: opposition to traditional bias (= dissimilarity to Christianity); coherence of sources (= multiple attestation combined with coherence); contextual appropriateness (= Palestinian context/environment); contextual distinctiveness.

S. E. Porter, *The Criteria for Authenticity in Historical Jesus Research*, 2000, evaluates several previously suggested criteria and offers the following new proposals: Greek language and its context; Greek textual variance; discourse features (comes near the criterion of dissimilarity to Christianity).

Foreshadowing the maturation of the discussion, Theissen and Winter put substantial effort into developing an ensemble usage of the criteria – that is, determining how the various criteria should best be applied in combination with each other. Porter too places weight on such questions. While Sanders and Davies and Meier still uphold the dissimilarity criterion in its double form, Theissen and Winter and Porter (in his evaluative discussion) reduce it to dissimilarity to Christianity. The latter solution has prevailed in the Third Quest (for reasons, see Holmén, "Doubts about Double Dissimilarity"). All these contributions are indicative of the more trustful attitude towards the historical reliability of the sources that also has prevailed in the Third Quest. The conviction of Sanders, "we know quite a lot" (*sc.* about Jesus) (Sanders 1993: 5), characterizes the majority of the Third Quest studies.

Theissen and Winter's criteriology is probably the best systematic compilation of all knowledge gained during more than a century of discussion about the criteria of authenticity. The following brief presentation of an authenticating method featuring the authenticity criteria is to a considerable degree commensurable with their ideas even though the more traditional nomenclature is preferred over against their new suggestions.

Some definitions

On the basic level, we can speak about "a piece of information" (*sc.* regarding the historical Jesus), the authenticity or inauthenticity of which should be determined. A piece of information in principle can take on two different forms and have three different types of contents.

As to its form, a piece of information can appear as an individual tradition or as a motif (/theme). An individual tradition is tied up with some certain words and shape while a particular motif can in principle be embodied in and expressed through several different individual traditions. For example, the individual tradition about the relation between Jesus' exorcisms and the kingdom of God can be found in Matt 12:28 and Luke 11:20, the overall basic motif of the kingdom of God, again, in numerous and highly diverse individual traditions. Obviously, then, motifs usually consist of more general kinds of information compared with individual traditions. Still, even motifs can be more specific than in the above example. For instance, Luke 17:20–21 and Matt 12:28/Luke 11:20, which display two different individual traditions, share not only the overall motif of the kingdom but also the more particular motif of Jesus speaking of the kingdom as present.

As to its contents, a piece of information can pertain to something Jesus said, something Jesus did or something that happened to Jesus. Here it should be noticed that the criteria of authenticity are not particularly suited to finding out the *ipsissima verba Jesu* – that is, determining the exact words Jesus spoke – and that even in cases of individual traditions reporting something Jesus said the criteria are not usually appealed to with such a purpose in view. Instead, it is the gist or main/general message of the traditions that the criteria seek to seize and evaluate.

A piece of information is "authentic" if it contains genuine, historically reliable knowledge about Jesus. However, "determining (establishing, verifying, etc.)" authenticity (or inauthenticity) by means of the "criteria of authenticity" means assessing probabilities. We should not assume that we ever can *prove* that some piece of information about Jesus is *certainly* authentic. Granted still that in the sources for Jesus there is both authentic and inauthentic material, we can define grounds by means of which we isolate the material that relatively has the best options of being Jesuanic, that is to say authentic. The criteria of authenticity should constitute such grounds. Scholarship has thereby endeavored to set terms for considering some particular piece of information more likely to be trustworthy. All claims made about Jesus should then rely on material assessable by these terms, or criteria, as "authentic," rather than on other types of material. The criteria of authenticity are therefore best characterized as tools in support of logic. It is exceptional that they should have conclusive power. (The word "criterion" may convey a sense of perfect certainty. Accordingly, for example, B. F. Meyer 1990, prefers "index." However, "criterion" is traditional, and when emphasizing that we are dealing with a range of probabilities, no change of terminology needs to be undertaken.)

The criteria of authenticity form the essential part of an "authenticity analysis." A full-scale authenticity analysis consists of three steps: (1) some preliminary considerations preparing for the use of the criteria; (2) the use of the criteria; (3) a general assessment. Formally and properly, judgments of authenticity should wait till the final step or phase of the authenticity analysis (hence, the careful expression "to have a claim to authenticity" is employed later).

The authenticity criteria articulated as a part of an authenticity analysis

There are, to be sure, many things involved in the mentioned beginning and concluding phases of the authenticity analysis that would also require detailed explication. However, the emphasis will here be on explaining the various criteria of authenticity.

Preliminary considerations

I shall confine myself to two major points.

First, the most fundamental preliminary issue, one that sets the criteria as a whole within a framework, is a general assessment of the historical value of the sources one intends to use in studying the historical Jesus. As two opposite ends, a source can be deemed as basically unreliable or basically reliable in historical respect. Shifting towards either end, this assessment has crucial corollaries to viewing the authenticity criteria: The more unreliable a source is deemed, the greater demands are placed on the criteria and the less probative they will appear. The more reliable a source is deemed, again, the more cogency with which the authenticity criteria can be invested.

It is important to recognize the deep impact of the framework within which one chooses to view the criteria of authenticity. The skepticism about the criteria sometimes voiced in scholarly debates ultimately derives from skepticism about the sources. Naturally, if sources are regarded as unreliable, even the strongest of criteria can hardly persuade. Involved here is also the question of the burden of proof. Scholars seeing the sources in dubious light regarding their historicity would place the burden of proof on showing authenticity. However, a burden of proof emerging from a full-blown skepticism about the sources cannot be borne by any single criterion, not even by all of them together. For there is to date no method of authentication available that could completely exclude the possibility of a secondary provenance of a piece of information. There will always be room for speculation. On the other hand, if the sources can instead be endowed with some credibility, the criteria, as tools in support of logic, can tell the relatively best options regarding where to find historically reliable material.

The lesson of a century of Jesus research employing criteria of authenticity seems to be that on at least one of the following points the scholar needs to have trust: He or she should – to a certain degree – trust either the sources themselves or the tools he or she uses to probe the sources for authentic material. To my estimation, the criteria that have been developed in Jesus research work well under the assumption that the sources they are applied to are to be characterized as reliable rather than unreliable. Questionable is, however,

whether any set of criteria can ever be developed that could suffice to revert the speculations and skepticism duly arising when the sources are regarded as unreliable rather than reliable. In my view, prospects of finding authenticity criteria that could make bad sources yield good results are either nil or unrealistic. Accordingly, it is but logical that those who cannot find the sources reliable enough find the pursuit of Jesus research irrelevant. Logically enough, then, the Third Quest interest in the historical figure of Jesus has displayed a rather positive view of the sources' historical reliability.

Second, now pertaining to individual cases, a measure that should be taken prior to using the criteria of authenticity is a balanced tradition-critical analysis by means of which secondary elements of a tradition are identified (and discarded) in order to reach towards an earlier form of the tradition. The Third Quest has entertained considerable reservedness about such an analysis. The reservedness can mostly be regarded as healthful, for there are no strict rules to follow in the tradition-critical "peeling-off" of a Jesus tradition, and the best that one normally can hope to accomplish is a reconstruction of a more or less hypothetical character. However, the question whether the tradition-critical analysis can ever be completely set aside is a tricky one. Having it means difficulties, while not having it is in most cases not an option at all, at least with the usual view of the sources. If, as usual, the traditions of the sources can be seen to contain later amendments resulting from the adaptation of earlier forms of the traditions to the various situations of the early Christian communities, refraining from a tradition-critical analysis risks getting misleading signals from the authenticity criteria. For when tools designed for identifying Jesuanic material are applied to later amendments they are bound to produce a negative result (only the I and the III criteria to be discussed below can sometimes be impervious in this respect). Presence of later elements in a tradition does not, however, mean that the whole tradition would be secondary. Therefore, in order to be able to use the criteria in a proper way, one has to become aware of these later amendments, and the only means by which even to attempt this is the tradition-critical analysis.

The picture is of course different if one thinks that the traditions do not at all contain later amendments or that the presence of later elements in a tradition should be considered to label the whole tradition as secondary. Neither of these views is, however, sustained in critical scholarship. The continuous striving for a balanced tradition-critical analysis, one that would allow for both the precariousness of the analysis and its necessity, is therefore to be seen as an inseparable part of an authenticating method.

The criteria and their use

The following compilation of criteria aspires to a maximum generalization of the logical principles on which the criteria are based. The aim is that each and every one of the various criteria would be based on a different and distinct logical principle. That is, none of the criteria should be part of or overlap with another. Quite naturally, one should avoid repetition of similar underlying principles. Only in this way, too, can it be accomplished that, basically, the probability of authenticity increases alongside the number of criteria suggesting authenticity.

The criteria are best explicated by describing their application and stating the reason and ground – the rationale – on which the criterion and its application relies.

I criterion: Recurrent attestation

(For the designation, see Allison forthcoming)

Rule of application: If a motif has gathered numerous recurrent attestations across the sources, it can be regarded as having a claim to authenticity.

Rationale: A greater dispersion of a motif suggests that the motif has landed in the Jesus tradition very early and through several tradents. It further suggests that already then the motif had been widely accepted and experienced as central. There are no better options for finding historically accurate reminiscences of Jesus.

Many earlier and also recent scholars have considered this criterion (or the logical principle the criterion builds upon) to lend an exceptionally strong support to authenticity. However, the applicability of the criterion is restricted in a particular way. It can be applied to motifs alone, not to individual traditions for, simply, appearances of one and the same tradition are never numerous enough in the sources to amount to a recurrent attestation. Herewith it is also clear that the criterion cannot be used to suggest authenticity of precisely those individual traditions that have been identified as giving expression to the recurrently attested motif. It is only the motif itself shared by all of these traditions that has a claim to

authenticity, not the individual traditions involved in the argument. For instance, one can quickly establish the motif of Jesus as a miracle worker and exorcist as being recurrently attested. The claim to authenticity the motif thus is endowed with cannot, however, be seen to pertain to the individual miracle or exorcism traditions. Naturally, this does not mean that individual miracle or exorcism traditions could not be authenticated on some other grounds.

Further, as this example also shows (cf. even the example about the overall motif of the kingdom of God given above), the recurrently attested motifs tend to be rather general ones. Consequently, the knowledge yielded by the criterion will usually remain on quite a general level. The composite picture of Jesus based solely on such knowledge, again, will turn out nonspecific and cursory. Most scholars would therefore prefer to use other criteria as well in addition to the criterion of recurrent attestation. Even though these cannot regularly be expected to provide arguments of equal strength, they would be necessary to complement the broad-brush portrait.

The criterion of recurrent attestation or its equivalent has often been lumped together with the criterion of multiple attestation (carrying the name of the latter criterion; cf. the III criterion below). However, these two criteria build on clearly different logical principles and should not be treated as one. They display considerable differences even as to their application. Their separation pursued here is the methodologically correct solution and also increases clarity.

II criterion: Dissimilarity to Christianity

Rule of application: If an individual tradition or a motif can be seen to be dissimilar to early Christian interests, views, practices and/or theological tendencies, etc., it can be regarded as having a claim to authenticity.

Rationale: The people behind the sources for Jesus (i.e. the early Christians) would not have created traditions about Jesus disadvantageous or with no particular (positive) value to themselves.

A modification – and, in fact, an antecedent – of the infamous criterion of double dissimilarity (demanding dissimilarity to both Judaism and Christianity), this criterion has stood, *inter alia*, the criticisms that have arisen at the final stages of the New Quest (Hooker) and on the route to maturation of the Third Quest (Theissen and Winter). Unlike as sometimes alleged, Hooker did not wish to discard the dissimilarity criterion for good but wanted to underline the relativity of the results arrived at by means of any of the criteria. "And what tools should he [the scholar] use in this task? He must, alas, use the tools we have been discussing, for there are no others, and there are unlikely to be any better ones discovered" (Hooker 1972: 580–81). The criteria she had been discussing were dissimilarity, coherence and multiple attestation. And unlike as often believed, Theissen and Winter do not discard the entire dissimilarity criterion but only the double dissimilarity version.

> The two aspects of the criterion of the plausibility of historical effects take up two traditional criteria (or three, depending on one's categories): on the one hand, the "criterion of dissimilarity" in its application to early Christianity ... , and, on the other hand, aspects of the criteria of "coherence" and "multiple attestation."
>
> (Theissen and Winter 179)

Quite in general, the Third Quest has – under varying names – endorsed the criterion of dissimilarity to Christianity.

While the rationale of the criterion of dissimilarity to Christianity is, as such, suited to yielding a strong support for authenticity, successful application of the criterion requires awareness of at least these observations:

The criterion must not be used negatively: that is, to suggest that those traditions or motifs which do *not* display dissimilarity to Christianity are inauthentic. There is no "criterion of similarity" suggesting that when a piece of information parallels the early Christian teachings it should be regarded as inauthentic. While it is reasonable to think that the early Christians would not invent teachings of Jesus they themselves disagreed with, we cannot conversely presume that they just could not willingly agree with anything he taught. Therefore, the criterion of dissimilarity to Christianity either supports or fails to support a given piece of information. It cannot rule it out.

Although in principle approved by scholars almost universally, this observation has proven surprisingly difficult to follow. Not seldom does one encounter the thought that a tradition or motif corresponds "too closely" to early Christian interests to be regarded as authentic. Especially liable to such reasoning appear to be instances where the tradition or motif serves the aims of the evangelist-redactor relating it. However, unless one thinks that the evangelists cannot have fully agreed with Jesus in anything, one has to postpone making judgments of authenticity till one has scrutinized the plausibility of the tradition or motif in question with respect to Jesus' context and situation. Mere similarity to early Christian thinking does not justify doubting the authenticity of a tradition or a motif. The estimate of authenticity naturally changes if the tradition or motif cannot be plausibly pictured within Jesus' surroundings. However, applicable then is not the criterion of dissimilarity to Christianity but that of implausibility (cf. the VI criterion).

Yet a further difficulty of applying the criterion of dissimilarity to Christianity one should observe is that because the criterion is able to identify as authentic such material only where Jesus differs from early Christian views, it cumulatively results in a biased picture of Jesus. The functionality of the criterion is restricted to a particular kind of material and, consequently, what it inevitably produces is a particular selection of authentic pieces of information. For this reason, when seeking to gather together authentic information about Jesus, this criterion should not be the only tool of authenticity applied. Criteria capable of probing the authenticity of such traditions or motifs, too, where Jesus appears to accord with early Christian views ought to accompany the criterion of dissimilarity to Christianity, so balancing its results. Let it be observed that the negative use of the criterion effectively precludes this balancing pursuit.

(For the problem of speculating with hypothetical branches of early Christianity whose interests and agendas could have accorded with a tradition or motif otherwise – i.e. on the basis of evidence from the available sources – displaying dissimilarity to Christianity, see Holmén 2001.)

As if compensating for these difficulties, the criterion of dissimilarity to Christianity can well be applied to all kinds of pieces of information: that is, to both individual traditions and motifs. It can also from time to time induce rather efficacious arguments for authenticity. For example, Mark 3:21 can be regarded as having a strong claim to authenticity because it casts the relatives of Jesus, highly respected in early Christianity, in such a bad light as suspecting Jesus of having gone haywire (to be sure, the passage casts doubts even on Jesus himself). Why would some early Christian have wished to make up a tradition like this? As to motifs, again, one could refer to Jesus' baptism by John the Baptist (Mark 1; Matt 3/Luke 3). Why would early Christians have invented Jesus' taking of a baptism of repentance for forgiveness of sins? As can be seen, the motifs seized by the criterion do not have to be particularly general.

The II criterion thus rather well complements the I criterion.

A word needs to be said about the so-called criterion of embarrassment. Being employed as part of a repertoire of criteria including not the criterion of dissimilarity to Christianity but the criterion of double dissimilarity, the criterion of embarrassment had something different to say: Irrespective of a tradition's or a motif's relation to Judaism, if the tradition or motif would seem to have been embarrassing to the early Christians, it can be regarded as having a claim to authenticity. Why? Because the early Christians would not have created traditions about Jesus embarrassing to themselves. However, it is easy to notice that this statement and the criterion of dissimilarity to Christianity rely on an essentially same rationale, embarrassment being a special case of dissimilarity. Hence, when the infamous double dissimilarity is reduced to dissimilarity to Christianity, there is no reason any more (and within a methodology reason translates to justification) to hold embarrassment as a criterion of its own.

III criterion: Multiple attestation

Rule of application: If an individual tradition or a motif appears in two or more independent sources, it can be regarded as having a claim to authenticity.

Rationale: An attestation in two or more independent sources means that the tradition or motif in question is earlier than these sources. An early tradition or motif, again, has on average a greater probability of authenticity than a later one.

A corresponding principle is commonly used as a tool of the inner criticism of general historiography and regarded to be of good worth. When applied in the gospels, however, the conclusiveness of the principle is considerably reduced. Here the sources are not "independent" in the sense that they might cherish different, maybe even opposite, opinions, or have substantially conflicting interests, etc. All the sources we utilize have too much in common regarding their interests and views to be characterized as "independent" in this sense. It is, then, only literary independence that is aimed at: Luke did not know Matthew (or vice versa), Mark did not utilize Q (or vice versa). Thus, the strongly persuasive sense "accepted by friend and foe" is gone (though not perhaps completely), and what the existence of a tradition or motif in, for example, both Q and Mark factually witnesses is that the tradition or motif in question antedates these two sources (cf. the rationale). One can also observe

that the functionality of the criterion is to an important degree dependent on source-critical solutions. As can be fathomed, the most favorable solution in view of the usability of the criterion is the Synoptic four-source hypothesis. Generally the Pauline letters and increasingly the Gospel of John are also regarded as independent sources. Still, choosing the Griesbach hypothesis or the like greatly disempowers the criterion.

The arguments generated by the criterion of multiple attestation are thus generally a lot weaker than those reached by means of the I and II criteria. Nevertheless, the cogency of the criterion varies depending on how the given attestations compare with each other. In order to explain this, a category known from previous scholarship needs to be rehearsed and developed further.

Scholarship has formerly distinguished a particular type of multiple attestation, namely that of literary forms (i.e. genres): that is, when one and the same tradition is independently attested in two or more different literary forms. For instance, Jesus' prohibition of divorce appears in Mark 10:2–9 as embedded in a pronouncement story, while in the Q-pericope Matt 5:31–32/Luke 16:18 it takes the literary form of a wisdom saying. The argument for the authenticity of the prohibition induced by an appeal to multiple attestation is hereby strengthened because traditions probably spread through different sources more easily by being copied than by being transformed into new forms. My proposal is now that instead of paying attention to different literary forms alone we should focus on differences in form in general. The greater the differences between the independent attestations of a tradition, the longer back in time and the tradition process we in principle can place a possible common point of origin of the tradition. In other words, great differences between the independent attestations of a tradition would, in principle, label the tradition as relatively early, thus also yielding a relatively strong argument for authenticity. More or less insignificant differences between the independent attestations of a tradition, again, would suggest that the common point of origin lies quite near and provide a weaker argument for authenticity. Well according with this proposal is also that scholars have generally regarded the arguments for authenticity provided by multiple attestations of motifs as stronger than those provided by multiple attestations of individual traditions. By definition, traditions which share only a common motif differ as to their forms.

Even at its best, however, the cogency of this criterion is usually outweighed by the two previous ones.

IV criterion: Coherence

Rule of application: If an individual tradition or a motif is coherent with what has already been deemed as authentic, it can be regarded as having a claim to authenticity

Rationale: On the basis of what we already know about Jesus, this is what we would expect him to say or do.

The support for authenticity provided by this criterion can be regarded as relatively good, although much depends on the issue where coherence between the different traditions or motifs is detected. To be sure, the fact that a tradition or a motif evinces trust in God, just like some other tradition or motif already determined as genuinely Jesuanic, does not bring forth a particularly strong argument for authenticity. However, a clearly more convincing argument ensues from the observation that the tradition forbidding swearing (Matt 5:33–37) displays just the particular kind of attitude towards the law discernible in the authentic tradition forbidding divorce (Matt 5:31–32; authenticity of this tradition is supposed here for the sake of argument). Thus, if attributes such as profiled, distinct or conspicuous can be related to the issue the assessment of coherence pertains to, this reinforces the resulting argument for authenticity.

The applicability of the criterion is limited by the demand that the tradition or motif to be tested should be compared with material the authenticity of which has already been determined. Thus, the criterion cannot be applied until some authentic material has already been identified. By the same token, the criterion is contingent upon the usability and cogency of the criteria by means of which the required authentic material is determined. Relevant here can be all of the criteria I–V. Hence, even the criterion of coherence itself can come into question. Provided is then, however, that the argument is not merely reversed. That is, for example, having argued for the authenticity of the prohibition of swearing on the basis of its coherence with the (supposedly) authentic tradition prohibiting divorce, one cannot assume that there has emerged a further argument for the authenticity of the prohibition of divorce because of its coherence with the now authenticated prohibition of swearing.

One also has to be wary of not mixing up the criterion of coherence with the criterion of multiple attestation. The (supposedly) authentic prohibition of divorce has provided an argument for the authenticity of the prohibition of swearing, for the latter tradition displays just the particular kind of attitude towards the law discernible in the former one. This is the criterion of coherence in operation. However, if we redirect our attention from the authenticity of the tradition about swearing to the authenticity of the *motif* shared by both traditions, the criterion of multiple attestation has become applicable: the particular kind of attitude towards the law is multiply attested for it can be found in two independent traditions, Mark 10:2–9 about divorce and Matt 5:33–37 about swearing (note, the Matthean texts about divorce would not clearly count as traditions independent of the swearing tradition).

The reason for such semi-interchangeability is that when two independent individual traditions give expression to a common motif – thus, a multiple attestation of some certain motif – the individual traditions in question are necessarily also coherent with each other, for otherwise they understandably could not give expression to a common motif. The difference between utilizing either one of the criteria is then twofold. The criterion of multiple attestation does not require that one of the traditions has already been deemed authentic. The argument of this criterion, however, pertains to the common motif alone, not to any of the individual traditions involved. The criterion of coherence, again, does require that one of the traditions has already been deemed as authentic and the argument applies to the tradition not yet authenticated.

V criterion: Historical intelligibility

Rule of application: If an individual tradition or a motif helps to explain and understand an authentic tradition or motif, it can be regarded as having a claim to authenticity.

Rationale: History can usually be assumed to be intelligible. It is practical to divide this rationale into two parts: (a) it is probable that Jesus usually had some reason for saying or doing something; (b) similarly, one can usually assume some cause behind what happened to Jesus.

This criterion consists partly of a principle lying behind what has varyingly been called the criterion of historical coherence (Evans 1995: 13–15) or the criterion of rejection and execution (Meier 1991: 177). A classical example pertaining to this part of the criterion is the temple action of Jesus (Mark 11:15–17) which scholars generally regard as what triggered the chain of events resulting in Jesus' execution. Here, thus, a piece of information (the temple action) can help to understand what we know happened to Jesus (execution) and can therefore be seen as having a claim to authenticity (cf. rationale (b)). However, the criterion suggested now accommodates even a further assumption, one that rests on the intelligibility of Jesus' words and deeds (cf. rationale (a)). For example, if Jesus' acceptance of the company of grievous sinners is considered to be authentic (as it regularly is), pieces of information that could explain such an acceptance would have a claim to authenticity. One can then discuss if the traditions Mark 2:17 and Luke 19:10 serve here best or whether some other and better explanation could be found in the sources. Whatever the solution, it seems sensible to think both that Jesus had some reason for this extraordinary mode of behavior of his and that where in the sources one finds such a reason one can justifiably suspect authenticity. Hence, in both of its parts the criterion involves an attempt to make history understandable (on the assumption that history basically and/or usually is).

The criterion of historical intelligibility comes rather close to the criterion of coherence. Usage of both requires a comparison to material the authenticity of which has already been determined. Therefore the criteria also share the limitations ensuing from the need for such a comparison.

At this point, an overarching consideration must be brought into view. All the criteria reviewed so far have been *positive* ones: that is, yielding arguments *for* authenticity. This observation is highly important. The criteria studied so far cannot indeed be used to suggest inauthenticity. In other words, what has above been said about the negative usage of the criterion of dissimilarity to Christianity applies basically to all criteria discussed so far: the fact that the authenticity of a tradition or a motif cannot be supported by these criteria must not be taken as an indication of the inauthenticity of the tradition or motif at issue. Precisely for this reason, however, criteria that would be suited to yielding arguments *against* authenticity – i.e. that would suggest inauthenticity – should be defined! The need to present such *negative* criteria as well is particularly urgent when one thinks that the burden of proof lies on showing inauthenticity. Failing then to state the criteria by means of which inauthenticity could be shown effectively invalidates one's authenticity analysis. Surprisingly enough, concentrating almost exclusively on positive criteria, today's discussion still tends to reflect the New Quest situation where the skepticism about the sources was allowed to adopt the role of the negative criteria: inauthenticity was assumed if not proven otherwise.

All in all, however, only two negative criteria are warranted:

VI criterion: Implausibility

Rule of application: If an individual tradition or a motif involves features integral to it that are incapable of being plausibly situated in the Palestine of Jesus' time, inauthenticity of the tradition or motif is suggested.

Rationale: Such features are by definition mislocations and/or anachronisms, and traditions or motifs which integrally depend on them can be deemed as mislocated and/or anachronistic traditions and motifs.

If a tradition or a motif appears to be clearly implausible with respect to Jesus' environment and time, its authenticity cannot be sustained any more. The criterion of implausibility can thus be regarded as quite an effective negative criterion. However, the formulation "features integral to a tradition or a motif" is important. For it is usual that an early tradition gathers secondary elements during the process of transmission. Because of their nature (adaptions to new situations), these elements can often include features not quite at home within the Palestine of Jesus' time. It would then be erroneous to deem the tradition as a whole as inauthentic on the grounds of such secondary elements. For this reason, one must find out whether a feature not properly suited to the Jesuanic context derives from later phases of the transmission process or if it in fact is integral to the tradition: that is, an indispensable part of it. The only way to find this out is the performance of a tradition-critical analysis. Appropriately, then, the analysis was, despite its many uncertainties underlined earlier above, a necessary preliminary measure to be taken.

There have been attempts to sustain a positive variation of this criterion, suggesting authenticity of traditions or motifs well at home in first-century Palestine (e.g. the criterion of "Palestinian context/environment;" Polkow, Meier). Suitability with respect to the Jesuanic context should, however, be seen as the precondition to which any piece of information should conform in order not to be disqualified as inauthentic (the underlying fundamental question at issue here is the endeavor, emphasized by the Third Quest, to view Jesus within the Judaism of his time). This is precisely how Theissen and Winter present their criterion of contextual appropriateness: being plausible with respect to Jesus' context forms the prerequisite to which all traditions and motifs to be considered authentic should acquiesce. Therefore, although taking a positive form, Theissen and Winter's contextual appropriateness works like the negative criterion of implausibility. Understandably, to be found implausible with respect to Jesus' Jewish context is equivalent to not fulfilling the precondition of being always plausible with respect to the context. Since the other positive criteria cannot be regarded as preconditions (for this would mean applying them negatively which, as stated above, must not be done), a "criterion of *im*plausibility" is to be preferred over against a "criterion of plausibility." Then all the criteria, both positive and negative, can be regarded as yielding an argument – for or against authenticity respectively – *when applicable*, but where they cannot be applied they do not turn to suggest otherwise. That is, the positive criteria when inapplicable do not suggest inauthenticity and, again, the negative criteria when inapplicable do not turn to suggest authenticity.

Let it be noted, further, that the negative use of the criterion of dissimilarity to Christianity (i.e. traditions or motifs displaying similarity to early Christian views and/or interests are considered inauthentic) – which thus must not be accepted – actually represents an incomplete form of the criterion of implausibility: traditions or motifs similar to early Christianity are, without further ado, treated as if they were mislocations or anachronisms. Naturally, mislocations and anachronisms do display similarity to early Christian views which they derive from, but above all they are also incapable of being situated within the Palestine of Jesus' time. The fallacious negative "criterion of similarity to Christianity" thus errs in not paying attention to whether the traditions or motifs deemed similar to Christianity could still also be seen as plausible with respect to Jesus' context.

VII criterion: Incoherence

Rule of application: If an individual tradition or a motif is incoherent with what has already been deemed as authentic, inauthenticity of the tradition or motif is suggested.

Rationale: On the basis of what we already know about Jesus, this is what we would not expect him to say or do.

The support for inauthenticity provided by this negative criterion is relatively weak. The criterion shares – *mutatis mutandis* – the restrictions of the criterion of coherence. Moreover, the concept of incoherence serves as a clearly weaker basis for inferences: (a) people tend to be inconsistent; (b) ancient Semitic thought differs from ours, for example by being more attracted to paradoxes and tensions; (c) when preaching on various occasions and for various people, Jesus probably did not aim at and could hardly accomplish a bulk of teaching which would be like a systematic presentation.

The criterion of incoherence does not actually equate with a negative use of the criterion of coherence. For besides being mutually coherent or incoherent, two issues can also be irrelevant to each other.

Too weak to be accepted for use – indeed, even misleading – would be a "criterion of unintelligibility" (cf. the V criterion) which could easily lead to a situation where everything not quite comprehensible in the light of scholars' theories, based on part of the source material, would be branded as inauthentic.

In general, the criteria should be used with great discrimination observing several different variables. First, the different criteria are not all of the same value in what comes to argumentative strength and cogency. There are criteria whose results are usually more convincing than the results reached by means of other criteria. For instance, the criterion of recurrent attestation (I) and the criterion of implausibility (VI), when applicable, yield relatively strong arguments, the former for authenticity, the latter against it (or for inauthenticity). The criterion of incoherence (VII), again, usually produces relatively weak arguments against authenticity.

Second, one should take account of the difference between the rationale upon which a criterion is based and the concrete implementation of the criterion. For instance, the rationale of the criterion of dissimilarity to Christianity is quite strong while the implementation of the criterion involves several difficulties. On the other hand, while the criterion of multiple attestation can be implemented relatively easily, the rationale the criterion builds on is not particularly convincing.

Lastly but not less importantly, the effectiveness and cogency of the different criteria vary from case to case. One cannot mechanically invest their results always with the same argumentative strength, but one should evaluate the tradition or motif under scrutiny with a view to knowing how well the rationales of the criteria can be assumed to work and what kind of difficulties if any will be involved in their implementation. This applies especially to the criterion of dissimilarity to Christianity and the criterion of coherence, but must be taken into consideration with respect to the other criteria as well.

General assessment

The general assessment is the phase of an authenticity analysis where the decisions of authenticity are properly made. This final phase involves many questions that should be taken into account but only some general remarks can now be made.

Of course, the more criteria one can appeal to for the authenticity of a tradition or a motif, the better. However, decisions must not be based on simple counting of the criteria but the variables spoken of above should be paid heed to (cf., in particular, the remarks that the criteria are not all of equal value in what comes to argumentative strength and that the cogency of the criteria varies from case to case). The best way to observe these considerations is an ensemble use of the criteria: that is, allowing flexibly for the whole repertoire of applicable criteria. If possible, one should first employ the overarching criterion of recurrent attestation so laying a securer basis for the utilization of the other criteria. Also, one should always find out whether the criterion of implausibility is applicable vis-à-vis the material under scrutiny. However, the ensemble usage of the criteria pertains not only to individual cases. Even on the whole, thinking of piling up of traditions and motifs deemed authentic, one should strive to include material authenticated with varying criteria. In particular, as stated earlier, one should try to see that all or most of the decisions for authenticity do not rely on the criterion of dissimilarity to Christianity alone.

In addition, the observations made in the preliminary phase should be carried over into the general assessment. One should evaluate the importance of the results of the tradition-critical analysis to the tradition or motif under scrutiny. Was the tradition-critical analysis particularly difficult and/or hypothetical? Are there some considerable question marks left? (To be sure, the tradition-critical analysis will in most cases be *somewhat* difficult and hypothetical and leave open questions of *some* significance.) Naturally, the view taken of the basic (un)reliability of the sources is also of substantial relevance here. The criteria can never with certainty prove that some particular piece of information is authentic but there will always be room for speculation. Whether such speculation mounts up to devastating measures or remains on a level which allows reasonable decision-making depends on how one views the sources.

In principle, not until all these considerations have been given their due attention can decisions regarding authenticity or inauthenticity be made.

Open issues naturally remain, for example the more exact way of using the criteria in combination. Further, a whole new set of problems is created by the question of how the usage of the criteria should be seen to be affected by the change of focus when, on the one hand, an overall picture of the historical Jesus is aimed at and, on the other, only a study of a particular aspect of Jesus' life and teaching is intended. Understandably, when focusing on a particular aspect, one simply cannot survey large sections of material in order to try to reach general impressions, much as such overarching approach would indeed provide relatively securer results (cf. the I criterion).

Moreover, one of the most burning issues will no doubt be the need to react determinedly on the change of attitude with respect to the historical reliability of the sources for Jesus. In the light of the predominantly skeptical view of the sources during the New Quest, the required tools were naturally those capable of identifying authentic material. Hence, the burden of proof was placed squarely on showing authenticity. Now that the predominant position has moved to somewhat more trusting direction, previous decisions must be reconsidered. The situation is now better in that the dilemma formed by overconfidence in the criteria of authenticity resulting from a lack of confidence in the sources is usually avoided. Most Third Quest scholars can accept that a probability of authenticity suffices to make a piece of information provided by the sources useable for historical Jesus study. As the flip side, however, an exclusive use of tools suited to identifying authentic material can no more count as an adequate authenticity analysis. More effort should therefore be put into defining negative criteria: that is, tools designed for identifying inauthentic material.

A related question is that of the burden of proof. Placing the burden on showing authenticity risks being a solution appropriate for a situation no longer prevailing. It could also once again tempt one to expect too much of what the criteria can accomplish. On the other hand, placing the burden of proof squarely on showing inauthenticity could possibly prompt branding the positive criteria as superfluous, hardly an appropriate solution either. And finally, the statement that the burden of proof lies on the one who wants to prove something, whether authenticity or inauthenticity, is mere semantics. Following this line of reasoning, a piece of information without proof of either authenticity or inauthenticity would still be treated as if it were inauthentic: that is, it will not be used in portraying a picture of the historical Jesus. The end of this matter: need for more research is clearly indicated.

The criteria of authenticity are and remain problematic and incomplete. At any event, however, if one is to assess authenticity, this will always be more sensibly done with the help of some explicitly stated tools and guidelines than without them.

TOM HOLMÉN

Further reading

Allison, D. C. *Jesus of Nazareth: Millenarian Prophet*, Minneapolis, MI: Fortress Press, 1998.
—— "How to Marginalize the Traditional Criteria of Authenticity," in T. Holmén and S. E. Porter (eds) *The Handbook of the Study of the Historical Jesus. Volume One: The Study of Jesus*, Leiden: Brill, forthcoming.
Boring, M. E. "The Historical-Critical Method's 'Criteria of Authenticity': The Beatitudes in Q and Thomas as a Test Case," *Semeia* 44 (1988) 9–44.
Bultmann, R. *The History of the Synoptic Tradition*, New York: Harper and Row, 1976.
Burkitt, F. C. *The Gospel History and its Transmission*, Edinburgh: T. & T. Clark, 1906.
Evans, C. A. "Authenticity Criteria in Life of Jesus Research," *CSR* 19 (1989) 6–31.
—— *Jesus and His Contemporaries: Comparative Studies*, Leiden: Brill, 1995.
France, R. T. "The Authenticity of the Sayings of Jesus," in C. Brown (ed.) *History, Criticism and Faith: Four Exploratory Studies*, London: InterVarsity Press, 1976, pp. 101–43.
Holmén, T. "Doubts about Double Dissimilarity: Restructuring the Main Criterion of Jesus-of-history research," in B. Chilton and C. A. Evans (eds) *Authenticating the Words of Jesus*, Leiden: Brill, 1999, pp. 47–80.
—— "Knowing about Q and Knowing about Jesus: Mutually Exclusive Undertakings?," in A. Lindemann (ed.) *The Sayings: Source Q and the Historical Jesus*, Leuven: Peeters, 2001, pp. 497–514.
—— "Review Article of G. Theissen and D. Winter: *The Quest for the Plausible Jesus*," *JTS* 55 (2004) 216–28.
Holmén, T. and S. E. Porter (eds) *The Handbook of the Study of the Historical Jesus. Volume One: The Study of Jesus*, Leiden: Brill, forthcoming.
Hooker, M. "Christology and Methodology," *NTS* 17 (1970–71) 480–87.
—— "On Using the Wrong Tool," *Theology* 75 (1972) 570–81.
Käsemann, E. "Das Problem des historischen Jesus," *ZTK* 51 (1954) 125–53.
Kümmel, W. G. "Jesu Antwort an Johannes den Täufer: ein Beispiel zum Methodenproblem in der Jesusforschung," in E. Grässer, O. Merk, and A. Fritz (eds) *Heilsgeschehen und Geschichte: Gesammelte Augsätze III/W. G. Kümmel*, Marburg: N. G. Elwert, 1978, pp. 177–200.
Meier, J. P. *A Marginal Jew: Rethinking the Historical Jesus. Volume One: The Roots of the Problem and the Person*, New York, Doubleday, 1991.
Meyer, B. F. "Objectivity and Subjectivity in Historical Criticism of the Gospels," in D. L. Dungan (ed.) *The Interrelations of the Gospels*, Leuven: Leuven University Press, 1990, pp. 546–65.
Perrin, N. *Rediscovering the Teaching of Jesus*, London: SCM Press, 1967.
Polkow, D. "Method and Criteria for Historical Jesus Research," *SBLSP* 26 (1987) 336–56.
Porter, S. E. *The Criteria for Authenticity in Historical-Jesus Research: Previous Discussion and New Proposals*, Sheffield: Sheffield Academic Press, 2000.
Sanders, E. P. *The Historical Figure of Jesus*, London: Allen Lane, 1993.
Sanders, E. P. and M. Davies. *Studying the Synoptic Gospels*, London: SCM Press, 1989.
Sanders, J. T. "The Criterion of Coherence and the Randomness of Charisma: Poring through some Aporias in the Jesus Tradition," *NTS* 44 (1998) 1–25.
Schmiedel, P. W. "Gospels," in T. K. Cheyne and J. S. Black (eds) *Encyclopaedia Biblica II*, London: A. & C. Black, 1901, pp. 1761–898.
Stein, R. H. "The 'Criteria' for Authenticity," *Gospel Perspectives* 1 (1983) 225–63.
Streeter, B. H. *The Four Gospels: A Study of Origins, Treating of the Manuscript Tradition, Sources, Authorship, and Dates*, London: Macmillan, 1924.
Theissen, G. "Historical Scepticism and the Criteria of Jesus Research," *SJT* 49 (1996) 147–76.
Theissen, G. and D. Winter. *Quest for the Plausible Jesus: The Question of Criteria*, Louisville, KY: John Knox, 2002.
Viviano, B. T. "The Historical Jesus in the Doubly Attested Sayings: An Experiment," *RevBib* 103 (1996) 367–410.
Walker, W. O. "The Quest for the Historical Jesus: A Discussion of Methodology," *ATR* 51 (1969) 38–56.

B

BAPTISM OF JESUS

In the Synoptic Gospels the baptism of Jesus marks the beginning of his public ministry. The story links Jesus to John the Baptist, his message of repentance and his baptismal practice. The main focus of the story, however, is not the act of baptism in itself, but the supernatural events connected with it: the opening of heaven, the Spirit coming down and the voice from heaven with its pregnant declaration about Jesus. This *theophany* reveals who Jesus is, and corresponds to the preceding prophecy: John baptizes with water, but the one who baptizes with Spirit is coming. The intention of the story is primarily Christological, but it may also have served as an explanation of the baptism as a rite of initiation in the early church.

The sources

The baptism of Jesus in Mark 1:9–11 is the first presentation of Jesus in this Gospel, and the theophany is here told as a vision of Jesus: "he saw" heaven being "split" or torn apart. The divine voice from heaven confirms that Jesus is the authorized Messiah and the Son of God in accordance with the headline of the gospel (1:1).

Compared to Mark, the accounts of Matthew and Luke have some "minor agreements" that may be remnants of a *common source Q* (e.g. heaven "opened", not "split"; the descent of the Spirit "on" *epi* Jesus, not "into" *eis* him). The existence of a Q version of the story is disputed, but it seems reasonable to assume that the hypothetical source Q had a story about

Jesus' baptism between its presentation of John's message and the temptation of Jesus, perhaps in a form very similar to Mark (Meier 103).

Matthew alone adds a dialogue between Jesus and the Baptist (3:14–15), implying that John recognizes Jesus as the stronger one bringing the baptism in Spirit that he had foretold. Therefore John objects to baptize Jesus: He himself needs to receive the baptism from Jesus. But Jesus argues that they should "fulfil all righteousness." Jesus is the obedient Son of God, a model for his followers who also are called to "righteousness" (Matt 5:20). In the Great Commission at the end of the gospel, the way to become a disciple is baptism (28:19). Jesus' baptism may therefore in Matthew also function as a model for Christian baptism: his followers should be baptized like him (Hartman 24f). Peculiar to Matthew is the third person in the voice from heaven, "this is my son ... " addressed to the audience or the readers of the gospel, instead of the second person in Mark and Luke, "you are my son ... " addressed to Jesus. This may be an adaptation to the heavenly voice at the transfiguration of Jesus (Mark 9:7).

Luke seems to reduce the role of the Baptist by telling of his imprisonment before the baptism of Jesus (3:19–22). This corresponds to his correction of the popular rumour in 3:15 that John may be the Messiah. The baptism of Jesus is only briefly mentioned, together with the baptism of "all the people." The focus is on the theophany. Luke alone mentions Jesus' prayer at this occasion, and makes clear that the Spirit came on him "in bodily form" like a dove. The following genealogy traces Jesus' ancestors back to Adam, the son of God, indicating the role of Jesus as a representative not only of Israel, but of all human beings.

The fourth Gospel does not present John as the "Baptist" and has no direct indication that Jesus was baptized by John. This does not mean that the role of John is reduced; on the contrary, he is the most prominent "witness" for Jesus, introduced already in the prologue. He was not the light, but a witness to the light (1:6–8), he was surpassed by him who came after him, but in fact was before him (1:15, 30). Three times his baptism in water is mentioned (1:26, 31, 33) but it is inferior to the coming Spirit baptism. John has seen the Spirit coming down from Heaven and remaining on Jesus, and he can testify: "This is the Son of God" (1:32–34). The combination of the gift of the Spirit with a declaration of sonship in this text is a clear indication that the fourth gospel knows the synoptic tradition of the baptism of Jesus. This is also probable from the often neglected remark in John 6:27, that God the Father has "put his seal" on Jesus. The seal is very early a symbol of the gift of the Spirit in baptism (2 Cor 1:22; 2 Clem 7:6; Herm 93). The subject of the sealing, however, is not John, but God the Father. In the fourth Gospel it is more important that Jesus is confirmed by God than that he was baptized by John. John's role is to identify Jesus as the Spirit baptizer and to testify to him as the Son of God. This Gospel alone informs us that Jesus baptized others in Judea before John was put in prison (3:22–26; 4:1–3). According to John 7:37–39 and 20:22, however, this cannot be the promised Spirit baptism. During his lifetime Jesus (or his disciples, some of whom were originally John's disciples 1:35–39) conducts a water baptism in line with John's own. This picture of a baptismal activity by Jesus parallel to that of John also seems to presuppose that Jesus had been baptized by John.

The baptism of Jesus is mentioned in the apocryphal *Gospels of the Ebionites* and of the Hebrews (mid-second century, texts in Aland's synopsis). They are evidently dependent on the synoptic versions, but have some peculiarities. In the gospel of the Ebionites a light enlightens the place of baptism, and *after* John has heard the voice from heaven he kneels before Jesus and asks him to baptize him. In one fragment of the *Gospel of Hebrews* the mother and the brothers of Jesus encourage him to be baptized by John, but he asks back: "What sin have I committed?" Here the embarrassment at the baptism of Jesus is expressed: How could the sinless undergo a baptism for remission of sins? In another fragment it is not the

voice from heaven but the Holy Spirit who addresses Jesus: he has being waiting for him in all the prophets, and now he can rest in him who is the firstborn son of the Spirit.

Ignatius of Antioch briefly mentions the baptism of Jesus in his letter to the Ephesians 18:2: "He was born and was baptized, that by his passion he might purify the water." Here the baptism of Jesus is seen as the preparation of the Christian baptism. This is probably also the implication of Justin's remark in *Dial.* 88:3: when Jesus entered the water "a fire was kindled in Jordan." Similar expressions are used when Justin describes his conversion in Dial. 4:1. They correspond to the designation of baptism as "enlightenment" *fotismos* (Apol. 61:12, cf. Dial. 39:2; 122:3–5). The baptism of Jesus is for Justin the beginning of the "fire" that later is given in Christian baptism as a metaphor for spiritual wisdom or "enlightenment".

The references to the baptism of Jesus in the *Testaments of the Twelve Patriarchs* (*T. Levi* 18:6–7 and *T. Jud.* 24:2–4) are Christian interpolations, perhaps from the early second century CE.

These later sources inform us about early Christian reflections on the meaning of the baptism of Jesus, but they do not supply us with historical information beyond the canonical gospels.

Historicity and significance

There are no good reasons to doubt that the baptism of Jesus by John is a historical fact. It is well attested in the Synoptic Gospels, probably with Q as an independent source in addition to Mark. It has been taken for granted in Christian tradition and is broadly accepted in modern scholarship (Meier 101). It is indirectly supported by many sayings of Jesus where John has a positive role as God's messenger and as a precursor of Jesus (Matt 11:1–19 par. Luke 7:18–35) and by his explicit reference to John's baptism as coming from God (Mark 11:27–33). The most decisive argument for its historicity is the embarrassment it evidently has evoked in the early church. If Jesus was baptized by John, it would be natural to regard John as the greater one. If Jesus was baptized with a baptism for repentance and remission of sins, Jesus must have been a sinner in need of repentance. This kind of logic would contradict the picture of Jesus in the early church and seems to be encountered in the gospels when John himself admits his need to be baptized by Jesus (Matthew) or when the active role of John as baptizer at this occasion is played down to a minimum (Luke) or to nothing (John). It is hardly possible to imagine a reason to "invent" a story that evidently created such problems. Jesus' baptism by John was in the Early Church a well-known fact that needed explanation, but that nobody could explain away.

From this historical fact we may deduce that Jesus accepted John as a prophet sent by God and his baptismal activity as a way of preparing the people of God for the coming judgement. It is historically more dubious whether John recognized and accepted Jesus as the "stronger one" he had prophesied. His question from his imprisonment: "Are you the one who was to come, or should we expect someone else?" (Matt 11:2–6; Luke 7:18–22) may be authentic, but his witness to Jesus as the Son of God and as the Lamb of God in the fourth gospel is probably due to theological reinterpretation.

That Jesus underwent a baptism to remission of sins does not necessarily imply that he saw himself as a sinner. John called the people of Israel as a whole to conversion and repentance. Jesus may have received his baptism because he identified himself with this prophetic call to the people, not because he had a burdened conscience or a personal need for remission of sins. His baptism is his identification both with John's message and with the people of Israel. The question of Jesus' sinlessness cannot be decided historically from the fact of his baptism alone, but should be considered theologically from the NT as a whole (Meier 111–16).

From a historical point of view we should distinguish between the fact of Jesus' baptism and the theophany linked to it. The latter cannot be conceived as a "public event" in the same manner as the water rite, which was visible and audible to everybody who might be present. Mark presents the theophany as a vision of Jesus. This may imply that others were not able to see the Spirit coming down or to hear the heavenly voice. In this respect the story may be comparable to the call of the prophets in the OT and the Damascus experience of Paul. Such experiences are hardly accessible to bystanders and in that respect not to historical investigation in a narrow sense. But they are historical by their impact on the persons involved and their consequences in their lives. For Jesus the theophany at his baptism functions as the decisive experience on his way to a public ministry.

The stories of the theophany at Jesus' baptism have no references to witnesses except Jesus himself and John. In this regard they are similar to the temptation stories, presented as an experience between Jesus and the devil, with no others present. Jesus has not yet called disciples to follow him, so they cannot be presupposed to have witnessed these events in the same way as they are present "the whole time the Lord Jesus went in and out among us, beginning from John's baptism to the time when Jesus was taken up from us" (Acts 1:21–22). Luke the historian has evidently reflected on the question of eyewitnesses to the life of Jesus (Luke 1:2), and this means that the historicity of the baptismal theophany and the temptation (and even more the infancy stories in Luke 1–2 and Matt 1–2) must be assessed differently from the public ministry of Jesus, where the disciples as eyewitnesses give a continuity to the traditions in the gospels.

The story of the transfiguration of Jesus (Mark 9:2–10; Matt 17:1–17; Luke 9:28–36) is different in so far as three disciples are mentioned as witnesses to the event. The heavenly voice here gives a similar declaration as at the baptism, but now in the third person in all the three gospels, and they all render an additional imperative addressed to the witnesses: "Hear him!" The role of the disciples as witnesses in this story is further elaborated in 2 Pet 1:16–18, pointing to its difference from "cleverly invented myths" because "we" were eyewitnesses and heard the heavenly voice on the holy mountain.

The theophany at the baptism can historically be seen either as a "Christian composition interpreting the significance of Jesus' person and mission vis-à-vis his potential rival John" (Meier 107, cf. Vögtle and Lentzen-Deis), or as a tradition based on Jesus' personal experience at his baptism (Dunn 23–37, DeMaris). If it is a Christian composition it cannot be a source to the historical Jesus, but to the development of the Christology of the early church. Even if it is based on based on a vision Jesus had in connection with his baptism, the form and words may have been influenced by the reflection of those who transmitted it.

The content of the story is confirmed by basic features in the picture of Jesus in the gospels. The descent of the Spirit points to his life as a man of the Spirit, guided by the Spirit and working in the power of the Spirit (Matt 12:28) until the Spirit is released to his disciples on the resurrection day (John 20:22) or at Pentecost (Acts 2). The voice from heaven points in a pregnant way to Jesus as fulfilment of Scripture. He is the Son of God, a title designating the Messiah or Davidic king as the adopted son of God (2 Sam 7:14; Ps 2:7). As Son of God Jesus is conscious of standing in a unique relationship to God as his Father (Matt 11:25–27; Luke 10:21–22). His basic trust in God leads him to teach his disciples to address God as their Father (Matt 6:9; Luke 11:2). As "beloved" son he is an antitype to Isaac in Gen 22, so that his baptism also may point forward to his passion, the last test of his obedience to God the loving Father. This direction may also be implied in the expression "in whom I am well pleased", which is taken from the first Servant song in Isaiah 42:1 and may connect Jesus with the suffering Servant in Isaiah 53. His way to the cross made him different from the messianic expectations of his contemporaries. He was sent to release his people not from their enemies, but from their sins.

We have no historical means to check out how many of these ideas were a part of Jesus' own self-consciousness, and even less to control whether they were there from the beginning of his ministry or gradually came to his mind and determined his way. But as far as such ideas can be accepted as important for the historical Jesus and his aims, it should also be possible to regard his experience at his baptism as a decisive sign to show him his way.

The baptism of Jesus was important for the early church not only to explain who Jesus was and is. It must very early have been seen as the source of and model for Christian baptism (Kvalbein). It also played a role in the development of the Trinitarian dogma. The baptism to the name of the Father, the Son and the Holy Spirit (Matt 28:19; *Did.* 7:1) could be seen as instituted in the baptism of Jesus, where the Father as the voice from heaven addressed his Son in the Jordan and bestowed on him the Holy Spirit. But these aspects of the story lead us beyond its possible significance for the historical Jesus.

HANS KVALBEIN

Further reading

Alands K. (ed.) *Synopsis Quattuor Evangeliorum* rev. ed., Stuttgard: Deutsche Bibelgesellschaft, 1985.

Beasley-Murray, G. R. *Baptism in the New Testament*. Grand Rapids, MI: Eerdmans, 1962, reprinted 1990.

Chilton, Bruce. *Jesus' Baptism and Jesus' Healing: His Personal Practice of Spirituality*, Harrisburg, PA: Trinity Press International, 1998.

DeMaris, Richard E. "The Baptism of Jesus: A Ritual-Critical Approach," in Wolfgang Stegemann, Bruce J. Malina, and Gerd Theissen (eds) *The Social Setting of Jesus and the Gospels*, Minneapolis, MN: Fortress Press, 2002, pp. 137–57.

Dunn, James D. G. *Baptism in the Holy Spirit: A Reexamination of the New Testament Teaching on the Gift of the Spirit in Relation to Pentecostalism Today*, Philadelphia, PA: Westminster Press, 1970.

Evans, Craig A. "The Baptism of John in a Typological Context," in Stanley E. Porter and Anthony R. Cross (eds) *Dimensions of Baptism: Biblical and Theological Studies*, JSNTSS 234, London: Sheffield Academic Press, 2002, pp. 45–71.

Hartman, Lars. *Into the Name of the Lord Jesus: Baptism in the Early Church*, Edinburgh: T. & T. Clark, 1997.

Kvalbein, Hans. "The Baptism of Jesus as a Model for Christian Baptism: Can the Idea be Traced Back to New Testament Times?" *ST* 50 (1996) 67–83.

Légasse, Simon. *Naissance du baptême*, Lectio Divina 153, Paris: Éditions du Cerf, 1993.

Lentzen-Deis, Fritzleo. *Die Taufe Jesu nach den Synoptikern*, Frankfurter Theologische Studien Vol. 4, Frankfurt: Knecht, 1970.

Meier, John P. *A Marginal Jew: Rethinking the Historical Jesus, Vol. 2: Mentor, Message and Miracles*, New York, London, Toronto, Sydney, Auckland: Doubleday, 1994.

Sanders, E. P. *The Historical Figure of Jesus*, London: Penguin, 1993.

Theissen, Gerd and Annette Merz. *Der historische Jesus: Ein Lehrbuch*, 2, Auflage Göttingen: Vandenhoeck & Ruprecht, 1997.

Vögtle, Anton. "Die sogenannte Taufperikope Mark 1,9–11. Zur Problematik der Herkunft und des ursprünglichen Sinns," in *Evangelisch-Katholischer Kommentar zum Neuen Testament. Vorarbeiten 4*, Neukirchen-Vluyn: Neukirchener, 1972.

BEATITUDES AND BLESSING

Beatitudes in Greek and Hebrew

The word 'beatitudes' is derived from Latin *beati*, meaning 'blessed' or 'happy'. It is often applied to pronouncements of blessing found in Jewish and Christian texts, both in Hebrew and Greek. Beatitudes found in Greek texts are also called makarisms, after the Greek word μακάριοι. The equivalent Hebrew word is אַשְׁרֵי. Beatitudes are found in the Old Testament (e.g. Isa 30:18; 56:2; Ps 1:1; 2:12; 32:1, 2; 119:1, 2), in Rabbinic sources (e.g. *b. Hag.* 14b; *b. Yoma* 87a), and in the New Testament (e.g. Rom 14:22; Jas 1:12; Rev 1:3 [see also later]).

Jesus' beatitudes in the Gospels

The New Testament Gospels contain many beatitudes spoken by Jesus (Matt 5:3, 4, 5, 6, 7, 8, 9, 10, 11; 11:6; 13:16; 16:17; 24:46; Luke 6:20, 21 [2x], 22; 7:23; 10:23; 11:28; 12:37, 43; John 20:29). Some are also found in the *Gospel of Thomas* (7, 19, 49, 54, 58, 68, 69 [2x], 79, 103), an apocryphon which some scholars believe to be dependent on the New Testament Gospels, although others regard it as an independent account of the sayings of Jesus.

The most well-known list of beatitudes presented as spoken by Jesus is found in the Gospel of Matthew, in Jesus' Sermon on the Mount (5:3–12). In the Gospel of Luke we find a shorter parallel list as part of Jesus' Sermon on the Plain (6:20–23; cf. Matt 5:3, 4, 6, 11–12). Each beatitude consists of the initial word μακάριοι (the plural form of the adjective 'blessed' in Greek), a description of those called 'blessed', followed by a clause stating the reason why these people are blessed.

The main variances between Matthew's and Luke's lists of beatitudes are as follows:

1 Matthew has a list of eight or nine beatitudes (nine, if one counts 5:11) whereas Luke a list of four.
2 Unlike Matthew's, Luke's list of beatitudes is followed by a list of woes (cf. 6:24–26).
3 Matthew uses the third person plural whereas Luke the second person plural.
4 'The poor' in Luke 6:20 are 'the poor in spirit' in Matt 5:3, to the former ones belongs 'the kingdom of God', to the latter ones 'the Kingdom of Heaven'.
5 'Those who are weeping' in Luke 6:21 are 'those who mourn' in Matt 5:4, the former ones 'will laugh', the latter ones 'will be comforted'.
6 'The hungry' in Luke 6:21 are 'those who hunger and thirst for righteousness' in Matt 5:6, the former ones 'will be satisfied', the latter ones 'will be filled'.
7 'Those hated, excluded and reviled on account of the Son of Man' in Luke 6:22 are 'those persecuted for righteousness' sake' in Matt 5:10 and 'those insulted, persecuted and falsely accused on account of Jesus' in Matt 5:11.

The first eight beatitudes in Matthew form a literary unit, as is indicated by the *inclusio* 'for theirs is the kingdom of heaven' (5:3, 10; cf. Luke 6:20). The promise is attached to all other beatitudes as well (Carson 1984: 132). Unlike the first eight, the last beatitude is a direct address in the second person plural, just like Luke's beatitudes, and could be seen as a summary statement of the preceding ones. The theme of the 'kingdom of God' was central to the message of the historical Jesus. 'kingdom of God' (Luke) and 'kingdom of heaven' (Matthew) can be treated as synonymous. Writing as a Jew for a Jewish audience, Matthew prefers using the latter in order to avoid the name of God (Harrington 1991: 79). It is a matter of debate whether the 'kingdom of God' is the transformation of this world (present or future) or the eschatological hope for the next world. In the list of beatitudes the mere use of the future tense in Greek indicates a futuristic aspect to the kingdom of God. Luke makes a deliberate contrast between the present state of the oppressed and their future reward by adding adverbs of time, i.e. 'now' (6:21 [2x]) versus 'in that day' (6:23), thereby making clear that the kingdom of God is still in anticipation. It

could be argued that Matthew may also add a present dimension to the kingdom of God, since the *inclusio* 'because theirs *is* the kingdom of heaven' (5:3, 10) suggests it has already arrived. Jesus has already effected God's redemptive reign.

Beatitude 1: 'Blessed are the poor in spirit, for theirs is the kingdom of heaven' (Matt 5:3) || 'Blessed are you who are poor, for yours is the kingdom of God' (Luke 6:20).

Some scholars would say that Matthew's 'poor in spirit' stands in contrast to 'the poor' of Luke (e.g. Schweizer 88). The antithetical parallel '(woe to) the rich' in Luke 6.24 suggests that Luke is referring to a socioeconomic status whereas Matthew seems to describe a virtue, a spiritual quality. In Luke's account, the kingdom of God is a promise to the oppressed that God in His compassion will vindicate them. Matthew, on the other hand, makes being 'poor in spirit' (often understood as meaning being 'humble') an ethical requirement to enter the Kingdom of Heaven. Scholars who seek to harmonize the two gospel accounts argue that 'the poor' and 'the poor in spirit' are one and the same category of people (e.g. Broer 71; Hagner 91–92). 'The poor in spirit' are also literally poor in the sense of economically deprived. Perhaps Matthew wishes to emphasize that this poverty is voluntary, chosen for spiritual reasons. The occurrence of the equivalent Hebrew expression in the Dead Sea Scrolls (עֲנוֵי רוּחַ, 1QM 14:7; cf. Isa 61:1) apparently in reference to the 'sons of light', may possibly support this harmonization, because these pious members of the Qumran community lived in voluntary poverty, entirely dependent on God (Harrington 78–79).

Beatitude 2: 'Blessed are those who mourn, for they will be comforted' (Matt 5:4) || 'Blessed are you who weep now, for you will laugh' (Luke 6:21).

Like 'the poor', 'those who weep' in Luke 6:21 are the needy who have been rejected by society, but who 'will laugh' when vindicated by God. Luke may be alluding to Ps 126:2–6. Matthew's word-choice (5.4), on the other hand, echoes Isa 61:2 (LXX), where 'those who mourn' bewail the loss of their nation as a result of sin and will be comforted by God (Guelich 1982: 100–1).

Beatitude 3: 'Blessed are the meek, for they will inherit the earth' (Matt 5:5).

Matthew's third beatitude is almost a quotation of Ps 37:11 (LXX): 'The meek will inherit the earth.'

Some say that 'the meek' refers to a socioeconomic status, 'those who have been humbled, oppressed'; others say it is expressing a spiritual quality, 'those humble before God'. 'The earth' is probably a reference to the (through God's intervention) 'regenerated earth' (Hagner 92), and thus can be seen as a parallel to the 'Kingdom of Heaven'.

Beatitude 4: 'Blessed are those who hunger and thirst for righteousness, for they will be filled' (Matt 5:6) || 'Blessed are you who hunger now, for you will be satisfied' (Luke 6:21).

'The hungry' in Luke 6:21 has an antithetical parallel in 6:25, 'the full' who are well off and have enough to eat; the socioeconomic status of the recipients of blessing and curse is described. Again, some view Matthew's redactional addition, 'those who hunger and thirst for righteousness' as a spiritualization of the original version. They interpret the word 'righteousness' as personal righteousness: in contrast to Luke, Matthew describes an ethical quality as prerequisite for entrance into the Kingdom, so they argue (e.g. Betz 129–32). Other scholars say, especially those who seek to harmonize the two Gospel accounts, that 'righteousness' here means 'social justice' (e.g. Hagner 93): in other words, those who have experienced injustice are longing for God to intervene.

Beatitude 5: 'Blessed are the merciful, for they will be shown mercy' (Matt 5:7).

Some would say 'the merciful' are those who show kindness to people in need (e.g. Hagner 93; cf. Prov 14:21); others believe it means those who do not judge and are forgiving towards others. It is God who will show them mercy in return, i.e. forgiveness (e.g. Guelich 1982: 104–5; cf. Matt 18:21–35; Luke 6:36).

Beatitude 6: 'Blessed are the pure in heart, for they will see God' (Matt 5:8).

'The pure in heart' are sincere and loyal before God, and therefore will be accepted into His presence (cf. Ps 24:4; Matt 7:16–20; 12.33–35; Luke 6:43–45).

Beatitude 7: 'Blessed are the peacemakers, for they will be called sons of God' (Matt 5:9).

'The peacemakers' are those who love their enemies, a love Jesus required to become sons of His Father (cf. Matt 5:43–48).

Beatitudes 8 and 9: 'Blessed are those who are persecuted because of righteousness, for theirs is the kingdom of heaven. Blessed are you when people insult you, persecute you and falsely say all kinds of evil against you because of me' (Matt 5:10, 11) || 'Blessed are you when men hate you, when they exclude you and insult you and reject your name as evil, because of the Son of Man' (Luke 6:22)

Matthew's 'righteousness' which leads to persecution is the godly behaviour of the recipients of blessing. By leading holy lives they become partakers of the kingdom of God. Luke's 'because of the Son of Man' expresses essentially the same notion as Matthew's 'because of righteousness' and 'because of me (Jesus)': believing in Christ and acting in a Christ-like manner leads to persecution. The blessed ones' 'reward in heaven' (Matt 5:12 || Luke 6:23) refers to their position in the kingdom of God.

The distinct variances among the evangelists raise the question whether these beatitudes are authentic sayings of Jesus. Most scholars would say that both Matthew and Luke have derived them from the Q document (see also Form criticism) and have modified them in order to suit their respective Gospel message. It is more likely that Jesus spoke the beatitudes in the second person plural which Matthew changed into third person plural in order to make clear the 'universal significance' of the teachings of Jesus (Hagner 90). So the exact wording of the beatitudes found in the Gospels may not be identical to the actual words spoken by the historical Jesus.

Jesus' beatitudes and the Qumran wisdom text 4QBeatitudes

Of Jewish beatitudes' lists at present knowable, those found in a Qumran wisdom text, 4Q525 (also known as 4QBeat), are probably the closest in date to those of Jesus, and therefore deserve special attention. We will compare them to the longer list of beatitudes in Matthew.

There are two main differences between the Qumran beatitudes and the Matthean makarisms. First of all, the Matthean makarisms do not mention 'the pursuit of wisdom'. In this regard they are in contrast with the Qumran beatitudes, those of Sir 14:20–27, and those of Prov 3:13; 8:32, 34 (Viviano 1993: 76). Second, each Matthean makarism gives a reason for the proclamation of blessedness whereas the Qumran beatitudes do not tell us why the person in question is blessed (Viviano 1992: 53–54).

The most obvious parallels between the Qumran and Matthean beatitudes are the following: the importance of a pure heart (4Q525, fr. 2 ii 1; Matt 5:8) and the emphasis on rejoicing in doing good, despite difficulties and trials (4Q525, fr. 2 ii 2–6; Matt 5.11–12) (Evans 142). In short, both emphasize the importance of sincerity and perseverance.

There are even more similarities between the two collections of beatitudes than one might think at first sight. This becomes clear when one looks at their function within their context. The Matthean makarisms may not have an explicit reference to the pursuit of wisdom. However, like the author of 4Q525, in one of his parables on the kingdom of heaven Matthew does make a distinction between the wise and the foolish. The five wise virgins entered the kingdom of heaven, but the five foolish virgins did not (Matt 25:1–13). In Matthew the phrase 'for theirs is the kingdom of heaven' (5:3–10) functions as an inclusio to the beatitudes. In the Matthean beatitudes the blessed ones are those to whom belongs 'the kingdom of heaven'. The parable of the ten virgins tells us that the wise enter the kingdom of heaven. So those blessed ones of Matthew 5 are the wise of Matthew 25. Likewise, in 4Q525 the wise are called blessed (fr. 2 ii 3).

In some ways the Qumran beatitudes relate in a similar manner to their context as do the Matthean makarisms. For they both point to the final outcome of one's actions in the day of judgment. Neither the author of 4Q525 nor Matthew refers to the day of judgment in their beatitudes. However, the Qumran beatitudes are placed in a context which speaks of this day designated (fr. 22). Likewise, Matthew has several references to 'the day' or 'the day of judgment' (7:22; 11:22, 24; 12:36; 24:36, 38, 50; 25:13). The blessed ones to whom the kingdom of heaven belongs (5:3–10) will inherit the kingdom on the day when the Son of Man will come to judge the righteous and the wicked. Then He will separate them like sheep from goats (Matt 25:31–46). The same division between the righteous and the wicked is made in 4Q525. The promised invitation in Matt 25:34 'Come, you blessed ones (οἱ εὐλογημένοι) of My Father, inherit the Kingdom prepared for you from the foundation of the world' brings to mind the promise made in 4Q525, fr. 14 ii 7 to those who have led wise lives: 'You shall be blessed (תתברך).' 'The accursed ones' who 'will go away into eternal punishment' in Matt 25:41, 46 remind us of 'those cursed of God continually' and 'the eternal curses' in 4Q525, frs 15 and 21. Moreover, the fire-imagery which is so vivid in 4Q525, i.e. 'flame[s of] death' (fr. 15 5, רשפ[י]מות) which fly about, 'flaming brimstone'

(fr. 15 6, להבי גו[פ]רית), also occurs in Matthew. It speaks of 'the eternal fire' into which 'the accursed ones' will go (25:41). In 7:13–14 Matthew refers to 'the way which leads to destruction' and 'the way which leads to life'. These expressions call to mind the contrast made in 4Q525 between 'the paths of folly' (fr. 2 ii 2) and 'the paths of life' (fr. 15 8). In chapter 25 Matthew makes explicit by the use of vivid imagery where those on the way to destruction and those on the way to life will end. Likewise, 4Q525 draws a clear picture of the place where those on the paths of folly will go, into 'the depth of the pit' (fr. 23 3), into 'the fiery furnace' (fr. 23 4).

The main difference between the Qumran beatitudes and the Matthean makarisms is that the latter are connected with Christ. When Jesus predicts the coming of the Son of Man in glory to separate the sheep from the goats, He is speaking of His own coming (25:31ff.). In Matthew it is Jesus who is pictured as Judge. In 4Q525, on the other hand, only God Himself is Judge (cf. 'those cursed of God con[tinually] ... '). This difference makes Matthew's beatitudes unique, despite the many similarities.

JACQUELINE DE ROO

Further reading

Albright, W. F. and C. S. Mann. *Matthew*, AB 26, New York: Doubleday, 1971.

Betz, H. D. *The Sermon on the Mount*, Minneapolis, MN: Fortress Press, 1995 [1985].

Broer, I. *Die Seligpreissungen der Bergpredigt*, BBT 61, Bonn: Peter Haustein, 1986.

Brooke, G. J. "The Wisdom of Matthew's Beatitudes," *ScrB* 19 (1988–89) 35–41.

—— *The Dead Sea Scrolls and the New Testament*, Minneapolis, MN: Fortress Press, 2005.

Carson, D. A. "Matthew," in F. E. Gaebelein (ed.) *The Expositor's Bible Commentary*, Grand Rapids, MI: Zondervan, 1984, Vol. 8.

Dupont, J. *Les Béatitudes*, 3 vols, Paris: Gabalda, 1969–73.

Evans, C. A. *Jesus and His Contemporaries: Comparative Studies*, Leiden: Brill, 1995.

Fabry, H. J. "Die Seligpreisungen in der Bibel und in Qumran," in C. Hempel, A. Lange, and H. Lichtenberger (eds) *The Wisdom Texts from Qumran and the Development of Sapiential Thought*, Leuven: Peeters, 2005, pp. 189–200.

Fitzmyer, J. A. "A Palestinian Collection of Beatitudes," in F. Van Segbroeck, C. M. Tuckett, J. Verheyden, and G. van Belle (eds) *The Four Gospels. Festschrift Frans Neirynck*, 4 vols, BETL 100, Louvain: Louvain University Press, 1992, Vol. 2, pp. 509–15.

Guelich, R. A. "The Matthean Beatitudes: 'Entrance Requirements' or Eschatological Blessings?" *JBL* 95 (1976) 415–34.

—— *The Sermon on the Mount*, Waco, TX: Word, 1982.

Hagner, D. A. *Matthew 1–13*, WBC 33A, Dallas, TX: Word, 1993.

Harrington, D. J. *The Gospel of Matthew*, Collegeville, PA: Liturgical Press, 1991.

Puech, E. "Un hymne essénien en partie retrouvé et les béatitudes," *RevQ* 13 (1988) 59–88.

—— "4Q525 et les péricopes des béatitudes en Ben Sira et Matthieu," *RB* 98 (1991) 80–106.

—— "The Collection of Beatitudes in Hebrew and in Greek (4Q525 1–4 and MT 5.3–12)," in F. Manns and E. Alliata (eds) *Early Christianity in Context. Monuments and Documents*, Jerusalem: Jerusalem Franciscan Printing Press, 1993, pp. 353–68.

Schweizer, E. *The Good News According to Matthew*, trans. D. E. Green, London: SPCK, 1976.

Viviano, B. T. "Beatitudes Found Among the Dead Sea Scrolls," *BAR* 18 (1992) 53–56.

—— "Eight Beatitudes at Qumran and in Matthew?," *SEÅ* 58 (1993) 71–84.

BETHANY AND BETHPHAGE

Bethany

Place (Hebr. *Bet Aniyya, Bet Hannanyah*; Gk. *Bēthania* "the house of the poor man" or "of Ananias").

Bethany was a small town or village on the eastern side of the Mount of Olives, about 2 miles (~15 stadia = 2.775 km) east of Jerusalem (John 11:18), near or on the Jericho road (Mark 11:1; Luke 19:29). Bethany was a lodging place for Jews visiting Jerusalem on pilgrimages.

Bethany is an important town in the ministry of Jesus – from a place of refugee to a place of commissioning. There are several significant events that occurred in Bethany during the ministry of Jesus. First, Jesus made Bethany his headquarters during his final week of ministry (see Mark 11:11, 12 and Matt 21:17 "[Jesus] spent the night there"; cf. Luke 19:29). Second, Jesus was anointed in the house of Simon the leper (Mark 14:3 = Matt 26:6; cf. John 12:1–9) by an unnamed woman. This woman is referred to as "Mary" in John's account. (Martha also served a meal on this occasion (see John 12:2), which may suggest that this may have been the same home as Simon's. Or there could be two different houses; cf. Luke 10:38–42. Mary and Martha's relationship to Simon is unclear, which may support two different houses.) It appears that the reference to Simon as "the leper" may be more of a nickname than an indication that he had the dreaded disease. Religious tradition prohibited any Jew to enter or reside in a home where a leper was present; perhaps Jesus had previously healed Simon, since He frequented the town often. Hence, the villagers knew Simon as "the leper." In any case, Jesus was anointed in his home. Third, and perhaps most significant, Jesus raises Lazarus from the dead (John 11:1–44). Lazarus and his sisters Mary and Martha are established in this town. Fourth, and final, Jesus, after his resurrection, blesses the disciples and ascends into heaven from Bethany (see Luke 24:50). Acts 1:6–12 seems to suggest that the ascension took place near or on the Mount of Olives, which would include Bethany.

The village is presently named El-'Aziriyeh or El-'Azir (the Arabic form of the name of "Lazarus") and has been a pilgrimage site since the fourth century, due in part to the supposed location of the tomb of Lazarus and the home of Simon the leper. Eusebius the Church historian (260–339 CE) mentions the legacy of Lazarus's tomb "There the place of Lazarus is still shown" (*Onomasticon*).

Bethany beyond the Jordan

There is another Bethany mentioned in John's Gospel "This took place in Bethany across the Jordan where John was baptizing" (1:28) on the east side of the Jordan River. There is some discrepancy about the actual name and place of the gospel's reference (the AV has "Bethabara," which is located on the west side of the Jordan; hence the confusion). Origen (3 CE) adopted a reading of "Bethabara," (followed by John Chrysostom 4/5th c.) since he knew of a few copies of manuscripts that had this word. Bethabara means "House of Preparation" which would seem to fit John's activity there (i.e. John's baptism of Jesus). B. Metzger concludes, however, that "Bethany" is established in the earliest manuscript (P[75]; 3 CE) and most widely attested reading (see Metzger).

Bethphage

Place (Hebr. *Bēth Paghāh* "house of unripe figs"; Gk. *Bēthphagē* "house of figs").

A village near or on the Mount of Olives, near Bethany, on the road going east from Jerusalem to Jericho (i.e. the Jericho road), where Jesus sent his disciples to secure a donkey for his triumphant entry into Jerusalem (Matt 21:11; Mark 11:1; Luke 19:29). It was also in the vicinity of Bethphage that Jesus cursed the barren fig tree (Matt 21:18–20; Mark 11:12–14, 20–21). In the Mishnah, there is an indication that Bethphage may have been a suburb of Jerusalem, surrounded perhaps by its own wall (see *m. Menahoth* 11.6). Many scholars locate Bethphage east of Bethany, because it is always listed before Bethany when the two are mentioned (see Mark 11:1; Luke 19:29). Beth-phage's exact location has never been determined.

JOSEPH B. MODICA

Further reading

Finegan, Jack. *The Archeology of the New Testament: The Life of Jesus and the Beginning of the Early Church*, revised edition, Princeton, NJ: Princeton University Press, 1992.
Metzfery, B. M., *A Textual Commentary on the Greek New Testament*, London and New York: United Bible Societies, 1971.

BETHLEHEM

The word "Bethlehem" consists of two Hebrew words, *beth*, which means "house," and *lechem*, which means "bread." Bethlehem of Judah, the Bethlehem familiar to readers of the gospel as the birthplace of Jesus, was situated in Judea around 10 km south of Jerusalem. It came to be of some importance when the Prophet Micah suggested that it would be there that the expected "Messiah" would be born (see Mic 5:2). The Bible also, however, knows of another town of the same name, in Zebulon (see Josh 19:15 and Jud 12:8–10) and a scant 7 miles from Nazareth. In connection with the Historical Jesus, however, this northern locale plays no part in spite of the suggestion of some (particularly most recently Bruce Chilton 2000: 8–9, 294) that the northern Bethlehem is the intended reference in Matthew's Gospel. Indeed, the fact that Matthew specifically says "of Judea" (2:1) is all that is needed to dismiss that suggestion.

The word "Bethlehem" occurs in Matt 2:1, 2:5, 2:6, 2:8, 2:16, Luke 2:4, 2:15, and finally John 7:42. It is Matthew who is predominantly concerned with this town and draws a connection to the prophetic indication of its importance in the life of Jesus. In contrast, Luke's interest is marginal and John's even more so.

Matthew's use of the word occurs only in the second chapter of his Gospel, in his telling of the events surrounding the birth of Jesus. The historical background provided there offers a number of important clues to the life of Jesus. First, Herod is the king when Jesus is born. Second, he is visited there by wise men from eastern lands. The number of wise men is unclear, though the plural *magoi* (magi) indicates that there were at least two. Tradition suggests that there were three, because three gifts were offered to the newborn king. But that is simply unsubstantiated speculation. Third, the wise men enquire of Herod the location of the king's birth. Fourth, Herod enquires of the priests and they suggest that Micah 5 offers the answer. Fifth,

the wise men depart and arrive in Bethlehem. Sixth, they present their gifts to the baby and his family. Seventh, they depart for home being sure to avoid a return through Jerusalem.

Matthew then relates that Jesus and his family flee to Egypt because Joseph has been warned of Herod's wrath. When next Bethlehem is mentioned (in 2:16) it is to inform the reader of what took place there: the "Slaughter of the Innocents." Though there is no extra-biblical evidence for this event, it certainly aligns quite nicely with what we know of Herod from Josephus, the Jewish historian. Matthew 2:17–18 relates this slaughter to a proclamation of Jeremiah that Rachel would weep because her children were destroyed (Jer 31:15).

In this account Matthew makes use of passages from the Hebrew Bible to confirm that Jesus is, in fact, the expected Messianic figure. Bethlehem figures as the central location for his birth and early life because, in Matthew's estimation, that is where the Savior would be born.

Luke's use of Bethlehem, too, ties in with prophetic expectation. In Luke 2:4, he makes it quite clear that Joseph went to Bethlehem to enroll for the tax lists because he was a descendent of David. That the census recorded by Luke didn't take place until 6 CE doesn't affect in any substantive way the theological significance of his telling of the tale of Jesus' birth. At 2:15 Luke relates that the shepherds who had been addressed by the angelic visitor make their way to Bethlehem because they have been told that the Savior would be there. They would find him in swaddling clothes, the clothing of the newborn, and lying in a feeding trough. In both Matthew and Luke, Bethlehem is the "Messianic" town and naturally the messiah would be born there.

The final passage in which Bethlehem occurs in the gospels (and in the New Testament as a whole) is John 7:42. The context is Jesus' speech on the "last day of the feast" where he utters the great invitation that all those who thirst may come to him and drink. In response to this invitation, the Gospel notes that some believed on him and others didn't. With John's usual sense of irony, those who reject Jesus' invitation protest that since he is from Galilee, he cannot be the Messiah, since the Messiah will come from Bethlehem. John 7:42 says, "doesn't the Scripture say that the Christ comes from the seed of David and from Bethlehem, David's town?" John and his readers know the answer is yes. And they also know that Jesus is that Messiah. The irony is that those who reject Jesus don't know so much about him as even where he was born.

JIM WEST

Further reading

Birdsall, J. N. "The Star of Bethlehem," *ExpTim* 114 (2002) 96–98.

Chilton, B. D. *Rabbi Jesus: An Intimate Biography. The Jewish Life and Teaching that Inspired Christianity*, New York: Doubleday, 2000.

de Cree, F. "History and Archaeology of the Bet Sahlur Region. A Preparatory Study for a Regional Survey (the Bethlehem archaeological project)," *ZDPV* 115 (1999) 59–84.

Deichmann, F. W. "Zur Erscheinung des Sternes von Bethlehem," in E. Dassmann and K. Thraede (eds) *Vivarium. Festschrift Theodor Klauser zum 90. Geburtstag*, Jahrbuch für Antike und Christentum: Ergänzungsband 11, Münster: Aschendorffsche Buchhandlung, 1984, pp. 98–106.

Derrett, J. D. M. "The Manger at Bethlehem: Light on St. Luke's Technique from Contemporary Jewish Religious Law," in *SNT* 2:2, Leiden: Brill, 1973/1978, pp. 39–47.

France, R. T. "Herod and the Children of Bethlehem," *NovT* 21 (1979) 98–120.

Maier, P. L. "Herod and the Infants of Bethlehem," in E. J. Vardaman (ed.) *Chronos, Kairos, Christos II. Chronological, Nativity, and Religious Studies in Memory of Ray Summers*, Macon, GA: Mercer University Press, 1998, pp. 169–89.

Pixner, B. and B. Bargil. "Die Nazoräer, Bethlehem und die Geburt Jesu," in R. Riesner (ed.) *Wege des Messias und Stätten der Urkirche: Jesus und das Judenchristentum im Licht neuer archäologischer Erkenntnisse*, Studien zur biblischen Archäologie und Zeitgeschichte 2, Gießen: Brunnen-Verlag, 1980/1991, pp. 23–41.

BETHSAIDA

Bethsaida is located on the northeast coast of the Sea of Galilee, a mile away from the sea shore and a few hundred feet east of the Jordan River. It is identified with a 20-acre mound named e-Tell. The mound rises to an elevation of 147 feet above the Bethsaida (or Batheiha) Plain.

Bethsaida is frequently mentioned in the New Testament as the birthplace of three Apostles, Peter, Andrew, and Philip, and a center of Jesus' ministry. Byzantine sources relate two more apostles, the Zebedee sons, James and John, to Bethsaida. Near Bethsaida, Jesus healed a blind man (Mark 8:22), performed the miracle of the multiplication of fish and loaves (Luke 9:11), and was seen walking on the sea (Mark 6:45). According to Matthew and Luke (Q sources), Jesus rebuked the cities of Bethsaida, Chorazin, and Capernaum for refusing to repent.

Josephus located Bethsaida in lower Gaulanitis near the estuary of the Jordan River. He asserted that Philip, the son of Herod the Great, who inherited Gaulanitis from his father, elevated the village of Bethsaida to the status of a Greek city, *polis*, and renamed it Julias. The notion that Julias was founded in the time of Tiberius was suggested

by Eusebius in his *Chronicles* and was strongly criticized by Schuerer in the twentieth century. However, numismatic and archaeological research has revealed that he was actually correct. This enhancement took place in the year 30 CE. Julia was the name of Julia/Livia, the wife of the emperor Augustus and the mother of incumbent emperor Tiberius. Since Julia/Livia had died a few months earlier, Philip's initiation can be explained as an attempt to participate in the Roman imperial cult. Remains of a small temple discovered at the site are attributed to this activity. Bethsaida probably failed as a *polis*. The founder, Philip, had died four years after this initiation, perhaps causing funds needed to build up the city to cease. Unlike most *poleis*, Bethsaida never minted coins, indicating that it never maintained a solid economy and never developed into a thriving community during the Roman period. All these facts are crucial in the attempt to identify the town.

Josephus recounted that one of the early skirmishes in the Jewish Roman war (perhaps in 65 CE) took place near Julias (Bethsaida). In this battle he was injured and evacuated to Capernaum. Josephus never revealed the fate of the city after this battle. Archaeological excavations discovered that there is no serious destruction layer at the site and the inhabitation continued to the fourth century CE.

Eusebius located Bethsaida 6 miles from Capernaum, and from the fourth century onward Bethsaida is frequently mentioned by Christian pilgrims. Willibald, an eighth-century German pilgrim, reported that he visited Bethsaida and saw there a church dedicated to Peter; he spent a night at the site and continued the next day to Capernaum. No Byzantine church was discovered at Bethsaida. However, this description fits better with Capernaum than Bethsaida. Apparently, the authentic identification of Bethsaida was lost beginning in the fourth century CE.

History of research

The search for Bethsaida was already initiated in the Renaissance period. Bethsaida was located on the maps of the period, occasionally on the west or on the east side of the Sea of Galilee. At the end of the nineteenth century, an idea emerged that there were perhaps two places named Bethsaida, one on the western side of the lake and one on the eastern side. The view that Bethsaida and Julias are two separate locations was proposed by Schumacher in the 1880s. This theory was widely accepted throughout the twentieth century. According to this view, Bethsaida should be identified with one of the ruins on the northern shore of the Sea of Galilee, while Julias, with the palace of Philip, would have been located on the mound of e-Tell. Archaeological surveys and researches have refuted these ideas. Consequently, there is only one Bethsaida. Julias and Bethsaida were the same place.

Bethsaida was first identified with e-Tell, the largest mound around the Sea of Galilee, by the German traveler Sitzen in the early nineteenth century and again in 1838 by E. Robinson, who bolstered this identification with a scrutiny of the historical sources. The French scholar Guerin suggested in the middle of the nineteenth century that Bethsaida should be identified with Tel Hum, (today's Capernaum). He suggested identifying Capernaum with Khirbet Minyeh, which dates only to the Umayyad period (eighth century CE). The German scholar G. Schumacher speculated in 1881 that Bethsaida should be located closer to the sea shore and should be identified with el Araj, a site close to the estuary of the Jordan River. He also suggested locating the palace of Philip, the son of Herod, on the top of the mound of e-Tell.

The excavations at Bethsaida have been conducted since 1987 under the direction of R. Arav. Since 1991, they have been carried out on behalf of the Consortium for the Bethsaida Excavations Project, headed by the University of Nebraska at Omaha.

The finds of the excavations

Geological investigations at the plain of Bethsaida reveal that it emerged out of the lake only in the past 2,000 years. Prior to this, the Sea of Galilee reached the southern slopes of the mound. Earthquakes and landslides in the Jordan rift caused blocking of the river, which produced overflow and embedment of the silt on the banks of the plain. This ultimately resulted in uplifting of the plain over the banks. At the end of the process the plain emerged above the level of the lake and the shoreline withdrew southward.

The excavations revealed that Bethsaida was founded at the tenth century BCE, most probably as the capital of the kingdom of Geshur. The city thrived through the eighth century BCE and during this period monumental structures were built at Bethsaida which included two sequent massive city walls, a large city gate complex, including outer and inner city gates, a spacious courtyard and a massive bastion. Inside the city there was a large palace built in the north Syrian style known as *bit Hilani*. The city was ultimately destroyed by the Assyrian king Tiglath Pileser III in 732 BCE.

After a few centuries of meager inhabitation, the settlement resumed during the late third century BCE, and a new village was built on top of the old Iron Age monumental remains. Since the Iron Age city walls were built massive and strong (18–24 ft wide) they were still standing up to a considerable elevation in the Hellenistic Roman periods and were put to use as back walls of buildings. The outcome of this resettlement was somewhat peculiar. To an outsider it looked like a fortified town. Inside it looked rather rural.

A few courtyard houses, lined up along partly cobbled stone lanes, were excavated. The houses were built in similar design, with small to medium-sized field stones and a few semi-dressed stones surrounding the entrances. Each house consisted of a spacious but poorly paved courtyard, surrounded by a dining room at the north and large kitchen at the east. Cooking ware, grinding stones, storage, and tableware were unearthed in the kitchens. Bedrooms were perhaps at the second floor and were approached by a ladder or a wooden staircase.

Apparently, the inhabitants of Bethsaida kept close connections with the Phoenician coast and perhaps this was the place of their origin. This conclusion is supported by number of finds including Phoenician glass, high-quality fine ware pottery, manufactured in the Phoenician coast, and coin finds showing that most of the coins were minted either in Tyre or Sidon. Particularly outstanding are two high-quality silver tetradrachmas minted around 300 BCE, one in Tyre and the other in Sidon. An outstanding stamped royal jar handle from Tyre dating from 125 BCE provides perhaps the best evidence for Phoenician origin of the inhabitants.

The main occupation of the Phoenician settlers was most probably the textile industry. Loom weights, bone loom shuttles, and spindle whorls, in addition to pollen analysis, indicating a massive presence of flax, testify to this conclusion. The increasing demand for dyed garments in the newly opened western markets required massive production of textiles. The Phoenician settlers of Bethsaida were probably quick to respond and provided linen to Tyre and Sidon, which was then dyed and sold for a high price in these markets. Silver coins, gold and silver jewelry, and high-quality wine imported from the island of Rhodes in large amphorae discovered at Bethsaida indicate that the village thrived and provided a well-to-do livelihood for the inhabitants.

The end of this prosperity came with the Hasmonean conquest of Galilee and Golan during the turn of the first century BCE. The conquest was followed by forced conversion into Judaism, and apparently unlike the Idumeans, who did not have anywhere to go and converted to Judaism, the Phoenician population of Bethsaida decided to leave and the site was abandoned for over than half a century.

The settlement of Bethsaida resumed once more during the reign of Herod the Great and can be explained as a result of his attempt to quell groups of bandits that roamed about the semi-deserted areas of his kingdom. Herod settled this region with people from his realm, namely Jews from Judea, and once more since the Iron Age Jews populated this region. Similar settlement pattern was discerned in places such as Capernaum, Nazareth, Nain, Cana, and other Galilean places, suggesting that the Jews were newcomers to Galilee.

The renaming and upgrading of Bethsaida to a *polis* by Philip the son of Herod the Great, in 30 CE, was followed by boosting the population and reinforcement of the fortification. New houses were built in the center of the mound and some old abandoned houses at the north part of the site were resettled. The old Iron Age city walls were still partially standing but large segments were destroyed, dismantled and fell into disuse, especially near the city gate. Philip repaired and rebuilt the walls, added buttresses in short intervals, but did not reconstruct the original width of the Iron Age walls. His course was only 5 ft wide.

However, Philip's main enterprise was not the city walls but, as the renaming of Julias would imply, establishing a temple for the Roman imperial cult at Bethsaida. The destruction of the Iron Age city gate left an elevated plateau of rubble and this place was used by Philip as a podium for the temple. Although the temple was modest (65 ft by 16 ft) it was the only structure at Bethsaida that was built of meticulously dressed basalt and limestone. It was decorated with floral and meander designs, similar to the stone decoration his father, Herod, had built for the Temple in Jerusalem and recalls contemporary Roman designs. The decoration included a lintel with a meander motif between two rosettes; a basalt door jamb with ivy and acanthus leaves; basalt friezes depicting acanthus leaves arranged in medallions surrounding a flower; basalt columns; drums and column bases; and a few limestone blocks and pilasters. The building included a porch, antechamber, holy of holies (*naos/cella*), and a back porch. Foundations of a column base were discovered in the area between the eastern *antae*. The temple was not well preserved. It went out of use in the third century CE and much of its walls were looted and carried away as *spolia*; only a few remains of the semi-dressed basalt stones were left *in situ*. A few nicely dressed stones were found in secondary use in Bedouin tombs near the temple. It has been suggested that the pediment with a three-dimensional eagle on its gable, discovered among the ruins of the synagogue at Chorazin, a few miles west of Bethsaida, was transported from the temple at Bethsaida.

A few figurines were found in the area of the temple and served presumably as offerings. One figurine depicts a female wearing a diadem on top of a cylindrical headgear covered with a veil. Another female wears a veil and is identified with Demeter/Ceres/Persephone/Kore, whose image was assumed by Livia/Julia.

Other finds around the temple include bronze incense shovels and a few coins minted by Philip in 30 CE. The coins commemorate the renaming of Bethsaida to Julias (which alludes to the date of the construction of the temple). To the south of the temple, there were a few more structures found. Some contained shards of limestone vessels, which indicate a Jewish presence.

The city gate from the Iron Age was thoroughly destroyed, yet the paved road leading to the city gate was still in service. During the Roman period a few tombs were excavated into it. The tombs were in a north–south orientation and did not contain any offerings. This entire area was covered with debris and boulders from the fourth century CE.

The economy of Bethsaida during this phase of occupation was also changed. Instead of the textile industry as in the Phoenician period, plenty of fishing implements indicate that fishing was the primary source of livelihood for the newly Jewish population. Fishing implements found at the dig include a large number of lead net weights, fish hooks, line sinkers, and basalt anchors. This implies that fishing was not a weekend hobby but was done professionally.

The end of the occupation at Bethsaida came during the fourth century CE when a major geological catastrophe, mentioned above, caused the north shoreline to retreat about one mile south, and the lagoons in the plains dried out almost completely. The fishermen apparently decided to move farther south and to locate their new site closer to the lake.

Applications for historical Jesus research

Bethsaida, according to the gospels and the historical documents, was an existing village that was elevated into a city, *polis*, in 30 CE and was dedicated to the imperial cult. It did not thrive into a successful *polis* and never minted coins. The remains at e-Tell support this data more than any other site in the proximity of e-Tell and suggest, therefore, that e-Tell should be identified with Bethsaida.

Bethsaida does not appear to be a Greco-Roman city built in a Hippodamean grid system, furnished with a theater, stadiums, bath houses, colonnaded streets, and porticos. It rather appears as a humble Jewish fishermen's village built of local basalt field stones; narrow lanes meander in between one- or two-storey buildings. No remains of Hellenization or Romanization were discerned except of the modest Roman imperial cult temple built by the authorities on the highest spot of the mound. Mark 8:22 is correct in referring to Bethsaida as a *kome*, village, and not as a *polis*, city, at the time of Jesus. It reconfirms the notion shared by many scholars that Jesus refrained from entering Greek *poleis*. Jesus' ministry at Bethsaida was addressed to a thoroughly un-Hellenized Jewish rural population.

Fishing plays a major role in the gospel narratives. Jesus recruited fishermen as his first followers and the terminology "fishermen of men" is applied to his disciples. The context of these narratives matches the reality of the Jewish fishermen settlers of Bethsaida during the Herodian dynasty.

Noteworthy is the gospels' view that Jesus' family originated from Judea. The family of Jesus migrated together with other Jewish families from Judea to Galilee as part of the Herodian attempt to settle Galilee with his constituencies. Although Luke's narrative of the census as the reason for Jesus' family travel to Bethlehem was largely found inaccurate, he was correct about the origin of the family.

There is a consensus among scholars that Bethsaida is the only site that is associated directly with the ministry of Jesus and is accessible to archaeological researches. Other places, such as Nazareth, Capernaum, and Chorazin, yielded extremely meager or almost no first-century finds. Therefore, the significance of Bethsaida to the Historical Jesus quest cannot be exaggerated.

RAMI ARAV

Further reading

Albright, W. F. "Among the Canaanite Mounds of Eastern Galilee," *BASOR* 29 (1928) 1–8.

Arav, R. "E-Tell and El Araj," *IEJ* 38:3 (1988) 187–88.

—— "E-Tell 1988," *IEJ* 39:1–2 (1989) 99–100.

—— "E-Tell (Bethsaida) 1988," *Hadshot Archeologiot* 93 (1989) 15 (in Hebrew).

—— "E-Tell (Bethsaida) 1989," *Excavations and Surveys in Israel* 9:2 (1989–90) Jerusalem, 98–99.

—— "Bethsaida 1989," *IEJ* 40:1–3 (1991), 184–86.

—— "Bethsaida 1992," *IEJ* 42 (1992) 252–54.

—— "Bethsaida 1990–91," *Hadshot Archeologiot* 99 (1993) 8–9 (in Hebrew).

—— "A Mamluk Drum from Bethsaida," *IEJ* 43 (1993) 241–45.

—— "Bethsaida 1992," *Hadshot Archeologiot* 101–2 (1994) 22–23 (in Hebrew).

—— "Bethsaida," in E. Meyers (ed.) *Encyclopedia for Archaeological Excavations in the Near East*, New York: Oxford University Press, 1996.

—— "Bethsaida 1996–98," *IEJ* 49:1–2 (1999) 128–36.

—— "New Testament Archaeology and the Case of Bethsaida," in M. Becker (ed.) *Das Ende der Tage und die Gegenwart Heils, H.-W. Kuhn Festschrift*, Leiden: Brill, 1999, pp. 75–91.

—— "Bethsaida Excavations," *IEJ* 51 (2001) 239–46.

—— "Bethsaida," in G. Fassbeck, S. Fortner, A. Rottlof, and J. Zangenberg (eds) *Leben am See Genesereth*, Mainz am Rhein: Philip von Zabern, 2003.

Arav, R. and M. Bernett. "An Egyptian Figurine of Pataikos at Bethsaida," *IEJ* 47:3–4 (1997) 198–213.

—— "The Bit Hilani at Bethsaida: Its Place in Aramean/Neo-Hittite and Israelite Palace Architecture in the Iron Age II," *IEJ* 50:1–2 (2000) 47–81.

Arav, R. and R. Freund (eds) *Bethsaida: A City by the Northern Shore of the Sea of Galilee*, Vol. 1, Kirksville, MO: Thomas Jefferson Press, 1996.

—— (eds) *Bethsaida: A City by the Northern Shore of the Sea of Galilee*, Vol. 2, Kirksville, MO: Thomas Jefferson Press, 1999.

—— (eds) *Bethsaida: A City by the Northern Shore of the Sea of Galilee*, Vol. 3, Kirksville, MO: Thomas Jefferson Press, 2004.

Arav, R., R. Freund, and J. Shroder. "Bethsaida Rediscovered," *BAR* 26:1 (January, 2000).

Avi-Yonah, M. *Gazetteer of Roman Palestine*, QEDEM 5, Jerusalem: Institute of Archaeology, 1976.

Baldi, D. *Enchiridion, Locurum Sanctorum*, Jerusalem: Franciscan Printing, 1982.

Bernett, M. and O. Keel. *Mond, Stier und Kult am Stadttor: Die Stele von Betsaida (et-Tell)*, Orbis Biblicus et Orientalis 161, Freiburg/Schweiz and Göttingen: Universitätsverlag and Vandenhoeck & Ruprecht, 1998.

Blomquist, Tina Haettner. *Gates and Gods: Cults in the City Gates of Iron Age Palestine: An Investigation of the Archaeological and Biblical Sources*, Stockholm: Almqvist & Wiksel International, 1999.

Dalman G. H. *Sacred Sites and Ways*, London: Macmillan, 1935.

Kochavi, M. (ed.) *Judea, Samaria and the Golan*, Jerusalem: Israel Antiquities Authority, 1972.

Kuhn, H.-W. and R. Arav. "Bethsaida Excavations, Historical and Archaeological Approaches," in B. A. Pearson (ed.) *The Future of Early Christianity: Essays in Honor of Helmut Koester*, Minneapolis, MN: Fortress Press, 1991, pp. 77–107.

McCowan, Ch. "The Problem of the Site of Bethsaida," *JPOS* 10 (1974–75) 32–58.

Na'aman, N. "In Search of Reality behind the Accounts of David's Wars with Israel's Neighbors," *IEJ* 52 (2002) 200–24.

Robinson, E. *Biblical Researches in Palestine, Mt Sinai and Arabia Petraea: A Journal of Travels in the Year 1838 by E. Robinson and E. Smith*, Vol. III, London: 1841.

Rousseau, J. J. and R. Arav. "Bethsaida, Ville Perdu et Retrouvée," *RB* Centième Année no. (Juillet, 1993) 415–28.

—— *Jesus and His World*, Minneapolis, MN: Fortress Press, 1995.

Schuerer, E. *A History of the Jewish People in the Time of Jesus Christ*, Edinburgh: T. & T. Clark, 1890, Vol. I, Division II, pp. 135–36.

Schumacher, G. *The Jaulan*, London: R. Bentley, 1888.

Strange, J. "Beth-Saida," in D. N. Friedman (ed.) *Anchor Bible Dictionary*, London: Doubleday, 1992.

Strickert, F. *Bethsaida, Home of the Apostles*, Collegeville, MN: Liturgical Press, 1998.

Urman, D. *The Golan*, BAR International Series 269, Oxford: BAR, 1985.

BIOGRAPHY

The world today is preoccupied with individuals, and the post-modern rejection of the 'big picture' has only intensified this with a fascination about others. Over the last 150 years, biography has become a major way of understanding people within society. Thus at a more academic level, biographies have sought to describe the life and times of significant persons, to set individuals in the context of major historical events during their lifetime, often at great length. On the other hand, popular literature is full of instant biographies which reflect the current obsession with so-called 'celebrities', with what they look like and speculations about their private life, rather than a concern for factual history. Both types are indebted to a post-Freudian interest in 'personality', to understand what makes an individual 'tick'. However, the ancients were more interested in 'character' and 'type', even stereotype, than the historical individual. Therefore when modern readers bring these expectations of contemporary biography to ancient texts like the gospels and to seek to understand historical figures like Jesus, problems can arise.

Instead of the canons of modern biography, it is important to understand how ancient writers viewed this form of literature. Classical literary critics and grammarians attempted to describe and classify the main features of key genres such as tragedy and history. However, these were never rigid rules and it is best to look at actual examples of each genre. This is particularly important in the case of ancient biography. The word *biographia* itself does not occur until the ninth-century writer, Photius of Constantinople (*Bibliotheca* 181 and 242; see Momigliano 12); works prior to that were called simply 'lives,' *bioi* or *vitae*. Ancient writers sometimes tried to distinguish *bioi* from other genres, especially history, as in Plutarch's famous introduction to his *Alexander*, 1.1–3: here, *historia* is concerned for great events and illustrious deeds, while *bios* is interested in a person's character, often revealed by

'little things'. However, this probably only reflects the fact that he cannot include all the historical material available in his shorter 'life' of Alexander. In fact, as Pelling's analysis of Plutarch has shown, some ancient biographies are quite historical, while others include features of philosophy, rhetoric, romance, religious or political works. Therefore, we must study the works themselves for a full picture to understand how biography relates to historical study of Jesus, or anyone else from the ancient world.

The growth of ancient biography

Greek biography

The origins of Greek biography lie in the Persian period with the travel writings of Skylax of Caryanda (*c.* 480 BC) and Ion of Chios (*c.* 440). The first surviving works to concentrate on a person's life are encomia, laudatory speeches, such as Isocrates' *Evagoras* and Xenophon's *Agesilaus* (370–360 BC). Another key factor came from the philosophical schools of the fourth century with works about Socrates and other thinkers. The third century was dominated by the house of Macedon, so Hellenistic accounts of Philip and Alexander the Great were composed. Meanwhile vast amounts of material were amassed for the libraries at Alexandria, leading to the production of books like Satyrus's *Lives of the Tragedians*, of which only parts of his *Euripides* survives.

Roman biography

Concern for the ancestors and for precedent led the Romans naturally towards biography. In the middle of the first century BC, Varro and Cornelius Nepos wrote accounts of famous leaders and generals, philosophers and writers, while political leaders like Caesar and Cicero published their memoirs. The first century AD provided opportunities for propagandistic accounts of early emperors like Augustus, as well as of political opponents like Cato the Younger. The period around 100 AD saw a flowering of biography with Tacitus's *Life of Agricola*, his father-in-law and governor of Britain from 77 to 84, Plutarch's *Parallel Lives*, comparing famous Greeks with Romans, and Suetonius's *Lives of the Caesars*, full of scandal and gossip. The second-century philosophical satirist, Lucian, composed lively accounts of various people. The third century saw Diogenes Laertius's compendium of *Lives of the Philosophers*, while Philostratus described the travels, teaching and miracles of *Apollonius of Tyana*. Biography then became an important tool in pagan–Christian debates around 300 AD with Iamblichus's *Pythagoras*, Porphyry's *Plotinus* and Eusebius's *Origen*. Political, philosophical and religious biography continued beyond the Roman empire and into the early middle ages with lives of emperors, kings and saints.

Jewish biography

There is some biographical material in the Old Testament about people like Moses, David and Elijah but this just forms part of the prophetic and historical books. Momigliano (35–36) points out that the nearest we come to ancient Jewish lives are autobiographical books written in the service of the Persian king, like that by Nehemiah. When Philo later writes his *Life of Moses* (*c.* 25–30 AD), it is consciously modelled upon the Greek biographical tradition, following the structure of Xenophon's *Agesilaus*. Biographical material is also preserved in the stories and anecdotes preserved in the rabbinic traditions, which are often compared with individual gospel passages. Thus the question about the greatest commandment in Mark 12:38–34 and parallels can be studied in the light of the famous story from the Babylonian Talmud, *Shabbat* 31A, of the differing reactions of Shammai and Hillel when asked to teach the whole law to a Gentile enquirer standing on one leg. However, it is significant that the ancient Jews never developed this material into actual biographies, even within the later rabbinical tradition. We shall return later to possible explanations for this omission.

Ways of classifying ancient biographies

Attempts to classify this wide range of ancient biographies with their different subjects and approaches have produced much debate among classical scholars. Leo's great analysis of Graeco-Roman biography attempted to distinguish two main groups: the *Plutarchian*, arranged chronologically for generals and politicians, and the *Suetonian*, more systematically ordered for literary men. Although Leo argued that the former came from the early philosophical schools and the latter from Alexandria, more recent work, particularly by Momigliano and Geiger, has shown that this distinction cannot be sustained. Talbert (93–98) proposed a five-fold classification of ancient biographies according to their social functions; however, most ancient lives had several purposes and cut across Talbert's categories. Instead, it is better to view ancient biography as a highly flexible genre, adapting to various cultures and growing through the centuries. It seems to occur naturally among those following or interested in particular people, such as leaders, teachers or writers, and it often functions within a context of didactic or philosophical debate and conflict.

The generic features of ancient biography

An alternative approach is to compare different works from different authors to illustrate the nature of the genre. 'Generic features' are embedded within any work's formal and structural composition (often called 'external features') and its content, style, mood and character ('internal features'). When taken all together, such features communicate the 'family resemblance' of a group of works and thus define its genre. Burridge has analysed a diverse group of ancient 'lives' of all types ranging from the fourth century BC to the third century AD. Despite such accounts comprising a flexible genre, there is a recognizable family resemblance in both form and content.

From the formal or structural perspective, they are written in continuous prose narrative, between 10,000 and 20,000 words in length – the amount on a typical scroll of about 30–35 feet in length. Unlike modern biographies, Graeco-Roman lives do not cover a person's whole life in chronological sequence, and have no psychological analysis of the subject's character. They may begin with a brief mention of the hero's ancestry, family or city, his birth and an occasional anecdote about his upbringing; but usually the narrative moves rapidly on to his public debut later in life. Accounts of generals, politicians or statesmen are more chronologically ordered, recounting their great deeds and virtues, while lives of philosophers, writers or thinkers tend to be more anecdotal, arranged topically around collections of material to display their ideas and teachings. While the author may claim to provide information about his subject, often his underlying aims may be apologetic, polemic or didactic. Many ancient biographies cover the subject's death in great detail, since here he reveals his true character, gives his definitive teaching or does his greatest deed. Finally, detailed analysis of the verbal structure of ancient biographies reveals another generic feature. While most narratives have a wide variety of subjects, it is characteristic of biography that attention stays focused on one particular person with a quarter to a third of the verbs dominated by the subject, while another 15 to 30 per cent occur in sayings, speeches or quotations from the person (see Burridge 2004: 308–21).

When the gospels are compared with such ancient lives, marked similarities of form and content demonstrate that they share both the external and internal generic features of ancient biographies, including the particular focus upon the main character, Jesus, shown by verbal analysis. As with other ancient biographies, Jesus' deeds and words are of vital importance for the evangelists' portraits of Jesus. Burridge's comparison of the gospels with Graeco-Roman *bioi*, originally published in 1992, established the Gospel genre as ancient biography, refuting the previous *sui generis* approach of the form critics. As this has been increasingly accepted, so the debate has moved on to the implications of this for their interpretation (see Burridge 2004: 252–88).

Implications for the historical Jesus

Given this understanding of ancient biography, it remains to explore briefly how seeing the Gospels within this genre helps to clarify our understanding of Jesus' teaching and activities.

The Christological claim

The subjects of Graeco-Roman lives were many and varied, but they were almost always from the upper levels of society and leaders in their field – kings, emperors, generals, statesmen, philosophers, poets, writers and so forth. To write a *bios* of Jesus of Nazareth is to make an implicit claim about the importance of his life and death, activities and teachings. Readers familiar with accounts of other teachers or religious philosophers might assume that Jesus is like them – but the Gospels constantly challenge the audience with the question of Jesus' identity: 'who then is this, that even wind and sea obey him?' (Mark 4:41). While the biographical genre is well suited to describing the great deeds and words of leading human beings, the Gospels take the genre and gently subvert it by suggesting that the only proper response is that of worship (Matt 14:33; John 20:28).

This is particularly significant in the Jewish context, given the absence of biographical works already noted. Jesus seems to have been the only first-century Jewish teacher about whom such *bioi* were written. If the Gospels are seen merely as a collection of such stories strung together like beads on a string, we might expect similar works to be constructed about Hillel, Shammai or other rabbis. Yet this is precisely what we do not find. Both Neusner (1984 and 1988) and Alexander have explored various reasons why there is nothing like

the Gospels in the rabbinic traditions. Although the rabbinic material is more anecdotal than are the Gospels and some ancient lives, it still contains enough biographical elements (through sage stories, narratives, precedents and death scenes) to enable an editor to compile a 'life of Hillel' or whoever. Such an account would have been recognizable as ancient biography and could have looked like Lucian's *Demonax*. Literary or generic reasons alone are therefore not sufficient to explain this curious absence of rabbinic biography. Burridge has argued that to write a biography is to use a genre which concentrates upon a person centre-stage; however, for the rabbis, this is where only the Torah should be (Burridge 2000: 155–56; 2004: 337–40). Therefore the biographical genre of the Gospels is making an explicit theological claim about the centrality of the historical Jesus – the Christological statement that God is revealed in the life, death and resurrection of this person.

Truth and historicity

Ancient biography also gives us a useful guide for the issue of truth in the search for the historical Jesus. Too often, this is conducted in twenty-first-century terms about facts and what a video-recorder might have recorded, and 'myth' is disparaged as unhistorical. However, the ancients were more interested in truth and meaning than mere facts – and myths were the means for communicating profound truth. Even ancient historiography included a significant amount of interpretation, with the licence given to the author to include speeches which may include what was said, but also what was 'needed' in the situation (see Thucydides' preface to his *History of the Peloponnesian War* 1.21–22). Nepos argues that 'narrating someone's life' must go beyond the mere recitation of his deeds, as in history, to the person's virtues (*Pelopidas* 1:1); Plutarch's concern for character as revealed in 'little things' (*Alex* 1:1) was noted at the beginning. In fact, ancient lives operated between the genres of history on one side, and legends, the novel and the encomium on the other. Therefore we should not expect the exacting criteria of modern historiography in the Gospels and other ancient lives, but nor wholesale fabrication: it was important for *bioi* that there was a correlation of the narrative account with the historical person (see further, Burridge 2005: 168–73).

The narrative context

Finally, the biographical approach to the gospels reminds us that the gospels are narratives about a person's life and death, his activities as well as his teaching. Too often the search for the historical Jesus has concentrated predominantly upon Jesus' teaching and words, searching for the *ipsissima vox*, for truly 'authentic' sayings. However, the gospels are not just collections of Jesus' sayings, in the manner we find in the *Gospel of Thomas* (or as Q is often reconstructed without a narrative). Central to all ancient biography is that the picture of the subject is built up through both their words *and* their deeds. So to find the heart of Jesus' message we need to consider both his teaching *and* his actual practice. Jesus' teaching is not a separate and discrete set of maxims, but is part of his proclamation of the kingdom of God. It is primarily intended to elicit a response from his hearers to live as disciples within the community of others who also respond and follow.

Ancient biographies held together both words and deeds in portraying their central subject often for exemplary purposes. Thus Xenophon described Agesilaus as a paradigm for others to follow to become better people (*Agesilaus* X.2). Similarly, Plutarch provides examples for the reader to imitate the virtues and avoid the vices described to improve moral character (*Pericles* 1; *Aemilius Paulus* 1). Equally in the gospels, the readers are exhorted to follow Jesus' example in accepting and welcoming others (Mark 1:17; Luke 6:36). Therefore, as befits a biographical narrative, it is not enough just to outline the main points of Jesus' teaching; any account of the historical Jesus must also include the call to follow his example.

RICHARD A. BURRIDGE

Further reading

Alexander, Philip S. "Rabbinic Biography and the Biography of Jesus: A Survey of the Evidence," in C. M. Tuckett (ed.) *Synoptic Studies: The Ampleforth Conferences of 1982 and 1983*, JSNTSS 7, Sheffield: JSOT Press, 1984, pp. 19–50.

Burridge, Richard A. "Gospel Genre, Christological Controversy and the Absence of Rabbinic Biography: Some Implications of the Biographical Hypothesis," in C. M. Tuckett and D. G. Horrell (eds), *Christology, Controversy and Community: New Testament Essays in Honour of David Catchpole*, Leiden: Brill, 2000, pp. 137–56.

—— *What are the Gospels? A Comparison with Graeco-Roman Biography*, SNTS MS 70, revised and updated edition, Grand Rapids, MI: Eerdmans, 2004 [first edition Cambridge: Cambridge University Press, 1992].

—— *Four Gospels, One Jesus? A Symbolic Reading*, revised and updated edition, Grand Rapids, MI: Eerdmans, 2005 [first edition London: SPCK, 1994].

Cox, Patricia. *Biography in Late Antiquity: A Quest for the Holy Man*, Berkeley, CA: University of California Press, 1983.

Geiger, Joseph. *Cornelius Nepos and Ancient Political Biography*, Historia Einzelschriften 47, Stuttgart: Franz Steiner, 1985.

Leo, Friedrich. *Die griechisch-römische Biographie nach ihrer literarischen Form*, Leipzig: Teubner, 1901.

Momigliano, Arnaldo. *The Development of Greek Biography*, Harvard, MA: Harvard University Press, 1971.

Neusner, Jacob. *In Search of Talmudic Biography: The Problem of the Attributed Saying*, Brown Judaic Studies 70, Chico, CA: Scholars Press, 1984.

—— *Why No Gospels in Talmudic Judaism?* Atlanta, GA: Scholars Press, 1988.

Pelling, Christopher B. R. "Plutarch's Method of Work in the Roman Lives," *JHS* 99 (1979) 74–96.

—— "Plutarch's Adaptation of his Source Material," *JHS* 100 (1980) 127–40.

Stuart, Duane Reed. *Epochs of Greek and Roman Biography*, Berkeley, CA: University of California Press, 1928.

Talbert, Charles H. *What is a Gospel? The Genre of the Canonical Gospels*, Philadelphia, PA: Fortress Press, 1977; London: SPCK, 1978.

BIRTH OF JESUS

Jesus was a historical person and not a mythical figure; as such he was undoubtedly born. However, the historical circumstances surrounding his birth are much disputed, particularly the claim made in the canonical gospels that he was born to a Galilean woman named Mary through a miraculous conception.

The birth narratives in Matthew and Luke

The Markan and Johannine Gospels do not include any account of Jesus' birth or formative period, in contrast to Matthew (1:18–2:23) and Luke (1:5–2:52) who supply details about Jesus' birth and childhood at the beginning of their volumes.

Matthew begins his Gospel with a genealogy emphasizing Jesus' Davidic lineage and the Gentiles in Jesus' heritage (Matt 1:1–17). The birth story is narrated in Matt 1:18–25 where Mary, though pledged to Joseph, was "found to be with child through the Holy Spirit" (Matt 1:18). Although Joseph was planning to divorce Mary during the betrothal period, probably on suspicion of infidelity, an angel of the Lord appeared to him in a dream and stated that "what is conceived in her is from the Holy Spirit" (Matt 1:20). The name of the child "Jesus" is given to Joseph by the angel. Matthew adds an editorial remark that Jesus' birth fulfilled the prophecy of Isa 7:14 about the virgin bearing a child who is called "Immanuel" (Matt 1:22 23). It is reported that Joseph does as he is commanded and takes Mary as his wife and Matthew emphasizes that "he had no union with her until she gave birth to a son" drawing attention to the supernatural nature of Jesus' birth. The actual birth of Jesus is described briefly in Matt 2:1. "Jesus was born in Bethlehem in Judea." This is followed by the story of the visit of the Magi (Matt 2:1–12), the escape to Egypt (Matt 2:13–18), and the return to Nazareth (Matt 2:19–23). Matthew understands the birth story as pointing to the fulfilment of Israel's Scriptures in Jesus Christ. The passages quoted (Isa 7:14 = Matt 1:23; Mic 5:2 = Matt 2:6; Hos 11:1 = Matt 2:15; Jer 31:15 = Matt 2:18; Isa 11:1 [?] = Matt 2:23) are interpreted either typologically or in a promise-fulfilment cycle where the prophetic hopes find realization in Jesus as Christ. The narrative exhibits several points of contact with exodus and exile traditions (Matt 1:17; 2:13–18) where Jesus' infancy recapitulates a *new exodus* and the *end of exile* marking him out further as the true representative of Israel. Unlike Luke, who concentrates on Mary, in Matthew it is Joseph who is the linchpin to the story, and he emerges as the model disciple and exemplary Israelite who is righteous and compassionate (Matt 1:19) and obedient to God (Matt 1:24; 2:14, 21).

Luke's narration of Jesus' birth is more complex than that of Matthew. Luke invests a lot of time into the characterization of Mary and Elizabeth and he develops his theological motifs in the *Magnificat* of Mary (Luke 1:46–55), *Benedictus* of Zechariah (Luke 1:67–79), and *Nunc Dimittis* of Simeon (Luke 2:29–32). The births of Jesus and John are also intertwined as part of the one saving purpose of God. Like Matthew, Luke emphasizes the virginity of Mary at several points (Luke 1:27, 34) and an angel reports to Mary that she will conceive through the Holy Spirit "which will come upon you" and the power of the Most High "will overshadow you" (Luke 1:35). The account of Jesus' birth is prefaced with a reference to a worldwide census during the reign of Augustus while Quirinius was governor of Syria (Luke 2:1–2), the substance of which is historically disputed. Joseph registers in his home town of Bethlehem and it is there that Mary gives birth to Jesus (Luke 2:4–7). The subsequent narrative includes the announcement to shepherds of the Messiah's birth (Luke 2:8–20), Jesus is presented in the temple for circumcision (Luke 2:21–40), and the description of Jesus' coming of age (Luke 2:41–52). The key emphases of Luke's account are liberation for the poor and oppressed, a radical reversal of fortunes for the marginalized and the powerful, the role of Mary as the vessel for God's Son entering the world, the coming of the age of salvation, a light for the Gentiles, and the presence of the Holy Spirit with God's people.

Critical issues pertaining to the birth narratives

In the course of surveying the birth narratives it is necessary to identify several points of critical discussion.

Sources

Scholars debate whether the birth stories derive from the theological creativity of the Evangelists, are based on fragmentary reports about Jesus that were subsequently embellished, or are rooted in historical tradition. On the assumption of the two-source hypothesis whereby Matthew and Luke used Mark and "Q" as their primary written sources (see Source criticism), the differences between Matthew and Luke in the birth narratives are so sharp that they probably wrote their accounts independently from one another and used different sources. At the same time there is an outline common to Matthew and Luke (Fitzmyer 307; Brown 34–35).

1 Jesus' birth in relation to the reign of Herod the Great (Matt 2:1; Luke 1:5).
2 Mary is a virgin, betrothed to Joseph, but their relationship is not yet consummated (Matt 1:18; Luke 1:27, 34; 2:5).
3 Joseph is of Davidic descent (Matt 1:16, 20; Luke 1:27; 2:4).
4 The birth is announced by angels (Matt 1:20–23; Luke 1:26–35).
5 Jesus is the Son of David (Matt 1:1; Luke 1:32).
6 Jesus is conceived by the Holy Spirit (Matt 1:18, 20; Luke 1:35).
7 Joseph plays no role in the conception (Matt 1:18–25; Luke 1:35).
8 The name "Jesus" is divinely given (Matt 1:21; Luke 1:31).
9 An angel refers to Jesus as "Saviour" (Matt 1:21; Luke 2:11).
10 Jesus is born after Mary and Joseph have come to live together (Matt 1:24–25; Luke 2:4–7).
11 Jesus is born in Bethlehem (Matt 2:1; Luke 2:4–7).
12 Jesus' family settles in Nazareth (Matt 2:22–23; Luke 2:39).

In the early church there may have circulated multiple traditions about Jesus' family and birth which the Evangelists had access to. If there is some historical basis to the events referred to, especially given the private nature of much of the story (e.g.

private conversations and dreams), it could conceivably stem from sources related to or dependent upon individual figures such as Joseph (used by Matthew) and Mary (used by Luke). This is moderately plausible since Mary (John 19:26–27; Acts 1:14) and Jesus' relatives were active in the early church (Acts 12:17; 15:13; 21:18; 1 Cor 9:5; 15:7; Gal 1:19; 2:9, 12; Jas 1:1; Jude 1:1). Others postulate a pre-gospel annunciation tradition shaped by OT narrative (e.g. Brown).

Genre

The birth stories are framed as the fulfilment of prophetic promises and typological patterns from Israel's sacred traditions. The birth stories have been compared to Graeco-Roman youth narratives that predict greatness for young nobles (Talbert) and to a form of Jewish interpretation known as Midrash (Gundry; Brown). The problem is that the birth narratives are different from any known form of ancient literature. While Matthew's version is not strictly a Midrash or Haggadah, it is *midrashic* to the extent that the OT quotations are of pivotal importance and it is *haggadic* to the degree that the story is not recounted for its own sake but for its particular theological significance (Hagner 16).

Use of the Old Testament

The birth narratives show signs of being influenced by reflection on the Jewish Scriptures. The Lucan annunciation narratives are heavily influenced by OT prototypes (e.g. Gen 17:15–21; Judg 13:2–7; and 1 Sam 1–3) and Matthew's depiction of Herod the Great parallels accounts of Pharaoh's cruelty to the Hebrews and Moses' birth as national deliverer (Exod 1–2). While it may be possible that early Christians created the birth narratives out of their meditation on OT passages in order to develop their Christology, this is not generally how primitive Christian exegesis operated. Instead, the OT provided the hermeneutical grid through which they interpreted and modelled traditional material rather than comprising the creative pool from which they formulated it. Matthew's citation of OT texts may appear haphazard at points, especially in Matt 1:23 with the reference to Isa 7:14, "Look, the virgin shall conceive and bear a son." Not only was this passage not regarded as messianic in Jewish interpretation which associated the son with a child born during the time of Ahaz and Isaiah, but the Hebrew word *'almâh* means a woman of marriageable age and not necessarily a virgin. The notion of virginity is probably imported from the

Septuagint through the word *parthenos* that implies more explicitly a "virgin." While *'almâh* is not a technical term for *virgo intacta* the idea of virginity could be connoted depending on the context. In any event, a virgin conception is clearly not predicted in the Hebrew text of Isa 7:14, but Matthew's citation does not demand an exact correspondence of events as much as it postulates a correlation of patterns or types between Isaiah's narrative and his own birth story. The coming of God's anointed, the manifestation of God's presence, and the rescue of Israel through a child born to a young girl brings to Matthew's mind Isaiah 7 as an obvious prophetic precedent again repeated at a new juncture of redemptive history.

Religionsgeschichte

In the sphere of the history of religions, certain religious sages or political heroes were said to have been born of miraculous circumstances involving gods (e.g. Perseus, Plato, Alexander, Buddha). That such stories were believed even among the educated elite is underscored by Josephus' account of how Decius Mundus disguised himself as the god Anubis in order to seduce the Roman noblewoman Paulina (*Ant.* 18:66–80). According to Suetonius (*Augustus* 94:4) the birth of Augustus came about by his mother being impregnated by the god Apollo. Based on these comparisons Crossan and Reed argue: "If you take Jesus' conception story literally, take Augustus' literary. If you take Jesus' conception story metaphorically, take Augustus' metaphorically" (Crossan and Reed 88). One should also keep in mind that analogy does not mean genealogy; there is no indication that Luke and Matthew use Graeco-Roman birth stories as their sources. The birth narratives also possess a distinctive Palestinian character and reflect the piety of Jewish Christianity (esp. the Lucan hymns). Additionally, other mythic birth stories like that of Augustus imply some human–divine sexual union which is absent from the Gospels. (For early Christian responses to pagan myths about human–divine intercourse, see Justin, *Dial.* 67–70, *Apol.* 1.33, and Origen, *Cels.* 1.37.)

The date of Jesus' birth

Due to a miscalculation by the sixth-century monk Dionysius, the given date of Jesus' birth is probably wrong. Jesus was most likely born prior to 1 CE since he was born during the reign of Herod the Great, who died in *c.* 4 BCE. Estimates of the date of Jesus' birth range from 6 to 4 BCE. The only other historical markers are that Jesus was "about" thirty years old when he commenced his ministry (Luke 3:23), John the Baptist was probably executed c. 29 CE, and Jesus was executed probably on the Passover of 30 CE. A rabbinic tradition also records that Jesus was thirty-three or thirty-four years old when he commenced his ministry (b. Sanh. 106b). Luke's reference to a census under Quirinius (Luke 2:1–2) who was, as far as is known from other sources, governor of Syria in 6 CE rather than 6 BCE complicates the dating further.

The place of Jesus' birth

According to the Evangelists, Jesus was born in Bethlehem, the city of David. Some scholars argue that this story was contrived in order to make Jesus fulfil the prophecy of Mic 5:2 (cf. John 7:41–42) and that the census was devised for the purpose of placing Mary and Joseph in Bethlehem at the time of Jesus' birth. Consequently the reference to Bethlehem is regarded as fictitious and some scholars think that Jesus was more probably born in Nazareth (e.g. Meier 214–16, 229; Brown 513–16). Yet belief that the Messiah would be born in Bethlehem was not a widespread element of Jewish messianic hopes so it is difficult to imagine Christians inventing the Bethlehem location for apologetic reasons.

Traditionally Jesus has been pictorialized as being born in the stable of an inn because Mary and Joseph could find no accommodation upon their arrival. Yet a small hamlet like Bethlehem did not have an assortment of inns with signs saying "no vacancy". Luke 2:4–7 does not say that Mary went into labour immediately upon arrival in Bethlehem, it was only sometime during the stay there that she gave birth. Furthermore, the word kataluma ordinarily means "guestroom" and so Jesus was probably born in the house of a family related to Joseph in a guestroom adjacent to an indoor stable. There are also some later traditions that speak of Jesus being born in a cave (Protoevangelium of James 18–19).

A virginal conception

According to the Apostles' Creed, Jesus "was conceived of the Holy Spirit, born of the Virgin Mary." By the time of Ignatius's martyrdom (c. 110–17 CE) belief in the virgin birth had become a standard part of Christian belief, at least in western Asia Minor (Ignatius, Eph. 18.2–19.1; Smyrn. 1.1–2). The proto-orthodox affirmation of the virgin birth in the second century was maintained amidst those who postulated a purely human birth (e.g. the Ebionites, Cerinthus, Carpocrates) and those who denied Jesus any human birth (e.g. Marcion). What one thinks of a virgin conception will depend largely upon what presuppositions one has and whether one believes in a God who can and does intervene in human affairs in such a way. On the one hand miraculous birth stories are not entirely unique in the sphere of religious history and they are invested with theological meaning by the Evangelists. Conversely, there is a sound array of evidence that could be said to imply a miraculous birth: (1) Paul speaks of Jesus as "born of woman" (Gal 4:4); (2) Jesus is called the "son of Mary" and not the son of Joseph in Mark 6:3; (3) there was a known Jewish polemic that presupposes that there was something suspicious about the circumstances about Jesus' birth including the insinuation that he was a mamzer or illegitimate (John 8:41; Gos. Thom. 105; Tertullian, De Spec. 30.6; Protoevangelium of James 13–16; Acts of Pilate 2.3) and born to a Roman soldier called "Panthera" (Origen, Cels. 1.28, 32; cf. Toledoth Yeshu); (4) ascription of Jesus' Davidic heritage is multiply attested in Mark, Matthew, Luke, Acts and by Paul, and was unlikely to be invented on the basis of belief in his resurrection (see Meier 218–19); and (5) there is no reason for taking the birth narratives as being altogether different from the rest of the gospels which contain historical narratives set in the parameters of a Graeco-Roman bios or vita. While the evidence does not prove a virgin birth, it is at least consistent with it. What we can say is that Jesus' paternity was enigmatic from the start (Bockmuehl 33). Whether one chooses to accept the virgin birth will depend upon one's theological and philosophical convictions as well as one's faith in the ancient church's witness to Jesus (cf. Meier 222; Brown). In the words of Machen (396), "even if the belief in the virgin birth is not necessary to every Christian, it is certainly necessary to Christianity."

MICHAEL F. BIRD

Further reading

Bockmuehl, Markus. This Jesus: Martyr, Lord, Messiah. London: T. & T. Clark, 1994.

Brown, Raymond. The Birth of the Messiah, ABRL, New York: Doubleday, 1993.

Crossan, John Dominic and Jonathan L. Reed. Excavating Jesus: Beneath the Stones, Behind the Texts, San Francisco, CA: Harper, 2001.

Gundry, Robert H. Matthew: A Commentary on His Handbook for a Mixed Church under Persecution, second edition, Grand Rapids, MI: Baker, 1994.

Fitzmyer, Joseph A. Luke, 2 vols, AB, New York: Doubleday, 1983.

Freed, E. *The Stories of Jesus' Birth: A Critical Introduction*, Sheffield: Sheffield Academic Press, 2001.

Hagner, D. A. *Matthew 1–14*, WBC, Dallas, TX: Word, 1993.

Labooy, Guus. "The Historicity of the Virginal Conception. A Study in Argumentation," *EJTh* 13 (2004) 91–101.

Lüdemann, Gerd. *Virgin Birth? The Real Story of Mary and her Son Jesus*, Harrisburg, PA: Trinity Press International, 1997.

Machen, J. G. *The Virgin Birth of Christ*, New York: Harper, 1930.

Meier, John P. *A Marginal Jew: Rethinking the Historical Jesus*, ABRL, New York: Doubleday, 1991.

Talbert, Charles. "Prophecies of Future Greatness: The Contributions of Greco-Roman Biographies to an Understanding of Luke 1:5–4:15," in J. L. Crenshaw and S. Sandmel (eds) *The Divine Helmsman*, New York: KTAV, 1980, pp. 129–41.

Witherington, Ben. "Birth of Jesus," in Joel B. Green, Scot McKnight and J. Howard Marshall (eds) *Dictionary of Jesus and the Gospels*, Downers Grove, IL: InterVarsity Press, 1992, pp. 60–74.

BLASPHEMY

"Blasphemy" is a religious word that expresses outrage over an action or statement thought to demean God or something sacred. In what follows the (1) usage and meaning of blasphemy and (2) the role of blasphemy in the life and death of Jesus will be reviewed.

Usage and meaning of blasphemy

In Second Temple Judaism, blasphemy covered a wide range of activity. There is little discussion of trials of blasphemy, though *Sanhedrin* 7:5 (Mishnah) does define a procedure for examining a charge and limits the offense to speaking the very Name of God. Leviticus 24:10–16 is discussed where blasphemy is presented (note Josephus, *Ant.* 4.202). Its ambiguities made defining blasphemy, especially where euphemisms were used, a subject of some rabbinic debate. Numbers 15:30–31 is often cited as an analogous situation to blasphemy with its Sabbath violation followed by a death penalty. To use the divine Name in an inappropriate way is certainly blasphemy and is punishable by death (Lev 24:10–16; *m. Sanh.* 6:4 and 7:5; Philo, *On the Life of Moses* 2:203–6). At the base of these ideas about blasphemy lies the command of Exodus 22:27 not to revile God nor the leaders he appointed for the nation.

Later rabbis debated whether the use of an alternative name qualifies as blasphemy, though some sentiment existed for including it (*m. Sheb.* 4:13; *b. Sheb.* 35a; *b. Sanh.* 55b–57a, 60a). Warnings were issued in such cases, but it does not appear, at least in the rabbinic period, to have carried an automatic death sentence.

What happened if a warning was ignored seems easy to determine, given the parallel with another warning involving the incorrigible son in *m. Sanh.* 8:4. Unheeded, potential liability came with the second offence. The official rabbinic position is that the use of the divine Name constitutes the only clear case of capital blasphemy (*m. Sanh.* 7:5). One is even to avoid blaspheming foreign deities as a sign of respect for the name of God (Josephus, *Ant.* 4.207; Philo, *Moses* 2.205; *Spec. Laws* 1.53).

There are acts of blasphemy. These include the use of substitute titles and a whole range of actions offensive to God. Their existence suggests a category of cultural blasphemy representing an offense against God.

Acts of blasphemy concentrate on idolatry, a show of arrogant disrespect toward God, or the insulting of his chosen leaders. Often those who blasphemed verbally also acted on their feelings. God manages to judge such offenses. Examples in Jewish exposition are Sisera (Judg 4:3 and *Numbers Rabbah* 10.2; disrespect toward God's people), Goliath (1 Sam 17 and Josephus, *Ant.* 6:183; disrespect towards God's people and worship of Dagon), Sennacherib (2 Kgs 18–19 = Isa 37:6, 23; disrespect for God's power), Belshazzar (Dan 3:29 Q [96] and Josephus, *Ant.* 10:233, 242, disrespect for God's presence in the use of temple utensils at a party), Manasseh (acting against the Torah; *Sifre* §112) and Titus (*b. Gittin* 56 and *Aboth Rabbi Nathan B* 7; entering, defaming the Temple, slicing open the curtain and taking the utensils away). Acting against the Temple is also blasphemous (1 Macc 2:6; Josephus, *Ant.* 12:406). Significantly, comparing oneself to God is also blasphemous reflecting arrogance according to Philo (*Dreams* 2:130–31; *Decalogue* 13–14, 61–64). At Qumran, unfaithfulness in moral action by those who pretend to lead the people (CD 5:12) or the act of speaking against God's people (1QpHab 10.13) are blasphemous. Within Israel, the outstanding example is the golden calf incident (Philo, *Moses* 2:159–66).

Blasphemy represents an offense against God and a violation of a fundamental principle of the faith. Sometimes God alone punishes the blasphemer (e.g. Pharaoh, Korah, Titus), while at other times the community executes judgment (the Israelite woman's son). Attacking God's people verbally is a second class of blasphemy (Sennacherib; Goliath). Those who challenge the leadership God has put in place for his people are also seen as attacking God himself. So blasphemy refers to a wide range of insulting speech or activity, crucial background to how blasphemy relates to Jesus.

The role of blasphemy in the life and death of Jesus

There are a few texts involving Jesus and blasphemy. The first major controversy surrounding Jesus appears in Mark 2:7, where he is charged with blasphemy for forgiving sin. The charge seems to revolve around Jesus' directly exercising an exclusively divine prerogative (Exod 34:7). Here Jesus gives forgiveness without any cultic requirements, an approach that points to Jesus' own authority. So forgiveness on his authority did not require priests, sacrifices, or rabbis (Ellis). The implications for religious authority structures are huge, since these authorities would believe that they bestowed forgiveness in line with divine instruction.

Two other relevant blasphemy texts appear in Mark. In each of these cases, it is others who blaspheme or risk blaspheming. In 3:29, Jesus warns about blaspheming the Spirit, as opposed to the other sins and blasphemies people might perform. Those who blaspheme the Spirit are guilty of a sin that cannot be forgiven, an "eternal sin." The remark comes in response to the claim that Jesus casts out demons by Beelzebul in 3:22 or by an unclean spirit in 3:30, texts that form an inclusio around the remark. The combination of 2:7 with 3:29 sets up a "battle of the blasphemies" in Mark, with each side accusing the other of offending God by their claims. Jesus meets the blasphemy accusation of the Jewish leadership in 2:7 and in 3:22 with his warning about blaspheming the Spirit. The fact that Jewish materials accuse Jesus of being a deceiver or sorcerer means that this "dispute" has a credible claim to be authentic (Stanton, as noted by Justin, *First Apology* 30, 108; *Contra Celsum* 1:28, 71; *Dialogue* 69:7; *b. Sanh.* 43a; 107b).

This leaves a final crucial text, Jesus' examination by the Jewish leadership and his reply appealing to a combination of Ps 110:1 and Daniel 7:13–14 (Mark 14:53–65). This passage has long been a topic of controversy concerning its authenticity. The debate has been traced in full elsewhere, but has a good claim to being authentic (Bock: 184–237; Ellis; Evans).

Jesus' blasphemy operated at two levels. (1) Jesus claimed he would exercise comprehensive authority from the side of God. Though Judaism might contemplate such a position for a few (*1 En.* 62; *Exagoge of Ezekiel* 69–82), the leaders did not think that this teacher from Galilee could be a candidate. As a result, his remark would have been seen as a self-claim that was an affront to God's presence. (2) Jesus also attacked the leadership, by implicitly claiming to be their future judge (or by claiming a vindication by him). They held him in violation of Exod 22:27, where God's leaders are not to be cursed. Jesus' claim that their authority was non-existent and that they would be accounted among the wicked is a total rejection of their authority. To the leadership, this was an affront to God as they were, in their own view, God's chosen leaders. Jesus' claim of authority led to his being taken before Rome on a socio-political charge, as well as constituting a religious offense seen as worthy of the death penalty. In the leadership's view, the socio-political threat to the Jewish people's stability was an underlying reason why this claim provoked a response (Gundry argues that Jesus did pronounce the divine name, violating *m. Sanh.* 7:5, a view that is less likely).

The scene as a summary of trial events has a strong claim to authenticity, a stronger claim to it than to the alternative that the scene was created by Mark or by the early church (Bock: 184–237; Evans).

DARRELL L. BOCK

Further reading

Bock, D. L. *Blasphemy and Exaltation in Judaism and the Jewish Examination of Jesus*, WUNT II/106, Tübingen: Mohr-Siebeck, 1998; *EDNT* Vol. 1, pp. 220–21.

Ellis, E. E. "Deity Christology in Mark 14:58," in Joel Green and Max Turner (eds) *Jesus of Nazareth Lord and Christ*, Grand Rapids, MI: Eerdmans, 1994, pp. 192–203.

Evans, C. A. "In What Sense 'Blasphemy'? Jesus Before Caiaphas in Mark 14:61–64," in Eugene H. Lovering, Jr (ed.) *Society of Biblical Literature 1991 Seminar Papers*, SBLSP 30, Atlanta, GA: Scholars Press, 1991, pp. 215–34.

Gundry, R. H. "Jesus' Blasphemy according to Mark 14:61b–64 and Mishnah Sanhedrin 7:5," in *The Old is Better*, WUNT 178, Tübingen: Mohr Siebeck, 2005, pp. 98–110.

Stanton, G. N. "Jesus of Nazareth: A Magician and a False Prophet," in Joel Green and Max Turner (eds) *Jesus of Nazareth Lord and Christ*, Grand Rapids, MI: Eerdmans, 1994, pp. 164–80; St-B Vol. 1, pp. 1007–24.

BORNKAMM, GÜNTHER

Günther Bornkamm (1905–90) was born in Görlitz, studied theology and philosophy at Marburg, Tübingen, Berlin, and Breslau, and became one of the early disciples of Rudolf Bultmann. His dissertation was entitled *Mythos und Legende in den apokryphen Thomas-Akten. Beiträge zur Geschichte der Gnosis und zur Vorgeschichte des Manichäismus* [*Myth and Legend in the Apocryphal Acts of Thomas: Contributions to the History of Gnosis and the Pre-History of Manichaeism*] (FRLANT 49, Göttingen: Vandenhoeck & Ruprecht, 1933). Very important for his development as a scholar was his relationship to German political history after 1933.

Because he was part of Germany's *Bekennende Kirche* ("Confessing Church") that opposed the *Deutsche Christen* ("German Christians") and their loyalty toward the political system, he was banned from the state university by revocation of his *venia legendi* ("permission for lecturing") in 1937 (Heidelberg). Moreover, his teaching at the Church University of Bethel (Bielefeld) came to an end, because the institution was closed by the Nazi government. Upon the end of the war and the defeat of the Nazi government, in 1946 Bornkamm became a professor in Göttingen and in 1949 moved to Heidelberg where he remained until his retirement in 1972.

Next to Jesus, a major part of Bornkamm's historical and theological focus was Paul, to whom he contributed several significant studies and a very helpful monograph (*Paulus* [Urban-Taschenbücher 119, Stuttgart: Kohlhammer, 1969]; English translation: *Paul* [London: Hodder and Stoughton, 1971]), which in some respects is similar to his *Jesus von Nazareth*. Other important areas of interest were the Gospel of John and Hebrews.

In the context of the so-called new or second quest for the historical Jesus it was Bornkamm who wrote the classic German monograph on Jesus. This book, along with Hans Conzelmann's lengthy encyclopedia article, which appeared in English as a book, became the definitive statement. Although Bornkamm's approach to the historical Jesus was not revolutionary as some scholars had wished, his monograph is an example of a well-founded, serious text that exhibited current thought in an accessible manner. The subsequent multitude of translations and editions testifies to the book's lasting value. For the tenth German edition, Bornkamm prepared a slightly revised version of the "classic 'Jesus book' of a whole generation" (Morgan 1998: 441); it is that edition to which this article refers.

In contrast to his teacher Bultmann, Bornkamm understood the role of historical knowledge in a different manner. So far as the gospels show that Christian faith grows out of a given history ("*die Evangelien bekunden, daß der Glaube von einer vorgegebenen Geschichte lebt*"; 1975: 30), the quest for historical events is important and possible. In his classic volume on Jesus of Nazareth, Bornkamm did not intend to provide in detail the life of Jesus, although it is important to note that he did provide a biographical sketch.

Bornkamm sought to present the appearance and deeds of Jesus according to his "unmistakable

uniqueness and particularity" ("*Jesu Gestalt und Wirken in ihrer unverwechselbaren Einmaligkeit und Besonderheit*"; 1975: 20, 23). It is possible to present such a portrait of Jesus through critical exegesis and because the early Christian reports on Jesus mentioned the uniqueness and particularity of his message and deeds in an authentic manner that preceded any faith-based understanding and interpretation (1975: 24). Although the proclamation of Jesus became valid through the experience of cross and resurrection, the pre-Easter history of Jesus is preserved in the gospel tradition (1975: 283).

This basic hermeneutical assumption shows one of the limits of the post-Bultmannian approach to Jesus, giving special emphasis on uniqueness and particularity for methodological reasons. Any reconstruction must differentiate the later early Christian Christology from its Jewish background, in order to consider the possibility that the peculiarity of the "historical" Jesus may fail to take into account the continuity of Jesus with his Jewish background and with later Christian reception guided by Easter faith. With regard to Judaism it can be shown that Jesus supersedes or contradicts Jewish thought and faith in different ways (e.g. the concept of election, 1975: 71; the model of retribution: 1956: 130) although Bornkamm admits that Jesus never abandoned the fundamental of Jewish faith and life (1975: 85). This remark shows that he was not unaware of the problem mentioned before.

It has to be further kept in mind, that Bornkamm defined Judaism, like most contemporary scholars searching for the historical Jesus, on the basis of Billerbeck's *Kommentar zum Neuen Testament aus Talmud und Midrasch* (München: Beck, 1926ff.). Like them he depended on (mostly) later sources and just one type of Judaism, in contrast to the picture presented in recent scholarship. Nevertheless, Bornkamm, referring to Jesus, portrayed Jesus against the background of contemporary Judaism. The new findings of Qumran were recognized but did not play an important role in his monograph, even in later revisions (see, however, 1975: 40).

As sources for his reconstruction of the life and teaching of the historical Jesus, Bornkamm used principally the Synoptic Gospels, although he was aware of the apocryphal early Christian literature from the start of his academic career. Regarding that kind of literature, which played an important role in recent discussion, he stated that the historical value of the generally late literature is small (1975: 195); only the *Gospel of Thomas* is named as a kind of exception containing some old Jesus tradition. The Gospel of John forms an example for secondary development of Jesus tradition, too.

As a tool for reconstructing early Jesus tradition, Bornkamm depended on the two-source hypothesis and the method of form criticism (since the third edition, Bornkamm has served as editor of Martin Dibelius, *Die Formgeschichte des Evangeliums*). On the recently debated character of Q he acknowledged a rather fluid nature as *Traditionsschicht* ("layered tradition") and not as a *fest-umrissene literarische Größe* ("fixed outline of a literary quantity"; 1958: 756; cf. 1975: 193). However – and in this it becomes a contradiction – Bornkamm determined a certain kind of Q theology of his own (1958: 759).

Bornkamm's main interest was in the teaching of Jesus. After a short description of the basic information on Jesus that could be reconstructed from the gospels, he focused on the message of Jesus, the dawn (*Anbruch*) of the kingdom of God and the proclamation of God's will, a chapter combining different important aspects of the teaching of Jesus, to build the main parts of his book. In agreement with Bultmann and his disciples Bornkamm discerned that Jesus did not employ any messianic title, although he awakened such an expectation and Jesus taught with "authority." This was a question he discussed at some length and to which he returned in one of his excursuses. Some important observations are that Bornkamm clearly acknowledged the authority with which Jesus preached without reflecting his own dignity and claiming to be the Messiah.

Jesus proclaimed the coming of the kingdom of God, which appears in his call to repent. We may find traits of Bultmann's existential philosophy in this assumption. In Jesus' claim the present opens the future and the future is not in contrast to the present (1975: 82–83). Regarding the deeds of Jesus we have also to mention some limits of Bornkamm's interpretation. Within this theological tradition, like his contemporary colleagues in Jesus-research, Bornkamm focused on the teaching of Jesus and less on his deeds. With the miracles in particular, as they were portrayed as a secondary christological formation, however, Bornkamm retains some kind of continuity between the proclamation and deeds of Jesus.

With regard to gospel studies Bornkamm became influential as one of the founders of the redaction criticism (*Redaktionsgeschichte*), mostly by encouraging his disciples with the well-known and influential collection *Überlieferung und Auslegung im Matthäus-Evangelium* (English translation: *Tradition and Interpretation in the Gospel of Matthew*). His paper, "Matthäus als Interpret der

Herrenworte" ("Matthew as Interpreter of the Lord's Words"), read previously in 1954, belonged to the earliest contributions on redaction criticism, especially with regard to Matthew. Matthew is an interpreter of Jesus tradition, who uses the words of Jesus to combine ecclesiology with eschatology.

MICHAEL LABAHN

Further reading

Bornkamm, Günther. "Matthäus als Interpret der Herrenworte," *TLZ* 79 (1954) 341–46.
—— *Jesus von Nazareth*, Urban-Taschenbücher 19, Stuttgart: Kohlhammer, 1956; 10th edition, Stuttgart: Kohlhammer, 1975; ET: *Jesus of Nazareth*, New York: Harper, 1960.
—— "Evangelien, synoptische," *Religion in Geschichte und Gegenwart*, third edition, Tübingen: J. C. B. Mohr, 1958, pp. 753–66.
—— "Glaube und Geschichte in den Evangelien," in Helmut Ristow and Karl Matthiae (eds) *Der historische Jesus und der kerygmatische Christus*, Berlin: Evangelische Verlagsanstalt, 1961, pp. 281–88.
—— "Die Bedeutung des historischen Jesus für den Glauben," in P. Rieger (ed.) *Die Frage nach dem historischen Jesus*, Göttingen: Vandenhoeck & Ruprecht, 1962, pp. 57–71.
—— "The Problem of the Historical Jesus and the Kerygmatic Christ," *SE* III, TU 88, Berlin: Akademie Verlag, 1964, pp. 33–44.
—— "Geschichte und Glaube im Neuen Testament. Ein Beitrag zur Frage der 'historischen' Begründung theologischer Aussagen," in *Geschichte und Glaube I. Gesammelte Aufsätze III*, BevTh 48, München: Kaiser, 1968, pp. 9–25.
Bornkamm, Günther, Gerhard Barth, and Heinz J. Held. *Überlieferung und Auslegung im Matthäus-Evangelium*, WMANT 1, Neukirchen: Neukirchener Verlag, 1960, pp. 13–47 ("Enderwartung und Kirche im Matthäusevangelium" [originally published 1956 in English]); 48–53 ("Die Sturmstillung im Matthäusevangelium" [originally published 1948]); ET: *Tradition and Interpretation in Matthew*, Philadelphia, PA: Westminster Press, 1963).
Dobbin, J. D. "Günther Bornkamm and the New Quest of the Historical Jesus," unpublished dissertation, Rome, 1970.
Keck, Leander E. "Bornkamm's Jesus of Nazareth Revisited," *JR* 49 (1969) 1–17.
Kümmel, Werner Georg. *40 Jahre Jesusforschung (1950–1990)*, ed. Helmut Merklein, second edition, Bonner Biblische Beiträge 60, Bonn: Hanstein, 1994, pp. 47–49.
Lührmann, Dieter. "Bornkamm's Response to Keck Revisited," in Abraham J. Malherbe and Wayne A. Meeks, *The Future of Christology: Essays in Honor of Leander E. Keck*, Minneapolis, MN: Fortress Press, 1993, pp. 66–78.
Morgan, Robert. "Günther Bornkamm in England," in Dieter Lührmann and Georg Strecker (eds) *Kirche*, FS Günther Bornkamm, Tübingen: Mohr Siebeck, 1980, pp. 491–506.
—— "Bornkamm, Günther," in Donald K. McKim (ed.) *Major Biblical Interpreters*, Downers Grove, IL: InterVarsity Press, 1998, pp. 439–44.

Rohde, Joachim. *Die redaktionsgeschichtliche Methode. Einführung und Sichtung des Forschungsstandes*, Hamburg: Furche-Verlag, 1966, pp. 44–49.

Theißen, Gerd. "Theologie und Exegese in den neutestamentlichen Arbeiten von Günther Bornkamm," *EvT* 51 (1991) 308–32.

Thielman, Frank S. "Bornkamm, Günther," *DBI* 1 (1999) 135f.

BUDDHIST THOUGHT AND JESUS

There are many interesting parallels between the lives and teachings of the fifth-century BCE Gautama Sakyamuni (the historical Buddha) and Jesus of Nazareth. The world was irrevocably changed because of the impact of these two individuals – a legacy that continues to resonate in our time. This article considers the topic from three perspectives. First, it sets down certain interesting parallels and similarities between the Buddha and Jesus in terms of background, ministry and teaching. Second, it indicates how the Buddhist saga may have been partially known (and therefore putatively influential) in the Mediterranean and Middle East of the early Christian centuries. Third, it acknowledges ways in which important contemporary Buddhist and Christian thinkers recognize the spiritual benefit that may arise from an empathetic inter-faith understanding of what these teachers of grace and wisdom had to so clearly have shared.

Turning to the first point, we are reminded at once of the historical and cultural divide that separates the Buddha and Jesus. In both instances, scholarship shows that despite certain embellishments, there is adequate reason to trust the basic records set down about the lives of these two masters. Gautama Sakyamuni was born into wealth, privilege and an educated environment in ancient India, exposed to the highly advanced metaphysics of Brahmanical Hinduism (e.g. the *Upanishads*, among the most sophisticated of scriptures in the history of religion), which he subjected to rigorous criticism. In due course, a whole new *dharma* or way of being religious emerged from this criticism. Buddhism is agnostic if not atheistic, focused on understanding the experience of living, especially the arising of painfulness (*dukkha*) and the role of several psycho-physical features (such as unconscious willing, *sankhāra*, and craving, *tanhā*) that lend the human condition both trouble and promise. Gautama is also identified with a wondrous story of escape from the princely life which prevented him from "seeing things as they really are" (*yathabhutam*). His ministry in the Gangetic plain as a celibate ascetic lasted fifty years, with an outreach to the powerful as well as the poor. On the other hand, Jesus of Nazareth was born into humble circumstances in Judea, a carpenter by trade. Consistent with Judaism's long tradition of prophetic reformers, Jesus' critique of his inherited faith was aimed at ethical practice. Like the Buddha *dharma*, Jesus too was intent on leaving behind the formalities of ritual worship for an interior sense of knowing one's relationship with the divine, the kingdom of God that is within (*entos hymon*, Luke 17:21) the human soul. Although both Gautama and Jesus were essentially teachers of wisdom and ethics, Jesus was also a social prophet who preached about the need for reform of political and economic conditions – something the Buddha did not do. His ministry, which encompassed only one to three years, was confined entirely to Palestine. Of special interest are the elements shared by the two great figures in terms of personal life-story and saving message. Both were considered to be avatars or specially anointed ones (with mothers who conceived by parthenogenesis), and both attracted large communities of adoring followers. Both focused on emptying the self of ego and finding true identity in a purer state of consciousness or experience. Both spoke in parables, not to obfuscate but to reflect local culture and surroundings as they sought to enlighten devotees about the path to purity. And both were miracle workers, but resisted any ultimate identification with these powers.

A second issue is whether the story of the Buddha may have been known to Jesus or to his immediate followers. There is little evidence that this could have been the case. This is not to deny that some fragmentary aspects of Asian lore were known in places like Greek-speaking Alexandria or Sepphoris during the time of Jesus. Alexander the Great's forays into the Punjab, three centuries before Jesus, opened a viaduct of sorts between East and West, the best example of which is the famous Buddhist text the *Milinda pañha*, or *Questions of King Menandros* (a second-century BCE Bactrian Greek figure who was assisted in a grave personal crisis by the Buddhist monk Nāgasena). In the first few centuries of the Christian era, noncanonical but important biographies of the Buddha (notably the *Buddhacarita* of Aśvaghosa) disseminated some elements of Gautama's legacy to the West. But to suggest that Jesus knew anything at all of the Buddha, or that in "the missing years" of his youth he visited India, or that perhaps the Essenes were crypto-Buddhists who influenced Jesus, is completely unfounded. Any similarity between the teachings of the two masters is one of coincidental spiritual insight alone. In the early medieval period, however, the rise of a popular hagiography in the Christian West associated with the story of Barlaam and Josaphat shows obvious Buddhist roots. Here, the young prince Josaphat (a word linguistically associated with *bodhisattva*, a "buddha-to-be") breaks out of his father's grip in a saga similar to that of Gautama Sakyamuni. Saved by an ascetic Christian monk (Barlaam), the figure of Josaphat had a significant impact on Christian devotees of the time. Though the story was shorn of any direct Buddhist references, it is an example of the engaging dimension of the Buddha's "Great Going Forth" in medieval Christian guise (see MacQueen 109).

Third, although clearly separate in obvious ways, the stories of the Buddha and Jesus evidently have spiritual crossing points that continue to be of inspiration. The great Cistercian monk and scholar Thomas Merton wrote extensively about this topic, "crossing over" in complete empathy and understanding to touch on the Buddhist "experience." Merton engaged in years of personal contact with Buddhist thinkers such as D. T. Suzuki, Thich Nhat Hanh, and the Dalai Lama. Perhaps this correspondence in turn precipitated these Buddhist thinkers to write sensitively and evocatively about the message of Jesus (e.g. Thich Nhat Hanh 1995, 1999; the Dalai Lama's *The Good Heart: A Buddhist Perspective on the Teachings of Jesus*, 1998). Merton provides the Christian with precise insights into the heart of the Buddha *dharma* (e.g. 1961, 1967, 1968, 1986: 212). Dom Aelred Graham's *Zen Catholicism* (1963) and Roy Amore's *Two Masters, One Faith* (1978) are other helpful examples. Marcus Borg has edited an interesting collection of teachings (2002), which emphasize "wisdom teachings" with the "same moral dimension" (notably compassion). These studies never aim to synthesize the stories and figures of the Buddha and Jesus in such fashion as to undermine their individual integrity and uniqueness. But they do show with dignity and thoughtfulness that spiritual yearning and insight in these two paradigmatic individuals share many themes.

BRUCE MATTHEWS

Further reading

Amore, Roy. *Two Masters, One Faith*, Nashville, TN: Abingdon, 1978.
Borg, Marcus. *Jesus and Buddha: The Parallel Sayings*, Berkeley, CA: Ulysses, 2002.
Graham, Dom Aelred. *Zen Catholicism*, New York: Harcourt Brace, 1963.
Hanh, Thich Nhat. *Living Buddha, Living Christ*, New York: Riverhead: 1995.
—— *Going Home: Jesus and Buddha as Brothers*, New York: Riverhead, 1999.
Lama, Dalai. *The Good Heart: A Buddhist Perspective on the Teachings of Jesus*, ed. Robert Kiely, Somerville. MA: Wisdom Publications, 1998.
MacQueen, Graeme. "The Killing Test: The Kinship of Living Beings and the Buddha Legend's First Journey to the West," *Journal of Buddhist Ethics* 9 (2002) 109–48.
Merton, Thomas. *Mystics and Zen Masters*, New York: Delta, 1961.
—— "Introduction" to Thich Nhat Hanh, *Vietnam: Lotus in a Sea of Fire*, New York: Hill and Wang, 1967.
—— *Zen and the Birds of Appetite*, New York: New Directions, 1968.
—— *The Asian Journal of Thomas Merton*, New York: New Directions, 1986.

BULTMANN, RUDOLF

It is no exaggeration to state that possibly no scholar has had more influence on the course of gospel research and, by extension, research on the historical Jesus than Rudolf Bultmann (1884–1976). His impact continues to the present. It was Bultmann who advanced the agenda of demythologizing, and his research has provided some of the major philosophic underpinnings for the work of other scholars, including Günther Bornkamm, Hans Conzelmann, and several of those participating in the Jesus Seminar.

Education and early life

Rudolf Bultmann was the son of a Lutheran pastor, and the grandson of a Lutheran missionary. His maternal grandfather was also a pastor. In his "Autobiographical Reflections," originally delivered in 1956, Bultmann notes that his early years were spent in a country parsonage. These were followed by attendance in the gymnasium, or school for preparing young people for university, at Oldenberg. In 1903, Bultmann commenced his study of theology, first at Tübingen, and later at Berlin and Marburg. He notes that those professors who made the greatest impact upon him were Adolf Jülicher and Johannes Weiss in New Testament, Hermann Gunkel in Old Testament, Wilhelm Herrman in systematic theology and Adolf Harnack in Church history (Bultmann 1960: 283–84).

The influence particularly of Gunkel, Weiss, and Jülicher may be discerned from a careful reading of Bultmann's studies. Gunkel's seminal research in Old Testament form criticism influenced Bultmann's application of the method to the gospel tradition. Likewise, Jülicher's analysis of Jesus' parables would provide much of the basis for Bultmann's own study both of the parables and the sayings of Jesus. Finally, Weiss's understanding of Jesus' conceptual world would provide the theoretical basis for Bultmann's insights into Jesus' apocalyptic preaching, and the need to apply the method of demythologizing if the essentials of that message were to be accepted by modern people.

Bultmann would receive his terminal degree (*Lic. Theol.*, an equivalent of a PhD) in 1910 from Marburg where his thesis, proposed by Johannes Weiss, was *Der Stil der paulinischen Predigt und Kynisch-stoische Diatribe* (*The Style of Pauline Preaching and Cynic-Stoic Diatribe*). In 1912, Bultmann completed his *Habilitationschrift*, the qualification for teaching in the German university system, under the title *Die Exegese des Theodor von Mopsuestia* (*The Exegesis of Theodore of Mopsuestia*). The subject of the latter work was proposed to Bultmann by Adolf Jülicher, and would be one of the few works Bultmann never published. From 1916 to 1920, Bultmann worked at Breslau. The years 1920–21 were spent at Giessen. From 1921 until his retirement in 1951, Bultmann taught at Marburg (Bultmann 1960: 284–85). It was at Marburg where he met some of the most important figures who would assist him in developing the distinctive elements of his theology. Most notably was his collaboration with the philosopher Martin Heidegger, resulting in Bultmann's emphasis on the importance of individual's existential appropriation of the gospel message, or *kerygma*.

Form criticism or form history

In 1921, Bultmann published one of his most important works, *Geschichte der synoptischen Tradition*, later translated under the title *History of the Synoptic Tradition*. Along with Martin Dibelius's *Formgeschichte des Evangeliums* (1919, translated in 1934 as *From Tradition to Gospel*), and K. L. Schmidt's *Rahmen der Geschichte Jesu* (1919), Bultmann's study provided one of the foundations for the practice of form critical, or, more accurately translated from the German, form historical, analysis of the gospel tradition. In *History of the Synoptic Tradition*, Bultmann utilized not only the findings of Schmidt and Dibelius, but also those of W. Wrede's *Messianic Secret* (1901) and J. Wellhausen's analysis of the gospels. From these scholars, Bultmann established the theoretical framework of his study which included: (1) the two-source hypothesis of gospel origins, including Markan priority and Matthew's and Luke's use of a saying source known as "Q"; (2) the possibility of establishing the earliest form of gospel narrative

or saying; (3) the reference to analogies derived from rabbinic and Hellenistic literature which demonstrate the ways in which traditions developed (Bultmann 1968: 6–7).

"The purpose of Form Criticism is to study the history of the Oral Tradition behind the gospels" (Bultmann 1934a: 11). In the quest for the underlying oral history of the gospel message, it was assumed that certain identifiable forms developed early, and had distinguishing characteristics. These traditions, however, did not necessarily derive from the historical Jesus. Rather, they are characteristic of the preaching of the early church, and contain much that originated in its early proclamation, or *kerygma*. Form criticism was a tool that identified the various strata of the gospel accounts, and identified their life situation, or *Sitz im Leben*, within the early church. The allusion to archaeology was not accidental, for as an archaeologist excavated the earth to find the remains of ancient civilizations, so the critic could dig through the accretions imbedded in the gospels to discover the original life setting of a story or account, and discover what, if anything, derived from the historical Jesus.

Bultmann first analyzed the stories about Jesus that concluded with an apophthegm, or short pithy saying of Jesus. In these cases, the story had an existence separate from the saying (Bultmann 1968: 61–69). Examples of healing stories to which a short saying of Jesus was added are Mark 3:1–6; Luke 14:1–6 (which Bultmann held to be a variant of the story in Mark); Luke 13:10–17 and Mark 3:22–30 (Bultmann 1968: 12–13). In controversy stories, such as Mark 2:23–28; 7:1–23, Bultmann understood the situations clearly to reflect the practice of the early church. A saying of Jesus was attached in order to defend the church's practices against criticism. Then, the whole incident was located in a setting within the life of Jesus (Bultmann 1968: 16–18). For instance, Mark 7:1–23 was considered one of the clearest examples for this type of activity, since Bultmann understood it would have been inconceivable that Pharisees would travel all the way from Jerusalem to Galilee to dispute something as minor as hand washing. In addition to controversy sayings, biographical apophthegms are also found, (see Luke 9:57–62; Mark 3:31–35), which have close parallel to rabbinic biographical stories, but which had their origin as illustrations for the preaching of the church (Bultmann 1968: 57–61). The stories connected with apophthegms as a general rule, therefore, had their primary origin in the life of the church.

The words ascribed to Jesus also circulated in other forms, such as: (1) logia, or wisdom sayings;

(2) prophetic or apocalyptic sayings; and (3) parables. Wisdom sayings were preserved primarily in the "Q" tradition, although a few are also preserved in Mark. With the exception of sayings such Mark 3:24–25; 8:35; Matt 7:13–14; Luke 14:11; 16:25, the wisdom sayings reflect little that is new. Others, such as Luke 14:8–10 are so typical of Jewish wisdom Bultmann wondered how they ever were attributed to Jesus. Both logia and apocalyptic or prophetic sayings originated as Jewish material acquired by the Church, and later ascribed to Jesus. Parables, on the other hand, do have their origin in Jesus' words. Yet the Church has modified Jesus' simple parables with allegorical additions (Bultmann 1968: 198). Here Jülicher's influence on Bultmann may be noted.

In addition to sayings, Bultmann analyzed the deeds of Jesus. Of the miracle stories, Bultmann noted different types, including exorcisms, healings, raisings of the dead, and nature miracles (Bultmann 1968: 231–44). While Jesus had a reputation in the Palestinian church of being a miracle worker, Bultmann concluded that the form of the stories in the gospels is undoubtedly Hellenistic (Bultmann 1968: 239–40). Yet the most coherent narrative of the events of Jesus' life was the passion narrative (Bultmann 1968: 275–91). The sequence was established very early, as is evidenced by 1 Cor 11:23–26 (Bultmann 1968: 275). Yet even here one finds legendary additions from the early church, such as the stories of the empty tomb (Bultmann 1968: 291).

Demythologizing

Bultmann's form criticism of the gospel tradition enabled him to embark on one of the tasks that became most associated with his name: demythologizing. Demythologizing was the means by which Bultmann endeavored to isolate the essential features of the *kerygma*, which remained relevant to the church of the modern age. Thus, those elements which reflected an ancient cosmology, such as a three-story universe, or the first-century understanding of the demonic origin of disease, could be safely discarded. In part, this task was possible because these characteristics were not part of the original preaching of Jesus. The agenda was also possible because "*[t]he message of Jesus* is a presupposition for the theology of the New Testament rather than a part of New Testament theology itself" (Bultmann 1951: 3, emphasis his). Theology actually consists of the *kerygma*, the preaching of the church, in which the individual attains an existential encounter with the living God. Thus, the specifics of the life of the historical

Jesus become. Rather, "Historical research can never lead to any result which could serve as a basis for faith, for *all its results have only relative validity*" (Bultmann 1969: 30, emphasis his). Thus, demythologizing is not only helpful but a necessity of the Church, in order to make the message of Jesus valid for the modern world.

One example of Bultmann's demythologizing agenda is in his understanding of Jesus' death on the cross. The traditional Christian proclamation of the cross is mythological in its cosmic dimensions. This proclamation is inadequate for the modern person. Rather, for Bultmann, the proclamation of the cross gains its legitimacy in that it "created a new historical situation." The hearer of the proclamation must appropriate that message by participating with Jesus in crucifixion, in being crucified with Christ (Bultmann 1984: 36). The significance for understanding the person of the historical Jesus is that God has acted decisively in space and time through the life of a historical person, Jesus of Nazareth. God continues to act through Jesus as the means by which people attain an existential encounter with God. God has not become imminent, but become flesh, and in that way history is affirmed (Bultmann 1984: 41–42).

Jesus and the Word

In light of his skepticism of specifics of the gospel tradition, as well as his agenda for demythologizing, one may well question whether Bultmann was actually concerned about the events of Jesus' life or the content of his preaching. In fact, Bultmann showed considerable interest in the historical Jesus, as demonstrated in his short book, *Jesus and the Word* (translated 1934). Bultmann's methodology was established in the first chapter (Bultmann 1934b: 3–15). Here, the "objective history" claimed by nineteenth-century studies was rejected. Rather than attempting to present an account of the facts of history as they "really happened," Bultmann focused upon a "dialog with history," since the historian does not stand outside the events of history, but within them. Bultmann also noted the importance of Schweitzer's *Quest of the Historical Jesus*, and therefore eschewed efforts to develop a comprehensive psychology of Jesus. He did not discuss Jesus' "genius" or "greatness." Rather, Bultmann restricted his psychological analysis to the conclusion that Jesus did not understand himself as the Messiah. This theme would also be developed later in Bultmann's famous dictum, "The proclaimer became the proclaimed" (see Bultmann 1951).

What picture of the historical Jesus then emerged? Jewish religion of Jesus' time bound hope with obedience to the law (Bultmann 1934b: 19). As such, it was legalistic. In this atmosphere, Jesus appeared preaching the kingdom of God, which is a wholly other, miraculous event (Bultmann 1934b: 37). In this respect, Jesus shares the apocalyptic world view of his contemporaries. Yet Jesus differed from other apocalyptic preachers, including John the Baptist, in that his understanding of the kingdom of God did not include a demand for asceticism. Rather, Jesus required obedience to God. But this obedience was consistent with the earlier message of the classical prophets of the Old Testament, which minimized cultic observance. Jesus recognized human sin, but did not propose to establish a new and better society. Such an ambition was precluded by his expectation of the imminent appearance of God's kingdom (Bultmann 1934b: 106–7). Thus, Jesus' focus was not on providing a new and better commandment, but presenting the standard of the commandment of love as normative (Bultmann 1934b: 110–32).

Finally, in contrast to Judaism's understanding of God as distant and remote, Jesus presented a God who was near at hand (Bultmann 1934b: 133–219). One manifestation of this difference was Jesus' understanding of God as the loving father. While Judaism and Stoicism both taught about a God who related to God's people as father, Jesus' unique contribution was to apply it to the individual's relationship with a heavenly parent (Bultmann 1934b: 191–94).

It is interesting that Bultmann's portrait of the historical Jesus, for all its reliance upon the findings of Schweitzer and Weiss along with the tools of form criticism, resembles nothing as much as the nineteenth-century romantic reconstructions of the historical Jesus. Again, we encounter a Jesus divorced from the Judaism of his heritage, preaching a message of an imminent, loving Father, as contrasted with a supposed Jewish legalism. It is a picture closely related to Bultmann's teacher Harnack's understanding of Jesus in *What is Christianity?* Thus, while Bultmann was able to transcend many of the foibles of the nineteenth-century lives of Jesus, he remained very much an heir to the liberal tradition that produced these works.

Evaluation

Bultmann's contribution to the study of the historical Jesus, as his influence upon the discipline of New Testament in general, is truly immense. Perhaps no other single person has so successfully set the agenda for further studies. Yet, as we approach the century mark since the appearance of *History of the Synoptic Tradition*, it may be time to look back and reconsider some of Bultmann's conclusions. His work on form criticism certainly alerted other scholars to the importance of oral tradition in the transmission of the gospel tradition.

Yet, at the same time, Bultmann failed to appreciate the Jewish nature of that tradition, locating much of it in the gentile Hellenistic–Roman church world. While Hengel (1974) is correct in stating that all Judaism of the first century was Hellenistic Judaism, it remained Jewish, and was a religious system not well understood by its Greco-Roman contemporaries. Perhaps one reason for this failure was that Bultmann shared with his contemporaries a view of Judaism that is little more than a caricature of the religion's true dynamic. The contrast between the legalism of Judaism and the religion of love preached by Jesus is no longer viable. Likewise, Bultmann's emphasis on demythologizing, in light of current anthropological and psychological studies, looks remarkably ethnocentric. One also wonders if Bultmann's modern person was his own construct, not to be found outside the hallowed halls of academia. Nevertheless, Bultmann cast a long shadow, which continues to influence scholars today. His studies remain foundational for the examination of the question of the historical Jesus.

RUSSELL MORTON

Further reading

Ashcraft, Morris. *Rudolf Bultmann*, Makers of the Modern Theological Mind, Waco, TX: Word, 1972.

Bultmann, R., *Der Stil der paulinischen Predigt und die Kynischtische Diatribe*, Göttingen: Vandenhoeck & Ruprecht, 1910.

—— *Jesus and the Word*, trans. Louise Pettibone Smith and Erminie Huntress Lantero, New York: Charles Scribner's Sons, 1934a.

—— "Study of the Synoptic Gospels," in Rudolf Bultmann and Karl Kundsin, *Form Criticism: Two Essays on New Testament Research*, trans. Frederic C. Grant, New York: Harper & Row, 1934b, pp. 11–76.

—— *Theology of the New Testament, Vol. 1*, trans. Kendrick Grobel, New York: Charles Scribner's Sons, 1951.

—— *Existence and Faith: Shorter Writings of Rudolf Bultmann*, selected, trans. and introduced by Schubert M. Ogden, London: Hodder and Stoughton, 1960.

—— *History of the Synoptic Tradition*, revised edition, trans. John Marsh, New York: Harper & Row, 1968.

—— *Faith and Understanding*, ed. with an introduction by Robert W. Funk, trans. Louise Pettibone Smith, Philadelphia, PA: Fortress Press, 1969.

—— *New Testament and Mythology: And Other Basic Writings*, selected, ed. and trans. Schubert M. Ogden, Philadelphia, PA: Fortress Press, 1984.

Bultmann, Rudolf, and Five Critics *Kerygma and Myth*, ed. Hans Werner Bartsch, New York: Harper & Row, 1961.

Funk, Robert (ed.) *The Bultmann School of Biblical Interpretation: New Directions?* JTC 1, New York: Harper & Row, 1965.

Harnack, Adolf von *What is Christianity? Lectures Delivered in the University of Berlin during the Winter-Term 1899–1900*, trans. Thomas Bailey Saunders, New York: Putnam's, 1901.

Hengel, Martin. *Judaism and Hellenism*, trans. John Bowden, Philadelphia, PA: Fortress Press, 1974.

Johnson, Roger A. *Rudolf Bultmann: Interpreting Faith for the Modern Era*, The Making of Modern Theology, London: Collins, 1987.

Jones, Gareth. *Bultmann: Towards a Critical Theology*, Cambridge: Polity Press, 1991.

Kay, James F. *Christus Praesens: A Reconsideration of Rudolf Bultmann's Christology*, Grand Rapids, MI: Eerdmans, 1994.

Perrin, Norman. *The Promise of Bultmann*, Philadelphia, PA: Fortress Press, 1978.

Roberts, Robert C. *Rudolf Bultmann's Theology: A Critical Interpretation*, Grand Rapids, MI: Eerdmans, 1976.

Thiselton, Anthony C. *The Two Horizons: New Testament Hermeneutics and Philosophical Description with Special Reference to Heidegger, Bultmann, Gadamer and Wittgenstein*, Grand Rapids, MI: Eerdmans, 1980.

C

CADBURY, HENRY J.

Although Henry J. Cadbury is most widely known for his contributions to the study of Luke—Acts and his leadership in the translation of the Revised Standard Version of the Bible (especially the Apocrypha), he was also a major contributor to historical Jesus studies. Cadbury's two books on Jesus, *The Peril of Modernizing Jesus* (1937) and *Jesus: What Manner of Man?* (1947), were actually published before the "New Quest" broke loose in the 1950s, and the field's indebtedness to his contributions to that transition has been underacknowledged. (Cadbury also wrote an essay on the obverse feature of his first book: "The Peril of Archaeizing Ourselves" [1949].)

On one hand, this is understandable. Cadbury's first book on Jesus emphasized the peril of trying to make Jesus relevant to our modern sensibilities and thus would have been seen as continuing Schweitzer's critique of the tendency to project our own interests onto Jesus rather than advocating a new quest. He certainly furthered the basis for historical-Jesus skepticism in his 1963 analysis, *The Eclipse of the Historical Jesus*, as well as other writings. On the other hand, Cadbury's work was not simply deconstructive. Because of his understated and modest claims, Cadbury actually sketched a more likely presentation of Jesus than interested interpreters might have done for themselves, and in this way he contributed several constructive elements.

For instance, rather than assuming Jesus had a programmatic goal, or set of intentional platforms and strategies, perhaps he simply responded to occasional needs as they presented themselves. And, rather than seeing himself as a social reformer, or as one setting out to change society, Jesus appears to have been driven by an apocalyptic vision of God's sovereign fulfillment of history. Further, rather than inferring Jesus had a set of doctrines to levy upon his followers, he appears primarily given to emphasizing human responsiveness to the divine will. Or, rather than being the sort of evangelist that sought to make converts, or a salesman peddling spiritual wares, he more characteristically sought to privilege the truth and authentic apprehensions of it, even challenging religious institutions and constructs as a result. In these and other ways, Cadbury not only challenged modernistic tendencies to create a Jesus in "our image," he also posed a more plausible set of ways to envision the epoch-changing stranger from Galilee.

More directly, though, Cadbury did argue that Jesus had an *emphasis*; or in Quaker terms, a "concern." The central concern of Jesus related primarily to "human conduct" and social ethics. Rather than focusing on the place, time, or setting of Jesus' teachings, the pressing *historical* interest lies in understanding his primary concerns for humanity: loving God and social justice. Likewise, noting his pointing to the center of the Jewish law shows us something not just about *what* Jesus taught, but *how*. By asking probing questions rather than giving answers, Jesus helped others discover the truth rather than propounding particular notions about it. This mode of operation continues to create new "learnings" and "understandings" transformatively, rather than seeing Jesus' teaching as a closed venture.

Cadbury also emphasizes the Jewishness of Jesus as a first-century prophet. Accordingly, Cadbury's Jesus was more of a conservative than a radical. In other words, in emphasizing the truth of the Hebrew prophets' message, Jesus can be seen as calling people *back to* covenant faithfulness, rather than inciting innovations. In that sense, Jesus also can be seen to be challenging the legalistic ways humans either seek to drive values home or seek to wriggle their way out of an ethical standard by means of parsing the letter of the law, pleading for exceptions to norms. Jesus likewise challenged cultic regulations within Judaism, extending implications to formalistic accretions within Christianity, as well. His association with John the Baptist also betrays a critique of religious assimilation with political power, so these features help us understand the sort of informal reformer Jesus was likely to have been – and why he raised the ire of contemporary authorities.

Cadbury's most sustained contribution to historical Jesus studies came in his second book on Jesus (1947), in which he questions "what manner of man" Jesus might have been. What were Jesus' interests? He called for following the way of the Kingdom, even if costly. Where did he get his wisdom? Some of it reflects conventional understandings, but it also suggests Jesus' own discoveries and observations about the ways things are. Why did he teach in parables? The parables conceal the reign of God as well as revealing it; they also connect the ways of God with the experiences of persons. What was the character of his new teaching and his authority? The impressive feature of his teaching is his self-assuredness rather than his originality. And, who can really claim to know Jesus? Much of what Jesus says on the subject questions people's claims to know; his mode of asking questions functioned to facilitate self-reliance and trusting in God rather than propping up religious or political authorities.

Jesus' ethic was not an "interim" one; rather, it assumed the divine will as a standard for all time. Rather than being a factor of outcomes or utilitarianism, Jesus' ethic called for holy obedience to the ways of God as a factor of truth's convincing power. Jesus challenged incongruity where he observed it, yet he also used superlatives as a means of emphasizing ideals. There is no such thing as "enough" faithfulness; it is a life-long vocation. His teachings appear to be ordered by cognitive reflection upon experience rather than by

reasoned argument, and his challenging of authorities made him controversial. The miracles of Jesus legitimated his Messianic identity, and his Messiahship bolstered the authority of his teachings. Finally, however, Jesus' authority lay in the veracity of his claims, finding resonance in the consciences of his audiences then and now.

Cadbury contributed to Jesus studies by his insistence upon limiting the interpreter's inferences to what the text actually says rather than filling in the gaps with either liberal or conservative speculation. Therefore, "Hades" replaces "Hell" in the RSV, the informality of early Christianity is highlighted, and his identification of Jesus within the mold of the Jewish prophet becomes formative for future Jesus studies. Motive-criticism provided windows into the works of ancient authors, as well as a means of critique for modern scholarship, and his introduction of form-criticism to the English-speaking world furthered the distinguishing of oral from written traditions in Gospel studies. Because of his reluctance to claim more than the evidence will substantiate, Henry J. Cadbury exercised impressive modesty of claim regarding what can be known about Jesus of Nazareth. In that sense, Cadbury contributes to what we can know about the Jesus of history precisely because he clarifies critically what we cannot.

PAUL N. ANDERSON

Further reading

Cadbury, Henry J. "Stumbling at Jesus," *Present Day Papers* 1 (1914) 140–45.
—— "Jesus and the Prophets," *JR* 5 (1925) 607–22.
—— "Jesus and John the Baptist," *JQR* 23 (1933) 373–76.
—— *The Peril of Modernizing Jesus*, New York and London: Macmillan, 1937; reprinted paperback edition, Eugene, OR: Wipf & Stock, 2007.
—— *Jesus: What Manner of Man?*, New York: Macmillan, 1947; reprinted paperback edition, London: SPCK, 1962.
—— "The Peril of Archaizing Ourselves," *Int* 3 (1949) 331–38.
—— "Intimations of Immortality in the Thought of Jesus," *HTR* 53 (1960) 1–26; reprinted in *SPCK Theological Collection 3*, London: SPCK, 1964, pp. 79–94.
—— *Jesus and Judaism and The Emphasis of Jesus*, Shrewsbury Lecture, Indianapolis, IN: John Woolman Press (1962), pp. 1–9 and 11–22.
—— *The Eclipse of the Historical Jesus*, Haverford Library Lectures, Pendle Hill Pamphlet 133, Wallingford, PA: Pendle Hill Publications, 1963.

CAESAREA MARITIMA

Caesarea Maritima, also known as Caesarea, was an ancient port city of great importance located on the Mediterranean coast approximately 25 miles south of modern-day Haifa and 30 north of Tel Aviv. The port was first established as a Phoenician colony and trading village named Strato's Tower. Its settlement most likely occurred in the middle of the fourth century BCE when a Sidonian king named Strato II built a coastal tower along the Phoenician–Egyptian trade route. The tower structure probably served as both a lighthouse for ships and a storage facility for goods.

In the Hellenistic period, Strato's Tower came under Ptolemaic control and consequently became a thoroughly Hellenized Greek *polis*. In fact, our earliest reference to Strato's Tower is found in the Zenon papyri. In 259 BCE Zeno, an agent of the Ptolemaic minister of finance in Egypt, listed Strato's Tower among a group of important Palestinian trading cities. In 198 BCE the Seleucids took control of Strato's Tower; yet, when Seleucid power waned late in the second century, a local ruler named Zoilus was able to seize control of Strato's Tower for a couple of decades. Notably, it was at this time that the fortification of the city was initiated. Soon thereafter in 103 BCE, Alexander Jannaeus of the Hasmonean Dynasty annexed Strato's Tower to his Jewish kingdom. The port city then remained under Hasmonean control until Pompey, a Roman general, claimed the entire region in 63 BCE and added Strato's Tower to the Roman province of Syria.

It was during the Roman period that Caesarea's prominence and fame as an international port city was most firmly established. First, in 30 BCE Octavian, later known as Augustus Caesar, transferred control of Strato's Tower from Syria to the Roman province of Palestine and Herod the Great, Rome's vassal king over the region. In gratitude to his powerful patron, Herod changed the name of the port city to Caesarea and elaborately rebuilt it as a monument to the Roman emperor. Over the next twelve years (22–10 BCE) Herod spared little expense or effort while completing this ambitious project.

Josephus, the Jewish historian who wrote in the latter half of the first century CE, describes Caesarea in great detail in both *The Jewish Wars* 1.408–15 and *The Antiquities of the Jews* 15.331–41. He indicates that Herod built numerous palaces, subterranean storerooms, a system of aqueducts that carried rainwater and human waste out to the sea, a theater, an amphitheater, and a large pagan temple dedicated to Rome and Caesar. Yet Josephus reserves his highest praise for the large harbor complex that Herod constructed, named Sebastos. To shield anchored ships from the dangerous south winds, Herod's workers placed large stones in a crescent-shaped pattern off Caesarea's shoreline in order to create a large sea wall below the surface of the water. Ships were then able to dock in multiple locations within and around the mole. Furthermore, a large dock ran along the top of the enormous sea wall and was equipped with watchtowers and arches under which sailors lodged.

Despite earlier skepticism, modern archaeologists have largely confirmed the accuracy of Josephus's reports. Much of the archaeological research on Caesarea chronicles the discovery of large structures (e.g. theater, amphitheater, hippodrome, palace, and temple) as well as the impressive engineering of the harbor complex and water systems. For instance, it appears that while constructing the sea wall the workers combined imported materials with advanced construction methods such as the use of hydraulic concrete.

Moreover, shortly after Herod's death, Caesarea's role in Roman politics, military campaigns, and culture increased markedly. In 6 CE, Caesarea became the capital and administrative center of the newly formed province of Judea. As a result, Roman governors or procurators took up residence in Caesarea and Roman troops were stationed there. Furthermore, Caesarea functioned as a cultural exemplar for the region, which was largely populated by Jews, Samaritans, and eventually Christians.

The writers of the New Testament clearly recognized Caesarea's importance at the time of Jesus. In the book of Acts, Luke indicates that Philip resided in Caesarea (8:40, 21:8); Peter traveled there and helped Cornelius, a Roman centurion, become the first Gentile convert to Christianity (10:1–48); and Paul was tried and imprisoned there for two years before being transferred to Rome (23:33–26:32). In addition, Pontius Pilate resided in Caesarea and only visited Jerusalem during important festivals and celebrations.

Unfortunately, conflict between a Jewish minority and the Roman majority in Caesarea increased sharply around 60 CE. After riots broke out, Nero declared the Jews guilty of disrupting the peace and reportedly 20,000 Jews were executed in Caesarea on one day. Moreover, this violence led to the beginning of the Jewish war against Rome that lasted from 66 to 73 CE and ended with a decisive Roman victory. During the war, however, both Vespasian and Titus directed the Roman war efforts from Caesarea. Afterward, Caesarea acquired even greater prominence. In 70 CE, Vespasian bestowed upon Caesarea the status of "colony," and even later (c. 231–32), Severus Alexander bestowed the status of "metropolis" upon the city.

Eventually, Caesarea reached its greatest size and perhaps its cultural apex in the third through sixth centuries CE. During this period Caesarea developed an astounding degree of ethnic, cultural, and religious diversity to accompany its status as a provincial capital and major port city. Significant numbers of Jews, Samaritans, and Christians all resided in the city and thrived intellectually. For instance, a robust rabbinic community grew up in Caesarea and significantly influenced the Babylonian and Jerusalem versions of the Talmud. Similarly, Origen's arrival in Caesarea in 231 CE helped to transform Caesarea into an important center of Christian education. Shortly thereafter, both Eusebius and Jerome extended the rich heritage of Christian learning in the city. In the middle ages, Caesarea declined significantly as control of the city alternated between warring Christians and Muslims. Finally, the city was completely destroyed in 1291 CE.

ANDREW ARTERBURY

Further reading

Donaldson, Terence L. (ed.) *Religious Rivalries and the Struggle for Success in Caesarea Maritima*, Studies in Christianity and Judaism 8, Waterloo, ON: published for the Canadian Corporation for Studies in Religion by Wilfrid Laurier University Press, 2000.

Fritsch, Charles T. (ed.) *Caesarea Studies: Studies in the History of Caesarea Maritima*, BASORSup 19, Missoula, MT: Scholars Press, 1975.

Hohlfelder, Robert L. "Caesarea," in David Noel Freedman (ed.) *The Anchor Bible Dictionary*, New York: Doubleday, 1992, Vol. I, pp. 798–803.

Holum, Kenneth G., Robert L. Hohlfelder, Robert J. Bull, and Avner Raban, *King Herod's Dream: Caesarea on the Sea*, New York: Norton, 1988.

Holum, Kenneth G., Avner Raban, and Joseph Patrich (eds) *Caesarea Papers 2: Herod's Temple, The Provincial Governor's Praetorium and Granaries, The Later Harbour, A Gold Coin Hoard, and Other Studies*, Journal of Roman Archaeology, Supplemental Series no. 35, Portsmouth, RI: Journal of Roman Archaeology, 1999.

Levine, Lee I. *Caesarea under Roman Rule*, SJLA 7, Leiden: Brill, 1975.

Raban, Avner and Kenneth G. Holum (eds) *Caesarea Maritima: A Retrospective after Two Millennia*, Leiden: Brill, 1996.

Stoutenburg, Dennis C. "Caesarea Maritima: Restoring a Former Glory," *Did* 5:2 (Spring 1994) 42–55.

Vann, Robert L. (ed.) *Caesarea Papers: Straton's Tower, Herod's Harbour, and Roman and Byzantine Caesarea*, Journal of Roman Archaeology, Supplement Series no. 5, Ann Arbor, MI: Journal of Roman Archaeology, 1992.

CAESAREA PHILIPPI

The area referred to twice in the New Testament as Caesarea Philippi, and known today as Banias, is located on a level plateau at the foot of the southwest slope of Mt Hermon. It is about 40 km north of the Sea of Galilee and 3 km east of the biblical site of Dan The main east–west trade route from Tyre to Damascus runs through the area. To the east and south one finds the Golan Heights while to the west there is the northern Jordan Valley. To the north of the urban area is a cave and a spring that is one of the sources of the Jordan River (cf. Pliny, *Nat.* 5.71). The area is such that Josephus comments on its natural beauty on more than one occasion (*Ant.* 15.364; *B.J.* 1.404, 3.514).

Before the area was settled there is evidence for the existence of a rural grotto dedicated to Pan, the half-human and half-goat god of shepherds and flocks, and the nymphs. The grotto was used primarily by local rural inhabitants of the area. Significant archaeological evidence such as pottery sherds suggest meals were held at the site, although it is not clear whether it involved ritual dining or informal picnicking.

Following the conquests of Alexander the Great, the area fell under Ptolemaic rule. It is possible that it was at this time that the grotto was developed into a more formal cult place for Pan. One of the earliest literary references to the site, which was called Panias, is Polybus' description of Antiochus III's victory here over the Ptolemaic general Scopas around 200 BCE (*Hist.* 16.18:2–3). As a result of this battle, Palestine came under Seleucid control.

With the coming of the Romans into the region under Pompey between 67 and 63 BCE Panias eventually became part of the territory of Herod the Great sometime around 20 BCE. As part of his wider building project, Herod built a temple there that opened onto the Panias cave and named it the Augusteion to honor the emperor (Josephus, *Ant.* 15.363). Following Herod's death c. 6–4 BCE and the division of his kingdom, his son Herod Philip took control of the territory of Trachonitis. He established a new urban center south of the sacred district of Panias and named it Caesarea Philippi, the first name in honor of the Roman emperor Caesar Augustus, the latter name distinguishing it from his father's civic jewel on the Mediterranean coast, named Caesarea Maritima.

Although Caesarea Philippi served as Philip's primary residence and place of governance, there is disagreement among archaeologists as to whether it was an administrative center or a city, primarily due to the paucity of archaeological evidence for residential buildings during Philip's reign. When Philip died in 33 CE he left no direct heir. Four years later, however, the emperor Caligula granted

Philip's territories to Philip's nephew, Agrippa I, who ruled them from Caesarea Philippi until 44 CE. After another period of direct Roman rule, in 53–54 CE Claudius granted Agrippa II these territories. It is at this point that the site seems to have been transformed from an administrative town into a Roman city. Agrippa II built a royal palace and renamed the city Neronias in honor of Nero (Josephus, *Ant.* 20.211). During this time the city seems to have remained modest in size at 150,000 sq m, although it had many monumental buildings.

Throughout the first century Caesarea Philippi was predominantly inhabited by Itureans and Phoenicians. The city had very few Jewish residents and a distinctly non-Jewish character. Some infer a Jewish population there from Jesus' visit, although this is not altogether clear. Josephus does mention in passing Jewish residents of Caesarea Philippi during Philip's reign (*Vit.* 13). During the Jewish War Vespasian rested his troops at Caesarea Philippi (Josephus, *B.J.* 3.443), and at the end of the war his son Titus stopped in Caesarea Philippi and held games in which many of his Jewish captives died violently (*B.J.* 7.23–24, 37–38). While Titus was in Caesarea Philippi he became interested in Berenice, Agrippa II's consort and half-sister, and took her back to Rome with him, only to send her back when she was met with disapproval at Rome because of her ethnicity (Suetonius, "Titus," 7.1). Towards the end of the first century, after the death of Agrippa II, the city and its territories were absorbed into the larger Roman province of Syria-Phoenicia.

The New Testament texts provide scant evidence concerning Caesarea Philippi other than to note Jesus' journey there from the Galilee. Even here, Jesus' precise destination is not clear as Matthew locates him "in the district of Caesarea Philippi" (16:13) while Mark has him visit "the villages of Caesarea Philippi" (8:27). It is en route to this location that one of the pivotal moments in Jesus' ministry is set – Peter's confession of Jesus' messianic identity and Jesus' subsequent proclamation of his destiny (Mark 8:27–33; Matt 16:13–23). Six days later the Transfiguration takes place upon a mountain, but the text is unclear as to whether Jesus and his followers have remained in the area of Caesarea Philippi. The next geographic marker in the texts is in Galilee (Matt 17:22), specifically Capernaum (Mark 9:33; Matt 17:24), thus presuming the return of Jesus from the northern territory. Interestingly, while Luke includes the same events he drops the specific mention of Caesarea Philippi, thus locating them in the Galilee (Luke 9:18–50).

It is not at all clear why Jesus took this trip to Caesarea Philippi we might also ask if one can find some specific connection associated with this location and the events recorded there. Some commentators suggest that Jesus has deliberately traveled to a place of ancient cultic significance (and away from Jerusalem) in order to undergo revelatory experiences connected to his identity. Others point to the imposing rock face as a possible backdrop for Jesus' metaphorical use of "upon this rock" (Matt 16:18). However, the distinctly non-Jewish nature of the site seems to mitigate such interpretations.

RICHARD S. ASCOUGH

Further reading

Berlin, Andrea M. "The Archaeology of Ritual: The Sanctuary of Pan at Banias/Caesarea Philippi," *BASOR* 315 (1999) 27–45.
Guttenberger, Gudrun. "Why *Caesarea Philippi* of All Sites? Some Reflections on the Political Background and Implications of Mark 8.27–30 for the Christology of Mark," in M. Labahn and J. Zangenberg (eds) *Zwischen den Reichen. Neues Testament und Römische Herrschaft,* TANZ 36, Tübingen and Basel: Francke, 2002, pp. 119–31.
Ma'oz, Zvi Uri. "Banias," in E. Stern, A. Lewinson-Gilboa, and J. Aviram (eds) *The New Encyclopedia of Archaeological Excavations in the Holy Land,* Jerusalem and New York: Israel Exploration Society, Carta, and Simon and Schuster, 1993, Vol. 1, pp. 136–43.
Tzaferis, Vassilios. "Cults and Deities Worshipped at Caesarea Philippi-Banias," in E. Ulrich, J. W. Wright, R. P. Carroll, and P. R. Davies (eds) *Priests, Prophets and Scribes: Essays on the Formation and Heritage of Second Temple Judaism in Honour of Joseph Blenkinsopp,* JSOTSup 149, Sheffield: JSOT Press, 1992, pp. 190–201.
Wilson, John F. *Caesarea Philippi: Banias, The Lost City of Pan,* London and New York: I. B. Tauris, 2004.
Wilson, John F. (ed.) *Rediscovering Caesarea Philippi: The Ancient City of Pan,* Malibu, CA: Pepperdine University Press, 2001.

CANA IN GALILEE

Three sources attest the existence of a village named Cana in Galilee in the first century CE. The first is Josephus reporting that he resided in Cana while living in the plain of Asochis (*Life* 16, 41). The second is the Fourth Gospel, which is the only one among the Gospels to mention the name of "Cana in Galilee," perhaps to distinguish it from Cana south of Tyre. According to John, Jesus performed two miracles at Cana, the changing water into wine (John 2:1–11), and the healing at a distance the son of an official (John 4:46–56). In the last chapter, generally recognized as a late addition, Cana is said to be the city of origin of the disciple Nathanael.

The third source is epigraphic; it was discovered in Caesarea Maritima and mentions a priestly family by the name of Elyashiv, native to Cana. This family is mentioned among other families who shared guard shifts at the Temple in Jerusalem.

The identification of the site and the archaeological research

The precise location of "Cana in Galilee" was debated during the nineteenth century when the traditional site, Kefar Kana, situated in the hillside of lower Galilee, in the hinterland of the city of Sepphoris and 5 miles northeast of Nazareth, was challenged by scholars such as E. Robinson and others. Robinson preferred a place called Khirbet el Kana, 9 miles north of Nazareth in the Beth Natofa valley to comply with Cana in Galilee and Cana in the plain of Asochis. He even reported in 1853 that Khirbet Cana was also called Kana el Jelil, Kana of Galilee, by his local guide.

Twentieth-century archaeological surveys did not help to determine which contender is Kana of the historical sources, but in the past few years this picture has been thoroughly changed due to archaeological excavations taking place in the two contenders.

In 1997 Fr Eugenio Alliata conducted excavations in the Franciscan church in Kefar Kana and discovered below it medieval and Byzantine remains, a few walls that he ascribed to the "first to the fourth centuries CE." No evidence follows his assertion.

Beginning in 1999, the Israel Antiquities Authority launched a series of excavations at Kefar Kana. Thus far, eleven areas have been excavated with the following settlement pattern.

The earliest occupation of the site dates from the Middle Bronze Age (twentieth–sixteenth centuries BCE). Only shards of pottery without architectural context were discovered from this occupation level. After a hiatus during the Late Bronze Age and Iron Age I (1550–1000 BCE), a small settlement resumed during Iron Age II (tenth–eighth centuries BCE). This occupation was destroyed, together with many Galilean sites, presumably as a result of the Tiglath Pileser III campaign in 732 BCE. Nevertheless, a small inhabitation continued to occupy the area throughout the Persian era.

A dramatic increase in population took place in the Hellenistic period (fourth century BCE), when new buildings covered the site, and it seems that the site thrived. However, prosperity did not last too long and as a result of the Hasmonean conquest the site of Cana declined during the first half of the first century.

The Herodian period brought a new wave of prosperity and the population increased once more. New buildings were constructed on the ruined Hellenistic structures and some old Hellenistic buildings were renovated and reoccupied. Noteworthy are a few Jewish immersion baths (*Miqvaot*). One of these baths measures 6 ft by 14 ft and was preserved to an elevation of 6 ft. Among the outstanding finds were plenty of limestone vessels known elsewhere, primarily from Jerusalem. A workshop for manufacturing of limestone vessels was discovered in a cave near the village of Reine, located between Kefar Cana and Nazareth. Ritual baths and limestone vessels are the hallmark of Jewish presence during the time of Jesus. Apparently, this wave of newcomers to Galilee was undoubtedly Jewish immigrants from Judea. This is not unique to Cana; settlements of Judean Jews, during the Herodian period, were discerned in other places such as Nazareth, Nain, Bethsaida, Capernaum, Yodfat, and Gamla.

The most extensive Early Roman settlement in Cana was discovered in the west outskirts of the modern Kefar Cana, in an area called Karm el Ras. The excavators believe that this is the location of Cana in Galilee.

Apparently, the First Jewish Revolt (66–70 CE) did not leave any scars in Cana as it did not leave marks in any other places in the hinterland of Sepphoris. The latter did not take part in the rebellion and it appears that the villages of its hinterland did not participate either. Yodfat, the headquarter of Josephus, and Gamla, located outside this hinterland, were exceptional.

The Jewish attitude towards the Romans was totally changed after the First Revolt, perhaps as a result of an influx of Jewish refugees from Jerusalem and Judea. In the sixty-year interval between the two revolts, the Galilean Jews made preparations for the Second Revolt (132–5 CE). An underground hideaway system of caves and tunnels was excavated in the soft local limestone of Cana, similar to the way the Jews had done in Judea. This fact points to the large scale of collaboration, coordination and preparation for the revolt, undertaken by the Jews in Galilee, Judea and presumably also in the Diaspora. The settlement in Cana suffered destruction and decline at the aftermath of the Second Revolt, but during the Byzantine period (fourth–sixth centuries CE) the settlement resumed and a synagogue which was replaced with a church in the sixth century. The synagogue contained an Aramaic mosaic inscription bearing a certain Yoseh the son of Tanhum.

Implication for the historical Jesus research

The archaeological picture thus far suggests that Kefar Cana should be identified with Cana in Galilee. Khirbat Cana did not yield Roman material. It seems, therefore, that the nineteenth-century debate has come to an end.

Cana appears to be a small Jewish village founded by Herod on the ruins of a Hellenistic settlement. Originating in Judea, the Jewish population of Cana was probably familiar with the Jewish population of other villages in Galilee, such as in Nazareth and Capernaum and Nain. Most probably they would invite each other to weddings and attended funerals. The proximity of these villages, the fact that they originated in Judea, the limestone vessels mentioned in John 2:11 that are common to this area, and the fact that the wedding at Cana took place on Tuesday (the third day of the week in a Jewish calendar), which is the most preferred day for Jewish weddings, implies that John's sources for these events were quite accurate.

RAMI ARAV

Further reading

Avi-Yonah, M. "Gazetteer of Roman Palestine," *Qedem* 5, 1976.
—— *The Holy Land from the Persian Period to the Arav Conquest*, Grand Rapids, MI: Eerdmans, 1977.
Bagatti, B. and S. Loffreda. "Le Antichità di Khirbet Qana e di Kefar Kanna in Galilea," *LASBF* 15 (1969) 251–92.
Mackowsky, R. M. "Scholars' Qanah: A Re-examination of the Evidence in Favor of Kirbet Qanah," *BZ* NF 23.2 (1979) 278–84.
Masterman, E. W. G. "Cana of Galilee," *Palestine Explorations Fund, Quarterly Statement* (1914) 179–83.
Pilter, W. T. "Where is Cana of Galilee?," *PEFQS* (1883) 143–48.
Storme, A. "Cana do Galilea: Lugar del primer milagro de Jesus," *Tierra Sancta* 66 (1991) 176–79.
Strange, J. F. "Cana of Galilee," in D. N. Freedman (ed.) *Anchor Bible Dictionary*, New York: Doubleday, 1992, Vol. I, p. 827.
http://198.62.75.1/www1/ofm/sbf/SBFCana97en.html
http://www.antiquities.org.il/search_heb.asp?q = %EB%F4%F8+%EB%F0%E0&x = 6&y = 6

CAPERNAUM

Capernaum was a fishing community on the northwest shore of the Sea of Galilee, located approximately 9 miles northeast of modern Tiberias. It is never mentioned in the Hebrew Bible and only limited archaeological evidence has been found for habitation prior to the Late Hellenistic period. The settlement began to grow in the late second century BCE, perhaps in conjunction with Hasmonean expansion into Galilee. In the early first century CE, it lay within the territory of the client king Herod Antipas, near the border with the territory of his brother Philip. The modern site, a major tourist attraction, is divided among the Franciscans, who are the guardians of the western portion, and the Greek Orthodox Church, who have custody of the eastern section.

All four of the canonical gospels attest to Jesus' activity at Capernaum. According to Mark, it was the hometown of Jesus' disciples Andrew, Simon, James, and John (1:29), though John states that Andrew and Philip came from nearby Bethsaida (1:44, 12:21). Stories situated in Capernaum include Jesus' call of the tax collector Levi (Mark 2:13–17/Luke 5:27–32) or Matthew (Matt 9:9–13); his preaching and performing an exorcism in a synagogue (Mark 1:21–28/Luke 4:33–37); his instruction to Peter to find payment of the Temple tax in the mouth of a fish (Matt 17:24–27); and his healings of a centurion's servant (Matt 8:5–13/Luke 7:1–10); a royal official's son, healed from a distance while Jesus was in Cana (John 4:46–54); a paralyzed man (Mark 2:1–12/Matt 9:1–9/Luke 5:17–26); and Simon's mother-in-law (Mark 1:32–34/Matt 8:16/Luke 4:40–41). Matthew goes so far as to suggest that Jesus made the village his home base for part of his ministry, calling it his "own city" (9:1; cf. 4:13, 9:8 and Mark 2:1) – a claim which, if accurate, would require modification of the thesis that Jesus' ministry was wholly itinerant in nature. Matthew also associates Jesus' presence at Capernaum with the prediction in Isaiah 9:1–2 that the people sitting in darkness in the land of the tribes of Zebulon and Naphtali would see a great light. Jesus' warning to Capernaum (Matt 11:23/Luke 10:15) that it would be brought down to Hades suggests that his message was not well received by its populace as a whole; some have argued that the saying reflects Galilean rejection of the Christian movement represented in Q (Reed).

Literary references to the village are not limited to the gospels. Josephus mentions Capernaum as the source of a spring (*J.W.* 3.519) and notes that he was taken there during the Jewish revolt after falling off his horse and breaking his ankle (*Life* 72). The few rabbinic references to the community utilize its Semitic name, Kefar Nahum (*Ecclesiastes Rabbah* 1:8, 4). Later Christian sources identify it as a destination for Christian pilgrims (Taylor 1989–90, 1993).

The cultural atmosphere of first-century CE Capernaum

Substantial remains from the Hellenistic, Roman, and later periods have been discovered at Capernaum. In the first century CE, the community occupied 17 hectares at most and had a population ranging from 600 to 1,500 (Reed). Pottery fragments reflect the usage of common wares made elsewhere in Galilee, not vessels imported from afar, and no luxury goods have been discovered in the early strata. Its mostly single-storey houses were constructed primarily of local basalt, with three or four typically grouped around a single courtyard. Despite the Franciscan excavators' characterization of these residential clusters as *insulae* and suggestion that the village layout reflects an orthogonal design, there is little evidence of civic planning in the first century (Reed). The Synoptic Gospels' references to Capernaum as a *polis* (Matt 9:1, 11:20; Mark 1:33; Luke 4:31) probably reflect the influence of the Septuagint's casual use of the term and should not be taken to indicate that local government was organized like a Greek city.

Like the rest of Galilee, Capernaum appears to have been predominantly Jewish. Though excavations have not yet discovered any ritual baths in Early Roman strata, they have recovered fragments of stone vessels, which Jews believed to be unsusceptible to ritual impurity. Mark 1:21, Luke 7:5, and John 6:59 refer to a synagogue there; for Luke, the referent is explicitly identified as a building, not merely an assembly of Jewish worshipers.

Occasional contact with gentiles was probably inevitable, given Capernaum's proximity to Philip's territory and the eastern side of the lake. Only one gospel pericope provides evidence for a gentile presence at the village itself, the story of Jesus' healing of a centurion's servant. Both Matthew and Luke utilize the story to illustrate the value of faith and foreshadow the inclusion of the gentiles (Matt 8:5–13/Luke 7:1–10). Luke highlights the centurion's pagan identity further by specifying that Jewish elders contacted Jesus on his behalf and reported that he had built the local synagogue. This story has often been regarded as evidence that Roman troops were garrisoned at Capernaum, perhaps to help gather customs tolls at the border between Antipas's and Philip's territories (cf. Mark 2:13–14). Others, however, argue that this interpretation is unpersuasive (Chancey 2002 and 2005; Reed). Though both versions of the story identify the officer as a gentile, they do not specify that he was a Roman. It was typical for client kings to organize their military along Roman lines, and Herodian armies are known to have included gentiles. Thus, it is more likely that this centurion was a gentile officer in the army of Antipas. Aside from the time of the First Revolt (66–70 CE), no Roman

legions were stationed in Galilee until *c.* 120 CE. The Roman milestone with a Latin inscription on display at modern Capernaum dates to the early second century CE, not to the time of Jesus. There is no evidence for the deployment of small units of Roman soldiers in Galilee in the early first century, and it is difficult to imagine why an imperial garrison would have been necessary at the border of two loyal client kings (and brothers). Extrapolating the presence of a Roman contingent at Capernaum from the story of the centurion's servant is thus problematic.

Capernaum after the first century CE

Capernaum grew throughout the Roman and Byzantine periods. A Roman-style bathhouse was constructed in the second or third century CE (Laughlin), though the identities of its builders and users are unknown. A mausoleum with several sarcophagi decorated with carvings attests to wealth on the part of some inhabitants.

Perhaps the most famous archaeological remain of Capernaum is its stunning synagogue, which stands today in reconstructed form. Early twentieth-century excavators identified it as the "centurion's synagogue" mentioned in Luke. Though some scholars later dated it on stylistic grounds to the late second or third century, most now agree on the basis of ceramic and coins (some of which were mixed into the mortar) that it was constructed in the late fourth or fifth century. Built of limestone, it stands in stark visual contrast to the basalt remains elsewhere at Capernaum. It is basilical in style, with two rows of columns creating three aisles. A columned courtyard stands adjacent. The synagogue was extensively decorated with painted plaster and a variety of carvings, including floral and geometric designs and depictions of Medusa or Helios, sea horses, and eagles. A Corinthian column capital is adorned with carvings of lions, a Menorah, a shofar, and an incense shovel.

Two of the synagogue's columns bear inscriptions, one in Greek ("Herod, son of Mo[ni]mos, and Justus his son, together with [his] children, erected this column"), the other in Aramaic ("Halfu, the son of Zebidah, the son of Yohanan, made this column. May he be blessed"). When archaeologists dated the synagogue to the second or third century, scholars often appealed to these inscriptions as evidence for the linguistic milieu of Galilee during the time of Jesus. Now that the synagogue has been dated to a later period, their importance for understanding Jesus' Galilee is lessened.

If the limestone edifice itself post-dates Jesus by centuries, the strata beneath it are more contemporaneous with his time period. Some excavators have suggested that the stone pavements, stairs, water channels, and basalt walls found there are remnants of a first-century CE synagogue, though others argue that they come from residences and perhaps some other type of public building. If these architectural fragments do come from a first-century CE synagogue, it would be the only one discovered thus far in Galilee and one of only a few discovered in all of Palestine. Systematic excavation of these strata, however, would endanger the later limestone synagogue, and so the precise identification of their contents is impossible, at least for the foreseeable future.

Franciscan excavators have famously claimed to have discovered evidence of continuous Jewish-Christian habitation at Capernaum from the first through the fifth centuries (Corbo 1969). As their primary evidence, they point to a structure approximately 30 m south of the limestone synagogue, a fifth-century octagonal church which they argue commemorates the site of Peter's house. This church, they argue, was constructed on top of a fourth-century house church, which was itself built on top of an extensively renovated residence that originally dates to the Late Hellenistic and Early Roman periods. This earlier residence, in their view, belonged to Peter and was used after his lifetime as a church for local Jewish-Christians. Graffiti in the fourth-century stratum demonstrate that by then the house had become a pilgrimage site. At least two of the graffiti, they suggest, refer explicitly to Peter; this evidence, combined with a report by the fourth-century Christian pilgrim Egeria to have visited the house of Peter, confirm their association of the structure with the disciple. Most of the 176 graffiti are in Greek, Syriac, and perhaps Latin, but the excavators identify ten as Aramaic; they cite these as strong evidence for the presence of Jewish-Christians. Rabbinic references to *minim* ("heretics") at Capernaum confirm the presence of Jewish-Christians there. According to Bellarmino Bagatti (1971), the Jewish-Christians there were part of a larger group whose roots go back to the original Jesus movement.

Joan E. Taylor (1989–90, 1993), however, has successfully challenged virtually every aspect of this thesis. She notes that there is little evidence for the use of this structure as a church until the fourth-century CE phase and thus little reason to believe that the earlier house was used for Christian gatherings.

Both the interpretation of graffiti as reference to Peter and the identification of some as Aramaic are questionable, in her view, and it is by no means clear that Egeria had this particular building in mind when referring to Peter's house. Thus, while the graffiti as a whole clearly attest to Christian pilgrimages to the church, they do not provide any association with Peter nor do they provide evidence for the presence of local Jewish-Christians. As for the rabbinic reference to *minim*, the context makes clear that the issue at stake was Sabbath observance, not belief in Jesus' messiahship. Lastly, Taylor notes that the fourth-century Christian heresiologist Epiphanius mentions only Jews, not Jewish-Christians, at Capernaum. Thus, there is little evidence for any continuation of Jesus' movement at Capernaum beyond the first century; the later church should be associated with the influx of Christians into the "Holy Land" after the reign of Emperor Constantine.

MARK A. CHANCEY

Further reading

Bagatti, Bellarmino. *The Church from the Circumcision*, trans. Eugene Hoade, Jerusalem: Franciscan Printing Press, 1971.

Chancey, Mark A. *The Myth of a Gentile Galilee*, SNTSMS 118, Cambridge: Cambridge University Press, 2002.

—— *Greco-Roman Culture and the Galilee of Jesus*, SNTSMS 134, Cambridge: Cambridge University Press, 2005.

Corbo, Virgilio C. *The House of St. Peter at Capharnaum*, trans. Sylvester Saller, Jerusalem: Franciscan Press, 1969.

—— "Capernaum," in D. N. Freedman (ed.) *The Anchor Bible Dictionary*, New York: Doubleday, 1990, Vol. 1, pp. 866–69.

Laughlin, John C. H. "Capernaum: From Jesus' Time and After," *BAR* 19:5 (1993) 54–61.

Loffreda, Stanislao. "Capernaum," in Ephraim Stern, Ayelet Lewinson-Gilboa, and Joseph Aviram (eds) *The New Encyclopedia of Archaeological Excavations in the Holy Land*, Jerusalem: Israel Exploration Society and Carta; New York: Simon & Schuster, 1993, Vol. 1, pp. 291–95.

—— *Recovering Capharnaum*, second edition, Jerusalem: Franciscan Printing Press, 1993.

Reed, Jonathan L. *Archaeology and the Galilean Jesus: A Re-examination of the Evidence*, Harrisburg, PA: Trinity Press International, 2000, pp. 139–69.

Strange, James F. and Hershel Shanks. "Has the House where Jesus Stayed in Capernaum been Found?," *BAR* 8:6 (1982) 26–37.

—— "Synagogue where Jesus Preached Found at Capernaum," *BAR* 9:6 (1983) 25–28.

Taylor, Joan E. "Capernaum and its 'Jewish-Christians': A Re-examination of the Franciscan Excavations," *BAIAS* 9 (1989–90) 7–28.

—— *Christians and the Holy Places: The Myth of Jewish-Christian Origins*, Oxford: Clarendon Press, 1993.

CHILD, CHILDREN

Jesus reflected the general attitudes of the Jewish people toward children but with some significant qualifications. Accordingly, it is important to look at the place of children in the Hebrew Scriptures to understand that context.

The place of children in the Hebrew Scriptures

In the Jewish world children were valued as gifts from God (Gen 17:16, 20; 33:5; 48:9; Josh 24:3–4; Ruth 4:13; Ps 127:3–5; 128:3–4; Prov 17:6; Isa 8:18). The patriarchs were promised a large progeny (Gen 12:2; 15:5; 22:17; 26:4, 24). Boys were circumcised on the eighth day after birth (Lev 12:3; Luke 1:59; 2:21). Girls were closely supervised until puberty, and fathers were concerned for their daughters' sexual purity (2 Macc 3:19; Sir 42:9–14). Children helped their parents with work, either at home or in the fields (Gen 29:6; Exod 2:16; 1 Sam 16:11; Jer 7:18). Childlessness was a grief and disappointment (Gen 29:32; 30:1–3; 1 Sam 1:6, 10–11), and barrenness considered a source of reproach and disgrace (Gen 16:2; 25:21; 30:22–23; 1 Sam 1:1–18; 2:5; Isa 4:1; Luke 1:25). The predicament of having no children was sometimes conquered by divine intervention (Gen 17:15–21; 25:21; Judg 13; 1 Sam 1:6–20; Luke 1:5–25). On the other hand, barrenness was viewed as a divine judgment (Gen 12:17; 20:17–18; cf. Lev 20:20–21; Jer 22:30).

Some children, like Samuel and John the Baptist, were dedicated to divine service by their parents (1 Sam 1:11; Luke 1:76–79). When parents died and children were left orphans, God was seen to be concerned for their welfare (Pss 10:14,17–18; 27:10; 68:5; 146:9; Hos 14:3; Mal 3:5). Like widows, defenseless children were to be cared for (Exod 22:22–24; Deut 10:18; 14:29; Job 29:12; Ps 68:5; Jer 49:11). Infanticide was strongly attacked (Lev 18:21; 20:2–5; Deut 12:31; 2 Chr 28:3; Isa 57:5; Jer 19:4–7).

Children were commanded to respect and honor their parents (Exod 20:12; Lev 19:3; Deut 5:16; cf. Sir 3:8; 7:27; Luke 2:51), a point repeatedly made in the wisdom literature (Prov 4:1–4, 10–11; 6:20; 10:1; 23:22; cf. Sir 3:1–17; 7:27–28). These commands were retained unchanged by Jesus and honored also in the life of the early church (Matt 15:4; 19:19; Mark. 10:19; Luke 18:20; Eph 6:2–3; 1 Tim 5:4). Stress upon dutiful obedience to parents is mentioned frequently (Balla 113–228), and later it is reasserted in the NT epistles (Eph 6:1–3; Col 3:20). On the other hand, parents were commanded to train their children in godly living,

reminding them of the mighty acts of God in Israel's history (Exod 12:25–27; 13:14; Deut 4:9–10; Josh 4:6–7, 21–24; Ps 78:1–8; Prov 19:18; 29:15; Isa 38:19).

There was no formal public education prior to the establishment of synagogues. Parents were expected to provide moral and religious instruction for their children (Exod 13:8–16; Deut 6:6–9; 11:19–21; 31:12–13; Josh 8:35; Isa 28:9–10; Joel 1:3; 2 Tim 3:15). Sometimes children were rebellious and disrespectful (Deut 21:18–21; 2 Kgs 2:23; Job 19:18). Children needed discipline, and parents were called to provide it (Prov 22:6,15; 13:24; 19:18; 23:13–14; 29:15, 17).

The Jewish perspective on home and family life is clearly reflected in the New Testament, though the presence of the "household tables" characteristic of the Hellenistic world is also in evidence in the epistles (Col 3:18–4:1; Eph 5:22–26:9; see Doty 58). The treatment of children by Jesus, however, calls for special comment.

References to children in the three Synoptic Gospels

The compassion of Jesus toward children and their parents is expressed in the healing miracles recorded in each of the gospels (Matt 8:5–13//Luke 7:1–10; Mark 10:46–52//Matt 20:29–34; Luke 18:35–43; Luke 7:11–17; John 4:46–54). For instance, Jesus addressed Jairus' daughter as "little girl" or "child," and restored her to her anxious parents (Mark 5:21–43//Matt 9:18–26; Luke 8:40–56).

All three Synoptic Gospels relate a case of healing that follows the Transfiguration account (Mark 9:14–29//Matt 17:14–21; Luke 9:37–43a), where "the boy"(Greek *pais*) was cured and restored to his father. Mark's account observes that the pitiful condition had existed "from childhood"(Mark 9:21), and notes the lack of faith or prayer as the reason the disciples were unable to help despite the father's urgent call to do so (Mark 9:14–19, 29; cf. Matt 17:14–17,20; Luke 9:37–41).

Sometimes Jesus referred to his followers as "these little ones who believe in me" (Mark 9:42; Matt 18:6), recognizing their vulnerability and fragility. Warnings are given to the community not to cause a member to stumble (Mark 9:42–50//Matt 18:6–9; Luke 17:1–2).

In Jewish society, young children were without status, completely dependent upon their parents. Jesus recognized children were vulnerable. When the disciples rebuked those who would bring children to him, Jesus was indignant and openly welcomed them (Mark 10:13–16//Matt 19:13–15; Luke

18:15–17). Jesus saw the receptivity of children as a picture of the complete childlike dependence required to enter the kingdom of God

In one incident the gospels mention the absence of children in a dispute Jesus had with the Sadducees, who rejected belief in the resurrection. Here the protection of property rights was the real issue at stake (Mark 12:18–27//Matt 22:23–33; Luke 20:27–40).

Mark, followed by Matthew, notes that the Jewish people were metaphorically called "children" in contrast to the Gentiles, who were traditionally dismissed as "dogs" (Mark 7:27f; Matt 15:26), though the incident in question closes with the granting of the Syrophoenician woman's request in response to her genuine faith (Mark 7:30; Matt 15:28). Those who followed Jesus were sometimes addressed affectionately as "children" (*tekna*, Mark 10:24; *paidia*, John 21:5).

References to children in Matthew and Luke

The so-called "Q" material (an abbreviation of the German word *Quelle* meaning "source," the roughly 250 verses that Matthew and Luke have in common), calls for some comment. For instance, both Matthew and Luke note John the Baptist's declaration that God was able "from these stones to raise up children to Abraham" (Matt 3:9//Luke 3:8). They also speak of the fact that parents "know how to give good gifts to their children" as a basis for suggesting how much more God, the heavenly Father, will bestow his blessings on those who ask him (Matt 7:11//Luke 11:13). This teaching method of arguing from the lesser to the greater was a favorite one often used by Jesus (e.g. Matt 6:26, 30; 10:25; 12:12; Luke 12:6–7, 24, 28). Similarly, another memorable incident is the plaintive lament over Jerusalem, where Jesus in the face of continued Jewish antagonism and unbelief comments: "How often have I desired to gather your children together as a hen gathers her brood under her wings, and you were not willing!" (Matt 23:37//Luke 13:34).

Matthew and Luke record Jesus' words about John the Baptist (Matt 11:2–19//Luke 7:18–35). Neither Jesus nor John suited their Jewish contemporaries – John was too strict and ascetic, Jesus was too permissive. Jesus compared the sulky attitudes of his contemporaries to that of "children sitting in the market places" playing entertaining games of weddings and funerals (Matt 11:16–19// Luke 7:31–34, one of the few passages in the Scriptures that refer to the play of children). When they didn't get the game they preferred, they refused to play at all. And yet, Jesus declared,

"wisdom is justified by all her children" (Luke 7:35; cf. Matt 16:19b).

Frequently in Jewish tradition wisdom was personified as a woman created by God and offered graciously to humanity; she invites the upright to follow her (Prov 8:1–36; 9:1–6; Sir 1:1–20; 4:11–19; 6:18–37; 14:20–15:10; 24:1–34). In Luke 7:35 she is presented as the mother of the upright. Jesus thanked God for revealing spiritual matters to "babes" or "infants" (*nēpioi*), when they had been hidden from "the wise" (Matt 11:25–27//Luke 10:21–22).

References to children in Matthew's Gospel

A parent's natural concern for offspring is reflected in Matthew's Gospel, where the slaughter of the innocents is noted as a fulfillment of Jeremiah's words about Rachel weeping for her children (Matt 2:18; Jer 31:15). The inextricable family bond is also strongly indicated in the parable of the unmerciful servant, where the master ordered that the servant be "sold, with his wife and children ... and payment ... be made" (Matt 18:25).

During Jesus' final trip to Jerusalem Matthew notes the loud praise he received in the Temple from the defenseless young children, the indignant response of the high priests and the scribes, and the scriptural defense offered on this memorable occasion (Matt 21:15–16; cf. Ps 8:2).

Matthew, probably writing against the background of internal Jewish debates (note the distancing of his community from traditional Jewish circles observable in the phrase "their synagogues" [Matt 4:23; 9:35; 10:17]), also includes the passage where the Jews in the crucifixion scene accept responsibility for Jesus' death – a passage that has often been mistakenly used to whip up anti-Semitic sentiments and actions (Matt 27:25). Here there is a reference to "our children," not embracing all Jews of subsequent times, but pointing to the generation following Jesus' death who would undergo suffering in the devastation of Jerusalem in 70 CE.

References to children in Luke's Gospel

Luke's Gospel predicts the key place that John the Baptist would occupy in holy history in leading a national back-to-God movement (Luke 1:16). Like Elijah, John would have a decisive prophetic role. He would prepare the way for the coming Messiah, turning "the hearts of parents to their children" and "the hearts of children to their parents," thereby achieving familial reconciliation (Luke 1:17; cf. Mal 4:5–6; Sir 48:10); John's ministry would result in "a people prepared for the Lord."

Luke has the only account of the childhood of Jesus in the canonical Gospels (Luke 2:39–40), followed by the striking incident of the youthful Jesus in the Temple in discussion with the Jewish teachers (Luke 2:41–52). Contrary to the fantastic pictures found in the Apocryphal Gospels (e.g. the Infancy Story of Thomas, where Jesus as a five-year-old boy took soft clay and fashioned it into twelve sparrows that flew away [Hennecke 1963: 393]), there is no indication here that the historical Jesus functioned as a wonder boy. The child Jesus returned to Nazareth with his parents "and was obedient to them" (Luke 2:51). Luke presented Jesus' personal development as involving mental, physical, spiritual, and social dimensions (Luke 2:52).

Luke also mentions a prayer parable of Jesus concerning a person calling a neighbor at midnight and asking for a loan of three loaves of bread to handle an emergency (Luke 11:5–8). A hostile response is given because meeting the request would disturb the whole household, including the children who have settled down for the night. The parable gives a lively insight into the typical Palestinian family of the first century CE.

Luke's passion story includes a striking reference to the women of Jerusalem who are told by Jesus, "Do not weep for me, but weep for yourselves and for your children" in view of the ominous things that were about to come on the holy city within their lifetime (Luke 23:28–31; cf. Joseph, *J.W.* 6.363–69; 6.392–408). A sense of foreboding is present that is a presentiment of evil things to follow within that generation.

References to children in John's Gospel

The only miracle recorded in all four Gospels is the feeding of the five thousand (Matt 14:13–21; Mark 6:30–44; Luke 9:10–17; John 6:1–14). John's account alone notes that: (1) it was Andrew who commented to Jesus on this occasion; (2) it was a little boy (the word *paidarion* is only used here in the NT of a "little boy," "a lad") who had the provisions; (3) the bread in question was "barley" loaves, the food commonly used by the poor (John 6:9). Jesus used the child's meager provisions in the remarkable feeding that followed (Mark 6:42; John 6:11).

Later in the Fourth Gospel Jesus challenges his Jewish critics by saying, "If you are Abraham's children, you would be doing what Abraham did, but now you are trying to kill me … This is not what Abraham did" (John 8:39–40). Their hostile behavior in attacking Jesus was not in keeping with their claim to be heirs of Abraham and genuine children of God.

Note also the prediction of Caiaphas, the high priest, that it was better "for one man to die than to have the whole nation destroyed" (John 11:50). John interprets this remark in more universal terms, so that Jesus' death is presented as significant not only for the Jewish nation but also for Gentiles – "to gather into one the dispersed children [people] of God" (John 11:51–52).

Summary of Jesus' teaching on the child and children

Jesus was basically a Jewish traditionalist in his views of children, teaching them to honor and respect their parents. While his teaching did not idealize childhood, he attacked the disciples' habit of restricting access to him and his movement. Instead he spoke of children, who were traditionally placed on the lowest level in society, as a symbol of the manner in which one should respond to the kingdom of God (Matt 11:25–27// Luke 10:21–22). Jesus showed sensitivity when he picked up a child in his arms and said, "Whoever welcomes one such child in my name welcomes me … and the one who sent me" (namely, God; Mark 9:37//Matt 18:5; Luke 9:48). Indeed, Jesus declared, "Whoever does not receive the kingdom of God as a little child will never enter it" (Mark 10:15//Luke 18:17; Matt 18:3–4). Jesus treated children with care, compassion, and respect, and taught his followers to practice the same virtues.

However, Jesus recognized that discipleship could be disruptive of family relationships (Mark 13:12//Matt 10:21; Luke 21:16; Luke 12:51–53// Matt 10:34–36; cf. *1 En.* 100:1–2). Balla argues plausibly that there are three types of passage discussed:

(1) divisions within a family can be a consequence of the disciples' commitment to Jesus (Matt 10:37; Luke 14:26); (2) some texts may refer to exceptional cases, i.e. they do not apply to all disciples (Mark 1:16–20// Matt 4:18–22; Luke 5:1–11); (3) some texts either refer to the end time (Mark 13:12–13//Luke 21:16–17; Matt 24:9b), or to the urgency of deciding upon priorities in the present (Matt 8:21–22//Luke 9:59–60).

(Balla 230)

Those who make sacrifices by following Jesus are promised "houses, brothers and sisters, mothers and children" "with persecutions – and in the age to come eternal life" (Mark 10:29–30//Matt 19:29; Luke 18:29–30). The true family of Jesus is "those who hear the word of God and do it" (Luke 8:19–21//Mark 3:31–35; Matt 12:46–50).

ALLISON A. TRITES

Further reading

Balla, P. *The Child–Parent Relationship in the New Testament and Its Environment*, Peabody, MA: Hendrickson, 2005.

Barton, S. C. "Child, Children," in J. B. Green and S. McKnight (eds) *Dictionary of Jesus and the Gospels*, Downers Grove, IL: InterVarsity Press, 1992, pp. 100–4.

Doty, W. G. *Letters in Primitive Christianity*, Philadelphia, PA: Fortress Press, 1973.

Francis, J. "Children, Childhood," in D. N. Freedman (ed.) *Eerdmans Dictionary of the Bible*, Grand Rapids, MI: Eerdmans, 2000, pp. 234–35.

Hennecke, E. *New Testament Apocrypha*, 2 vols, ed. W. Schneemelcher, *Vol. 1: Gospels and Related Writings*, Philadelphia, PA: Westminster Press, 1963, pp. 392–401.

Léon-Dufour, X. *Dictionary of the New Testament*, San Francisco, CA: Harper & Row, 1980.

McKenzie, J. L. *Dictionary of the Bible*, New York: Macmillan, 1965, 129–30.

Mawhinney, A. "Children in the Bible," in P. Gardiner (ed.) *The Complete Who's Who in the Bible*, London: Marshall Pickering, 1995, pp. 99–101.

Osiek, C. and M. Y. MacDonald, with J. H. Tulloch. *A Woman's Place: House Churches in Earliest Christianity*, Minneapolis, MN: Fortress Press, 2005.

Robinson, D. W. B. "Family in the New Testament," in J. D. Douglas (ed.) *The New Bible Dictionary*, London: InterVarsity Fellowship, 1962, pp. 417–18.

Stamps, D. L. "Children in Late Antiquity," in C. A. Evans and S. E. Porter (eds) *Dictionary of New Testament Backgrounds*, Downers Grove, IL: InterVarsity Press, 2000, pp. 197–200.

Watson, D. F. "Childhood of Jesus," in J. B. Green and S. McKnight (eds) *Dictionary of Jesus and the Gospels*, Downers Grove, IL: InterVarsity Press, 1992, pp. 104–6.

Wilson, R. R. "Child, Children," in P. J. Achtemeier (ed.) *Harper's Bible Dictionary*, San Francisco, CA: Harper & Row, 1985, pp. 161–62.

CHORAZIN

Chorazin was one of the three Galilean villages (along with Capernaum and Bethsaida) that were cursed by Jesus for failing to repent after Jesus performed "mighty works" (Matt 11:21; Luke 10:13). Chorazin is also mentioned in early rabbinic literature. In the Babylonian Talmud (*Menahot* 85a) it is cited in association with the first harvest offering and in Tosefta (*Makkot* 3:8) it is described as a "medium-sized town" of Palestine. The early Christian writer Eusebius in compiling a guide to the biblical sites in Palestine (*Onomasticon*) in the early fourth century noted (*Onom.* 174:23) that Chorazin was located two Roman miles from Capernaum and was in ruins.

Although efforts to unearth the first-century village have not been successful, the remains of the town cited in the rabbinic literature (third–fourth century) have been identified and partially excavated. Khirbet Karazeh, a site with substantial remains, and situated just north of Capernaum, was first identified as ancient Chorazin by Charles Wilson in 1869. In 1905, the German team of Heinrich Kohl and Carl Watzinger identified the remnants of an ancient synagogue at Chorazin. In 1926, Na'im Makhouly and Jacob Ory working on behalf of the Department of Antiquities removed a later building that partially covered the synagogue and collected architectural fragments from the synagogue that had been strewn over the site. A true excavation of the site began in 1962 under the direction of Zeev Yeivin. Yeivin continued the excavations until 1965 and then again from 1980 to 1986. The Israel Department of Antiquities and the National Parks Authority have joined to preserve the site and have restored a few of the ancient structures. Visitors to this site will encounter the remains of a town which was certainly larger than the one in the time of Jesus but nevertheless can gain an impression of the layout and some of the architectural features of a first-century village that overlooked the Sea of Galilee.

The town had been constructed along the southern and western slopes of a basalt plateau that rises some 270 m above the Sea of Galilee. Nearby is the Bir Karazeh spring that flows along the eastern perimeter of the town. Just to the north, the ancient Ptolemais–Bethsaida road crossed the Jordan River and continued on to join the major road to Damascus. The excavations, which have focused on the synagogue and the town center, have exposed a town that flourished in the third and early fourth century CE and was badly damaged (earthquake?) in the early fourth century. There is evidence of partial restoration in the late fourth century and continued habitation into the ninth century. In addition to the synagogue, the excavations have exposed two domestic areas, and a large public building that housed a sizeable bathing installation that Yeivin identified as a Jewish ritual bath or *mikveh*. The excavations have also recovered three olive oil installations, the oldest dating to the second century.

The synagogue that Yeivin described as a "masterpiece of stonework" was built entirely of local basalt ashlars. It appears to have been founded in the late third or early fourth century and follows the plan of the Galilean-type synagogue. The three entrances lead to a main hall (65 ft long and 45 ft wide) that is divided into a nave and three aisles. The roof was supported by a plain architrave and a richly decorated (geometric and floral patterns in addition to human reliefs) frieze. The excavators also found architectural fragments of what they believe to be the platform for the Torah ark and a platform for the Torah reader. Both platforms were built into niches along the southern wall on either side of the entrance to the synagogue. In the course of excavating the floor of the synagogue, a deposit of 2,000 coins was found in the earth floor that had replaced an earlier plaster floor. The coins ranged in date from the late fourth century to the early seventh century. Given the tremendous range of dates for the coins, the excavators concluded it could not have been a horde hidden at one point in the history of the community. They suggest that coins were tossed onto the synagogue floor by pilgrims, and especially Christian pilgrims, who had come to view the fulfillment of Jesus's prediction of woe.

One other particularly interesting find from the synagogue was a basalt chair that was recovered in 1927 by Ory in the rubble inside the synagogue. On the lower front panel of the chair a four-line dedicatory Aramaic inscription had been incised referring to a Yodan ben Yishma'el who had made (or donated) the chair and the steps leading to it. The chair was found close to the area of the synagogue later identified as the reader's platform. Given its location and similarity of design to chairs found at the synagogues of Hammat Tiberius and 'Ein Gedi, the chair is presumed to be an example of the "Seat of Moses." Jesus refers to "Moses' seat" in Matt 23:2–3 and to a seat of honor in Luke 14:7–11. No "seat of Moses" has been recovered in a first-century context (possibly because they were made from wood) but the recovery of the Chorazin chair (in conjunction with the finds at H. Tiberius and 'Ein Gedi) may shed some light on Jesus's references to this piece of synagogue and banquet furniture. In some cases the "Seat of Moses" may have been an actual seat for a synagogue dignitary (e.g. *archisynagoge*) or the one being honored at a banquet. The text in Luke would imply such as it makes a case for the value of humility. In other cases, as in the case of the seat found at Chorazin, the seat may have been occupied by the reader or the interpreter of the Torah or the prophets (*haftorah*). This sense of the seat of Moses would appear to underlie the reference in Matthew as the text refers to someone sitting and teaching from the seat.

C. THOMAS MCCOLLOUGH

Further reading

Fine, Steven. "Chorazin," in *The Oxford Encyclopedia of Archaeology in the Near East*, Oxford: Oxford University Press, 1997, Vol. 1, pp. 490–91.

Rahmani, L. Y. "Stone Synagogue Chairs: Their Identification, Use and Significance," *IEJ* 40 (1990) 192–214.

Rousseau, John and Rami Arav. *Jesus and His World: An Archaeological and Cultural Dictionary*, Minneapolis, MN: Fortress Press, 1995.

Yeivin, Zeev. "Ancient Chorazin Comes Back to Life," *BAR* 13 (1987) 22–36.

—— "Chorazin," in E. Stern, A. Lewinson-Gilboa, and J. Aviram (eds) *New Encyclopedia for Archaeological Excavations in the Holy Land*, Jerusalem and New York: Israel Exploration Society, Carta, and Simon and Schuster, 1993, Vol. 1, pp. 301–4.

CHREIA, APOPHTHEGM

Terminological and methodological considerations

Chreia, also spelt as *chria*, is a Greek term meaning "usage;" it is related to the Greek term *chreiodes*, meaning "useful." *Chreia* was a rhetorical device in ancient literature, employing a saying, aphorism, or even a deed of a well-known, authoritative figure to amplify one's own statement (see Quintilian, *Inst.* 1.9:4). Some New Testament scholars apply this term of ancient rhetoric to certain sayings of Jesus, while others prefer different terms: for example, paradigm (suggested by Dibelius), pronouncement story (a term preferred by Vincent Taylor), or apophthegm (used by Bultmann and many others). The latter Greek term means "statement," or "utterance," and it has the advantage that it is always attributed to one particular person; thus, in the case of the New Testament, the connection of the saying to Jesus is emphasized (see Theissen and Merz: 191).

Form criticism, as an approach in Historical Jesus research, focuses its study especially on the various forms in which the sayings of Jesus have been transmitted. The early phase of form criticism in the New Testament can be connected to three German works, two of which have been later translated into English as well, and have become influential in world-wide scholarship. A work of Karl Ludwig Schmidt, published in 1919, initiated in Jesus research the focusing on the first stage of the transmission of the Gospel material, i.e. the stage of oral transmission: *Der Rahmen der Geschichte Jesu* (the title of this German work means, "The Framework of the Story of Jesus"). Schmidt argued that individual units can be distinguished from the Markan framework within the Gospel, and thus prepared the way for others to study these units in more detail.

In the same year, Martin Dibelius published a work in which he proposed various categories to distinguish among the sayings of Jesus on the basis of the form of the saying and of the role it played in the life of the early church. From the German title of his book, *Die Formgeschichte des Evangeliums*, the term *Formgeschichte* ("form history") has become the name of the approach in biblical scholarship in German-speaking countries, while "form criticism" is used for it in English. Dibelius gave the following names to the classified sayings of Jesus: paradigm, tales, legends, myth, sayings. In this classification, the term "paradigm" is used for what others refer to as *chreia* and apophthegm.

In 1921 Rudolf Bultmann published his analysis of the forms in the Synoptic Gospels, *Die Geschichte der synoptischen Tradition* (English Translation: *History of the Synoptic Tradition*). While Dibelius focused on the role of the sayings in the life-setting (sometimes referred to as the "life-situation") of the early church (in German: *Sitz im Leben*), Bultmann's analysis was based on the identification of the individual units on the basis of their forms. He divided the discourses of Jesus into two main groups: apophthegms and dominical sayings, but he differentiated further sub-categories under these two main headings. Under apophthegm, he classified three sub-categories on the basis of the different settings or causes for the sayings: controversy dialogue, scholastic dialogue, and biographical apophthegm. Under dominical sayings, he categorized proverbs, prophetic and apocalyptic sayings, laws (of Jewish piety) and regulations (of the early Christian community). Bultmann offered a special treatment of two further types of the dominical sayings: the "I sayings" and the parables as well. Bultmann's apophthegm category is basically the same as the paradigms in Dibelius's classification. In what follows, we use apophthegm to refer to certain sayings of Jesus. We note that this term was already used by J. G. Herder in 1797, who argued that apophthegms were easier to be remembered by the apostles than composite speeches (see in Berger 64; Berger uses *chreia* and apophthegm as equivalents, see e.g. his usage "Chrie/Apophthegma" in his German textbook on form criticism: 77, 219).

Before mentioning examples of apophthegms, certain presuppositions and axioms of form criticism have to be summarized, because the use of this approach has an impact on the Historical Jesus research inasmuch as scholars differ in their views on the authenticity (historicity) of certain sayings of Jesus that are classified as apophthegms. It is interesting to observe that these presuppositions are not discussed at length by Dibelius and Bultmann; rather, they can be found only in some preliminary sentences of their works (cf. also Bock 2001: 124, n. 6; the following listing of the basic axioms of form criticism is based on Bock 2001: 108–10; see also McKnight 17–20 and Travis 153–55).

1   The gospels are not primarily the work of one person, but they are "popular" literature; they belong to communities. The needs of the community shaped the form of the sayings.
2   The material circulated in oral form for at least two decades. The sayings material was transmitted at this oral stage as individual units. The only exception is the Passion Narrative, which was a continuous tradition from very early on. It is worth noting that Schmidt, Dibelius, and Bultmann also acknowledged that some pericopae (individual units of tradition) were grouped together already at the oral stage even outside the Passion material (see e.g. the interweaving of the story of Jairus with the story of the woman with the hemorrhage, Mark 5:21–43 par. Matt 9:18–26 and Luke 8:40–56).
3   The short individual units were used as the need in the congregation required; it was their usefulness that caused them to be transmitted.
4   The various forms of the material corresponded to the setting in which they were used. From the form one can conclude as regards the function of the material unit in the life of the congregation.
5   The approach of form criticism is usually combined with the appropriation of the Two Document Hypothesis; i.e. Markan priority is presupposed.
6   Form critics tended to assume that the shorter, simpler forms are older, and that during the course of transmission the accounts expanded, and more complex forms were created.

These axioms of form criticism are not without problems. Already during the first stage of the application of the approach, reservations were expressed, for example, by Vincent Taylor, who was the first in Britain to write an extensive work on the method, entitled, *The Formation of the Gospel Tradition* (1933). Detailed criticisms are presented, for example, by Ladd, Travis, Muddiman, and Bock. The latter emphasizes that the study of form remains helpful and even necessary even if one does not subscribe to the Two Document Hypothesis, or does not see the congregation as active in transforming and even creating sayings and placing them into the mouth of Jesus, as many of the early and even present-day form critics would suggest (see e.g. Bock 2001: 111). Theissen and Merz argue against the unjustified, over-critical skepticism in some historical Jesus scholarship (see Ch. 4 of their book, pp. 90–124), and they emphasize that especially with regard to the apophthegms, one can hold that they "contain something of Jesus' character" (p. 192). They affirm that "The content of many apophthegms also suggests a historical background" (ibid.). Students of the gospels will meet different views as regards the historicity of certain apophthegms; they should always reflect on the axioms and hypotheses involved in reaching those conclusions.

Examples

It is not always self-evident, which units of the gospel tradition should be classified as apophthegms. On occasion, there are pericopae in which more than one form appears, and scholars even speak of mixed forms (see e.g. Travis 159, who warns against the self-confidence in proposing "pure forms"). However, in general an apophthegm is a saying of Jesus set in a brief context. Jesus usually responds with a saying at the end of the unit. The saying can be one sentence or a combination of ideas, but the point of the account is Jesus' response. In the Gospel of Mark, there are three large blocks of apophthegms: Mark 2:1–3:5 (in Galilee); 10:1–45 (on a journey from Galilee to Jerusalem); 12:13–44 (in Jerusalem). In the following, we consider some examples of apophthegms, following the threefold subdivision proposed by Bultmann.

The first category is that of the controversy dialogues; these are usually occasioned by conflict over Jesus' healings or the conduct of Jesus and his disciples. For Bultmann, the *Sitz im Leben* of these apophthegms is the polemic atmosphere of the early church. The pericope on the disciples plucking corn on the Sabbath is an example of it. We quote the apophthegm from Mark 2:23–28, and we observe how Jesus' saying concludes the account as its didactic key point – in this case the saying contains more than one idea (RSV):

> One sabbath he was going through the grainfields; and as they made their way his disciples began to pluck heads of grain. 24 And the Pharisees said to him, "Look, why are they doing what is not lawful on the sabbath?" 25 And he said to them, "Have you never read what David did, when he was in need and was hungry, he and those who were with him: 26 how he entered the house of God, when Abiathar was high priest, and ate the bread of the Presence, which it is not lawful for any but the priests to eat, and also gave it to those who were

> with him?" 27 And he said to them, "The sabbath was made for man, not man for the sabbath; 28 so the Son of man is lord even of the sabbath."

It is worth noting that the parallel versions (Luke 6:5 and Matt 12:8) have only one of the two ideas of Jesus at end of the pericope: "The Son of man is lord of the sabbath."

The healing of the man with the withered hand on a Sabbath is another example of a controversy dialogue: Mark 3:1–6 contains both a short scene and the saying of Jesus. In this case, the saying is not the last sentence of the unit. To quote it in full (RSV):

> Again he entered the synagogue, and a man was there who had a withered hand. 2 And they watched him, to see whether he would heal him on the sabbath, so that they might accuse him. 3 And he said to the man who had the withered hand, "Come here." 4 And he said to them, "Is it lawful on the sabbath to do good or to do harm, to save life or to kill?" But they were silent. 5 And he looked around at them with anger, grieved at their hardness of heart, and said to the man, "Stretch out your hand." He stretched it out, and his hand was restored. 6 The Pharisees went out, and immediately held counsel with the Herodians against him, how to destroy him.

In Bultmann's classification, the second subgroup among apophthegms is that of the scholastic dialogue. This kind of apophthegm has a certain similarity to the controversy dialogue; the main difference is that here the scene does not concern the opponents of Jesus, but Jesus is usually asked by his disciples or by someone seeking knowledge. The question concerning the chief commandment is an example of the category of the scholastic dialogue. In Mark 12:28–34 we read (RSV):

> And one of the scribes came up and heard them disputing with one another, and seeing that he answered them well, asked him, "Which commandment is the first of all?" 29 Jesus answered, "The first is, 'Hear, O Israel: The Lord our God, the Lord is one; 30 and you shall love the Lord your God with all your heart, and with all your soul, and with all your mind, and with all your strength.' 31 The second is this, 'You shall love your neighbor as yourself.' There is no other commandment greater than these." 32 And the scribe said to him, "You are right, Teacher; you have truly said that he is one, and there is no other but he; 33 and to love him with all the heart, and with all the understanding, and with all the strength, and to love one's neighbor as oneself, is much more than all whole burnt offerings and sacrifices." 34 And when Jesus saw that he answered wisely, he said to him, "You are not far from the kingdom of God." And after that no one dared to ask him any question.

Another example of the scholastic dialogue is the well-known pericope about the rich young man (Mark 10:17–27 par. Matt 19:16–26 and Luke 18:18–27). May it suffice here to quote its concluding saying (Mark 10:27): "With men it is impossible, but not with God; for all things are possible with God." We note that some scholars regard the following pericope (concerning the disciples leaving everything for Jesus, Mark 10:28–31 par.) as belonging to this apophthegm (so e.g. Bock 2001: 112). Most form critics agree in general that the forms developed during the course of the transmission, and this applies to the apophthegms as well (see e.g. Berger 219–20). The development could include more precision as regards the questioners in the apophthegm, or even in the formulation of the statement (see e.g. McKnight 27).

The last category in Bultmann's terminology is that of the biographical apophthegm. These apophthegms contain some information about Jesus; they are little scenes from his life. One example may be Luke 9:57–62, where we read about Jesus' encounter with three would-be disciples (RSV):

> As they were going along the road, a man said to him, "I will follow you wherever you go." [58] And Jesus said to him, "Foxes have holes, and birds of the air have nests; but the Son of man has nowhere to lay his head." [59] To another he said, "Follow me." But he said, "Lord, let me first go and bury my father." [60] But he said to him, "Leave the dead to bury their own dead; but as for you, go and proclaim the kingdom of God." [61] Another said, "I will follow you, Lord; but let me first say farewell to those at my home." [62] Jesus said to him, "No one who puts his hand to the plow and looks back is fit for the kingdom of God."

Another example of the biographical apophthegm is Jesus' discourse with the two sisters, Mary and Martha, in their home, as narrated in Luke 10:38–42 (RSV):

> Now as they went on their way, he entered a village; and a woman named Martha received him into her house. [39] And she had a sister called Mary, who sat at the Lord's feet and listened to his teaching. [40] But Martha was distracted with much serving; and she went to him and said, "Lord, do you not care that my sister has left me to serve alone? Tell her then to help me." [41] But the Lord answered her, "Martha, Martha, you are anxious and troubled about many things; [42] one thing is needful. Mary has chosen the good portion, which shall not be taken away from her."

To sum up, a *chreia* or an apophthegm tells us "something about the historical Jesus – and about Jesus in his relationships" (Theissen and Merz 193). Although the question of authenticity is discussed by scholars in the case of certain apophthegms, and the possibility of a creative role of the first Christian congregations is raised by form critics, in general the apophthegms may be seen as – at least in their core – reliable memories of the historical Jesus treasured and transmitted by the early church.

PETER BALLA

Further reading

Berger, Klaus. *Einführung in die Formgeschichte*, Tübingen: Francke Verlag, 1987.

Bock, Darrell L. "Form Criticism," in D. A. Black and D. S. Dockery (eds) *Interpreting the New Testament: Essays on Methods and Issues*, Nashville, TN: Broadman & Holman, 2001, pp. 106–27 (revised edition of *New Testament Criticism and Interpretation*, 1991, in which Bock has a somewhat different form of this chapter under the same title).

—— *Studying the Historical Jesus: A Guide to Sources and Methods*, Grand Rapids, MI: Baker Academic, 2002 (esp. Ch. 8 on Form Criticism, pp. 181–87).

Bultmann, Rudolf. *Die Geschichte der synoptischen Tradition*, Göttingen: Vandenhoeck & Ruprecht, 1921; ET of the third edition (1958) by J. Marsh, *History of the Synoptic Tradition*, New York: Harper & Row, 1963.

Dibelius, Martin. *Die Formgeschichte des Evangeliums*, Tübingen: J. C. B. Mohr, 1919; ET of the second German edition (1933) by B. L. Woolf, *From Tradition to Gospel*, New York: Charles Scribner's Sons, 1934, repr. 1971.

Ladd, George Eldon. *The New Testament and Criticism*, Grand Rapids, MI: Eerdmans, 1967 (repr. 1989; esp. Ch. 6 on Form Criticism, pp. 141–69).

McKnight, Edgar V. *What is Form Criticism?* Philadelphia, PA: Fortress Press, 1978 (seventh printing of 1969 orig.).

Muddiman, John. "Form Criticism," in R. J. Coggins and J. L. Houlden (eds) *A Dictionary of Biblical Interpretation*, London: SCM Press, 1990, pp. 240–43.

Schmidt, Karl Ludwig. *Der Rahmen der Geschichte Jesu. Literarkritische Untersuchungen zur ältesten Jesusüberlieferung*, Berlin: Trowitzsch und Sohn, 1919.

Taylor, Vincent. *The Formation of the Gospel Tradition: Eight Lectures*, London: Macmillan, 1933 (second edition 1935, reprint 1949).

Theissen, Gerd and Annette, Merz. *The Historical Jesus: A Comprehensive Guide*, trans. J. Bowden (from 1996 German orig.), Minneapolis, MN: Fortress Press, 1998 (see esp. Ch. 8, "Jesus as a Charismatic: Jesus and his Social Relationships," pp. 185–239, where many apophthegms are discussed).

Travis, Stephan H. "Form Criticism," in I. Howard Marshall (ed.) *New Testament Interpretation: Essays on Principles and Methods*, Carlisle: Paternoster, 1977, pp. 153–64 (revised 1979, 1985; repr. 1992).

For *chreia* in the rhetoric of the classical literature, with examples, see the website "Silva Rhetoricae" at http://rhetoric.byu.edu

CHRIST, MESSIAH

"Christ" is among the most familiar designations of Jesus in the NT and in subsequent Christian tradition. Χριστός (*christos*), the Greek term transliterated as "Christ," appears 529 times in the NT (NA[27]) and, among the NT books, is missing only in 3 John. It designates Jesus of Nazareth as the divinely appointed mediator of eschatological salvation.

So pervasive is the title in early Christian literature that we might easily conclude that the term was widespread and had a stable meaning in the literature of Second Temple Judaism, and that the significance allotted the title in Christian usage was explicitly anticipated in Israel's Scriptures. This is not the case. Consequently, it is important to grasp how the term is used when applied to Jesus in the NT, and then to discern potential warrants for such usage in the various strands of messianism we find in the Second Temple period as well as background ideas in the OT. In what sense might it be claimed that the historical Jesus "fulfilled" Jewish messianic expectations?

Parsing the evidence is not a straightforward task for at least four reasons. First, the term Χριστός and its Hebrew antecedent מָשִׁיחַ (*māšîªḥ*, transliterated in John 1:41; 4:25 as μεσσίας, *messias*) have a basic meaning of "anointed (with ointment or oil)" and need not necessarily designate a christ- or messianic-figure. Second, we must distinguish between uses of the terms on the one hand, and, on the other, the various forms of "messianic expectation" that may or may not have used these characteristic terms. *Messianism* refers to the expectation of a figure to restore Israel, typically in the context of the end-time rule of God, irrespective of whether the term "messiah" or "Christ" is used. Third, the variety of expressions of Judaism in the Second Temple period, as well as diverse theological strands within Israel's Scriptures, should alert us against assuming that we can generalize from one text or group of texts, or from one Jewish sect to all of Judaism, in order to achieve a homogeneous perspective. Fourth, we have no reason to expect that the attribution of the term "Christ" to Jesus promulgated so widely in early Christianity can be traced either in its nuances or breadth of meaning or in its volume of usage to contemporary Jewish expectation. We must remain open, that is, to creativity and development of the title and its significance among Jesus' earliest followers.

The messiah and messianic ideas in Israel's Scriptures

The term מָשִׁיחַ is found thirty-eight times in the Hebrew Bible, never with reference to the expectation of a divinely appointed agent of salvation. Most commonly, it appears in fixed expressions in association with the God of Israel: "the anointed of Yahweh" (1 Sam 24:7 [2x], 11; 26:9, 11, 16, 23; 2 Sam 1:14, 16; 19:22; Lam 4:20), "his (my, your) anointed one" (1 Sam 2:10, 35; 12:3, 5; 16:6; 2 Sam 22:51; Isa 45:1; Hab 3:13; Pss 2:2; 18:51; 20:7; 28:8; 84:10; 89:39, 52; 132:10, 17; 2 Chr 6:42), and "the anointed of the God of Jacob" (2 Sam 23:1). Many of these occur in stories of David and his succession, or in poetic celebrations of or commentary on David and his progeny. Indeed, with only one exception (Isa 45:1), these phrases refer to the king of Israel. This underscores the almost-exclusive relationship between Yahweh and his "anointed one," and signals the status of the king as the (singular) agent of God's beneficence and rule. Among these texts, 1 Sam 16:1–13 is of special interest for its formulation of royal selection and anointing: (1) the choice of a ruler is Yahweh's, so the act of anointing is Israel's recognition of divine election; (2) Yahweh's representative is sent to perform the ritual act of anointing by which the divine call and mission of the king are embraced and conveyed; and (3) the spirit of Yahweh endows the king for service. Isaiah 45:1 names Cyrus as Yahweh's anointed one, appointed to serve on God's behalf in a way analogous to the Israelite kings – namely, to mediate salvation to Israel. In none of these instances does "messiah" refer to a future figure who would inaugurate the age of salvation.

The verbal root מָשַׁח (*māšaḥ*), "to anoint or to smear with oil," was used in a variety of ways, with reference to inanimate objects like walls (Jer 22:14) or pillars (Gen 31:13), but also of persons, especially kings (e.g. 1 Sam 9:9, 16; 10:1; 16:3, 12–13; 2 Sam 19:10; 1 Kgs 1:34, 39, 45) and priests (e.g. Exod 29; Lev 4:3, 5). Whether prophets were anointed is debated, but 1 Kgs 19:15–16 assumes that this is the case (see also Sir 48:8), and this practice would prepare for later references to the anointing of prophets with God's spirit (Isa 61:1–2; Joel 2:28–29; cf. Luke 4:18–19). In Ps 105:15 (also 1 Chr 16:22), Yahweh refers to the patriarchs as "my anointed ... my prophets."

With the benefit of hindsight we can refer to such usage as laying the groundwork for later theologies of the Messiah, but it would be too much to say that such texts intend or themselves anticipate an eschatological savior. Nevertheless, they do identify particular persons who serve as agents of divine activity and thus firmly establish the notion of such agentry in Israel's history and theology. Yahweh delegates divine authority to the king, who executes the will of Yahweh over Israel and the nations (Ps 2). Derivative of Yahweh's rule, royal rule was constrained by Yahweh's interests. As Yahweh's agent, the king was to execute justice and uphold righteousness, lead the people as a shepherd leads the flock, and defend those on the margins of society (see the royal psalms and prophetic oracles – e.g. Pss 45; 72; Isa 9:1–7; 11; Ezek 34) that is, through the faithful service of the king Yahweh's own rule would be actualized on earth. Virtually by definition, priests mediated the divine presence, together with Yahweh's blessing and forgiveness. In time, priests would become prominent as political leaders whose competence expanded as they stepped into roles as divine agents for delivering and gathering Israel. As spokespersons for God, prophets participated in the divine council (cf. Jer 23:16–22), and as bearers of God's spirit they were empowered to speak God's word and thus to put his purpose into action (cf. Isa 55). Not surprisingly, then, when God's people envisioned the divine appointment of a mediator of salvation, it is from rich traditions surrounding these human intermediaries that they drew their inspiration.

Not all agents of God's activity were human, however. Borrowing from passages in Israel's Scriptures, often from some of its more enigmatic texts, God's people identified transcendent figures as eschatological agents of salvation. These include Melchizedek, "priest of God Most High" (Gen 14:18–19), about whom almost nothing is known, but who reappears in Second Temple Jewish literature as a messianic figure; and "One Like a Son of Man," apparently Yahweh's authorized viceregent: "To him was given dominion and glory and kingship, that all peoples, nations, and languages should serve him. His dominion is an everlasting dominion that shall not pass away, and his kingship is one that shall never be destroyed" (Dan 7:13–14).

In the tumultuous context of oppressive Greek and Roman occupation of Israel, messianic hopes began to surface more explicitly in the second or third century BC. Not coincidentally, these would also have been years during which no Israelite was anointed king and for which there is no evidence that priests were being anointed for service. In contrast to the scriptural record of a lineage of persons chosen by Yahweh and anointed for service on his behalf, then, among the people of Israel of this period there were no anointed ones. Interestingly, when later interpreters turned to Israel's Scriptures for messianic portents, they drew only partially from the well of texts in which the term "messiah" is found. Instead, they tended to ground the development of messianic expectation in biblical passages in which the potential of eschatological significance is strong even when the terminology of messianism is lacking.

Among the scriptural texts that do refer to Yahweh's anointed one and which were mined for their significance for unfolding messianism, none is more important than Ps 2, with its vision of royal enthronement in the service of Yahweh's dynastic promise to David – motifs that are further developed in texts that would figure strongly in messianic interpretation of Israel's Scriptures (especially 2 Sam 7:4–17; Ps 110; Isa 9:1–7; 11:1–6). Though these promises and invitations were given to particular rulers and their subjects, together they reflect a royal theology that was to be embodied and promulgated among the people of Yahweh in Israel and Judah. These include the divine choice of David and his lineage to occupy the throne, and the choice of Zion as the seat of that everlasting dynasty. The conjunction of these two notions of election and eternal dynasty flow together with a third motif, the international and even cosmic significance allocated the enthronement of Israel's king. Israel's ruler is a "star" from Jacob (Num 24:17) and his "origin is from of old, from ancient days" (Mic 5:2); his righteous reign signals a paradisal state even among the animals (Isa 11; 66:25). These three motifs then ground the later interpretation of these and related texts in terms of the inauguration of the messianic age by a scion of David. Psalm 89 bears witness to a persistent belief in the eternal viability of Yahweh's promise to David, entreating Yahweh to restore the Davidic dynasty and install his anointed one. Indeed, with God's promise to David read as an everlasting commitment, in times of crisis Israel had good reason for nurturing its hope in the coming of a "new David" (whether an actual descendent of David or a ruler who lived up to the Davidic ideal) through whom God would restore the people. Often interpreted with reference to a faithful remnant of Israel, rather than Israel as a whole, the recovery of the throne of David was nonetheless associated with the renewal of justice and revival of Israel's integrity and dominance as a people.

Texts that do not refer to Yahweh's anointed one could nonetheless be read as indirect witnesses to an eschatological messiah. Two passages that served in this way both in Second Temple Jewish and in early Christian literature are Gen 49:10 ("The scepter shall not depart from Judah, nor the ruler's staff from between his feet, until tribute comes to him; and the obedience of the peoples is his"); and Num 24:17 ("I see him, but not now; I behold him, but not near – a star shall come out of

Jacob, and a scepter shall rise out of Israel"). Read in terms of messianic anticipation, both texts point to the king's function in execution of God's justice in the eschatological age. In the case of Gen 49:10, the LXX may already press in the direction of messianic interpretation. Messianic readings of both texts are indisputable in the targumim, among the Dead Sea Scrolls, and other Second Temple Jewish literature (with regard to Gen 49:9–10, e.g. 4Q252 5:1–7; *T. Jud.* 1:6; 22:3; with regard to Num 24:17, e.g. CD 7:20; 1QM1 1:4–9; 4Q175 1:9–13; *T. Jud.* 24:1–6). Among NT texts, Rev 22:16 is remarkable for its fusion of Num 24:17 with Isa 11:1: "It is I, Jesus, ... I am the root and the descendant of David, the bright morning star."

The messiah and messianic ideas in the Second Temple period

Although it is possible to find some degree of coherence among the strands of messianic ideas among Jews of the Second Temple period, we should be wary of two potential hyperboles. The first is signaled by such phrases as "the Jewish Messiah" or "Jewish expectation of a messianic deliverer." The unity of thought that surfaces in these phrases fails to account for the variegated countenance of Judaism that emerged through myriad forms of response to the crises of exile, foreign occupation, and dismantling of such world-defining institutions as monarchy and temple. In the same way that, early on, followers of Jesus comprised a "sect" within Judaism (e.g. Acts 24:5, 14), with its own practices and beliefs, so other groups would have had their distinguishing practices and beliefs, including hope for (or rejection of belief in) an eschatological agent of divine deliverance. The second is the possible claim that messianic expectation pervaded the Jewish people in the years leading up to the advent of Jesus of Nazareth. Messianic hope probably arose in the third – and if not the third, then the second – century BC, with the earliest evidence derived from the translation into Greek of the Pentateuch. But throughout the period in question, the most pervasive view focused on God's intervention to restore Israel – God's intervention directly, apart from an intermediary figure.

Among those texts that are significant in the discernment of an emerging messianic expectation are the following.

LXX

In many ways, Greek translations of the Hebrew Scriptures followed the Hebrew text, translating משׁח (*mšḥ*) and its cognates with χρίω (*chriō*) and its derivatives; the basic sense of both is "to anoint." Clear departures from the Hebrew text occur at some points that suggest a developing messianism. This is possibly true in the introduction of "his Christ" or "to anoint" in the Greek texts of Ezek. 43:3; Amos 4:13; Hos 8:10, but more plain in Num 24:7 LXX ("A person will come forth from his seed, and rule over many nations; and the kingdom of Gog shall be exalted, and his kingdom shall be increased") and 24:17 LXX ("I will make him known, but not now; I bless him, but he does not draw near; a star will rise out of Jacob, a person shall rise up out of Israel and shatter the leaders of Moab, and plunder all the sons of Seth"), where an eschatological king may well be in view.

Dead Sea Scrolls

Our awareness of the importance of messianic hope in Second Temple Judaism was significantly enhanced with the discovery of the Dead Sea Scrolls in the mid-twentieth century. The relevant writings probably reflect the Hasmonean period, from the early second century to the mid-first century BC. Messianism is prominent in a number of texts – sometimes portraying the Messiah as a singular figure, kingly, victorious, and Davidic; and at other times imagining two or possibly even three messianic figures. These were the royal (e.g. "Branch of David," "Messiah of Israel," "Scepter") and priestly (e.g. "Priest," "Messiah of Aaron," "Interpreter of the Law") messiahs, and, explicitly in one text, the Prophet (1QS 9:11: "until the coming of the prophet and the anointed ones of Aaron and of Israel"). In accordance with the theology of a priestly community like Qumran (e.g. 1QS 6:3–5), the Priest was the lead figure. The royal Messiah would defer to the Priest in matters of instruction and legal interpretation (CD 6:11; 1QSa 2:20; 4Q161), and the Priest would preside over the liturgy of battle (1QM 15:4; 16:13; 18:5) as well as the end-time banquet (1QSa 2:17–21). The possibility of two (or three) messianic figures, although remarkable in Second Temple Judaism, is not the novelty it might at first seem; potential precursors can be found in Zech 4:11–14; 6:12–13 (the latter portends the coming of "Branch" who will build the temple and be joined by a priest) and Jer 33:15–18 (anticipating a righteous Branch of David and a priest).

The Dead Sea Scrolls may provide little evidence for a prophetic messiah, but such a figure is otherwise well-attested. Testimony is found in the

NT and in documents predating the NT, whether as a forerunner to the Messiah (based on Mal 4:5; see *1 En.* 40:31, 37; Matt 11:13–14; 17:10–12) or as the Messiah (e.g. 1 Macc 4:46; 14:41; Luke 7:16; John 1:21; 6:14). This is the "prophet like Moses," promised by God in Deut 18:15–18 (cf. Acts 3:19–23; 7:37). Among the Dead Sea Scrolls, the promise from Deuteronomy is included in an anthology of messianic texts known as *Testimonia* (4Q175) where it is cited alongside Num 24:15–17 (portending a royal messianic figure) and Deut 33–11 (in support of a priestly messiah).

Messianic expectations can be indexed through a plethora of additional texts (see Evans 701–2). Attempts to find a "slain and executed messiah" at Qumran in 4Q285 were based on an erroneous reading of the text and are contradicted by the immediate context of the passage.

OT Pseudepigrapha

Among the fifty-plus documents generally classified as OT Pseudepigrapha, four are of immediate relevance – both because they predate the close of the first century AD and because they include major references to a messiah. The first of these is *Psalms of Solomon* (first century BC) which, in an extended passage in chs 17–18, longs for the overthrowing of the Romans at the hands of the much-anticipated Messiah. The Messiah is a royal figure in the lineage of David who will rule over Israel, destroy the unrighteous rulers, purge Jerusalem of sinners, and gather a holy people whom he will judge and lead.

First Enoch 37–71, usually dated to roughly the first half of the first century AD, sometimes earlier, refers to the Messiah in 48:10 and 52:14. The Enochian material is not as forthcoming as *Psalms of Solomon* with regard to the particular role(s) of the Messiah, referring more generally to his achieving end-time harmony throughout the cosmos. Of greater significance is the portrayal in *1 En.* 37–71 of an astounding agent of divine activity, variously known as "Son of Man," "Chosen One," and "Righteous One." His portrait draws from a number of motifs in Israel's Scripture, including material related to the Isaianic Servant of Yahweh (Isa 42, 49, 52–53), the coming of the "One Like a Son of Man" in Dan 7, the kingly Davidic tradition (e.g. Ps 2; Isa 11), and the emerging hypostatization of divine Wisdom (Nickelsburg 104–6). Drawing together aspects of both human and transcendent intermediaries, this figure is identified as servant and priest, royal and prophetic, transcendent and human. His primary role is to execute eschatological justice: the separation of the righteous

from the wicked, with the oppressed vindicated and the rich and powerful sent to destruction (62:13–16).

For our purposes, the significance of 4 *Ezra* is not easy to assess, both because of textual ambiguities and because it postdates the fall of Jerusalem and can be viewed as responding at some points to emerging Christian thought. In ch. 7 the Messiah dies without having inaugurated a messianic age, whereas in chs 11–12 the Messiah, a descendent of David, is warrior and judge; and in 13:1–14:9 a messianic figure engages Rome in war, though without the usual armaments of warfare. Also dating from the latter part of the first century AD is *2 Baruch*, which mentions the Messiah on five occasions: 29:3; 30:1; 39:7; 40:1; 72:2. Taken together, these portray the Messiah in military cloth, slaying Israel's enemies and inaugurating an eternal, paradisal dominion.

Other texts

Examination of other texts would include attention to the targumim, the respective works of Philo and Josephus, and rabbinic literature. Among these, the targumim and rabbinic literature require an especially critical eye since, though they *may* reflect traditions from the Second Temple period, this cannot be assumed. Both sets of documents testify to a blossoming and codification of messianic ideas, and this speaks to their later provenance. Josephus is of interest primarily for his accounts of revolutionary movements, sometimes labeled "messianic movements," involving peasant leaders (whether messianic pretenders or prophets) and sometimes thousands of the populace bent on overthrowing Roman domination. Josephus' records illustrate the turmoil that simmered just below the surface of Roman "peace," the pervasiveness among the masses of dissatisfaction with Roman overlordship and concomitant hope for divine deliverance, and the lengths to which Rome would go to demolish any attempt at revolt (e.g. *J.W.* 2.4.1:55–56; 2.13.4:259; 2.17.8:433–34; *Ant.* 17.10.5–8:271–85; 20.5.1:97–98; cf. Acts 5:34–40; 21:38). As in other aspects of his exegesis, Philo's messianism moves us from the realm of social, political, and religious struggle, such as one finds in Josephus' prophets and kingly aspirants, to the personal experience of inner transformation.

Messianic woes

Finally, by way of contextualizing ideas of an end-time mediator of salvation, we should note that a number of apocalyptic texts wrap their expectation of the eschaton with references to catastrophes and/or a great tribulation expected to precede the final judgment (e.g. Dan 12:1; 1 QH 11:3–18; *2 Bar.* 25–32; 53–76; *Jub.* 23; cf. Mark 13; Revelation). Such texts do more than describe the coming horror, but also put it in perspective. These trials and tribulations are interpreted as "woes" that accompany the birth of the messianic age. In other words, Israel's deliverance would come by means of great suffering.

Jesus as Christ

In the earliest NT materials, the Pauline letters, Χριστός (*Christos*, "Christ") occurs 382 times, and is already a title functioning in many instances as a virtual "second name": Jesus Christ. Indeed, the identification of Jesus as "Christ" (or "Messiah") was persistent and routinized enough that the title, by itself, could be used to refer to him. Very early on, among his followers, the attribution to Jesus of the title "the Christ" did not require proof but was simply taken for granted.

The widespread use of "Christ" might be expected in circles of Jewish Christians, for whom the designation would have served as a translation of מָשִׁיחַ (*māšîᵃh*, "messiah") and connected in some way with usage in Israel's Scriptures and subsequent messianic speculation. Further definition was necessary, since, as we have seen, "messiah" was capable of a range of possible interpretations; messianic categories were at least known among such Christians, however. More telling is the title's pervasiveness in the Pauline mission, oriented as it was primarily toward Gentiles. Although one of the apostle's more significant roles was his induction of Gentile Christians into the story of God as this is told in Israel's Scriptures, his audiences generally would not have been familiar with the messianism of the Second Temple period. Even more than in the case of predominately Jewish Christian communities, for them "Christ" would have been a vessel ready to be filled with content. How does the attribution of "Christ" to Jesus of Nazareth relate to the wider horizons of messianic ideas in the Second Temple period? The relationship is a complex one, with points of congruence and transformation. Nevertheless, the lack of consistency among portraits of messianic figures in contemporary Jewish speculation makes room for the exploration of Christian reflection on the messiahship of Jesus within the matrix of messianic ideas. Points of contact would include:

1 recognition of Jesus' royal, Davidic ancestry – affirmed in an early creed cited by Paul (Rom 1:3); witnessed in the gospel tradition most powerfully in accounts of Jesus' triumphal entry into Jerusalem (Mark 11:1–10 pars.), with Jesus riding on a colt as the victorious yet humble king (Zech 9:9) and acclaimed by the crowds as king with words borrowed from Ps 118 (see also 2 Kgs 9:13); but also attested in the narratives of Jesus' birth (Matt 1–2; Luke 1–2), baptism (Mark 1:11 pars.; citing Ps 2:7; cf. Heb 5:5), and ministry of healing (e.g. Matt 12:23; Mark 10:47). Related to this is Jesus' execution as a pretender to the throne, "the king of the Jews" (e.g. Matt 27:11, 29, 37 pars.);

2 recognition of Jesus' priesthood "in the order of Melchizedek" (recall that Melchizedek was named as a messianic figure in 11QMelch) – witnessed explicitly in Hebrews (e.g. 5:6, 10; 6:10; 7), but also in his atoning sacrifice and exaltation to God's right hand where he makes priestly intercession (Ps 110:1, 4; Heb 1:3; 2:17; 5:10; 9:11–14; cf. Rom 8:34);

3 recognition of Jesus' status as a prophet (e.g. Mark 6:4 pars.; Luke 4:18–19, citing Luke 61:1–2), including acclamation of Jesus as the eschatological prophet (e.g. Luke 7:16; John 6:14) and his identification as the messianic prophet-like-Moses (e.g. Acts 3:19–26); and

4 recognition of the coalescing of messianic ideas in early Christian understanding of Jesus in ways following the kind of path already opened in *1 En.* 37–71 but also reminiscent of the tale of the Suffering Righteous One in Wis 2, 4–5. Here we find already the combination of such tropes as servant, king, and prophet, together with earthly life and death leading to exaltation and enthronement. These precursors suggest the Jewish grounding of early christological thought in relation to Jesus even if the particular combination of motifs found in developing understandings of Jesus is without direct precedent.

Perhaps the most characteristic feature of the attribution of "Christ" to Jesus in early Christianity is its close association with the death and resurrection of Jesus (e.g. Rom 5:6, 8; 8:34; 14:9; 2 Cor 5:14–15). This includes the earliest confessional materials to which we have access (e.g. 1 Cor 15:3–5). In the world of Jesus and his first followers, this combination of terms, "Christ" and "crucified" (e.g. Acts 4:10; 1 Cor 1:23; 2:2; 3:1), would have been especially jarring. This is because, for both Jew and Gentile, Jesus' crucifixion would have marked him in the most ignoble terms (e.g. 1 Cor 1:23; see Deut 21:22–23), whereas "Christ" has the basic sense of "anointed one" and, in traditions that had developed from the Scriptures of Israel, would have signified honorable status as God's envoy.

Although never sundered from the basic Jewish sense of God's end-time mediator of salvation, "Christ" among Christians became the focus of devotion in a way unparalleled in previous and contemporary Jewish literature. Among contemporary Jews whose expectations for God's intervention to restore Israel included a messianic figure (or figures), such hopes were invariably set within a larger network of expectation regarding God's eschatological intervention to vindicate his people. Among Jesus' followers, however, the person of Jesus himself was central. This was true to such a degree that, irrespective of how they might have spoken of themselves, they quickly became known as "Christians" (1 Pet 4:16; Acts 11:26; 26:28). Speaking of the fire of Rome, Tacitus reports that:

> Nero fastened the guilt and inflicted the most exquisite tortures on a class hated for their abominations, called Christians by the populace. Christus, from whom the name had its origin, suffered the extreme penalty during the reign of Tiberius at the hands of one of our procurators, Pontius Pilatus, and a most mischievous superstition, thus checked for the moment, again broke out not only in Judaea, the first source of the evil, but even in Rome, where all things hideous and shameful from every part of the world find their center and become popular.
>
> (*Ann.* 15.44)

Though among his followers, the label "Christian" would be embraced as a honorable way to identify and to be identified with Christ, it was coined by persons hostile to Jesus' followers by way of denigrating them for their worship of one who experienced the ultimate humiliation of execution as a criminal on a Roman cross.

Did Jesus think of himself in messianic terms? The question is difficult, given the range of messianic ideas among Jews of the first century. Certainly, there is no unambiguous evidence that Jesus used the term "Christ" of himself (cf. Mark 9:41), and when he apparently allowed or affirmed its use by others he did so by immediately defining it with reference to suffering and the tradition of God's vindication of the suffering righteous (e.g. Matt 26:63 pars.; Mark 8:27–38 pars.). Most scholars now agree that Jesus regarded his mission as that of restoring Israel (or a remnant of Israel), a role

that could have included messianic ideas. In addition, we may take as axiomatic that Jesus did anticipate his death; in the charged environment of Roman Palestine how could he not have done so? To admit this is to open the door to its corollary – namely, the probability that he reflected on its significance and did so in a way that intimately related it to his mission to redeem the people of God. Certainly, the interpretive resources were available to Jesus for him both to anticipate his violent death and his vindication by God, and to do so in ways congruent with his recognition of himself as the divinely appointed mediator of eschatological salvation.

JOEL B. GREEN

Further reading

Allison, Dale C. *The End of the Ages Has Come: An Early Interpretation of the Passion and Resurrection of Jesus*, Philadelphia, PA: Fortress Press, 1985.

Charlesworth, James H. (ed.) *The Messiah: Developments in Earliest Judaism and Christianity*, The First Princeton Symposium on Judaism and Christian Origins, Minneapolis, MN: Fortress Press, 1992.

Evans, Craig A. "Messianism," in Craig A. Evans and Stanley E. Porter, *Dictionary of New Testament Background*, Downers Grove, IL: InterVarsity Press, 2000, pp. 698–707.

Fabry, Heinz-Josef. "Messianism in the Septuagint," in Wolfgang Kraus and R. Glenn Wooden (eds) *Septuagint Research: Issues and Challenges in the Study of the Greek Jewish Scriptures*, Septuagint and Cognate Studies 53, Atlanta, GA: SBL, 2006, pp. 193–205.

Longenecker, Richard N. *Contours of Christology in the New Testament*, McMaster New Testament Studies, Grand Rapids, MI: Eerdmans, 2005.

Neusner, Jacob, William Scott Green, and Ernest S. Frerichs (eds) *Judaisms and Their Messiahs at the Turn of the Christian Era*, Cambridge: Cambridge University Press, 1987.

Nickelsburg, George W. E. *Ancient Judaism and Christian Origins: Diversity, Continuity, and Transformation*, Minneapolis, MN: Fortress Press, 2003.

CHRISTOLOGY

Christology attempts to trace how the early Christians came to understand Jesus the man as Christ the Messiah. From the witness of the books of the New Testament, Christology attempts to trace how Jesus of Nazareth could be proclaimed Jesus the Christ.

Components and procedure

There are three key components for the investigation of the development of Christology. The first component is the expectation of a redeemer figure within Judaism, an expectation shared by Jesus and the Jewish Christians. The Jewish expectation of a redeemer was diverse, being both religious and political. This expectation included a priest, a prophet like Moses, and a liberating king – whether human or divine. With his teaching and ministry, Jesus implicitly and explicitly tied aspects of these expectations to himself.

The second component is the influence of Jesus' ministry, crucifixion, resurrection, and post-resurrection appearances to his followers. These events are crucial to the early Christians' understanding of the nature of Jesus. As early Christians sought to understand Jesus as Christ they further developed the expectations of a redeemer figure in light of the events of Jesus' life, a process that eventually resulted in formal creeds.

The third component is the translation of the terminology of Christology from Hebrew and Aramaic to *koinē* Greek. While the terminology derives from the Old Testament and Jewish tradition, the language in which it found final expression was Greek. Language is culturally embedded and the meaning of the Greek terminology is partly supplied by the Hellenistic world. In other words, Christology can be understood as a process influenced by the religious, political, and cultural environment of early Christianity, both Jewish and Hellenistic.

A typical approach to Christology is to study the titles that the early Christians attributed to Jesus. These titles have deep roots in the Old Testament and Jewish tradition and have many associated expectations. Early Christians believed that these titles were appropriate to assign to Jesus. In other words, this approach seeks to understand how the early Christians understood Jesus by the titles they gave to him.

While the examination of titles is important, it is only one aspect of Christology. In this article we will examine Christology by tracing traditions and their development within segments of early Christianity. We will trace the movement from Jewish expectations for a redeemer, through the teaching and ministry of Jesus, to the christological witness of the early church as attested by the books of the New Testament. We will examine the New Testament books to determine what the segments of early Christianity that produced them contributed to the development of Christology.

Obviously the New Testament preserves the Christology of what is known as orthodoxy and does not represent the full range of Christology that emerged in the early church. For the purposes of this discussion, we will not be examining the

Christology of Gnosticism as well as other Christologies that early Christians eventually judged as not adequately reflecting the nature of Jesus as the Christ.

Jewish expectation

The Jewish expectations and traditions for a coming prophet, priest, and king as found in the Old Testament and Jewish tradition are primary for Christology. They were resources for Jesus' understanding of his mission and identity, as well as for the early Christians as they sought to understand Jesus' significance.

Within Judaism the expectation of a prophet was multifaceted and included a prophet like Moses (Deut 18:15, 18), the return of Elijah (Mal 4:5; Sir 48:9–10), and the appearance of an eschatological prophet (Isa 61:1–2; 1QS 9:11). Jesus was identified as a prophet, one of the ancient prophets, Elijah, and the prophet like Moses (Mark 6:15 = Luke 9:8.; 8:28 = Matt 16:14 = Luke 9:19; John 6:14). There is evidence that Jesus accepted this title (Mark 6:4 = Matt 13:57). He used Isa 61:1–2 pertaining to the eschatological prophet as a programmatic statement for his ministry (Matt 5:3–4 = Luke 6:20–21; Matt 11:2–6 = Luke 7:18–23; Luke 4:16–21).

His actions too would indicate to those who witnessed them that he was a prophet. The cleansing of the Temple in Jerusalem and the pronouncement of its destruction is one of many examples of a prophetic act. However, there was also indication that he was more than a prophet. He spoke as one having his own authority, not as one whose role was solely as a mouthpiece for God (Mark 1:27 = Luke 4:36; Mark 6:1–6 = Matt 13:53–58).

Within some circles of Judaism there was a tradition of a priestly messiah (1QSa 2:11–22). However, this tradition was not used to shape Christology because Jesus was not born of the priestly tribe of Levi. Also, given the current political subjugation of the Mediterranean region by the Romans, expectations of a priestly messiah would not be as appealing for the development of Christology as those of a kingly or military messiah.

The royal or kingly messiah was the most popular of the messianic expectations of Jesus' contemporaries (Isa 11:1–16; *Pss. Sol.* 17:21–25). Judaism had been subject to Roman occupation since 63 BCE and the desire for political independence was strong. There was a great hope that a son of David would arise and re-establish Jewish independence. The fact that Jesus was executed as

King of the Jews (Mark 15:26 = Matt 27:37) indicates that this expectation was prominent during his lifetime. His own actions, like those of cleansing the temple and riding a donkey into Jerusalem, also had overtones of kingship.

Jesus did not reject the title of messiah itself (Mark 8:29–30 = Matt 16:18, 20; Mark 14:61–62 = Matt 26:63–64; Mark 15:2 = Matt 27:11 = Luke 23:3), but did reject the popular expectation that came with it (Mark 6:45; 8:30–33). The full meaning of role of the messiah was not going to be clear until after his crucifixion and resurrection transformed the role of the kingly messiah to include suffering and cosmic sovereignty.

Jesus' understanding of his identity

By the titles that he used to refer to himself, it appears that Jesus understood his mission as one ushering in the eschatological age to fulfill God's promises to Israel. Two of Jesus' self-designations are central to his self-understanding: Son of God and Son of Man.

The title "Son of God" could designate a king (Ps 2:7), the people of Israel (Hos 11:1), and the heavenly host (Gen 6:1–4). In the latest gospel, the Gospel of John, Jesus designates himself as the Son of God over 100 times. Since the Gospel of John is a unique and purposeful blending of the words of Jesus and the theological reflection of the early church, this usage indicates that by the end of the first century the church was claiming this title to designate Jesus as the divine son of God. Perhaps this reflection is rooted in Jesus' practice of addressing God as Father (*abba*) in his prayers (Mark 14:36) and addressing God in the presence of his disciples (Matt 11:25–27 = Luke 10:21–22).

The most common form of Jesus' self-designation in the Gospels is "the Son of Man." This title is used only by Jesus and no one else applies it to him (e.g. Mark 2:10; 8:31; 14:62). The title may be rooted in Jesus' own words and deeds because it is confined to the Jesus tradition. Except for a few exceptions (Acts 7:56; Rev 1:13, 14:14), it did not become a part of Christology outside the Jesus tradition. The title designates Jesus as a human being, member of the human race (Ps 8:4).

Although debated, the title "Son of Man" may also derive from Dan 7:13. Jewish tradition understood this figure to refer to a heavenly eschatological redeemer figure that brings deliverance and judgment. It is debated whether Jesus applied this title to himself or understood it in this eschatological sense, although the New Testament writers developed their Christology in full light of the Jewish tradition – especially Jesus as judge.

From the experience of Jesus to Christology proper

The teachings and ministry of Jesus had many connections with Jewish expectations for a redeemer and messiah. However, it was the resurrection, the subsequent experience of the Holy Spirit, preaching needs, and eschatological expectation that were the catalysts that prompted the early Christians to formulate a fuller understanding of Jesus' nature and mission. Without these experiences Jesus could have gone down in history as just another messianic pretender rather than Jesus the Christ.

The resurrection

The firm belief in God's resurrection of Jesus from the dead is the bedrock of Christology. It is central to the earliest Christian creeds as found in Paul's letters in the 50s and 60s CE which indicates just how early they were formulated (Rom 8:11; 10:9; Gal 1:1; Col 2:12; 1 Thess 1:10). Paul also stressed the centrality of God raising Jesus from the dead in his own discussion of the resurrection (1 Cor 15:12–28; Phil 2:9–11). The sermons and speeches of Acts describe the significance of key events in the early church, and the centrality of the resurrection of Jesus to this proclamation indicates just how important this topic was to the faith of the earliest Christians (Acts 2:24–32; 4:1–2, 33; 10:39–41; 13:30–37; 17:30–31).

The resurrection of Jesus is the culmination of the rhetorical scheme of all four gospels. One of the best-known examples is the messianic secret in Mark's Gospel. In this motif, Jesus works to keep his full identity secret until the resurrection which reveals his true nature in full (Mark 9:9). In John the resurrection is the event that clarifies Jesus' teaching about himself (2:22).

Experience of the Spirit

The understanding of the early Christians that they experienced the outpouring of the Holy Spirit of the last days had an influence on early Christology. John the Baptist proclaimed that his successor would be responsible for the outpouring of the Spirit (Mark 1:8). This outpouring was attributed to the exalted Jesus (Acts 2:33), and the Spirit itself was considered to be the Spirit of Jesus (Acts 16:7; 1 Pet 1:11). The understanding that the role of the Spirit was to witness to Christ also was part of the development of Christology (Acts 5:32; 1 Pet 1:12; 1 John 5:6–8). This is particularly true of the

Gospel of John where the sending of the Spirit after the ascension is understood as partly to help the disciples recall what they had seen and heard. The Johannine community in Ephesus understood that the risen Christ, through the Holy Spirit and the prophets of the church, helped it interpret the words and deeds of the earthly Jesus (John 14:25–26; 15:26–27; 16:12–15).

The needs of preaching and evangelism

The early church had to prove, especially to its initial Jewish audience, that a dead man, a crucified man could qualify as the messiah. Popular Jewish messianic expectation anticipated the opposite – that the messiah was to remain and lead Israel and that one who hung on a tree was cursed (Deut 21:22–23). To meet this apologetic need, the early church naturally turned to the Old Testament. The third and fourth servant songs of Isaiah proved particularly helpful (50:4–11; 52:13–53:12; Rom 4:25; 1 Cor 15:3; 1 Pet 2:24–25). This use of the suffering servant built upon what may have been Jesus' allusion to the servant in his own teaching that he must "suffer" (Mark 9:12 = Matt 17:12; Mark 8:31 = Matt 16:21 = Luke 9:22).

The early Christians also had to give clarity to Christ's exaltation. They conscripted the royal psalms used to celebrate the coronation of kings. Pslm 110 was a favorite messianic text, especially verse 1, that proclaimed the king or lord as seated on God's right hand (Acts 2:34; Rom 8:34; 1 Cor 15:25; Heb 1:3, 13; 1 Pet 3:22). Psalm 2 was another favorite, especially verse 7, which calls the king God's "son" (Acts 13:33; Heb 5:5). These associations of Jesus with the Lord and Son of God may have come from the Jesus tradition itself (Mark 1:11; 12:35–37; 14:62). In any event, it allowed the Christian message to communicate with the wider Greco-Roman world using the titles Jesus as Lord and Son of God that were familiar from its own religious terminology and conceptions.

Essential to the Christology of the first century was imminent eschatology, the expectation that Jesus would return within a very short time. This is reflected in the Son of Man sayings in Q in which the Son of Man expected to return in judgment (Matt 24:27; Luke 17:24) as well as in several New Testament books (1 Cor 16:22; 1 Thess 1:9–10). The expectation was strong in Jewish-Christian congregations in Palestine (Jude) and in the dispersed Jewish Hellenist communities (Jas 5:7–8), Paul's gentile congregations (1 Thess 4:13–18), Johannine churches at Ephesus (Revelation, 1 John), and the churches at Rome (2 Pet 3:1–13).

Except for the book of Hebrews, this imminent expectation steered early Christology away from developing a detailed picture of Christ's role as heavenly intermediator.

The Christology in the Pauline and Deutero-Pauline Epistles

Paul's Christology is rooted in the Jewish expectations of a messianic figure that were familiar to him from Judaism, his conversion experience on the Damascus Road (Gal 1:16), and conceptions of Christology that were already being formulated in early Christianity.

Jesus as Lord is a central affirmation of Pauline Christology (Rom 10:9; 1 Cor 12:3; Phil 2:11). Paul could take Old Testament texts that applied to God as Lord and apply them to Jesus (Rom 10:13; 1 Cor 2:16; Phil 2:10–11). Paul did not seem to think that the title "Lord" ascribed to Jesus was an affront to Jewish monotheism (1 Cor 8:6). In Phil 2:6–7 he affirms the pre-existence of Jesus and his equality with God. It is possible that Paul even calls Jesus "God" in Rom 9:5, depending on how the punctuation is placed. This Christology was useful in relating to Hellenistic culture that had similar terminology for the gods of their cults.

Paul was also a creative individual and made his own important contributions to budding Christology. His contributions can be categorized as Adam-Christ, Wisdom, and Spirit Christologies. Regarding Adam-Christ Christology, Paul understood Jesus to be fully human. Jesus came in the "likeness of sinful flesh" (Rom 8:3), "born of a woman" (Gal 4:4), and "being born in human likeness, and being found in human form" (Phil 2:7). This is the foundational premise of his Adam-Christ Christology. Through the sin of the first man, Adam, death came to have dominion over all humanity. Through the obedience of the man Jesus grace now has dominion, bringing life, justification, and righteousness for all humanity (Rom 5:12–21; 1 Cor 15:20–22, 45–49).

Christ's death and resurrection is the key to the Adam-Christ Christology. As Christ died, so all die. Christ's death and resurrection is a conquest of death that all can experience (2 Cor 5:14–15). Christ's death and resurrection has the far-reaching effect of enabling humanity to escape the finality of death and come to experience life. Christ experiences the full effect of sin – death – for humanity so that he may conquer it through resurrection and lead humanity through death to life (Rom 6:5–11; Phil 3:10–11). Through his sacrifice and resurrection Christ both embraces the death shared by humanity because of Adam's sin and creates a new humanity no longer under the curse of death (Rom 8:29; 1 Cor 15:21–22). The obedience of Christ and his obedience even to death stands in contrast to Adam's disobedience and in effect nullifies its effects (Rom 5:19).

Regarding wisdom Christology, in Judaism prior to Jesus, wisdom had come to signify God in his creative and revelatory nature. For Paul, Christ was God's wisdom: that is, he was the creator and revealer of God in creation (1 Cor 1:24, 30; 8:6; Col 1:15–17). Christ as crucified is the essence of divine wisdom (1 Cor 1:23–25) and the key revelation of God's work of salvation to the world (2 Cor 5:19).

Whereas the role of wisdom in creation in Jewish thought made for a natural identification of Christ as the wisdom of God, the identification of Christ as the Spirit of God was not. In Paul's Christology the close association of Christ with the Spirit began at the resurrection (Rom 1:3–4; 1 Cor 15:45). The experience of Christ and the Spirit overlap, for the Christian experiences Christ through the Spirit and as the Spirit of God (Rom 8:9–11; 1 Cor 6:17; 12:4–6). The Spirit is the Spirit of Christ (Rom 8:9; Gal 4:6; Phil 1:19), but the Spirit remains primarily the Spirit of God (Rom 8:9–11, 14).

The Deutero-Pauline Epistles do not significantly advance Christology. In Colossians (1:25–27; 2:2–3) and Ephesians (3:1–13), Christ is the revelation of God's purposes. This emphasis is an extension of Paul's wisdom Christology. There is little development of Christology in the Pastoral Epistles. The Adam-Christ Christology reappears as Christ abolishes death and brings life (2 Tim 1:9–10). Christ fulfills God's purposes for salvation (2 Tim 1:9–10; Titus 1:2–3). Christology is mainly found in creeds and hymns (1 Tim 1:15; 2:5–6; 3:16; Titus 3:5–7).

Mark and Matthew

In Mark's Christology, the title "Son of God" is used by God at Jesus' baptism in words that designate Jesus as king and turn his baptism into an enthronement (1:9–11; cf. Isa 40:1; Ps 2:7). The title "Son of Man" is used in relation to Jesus' authority as servant of God (2:10), his suffering (8:31), and his role as eschatological deliverer and judge (14:62). Mark creates a literary motif of the messianic secret that Jesus did not want his identify as Christ known prior to his passion (8:29) in order to demonstrate that the true nature of Jesus as the Christ was not understood fully until after the crucifixion and resurrection.

Matthew's Christology is built upon an overlapping understanding of Jesus as Son of God and Son of Man. With the "Son of God" title, Matthew stresses Jesus' origin and family relationship with God and the suffering role of the Son (12:18–21; 27:40, 43). The title "Son of Man" gives further meaning to the title "Son of God" (26:63–64). It describes Jesus much as it does in Mark, as an authoritative servant of God (9:6), suffering servant of God who dies and rises as a ransom for others (17:22–23; 20:17–28; 26:2) and as the eschatological deliverer and judge (10:23; 16:27–28; 24:30–31, 36).

Luke–Acts

Luke and Acts offer us a picture of Christology in the period of 70–85 CE. Within Luke's salvation history scheme, Jesus is the fulfillment of God's promises and purposes through Israel. The Jewish expectation of a prophet like Moses characterizes earliest Christianity (Luke 24:19; Acts 3:22; 7:37). Luke emphasizes that Jesus is the Savior of the House of David (Luke 1:69; 2:11, 30; 3:6; Acts 5:31; 13:23), but there is no doctrine of atonement. Luke establishes that Jesus' death was foretold and necessary, but not how his death secures atonement. Atonement is not one of vicarious suffering, but of a Servant who suffers and is raised by God (Acts 3:13–15, 26; 4:25–27, 30; 10:39–40; 13:29–30). By virtue of his resurrection, Jesus is installed as Lord and Christ (Acts 2:34–36); leader and savior who gives repentance and forgiveness of sins (Acts 5:31) and salvation (4:10–12); and eschatological judge who forgives sin (Acts 10:42–43).

The Johannine literature

The Gospel and Epistles of John and the book of Revelation all derive from the Johannine Community and were written between 80 and 110 CE. Their Christology is best studied together, beginning with the earliest work, the Gospel of John.

The Gospel of John (80s CE) presents the most developed Christology in the New Testament. While it has roots in the Jesus tradition, it reflects considerable development of that tradition. The Christology consistently presents Jesus as the pre-existent Son of God who descended to earth as the Son of Man with a mission that ended in his ascent back to heaven. John introduces many of his christological themes in the prologue (1:1–18) which may be a hymn encapsulating the Christology of the Johannine Community. John extends the wisdom Christology, replacing wisdom with "word" (*logos*), a shift of terminology that better enables John to proclaim the gospel to the gentile world. Like wisdom, word is the effective self-revelation of God to humankind. It is God's power to create and reveal. This word is incarnate in Jesus Christ who reveals God in every aspect of his words and deeds (vv. 1, 14). The Word is the mediator in creation (vv. 1, 10), revelation (vv. 4, 18), and salvation (vv. 12–13, 16–17).

The remainder of the Gospel of John is a narrative of the revelation of God through Jesus the Word. Jesus' unique position to reveal God comes from his heavenly pre-existence. Having been in heaven, he can reveal heavenly things (3:11–13, 31–32) and God whom he has seen (1:18). This unique status held by Jesus alone comes to the fore in the "I am" sayings. These combine the wisdom themes with the divine self-designation of God as "I am" (Exod 3:14; Isa 43:10). In these sayings Jesus is God in his creative and revelatory glory (8:12, 24, 28, 58). Jesus was God making himself known in the world (1:18, 20:28).

The most comprehensive title for Jesus in John's Gospel, "Son of God," emphasizes the basis for Jesus' revelation of God and his authority to do so (20:31). It is a unique status since he is the only begotten (*monogenēs*) of God (1:14, 18; 3:16, 18). This identification of Jesus with God is so strong that to see Jesus is to see his Father (14:9); to know him is to know the Father (8:19; 14:6–7). Jesus and his Father are one (10:30). In John's Christology we see the beginnings of the reformulation of Jewish monotheism. However, John was careful to emphasize that Jesus was not just God in human form, but was in fact incarnate. The Word became flesh (1:13–14; 3:6) and his death on the cross was a real physical death (19:34–35).

First and Second John written after the Gospel of John (90–100 CE) indicate that the christological formulations of the Gospel were subject to further modification by the Johannine Community. A secession occurred in the community; a secession centered on Christology. The secessionists hesitated to identify Jesus with the Christ. They drew out the implications of the high Christology of the Johannine tradition, particularly its emphasis upon an incarnation based on pre-existence. The tradition speaks of Jesus' earthly ministry as a revelation of God's glory and the crucifixion as a continuation of that revelation (John 1:14; 14:9). The secessionists minimized the salvific significance of Jesus' earthly ministry, denying that Jesus was the Christ, the Son of God, come in the flesh, and come by water and blood (1 John 2:22–23; 4:2–3; 5:1, 5–6, 20; 2 John 7). For them, the baptism of John initiated

the revelation of God's glory in Jesus and the crucifixion was merely the continuation of this initial revelation. If the incarnation brought eternal life into the world, then the death of Jesus on the cross was not salvific.

Such a position by the secessionists would explain the Elder's stress upon the salvific nature of Jesus' earthly life (1 John 1:7–9; 2:2, 12; 3:5, 8, 16; 4:9–10) and upon his death (1 John 5:6). Jesus was pre-existent and then incarnate (1:1–3). He is the divine Son who was revealed (1:1–3, 7; 3:5, 8, 23; 4:15; 5:1, 9–13, 20). His revelation was experienced by the founders of the churches and is the basis of the community's Christology (1:1–3). Jesus was revealed to take away sin (3:5, 8). His death was an atoning sacrifice that cleanses from sin (1:5–2:2; 4:10). Belief that Jesus is the Christ is necessary for salvation and fellowship with God (1:1–3; 5:1, 9–13). Jesus is now an advocate between the Christian and God (2:1).

The book of Revelation (written mid-90s CE) contains a high Christology like its predecessor, the Gospel of John. It is well grounded in Jewish Scriptures and tradition. The author addresses the large question, "Who is Lord?" He seeks to persuade his churches to remain faithful to God and Christ, and not succumb to the demands of the emperor cult that the emperor be worshiped as Lord and God. Only God and Christ deserve worship and allegiance (5:6–14; 7:10). He holds up Christ as a slain, yet victorious lamb as a model for Christians to follow in a turbulent time of persecution. As Christ faithfully proclaimed the gospel, died by the hands of the Romans, and was subsequently exalted, so should the Christians be faithful (5:6–14; 11:8–11).

Christ appropriates the dignity of God. The kingdom belongs to both God and Christ (11:15; 12:10). Both God and Christ are the "Alpha and the Omega" (1:8; 22:12–13). The theophany of Christ that opens the book describes Christ with language borrowed from Old Testament theophanies of God (1:9–20). Christ is the voice of prophecy (2:7, 11) and who dispenses future judgment and reward (2:7, 10, 17, 22–28). Christ as the slain Lamb is the image of redemption in Revelation. He frees humanity from sin with his blood (1:5–6; 7:14; 12:11). He conquered sin through being slaughtered and ransoming saints with his blood (5:9–10).

Hebrews and the General Epistles

An early development in Christology in Jewish Christian churches was to associate Christ with

God of the Old Testament. We see this development in James and Jude, both of which were probably written in the 50s CE in early Jewish Christian contexts. In James, Jesus is given the title "Lord" used of God in the Old Testament, being called the "Lord Jesus Christ" (1:1; 2:1). Jesus also exhibits some of the corresponding attributes of God as Lord. He is the Lord in whose name the prophets spoke and is compassionate and merciful (5:10–11). He is the Lord who governs the lives of Christians (4:15), saves and raises the sick and forgives their sin (5:13–15), and returns as Judge (5:7–9). James also alludes to Christ's pre-existence, for the Spirit of Christ inspired the prophets (1:11). Besides a reference to pre-existence, this is another example of the lack of distinction in early Christianity between Christ and the Spirit.

In Jude we find the titles typically attributed to God: "Master and Lord, Jesus Christ" (v. 4), Lord Jesus Christ (vv. 17, 21) and Jesus Christ our Lord (v. 25). However, when Lord is used of the saving of Israel out of Egypt (v. 5) and the archangel's invoking of the Lord (v. 9), the referent is probably still God. In the prophecy of the coming of the Lord in judgment (vv. 14–15), we see the referent of "Lord" shifting from God coming on the Day of the Lord to Christ coming at the Parousia.

First Peter places his Christology within the context of the plan of God. It shares the early conviction that God predestined Christ for his redemptive mission before the foundation of the world (1:20). However, 1 Peter emphasizes that Christ's redemptive work included suffering prophesied by Old Testament prophets (1:10–11). Christ's suffering and death culminated in the resurrection which makes his suffering effective for salvation and conquest of evil (1:3; 3:18–22). Christ is enthroned in heaven at God's right hand above angels, authorities, and powers (3:22).

First Peter has the fullest use of the Suffering Servant Song of Isa 52:13–53:12, emphasizing the vicarious nature of Christ's death to free humanity from sin (2:21–25; 3:18–22). His suffering is portrayed using imagery of sacrifice from Jewish tradition. Christians are ransomed from their futile ways with the blood of Christ, "like that of a lamb without defect or blemish" (1:18–19), imagery that makes Christ the Passover Lamb (Exod 12:5). Christians are sprinkled with Christ's blood (1:3), imagery of Christ as the sacrificial animal whose blood is sprinkled for cleansing purposes (Exod 29:19–21; Lev 4:3–6, 13–17; 14:5–7; Num 19)

Also in 1 Peter, Christians are chosen by God in his foreknowledge to be obedient to Jesus Christ (1:3). God's mercy gives the Christian new birth and inheritance as his children through his resurrection of Jesus Christ (1:4–5, 21), a resurrection that makes baptism effective (3:21). Jesus Christ is the mediator of spiritual sacrifices made by Christians to God (2:4–5).

Second Peter (80s CE) attributes these titles to Jesus: "Lord Jesus Christ" (1:8, 14, 16), "Lord and Savior Jesus Christ" (1:11; 2:20; 3:18), and "Lord and Savior" (3:2). The title "God and Savior Jesus Christ" in 1:1 may refer to God and Jesus individually or be two designations for Jesus alone. Jesus is the Son of God as repetition of the Jesus tradition of the transfiguration makes clear (1:16–18). The redemptive work of Christ is defined a "master who bought the Christians" (2:1), a use of the imagery of sacral manumission in which Jesus is portrayed as a master who buys slaves out of slavery to serve him. Eschatological expectation has weakened as the scoffing of the opponents indicates (3:1–4), but the author still expects that his audience will experience the coming of the Lord (3:14–18). Since the author has previously understood the coming of the Lord as referring to Christ (1:16; 3:4), it is possible that reference to the "day of God" (3:12) blurs the distinction between God and Christ.

The book of Hebrews has an elaborate Christology. It contains both Adam-Christ (2:5–18) and wisdom Christologies (1:1–4). It concentrates on demonstrating that Christ is superior to any other mediator figure such as prophets (1:1–2), angels (1:4–14), Moses (3:1–18), and the levitical priesthood (4:14–15:10). The latter receives emphasis. Christ is the high priest, not of the fallible and mortal line of Aaron, but, as the divine Son (5:5–10; 7:28) and of the immortal line of Melchizedek (Pss 110:4, 5:6; 7:1–28). He is also the perfect sacrifice, one that is sacrificed once for all to effect a new covenant (chs 8–10). As well as being the divine Son, Jesus shares human nature. It is in sharing human nature that he is able to die and destroy the power of death, become an atoning sacrifice for sin, and become an emphatic high priest who has suffered like those for whom he mediates (2:14–18).

Conclusion

The Christology of the New Testament is deeply rooted in and builds upon Old Testament and Jewish tradition, as well as that tradition as appropriated by Jesus. Christology focuses these diverse expectations on Jesus Christ and molds them in light of the ministry and teachings of Jesus. Thus Jesus can be identified with a variety of Jewish figures and images including God, Lord, Son of God, messiah, Son of Man, suffering servant, atoning sacrifice, high priest, word, wisdom, and savior. Many of these figures and images also had usage in the wider Greco-Roman world, and that usage had some influence on Judaism prior to Christianity. However, the usage of these figures and images in New Testament Christology remains largely rooted in their Jewish counterparts.

The heart of Christology in the New Testament is the claim that Jesus is the definitive manifestation of God to humanity. Jesus' death, resurrection, and exaltation bring salvation to creation and humankind. However, individual authors of the New Testament have differing ways of expressing Christology and emphasize different aspects of it depending on the exigencies they addressed. As Christianity progressed, not all of these conceptions were maintained. The wisdom and word Christologies of Paul and John became prominent, while any formulation hinting of adoptionist Christology was abandoned. It took subsequent centuries to mold Christology into a Trinitarian formulation that balanced the claims of monotheism with the attributions to Christ that seemed to substitute binitarianism for monotheism, such as the title "Lord" used of God in the Old Testament.

DUANE F. WATSON

Further reading

Brown, Raymond E. *An Introduction to New Testament Christology*, New York: Paulist Press, 1994.

De Jonge, Martinus. *Christology in Context: The Earliest Christian Response to Jesus*, Philadelphia, PA: Westminster, 1988.

Dunn, James D. G. *Christology in the Making: A New Testament Inquiry into the Origins of the Doctrine of the Incarnation*, Philadelphia, PA: Westminster, 1980.

—— *Jesus Remembered: Christology in the Making*, Vol. 1, Grand Rapids, MI: Eerdmans, 2003.

Green, Joel B. and Max Turner (eds) *Jesus of Nazareth, Lord and Christ: Essays on the Historical Jesus and New Testament Christology*, Grand Rapids, MI: Eerdmans, 1994.

Hultgren, Arland J. *Christ and His Benefits: Christology and Redemption in the New Testament*, Philadelphia, PA: Fortress Press, 1987.

Hurtado, Larry W. *Lord Jesus Christ: Devotion to Jesus in Earliest Christianity*, Grand Rapids, MI: Eerdmans, 2003.

—— *How on Earth Did Jesus Become a God? Historical Questions about Earliest Devotion to Jesus*, Grand Rapids, MI: Eerdmans, 2005.

Matera, Frank J. *New Testament Christology*, Louisville, KY: Westminster John Knox Press, 1999.

O'Collins, Gerald. *Christology: A Biblical, Historical, and Systematic Study of Jesus*, Oxford: Oxford University Press, 1995.

Schnackenburg, Rudolf. *Jesus in the Gospels: A Biblical Christology*, trans. O. C. Dean, Jr, Louisville, KY: Westminster John Knox, 1995.

Scroggs, Robin. *Christology in Paul and John*, Proclamation Commentaries, Philadelphia, PA: Fortress Press, 1988.

Tuckett, Christopher M. *Christology and the New Testament: Jesus and His Earliest Followers*, Louisville, KY: Westminster John Knox, 2001.

Witherington, Ben. *The Christology of Jesus*, Minneapolis, MN: Fortress Press, 1991.

—— *The Many Faces of Christ: The Christologies of the New Testament and Beyond*, Companions to the New Testament, New York: Crossroad, 1998.

CHRONOLOGY

The birth of Jesus

Since early Christians were more concerned with the fact of Jesus' birth and not the exact date, the time of his birth can be best determined by considering the year of Herod's death, the census of Quirinius, and the star of the Magi.

The death of Herod

The Scriptures note that Jesus was born before Herod the Great died (Matt 2:15–16, 19–20) which, according to Josephus, was preceded by a lunar eclipse (Josephus *A.J.* 17.6.4:167) occurring on 12/13 March 4 BC. Soon after his death a Passover took place on 11 April 4 BC, placing Herod's death between 12 March and 11 April 4 BC, thus setting Jesus' birth no later than March/April of 4 BC.

The census of Quirinius

Prior to Jesus' birth Augustus decreed a worldwide census, the first of which occurred during the time when Quirinius was governor of Syria (Luke 2:1–5). It is difficult to pinpoint the exact date of this census. Certainly it is not the same one organized by Quirinius in AD 6 because that one occurred immediately after the deposition of Herod's son Archelaus (Acts 5:37), whereas the census of Luke 2 was in the context of the birth narrative of Jesus in the days of Herod the Great (Luke 1:5). There has been much discussion regarding the adjective "first" in connection with the census in Luke 2:2. Most likely the solution lies in considering that the adjective "first" is used adverbially thus, "This census occurred *before* Quirinius was governor of Syria." Possibly then this census occurred when Herod the Great was in a weakened state politically and healthwise, sometime around 6 to 4 BC.

The star of the Magi

According to Matt 2:1–12, the Magi (astrologers) from the East came to Jerusalem searching for

Jesus because they had seen a star at its rising. Modern astronomers note that a massing of the planets Jupiter and Saturn with Mars (which occurs every 805 years) occurred in February 6 BC and would have alerted the Magi that something significant was about to occur. About a year later, March/April of 5 BC, the Magi observed the star mentioned in Matt 2:2 and traveled to Israel. As they arrived they saw once again the star they had seen in the East standing over where Jesus was, namely, Bethlehem (2:9). This star was not the massing of planets mentioned above because this phenomenon was too far removed from the earth to have led the Magi and to have stood precisely over Bethlehem. On the other hand, a comet would have been clearly visible to the naked eye for a prolonged period of time. It has been recorded that during that time a tailed comet was visible for seventy days. It is likely that this what was first seen in the East in March/April of 5 BC and would have been visible in Bethlehem in April/May.

Therefore, the preceding astrological information, along with the census having occurred between 6 and 4 BC and Herod's death having occurred in the spring of 4 BC, all point to the conclusion that Jesus was born in the spring of 5 BC.

The commencement of Jesus' ministry

The beginning of Jesus' ministry is indicated by three chronological markers: the beginning of John the Baptist's ministry, the beginning of Jesus' ministry, and the first Passover of Jesus' ministry.

The commencement of John the Baptist's ministry

Luke 3:1–3 specifically states that John the Baptist's ministry began in the fifteenth year of Tiberius. But to which calendar was Luke referring? The fifteenth year of the Julian calendar would have been 1 January to 31 December AD 29 but if reckoned from Tiberius' regnal year, the normal Roman method, the fifteenth year would be 19 August AD 28 to 18 August 29. Using either one of these calendars, the fifteenth year of Tiberius would have occurred sometime between 19 August 28 and 31 December 29. At some point during this period John the Baptist's ministry began.

The commencement of Jesus' ministry

Sometime after the beginning of John the Baptist's ministry Jesus was baptized and began his ministry at "'about' thirty years of age" (Luke 3:23). If Jesus had been born in the spring of 5 BC and was

baptized in the summer or autumn of AD 29, he would have been thirty-three years of age, agreeing with Luke's statement that Jesus was "about" thirty years old when he began his ministry.

The first Passover of Jesus' ministry

Not long after his baptism, the first recorded visit of Jesus to Jerusalem (John 2:13–3:21) marked the first Passover of his ministry. It was on this occasion that the Jews mentioned that Herod's temple had been constructed forty-six years earlier (John 2:20). According to Josephus the temple construction began in Herod's eighteenth year (*A.J.* 15.11.1:380) coinciding with the arrival of Augustus in Syria (*A.J.* 15.10.3:354) which, according to Dio Cassius, occurred in spring or summer of 20 BC (Dio Cass. 54.7.4–6). Significantly, there are two Greek words for temple. The first word, *hieron*, refers to the whole sacred area which included the three courts – court of the Gentiles, court of the women, and the priests' court (completed in AD 63). The second term for the temple, *naos*, was located within the priests' court and was completed by the priests in one year and six months (Josephus *A.J.* 15.11.6:421). This distinction is consistently maintained by Josephus and the New Testament. In discussing the temple with Jesus, the Jews were referring to the *naos* as having stood for forty-six years. Thus, if the construction of the *naos* commenced in 20/19 BC and was completed in one year and six months (18/17 BC), forty-six years later would be the year AD 29/30. This places the first Passover of Jesus' ministry in the spring of AD 30.

In conclusion, the fifteenth year of Tiberius, AD 28–29, marked the beginning of the ministry of John the Baptist. If John began his ministry in the first part of AD 29 and Jesus was baptized in the summer or autumn of that year, Jesus would have been thirty-three years old. His first Passover in AD 30 would have been four to nine months after he began his ministry, which was forty-six years after the *naos* had been completed. Thus, Jesus began his ministry sometime in the summer or autumn of AD 29.

The duration of Jesus' ministry

Although the gospel writers never specifically state the duration of Jesus' ministry, the three Passovers mentioned in the Gospel of John (2:13; 6:4; 11:55) indicate that his ministry spanned at least two years in addition to the time between his baptism and the first Passover of his ministry in AD 30, as mentioned above. However, there is a reasonable basis for the inclusion of an additional year of ministry between the Passovers of John 2:13 and 6:4. The Passover of John 6:4 occurred about the time he fed the 5,000, the only miracle mentioned in all four gospels. Previous to this event the Synoptic Gospels speak of the disciples plucking grain in Galilee (Matt 12:1; Mark 2:23; Luke 6:1) which would point to the harvest season a year earlier. Yet the Passover of John 2:13 is too early for this incident to have occurred because the Passover of John 2:13 occurred shortly after Jesus had been baptized and had started his ministry. Also, after the Passover of John 2:13 his ministry was in Judea, whereas the plucking of grain occurred after he arrived in Galilee. Hence, the plucking of the grain fits well with the Passover between the Passovers mentioned in John 2:13 and 6:4.

Two additional time notes substantiate an additional year between these two Passovers. First, after the first Passover of John 2:13 Jesus ministered in Judea and then went into Samaria, during which time he noted that there were four months until harvest (John 4:35), pointing to the following January/February. Second, there is another feast mentioned in John 5:1. Although not specified and some think it refers to another Passover, it more likely refers to the Feast of Tabernacles. These two time notes substantiate the need for another Passover between the Passovers of John 2:13 and 6:4. Consequently, this suggests that there were four Passovers during Jesus' public ministry which would make possible a span of three and a half or three and three-quarter years.

The death of Jesus

This is divided into two parts: the day of Jesus' death and the year of his death.

The day of Jesus' death

Although most think that Jesus died on the Friday of passion week, some propose that he died either on Wednesday or Thursday because of his statement that he would be three days and three nights in the heart of the earth (Matt 12:40). However, when one considers that the Jews reckoned a part of a day as a whole day, there would be no problem of Jesus' death having occurred on Friday. Furthermore, repeatedly there is mention that Jesus' resurrection occurred on the third day (not on the fourth day) (e.g. Matt 16:21; 17:23; Luke 9:22; 18:33; Acts 10:40; 1 Cor 15:4). Also, the gospels specifically state that the day before the Sabbath was the day of his death (Matt 27:62; Mark 15:42; Luke 23:54; John 19:14, 31, 42). Therefore, the

scriptural evidence would indicate that Friday was the day of the week on which Jesus died.

A problem to be resolved is whether or not Jesus ate the Passover. All the gospels mention that on the day before his crucifixion, Jesus ate the Last Supper (Matt 26:20; Mark 14:17; Luke 22:14; John 13:2; cf. also 1 Cor 11:23). On the one hand, the Synoptic Gospels (Matt 26:17; Mark 14:12; Luke 22:7–8) report that the Last Supper was the Passover meal celebrated on Thursday evening, Nisan 14, and that Jesus was crucified the following day, namely, Friday Nisan 15. On the other hand, John mentions that the Jews who took Jesus to the Praetorium did not enter it "in order that they might not be defiled but might eat the Passover" (John 18:28) and that Jesus' trial was on the "day of preparation for the Passover," not after the eating of the Passover (John 19:14). This implies that Jesus' Last Supper (which occurred on Thursday night, Nisan 13) was not a Passover and that Jesus was tried and crucified on Friday Nisan 14, just before the eating of the Jewish Passover. Several suggestions have been proposed to resolve the difference between the Synoptic Gospels and the Gospel of John. First, some propose that the Last Supper was not a Passover meal but a meal the night before the Jewish Passover (John 13:1, 29), yet the Synoptic Gospels explicitly state that the Last Supper was a Passover (Matt 26:2, 17, 18, 19; Mark 14:1, 12, 14, 16; Luke 22:1, 7, 8, 13, 15). Second, some think that Jesus and his disciples had a private Passover. But this would not be possible because the Passover lamb would be slaughtered within the temple precincts and the priests would not have allowed the slaughter of a Paschal lamb for a private Passover. Third, some think that Jesus and his disciples celebrated the Passover according to the Qumran calendar, but there is no evidence that they followed the Qumran calendar. Fourth, some suggest that the Passover was celebrated on two consecutive days since it would have been impossible to slaughter all the Passover lambs on one day. Fifth is the proposal that different calendars were used. On the one hand the Synoptic Gospels used the method of the Galileans and the Pharisees in reckoning the day from sunrise to sunrise, thus Jesus and his disciples had the Paschal lamb slaughtered in the late afternoon of Thursday Nisan 14, and later that evening they ate the Passover with the unleavened bread. On the other hand, John's Gospel seems to have followed the method of the Judeans by reckoning the day from sunset to sunset, allowing the Judean Jews to have the Paschal lamb slaughtered in the late afternoon of Friday Nisan 14 and eaten it for

Passover with the unleavened bread that night, Nisan 15. Thus, Jesus had eaten the Passover meal when his enemies, who had not as yet had the Passover, arrested him. This last view best resolves the difference between the Synoptic Gospels and John's Gospel.

The year of Jesus' death

Although the proposed years of Jesus' death range from AD 21 to AD 36, they can be narrowed by several considerations.

The officials of the trial

The three officials involved in the trial of Jesus were Caiaphas, the high priest (Matt 26:3, 57; John 11:49–53; 18:13–14), who served from AD 18 to Passover of AD 37 (Josephus *A.J.* 18.2. 2:35; 4. 3:90–95); Pilate, prefect of Judea (Matt 27:2–26; Mark 15:1–15; Luke 23:1–25; John 18:28–19:16; Acts 3:13; 4:27; 13:28; 1 Tim 6:13), who ruled from AD 26 to 36 (Josephus *A.J.* 18.2.2:35; 18.4.2:89); and Herod Antipas, tetrarch of Galilee and Perea (Luke 23:6–12), who reigned from 4 BC until AD 39 (Josephus *A.J.* 17.11.4:317–18; 18.7.2:252; 19.8.2:351). Hence, Jesus' trial must have occurred between AD 26 and 36.

The contribution of astronomy

Since it was concluded that Jesus was crucified on Friday Nisan 14, there is a need to determine when Nisan 14 fell on Friday within AD 26–36. Studies indicate the only possible years are AD 27, 30, 33, and 36. Of these, AD 27 is the least likely astronomically, and it is questionable as to whether or not Nisan 14 fell on Friday in AD 30 and 36. The least problematic date astronomically is AD 33.

The ministry of Jesus

Having discussed the ministry of Jesus earlier, it is safe to eliminate AD 27 and 36 because neither fit within the time frame of his ministry. Although many accept an AD 30 date for Jesus' crucifixion this presents a problem if the beginning of John the Baptist's ministry occurred in the fifteenth year of Tiberius, AD 29 (Luke 3:1–3), for this would mean that Jesus' ministry could not have lasted more than one year which, as discussed earlier, is not possible. Hence, the AD 33 seems to fit the evidence best.

The confirmation of history

Pilate is portrayed by his contemporary Philo (*Legat.* 301–2) and later by Josephus (*A.J.* 18.3.1:55–59;

B.J. 2.9.2–4:167–77) as one who was greedy, inflexible, and cruel and who resorted to robbery and oppression. This is in keeping with his portrayal in Luke 13:1 where he mixed the blood of the Galileans with their sacrifices. Yet, when he tried Jesus, Pilate is portrayed as one who submitted to the pressures of the religious leaders who were insisting that Jesus be handed over to them.

It is important to explain this change in attitude. Initially, it must be remembered that Pilate was probably appointed prefect of Judea through the intervention of Lucius Aelius Sejanus, a confident of Tiberius, the prefect of the Praetorian Guard, and a devoted anti-Semite who wanted to exterminate the Jewish race (Philo *Flacc.* 1; *Legat.* 159–61). When Pilate instigated any problems with the Jews in Israel, Sejanus would not report it to Tiberius who resided on the Island of Capri. However, when Sejanus was deposed and executed by Tiberius on 18 October AD 31, Pilate no longer had the protection of his mentor in Rome. Later, it is most likely that Herod Antipas reported to Tiberius that Pilate had brought votive shields to Jerusalem, causing a riot among the Jews, probably during the time of the Feast of Tabernacles in AD 32 (Philo *Legat.* 299–305). Tiberius had ordered their immediate removal from Jerusalem. Now that Herod Antipas "had one" on Pilate, it is understandable that in the midst of the trial of Jesus when there was mention that Jesus was from Herod Antipas' territory of Galilee, Pilate was eager to have Herod Antipas, who was in Jerusalem, take part in the trial (Luke 23:6–12). In light of these factors, the AD 33 date for the trial makes good sense for three reasons: (1) Pilate's move to hand Jesus over to Antipas, although not required by Roman law, ingratiated himself to Antipas preventing another negative report of Pilate to the Emperor; (2) the seeming lack of progress of the trial in Luke 23:6–12 is understandable because Antipas' refusal to make a judgment prevented Pilate from making a bad report about him; and (3) the mention in Luke 23:12 that Pilate and Antipas were friends from that day onward would be inaccurate if the crucifixion were in AD 30 because at that time they were extremely at odds with each other in AD 32. Therefore, the AD 33 date fits best historically.

Conclusion

Having examined the data regarding the day of the week and month as well as the year of his death, the evidence points to Jesus' death having occurred on Friday Nisan 14, 3 April AD 33.

Summary of the dates

The birth, life, and death of Jesus can be charted as in Table 1.

Table 1 Chronology

Jesus' birth	spring 5 BC
Herod the Great's death	March/April BC
Jesus at the temple when twelve	Passover, 29 April AD 8
Commencement of John the Baptist's ministry	AD 29
Commencement of Jesus' ministry	summer/autumn AD 29
Jesus' first Passover (John 2:13)	7 April 30
Jesus' second Passover	25 April 31
Jesus at the Feast of Tabernacles (John 5:1)	21–28 October 31
Jesus' third Passover (John 6:4)	13/14 April 32
Jesus at the Feast of Tabernacles (John 7:2, 10)	10–17 September 32
Jesus at the Feast of Dedication (John 10:22–39)	18 December 32
Jesus' death	Friday, 3 April 33
Jesus' resurrection	Sunday, 5 April 33
Jesus' ascension (Acts 1)	Thursday, 14 May 33
Day of Pentecost (Acts 2)	Sunday, 24 May 33

HAROLD W. HOEHNER

Further reading

Beckwith, Roger T. *Calendar and Chronology, Jewish and Christian: Biblical, Intertestamental and Patristic Studies,* Arbeiten zur Geschichte des Antiken Judentums und des Urchristentums, ed. Martin Hengel, Vol. 33, Leiden: Brill, 1996.

Donfried, Karl P. "Chronology: New Testament," in David Noel Freedman (ed.) *Anchor Bible Dictionary,* New York: Doubleday, 1992, Vol. 1, pp. 1011–22.

Finegan, Jack. *Handbook of Biblical Chronology: Principles of Time Reckoning in the Ancient World and Problems of Chronology in the Bible,* revised edition, Peabody, MA: Hendrickson, 1998.

Hoehner, Harold W. *Chronological Aspects of the Life of Christ,* Grand Rapids, MI: Zondervan, 1977.

—— "The Date of the Death of Herod the Great," in Jerry Vardaman and Edwin M. Yamauchi (eds) *Chronos, Kairos, Christos: Nativity and Chronological Studies Presented to Jack Finegan,* Winona Lake, IN: Eisenbrauns, 1989, pp. 101–11.

Humphreys, Colin J. "The Star of Bethlehem, a Comet in 5 BC and the Date of Christ's Birth," *TynBul* 43:1 (May 1992) 31–56.

Humphreys, Colin J., and W. G. Waddington. "The Jewish Calendar, a Lunar Eclipse and the Date of Christ's Crucifixion," *TynBul* 43:2 (November 1992): 331–51.

Instone-Brewer, David. "Jesus's Last Passover: The Synoptics and John," *ExpTim* 112 (January 2001) 122–23.

Jeremias, Joachim. *The Eucharistic Words of Jesus,* trans. Norman Perrin, third edition, New Testament Library, London: SCM Press, 1966.

Maier, Paul L. "Sejanus, Pilate, and the Date of the Crucifixion," *CH* 37 (March 1968) 3–13.

—— *In the Fulness of Time: A Historian Looks at Christmas, Easter, and the Early Church,* San Francisco, CA: Harper, 1991.

Ogg, George. *The Chronology of the Public Ministry of Jesus,* Cambridge: Cambridge University Press, 1940.

Porter, Stanley E. "Chronology, New Testament," in Craig A. Evans and Stanley E. Porter (eds) *Dictionary of New Testament Background,* Downers Grove, IL: InterVarsity Press, 2000, pp. 201–8.

—— "The Reasons for the Lukan Census," in Alf Christophersen, Carsten Claussen, Jörg Frey, and Bruce Longenecker (eds) *Paul, Luke and the Graeco-Roman World: Essays in Honour of Alexander J. M. Wedderburn,* JSNTSup. 217, London: Sheffield Academic Press, 2002, pp. 165–88.

COINAGE, JEWISH

During Jesus' lifetime, a complex mixture of Greek, Roman, Phoenician, and Jewish coins circulated in Galilee and Judea. Both coins bearing the provincial name of Judea and coins issued by Jewish authorities can be considered Jewish. The earliest Jewish coins in the first sense were minted under Persian rule in or near Jerusalem for local use. These small silver coins weighing less than a gram imitate Greek designs but carry the Aramaic inscription "Yehud" (Judea). Neighboring regions, including Gaza and Samaria, produced similar issues. Larger denominations in silver and gold were produced only in central mints. A few coins in the Yehud series bearing the name of a governor or high priest may reflect periods of revolt against Persia.

Similar coins were produced under early Ptolemaic rule, although the ethnic was changed to the Hebrew "Yehudah." A portrait of Ptolemy I was added to this series under Ptolemy II Philadelphus. A few larger half-drachma coins bearing this portrait have been found. These early Jewish coins had probably disappeared from circulation before the time of Jesus. Under the later Ptolemies and Seleucids no Jewish coins in either sense were minted.

Hasmonean kings, beginning with John Hyrcanus I (135–104 BCE), or more likely Alexander Jannaeus (103–76 BCE), issued Jewish coins in the second sense, but only in bronze. Values ranging from the half-shekel down to the *prutah* (one sixty-fourth shekel), which could weigh as little as 0.2 grams. The first Hasmonean coins were important signs of autonomy. Their legends read "Yehonatan the King" in Hebrew on the obverse and "of King Alexander" in Greek on the reverse. The designs followed late Seleucid issues; lilies, stars, cornucopia, and anchors dominate. Many of these coins were later overstruck with "Yehonatan the High Priest and the Community of the Jews." Judas Aristobolus II (66–63 BCE) used designs as did John Hyrcanus II (63–40 BCE) until 47 BCE. When he received the title *ethnarch* from Julius Caesar, he modified the inscription to read "Yehohanan the High Priest, Head of the Community of the Jews." Mattathias Antigonus spent most of his reign (40–37 BCE) fighting with Herod for control of the region. His coins restore the title "king" in both Greek and Hebrew. His last issues introduced explicitly Jewish symbols: the menorah and showbread table. Many Hasmonean coins remained in circulation in New Testament times. During the Hasmonean period silver and gold denominations from the neighboring Hellenistic kingdoms remained in use. Tyre had begun minting silver shekels roughly equivalent in value to four Greek drachmas in the mid-second century BCE.

Under the Roman Empire only a few cities, including Tyre, were allowed to strike silver coins alongside the imperial mints. The Roman denarius and the slightly heavier Greek drachma are treated as interchangeable in New Testament texts. Each was roughly equivalent to a day's wage. Regional mints produced small bronze coins for use in everyday transactions. Most of the bronze coins produced in Judea and Galilee during the time of Jesus show an unusual deference to Jewish sensibilities in their imagery.

Herod the Great (37–4 BCE), as a client king, issued bronze coins on the Roman standard which can be considered Jewish in both senses. They carried the inscription "King Herod" in Greek, and the earliest issues gave the year of his reign. Herod employed mostly neutral emblems such palm branches, pomegranates, and anchors. Some images such as shields, helmets, the winged caduceus and tripod did suggest the Roman power behind his throne, but he avoided more offensive symbols such as the imperial portraits and Roman divinities typically found on provincial bronzes.

Later Herodians also issued bronze coins on the Roman standard. Herod Archaelaus (4 BCE–6 CE) controlled the Jerusalem mint and used designs similar to his father's.

Herod Antipas (4 BCE–39 CE) minted coins in Tiberias starting in the twenty-fourth year of his reign. He used only designs such as palm branches and clusters of dates that had associations with the land. Herod Phillip II (4 BCE–33 CE) ruled a region dominated by Gentiles and produced bronze coins that were typical of Roman provinces displaying the bust of the emperor, a Roman temple, and the emperor's name in Greek. In the decades after Jesus, Herod Agrippa I (37–44 CE) produced coins on both the Jewish and gentile patterns, probably for use in different parts of his territory. He was the first Herodian to put his own image on a coin. Agrippa II (50–95 CE) issued coins typical of provincial issues.

Five of the thirteen Roman procurators in Judea minted bronze coins for local use. They usually employed neutral symbols similar to those used by Herod the Great. Pilate, who depicted Roman religious implements, on some of his coins, was the exception.

The foreign character of gold (talents) and silver (stater, denarius, drachma) coins remained offensive to the most nationalistic portions of the Jewish population. That offense was compounded by the imperial imagery and inscriptions on the denarius (Matt 22:19–22; Mark 12:15). However, many of the bronze coins in circulation could be considered Jewish. The *as* (Matt 10:29; Luke 12:6) equal to one-tenth of a denarius and *quadrans* (Matt 5:26; Mark 12:42) equal to one-quarter *as* are Roman denominations but would include Herodian and provincial issues. The *lepton* (Mark 12:42; Luke 12:59, 21:2) can be understood as either the smallest Greek coin or the Hasmonean *prutah*. Thus, references to these coins and as to bronze coins in general (Mark 6:8) or small coins (John 2:15) are not specific. The widow's "mite" (*lepton*) in Mark 12:42 should probably be understood as the *prutah*, since two of them would equal the Roman *quadrans*, while the Greek *lepton* was only half as large.

Jewish coins, and especially their absence in the larger denominations, remained symbolically important in the generations after Jesus. During the revolt of 66–70 CE, both silver coins bearing the legend "Shekel of Israel" and bronze issues were minted. During the Bar Kochba revolt (132–35 CE) Roman coins were filed down and restamped with distinctively Jewish designs and legends.

ROBERT F. STOOPS

Further reading

Barag, D. and S. Qedar. "The Beginning of the Hasmonean Coinage," *Israel Numismatic Journal* 4 (1980) 8–21.

Betlyon, J. W. "Coinage," in D. N. Freedman (ed.) *The Anchor Bible Dictionary*, New York: Doubleday, 1992, Vol. 1, pp. 1076–89.

Hendin, D. *Guide to Ancient Jewish Coins*, New York: Attic Books, 1976.

Meshorer, Y. *Ancient Jewish Coinage*, 2 vols, Dix Hills, NY: Amphora Books, 1982.

—— "Jewish Numismatics," in R. A. Kraft and G. W. E. Nickelsburg (eds) *Early Judaism and its Modern Interpreters*, Atlanta, GA: Scholars Press, 1986, pp. 211–20.

Mildenberg, L. *The Coinage of the Bar Kokhba War*, ed. and trans. P. Mottahedeh, Typos Monographien zur antiken Numismatic 6, Aarau: Sauerländer, 1984.

Rappaport, U. "Numismatics," in W. D. Davies and L. Finkelstein (eds) *The Cambridge History of Judaism*, Cambridge: Cambridge University, 1984, Vol. 1, pp. 25–59.

COINAGE, ROMAN

Diversity characterized the coinage of the Roman East. Coins emanated from a variety of minting authorities (Roman imperial mints, individual Roman governors, client kings, and cities) and were struck on different monetary standards (Roman, Greek, and Phoenician). Most coins lacked inscriptions identifying their value, which complicates the archaeologist's task of determining their denominations.

At the top of the value system stood gold and silver. Almost all gold coins in circulation throughout the Empire were struck at imperial mints. Relatively few have been found in Palestine, presumably because they were less likely to be lost in antiquity and more likely to be melted down later.

In the early first century CE, most of Palestine's silver consisted of shekels and half-shekels struck at Tyre and, to a lesser extent, Sidon. Though Tyre's silver coins were decorated with its patron deity, Hercules-Melqart, on one side and an eagle on the other, they were nonetheless the coinage required for payment of the Jewish temple tax. This preference for Tyrian silver is sometimes attributed to its exceptionally high level of purity. Alternatively, the custom may derive from the fact that Tyre provided most of the region's silver when the tax was instituted in the Hasmonean period and for the entirety of the time it was collected. Josephus (*Ant.* 18.312) and Matthew (17:24–27) both refer to this tax as a didrachma tax, thus showing that two drachms (a Greek unit) were equivalent to a half-shekel (a Phoenician unit). Matthew identifies the coin Peter pulled from a fish's mouth as a *stater*, a general reference for a gold or silver coin. Sidon ceased producing silver coins in 43/44 CE, and Tyre did likewise in the 60s CE.

From that time on, the primary silver coinage consisted of tetradrachms from Roman imperial mints. Antioch provided most of these tetradrachms, though some came from other mints, such as Alexandria. Archaeological discovery of denarii is less frequent than that of other silver coins, suggesting that they were uncommon in Palestine, perhaps because they were usually struck at distant western mints like Rome. Thus, the easy availability of one when Jesus requested it to respond to a question about the census tax is somewhat curious (Mark 12:13–17 and parallels). The numerous references to denarii elsewhere in the gospels may reflect the gospels' provenances more than they do the monetary situation of early first-century CE Palestine. Matthew's reference to Judas's thirty pieces of silver (26:15, 27:3–10) does not identify a particular denomination, perhaps to maintain the clarity of the allusion to Zechariah 11:12–13. The *mina* (Luke 19:12–17) and talent (Matt 18:24) were older and larger units of measurement; by one estimate, they corresponded in value to approximately 600 and 6,000 denarii, respectively.

Most coins were of lesser value bronze. Old Hasmonean currency was still in circulation, as were newer issues of the Herodian rulers. Tyre, Sidon, and the imperial mint at Antioch provided a considerable amount of the region's bronzes. Cities in Palestine that struck bronze coinage during the first century included Ashkelon, Gaza, Caesarea Maritima, Ptolemais, Gerasa, and Scythopolis. Not until after the time of Jesus did Galilean cities strike civic coins; Tiberias struck its first in 53 CE, Sepphoris in 68 CE. Procuratorial coinage struck in Jerusalem circulated primarily within Judea, rarely reaching Galilee.

The gospels reflect the complexity of the region's monetary system, referring to a variety of bronze denominations. Thus, Mark's version of the story of the "widow's mite" (12:42) explains that two *lepta* (a Greek unit) equal a *quadrans* (a Roman unit); the Lukan parallel (21:2) omits the reference to the *quadrans*. In reporting Jesus' advice that one should settle one's differences with an opponent rather than risk losing one's last coin in court, Luke again uses Greek denomination, the *lepton*, while Matthew 5:26 refers to a *quadrans*. Other bronze coins mentioned in the gospels include the *as*, a Roman *assarion* (Luke 12:6/Matt 10:29) and the drachma (Luke 15:8–9).

The majority of coins, even those struck by the procurators in Jerusalem and by eastern imperial mints, employed Greek inscriptions, a custom that was the numismatic norm for the Roman East. In contrast, denarii bore Latin inscriptions. Occasionally, a city might place Latin upon its coins, as Ptolemais, newly re-founded as a Roman colony, did during the reign of Emperor Nero (54–68 CE). Such a choice reflected a strong statement of Roman identity. Coins would have been the primary means of exposure to Greek and Latin inscriptions for most people. Because the literacy rate was so low, however, most would not have been able to read them.

The designs of coins reflected the values of their minting authorities, and on some level they served as propaganda. The obverses of imperial tetradrachms and denarii bore the emperor's bust, a fact providing the context for Jesus' command to "render to Caesar the things that are Caesar's" (Mark 12:13–17 and parallels). Given the rarity of statues in the Jewish parts of Palestine, numismatic images would have been the main means there of propagating the imperial image. A variety of images were found on the reverses of coins produced at imperial mints, such as an eagle or deity. As for city coins, their obverses usually depicted the emperor, while their reverses often bore images of local significance, such as a galley for coastal cities. Some depicted patron deities, such as Dionysos for Scythopolis, Artemis for Gadara, or Tyche for many cities. In contrast, the designs of Judea's procuratorial coinage avoided anthropomorphic and zoomorphic imagery, perhaps in deference to Jewish sensibilities regarding graven images. Many bore plant imagery, such as an ear of grain, a palm tree, lilies, or a palm branch. Some coins of Pilate depicted a *lituus* and a *simpulum*, vessels associated with Roman cultic practices. After the first Jewish revolt, the Romans advertised their victory by striking coins at Caesarea Maritima and throughout the Empire depicting a captive Jew, the deity Nike, a military trophy, or similar martial imagery.

MARK A. CHANCEY

Further reading

Burnett, A. and M. Amandry (eds) *Roman Provincial Coinage*, Vols. 1–2, London: British Museum Press; Paris: Bibliothèque Nationale, 1992, 1999.

Chancey, M. A. "City Coins and Roman Power in Palestine: From Pompey to the Great Revolt," in Douglas R. Edwards (ed.) *Religion and Society in Roman Palestine: Old Questions, New Approaches*, New York and London: Routledge, 2004, pp. 103–12.

—— *Greco-Roman Culture and the Galilee of Jesus*, NTSMS 134, Cambridge: Cambridge University Press, 2005.

Kreitzer, L. *Striking New Images: Roman Imperial Coinage and the New Testament World*, Sheffield: Sheffield Academic Press, 1996.

Meshorer, Y. *City-Coins of Eretz Israel and the Decapolis in the Roman Period*, Jerusalem: Israel Museum, 1985.

—— *A Treasury of Jewish Coins*, Jerusalem: Yad Ben Zvi Press; Nyack, NY: Amphora Books, 2001.

Powell, M. A. "Weights and Measures," in David Noel Freedman (ed.) *The Anchor Bible Dictionary*, New York: Doubleday, 1992, Vol. 6, pp. 897–908.

Spijkerman, A. *The Coins of the Decapolis and Provincia Arabia*, Jerusalem: Franciscan Press, 1978.

COMPASSION ON THE POOR

In the NT the term most frequently used for "poor" is πτωχός; it occurs thirty-seven times. Twenty-four of its occurrences appear in the gospels: five in Mark (10:21; 12:42–43; 14:5, 7), five in Matthew (5:3; 11:5; 19:21; 26:9, 11), ten in Luke (4:18; 6:20; 7:22; 14:13, 21; 16:20, 22; 18:22; 19:8; 21:3), and four in John (12:5, 6, 8; 13:29). Elsewhere πτωχός occurs in Rom 15:26; 2 Cor 6:10; 8:2, 9; Gal 2:10; 4:9; Jas 2:2–3, 5–6; and Rev 2:9; 3:17; 13:16.

A comparison of the uses of πτωχός in the gospels suggests that Mark is the probable source for twelve occurrences: in Matt 19:21 and Luke 18:22 (cf. Mark 10:21, the rich young man), in Matt 26:9, 11 and John 12:5, 8 (cf. Mark 14:5, 7, the anointing at Bethany), and in Luke 21:2–3 (cf. Mark 12:42–43, the widow's offering. Note that Luke 21:2 replaces πτωχός with the rare synonym πενιχρός in the phrase "a poor widow"). Of the twelve remaining instances of πτωχός in the gospels, four are found in Q (Matt 5:3; 11:5; Luke 6:20; 7:22), six are peculiar to Luke (4:18; 14:13, 21; 16:20, 22; 19:8), and two are peculiar to John (12:6, 13:29).

As the foregoing references make clear, Jesus' compassion for the poor is well attested in the words and deeds attributed to him. Not only did he herald the good news of God's coming kingdom for the poor (Luke 4:18; 6:20; 7:22; Matt 5:3; 11:5), he also actively cared for them (Luke 7:21) and directed his disciples to do the same (Luke 14:13; 16:20–22; 18:22; see also Matt 25:31–46; Acts 11:27–30; 2 Cor 6:10; and for the only occurrence of πένης, "poor," "needy," in the NT, see 2 Cor 9:9; cf. Ps 111:9). Accordingly, Jesus' compassion on the poor mirrored that of the Holy One of Israel (see Luke 14:13), which is reflected in the Law (Exod 23:6, πένης; 23:11, πτωχός), the prophets (Amos 2:6, πένης; 2:7, πτωχός; cf. Isa 3:14–15; 10:2) and the Psalms (LXX Pss 71:2, 4, 12, 13; 81:3–4; 131:15; 139:13). Indeed, it appears that only in sayings attributed to Jesus are the poor actually promised the kingdom (Matt 5:3; Luke 6:20b; cf. James 2:5; Polycarp, *Phil.* 2:3; and *Gos. Thom.* 54). Some scholars question the authenticity of some of the sayings and deeds attributed to Jesus regarding the poor, but that Jesus had compassion on the poor is accepted universally and enthusiastically.

But who were the poor? They were for the most part literally poor, both economically and socially. They lacked not only material means, but also status and power within their society and culture (see Matt 5:3–5; Luke 21:2–3; cf. LXX Ps 67:6).

Observing the frequency of πτωχός in the NT and its typical use in Greek parlance as a term for "the beggarly poor," and the concomitant infrequency of the term πένης, and its common meaning, "a day laborer," some scholars hold that the poor on whom Jesus had compassion were only the poorest of the poor. This seems improbable, however, for several reasons. On the one hand, the terminology in question is ambiguous. Already in the LXX, as even the few references above make clear, the distinction between πτωχός and πένης was blurred, just as it is in the NT. Further, there is nothing in the Jesus tradition that requires such a narrow understanding of πτωχός. On the other hand, while the economic and social aspects of poverty are never lost in the sayings and concern of Jesus, the religious dimensions of the term "poor" appear to be just as important.

At least as early as some of the Psalms, both πτωχός and πένης, and related terms, such as ταπεινός, "humble, lowly" (LXX Pss 71:4, 12–13; 81:3), were understood as references not just for those who were literally poor, but also for those who trusted in and depended upon God. These were the pious poor, those who loved and obeyed God (Ps Sol. 15:1–3). Moreover, while some of them were destitute, others of them were not. The tradition of the pious poor was very important in the Jesus tradition, just as it was in Israel's scripture before him and in the church after him. Accordingly, the eschatological reversal in Luke 6:20b//Matt 5:3 and James 2:5 is not a heavenly reward for earthly poverty; rather is it God's gracious promise to the poor who trust in and depend upon God. Within the tradition of the piety of the poor, the opposite of "poor" is not necessarily "rich" but "wicked" or "sinner" (LXX Pss 9:23; 81:3). It appears that Jesus' blessing of the poor (Luke 6:20b//Matt 5:3) was correlative to his warning of the rich (Luke 16:13//Matt 6:24; Mark 10:23–26//Matt 19:23–26. Luke 6:24, "woe to you ... rich," is probably a creation of the evangelist, but it does not distort Jesus' compassion for the rich). It would seem unwise, therefore, to separate Jesus's compassion on the poor from his compassion on the rich. Indeed, the God whom Jesus proclaimed is the maker and just judge of both the rich and the poor (1 Sam 2:7–8; cf. Lev 19:15, 18).

Some groups within Jesus' milieu referred to themselves as "the poor" of God (see 1QpHab 12:3, 6, 10), but Jesus apparently did not refer to himself or his disciples in this fashion. If he really was a "carpenter" (Mark 6:3), and there appears to be no significant historical reason to doubt that he

was, then, though he would hardly be well off economically, he would not be among the poorest of the poor. The poverty that he endured as a peripatetic prophet and teacher would have been voluntary, assumed for the sake of his mission (Luke 9:58//Matt 8:20). That he had supporters who had material means and shared hospitality with him (for example, Zacchaeus, Luke 19:1–10), would further suggest that while his compassion for the literally poor was fundamental to his message and mission, it was not the whole of either.

WESLEY H. WACHOB

Further reading

Betz, Hans Dieter. *The Sermon on the Mount*, Hermeneia, Minneapolis, MN: Fortress Press, 1995.
Crossan, John Dominic. *The Historical Jesus: The Life of a Mediterranean Jewish Peasant*, San Francisco, CA: Harper & Row, 1991.
Davies, W. D. and Dale Allison. *A Critical and Exegetical Commentary on the Gospel According to Saint Matthew*, 3 vols, Edinburgh: T. & T. Clark, 1988–97.
Keck, Leander E. *Who is Jesus? History in the Perfect Tense*, Columbia, SC: University of South Carolina Press, 2000.
Meier, John P. *A Marginal Jew: Rethinking the Historical Jesus*, 3 vols, ABRL, New York: Doubleday, 1991–2001.

CONZELMANN, HANS

Born in the small town of Tailfingen in Württemberg, Hans Conzelmann (1915–89) studied theology in Tübingen and Marburg where he became acquainted with Hans von Soden and Rudolf Bultmann. His first examination by the local church was in Tübingen, where he became part of the "Würtembergische Sozietät" which was in opposition to the Nazi government and the church of Würtemberg under its bishop Wurm. Conzelmann's theological education was interrupted by military service where he suffered serious wounds. His dissertation on the Geography of Luke was accepted in 1951 followed by his rehabilitation in 1952 (Heidelberg). In 1954 he became a professor in Zürich. He spent the main part of his career as professor in Göttingen from 1960 to 1978. During that time he wrote different textbooks on the history of Early Christianity, New Testament Theology, and his major commentary on 1 Corinthians (*Der erste Brief an die Korinther* [KEK 5; Göttingen: Vandenhoeck & Ruprecht, 1969]; English translation: 1988).

Like his German contemporaries, Conzelmann contributed to a constructive dialogue with Bultmann's theology of the study of the historical Jesus and to redaction criticism. His approach was based on the theological, philosophical, and form-historical suppositions of Bultmann. Conzelmann adopted these in his own way for the quest for Jesus and the interpretation of the Lukan writings which were composed from the currently respected tradition.

Conzelmann's longer article on Jesus first appeared in the third edition of *Religion in Geschichte und Gegenwart* ("Religion in Past and Present"). This article subsequently was edited and translated into English, which is the only other complete research of Jesus and his life that German scholars belonging to new or second quest for Jesus produced.

Conzelmann may be one of those scholars who understood most clearly that the new approach to the historical Jesus needed a verifiable methodology. Criticizing his contemporaries for their lack of methodology (1974: 24: "*Schluß mit der methodischen Anarchie!*" = "An end to methodological anarchy!"), he tried to establish appropriate criteria. A starting point for this reconstruction could be a critically evaluated core of the parables of Jesus (1974: 25) that could be used as a critical tool for authenticating the words of Jesus. Although clearly acknowledging that Jesus was part of ancient Palestinian Judaism, Conzelmann particularly adopted the criterion of double dissimilarity (1959: 623), which was defined as only those materials that could not be derived from Jewish thinking or from the faith and theology of the later Christian community could be authentic (1959: 623). In that strict sense, of course, the reconstruction would not lead to a reliable picture of the historical Jesus but instead into a dogmatic and artificial construction in danger of separating Jesus, the creative Jew, from his historic background and, second, from his effect on the early Christian community.

According to Conzelmann, any historian could hypothesize about the historical Jesus and his proclamation. Nevertheless – and here Conzelmann clearly followed Bultmann's theological concept – the historical investigation of Jesus did not undermine the basis of Christian faith (1959: 648–51). Conzelmann repeated Bultmann's dictum that the only thing of relevance is the naked fact of the presence of Jesus (1959: 651): "*so kann der Bezug des Glaubens auf den historischen J. nur ein jeweilig-punktueller sein: der einzige historische Fixpunkt ist in der Tat das nackte Daß des Dagewesenseins Jesu*" (= "then the relationship of faith to the historical Jesus can only be a specific punctiliar one: The single historical fixed point is in fact the naked 'that' of the existence of Jesus").

Regarding the sources for the Jesus quest, Conzelmann focuses on the Synoptic Gospels and attributes some additional relevance to the "agrapha" (sayings of Jesus not found in the canonical gospels) and to kerygmatic formulas. A major topic in the proclamation of Jesus is God's coming kingdom. As a disciple of Bultmann, Conzelmann understood Jesus' teaching about God's kingdom in an existential philosophical manner. Jesus did not teach about any specific understanding of the future, but he focused on the person and it was Jesus, and he alone, that asked a person for immediate repentance (1974: 53). There is nothing about the future that is not a decisive determination of one's current situation (1959: 644). Within the teaching of Jesus, in contrast to John the Baptist, the theme of salvation became a central aspect: the primary element is the absolute focus on the promise of salvation ("*Absolutheit der Heilszusage*"; 1959: 633). Important is the inseparable connection with the person who proclaimed Jesus ("*unlösbar mit seiner Person verbunden*"; 1974: 52). There is little known about any passage of time, but Jesus' claim confronted the addressees and led them to a decision. In this way Jesus reduced all speculation by his approach into a "*punctum mathematicum*" (1974: 54). By this, Conzelmann accepted an indirect christological appeal which was visible in Jesus' immediate confrontation with God (cf. 1954: 25). Both the coming events and the person have to be brought into an essential unity, however; no christological titles were used by Jesus, even the future Son of Man sayings were not in accordance with the core of Jesus' teaching (1974: 46–47).

Conzelmann's main contribution was to redaction criticism of the Gospel of Luke. In the first major contribution, in which he applied the method to Luke, he enriched the scholarly discussion with his still influential and controversially discussed thesis that in the Lukan portrait, Jesus was the "middle of time" ("*Mitte der Zeit*"). With reference to Acts, Luke reacted to the belated parousia of Jesus by understanding the time of the church as a time governed by the Spirit. The time of Jesus was a time free from Satan (cf. Luke 4:13; 10:18), a time of salvation. The times of the Old Testament prophets separated from the time of Jesus reached up to and includes John the Baptist (Luke 16:16). The time of the church, which is still open for future events (Acts 28:31), started after Jesus. Conzelmann further elaborated this theological program in his commentary on Acts (1972). It is questionable if the model of periodization of time could be used so strictly because according to Luke 1–3, John the Baptist and Jesus are paralleled.

Conzelmann's redaction-critical were insights exhibited in his *Grundriß der Theologie des Neuen Testaments* (English translation: *An Outline of the Theology of the New Testament*) that he published first in 1968. Together with his disciple Andreas Lindemann, he edited a major textbook on New Testament method, reflecting and teaching the method of redaction criticism to New Testament students. It was based on the insight of the gospels as being not only a further process of gathering tradition, but an act of intentional formation based on a genuine concept of theology in that each writing of the New Testament exegesis benefits from his idea leading into modern text orientated methodologies. The program of redaction criticism inaugurated by scholars like Conzelmann, however, was correctly aware that behind the unity of gospel narrative stood a process of reshaping tradition.

MICHAEL LABAHN

Further reading

Conzelmann, Hans. "Die geographischen Vorstellungen im Lukasevangelium," diss. Masch., Tübingen, 1951.
—— *Die Mitte der Zeit. Studien zur Theologie des Lukas*, BHTh 17, Tübingen: Mohr Siebeck, 1954; seventh edition, 1993; ET: *The Theology of Saint Luke*, London: Faber & Faber, 1960.
—— *Jesus. Religion in Geschichte und Gegenwart*, third edition, Tübingen: Mohr Siebeck, 1959; ET: *Jesus: The Classic Article from RGG, Expanded and Updated*, Philadelphia, PA: Fortress Press, 1973.
—— *Die Apostelgeschichte*, HNT 7, Tübingen: Mohr Siebeck, 1963; second edition 1972; ET: *Acts of the Apostles*, Hermeneia, Philadelphia, PA: Fortress Press, 1987.
—— *Grundriß der Theologie des Neuen Testaments*, Einführung in die evangelische Theologie 2, Munich, Kaiser, 1967; fourth new revised version by Andreas Lindemann, UTB 1446, Tübingen: Mohr Siebeck, 1987; ET: *An Outline of the Theology of the New Testament*, New York: Harper & Row, 1969.
—— *Theologie als Schriftauslegung: Aufsätze zum Neuen Testament*, BevT, 65, Munich: Kaiser, 1974, pp. 18–29 ("Zur Methode der Leben-Jesu-Forschung" [originally published in 1959]), pp. 30–41 ("Das Selbstbewußtsein Jesu" [originally published in 1963/4]), pp. 42–61 ("Gegenwart und Zukunft in der synoptischen Tradition" [originally published in 1957]).
Lindemann, Andreas. *Arbeitsbuch zum Neuen Testament*, Tübingen: Mohr Siebeck, 1975; ET: *Interpreting the New Testament*, Peabody, MA: Hendrickson, 1988.
—— "Conzelmann, Hans," *Biograpisch-Bibliographisches Kirchenlexikon XXIII*, Nordhausen: Verlag Traugott Bautz, 2004, cols 239–43.
Lohse, Eduard. "Theologie als Schriftauslegung. Zum Gedenken von Hans Conzelmann," *TLZ* 115 (1990) 865–911.
Plümacher, Eckhard. "Conzelmann, Hans," *RGG*, fourth edition, 1999, Vol. 2, pp. 456–57.
Robinson, William C. *Der Weg des Herrn. Studien zur Geschichte und Eschatologie im Lukas-Evangelium. Ein Gespräch mit Hans Conzelmann*, Hamburg: Herbert Reich, 1964.
Rohde, Joachim. *Die redaktionsgeschichtliche Methode. Einführung und Sichtung des Forschungsstandes*, Hamburg: Furche-Verlag, 1966, pp. 125–44.
Talbert, Charles H. "Conzelmann, Hans Georg," in Donald K. McKim (ed.) *Major Biblical Interpreters*, Downers Grove, IL: InterVarsity Press, 1998, pp. 462–67.

CURSES AND WOE

No formal curses appear in the Jesus tradition. The three explicit usages of the Greek verb *kataraomai*, "to curse," are references to Jesus' words to a fig tree in Mark 11:14 (called a curse by Peter in Mark 11:21), to people who are cursing others (within an explication of the command to love one's enemies in Luke 6:28), and to the state of being cursed (uttered by the "King" to those at his left hand in Matt 25:41). Even when probing the tradition for instances which *de facto* could be understood as curses, the result is meager. The interpretation of the statement "may no one ever eat fruit from you again" (Mark 11:14), with its immediate outcome (cf. Mark 11:20), as a cursing of the fig tree can perhaps be accepted. However, the story in Mark 11:12–14, 20–21 is probably inauthentic. One also has to be careful not to turn all threatening words into curses. For instance, it is hardly accurate to label Jesus' prediction of the destruction of the Temple in Mark 13:1–2 as a curse. A sound basis of classification could be that a curse should take the form of a wish. So being, however, besides the fig tree story no actual curses can be found in the Jesus tradition, not among the woes either although a part of them do pronounce a judgment, even declare doom.

Hence, the historical Jesus most likely did not utter curses. Appropriately, then, Luke 9:54–55 tells of Jesus rebuking James and John for wishing to do so (cf. Mark 3:17). [Matt 27:25 has sometimes been interpreted as a self-curse of the people, but this probably reflects later hermeneutics. For self-curses inherent in making oaths or swearing (cf. Mark 14:71; par. Matt 26:74; see Oaths and swearing.]

Unlike curses, woes (expressed through the Greek interjection *ouai*, "woe," "alas"; cf. Hebr. *hoy*, *'oy*) are numerous in the Jesus tradition. Woes appear in Q (Matt 11:21/Luke 10:13; Matt 23/Luke 11; Matt 18:7/Luke 17:1) and Mark (Mark 13:17; 14:21; cf. 15:29). Additionally, there are some woes unique to Matthew or to Luke which, however, may almost all come from Q. Mark recounts only two woes uttered by Jesus, namely on those who are pregnant and nursing infants (Mark 13:17; cf.

Matt 24:19; Luke 21:23) and on the one who will betray the Son of Man (Mark 14:21; cf. Matt 26:24; and Luke 22:22). From Q, Matthew and Luke have both included woes on Chorazin and Bethsaida (Matt 11:21–22/Luke 10:12–14), about tithing (Matt 23:23/Luke 11:42), being tombs (Matt 23:27/Luke 11:44), building tombs (Matt 23:29–31/Luke 11:47–48), the kingdom of heaven/the key of knowledge (Matt 23:13/Luke 11:52), and about temptations to sin (Matt 18:7/Luke 17:1). Within the Q-block of Matt 23/Luke 11, Matthew includes even woes dealing with making a proselyte (Matt 23:15), swearing (Matt 23:16–22; cf. Matt 5:33–36), and cleaning the cup (Matt 23:25–26; cf. Luke 11:39–41). Luke, again, includes woes about best seats (Luke 11:43; cf. Matt 23:6–7) and burdens (Luke 11:46; cf. Matt 23:4). Matthew adds a second woe, namely on the world, to the Q-saying in Matt 18:7/Luke 17:1. Finally, after his account of the Beatitudes, Luke adds woes on those who are rich and full, who laugh and are spoken well of by all people (Luke 6:24–26).

Considering the broad attestation, woes as a form of speech can safely be attributed to Jesus himself. Woes represent a characteristically prophetic means of expression in the Old Testament, often used to voice anger for sins and wrongdoings (see, for example, Isa 5:8, 11, 18, 20, 21, 22; Hab 2:9, 12, 15, 19), sometimes grief on account of befallen or anticipated misfortunes and calamities (e.g. Isa 1:4; Jer 13:27; Zech 2:11[7]). Uttering woes goes thus well together both with Jesus' prophetic self-understanding and the element of judgment in his proclamation. The woes of Q may originally have existed as independent sayings. However, there is no reason why Jesus could not at times have delivered even series of woes. Models for such speeches were available in the Old Testament (cf. Isa 5 and Hab 2). And later in Judaism *1 En.* 94–100, for example, presents several lists of woes (see even Sir 2:12–14).

As to the historicity of the main bulk of the woes, i.e. those in Matt 23 and Luke 11, a central question is whether the allegations and polemics present in them can be situated in Jesus' time and place or whether they should rather be seen as reflecting a later Christian *Sitz im Leben.* The Matthean stereotypical phrase, "woe to you, scribes and Pharisees, hypocrites!" (Matt 23:13, 15, 23, 25, 27, 29), has usually been regarded as secondary. Its tendency to lump all Jews together (see also Matt 23:33–39) branding them as hypocrites betrays a later development of the tradition (cf. Matt 6:2, 5, 16). Initially, however, the woes probably targeted one particular group alone, as in

Luke (although Luke also presents lawyers/scribes as intervening the debate; cf. Luke 11:45; 11:53). As such, then, they are well understandable as an expression of an inner-Jewish controversy originating in Jesus' situation. In early Judaism, disparagement between the many different religious movements was usual. In fact, criticism similar to that in Matt 23/Luke 11, leveled by one Jewish group against another (probably precisely against the Pharisees), can be found in Qumran (4QpNah 1.3–4, 7; 2.8–9; 3.6–7; 1QH 10.31–34).

The woes in the Jesus tradition differ as to their targets, causes, and purposes. While the targets and causes are many, the purposes the woes are uttered with are basically two: to express sorrow or to pronounce a judgment. The purposes depend on who or what is targeted and for what cause.

1   **target** (woe on ...) – those who are pregnant and nursing infants (Mark 13:17)
    cause (because of ...) – the great distress that will befall (their not being able to flee)
    purpose – sorrow
    target (woe on ...) – the one who will betray the Son of Man (Mark 14:21)
    cause (because of ...) – betraying the Son of Man
    purpose – judgment: it would be better to be cast into the sea with a millstone round the neck

3   **target** (woe on ...) – the towns of Chorazin and Bethsaida (Matt 11:21–22/Luke 10:12–14)
    cause (because of ...) – not repenting
    purpose – judgment: even Tyre and Sidon will be better off on the judgment day

4   **target** (woe on ...) – the world (Matt 18:7)
    cause (because of ...) – temptations to sin with which it will be confronted
    purpose – sorrow

5   **target** (woe on ...) – the Pharisees/the Pharisees and the Scribes (Matt 23:23–31/Luke 11:42–52)
    5.1 **cause** (because of ...) – meticulous observance of tithes while neglecting justice, mercy, faith, and love of God
        purpose – judgment
    5.2 **cause** (because of ...) – being like whitewashed/unmarked tombs (Matt: thus unclean)
        purpose – judgment
    5.3 **cause** (because of ...) – building tombs of the prophets so agreeing with those who killed the prophets
        purpose – judgment
    5.4 **cause** (because of ...) – shutting the kingdom of heaven/having taken away

the key of knowledge and not entering even themselves

purpose – judgment

5.5 **cause** (because of ...) – making proselytes children of hell and being such even themselves

purpose – judgment

5.6 **cause** (because of ...) – teaching falsely on swearing

purpose – judgment

5.7 **cause** (because of ...) – cleaning the outside of the cup and the plate while being full of extortion and dissipation inside

purpose – judgment

5.8 **cause** (because of ...) – loving best seats and salutations

purpose – judgment

5.9 **cause** (because of ...) – loading men with heavy burdens

purpose – judgment

6 **target** (woe on ...) – the one by whom temptations to sin will come (Matt 18:7/Luke 17:1)

cause (because of ...) – ushering in the temptations to sin

purpose – judgment: it would be better not to have been born.

In three cases (cf. 2, 3, and 6) the judgment concerns doom that will befall sometime in the future. It is interesting to notice that both in Mark and Q the doom is described indirectly, using a periphrasis. This deviates somewhat from the way common in the Old Testament to supply the woes with squarely stated descriptions of doom (see even the woes in *1 En.* 94–100). In the woes addressed to the Pharisees/the Pharisees and the scribes (cf. 5), the judgment is akin to criticism and disparagement and appears (rather naturally) as embedded in the statements of the causes for the woes. In the woes expressing sorrow (cf. 1 and 4), again, the judgment has actually become the cause: those addressed are pitied because of the things they will have to suffer. Considering this last group of woes and the way their purpose is manifested, two of the four woes in Luke 6:24–26 (not included in the above chart), a

section clearly meant as pronouncing judgment, appear peculiar. In the second and the third woe of the section, the cause is formed by the judgment itself but still the purpose of the woes is not to express sorrow. Taken in isolation, uttering woes on full and happy people because they will have to hunger, mourn and weep (Luke 6:25) is actually well comparable to uttering a woe on pregnant and nursing people because they will be in great trouble in the coming tribulation (1). In other words, in themselves the two Lukan woes do not clearly reveal whether they aim to condemn or pity those who are going to suffer. The judgmental purpose of the woes is fully understandable only when they are viewed within their Lukan context, in particular, as being preceded by the Beatitudes (cf. Luke 6:20–23).

Hence, Jesus used not to utter curses. Still, woes seem to have served as a fairly regular means of expression for him. Maybe more can be seen here than a mere casual preference for one way of speech over another. Even when uttered with the purpose of pronouncing a judgment, there is often a warning aspect to the woes. Curses, instead, display an aspect of finality (or immediacy; see Mark 11:20; cf. also Luke 9:54 and 2 Kgs 1:10, 12) not usually found in the woes (cf., however, 2 and 6). Perhaps we see here the teaching of Luke 13:6–9 put into practice (cf. Matt 3:10/Luke 3:9; see even Matt 25:41 describing the judgment day).

TOM HOLMÉN

Further reading

Garland, D. E. *The Intention of Matthew 23*. Leiden: Brill, 1979.

Johnson, L. T. "The New Testament's Anti-Jewish Slander and the Conventions of Ancient Polemic," *JBL* 108 (1989) 419–41.

Meier, J. P. *A Marginal Jew: Rethinking the Historical Jesus. Volume II. Mentor, Message and Miracles*, New York: Doubleday, 1994.

Newport, K. G. C. *Sources and Sitz im Leben of Matthew 23*, Sheffield: Sheffield Academic Press, 1995.

Reiser, M. *Jesus and Judgment: The Eschatological Proclamation in its Jewish Context*, Minneapolis, MN: Fortress Press, 1997.

Weinfeld, M. "The Charge of Hypocrisy in Matthew 23 and in Jewish Sources," *Imm* 24/25 (1990) 52–58.

D

DAHL, NILS ALSTRUP

Dahl was born in Oslo, Norway, 25 June 1911. He was professor of New Testament at the University of Oslo 1946–65; professor of New Testament at Yale University, USA, 1965–80, and active as scholar and author in Oslo from 1980 till his death 2 July 2001. He published widely, mainly articles, on Paul, the concept of the church in the New Testament, and especially on the historical Jesus and Christology.

Dahl finished his doctoral dissertation, *Das Volk Gottes (The People of God)*, during the dramatic months following the German occupation of Norway 9 April 1940. Equally dramatic were the circumstances surrounding the publication of the book in 1941, and Dahl's doctoral disputation the same year. The great majority of the printed copies were confiscated by the German authorities, and the disputation took place one day after the Nazis had arrested the president of the University of Oslo and several of the professors. In 1944 Dahl himself was deposed and had to take refuge in Sweden.

These dramatic events were not completely unrelated to the contents of Dahl's dissertation. In this pioneering study he laid bare the deep Jewish roots of Jesus' thinking about the *ekklesia*, the renewed Israel that would result from his ministry. Dahl was influenced towards this point of view by German theologians, oppositional towards the Nazi regime, as well as by Swedish scholars, some of whom belonged to an ecclesiastical group advocating a new ecclesiastical consciousness in theology. His choice of subject for his dissertation was not unrelated to these biographical data.

In 1946 Dahl was appointed professor of New Testament at the Faculty of Theology, University of Oslo. He now turned his attention more fully to the problem that had been one of the sub-themes of his dissertation: the problem of the "historical Jesus." Typical of Dahl, he did not address the problem in a major monograph, but in several seminal articles, some of which were first published in Norwegian, and for a general audience. This is the case with his major contribution from 1953, "The Problem of the Historical Jesus." This article, later published in an English version in 1962, reopened the question of the historical Jesus in the wake of Bultmann's proscription of the issue, and did so one year before Ernst Käsemann's famous challenge to the Bultmann school in his "Das Problem des historischen Jesus." Unlike Käsemann, Dahl did not believe the way forward in Jesus research was to start exclusively from "a critically secured minimum" of authentic sayings of Jesus. He also doubted the validity of a mechanical use of the double criterion of difference (a saying of Jesus is authentic if it stands in clear contrast to contemporary Judaism as well as to the theology of the early community of disciples). He advocated instead an approach based on "cross-sections" in all layers of gospel traditions, combined with "longitudinal lines" that placed the sayings of Jesus within a continuum between the Judaism of his time and the theology of the first and later communities of believers. (At this point he acknowledges his debt to Julius Schniewind.)

Dahl was skeptical of any attempt to extricate a "historical Jesus" at complete variance with the memory Jesus had left in the available sources.

> In no case can any distinct separation be achieved between the genuine words of Jesus and constructions of the community. We do not escape the fact that we know Jesus only as the disciples remembered him. Whoever thinks that the disciples completely misunderstood their Master or even consciously falsifies his picture may give fantasy free reign. From a purely scientific point of view, however, it is logical to assume that the Master can be known through his disciples' words about him and their historical influence.
>
> (*The Crucified Messiah*, 67)

It seems fair to say that Dahl in his 1953 article anticipated insights spelled out more fully, e.g. in James Dunn's recent *Jesus Remembered*.

Unlike Bultmann, Dahl also recognized that Jesus accorded his own mission and his own person a decisive significance, albeit indirectly, in all of his public teaching, not least in his parables. Later Christology is not entirely without foundation in Jesus' own thinking. Historically speaking, the most certain fact we know about Jesus is that he was crucified as a messianic pretender. That is not an accidental fact about him; his life and mission are incomprehensible unless they made him "crucifiable." Dahl spelled this out in another article (first published in German in 1960), the title of which also became the title of his first collection of articles on Christology: "The Crucified Messiah."

In 1965 Dahl became professor of New Testament at Yale University, a position he held until he returned to Oslo in 1980. His teaching at Yale proved a great inspiration for many aspiring scholars, and many are those who proudly call him their teacher. During these years his many articles on Jesus and Christology were published in English in two volumes: *The Crucified Messiah and Other Essays* (1974); *Jesus in the Memory of the Early Church* (1976); followed up in 1991 by *Jesus the Christ: The Historical Origins of Christological Doctrine* (ed. Donald H. Juel).

After his return to Oslo, Dahl again turned his main attention to Pauline studies, a life-long interest with him. During his Yale years he had published *Studies in Paul: Theology for the Early Christian Mission* (1977). Now, in his 89th year, he published an entirely fresh collection of pioneering *Studies in Ephesians* (2000).

Dahl represented a rare combination of deep Christian piety and a critically acute mind. In him, historical criticism of the most rigorous kind coexisted with an ecclesiastically committed theology in an apparently effortless harmony.

OSKAR SKARSAUNE

Further reading

Borgen, Peder J. "Minnetale" [obituary], in *Det Norske Videnskaps-Akademi: Årbok 2002*, Oslo: Det Norske Videnskaps-Akademi, Novus Forlag, 2004, pp. 143–9 [in Norwegian].

Dahl, Nils Alstrup. *Das Volk Gottes: Eine Untersuchung zum Kirchenbewusstsein des Urchristentums*, Skrifter utgitt av Det Norske Vitenskapsakademi, II. Historisk-Filosofisk Klasse, No. 2, Oslo, 1941; repr. Darmstadt: Wissenschaftliche Buchgesellschaft, 1962.

—— *Kurze Auslegung des Epheserbriefes*, Göttingen: Vandenhoeck & Ruprecht, 1965.

—— *The Crucified Messiah and Other Essays*, Minneapolis, MN: Augsburg, 1974.

—— *Jesus in the Memory of the Early Church*, Minneapolis, MN: Augsburg, 1976.

—— *Studies in Paul: Theology for the Early Christian Mission*, Minneapolis, MN: Augsburg, 1977.

—— *Jesus the Christ: The Historical Origins of Christological Doctrine*, ed. Donald H. Juel, Minneapolis, MN: Fortress Press, 1991.

—— *Studies in Ephesians: Introductory Questions, Text- and Edition-Critical Issues, Interpretation of Texts and Themes*, WUNT 131, Tübingen: Mohr Siebeck, 2000.

Jervell, Jacob and Wayne A. Meeks (eds) *God's Christ and His People: Studies in Honour of Nils Alstrup Dahl*, Oslo: Universitetsforlaget, 1977.

Juel, Donald H. "Foreword," in N. A. Dahl, *Jesus the Christ: The Historical Origins of Christological Doctrine*, Minneapolis, MN: Fortress Press, 1991, pp. 7–9.

Mæland, Bård and Fredrik Saxegaard. "Nils Alstrup Dahl," *Ung Teologi* 26.2 (1993) 49–61 [in Norwegian].

Moxnes, Halvor. "Dahl, Nils Alstrup," in *Norsk Biografisk Leksikon Vol. 3*, Oslo: Aschehoug, 2000, pp. 274–6 [in Norwegian].

DANIEL

The name "Daniel" (דָּנִיֵּאל, "my judge is El") is very old (Noth, 35), appearing in OB cuneiform texts as early as the eighteenth century (*da-ni-èl*, *ARM* VII 263 iii 23') and Canaanite cuneiform texts from the fourteenth century BCE (e.g. *Dnil* in *CAT* 1.17 i 6). In the *Aqhat* myth from Ugarit a king named *Dnil* enacts the role of a "childless patriarch" unable to sire children apart from the gracious intervention of a benevolent deity (McAfee). Most interpreters recognize this role as strikingly similar to those enacted by Kirta (another Canaanite king, *CAT* 1.14 i 1–25) and Abraham (Gen 15:2; Hendel, 37–59). Opinions divide, however, over (a) the characteristics of this *Dnil* vis-à-vis those of דָּנִאֵל in Ezek 14:14–20, as well as (b) the degree to which either figure reflects the characteristics of the young protagonist in MT *Daniel*. Many interpreters believe they do because "righteousness" (צדקה, Ezek 14:14; *CAT* 1.17 v 7–8) and "(mantic) wisdom" play such obvious roles (חכם, Ezek 28:3; *CAT* 1.19 i 38–42; Müller 93–4; Day 181)

Some inevitably disagree, however (Dressler, Ferch), even though "righteousness" and "wisdom" also figure prominently in the character of the young "aristocrat" introduced in Dan 1:3 (הפרתמים = "the first" in Old Persian; Gehman 327). God gifts this young man with "knowledge and skill in all literature and wisdom" (מדע והשכל בכל־ספר וחכמה, Dan 1:17b), as well as the ability to "interpret" (פשׁר; lit. "unravel") "visions and dreams" (חזון וחלמות, Dan 1:17c). The apocryphal books Bel and the Dragon and Susanna emphasize the wisdom/knowledge/judgment component (particularly in Theodotion's recension; McLay 15), while MT Daniel is the major source of information about Daniel's oneiromantic skills, even as the visions in Dan 7–12 reflect an awareness of prophetic/sapiential traditions elsewhere in the Hebrew Bible (Lucas 69; Moore 1983: 29–32).

Whether the deepest roots of these images originate in Babylonian (Gunkel 323–55), Canaanite (Emerton 241–2), or Jungian myth (Wink 83–117), the images themselves fuse over time with those of other seers (Moore 1990: 41–4, 66–86, 123) to create the black-and-white framework which is apocalyptic Judaism. Within this framework the "Son of Man" vision in Dan 7:13–14 virtually colorizes everything it touches as an apocalyptic trajectory begins to form – a trajectory which arcs its way through 2 Esdra 13:1–13; *1 En.* 46:1; 47:3; 71:14, and several Danielic texts from Qumran (Flint). The ambiguity shrouding these images continues to lure interpreters into guessing the "identity" of Daniel's בר אנשׁ ("Son of Man" in Aramaic), either as (a) a specific entity (e.g. the archangel Michael; Collins 1993: 304–10), or (b) a non-specific "impulse" (Wink 83).

At any rate, the early Nazarenes, like the Enochian (*1 En.* 71:14; yet cf. 70:1) and Essene communities before them (4Q246 ii 1; Collins 1997), seize on this mythological imagery to explicate the character of *their* founder, Jesus of Nazareth. Whereas the Johannine community uses it to help explain the mystery of the Incarnation (Moloney; Pryor) the Synoptics use it to describe Jesus' "heavenly throne" (Matt 19:28), his "seat at the right hand of Power" (26:64), his "lordship" over the "angels" (13:41), his "lordship" over the Law (the Sabbath, Matt 12:8), his heavenly "glory" (25:31), and his "coming on the clouds of heaven" (24:30). All these images flow out of the "Son of Man"

vision in Dan 7:13–14, whether or not the Nazarenes sift it through Danielic, Enochian, or recombinant filters (Stuckenbruck; Boccaccini). In short, while some interpreters continue to view the "Son of Man" figure in the NT as (a) the Coming One, (b) the Suffering/Risen One, or (c) as the Present One (Bultmann 1.30), textual discoveries in the Judean Desert since 1947 are leading most contemporary interpreters to view it as (a) directly related, (b) indirectly related, or (c) unrelated to the "Son of Man" described in Dan 7:13–14 (Vermes 177–86).

In Matthew's "little apocalypse" (chapter 24) Jesus warns his disciples to flee from an impending disaster for which the eschatological trigger is the appearance of a "desolating sacrilege" (τὸ βδέλυγμα τῆς ἐρημώσεως) "standing in the holy place, as was spoken of by the prophet Daniel" (Matt 24:15–18). Most interpreters agree that the historical referent to this "sacrilege" is the השקוץ משומם described in Dan 11:31 (OG); i.e. the pig slaughtered on the altar of Zeus within the precincts of the Temple (1 Macc. 1:54). That the Matthean Jesus reflects on this catastrophe in order to predict another one probably reflects widespread dread of war with Rome, a feeling which becomes painful reality with the arrival of Vespasian's legions (Price 265–7). Dismissing the radical narcissism driving contemporary Western apocalypticism (Boyer 299), historians find the most likely options for this "sacrilege" to be (a) the erection of a statue to the emperor within Temple precincts, and/or (b) the public defrocking of the High Priest (Josephus, *J.W.* 4.150–7).

MICHAEL S. MOORE

Further reading

Boccaccini, G. *Roots of Rabbinic Judaism: An Intellectual History from Ezekiel to Daniel*, Grand Rapids, MI: Eerdmans, 2002.

Boyer, P. *When Time Shall Be No More: Prophecy Belief in Modern American Culture*, Cambridge, MA: Belknap Press of Harvard University, 1992.

Bultmann, R. *Theology of the New Testament*, New York: Scribner's, 1951.

Collins, J. J. *Daniel*, Hermeneia, Minneapolis, MN: Fortress Press, 1993.

—— "The Background of the 'Son of God' Text," *BBR* 7 (1997) 51–61.

Day, J. "The Daniel of Ugarit and Ezekiel and the Hero of the Book of Daniel," *VT* 30 (1980) 174–84.

Dressler, H. H. P. "The Identification of the Ugaritic Daniel with the Daniel of Ezekiel," *VT* 29 (1979) 152–61.

Emerton, J. A. "The Origin of the Son of Man Imagery," *JTS* 9 (1958) 225–42.

Ferch, A. J. "Daniel 7 and Ugarit: A Reassessment," *JBL* 99 (1980) 75–86.

Flint, P. W. "The Daniel Tradition at Qumran," in J. Collins and P. W. Flint (eds) *The Book of Daniel: Composition and Reception, Vol. 2*, VTSupp 83:2, Leiden: Brill, 2003, pp. 329–67.

Gehman, H. S. "Notes on the Persian Words in the Book of Esther," *JBL* 43 (1924) 321–8.

Gunkel, H. *Schöpfung und Chaos in Urzeit und Endzeit*, Göttingen: Vandenhoeck & Ruprecht, 1895.

Hendel, R. S. *The Epic of the Patriarch: The Jacob Cycle and the Narrative Traditions of Canaan and Israel*, HSM 42, Atlanta, GA: Scholars Press, 1987.

Lucas, E. "Daniel: Resolving the Enigma," *VT* 50 (2000) 66–80.

McAfee, E. C. "The Patriarch's Longed-for Son: Biological and Social Reproduction in Ugaritic and Hebrew Epic," unpublished ThD dissertation, Cambridge, MA: Harvard, 1996.

McLay, T. *The OG and Th Versions of Daniel*, SBLSCS 43 Atlanta, GA: Scholars Press, 1996.

Moloney, F. J. *The Johannine Son of Man*, Rome: LAS, 1976.

Moore, M. S. "Resurrection and Immortality: Two Motifs Navigating Confluent Theological Streams in the Old Testament (Dan 12:1–4)," *Theologische Zeitschrift* 39 (1983) 17–34.

—— *The Balaam Traditions: Their Character and Development*, SBLDS 113, Atlanta, GA: Scholars Press, 1990.

Müller, H. P. "Magische-mantische Weisheit und die Gestalt Daniels," *UF* 1 (1969) 79–94.

Noth, M. *Die Israelitischen Personennamen im Rahmen der Gemeinsemitischen Namengebung*, Stuttgart: Kohlhammer, 1928.

Price, J. J. *Jerusalem Under Siege: The Collapse of the Jewish State*, Leiden: Brill, 1992.

Pryor, J. W. "The Johannine Son of Man and the Descent-Ascent Motif," *JETS* 34 (1991) 341–51.

Stuckenbruck, L. T. "Daniel and Early Enoch Traditions in the Dead Sea Scrolls," in J. Collins and P. W. Flint (eds) *The Book of Daniel: Composition and Reception, Vol. 2*, VTSupp 83.2, Leiden: Brill, 2003, pp. 368–86.

Vermes, G. *Jesus the Jew*, Philadelphia, PA: Fortress Press, 1973.

Wink, W. *The Human Being: Jesus and the Enigma of the Son of Man*, Minneapolis, MN: Fortress Press, 2002.

DAVID

David's anointing as king over Israel and Judah along with the establishment of Jerusalem as his capital is the climax of his rise to power (2 Sam 5). David's great political success, which saw the establishment of an empire that lasted forty years (c. 1010–1970 BCE) and stretched from Egypt to Mesopotamia, is matched by his spiritual success which saw a return of the ark to Jerusalem and an establishment of a covenant with YHWH that would ensure a perpetual dynasty. Despite personal and political failures, David emerges in Samuel as a repentant figure who seeks the will and relationship of YHWH – "a man after God's own heart" (1 Sam 13:14; cf. Acts 13:22). In the Chronicles narratives, latter Prophets, and the Writings, historical

portrayals of David along with his personal indiscretions appear unimportant. Instead, David is portrayed as a symbol of the ideal king whose intimacy with God (e.g. "son" in Ps 2:7) assures Israel of its favored status. The idealizations of David also play an important eschatological role especially during times of oppression when messianic expectations and hopes of liberation ran high.

Messianic expectations, however, do not imply a "generic" or only a royal messiah (in the line of David). During the Second Temple period, texts from the Scrolls and Pseudepigrapha, though arguably representative of the scribal class, convey that various messianic paradigms were at play which included not only that of king, but also that of priest, prophet, heavenly messiah, and various combinations of these (Collins 195–203). After the death of Herod the Great (4 BCE), those who placed themselves within the royal messianic paradigm as restorers of the Davidic line – and not all kingly aspirants did – were committed to the military overthrow of Roman occupation and are portrayed as bandits by Josephus, our best source, due to the devastating impact that armed resistance had on their own countrymen and on the disruption of the *pax Romana* (e.g. *Ant.* 17.278–85). Although Josephus refers to these charismatic aspirants using language such as "king," "kingship," and "diadem," he avoids, perhaps purposely, messianic language such as "branch," "son of David," and "messiah" (Horsley and Hanson 114). In deference to the Romans, Josephus emphasized David's literary accomplishments, wisdom, and fairness, while downplaying David's revolutionary hopes and connections with messianic expectations (Feldman). It is difficult to know whether all the aspirants actually identified themselves with David. On the one hand, there is some indication in the Roman period (e.g. 4Q246; *Pss. Sol.* 17) that popular Jewish eschatological hopes of liberation would be achieved militarily by an ideal Davidic king. Thus, it is possible that the royal aspirants in Josephus' accounts identified with such an ideal. On the other hand, apart from generic similarities, early Jewish texts which interpret the Davidic dynasty messianically (e.g. *Pss. Sol.* 17; 4QpGen^a, 4QFlor, *4 Ezra*) do not consistently ascribe the same function to the Davidic messiah. For example, the apocalyptic messiah in *4 Ezra* 12:32 who "will arise from the posterity of David" appears closer to Daniel's Son of Man coming as a warrior on the clouds to deliver the righteous remnant and judge the wicked. More recently, some scholars have pointed to 4Q521 which refers to the age of the Messiah when the dead will rise, the afflicted will be healed, and the good news will be preached. The events remarkably parallel Jesus' response to the Baptist in Matt 11:2–5 and bolster the suggestion that if Jesus understood himself as messiah, he may have done so within the charismatic eschatological prophet paradigm (Hengel 19–22). Likewise, the messiah in 4Q521 is not a Davidic king. In short, expectations of a Davidic messiah in the first century do not appear to be, in Pomykala's words, "continuous, widespread, or dominant" (270).

For the early Christians, David stands at the mid point of an unbroken continuity between Abraham and Jesus. The promise of descendents (and a great nation) made to Abraham corresponds to David, and finds its ultimate typological fulfillment in Jesus whose messianic work is for the benefit of the world. The connection is immediate in Matthew's genealogy (1:2–17) which is carefully structured into three sets of fourteen generations from Abraham to Jesus, with David's name appearing once before the list and twice at the end. Most contemporary scholars explain Matthew's deliberate structure in light of *gematria*, the practice of numerical values to Hebrew letters. Thus, when the three consonants in David's name are added together, their total is fourteen. Moreover, David's name in the list is in the fourteenth position. Jesus as "son of David" in Matthew, as well as elsewhere in the New Testament (e.g. Mark 10:46–52), may have a double meaning, referring to both Jesus as messiah and Jesus as the ideal Solomon who was connected not only with healing powers in the first century, but with the eternal kingdom in light of 2 Sam 7 (e.g. *T. Sol.*; 4Q521; Charlesworth). For Paul, Jesus is "descended from David according to the flesh, established as Son of God in power according to the spirit of holiness through resurrection from the dead" (Rom 13–14). However, since there is no precedent in early Judaism for resurrection as a basis for messianic status, Paul's understanding should probably be taken in a broad sense which encompasses Jesus' heavenly kingship (Collins 204) or even his superiority as son of God and lord of the world over and against Caesar (Wright 242–3).

Although there is no question that several Christian groups and individuals portrayed Jesus as the Davidic ideal and reinterpreted this ideal in theological categories, historians are divided whether Jesus himself identified with the messianic Davidic ideal given its military connotations. Among the three independent sources most often consulted in reconstructions of Jesus – Q, the Gospel of Mark and the *Gospel of Thomas* – Mark is the only one which refers to David (or son of David). Of the seven references, four are placed on Jesus' lips as appeals to scripture in contexts of debate with religious authorities (2:25; 12:35, 36, 37), and three appear on the lips of others addressing Jesus (Bartimaeus in 10:47 and 48, and the welcoming crowd in 11:10). While Jesus does not explicitly claim to be David or the son of David, he at the same time does not deny it. S. H. Smith has argued that the Davidic title is not politically charged in Mark. But in light of Mark's narrative, Jesus' ambiguous connection with the title should be better understood in light of the future coming of the Son of Man (8:38; 13:26; 14:62), the royal/ messianic attributions by the voice from heaven (1:11; cf. Ps 2:7), the narrator and Centurion (1:1; 15:39), by Peter (8:29), and by the antagonists in the passion account wherein he is mocked as a king by Pilate, the crowd, and the soldiers (e.g. 15:9, 18), and is crucified as "king of the Jews" (15:26). Although all of these references underscore that Mark aims to present Jesus as a kingly messiah, it is much more difficult to say that the evangelist, who is engaged in apologetic polemic, preserves material that goes back to Jesus. Yet at the same time it is doubtful that royal messianic titles, which were so politically charged, would have been attributed to Jesus if they had no basis in his life (Evans 272–5). One example is the independent references to Jesus as one who dies as "king of the Jews" (Juel). The problem, in short, which was already recognized by Schweitzer is that Jesus' public life, which was non-violent and non-militaristic, does not coincide with the evangelist's Davidic/messianic claim for him. The only exception may be Jesus' triumphal entrance into Jerusalem, but given that (1) it fits a biblical paradigm (Zech 9:9), (2) the crowd's welcome may have been extended to all pilgrims, and (3) the "crowd" quickly turns against him for no apparent reason, the historicity is difficult to establish. The apparent inconsistency has led some like Dunn to argue that Jesus did not look to the royal messiah paradigm to define his mission and identity (380). In the end, whether Jesus viewed himself as a Davidic messiah is difficult to determine. If he did, he would have had to redefine the title at the risk of incomprehension. Furthermore, if he viewed himself as a Davidic messiah, historians are faced with the difficulty of ascertaining Jesus' political mission. Was his goal utopia, the overthrow of the Romans, a theocracy, social justice, or something else?

THOMAS R. HATINA

Further reading

Brueggemann, W. *David's Truth in Israel's Imagination and Memory*, Philadelphia, PA: Fortress Press; 1985.

Charlesworth, J. H. "Solomon and Jesus: The Son of David in Ante-Markan Traditions (Mark 10:47)," in L. B. Elder, D. L. Barr, and E. S. Malbon (eds) *Biblical and Humane: A Festschrift for J. F. Priest*, Homage 20, Atlanta, GA: Scholars Press, 1996, pp. 125–51.

Collins, J. J. *The Scepter and the Star: The Messiahs of the Dead Sea Scrolls and Other Ancient Literature*, ABRL, New York: Doubleday, 1995.

Dunn, J. D. G. "Messianic Ideas and Their Influence on the Jesus of History," in J. H. Charlesworth (ed.) *The Messiah: Developments in Earliest Judaism and Christianity*, Minneapolis, MN: Fortress Press, 1992, pp. 365–81.

Evans, C. A. *Mark 8:27–16:20*, WBC 34B, Nashville, TN: Thomas Nelson, 2001.

Feldman, L. H. "Josephus' Portrait of David," *Hebrew Union College Annual* 60 (1989) 129–74.

Hengel, M. *The Charismatic Leader and His Followers*, trans. J. C. G. Greig, Edinburgh: T. & T. Clark, 1981.

Horsley, R. A. and J. S. Hanson. *Bandits, Prophets, and Messiahs: Popular Movements at the Time of Jesus*, New York: HarperCollins, 1985.

Howard, D. M., Jr. "David," in David Noel Freedman (ed.) *The Anchor Bible Dictionary*, New York: Doubleday, 1992, Vol. 2, pp. 41–49.

Juel, D. H. "The Origin of Mark's Christology," in J. H. Charlesworth (ed.) *The Messiah: Developments in Earliest Judaism and Christianity*, Minneapolis, MN: Fortress Press, 1992, pp. 449–60.

Neusner, J., W. S. Green and E. Frerichs (eds) *Judaisms and Their Messiahs at the Turn of the Christian Era*, Cambridge: Cambridge University Press, 1987.

Pomykala, K. E. *The Davidic Dynasty Tradition in Early Judaism: Its History and Significance for Messianism*, SBLEJ 7, Atlanta, GA: Scholars Press, 1995.

Schweitzer, A. *The Quest of the Historical Jesus: A Critical Study of its Progress from Reimarus to Wrede*, trans. W. Montgomery, third edition, London: Adam and Charles Black, 1954.

Smith, S. H. "The Function of the Son of David Tradition in Mark's Gospel," *NTS* 42 (1996) 523–39.

Wright, N. T. *The Resurrection of the Son of God*, Christian Origins and the Question of God: Volume 3, Minneapolis, MN: Fortress Press, 2003.

DEAD SEA SCROLLS

Discovered more than a half century ago, the Dead Sea Scrolls have shed a great deal of light on Jewish beliefs at the turn of the era. The Scrolls are widely regarded as the most important find ever made relating to the Bible and Jewish and Christian origins. The Scrolls shed light on several significant aspects of early Christian teaching, including the teaching of Jesus and the teachings of Paul and other New Testament writers.

Two the most important themes in Jesus' preaching are his announcement of the kingdom (or rule) of God and his announcement of jubilee, the forgiveness of sin and debt. These are closely related themes and both are clarified by important parallels with the Dead Sea Scrolls.

The kingdom of God

It is widely accepted (Chilton 1994) that Jesus proclaimed the "kingdom of God" (ἡ βασιλεία τοῦ θεοῦ). His proclamation is consistent with ideas about the kingdom expressed in the Scrolls and the Aramaic paraphrase of Isaiah. But Jesus' proclamation is also rooted in the Scriptures themselves, an important point not always sufficiently appreciated. In the Scriptures there is present a shift from the kingdom *of David* or the kingdom *of Israel* to kingdom *of God*. A superficial survey of the data bears this out: In 1 Sam 28:17 God gives the kingdom to David.

Israel's ancient story speaks of the kingdom as belonging to David (e.g. 2 Sam 3:28: "my kingdom"; 2 Sam 5:12: "his kingdom"; cf. 1 Kgs 2:12, where Solomon sits on David's throne and "his kingdom" is firmly established). But this picture changes in the Chronicler, who speaks of the Lord's kingdom and the Lord's throne (cf. 1 Chr 17:14 "my kingdom"; 1 Chr 29:23: "the throne of the Lord"; 1 Chr 28:5 and 2 Chr 13:8 "the kingdom of the Lord"). In the book of Daniel God himself is depicted as king over all of humanity, whose kingdom will displace all previous human kingdoms (cf. Dan 4:3, 17, 34; 6:26).

Elsewhere Scripture makes reference to God's kingdom using personal pronouns or equivalents (e.g. Pss 22:28; 103:19; 145:11, 12, 13; Obad. 21; 1 Chr 29:11). Accordingly, Dennis Duling (50) comments that

> These passages indicate that God was imagined as the reigning king over Israel, all peoples, and, indeed, nature itself. Thus, other scholars have concluded that although the exact phrase [viz. kingdom of God] is missing, the *idea* of the kingdom of God is present, indeed even widespread, in the Hebrew Scriptures.

In later literature the idea of the kingdom of God becomes more explicit. According to *Jub.* 1:28 God rules from Mount Zion, while in *Pss. Sol.* 17:3 we encounter the exact phrase "kingdom of God" (ἡ βασιλεία τοῦ θεοῦ) and in *T. Benj.* 9.1 the synonymous phrase "kingdom of the Lord" (ἡ βασιλεία κυρίου). In many passages in *1 En.* God is depicted as king and as ruling the world. The author of the *Testament of Moses* anticipates the appearance of the kingdom of God and the demise of the Devil (*T. Moses* 10:1–3).

The Dead Sea Scrolls present ideas that are consistent with these ideas (Viviano). Hope of a "kingdom of God" is expressed in the War Scroll: "And to the God of Israel shall be the kingdom, and by the saints of his people will he display might" (1QM 6:6); and "You, O God, resplendent in the glory of your kingdom [מלכותכה]" (1QM 12:7). The reference to "his kingdom" in 1QH 11 i 4–7 should probably be understood in the same way. In 4Q491, which is related in some way to the War Scroll, is: "And [the kingdo]m shall be for God and the salvatio[n] for His people" (11 ii 17). This text appears to cohere with the eschatological dimension of Jesus' proclamation of the kingdom.

In the Rule of Blessing the following is said of the High Priest: "May you serve in the Temple of the kingdom [בהיכל מלכות]" (1QSb 4:25–26). This is the prayer of blessing for the priest who will serve when Israel is restored and the Messiah takes his place. The last column of 1QSb blesses this figure as well. Part of the blessing says: "And he shall renew for him the covenant of the community, so as to establish the kingdom of His people [מלכות עמו] forever" (1QSb 5:21). The passage goes on to quote parts of Isaiah 11 and apply them to the awaited Messiah. (See also 4Q286 7 i 5, which speaks of God supporting "your kingdom [מלכותכה] in the midst of ... " The singular suffix probably refers to the anticipated Messiah.)

No texts more than the Songs of the Sabbath have extolled the glory of the kingdom of heaven. We find more than twenty references to the celestial kingdom in these fragmentary scrolls. Although in no one instance do we have the exact phrase "kingdom of God," it is nevertheless about the kingdom of God that these texts speak. The pronouns appear in the second and third persons: " [Your] lofty kingdom" (4Q400 1 ii 1); "His lofty kingdom" (4Q403 1 i 8; 1 i 14; 4Q405 3 ii 4; Mas-ShirShab 2:20); "the beauty of Your kingdom" (4Q400 1 ii 3); "the praiseworthiness of Your kingdom among the holiest of the h[oly ones]" (4Q400 1 ii 3; 2 1; 4Q401 14 i 7); "and they declare His kingdom" (4Q400 2:3); "the heavens of Your glor[ious] kingdom" (4Q401 14 i 6); "[in all] the heavens of His kingdom" (4Q400 2:3–4); "[who pr]aise His glorious kingdom" (4Q403 1 i 25); "in the splendor of praise is the glory of His kingdom" (4Q403 1 i 32); "the praises of all the gods together with the splendor of all His kingdom" (4Q403 1 i 32–33); "And the tabernacle of highest loftiness, the glory of His kingdom" (4Q403 1 ii 10); "a seat like the throne of His kingdom" (4Q405 20–22 ii 2); "the kingdom glorious seats of the chariot thrones" (4Q405 20–22 ii 4); "the throne of His glorious kingdom" (4Q405 23 i 3); "the chiefs of the realm of the holy ones of the King of holiness in all the heights

of the sanctuaries of His glorious kingdom" (4Q405 23 ii 11–12); and "the glorious kingdom of the King of all the g[ods]" (4Q405 24:3) are among the best preserved texts that speak of the divine kingdom (for texts and critical discussion, see Newsom 1985).

These materials indicate that Jesus' idea of God as king, or the kingdom of God in the sense of the sphere in which God rules, or in the sense that God rules over humanity and the cosmos, is hardly distinctive of Jesus and hardly need be explained by an appeal to Hellenism, as a few scholars have suggested (e.g. Mack). Jesus' proclamation of God's rule is consistent with the expressions found in the Dead Sea Scrolls, in Old Testament Scripture itself, and in the Aramaic paraphrase of Scripture (e.g. *Tg. Isa* 40:9; 52:7; *Tg. Mic* 4:7–8; *Tg. Zech* 14:9; on the kingdom of God in the Aramaic, see Chilton 1979: 86–90; 1982: 77–81).

Jesus' proclamation of the kingdom of God is thus coherent with important Jewish traditions. These traditions envision God as king, as well as a kingdom of God that will supersede all of the human kingdoms. In this respect, Jesus' proclamation is no different. Yet Jesus' proclamation is somewhat distinctive. The author of Daniel, authors of some of the Dead Sea Scrolls, and the Aramaic paraphrase of Isaiah anticipate *the coming* of the kingdom of God. Jesus proclaims it *as having come*. This sense of fulfillment, which Jesus apparently linked to his own ministry and to his own time, involves some interesting, perhaps unique features.

Jubilee proclamation

Ancient Israel's tradition about the jubilee, in which one's debts are forgiven, is found in Lev 25:13–17 ("In this year of jubilee each of you shall return to his property ..."). Jesus' sermon at Nazareth (Luke 4:16–30), in which he cites and expounds Isa 61:1–2, is understood by many to have an announcement of jubilee. Important parallels with the Dead Sea Scrolls have borne this out.

One of the most important passages in the dominical tradition is the exchange between Jesus and the questioning, imprisoned John the Baptist. The tradition has been preserved in Q (the non-Markan material that Matthew and Luke have in common) and is accepted by most as authentic (Matt 11:2–6 = Luke 7:19–23):

[John] sent word by his disciples and said to him, "Are you he who is to come, or shall we look for another?" And Jesus answered them, "Go and tell John what you hear and see: the blind receive their sight and the lame walk, lepers are cleansed and the deaf hear, and the dead are raised up, and the poor have good news preached to them. And blessed is he who takes no offense at me."

The allusions to words and phrases from Isaiah (e.g. Isa 26:19; 35:5–6; 61:1–2) have intrigued interpreters. One of the more celebrated of the recently published Scrolls, 4Q521, may help us answer these questions. According to 4Q521 2 + 4 ii 1–13 (following Wise *et al.* 421):

> [1][... For the hea]vens and the earth shall listen to his Messiah [2][and all w]hich is in them shall not turn away from the commandments of the holy ones. [3]Strengthen yourselves, O you who seek the Lord, in his service. (*vacat*) [4]Will you not find the Lord in this, all those who hope in their heart? [5]For the Lord seeks the pious and calls the righteous by name. [6]Over the humble his spirit hovers, and he renews the faithful in his strength. [7]For he will honor the pious upon the th[ro]ne of the eternal kingdom, [8]setting prisoners free, opening the eyes of the blind, raising up those who are bo[wed down.] [9]And for [ev]er (?) I (?) shall hold fast [to]the [ho]peful and pious [...] [10][...]..shall not be delayed [...] [11]and the Lord shall do glorious things which have not been done, just as he said. [12]For he will heal the critically wounded, he shall revive the dead, he shall proclaim good news to the afflicted, [13]he shall [... the ...], he shall lead the [...], and the hungry he shall enrich (?).

This text borrows words and phrases from Ps 146:6–8 ("heaven and earth ... and all that is in them ... the Lord opens the eyes of the blind"), Isa 35:5 ("the eyes of the blind shall be opened"), 26:19 ("he shall revive the dead"), and 61:1 ("anointed ... to proclaim good news to the afflicted ... liberty to prisoners ... opening of the eyes"). The parallels between 4Q521 and Jesus' reply to John are remarkable (for detailed analysis, see Zimmermann 344–7).

In 11Q13 (a.k.a. 11QMelch) there is an explicit link between the jubilee legislation of Lev 25 and that of Isa 61:1–3 which declares that it is to be fulfilled "in the last days" (2:4). Scholars have rightly studied this text as a possible backdrop to Jesus' use of Isaiah 61 (as in Matt 11:5 = Luke 7:22; cf. Luke 4:16–30) and his pronouncements of the forgiveness of debts/sins (cf. Mark 2:5; Luke 7:36–50). The eschatological figure envisioned in 11Q13 is probably based on the expected prophet like Moses and/or the second coming of Elijah (for critical discussion of this scroll, see Zimmermann 389–412).

As part of the eschatological jubilee, Jesus is able to pronounce blessings on the "poor," the "merciful," the "meek," the "peacemakers," and those "persecuted for the sake of righteousness," as seen in the Beatitudes (Matt 5:1–12). The poor and the suffering are blessed because of the coming reign of God. For then they will inherit the kingdom, be comforted, be satisfied, obtain mercy, and see God.

Prior to the discovery of the Dead Sea Scrolls, Jesus' string of nine (or ten) beatitudes was unparalleled. But among the fragments of leather that make up 4Q525, we now have a such a string (4Q525 frag. 2 ii + 3:1–10):

> [Blessed is the one who ...] with a clean heart and does not slander with his tongue.
>
> Blessed are those who hold fast to its statutes and do not hold fast to the ways of injustice.
>
> Ble[ssed] are those who rejoice in it, and do not burst forth on paths of folly.
>
> Blessed are those who seek it with pure hands, and do not search for it with a deceitful [hea]rt.
>
> Blessed is the man who attains wisdom, and walks in the law of the Most High: establishes his heart in its ways, restrains himself by its corrections, is continually satisfied with its punishments, does not forsake it in the face of [his] trials, at the time of distress he does not abandon it, does not forget it [in the day of] terror, and in the humility of his soul he does not abhor it. But he meditates on it continually, and in his trial he reflects [on the law, and with al]l his being [he gains understanding] in it, [and he establishes it] before his eyes so as not to walk in the ways [of injustice, and ... and ...] together, and perfects his heart by it, [and ... and ... places a crown of ... upon] his [hea]d, and with kings it shall se[at him, and ... and ...] brothers shall [...].
>
> (trans. Wise *et al.* 423–4)

Because the beginning of this fragment is missing, we do not know how many beatitudes originally made up this string. Scholars have suggested seven. In any case, we now know that a string of beatitudes would not have struck Jesus' hearers as novel in itself. However, the beatitudes of 4Q525 focus on wisdom, not on eschatology, and herein lies an important difference. For Jesus, the righteous one is blessed, because of the kingdom of God. For the author of 4Q525, the righteous one is blessed, because he has attained wisdom. Thus we find that the differences can be just as informative as the similarities.

Another part of the jubilee is the announcement of liberation from Satan. The exorcisms were for Jesus evidence of the powerful presence of the kingdom of God and of the binding and defeat of Satan. In perhaps his most distinctive saying, Jesus is remembered to have said: "If it is by the finger of God that I cast out demons, then the kingdom of God has come upon you" (Luke 11:20). Here again we have another important parallel with Qumran (1Q27 1 i 5–8):

> [5]This shall be the sign that this shall come to pass: when the sources of evil are shut up and wickedness is banished in the presence of righteousness, as darkness in the presence of [6]light, or as smoke vanishes and is no more, in the same way wickedness will vanish forever and righteousness will be manifest like the sun. [7]The world will be made firm and all the adherents of the secrets of sin [MS: wonder] shall be no more. True knowledge shall fill the world and there will never be any more folly. [8]This is all ready to happen, it is a true oracle, and by this it shall be known to you that it cannot be averted.
>
> (trans. Wise et al. 176)

The "sign" of the eschatological moment, according to this text, is "when the sources of evil are shut up." Admittedly the "evil" and "wickedness" envisioned in this text are probably to be understood as human beings – wicked Gentiles and apostate Israelites – but elsewhere Qumran teaches that Satan (or Belial) and his minions are the ultimate source of human evil. For Jesus, too, the sign of the eschatological moment is the shutting up of evil. But for Jesus this means the liberation of humans who are held in bondage to evil.

According to T. Mos. 10:1, which some think may have originally been an Essene document, the appearance of the kingdom of God means the end of the kingdom of Satan: "Then his [viz. God's] kingdom will appear throughout his whole creation. Then the devil will have an end." The linkage between the appearance of the kingdom of God and the demise of Satan is presupposed in Jesus' teaching also. In Mark 3:23–27 Jesus counters the charge that he is casting out evil spirits through the power of Satan: "If Satan has risen up against himself and is divided, he cannot stand, but has an end." The last part of this saying, "has an end" (τέλος ἔχει), is the equivalent of the Latin's "will have an end" (finem habebit) of the Testament of Moses. This is a remarkable parallel.

Jesus' proclamation of the kingdom of God, informed by ideas of forgiveness of debts/sins, form a coherent and calculated agenda; these elements should not be viewed as ad hoc, spontaneous, or unrelated. These integrated elements comprise the aims of Jesus, whose central goal was the restoration of Israel. The Covenanters of Qumran nurtured similar aims. These men also spoke of a celestial kingdom, and anticipated the overthrow of the corrupt Temple establishment and the inauguration of a restorative, rectifying jubilee.

See 1QSa (Rule of the Congregation); 4Q246 (Son of God Text); 4Q491c (Hymn of Self-Glorification); 4Q521 (Messianic Apocalypse); Exorcisms and Healings.

CRAIG A. EVANS

Further reading

Chilton, B. D. God in Strength: Jesus' Announcement of the Kingdom, SNTU 1, Freistadt: Plöchl, 1979; repr. BibSem 8, Sheffield: JSOT Press, 1987.

—— The Glory of Israel: The Theology and Provenience of the Isaiah Targum, JSOTSup 23, Sheffield: JSOT Press, 1982).

—— "The kingdom of God in Recent Discussion," in B. D. Chilton and C. A. Evans (eds) Studying the Historical Jesus: Evaluations of the State of Current Research, NTTS 19; Leiden: Brill, 1994, pp. 255–80.

Duling, D. C. "kingdom of God, Kingdom of Heaven," in D. N. Freedman (ed.) The Anchor Bible Dictionary, 6 vols, New York: Doubleday, 1992, Vol. 4, pp. 49–56.

Mack, B. L. "The Kingdom Sayings in Mark," Forum 3:1 (1987) 3–47.

Newsom, C. A. Song of the Sabbath Sacrifice: A Critical Edition, HSS 27, Atlanta, GA: Scholars Press, 1985.

Viviano, B. T. "The kingdom of God in the Qumran Literature," in W. Willis (ed.) The kingdom of God in 20th Century Interpretation, Peabody, MA: Hendrickson, 1987, pp. 97–107.

Wise, M. O., Abegg, M. G. Jr., and Cook, E. M. The Dead Sea Scrolls: A New Translation, San Francisco, CA: HarperCollins, 1996.

Zimmermann, J. Messianische Texte aus Qumran: Königliche, priesterliche und prophetische Messiasvorstellungen in den Schriftfunden von Qumran, WUNT 2/104, Tübingen: Mohr Siebeck, 1998.

DEAD SEA SCROLLS: BEGOTTEN MESSIAH TEXT (1Q28A = 1QSA)

The Rule of the Congregation (sometimes called The Messianic Rule), 1QSa (or 1Q28a), was found in Cave 1 at Qumran. The one extant copy is complete (though difficult to read in places) and, along with 1QSb (The Rule of Benedictions), the scroll was one of two appendixes to 1QS (The Rule of the Community). F. M. Cross dated the three texts to 100–75 BCE, but it is widely held that each of these Rules scrolls existed prior to their compilation as a more or less unified corpus.

The editio princeps of 1QSa was edited by D. Barthelemy and published in 1955. The scroll was named for its first words, "And this is the rule of all the congregation of Israel in the final days ... " The work has been read variously as a description of the eschaton (Barthelemy and Milik 1955), of the present age (Stegemann 1996), or as a present enactment of an expected future event (Schiffman 1989). The majority view is that the text is eschatological, "picturing the ideal constitution of the sect in the end of days" (Schiffman 1989: 8).

Scroll 1QSa consists of fifty-one lines of text in two columns. It has been outlined as follows:

1 Introduction (1:1–5)
2 Stages of life for men of the congregation (1:6–22)
3 The council of the community (1:23–2:3)
4 Exclusion from the council (2:4–11)
5 The Messianic Banquet (2:11–22)

In each of these sections the *Rule of the Congregation* bears some striking similarities to other sectarian writings of the Qumran community. The "stages of life" passage has parallels in several other key scrolls (cf. the age of twenty in 11QTemple 17:8; the age of twenty-five in 1QM 7:2–3, CD 10:4–10; the age of thirty in CD 14:6–9, 1QM 6:12–13; and the elderly in CD 10:4–10 and 1QM 7:1–2). The lines dealing with the council of the community share aspects of the regulations of 1QS 6:8–13 as well as CD 12:23–3:7. In the section detailing those who are excluded from the council and from battle the *Rule* contains proscriptions like those of 1QM 7:3–6 and 11QTemple 45:7–12. Likewise, the Messianic Banquet closely resembles 1QS 6:3–8, containing such similar elements as ten men, a meal with bread and wine, the presence of a priest, and the reading of the law.

There are also notable differences. Whereas women are not in the purview of 1QS, they are clearly a part of the life of the community envisaged in 1QSa. In earlier work many scholars concluded that 1QS was the rule for the (celibate and male) Qumran community, while the *Damascus Document* was normative for the wider Essene group that existed in cities and towns. The role of women in 1QSa has made it clear that another explanation needs to be postulated.

Some scholars have made a strict distinction between the "congregation" and the "community," allowing for the presence of women in the congregation but not necessarily the community. This deserves further study, but some passages in 1QSa caution against too sharp a distinction (2:21; cf. 1:9–10 with 1:12–13).

A more debatable difference involves the presence of two messiahs at the meal described in 1QSa 2:11–22. Passages like 1QS 9:11 and CD 12:23–13:1, 14:19, 19:10–11, and 20:1 have made it clear that the Qumran community held expectations for two messianic figures, one priestly and one non-priestly (see 1QS 9:11: "the Messiahs of Aaron and Israel"). 1QSa mentions "the messiah" (2:11, 14) and a "priest" (2:12, perhaps "chief priest"), but does not use the term "messiah" with

reference to this figure. Nevertheless, most scholars have understood this to indicate the presence of two messiahs in this scene. This view has recently been challenged with the suggestion that 1QSa comes from a time before the development of the idea of a priestly messiah (Stegemann).

The greatest significance of the *Rule of the Congregation* for the study of the New Testament and Jesus is found in the very controversial passage beginning at the end of 2:11. In Barthelemy's edition the last word in the line (which is difficult to read) was *yôlid*, which resulted in God "begetting" the Messiah. If in pre-Christian Judaism there is an explicit expectation of a Messiah begotten by God this is obviously significant. However, the reading has not gone unchallenged. Many emendations have been suggested, including *yôlik* (Charlesworth), *ytglh* (Puech), *ywklw* (Stegemann), and *ytw'd* (Schiffman, following J. Licht). Missing fragments and damage to the scroll have made it one of the longest-running discussions in Scrolls research, and recent technological advances do not seem to be hastening a satisfactory answer. Perhaps the strongest argument in favor of Barthelemy's original reading (which is still accepted by many – see, e.g., the recent English translations of both Vermes and García-Martínez) is that there was such unanimity amongst the scholars who saw the scroll in the early 1950s.

If *yôlid* is the accepted reading, it should probably be read as an updated understanding of the idea contained in Ps 2:7 ("You are my son; today I have begotten you") of God begetting the Messiah (Ps 2:2). Early Christians applied this Psalm to Jesus (Acts 13:33; Heb. 1:5), and in rabbinic writings (*b. Suk.* 52a; *Midr. Ps* 2.9 [on Ps 2:7]) it was also understood in a messianic sense. This claim may not be intended to be taken literally; it might simply mean that God will raise up a messianic figure for the community (Evans).

SCOTT A. KOHLER

Further reading

Barthelemy, D. "Le Règle de la congregation (1QSa)," in D. Barthelemy and J. T. Milik (eds) *Qumran Cave 1*, DJD 1, Oxford: Clarendon Press, 1955, pp. 107–18, plates XXII–XXIV.
Charlesworth, James H. and Stuckenbruck, Loren. "The Rule of the Congregation," in James H. Charlesworth (ed.) *The Dead Sea Scrolls 1: Rule of the Community and Related Documents*, Tubingen: Mohr Siebeck; Louisville, KY: Westminster, 1994, pp. 108–17.
Davies, P. R. and Taylor, J. E. "On the Testimony of Women in 1Qsa," *DSD* 3 (1996): 223–35.
García, Martínez, F., Tigchelaar, E. J. C. *The Dead Sea Scrolls Study Edition. Volume one: 1Q1–4Q273*, Leiden: Brill, 1997.

Evans, Craig A. "A Note on the 'First-Born Son' of 4Q369," *DSD* 2 (1995) 185–201.

Puech, É. "Préséance sacerdotale et messie-roi dans la Règle de la Congrégation (1QSa ii 11–22)," *RevQ* 16 (1994) 351–65.

Schiffman, Lawrence H. *The Eschatological Community of the Dead Sea Scrolls: A Study of the Rule of the Congregation*, SBLMS 38, Atlanta, GA: Scholars Press, 1989.

Stegemann, Hartmut. "Some Remarks to 1QSa, to 1QSb and to Qumran Messianism," *RevQ* 17 (1996) 479–505.

Vermes, G., *The Dead Sea Scrolls in English*, 4th ed. London and New York: Penguin, 1994.

DEAD SEA SCROLLS: JERUSALEM PRIESTHOOD IN THE SCROLLS

There are indications that the Dead Sea Scrolls and the New Testament accounts of Jesus share a common view regarding the Jerusalem priesthood. Both literary corpora speak of the character and activities of the Jerusalem priesthood, but almost entirely in polemical ways.

The Jerusalem priesthood in the Dead Sea Scrolls reflects the Hasmonean and Herodian periods (150 BCE to 68 CE). The latter half of this period overlaps with the ministry of Jesus and the emergence of the Christian Church. Similar to the polemic articulated in the scrolls, Jesus, too, is described as sharply opposing the character and teaching of the Jerusalem priesthood.

In the gospel accounts criticism is directed against the chief priests and their Sadducean allies, as well as against the Pharisees, bitter rivals of the Sadducees. They are described as self-righteous and overly critical in their judgment of others (including and sometimes especially Jesus), which often occasioned negative exchanges between them and Jesus (e.g. Matt 9:11, 34; 12:1–2, 22–24, 38; 15:1–2; 16:1, 6, 11–12; 19:3; 22:15–18, 23–28; 34–36; Mark 11:27–33; Luke 20:1–2; John 8:13; 9:13ff.). According to Matthew 21:23–46, when Jesus is questioned about the authenticity and authority of his teachings, he in turn accuses the Jerusalem priesthood of self-serving intentions. The Jerusalem priesthood responds to Jesus in negative and ultimately threatening ways (e.g. Matt 12:14; 21:15, 45–46; 22:15–18; 26:3–5, 59–66; 27:1–2, 20, 41–43, 62–64; 28:11–15; Mark 11:18; 12:12, 13–16, 18–23; 14:1–2, 53–64; 15:1–13; Luke 19:47–48; 20:19–20; John 7:32; 8:3–9; 11:46–53, 57). The priesthood even conspires with one of Jesus' disciples to betray and kill him (Matt 26:14–16, 46–47; Mark 14:10–11; Luke 22:2–6 and John 18:3). Sources outside the New Testament Gospels (such as the writings of Josephus or early rabbinic literature) offer important support to most aspects of this tradition.

The Pharisees and Sadducees, both of whom interchangeably supplied priests during the intertestamental period, are characterized as hypocrites (Matt 15:6–9; 22:15–18; 23:13, 15, 23, 25, 27–29). Although they taught and enforced strict laws, they themselves failed to adhere to these laws – so goes the criticism (Matt 23:1–33; Luke 11:39–54). Colorful epithets are employed. For example, the Pharisees are called vipers and snakes (Matt 3:7; 12:34; 23:33; Luke 3:7), blind guides and fools (Matt 15:12; 23:16–19, 24, 26; Luke 11:40; John 9:39–41), and whitewashed tombs (Matt 23:27; Luke 11:44). Jesus warned his disciples not to emulate the behavior of the Pharisees.

Throughout the Dead Sea Scrolls, the Jerusalem priesthood is similarly described with incendiary language. In the sectarian Dead Sea texts, reference to the Jerusalem priesthood is given from the perspective of a particular community. The community of the scrolls viewed itself as priestly, consisting of priests, Levites, and the "sons of Zadok" (CD 3:21–24:4a). This community described itself as being raised up from Aaron (CD 6:2). The community members are described as being God's remnant, called out from Jerusalem due to their steadfastness to God's precepts. This portrayal of the remnant community is set in contrast to the illegitimate priestly establishment in Jerusalem. Here we find criticism leveled against the Jerusalem priesthood in reference to regulations concerning purification, sacrifices, and calendar. According to the *Damascus Document* (6:14–20a), the remnant community is instructed to (1) abstain from the wicked wealth which defiles the temple, (2) separate the clean from the unclean, (3) differentiate between the holy and the common, (4) keep the Sabbath day and set apart holy portions according to the exact interpretation and (5) keep the festivals and day of fasting. Hence, the remnant community is noted as leaving the land of Judah (i.e. Jerusalem in particular) for these reasons.

The appellation "sons of Zadok" is in reference to the remnant community. The "sons of Zadok" presumably claimed literal descent from Zadok, the priest whom David appointed during his reign. This epithet is found in the *Damascus Document*, *Serekh Damascus*, the *Rule of the Community*, the *Rule of the Congregation*, *4QFlorilegium* and *Pesher Isaiah^c*. Moreover, some of these texts refer to the leader of the community as the Teacher of Righteousness. This priestly teacher is the counterpart to the Wicked Priest, who according to 1QpHab 8:8–13 once was accepted by the community. In 1QpHab 11:4–8, the Wicked Priest is described as pursuing the priestly Teacher on the

Day of Atonement to consume him. The Day of Atonement is identified as a point of contention, particularly regarding the calendrical observance of certain holy days and festivals.

The critical stance of the "sons of Zadok," or the men of the Community of the restored Covenant, over against the priestly regime of Jerusalem provides an important backdrop for our understanding of the historical Jesus. The critical issues attested in the Scrolls and here or there in the New Testament Gospels are only representative of much larger, contentious issues that separated the ruling priests of Jerusalem from significant constituencies throughout Jewish Palestine. Jesus' protest in the temple precincts, which resulted in his arrest and execution, must be interpreted in the light of this backdrop.

JAMAL-DOMINIQUE HOPKINS

Further reading

Brooke, G. J. "The Messiah of Aaron in the Damascus Document," *RevQ* 15 (1991) 215–30.

Evans, C. A. "Jesus' Action in the Temple: Cleansing or Portent of Destruction?" *CBQ* 51 (1989) 237–70.

Gärtner, B. *The Temple and the Community in Qumran and the New Testament*, SNTSMS 1, Cambridge: Cambridge University Press, 1965, pp. 4–15.

Kugler, R. A. "A Note on 1QS 9.14: The Sons of Righteousness or the Sons of Zadok," *DSD* 3 (1996) 315–20.

—— "The Priesthood at Qumran: The Evidence of References to Levi and the Levites," in D. Parry and E. Ulrich (eds) *The Provo International Conference on the Dead Sea Scrolls*, STDJ 30, Leiden: Brill, 1999, pp. 465–79.

Liver, J. "The Sons of Zadok, the Priests in the Dead Sea Sect," *RevQ* 6 (1967) 3–30.

Schiffman, L. H. *Reclaiming the Dead Sea Scrolls: The History of Judaism, the Background of Christianity, the Lost Library at Qumran*, Philadelphia, PA: Jewish Publication Society, 1994, pp. 83–126.

Schwartz, D. R. "On Two Aspects of a Priestly View of Descent at Qumran," in L. H. Schiffman (ed.) *Archaeology and History in the Dead Sea Scrolls: The New York University Conference in Memory of Yigael Yadin*, JSPSup 8, Sheffield: JSOT Press, 1990, pp. 157–79.

Van der Woude, A. S. "Wicked Priest or Wicked Priests? Reflections on the Identification of the Wicked Priest in the Habakkuk Commentary," *JJS* 33 (1982) 349–59.

DEAD SEA SCROLLS: MESSIANIC APOCALYPSE (4Q521)

4Q521, variously called *Messianic Apocalypse*, the *Works of the Messiah*, or *On Resurrection*, is a Hebrew text preserved in sixteen to eighteen fragments, in which a messianic figure is mentioned. It is of special interest to historical Jesus studies because of its parallel with the dominical reply to the imprisoned John the Baptist.

The text has been paleographically dated within the Hasmonean era to 100–80 BCE (Puech 1997: 1–38), with carbon dating supporting this range (Jull *et al.* 14). There is no scholarly consensus regarding genre, provenance, and interpretation. The proposed apocalyptic identification, as John J. Collins has remarked, "is at best an approximate indication of generic affinity. The extant fragments show none of the formal marks of apocalyptic revelation" (Collins 1994: 98). In his translation of the scrolls Florentino García Martínez identified 4Q521 as a sapiential work (García Martínez and Watson 394–5). This designation has been followed, with some modification, by Géza Xeravits, who characterizes 4Q521 as "an apocalyptic poem containing eschatological wisdom material" (Xeravits 188).

Émile Puech believes the text originated within the Qumran community because it is not the original copy and it suppresses the tetragrammaton (Puech 1999: 552). Collins does not think it originated with the Essenes because of its reference to resurrection, otherwise scant in the Qumran texts, and because its eschatological reading of Isa 61:1–3 was common in wider Judaism (Collins 1997: 238).

Parallels

Due to the fragmentary condition of 4Q521 the identity of the messianic figure is uncertain. Puech finds multiple messiahs in the text, with both the eschatological Elijah and the priestly messiah being mentioned at fr. 2 ii lines 1–2 (Puech 1999: 560–1). Collins, preferring a singular anointed figure, has posited the eschatological Prophet like Elijah, noting the use of Mal 4:5–6 in frag. 2 col. iii line 2 (Collins 1994). García Martínez understands the anointed one as the kingly Messiah of Israel (García Martínez 168–70). More recently John Poirier has argued that the anointed figure is the priestly Messiah who was fashioned after Elijah, the eschatological priestly messiah in several rabbinic sources (Poirier).

The "wondrous things" that the Lord does through his messianic agent are described in frag. 2 col. ii; it is this section that parallels Q material found in Matt 11:5 = Luke 7:21–22. These eschatological deeds reflect the blessings described in Isaiah and the parallels in Ps 146. They may be tabulated as in Table 2.

The parallels are impressive. Collins remarks: "[T]his can hardly be coincidental. It is quite possible that the author of the Sayings source knew 4Q521; at the least he drew on a common tradition" (Collins 1994: 107).

Table 2 Parallels

Q (Matt 11:5 = Luke 7:21–22)	OT allusions	4Q521 parallels
He cured many of diseases		Heal the wounded
Blind receive sight	Blind receive sight (Ps 146:8, Isa 35:5)	Make blind see
Lame walk	Lame walk (Isa 35:6)	
Lepers are cleansed	Isa 53:4 stricken(?); cf. Lev 14:3 (stricken with leprosy)	
Deaf hear	Deaf hear (Isa 29:18–19; 35:5)	
Dead are raised up	Their dead bodies will rise (Isa 26:19; Dan 12:2)	Revive the dead
Poor have good news preached to them	Poor have good news preached to them (Isa 61:1)	The afflicted have good news sent to them
	Setting prisoners free (Ps 146:7)	Setting prisoners free
	Lifting those who are bowed down (Ps 146:8)	Lifting those who are bowed down

Relation to the historical Jesus

Jesus responds to John's question with a series of words and phrases taken from the prophecy of Isaiah. The table above shows that "setting prisoners free" was part of the tradition in 4Q521, and it is the absence of this not only in Jesus' reply, but in his ministry as well, that may have caused John to question him in the first place. After all, John was in Herod's custody awaiting vindication – at least according to Isaiah. John the Baptist may well have been familiar with this prophetic tradition, and wondered why the promised deed of emancipating prisoners was not being fulfilled.

John Meier has argued for the historicity of John's question and Jesus' reply. He offers six supporting arguments: (1) the exchange belongs to the earliest strata of gospel material; (2) there is a lack of christological titles that would otherwise be expected in later material, the "coming one" (Matt 11:3 = Luke 7:19) being a vague title; (3) common themes like kingdom, miracles, and a beatitude are at home in the dominical tradition; (4) the allusion and use of Isaiah is coherent with Jesus material elsewhere; (5) the criterion of embarrassment applies to this scene, since the forerunner of Jesus is expressing doubt in Jesus; (6) the silence of John is discontinuous with gospel material that elsewhere has John leaping in the womb, confessing his need to be baptized by Jesus, and declaring that Jesus is the lamb of God who takes away the sin of the world (Meier 130–6).

The presence of this material in Q supports authenticity as well. Q contains only the barest amount of narrative, and almost no accounts of healing or miracles, so the creation and/or circulation of this material bears little resonance with the rest of Q. That Matthew and Luke chose to include this material also indicates a fixed and well-known tradition; the narrative of Matthew only has one resuscitative miracle in the entire story, and Luke has only one resuscitative miracle before 7:18–23. It is hard to explain why the evangelists would have Jesus say "the dead [pl.] are raised" (Matt 11:5//Luke 7:22), when it stands in tension with their individual narratives. The evangelists preserved this material because it was an early and well-known tradition.

The parallel of 4Q521 with Jesus' reply to John the Baptist suggests that the historical Jesus possessed messianic self-awareness: "4Q521 provides compelling evidence that Jesus' understanding of his mission was messianic, though precisely in what sense messianic needs to be carefully nuanced" (Evans 1999: 588). The uncertain identity of 4Q521's anointed figure(s) cannot help clarify Jesus' messianic self-awareness, and the 100+ years between 4Q521 and Jesus' ministry undoubtedly witnessed a transformation of Jewish understanding of the coming messiah anyway. Nonetheless, 4Q521 provides compelling evidence that Jesus understood himself performing the deeds of a messiah.

DANNY ZACHARIAS

Further reading

Collins, John J. "The Works of the Messiah," *DSD* 1 (1994) 98–112.
—— "A Herald of Good Tidings: Isaiah 61:1–3 and its Actualization in the Dead Sea Scrolls," in Craig A. Evans and Shemaryahu Talmon (eds) *The Quest for*

Context and Meaning: Studies in Biblical Intertextuality in Honor of James A. Sanders, Leiden: Brill, 1997, pp. 225–40.

Evans, Craig A. "Jesus and the Dead Sea Scrolls," in Peter W. Flint and James C. VanderKam (eds) *Dead Sea Scrolls after Fifty Years*, Boston, MA and Leiden: Brill, 1999, pp. 573–98.

—— "Messianic Apocalypse (4Q521)," in Craig A. Evans and Stanley E. Porter (eds) *Dictionary of New Testament Background on CD-ROM*, Accordance Bible Software; print edition, *Dictionary of New Testament Background*, Downers Grove, IL: InterVarsity Press, 2000.

—— "The Messiah in the Dead Sea Scrolls," in Richard S. Hess and Daniel Carroll (eds) *Israel's Messiah in the Bible and the Dead Sea Scrolls*, Grand Rapids, MI: Baker, 2003, pp. 85–101.

Garcia Martinez, Florentino. "Messianic Hopes in the Qumran Writings," in Florentino Garcia Martinez and Julio Trebolle Barrera (eds) *The People of the Dead Sea Scrolls*, New York: Brill, 1995, pp. 159–89.

Garcia Martinez, Florentino and Watson, W. G. E. *The Dead Sea Scrolls Translated: The Qumran Texts in English*, Leiden: Brill, 1997.

Jull, A. J. Timothy, Donahue, Douglas J., Broshi, Magen and Tov, Emanuel. "Radiocarbon Dating of Scrolls and Linen Fragments from the Judean Desert," *Radiocarbon* 37 (1995) 11–19.

Labahn, Michael. "The Significance of Signs in Luke 7:22–23 in the Light of Isaiah 61 and the Messianic Apocalypse," in Craig A. Evans (ed.) *From Prophecy to Testament: The Function of the Old Testament in the New*, Peabody, MA: Hendrickson, 2004, pp. 146–68.

Meier, John P. *A Marginal Jew: Rethinking the Historical Jesus*. Volume Two: *Mentor, Message, and Miracles*, ABRL, New York: Doubleday, 1994.

Poirier, John C. "The Endtime Return of Elijah and Moses at Qumran," *DSD* 10 (2003) 221–42.

Puech, Émile. *Textes Hebreux (4Q521 4Q528, 4Q576–4Q579) Qumran Cave 4 XVIII*, Oxford: Clarendon, 1997.

—— "Some Remarks on 4Q246 and 4Q521 and Qumran Messianism," in Donald W. Parry and Eugene Ulrich (eds) *The Provo International Conference on the Dead Sea Scrolls: Technological Innovations, New Texts, and Reformulated Issues*, Boston, MA: Brill, 1999, pp. 545–65.

—— "Messianic Apocalypse," in Lawrence H. Schiffman and James C. VanderKam (eds) *Encyclopedia of the Dead Sea Scrolls*, 2 vols, Oxford: Oxford University Press, 2000, Vol. 1, pp. 543–4.

Xeravits, Géza G. "Wisdom Traits in the Qumranic Presentation of the Eschatological Prophet," in F. Garcia Martinez (ed.) *Wisdom and Apocalypticism in the Dead Sea Scrolls and in the Biblical Tradition*, Leuven: Leuven University Press, 2002, pp. 185–92.

DEAD SEA SCROLLS: SELF-GLORIFICATION HYMN (4Q491C)

Maurice Baillet believed that 4Q491c was a fragment of the War Scroll (i.e. 1QM and related materials) and that the speaker was the archangel Michael who plays a major role in the anticipated eschatological war (Baillet). The speaker in this fragment boasts that his "glory is incomparable" and that beside him "no one is exalted." Indeed, his knowledge and wisdom are unequalled and his habitation is heaven itself. Baillet believed that the speaker could only be an angelic being, so he labeled the fragment "Cantique de Michel" (or "Song of Michael"). However, further examination of other fragments found in Cave 4 has led some to conclude that 4Q491c is a fragment from the *Thanksgiving Psalms*, especially when compared with 4Q427 fragment 7 column 1 and 4Q471b (cf. Abegg).

The extravagant speech in 4Q491c is not easily explained. Even with the help of 4Q427 and 4Q471b the identity of the boastful speaker remains unclear. Israel Knoll rightly remarks that in the Dead Sea literature "there is nothing remotely like this hymn written in the first person" (Knoll 19).

The speaker in 4Q491c claims to be enthroned in heaven upon a throne on which no ancient king shall sit (line 12). John Collins writes, "If we may assume that the mighty throne is where the speaker takes his seat, then this is the only passage in the Dead Sea Scrolls that speaks of an individual other than God being enthroned in heaven" (Collins and Kugler 25). From this statement it is obvious that this person receives unparalleled honor. King David, Solomon, Hezekiah, Josiah – all of Israel's great kings – are overshadowed by this individual taking a throne that surpasses them so greatly that it resides in heaven.

Three times the speaker asserts that he is reckoned with the gods (lines 12, 14, and 18) but he also boasts that his "abode is in the holy congregation" (line 14). This is significant to note because "it seems to be a rule in the scrolls that the earthly congregation is described as Holy, using singular adjective, and the heavenly Congregation is described as consisting of the Holy Ones or of the gods in the plural" (O'Neill 24). Therefore what we have is a speaker who is not simply boasting about his status in heaven; he is also boasting that he is important in the context of earthly gatherings.

Line 14 also reveals that his "desire is not according to the flesh," which implies that "he was a human being whose desire could have been according to the flesh, but was not" (O'Neill 26). This again argues for a dual status between earth and heaven.

Even more mystery is added when we take notice that the speaker boasts of his sufferings. This may have relevance for New Testament interpretation. There we are told that the sufferings of Jesus are a "stumbling block to Jews" (1 Cor 1:23;

cf. Mark 8:33, where Peter is sharply rebuked when he questioned the need for Jesus' sufferings). Now through the discovery of 4Q491c we know that there was a person, whether real or fictive, who claimed divinity and at the same time boasted of great sufferings. The claims of the speaker in 4Q491c are comparable with those of the suffering servant in Isaiah 53, a passage that in places in the New Testament is applied to Jesus.

Who was this person who made all of these claims decades before the life and activities of Jesus of Nazareth? As mentioned, Maurice Baillet believed that he was the archangel Michael. The name Michael does mean, "who is like God," which offers a measure of support to Baillet's suggestion, but it is unlikely that an angel would claim to possess attributes that belong to God alone (lines 13, 15) or need to explain that his desires are not "according to the flesh" (line 14). Accordingly, it seems best to conclude that the speaker is a human being.

Of course, we must now ask: in what sense would a human being speak in such a manner? John Collins shows that it is not an impossible idea that a human can be given the attributes of a god; he refers to Exod 7:1, where it is said that Moses was "made like God to Pharaoh" (cf. 4Q374: "he made him as God to the mighty ones and a cause of reeling to Pharaoh"). Also, as Collins further notes, we have the work of Ezekiel the playwright, in which Moses sits on God's throne (Collins 23).

The suggestion that the speaker is the Messiah is not a perfect solution because we cannot say for certain that the authors of the scrolls believed the Messiah was to be divine. Certainly the Sanhedrin at Jesus' trial did not think it was right for any human to claim divinity (Mark 14:61–64). However, this alone cannot rule out the possibility. There is evidence from the Dead Sea Scrolls that some Jews did believe that at least the Davidic Messiah was regarded as divine (e.g. 4Q246). The New Testament also provides examples that the Hebrew Scriptures can be used to prove that Jesus was both the Messiah and divine.

Martin Abegg has suggested that the speaker is the Teacher of Righteousness, a figure who played an important role in the founding of the community, which is probably to be identified with the Essenes and left behind the scrolls found at Qumran and other locations nearby (Abegg).

The final possibility to note here is the suggestion that the speaker is Melchizedek. Collins remarks that in "the Melchizedek Scroll ... he is *Elohim,* god, or divine being, and not *adam* or human" (Collins 19). For a helpful study on the problem,

see J. C. O'Neill. In this study O'Neill identifies comparisons between 4Q491c and the Melchizedek Scroll (11Q13). The latter scroll is helpful, but does not offer parallels to the remarkable claims found in the former scroll.

The speaker of 4Q491c may never be identified, but his language may well be of some help in the study of the historical Jesus. At the very least it shows that Jesus could have replied to the Jewish high priest as related in the gospels.

JEFF SEARS

Further reading

Abegg, Martin G. "Who Ascended to Heaven? 4Q491, 4Q427, and the Teacher of Righteousness," in C. A. Evans and P. W. Flint (eds) *Eschatology, Messianism, and the Dead Sea Scrolls,* Studies in the Dead Sea Scrolls and Related Literature, Grand Rapids, MI: Eerdmans, 1997, pp. 61–73.

Baillet, Maurice. *Qumrân Grotte 4. III (4Q482–4Q520),* DJD 7, Oxford: Clarendon, 1982.

Collins, John J. *The Scepter and the Star: The Messiahs of the Dead Sea Scrolls and Other Ancient Literature.* New York: Doubleday, 1995.

Collins, John J. and Robert A. Kugler. *Religion in the Dead Sea Scrolls,* Grand Rapids, MI: Eerdmans, 2000.

Dimant, Devorah. "A Synoptic Comparison of Parallel Sections in 4Q427 7, 4Q491 11 and 4Q471B," *JQR* 85 (1994) 157–61.

Hess, Richard S., and M. Daniel Carroll R. (eds) *Israel's Messiah in the Bible and the Dead Sea Scrolls,* Grand Rapids, MI: Baker Academic, 2003.

Knoll, Israel. *The Messiah before Jesus: The Suffering Servant of the Dead Sea Scrolls,* Berkeley, CA: University of California Press, 2000.

O'Neill, J. C. "'Who is Comparable to Me in My Glory?' 4Q491 fragment 11 (4Q491C) and the New Testament," *NovT* 42 (2000) 24–38.

Schiffman, Lawrence H. and James C. VanderKam (eds) *Encyclopedia of the Dead Sea Scrolls,* 2 vols, Oxford: Oxford University Press, 2000.

Wise, Michael, Martin Abegg, Jr, and Edward Cook. *Dead Sea Scrolls: A New Translation,* New York: HarperCollins, 1996.

DEAD SEA SCROLLS: SON OF GOD TEXT (4Q246)

The *Son of God* text, 4Q246, comprises a single fragment of Aramaic text, which dates to the first century BCE. A portion of the text was published by J. A. Fitzmyer in 1974 (reprinted in 1979: 92–3), but E. Puech's official edition was not released until 1992.

According to 4Q246 a seer interprets the vision of a distressed king (1.1–3), who has observed the destruction and carnage wreaked by oppressive foreign powers (1:4–8; cf. 2:2–3, 8–9). The most noted aspect of the king's vision, however, is a figure entitled "son of God" and "son of the Most High" (2:1). The identity of this figure is the subject of debate, since scholars disagree as to whether the "son of God" is responsible for the violence in the vision, and what relationship he has to the rise God's people (2:4–6).

History of interpretation

D. Flusser contends that 4Q246 testifies to a pre-Christian antichrist (Flusser 31–7), analogous to the figure described in the NT as "a son of perdition who opposes and exalts himself against every so-called god or object of worship … proclaiming himself to be God" (2 Thess 2:3–4; cf. *Mart. Ascen. Isa* 4:2–16; *Did.* 16:4; *T. Mos.* 9:6–7; the *Oracle of Hystapses*). There are two difficulties with this interpretation. First, there is limited value in Christian or post-Christian documents as parallels to 4Q246 (Cook 61). Second, a key aspect of Flusser's interpretation depends on the translation of the Aramaic verb, "they will serve" (1:8), with the Hebraism, "they will worship" (Fitzmyer 1993: 169).

J. T. Milik also suggests the "son of God" is an oppressive figure, and believes it is the Seleucid king, Alexander Balas (Milik 1976: 60; Fitzmyer 1979: 85–113). While Balas did inscribe coins with divine epithets, there is nothing specifically tying 4Q246 to his reign. Furthermore, Josephus notes that Balas installed Jonathan as high priest (*Ant.* 13.2.2:45), making it unlikely he would be regarded as Israel's enemy (Fitzmyer 1993: 168).

E. M. Cook (43–66) has proposed another Seleucid king, Antiochus Epiphanes, as the negative inspiration behind the "son of God," and also suggests that that certain Akkadian prophecies shed light on 4Q246. These prophecies describe the chaotic reigns of a series of unnamed rulers, the last of whom ushers in an era of peace. This last reign is paralleled in 4Q246 in the rise of the people of God, and their ensuing governance of the kingdom (2:4–5), which ends the rule of the blasphemous "son of God," Antiochus. In response, it has been observed that the parallels between 4Q246 and the Akkadian literature are too general to establish a direct relationship, and that the historical record is damaging to many of Cook's arguments. Moreover, the proposal depends on a restoration of the text: without Cook's addition of "likewise his son" (1:9), the dynastic father-son succession motif of the Akkadian prophecies is not to be found in 4Q246, further weakening the link to Antiochus (Collins 1997: 51–8).

F. Garcia Martinez (1992: 162–79) has argued for an angelic interpretation of the "son of God."

4Q246, then, is similar to 11QMelch, which describes an eschatological battle fought by the "sons of God" (11Q13 2:14), and also ends with the peaceful reign of Israel. But this understanding is problematic: if the "son of God" is an angel, and "the great God himself is his might" (2:7) is a reference to this figure, the description is peculiar, as normally it is said that angels support Israel. Moreover, while angels are called "*sons* of God" at Qumran, the singular "son of God" is not a title associated with the principal angel figure (Collins 1994: 161–3).

J. D. G. Dunn has posited a collective interpretation of the "son of God" (198–210), suggesting that 4Q246 is a amalgam of the expectations of 2 Sam 7:10–14 and Dan 7, where the "son of God" people of God" in 2:1, 4 are deliberate echoes of the parallel between the "son of man"/ people of the saints of the Most High" in Dan 7:13, 27. Since in its original context Daniel 7 represents the triumph of the Jewish people, 4Q246 and the "son of God" are primarily intended to convey the collective victory of Israel over her enemies.

J. J. Collins (1997: 51–61), J. Zimmermann (173–90), and others interpret the "son of God" as a messianic figure. In light of 4Q174 3:10–13, where the messiah is described in terms of the divine sonship of 2 Sam 7:14 (cf. 1QSa 2:11–12), it is overwhelmingly probable that the "son of God" of 4Q246 was intended to represent a messianic deliverer of God's people (cf. Fitzmyer 1993: 171–4). The use of identical language by the Lukan evangelist strengthens this probability, as Luke would not have used the "son of God" epithet if had been associated with a blasphemous figure (see below). The close linguistic parallels of 4Q246 with Daniel 7 (Xeravits 86) may also suggest that the "son of God" figure is an implicit *individualistic and messianic* reworking of coming of the "son of man" of Dan 7:13–14 (cf. Dunn 198–210; Collins 2000a: 9–28).

4Q246 and the Gospel of Luke

The relevance of 4Q246 is seen in the significant parallels with the language of annunciation in the Lukan infancy narrative. These parallels seem to confirm that this language is indeed messianic: God will give Jesus "the throne of his father, David" (Luke 1:32): "he will be great" (1:7; cf. Luke 1:32); "he will be called 'son of the Most High'" (2:1; cf. Luke 1:32); "he will be called 'son of God'" (2:1; cf. Luke 1:32); and "his kingdom will be an everlasting kingdom" (2:5; cf. Luke 1:33).

Furthermore, the appearance of the epithets "son of God" and "son of the Most High" in a first-century BCE Jewish Aramaic text argues against assumptions made in the past that the use of such language in developing Christology arose because of the influence of Greco-Roman ideas of the divine ruler; 4Q246 testifies that messianic divine sonship was a familiar concept in pre-Christian Palestinian Judaism.

It also demonstrates an early willingness to amalgamate the apocalyptic imagery of Daniel 7 with the expectations of Davidic messianism. This combination is especially important in Jesus' response to the High Priest regarding his messianic status (cf. Mark 14:61–62; Luke 22:67–70; Matt 26:63–64).

MATTHEW L. WALSH

Further reading

Collins, J. J. *Daniel: A Commentary on the Book of Daniel*, Hermenia, Minneapolis, MN: Fortress Press, 1993, pp. 277–324.

—— *The Scepter and the Star: Messiahs of the Dead Sea Scrolls and Other Ancient Literature*, ABRL; New York: Doubleday, 1993, pp. 154–72.

—— "The Son of God Text from Qumran," in M. C. De Boer (ed.) *From Jesus to John: Essays on Jesus and New Testament Christology in Honor of Marinus de Jong*, JSNTSup 84, Sheffield: JSOT, 1993, pp. 65–82.

—— "The Works of the Messiah," *DSD* 1 (1994) 98–112.

—— "The Background of the 'Son of God' Text," *BBR* 7 (1997) 51–61.

—— "God, Gods, and Angels in the Dead Sea Scrolls," in J. J. Collins and R. A. Kugler (eds) *Religion in the Dead Sea Scrolls*, Grand Rapids, MI: Eerdmans, 2000a, pp. 9–28.

—— "The Nature of Messianism in Light of the Dead Sea Scrolls," in T. H. Lim (ed.) *The Dead Sea Scrolls in their Historical Context*, Edinburgh: T. & T. Clark, 2000b, pp. 199–217.

Cook, E. M. "4Q246," *BBS* 5 (1995) 43–66.

Cross, F. M. "Notes on the Doctrine of the Two Messiahs at Qumran and the Extracanonical Daniel Apocalypse (4Q246)," in D. W. Parry and S. D. Ricks (eds) *Current Research and Technological Developments on the Dead Sea Scrolls: Conference on the Texts from the Judean Desert, Jerusalem, 30 April 1995*, STDJ 20; Leiden: Brill, 1996, pp. 1–13.

—— "The Structure of the Apocalypse of 'Son of God'," in S. M. Paul, R. A. Kraft, L. H. Schiffman and W. W. Fields (eds) *Emanuel: Studies in Hebrew Bible, Septuagint, and Dead Sea Scrolls in Honor of Emanuel Tov*, Leiden: Brill, 2003, pp. 153–4.

Dunn, J. D. G. "'Son of God' as 'Son of Man' in the Dead Sea Scrolls? A Response to John Collins on 4Q246," in S. E. Porter and C. A. Evans (eds) *The Scrolls and the Scriptures: Qumran Fifty Years After*, JSPSup 26, Sheffield: Sheffield Academic Press, 1997, pp. 198–210.

Evans, C. A. "Jesus and Dead Sea Scrolls from Qumran Cave 4," in C. A. Evans and P. W. Flint (eds) *Eschatology, Messianism, and the Dead Sea Scrolls*, Grand Rapids, MI: Eerdmans, 1997, pp. 91–100.

Fitzmyer, J. A. "The Contribution of Qumran Aramaic to New Testament Studies," in *A Wandering Aramean: Collected Aramaic Essays*, SBLMS 25, Chico, CA: Scholars Press, 1979, pp. 85–113.

—— "4Q246: The 'Son of God' Document from Qumran," *Bib* 74 (1993) 153–74.

—— "The Aramaic 'Son of God' Document from Qumran," in M. O. Wise, N. Golb, J. J. Collins, and D. G. Pardee (eds) *Methods of Investigation of the Dead Sea Scrolls and Khirbet Qumran Site: Present Realities and Future Prospects*, ANYAS 722, New York: New York Academy of Sciences, 1994, pp. 163–78.

Flusser, D. "The Hubris of the Antichrist in a Fragment from Qumran," *Immanuel* 10 (1980) 31–7.

Garcia Martinez, F. "The Eschatological Figure of 4Q246," in *Qumran and Apocalyptic: Studies on the Aramaic Texts from Qumran*, STDJ 9, Leiden: Brill, 1992, pp. 162–79.

—— "Messianische Erwartungen in den Qumranschriften," *JBTh* 98 (1993) 171–208.

Hengel, M. *The Son of God: The Origin of Christology and the History of Jewish-Hellenistic Religion*, Philadelphia, PA: Fortress Press, 1976, pp. 44–5.

Kim, S. "'The Son of Man' as the Son of God", WUNT 30, J. C. B. Mohr [Paul Siebeck]: Tubingen, 1983, pp. 20–2.

Milik, J. T. *The Books of Enoch: Aramaic Fragments of Qumran Cave 4*, Oxford: Oxford University Press, 1976, p. 60.

—— "Les Modèles Aramens du Livre d'Esther dans la Brotte 4 de Qumran," *RevQ* 15 (1992) 321–99.

Puech, E. "Fragment d'une Apocalypse en Araméen (4Q246 = pseudo-Dand) et le 'Royaume de Dieu'," *RB* 99 (1992) 98–131.

—— "Les manuscripts de la mer Morte et le Nouveau Testament," *MdB* 86 (1994) 34–41.

—— "Notes sur le fragment d'apocalypse 4Q246 – 'le fils de Dieu'," *RB* 101 (1994) 533–58.

—— "246. 4QApocryphe de Daniel ar (Pl. XI)," in G. J. Brooke (edn) *Qumran Cave 4.XVII: Parabiblical Texts, Part III*, DJD 22, Oxford: Oxford University Press, 1997, pp. 165–84.

Steudel, A. "The Eternal Reign of the People of God – Collective Expectation in Qumran Texts (4Q246 and 1QM)," *RevQ* 17 (1996) 509–21.

Xeravits, G. G. *King, Priest, Prophet: Positive Eschatological Protagonists of the Qumran Library*, STDJ 47, Leiden: Brill, 2003, p. 86.

Zimmermann, J. "Observations on 4Q246 – The 'Son of God'," in J. H. Charlesworth, H. Lichtenberger, and G. S. Oegema (eds) *Qumran-Messianism*, Tubingen: Mohr Siebeck, 1998, pp. 175–90.

DEATH AND BURIAL OF JESUS

Jesus died in Jerusalem in either the year 30 or 33. He was executed by crucifixion as a criminal. The factors that led up to his arrest and execution are disputed. Recently at least one scholar has raised doubts about the burial of Jesus. Primary literature from late antiquity, including the Dead Sea Scrolls, and recent archaeological findings shed light on the manner of Jesus' death and on the high probability that he was buried in accordance with Jewish burial traditions.

Factors leading to the death of Jesus

Jesus' death was the result of his entry into Jerusalem, where he threatened the ruling priestly establishment. Jesus' controversial teachings regarding Sabbath, purity, and forgiveness seem to have played little or no role in his arrest and execution.

Jesus' entry probably was guided by and interpreted in the light of passages from Zechariah and Pslm 118, evidently as nuanced in the setting of the Aramaic-speaking synagogue (Mark 11:1–11; cf. Zech 9:9; Ps 118:25–26). These Scriptures continue to play a role in Passion Week, with Jesus forbidding commercial traffic in the temple precincts (Mark 11:15–18; cf. Zech 14:20–21), identifying himself as the stone rejected by the builders (Mark 12:10–12; cf. Ps 118:22–23), and as the shepherd struck down by God (Mark 14:26–27; cf. Zech 13:7). The Words of Institution probably also allude to Zechariah (Mark 14:24; cf. Zech 9:11). Although it is true that the later evangelists, especially Matthew, embellish these allusions, sometimes upgrading them to formal quotations (as in Matt 21:4–5; John 12:14–15), their allusive presence in Mark suggests that they were part of the earliest tradition and probably derived from the words and actions of Jesus himself.

Whether Jesus anticipated his death and resurrection remains an item of debate. His anticipation of death seems probable, for the violent fate of John the Baptist surely impressed itself on Jesus (Mark 6:14–29; 9:13). What is more compelling is the scene in Gethsemane, in which the frightened Jesus falls on his face, begging God to take away the cup of suffering (Mark 14:33–36). This is not the stuff of pious fiction or dogma. Indeed, it stands in stark contrast to the serene Jesus portrayed in John 17.

Of course, if Jesus anticipated his death, it is probable that he attempted to find meaning in it. The words of institution should be interpreted in this light. In the shedding of his blood, Jesus finds guarantee of the covenant and the kingdom of God (Mark 14:22–25). Luke's addition of "new," as in "the new covenant" (Luke 22:20), is redactional, to be sure, but it probably correctly captures the sense of Jesus' words. The "new covenant" hearkens back to the promise of Jer 31:31. The new covenant cannot be established until the blood of God's Son, Israel's Messiah, is shed.

The idea of the saving benefit of a righteous man's death is hardly unusual in the Jewish world, or in the Mediterranean world in general for that matter. There are several expressions of the belief that the death of the righteous will benefit, or even

save, God's people (e.g. 1 Macc 6:44; 4 Macc 1:11; 17:21–22; 18:3–4; *T. Mos.* 9–10; Ps-Philo, *Bib. Ant.* 18:5). Among the most important are traditions associated with the torture and death of the Maccabean martyrs.

> If our living Lord is angry for a little while, to rebuke and discipline us, he will again be reconciled with his own servants ... I, like my brothers, give up body and life for the laws of our fathers, appealing to God to show mercy soon to our nature ... and *through me and my brothers* to bring to an end the wrath of the Almighty which has justly fallen on our whole nation.
> (2 Macc 7:33, 37–38, emphasis added)

Similarly, Jesus believed that God was angry with his people for having rejected his message. We see this in Jesus' weeping over the city (Luke 19:41–44; Matt 23:37–39 = Luke 13:34–35) and in his ominous allusion to the shepherd in Zech 13:7.

If Jesus did anticipate his death, did he anticipate his resurrection as well? Had he not anticipated it, it would have been very strange, for pious Jews very much believed in the resurrection (Dan 12:1–3; *1 En.* 22–27; 92–105; *Jub.* 23:11–31; *4 Macc* 7:3; *4 Ezra* 7:26–42; *2 Bar.* 21:23; 30:2–5; Josephus, *J.W.* 2.154, 165–66; *Ant.* 18.14, 16, 18). One is reminded of the seven martyred sons and their mother, several of whom expressed their firmest conviction of the resurrection (2 Macc 7:14, 23, 29; cf. *4 Macc.* 8–17). Would Jesus have faced death and then, having earlier affirmed his belief in the resurrection (Mark 12:18–27), have expressed no faith in his own vindication? Surely not. It seems probable that Jesus would have reassured his disciples (and himself) with a confident prediction of his resurrection.

The words of Jesus, "after three days rise again" (Mark 8:31) and – in the other gospels – "on the third day" (Matt 16:21; Luke 9:22; cf. 1 Cor 15:4), probably allude to the oracle of Hosea that promised the renewal of Israel: "After two days he will revive us; on the third day he will raise us up, that we may live before him" (6:2), though, again, as refracted through the Aramaic tradition: "He will revive us *in the days of consolations that will come; on the day of the resurrection of the dead* he will raise us up and we shall live before him" (*Tg. Hos* 6:2, with italicized portion indicating differences in the Aramaic). Not only has the text been paraphrased to give expression to the resurrection (which was not the original meaning of the underlying Hebrew), it has also taken on a messianic nuance with the words, "in the days of consolations" (cf. *Tg. 2 Sam* 23:1). The coherence of Jesus' words with the Aramaic tradition is striking.

The juridical process that overtook Jesus (arrest, interrogation by Jewish authorities, delivery to Roman authorities with recommendation of execution, interrogation by Roman, scourging, execution) corresponds with what we know of other cases. Indeed, the experience of Jesus of Nazareth parallels quite closely the experience of Jesus ben Ananias, who some thirty years later uttered oracles of doom in the city of Jerusalem and in the temple precincts themselves. Like Jesus of Nazareth (Mark 11:17; cf. Jer 7:11), Jesus ben Ananias alluded to Jeremiah 7, while in the vicinity of the Temple (Josephus, *J.W.* 6.300–305; cf. Jer 7:34). Unlike Jesus of Nazareth, Jesus ben Ananias was not executed (despite calls from religious leaders that he be put to death), but was released.

The crucifixion of Jesus

Jesus was put to death by crucifixion, a form of execution practiced in late antiquity, whereby a person was tied or nailed to a pole or cross. Crucifixion was practiced in the eastern Mediterranean long before the Romans adopted the practice. It was practiced by Persians (cf. Herodotus 1.128.2; 3.125.3) and other peoples, such as Assyrian, Scythians, and Thracians. Alexander the Great is said to have crucified thousands (cf. Curtius Rufus, *Hist. Alex.* 4.4.17). His successors continued the practice. It is not surprising that in time the Romans adopted this form of execution. It was primarily reserved for murderous or rebellious slaves (and for this reason was known as "slaves' punishment"; Latin: *servile supplicium*).

Jewish authorities before the Roman period also practiced crucifixion. Most notorious was Alexander Jannaeus (ruled 102–76 BCE), who, Josephus tells us, on one occasion crucified a large number of Pharisees who had opposed him and had allied themselves to a foreign enemy (*J.W.* 1.97–98; cf. *Ant.* 13.380). Josephus' testimony helps explain a reference in the Dead Sea Scrolls, where in one of the *pesharim* there is reference to the "Lion of Wrath" (understood to be Alexander Jannaeus) who "used to hang men alive" (4Q169 3–4 i 7). This may well be in reference to the incident mentioned by Josephus.

The Romans placed crosses along well-traveled highways, on tops of hills, and at city gates. The condemned man usually carried the cross-beam, or *patibulum* (cf. Plautus, *Carbonaria* 2; *Mil. glor.* 2.4.6–7:359–360; Plutarch, *Mor.* 554A–B; Mark 15:21), sometimes with a *titulus* around his neck, declaring his name and punishment, later to be affixed to the upright cross (cf. Suetonius, *Caligula*

32.2; Dio Cassius 54.3.6–7). This cruel punishment later also befell Christians. Fourth-century church historian and apologist Eusebius tells of one Attalus the Christian, who "was led around the amphitheatre and a placard was carried before him on which was written in Latin, 'This is Attalus, the Christian'" (*Hist. eccl.* 5.1.44).

According to Mark 15:21, the Romans "compelled a passer-by, Simon of Cyrene, who was coming in from the country, the father of Alexander and Rufus, to carry his cross." The authenticity of this scene is supported by the observation that Jesus had earlier instructed his disciples to be ready and willing to take up the cross and come after him (Mark 8:34). It is not likely early Christians would invent a story about Jesus being unable to follow his own instruction to the letter.

Interestingly enough, the ossuary (or bone box) of Alexander, son of Simon, may have been found. Inscribed on the back of the ossuary (in Greek) are the names "Alexander of Simon" and on the lid (in Aramaic) "Alexander the Cyrenite" (for further discussion, see Evans 2006: 338–40).

The gospels say that a *titulus* was placed on the cross of Jesus (cf. John 19:19; Matt 27:37; Mark 15:26; Luke 23:38) and that it was written in more than one language, describing Jesus as "king of the Jews." The epithet "king of the Jews" is Roman and was originally applied to Herod the Great (cf. Josephus, *Ant.* 15.409: "the king of the Jews, Herod").

As a prelude to his crucifixion, Jesus is scourged (the Latin loan word *phragellosas* in Mark 15:15 and Matt 27:26; forms of the Greek *mastigoun* in Luke 18:33 and John 19:1; in the Passion predictions in Mark 10:34 and Matt 20:19). Scourging was apparently standard pre-crucifixion procedure in Roman times (cf. *Digesta* 48.19.8.3; Josephus, *J.W.* 2.306). It was done with a whip made of several leather straps, to which were attached sharp, abrasive items, such as nails, glass, or rocks. Scourging resulted in severe laceration of the skin and damage to the flesh beneath. Josephus tells of one Jesus son of Ananias (*c.* 62 CE), whose prophecies of Jerusalem's doom resulted in his being brought before the Roman governor. Although in the end the man was not executed (as the ruling priests wished), he was "flayed to the bone with scourges [*mastixi mechri osteon xainomenos*]" (*J.W.* 6.304). Jesus of Nazareth warned his followers that they too face the danger of scourging (cf. Matt 10:17; 23:34).

Paul is threatened with beating (Acts 16:22; 22:24–25; cf. 2 Cor 11:25). Rabbinic law in late antiquity laid down rules regarding scourging (cf. *m. Sanh.* 1:2; *b. Sanh.* 10a). Scourging could be meted out in the local synagogue (cf. *m. Mak.* 3:10; Epiphanius, *Haer.* 30.11; Eusebius, *Hist. eccl.* 5.16.12; where Christian converts are beaten in the synagogue).

In the Greek version of the Old Testament *mastigoun* is found in reference to persons who are punished with floggings (cf. Deut 25:2–3; Josephus, *Ant.* 4.238). The word is sometimes used metaphorically in reference to discipline: "for the LORD whips him whom he loves, as a father the son in whom he delights" (Prov 3:12; cf. 19:25; 27:22); as well as punishment: "O LORD, do not thy eyes look for truth? Thou hast scourged them, but they felt no anguish; thou hast consumed them, but they refused to take correction" (Jer 5:3).

Oftentimes crucifixion victims were mocked, before and during execution. Jesus was mocked by the Jewish council. His face is covered and he is ordered to "prophesy" (Mark 14:65). The soldiers under the command of Governor Pilate also mocked Jesus: "They clothed him in a purple cloak, and plaiting a crown of thorns they put it on him. And they began to salute him, 'Hail, King of the Jews!' And they struck his head with a reed, and spat upon him, and they knelt down in homage to him" (Mark 15:17–19). The mockery of the soldiers is modeled after the homage paid to Caesar. The crown of thorns, meant to resemble a wreath of laurel worn by Caesar, is part of the mockery of Jesus. This mockery includes a purple cloak, a reed (symbolizing the scepter), and being addressed as a king (Mark 15:18–19). Sources from late antiquity describe others mocked in a similar fashion.

The mockery of Jesus as a Jewish king finds an approximate parallel in Philo, *Flacc.* 36–39. It was on the occasion of King Agrippa's visit to Alexandria, where the people seized a lunatic named Carabas, a street person who was often made sport of. They

> drove the poor fellow into the gymnasium ands set him up high to be seen by all and put on his head a sheet of byblus spread out wide for a diadem, clothed the rest of his body with a rug for a royal robe, while someone who had noticed a piece of the native papyrus thrown away in the road gave it to him for his scepter. And when as in some theatrical farce he had received the insignia of kingship and had been tricked out as a king, young men carrying rods on their shoulders as spearmen stood on either side of him in imitation of a bodyguard. Then others approached him, some pretending to salute him, others to sue for justice, others to consult him on state affairs. Then from the multitudes there rang out a tremendous shout hailing him as *Mari* [Aramaic: "My lord"], which is said to be the name for "lord" with the Syrians.

The mockery of Agrippa I is quite significant, well illustrating the mockery to which Jesus was subjected. It does not, however, require us to conclude that Mark is dependent in some way on this incident or on Philo's work itself. Other incidents approximate the mockery of Jesus. One thinks of harsh and humiliating treatment of deposed Vitellius (69 CE) at the hands of Roman soldiers, who mockingly made the former emperor revisit various stations where at one time he was held in honor (cf. Dio Cassius 64.20–21).

The mockery of Jesus also mimics aspects of the Roman triumph (see Schmidt), whereby Caesar is hailed as emperor and receives homage. The purple cloak, the crown of thorns (resembling the crown of ivy), the reed, with which Jesus is struck on the head, and the bowing in mock homage are all components of the apparel worn and homage received by the Roman emperor, who at the triumph wore a purple robe and laurel wreath and held a scepter (e.g. Dio Cassius 6.23; 44.11 [Julius Caesar]; Appian, *Bell. Civ.* 5.130 [Augustus]; Dio Cassius 59.25.3 [Gaius Caligula]; see Schmidt: 2–4 nn. 6–12). Being dressed in purple would also recall the attire of Hellenistic kings of an earlier period (cf. 1 Macc 10:20 ["purple robe and golden crown"], 62 ["clothe him in purple"]; 11:58 ["to dress in purple"]; 14:43–44 ["clothed in purple"]; Luke 16:19 ["dressed in purple"]).

We think too of the savage and humiliating treatment of Eleazar who was stripped, scourged, tortured, and then in his dying breath prayed for the salvation of Israel (*4 Macc.* 6:1–30). One is also reminded of the deposition recording the words of the new emperor Hadrian and a Jewish embassy, with reference to the Jewish revolt that occurred toward the end of Trajan's reign (115–17 CE). In this fragmentary document mention is made of the mockery of a would-be monarch: "Paulus [spoke] about the king, how they brought him forth and [mocked him?]; and Theon read the edict of Lupus ordering them to lead him forth for Lupus to make fun of the king" (P.Louvre 68 1.1–7). Plutarch (*Pomp.* 24.7–8) relates a story in which pirates mocked a prisoner who had claimed the rights of Roman citizenship. They dressed him up ("threw a toga on him"), extended to him various honors (including falling to their knees), then finally made him walk the plank.

Normally crucifixion victims were left to die, however long that took (sometimes several days). Sometimes friends and relatives were allowed to feed their loved one (cf. Matt 27:34; Mark 15:23; John 19:28–29). Guards were stationed until the victim expired. Occasionally friends or relatives attempted to rescue the victim. The bodies of the crucified were usually left unburied, to rot and to be picked apart by birds and animals (though Roman law did permit bodies to be taken down and buried; cf. *Digesta* 48.24.1, 3; Josephus, *Life* 420–21).

According to Cicero (*Ag. Verr.* 2.5.168) and Josephus (*J.W.* 7.203), crucifixion was the worst form of death (see also the disturbing comments in Juvenal, *Sat.* 14.77–78; Suetonius, *Aug.* 13.1–2; Horace, *Ep.* 1.16.48; Seneca, *Dial.* 3.2.2; 6.20.3; Isidore of Seville, *Etymologia* 5.27.34; *Mek.* on Exod 15:18 [*Shirata* §10]). Indeed, the words *cross* and *crucify* actually derive from the word *torture* (Latin: *cruciare*). The primary political and social purpose of crucifixion was deterrence: "Whenever we crucify the condemned, the most crowded roads are chosen, where the most people can see and be moved by this terror. For penalties relate not so much to retribution as to their exemplary effect" (Ps-Quintilian, *Decl.* 274; Aristophanes, *Thesm.* 1029 and Ps-Manetho, *Apostelesmatica* 4.198–200; cf. Josephus, *J.W.* 5.450–51).

In the gospels the soldiers who crucify Jesus divide his garments among themselves (Matt 27:35; Mark 15:24; Luke 23:34; John 19:23–24). This is consistent with Roman practice (cf. *Digesta*) 48.20.1; Tacitus, *Ann.* 6.29: "people sentenced to death forfeited their property").

The necessity of burial

In the Mediterranean world of late antiquity proper burial of the dead was regarded as sacred duty, especially so in the culture and religion of the Jewish people. The *first reason* for providing proper burial was for the sake of the dead themselves. The importance of care for the dead and their proper burial is well attested in Scripture, from the amount of attention given to the story of Abraham's purchase of a cave for the burial of Sarah (Gen 23:4–19), to the burial accounts of the patriarchs and monarchs of Israel. Of special interest is the story of Jacob's body taken to the land of Canaan, to be buried in a tomb that he had hewn (Gen 50:4–14). So also Joseph; though buried in Egypt, his bones are exhumed, taken with the Israelites at the time of the exodus and are eventually buried in Canaan (Gen 50:22–26; Josh 24:32). The bones of the slain Saul and his sons are buried in Jabesh (1 Sam 31:12–13). David later commends the men who did this (2 Sam 2:4–5: "May you be blessed by the Lord, because you showed this loyalty to Saul your lord, and buried him!"). Saul's bones are later taken to the land of

Benjamin (2 Sam 21:12–14). Even the wicked and divinely judged are buried, too, such as those in the wilderness who were greedy for meat (Num 11:33–34), or individual criminals who are executed (Deut 21:22–23). Israel's enemies, slain in battle, are buried (1 Kgs 11:15), including the eschatological enemy hosts of Gog (Ezek 39:11–16).

The great importance of proper burial provides the backdrop for the passages that speak of those who will *not be buried*, usually because of sin and divine judgment. Moses warns the Israelites that if they disobey the covenant, their enemies will slay them and their unburied bodies will be food for birds and animals (Deut 28:25–26). Generations later this judgment befell the families of the wicked kings Jeroboam (1 Kgs 14:11) and Ahab (1 Kgs 21:24). According to the prophetic warning, one from these families "who dies in the city the dogs shall eat; and any one who dies in the open country the birds of the air shall eat." Jezebel herself is eaten by dogs and becomes "dung upon the fields" (1 Kgs 21:23; 2 Kgs 9:33–37); that is, she has been eaten and then defecated. There will be no marker that says, "This is Jezebel." Jeremiah warns his own generation with the same disturbing imagery:

> And the dead bodies of this people will be food for the birds of the air, and for the beasts of the earth; and none will frighten them away … and they shall not be gathered or buried; they shall be as dung on the surface of the ground.
>
> (Jer 7:33; 8:2)

(Cf. Jer 14:16; 16:4; 20:6; 22:19; 25:33; cf. Ps 79:2–3; Ezek 29:5; Josephus, *J.W.* 1.594: "he would have her body torn to pieces by torments, and leave no part of it to be buried")

The ghastly image of Jews in exile, murdered and then left unburied beside the road or flung outside the city walls, is reflected in the book of Tobit. The book's namesake is a righteous man, who keeps *kashruth*, shares food and clothing with the poor, and buries the dead, even at great personal risk. The theme of Tobit burying the dead may well reflect Jeremiah's earlier warning.

Of all Tobit's virtues, it is his burying the dead that is his greatest (1:18–20; 2:3–8; 4:3–4; 6:15; 14:10–13). Some of the persons whose bodies Tobit buries evidently had been executed by state authority, and not simply murdered: "And if Sennacherib the king put to death any who came fleeing from Judea, I buried [ἔθαψα] them secretly. … When the bodies were sought by the king, they were not found" (1:18). The dead man mentioned in 2:3, whom Tobit also buries, was also executed, either strangled (so the RSV) or "exposed," in the

147

sense of being publicly hanged (as Moore argues). This Jewish sense of obligation that Jews executed by gentile authorities must be buried, even at personal risk, is very significant for the present study.

Josephus' perspective is consistent with that expressed in Tobit. Explaining Jewish ethical obligations, Josephus states: "We must furnish fire, water, food to all who ask for them, point out the road, not leave a corpse unburied [ἄταφον], show consideration even to declared enemies" (*C. Ap.* 2.211; cf. 2.205).

Perhaps Philo gives the most eloquent expression to Jewish sensitivities on this question, in his imaginative recounting of Jacob's grief over the report that his son Joseph had been killed and devoured by wild animals. The patriarch laments:

Child, it is not your death that grieves me, but the manner of it. If you had been buried [ἐτάφης] in your own land, I should have been comforted and watched and nursed your sick-bed, exchanged the last farewells as you died, closed your eyes, wept over your body as it lay there, given it a costly funeral and left none of the customary rites undone.

(*Ios.* 22–23)

The imaginative dirge goes on to speak of the importance of proper burial:

And, indeed, if you had to die by violence or through premeditation, it would have been a lighter ill to me, slain as you would have been by human beings, who would have pitied their dead victim, gathered some dust and covered the corpse. And then if they had been the cruelest of men, what more could they have done but cast it out unburied and go their way, and then perhaps some passer-by would have stayed his steps, and, as he looked, felt pity for our common nature and deemed the custom of burial to be its due.

(25)

Jacob concludes his lament by saying that he has experienced no greater tragedy, in that nothing of Joseph remains and that there is no possibility of burial (26–27).

Concern with proper burial continues beyond the first century. For the Rabbis burial of the dead, according to George Foot Moore (71), "was regarded as a duty of the highest obligation." He cites *b. Meg.* 3b, where this duty ("law of the dead") takes precedence in the study of the law, the circumcision of one's son, or in the offering of the Passover lamb, and *Sipre Num* §26 (on Num 6:6–8), where even a high priest or a Nazirite has the obligation to bury a "neglected corpse," since there is no one else to do it.

A second reason for burying the dead is to avoid defilement of the land of Israel. This requirement is grounded in the Mosaic law:

And if a man has committed a crime punishable by death and he is put to death, and you hang him on a tree, his body shall not remain all night upon the tree, but you shall bury him the same day, for a hanged man is accursed by God; you shall not defile your land which the Lord your God gives you for an inheritance.

(Deut 21:22–23)

It is also expressed in Ezekiel: "They will set apart men to pass through the land continually and bury those remaining upon the face of the land, so as to cleanse it ... Thus shall they cleanse the land" (Ezek 39:14, 16).

This tradition remained current at the turn of the era, as seen in its elaboration in the *Temple Scroll*, where we read:

If a man is a traitor against his people and gives them up to a foreign nation, so doing evil to his people, *you are to hang him on a tree until dead.* On the testimony of two or three witnesses he will be put to death, and they themselves shall hang him on the tree. If a man is convicted of a capital crime and flees to the nations, cursing his people and the children of Israel, *you are to hang him, also, upon a tree until dead.* But you must not let their bodies remain on the tree overnight; you shall most certainly bury them that very day. Indeed, anyone hung on a tree is accursed of God and men, but you are not to defile the land that I am about to give you as an inheritance [Deut 21:22–23].

(11QT 64:7–13a = 4Q524 frag. 14, lines 2–4; with emphasis added)

Whereas Deut 21:22–23 speaks of one put to death and then hanged, 11QTemple speaks of one hanged "until dead." Most think crucifixion is in view (as also in 4QpNah 3–4 i 6–8). It is also important to note that this form of execution is linked to treason.

It should also be observed that the requirement to bury the executed person *the day of his death* is emphasized. In Deuteronomy it simply says, "you shall bury him the same day"; but the *Temple Scroll* adds "you must not let their bodies remain on the tree overnight." The reason given for taking the bodies down and burying them the day (or evening) of death is to avoid defiling the land, for the executed person is "cursed of God." This is probably the rationale that lies behind the concern regarding slain enemy soldiers.

In the fragmentary conclusion of the *War Scroll* we have reference to the fallen Kittim (i.e. Romans) and their allies. Their corpses lie on the field of battle, unburied. Priests, including the high priest, stand over the corpses and praise God. What is said is not preserved (1QM 19:9–14 = 4Q492 frag. 1 lines 8–13), but it is probable that the priests oversee burial of the corpses and cleansing of the land. The related 4Q285, which is also fragmentary, supports this interpretation. It seems to say that while Israel celebrates victory over the Kittim (with women beating timbrels and dancing, as in the great victories recounted in Scripture; cf. Exod 15:20; Judg 11:34; perhaps also 4QpIsa^c 25 iii 1–3), the high priest shall give orders for the disposal of the corpses, evidently to avoid corpse impurity (4Q285 frag. 7, lines 1–6, esp. lines 5–6; cf. frag. 10, lines 4–6: "and you shall eat [the spoil of your enemy . . . and they shall dig] graves for them [and you shall cleanse yourselves from al]l their corpses . . . "). This then explains the meaning in 1QM 7:2–3, which refers to the men who "strip the slain, plunder the spoil, cleanse the land." Cleansing the land would include burying the corpses of the enemy.

In a section concerned with holiness, the *Temple Scroll* enjoins Israel:

> "for you are a people holy to the Lord your God" [Deut 14:2]. "Thus you shall not defile your land" [Num 35:34]. You are not to do as the nations do: they bury their dead everywhere, even inside their homes. Rather, you must set apart places in your land where you will bury your dead. For every four cities you must designate one burial ground.
>
> (11QT 48:10–14)

What is important here is that even in the case of the executed criminal, proper burial was anticipated. Various restrictions may have applied, such as being forbidden burial in one's family tomb – at least until the flesh had decomposed – or not being allowed to mourn publicly, but burial was to take place, in keeping with the scriptural command of Deut 21:22–23 and the Jewish customs that had grown up alongside it.

The commands of Scripture, taken with traditions regarding piety (as especially exemplified in Tobit), corpse impurity, and the avoidance of the defilement of the land, strongly suggest that under normal circumstances (i.e. peacetime) no corpse would remain unburied – neither Jew nor Gentile, neither innocent nor guilty. All were to be buried. What is especially interesting is that some of the tradition reviewed may have been specifically linked to, even produced by, priests (as in the materials from Qumran). If this is the case, then the relevance of these laws and traditions for the execution of Jesus of Nazareth and its aftermath becomes more evident.

The burial of Jesus

According to the Gospels, Jesus was taken down from the cross the very day he was crucified. To hasten the deaths of the two men crucified with Jesus, their legs were broken. In 1968 an ossuary was found at Giv'at ha-Mivtar, just north of Jerusalem (i.e. ossuary no. 4), which contained three skeletons (see Naveh; Zias and Sekeles; Zias and Charlesworth). One of the skeletons was of a man who had been crucified, for an iron spike still transfixed the right heel bone. Fragments of wood at both ends of the spike were present. Moreover, the man's legs had been broken. The skeleton of the crucified man has been dated to the late 20s CE, when Judaea and Samaria were administered by the Roman prefect Pontius Pilate. The crucified remains prove that Pilate permitted crucified Jewish criminals proper burial (as the Gospels say was the case of Jesus of Nazareth) and – if the broken leg bones are relevant – allowed them to be buried before sundown, contrary to normal Roman practice but in keeping with Jewish law and sensitivities (Evans 2005).

The major difference between Jewish crucifixion and later Roman crucifixion is that in the case of the former the bodies were taken down, at least if they had been crucified in lands inhabited by Jews (cf. Philo, *Flacc.* 10.83). No corpse in the vicinity of a Jewish city was left unburied at sundown, in keeping with Mosaic law (cf. Deut 21:23). Moreover, strict Jewish laws regarding corpse impurity, as well as pious devotion to the dead, even criminal dead, would make it unthinkable to leave unburied bodies just outside the walls and gates of Jerusalem.

Jesus was taken down from the cross before nightfall and was buried according to Jesus customs (Mark 15:42–16:4). Jesus was put to death as a criminal and he was buried accordingly (*m. Sanh.* 6:5; *Semahot* 13.7). The novel suggestion that perhaps Jesus was left on the cross, unburied (as was usually the case outside Israel; cf. Suetonius, *Aug.* 13.1–2; Petronius, *Sat.* 111), or that his corpse was thrown into a ditch, covered with lime, and left for animals to maul, is wholly implausible. Obligations to bury the dead properly, before sundown, were keenly felt by Jews of late antiquity.

Accordingly we have every reason to conclude that Jesus was properly buried the very day of his death. It is further concluded that it is very probable that some of Jesus' followers (such as the women mentioned in the Gospel accounts) knew where Jesus' body had been placed and intended to mark the location, perfume his body, and mourn, in keeping with Jewish customs. The intention was to take possession of Jesus' remains, at some point in the future, and transfer them to his family burial place.

CRAIG A. EVANS

Further reading

Bonner, C. "The Crown of Thorns," *HTR* 46 (1953) 47–8.

Brown, R. E. *The Death of the Messiah: From Gethsemane to the Grave. A Commentary on the Passion Narratives in the Four Gospels*, 2 vols, ABRL, New York: Doubleday, 1994.

Evans, C. A. "Jewish Burial Traditions and the Resurrection of Jesus," *Journal for the Study of the Historical Jesus* 3 (2005) 233–48.

—— "Excavating Caiaphas, Pilate, and Simon of Cyrene: Assessing the Literary and Archaeological Evidence," in James H. Charlesworth (ed.) *Jesus and Archaeology*, Grand Rapids, MI: Eerdmans, 2006, pp. 323–40.

Fitzmyer, J. A. "Crucifixion in Ancient Palestine, Qumran Literature, and the New Testament," *CBQ* 40 (1978) 493–513.

Goodenough, E. R. and C. B. Welles. "The Crown of Acanthus (?)," *HTR* 46 (1953) 241–2.

Hengel, M. *Crucifixion: In the Ancient World and the Folly of the Message of the Cross*, London: SCM Press; Philadelphia, PA: Fortress Press, 1977.

Hewitt, J. W. "The Use of Nails in the Crucifixion," *HTR* 25 (1932) 29–45.

Moore, G. F. *Judaism in the First Centuries of the Christian Era: The Age of the Tannaim*, 3 vols, Cambridge, MA: Harvard University Press, 1927–30.

Naveh, J. "The Ossuary Inscriptions from Giv'at ha-Mivtar, Jerusalem," *IEJ* 20 (1970) 33–7.

Osiek, C. "The Women at the Tomb: What are They Doing There?" in A. Levine (ed.) *A Feminist Companion to Matthew*, Cleveland: Pilgrim Press, 2004, pp. 205–20.

Schmidt, T. E. "Mark 15.16–32: The Crucifixion Narrative and the Roman Triumphal Procession," *NTS* 41 (1995) 1–18.

Zias, J. and J. H. Charlesworth. "Crucifixion: Archaeology, Jesus, and the Dead Sea Scrolls," in J. H. Charlesworth (ed.) *Jesus and the Dead Sea Scrolls*, New York: Doubleday, 1992, pp. 273–89 and plates following p. 184.

Zias, J. and E. Sekeles. "The Crucified Man from Giv'at ha-Mivtar: A Reappraisal," *IEJ* 35 (1985) 22–7.

DECAPOLIS

The Decapolis is a region consisting of approximately ten Hellenistic cities in the northern Transjordan area of Palestine. Though the word *Dekapolis* in Greek literally means "ten cities," the exact number of cities belonging to the group varied. Pliny the Elder is the earliest extant source to list the towns of the Decapolis (*Nat.* 5.16:74). He explains that there were differing lists at his time of writing, but gives what he saw to be the most common: Damascus, Philadelphia, Raphana, Scythopolis (Beth-Shean), Gadara, Hippus, Dium, Pella, Galasa (Gerasa), and Canatha. The list is expanded by Ptolemy, who adds: Heliopolis, Abila Lysinias, Saana, Ina, Samulis, Abida (Abila), Capitolias, Adra, and Gadora (*Geog.* 5.15:22–23). Since Ptolemy does not list Raphana, the number of unique cities listed between the two sources is nineteen. In the fourth century CE, Eusebius states

that the Decapolis is the region in Perea which encompasses Hippus, Pella, and Gadara (*Onom.* 396/80:16). Of all the cities listed, Scythopolis is the only one west of the Jordan River.

Most of the cities were granted independence by Pompey in 63 BCE, and were absorbed into the province of Syria (Josephus, *Ant.* 14.4.4:75–76; *J.W.* 1.7.7:155–157). They were likely grouped as the Decapolis at this period. Previous scholarship had assumed that the Decapolis was a league or confederation of cities, but more recently as an administrative region connected to the province of Syria (Parker 128).

Mark is the earliest extant source to mention the term *Decapolis* (5:20; 7:31), and Matthew is the only other New Testament author to use it (4:25). Early on in Jesus' ministry, the multitude following him was comprised of people from various parts of Palestine, including those of the Decapolis (Matt 4:25; cf. Mark 3:8).

The most prominent event in the Decapolis associated with Jesus is the pericope of the Gerasene Demoniac (Mark 5:1–20; Matt 8:28–34; Luke 8:26–39). Mark places its setting in the "region of the Gerasenes," that is, somewhere near the city of Gerasa (Jerash). Even in the first century, the pericope's location was disputed. Matthew, according to the best manuscripts, places it in the region of the "Gadarenes." Origen suggests the correct reading should be "Gergesenes" (*Comm. Jo.* 6.24), supported by some manuscripts (possibly on account of Origen's suggestion), but ultimately not the best reading in any gospel. Both readings, Gerasa and Gadara, are part of the Decapolis and thus relevant to the discussion here. What made Gergese a lucrative choice for Origen and others is its location on the Sea of Galilee, a necessary component for this pericope. Both the cities of Gerasa and Gadara are removed from the sea by a number a miles, though the territory belonging to Gadara stretched to the sea, which is observable by images of ships on its coins (Schürer 136).

In Mark's Gospel Jesus arrives in the region of Gerasa and immediately meets an unrestrainable demoniac living among tombs. The demoniac recognizes Jesus as the "Son of the Most High God." Jesus asks his name, to which the demoniac replies, "My name is Legion, for we are many." Seeing a herd of swine, the unclean spirits beg Jesus to send them into the swine instead of casting them out of the country. Jesus agrees and the spirits are sent into the swine, about two thousand in number, and immediately they rush down a steep bank and drown in the sea. People hurry to find the demoniac sitting, clothed, and sane. The people, seized with fear, ask Jesus to leave; but as he departs, he tells the demoniac to proclaim what God has done for him. The demoniac spreads the word in the Decapolis, astonishing everyone.

Luke's version varies slightly from Mark. The unclean spirits are not afraid of being cast out of the country, but of returning to the abyss. Additionally, Luke removes Mark's fantastic number of swine and leaves the number ambiguous. More fascinating is Luke's change of the location; Mark states that the location of the demoniac's proclamation is "in the Decapolis," but Luke removes the reference to the Decapolis and changes it to "throughout the city." Luke's failure to set the story in the Decapolis varies from his normal considerable interest in the interaction between Jesus and the Gentiles.

Matthew's version is strikingly different from both Mark and Luke. Now the setting is the region of the Gadarenes, and Jesus confronts two demoniacs instead of one. Similarly, the demons depart into the swine that ultimately drown, but unlike in Mark and Luke, however, Matthew's version ends on a negative note with Jesus being asked to leave their district.

The other clear reference to the Decapolis in Mark's Gospel is 7:31. Jesus, after healing the Syrophoenician's daughter in the region of Tyre, travels to the Sea of Galilee by way of the Decapolis. While in the Decapolis (7:32–37) he heals a deaf man by unconventional means and amazes the crowd that affirms his ability to heal.

Early tradition describes a flight to Pella by Christians in Jerusalem to avoid God's pending judgment on that city (Eusebius, *Hist. eccl.* 3.5.3; Epiphanius, *Pan.* 29.7.7–8; 30.20.7; *De Mens. et Pond.* 15; cf. Pseudo-Clementines *Recog.* 1.37.2; 1.39.3). Scholars are divided on whether this tradition has any historical correlation to Jesus' apocalyptic statement, "let those in Judea flee to the mountains" (Mark 13:14; Matt 24:16; Luke 21:21). Mark first connects this statement with the desolating sacrilege. Luke clearly links the saying with the siege of Jerusalem in 70 CE by including a remark about Jerusalem surrounded by armies (21:20).

The association between Jesus and the Decapolis mostly occurs in the Synoptic Gospels; yet John's Gospel may indirectly refer to the Decapolis as well. In 3:23, John the Baptist performs baptisms at Aenon near Salim, which was possibly located within the region of Scythopolis. Additionally, Greeks attending the feast in Jerusalem seek after Jesus (12:20–25). Although they may have come from the Decapolis, John does not mention their place of origin and it remains speculative at best.

The Decapolis is an important region for historical Jesus research. Not only were there followers of Jesus among its residents, but significant pericopae of healing and exorcism find their settings there. Since the Decapolis cities were mostly Hellenistic, these pericopae show interconnections between Jesus' activities and the greater Hellenistic society, a precursor for Christianity's spread throughout the Gentile world.

BRANDON C. WASON

Further reading:

Baarda, Tj. "Gadarenes, Gerasenes, Gergesenes and the 'Diatessaron' Traditions," in E. Earle Ellis and Max Wilcox (eds) *Neotestamentica et Semitica: Studies in Honour of Matthew Black*, Edinburgh: T. & T. Clark, 1969, pp. 181–97.

Koester, Craig. "The Origin and Significance of the Flight to Pella Tradition," *CBQ* 51:1 (1989) 90–106.

Parker, S. Thomas. "Decapolis," in Eric M. Meyers (ed.) *The Oxford Encyclopedia of Archaeology in the Near East*, New York: Oxford University Press, 1997, Vol. 2, pp. 127–30.

Rey-Coquais, Jean-Paul. "Decapolis," in David Noel Freedman (ed.) *The Anchor Bible Dictionary*, New York: Doubleday, 1992, Vol. 2, pp. 116–21.

Schürer, Emil. *The History of the Jewish People in the Age of Jesus Christ (175 BC–AD 135)*, revised and ed. Geza Vermes, Fergus Millar, and Matthew Black, Edinburgh: T. & T. Clark, 1979, Vol. II.

DEMONS AND EXORCISM

Although in earlier times views on demons were not always clear, perhaps because of contact with other cultures (cf. *2 Bar.* 48:1–24; Tob 3:1–6; 13:1–15), by the New Testament era demons were evil or unclean spiritual entities under the leadership of Satan and could cause personal harm or illness as well as immorality and false belief. Exorcism has been practiced from antiquity and, although not common among the Greeks, Jews in the time of Jesus were famous for their demonology and exorcisms.

Old Testament

The Hebrew Bible has no single concept corresponding to "demon." Instead, in a way widely reflected in the ancient world (e.g. Aeschylus, *Agam.* 160–6; Pindar, *Pyth.* 5.122–3), early stories in the Old Testament depict God as responsible for both good and bad spirits (1 Kgs 22:21–23), sending his spirit or a divine spirit (Exod 31:3), as well as an evil spirit that could cause suffering for a person (1 Sam 16:13–23) or in a relationship (Judg 9:23). Nevertheless, for example, Azazel (Lev 16:8, 10, 26) may have had evil connotations and was certainly later demonized (e.g. *1 En.* 10:4–8) to become a name used for the chief demon (e.g. *1 En.* 54:5). Also, the "lilith" (Isa 34:14), probably a desert-dwelling animal, may always have had evil associations not only because Mesopotamians located the demonic in animals but also because it is the Hebrew form of the Akkadian female demon *liltu* (*CAD* 9:190) and is another figure that increased in demonic status (see 4Q511 10.1). The LXX provides important background against which the New Testament was written in portraying pagan gods (e.g. Deut 32:17; Ps 105 [106]:37; Bar 4:7) and the sources of threat in Ps 90 (91):6 as demonic, and in having an evil demon or spirit sent away by the smoke of burning fish (Tob 3:8; 6:8).

The New Testament world

The ministry of Jesus took place in a society with a highly developed demonology in which Belial (e.g. *Jub.* 1:20), Mastema (e.g. CD 16:5), Melcheresa (4Q280 1:2), Azazel (*1 En.* 54:1–6) or Satan (*Jub.* 10:11; 11Q5 19:15) were names used for the head of the evil spirits or demons. Beelzebul ("Baal-Prince," Mark 3:22) was the name Jesus' opponents used in charging him with exorcism by the chief of the demons, probably because the pagan god Baal was associated with exorcism (*KTU* 1:169) and pagan gods were considered demons (e.g. 1 Cor 10:20). Demons were thought to inflict harm (*1 En.* 15:8–11), lead people astray (1QS 3:20–26; 1 Tim 4:1; 1 John 4:1–6), cause illness (*Jub.* 10:1, 12), and were associated with physical (1QS28 2:3–10; Luke 13:2) and ritual (Num 19:16; Mark 5:2), as well as theological (1 John 4:1–2; cf. Zech 13:2) and ethical impurity (2 Tim 2:26).

Those around Jesus were familiar with a range of kinds of exorcisms that expressed varying understandings of the relative importance of the exorcist, the power-authority and the methods used to enlist the power-authority to evict the demon. At one end of this spectrum are those most commonly known exorcisms that were thought to be successful because of what was said and done rather than because of who performed them. Notably, a text in the magical papyri says the exorcist stood behind the sufferer and, using a whip, recited words that were thought to co-opt a god to drive away the demon (*PGM* IV.1227–64; cf. V.96–172). Also, Josephus tells of Eleazar, a Jew, putting a ring to the nose of the sufferer and, as the demon-possessed man smelled the roots in it, drew out the demon and then, when the demon had left, he "adjured the demon never to come back into him, speaking Solomon's name and

reciting the poems which he had composed" (*Ant.* 8.47). Similar approaches to exorcism are seen in the story of the unknown exorcist (Mark 9:38/Luke 9:49) and the seven sons of Sceva (Acts 19:13–19) who may provide evidence of exorcists having apprentices (cf. Matt 12:27/Luke 11:19).

Further along this spectrum were other exorcisms thought to be successful because they combined particular methods with the personal force of the healer. In the *Genesis Apocryphon* from Qumran, the identity of Abraham the exorcist is important, for the point of the story is to glorify him. But he is also said to pray and lay hands on the king to cause the evil spirit to leave (1Q20 20.28–9). Josephus tells a story of David in which it was not only David's presence but also his playing lyre that was considered important in removing an evil spirit from Saul (*Ant.* 16.166–9). It is these kinds of exorcisms – those dependent on the person of the exorcist as well as a dependence on an outside power-authority – that provide the closest examples of Jesus as an exorcist.

Jesus

We know of no other miracle worker in antiquity who conducted so many exorcisms and for whom exorcism was as important as it was for Jesus (e.g. Matt 12:28/Luke 11:20). In light of the demoniac in the Capernaum synagogue said to scream out when he confronts Jesus (Mark 1:24) and the Gadarene demoniac falling on his knees shouting in front of Jesus (5:6–7; cf. 9:2), his exorcisms can be understood as power encounters between God and the demonic. Also, in his exorcisms Jesus is reported to have use well-known formulae: "Be silent" or "Be bound" (Mark 1:25; cf. *PGM* IX.9; XXXVI.164); "Come out" (1:25; 5:8 and 9:25; cf. *PGM* IV.1239–41; Lucian, *Philops.* 11, 16) and to ask for the name of the demon (Mark 5:9; cf. Philostratus, *Vit. Apoll.* IV.20), as well as forbidding a demon to return to the person (Mark 9:25; Josephus, *Ant.* 8.46–49). There is even an example of Jesus transferring demons from a person to some pigs (Mark 5:12–14) in a way that other exorcists would transfer demons into objects and then dispose of them to destroy the demons (Josephus, *Ant.* 8.46–49; *PGM* IV.1254, 3024–25). In a number of stories the violence we see in other exorcisms (Josephus, *Ant.* 8.49; cf. *PGM* IV.1248–52) is also reflected in those of Jesus (Mark 1:26; 9:26).

Even though Jesus is not reported to have mentioned any power-authority when he conducted an exorcism, saying that he cast out demons "by the Spirit (or finger) of God" (Matt 12:28/Luke 11:20;

cf. Mark 3:28–30), like other exorcists of the time, shows he understood that he was not operating unaided or relying only on his personal force or presence, but was also using a power-authority, the Spirit or finger of God. However, over against many of his contemporaries, there is no evidence Jesus collected or (apart from the episode of the pigs) used artifacts or a library of incantations. Also, having conducted an exorcism, Jesus expressed no particular interest in the control of, and protection from, unwanted demons that is frequently found in ancient magic. Also, Jesus shows no interest in exorcising buildings or places. Further, at no point is Jesus shown to use prayer as part of his exorcistic technique.

Since exorcisms were so common, and Jews did not consider exorcism to be eschatologically significant, it is remarkable that Jesus claimed that his particular exorcisms – and those of his followers (Luke 10:17–19) – were not only the first of a two-stage battle with Satan (the second stage to take place at the eschaton; cf. Isa 24:21–22; Matt 13:24–30), but were also the actual coming or operation of the kingdom of God itself.

GRAHAM H. TWELFTREE

Further reading

Alexander, P. S. "The Demonology of the Dead Sea Scrolls," in Peter W. Flint and James C. Vanderkam (eds) *The Dead Sea Scrolls after Fifty Years: A Comprehensive Assessment*, 2 vols. Leiden: Brill, 1999. Vol. 2, pp. 331–53.

Aune, D. E. "Magic in Early Christianity," *ANRW* II.23:2 (1980) 1507–57.

Betz, H. D. *The Greek Magical Papyri in Translation Including the Demotic Spells, Vol. I: Texts*, second edition, Chicago, IL and London: University of Chicago Press, 1992.

Brenk, F. E. "In the Light of the Moon: Demonology in the Early Imperial Period," *ANRW* II.16:3 (1986) 2068–145.

Eitrem, S. *Some Notes on the Demonology in the New Testament*, SO Supp. 20, Oslo: Universitetsforlaget, 1966.

Foerster, W. "δαίμων, δαιμόνιον," in Gerhard Kittel (ed.) *Theological Dictionary of the New Testament. Vol. 2*, trans. and ed. Geoffrey W. Bromiley, Grand Rapids, MI: Eerdmans, 1965, pp. 1–20.

Lange, A., H. Lichtenberger, and K. F. D. Römheld (eds) *Die Dämonen (Demons)*, Tübingen: Mohr Siebeck, 2003.

Sorensen, E. *Possession and Exorcism in the New Testament and Early Christianity*, WUNT 2/157, Tübingen: Mohr Siebeck, 2002.

Twelftree, G. H. *Jesus the Exorcist: A Contribution to the Study of the Historical Jesus*, WUNT 2/54, Tübingen: J. C. B. Mohr, 1993.

DEMYTHOLOGIZATION

In biblical scholarship, demythologization is generally associated with the theological contributions of Rudolf Bultmann (1884–1976), who began this modern theological discussion in 1941 with his significant essay, "The New Testament and Mythology." That essay initiated theological debates about the ministry, fate, and activity of Jesus and the proclamation of the New Testament about him. The early debate continued through the 1970s, and still sparks significant discussion and debate among biblical scholars in what is commonly called the "third quest of the historical Jesus." Hans Jonas originally coined the term "demythologizing" (German: *Entmythologisierung*) to characterize the elimination of myth, but later, Bultmann employed it as a hermeneutical tool to argue his historical and theological interpretation of the New Testament proclamation. He wrote a subsequent essay to support his enterprise, entitled "Jesus Christ and Mythology," that was published in the first of six volumes edited by H.-W. Bartsch called *Kerygma und Mythos* (1948ff., English translation: *Kerygma and Myth*).

Bultmann used the term to identify what he called the false stumbling block (see 1 Cor 1:23) of the New Testament that prevented modern humanity from appropriating what he believed was the true meaning of the New Testament message that speaks of authentic self-understanding. Because of his agreement with the positivistic approach to history that denied in principle the existence of miracles and all divine intervention into the historical causal-nexus, Bultmann rejected the world of nature miracles such as the virgin birth of Jesus, Jesus walking on the water, all stories of divine interventions in human history that violated natural laws, including the resurrection of Jesus from the dead and his return to earth with the "clouds of heaven." He rejected a three-tiered universe, biblical notions of heaven and hell, substitutionary atonement, and the second coming of Christ (*Jesus Christ and Mythology*, 13).

Bultmann contended that Jesus' and his disciples' belief in the imminent emergence of the kingdom of God simply did not happen and the world order continues today with no change. Like all ancient mythological notions, they needed to be translated into meaningful language of human existence. This translation enterprise is what he called "demythologizing" the New Testament proclamation. For him, the mythical worldview was refuted by history and it was also contrary to the modern worldview that has been developed by science. He further added, "if the truth of the New Testament proclamation is to be preserved, the only way is to demythologize it" ("The New Testament and Mythology," 10).

To the extent that the New Testament proclamation is bound to an antiquated worldview (*Weltanschauung*), Bultmann insisted that it is "incredible to modern man, for he is convinced that the mythical view of the world is obsolete." He adds that, "an historical fact which involves a resurrection from the dead is utterly inconceivable" ("New Testament and Mythology," 15 and 39, respectively). Such beliefs, he claims, contradict both human experience and rational thought. To this extent, Bultmann was a modernist apologist for Christian faith. He believed that the New Testament, when its mythological proclamation is properly interpreted, continues to have a vital message for all humanity today.

Bultmann's understanding of myth is central to understanding his demythologizing. Myth, he argued, is a form of expression in which humankind, not yet awakened to reason, expresses an understanding of the world and of humanity. It is the expression of the "other worldly" in terms of "this worldly" language. Myth expresses humanity's belief that the origin and purpose of the world is to be sought beyond it, that is, beyond the tangible realm that is dominated by mysterious powers. For Bultmann, myth is an expression of man's awareness that he is not lord of his own being, and the purpose of myth is to "speak of a transcendent power which controls the world and man, but that purpose is impeded and obscured by the terms in which it is expressed" ("New Testament and Mythology," 11). He contends that the real *kerygma* or proclamation in the New Testament is about an understanding of human existence and that it is not bound to the myth that contains it.

Myth, he claimed, speaks of God's objectifying activity in human history, but God acts only in hidden ways *in history*. That conclusion led him to distinguish two German words for history, namely *historisch* and *geschichtlich* (he did not use *historie* and *geschichte* to distinguish these two realities). In modern German, there is essentially no difference between these two terms, but in theology they offered Bultmann an opportunity to argue for two kinds of historical reality, namely the actual event (*historisch*) and its significance or meaning (*geschichtlich*). There can be no *geschichtlich* that is not connected to an actual event of history (*historisch*) and this recognizes that God acts in hidden ways in and through acts of history. In the case of Jesus, Bultmann contended that God acted in the cross of Jesus in ways that were not revealed to others, but were disclosed to his disciples through the eyes of faith. Easter faith for Bultmann was essentially the rise of faith in Jesus' disciples,

occasioned by a new understanding of the cross that was divinely disclosed to them. Unlike his predecessors who rejected and eliminated the myth of the New Testament, Bultmann interpreted it in terms of human existence. The existential categories that he utilized in this process were developed by his colleague at Marburg, Martin Heidegger (1889–1976; see his *Sein und Zeit*; English translation: *Being and Time*) as well as by the earlier Wilhelm Dilthey (1833–1911; see his *Introduction to Human Sciences*).

Bultmann appealed to Paul for support for rejecting the ancient world's belief in mythological activity. Paul claimed that he was determined to know nothing among the Corinthian believers except Jesus Christ and him crucified (1 Cor 2:2). Paul centered God's activity in a historical event in which God acted in hidden ways to reveal himself to the eye of faith. While objective observers only saw the crucifixion of a Jewish man, the followers of Jesus discerned in the crucifixion by God's revelation the activity of God. God acted in hidden ways in this historic (*historisch*) event, and its significance for faith (*geschichtlich*) was revealed only to the eyes of faith. The primary important historical fact about Jesus that is essential for Christian faith, according to Bultmann, was his "thatness" (German: *dass*), but his demythologizing enterprise also depends significantly on the death of Jesus on the cross. If historians could disprove that, the credibility of Christian faith, Bultmann agreed, would be adversely affected.

Bultmann's general lack of interest in the life of Jesus is again rooted in Paul. He argues that Paul was uninterested in the historical Jesus and only proclaimed the crucified Christ who comes to the individual through faith. He says that Paul rejected the value of knowing "Christ according to the flesh" or "from a human point of view" (2 Cor 5:16). He adds that Paul also demythologized the coming of Christ when he claimed: "the kingdom of God is not food and drink, but righteousness and peace and joy in the Holy Spirit" (Rom 14:17). According to Bultmann, Paul taught that new life in Christ begins when one is united with Christ by faith (2 Cor 5:17). As further biblical justification for his demythologizing enterprise, he claimed that John translated the return of Christ into language of the presence of eternity in the here and now (John 1:12; 10:10; 1 John 1:1–4). For Bultmann, the old worldview of biblical times is outmoded and needs replacing if the Christian proclamation is to have any relevance for contemporary humanity. The divine–human relationship that the New Testament proclaims has to be reinterpreted if it is to be relevant and acceptable to modern humanity.

By translating the New Testament into existentialist categories, Bultmann contended that he had achieved the same goal that the original followers of Jesus had, even if it is not readily apparent. In order to arrive at the appropriate understanding of this myth, he argued that it is important to ask what ideas of human existence are contained within the mythical expressions. If followed carefully, Bultmann contended that those mythical elements, that otherwise only puzzle modern man, now become understandable and relevant when demythologized. He aimed at interpreting ancient mythology into meaningful terms that can be readily understood and accepted by modern man. This, he claimed, allowed the true meaning of the New Testament proclamation to have continuing relevance to modern humanity. As a contemporary apologist of the Christian faith, he wanted the Christian proclamation to appeal to his modern scientific generation.

The "real scandal" of Christian faith, for Bultmann, was not its mythological worldview, but giving up of one's life in order to save it (Mark 8:34–35). This is seen in the scandal of Jesus laying down his life (1 Cor 1:18–25). Bultmann translated what he called the biblical myths in terms of a view of existence that myths themselves inadequately express. The real intention of demythologizing is to interpret in meaningful language the categories of human existence expressed in mythological language. The true activity of God takes place in hidden ways in human existence, but when perceived by the pre-enlightened followers of Jesus, they conceptualized it in terms of the concrete activity of a resurrection from the dead, or more precisely, in terms of mythological language. Bultmann believed that God has revealed himself to humanity through humanity's obedience to the call of God that comes through the Christian proclamation. Since the language of the New Testament was born in a pre-enlightened era it could not adequately express for modern humanity its intended understanding. For him, the Christian message speaks of a divine–human relationship that can be translated out of its pre-enlightened mythological thought categories in order to make it intelligible.

By demythologizing the Christian proclamation, Bultmann did not intend to eliminate what he identified as myth, but rather he reinterpreted it in terms of human self-understanding. All divine–human encounters, he argued, take place in the *hidden* activity of God that cannot be examined or objectified by the historian's craft. He claimed that the Christian proclamation has a deeper meaning that mythology conceals and that it only becomes clear and relevant by translating it in terms of human existential self-understanding. Bultmann wanted to free the essential Christian message from its pre-enlightened framework and mythological worldview and thereby identify its true meaning. That is the essence of his demythologizing enterprise.

LEE MARTIN MCDONALD

Further reading

Primary sources – works by Rudolf Bultmann

"The New Testament and Mythology," in Hans-Werner Bartsch (ed.) *Kerygma and Myth*, trans. R. H. Fuller, New York: Harper & Row, 1961 (German: *Kerygma und Mythos*, Hamburg-Volksdorf: Herbert Reich, 1953).
History and Eschatology: The Presence of Eternity, New York: Harper & Row, 1957.
Jesus and the Word, New York: Scribner's, 1958 (German: *Jesus*, Tübingen: J. C. B. Mohr, 1926, 1934, 1964).
Jesus Christ and Mythology, London: SCM Press, 1966.
Faith and Understanding, ed. R. W. Funk, London: Harper & Row, 1969 (German: *Glauben und Verstehen*, I, Tübingen: J. C. B. Mohr, 1966).
Karl Barth – Rudolf Bultmann: Letters 1922–1966, ed. B. Jaspert and G. E. Bromiley, Grand Rapids, MI: Eerdmans, 1981 (German: *Karl Barth–Rudolf Bultmann: Briefwechsel, 1922–1966*, Vol. 1 of the *Karl Barth Gesamtausgabe*, Zurich: Theologischer Verlag, 1971).

Secondary sources

Heidegger, Martin. *On the Way to Language*, New York: Harper & Row, 1982 [1959].
Henderson, Ian. *Rudolf Bultmann*, Makers of Contemporary Theology, Richmond, VA: John Knox Press; London: Lutterworth Press, 1965.
Hübner, Hans. "Demythologizing," in Erwin Fahlbusch, J. M. Lochman, J. Mbiti, J. J. Pelikan, and L. Vischer (eds) *The Encyclopedia of Christianity*, Grand Rapids, MI and Cambridge: Eerdmans/Brill, 1999, Vol. 1, pp. 795–7 (originally published in German as *Evangelisches Kirchenlexikon*, Dritte Auflage 1986, 1989, 1992, 1997).
Johnson, R. A. *The Origins of Demythologizing: Philosophy and Historiography in the Theology of Rudolf Bultmann*, Leiden: Brill, 1974.
Jones, G. *Bultmann: Towards a Critical Theology*, New York and Oxford: University Press, 1991.
Kähler, Martin. *The So-Called Historical Jesus and the Historic Biblical Christ*, trans. and ed. C. E. Braaten, Philadelphia, PA: Fortress Press, 1964 (German: *Der sogenannte historische Jesus und der geschichtliche, biblische Christus*, 1896).
MacQuarrie, John. *The Scope of Demythologizing*, London: SCM Press, 1960.
Morgan, R. "Bultmann, Rudolf Karl," in John G. Hayes (ed.) *Dictionary of Biblical Interpretation*, Nashville, TN: Abingdon, 1999, Vol. 1, pp. 148–9.
Perrin, Norman. *The Promise of Bultmann, The Promise of Theology*, Philadelphia, PA and New York: J. B. Lippincott, 1969.

DIASPORA

At the time of Jesus, many Jews lived outside of the land of Palestine, in the Jewish Diaspora. Our sources for these communities include Jewish texts, inscriptions and papyri, Jewish synagogue buildings, and information provided by non-Jewish authors.

Geography and history

By the first century CE, there were significant Jewish communities throughout the Greco-Roman world (see e.g. Philo, *Legat.* 214, 281–3). Particularly noteworthy communities lived in Babylon, Antioch, Alexandria, parts of Asia Minor and Rome. The origin of the communities varied. For example, the Jewish community in Babylonia had its origins in people exiled to the area by the Babylonians in 587 BCE who stayed on after some Jews returned to Palestine in 538. The origin of the Jewish communities in Asia Minor probably stemmed from the actions of Antiochus III, who in 210–205 BCE transferred two thousand Jewish families from Mesopotamia and Babylonia to Lydia and Phrygia as military settlers. It is clear that, by the first century CE, many Diaspora Jewish communities had been established in their cities for many years.

It is very difficult to judge the size of the Jewish Diaspora in this period, but it is clear that Jews were a major ethnic group within the Roman Empire, and were perhaps 5 to 7 percent of the population.

Significant Diaspora Jewish texts which have been preserved include the *Letter of Aristeas, Joseph and Aseneth, 3* and *4 Maccabees, The Sibylline Oracles, The Testament of Abraham* and *Wisdom of Solomon* and works by Aristobulus, Artapanus, Demetrius, Ezekiel the Tragedian, Josephus, Philo and Pseudo-Phocylides.

Facets of Jewish identity in the Diaspora

Although Diaspora Judaism was clearly diverse, there were common elements that enabled Jewish communities to endure as coherent entities, and that made the difference between a Jew and a non-Jew clear to both groups. We note the sense of ethnicity, the strength of the local community and its communal life, the link to Jerusalem and to other Diaspora communities, the commitment to Torah (in Greek translation), and Jewish practices and beliefs, most notably worship of the one God, dietary laws, circumcision and Sabbath.

Diaspora communities in the Greek cities

While there was considerable variety in this regard among Diaspora Jewish communities, it is clear that some Jewish communities held a respected place in their cities and saw themselves as "at home" in the Diaspora. They were not aloof, or marginalized, but rather participated in many facets of the life of the city. And yet they did so as Jews, who actively maintained many features of their Jewish identity.

The historical Jesus and the Diaspora

Some sayings or actions of Jesus in the Gospels relate to the Jewish Diaspora. For example, in Matt 8:11 Jesus speaks of many coming from "east and west" and sitting at table with Abraham, Isaac and Jacob in the Kingdom of heaven (cf. Luke 13:29). The allusion to Isa 43:5; Zech 8:7 and Ps 107:3 here suggests he is probably speaking of the Jewish Diaspora. Jesus' calling of the Twelve also points to the restoration of all of Israel, including the ten currently "lost" tribes.

The Diaspora and historical Jesus studies

The study of the Jewish Diaspora is of relevance to the study of the historical Jesus in a number of ways. It is likely that each of our canonical gospels was written in a city outside of Palestine (for example, Matthew probably in Antioch, Mark probably in Rome). Many scholars would argue that the final shape of at least some of the Gospels reflects the tensions between Christian and Diaspora Jewish communities, both prior to and at the time of writing. These tensions have led to the selection of particular pericopes, as well as the shaping during oral transmission of some pericopes in the light of Jewish–Christian tensions and disagreements. Thus, for example, scholars have debated whether Matthew sees himself as still within Judaism, or whether the Gospel reflects a recent separation from Judaism, in which case the author would see himself as belonging to a separate community which is defining itself over against Judaism. The latter is more likely, but in either case the controversy with Jewish communities has left its imprint on the Gospel. While it is likely that much of this controversy is with Diaspora Jewish communities, we should note that developments within Palestinian Judaism were probably also significant factors in the controversies. In seeking to use the Gospels as sources for the historical Jesus, we need then to become aware of the impact of interactions between Christian and Diaspora Jewish communities on the Gospels.

Josephus and Philo are significant Diaspora Jewish authors (although Josephus also belongs with Palestinian Judaism, and shows that the division between the Diaspora and Palestine is problematic at times). In *Ant.* XVIII.116–19, Josephus gives invaluable information about John the Baptist, which provides independent attestation of his considerable impact. In *Ant.* XVIII.63–4 Josephus gives his well-known reference to Jesus. Although this passage has clearly been edited by a Christian, many scholars have argued that some features of what Josephus originally wrote can still be discerned, and so the passage provides significant evidence for the historical Jesus. Much else that Josephus writes sheds light on the historical Jesus and the contemporary social and political situation. Philo is drawn on less in studies of the historical Jesus, but he still gives valuable evidence for a range of issues. For example, Philo writes about the corruption and cruelty of Pilate in *Legat. 299–305.*

Other Diaspora Jewish texts are also valuable. The use of immersion in conjunction with forgiveness and an implicit criticism of the Temple, elements which are both found in John the Baptist's teaching, are also seen in *Sib. Or.* 4:8, 27–30, 162–70. Jesus spoke of men and women who are peacemakers and who love their enemies being children of God (see Matt 5:9, 44–45); similarly, Diaspora texts connect righteousness or particular behaviour with being children of God (see Wis 2:18; Philo *Spec.* 1, 317–18; see also *Jos. Asen.* 6:3–5; 21:4; 23:10). The use of kingdom and kingship imagery in relation to God's rule in the Wisdom of Solomon provides a helpful background to Jesus' message (see Wis 3:8; 10:10, 14; cf. 6:20–21).

A range of matters mentioned by Jesus in the gospels were also of significance to Diaspora Jews (as well as Palestinian Jews). For example, the temple and the temple tax, Sabbath, tithing, table fellowship and Jewish festivals were all of significance for Diaspora Jews. Yet because of their different situations, Diaspora Jewish communities sometimes had different emphases or different ways of expressing the importance of these matters from Palestinian Jews. The gospel texts which discuss these matters in connection with the historical Jesus can thus be illuminated by Diaspora Jewish texts.

PAUL TREBILCO

Further reading

Ameling, W. *Inscriptiones Judaicae Orientis Band ii: Kleinasien*, TSAJ 99, Tübingen: Mohr Siebeck, 2004.

Barclay, J. M. G. *Jews in the Mediterranean Diaspora from Alexander to Trajan (323 BCE–117 CE)*, Edinburgh: T. & T. Clark, 1996.
—— (ed.) *Negotiating Diaspora: Jewish Strategies in the Roman Empire*, Library of Second Temple Studies 45, London: T. & T. Clark International, 2004.
Bartlett, J. R. (ed.) *Jews in the Hellenistic and Roman Cities*, London and New York: Routledge, 2002.
Collins, J. J. *Between Athens and Jerusalem: Jewish Identity in the Hellenistic Diaspora*, second edition, Grand Rapids, MI: Eerdmans, 2000.
Feldman, L. H. *Jew and Gentile in the Ancient World. Attitudes and Interactions from Alexander to Justinian*, Princeton, NJ: Princeton University Press, 1993.
Gruen, E. S. *Diaspora: Jews amidst Greeks and Romans*, Cambridge, MA: Harvard University Press, 2002.
Hachlili, R. *Ancient Jewish Art and Archaeology in the Diaspora*, HO 35, Leiden: Brill, 1998.
Horbury, W. and D. Noy (eds) *Jewish Inscriptions of Graeco-Roman Egypt*, Cambridge: Cambridge University Press, 1992.
Noy, D. *Jewish Inscriptions of Western Europe. Volume 1: Italy (excluding the City of Rome), Spain and Gaul*, Cambridge: Cambridge University Press, 1993; *Volume 2: The City of Rome*, Cambridge: Cambridge University Press, 1995.
Noy, D. and Bloedhorn, H. (eds) *Inscriptiones Judaicae Orientis Volume III: Syria and Cyprus*, TSAJ 102, Tübingen: Mohr Siebeck, 2004.
Noy, D., Panayotov, A. and Bloedhorn, H. (eds) *Inscriptiones Judaicae Orientis Volume I: Eastern Europe*, TSAJ 101, Tübingen: Mohr Siebeck, 2004.
Overman, J. A. and MacLennan, R. S. *Diaspora Jews and Judaism. Essays in Honor of, and in Dialogue with, A. Thomas Kraabel*, South Florida Studies in the History of Judaism 41, Atlanta, GA: Scholars Press, 1992.
Rajak, T. *The Jewish Dialogue with Greece and Rome. Studies in Cultural and Social Interaction*, AGJU 48, Leiden: Brill, 2001.
Schürer, E. *The History of the Jewish People in the Age of Jesus Christ (175 BC–AD 135)*, 3 vols, revised and ed. G. Vermes, F. Millar, M. Black, and M. Goodman, Edinburgh: T. & T. Clark, 1973–87.
Stern, M. *Greek and Latin Authors on Jews and Judaism*, 3 vols, Jerusalem: Israel Academy of Sciences and Humanities, 1974, 1981, 1984.
Trebilco, P. R. *Jewish Communities in Asia Minor*, SNTSMS 69, Cambridge: Cambridge University Press, 1991.
Williams, M. H. *The Jews among the Greeks and Romans. A Diasporan Sourcebook*, London: Duckworth, 1998.

DIBELIUS, MARTIN

Martin Dibelius (1883–1947) was born the son of a protestant minister in Dresden. Studying theology and philosophy in Neuchâtel, Leipzig, Tübingen, and Berlin, he was especially influenced by Adolf (von) Harnack and by Hermann Gunkel. In 1905 he received his philosophical doctorate on an Old Testament subject *Die Lade Jahves* ["The Ark of Yahweh"] (FRLANT 7, Göttingen: Vandenhoeck & Ruprecht, 1906), in 1908 his *Lizenziat* and finished in 1909 his habilitation on "Das Selbstzeugnis des Paulus von seiner Bekehrung und Sendung" ["Paul's Own Witness with respect to his Conversion and Mission"] in Berlin (unpublished).

In 1915 Dibelius obtained a full professorship in Heidelberg. He was active both in the ecumenical movement and, from 1918, in political affairs pronouncing democratic values. It was because of these values that he did not succumb to the influences of German National Socialism. Dibelius was a scholar with broad interests in the field of New Testament, early Christian literature, and the religious and social environment of Early Christianity. His particular interests were in three fields: the religio-historical, the oral tradition of the Gospel literature and the Early Christian ethos (1929: 13–17) including the relevance of past moral teaching for present-time ethics: "*Ein Christentum, dem die Heiligkeit des eigenen abgeschlossenen Bezirks höher steht als die Verantwortung für die Welt, ist mir persönlich fremd geblieben*" (= "A Christianity, for which salvation of the exclusive, closed constituency is more important than justification for the world, remains strange to me"; 1929: 4).

For Dibelius, the importance of gospel and Jesus studies mostly referred to him as being together with Rudolf Bultmann, one of the German fathers of the *Formgeschichte* (lit. "form history" = "form criticism"). Form history tried to explore the pre-history of the Gospel tradition with regard to oral histories and its popular rules of transmission (cf. already 1911). Compared to Bultmann, Dibelius chose a different approach in terminology and methodology in classifying and reconstructing the oral pre-history of the gospel tradition. Dibelius reconstructed the gospels' pre-history by approaching it with the general theory that the transmission of Jesus tradition was based in the Early Christian proclamation (1933: 12, 23ff.; 1985: 27ff.). In Dibelius' concept, proclamation was a wide-ranging term that included all kinds of preaching within Christian communities as well as the whole range of missionary activities. The form-critical terminology mirrors the constructive momentum of his theory that most of the different forms were grounded in the activity of Early Christian proclamation.

As for the tradition of communication of Jesus' words, Dibelius referred to the exhortation of the Early Christian community. In this he used the term "paraenesis" and supposed that material from this genre mostly shaped the sayings of the "Gospel" Q. The sayings of Jesus, however, exist in different forms such as *parables* and *apocalyptic* or *prophetic words*. The terminology used for the

small genres of sayings is similar to that of Bultmann. However, differences are seen in the identifications of narrative genres: *paradigm* (Bultmann used *apophthegma*) as the oldest narrative genre is built around a saying of Jesus used for preaching, its basic shape nearly uninfluenced by Hellenistic patterns and therefore, although Dibelius does not ignore the creative character of the transmitting community, of a relatively high value for historical reconstruction. Another narrative genre is the so-called *tale* ("*Novelle*") which includes healing stories whose historical value needs to be evaluated time by time, as some of those tales attribute non-Christian motifs to Jesus. There are also *examples* and *legends* serving the needs of early Christian communities. The longest narrative unit found in early Christian literature is the Passion Narrative. Although Dibelius acknowledged christological interpretation and re-workings by using proof from Scripture, he judged the basic elements of the Passion Narrative, which may belong to old tradition, as historically reliable. Dibelius' approach was not one of an aesthetic description of forms, but instead an approach that looked centrally for historical reconstruction and development (1985: 24–25) and for theological interpretation.

Dibelius, like his counterpart Bultmann, started his analysis with small forms, finally reaching the gospel genre. Like Bultmann, he questioned the tendencies in collecting and interpreting the tradition within the different gospel texts and, herewith, he opened a path for later redaction critical studies.

Modern critics of the old approach of *Formgeschichte* criticized the confidence in reconstructing older texts and units pointing to discontinuity within the process of transmission or by reshaping the tradition in being written down. In any case, the process of transmission is a more fluid process of transmission than acknowledged by the fathers of *Formgeschichte* who used mostly the same methods for reconstructing oral tradition as for literary sources. Nevertheless, there is no need to view this dichotomy as complete discontinuity in the process of transmission (Labahn 1999).

Dibelius also wrote a short and popular book on Jesus accompanied by a companion volume on Paul that was posthumously edited by Werner Georg Kümmel (*Paulus* [Sammlung Göschen 1160, Berlin: de Gruyter, 1951]; English translation: *Paul* [London: Longmans, Green, 1953]). The short but masterly written volume on Jesus was one of those contributions of the middle of the last century which explicitly intended to keep the question for the historical Jesus alive (1960: 9). Although not very often referred to within the history of research for the historical Jesus, it is an important volume because it draws consequences of a form-historical approach without being bound to the specific theological presupposition of Bultmann. Dibelius' appeal for the quest of a historical Jesus, being both possible and important for faith, at points paralleled the insights of scholars from the later second or new quest for Jesus, such as Ernst Käsemann or Günther Bornkamm.

Mostly concerned with the subjects of Jesus' teaching, Dibelius did not present a biography *en detail* but placed Jesus in a historical and social environment as well as adding a brief sketch of Jesus' life and movement. Altogether, Dibelius' book on Jesus is an interesting presentation of Jesus' life and teachings based on the historical analysis of the Synoptic Gospels as the main source. It should be added that Dibelius viewed the apocryphal Jesus tradition as part of the oral transmission of Jesus tradition but thought it unreliable because of the lack of documentation relative to its transmission (1975: 48). Dibelius refused general historical judgment about this literature but he was willing to find old, possibly authentic traditions especially within the so-called agrapha (sayings not included in the canonical gospels) of Jesus.

The center of Jesus' teaching was the kingdom of God, which will come in future (1960: 53–4) but it is also something that is becoming present by Jesus' words and in his deeds. With the actual appearance in his preaching and his deeds, Jesus started the fulfillment of time, "the *yet* of the immediately arriving dawn of the kingdom of God" (1960: 55). That claim revealed an authority present in Jesus' preaching, which urged people to understand the signs of their time and draw right conclusions from them and thus become witnesses of God's work in Jesus' deeds and speech (1960: 103). In the sense of stressing this kind of authority, Jesus may have considered himself as the Son of Man and as the Messiah, but not in a classical political manner and without emphasizing the titles as center of his appearance (1960: 84–5).

With his popular but still important volume, *Geschichte der urchristlichen Literatur* [= "History of Early Christian Literature"] (Walter de Gruyter, 1926), which had its origin in a lecture in 1915, Dibelius made an important contribution to the understanding of how early Christian literature, including the gospels, came into being and which ones were the leading forces He also wanted to show in which way this literature was related to the needs of the situation of its origin (1975: 15). Following his teacher Gunkel, Dibelius in his study

included oral forms of tradition that were later fixed in written texts, although he intentionally ignored the borders of New Testament canon.

MICHAEL LABAHN

Further reading

Baird, William. *History of New Testament Research II: From Jonathan Edwards to Rudolf Bultmann*, Minneapolis, MN: Fortress Press, 2003.

Bringeland, Hans. "Dibelius, Martin," *DBI* 1 (1999) 296–7.

Dibelius, Martin. *Die urchristliche Überlieferung von Johannes dem Täufe*, FRLANT 15, Göttingen: Vandenhoeck & Ruprecht, 1911.

—— "Martin Dibelius," in Erich Stange (ed.) *Die Religionswissenschaft der Gegenwart in Selbstdarstellungen V: Dibelius, Feine, Kattenbusch, Mayer, Staerk, Wernle*, Leipzig: Meiner, 1929, pp. 1–37.

—— *Die Formgeschichte des Evangeliums*, second revised edition, Tübingen: Mohr Siebeck, 1933 [1919; third edition, ed. Günther Bornkamm, 1959; ET: *From Tradition to Gospel*, New York: Scribner's, 1971].

—— *Die Botschaft von Jesus Christus. Die alte Überlieferung der Gemeinde in Geschichten, Sprüchen u. Reden. Wiederhergestellt und verdeutscht*, Tübingen: Mohr, 1935; ET: *The Message of Jesus Christ: The Tradition of the Early Christian Communities*, Library of Christian Knowledge, New York: Scribner's, 1939.

—— *Paulus*, ed. by W. G. Kümmel, Berlin: W. de Gruyter, 1951.

—— *Botschaft und Geschichte. Gesammelte Aufsätze. Erster Band: Zur Evangelienforschung*, in connection with Heinz Kraft, ed. Günther Bornkamm, Tübingen: Mohr Siebeck, 1953.

—— *Jesus*, third edition with an addendum by Werner Georg Kümmel, Sammlung Göschen 1130, Berlin: de Gruyter, 1960 [1939; ET: *Jesus*. Philadelphia, PA: Westminster Press, 1949].

—— *Geschichte der urchristlichen Literatur*, Sammlung Göschen 934/935, Berlin: de Gruyter, 1926; Neudruck der Erstausgabe von 1926 unter Berücksichtigung der Änderungen d. englischen Übersetzung von 1936, ed. Ferdinand Hahn, Theologische Bücherei 58, München: Kaiser, 1975.

—— "Zur Formgeschichte der Evangelien," in Ferdinand Hahn (ed.) *Zur Formgeschichte des Evangeliums*, Wege der Forschung 81, Darmstadt: Wissenschaftliche Buchgesellschaft, 1985, pp. 21–52 [1929].

Geiser, Stefan. *Verantwortung und Schuld. Studien zu Martin Dibelius*, Münster: LIT, 2001.

Kümmel, Werner Georg. "Martin Dibelius als Theologe," in *Heilsgeschehen und Geschichte. Gesammelte Aufsätze 1933–1964*, ed. Erich Grässer, Otto Merk, and Adolf Fritz, Marburger Theologische Studien 3, Marburg: Elwert, 1965, pp. 192–206.

Labahn, Michael. *Jesus als Lebensspender: Untersuchungen zu einer Geschichte der johanneischen Tradition anhand ihrer Wundergeschichten*, BZNW 98, Berlin, New York: de Gruyter, 1999.

Theissen, Gerd. "Die 'Formgeschichte des Evangeliums' von Martin Dibelius und ihre gegenwärtige Bedeutung," in Christoph Burchard and Gerd Theissen (eds) *Lese-Zeichen für Annelies Findeiß zum 65. Geburtstag am 15.*

März 1984, DBAT, Beiheft 3, Heidelberg: Wiss.-Theol. Seminar der Theolgischen Fakultät, 1984, pp. 143–58.

Van Oyen, Geert. *De Studie van de Marcusredactie in de Twintigste Eeuw*, SNTA 18, Leuven: Peeters, 1993.

Wolfes, Matthias. "Schuld und Verantwortung. Die Auseinandersetzung des Heidelberger Theologen Martin Dibelius mit dem Dritten Reich. Mit einer aus dem Nachlaß herausgegebenen 'Lebensbeschreibung' aus dem Jahre 1946," *ZKG* 111 (2000) 185–209.

DISCIPLES, DISCIPLESHIP

Within the New Testament, the word *mathētēs*, normally translated "disciple," occurs only in the gospels and Acts. Since the New Testament does not utilize a Greek term for the notion that in English we would refer to as "discipleship," the meaning of "discipleship" in the New Testament must be inferred from its usage of *mathētēs* and related words or expression such as "to be with," "to follow," "to come after." The connection of *mathētēs* terminology with this related nomenclature also can provide some basis for determining what constitutes a "disciple" in those books of the New Testament which do not employ the term. Considerations of space preclude discussion of disciples/discipleship outside of the gospels and Acts (but see Longenecker).

General characteristics of disciples in the New Testament

Although those described as called to follow Jesus in the New Testament are sometimes relatively prosperous, they are not, apparently, extraordinarily wealthy, remarkably influential, or generally distinguished for intellectual brilliance. Likewise, during the ministry of Jesus and events leading to his crucifixion, they are not always faithful and often seem lacking in understanding of Jesus' message. The Gospels, Acts, and undisputed letters of Paul indicate that Peter emerged as a spokesperson/leader among the disciples, despite the fact that the gospel tradition is unanimous in portraying his denial of Jesus. Many, perhaps most, New Testament scholars conclude that the unfaithfulness of the disciples, most prominently Peter, reflects the historical situation of the time of Jesus.

During the time of Jesus the practice of seeking a master for instruction was not uncommon, both among Jews desiring learning in Torah and those in Hellenistic society interested either in intellectual guidance from an adherent of one of the philosophical schools of thought or initiation into the mystery religions. The person seeking instruction was frequently referred to as a disciple who sought instruction from a teacher. Among some Greek philosophers, the disciple was expected to provide (sometimes very substantial) financial compensation to the teacher for services rendered. A common element in all these situations was that the relationship was initiated by the person seeking knowledge.

K. H. Rengstorf has pointed out that while the New Testament depiction of discipleship shares some characteristics of similar contemporaneous non-Christian affiliations, in contrast, all of the gospels make clear that it is Jesus who initiates the master–disciple relationship. However, there are also indications that those whom Jesus calls already have some knowledge of him, and therefore openness. Though the synoptic accounts of the call of the first disciples are often compared to Elijah's call of Elisha, a striking difference is that, unlike Elisha, these disciples respond to Jesus by leaving all without stopping to say farewells (Donahue and Harrington). The commitment of Jesus' followers to him personally is apparent not only in the gospel call accounts, but in the assertion of Paul in Gal 2:20–21. Being a disciple of Jesus is portrayed as a lifetime commitment rather than a temporary situation. In following Jesus, disciples are called both to be with him and to do as he does, even to the point of following him to a humiliating death. After the death of Jesus, his message alone is not enough to console his followers. The risen Jesus once again takes the initiative in re-establishing the relationship of fellowship, which has been strained both by his death and by the unfaithfulness of many of his disciples.

Within the gospels (including Q), Acts, and Paul, there are references to a group of "the twelve" who are selected by Jesus from among the larger group of disciples. The Markan and Matthean evangelists, in addition, make occasional reference to "the twelve apostles" in connection with their missionary activity, but only the author of Luke–Acts specifies criteria for belonging to this group. This peculiar use in Luke–Acts, coupled with Paul's insistence on identifying himself as an apostle and occasional references to Paul as such in Luke–Acts, suggest that "the twelve apostles" is a literary creation of Luke. However, since at least the mid-twentieth century, the criteria of multiple attestation and embarrassment (Judas is one of the twelve; the lists of their names are inconsistent) makes most scholars more inclined to believe that the existence of a group of twelve goes back to the ministry of the historical Jesus.

Disciples/discipleship in Mark

In addition to those specifically called by Jesus, a number of individuals mentioned by the Markan evangelist, such as Peter's mother-in-law, Joseph of Arimathea, and the women mentioned in 15:41 who had followed Jesus and ministered to him, seem to function as disciples, and 13:37 indicates that Jesus' words are intended for all who are willing to accept them. Nonetheless, the Markan Gospel depicts the call of particular disciples in 1:16–20 and 2:14. In 3:13 Jesus summons a company of "those whom he wanted" and makes specific appointments for a smaller group of twelve. In 6:7 Jesus gives the twelve authority over unclean spirits and sends them on a mission, which, according to 6:12, seems to have included a commission to preach repentance as well as to exorcise.

It is commonly said that the Markan Gospel does not appear to stress any theological significance of this group. However, it may be suggested that "the twelve" for Mark are a representative group, as Peter is an individual representative, of what the disciples should be and do as well as of how they fail. In 6:12–13, they are represented as doing what Jesus did: preaching repentance, exorcising, and healing. Yet John Donahue and Daniel Harrington point out that the disciples' original commission in 3:13–19 already foreshadows their ultimate goal, to follow Jesus in the way of the cross. The commission "to be with him" takes place on a mountain; it is from a mountain that Jesus will go to his suffering and death. The last named of the twelve is Judas, who will betray him. Mark 8:27–38 and the other two passion predictions make clear that while for the author of Mark's Gospel disciples are called to preach, heal, and exorcise as Jesus did, the overwhelming challenge for the disciple is to keep on following Jesus even when faithful following leads to persecution and death. Morna Hooker observes that even if the passion predictions display the influence of the early church, there is no reason to exclude the possibility that Jesus spoke of his rejection, at least in general terms, and also expressed confidence in his vindication.

Discussions of the portrait of the disciples in the Markan Gospel often perhaps overemphasize the negative aspects such as their lack of understanding of Jesus' message and their failure to remain with him during his suffering and death, but recent commentaries such as those by Hooker and Donahue and Harrington point out positive aspects as well. Many maintain that the unflattering portrayal of the disciples and Jesus' family is a

contemporaneous literary device intended to highlight the main character. Donahue and Harrington suggest in addition that an Old Testament theme such as the constantly renewed graciousness of God in response to the frequent failings of God's people might be in the background, with the purpose of sustaining the community for which the gospel was written, a community in which many members may have found it difficult to remain faithful in face of persecution.

Disciples/discipleship in Matthew

The passion predictions and Jesus' teaching his disciples of the necessity of suffering for his sake, together with the emphasis on persecution both in the beatitudes and in 10:17–18, make clear that the Matthean evangelist shares the more general gospel tradition that the followers of Jesus can expect to share in his suffering. Though acknowledging the influence of the early church on the persecution sayings in the Matthean gospel, Jan Lambrecht insists on leaving open the possibility that the root of the beatitude on suffering goes back to Jesus himself.

As is the case with the Markan evangelist, the Matthean portrayal of the disciples includes a group of twelve, presumably chosen from the larger group of disciples, referred to rather peculiarly as "the twelve disciples" in 10:1 and possibly 20:17. The term "twelve apostles" in 10:2 is used in connection with the mission pericope (compare Mark 6:30), and does not appear to be of significant importance. However in 19:28, in a text generally attributed to Q, the mention of sitting on twelve thrones and having some sort of authority over the twelve tribes of Israel clearly refers to the group of the twelve, and, according to Harrington, may reflect a concern of Matthew's Jewish-Christian community.

While the Matthean evangelist's account of the call of the first four disciples in 4:18–22 is similar to that of the Markan evangelist in its placement immediately after Jesus' initial call to repentance and in its general structure, W. D. Davies and Dale Allison present forceful arguments that the radicalness of the demand and the obedient response of the disciples in leaving family and livelihood go back to the time of the historical Jesus. Nonetheless, the Matthean Gospel does not seem to preclude the existence of disciples of Jesus among the relatively wealthy. It is difficult for the rich person to enter the kingdom of heaven, but not impossible. This qualification is one indication that the community for which this gospel was written included people of relative wealth, who are nevertheless reminded that they will be judged on how they have treated "the least."

A strongly accentuated feature of the role of a disciple of Jesus in the Matthean Gospel is that the disciple is one who is to teach as Jesus taught. While this aspect does appear in the Markan mission pericope, in the Matthean Gospel the final commission of the risen Jesus to his followers is that they in turn must make disciples of all nations/Gentiles, baptizing them in the name of the Father and the Son and the Holy Spirit, and teaching them to observe all that Jesus has commanded. The disciples have been prepared for this teaching mission by Jesus earlier in the gospel, which makes clear at the beginning of chapter 5 that Jesus teaches the disciples and the crowds. At other points in the gospel Jesus gives his disciples additional teaching not given to the crowds, and they are portrayed as understanding him, if not totally, at least to some degree. The baptism in the name of the Father, the Son, and the Holy Spirit, found also in the *Didache*, is generally thought to reflect a baptismal formula of the Early Church and perhaps may be meant to recall the presence of the Father, Son, and Spirit at the baptism of Jesus. It might be asked why the disciples are commissioned to baptize, if generally they are to do as Jesus did, and neither the Matthean Gospel nor the other Synoptic Gospels portray Jesus as baptizing. Commentators on John 4:2 seem more inclined to view the remark there that Jesus did not baptize as a later editorial comment, which clearly contradicts the earlier assertions in that gospel that Jesus and his disciples baptized (Brown). In view of John 1–3, and the Synoptic Tradition that Jesus was to baptize with the (Holy) Spirit, it cannot be ruled out that Jesus did baptize and that here, as well, his disciples are commissioned to do as he did.

Disciples/discipleship in Luke–Acts

The portrayal of the disciples found in Luke–Acts has some distinctive features. In addition to the response of disciples common to other New Testament writers, such as faith, repentance/conversion, and baptism, Joseph A. Fitzmyer points out characteristics that have been frequently noted by Lukan scholars: (1) The following of Jesus generally expected of a disciple acquires a geographical and spatial stance; the disciple literally walks the journey to Jerusalem with Jesus. In Acts, the designation "the Way," used to describe the early Palestinian Christian community, adds a corporate sense to the notion of following Jesus. (2) Beginning in the last chapter of the Gospel, the theme of disciple as witness to the risen Christ is carried out through Acts. (3) Jesus is often depicted as praying, and, unique to the Lukan Gospel, the disciples ask Jesus to teach them how to pray. (4) Throughout Luke–Acts, there is a strong emphasis on the way in which disciples should use material possessions.

In the Gospel, the call of the first disciples becomes the call of the first disciple, Simon, and is combined with a narrative of a miraculous catch of fish. The prediction of Jesus that Peter will catch people is portrayed in great detail in Acts, where Peter and Paul both preach as Jesus did and perform miracles that parallel those of Jesus. This suggests that the Lukan evangelist viewed Paul as a disciple.

Although all of the gospels witness to the fact that there were both women and men disciples, since the 1980s intense discussion has arisen regarding the portrayal of women disciples in Luke–Acts. Prior to this, commentators generally remarked that the author of Luke–Acts portrayed women disciples very favorably. A. Plummer (528), for example, refers to the third gospel as the "Gospel of Womanhood." Recent studies (e.g. Levine, Price), challenge this view, asserting that women in Luke–Acts are clearly portrayed as disciples, but not in positions of leadership. Whether this reflects the view of the author of Luke–Acts or an early church situation is disputed.

Disciples/discipleship in John

Raymond E. Brown has noted that in the fourth gospel "Becoming or being a disciple is the same as being or remaining in Jesus" (663), and also, that, though in both the Synoptic and Johannine traditions the saying about following Jesus (John 12:26) implies willingness to suffer and die, the author of the fourth gospel refers to those who would "serve" Jesus, while the Synoptic Tradition refers to serving others. Brown suggests that the Johannine version may be more ancient, since the women who followed Jesus are described as serving him in Mark 14:41 and Luke 10:40. Raymond F. Collins has noted a pattern of discipleship in the early chapters of John's gospel: (1) prospective disciples encounter Jesus; (2) Jesus invites them to be with him; (3) they spend time with him; (4) they bring others to him. Francis Moloney, among others, has pointed out that, despite their positive initial response, these disciples do not fully understand Jesus immediately.

In the fourth gospel, some would-be disciples turn away from the hard sayings of Jesus, while some persist and gradually grow in understanding. The pattern depicted in the beginning of the gospel is reflected with later characters such as Nicodemus, who possibly remains a disciple, but more clearly in the Samaritan woman. Women disciples are prominent in the fourth gospel. I suggest that the mother of Jesus and Mary Magdalen are among those who have gradually grown to understand Jesus (Koperski 2006–7). In this sense, the New Testament portrayal of discipleship in general offers encouragement not only to its first hearers/readers, but to would-be disciples today who strive to understand Jesus more fully despite weakness, failure, and the specter of suffering.

VERONICA KOPERSKI

Further reading

Brown, Raymond E. *The Gospel According to John*, AB 29, 29A, Garden City, NY: Doubleday, 1970 [1966].

Collins, Raymond F. *These Things Have Been Written: Studies on the Fourth Gospel*, Louvain Theological and Pastoral Monographs 2, Louvain and Grand Rapids, MI: Peeters, Eerdmans, 1990.

Davies, W. D. and Allison, Dale C. Jr. *A Critical and Exegetical Commentary on the Gospel according to Saint Matthew*, ICC, Edinburgh: T. & T. Clark, 1997 [1988].

Fitzmyer, Joseph A. *The Gospel According to Luke*, AB 28, 28A, Garden City, NY: Doubleday, 1985 [1981], pp. 235–57.

Donahue, John R. and Harrington, Daniel J. *The Gospel of Mark*, SP 2, Collegeville, MN: Liturgical Press, 2002.

Harrington, Daniel J. *The Gospel of Matthew*, SP 1, Collegeville, MN: Liturgical Press, 1991.

Hooker, Morna. *The Gospel according to Saint Mark*, BNTC, London and Peabody, MA: A. & C. Black/Hendrickson, 1991, pp. 204–5.

Karris, R. J. "Women and Discipleship in Luke," *CBQ* 56:1 (1994) 1–20.

Koperski, Veronica. "Is 'Luke' a Feminist or Not? Female–Male Parallels in Luke–Acts," in R. Bieringer, G. Van Belle, and J. Verheyden (eds) *Luke and His Readers. Festschrift A. Denaux*, BETL 182, Leuven: University Press/Peeters, 2005, pp. 25–48.

—— "The Mother of Jesus and Mary Magdalene: Looking Back and Forward from the Foot of the Cross in John 19,25–27," in G. Van Belle (ed.) *The Death of Jesus in the Fourth Gospel*, BETL 200, Leuven: University Press/Peeters, forthcoming.

Lambrecht, Jan. *The Sermon on the Mount: Proclamation and Exhortation*, GNS 14, Wilmington, DE: Michael Glazier, 1985, p. 54

Levine, Amy-Jill (ed.) *A Feminist Companion to Luke*, London, New York: Sheffield Academic Press, 2002.

Longenecker, Richard (ed.) *Patterns of Discipleship in the New Testament*, McMaster New Testament Studies, Grand Rapids, MI: Eerdmans, 1996.

Marshall, I. Howard. *Commentary on Luke*, NIGTC, Grand Rapids, MI: Eerdmans, 1978.

Moloney, Francis J. *The Gospel of John*, SP 4, Collegeville, MN: Liturgical Press, 1998.

Plummer, A. *A Critical and Exegetical Commentary on the Gospel According to St Luke*, ICC, Edinburgh, T. & T. Clark, 1969 [1896].

Price, R. M. *The Widow Traditions in Luke–Acts. A Feminist-Critical Survey*, SBLDS 155, Atlanta, GA: Scholars Press, 1997.

Rengstorf, K. H. "*Mathetes*," in Gerhard Kittel (ed.) *Theological Dictionary of the New Testament. Vol. IV*, trans. and ed. Geoffrey W. Bromiley, Grand Rapids, MI: Eerdmans, 1967, pp. 415–59.

DISEASE, HEALTH, LONGEVITY

To deal with the misfortunes of pain and an accompanying sickening process, people throughout history have developed various "health care delivery systems" that offered ways to explain, predict, and control the symptoms of sickness. The word "disease" is one of the interpretative concepts used to describe the source of physical and psychological sickness. Disease is based on an explanatory framework that seeks the immediate adequate cause of the sickening in terms of the malfunction of some physical or psychological system. Such malfunction is due either to functional failure or disruption of an organism caused by external or internal sources (for example, bacteria, viruses, and gunshots invade from outside; cancerous growths are internal sources). Explaining human sickness in terms of disease and its symptoms is a recent phenomenon (eighteenth century) that now forms the bedrock of a medicocentric worldview typical of Western societies: The task of physicians is to cure disease. Curing involves adopting a strategy of destroying or checking a pathogen, removing (or replacing) a malfunctioning or non-functioning organ, and thus enabling the human organism to restore its "health," demonstrated by proper organic functioning. Without anachronism, this medicocentric perspective is not found in the Bible.

Traditionally in the Mediterranean culture area, people explained sickening in terms of an ill-being process, a process that forced out and attempted to eliminate well-being. The result was illness, an explanatory concept that ascribed ill-being largely to some personal cause, whether the sick persons themselves or other persons, both visible humans (attack or evil eye) or non-visible beings (such as the dead, spirits, demons or angels, and ultimately God [or gods]). Healing an illness dealt with working out a compromise with or banishing the personal causes of the misfortune and restoring the afflicted person to his or her social standing. Thus while the pain symptomatic of some sickness is quite real, the assessment of the meaning and treatment of sickness are derived from social systems and their culturally specific interpretations in terms of disease or illness.

Illness as described in the Bible is not so much a biomedical matter as it is a social one, attributable to social or interpersonal, not physical causes. Since people in antiquity paid little attention to impersonal cause–effect relationships, healers focused on sick persons in their social settings rather than on organs. When a person felt pain and began to sicken, the normal question was "who is doing this?" not "what is causing this?" The ancient concern was not so much with getting sick, but with "why me?" – something unanswered by modern medicine. Since illness was a matter of deviation from cultural norms and values, healing entailed a strategy of restoring social and personal meaning in face of the problems that accompanied a person afflicted with physical misfortunes.

The health care system of antiquity had three overlapping sectors: professional, popular, and folk. The professional sector included philosophically oriented "physicians" who studied the behavior of sick people, their symptoms and complaints, and developed theories to explain illness. Professionals never physically ministered to the sick. To this end they used slaves, who were duly punished should the sick person die.

The popular sector embraced the household, social network, and community and their respective beliefs and activities. A variety of demons and deities associated with healing shrines, shrine personnel, and apotropaic rituals belonged to this category. Circum-Mediterranean traditional cultures in general tended to adopt an attitude of being subservient to nature (the US value is to control nature). Peasant populations certainly knew they could not master or control nature (e.g. Mark 4:1–9), though they did learn how to live in harmony with it (e.g. Mark 2:22). Pain and suffering were considered part and parcel of a devolving universe and defective nature (Gen 3). Pain could be alleviated, but not eliminated. The principal concern of popular culture was health and health maintenance, a concern which sensitized people to notice deviance from the culturally defined norm known as "health." Therefore, it is in this popular sector that the deviant condition known as "illness" is first observed, defined, and treated, with attention to how illness affected and involved everyone in the kinship group and wider community. The consequences of healing therefore affect this wider group as well.

The folk healer was a person recognized by people in a community as having a divinely endowed ability to restore people to health. Holy men in contact with the realm of God, such as Elijah, Elisha, and Jesus, were folk healers whose "license to practice" was tacitly granted and acknowledged by success with each individual sick person in the local community. These healers shared the significant elements of the constituency's world view and health concepts. They accepted everything that was presented to them as naturally co-occurring elements of a syndrome (see notably John 9:1–34). Clients were "outpatients," in the public gaze typical of honor-oriented people. They took the patient's view of illness at face value, rarely ignoring or correcting the symptoms as communicated by the sick person or surrogate. The vocabulary folk healers used to describe an illness was that of the sick person's everyday experiences and belief system. Finally, since folk healers were native to the community and knew its mores, history, and scandals well, they made special use of the historical and social context of each illness.

Health is the cultural assessment that one is well. The World Health Organization defines health as "a state of complete physical, mental and social well-being and not merely the absence of disease and infirmity." Allied to health is peace: a condition that supports total social well-being, not merely the absence of war.

Lifespan is less a question of health care than of diet. Hence it is no surprise that in antiquity, elites lived longer than the 98 percent non-elite population. Experts tell us that average life expectancy was short, roughly twenty-five to thirty years. Fifty percent did not pass age ten, and of elites who did, 50 percent might attain to fifty; 33 percent to sixty; and 16 percent to seventy. At twenty, expectancy was thirty-one more years, at thirty add twenty-six.

BRUCE J. MALINA

Further reading

Murdock, George Peter. *Theories of Illness: A World Survey.* Pittsburgh, PA: University of Pittsburgh Press, 1980.

Pilch, John J. *Healing in the New Testament: Insights from Medical and Mediterranean Anthropology.* Minneapolis, MN: Fortress Press, 2000.

Saller, Richard. *Patriarchy, Property and Death in the Roman Family.* Cambridge: Cambridge University Press, 1994.

Worsley, Peter. "Non-Western Medical Systems," *Annual Review of Anthropology* 11 (1982) 315–48.

Young, Allan. "The Anthropologies of Illness and Sickness," *Annual Revue of Anthropology* 11 (1982) 257–85.

DIVINE MAN/*THEIOS ANĒR*

In classical studies and in research into the origins of Christianity "divine man," or its Greek counterpart, *theios anēr*, refers to a type of religious virtuoso who was regarded as divine on the basis of his supernatural powers, especially numinous wisdom and miracle-working prowess. The isolation of this figure is usually credited to the giants of the History-of-Religions School, particularly R. Reitzenstein, who in 1910 spoke of

[a] general conception of the θεῖς ἄνθρωπος [divine human] ... , according to which such a divine man combines within himself, on the basis of a higher nature and personal holiness, the profoundest knowledge, vision, and the power to work miracles.

(26)

Successive classical scholars, such as G. P. Wetter (1916), Otto Weinreich (1926), Hans Windisch (1934), and especially Ludwig Bieler (1935–6), further explored this type and changed Reitzenstein's nomenclature to θεῖος ἀνήρ (*theios anēr*).

Development of the "divine man" hypothesis

The notion of the "divine man" came to exercise enormous influence in New Testament studies through the two most famous works of the German Form-Critical School, produced by Martin Dibelius (*From Tradition to Gospel*, 1919) and Rudolf Bultmann (*History of the Synoptic Tradition*, 1921). In particular, these pioneers utilized the "divine man" to explain the origin and significance of the miracle stories of the canonical gospels. Bultmann, for example, asserted that while Jesus in Q was the "preacher of repentance and salvation," in the Gospel of Mark he appears as a θεῖως ἄνθρωπος (divine human), and this largely on account of the miracle stories (241). Dibelius and Bultmann believed that most of the miracle stories in the canonical gospels were created or at least formulated in an Hellenistic environment by gentile Christians who used such stories as propaganda in the effort to win converts to the Lord Jesus Christ, the superior "divine man." This view of the *Sitz im Leben*, or life-setting, of the miracle stories in the early church, with the concomitant judgment that they were relatively late and not, at least for the most part, based on historical reminiscence, continues to be attractive to this day.

Although Dibelius and Bultmann implied that it was in the literary forms that they, respectively, identified as Tales (*Novellen*) and Miracle Stories (*Wundergeschichten*) that the "divine man" made its deepest inroads, various scholars have detected its influence in other miraculous traditions. These would include Jesus' miraculous conception, his preternatural knowledge at age twelve, the visionary experiences at his baptism, his supernatural perception of otherwise unknowable past and present realities, his transfiguration, the discovery of his empty tomb, and his ascension.

In 1963 Ferdinand Hahn refined the earlier Form-Critical appropriation of the "divine man" concept. Believing that there was a significant difference between Palestinian and Hellenistic Judaism, Hahn argued that prior to the appearance of Jesus, Hellenistic Jews, such as Philo and Artapanus (and later Josephus), portrayed Israel's heroes – above all Moses – as "divine men." Thus Hahn held that it was first through Hellenistic Jewish Christians that the "divine man" concept begin to work its magic on the traditions of the earthly life of Jesus. Though this modification was widely hailed as positive refinement, it had little effect on the overall negative assessment of the historicity of the miracle traditions appearing in the gospels. Most scholars agreed with Bultmann that Jesus performed what he and many onlookers viewed as healings and exorcisms (since such could be deduced from authentic sayings of Jesus), but were loath to believe that many of the specific incidents appearing in the gospels were rooted in memory.

Another significant refinement of the "divine man" hypothesis was offered in 1972 by David Tiede, who demonstrated that until the time of Philostratus's biography of Apollonius of Tyana (early third century CE), the "divine men" of the Greco-Roman world were authenticated on the basis of *either* their supernatural powers *or* their wisdom, but not both. This thesis had the effect of ever more tightly connecting the miracle traditions surrounding Jesus with an early Christian "divine man" Christology.

In more recent decades, scholars who are enthusiastic about the heuristic value of the "divine man" concept for understanding Christian origins have identified its earliest literary deposits in the putative catenae of miracle stories incorporated into the Gospels of Mark and John. The catena in the latter gospel, of course, has been dubbed the Signs Source. Almost no one doubts that the historical Jesus performed what he and others viewed as miraculous healings and exorcisms; in other words, he was a noted miracle worker. However, the miracle *stories* in the catenae (as well as the catenae themselves) were formulated, so the theory goes, when certain Hellenistic Jewish Christians attempted to win converts in the wider pagan world. Such demonstrations of divine power would have impressed other Hellenistic Jews and pagans, convincing them that they, too, could have access to present blessings through the Lord Jesus or his miracle-working emissaries. At this stage the miracle stories would not only have been influenced and modeled after stories of prophets and other miracle-working figures in the OT and Judaism, but also the famous "divine men" of the Hellenistic world. In 1964 D. Georgi (*The Opponents of Paul in Second Corinthians*) argued that the Hellenistic Jewish Christians responsible for propagandizing with the miracle stories in the catenae were somehow related to the Hellenistic Jewish Christian missionaries whom Paul battled in 2 Corinthians. The latter, Georgi argued, made use of "letters of recommendation" (2 Cor 3:1), which contained reports of their miracles and other sensational accomplishments.

Advocates of the existence of such a "divine man" Christology typically maintain that this naïve Christology of the miracle catenae and other miracle stories and traditions similar to the ones comprising them was adopted but modified by each of the canonical gospels.

H. D. Betz, for example, believes that Mark accepted the "divine man" Christology, but subjected it to the cross and resurrection. For Matthew, Jesus is the divine Messiah, whose miracles fulfill scripture and prove his messiahship. In Luke–Acts, Jesus is the "divine man" *par excellence* during his earthly ministry; the ascended Jesus continues to work through his "name," Spirit, and apostles, who are, themselves, "divine men." The author of John combines the "divine man" Christology with the descending/ascending Logos Christology. In this way Betz concludes that "the Gospels and their source materials represent five different versions of the Divine Man Christology" (129).

Pillars of the "divine man" hypothesis

Evidence that the miracle traditions of the canonical gospels express a "divine man" Christology falls into three categories. First, these traditions betray reflection on Jesus' divine nature. U. Luz, for example, speaks of a mixture of the human and the divine in the Markan miracle stories that was characteristic of the Hellenistic "divine men." As examples he pointed to the motifs of prostration (in worship) and theophany. An excellent example of the latter would be the story of Jesus Walking on the Sea appearing in Mark 6:45–52. Since several theophanic motifs appearing in the OT are transferred to Jesus, some scholars doubt whether such a story could have been formulated in the pronounced monotheism of the earliest Aramaic-speaking church. According to this perspective,

such a development must have been effected by Hellenistic Jewish Christians or possibly Christian gentiles well versed in the OT.

The second category of evidence includes the many parallels in themes and motifs between the miracle traditions connected to Jesus and those associated with pagan miracle workers and magicians of the Greco-Roman world. Long ago, Bultmann collected many of these and made them conveniently accessible to NT scholars in his *History of the Synoptic Tradition* (218–44). The most impressive cases exist where Jewish parallels are few but pagan ones are numerous. Several such cases appear in the stories found in Mark 7:31–37 and 8:22–26: the use of spittle, manipulations with the hand, sighing, and a miracle-working command in a foreign language (*rhesis barbarike*). Moreover, the *Papyri Graecae Magicae*, as well as other Greco-Roman texts, has furnished parallels to many of the exorcistic motifs appearing in the gospels: the apotropaic use of the opponent's name, a "binding" command using the Greek verbs *phimoō*, *deō*, or *katadeō*, a formula of exorcism employing the command *exelthe*, and the banishment of the demon (the so-called *epipompe*).

Third, there is a remarkable formal resemblance between the Jesuan miracle stories and stories that narrate the miracles of pagan miracle workers, especially Pythagoras and Apollonius of Tyana. Time and again there is a three-fold structure: (1) the problem needing rectification is described, (2) the miracle is narrated, and (3) there is a conclusion that attests the effectiveness or impressiveness of the miraculous deed. These three categories of evidence have convinced generations of scholars that the gospel miracle traditions (especially the miracle stories) bear the heavy impress of the "divine man," and as such are historically suspect.

Critique of the "divine man" hypothesis

During the second half of the twentieth century there appeared a spate of studies which called into question the existence of a "divine man" concept in the Greco-Roman world and/or the usefulness of such a concept as an analytic tool in the study of Christian origins. In 1969 P. W. von Martitz concluded "that θεῖος ἀνήρ is by no means a fixed expression at least in the pre-Christian era," and that "[t]he features of θεῖος in later antiquity [illustrated by the *vitae* of Pythagoras composed by Porphyry and Iamblichus and the *vita* of Apollonius of Tyana] cannot be traced back smoothly to the earlier period" (338–9). This latter judgment received support in 1972 from Otto Betz, who argued against the existence of a "divine man" Christology in Mark by positing an early Palestinian-Jewish provenance for the miracle stories appearing in Mark 4:35–41 and 5:1–20, two traditions that had previously often been subsumed under the "divine man" rubric. H. C. Kee perpetuated a similar line of attack in several articles and books published in the 1970s and 1980s. In particular, he called attention to a Jewish hope for an eschatological Mosaic prophet, whose signs and wonders would herald the Eschaton. Moreover, Kee acknowledged that there were pagan miracle stories that closely resembled the miracle stories in the gospels in both *form* and *content*; nevertheless, their *function* would be determined by the specific cultural-religious milieu in which they originated. Thus while in certain pagan settings miracles might be narrated to document a thaumaturge's divinity, such a purpose need not be attributed to miracle stories circulating in early Christianity. Eugene Gallagher's 1982 study of the christological debate between Origen and Celsus raised further doubt whether "there was a *native* Hellenistic conception of the divine man," but if so "it was certainly a more fluid conception than is portrayed in much contemporary scholarship" (177). "[C]ontemporaries . . . of candidates for divine status in Late Antiquity" did not employ "a single, rigid 'Hellenistic concept of the divine man' as their guideline for evaluation, but rather a shifting and flexible collection of categories and criteria which could be adapted to fit the demands of particular situations" (176f.).

Inasmuch as most advocates of the influence of the "divine man" on early Christology held that Hellenistic Judaism was the mediating link between paganism and early Christianity, the publication (in 1977) of Carl Holladay's Cambridge thesis proved troublesome. On the basis of a study of Artapanus, Philo, and Josephus, he concluded that these authors provide no evidence "that during the Hellenistic era there occurs a significant shift in Jewish thinking which enables Jews more easily to attribute divinity to their Biblical heroes for propagandistic purposes," or "that Hellenistic Jews, in an effort to propagate their faith to Gentiles, tended to heighten thaumaturgic motifs, either in their portrayals of Israel's heroes or in their understanding of history" (236, 238).

The decade of the 1990s saw the appearance of three major critiques of the application of the "divine man" concept to the study of Christian origins. Barry Blackburn conducted a survey of the human figures in the Greco-Roman world to whom both miracles and divinity were credited. He concluded that these figures do not "constitute

anything like a fixed type whose representatives share a set of several characteristics" (94). There was "no standard or customary designation, including θεῖος ἀνήρ, for these miracle workers" (94), "there was no uniform manner of expressing their divine status" (95), and their miraculous activities were wildly diverse. In addition, Blackburn's analysis of the Markan miracle traditions against their Old Testament/Jewish background led him to conclude that none of the so-called "divine man" elements – the "divinity" of Jesus, the themes and motifs of the miracle traditions, and the miracle story genre – *requires* the conclusion that "the miracle traditions incorporated into Mark [have] been influenced by distinctively Hellenistic traditions or notions respecting miracles or miracle-working" (264).

Erkki Koskenniemi's research on Philostratus's *Life of Apollonius of Tyana* led him to indict the "divine man" hypothesis. He has observed that several of the features of the "divine man" pattern, especially those identified much earlier by L. Bieler, were abstracted from two figures: Jesus in the canonical gospels and Apollonius in the Philostratean *vita*. This is problematic, according to Koskenniemi, since the Apollonius encountered in Philostratus's work is essentially a third-century product with little claim to historicity.

Finally, David du Toit claims to have decisively cut the link between the "divine man" hypothesis and "θεῖος ἄνθρωπος terminology" (i.e. the adjectives θεῖος, δαιμόνιος, θεσπέσιος). During the Greco-Roman period this terminology was used within the semantic field of epistemology or ethics, but not anthropology: these terms denote, not God-men [*Gottmenschen*] or charismatic miracle workers, but founders and/or guarantors of an epistemology, or they function as qualitative adjectives which emphasize the special piety of the person in question" (402). If the θεῖος ἄνθρωπος terminology is not the linguistic bearer of the "divine man" concept, then either the concept itself will have to be renounced or other, successfully tested terminology will have to be discovered to take its place.

The "divine man" hypothesis in recent *Leben Jesu* research

A perusal of major monographs on the historical Jesus published during the last twenty-five years demonstrates that scholars have made little use of the "divine man" concept in their efforts to identify Jesus' authentic teachings and activities. It is telling, indeed, that neither "divine man" nor "theios anēr" appears in the subject indexes of the most significant books on the historical Jesus by E. P. Sanders, Geza Vermes (*The Changing Faces of Jesus*, 2000), Marcus Borg, Marinus de Jonge, N. T. Wright, and Paula Fredriksen. No subject index appears in J. D. Crossan's major work on Jesus, but he speaks of Jesus as "magician" rather than "divine man." However, Crossan avers that the type of magician that Jesus approximated was closer to that represented by Elijah, Elisha, Honi the Circle Drawer, and Hanina ben Dosa than to the practitioners of the kinds of spells appearing in the magical papyri. Hence, in calling Jesus a "magician," Crossan underscores, not the influence of alien Hellenistic notions on an authentic Jesus tradition, but the fact that the historical Jesus himself was an excellent representative of those figures who offered personal, individual power, which, of course, was disapproved by the communal and ritual power represented by priest and temple. John Meier prefaces his lengthy analysis of the gospel miracle tradition with a brief discussion of the "divine man" hypothesis, which, however, he decisively rejects as a helpful instrument in the quest for the historical Jesus

Of authors of major books on the historical Jesus, only Gerd Theissen and Annette Merz are willing to affirm the *possibility* "that the picture of Jesus in the tradition has been assimilated at a secondary stage to such motifs [represented by the term 'divine man']" (305). Yet even here, they acknowledge that "it is disputed whether we have here [in the term 'divine man'] a clearly definable type of miracle-worker or merely a collection of motifs."

Contemporary scholars virtually unanimously agree that the historical Jesus performed healings and exorcisms. (A few, e.g. Meier, would even argue that some or all of the accounts of his raising of the dead are based on actual events.) However, most critics, even in the wake of the eclipse of the "divine man" hypothesis, would still agree that while some of the healing and exorcism stories probably rest on memory, most of them resist a firm historical verdict.

BARRY L. BLACKBURN, SR

Further reading

Betz, Hans Dieter. "Jesus as Divine Man," in F. Trotter (ed.) *Jesus and the Historian*, Philadelphia. PA: Westminster, 1968, pp. 114–33.
—— "Gottmensch II," *RAC* 12 (1983) 234–312.
Betz, Otto. "The Concept of the So-called 'Divine Man' in Mark's Christology," in D. Aune (ed.) *Studies in New*

Testament and Early Christian Literature, Leiden: Brill, 1972, pp. 229–40.
Bieler, Ludwig. ΘΕΙΟΣ ANHP, 2 vols, Vienna: Oskar Höfels, 1935–36.
Blackburn, Barry. *Theios Anēr and the Markan Miracle Traditions*, WUNT 2:40, Tübingen: Mohr, 1991.
Bultmann, Rudolf. *History of the Synoptic Tradition*, trans. John Marsh. New York: Harper & Row, 1963.
Corrington, Gail P. *The "Divine Man": His Origin and Function in Hellenistic Popular Religion*, New York: Peter Lang, 1986.
du Toit, David. *Theios Anthrōpon*, WUNT 2:91, Tübingen: Mohr, 1997.
Gallagher, Eugene V. *Divine Man or Magician? Celsus and Origen on Jesus*, SBLDS 64, Chico, CA: Scholars Press, 1982.
Hahn, Ferdinand. *The Titles of Jesus in Christology*, trans. H. Knight and G. Ogg, London: Lutterworth Press, 1969.
Holladay, Carl. *Theios Aner in Hellenistic Judaism*, SBLDS 40, Missoula, MT: Scholars Press, 1977.
Kee, Howard Clark. *Miracle in the Early Christian World*, New Haven, CT: Yale University Press, 1983.
Koskenniemi, Erkki. "Apollonius of Tyana: A Typical ΘΕΙΟΣ ANHP?" *JBL* 117.3 (1998) 455–67.
Luz, Ulrich. "Das Jesusbild der vormarkinischen Tradition," in G. Strecker (ed.) *Jesus Christus in Historie und Theologie*, Tübingen: Mohr, 1975, pp. 347–74.
Reitzenstein, Richard. *Hellenistic Mystery-Religions*, trans. J. Steely, PTMS 15, Pittsburgh, PA: Pickwick Press, 1978.
Theissen, Gerd and Merz, Annette. *The Historical Jesus*, trans. John Bowden, Minneapolis, MN: Fortress Press, 1998.
Tiede, David L. *The Charismatic Figure as Miracle Worker*, SBLDS 1, Missoula, MT: Scholars Press, 1972.
von Martitz, P. Wülfing. "υἱός (in Greek)," in G. Kittel (ed.) *Theological Dictionary of the New Testament, Vol. 8*, Grand Rapids, MI: Eerdmans, 1972, pp. 334–40.

DIVORCE AND REMARRIAGE

Questions of divorce and remarriage carried a similar emotional fervor in the first century as they do in our own day. Marriage was understood as the foundation of society by both Jewish and Hellenistic-Roman writers. At the same time, it was recognized that marriages failed, and divorce was an acceptable escape clause in both societies. Jesus' strict stand on divorce as recorded in Matt 5:31–32//Luke 16:18; Mark 10:2–12//Matt 19:2–12 and 1 Cor 7:12–14 is, therefore, truly exceptional.

Jewish teaching on divorce

Marriage and divorce in the Mishnah

As was common practice in the ancient world, Jewish marriages were arranged by families. Girls married young, usually at around twelve or twelve and half (*m. Ketub.* 4:4–5). Men married at about eighteen. The arrangement began when the two families arranged a betrothal, which was less than a marriage but more than the modern engagement. It could only be broken by a formal divorce. The bride's family would pay a dowry, or *Ketubah*, a term that originally referred to the marriage contract (Tob 7:11–15). The contract outlined the payments in property and money, so eventually the term *Ketubah* applied to the dowry itself (Instone-Brewer 82). In the Mishnah, the dowry for a virgin was 200 *zuz*, or denars, while for a widow or a divorced woman it was 100 *zuz*. The dowry was the property of the wife, but would be used by the couple while they were married. If the woman is widowed or divorced, the money returned to her (*m. Ketub.* 5:1, see Instone-Brewer 83). This custom functioned as a discouragement to divorce by making it costly.

Divorce, while costly, was recognized as legitimate, based on Deut 24:1–4. While this passage actually discussed the unlawful remarriage of a divorced wife, Deut 24:1 mentioned that if a husband found something objectionable in his wife he could then write a certificate of divorce, or a *get*, to dismiss her. Later rabbinic tradition would devote an entire tract of the Mishnah to the *gittin* elaborating the lawful means of writing and delivering these documents. In rabbinic custom, divorce was exclusively the prerogative of the husband, who upon writing up the *get* and sending his wife away declared her freedom to marry another man (*m. Git.* 9:1). The vague language of Deut 24:1 led to a dispute between the rabbinic schools on the grounds of divorce, with the House of Shammai restricting it to unchastity on the part of the wife, while the House of Hillel allowed it for even trivial matters, such as spoiling the husband's dinner (*m. Git.* 9:10). One should not conclude, however, that divorce was common. The very regulations found in the Mishnah tractate *Gittin*, as well as the requirement of the return of the dowry, would have been mitigating factors.

The emphasis on divorce resulted, in part, from the changing circumstances of the Second Temple period. While polygamy was permitted in Judaism, by the time of Jesus monogamy was generally the rule. Thus, regulations on divorce became more important. In the cases of infertility of a wife or of adultery on the part of the wife or the betrothed, the husband would be expected to divorce his wife. One example is found in the case of Joseph when he suspected Mary of unchastity and planned to initiate a quiet divorce (Matt 1:18–19). After 30 CE, rabbinic custom would require the divorce of an adulterous wife (*m. Sotah* 6:1) While in rabbinic custom divorce was the husband's prerogative,

evidence exists of women initiating divorce even in Palestine. One instance has been found among the documents found in the caves at Murabb'at, known as the Se'elim *get* or Papyrus Se'elim 13. Published in 1995, this document clearly demonstrates the woman initiating divorce (Instone-Brewer 87–9). Furthermore, marriage certificates from the Jewish colony of Elephantine in Egypt show both men and women as having equal right to divorce (Instone-Brewer 89–90).

Marriage and divorce at Qumran

Our understanding of marriage and divorce among the Qumran sectarians, likely members of the Essene sect of Judaism, derives from two documents in particular. The first is from the *Damascus Document* or *Covenant of Damascus* (CD). CD 4:20–25:6 specifically prohibits royal polygamy on the basis of Gen 1:27 and Deut 17:17. David's polygamy is excused on the basis that the law was sealed from him and he was unaware of the prohibition. In the *Temple Scroll* 54:5 refers to the vow of a widow or a divorced woman, which cannot be abrogated. This passage is a quote from Num 30:9.

How the Qumran community understood polygamy or divorce within the context of their own community, however, is more difficult to assess. According to Pliny the Elder *Nat.* 5.73, the Essenes who live by the Dead Sea abstained from marriage and every form of sexual desire. Likewise, Josephus, in *Jewish War* 2.120 states that the Essenes scorn marriage, but will adopt young children and instruct them in their way of life. Yet in *J.W.* 2.161 Josephus also mentions a second order of Essenes, who practice marriage for the purpose of procreation. The Essene scroll known as the *Manual of Discipline* provides regulations for virtually every aspect of Essene society, but neglects mention of marriage and family. Thus, some scholars assume that the Essene group at Qumran were celibate (VanderKam 91). The evidence is further complicated by the presence of the skeletons of women and children outside the main burial ground at Qumran.

Perhaps the best conclusion is that the majority of Essenes were celibate. Their lifestyle reflected their preparation for the eschatological battle as outlined in the *War Scroll* (1QM). Their need to remain celibate is preparation for participation in the final eschatological battle, according to the regulations of holy war as dictated in Deut 20:1–9. Nevertheless, there is no evidence that either divorce or remarriage were rejected in theory at Qumran.

Marriage and divorce in the Greco-Roman world

The Hellenistic/Roman world understood marriage not in terms of a love match between two individuals, but as an alliance of families and combining of resources. In the upper classes, the average age for first marriages varied greatly between men and women. A man's first marriage occurred usually occurred around the age of thirty, while women usually married young, from between fourteen and eighteen (Osiek and Balch 62). When a woman married, she had the option of either coming under the authority (*manus* or "hand") of her husband, or remaining under the authority of her father. If she remained under her father's authority, she retained greater autonomy and could initiate a divorce. A Roman head of household or *paterfamilias* could also compel the divorce of his son, as Augustus did with Tiberius. From early times, Roman law allowed for divorce in the case of adultery, but the first precedent noted was in 230 BC. By the first century, divorce was understood as an agreement between the two parties, and did not require legal action except for property disputes. It could be initiated by either the man or the woman (Dixon 45), and neither divorce nor remarriage were stigmatized. Even Augustus, who attempted to combat the sense of moral decay through marriage legislation, was divorced and married the divorced Livia.

Jesus' teaching on divorce and remarriage

In contrast to the easy divorce of much of antiquity, Jesus' view was uncompromising, rooted in the creation story of Gen 1:27; 2:24. Jesus' views are attested early, not only in the gospels but also by Paul, in 1 Cor 7:10–11. Here the apostle quoted the authority of "the Lord" to state that believers should not divorce, and in 7:12–14 extrapolated that they should not initiate a divorce of unbelieving spouses.

In the gospels, the earliest tradition of Jesus' views on divorce derives from the Q tradition preserved in Matthew and Luke (Luke 16:18//Matt 5:32). It is likely that Luke 16:18 is the more original form of Jesus' statement (Fitzmyer 82–3). The gist of this saying is also preserved in 1 Cor 7:10–11 as well as the prohibitions of Matt 5:32b and Mark. 10:11//Matt 19:9). The prohibition on divorce is absolute, and stands in contrast both to Jewish and Hellenistic practice. That it is attested in numerous sources, including Mark, "Q," and Paul, enhances the likelihood that the historical Jesus prohibited divorce.

In Luke 16:18, Jesus bluntly stated that every man who divorced his wife and married another committed adultery. Furthermore, it was said that the male who married a divorced woman committed adultery. The saying appears straightforward. Nevertheless, there are ambiguities. Is the act of adultery found in the act of divorce, or in remarriage? Is remarriage after divorce adulterous because of the divorce itself, or because the divorce was procured strictly for the sake of marrying another (cf. Matt 5:28)? In rabbinic tradition, if a woman was not properly divorced, her first marriage was still binding (see Instone-Brewer 125–32). If she remarried, she and her new husband were technically guilty of adultery (*m. Git.* 8.5). So, Jesus' statement could be understood as prohibiting divorce for the sake of remarriage. Such divorces were, by definition, invalid.

Jesus' prohibition on divorce, therefore, may correspond to certain aspects of Jewish law. It certainly applied to the case where a man divorced his wife for the express purpose of remarriage to another. On the basis of Matt 5:28, this would have been viewed by Jesus as adulterous. The application of Jesus' teaching, however, remained problematic for the church from its earliest times. In 1 Cor 7:12–16, Paul addresses the tense situation of a marriage where one partner has become a Christian and the other has not. Jesus' commandment (see 1 Cor 7:8–11), had not addressed this situation. Paul recognized that in these circumstances, the believer was not bound by the decision of the unbeliever. In such a mixed marriage, Paul allowed for a divorce when it came at the insistence of the unbelieving partner.

In Matthew and Mark, further adjustment to Jesus' teaching may be observed. Both Mark 10:2–9 and Matt 19:2–9 place Jesus' teaching in the context of a dispute with the Pharisees. The question possibly arose from what was already known of Jesus' teaching as reflected in Luke 16:18. In Mark 10:6–9, we see the reason for Jesus' prohibition of divorce. It was based on God's original intention of creation. In a combination of Gen 1:27; 2:24, it was noted that God ordained that man and woman would be united in marriage, with the two becoming one flesh. The quotation of Gen 2:24 in Mark 10:7 is from the LXX. Some scholars have seen this fact as evidence that the scriptural evidence was a secondary feature added by the early church. Mark may, however, simply be quoting scripture from the version most familiar to his implied readers.

What is remarkable is Jesus' private teaching with his disciples in Mark 10:10–12, where the

Markan Jesus noted that if a man divorced his wife to marry another he commits adultery against her, and if a woman divorced her husband to marry another, she committed adultery. The language of the prohibition of divorce for the purpose of remarriage is similar to that of Luke 16:18. More noteworthy is the statement that if a husband carried through with plans to divorce he committed adultery against his wife. In the patriarchal society of first-century Palestine, where polygamy was at least a theoretical option, adultery was an offense against the aggrieved husband, not against the wife. The unexpected and radical nature of this statement, which elevated the status of the wife beyond the norm of both Jewish and Hellenistic/Roman society, enhance the likelihood that it derived from the lips of the historical Jesus.

More problematic is Mark. 10:12, where the woman divorces the husband. Josephus noted the examples of Salome (Josephus, *Ant.* 15.259–60) and Herodias (Josephus, *Ant.* 109–11) who divorced their husbands, but he also mentioned that they were following Roman rather than Jewish practice. While we noted that in some cases it appears women could initiate divorce in Palestinian Judaism, the evidence is later than the time of Jesus. Thus, Mark. 10:12 is likely an addition to the words of Jesus to make his statement more applicable to the Greco-Roman world. Likewise, the "Matthean exception" of divorce for the sake of adultery (Matt 5:32b; 19:9) is likely an addition by the early church.

Why would Jesus' teaching on divorce stand in such contrast to his social setting? The answer may come from the appeal in Mark. 10:6–9 to the creation story, in the context of Jesus' teaching on the impending arrival of God's kingdom or reign. If Jesus taught that the kingdom of God was near (see Mark 1:15), then it is likely that a significant element of his preaching was God's restoration of the created order, beginning with his own ministry. One ramification of this restoration was the return of marriage to its proper role, and the annulment of the temporary provision of divorce, which was allowed solely for human "hardness of heart" (Mark. 10:5//Matt 19:8).

Conclusions

Jesus' teaching on divorce is uncompromising, and intimately linked with his preaching of God's kingdom. Yet, even within the first century the church needed to adjust the ideal to the real, as can be seen in Paul's advice in 1 Cor 7:8–11, and the Matthean exception in Matt 5:32b; 19:9. It is likely Jesus linked the indissolubility of marriage to God's purpose in creation. The restoration of creation is then associated with his preaching of the impending kingdom of God. Jesus' teaching does, however, contain major ambiguities. Was Jesus' prohibition on divorce meant absolutely? Was it primarily directed to the problem of a man divorcing his wife with the specific intent of marrying another? If the latter is the case, may we understand the intention of Jesus' teaching to be protection of the woman? In a patriarchal society, the onus of Jesus' words would fall on the man, who would be required to maintain his obligations to support and care for his wife. If the words of Mark 10:11–12 do go back to Jesus, such a conclusion is warranted. Here we find Jesus introducing what would, in his society, be revolutionary: that the husband who divorces his wife to marry another is guilty of adultery against his first wife.

In this light, Jesus' teaching is oriented not so much to the protection of the institution of marriage as to secure the safety of individuals, particularly the wife. Perhaps this is why Paul could feel free to expand on Jesus' advice in 1 Cor 7. In any case, there is no evidence that Jesus intended wives to remain in abusive marriages solely for the sake of preservation of the marriage. How Christians today are to appropriate this teaching has been discussed by several very good studies (see Collins, Instone-Brewer and Keener).

RUSSELL MORTON

Further reading

Bockmuehl, Markus. *Jewish Law in Gentile Churches: Halakhah and the Beginning of Christian Public Ethics*, Grand Rapids, MI: Baker Academic Press, 2000.

Collins, Raymond F. *Divorce in the New Testament*, GNS, Collegeville, MN: Liturgical Press, 1992.

Corbier, Mireille. "Divorce and Adoption as Roman Familial Strategies," in Beryl Rawson (ed.) *Marriage, Divorce and Children in Ancient Rome*, Canberra: Humanities Research Centre; Oxford: Clarendon Press, 1991, pp. 47–78.

Davies, W. D. and Dale C. Allison. *Matthew*, ICC, Edinburgh: T. & T. Clark, 1988–97.

deSilva, David A. *Honor, Patronage, Kinship and Purity: Unlocking New Testament Culture*, Downers Grove, IL: InterVarsity Press, 2000.

Dixon, Suzanne. *The Roman Family*, Baltimore, MD: Johns Hopkins University Press, 1992.

Dunn, James D. G. *Jesus Remembered*, Christianity in the Making 1, Grand Rapids, MI: Eerdmans, 2003.

Fitzmyer, Joseph A. "The Matthean Divorce Texts and Some New Palestinian Evidence," in *To Advance the Gospel: New Testament Studies*, second edition. Grand Rapids, MI: Eerdmans, 1998.

Hanson, K. C. and Douglas E. Oakman. *Palestine in the Time of Jesus: Social Structures and Social Conflicts*, Minneapolis, MN: Fortress Press, 2002 [1998].

Instone-Brewer, David. *Divorce and Remarriage in the Bible: The Social and Literary Context*, Grand Rapids, MI: Eerdmans, 2002.

Keener, Craig S. *And Marries Another: Divorce and Remarriage in the Teaching of the New Testament*, Peabody, MA: Hendrickson, 1991.

Levine, Amy-Jill. "The Word Become Flesh: Jesus, Gender, and Sexuality," in James D. G. Dunn and Scot McKnight (eds) *The Historical Jesus in Recent Research*, Winona Lake, IN: Eisenbrauns, 2005, pp. 509–23.

Luz, Ulrich. "Matthew 1–7," CC, Minneapolis, MN: Fortress Press, 1992.

—— "Matthew 8–20," *Hermeneia*, Minneapolis, MN: Fortress Press, 2001.

Neusner, Jacob (trans.) *The Mishnah: A New Translation*, New Haven, CT: Yale University Press, 1988.

Osiek, Carolyn and David L. Balch. *Families in the New Testament World, Households and House Churches*, Louisville, KY: Westminster/John Knox Press, 1997.

Sanders, E. P. *Jesus and Judaism*, Philadelphia, PA: Fortress Press, 1985.

Sigal, Phillip. *The Hallakah of Jesus of Nazareth According to the Gospel of Matthew*, Lanham, MD: University Press of America, 1986.

Treggiari, Susan. "Divorce Roman Style: How Easy and How Frequent Was It?" in Beryl R. Rawson (ed.) *Marriage, Divorce and Children in Ancient Rome*, Canberra: Humanities Research Centre; Oxford: Clarendon Press, 1991, pp. 31–46.

VanderKam, James, *The Dead Sea Scrolls Today*, Grand Rapids, MI: Eerdmans, 1994.

Vermes, Géza (ed.) *The Complete Dead Sea Scrolls in English*, New York: Allen Lane, Penguin Press, 1997.

Wright, N. T. "Jesus and the Victory of God," *Christian Origins and the Question of God* 2, Minneapolis, MN: Fortress Press, 1996.

DODD, CHARLES HAROLD

Charles Harold Dodd was born in Wrexham, North Wales, in 1884. He had an outstanding career in Oxford, studying at University and Magdalen Colleges, plus a brief time of study in Berlin. While at Oxford Dodd studied theology at Mansfield College, and returned there to teach in 1915 after three years of pastoral work at Warwick. His biblical expertise was recognized, and in 1930 he was appointed to the Rylands chair in Biblical Criticism and Exegesis at Manchester, moving to Cambridge in 1935 to become the Norse-Hulse Professor of Divinity. He also held lectureships in Yale and Harvard.

Dodd used his literary, linguistic, theological, and historical skills to study the NT documents and their background in Jewish and Hellenistic settings. By a rigorous use of critical biblical study he engaged in the pursuit of truth, at the same time utilizing his skill as an expositor to interpret the Bible in gripping language to a wide audience (e.g. *The Authority of the Bible* [1928], *The Johannine Epistles* [1946]).

While much of Dodd's earlier work was on Paul (e.g. *The Meaning of Paul for Today* [1920] and his classic commentary *The Epistle of Paul to the Romans* [1932]), one of his most influential works was *The Parables of the Kingdom* (1935), a groundbreaking study devoted to the teaching of Jesus. After taking account of the changes in interpretation that had taken place during the oral period and setting aside the work of later interpreters, Dodd searched for the original teaching given by the historical Jesus, an enterprise carried even further by Joachim Jeremias. In particular, Dodd noted the indications in the parables and elsewhere in the gospel traditions that the Kingdom (or "rule of God") was for Jesus a present reality, the claim commonly known as "realized eschatology." Dodd saw in Jesus' coming and in his ministry of healing and preaching, that the reign of God had arrived. The repeated predictions of the coming of the Son of Man were seen as fulfilled in the resurrection and subsequent events, and any passages pointing to a "second coming" at the end of time were dismissed as misunderstandings or reinterpretations. Many other scholars have questioned Dodd's assessment of eschatology and viewed parts of his exegesis as one-sided (e.g. Beasley-Murray, *Jesus and the kingdom of God*), but his emphasis on the theme of fulfillment is of enduring significance. The search for a firm historical basis for the life of Jesus in accordance with critical principles was carried further in his work *History and the Gospel* (1938; note also his perceptive essay on form criticism, "The Appearances of the Risen Christ … " in *Studies in the Gospels*, ed. D. E. Nineham [1955]).

Dodd reviewed early Christian proclamation in *The Apostolic Preaching and Its Developments* (1936). Despite some prevailing skepticism about the picture painted in Acts, Dodd found in Paul's writings important historical evidence of the character of the apostolic preaching or *kerygma*, a word that he popularized. This *kerygma* had a definite pattern: (1) the Old Testament promises had been fulfilled; (2) this had taken place in the life, death, resurrection, and exaltation of Jesus Christ; (3) God had appointed Jesus by the resurrection to be the Messiah, the head of the new Israel; (4) the proper response to this Good News was repentance from sin and faith in Jesus; (5) the Holy Spirit was promised to those who responded positively to this offer of forgiveness and new life in Christ. The one element that Dodd surprisingly overlooked in the apostolic preaching was the importance of witnesses, for the apostles functioned both as eye-witnesses of all the public ministry of Jesus, and also as divinely appointed advocates of their Lord (Luke 24:48; John 15:27; 1 John 1:1–3; Acts 1:22; 2:32; 3:15; 4:33; 5:32; 10:39–43).

The apostolic preaching received further attention in *According to the Scriptures* (1952), which followed up lines of research developed by J. Rendel Harris, who proposed that the early church had developed collections of Hebrew Bible texts that it employed as "testimonies" in defending and promoting its faith. Dodd conducted a meticulous analysis of these *testimonia* used by various NT writers. His study revealed the use of such *testimonia* illustrated basic articles of faith, and argued that these convictions must accordingly have been held at a very early date.

Dodd's most massive work was *The Interpretation of the Fourth Gospel* (1953). This book broadly canvassed the religious writings of the ancient world, including Gnostic, Mandaean, and Hermetic literature – all to shed possible light on the major Johannine themes. Dodd's prodigious scholarship is supremely evident in this work. However, Dodd did not neglect John's ties with primitive Christian traditions. In his companion volume, *Historical Tradition and the Fourth Gospel* (1963), he vigorously defended the integrity and basic unity of the Fourth Gospel, showing detailed parallels between John and the Synoptics. This careful comparative study led him to argue that John represented an important, early, independent Palestinian tradition that was not dependent on the Synoptics.

Dodd's final book was *The Founder of Christianity* (1970). Without adopting the extreme positions that emerged later in the Jesus Seminar, Dodd lucidly expounded his view of Jesus' life and teaching in a paperback that would be both useful to the average reader and still faithful to the insights and methods of biblical criticism.

Dodd was one of the leading NT scholars of the twentieth century. To the general public he is perhaps best remembered as the Joint Director of the *New English Bible* (1970), a project to which he gave himself unstintingly following his retirement in 1949. A Cambridge don has captured the admiration in which Dodd was held: "He combined magisterial knowledge with modest and tolerant gentleness, a lively wit with deep seriousness, a loyalty to the truth with pastoral warmth and ... zeal, and much practical common sense with just a touch of otherworldly eccentricity" (Styler 305).

ALLISON A. TRITES

Further reading

Beasley-Murray, G. R., Jesus and the Kingdom of God, Grand Rapids, MI: Eerdmans, 1986.

Bruce, F. F. "C. H. Dodd," in P. E. Hughes (ed.) *Creative Minds in Contemporary Theology*, Grand Rapids, MI: Eerdmans, 1973, pp. 239–69.
Davies, W. D. and D. Daube (eds) *The Background of the New Testament and Its Eschatology: Studies in Honour of C. H. Dodd*, Cambridge: Cambridge University Press, 1954.
Dodd, C. H., *According to the Scriptures: The Sub-Structure of New Testament Theology*, London: Nisbet, 1952.
—— "The Appearances of the Risen Christ: An Essay in Form-Criticism of the Gospels," in D. E. Nineham, ed., *Studies in the Gospels: Essays in Memory of R. H. Lightfoot*, Oxford: Basil Blackwell, 1955, 9–35.
—— *The Authority of the Bible*, London: Nisbet, 1928.
—— *The Epistle of Paul to the Romans*, MNTC, London: Hodder and Stoughton, 1932.
—— *The Founder of Christianity*, London: Collins, 1971.
—— *Historical Tradition in the Fourth Gospel*, Cambridge: Cambridge University Press, 1963.
—— *History and the Gospel*, London: Nisbet, 1938.
—— *The Interpretation of the Fourth Gospel*, Cambridge: Cambridge University Press, 1953.
—— *The Johannine Epistles*, MNTC, London: Hodder and Stoughton, 1946.
—— *The Meaning of Paul for Today*, London: Swarthmore, 1920.
—— *The Parables of the Kingdom*, London: Nisbet, 1935.
Dillistone, F. W. *C. H. Dodd: Interpreter of the New Testament*, Grand Rapids, MI: Eerdmans, 1977.
Heaton, E. W. "Dodd, Charles Harold," in *Dictionary of National Biography*, Supplement 9, Oxford: Oxford University Press, 1986, pp. 243–4.
Styler, G. M. "Dodd, Charles Harold," in J. H. Hayes (ed.) *Dictionary of Biblical Interpretation*, Nashville, TN: Abingdon Press, 1999, pp. 304–5.

DUNN, JAMES D. G.

Now Emeritus Lightfoot Professor of Divinity at the University of Durham, James Dunn (1939–) has been a major contributor to the quest for the historical Jesus. He has written over thirty books, articles, and essays related to the quest. The most significant and most recent of these is his *Jesus Remembered* (2003).

Dunn's approach was heavily influenced by Martin Kähler's observation that attempts to discover a historical Jesus in the gospel traditions who is significantly different from the Jesus portrayed in the gospels are absurd. One cannot hope to recover the real Jesus by stripping away the theological impact that he had on his disciples since this impact is to a large degree the result of his life. The Jesus that can be recovered by modern historians is Jesus as remembered by his earliest disciples.

Dunn felt that the most distinctive feature of his study was his fresh assessment of the importance of the oral tradition of Jesus' mission. Dunn suggested that the Synoptic Gospels bear testimony to a pattern and technique of oral transmission that ensured a greater stability and continuity in the Jesus tradition than has thus far been generally appreciated. In this he shows the influence of Kenneth Bailey who sought to demonstrate that the oral tradition behind the gospels was informal but controlled, i.e. that some elements of the tradition were flexible but that the core was faithfully preserved.

According to Dunn, the focus of Jesus' teaching was the kingdom of God. This kingdom would consist of an eschatological reversal in which those who had lived in humiliation would be exalted, but those who assumed that their future status was secure would face unexpected judgment. Jesus' teaching often portrayed this judgment as final judgment which would result in persons being welcomed into the kingdom, heaven itself, or excluded from the kingdom and banished to hell. Jesus stressed the imminence of the coming eschatological crisis and the kingdom. However, he also stressed that the kingdom was in some sense already present. Jesus was remembered by his earliest followers as a great exorcist whose exorcisms bound Satan in demonstration that the final exercise of God's rule was already in effect.

Jesus' kingdom preaching cannot be disentangled from imminent expectation. However, Jesus' expectation of an imminent end has been proven wrong by history. These inaccuracies did not prompt rejection of Jesus' message by his disciples since the prophetic tradition had learned to live with the failure of prophecy without denigrating the prophecies themselves. The ultimate question for Jesus' early followers was not whether Jesus was right about the time of the kingdom but whether he was right about the God whom he imaged as king and father.

Jesus' vision for the present was that his disciples live in the light of the coming kingdom. Jesus was remembered as expecting the community that he founded to practice forgiveness, shun exclusive boundaries, celebrate God's goodness in open table-fellowship, and express love to others. In general, Jesus urged his disciples to seek to order society in anticipation of that moment when God's will would be done on earth as it is in heaven.

Against Wrede, Dunn argued that Jesus was recognized as royal Messiah by his earliest followers even before his resurrection. Jesus personally, however, saw the role of royal Messiah as a false characterization of his mission. The first Christians were able to use the title of Jesus only after first transforming its meaning in light of Jesus' teaching and death.

Jesus' earliest disciples viewed him as an exorcist and miracle-worker. Jesus' reputation as an exorcist and miracle-worker is so firm and so early as to preclude notions that natural events were later interpreted as having supernatural significance. Rather, witnesses saw genuine healing and deliverances that they immediately ascribed to the power of God flowing through Jesus.

Jesus' earliest disciples recognized him as a prophet, but also as one who transcended even the greatest of the Old Testament prophets. His "I say to you" surpassed the typically prophetic "Thus says the Lord" and identifies Jesus as God's unique emissary. Jesus was remembered as addressing God as Abba, since Pauline references to God as Abba presume that this address was a distinctive mark of Christian worship. Jesus likely had a profound sense of an intimate relationship with the Father that was crucial to his own self-understanding.

Jesus referred to himself as the son of man, but primarily did so in a general and self-referential way meaning "a man like me" or "one." Jesus' use likely included some reference to the similar phrase in Daniel 7:13, but may have simply been an allusion to the "vindication-following-suffering role" which the figure represented for faithful Israel.

Jesus' arrest was motivated by two factors. Jesus offered forgiveness apart from the Temple cultus and had a casual attitude toward purity rituals. This stirred the anger of Temple authorities. Jesus anticipated that his mission would not be accepted in Jerusalem and that he would be arrested and executed. However, one cannot form a convincing case that Jesus saw his death as vicarious or as the fulfillment of Isaiah 53. Jesus did, however, expect to be vindicated after his death and to share in the general and final resurrection of the dead. Jesus' earliest disciples saw him after his death and burial beginning on the first Sunday after his crucifixion. Dunn argued that the claim that the first believers experienced "resurrection appearances" was so enshrined in the tradition as to be "beyond reasonable doubt."

Criticisms of Dunn's work have focused primarily on the aim and method of his research. Regarding aim, some scholars have argued that true historiography seeks to discover events as they actually occurred and not merely as they were remembered. Dunn himself seems unable to resist moving from his "remembered Jesus" to the "real Jesus" at many points. Others have been hesitant to adopt Dunn's view that differences between the Synoptic accounts occurred mainly at the level of oral tradition rather than editing of written sources. Perhaps most importantly, Dunn's treatment of the gospel accounts of Jesus' life and teaching overlooks that degree of control that eye-witnesses must have exercised over the tradition during the relatively brief period of time between the composition of the gospels and the events that they record. Despite these criticisms, Dunn's massive work remains one of the most significant contributions to historical Jesus research in this generation.

CHARLES L. QUARLES

Further reading

Dunn, J. D. G. *Baptism in the Holy Spirit*, London: SCM Press, 1970.

—— "The Messianic Secret in Mark," *TynBul* 21 (1970) 92–117.

—— "Spirit-and-Fire Baptism," *NovT* 14 (1972) 81–92.

—— *Jesus and the Spirit: A Study of the Religious and Charismatic Experience of Jesus and the First Christians as Reflected in the New Testament*, London: SCM Press, 1975.

—— "Demythologizing – The Problem of Myth in the New Testament," in I. H. Marshall (ed.) *New Testament Interpretation: Essays on Principles and Methods*, Exeter: Paternoster, 1977, pp. 285–307.

—— *Unity and Diversity in the New Testament*, London: SCM Press, 1977.

—— "Prophetic 'I'-Sayings and the Jesus Tradition: The Importance of Testing Prophetic Utterances within Early Christianity," *NTS* 24 (1977–78) 175–98.

—— *Christology in the Making*, London: SCM Press, 1980.

—— *The Evidence for Jesus*, London: SCM Press, 1985.

—— *The Living Word*, London: SCM Press, 1987.

—— "Jesus and Ritual Purity: A Study of the Tradition-History of Mark 7.15," in *Jesus, Paul and the Law*, London: SPCK, 1990, pp. 37–60.

—— *Jesus, Paul and the Law: Studies in Mark and Galatians*, London: SPCK, 1990.

—— "John and the Oral Gospel Tradition," in H. Wansbrough (ed.) *Jesus and the Oral Gospel Tradition*, Sheffield: JSOT, 1991, pp. 351–79.

—— *The Parting of the Ways between Christianity and Judaism*, London: SCM Press, 1991.

—— *Jesus' Call to Discipleship*, Cambridge: Cambridge University, 1992.

—— "Jesus, Table-Fellowship, and Qumran," in J. H. Charlesworth (ed.) *Jesus and the Dead Sea Scrolls*, New York: Doubleday, 1992, pp. 254–72.

—— "Matthew's Awareness of Markan Redaction," in F. van Segbroeck, C. M. Tuckett, J. Van Belle, and J. Verheyden (eds) *The Four Gospels*, Leuven: Leuven University Press, 1992, pp. 1349–59.

—— "Messianic Ideas and Their Influence on the Jesus of History," in J. H. Charlesworth (ed.) *The Messiah: Developments in Earliest Judaism and Christianity*, Minneapolis, MN: Fortress Press, 1992, pp. 365–81.

—— "The Question of Antisemitism in the New Testament Writings," in J. D. G. Dunn (ed.) *Jews and Christians: The Parting of the Ways AD 70 to 135*, Tübingen: Mohr Siebeck, 1992, pp. 177–211.

—— "John the Baptist's Use of Scripture," in C. A. Evans and W. R. Stegner (eds) *The Gospels and the Scriptures of Israel*, Sheffield: Sheffield Academic, 1994, pp. 118–29.

—— "Jesus Tradition in Paul," in B. Chilton and C. A. Evans (eds) *Studying the Historical Jesus*, Leiden: Brill, 1994, pp. 155–78.

—— "Judaism in the Land of Israel in the First Century," in J. Neusner (ed.) *Judaism in Late Antiquity*, Leiden: Brill, 1995, pp. 229–61.

—— "Jesus and Factionalism in Early Judaism," in J. H. Charlesworth and L. L. Johns (eds) *Hillel and Jesus*, Minneapolis, MN: Fortress Press, 1997, pp. 156–75.

—— "'Son of God' as 'Son of Man' in the Dead Sea Scrolls? A Response to John Collins on 4Q246," in S. E. Porter and C. A. Evans (eds) *The Scrolls and the Scriptures: Qumran Fifty Years After*, Sheffield: Sheffield Academic, 1997, pp. 198–210.

—— *The Christ and the Spirit*, Grand Rapids, MI: Eerdmans, 1998.

—— "Can the Third Quest Hope to Succeed?," in B. Chilton and C. A. Evans (eds) *Authenticating the Activities of Jesus*, Leiden: Brill, 1999, pp. 31–48.

—— "Are You the Messiah?' Is the Crux of Mark 14:61–62 Resolvable?" in D. G. Horrell and C. M. Tuckett (eds) *Christology, Controversy and Community*, Leiden: Brill, 2000, pp. 1–22.

—— "The Danielic Son of Man in the New Testament," in J. J. Collins and P. W. Flint (eds) *The Book of Daniel: Composition and Reception*, Leiden: Brill, 2001, pp. 528–49.

—— "Jesus and Purity: An Ongoing Debate," *NTS* 48 (2002) 449–67.

—— *Jesus Remembered*, Grand Rapids, MI: Eerdmans, 2003.

E

ELDERS

An "elder" (זָקֵן) was a respected member of Israelite society who initially governed families and clans. They developed the role of an official governing figure in Israelite society (cf. Exod 3:16; 18:12), receiving the Holy Spirit to commission them for their task (Num 11:16, 24–25) of assisting Moses in his leadership of the community. They always ruled as a group, representing the people under the authority of the divinely appointed leader, such as Moses (Exod 3:16, 18; 18:12). They were important witnesses to key events, such as Moses' striking of the rock (Exod 17:5–6), a covenant ceremony (Exod 24:1, 9), and the fate of Datham and Abiram (Num 6:25). They presided over disputes while Moses was away (Exod 24:14) and were responsible for laying hands on the sin offering on behalf of the entire congregation (Lev 4:15). They would govern within a dynasty of a king, such as Pharaoh (Gen 50:7; Ps 105:22) or David (2 Sam 12:17; cf. 2 Sam 19:11). They also served as a ruling body within an Israelite city or one of its neighboring peoples (cf. Num 22:4, 7; Josh 9:11; 1 Kgs 20:7; 21:8). Their posture of governing was frequently depicted as sitting at the gate of a city (Deut 21:19; 22:15; Prov 31:23; Lam 5:14). Their role was to function as a governing body (Ruth 4:2) to preside over civil and criminal hearings among a community, such as the trying of a murder case (Deut 19:12; 21:1ff.; Josh 20:4), the ratification of property and inheritance agreements (Ruth 4:9, 11) and even disputes concerning the virginity of a woman (Deut 22:15). It was the elders who requested a king for Israel (1 Sam 8:4) and made a covenant with David (2 Sam 5:3; cf. Josh 8:33; 23:2; 24:1; 2 Kgs 23:1). Subsequent to the conquest of Canaan, the role of elders shifted from solely judicial authority to those of political and military leadership of Israel (1 Sam 4:3; 8:4–9). Saul sought their favor (1 Sam 15:30), and both David (2 Sam 3:17; 5:3) and Rehoboam (1 Kgs 12:6–8) turned to the elders when seeking the throne.

Elders continued to be influential even during the exilic (Jer 29:1; Ezek 8:1; 14:1; 20:1) and post-exilic community (Ezra 10:8, 14). The destabilization of the monarchy in exilic and postexilic Israel gave room for the elevation of the status of elders (Jer 29:1; Ezek 8:1; 14:1), not so much as a body of leaders but as influential heads of influential families within their respective communities (cf. Ezra 10:14, 16; Neh 5:7; 7:5). They led in the reconstruction of the Temple (cf. Ezra 5:9; 6:6–15). This council of elders eventually formed a static company that originally consisted of twelve men (Ezra 2:2; Neh 7:7), but eventually expanded to seventy (m. Sanh. 1.6; Joseph, B.J. 2.18.6:482) of varying responsibility and degree of authority during the so-called "intertestamental" period.

"Elders" in the NT (πρεσβύτεροι) are divided into two groups. First is the religious figure among the Jewish leadership. They confront Jesus' disciples when the latter break the "tradition of the elders" regarding hand washing (Matt 15:2; Mark 7:3, 5). In his passion predictions, Jesus anticipates suffering not only at the hands of the chief priests and teachers of the law, but also of the elders

(Matt 16:21; Mark 8:31; Luke 9:22). His authority is challenged by them and the chief priests (Matt 21:23; Mark 11:27; Luke 20:1) while teaching in the temple courts. The same gathered to Caiaphas to testify against Jesus (Matt 26:3, 57; 27:12) to put him to death (Matt 27:1; cf. Matt 27:3, 20, 41; 28:12; Mark 15:1; Luke 22:52, 66). The crowd that came to arrest Jesus was from the chief priests and "elders of the people" (Matt 26:47; Mark 14:43, 53). At one point they were summoned by a centurion to ask Jesus to heal the centurion's servant (Luke 7:3).

The second category of elders in the NT is those serving in Christian churches. In Acts, the identity of the elders switches. At first, they are the Jewish ruling class of the gospels. They are grouped with the rulers and teachers of the law who met in Jerusalem (Acts 4:5). Peter addresses them, along with the rulers (Acts 4:8; cf. v. 23). They seem to be equated with the Sanhedrin, who interrogated the imprisoned apostles (Acts 5:21). Rather than enticing the people, it was representatives from the "Synagogue of the Freedmen (as it was called) – Jews of Cyrene and Alexandria as well as the provinces of Cilicia and Asia" (Acts 6:9, NIV) who stirred up the elders, the people, and teachers of the law against Stephen (Acts 6:12). They, along with the chief priests, remained antagonists for the fledgling church (Acts 23:14; 24:1; 25:15).

For the remainder of Acts, however, πρεσβύτεροι are mostly church officers. The elders in Judea received gifts by Barnabas and Saul (Acts 11:30). Elders were appointed in each church founded by Paul and Barnabas (Acts 14:23; 21:17, 18; cf. Tit 1:5). The question about obligations for gentile believers was taken before the "apostles and elders" (Acts 15:2, 4, 6, 22, 23; 16:4). Elders in the church are absent from Pauline writings, save the pastoral epistles, where they are said to have laid hands on Timothy in conveyance of his gift (1 Tim 4:14), to direct the affairs of the church (1 Tim 5:17), to be worthy of particular respect (1 Tim 5:17, 19), and to be morally above reproach (Titus 1:6). Elsewhere in the NT, elders were to be called to pray over the sick (Jas 5:14). The author of 1 Peter claims to be an elder, who writes to elders (1 Peter 5:1; cf. also 2 John 1; 3 John 1). In Revelation there are twenty-four elders sitting on as many thrones (Rev 4:4; 5:11; cf. 14:3) who fall down and worship the lamb (4:10; 5:8, 14; 7:11; cf. 11:16; 19:4) and encircle the lamb (5:6). One of the elders speaks to John (5:5; 7:13). Their role in historical Jesus studies is primarily, along with other Jewish religious leaders, one of illustrating tensions and conflict with Jesus.

DANIEL M. GURTNER

Further reading

Bornkamm, G. "πρεσβύτερος," TDNT 6 (1968) 651–83.
Harris, R. Laird, Gleason L. Archer, Jr, and Bruce K. Waltke. Theological Wordbook of the Old Testament, 2 vols, Chicago, IL: Moody Press, 1980.
Harvey, A. E. "Elders," JTS n.s. 25 (1974) 318–32.
Reicke, B. "The Constitution of the Primitive Church in the Light of Jewish Documents," in K. Stendahl (ed.) The Scrolls and the NT, New York: Harper, 1957, pp. 143–56, 275–76.
Safrai, S. "Jewish Self-Government," in S. Safrai and M. Stern (eds) The Jewish People in the First Century, Philadelphia, PA: Fortress Press, 1974, pp. 377–419.
Schürer, E. History of the Jewish People in the Age of Jesus Christ, 4 vols, Edinburgh: T. & T. Clark, 1984.
Schweizer, E. Church Order in the New Testament, London: SCM Press, 1961.

ELIJAH AND ELISHA

Elijah was a major ninth-century prophet (1 Kgs 17–2 Kgs 2) who was expected to return before the Day of the Lord (Mal 4:5). Although John 1:19–27 has the Baptist deny that he is the returning Elijah, other texts encourage readers to associate the two figures. Luke 1:17 speaks of the Baptist coming in "the spirit and power of Elijah." The description of John's clothing in Matt 3:4 and Mark 1:6 matches the account of the prophet's garments in 1 Kgs 1:8 LXX. According to Mark 6:15 and Luke 9:8, some believed that John might be Elijah. Matt 11:14 has Jesus himself identify John with the eschatological Elijah prophesied in Mal 4:5, and the equation is implicit in Mark 9:13 (cf. Matt 17:13).

Despite John's sometime identity as a new or returned Elijah, the gospels also contain texts in which Jesus resembles Elijah. Luke 4:25–26 likens the circumstances of Elijah's time and place to those of Jesus. The story of the widow of Nain in Luke 7:11–17 makes Jesus rather like Elijah because it is clearly modeled upon 1 Kgs 17:8–24: in both cases a healer approaches a city gate; in both a widow's son has died; in both the healer brings the son back to life; and in both the phrase, "gives him back to his mother," occurs.

In Luke 9:52–56, the disciples ask Jesus if he will not call down fire from heaven and so, as the textual variant has it, act "as also Elijah did" when he called down fire upon his enemies (2 Kgs 1:9–12). The accounts of Jesus calling disciples in Mark 1:16–20 par.; 2:13–14 par.; and Matt 8:18–22 = Luke 9:57–62 are all modeled upon Elijah's calling of Elisha (1 Kgs 19:19–21). Matt 16:14; Mark 8:28; and Luke 9:19 purport that some of Jesus' contemporaries took him to be the eschatological Elijah. Interpreters have also often found echoes of Elijah's ascent (2 Kgs 2:9–12) in Jesus' ascension according to Luke 24 and Acts 1. It may even be that Luke–Acts as a whole is designed to recall the story of Elijah. 1 Kgs 16–2 Kgs 13 recounts the story of Elijah, narrates his ascension, then tells us about his miracle-working successor, Elisha, whereas Luke–Acts recounts the story of Jesus, narrates his ascension, then tells us about his miracle-working successors.

In addition to serving as a type for both Jesus and John, Elijah explicitly appears in the gospels on three occasions. First, he is present at the transfiguration (Matt 17:1–9; Mark 9:2–10; Luke 9:28–36). Although commentators often interpret his presence here as representing the prophets (with Moses representing the law), Elijah and Moses are the only figures in the Hebrew Bible to speak with God on Mount Sinai (called Horeb in Kings); and given the many parallels between Jesus' transfiguration and Moses' experience on Sinai, the presence of the latter with Elijah moves readers to think of the earlier epiphanies on that mountain.

Second, after the transfiguration, the disciples in Matt 17:10–13 and Mark 9:11–13 ask Jesus why scribes say "Elijah must come first." The question is of uncertain import because the precise nature of Elijah's task of restoration is left unstated, and there were differing notions. Mal 4:5–6 has Elijah reconciling families. The LXX (3:22–23) adds that he will also reconcile "the heart of a man with his neighbor." In Luke 1:17, the Elijah-like John will turn "the disobedient to the wisdom of the just, to make ready for the Lord a people prepared" (cf. Eccl 48:10–11). The idea that Elijah will preach eschatological repentance was presumably common (cf. Rev 11:1–13; *Pirqe R. El.* 43). In Eccl 48:10, he is expected "to restore the tribes of Jacob," which may mean ingathering the diaspora or purifying a remnant. According to rabbinic texts he will explain controverted items in the Torah (*m. Šeqal.* 2:5). There are also places where Elijah is expected to restore certain holy utensils long lost (e.g. *Mek.* on Exod 16.33). Finally, already by the first century Elijah – who in the Hebrew Bible raises the dead – may have been expected to inaugurate the resurrection or reawaken the dead (*m. Sota* 9:15). (In Matt 17:10 and Mark 9:11, the disciples' question about Elijah directly follows a reference to the resurrection of the dead.)

Third, in Matt 27:47, 49 and Mark 15:35–36, observers of Jesus' crucifixion wrongly imagine he is calling Elijah. This is presumably the earliest example of the belief that Elijah can aid people in trouble (cf. *b. Šabb.* 109b; *b. 'Aobd. Zar.* 17b–18a).

Given the conflicting indicators, it is very difficult to determine what Jesus believed about Elijah, himself, the Baptist, and Mal 4:5. One possibility is that he thought of himself as, among other things, an eschatological prophet like Elijah, and maybe he thought of John in a similar way. But perhaps the church first explicitly identified the Baptist as the fulfillment of Mal 4:5.

Elisha, whose story told is told in 1 Kgs 19:16–21 and 2 Kgs 2–13, is mentioned only once in the early Jesus tradition: Luke 4:27 compares Jesus' situation with that of Elisha. In several stories, however, Jesus looks very much like Elisha, who worked in the Northern kingdom, performed many miracles (cf. Eccl 48:12–14), and always sought to help the poor and needy. The story of Jesus feeding 5,000 in Mark 6:30–44 par. is modeled upon 2 Kgs 4:42–44: in both a prophet takes bread and commands that it be given to a crowd, and after someone objects that so little cannot feed so many, the people eat and food is left over. In John 6:9, moreover, the bread is barley bread, as in 2 Kgs 4:42–44. In Luke 10:4, Jesus commands his missionaries not to greet anyone on the way, which has often reminded commentators of 2 Kgs 4:29, where Elisha says to his servant, "If you meet anyone, give no greeting, and if anyone greets you, do not answer." It is also noteworthy that Elisha raised the dead (2 Kgs 4:8–37) and healed a leper (2 Kgs 5:1–19), and that Jesus was remembered as having worked both sorts of miracles (Mark 1:40–45 par.; Matt 11:4–5 = Luke 7:21–22; etc.).

Although the evidence is sparse, Jesus or some of his early followers could have understood his relationship to John as analogous to that of Elisha to Elijah, Jesus being the successor with a double portion of his predecessor's spirit (cf. 2 Kgs 2:9–10). But if so, that conception was soon eclipsed by more exalted christologies.

DALE C. ALLISON, JR

Further reading

Brodie, Thomas L. *The Crucial Bridge: The Elijah–Elisha Narrative as an Interpretive Synthesis of Genesis–Kgs and a Literary Model for the Gospels*, Collegeville, MN: Liturgical Press, 2000.
Brown, Raymond E. "Jesus and Elisha," *Perspectives* 12 (1971) 86–104.
Martyn, J. Louis. "'We Have Found Elijah'," in *The Gospel of John in Christian History*, New York: Paulist Press, 1978, pp. 9–54.
Öhler, Markus. *Elia im Neuen Testament*, BZNW 88, Berlin: de Gruyter, 1997.

ENTRY INTO JERUSALEM

Jesus' entrance into Jerusalem marks the beginning of Passion Week (Mark 11–15). Jesus directs his disciples to enter a nearby village, where they will find a colt. They are to take possession of it, and if any questions them, they are to reply as Jesus instructed them. The disciples follow Jesus' instructions and all works out as planned. Jesus mounts the colt, his disciples and others create a procession, with garments and branches paving the way. Amidst shouts of "Hosanna" and references to the coming kingdom of David, Jesus and his disciples wend their way into the ancient city of Jerusalem (Mark 11:1–11).

A history of triumphal entries

Catchpole (319–21) cites twelve examples of celebrated entries, six from 1 and 2 Maccabees, and six from Josephus, of a "more or less fixed pattern of entry." Entries involving major figures include Alexander who enters Jerusalem, is greeted with ceremony, and is escorted into the city where he participates in cultic activity (Josephus, *Ant.* 11.325–39); Apollonius who enters Jerusalem accompanied by torches and shouts (2 Macc 4:21–22); Judas Maccabeus who returns home from a military victory and is greeted with hymns and "praising God" (1 Macc 4:19–25; Josephus, *Ant.* 12.312); Judas Maccabeus, again, who returns from battle and enters Jerusalem amidst singing and merrymaking, followed by sacrifice (1 Macc 5:45–54; Josephus, *Ant.* 12.348–9); Jonathan brother of Judas, who is greeted by the men of Askalon "with great pomp" (1 Macc 10:86); Simon brother of Judas, who enters Gaza, expels idolatrous inhabitants, cleanses idolatrous houses, and enters the city "with hymns and praise" (1 Macc 13:43–48); Simon brother of Judas, again, who enters Jerusalem and is met by crowds "with praise and palm branches, and with harps and cymbals and stringed instruments and with hymns and songs" (1 Macc 13:49–51); Antigonus who with pomp enters Jerusalem, then the Temple precincts, but with so much pomp and self-importance he is criticized by some for imagining that he himself was "king" (Josephus, *J.W.* 1.73–74; *Ant.* 13. 304–6); Marcus Agrippa who enters Jerusalem, is met by Herod, and is welcomed by the people with acclamations (Josephus, *Ant.* 16.12–15); and Archelaus who hoping to confirm his kingship journeys to and enters Jerusalem amidst acclamation of his procession (Josephus, *Ant.* 17.194–239).

The elements that make up this pattern include: (a) a victory already achieved and a status already recognized for the central person; (b) a formal and ceremonial entry; (c) greetings and/or acclamations together with invocations of God; (d) entry to the city climaxed by entry to temple, if the city in question has one; (e) cultic activity, either positive (e.g. offering of sacrifice), or negative (e.g. expulsion of objectionable persons and the cleansing away of uncleanness). Catchpole remarks:

> Mark 11 contains all of these major and recurrent features. It also contains minor agreements with occasional features of some of the other stories, for example, the reference to the royal animal … Mark's story thus conforms to a familiar pattern in respect of both its determinative shape and some of its incidental details.
>
> (321)

The entry in Mark

The Markan entrance narrative, in which Jesus mounts a colt, appears to be deliberately modeled after Zech 9:9: "Tell the daughter of Zion, Behold, your king is coming to you, humble, and mounted on an ass, and on a colt, the foal of an ass." Other scriptural influences have been suggested, such as 1 Sam 10:2–10. But this act is to be traced to Jesus, not to a community imagination inspired by the prophetic scriptures. Mark's account (Mark 11:1–11) does not quote the passage from Zechariah, but the Matthean and Johannine accounts do (Matt 21:4–5; John 12:14–15). Mark's failure to exploit an important proof text argues both for his Gospel's priority and for the essential historicity of the account, as is rightly maintained by several commentators. The explicit and formal quotation of Zech 9:9 in Matthew and John is consistent with their scriptural apologetic, an apologetic that seems to be primarily fashioned with the synagogue in mind.

Commentators are divided over the question of the original significance of the entrance, with many seeing it as messianic and many suggesting that the messianic significance is later interpretation. The view taken here is that the act was indeed originally messianic, which in later tradition was exaggerated.

The shouts of the crowd, which allude to Ps 118:26 ("Blessed is he who comes in the name of the Lord"), are consistent with the imagery of Jesus mounted on the royal mule, much as Solomon did shortly before the death of his father David (1 Kgs 1:32–40). The crowd interpretively adds to Pslm 118 the words: "Blessed is the kingdom of our father David that is coming!" (Mark 11:10). In the Aramaic Pslm 118 is understood to be speaking of David "who is worthy to be ruler and king." The coherence of Aramaic Psalm 118 with Jesus' Zechariah-inspired action of mounting the colt argues for antiquity of the tradition, as well as its authenticity. The explicit quotation of Zech 9:9 in Matthew points to later elaboration and apologetic. The rephrasing of the shout of the crowd in Matt 21:9 draws the parallel closer to the text of Ps 118:26, chiefly through simplification of Mark's clumsy version, and explicitly identifies Jesus as the "son of David." The shouts of "hosanna" stand a "good chance of representing a genuine primitive Christian recollection of what was shouted to Jesus on the occasion of his entry into Jerusalem" (Fitzmyer 111).

The meaning of the entry for Jesus

Jesus' entry in Jerusalem marks in dramatic fashion the beginning of Passion Week. He is recognized in terms that hint at his royal messianic identity (riding on the colt, calls for the coming of the kingdom of David), an identity which will become explicit at the end of the week, in his confession before the High Priest (Mark 14:61–62, "Are you the Messiah, the Son of the Blessed?" "I am") and in his crucifixion by the Romans as "king of the Jews" (Mark 15:26). Thus Passion Week opens and closes with royal messianic themes. But these parallels also entail dramatic contrasts, for Jesus enters Jerusalem amidst shouts of joy and adulation, but he will exit the city amidst shouts of ridicule and torment.

The entry also sets the stage for the unfolding drama involving Jesus and the Temple establishment. He enters the Temple precincts and "looks around at everything" (Mark 11:11), thus hinting that Jesus has taken full stock of Jerusalem's religious condition. That he did not like all that he saw will become evident in the pericopes that follow, in which Jesus curses the fruitless fig tree (11:12–14), demonstrates in the precincts (11:15–18), criticizes various aspects of Temple polity and religious practice (12:1–44), and then finally predicts the Temple's destruction (13:1–2).

Jesus' entry into the city and into the sacred precincts of the Temple may well have been part of a diarchic understanding of messianism, by which Jesus as the humble, anointed king presented himself to Caiaphas, the anointed high priest. This diarchic messianism is presented explicitly in prophetic literature (e.g. Zech 4:14) and clearly underlies the eschatology of the Essenes, as we find it expressed in some of the Scrolls from Qumran: "until there come the Prophet and the Messiahs of Aaron and Israel" (1QS 9:11). The Messiahs of Aaron and Israel refer to the anointed high priest and the anointed king. Indeed, we find a quotation of Zech 4:14 ("the two sons of oil") in the context of a commentary on Gen 49:5–12, Jacob's blessing on his sons Levi and Judah (cf. 4Q254). What

precisely Jesus intended in his entry into Jerusalem and into the sacred precincts may never be known, for his overtures were rejected and his subsequent criticisms were deeply resented.

CRAIG A. EVANS

Further reading

Bruce, F. F. "The Book of Zechariah and the Passion Narrative," *BJRL* 43 (1960–61) 336–53.
Catchpole, D. R. "The 'Triumphal' Entry," in E. Bammel and C. F. D. Moule (eds) *Jesus and the Politics of His Day*, Cambridge: Cambridge University Press, 1984, pp. 319–35.
Evans, C. A. "Diarchic Messianism in the Dead Sea Scrolls and the Messianism of Jesus of Nazareth," in L. H. Schiffman, E. Tov, and J. C. VanderKam (eds) *The Dead Sea Scrolls: Fifty Years after Their Discovery. Proceedings of the Jerusalem Congress, July 20–25, 1997*, Jerusalem: Israel Exploration Society and the Israel Antiquities Authority, 2000, pp. 558–67.
Fitzmyer, J. A. "Aramaic Evidence Affecting the Interpretation of *Hosanna* in the New Testament," in G. F. Hawthorne and O. Betz (eds) *Tradition and Interpretation in the New Testament*, Tübingen: Mohr Siebeck; Grand Rapids, MI: Eerdmans, 1987, pp. 110–18.
Kuhn, H.-W. "Das Reittier Jesu in der Einzugsgeschichte des Markusevangeliums," *ZNW* 50 (1959) 82–91.
März, C.-P. *"Siehe, dein König kommt zu Dir ... " Eine traditionsgeschichtliche Untersuchung zur Einzugsperikope*, Leipzig: St Benno, 1980.
Mastin, B. A. "The Date of the Triumphal Entry," *NTS* 16 (1969) 76–82.
Sanders, J. A. "A New Testament Hermeneutic Fabric: Pslm 118 in the Entrance Narrative," in C. A. Evans and W. F. Stinesping (eds) *Early Jewish and Christian Exegesis*, Homage 10, Atlanta, GA: Scholars Press, 1987, pp. 177–90.

ESCHATOLOGY

Derived from the Greek ἔσχατον, "last," eschatology is traditionally understood as the study of the "last things." Central to this concept in the New Testament is the person and work of Jesus, as eschatology is thought to lie at the core of the New Testament in general and Jesus' teachings in particular. Its origins likely stem from discussion of the future "last days" or the "day of the Lord" of Israelite prophetic tradition (cf. Isa 2:2; Dan 11:6; Hos 3:5; Mic 4:1). These traditions promise, among other things, the suffering of exile (Jer 23:20) and persecution (Ezek 38:14–17; Dan 11:27–12:10) for God's people. Yet after these sufferings will come a time of deliverance for the faithful (Ezek 38:14–16; Dan 10:14; 12:1–13) and judgment for God's enemies (Ezek 38:14–16; Dan 10:14; 10:40–45). Such deliverance and vindication will be accomplished by an eschatological, anointed figure, the Messiah (Gen 49:1, 8–12; Num 24:14–19;

Isa 2:2–4; Mic 4:1–3), and a new covenant will be established (Jer 31:31–34).

For Paul, the arrival of the *eschaton* was assumed (1 Cor 10:11), inaugurated by the arrival of Jesus in the "fullness of time" (Gal 4:4; Eph 1:7–10; 1:20–22:6). Looking to the OT (cf. Isa 43; 65–66), Paul also saw the death and resurrection of Jesus as fulfillment of end-time prophecies (2 Cor 5:17). In Acts, the speaking of tongues at Pentecost was seen as a fulfillment of Joel 2:28, prophesying an event thought to occur in the "last days." The author of Hebrews presumes the last days to be upon him (Heb 1:2). Eschatological dimensions are found in each of the respective gospels. Each of them, in varying degrees, sees eschatology as, in some sense, future. Much of Markan future eschatology is found in Mark 13, the so-called "Little Apocalypse." It predicts trial and hardship, even among the faithful (13:9–13): the appearance of false prophets (13:5–6), wars, famines, and earthquakes (13:7–8; cf. 14–23). After the appearance of heavenly signs (13:24–25), the "son of Man" will appear "in clouds with great glory and power" (13:26 RSV) to gather the elect (13:27). Matthew's future eschatology is heavily dependent on that of Mark, though the former is more explicit than that latter on the role of the "son of man" in eschatological judgment (Matt 13:41; 16:28; 25:31). For Luke's future eschatology one must include the book of Acts in consideration. For there it is apparent that Luke expected that Jesus would return (Acts 1:11) and inaugurate the age of God's judgment (Acts 17:31). John has remarkably little to say about future eschatology, save a single reference to the "last day" (John 6:39) at which the resurrection will occur (5:28–29; 6:39–40).

NT eschatology in the gospels suggests the kingdom is near (Matt 4:23; 9:35; Mark 1:15; 8:11; 14:25; Luke 4:43; 8:1). However, the gospels do not simply look to the future, but have much to say about the inauguration of the eschatological future, begun in the life and ministry of Jesus. For Mark, this inauguration began with Jesus (1:14–15). Indeed, many of the events he foresaw happening at the end are depicted as occurring in the life of Jesus. Eschatological darkness, anticipated at the end of the age (13:24) was present at the crucifixion (15:33). Jesus warns his disciples to be watchful, lest the master come and find them sleeping (13:35–36), yet finds them asleep on their watch in Gethsemane (14:34, 37). Not only will the disciples be "delivered up" and beaten (13:9), but Jesus himself was likewise "delivered up" (14:10, 18, 21, 41) and beaten (14:65). Similarly, the disciples should expect to stand before civil authorities (13:9), as Jesus was before Pilate (15:1–15). In these parallels, Mark seems to indicate that he sees future eschatological events occurring in the present experience of Jesus.

Matthew appropriates the realization of the Eschaton not with parallels between the end experience of the disciples and the present experiences of Jesus, as in Mark, but primarily by his appropriation of OT eschatological texts to the life and ministry of Jesus. Most pronounced of these are his so-called formula quotations, which will highlight an event or teaching in Jesus' life and follow it with a statement like "All this took place to fulfill what the Lord had spoken by the prophet" (Matt 1:22 RSV). This is then followed by a citation from an OT text. Thus Jesus is repeatedly depicted as the realization of eschatological hopes from the Jewish scriptures. Furthermore, Jesus' death is depicting the inauguration of the eschatological age by means of the graphic images following his death and the rending of the veil (27:51b–53). Here, occasioned by the death of Jesus, stones are split, the dead rise and enter into the holy city, etc., in a vision revealed by the rending of the veil and witnessed by the centurion (27:54). These images are drawn from various texts in the OT (Zech 14; Ezek 37; Dan 12) and depict, in part, that the death of Jesus has inaugurated the dawning of the eschatological age predicted in these important prophetic texts (Gurtner). Christ's subsequent resurrection is but the "first fruits" of the general resurrection (1 Cor 15:20; cf. Rom 3:3–4). Additionally the presence of God, in Jesus, with his people (1:23; 18:20; 28:20) is among the important features Jews would have seen as integral to the last days (Zech 8:23; Ezek 37:26–28). Even Jesus' casting out of demons demonstrates the presence of the kingdom (Matt 12:28).

Some would see Luke's eschatology as being less organically connected with Jesus, and seeing a delay in the Parousia from what Jesus originally expected (12:45; 19:11). Nevertheless, for Luke also the Eschaton is at hand (3:9; 18:7–8; 21:31–32). H. Conzelmann categorized Jesus' death and resurrection, according to his scheme, as an event of the past and not, properly speaking, of the eschatological future. This view has been challenged by some more recent scholars, and may not take into account the fullest use of Lukan evidence. For while it may be true that Luke is not as systematic in his chronicling of eschatological future events, he clearly sees Jesus as the center of those events where mentioned. Similar to Matthew, Luke does so initially in his appropriation of the OT in the famous synagogue citation of Isa 61 in Luke 4. In

Luke 4:17–21, Jesus is said to read a portion of Isaiah, which is really a compilation of Isa 61:1–2 and Isa 58:6. Together these texts resonate with language of the Year of Jubilee from Lev 25 and seem to be appropriated by some Second Temple Jewish sects (Qumran, cf. 11QMelch 20) toward the arrival of an eschatological deliverer from bondage. That Jesus applies these texts to himself (Luke 7:22) suggests that he may see himself in the role of that deliverer, characterized by such traits as healing, preaching good news to the poor, etc., which are known concerns in Luke–Acts. So, it seems plausible, then, that Luke sees Jesus' ministry as the fulcrum for the dawning of the eschatological age. John's Gospel betrays a high degree of "realized" eschatology (Dodd 1937). End-time judgment is already in the hands of Jesus (John 9:35–39; 12:30–34). He is already exalted (3:14), and through him key eschatological features are already in place, notably eternal life (6:47; 3:16–17) and resurrection (5:25).

J. Weiss argued that the kingdom which Jesus proclaimed is entirely future. A. Schweitzer, building on the work of Weiss, traced an eschatological thread through the life of Jesus to propose that Jesus held a "thoroughgoing eschatology" (*konsequente Eschatologie*). Jesus, in Schweitzer's view, thought himself to be the one to bring about the kingdom. So imminent was the kingdom's arrival that Jesus instituted an "interim ethic," largely in the Sermon on the Mount, which was only intended to apply for the short period between Jesus' proclamation of the kingdom and its actual arrival. Jesus sends out his disciples (Matt 10), not expecting them to return (Matt 10:23). When they did return and no kingdom was apparent, Jesus entered Jerusalem to incite the process of the kingdom's arrival. This inevitably led to his arrest and crucifixion, from which Jesus died in despair. Schweitzer argued that Jesus expected and preached the imminence of the kingdom of God's arrival, but was simply wrong. For Jesus, eschatology was tied up with the arrival of the "Day of the Lord," or the "kingdom of God" and was associated with the future. Looking toward the future, Jesus anticipated an end-time judgment for the wicked (Luke 6:46–49; 10:13–15; 11:31–32) and rewards for the righteous (Luke 6:20–23), with one's relationship to himself the deciding factor of in which lot one fell (Luke 12:8–9). The dawning of these events would be preceded by tribulation for the faithful (Luke 12:49–53) and dramatic natural disasters (Mark 13:24–25). He also anticipated the resurrection of the dead (Mark 12:18–27). When Jesus was wrong in this prediction, Schweitzer

claimed, the early church developed a preaching that de-eschatologized that of Jesus (Paul).

C. H. Dodd (1935) countered with the notion of "realized eschatology," positing that the future arrival of the kingdom had, in fact, come in Jesus. The kingdom was present in Jesus' own time (Luke 11:20), and signs abound indicating that reality (Luke 10:18; 11:22; cf. Mark 2:18–20, 22; 4:11–12, 26–29). A mediating position is now more accepted: that is, the kingdom has come, in part, in Jesus, yet awaits its final consummation. Thus the phrase "already-and-not-yet" is widely employed. NT eschatology finds its roots in the OT and, in part, subsequent Jewish traditions. It is a Christian innovation, it seems, that sees OT prophecies concerning the two comings of the Messiah. Instead, it is more helpful to think of some prophecies fulfilled in Jesus (Luke 17:18–23) while others remain unfulfilled (cf. Mark 9:31).

Right or wrong about the imminence of the arrival of the kingdom, Jesus regularly underscored his rejection of attempts to calculate its arrival (Luke 17:20–21), as he himself did not know (Mark 13:32) and perhaps it was not yet determined (Mark 13:20; Luke 13:6–9). References such as Mark 9:1 (par; cf. Acts 1:7) pertaining to some not tasting death before seeing the kingdom come in power, are best seen in reference to the subsequent events of the transfiguration. Some Historical Jesus scholars, largely influenced by J. Weiss, contend that material attributed to Jesus that looked for the near consummation of the kingdom of God was most likely authentic. When the kingdom failed to come, Jesus died a disillusioned apocalyptic (Schweitzer). Not all agree. Moreover, the gospels are far from providing a roadmap by which to produce a calendar of end-time events. Instead, they point early Christians to follow the teachings of Jesus.

DANIEL M. GURTNER

Further reading

Allison, D. C., Jr. *The End of the Ages Has Come*, Philadelphia, PA: Fortress Press, 1985.

Beale, G. K. "The Old Testament Background of Reconciliation in 2 Corinthians 5–7 and Its Bearing on the Literary Problem of 2 Corinthians 6:14–18," *NTS* (1989) 550–81.

Beasley-Murray, G. R. *Jesus and the kingdom of God*, Grand Rapids, MI: Eerdmans, 1986.

Brown, C. "Jesus in European Protestant Thought, 1778–1860," SHT 1, Durham, NC: Labyrinth, 1985.

Conzelmann, H. *The Theology of St Luke*, London: Faber & Faber, 1960.

Dodd, C. H. *The Parables of the Kingdom*, London: Nisbet, 1935.

—— *The Apostolic Preaching and Its Developments*, New York: Willett, Clark, 1937.

Gurtner, Daniel M. "The Torn Veil: Matthew's Exposition of the Death of Jesus," SNTSMS, Cambridge: Cambridge University Press, forthcoming.

Hoekema, Anthony A. *The Bible and the Future*, Grand Rapids, MI: Eerdmans, 1979.

Jeremias, J. *The Parables of Jesus*, second revised edition, New York: Charles Scribner's Sons, 1972.

McCown, C. C. *The Search for the Real Jesus: A Century of Historical Study*, New York: Scribner's, 1940.

Perrin, N. *Jesus and the Language of the Kingdom*, Philadelphia, PA: Fortress Press, 1976.

Sanders, E. P. *Jesus and Judaism*, Philadelphia, PA: Fortress Press/London: SCM Press, 1985.

Schweitzer, Albert. *The Quest of the Historical Jesus*, Minneapolis, MN: Fortress Press, 2001.

Weiss, J. *Jesus' Proclamation of the kingdom of God*, trans. R. H. Hiers and D. L. Holland, Lives of Jesus Series, Philadelphia, PA: Fortress Press, 1971.

ETERNAL LIFE

Life (ζωή) occurs 135 times in the NT, of which forty-three occur in the phrase "eternal life" (ἡ αἰώνιος ζωή or ζωή αἰώνιος), two in Mark (10:17, 30), three in Matthew (19:16, 29; 25:46), three in Luke (10:25; 18:18, 30), seventeen in John (3:15, 16, 36; 4:14, 36; 5:24, 39; 6:27, 40, 47, 54, 68; 8:28; 12:25, 50; 17:2, 3), seven in 1 John, two in Acts, eight in the letters attributed to Paul, and one in Jude. Eternal life is a Johannine characteristic, with the Gospel and 1 John accounting for twenty-four of the forty-three uses. In the gospels, reference to entering into life implies eternal life so that Mark's other two uses of ζωή (9:43, 45) are to be understood in this way as are Matthew's four remaining uses (7:14; 18:8, 9; 19:17). This takes Matthew's use to seven and Mark's to four. In John the strong concentration is enhanced by fifteen cases where ζωή means eternal life (3:36; 5:24, 29, 40; 6:33, 35, 48, 51, 53, 63; 8:12; 10:10; 11:25; 14:6; 20:31). This stands out from the earlier Jesus tradition of the Synoptics and from the early church tradition found in Acts and Paul.

Jewish source

Although eternal life has Jewish roots in the language of the life of the age to come, there is only one reference to eternal life in the Jewish Scriptures (Dan 12:2, LXX) and a handful in the Pseudepigrapha (*Pss. Sol.* 3:12; 13:11; 14:10; *1 En.* 37:4; 58:3; *Jos. Asen.* 8:10; 15:4). There are also a few references in the Sectarian writings from Qumran, such as 1QS 4:7–14, which could be a development of Dan 12:2. But there are modifications. The lot of the wicked is ambiguously described as eternal torment (as in Dan 12:2) and annihilation or extinction. The lot of the righteous is both "healing, great peace in a long life" (like Deut 30:15–20) and "every everlasting blessing and eternal joy in life without end," a development of the tradition in Dan 12:2. There is no evidence of a Greek background for this motif. The evidence, such as it is, points in a Jewish direction.

Eternal life and the kingdom of God in the gospels

In the Synoptics, eternal life is used rarely compared with Jesus' teaching about the kingdom of God. If Markan priority is accepted, much of the Synoptic use comes from Mark (Mark 9:43, 45 = Matt 18:8, 9; Mark 10:17, 30 = Matt 19:16[17], 29 = Luke 18:18, 30 [10:25]). Mark 10:17–31 is important because in it eternal life is identified as the life of the kingdom (10:17, 23, 24, 30), which is "treasure in heaven" (10:21). The Markan narrative suggests kingdom of God is the preferred idiom of Jesus and that eternal life clarifies the life of the kingdom. Jesus speaks of entering life (Mark 9:43, 45) in the way he speaks of entering the kingdom (10:23, 24), both with a future reference so that eternal life is future (Mark 9:43, 45; 10:17, 30 and parallels; Matt 7:14; 25:46) as it is in Dan 12:2.

In John eternal life is also experienced in the present (John 5:24). Only two uses of kingdom of God occur, both in Jesus' conversation with Nicodemus (John 3:3, 5) where Jesus sets out the conditions of entry into the kingdom (cf. Mark 10:23–25 and Mark 9:43, 45). He speaks of entry (3:5) first in terms of seeing (= experiencing, 3:3), and describes the condition first as birth from above (a circumlocution for God cf. 1:13) before referring to water and Spirit (3:5). Birth images imply life, and the theme that emerges for the first time when Jesus and Nicodemus have disappeared from centre-stage (3:15–17, 36) is eternal life (3:15, 16, 36). These texts imply a reality experienced by believers in the present (cf. 5:24).

In John, apart from the narrator's words in 3:15, 16, 36; 20:31, Jesus expounds the theme of eternal life (as in the Synoptics). The narrator's role is critical because he introduces this key motif (3:15) and provides the closing reference to it in the planned conclusion of the Gospel (20:31). He asserts that, of the many signs Jesus performed in the presence of his disciples, those narrated in this book have the power to lead to a believing response and the experience of eternal life. If birth from God is a condition of eternal life, a believing response to Jesus is a condition of birth from above (1:12–13; 3:15–17, 36).

Future and present in the teaching of Jesus

In the Synoptics, as in Daniel 12:2, eternal life is the reward of the righteous at the end-time judgement. But there are aspects of Jesus' teaching that suggest the kingdom of God is dawning already in his ministry. Mark (1:14–15) gives a summary account of Jesus' preaching, "The time is fulfilled, the kingdom of God is at hand; repent and believe the gospel." In a passage peculiar to Matthew and Luke (Q?), Jesus responds to messengers from John (the Baptist) in prison asking Jesus, "Are you the coming one, or do we look for another?" Jesus responds,

> Go and report to John what you hear and see; the blind see and the lame walk, the lepers are cleansed and the deaf hear, and dead are raised and poor [have] good news proclaimed [to them]; and blessed is the one whoever is not scandalised by me.
>
> (Matt 11:2–6 = Luke 7:18–23; and see Isa 35:5; 61:1; Luke 4:18)

In another Q passage Jesus responds to the charge that he is casting out demons by the power of the prince of demons, "If I by the Spirit of God [Luke has "finger of God"] cast out demons, then the kingdom of God has dawned upon you" (ἔφθασεν, Matt 12:28; Luke 11:21; cf. ἤγγικεν in Mark 1:15). Jesus taught that the blessings of the kingdom were already present in his teaching and healing ministry. He also taught that the way of discipleship was fraught with hardship, danger, suffering, and even death, with the promise of eternal life in the age to come (Mark 10:29–30 = Matt 19:28–29 = Luke 18:29–30).

Future and present in John

In John the balance has changed. As in Dan 12:2, the Jesus of John looks to the imminent time when all in the tombs will hear the voice of the Son of Man and those doing good will come out to a resurrection of life, but those doing evil to a resurrection of judgement (5:28–29). The dominant perspective is found just a few verses earlier, "Truly, truly I tell you, the one who hears my words and believes in the one who sent me has eternal life and will not come into judgement, but has passed out of death into life" (5:24). For the Jesus and narrator of John, the presence of Jesus in the world has transformed the situation, from one characterised by hope and directed to the future, to a realisation in the present that guarantees the future. Jesus reveals the ground for this change, "Even as the Father has life in himself, in the same way he has given to Son [the power? authority?] to have life in himself" (5:26). This theme is already present in the Prologue (1:4; cf. 8:12; 11:25; 14:6).

These texts refer to Jesus' life-giving power, and his signs reveal different aspects of it. At the beginning of the story of the healing of the blind man Jesus says, "We must work the works of the one who sent me while it is day ... As long as I am in the world, I am the light of the world" (9:4–5). The healing of the blind man not only gives sight to his eyes, but also opens his eye of faith so that he believes in Jesus. It is a blinding light to those who refuse to believe (9:35–41).

As the expression of God's love for the world, Jesus came to bring life to the world (3:16), and his signs are signs of the life that he brings. The narration of the signs is life-giving because it has the power to evoke belief in Jesus as the source of the life (20:30–31), which has its source in God. "This is eternal life, to know you, the only true God, and Jesus Christ whom you have sent" (17:3). What is revealed in Jesus is God's love for the world, which realises its goal in those who recognise and respond to that love. The self-giving love of Jesus is revealed in his life as a whole, and is focused in the narrative of the foot-washing (13:1–17). It is the basis for the new commandment (13:34–35), the fulfilment of which is the basis for the continuing hope for the world. In John the mission of Jesus to bring eternal life is the ground of the mission of believers in the world upon which its hope of life (which has its source in God) hangs (17:20–26).

JOHN PAINTER

Further reading

Dodd, C. H. *The Interpretation of the Fourth Gospel*, Cambridge: Cambridge University Press, 1953, pp. 144–50, 318–54, 363–79.

Painter, John. "Jesus and the Quest for Eternal Life," in R. Alan Culpepper (ed.) *Critical Readings of John 6*, Leiden: Brill, 1997, pp. 61–94.

—— "God and the Quest for Eternal Life," *St Mark's Review* (Autumn 1998) 10–16.

ETHICS OF JESUS

The moral life is prescribed by Jesus for himself and for all those who wanted to follow him by association with him. As Leander Keck has put it well, when we are dealing with what Jesus said about "ethics" we are actually looking at a "moral life":

> The moral life is both broader and deeper than morality (patterned behavior) or morals (actions deemed right by a community), for it has to do with the sort of person one is (the doer) as well as with the grounding of what is to be done or not done (the deed).
>
> (152)

In fact, some prefer not to call Jesus' "moral life" the "ethics of Jesus," since ethics more narrowly refers to philosophical and critical reflection on right behavior, something more akin to Aristotle's *Nicomachean Ethics*. Commonly, however, the "ethics of Jesus" or the "ethic of Jesus" is used for what Jesus said about the moral life. The topic is immense, and only some of the specific lines of thinking can be brought up here (see 2003).

The ethics of Jesus in discussion

The ethics of Jesus are tied to the eschatology of Jesus, and how one defines that eschatology shapes how one understands his ethics (Schnackenburg; Hurst 211–14). In fact, Jesus believed that a new day had arrived and that the Torah was now fulfilled in his teachings and by following him (cf. Matt 5:17–48; 12:1–14; Luke 9:57–62).

Albert Schweitzer famously argued Jesus thought the world was about to come to a close and that meant the ethics of Jesus were little more than "emergency ethics" or an ethic for the "interim." L. D. Hurst (210) calls this a "colossal blunder," not only for its failure the exegesis of texts but also (in my estimation) for not dealing with the living reality of the ethics of Jesus for those who were not tied into such a radical eschatology. The ethic must be tied to eschatology, but the construction of Jesus' eschatology along "inaugurated" lines (see kingdom of God) cuts the legs off Schweitzer's famous proposal (McKnight 1999: 156–237).

In many ways, Schweitzer's theory provided a case for the classical "evangelical counsels" of Roman Catholicism: Schweitzer was a Lutheran, and Luther grounded ethics in grace radically as a reaction to the Roman Catholic "two-level ethic": one for the "religious" and one for "laity." Schweitzer, it might be said, laicized the ethics of Jesus – except his view was that they were only for the "interim." The classical Roman Catholic interpretation of the ethics of Jesus, however, remained even if since Vatican II the "evangelical counsels" have become more and more appropriated for the laity while the rigor of the evangelical counsels have not been relaxed for the priests and nuns (see Boyle vi).

Alongside this classical appropriation of the ethics of Jesus in Roman Catholicism is the Reformation view, however simplistically sketched here, that texts like the Sermon on the Mount are a heightened form of the Torah of Moses in order to drive the human to sense his or her own guilt before God and seek to be rectified before God by grace through faith. Following the Reformers were the Anabaptists: they repudiated the "evangelical counsel" approach as well as the admission by (especially) the Lutherans that the teachings of Jesus were impracticable, and they committed themselves to radical discipleship, hoping to form communities wherein the teachings of Jesus were established. Which leads us to Protestant liberalism, which steered away from each of the above views to focus more narrowly on "intention" and "disposition" (1957: 71–72). At the hand of R. Bultmann, the "intention" became the "existential moment" of confronting God (Bultmann).

Historical Jesus scholars find themselves in one of these approaches. In spite of the particularities that arise as a result of determining what is and what is not authentic, and the overall unique synthesis that results from such judgments, historical Jesus scholars have had little impact on the general direction of the ethics of Jesus: the general themes remain standing, even if slightly burned.

A useful way of categorizing the ethics of Jesus is to approach them, as was established by L. Goppelt, as relational ethics. This article will examine the ethics of Jesus in three major relationships: to God, to self, and to others.

The ethics of Jesus and God

Jews would not have distinguished the so-called attributes of God the way Christian theologians have, and neither would Jesus. To speak of the priority of either God's love or God's holiness is a mistake. God is God, and that One God is both love and holiness at the same time always and forever. Similarly, Jesus' moral life and his ethics were attempts to articulate this singular loving holiness of God for human behavior. Two words in the gospels bring this to the surface: righteousness and love.

Righteousness (*t-d-q*) in the Hebrew Bible and Judaism always described a person whose life conformed to the Torah (McKnight 1999: 200–6). It was the Pauline innovative emphasis of "righteousness" (Gk. *dikaiosune*) being a "declared status" that prevents many from hearing how Jesus would have used the term. For him, as for Judaism, "righteousness" described a condition of conformity to the Torah. An example would be Matthew's description of Joseph as a *tsadiq*, or righteous man (Matt 1:19). Inasmuch as righteousness describes conformity to the Torah, it always took on conformity to *one interpretation* of the Torah – with the clear implication that Pharisees and Essenes would have identified a "righteous" person by a differing set of categories (1QS 3:20–23; 4QMMT;

Matt 5:17–48; *m. Sanh.* 6:5; 8:5). Consequently, it is nothing unusual when Jesus defines "righteousness" by those who follow his teaching. This, depending of course on how much one judges to be authentic, is the singular focus of the so-called antitheses of Matthew 5:17–48. Here Jesus virtually defines what "righteousness" will look like for his followers: both dispositionally and behaviorally. Those who do follow Jesus' teachings are blessed (5:6, 10) and will be found in the right at the final judgment (7:15–27). To be righteous, then, in one's relationship with God is to follow the teachings of Jesus from the heart.

It is not common in the Hebrew Bible, in Judaism, in Jesus, or in earliest Christianity to turn one's duty before God into loving God. Not common may be accurate in its description of what texts say, but the observant Jew knew that reciting the *Shema* (Deut 6:4–9) was insufficient alone (cf. Jas 2:19). It is not clear today just what the observant Jew recited in the twice-daily sacred rhythm, because such a duty may have involved other texts (e.g. 11:13–21; Num 15:37–41 were eventually added, as were the Ten Commandments according to the Nash papyrus), but it is reasonably clear that observant Jews repeated *Shema* (Ps 55:18; Dan 6:10; Matt 6:5; Acts 3:1; *Did.* 1:2). It is clear also that early Christians were attached to the *Shema* in what I have elsewhere called the "Jesus Creed" (cf. Jas 2:8, 18–19; Gal 5:13–14; Rom 13:8–10; John 13:34–35; 1 John 3:11, 14, 23; 4:21; 5:2). Loving God was the fundamental core of the Jewish relationship to God, and Jesus carried this on with his followers. It is a risk to define the indefinable, but I shall offer this as a rough and ready place to begin: to love God is yearn for, pray for, and to work for God's glory in the context of knowing God from the heart and soul.

The ethics of Jesus and self

What is boilerplate in our world, self-esteem, was unheard of in Jesus' world. Nonetheless, self-love was assumed – perhaps radically so as an assumption. Twice Jesus grounds his central teaching in self-love. The first is the Golden Rule: "In everything do to others as you would have them do to you; for this is the law and the prophets" (Matt 7:12). And then the second of the (two) Great Commandments: "You shall love your neighbor as yourself" (Mark 12:31). In each case, his followers' fundamental dispositional and behavioral shape is rooted in self-love. Jesus assumes people love themselves and care for themselves. On top of that assumption he constructs the notion that his followers will look after others the way they look after themselves.

Jesus was well aware of the danger of *self-deception*, and some of his most famous sayings emerge from that very concern. The self, for Jesus, in spite of the Golden Rule and Great Commandments, was never the sole foundation for constructing ethics. Although some sayings may have been redacted, very few would question that Jesus had stiff warnings about hypocrisy: and his favorite target was the religious elites of his day, the scribes and Pharisees (e.g. Matt 6:1–18; 23:1–39; Mark 7:1–20). Jesus' teachings on humility (Matt 5:5, 8; Luke 14:7–14), trust (Matt 6:25–34; Mark 1:15), and denial of self (Mark 8:34–38) in their own way spring from the problems of self-deception and self-aggrandizement and pride.

Knowing self-deception doesn't turn Jesus into a cynic: he believes humans can be transformed from the center out, that the self can be restored. That is why he summons his followers to inner renewal (cf. Jer 31:31–34; Mark 7:17–23; Matt 5:8).

At the core of what Jesus thinks about the self is his teaching that the kingdom of God has come to empower people to live out the will of God in this world (Mark 1:14–20), and his conviction, though not often expressed, that the Holy Spirit is available for renewal (Mark 1:9–11; 3:22–30; Matt 12:28; Barrett).

The ethics of Jesus and others

At the core of Jesus' ethical teachings is loving others. The distinguishing feature of Jesus' version of the *Shema* was the addition of Leviticus 19:18 to the daily recitation of the *Shema* (cf. Mark 12:28–32). Luke's Gospel records that it was a scribe who added these words to the *Shema*, but many would explain that text as the scribe either saying what he had heard Jesus teaching or Luke attributing to the scribe what Jesus was teaching (10:25–28). The issue is hardly who said what first, but what was emphatic for Jesus: Leviticus 19:18 is a text not found attached to the *Shema* prior to Jesus, a text not cited in other literature prior to Jesus (cf. however *T. Iss.* 5:2; 7:6; *T. Dan* 5:3; [*T. Napht.* 8:9?], and which shows up centrally in earliest Christianity (Jas 2:8; Gal 5:13–14; Rom 13:8–10). The best explanation is that Leviticus 19:18, even more so than Deuteronomy 6:4–5, was at the center of Jesus' teachings. To hazard another definition: to love your neighbor is to yearn for, pray for, and work for what God desires for that neighbor.

For Jesus, love of neighbor shows two dramatic breakthroughs. First, when the scribe asked, "Who is my neighbor?" (Luke 10:29), Jesus' use of the parable of the Good Samaritan was intended to show that "neighbor" means anyone in need, even if they are defiled, impure, and dead (10:30–37). Second, the "neighbor" is not only the defiled, but also the "enemy," which in Jesus' day would no doubt have been Roman soldiers and Romans. Hence, "Love your enemies and pray for those who persecute you" (Matt 5:44) – and this grounded not in self-love as in the Golden Rule or Great Commandment but in God's love as seen in general providence (5:45). Such behavior imitated not only God's love for all, but also Jesus' regular mixing with the unclean and sinful (Mark 2:13–17).

In relation to others, the followers of Jesus were to express that love by forgiveness. While some have contended that the Jubilee expectations were what Jesus often has in mind (Lev 25; Luke 4:16–30), what Jesus has in mind is probably less specific and more comprehensive. He expected his followers to forgive others as God had forgiven them (Luke 11:4). In fact, forgiving others conditioned God's forgiveness in this text (cf. Mark 11:25–26). Jesus' parable of the Unforgiving Servant demonstrates that for him forgiving others was so central that those who didn't were not genuine followers (Matt 18:21–35). The sinful woman who lavished her oils on Jesus demonstrated that love for Jesus and forgiveness were integrally related (Luke 7:36–50).

Those who loved others sought for peace. Hence, Jesus blessed those who were known for pursuing peace (Matt 5:9). They are those who hunger for what is right (Dunn 563–83). Undoubtedly, though we cannot be more specific than the text states, such a blessing on Jesus' part would pit him against the Zealot-types of his day and place him in the camp of those who thought the way to find peace in the world was through loving others and negotiating at tables. Peace, which is anticipated as a messianic blessing (Isa 60:17–18), transcends the notion of internal content and finds its most complete expression in social tranquility and good relations with others. Jesus can call his followers "sons of peace" (Luke 10:5–6).

Yet another expression of one's loving relationship with others is in Jesus' constant exhibition and teaching of being "merciful" and "compassionate." Those who are merciful to those in need – and Jesus' perception of "need" was very, very wide – were blessed by Jesus (Matt 5:7), and he called his followers to be compassionate as the Good Samaritan was compassionate to those in need (Luke 10:30–37). Jesus' table fellowship with undesirables embodies what he meant by mercy (Luke 15:1–2; 19:1–10).

It goes beyond the scope of this entry, but Jesus' teachings on loving others created what was soon to be called the "church." In Jesus' day it was an informal fellowship of those who believed in Jesus they would enter into the eschatological kingdom (cf. Mark 14:12–25). They are what N. T. Wright calls "the real, the true, Israel" (Wright 443).

The ethics of Jesus, cost and reward

The "Christology" of Jesus' ethics is not without import. What kind of person, a historian might ask, would ask people to follow him as the sole means of life (cf. Matt 10:26–32)? Did Jesus think he was the New Moses (cf. Matt 5–7)? Did he think he was the Messiah? The expected prophet? However we answer that question, the ethics of Jesus are a clue that Jesus thought he revealed God and that following him was now the central obligation if Israel was to be restored and saved from its condition. (On this, Evans 437–56.)

So central did Jesus think his teachings were that he summoned all to abandon whatever got in the way. He summoned folks out of their vocations (Mark 1:16–20; 2:13–17), out of their families and the honor system they sustained (John 2:1–11; Mark 3:31–35; Luke 9:57–62; Matt 19:10–12), out of their financial security (Matt 6:25–34; Luke 9:57–62; 14:33), out of their physical securities (Matt 8:19–20; 10:17–22), and out of social and religious observances (Luke 9:59–60; Matt 9:14–17; 12:1–14; 15:1–20). In fact, Jesus summoned his followers to follow him at the very cost of the "self" (Luke 9:23–25; 14:33). Nothing was permitted to stand in the way of following Jesus.

In an age of altruism, the emphasis Jesus gives to rewards troubles many. Jesus did teach disinterested goodness (Matt 5:41; Luke 14:12–14), and he harped on the importance of character coming to fruition in good deeds (Matt 7:16–20). Furthermore, he disabused his contemporaries of the notion that reward came from a "contractual relationship with God" (Matt 20:1–16). Nonetheless, Jesus taught that what is done now will receive its just and inevitable reward (Matt 25:31–46). Why? Because God is both gracious and just: the reward will transcend what one receives, but the reward is shaped by how one has treated others (see Hurst 214–17).

The ethics of Jesus and their inception

How then does one become a follower of Jesus? This question could be answered in as many ways as Jesus encountered people, for his practice was not to apply a systemic approach but a personal-occasional approach. Conversion for Jesus was a process for each person, involving context, crisis, quest, interaction, commitment, and consequences (McKnight 2002). There are two elements to this process: the negative dimension of saying no to self and sin (repentance) and the positive dimension of saying yes to God through Jesus (faith).

One repents internally through self-denial (Mark 8:34–38) and externally by denying the world (see last paragraph of previous section). And one has faith by decision (Mark 1:15), deliberation (Luke 14:28–33), public identification with Jesus (Matt 10:32–33) and obedience (Matt 7:24–27; Luke 11:28; John 14:15–17).

SCOT MCKNIGHT

Further reading

Barrett, C. K. *The Holy Spirit and the Gospel Tradition*, London: SPCK, 1947.

Boyle, J. L. in E. Cothenet, *Imitating Christ*, St Meinrad, IN: Abbey, 1974. A translation of "Imitation du Christ (Livre)," from *Dictionnaire de spiritualité ascétique et mystique: Doctrine et histoire*, ed. by M. Viller *et al.*, 17 vols in 21 parts, Paris: G. Beauchesue, 1937–1995. Vol. 7.2, cols 1536–601, 2355–68.

Bultmann, R. *Jesus and the Word*, New York: Charles Scribner's, 1958.

Dunn, J. D. G. *Remembering Jesus*, Grand Rapids, MI: Eerdmans, 2003.

Evans, C. A. *Jesus and His Contemporaries: Comparative Studies*, Leiden: Brill, 1995.

Goppelt, L. *Theology of the New Testament*, Grand Rapids, MI: Eerdmans, 1981.

Harnack, A. *What is Christianity?*, New York: Harper, 1957.

Hurst, L. D. "Ethics of Jesus," in J. B. Green, S. McKnight, and I. H. Marshall (eds) *The Dictionary of Jesus and the Gospels*, Downers Grove, IL: InterVarsity Press, 1992, pp. 210–22.

Keck, L. *Who is Jesus? History in Perfect Tense*, Columbia, SC: University of South Carolina Press, 2000.

McKnight, S. *A New Vision for Israel*, Grand Rapids, MI: Eerdmans, 1999.

—— *Turning to Jesus: The Sociology of Conversion in the Gospels*, Louisville, KY: WJKP, 2002.

Schnackenburg, R. *The Moral Teaching of the New Testament*, New York: Seabury, 1965.

Wright, N. T. *Jesus and the Victory of God*, Minneapolis, MN: Fortress Press, 1996.

EXORCISMS AND HEALINGS

Jesus' ability to heal and exorcize was a very significant facet of his ministry, a facet that impacted his contemporaries enormously, not only during the pre-Easter ministry itself, but for generations after. For Jesus, healing and exorcism demonstrated the reality of the rule of God, a reality that lay at the very heart of his proclamation (cf. Mark 1:14–15; Luke 11:20). For the disciples of Jesus, healing and exorcism continued to demonstrate the reality of the proclamation of Jesus and even provide proof of the divine authority of Jesus himself. Even long after the time of Jesus and his original followers, his name was invoked by exorcists and healers.

Exorcism and healing in the ministry of Jesus

His surprising ability to heal and exorcize, noted by Josephus and other non-Christians, placed Jesus in a class by himself. Jesus' authority to heal and cast out demons is seen at the very beginning of his ministry. The first story of exorcism recounted by the Markan evangelist reads as follows (Mark 1:21–27):

> [21]And they went into Capernaum; and immediately on the sabbath he entered the synagogue and taught. [22]And they were astonished at his teaching, for he taught them as one who had authority, and not as the scribes. [23]And immediately there was in their synagogue a man with an unclean spirit; [24]and he cried out, "What have you to do with us, Jesus of Nazareth? Have you come to destroy us? I know who you are, the Holy One of God." [25]But Jesus rebuked him, saying, "Be silent, and come out of him!" [26]And the unclean spirit, convulsing him and crying with a loud voice, came out of him. [27]And they were all amazed, so that they questioned among themselves, saying, "What is this? A new teaching! With authority he commands even the unclean spirits, and they obey him."

This initial exorcism alludes to the eschatological implications of Jesus' proclamation: "The time is fulfilled, and the kingdom of God is at hand; repent, and believe in the gospel" (Mark 1:15). Moreover, only shortly before, the evangelist had narrated Jesus' wilderness encounter with Satan and his allies: "And he was in the wilderness forty days, tempted by Satan; and he was with the wild beasts; and the angels ministered to him" (Mark 1:13). Accordingly, when the frightened spirit asks Jesus, "What have you to do with us, Jesus of Nazareth? Have you come to destroy us? I know who you are, the Holy One of God" (1:24), he has acknowledged Jesus' role as Satan's eschatological adversary. The unclean spirit knows who Jesus is and therefore knows what Jesus intends to do.

Why Jesus rebuked the spirit and commanded it to "be silent" (1:25) is made clear in the next exorcism to be narrated: "And he healed many who were sick with various diseases, and cast out many demons; and he would not permit the demons to speak, because they knew him" (1:34). Jesus silences the evil spirits, "because they knew him," as seen in the earlier exorcism: "I know who you are, the Holy One of God" (1:24). There is no messianic secrecy theme at work here. The explanation has to do with exorcism. The spirit's declaration that it knows who Jesus is is meant as a threat. Knowing the name of the exorcist affords the evil spirit the opportunity to thwart, perhaps even harm the exorcist (just as knowing the name of the evil spirit aids the exorcist). But Jesus silences the spirit and orders its immediate departure.

Jesus needs no exorcistic formula and no paraphernalia, as do other exorcists (as will be seen in the examples considered below). He orders the spirit to come out of the afflicted person and the spirit obeys (1:26–27). The onlookers are astonished, not because the exorcism is successful, but because Jesus achieved it with a spoken word and without supporting gimmickry. It is no wonder that Jesus' word and action are dubbed "A new teaching [*didache*] with authority" (1:27). Years later, when Paul defeats his opponent Bar-Jesus, the Roman consul similarly is astonished at "the teaching [*didache*] of the Lord" (Acts 13:12).

The power and reputation of Jesus are such that unclean spirits fall before him and confess him as "the Son of God" (Mark 3:11). These spirits not only know who Jesus is, they fear and respect him. Jesus' critics, however, view his success in a very different light: "And the scribes who came down from Jerusalem said, 'He is possessed by Beelzebul, and by the prince of demons he casts out the demons'" (3:22). Jesus attacks the logic of the accusation, concluding that "if Satan has risen up against himself and is divided, he cannot stand, but has an end" (3:26). Although in the RSV the last part of the statement is rendered "is coming to an end," the Greek literally reads: "has an end [τέλος ἔχει]." We have an exact parallel in the *Testament of Moses*, a Palestinian document that originated sometime around 30 CE, or shortly before. After a period of suffering, the kingdom of God will appear and the power of Satan will be broken: "And then His kingdom shall appear throughout all His creation, and then Satan will have an end" (10:1). The second line, "will have an end [*finem habebit*]," which is in the future tense, anticipates what Jesus says is happening in his ministry, a ministry in which the rule of God is proclaimed and the demise of the rule of Satan is demonstrated through exorcism. (Evans 2005: 62, 67).

Jesus' power over Satan's kingdom is dramatically illustrated in the story of the demonized man in Mark 5:1–20. Part of the story reads:

> [2]And when he had come out of the boat, there met him out of the tombs a man with an unclean spirit, [3]who lived among the tombs; and no one could bind him any more, even with a chain; [4]for he had often been bound with fetters and chains, but the chains he wrenched apart, and the fetters he broke in pieces; and no one had the strength to subdue him. [5]Night and day among the tombs and on the mountains he was always crying out, and bruising himself with stones. [6]And when he saw Jesus from afar, he ran and worshiped him; [7]and crying out with a loud voice, he said, "What have you to do with me, Jesus, Son of the Most High God? I adjure you by God, do not torment me." [8]For he had said to him, "Come out of the man, you unclean spirit!" [9]And Jesus asked him, "What is your name?" He replied, "My name is Legion; for we are many."
>
> (5:2–9)

People of Jesus' time would have found this description of the demonized man terrifying. In some incantation texts the demons are said to be "bound with chains" (e.g. Gordon 278: "Bound is the bewitching lilith ... with a chain of iron on her neck"). Accordingly, the claim that not even chains and fetters could restrain the demonized man would have been very frightening to Jesus' contemporaries and Mark's original readers. Indeed, his amazing strength may have recalled Samson, a biblical hero renown for his great strength (see Aus 25–30).

Furthermore, the macabre details of this man's existence – living among tombs and howling night and day – would have added to the frightening picture. The people of late antiquity, including Jews, believed that the cemetery and necropolis were the haunts of ghosts and demons (cf. LXX Ps 67:6; Isa 65:1–7). And finally, the name "Legion" (Gk. λεγιών) itself would have brought to mind the feared Roman legion (Latin: *legio*). A demonized man such as this presented Jesus with a formidable opponent. And yet it is Jesus who frightens the man possessed with the demonic legion. He implores Jesus: "I adjure you by God, do not torment me" (5:7).

Jesus shares his remarkable power with his apostles:

> And he appointed twelve, to be with him, and to be sent out to preach and have authority to cast out demons ... And he called to him the twelve, and began to send them out two by two, and gave them authority over the unclean spirits.
>
> (Mark 3:14–15; 6:7)

Jesus' ministry of healing and exorcism, now multiplied through his apostles, becomes known throughout Galilee. Reports of his ministry even reach the ears of the tetrarch Herod (Mark 6:13–16):

¹⁴King Herod heard of it; for Jesus' name had become known. Some said, "John the baptizer has been raised from the dead; that is why these powers are at work in him." ¹⁵But others said, "It is Elijah." And others said, "It is a prophet, like one of the prophets of old." ¹⁶But when Herod heard of it he said, "John, whom I beheaded, has been raised."

Herod's conjecture that Jesus must be John the Baptist, whom he earlier had beheaded but now has returned from the dead, is amazing. Evidently, Herod thinks that the power of Jesus is so great, it can only be explained as a power that has been brought back from the unseen world of spirit. To be sure, Herod's conclusion is faulty, but it does bear significant witness to Jesus.

Jesus' reputation continues to grow, to the point that he cannot be in public without being recognized and pursued (Mark 6:54–56; cf. 5:27–29). The power of Jesus is such that he can heal and exorcize at a distance (Mark 7:24–30; John 4:46–54) and cast out a troublesome demon that had withstood other exorcists for years and could even hold its own against the disciples of Jesus (Mark 9:14–29).

At least one contemporary professional exorcist began making use of Jesus' name during his lifetime. In Mark 9:38–40 we learn of an exorcist, outside Jesus' following, who casts out demons in the name of Jesus.

³⁸John said to him, "Teacher, we saw a man casting out demons in your name [ἐν τῷ ὀνόματί σου ἐκβάλλοντα δαιμόνια], and we forbade him, because he was not following us." ³⁹But Jesus said, "Do not forbid him; for no one who does a mighty work in my name will be able soon after to speak evil of me. ⁴⁰For he that is not against us is for us."

What is remarkable is that this activity evidently was taking place during the pre-Easter ministry. The probability that this is authentic pre-Easter tradition is seen in the remarkable response of Jesus, which stands in tension with early Christian teaching and practice, in which only *Christian* leaders, especially the apostles, have the authority to invoke the name of Jesus for purposes of healing and exorcism. This point is dramatically illustrated in Acts, in the story of the young slave girl with the python spirit (Acts 16:16–18) and in the story of the seven sons of Sceva, the Jewish high priest (Acts 19:13–20). Not just anyone can invoke the name of Jesus, even professional soothsayers and exorcists. Given the probability that we have here the post-Easter Christian perspective, it is more than probable that the story found in Mark 9 represents genuine pre-Easter tradition.

In a lengthy section in which he is accused of being in league with Beelzebul (Matt 12:22–45), Jesus asserts: "Behold, something greater than Solomon is here [πλεῖον Σολομῶνος ὧδε]!" (Matt 12:42). The assertion that someone important is "here" (ὧδε) is echoed in many incantations considered (e.g. "Abraham dwells here [ὧδε]"). The comparison with Solomon seems to imply that Jesus is greater than Solomon, not simply in wisdom but also in matters of healing and exorcism, for which Israel's famous monarch was well known.

There are many traditions in late antiquity, in which reference is made to Solomon and his authority over evil spirits. One well-known story, in which Solomon the master exorcist appears, is related by Josephus (*Ant.* 8.46–49):

I have observed a certain Eleazar, of my race, in the presence of Vespasian, his sons, tribunes and a number of other soldiers, release people possessed by demons [ὑπὸ τῶν δαιμονίων λαμβανομένους ἀπολύοντα τούτων]. Now this was the manner of the cure: Placing to the nostrils of the demon possessed person the ring which had under the seal a root which Solomon had prescribed [τὸν δακτύλιον ἔχοντα ὑπὸ τῇ σφραγίδι ῥίζαν ἐξ ὧν ὑπέδειξε Σολόμων], he then, as the person smelled it, drew out the demon through the nostrils. When the person fell down, he adjured the demon, speaking Solomon's name and repeating the incantations that he had composed, never to re-enter him. Then, wishing to persuade and to prove to those present that he had this ability, Eleazar would place at a small distance either a cup full of water or a foot basin and command the demon while going out of the human to overturn it and to make known to those watching that he had left him. And when this happened, the understanding and wisdom of Solomon were clearly revealed, on account of which we felt compelled to speak in order that all might know of the greatness of his nature and divine favor, and that the surpassing virtue of the king might not be forgotten by anyone.

The ring, the seal, and the name of Solomon all appear in various exorcistic traditions, including various incantations and spells and the pseudepigraphal work known as the *Testament of Solomon* (see Duling 1985; Gordon 273–76).

Exorcism and healing in the name of Jesus

Jesus' fame as exorcist and healer lived on. Pagans and Jews, as well as Christians, invoked his name in a variety of incantations, amulets, and magical papyri. One pagan charm instructs the patient to conjure, by saying: "I adjure you by the God of the Hebrews, Jesus ... " The charm goes on to appeal to the seal (ring) of Solomon (*PGM* IV.3007–41).

A phylactery appeals: "[The] one God and his Christ, help Alexandra" (Louvre Museum no. MND 274.6). Another charm warns an evil spirit: "In the name of the Lord Jesus Christ, I denounce you, most foul spirit of Tartarus, whom the angel Gabriel bound with burning fetters" (*CIL* III.961). An exorcistic incantation appeals to Jesus Christ, the Nazarene and to his holy apostles and angels to drive out an evil spirit (Froehner no. 1212). Yet another amulet, worded as a prayer, petitions Jesus: "Protect, Lord, son of David according to the flesh [cf. Rom 1:3–4], the one birthed by the holy virgin Mary, holy, most high God, from holy Spirit" (P.Oslo gr. 5). Many more can be cited (for original language, bibliography, and comments on the texts that have been cited, see Betz; Kotansky 1994).

What we see in these incantations, prayers, and curses, many of which date to three or more centuries after the time of Jesus, is a continuation of a tradition that had its origins in the time of Jesus' ministry. Long before Easter and the Christian movement's proclamation of the resurrection and heavenly enthronement of its Lord and Master, professional healers and exorcists of all stripes had begun to invoke the name of Jesus. One of the elements of Jesus' ministry that impacted his contemporaries, for which he would be remembered by many succeeding generations, was his ability to heal and cast out evil spirits.

CRAIG A. EVANS

Further reading

Aus, R. D. "My Name is 'Legion': Palestinian Judaic Traditions in Mark 5:1–20 and Other Gospel Texts," *SJLA*, Lanham, MD: University Press of America, 2003.

Betz, H. D. (ed.) *The Greek Magical Papyri in Translation, Including the Demotic Spells: Volume One: Texts*, second edition, Chicago, IL: University of Chicago Press, 1992.

Brown, C. *Miracles and the Critical Mind*, Grand Rapids, MI: Eerdmans, 1984.

Duling, D. C. "Solomon, Exorcism, and the Son of David," *HTR* 68 (1975) 235–52.

—— "The Eleazar Miracle and Solomon's Magical Wisdom in Flavius Josephus's *Antiquitates Judaicae* 8:42–49," *HTR* 78 (1985) 1–25.

Chilton, B. D. *Jesus' Baptism and Jesus' Healing: His Personal Practice of Spirituality*, Harrisburg, PA: Trinity Press International, 1998.

Evans, C. A. "Defeating Satan and Liberating Israel: Jesus and Daniel's Visions," *Journal for the Study of the Historical Jesus* 1 (2003) 161–70.

—— "Inaugurating the kingdom of God and Defeating the Kingdom of Satan," *BBR* 15 (2005) 49–75.

—— "Jesus' Exorcisms and Proclamation of the kingdom of God in the Light of the Testaments," in I. H. Henderson and G. S. Oegema (eds) *The Changing Face of Judaism, Christianity, and Other Greco-Roman Religions in Antiquity*, Studien zu den Jüdischen Schriften aus hellenistisch-römischer Zeit 2, Gütersloh: Gütersloher Verlagshaus, 2006, pp. 210–33.

Eve, D. *The Jewish Context of Jesus' Miracles*, JSNTSup 231, London and New York: Sheffield Academic Press, 2002.

Gordon, C. H. "Aramaic Incantation Bowls," *Orientalia* 10 (1991) 116–41, 272–80.

Kotansky, R. D. *Greek Magical Amulets: The Inscribed Gold, Silver, Copper, and Bronze Lamellae*. Part I: *Published Texts of Known Provenance*, Sonderreihe Papyrologica Coloniensia 22/1, Opladen: Westdeutscher Verlag, 1994.

Labahn, M. and Peerbolte, B. J. L. (eds) *Wonders Never Cease: The Purpose of Narrating Miracle Stories in the New Testament and Its Religious Environment*, LNTS 288, London and New York: T. & T. Clark International, 2006.

Latourelle, R. *The Miracles of Jesus and the Theology of Miracles*, New York: Paulist, 1988.

Meier, J. P. *A Marginal Jew: Rethinking the Historical Jesus*. Volume Two: *Mentor, Message, and Miracles*, ABRL 9; New York: Doubleday, 1994.

Moule, C. F. D. (ed.) *Miracles: Cambridge Studies in their Philosophy and History*, London: Mowbray, 1965.

Pilch, J. J. *Healing in the New Testament: Insights from Medical and Mediterranean Anthropology*, Minneapolis, MN: Fortress Press, 2000.

Preisendanz, K. *Papyri Graecae Magicae: Die griechischen Zuaberpapyri*, 2 vols, Stuttgart: Teubner, 1973–74.

Shel, E. "Jesus the Exorcist in Light of Epigraphic Sources," in J. H. Charlesworth (ed.) *Jesus and Archaeology*, Grand Rapids, MI: Eerdmans, 2006, pp. 178–85.

Twelftree, G. H. *Jesus the Exorcist: A Contribution to the Study of the Historical Jesus*, WUNT 2.54, Tübingen: Mohr Siebeck, 1993; repr. Peabody, MA: Hendrickson, 1993.

—— *Jesus the Miracle Worker: A Historical and Theological Study*, Downers Grove, IL: InterVarsity Press, 1999.

Wenham, D. and C. L. Blomberg (eds) *The Miracles of Jesus*, Gospel Perspectives 6, Sheffield: JSOT Press, 1986.

F

FAITH

The NT use of faith/believing draws on the OT/ Jewish and the Greek/Hellenistic uses. On the Jewish side, the centrality of the Law was influential, and faith/believing was imbued with the sense of obedience, loyalty, and trust. Nevertheless, faith/believing is much more central in the NT, and its writings show preference for either the verb (believe πιστεύω) or the noun (faith πίστις), yet the total uses of each word are almost exactly the same. John and Paul are the big users of this language. John uses the verb exclusively and Paul strongly favours the use of the noun. Of the rest, only Acts and Hebrews are frequent users. The former favours the verb and the latter the noun. Considering its brevity, James should be added to this list as one who strongly favours the noun.

The Synoptic Gospels are significant but not frequent users of this language. In the Gospels faith is frequently depicted without using the vocabulary. The article takes account of this but focuses on the use of the vocabulary of faith/ believing. Apart from Mark, who favours the verb by a ratio of 2 to 1, there is not much difference between the use of verb and noun. Though Luke slightly favours the noun, Acts favours the verb by a ratio of better than 2 to 1. Given the high use of the verb by John, the absence of the noun suggests a conscious decision by the author (see Table 3).

The relatively small use of faith/believing in the synoptics is in contrast with the emphasis on this motif in Paul and John. A careful analysis of the synoptic evidence forms the basis for understanding the teaching of Jesus in John and faith in the teaching of the historical Jesus. Overlapping traditions confirm that Jesus called on his hearers to believe the message of the kingdom of God that he preached, and thus to believe the messenger.

Mark and the synoptics

Though it overlaps Matt 4:12, 17, Mark 1:14–15 distinctively narrates the opening proclamation of Jesus. For Mark, this beginning is marked by the arrest of John (the Baptist). John and Jesus represent two different eras. Matthew has John and Jesus proclaim the same message (Matt 3:2; 4:17), with no mention of gospel or believing. Mark carefully distinguishes the activity of John and

Table 3 Use of the vocabulary of faith/believing

	John	Synoptics	Matt	Mark	Luke	1 John	Paul	Others	NT total
believe	98	30	11	10	9	9	54	48	239
faith	0	24	8	5	11	1	142	76	243
Others =	Acts	Heb	James	1 Peter	2 Peter	Jude	Rev	Others total	
believe	39	2	3	3	0	1	0	48	
faith	15	32	16	5	2	2	4	76	

Jesus in time and message. He names the activity of Jesus as "announcing *the gospel of God*," before reporting Jesus' own words, "*The time is fulfilled, the kingdom of God is at hand; repent and believe in the gospel*." The gospel here is what Jesus preached, though in Mark 1:1 it is what Mark has written. In contrast with John's message (according to Q, Matt 3:11–12 = Luke 3:16–17) of fiery judgement, Jesus preached the good news of the dawning of the kingdom of God and called for repentance and belief. Mark's distinctive view is expressed in the nature of the gospel to be believed. It is the gospel of God and concerns the dawning of the kingdom of God in the presence of Jesus impinging on human life in the world. Jesus' call for *conversion* (repent and believe involves turning from the old and commitment to the new) sets the tone for understanding believing in Mark.

Mark 2:5 (= Matt 9:2 = Luke 5:20) refers to Jesus seeing the faith of those who brought a paralytic to him for healing. This faith is the basis for his healing activity. See also Mark 5:34 = Matt 8:26 = Luke 8:48; Mark 10:52 = Matt 20:34 (omits 'faith) = Luke 18:42; and Matt 9:28. Similarly, when the disciples are afraid in the midst of a storm at sea, having dealt with the situation Jesus asks them, "Why are you fearful? Do you not yet have faith?" Mark 4:40 = Matt 8:26 (omits faith) = Luke 8:25. In these references faith has the sense of trust and reliance. See also Mark 5:36 = Luke 8:50; Mark 9:23–24; 9:42 = Matt 18:6 = Luke 17:1 [lacks believe]). Without using the vocabulary of faith the Jesus of Matthew teaches trustful reliance on God for all the necessities of life (Matt 6:25–34). On the lack of faith, see references to faithless (Mark 6:6; 9:19, 24; cf. Matt 13:58) and little faith (Matt 6:30; 8:26; 14:31; 18:8; 17:20; Luke 12:28), which seems to be no different from no faith.

In Mark 11:31 = Matt 21:25 = Luke 20:5 Jesus corners the Jewish authorities with a question about John which they know they cannot answer because the popular answer would lead to the question, "Why did you not believe him?" Here believe means to accept his message and obey it. See also Mark 13:21 = Matt 24:23; 24:26; Matt 24:32; Luke 1:20; 1:45; 22:67; 24:25. In explaining the parable of the seed (the Sower in Matthew; the soil in Mark) only Luke puts the language of believing on the lips of Jesus, Luke 8. 12–13. The snatching away of the seed (= the word) prevents belief, and the stony ground allows no roots to develop so that such belief in the word as may develop does not survive the test of time.

In Mark 11:22–24 = Matt 21:21–22 Jesus' cursing of the fig tree followed by the disciples'

observation that it was dead led Jesus to say, "Have faith [in the word] of God." Here again the sense of trust seems to be paramount. The incident is followed by sayings of Jesus about the effectiveness of their prayers if they ask with unwavering belief (compare Matt 17:20 = Luke 17:6 (Q?)). Had these sayings not followed the reference to God they would be open to an interpretation of self-confidence but, in context, must be read in terms of confidence in God.

In Mark 15:32 = Matt 27:42 = Luke 23:35 (lacks believe) the Jewish leaders call on Jesus to come down from his cross that they may see and believe that he is the Christ the king of Israel. This mocking taunt has no expectation of fulfilment.

In Matt 8:10 = Luke 7:9 (Q?) Jesus is approached by a centurion (a nobleman in Luke) who showed such faith that Jesus remarked that he had not found such faith in Israel. This is again the trust that is the basis of a healing act but exceeds other examples. Compare Matt 15:28 = Mark 7:29. Mark lacks the use of faith though recording the commendation of the woman and the healing of her daughter. Matt 23:23 (= Luke 11:42 omits faith) lists faith as a virtue alongside justice and mercy. Here faith has the Hebraic sense of faithfulness, trustworthiness. See also Luke 16:11. This theme in Matthew balances the prohibition of Gentile mission in 10:5 but needs to be understood in relation to gentile converts to Judaism and the terms of the mission to the nations in 28:19–20.

In Luke 22:32 Jesus tells Simon (Peter) that he has prayed for him that his faith may not fail. Although the context of the words is found in the other gospels, Luke 22:31–32 has no parallel. Here faith has the sense of commitment and faithfulness. This suggests that Peter's faithlessness be understood as temporary and supports the view that discipleship in the Synoptics involves faith, that is, believing the message Jesus preached and accepting the reign of God revealed in his activity. It is trusting in God whose loving rule was revealed in Jesus. In this sense, though the language of faith and belief is not used of Jesus in the Synoptics, Jesus is the exemplar par. excellence of the life of faithful trust in God. Implicitly, believing in the gospel of God proclaimed by Jesus was a transformation of the understanding of God (see Matt 6:43–48).

John

John stands out from the other gospels with ninety-eight uses of believe, especially as the Jesus of John seems to be preoccupied with the necessity of believing in him. Almost half of the uses of the verb in the NT occur in John, providing a full range of syntactical constructions: to believe, with no stated object often expresses genuine faith at the time; or followed by prepositions "in" and "into" to express the personal faith relationship; followed by "that," to introduce a theological view such as "that Jesus is the Christ"; followed by the dative case, often to indicates believing a speaker. Thus believing involves a degree of perception into the mystery of Jesus, a commitment to him involving faithful following, a trust in God revealed in Jesus in the obedience of faith.

John 2:23–24 provides two related uses of the verb. First, "Many believed on his name seeing the signs that he did" (cf. 1:12). The description looks like a genuine deep commitment of faith. Two things warn the reader familiar with John that all is not quite as it seems. This is belief based on seeing signs and further evidence proves such belief to be unstable (4:48; 6:26–27, 30; 20:29). And yet the narrative account of the signs of Jesus has the potential to initiate belief that leads to eternal life (20:30–31). The conclusive warning is in 2:24. Though they believed in him Jesus did not believe in them. He did not trust them.

The narrator and Jesus are the two large-scale discoursers about the nature and purpose of believing. Many of the characters in the gospel story also speak about believing in Jesus, the Samaritans (4:42); the once blind man (9:36, 38); the crowd (6:30); Peter for the disciples (6:69); Martha (11:27); Thomas (20:25). There are also important expressions of believing that do not use this vocabulary, such as Andrew's report to Simon/Peter, "We have found the Messiah" (1:41), and Nathanael's response, "Rabbi, you are the Son of God, you are the king of Israel" (1:49). The narrator sums up the purposes of the written gospel, which is understood as a narration of signs. The purpose was to lead readers to believe that Jesus is the Christ the Son of God, to believe in his name. This purpose serves another, to realise God's gift of eternal life (20:30–31).

In John 14:1 Jesus tells his disciples "you believe in God, believe also in me." Belief in Jesus is coordinated with belief in God. In John believing and knowing are coordinated in a way that the one illuminates the other. Thus in John 17:3 Jesus says, "This is eternal life, to know you, the only true God, and Jesus Christ whom you have sent." Distinctive to John is Jesus' reference to God as "the Father who sent me" (5:23, 24, 30, 37; 6:38, 39, 44; 7:16, 18, 28, 33; etc.), which underlies his claim to do the work of God (5:17; 9:4). Jesus does only what he sees God (his Father) doing, and the Father reveals to him all that he does (5:19–20), he has given all things into his hand (3:35). Jesus speaks only what he hears from the Father (3:34). Jesus is sustained by doing the will of the Father (4:34). Consequently to believe in Jesus is to believe in the Father who sent him (5:24).

The Johannine concentration on belief in Jesus can be seen as a massive theological development of the Synoptic account of Jesus as the proclaimer of the gospel of God. By announcing the dawning of the kingdom of God in his own ministry and calling on his hearers to repent and believe the gospel, the Jesus of the Synoptics, as much as the Jesus of John, proclaimed a revolutionary understanding of God, though John has more consistently developed this in terms of God's love for the world (3:16) and by making the fulfilment of the love command the basis for the recognition of his disciples in the world (13:34–35) by which the world may come to believe and know Jesus as the one sent by the Father in love for the world (17:20–26, especially 21, 23, 26; cf. 17:18; 20:21). What is implicit in the belief of the Synoptics is explicit in John's understanding of God.

JOHN PAINTER

Further reading

Bultmann, R and A. Weiser, "πιστεύω κτλ.," in Gerhard Kittel (ed.) *Theological Dictionary of the New Testament*, Grand Rapids, MI: Eerdmans, 1964–76, Vol. VI, pp. 174–228.

Painter, J., *John Witness and Theologian*, London: SPCK, 1979, 71–100.

——"Eschatological Faith in the Gospel of John," in R. Banks (ed.) *Reconciliation and Hope*, Grand Rapids, MI: Eerdmans, 1974, pp. 36–52.

—— *The Quest for the Messiah*, Nashville, TN: Abingdon, 2005, pp. 226–49.

FAMILY

In Jesus' day, social life revolved about two major poles: politics and kinship, realized in city/town and house/household (the usual words for "family"). As the Alexandrian Philo observed: "There are two types of organized communities (*poleis*): the larger and the smaller. The larger ones are called 'cities,' (Gk. *astê*) and the smaller ones 'households' (Gk. *oikiai*)" (*Spec. Laws* 3.169). Religion and economics were embedded in each. There was political religion (the Jerusalem Temple) and political economy (Temple and elite production and consumption) as well as domestic religion (ancestor reverence, Sabbath and daily prayers) and domestic economy (family production and consumption).

Family analysis has two conceptual dimensions: the family of orientation and the family of reproduction. The former consists of the whole kin group into which a person is born, the latter consists of self and spouse, offspring and (grand)parents. Given the fact that Western society is largely individualistic, talk of "family" means family of reproduction. For collectivistic societies such as those of Jesus' times, "house/household" meant family of orientation, the whole kin group, including the family of reproduction. In Israel, the family was patriarchal, patrilineal and patrilocal. Ideally, the patriarchal family arranged largely endogamous and customarily monogamous marriages, and at times insisted on divorce. This family type was characterized by a moral division of labor, with men's work outside the residence, facing outward, and women's work largely confined to the residence, facing inward.

> Marketplaces and council chambers, and courts of justice, and large groups and assemblies of crowds, and a life in the open-air full of arguments and actions relating to war and peace are suited to men. But taking care of the house and remaining at home are the proper duties of women; the virgins having their rooms in the center of the house within the innermost doors and the full-grown women not going beyond the vestibule and outer courts.
>
> (Philo, *Spec. Laws* 3.169)

The gender-divided world endowed the male line (males and females) with entitlements, inheritance, obligation to maintain family honor. The wife's family had no obligations to her and her children apart from ties of affection. Within the family, the closest *bonds of obligation* were to father and mother, who were to be maintained and obeyed. However *bonds of affection and support* ranked siblings first; then mother and oldest son, married or not; mother and other children; then wife and husband; and father and children. First cousins were as close as siblings in Western society. (Consider the relation of Jesus and John the Baptist in Luke, Jesus and his mother, James the brother of Jesus in Acts.) Oldest males might put off marriage to help support younger siblings – which perhaps best explains Jesus' unmarried condition at the time of his divine call.

Archaeological evidence from the Galilee of Jesus' day attests to four types of family dwellings, hence four types of family. The least usual type (perhaps 1 percent) might be called the mansion, a very large house with room for the ideal extended family: father, mother, unmarried children, one or more married sons with wives and children, other family members (e.g. parents), and a number of slaves or indentured servants, with outbuildings for animals and storage. This house indicated a household of a wealthy landowner and/or local ruler (family of Herod Antipas in Mark 6:21; the great ones and the seventy or so leading families of Galilee noted by Josephus, *Life* 14.79; 44.220). The stories of slaves in the gospels use scenarios of the greedy rich and their large houses.

The second type (about 9 percent) was the courtyard house which was residence to multiple conjugal units of brothers, their wives and children, and the parents of the brothers. Each of the conjugal units had their own living quarters abutting on and facing a common space, the courtyard with its oven, barn, silo, well, and the like. Such houses were the majority in medium-sized towns such as Capernaum and Bethsaida, border towns inhabited by tax collectors, soldiers, merchants, fishermen as well as farmers (see Mark 1:16–20; 2:14; Luke 7:1–10).

The third type (70–75 percent) was the one-room house, made of sun-dried brick, offering housing and minimal storage for a nucleated family and its animals (if any). Common ovens and common wells served a village full of such families. These were the houses of small farmers and day laborers. Such families are called nucleated since they were largely cut off from their traditional land holdings by the taxation and usurpation of the greedy rich. They were simply unable to attain the ideal of an extended family in its own courtyard house or mansion. Family members numbered from four to six. To this category belonged the crowds that followed Jesus (see Mark 12:1–11; Matt 20:1–16).

The fourth type (15–20 percent) was the place where homeless people might congregate: caves, groves near cities, or on city streets if possible. This category included the permanently sick, beggars from disbanded nucleated families, widows and orphans without relatives, bandits and thieves, the disinherited. These were socially throw-away people.

Jesus was closely linked largely with persons of the multiple unit courtyard families, it seems. When he needed assistance, he recruited two sets of brothers, Simon and Andrew and John and James (Mark 1:16–20; Matt 4:18–22; Luke 5:1–11); Simon's mother-in-law lived with them (Mark 1:29–31; Matt 8:14–15; Luke 4:38–39), and soon after a well-situated tax collector (Mark 2:13–15; Matt 9:9–10; Luke 5:27–29). In response to Peter's reminder that the disciples assisting Jesus had left everything worthwhile in collectivistic society, Jesus answers:

Truly, I say to you, there is no one who has left house or brothers or sisters or mother or father or children or lands, for my sake and for the gospel, who will not receive a hundredfold now in this time, houses and brothers and sisters and mothers and children and lands, with persecutions, and in the age to come eternal life.

(Mark 10:29–30; Matt 19:29 and Luke 18:29–30 are truncated)

Note the absence of a father in the list of promised relations. Perhaps this is behind the saying in Matt 23:9: "and call no man your father on earth, for you have on Father who is in heaven," and in the previous verse: "you are all brothers." The list of what one has left fits the multiple family. The absent son-in-law in the Q saying about household division indicates that daughters marry out: "they will be divided, father against son and son against father, mother against daughter and daughter against her mother, mother-in-law against daughter-in-law and daughter-in-law against her mother-in-law" (Luke 12:53; Matt 10:35).

Jesus' real family is a fictive kin group: "Whoever does the will of God is my brother and sister and mother" (Mark 3:35; Matt 12:50; Luke 8:21 leaves out sister). While Jesus addressed his fellows in the house of Israel as brothers and sisters, by the second and third generation the Synoptic Gospels indicate that members of Jesus's following were "brothers and sisters" (for example, throughout the Sermon on the Mount/Plain, Matt 5–7 and Luke 6:20–49).

Jesus' advice to his disciples is that they are to serve, "whoever would be great among you must be your servant, and whoever would be first among you must be your slave of all" (Mark 10:43–44; 9:35; Matt 20:26–27; 23:11). They are to be as Jesus himself who came "as one who serves" (Luke 22:26–27 and John 13:12–17). This reversal of patriarchal entitlement would place the disciples among brothers in the matriline, e.g. the maternal uncle (Greek: *mêtrôs*, Latin: *avunculus*, English: *uncle*, German: *oheim*). The mother's brother related to his sister and her children without entitlement or precedence. And just as females were always embedded in some male (father, brothers, husband), so too males were always embedded in father and paternal uncles or in higher-status fictive kin such as patrons. It is this mother's brother role rather than patriarchal role that Jesus asks of his first disciples.

BRUCE J. MALINA

Further reading

Guijarro, Santiago. "The Family in First-Century Galilee," in Halvor Moxnes (ed.) *Constructing Early Christian Families: Family as Social Reality and Metaphor*, New York and London: Routledge, 1997, pp. 42–65.

Hanson, K. C. and Douglas E. Oakman. *Palestine in the Time of Jesus: Social Structures and Social Conflicts*, Minneapolis, MN: Fortress Press, 1998.

Pilch, John J. "A Window into the Biblical World: The Family: Status and Roles," *TBT* 40:6 (2002) 386–91.

Williams, Ritva H. *Stewards, Prophets, Keepers of the World: Leadership in the Early Church*, Peabody, MA: Hendrickson, 2006, pp. 9–56.

FASTING

People say things with goods. And food has always been a symbolic medium of communication, from feasting to fasting. Fasting refers to refraining from food and drink over a period of time. Such behavior can be directed either to oneself or to others. When directed to oneself such behavior is functional and is better called dieting (for weight control) or abstaining from food (in preparation for a medical procedure, or a vision). When not eating or drinking is directed to others, it is a form of symbolic behavior that is intended to communicate one's condition of distress, usually with a view to obtaining alleviation and support from another. It is a form of negative communication, saying something by not speaking, such as the silent treatment intended to communicate one's feelings and judgment to another by saying nothing in circumstances that warrant comment or conversation. Thus as a category of negative communication, fasting is to be distinguished from other forms of refraining from eating and drinking, and considered a form of social communication. For example, political prisoners who have access to reporters will undertake a fast to say something to the public about their unjust plight.

As is commonly known, all theology (reasoned understandings of God) as well as all forms of interacting with God (worship forms) are based upon analogies or comparisons. God is always "like" someone in human experience, for example a father, a loving person, an omnipotent king, and the like. Similarly, interacting with God follows the behaviors humans employ in having an effect on their higher status fellows. Such behaviors include modes of access to higher status persons (ritual), modes of making requests or petitions (prayer), and the like. In the Bible, popular analogical behaviors for approaching God include taking on the role of a mourner or a beggar. The reason for this is that in Mediterranean societies, when people mourn they receive assistance and support from their family, friends, and village mates. And for people to beg is to humiliate themselves in face of their fellows, who invariably lend assistance in face of such willingness to dishonor oneself. The belief was that if people are willing to offer help to mourners and beggars, so too God, and this all the more so.

Thus, as a ritual practice directed to God, voluntary fasting works by analogy with the involuntary fasting of people afflicted with social evil (e.g. death of a spouse, of one's child, war, the prospect of famine) or in a permanent state of distress and humiliation (e.g. beggars). These socially afflicted people either cannot eat or do not have anything to eat; they are disheveled, unconcerned about their looks or unable to wash or dress properly. Ritual mourning before God includes not sleeping (keeping vigil), not eating or drinking, unconcern with dress or grooming, and lamenting. When focus is on seeking assistance from God, the adoption of a beggar's sackcloth and unwashed appearance (ashes), coupled with not eating or drinking and begging (prayer) is ritually appropriate.

This fasting form of communication addressed to the God of Israel with a view to assistance is well attested from the Persian period on. In Leviticus 23: 27, 29, 32, the Day of Atonement involves self-affliction (another name for the mourning/fasting ritual, see Num 29:7; Ps 35:13). The story in 2 Sam 12:16–23 tells of David fasting when his child became ill, then abruptly stopping when the child died. 1 Kgs 21:9–27 tells of Jezebel, in King Achab's name, calling a fast obliging the whole populace in the face of the alleged evil done by Naboth, namely that "Naboth cursed God and the king" (1 Kgs 21:13). The real evil, of course, was Jezebel and Achab's desire for Naboth's vineyard and their killing him. Well known is the passage in Joel in which the prophet urges proclaiming a fast in face of the drought afflicting the land (Joel 1:14), during which ministers of the altar are to put on sackcloth and spend the night in sackcloth and lament (Joel 1:13; 2:12–15). In the Israelite tradition, references to fasting behaviors in face of social evil are quite numerous (Judg 20:26; 1 Sam 7:6; 31:13; Ezra 8:21.23; 9:5; Neh 1:4–5; 9:1; Esther 4:3.15; 9:31). Fasting is a form of self-humiliation (Isa 58:3.5; Ps 69:10; Jdt 4:9). One must set aside sense of honor expressed by self-composure, food and clothing since one fasts while dressed in sackcloth with ashes on the head (1 Macc 3:47); weeping and lying prostrate (2 Macc 13:12; Bar 1:5). Popular piety is expressed in Tobit 12:8: "Prayer is good when accompanied by fasting, almsgiving, and righteousness," a collocation found also in Matt 6. On the other hand, Isaiah 58:3–6 offers a penetrating critique of those who fast in face of social evil but continue to act

immorally toward their fellows (see also Zech 7:3–5; see Jer 14:12).

Interestingly a passage in *4 Ezra* 5 connects fasting with the dieting practiced by persons seeking altered state of consciousness experiences, in this case access to the celestial "presence of the Most High." Such an experience, part of his holy man formation, is ascribed to Jesus in the Q temptation accounts (Luke 4:1–13 where Luke refers to dieting, "he ate nothing," and Matt 4:1–11 refers to "fasting").

As is well known, the passage in Mark 2:18–19 resolutely describes Jesus as a non-fasting person, unlike Pharisee and John the Baptist groups (who fasted twice weekly aside from the Day of Atonement). By all criteria, this posture of Jesus is judged to be quite authentic. Jesus' wedding parable in v. 20 presumes that fasting communicates a protest to God about the presence of evil, hence one can imagine the insult to honor that fasting at a wedding feast would provoke. The allusion presumes that the events surrounding Jesus' activities are something like a wedding feast – a time of rejoicing, enjoyment, exuberance, and social pleasure.

On the other hand, as Mark 2:20b indicates, early Jesus groups fasted. What did that fasting mean? Paul expected mourning behavior rather than arrogance in face of Corinthian support for the man who married his step-mother (1 Cor 5:2). The beatitudes in Matthew's Sermon on the Mount point to those who fast and mourn before God, protesting the absence of righteousness in Israel (Matt 5:4.6). However Luke's beatitudes describe Jesus' consoling those in continual humiliation due to social conditions, a situating better befitting Jesus' activity (Luke 6:21–25).

BRUCE J. MALINA

Further reading

Malina. Bruce J. *Christian Origins and Cultural Anthropology: Practical Models for Biblical Interpretation*, Philadelphia. PA: John Knox. 1986.

FELLOWSHIP, SHARING

The historical Jesus was not a lonely wanderer in his ministry. Although he sometimes withdrew, the sources depict him as surrounded by disciples and sometimes also a wider audience. Hence the topic of fellowship and sharing develops naturally from our knowledge of the historical Jesus, albeit the topic is not easily connected with particular keywords.

Fellowship and sharing as life-style

Two kinds of followers

The Synoptic Gospels unanimously depict Jesus as master of a group of disciples. These formed the inner circle of his friends. They left behind their domestic life to follow Jesus (Moxnes 2003: 46–71). The life of discipleship implied renouncing the means of a secure life. Following Jesus meant spending time together with him and fellow-disciples, as well as sharing with them the available sources. This "*Wanderradikalismus*" (Theissen 1977) brings to mind OT prophets, cynic philosophers as well as the ideal of friendship in Antiquity (Sandnes). "Following" (Gk. *akolouthein*) implies living according to a given ethical standard, which in Jesus' life becomes visible in the so-called Sermon on the Mount. Radical sharing here stands out as the ideal of a disciple.

This kind of discipleship was, however, dependent upon the loyalty within the group itself as well as the support of outsiders or residents who sympathized with the movement (Theissen 1977). Jesus was received in the homes of such followers (Mark 1:29 and parallels; Luke 10:38–42). Luke 8:1–2 holds a key position in the reconstruction of a double discipleship in the life of the historical Jesus. Here it says that some women served (*diakonein*) Jesus and his disciples with their resources. Thus sharing and fellowship were key values on which the whole project of Jesus depended, inside the inner circle as well as between the two kinds of followers.

Table-fellowship

Jesus' association with sinners and tax-collectors, which is witnessed in all strata of the sources, has some important bearings on the topics of fellowship and sharing. Jesus was polemically addressed as a glutton and drunkard, a friend of sinners and tax-collectors (Matt 11:19 and parallel). In Luke's Gospel this picture becomes a symbol of Jesus' ministry (Smith), but *in nuce* this symbol-making is present in the life of Jesus as well (Sanders). This fellowship brought him into conflict with the Pharisees, due to questions of cleanliness. For the present entry, however, two aspects are of special relevance. The table-fellowship with the outcasts is seen as an act of friendship (Gk. *philia*) towards them. The ancient ideal of friendship involved sharing. The sharing of time and providing necessary help were characteristics of friendship (Sandnes). In John's Gospel (15:15) the sharing of a friend extends even to laying down one's life – a traditional motif in ancient texts about friends. Jesus' fellowship with the marginalized implies a sharing beyond socially accepted conventions, thus bringing to mind the radical sharing which is called for in the Sermon on the Mount (see below).

In Greco-Roman sources, table talk is often a mode of teaching (Smith). In Jesus' ministry, his sharing meals carry symbolic meaning (cf. the symbolic actions of OT prophets). His eating with tax-collectors and sinners probably prefigured their inclusion into the kingdom of God. Thus the meals pointed towards the messianic banquet (Isa 25:6–8; Q 13:28–29). Hence, the sharing of a meal becomes a key notion in Jesus' parables, most vividly expressed in Luke 14:15–24 (cf. *Gos. Thom.* 64). In Luke, the fellowship with these groups encapsulates the meaning of Jesus' ministry. This fellowship also implies an agenda for the life of Jesus' followers, namely to put into practice a sharing fellowship according to the boundary-breaking nature of Jesus' table-fellowship. Luke is here more vocal than the other sources. Luke 7:36–50 speaks of a loving fellowship which forgiveness brings about (see also below).

Teaching fellowship and sharing

Fellowship and sharing in the Sermon on the Mount

Although Matthew's version of this sermon is due to considerable editorial work, it still conveys a core of Jesus' teaching on the topic of the present entry. Matt 5:38–6:3, 19–21; 7:12, with some synoptic parallels in Luke, pave the way to the centre of Jesus' notion of sharing. The treasures to be sought are to be found in heaven, and a sharing life is the means of finding them. A scribe is asked to give to the needy what he owns in order to find this treasure (Mark 10:17–31). Jesus opposes the ethic of revenge (an eye for an eye, etc.) found in the OT. He urges his disciples to share, making no distinctions between enemy and neighbour. The love and care usually shown for family and fellowmen is extended even to enemies (H. D. Betz). In Matt 7:12 (Luke 6:31) he coins the so-called Golden Rule, which has analogies in Greco-Roman as well as in Jewish texts (P. S. Alexander), albeit mostly formulated in terms of what to avoid.

Imitatio Dei

Jesus teaches a fellowship and sharing which takes God's impartiality as example to be imitated. He teaches an *imitatio Dei*, taking as example God as the protector and helper of the poor, the orphans, widows and helpless among the people in the OT. This kind of fellowship challenges obligations of reciprocity and mutuality between benefactor and beneficiary (Luke 14:7–14; Moxnes 1988). In this text, the nature of the kingdom of God is also indicative of an altruistic lifestyle.

From this it follows that Jesus saw neglecting the poor as well as greed as amounting to abandoning the God of the fathers and mistrust towards him (Luke 12:13–33; 16:19–31). This teaching is inspired by OT texts on the year of jubilee, in which there will be no needy among God's people, and as for the greed, the discourse on mastering the desires in Greco-Roman philosophy is a relevant analogy.

Jesus identifies with those in need. Benefactions shown against his emissaries are, in fact, services rendered to himself (Matt 10: 40–42; Luke 10:16). According to Matt 25:31–46, Jesus speaks in the same vein, although "the little ones" with whom Jesus identify might here include all people in need.

KARL OLAV SANDNES

Further reading

Alexander, Philip S. "Jesus and the Golden Rule," in J. D. G. Dunn and S. McKnight (eds) *The Historical Jesus in Recent Research*, Winona Lake, IN: Eisenbrauns, 2005, pp. 489–508.

Betz, Hans Dieter. "The Sermon on the Mount: A Commentary on the Sermon on the Mount, including the Sermon on the Plain (Matthew 5:3–7:27 and Luke 6:20–49)," *Hermeneia*, Minneapolis, MN: Fortress Press, 1995.

Moxnes, Halvor. *The Economy of the Kingdom. Social Conflict and Economic Relations in Luke's Gospel*, Philadelphia, PA: Fortress Press, 1988.

—— *Putting Jesus in His Place: A Radical Vision of Household and Kingdom*, Louisville, KY: Westminster John Knox, 2003.

Sanders, E. P. "Jesus and the Sinners," in C. A. Evans and S. E. Porter (eds) *The Historical Jesus*, Sheffield: Sheffield Academic Press, 2001, pp. 29–60.

Sandnes, Karl Olav. "'I Have Called You Friends': An Aspect of the Christian Fellowship within the Context of the Antique Family," in *The New Testament in Its Hellenistic Context*, Studia theologica islandica 10, Reykjavik, 1996, pp. 95–111.

Smith, D. E. "Table Fellowship as a Literary Motif in the Gospel of Luke," *JBL* 106 (1987) 613–38.

Theissen, Gerd. *Soziologie der Jesusbewegung*, München: Chr. Kaizer Verlag 1977.

—— *Die Jesusbewegung: Sozialgeschichte einer Revolution der Werte*, Gütersloh: Gütersloher Verlagshaus, 2004.

FESTIVALS AND FEASTS, JEWISH

Jewish feasts and festivals are deeply rooted in the annual cycle of harvests and interpreted in light of Israel's covenantal history. Beside the weekly Sabbath (Shabbat) and the monthly New Moon (Rosh Kodesh) the main agriculture-related festivals are the springtime Feast of Unleavened Bread (Mazzot), of Weeks (Pentecost or Shavuot) early in summer and of Tabernacles (also Booths or Sukkoth) in fall. All three are also main feasts of pilgrimage. In addition to these there are the Feasts of Passover (Pessach) and a number of other notable days like the Feast of Dedication (also Feast of Lights or Hanukkah), the Feast of Lots (Purim), the Day of Atonement (Yom Kippur) or the celebration of the Jewish New Year (Rosh HaShannah).

In the NT only the Jewish feasts of Passover, Weeks, Tabernacles and Dedication are mentioned. They reveal on the one hand how Jesus and his followers were engaged with the Jewish calendar of their time and on the other how little the early Christian authors of the NT were interested in the Jewish festal calendar.

The festal calendar of ancient Judaism

The probably earliest festal calendars of Israel (Exod 23:14–17; 34:18, 22f.) only know of the aforementioned three great pilgrimage festivals. An enlarged calendar appears in the book of Leviticus (Lev 23:1–44) and a somehow final festival calendar within the Pentateuch appears in the book of Numbers (Num 28f.). The festivals which are to be celebrated with a "holy convocation" (Lev 23:3, 7f., 21, etc.; Num 28:18, 25f.; 29:1, etc.) include the weekly Sabbath (Lev 23:3; cf. Num 28:9–10) and every year altogether seven feast days: Passover and Unleavened Bread (Lev 23:5–8; cf. Num 28:16–25), Omer/First Fruits of Barley (Lev 23:9–14), Weeks (Lev 23:15–22; cf. Num 28:26–31), New Year (Lev 23:24–25; cf. Num 29:1–6), the Day of Atonement (Lev 23:27–32 cf. Num 29:7–11) and the first and the eighth day of Tabernacles (Lev 23:34–36, 39–43; cf. Num 29:12–34). In addition to the feasts also mentioned in Lev 23, the Feast of New Moon (Num 28:11–15) is added in Numbers where the Feast of Omer is missing (cf. Lev 23:10–14; cf. also the much shorter calendars in Deut 16. and Ezek 45). The Feasts of Dedication (1 Macc 4:36–59) and of Lots (Esth 9:16–32) are of later post-exilic origin. Philo has a list of altogether ten feasts (Philo *Spec. Laws* 2 11.41) starting with "every day" as a festival. Only introduced during the later Rabbinic Period and thus not known in Jesus' time are the Feasts of Simchat Torah ("Rejoicing in the Torah") and Tish B'Av ("ninth day of the month of Av"). The different festal calendars should remind readers of the NT that the Jewish festival procedures of the first century CE were not uniform. The following treatment is limited to the main feasts and those which are relevant for the historical Jesus.

The Jewish feasts and festivals in the time of Jesus

Sabbath

In Judaism the Sabbath or Shabbat as the last day of the week is the only one with a name, while the other days are merely numbered. As being mentioned in the Decalogue (Exod 20:8-11 par. Deut 5:12-15) it is considered the day of absolute rest without any exceptions. This is reinforced many times throughout the OT (Exod 23:12; 34:21; Lev 23:3). The reason given for this is the resting of God at the end of week of creation (Exod 20:11; 31:17; cf. Gen 2:1-3; different Deut 5:15 where the Exodus from Egypt is given as a reason for the Sabbath rest). A notable exception from the prohibition of work on the Sabbath is well established when human life is in danger (1 Macc 2:29-41).

During Second Temple Judaism Sabbath observance had become a Jewish identity marker (cf. J. D. G. Dunn), which by outsiders was sometimes admired (Josephus *Ag. Ap.* 2.40:282; Philo *Vit. Mos.* 2.21), sometimes viewed with scorn (Josephus *Ag. Ap.* 2.2:20-21). It led to the excusal from military service (Josephus *Ant.* 14.10.12:226f.) since Jews would not march forbidden lengths nor carry arms on this day.

The NT Gospels portray Jesus as customarily going to the synagogue on the Sabbath day (Mark 1:21, 29; 3:1; Luke 4:16, 44; 13:10 etc.). This indicates that Sabbath worship was part of his weekly routine. However, among the eight Sabbath incidents which are recorded in the four gospels, altogether six times Jesus appears to be in conflict with Sabbath *halakah*. These are: the plucking of grain by his disciples (Matt 12:1-8//Mark 2:23-28//Luke 6:1-5), the healing of the withered hand (Matt 12:9-14//Mark 3:1-6//Luke 6:6-11), of the crippled woman (Luke 13:10-17), of a man with dropsy (Luke 14:1-6), of a lame man at the pool of Bethzatha (John 5:1-18) and of a man born blind (John 9:1-41). For other reasons his rejection at his inaugural sermon at his home synagogue in Nazareth provides another example of Jesus in conflict on a Sabbath. Only Jesus' exorcism in the Capernaum synagogue (Mark 1:21-28//Luke 4:31-37) and the healing of Peter's mother-in-law (Mark 1:29-31) do not contain any controversy over the Sabbath. However, one should not make the mistake of concluding that Jesus' actions overthrow the Sabbath altogether. Jesus' pronouncement that "the Sabbath was made for humankind, and not humankind for the sabbath; so then the Son of Man is lord even of the sabbath" (Mark 2:27f., NRSV) indicates that Jesus" rather rejects Sabbath *halakah* in order to restore the Sabbath to its original function to serve humankind and not vice versa.

Passover

What may originally have been an ancient rite of shepherds at the beginning of leading their herds to the summer meadows (Rost) was later transformed to commemorate the Exodus from Egypt. The earliest occurrence in the OT is Exod 12:21-23, 27. The blood sprinkled at the entrances of the dwelling places of the Israelites (Exod 12:12f., 23) in order to avert the destroyer identifies the origin of Passover as an apotropaic rite. It was originally celebrated in each family's home. An unblemished lamb was slaughtered in the afternoon of the 14th of Abib/Nisan, which is called the "Day of Preparation." Then just after sunset, i.e. the beginning of the 15th of Abib/Nisan, the lamb is eaten. Anyone who was unclean or away on a journey at Passover had to celebrate a second Passover (Num 9:9-12).

During the Second Temple period large numbers of pilgrims went up to Jerusalem (Josephus *J.W.* 6.420f.), as did Jesus' parents each year (Luke 2:41f.). While Jesus and his disciples are portrayed in the Synoptic Gospels as celebrating only one Passover (Matt 26:2//Mark 14:1//Luke 22:1, etc.), the Fourth Gospel portrays them at three different Passovers (John 2:13; 6:4; 11:55; cf. 12:1, 12, 20; 13:1; 18:28). The practice of the Roman governor to release an imprisoned Jew at Passover (Matt 27:15; John 18:39) is otherwise without attestation.

According to the Synoptic Gospels, Jesus' final meal with his disciples (Matt 26:26-29//Mark 14:22-25//Luke 22:15-20) was a Passover meal. This is even emphasized in Luke where Jesus says: "I have eagerly desired to eat this Passover with you before I suffer" (Luke 22:15, NRSV). In early Christianity this Passover meal of Jesus and his disciples was interpreted as the installation of Lord's Supper (cf. 1 Cor 11:23-26). In contrast to the Synoptic account John dates Jesus' farewell meal one day earlier, i.e. the "Day of Preparation". According to John, Jesus dies precisely at the time when the Passover lambs are slaughtered in the Temple (John 13:1f.; 18:28; 19:31-34; cf. the Passover typology in John 1:29, 36; 19:36 and the comparison between Jesus and the paschal lamb in 1 Cor 5:7; 1 Pet 1:19; Rev 5:6, 9, 12). These different chronologies cannot be reconciled historically.

Unleavened bread

The Feast of Unleavened Bread for seven days in the month of Abib/Nisan (Exod 23:15; 34:18) also commemorates the exodus from Egypt (Exod 13:3–10; Deut 16:3f., etc.). It marks the beginning of the barley harvest in spring. During this week yeast is removed and thus only unleavened bread consumed. Later rabbinic practice (*m. Pesah* 1:1–4) puts emphasis on the removal of leaven from each Jewish household.

While in pre-Deuteronomic times a separate feast (Lev 23:4–7 cf. Josephus *J.W.* 2:280; 6:423–24), the Feast of Unleavened Bread was integrated into the Passover (Deut 16:1–8; cf. Josephus *Ant.* 17:213; 18:29; 20:106). While it would be more accurate to say that the Feast of Unleavened Bread begins only after the Passover, the NT Gospels basically identify both (Matt 26:17; Mark 14:1// Luke 22:1; Mark 14:12//22:7).

Weeks

The completion of the grain harvest is celebrated with the Festival of Weeks (Deut 16:9), also called Pentecost or Shavuot. Its Greek name Pentecost reflects its date of seven weeks, i.e. fifty days in Hebrew counting, after the entire festival of Passover and Unleavened Bread (Lev 23:15–21; Num 28:26; Deut 16:9–12). Later by the time of the book of Jubilees (second century BCE) it had also adopted the commemoration of the Mosaic covenant and the giving of the Torah to Moses on Mount Sinai (*Jub.* 1:1–26; Exod 19–20) as well as with the covenants of Noah (*Jub.* 6:1, 10f., 17–19) and of Abraham (*Jub.* 15:1–16). In the NT the name Pentecost occurs only in Acts 2:1; 20:16; 1 Cor 16:8.

New Year

The first day of the seventh month, called Tishri, is celebrated with a blowing of the Shofar (Lev 23:24; Num 29:1), Sabbath rest and a "holy convocation" (Lev 23:23–25; cf. Num 29:1). After the Babylonian exile the burnt offerings were reestablished by Ezra "on the first day of the seventh month" (Ezra 3:6; Neh 8:2). The Mishnah knows four different beginnings of the Jewish year (*m. Roš Haš.* I,1): the 1st of Nisan (in March) as new year for counting the years of reign of Israelite kings and of feasts; the 1st of Elul (in August) for the tithe of cattle;

the 1st of Tishri (in September) for counting the years of foreign eras; the 1st of Shebat (in February) for trees, in order to know when their fruit is ripe enough to be eaten.

Day of Atonement

Celebrated as a day of rest, fasting and sacrifice, the annual Day of Atonement or Yom Kippur is meant to serve the purification of the temple, land and people of Israel (Lev 16:1–34; 23:26–32; Num 29:7–11). Outside the priestly source of the Pentateuch the earliest mention of the Day of Atonement is in the second-century BCE book of Jubilees (*Jub.* 34:17–19; cf. 1QpHab 11:6–8).

Although the Day of Atonement is not mentioned in the NT its imagery is adapted to interpret the death of Jesus as atonement for sins (Rom 3:25; Heb 2:17).

Tabernacles

Tabernacles, also referred to as The Feast of Booths or Sukkoth, appears in the earliest OT festal calendars as "festival of ingathering at the end of the year" (Exod 23:16; 34:22). Its date is a full week from the 15th of the month of Tishri onwards with "holy convocations" on the first and eighth days (Lev 23:35f.). At this time of the year grapes and olives were taken in. It is a feast of great joy and the best-attended of the pilgrimages (Josephus *Ant.* 8:100). As the principal festival of ancient Israel it is sometimes referred to as the "Feast of the Lord" (Lev 23:39; Judg 21:19) without any further specification.

The Feast of Tabernacles may predate Israel (Judg 9:29), but for Israel it became a commemoration of the forty years of wandering in the desert where the Israelites had to live in booths (Lev 23:33–36, 39–43; Deut 16:13–15). During the Second Temple period the most outstanding features of the festival were, besides the camping out in huts, the ceremonial drawing of water each morning from the pool of Siloam and the light provided by large lamps which were lit every night in the court of the women. In the Johannine narrative the Feast of Tabernacles provides the background for one of Jesus' visits to Jerusalem (John 7:2) and also the imagery for Jesus' self-revelation as the one who brings salvation: outpoured water (cf. John 7:37f.) and light (cf. John 8:12) become metaphors for Jesus. The identification of the unspecified feast mentioned in John 5:1 with the Feast of Tabernacles (*v.l.* inserts Feast of Tabernacles or Unleavened Bread) is unwarranted.

Dedication

The Seleucid Ruler Antochus IV Epiphanes dese-crated the Jerusalem temple in 167 BCE. However, after the success of the Maccabean Revolt the temple was cleansed and rededicated in 164 BCE (1 Macc 4:36–59; 2 Macc 10:1–8; Josephus *Ant.* 12 316–22). This event was to be remembered by an annual Feast of Dedication, of Lights or simply Hanukkah. The festival is celebrated among other rituals with the lighting of lamps (2 Macc 1:8, 18ff. cf. 1 Macc 4:50).

In the NT the Festival of Dedication is briefly mentioned in John 10:22.

Lots

The Feast of Lots or Purim commemorates Esther's deliverance from Haman's plan to kill all Persian Jews (Esth 9:20–28). According to Josephus it is celebrated on the 14th and 15th of the month of Adar in order to commemorate the revenge of the Persian Jews against their enemies (Josephus *Ant.* 11.291–92). Outside the book of Esther the Feast of Lots is also mentioned in 2 Macc 15:36 as Morde-cai's day (cf. Esth 3:7; 9:20–23; 10:3).

The identification of the unspecified feast men-tioned in John 5:1 (*v.l.* inserts) with the Feast of Lots (as with any other Jewish feast) is unwarranted.

CARSTEN CLAUSSEN

Further reading

Bloch, A. P. *The Biblical and Historical Background of the Jewish Holy Days*, second edition, New York: KTAV, 1980.

Chilton, B. D. "Festivals and Holy Days: Jewish." in C. A. Evans and S. E. Porter (eds) *Dictionary of New Testament Background: A Compendium of Contemporary Biblical Scholarship*, IVP Bible Dictionary Series, Downers Grove, IL: InterVarsity Press, 2000.

Elbogen, I. *Jewish Liturgy: A Comprehensive History*, trans. Raymond P. Scheindlin, Philadelphia, PA: Jewish Publication Society and New York: Jewish Theological Seminary of America, 1993.

Hoffman, L. A. *The Canonization of the Synagogue Service*, Notre Dame, IN, and London: University of Notre Dame Press, 1979.

Rabello, A. M. "L'observances des fêtes juives hébraiques dans l'Empire Romain." *ANRW* II.21:2, Berlin and New York: De Gruyter, 1983, pp. 1288–312.

Rochber-Halton, F. "Calendars." *ABD* 1 (1998) 810–14.

Rost, L. *Das kleine Credo und andere Studien zum Alten Testament*, Heidelberg: Quelle & Meyer, 1965, pp. 101ff.

Schauss, H. *The Jewish Festivals: History and Observance*, New York: Schocken, 1962.

FOOD, HUNGER

Normal foods in Palestine included meat, fruit and vegetables though the staple diet was derived from a variety of grains. Meat was rare for the common people. Galilee was the grain bowl for Palestine. In the Roman Empire generally, large landholders who were often absentee farmers swallowed up small farms. In Palestine, because of taxes and other difficulties, small landholders were losing their farms through inability to repay debt. Unskilled workers found difficulty in finding work, and poverty was widespread. Against this back-ground it is not surprising that the teaching of Jesus included a significant focus on poverty and wealth as well as food and hunger.

Terminology

The word most used in the NT to denote food is ἄρτος, which literally means bread but, as the staple diet, comes to mean food generally (Hebr. לחם) (see Table 4).

Food language is concentrated in the gospels, though there is a concentration in 1 Cor 10–11 in dealing with the Lord's Supper. Four uses of ἄρτος in Acts may also refer to this observance. The fifth has a eucharistic resonance because the Last Supper was a characteristic Jewish meal in which Jesus gave thanks for the bread as Paul does in Acts 27:35. The Last Supper reminds us of Jesus' practice of sharing meals with his disciples. It is distinctive in that it was the last time he did this, and in that meal his foreboding vision was expressed in ways that became a foundation for the life of those who came to believe in his risen presence with them.

The Gospels provide examples of Jesus' practice of sharing meals (Mark 2:13–17 = Matt 9:9–13 = Luke 5:27–32; Mark 14:3–9 = Matt 26:6–13; Luke 7:36–50; John 12:1–8). On this basis his opponents, who dismissed John the Baptist as an ascetic extremist. labelled Jesus a drunken glutton (Matt 11:19 = Luke 7:34). Though Jesus had a serious concern for the plight of the poor, and he made pro-vision for the poor (John 12:5–6), he also affirmed the place of enjoying the good things of life.

The teaching of Jesus in Luke 6:20–21 reinforces his concern for the poor, "Blessed are you poor, because yours is the kingdom of God. Blessed are

Table 4 Use of ἄρτος in the New Testament

	Mark	Matt	Luke	John	Acts	Paul	Heb	Jas	NT total
ἄρτος	21	21	15	24	5	10	1		97
τροφή		4	1	1	7		2	1	16
βρῶμα	1	1	2	1		10	2		17
βρῶσις		2	4			4	1		11

you who hunger now, because you will be satisfied." In Luke Jesus addresses himself to those who are materially poor and physically hungry. But unless Jesus believed the coming kingdom was imminent this was cold comfort. His words to the rich and satisfied stand under the same eschatological threat (Luke 6:24–25). Yet Jesus pronounces a present blessing on the poor and hungry.

There is a concentration of feeding stories in the gospels. Mark narrates two feeding stories to a Jewish crowd of 5,000 (Mark 6:30–44 = Matt 14:13–21 = Luke 9:10–17; John 6:1–14) and a crowd of 4,000 in gentile territory (Mark 8:1–10 = Matt 15:32–39). While these accounts might have arisen from one feeding story, it coheres well with the picture of Jesus as one concerned about the physical welfare of those who followed him. In the shorter form of the prayer he taught his disciples (Luke 11:2–4), after the petitions about the hallowing of God's name and the coming of the kingdom, next is the petition for bread for today (cf. Matt 6:9–13 which may have Matthean elaborations).

Matthew's version of beatitudes (5:3, 6) varies from Luke in a number of ways. They are not addressed to such people but characterise them. They are not about material poverty and physical hunger but about spiritual qualities. "Blessed are the poor in spirit, because theirs is the kingdom of heaven." "Blessed are those who hunger and thirst after righteousness, because they shall be satisfied." Even so, the fulfilment remains future.

Matthew's spiritualised form of the beatitudes might arise from the Deuteronomic tradition that the testing of Israel in the wilderness was to teach them that "one does not live by bread alone but by every word that proceeds from the mouth of God" (8:3). It is fitting that, according to Matthew and Luke, the first temptation of Jesus in the wilderness was to turn stones into bread in order to satisfy his hunger. Jesus answered the tempter with the words of Deut 8:3 (Matt 4:4 and cf. Luke 4:4). Though Jesus asserted that there is more to life than bread, this recognition led to a symbolic development based on the analogy that, just as bread sustains the physical life, so there is spiritual bread that sustains the spiritual life.

By the time of Jesus bread had already become a symbol for that which sustains the spiritual life. Within Judaism bread, the manna, had become a symbol of the Law and of Wisdom. Against this background the Jesus of John says, "I am the bread of life, the one who comes to me shall not hunger, the one who believes in me shall never thirst" (John 6:35). The discourse, of which this saying is part (perhaps the text), follows John's

account of the feeding of the 5,000. Because the crowd Jesus had fed misunderstood his vocation, he separated himself from the crowd. When they again sought him the next day, Jesus at once distinguishes between the loaves they had eaten the day before and the food that abides to eternal life that the Son of Man will give them (John 6:26–27). They think that this is a reference to the manna, "bread from heaven" (Ps 78:24). Jesus then claims that God gives the true bread from heaven (John 6:31–33) and when they ask him to give them that bread he replies, "I am the bread of life ...," that is, the bread from heaven (6:34–35). This forms the basis of the following dialogue and discourse.

Though poverty and physical hunger were significant problems for the ordinary people amongst whom Jesus ministered, the gospels make quite clear that his concern went far beyond the physical survival of people. Material wealth and physical wellbeing fall behind hallowing the name of God, praying and working for the coming of the kingdom, listening to God's word and seeking to do God's will. But, for Jesus, these priorities could not become an excuse for ignoring the exploitation of the poor and the weak because such exploitation is contrary to God's will.

JOHN PAINTER

Further reading

Barrett, C. K. *The Gospel According to St John*, second edition, London: SPCK, 1978.

Behm, J. "ἄρτος," in Gerhard Kittel (ed.) *Theological Dictionary of the New Testament*, Grand Rapids, MI: Eerdmans, 1964–76, Vol. 1, pp. 477–78.

Borgen, P. *Bread from Heaven: On the Midrashic Exposition of the Manna Pericopae in the Homilies of Philo and the Gospel of John*, Leiden: Brill, 1965.

Painter, J. *The Quest for the Messiah: The History, Literature and Theology of the Johannine Community*, Nashville, TN: Abingdon, 1993, Ch. 6.

FORM CRITICISM

Form criticism is the English approximation of the German word *Formgeschichte*, which literally means "form history," and implies the critical study of the history of the development and use of literary forms, from the oral stage to the written stage. Classically understood, form criticism focuses upon the pre-literary stage of the tradition. By identifying the form, or genre, both of the literary subunits that make up a biblical book and of the book as a whole, interpreters hope to be able to understand the function that these discrete units and books had in the history of Israel and of the early church. Form criticism has been especially important in the study of the New Testament gospel and the origins and transmission of the Jesus tradition. As a discipline, form criticism developed first in Old Testament study, and then was adapted by New Testament critics. To understand the application of form criticism to the gospels, it is necessary to survey the method as it applies to all of biblical literature: Old Testament form criticism; and New Testament form criticism covering gospels, epistles and apocalyptic.

Old Testament form criticism

Old Testament form criticism has its roots in what Hermann Gunkel (1862–1932) called *Gattungsgeschichte* (lit. "analysis of genre"). Building upon the source-critical results of Karl Heinrich Graf (1815–69) and Julius Wellhausen (1844–1914), Gunkel attempted to identify distinctive literary genres within Hebrew Scripture. In his work on Genesis (1901), Gunkel believed that he could isolate legendary materials that reflected various aspects of ancient Israel's beliefs about God. He and others recognized that instead of formulating doctrines about the deity, the ancients told stories about the deity's interaction with human beings. In his work on the Psalms (1967), Gunkel attempted to identify several genres that reflected the mood or purpose of the individuals who composed the psalms (such as lament, imprecation, hymns, thanksgiving, royal psalms). Gunkel's student Sigmund Mowinckel (1884–1965) made further important contributions to form criticism, though sometimes coming to different conclusions. Contrary to his teacher, Mowinckel believed that the Psalms reflected communal worship.

Form criticism was soon applied to all of the literature of the Old Testament. Within the Pentateuch various forms have been identified, such as law, myth, folktale, saga, history, and legend, each with differing functions in the life of the community. The prophets (and here Gunkel and Mowinckel again were seminal) were recognized as presenting their oracles and compositions in certain set forms. Early on these forms were identified as threat, promise, and invective, though in more recent study, scholars speak of accounts, prayers, and speeches, with most of the material falling under the last heading. Under the first heading, one may regard the call narrative as a special subcategory. Acting out signs may be another type of account. One thinks of Isa 8:1–4; Jer 19.15, Ezek 4–5. One thinks especially of the call of Isaiah (cf. Isa 6). Speeches often entail announcements of judgment and salvation.

Wisdom literature in the Old Testament includes Proverbs, Job, Qoheleth, Sirach, and Wisdom of Solomon, though it is represented in some Psalms and in portions of Tobit, Judith, and 1 Esdras. Broadly speaking, wisdom literature falls into four categories: (1) juridical; (2) nature; (3) practical; and (4) theological. Wisdom tradition grew up in the family and the small village and reflects an agrarian and rural culture. It was imported into and stylized in the royal court setting. Wisdom literature is presented in various forms, not always easily recognizable. We have found proverbs, which are brief pithy aphorisms, didactic poetry and narrative, riddles, fables and allegories, hymns and prayers, dialogues, confessions, and lists. One should consult the volumes produced in R. Knierim's Formation of Old Testament Literature series (Eerdmans). Though dated, the collection edited by J. H. Hayes (1974) remains very useful.

New Testament form criticism

Gospels

New Testament form criticism found its origins in the work of Wellhausen, who in his commentaries and introduction in the early twentieth century applied Gunkel's form-critical insights to the Synoptic Gospels. Two important books appeared in 1919 that set New Testament form criticism on a path that has been followed by interpreters ever since. In *Der Rahmen der Geschichte Jesu* ("The Framework of the Story of Jesus") Karl Ludwig Schmidt (1891–1956) emphasized the relative independence of the units of tradition that make up the Synoptic Gospels. He concluded that the gospel stories for the most part are not in chronological order, but have been edited and placed into a narrative framework by the evangelists themselves. He conceded that the Passion Narrative was an exception, having taken its shape at a very early stage in the development and transmission of the Jesus story. That same year Martin Dibelius (1883–1947) published *Die Formgeschichte des Evangeliums* ("The Form History of the Gospel"), whose title gave the new critical method its name. Like Schmidt, Dibelius presupposed the results of Synoptic Source Criticism, namely the priority of Mark, and Matthean and Lukan use of Mark and Q. Forms identified by Dibelius included paradigms, tales, legends, myth, and sayings. Paradigms clarify doctrine, for example, the teaching concerning payment of tribute (Mark 12:13–17) or the pronouncement of the authority to forgive sins (Mark 2:1–12). Dibelius classified most of the miracle stories as tales, such as the cleansing of the leper (Mark 1:40–45) or the stilling of the storm (Mark 4:35–41). Some of these tales were extensions or embellishments of paradigms; some were foreign imports. Legends serve as "religious narratives of a saintly man" (Dibelius 1934: 104), in whose life hearers and readers take interest. The story of the boy Jesus in the Temple (Luke 2:41–49) is cited as an example. Dibelius identified only a few stories as examples of myth. These are the story of the heavenly vision and voice at the baptism (Mark 1:9–11 and parallels), the temptation of Jesus (Mark 1:12–13 and parallels), and the transfiguration (Mark 9:2–8 and parallels). Finally, Dibelius considered the sayings of Jesus, emphasizing their hortatory and paraenetic character, with the view of making Jesus' sayings apply to the questions and issues with which the early Christian community grappled.

In 1921 Rudolf Bultmann (1884–1976) published the first edition of his *Geschichte der synoptischen Tradition* ("History of the Synoptic Tradition") offering a comprehensive analysis of the Synoptic Gospels. Bultmann divided the tradition into discourse and narrative. The latter was further subdivided into historical narratives, miracle stories, and legends. Bultmann identified several forms. These included apophthegms (the approximate equivalent of Dibelius's paradigms), which may be further subdivided as controversy dialogues, scholastic dialogues, and biographical apophthegms. In Bultmann's opinion, apophthegms reflected ideal portraits. As such, they were not derived from the *Sitz im Leben Jesu* ("setting in the life of Jesus"); rather, they arose in the *Sitz im Leben der Kirche* ("setting in the life of the church"). Bultmann also identified dominical sayings, which he further subdivided into proverbs, prophetic and apocalyptic sayings, and laws and community rules. Of these the authenticity of the proverbs was the least certain, for many of Jesus' proverbial sayings parallel Jewish proverbs and may therefore have been borrowed. The prophetic and apocalyptic sayings revolved around Jesus' proclamation of the kingdom of God and his expectation of the coming "son of man." Bultmann judged many of the miracle stories (what are called tales by Dibelius) as derived from Hellenistic stories of divine men. Throughout his work Bultmann employed the criterion of double dissimilarity whereby it was argued that material that may be judged as authentic should be dissimilar to known tendencies in the Judaism of Jesus' day and to the interests and emphases of the early church.

In 1932 C. H. Dodd (1884–1973) challenged Schmidt's analysis of the Synoptic Tradition by arguing that although many pericopes circulated independently, there were larger complexes of material and a general outline of the whole of Jesus' ministry that reached back to eyewitness testimony. Two years later Vincent Taylor (1887–1968) responded to what he judged to be the excessive skepticism and highly subjective and speculative proposals of Bultmann. He admitted that form criticism had much to offer gospel study and that some of the tradition originated in the early church. But Taylor thought a great deal more of the material reaches back to Jesus and reflected accurately its original context and meaning.

The recent work of Martin Hengel (1926–) and James D. G. Dunn (1939–) contends for the great antiquity of much of the Jesus tradition, particularly the material thought to have made up the source ("Q") used by Matthew and Luke. In short, Hengel and Dunn believe that the character of the Jesus tradition clearly reflects a pre-Easter setting. This then explains the lack of material that reflects Jesus' passion, or the Easter event itself. Hengel and Dunn focus on the oral tradition, seeking to identify that which is characteristic of Jesus, rather than material thought distinctive (as in much of the earlier form-critical work). Richard Bauckham (1946–) has also called into question the attempts of many form and redaction critics who think they can recover hypothetical "communities" reflected in the respective New Testament Gospels and/or their sources.

Years ago scholars criticized the criterion of double dissimilarity, rightly contending that one should expect that Jesus' sayings should reflect the world and language of Jewish Palestine (see Theissen and Winter). In more recent years this criticism has been pressed forward even more vigorously, especially with reference to suggestions that Jesus' thought and lifestyle are better understood in the light of Hellenism and Cynicism (as has been proposed in some of the publications emanating from members of the Jesus Seminar). Scholarship today is more inclined to view the Synoptic Tradition as essentially authentic, even if edited and recontextualized.

Form-critical work on the New Testament Gospels has also progressed in the area of identifying the literary form of the gospels in their complete form (Burridge, Talbert). The gospels are no longer viewed as literary nova, wholly subordinated to the proclamation of the Christian message (as, for example, in Bultmann), but as instances of popular biography, exhibiting characteristic traits of this genre at many points.

Epistles

At about the same time that form-critical research of the gospels began, it was recognized that papyri found in Egypt in the late nineteenth century clarified in important ways the literary form of the Epistles in the New Testament. The work of (Gustav) Adolf Deissmann (1866–1937) was especially influential (1927: 227–45). Among other things, Deissmann was able to show that the Epistles of the New Testament followed epistolary convention in Greco-Roman late antiquity.

Recent studies have taken into account the thousands of papyri that have been published over the last 100 years. Whereas Deissmann had attempted to distinguish letters (less formal) from epistles (more stylized and artistic), recent form-critical research into epistles and letters of late antiquity (e.g. Doty, White) distinguishes several forms, such as the business letter, the official letter, the public letter, and other types. Common elements are (1) introduction (usually comprising a salutation), which includes the names of the sender and addressee, greetings, and often a prayer or wish for the addressee's good health; (2) body; and (3) conclusion, which usually includes greetings, expressions of good will, a benediction, and sometimes a date and mention of the courier.

Paul's letters reveal rhetorical devices and strategies (see Betz 1979) and contain autobiographical elements, apocalyptic, lists of vices and virtues, catechesis, confessional and hymnic materials. Sometimes it is suspected that some of Paul's letters may be composite (e.g. 2 Cor; see Betz 1985) and perhaps may even contain non-Pauline interpolations. Pseudonymity is another issue that bears on the question of epistolary form.

Apocalyptic

Another important element in both Testaments is apocalyptic. In the Old Testament it is found in Daniel, Zechariah, and Isaiah 24–27, while in the New Testament it is found in Mark 13 (and Matthew 24–25 and various places in Luke), here and there in the Pauline and General Epistles, and constitutes almost the whole of the book of Revelation. Apocalyptic material in the New Testament exhibits many of the features found in Jewish apocalyptic from the intertestamental and New Testament periods, such as *1 Enoch* and the *Testaments of the Twelve Patriarchs*. Apocalyptic often entails heavenly settings, the appearance and speeches of angels, visual overviews of human history, especially involving Israel, colorful symbolism that

often involves exotic creatures, and graphic descriptions of the horrors of hell and the joys of heaven. The purpose of apocalyptic varies, sometimes promising an end to suffering and, conversely, promising certain judgment upon the wicked. A decisive climax of human history is usually envisioned. In Jewish texts this is usually the end of evil and the restoration of Israel (with or without the appearance of a messiah), while in Christian apocalyptic the appearance of the glorified and reigning Christ, followed by resurrection and final judgment, is the usual scenario.

For more recent treatments of New Testament literary forms, one should see Aune and Berger.

CRAIG A. EVANS

Further reading

Aune, D. E. *The New Testament in Its Literary Environment*, Philadelphia, PA: Fortress Press, 1987.

Bauckham, R. J. *The Gospels for All Christians: Rethinking the Gospel Audiences*, Grand Rapids, MI: Eerdmans, 1998.

Berger, K. *Formgeschichte des Neuen Testaments*, Heidelberg: Quelle & Meyer, 1984.

Betz, H. D. "Galatians," *Hermeneia*, Philadelphia, PA: Fortress Press, 1979.

—— "2 Corinthians 8 and 9," *Hermeneia*, Philadelphia, PA: Fortress Press, 1985.

Bultmann, R. *The History of the Synoptic Tradition*, Oxford: Blackwell, 1972 [1919; second edition 1931].

Bultmann, R. and Kundsin, K. *Form Criticism: Two Essays on New Testament Research*, New York: Willett Clark, 1934 [1925].

Burridge, R. A. *What Are the Gospels? A Comparison with Graeco-Roman Biography*, second edition, Grand Rapids, MI: Eerdmans, 2004.

Childs, B. S. *Introduction to the Old Testament as Scripture*, Philadelphia, PA: Fortress Press, 1979.

Collins, J. J. (ed.) *Apocalypse: The Morphology of a Genre*, Semeia 14, Missoula, MT: Scholars Press, 1979.

Deissmann, A. *Light from the Ancient East*, London: Hodder & Stoughton; New York: George H. Doran, 1927 [1908; fourth edition 1923]; repr. Peabody, MA: Hendrickson, 1995.

Dibelius, M. *From Tradition to Gospel*, New York: Charles Scribner's Sons, 1934 [1919; second edition 1933]; repr. Cambridge and London: James Clarke, 1971.

Dodd, C. H. "The Framework of the Gospel Narrative," *ExpTim* 43 (1932) 396–400; repr. in *NTS*, Manchester: Manchester University Press, 1953, pp. 1–11.

Doty, W. G. *Letters in Primitive Christianity*, Philadelphia, PA: Fortress Press, 1977.

Dunn, J. D. G. *Jesus Remembered*, Christianity in the Making 1, Grand Rapids, MI: Eerdmans, 2003.

Gunkel, H. *The Legends of Genesis*, Chicago, IL: Open Court, 1901.

—— *The Psalms*, Philadelphia, PA: Fortress Press, 1967.

Hayes, J. *Old Testament Form Criticism*, San Antonio, TX: Trinity University Press, 1974.

Hengel, M. *The Four Gospels and the One Gospel of Jesus Christ: An Investigation of the Collection and Origin of the Canonical Gospels*, Harrisburg, PA: Trinity Press International, 2000.

McKnight, E. *What is Form Criticism?* Philadelphia, PA: Fortress Press, 1969.

Porter, S. E. and D. Tombs (eds) *Approaches to New Testament Study*, JSNTSup 120, Sheffield: Sheffield Academic Press, 1995.

Schmidt, K. L. *Der Rahmen der Geschichte Jesu: Literarkritische Untersuchungen zur ältesten Jesusüberlieferung*, Berlin: Trowitzsch & Sohn, 1919.

Taylor, V. *The Formation of the Gospel Tradition*, London: Macmillan, 1935.

Talbert, C. H. *What is a Gospel? The Genre of the Canonical Gospels*, Philadelphia, PA: Fortress Press, 1977.

Theissen, G. and D. Winter. *The Quest for the Plausible Jesus: The Question of Criteria*, Louisville, KY: Westminster John Knox Press, 2002.

Tucker, G. M. *Form Criticism of the Old Testament*, Philadelphia, PA: Fortress Press, 1971.

Westermann, C. *Basic Forms of Prophetic Speech*, Cambridge: Lutterworth Press; Westminster John Knox Press, 1991.

White, J. L. *Light from Ancient Letters*, Philadelphia, PA: Fortress Press, 1986.

FUCHS, ERNST

Ernst Fuchs (1903–83) was born in Heilbronn. After his education and military service he began the study of law in Tübingen. As a consequence of hearing Adolf Schlatter and because of his unsatisfied interest in the quest for justice (1965b: 136–37; letters of Fuchs quoted in Möller 2003: 15), he began the study of theology in Tübingen (1922–24, 1925–27) and in Marburg (1924–25, 1927–29) where he was influenced by Rudolf Bultmann. In Marburg he also witnessed the fruitful discussion between Bultmann and Martin Heidegger. In 1929 he finished his doctoral thesis "Das Verhältnis des Glaubens zur Tat im Hermasbuch" (published under the title *Glaube und Tat in den Mandata des Hirten des Hermas* [Marburg: Bauer, 1931]) and as assistant of Karl Ludwig Schmidt (Bonn) he completed in 1932 his *Christus und der Geist bei Paulus. Eine biblisch-theologische Untersuchung* (Untersuchungen zum Neuen Testament 23; Leipzig: Hinrichs, 1932). Like Karl Barth he was dismissed from his position as *Privatdozent* for political reasons on 23 September 1933.

Fuchs became a pastor in the church of Württemberg, where he would become part of the opposition to national socialism. For a short period he lived in Freudenstadt, then in Winzerhausen (until 1938, expelled under influence of national socialistic forces), and still later he lived in Oberaspach (1938–51). While still serving as a pastor in 1949 he returned to academic life, accepting an appointment as *Dozent* in Tübingen, and in 1953 he was appointed *extraordinarius* for New Testament. During that time he faced serious opposition because of his support of Bultmann in the controversial and sometimes heated discussion on demythologization. In 1955 he became full professor at the Kirchliche Hochschule of Berlin and from 1961 professor of New Testament and Hermeneutics in Marburg in Bultmann's old chair. Fuchs remained at Marburg until he retired in 1970 and moved back to his native region Württemberg, where he lived until his death in 1983.

According to Fuchs, the new quest for Jesus entailed not only a new historical approach but also a new hermeneutic (1971: 135–37). Accordingly, Fuchs was not only a protagonist of the new quest as a disciple of Bultmann but also was engaged in the debate about hermeneutics especially within the discussion on existential hermeneutics and demythologization. The final aim of his theory of hermeneutic and exegetical analysis was Christian preaching (1971: 140). For that reason he wrote textbooks on hermeneutics as early as 1954 and again in 1964. In Fuchs's thinking theological hermeneutics is dealing with the language of faith. Language is a site for understanding.

Fuchs is one of those scholars in the new quest (like, e.g., Gerhard Ebeling or Willi Marxsen) who reflect on the relationship between the faith in Jesus before Easter and the faith that grew out of the Easter event. The Christian *kerygma* ("proclamation") tells something new, something that Jesus could not tell (1965b: 239), but that does not mean that there is no continuity between the faith before Easter and the faith after Easter. The experience of Easter leads the followers of Jesus into "a new proof of worth" of their faith ("*eine neue Bewährung des in die Nachfolge schon eingetretenen Glaubens*"; 1965b: 188) and into a full understanding of Jesus (1965b: 241). It is apparent that Fuchs's questioning is provoked by Bultmann's own contradictions regarding the quest for Jesus and the foundation of Christology (cf. Harnisch 263) and are answered by the originality of Fuchs as a Christian theologian.

According to Fuchs, interpretation of the *kerygma* and of the historical Jesus could not be separated: "*Der sogenannte Christus des Glaubens ist in der Tat kein anderer als der historische Jesus*" (1965a: 166). No interpretation of the historical Jesus is possible beyond the earliest interpretation ascribed to Jesus himself (1965b: 447: "*Und Jesus auslegen kann man dann gerade aus historischen Gründen offenbar nur in der Auseinandersetzung mit denjenigen Auslegungen, die das Neue Testament Jesus zugeschrieben hat*"). Early Christian proclamation of Jesus who had himself spoken of one's relationship to God demanded a decision from all who heard.

Fuchs plays an important role in the hermeneutical discussion about the parables of Jesus. Although Jesus' preaching in parables refers to everyday life, the extraordinary appeal of his message completely changes the world. The authorization of this appeal is the presence of God's kingdom, which Jesus proclaims in his parables. The principal subject of that kingdom is, according to Fuchs, the presence of God's power of love (e.g. 1979: 138). "Love" is that behavior in which people may imitate God (1965a: 155). The central term used by Fuchs is *Sprachereignis* (language event): The function of language is not only to describe things; it leads to and constitutes an event. In this way language comes to its real and true substance (Harnisch 264). This happens when it evokes permission and freedom (1959: 283). By using parables, Jesus uses the power of language to open an entrance for his hearers to a place where people are placed by God's own speaking. This is so because people are addressed by God (1971: 91). Jesus' proclamation starts with language and returns to language by means of confessing. To the extent that faith works its way into language it becomes an "existential possibility within language" (Soulen 1999: 423).

For historians, there is of course great interest in both deeds and words of any historic figure. Fuchs understands that there is a kind of integrity between words and deeds. The words and deeds of Jesus in combination represent Jesus' *behavior* (*"Jesu Verhalten"*). It is the behavior of a man who dares to work on behalf of God (*"der es wagt, an Gottes Stelle zu handeln"*) that frightens people, who as sinners flee from the presence of God (1965a: 155–56). The behavior of Jesus is a key to understanding the historical Jesus. As far as Jesus' behavior is drawn back to his decision and his obedience toward God, including his acceptance of suffering, the hearers of his proclamation are also forced into a decision (*"Entscheidung"*) in their situation in the presence of God (1965a: 157–66; 1965b: 243–45). In Jesus' deeds the love of God became visible. We see this in the meals with sinners and tax collectors (Matt 11:19 par.), meals that are part of the eschatological proclamation. The kingdom to come is already present in Jesus' behavior. The reality to come is already present in contrast to the reality of the current world, which is going to vanish (1965b: 410).

With regard to method, Fuchs suggests that post-Easter discussions within the Christian community recall Jesus' behavior, even if the words are not authentic, for behavior encourages imitation (1965a: 156). As sources for the quest for Jesus he refers mainly to the Synoptic Gospels, accepting some historical information from the Gospel of John. Fuchs does not, however, make use of apocryphal Jesus tradition (e.g. 1965a: 153).

In Fuchs's original contribution to the quest for Jesus there are a lot of important aspects which are worth bearing in mind. Of major importance is his urging hermeneutical reflection. The quest for Jesus needs to give careful consideration to the method and means of the search itself, as well as its aims.

MICHAEL LABAHN

Further reading

Brantschen, Johannes. *Zeit zu verstehen: Wege und Umwege heutiger Theologie zu einer Ortsbestimmung der Theologie von Ernst Fuchs.* Ökumenische Beihefte zur Freiburger Zeitschrift für Philosophie und Theologie 9, Zürich: Theologischer Verlag, 1974.

Conrad, Joachim. "Ernst Fuchs (1903–1983)," in Rainer Lächele and Jörg Thierfelder (eds) *Wir konnten uns nicht entziehen. Dreißig Portraits zu Kirche und Nationalsozialismus in Württemberg,* Stuttgart: Quelle, 1998, pp. 451–68.

Fangmeier, Jürgen. "Ernst Fuchs. Versuch einer Orientierung. (Ein Referat aus Basel)," ThSt 80, Zürich: TVZ, 1964.

Fuchs, Ernst. *Hermeneutik,* Stuttgart: Müllerschön, 1954; third edition Bad Cannstadt, Müllerschön, 1963.

—— *Zum hermeneutischen Problem in der Theologie. Die existentiale Interpretation. Gesammelte Aufsätze 1,* Tübingen: Mohr Siebeck, 1959.

—— *Marburger Hermeneutik,* HUTh, 9, Tübingen: Mohr Siebeck, 1964.

—— *Studies of the Historical Jesus,* London: SCM Press, 1964.

—— *Glaube und Erfahrung. Zum christologischen Problem im Neuen Testament. Gesammelte Aufsätze 3,* Tübingen: Mohr Siebeck, 1965a.

—— *Zur Frage nach dem historischen Jesus. Gesammelte Aufsätze 2,* second edition, Tübingen: Mohr Siebeck, 1965b [1960].

—— *Jesus. Wort und Tat,* Vorlesungen zum Neuen Testament 1, Tübingen: Mohr Siebeck, 1971.

—— *Wagnis des Glaubens. Aufsätze und Vorträge,* ed. Eberhard Grötzinger, Neukirchen-Vluyn: Neukirchener Verlag, 1979.

Fuchs, Frank. *Konkretionen des Narrativen. Am Beispiel von Eberhard Jüngels Theologie und Predigten unter Einbeziehung der Hermeneutik Paul Ricoeurs sowie der Textlinguistik Klaus Brinkers,* Theologie 54, Münster: LIT, 2004, pp. 36–40.

Harnisch, Wolfgang. "Freude an der Liebe. Skizze zu einem Portrait des Theologen Ernst Fuchs," *Berliner theologische Zeitschrift* 4 (1987) 252–68.

Jüngel, Eberhard and Gerd Schunack (eds) *Ernst Fuchs Lesebuch. Ausgewählte Texte,* Tübingen: Mohr Siebeck, 2003.

Möller, Christian (ed.) *Freude an Gott. Hermeneutische Spätlese bei Ernst Fuchs,* Waltrop: Spenner, 2003.

Soulen, Richard N. "Ernst Fuchs: New Testament Theologian," *JAAR* 39 (1971) 467–87.

—— "Fuchs, Ernst," *DBI* 1 (1999) 422–23.

G

GENEALOGIES

Genealogies are records of a person's ancestry. Far from simply a list of names, genealogies, as used in the OT, made assertions about a person's identity, territory, or relationships (Knoppers 18). They were used in Genesis (cf. 1:1–11:26), for example, to provide a structural framework for the narrative of the book. In the NT we find two such accounts of Jesus, in Matthew (1:1–17) and Luke (3:23–38).

Matthew

Matthew's genealogy follows an OT pattern, "book of the generations of ..." (βίβλος γενέσεως; see Gen 2:4; 5:1 LXX), which serves as the heading for Matthew's genealogy, perhaps even the entire first gospel. What strikes the reader as odd is the structural indicators found in this genealogy, namely the designation of three distinct lists of fourteen persons: "So all the generations from Abraham to David are fourteen generations; from David to the deportation to Babylon, fourteen generations; and from the deportation to Babylon to the Messiah, fourteen generations" (1:17 NAS; though the last names only thirteen). Moreover, the author seems to indicate the list is arranged – in some sense – with respect to the Babylonian captivity. Explanations of these features vary, with the most plausible positing that a Semitic literary device, known as *grammatria*, is employed here. This feature assigns numerical values to Hebrew consonants, here King David's name: d = 4, v = 6, d = 4. So, d + v + d = 4 + 6 + 4 = 14, and serves

to underscore Jesus' Davidic origins. This view resonates with other texts in the first gospel which seem to use "Son of David" as a Messianic title (Matt 9:27; 12:23; 15:22; 20:30–31; 21:9, 15). Others suggest this arrangement simply depicts Matthew's affinity with symmetry, while still others would argue that such symmetry betrays Matthew's view that history is chronicled and organized with respect to the Messiah.

Whatever else is occurring in Matthew's genealogy, he is surely not intending to be exhaustive in his account. Following the accounts of the Davidic kings in the OT (1 Chr 3:11–12, 15–16; 2 Kgs 8:16–15:7), it is apparent that the evangelist has omitted four names from his second grouping (Ahaziah, Jehoash [Joash], Aniaziah, and Eliakim [Jehoiakim]). Such omissions are by no means unprecedented in biblical genealogies (cf. 1 Chr 6:3–15; Ezra 7:1–5), and suggestions that Matthew simply erred in his account are therefore unlikely. Instead, scholars have posited that the omissions were because of a curse on those individuals (cf. Exod 20:5; 1 Kgs 21:21; 2 Chr 22:7–9; 24:22–24; 25:14–28; Jer 22:28–30), though other reasons have been proposed. While Matthean omissions from the genealogies are rather curious, even more strange is his rather unusual inclusions. For example, he mentions three sets of brothers (Zerah, the brothers of Judah, and those of Jeconiah) and five women (Tamar, 1:3, Rahab, 1:5, Ruth, 1:5, Bathsheba, the wife of Uriah, 1:6, and Mary, 1:16). Women in particular were not normally accounted for in biblical genealogies, though such a practice is not unheard of (Gen 22:20–24; 25:1–6; 36: 1–14;

1 Chr 2:3–4, 18–20, 46–47; 3:1–9). What do they share in common that would cause them to be included in such a selective list? The four OT women may have been included because of their sinful lives from which Jesus came to deliver them (Jerome). Another suggestion is that the four OT women are Gentiles, listed to prefigure the extension of the kingdom through Jesus to include Gentiles (Luther). More promising is the proposal that for each woman there was something extraordinary about her union with a man. Moreover, they were given a role in God's plan of redemptive history (Brown). More recently, it has been suggested that these four women were lauded in Pharisaic circles regarding their role in the ancestry of the Messiah (Johnson), and that Matthew's inclusion of them underscores Jesus' fulfillment of their messianic expectations on this point.

Luke

Luke's account of the genealogy of Jesus (Luke 3:23–38) is found not at the beginning of his book (like that of Matthew) but rather after a lengthy introduction (1:1–3:22). Here it is immediately after Jesus' baptism and before his temptation in the wilderness. Unlike Matthew's genealogy of Jesus, Luke's contains a seemingly unstructured list of fifty-six men (no women, no brothers). Moreover, Luke's account contains no thematic commentary, such as Matthew's breaks at the Babylonian captivity and three lists of fourteen. Instead, Luke concludes his genealogy with the statement of Jesus "being the son (as was supposed) of Joseph" (Luke 3:23). Like Matthew, Luke is concerned to demonstrate Jesus' Davidic sonship (3:31; also 1:27, 36, 69; 2:4; 18:38–39), though he does so not through Solomon but through Nathan.

It has been widely seen that Luke's genealogy is more comprehensive – reaching back beyond Abraham (as Matthew has) to Adam, and then to God. This resonates with the declaration of Jesus' divine sonship in the Lukan baptismal account (3:22), and is raised again at the temptation immediately subsequent to the genealogy (Luke 4:3, 9). Moreover, the question of divine sonship, aside from these texts, is raised in Luke only by angelic hosts (Luke 1:32, 35) and demons (Luke 4:41; 8:28). Some see Luke's extension of the genealogy to Adam to thus identify the lineage of Jesus with all people. This is congruent with the universality of his understanding of Jesus' saving activity and subsequent mission of the church in the book of Acts (Acts 1:8).

Analysis

After David, the most dramatic distinctions arise between the Matthean and Lukan accounts. One of two solutions is typically adopted. The first, initially proposed by Julius Africanus (c. 170–245 CE), suggests both accounts provide Joseph's lineage, though Matthew gives the biological lineage while Luke the legal lineage (cf. Eusebius, *Hist. eccl.* 1.7). Yet this view seems to violate the plain sense of Matthew's "begat" language (esp. 1:16), which would insist all relationships in the list are biological. More plausible is a view proposed by Annius of Viterbo (c. 1490 CE) and adopted by Martin Luther and others, which takes Matthew's genealogy as reflective of Joseph, while Luke's comes from Mary. Regardless of if and how the tensions may be resolved, it is clear from the respective genealogical accounts that neither intend to be exhaustive, and that each is compiled with a thematic message in mind. Modern scholars recognize that Semitic genealogies are not typically intended to chronicle exhaustive ancestral lists (cf. Ezra 2:62; 8:1), and can be used to authenticate credentials of their subject, here Jesus, for the task articulated in the full narrative, such as those of Noah (Gen 5:1–32) and Abraham (11:10–32). For Matthew, Jesus is the Davidic (Messianic) King, tracing his ancestry to the father of Judaism: Abraham himself. For Luke, however, Jesus' lineage reaches back to Adam, the father of all humanity and therefore Jesus bears a degree of siblinghood with all people. Luke's Jesus is underscored as the son of God offering salvation to all. While by no means able to be dismissed for their historical veracity, genealogies of Jesus have received little attention in historical Jesus studies.

DANIEL M. GURTNER

Further reading

Brown, R. E. *The Birth of the Messiah*, Garden City, NY: Doubleday, 1977.

Carr, D. "Βίβλος γενέσεως Revisited: A Synchronic Analysis of Patterns in Genesis as Part of the Torah," *ZAW* 110 (1998) 159–72, 327–47.

Hess, R. S. "The Genealogies of Genesis 1–11 and Comparative Literature," in R. Hess and D. T. Tsumura (eds) *"I Studied Inscriptions from Before the Flood": Ancient Near Eastern, Literary, and Linguistic Approaches to Genesis 1–11*, SBTS 4, Winona Lake, IN: Eisenbrauns, 1994, pp. 58–72.

Hood, R. T. "The Genealogies of Jesus," in A. Wikgren (ed.) *Early Christian Origins*, Chicago, IL: Quadrangle, 1961, pp. 1–15.

Johnson, M. D. *The Purpose of Biblical Genealogies*, SNTSMS 8, second edition, Cambridge: Cambridge University Press, 1988.

Knoppers, G. N. "Intermarriage, Social Complexity, and Ethnic Diversity in the Genealogy of Judah," *JBL* 120 (2001) 15–30.

Nolan, B. M. *The Royal Son of God: The Christology of Matthew 1–2 in Its Gospel Setting*, OBO 23, Göttingen: Vandenhoeck & Ruprecht, 1979.

Overstreet, R. L. "Difficulties of New Testament Genealogies," *GTJ* 2 (1981) 303–26.

GENTILES

Gentiles did not figure prominently in the message and ministry of Jesus because his mission was focused on Israel. Even so, there is ample material in the Jesus tradition that attests Jesus' perspective about the place of the Gentiles in the kingdom of God. In accordance with Israel's scriptures, Jesus appears to have taught that Gentiles would experience salvation through incorporation into the restored Israel. It is in Jesus' understanding of Israel's role vis-à-vis the world that one finds the germinal roots of the Christian Gentile mission.

Jesus, Gentiles, and scholarship

The relationship of the historical Jesus to the Gentile mission of the early church has spawned a range of proposals (see Bird 2005). Late nineteenth-century scholarship, exemplified by David Strauss and Ernst Renan, saw Jesus as initiating a universal religion of love in contrast to Jewish legalism and xenophobia. Early twentieth-century discussion seems to have been concerned as to whether or not Jesus possessed a universalist or particularist perspective. Adolf von Harnack, Max Meinertz, and Maurice Goguel believed that Jesus had no vision of a Gentile mission, though he did exhibit an implicit universalism. Friedrich Spitta saw Jesus as influenced by the multi-ethnic Galilean environment to the point that Jesus was already concerned with closing the Jew–Gentile divide and was arguably the first Gentile missionary. Albert Schweitzer understood Jesus as universalistic in orientation, but particularist in demonstration as elect Gentiles would replace unbelieving Jews.

Discussion was invigorated by the proposal of Bengst Sundkler who advocated that the particularist or universalist question rested on a false dichotomy. Jesus did not conceive of his relationship with the Gentiles in horizontal dimensions of universalism, but vertically via the matrix of "salvation history". What happens in Jerusalem affects the entire cosmos. This led to Sundkler's dictum that Jesus was a "universalist only because he was also a particularist" (Sundkler 36). The salvation

history approach was developed further by David Bosch, G. B. Caird, T. W. Manson, Johannes Munck, and Joachim Jeremias. Jeremias argued that Jesus did not envisage a Gentile mission but believed that the Gentiles would be saved directly by God at the eschaton. This conclusion has dominated scholarship for the last fifty years and has only been contested by a relative few such as Schnabel (1994, 2004) who saw Jesus as initiator of a world-wide missionary movement. In the "Third Quest" two major approaches seem to have emerged. First, those who hold that Jesus did not sanction or intimate a Gentile mission but held to a general Jewish hope that the Gentiles would be saved in some form (Martin Hengel, E. P. Sanders, Geza Vermes, John Meier, James Dunn), and others who have been willing to posit a stronger connection between the restoration of Israel and the salvation of the Gentiles (Ben F. Meyer, N. T. Wright, Sean Freyne, Michael F. Bird).

Jesus' teaching about Gentiles

In the gospels there are several complexes that demonstrate Jesus' convictions about the Gentiles and their relationship to the kingdom.

The negative remarks about pagan ethics and religiosity (Mark 7:27; 10:41–45; Matt 6:7; 7:6; 18:17; Luke 12:30–31/Matt 6:32–33) are not attributable to an anti-Gentile ethos, but are indicative of the prophetic tradition (like Isaiah) that could condemn pagan religious practices but simultaneously hold out a hope for the inclusion of the Gentiles in the divine design.

Jesus is remembered for contrasting Gentiles of Israel's antiquity with the present faithlessness of Israel. In one complex (Luke 11:29–32/Matt 12:38–42) the Queen of the South and the men of Nineveh will "rise up" and condemn "this generation" for requesting a sign from Jesus. Jesus conceives of Gentiles, at least hypothetically, participating in a future kingdom over and against the current audience who have not responded positively to his message. Jesus likens himself to a Jewish king (Solomon) and a Galilean prophet (Jonah) known for their interaction with Gentiles. The memory of Jesus' woes oracles against Chorazin, Bethsaida, and Capernaum (Luke 10:12/Matt 10:15 and Luke 10:13–15/Matt 11:20–24), provocatively proposes that the notorious gentile cities of Sodom, Gomorrah, Tyre, and Sidon will fare better in the final judgment than a recalcitrant Israel. In response to the rejection of his Nazareth sermon (Luke 4:16–21), Jesus launches into a tirade against his audience and refers to the ministries of Elijah to the widow of Zarephath, and Elisha to Naaman the Syrian (Luke 4:25–27; cf. 1 Kgs 17:1–24; 2 Kgs 5:1–14). The juxtaposition of Isaiah 61 and the Elijah–Elisha narratives represents a form of "prophetic criticism" that seeks to redefine the boundaries of Israel's election, emphasizes that present opportunities of salvation are going unfulfilled for Israel, and comprises a parabolic defence of Jesus' willingness to minister to those outside the covenant boundaries because of the new eschatological situation created by the in-breaking of the kingdom.

Several parables arguably exhibit a reference (though sometimes obliquely) to the salvation of the Gentiles. The parable of the mustard seed (Mark 4:30–32; Luke 13:18–19/Matt 13:31–32; *Gos. Thom.* 20) reckons with the kingdom growing into a large tree and the birds of heaven nesting in its branches. In Jewish tradition "birds" is often a symbol for Gentiles (Ezek 17:22–24; 31:6; *1 En.* 90:30; *4 Ezra* 5:26). Wright (241) states: "The ministry of Jesus, which does not look like the expected coming kingdom, is in fact its strange beginning … when Israel becomes what her God intends her to become – others presumably Gentiles, will come to share in her blessing." The intertextual echoes suggest that when Israel was restored (became a great tree), Gentiles (like birds) would participate in the blessings of its arrival. When read as a defence of Jesus' ministry, the point of the parable is that the nuisance mustard tree is *already* growing (in the manner of a pesky weed) and the despicable birds are *already* beginning to take shelter in its branches. The parable of the great banquet (Luke 14:15–24; Matt 22:1–13; *Gos. Thom.* 64) implies that the participants of the banquet will be those regarded as being beyond the outer markers of the covenant. The banquet parable constitutes a parabolic defence of Jesus' table fellowship with sinners and implies that the mission of inviting outsiders to the banquet must continue in the future.

This logion found in Luke 13:28–30/Matt 8:11–12 ("many will come from the east and the west and will recline with Abraham, Isaac and Jacob in the kingdom of heaven") is the primary saying for exploring the historical Jesus' view of the future of the Gentiles. Scholars frequently privilege the Matthean version, which places the logion as the climax of Jesus' healings of the centurion's servant. However, the Lucan account of the logion occurs in a non-Gentile context in Luke 13:22–30 and there is no substantial proof that the "many/they" are Gentiles. Consequently several scholars (E. P. Sanders, Dale C. Allison, John Nolland, Richard Horsley) argue that the imagery correlates more

properly to traditions in Jewish literature hoping for the return of the Diaspora to Israel (Ps 107:2–3; Isa 43:5–6; Zech 8:7–8; Barn 4:36–37; 5:5; *1 En.* 57:1; *Pss. Sol.* 11:1–3). This may be true; however, the motifs of Israel's regathering and the eschatological pilgrimage of the Gentiles are sometimes combined where the Gentiles converge on Jerusalem on the coat tails of the regathered Israel or else the return of the exiles is contingent upon the repentance and conversion of the Gentiles (Jer 3:17–18; Isa 66:20–21; Zech 8:7–8, 20–23; *T. Benj.* 9:2; *1 En.* 90:33; *Pss. Sol.* 17:26, 31; Tob 13:5, 11; 14:5–7). The presence of Abraham at the banquet may also involve a broader ethnic group that constitute the "many" who participate in the banquet since Abraham was regarded as the link between Israel and the Gentiles (Gen 15–21; Rom 4:1–25; Gal 3:6–29; Josephus, *Ant.* 1:161–67; *T. Benj.* 10:5–6; *b. Hag.* 3a; *Gen. Rab.* 14:6). Additionally, the logion coheres with the widely attested theme in the Jesus tradition of eschatological reversal. It seems strange to regard Jews of the Diaspora as an unexpected group that is vindicated in the future age, as there was no cause for doubt as to whether Jews of the Diaspora would participate in the eschatological kingdom. The logion is a threat to Jesus' audience about exclusion from the kingdom, but at another level it is a description of what is already happening in his ministry. In the call of the twelve disciples, in Jesus' proclamation to the poor, in his healing and exorcism of the afflicting, the Kingdom is coming and restoration beckoning, and so many already are coming from near and far (Jews and non-Jews) and experiencing the saving power of the kingdom. Although Matthew's placement of the logion with the narrative of the centurion may be redactional, it remains in accordance with the inter-textual echoes of the saying that anticipates the regathering of Jews to the homeland and the eschatological pilgrimage of the Gentiles.

In the discourse of John 10, the Johannine Jesus informs his disciples that he has "other sheep" (possibly Gentiles) which need to be brought in. The passage has points of contact with the shepherd metaphors of the synoptic tradition (Mark 6:34; 14:27; Matt 2:6; 18:12; 25:32) and messianic connotations for shepherd in Jewish literature (Isa 44:28; Jer 23:4; Ezek 34:15, 23–24; *4 Ezra* 2:34). The saying represents a Johannine interpretation of the significance of Jesus' messiahship for the Gentiles.

The Olivet Discourse includes the saying attributed to Jesus that "the good news must first be proclaimed to all nations" (Mark 13:10; cf. 14:9;

Matt 24:14). This verse is the clearest reference to a preaching mission to Gentiles attributed to Jesus in a pre-Easter setting. The verse represents a plethora of textual and historical problems; not the least is that its authenticity is questioned on the grounds that it sounds too much like the mission theology of the early church. If Jesus spoke so clearly of a Gentile mission it begs the question as to why there was some stagnation in the early church before a Gentile mission got underway. The authenticity of the passage is moot; even so the verse does cohere with other material that links mission with persecution (Mark 8:35–38; Matt 10:16–25; Luke 11:49; 21:12–13).

The temple episode (Mark 11:15–17) sheds further light on Jesus' view of the Gentiles. Jesus' action in the Temple represents a brief and dramatic foreshadowing of judgment on the institution. One of the reasons for the demonstration was to attack the role of the Temple in fostering nationalistic violence and the limitation placed on gentile participation in cultus. Instead of being a magnet to the nations, the Temple had become a talisman thought to ensure victory over pagan Rome. The midrashic juxtaposition of Isa 56:7 and Jer 7:11 implies that the current Temple has failed to be the eschatological temple, in that it has failed to realize the universal role of the temple in drawing the nations to worship God (cf. 1 Kgs 8:41–43) and it had degenerated into an enclave of zealot theology. Craig Evans notes:

> If this interpretation is correct, then we may have here an important piece of evidence that suggests that Jesus' messianic mission included the Gentiles and that part of his criticism of the Temple establishment was in response to its failure to maintain a proper witness for the Lord.
>
> (Evans 440)

Jesus' encounters with Gentiles

In the Gospels there are several reported encounters between Jesus and gentile figures: the demoniac in the Decapolis (Mark 5:1–20; Matt 8:28–34; Luke 8:26–39), the deaf and mute man (Mark 7:31–37; Matt 15:29–31), the feeding miracle on the gentile side of the Sea of Galilee (Mark 8:1–10; Matt 15:32–39), the Syrophoenician/Canaanite woman in Tyre (Mark 7:24–30; Matt 15:21–28), the centurion in Capernaum (Luke 7:1–10/Matt 8:5–13 = John 4:46–54?), and the request of Greeks to meet Jesus (John 12:20–23). Although these narratives are often regarded as projections of the mission theology of the early church onto Jesus this seems unlikely because: (1) Jesus never seeks out Gentiles

and the gentile characters usually take the initiative in finding him; (2) none of the Gentiles that Jesus meets becomes a disciple; (3) in most cases, the healed person remains at a distance from Jesus; (4) several of the stories contain features that were potentially embarrassing, such as Jesus' stern reply to the Syrophoenician woman (Mark 7:27), Jesus' initial reluctance to go to the house of the Centurion (Matt 8:7), and the fact that he does not grant the request of the Greeks to meet him (John 12:20–23); (5) none of these narratives deals with the question of circumcision, law-observance for Gentiles, or disputes over Jew–Gentile fellowship. This confirms the words of Schnabel (1994: 47) that "this nexus between Jesus and mission among the Gentiles cannot simply be ascribed to the aetiological interests of the Gospel writers" (see Wright 431, 445). Jesus' movements into gentile territory were probably for respite rather than for mission. Although these encounters are exceptional and *ad hoc* they demonstrate that the saving power of the kingdom can already be extended to Gentiles prior to the eschatological consummation.

Factors leading towards a gentile mission

It is crucial to note that the gentile mission did not begin by way of reference to the dominical tradition, but instead it was born out of the belief that the eschaton had dawned in Jesus' resurrection, the experience of the Spirit at Pentecost, and reading the Septuagint in light of those two beliefs. Nevertheless, the early Christian mission is part of the *effective history* of Jesus and has clear pre-Easter antecedents in Jesus' itinerant ministry, the call to discipleship as a call to mission, Jesus' openness towards Gentiles, and commission of the disciples to replicate the universal role of Israel and the Temple in being "a light to the nations" and "a house of prayer for all nations". The early church followed this program with the new eschatological consciousness created by the belief that Jesus had been resurrected. Jesus probably did not envisage a *Torah*-free gentile mission that ran as a sequel to an abandoned Jewish mission, but he did intimate that a transformed Israel would transform the world (Manson).

MICHAEL F. BIRD

Further reading

Bird, Michael F. "Jesus and the Gentiles since Jeremias. Problems and Prospects," *CBR* 4 (2005) 83–108.
—— "Who Comes from the East and the West? Matt 8:11–12/Luke 13:28–39 and the Historical Jesus," *NTS* 52:4 (2006) 441–57.

—— *Jesus and the Origins of the Gentile Mission*, LHJS, Edinburgh: T. & T. Clark/Continuum, 2007.

Evans, Craig A. "From 'House of Prayer' to 'Cave of Robbers': Jesus' Prophetic Criticism of the Temple Establishment," in Craig A. Evans and S. Talmon (eds) *The Quest for Context and Meaning*, BIS 28, Leiden: Brill, 1997, pp. 417–42.

Hahn, Ferdinand. *Mission in the New Testament*, London: SCM Press, 1965.

Jeremias, Joachim. *Jesus' Promise to the Nations*, London: SCM Press, 1958 [1956].

McKnight, Scot. "Gentiles," in Joel B. Green, Scot McKnight, and I. Howard Marshall (eds) *DJG*, Downers Grove, IL: InterVarsity Press, 1992, pp. 259–65.

Manson, T. W. *Only to the House of Israel? Jesus and the Non-Jews*, Philadelphia, PA: Fortress Press, 1964.

Schnabel, Eckhard J. "Jesus and the Beginnings of the Mission to the Gentiles," in Joel B. Green and Max Turner (eds) *Jesus of Nazareth, Lord and Christ*, Grand Rapids, MI: Eerdmans, 1994, pp. 37–58.

—— *The Early Christian Mission*, 2 vols, Downers Grove, IL: InterVarsity Press, 2004, Vol. 1, pp. 327–82.

Sundkler, Bengst. "Jésus et les païens," *Arbeiten und Mitteilungen aus dem neutestamentlichen Seminar zu Uppsala* 6 (1937) 1–38.

Wilk, Florian. *Jesus und die Völker in der Sicht der Synoptiker*, Berlin: Walter de Gruyter, 2002.

Wright, N. T. *Jesus and the Victory of God*, Minneapolis, MN: Fortress Press, 1996.

GEOGRAPHY OF GALILEE AND JUDEA

Physical, political and theological geography

The main landscapes

The biblical Land of Israel is divided from west to east in four great regions. The Coastal Plain of the Mediterranean Sea broadens from north to south. The mountain range west of it descends from the Lebanon Mountains (1,940 m) to the hills of Upper Galilee (Meron 1,208 m) and Lower Galilee (Tabor 588 m). The Jezreel valley divides the Galilean Highs from the Carmel (546 m) and the Mountains of Samaria (Ebal 940 m, Garizim 881 m) that continue in the Judean Mountains (1,016 m near Ephraim, 821 m near Jerusalem, 1,019 m near Hebron), descending to the Negeb Desert. A big rift valley starts in the Beqaa Plain in Lebanon and continues through the Upper Jordan Valley with the Sea of Galilee (*c.* −210 m). The Lower Jordan Valley is about 100 km long and ends in the Dead Sea, the lowest point on earth (*c.* −390 m). The mountain range east of the Jordan lowers from Hermon (2,814 m) to the Gaulanitis (Golan Highs 1,204 m), and to the high plateaus of Trachonitis, Batanaea and Hauran. Then, to the south the Jordanian Mountains rise

(1,247 m near Gerasa, 1,065 m above the Dead Sea). The main roads went from north to south through the Coastal Plain, above the ridge of the Samaritan–Judean Mountains, through the Jordan Valley and on the western edge of the Jordanian Mountains. Another main road from east to west went from the Jordan Valley through the Jezreel Plain to the Mediterranean Sea. Secondary roads crossed the Samaritan–Judean Mountains near Shechem and Jerusalem.

The Coastal Plain, the western slope of the Samaritan–Judean Mountains and Galilee have a Mediterranean climate, the Jordan Valley a sub-tropical climate. There a partly very intense agriculture was possible (Josephus, *J.W.* 3:42–45), mainly corn (Mark 4:3–8; Luke 12:16–18), wine (Mark 12:1–9), olive (Mark 13:28) and fig trees (Mark 11:12–13; Luke 13:6–9). In biblical times the higher mountains were covered by woods (*J.W.* 3:49). Most of the other regions have a steppe climate and were only suitable for sheep and goats (Luke 15:4–7). The Lowest Jordan Valley (Mark 1:4–5) and the region around the Dead Sea were desert. Of outstanding economic importance was the fishing at the Sea of Galilee (Josephus, *J.W.* 3:508; cf. Mark 1:16–20; John 21:1–8).

Political geography

Flavius Josephus gave a rather comprehensive description of the Holy Land in NT times (*J.W.* 3:35–58). The tetrarchy of Herod's son Antipas comprised two separated territories, Galilee and Peraea. The borders of the totally Jewish Galilee lay to the east, against the Gaulanitis, the Upper Jordan, and the western shore of Lake Gennesaret. In the south they reached the Decapolis, Samaria, and the Jezreel Plain. In the north they reached the territory of the city of Tyre and the edge of the Coastal Plain, while in the north these borders extended to the Upper Galilean Mountains (*J.W.* 3:35–40). Some think of a Galilean regionalism with Upper Galilee more closed to external influences. Indeed, the city of Gischala, the original home of Paul's parents (Jerome, *De vir. ill.* 5), was a Zealots' centre (*J.W.* 2:585–89; 4:84–120). Peraea stretched east of the Lower Jordan for about 100 km from south of Pella to Machaerus upon the eastern shore of the Dead Sea (*J.W.* 3:44–47). The tetrarchy of Herod's other son, Philippus, comprised the northern territories of Gaulanitis, Trachonitis and Batanaea with a mixed population of Jews and Syrians (*J.W.* 3:56–57). The Gaulanite city of Gamala with its first-century BCE synagogue was a Zealot stronghold (*J.W.* 4:1–83). To the south of Philippus' tetrarchy stretched the Decapolis, a region of Hellenistic cities, with a Jewish minority. Most of them were situated east of the Jordan (Hippos, Gadara, Pella, Gerasa, Philadelphia [Amman], etc.), with only Scythopolis/Bet Shean at its western bank.

After Herod's son Archelaus lost his kingdom in 6 AD, Samaria and Judea formed one territory under direct Roman rule (*J.W.* 2:117). Nevertheless, both remained separated by people and religion (John 4:9). Samaria, bordering to the Mediterranean in the west, comprised the Sharon coastal plain from Caesarea to Antipatris and the highlands north of Arimathaea and Acrabetta, bordering in the east to the middle Lower Jordan Valley and in the north to the Jezreel Plain (*J.W.* 3:48–50). Judea comprised the big oasis of Jericho in the Lowest Jordan Valley, the eastern shore of the Dead Sea with En-Gedi and Masada, the Judean Mountains from Alexandreion to Hebron with Jerusalem in the middle, and also the eastern parts of the Coastal Plain with Emmaus, Lydda, Joppa and also in the far south the half-desert Idumea (*J.W.* 3:51–55). In the south, Judea bordered the Nabatean kingdom and in the southeast the territories of the free cities Ascalon and Gaza.

Gospel geography

Using the symbolical number five, Matt 4:25 states that Jesus reached people from all parts of the Holy Land with Jews as a majority or minority: "Galilee, Decapolis, Jerusalem, Judea and Trans-Jordan (πέραν τοῦ Ἰορδάνου)." Mark 3:7–8 gives seven regions, apparently, including the Decapolis in Trans-Jordan, but adding "Idumea, Tyre and Sidon." Both lists exclude Samaria. Either Luke, the Antiochene, or his Jewish Christian tradition shows an interest in the north, mentioning besides "Judea and Galilee" the tetrarchies of Philippus as "Ituraea and Trachonitis" and of Lysanias as "Abilene" (Luke 3:1). The fulfilment of three Messianic expectations through Jesus according to John 1:19–21 may also cover the main biblical regions: Davidic Messiah (Judea/Jerusalem), prophets like Moses (Samaria) and Elijah (Galilee and Northern Trans-Jordan).

Gospel geography has two dimensions. First, some places and regions have from the OT and Jewish tradition a symbolical meaning implied by the Evangelists, their traditions or Jesus himself. Second, concrete place names show how deeply the tradition is rooted in the Land of Israel and in the history of Jesus. When the Gospels (except Luke 5:1) speak about the "Sea (θάλασσα) of Galilee,"

this has a local colour (Mark 1:16; Matt 4:18; John 6:1, etc.). That in Galilee one had to "descend" from Cana to Capernaum (John 4:46–47), but "to ascend" to Jerusalem from all other parts of the land, betrays local knowledge (Mark 10:32–33; John 2:13). Matt 28:16–20 has only a Galilean and Luke 24 only Judean resurrection appearance(s). There are other indications that Luke used a tradition preserved in the south, whereas the Matthean community lived rather in the north of the Holy Land (cf. Matt 4:24; 9:1).

Geography of John the Baptist

Birth and education

John was born (Luke 1:39) in "the town of Juda in the hill country (εἰς τὴν ὀρεινὴν μετὰ σπουδῆς εἰς πόλιν Ἰούδα)." Pliny called the district around Jerusalem *orine* (*Nat.* 5:14) and the town is identified by tradition with Ain Karim (Theodosius, *De situ terrae sanctae* 6) 7 km west of the Holy City. That a nearby cave served for John's baptism is not proven by the archaeological evidence. The "wilderness" (ἐρήμοι) where John lived as a child (Luke 1:80) could have been an Essene settlement like Qumran; the Essenes adopted boys to give them a religious education (*J.W.* 2:120; cf. 1QH 9:35–36). If so, the choice of the places for baptism showed that after his prophetic call (Luke 3:1–3) John broke with Essene exclusivism to reach as many people as possible "in all the region around the Jordan" (Luke 3:3).

Places of baptism

Recent excavations have confirmed the tradition for the place of Jesus' baptism (Eusebius, *Onomast.* 59). It was opposite Jericho (cf. Mark 1:4–9) on the eastern bank of the River Jordan, near one of the most frequented fords. Jewish tradition (cf. Pilgrim of Bordeaux, *Itin.* 19) remembered here Israel's crossing of the Jordan (Josh 3:14–17) and Elijah's ascent to heaven (2 Kgs 2:4–15). John's baptism re-enacted the entry in the Promised Land because, through God's judgment, the Jewish people had lost their status of salvation (Matt 3:9–10). Another place of baptism was a strong "spring" (Αἰνών from עינן) "near Salim" (John 3:23), not to be identified with the nearly waterless Salim 5 km east of Shechem, but with Tel Shalem, 12 km south of Scythopolis (Eusebius, *Onom.* 40:1–4). Nearby was Abel Mehola where Elijah called Elisa (1 Kgs 19:16–21). The riddle of "Bethany (Βηθανία) beyond the Jordan" (John 1:28) has already been discussed by Origen (*Comm. Jo.* 6:204). This was not the place of Jesus' baptism (cf. John 1:29–34), but must have been in the north nearer to Galilee as the temporal and geographical indications in John 1–2 and 11 show. This "Bethany" may be identified with the Trans-Jordan region of Batanaea. Some Jews expected the return of Elijah (cf. Mark 9:2–13) in the north-east (*Sifre Deut* 41 [79b]; cf. 1 Kgs 19:15; *CD* 7:18–19).

Death and burial

That John was also active in the tetrarchy of Antipas is shown by the fact that this king condemned him to death (Mark 6:14–29). The baptizer was beheaded at the fortress Machaerus in Perea (Josephus, *Ant.* 18:119). The tomb of John was shown in Samaria/Sebaste (Jerome, *Ep.* 43:13; 108:13) where Jewish tradition venerated the tomb of Elisa (*Vit. Proph.* 95:6). The prominence of places connected with Elijah/Elisa may point to John's self-consciousness as the eschatological Elijah (Mark 1:6 [2 Kgs 1:8]; Luke 1:17; but John 1:19–21).

Jesus in Galilee

Nazareth

Most of his life (Mark 6:1; Luke 4:16) Jesus spent in the village of Nazareth (Ναζαρέτ) situated at about 350 m on a fertile high plain in Lower Galilee. In the nineteenth century the existence of Nazareth was doubted, because it is not mentioned in the OT or Jewish literature. But its name is verified by a list of priestly settlements from the third/fourth century (IEJ 12 (1962) 137–39). Excavations brought to light the remains of a first-century Jewish village. The caves found were not human habitations, but served as stables and cellars. Older drawings show that the village was erected on a rocky promontory (Luke 4:29). Julius Africanus says that the extended family of Jesus settled in Nazareth and Cochaba (Eusebius, *Hist. eccl.* 1:7.6–12). The names recall two of the most important messianic promises, the "star" (כוכב) of Num 24:17 and the "branch" (נצר) of Isa 11:1 (cf. Matt 2:22–23). Apparently, Nazareth was inhabited by descendants of David hoping for the restoration of the Israelite kingdom (cf. Luke 1:78). Nearby in Gubetha/Gath Hepher (2 Kgs 14:25), the tomb of the prophet Jonah was venerated (cf. Matt 12:39–41; 16:4). Only one hour's walk away was the ancient Galilean capital Sepphoris. So, one should not think of Jesus' outlook on the world as too narrow.

On pilgrimages to Jerusalem (Luke 2:41–51), he could hear famous teachers and have contacts with Jews from all parts of the ancient world.

Concentration on Galilee

The Synoptics presuppose that Jesus often visited Jerusalem (Matt 23:37) as John plainly says (John 2:13; 5:1; 7:10). Nevertheless, Jesus first concentrated his activity on Galilee. According to Matt 4:12–17 this was a messianic sign acted by him: the prophet had foreseen that the eschatological salvation would start where the judgement on Israel began with the downfall of the Northern Kingdom in 722/21 BCE, namely in "the land of Zebulun and Naphtali ... the way of the sea, the land beyond the Jordan, Galilee of the nations (גליל הגוים, LXX Γαλιλαία τῶν ἐθνῶν)" (Isa 8:23 [9:1]). This is confirmed by the fact that after his call to repentance failed, Jesus condemned the Galilean villages with an apodictic eschatological judgement (Matt 11:20–24; Luke 10:13–15). The gospels do not mention any activities in the capital Tiberias or in Sepphoris, cities with 10,000–20,000 inhabitants. Some explain this by the antipathy of a conservative Jewish countryman, but only Tiberias was partly Hellenized (*Ant.* 18:37), whereas Sepphoris, according to modern excavations, was strongly Jewish. Also, there are no hints that an unsuccessful mission was suppressed in the tradition. Probably Jesus avoided both cities because initially he did not wish to become a target of Antipas (cf. Luke 13:31–33).

Capernaum

Jesus centred his activity on Capernaum (Καφαρναούμ, כפר נחום) at the north-western shore of Lake Gennesaret, which with about 1,500–2,000 people was one of the greatest villages of Galilee and a considerable fishing harbour (Matt 4:13; 9:1). Sparse remains of a first-century synagogue (Mark 1:21; Luke 7:1–5) testify to the piety of the inhabitants. The toll station served to collect either sea toll or toll at the nearby border to Philippus' tetrarchy (Mark 2:14). Excavations show a building continuity from a first-century Jewish fisherhouse, early on converted into a religious assembly room, then into a fourth-century house church and then a fifth-century basilica. The uninterrupted presence of Jewish Christians until the fourth century (*Midr. Qoh.* 1:8 [9a]; 7:26 [38a]) enables the identification with Peter's house (Mark 1:29–33; 2:1). Separated from the Jewish village (cf. Luke 7:6), a Roman building complex may have housed a centurion and other pagan mercenaries of Antipas (Matt 8:5–13).

Strong springs, 2 km southwest of Capernaum and today called Tabhga (Arabized from the Greek *Heptapēgōn*, "seven springs"), were even thought by some to be one of the origins of the River Nile (*J.W.* 3:519 20). Early tradition (Egeria, *Itin.* [CSEL 39:112]) connected that place with the Feeding of the 5,000 (Mark 6:32–44), the Sermon on the Mount/Plain (Matt 5:1–2; Luke 6:12, 17) and a resurrection appearance (John 21). Indeed, it would have been an ideal gathering place for large crowds at the strongly frequented pilgrims' route from the Eastern Diaspora via Damascus to Jerusalem (cf. Josephus, *Ant.* 17:26). Jesus attracted people from the whole Land of Israel (Mark 3:7–8; Matt 4:24 25). About 1 km east of Capernaum, a little bay forms a natural theatre with good acoustic capacities for someone speaking from a boat (Mark 4:1–2). The unknown parallel toponyms Dalmanutha (Mark 8:10) and Magadan (Matt 15:39) are not corruptions of Magdala (despite some late variants to Matt 15:39) but Semitic names of a place either north of Magdala (Wadi Salmon) or near Capernaum (Tabgha).

Other Galilean villages

Not only summaries (Mark 1:38 39; Matt 4:23) but also isolated traditions show that Jesus' preaching reached all parts of Galilee. His fame spread to the whole "Land of Gennesaret" (Mark 6:53–56), a very fertile plain on the western shore of the Lake which Josephus was so fond of (*J.W.* 3:516–21). One of the most important woman followers, Mary Magdalene (Mark 15:40, 47; John 20:1, 18), was from Magdala/Tarichaeae. This little city in the Gennesaret Plain was apparently more hellenized (*J.W.* 2:599) and was famous for its industry of pickled fish (Strabo 16:3.4). Jesus also attracted hearers from the capital Tiberias (John 6:23) and he preached in his home town, Nazareth (Mark 6:1–6). Another important place of his activity was Cana (John 2:1–12; 4:46–54; 21:2), to be identified with Khirbet Qana and not with Kafr Kenna, as a very late tradition has it. Cana is situated on the northern edge of the fertile Netopha plain and near to Josephus' last stronghold Jotapata (*Vita* 86). Recent excavations have unearthed a big Jewish village, but no trace of a Dionysiac cult. Through the Netopha Plain went an important long trade road from the Lake of Gennesaret to Ptolemais (Acts 21:7) at the Mediterranean Sea.

Some identify the village of Nain with a town in Judea (*J.W.* 4:511), but the text of Josephus is here corrupted (cf. Josh 15:32; 19:7). The literary/geographical context and the Elisa/Elijah typology of the healing narrative (Luke 7:11–17) point to a northern location. Nain is situated about 8 km south-east of Nazareth at the edge of the Jezreel Plain (*Gen. Rabba* 31 [62a]; Eusebius, *Onom.* 140:3) and not far from Shunem, where Elijah resurrected a boy (2 Kgs 4:18–37). That Luke called towns like Nain or Nazareth a "city" (πόλις) might be explained by the fact that he had visited Jerusalem and the Coastal Plain (Acts 21:7–17) but not Galilee. Near Nain Galilee bordered Samaria and one healing story is located in this border territory (Luke 17:11 19). Corazin lies on the way from Capernaum (Matt 11:21; Luke 10:13) to Upper Galilee, called in Mark 7:24 "the hills (ὅρια) of Tyre". At the end of his Galilean activity Jesus sent the disciples to preach the kingdom of God and repentance "in every town" (Luke 10:1). Any location in Galilee could be reached in no more than a two-day journey; from southern Galilee to Jerusalem it took three days (Josephus, *Life* 269–70; cf. Luke 13:32–33).

Bethsaida

Josephus located this to the north-east of Capernaum (*J.W.* 3:515), only the Crusaders invented a location south of it. Today there are two candidates, the ruin hill et-Tel 2 km distant from the Lake with some Hellenistic-Roman city walls and buildings, and the unexcavated ruin field el-Aradj at the shore where stray finds from Second Temple times can be found. Bethsaida had a harbour (Josephus, *Life* 407). It is possible that in NT times the Jordan River flowed not to the west of el-Aradj, as today, but to the east of it, and this would make the place belong to Galilee. The tetrarch Philippus converted Bethsaida in the *polis* Julias (*Ant.* 18:28), placing this settlement east of the Jordan in the Gaulanitis and making an identification with et-Tel plausible. Perhaps a Jewish fishing village of Bethsaida existed to both sides of the influx of the Jordan. The eastern part could have been the ruin field of el-Mesadiye, with finds from the early Roman period. After the death of Herod in 4 BCE the Jordan became the border between the tetrarchies of Antipas and Philippus. In this case el-Aradj could have been called "Bethsaida in Galilee" (John 12:28) and a "village" (κώμη: Mark 8:23, 28). But sometimes the Gaulanitis was reckoned as part of Galilee (Josephus, *J.W.* 2:118; Ptol., *Geog.* 5:15.3). Apparently the Jews of Bethsaida were more Hellenized than those of Capernaum. Jesus' disciples Andrew and Philippus, stemming from Bethsaida, bore Greek names (John 1:44 cf. 12:20–22). The stress on Bethsaida and Cana in John may point to the existence of post-Easter Johannine communities there. The Petrine/Markan tradition (Papias in Eusebius, *Hist. eccl.* 3:39.14) was more interested in Peter's dwelling-place, Capernaum.

Jesus in the north

Jesus' stay in the territories north of Galilee was, for the Evangelists, a foreshadowing of the mission to the Gentiles – but they did not invent it. Since, after the mission of the disciples in Galilee, Jesus had to fear death at the hands of Antipas (Mark 6:14–29), he withdrew to the territories of the free cities Tyre and Sidon (Mark 7:24–31). Jesus was also safe in the vicinity of Caesarea Philippi (Mark 8:27), the capital of the mild Philippus (*Ant.* 18:106–7). The transfiguration (Mark 9:2; Matt 16:13) is placed on a "very high mountain" (ὄρος ὑψηλός). Comparable expressions (Deut 4:48; *T. Levi* 2:5) and the proximity to Caesarea Philippi point to Mount Hermon. Indeed, the oldest church tradition identified it as the place of the transfiguration, and not Mount Tabor (Eusebius, *In. Ps.* 88:13). Initially, the resurrection appearance on the "mountain in Galilee" (Matt 28:16–20) was localized to Tabor (Theodosius, *De situ terrae sanctae* 4). Before 70 AD Jewish groups expected that end-time events would start between Mount Hermon and Damascus (*CD* 7:12–21; *Sifre Deut* 1:1 [65a]; cf. *T. Levi* 2–6). That the messianic confession of Peter (Mark 8:27–30), the revelation of Jesus' path to the Passion (Mark 8:31–33) and the transfiguration (Mark 9:2–13) all took place in this northern region also had a Messianic/typological meaning.

Jesus in the Decapolis

In Hellenistic-Roman times there was much traffic between the western Jewish shore of the Sea of Galilee and the eastern shore belonging to the mostly pagan Decapolis (*Gen. Rabba* 31 [62a]). The "city" nearby in which Jesus performed an exorcism (Mark 5:1–20) must have been Hippos, which was in a commanding position upon the Lake. It could not have been Gerasa, about 40 km distant from the Lake. Ancient local tradition (Origen, *Comm. Jo.* 6:24; Eusebius, *Onom.* 74:13) together with some archaeological corroboration identifies the place as el-Kursi at the border between the Gaulanitis and the Decapolis. The "Land of the Gerasenes/Gergesenes" (Mark 5:1; Luke 8:26 Sin.) may point to apocalyptic expectations. Some rabbis

thought that Gog and Magog (Ezek 39:11) would be buried in this region (*Cant. Zuta* 1,1 [2a]). Whereas the pre-Israelite Geshurites (Deut 3:14 LXX Γάργασι) inhabiting the eastern shore (*y. Sheviit* 6:1 [36c]) were expelled by Joshua (Josh 12:5), Jesus accepted the healed pagan. The alternative name "Land of the Gadarenes" (Matt 8:28) refers to the fact that, according to numismatic evidence, the city of Gadara possessed a stretch of the south-eastern shore. Apparently Matt 15:32–39 and Mark 8:1–10 presuppose that the Feeding of the 4,000, taking place in the Decapolis (Mark 8:31), included Jews and Gentiles (Matt 15:31). Possibly, old church tradition placed it near el-Kursi (Baldi 278).

Jesus in Samaria

It is one of the agreements between the Lucan special tradition and John that Jesus also visited Samaria. Luke 9:51–56 reflects the tensions between the Samaritans and Jewish pilgrims, one of the causes for the outbreak of the Jewish War in 66 (*J.W.* 20:118). John 4:4–6 shows considerable local knowledge: Sychar and not the totally Hellenized city of Samaria formed the centre of the Samaritan religion. Jacob's Well was near to the Tomb of Joseph, and from there one could see Garizim, the holy mountain of the Samaritans (John 4:20). Because Jesus was "sent only to the lost sheep of Israel" he did not send his disciples to Samaria (Matt 10:5–6). The contacts with Samaritans were exceptions, as were those with pagans (Mark 7:24–30; Matt 8:5–13).

Jesus in Judea

Bethlehem

Although there was a Bethlehem in Galilee (Josh 19:15), the Matthean and Lukan tradition independently identify the Davidic Judean city (Mic 5:1) as the birth-place of Jesus (Matt 2:1; Luke 2:1–7). Already before the Bar-Kokhba war (132–35) a stable-cave was shown (Justin, *Dial.* 78) as the place of the "manger" (Luke 2:7) whose clay-wall was still known to Jerome (Baldi 91). If the "Star of Bethlehem" is identified with a conjunction of Jupiter and Saturn in 7 BCE it is interesting that the Zodiacal light fell on the city (cf. Matt 2:9). The "dwelling" of the shepherds (Luke 2:8) might have been connected to a "Tower of the Flock" (*migdal eder*) east of Bethlehem (Eusebius, *Ep.* 108:10) where some awaited the Messiah (*Tg. Ps.-J.* Gen 35:21; *Tg. Neb.* Mic 4:8;

5:1). One tradition (Gen 35:19; 48:7) localized the Tomb of Rahel near Bethlehem (cf. Matt 2:17–18).

Ephraim

The Johannine tradition presupposes that Jesus was also active in Judea and had followers there who could give him shelter. "Ephraim near the desert" (John 11:54) is to be identified with OT Ophra (Josh 18:23; cf. *J.W.* 4:551) and today's Arab-Christian village et-Taybe, formerly called Afra (Eusebius, *Onom.* 29:4; 86:1). Apparently in former times Ephraim belonged to Samaria (cf. 1 Macc 11:34).

Jericho

The Lukan special tradition knew that a dangerous road "descended" from Jerusalem to Jericho, with its colony of priests (Luke 10:30–31). As a strongly Hellenized and rich border city (*Ant.* 15:54; 17:340) it was the seat of a "chief tax collector" (Luke 19:1–2). That Luke 18:35 narrates the healing of a blind man in front of Jericho, but Mark 10:46 when leaving Jericho, was sometimes explained in that the former meant the Hellenistic-Roman and the latter the ruined OT city. But Josephus distinguished both (*J.W.* 4:459) and tradition unambiguously pointed to the exit of the city to Jerusalem (Jerome, *Ep.* 108:12).

Mount of Olives

This mountain east of Jerusalem, separated from the city by the Kidron Valley, was a place of fierce apocalyptic hopes (*b. Keth.* 111a; *Tg. Cant.* 8:5; cf. Ezek 11:23; Zech 14:4–5) and of apocalyptic uprisings (*J.W.* 2:261–63; cf. Acts 21:23). The disciples expected the inbreaking kingdom of God when ascending the Mount of Olives (Luke 19:11–38). There, Jesus wept prophetically over Jerusalem (Luke 19:41–44) and uttered apocalyptic teachings (Mark 13:3). This revelation has been localized to a cave on the mountain (Eusebius, *Vit. Const.* 3:41; cf. *Acts John* 97) and it was believed that nearby was the place of Jesus' ascension (Eusebius, *Dem. Ev.* 6:18; cf. Luke 24:50; Acts 1:12). On the eastern slope of the Mount of Olives "15 stadia from Jerusalem" (John 11:18) was located Bethany, where Jesus found hospitality and safety (Mark 11:1–12; John 11–12). Bethany, partly excavated, may have been one of the places the Temple Scroll of Qumran assigned for lepers (11QMiqd. 46:16–47:5; cf. Mark 14:3). On top of the mountain was the village of Bethphage (Mark 11:1), included by

halakha into the urban area of Jerusalem (*m. Menah.* 11:2).

Jerusalem

The centre of the Holy City was the Temple, where Jesus taught and debated (Mark 11–12), sometimes in the eastern "Portico of Solomon" (John 10:23). Probably the Messianic sign of the cleansing (Mark 11:15–18) was acted in the market hall in the southern "Royal Stoa." The healing of a lame man took place at the "Sheep Pool near Bethesda" (John 5:2; variants *Bethsaida, Bethzatha*). The double pool north of the Temple (cf. Isa 7:3; Sir 50:3) and some Jewish baths were excavated. The "Pool of Siloam" (John 9:7, 11), where Jesus sent a blind man, was recently discovered. It was fed by Ezekia's Tunnel and reputed to be the Spring of Gihon (*J.W.* 5:140–45) where Solomon was anointed king (1 Kgs 1:38–40). Probably, Jesus' Messianic entrance was through the gate near to it (cf. Mark 11:7–11). The interpretation of Siloam as "Sent" (John 9:7) followed local Jewish tradition (*Vit. Proph.* 13), pointing to the Messianic promise of Genesis 49:10 (cf. 4Qpatr 2:4). Sparse remains of the "Tower of Siloam" (Luke 13:4) and the Greek-speaking "Synagogue of the Freedmen", which Paul attended (Acts 6:9; 7:58), were also found nearby. Since both pools are mentioned in the Copper Scroll of Qumran (3Q15 10:15–16; 11:12) an Essene presence seems possible.

Luke identified the "Upper Room" (ἀνάγαιον) of Jesus' last Passover meal (Luke 22:12) with the first assembly room (ὑπερῷον) of the Primitive community (Acts 1:13). A Jewish-Christian synagogue from before 130 AD (Epiphanius, *De mensuris* 14), whose walls are part of the so-called Tomb of David, commemorated the place on the South-western Hill, today's Mount Zion. Jerusalem's Essene Quarter (cf. *J.W.* 5:145; 11QMiqd 46:13–15) was nearby (cf. Acts 2:5; 6:7). Leaving the city, Jesus passed the burial place "Akeldamah at the Potter's Field" (Matt 27:7–8; Acts 1:18–19) on the southern slope of the Hinnom Valley (cf. Jer 19:2), which was a symbol for hell (Matt 5:22). The prophecy of the "struck shepherd" (Mark 14:27; cf. Zech 13:7) might have been uttered in front of the traditional Tomb of Zechariah (*Vit. Proph.* 88:3–4), opposite the "Pinnacle of the Temple" (Matt 4:5). To reach Gethsemane (Mark 14:26, 32), a garden with an olive press at the foot of Mount Olives (Eusebius, *Onomast.* 74; cf. Luke 22:39), Jesus had to cross the Kidron Valley (John 18:1) like the refused David (2 Sam 15:23). The oldest tradition for the High

Priest's Palace (Mark 14:54) points to the present church of St Peter on the eastern edge of Mount Zion (Pilgrim of Bordeaux, *Itin.* 16). The assembly place of the Sanhedrin (Mark 15:1) could have been in the "Masonic Hall" left of the "Wailing Wall". The Praetorium of Pilate (Mark 15:16) was neither in the Antonia Fortress, as the Crusaders thought, nor in the Upper Herodian Palace (Citadel) for which there is no tradition at all. Earliest tradition (Pilgrim of Bordeaux, *Itin.* 17) identified it with the Hasmonean Palace on the rocky cliff (Gabbatha?) opposite the Temple Mount, whose traces, including the pavement "Lithostrotos" (John 19:13), may be seen in the "Herodian Mansion". "Golgotha", Aramaic גלגלת "the Skull" (John 19:17), was an artificially hewn rock in a big quarry in the north-west angle of the First and Second Walls near the Gennath Gate (*J.W.* 5:146; cf. John 19:20; Heb 13:12–13). Photogrammetric examinations demonstrated that the tomb under the nearby cupola of the Church of the Holy Sepulchre is characteristic of Second Temple times. The gospels point to an early veneration of the empty tomb of Jesus (Mark 16:5–6; John 19:41–42).

Emmaus

This "village about 60 (P[75]; B)/160 (Sin.) stadia from Jerusalem" (Luke 24:13) was the dwelling-place of pre-Easter followers of Jesus (Luke 24:28–30). Some identify it with Qalunya 6 km west of Jerusalem, a former Roman veteran colony, called *Ammaous* by the Greek text of Josephus (*J.W.* 7:217). But as the Latin tradition shows, this is a secondary variant, possibly influenced by Christian copyists. From OT times (Josh 18:26) until the Talmudic period (*m. Sukk.* 4:5; *y. Sukk.* 4:3 [54b]) the place was ever called Moza. Old church tradition unanimously points to Emmaus-Nicopolis (Eusebius, *Onom.* 90:15–17), 23 km west of Jerusalem, today's ruined Arab village of Amwas. There is a building continuity from a first-century house to fourth/fifth-century churches. Luke 24:13, 28 could call Emmaus a "village" because it suffered destruction after an uprising against the Romans in 4 BCE (*J.W.* 2:69–71) and had no city rights. The expression "redemption of Israel" (Luke 24:21) may allude to the great Maccabean victory over a Syrian army at Emmaus (1 Macc 4:11).

Other cities of the Coastal Plain

According to Sozomenos Jesus visited Emmaus before Easter (*Hist. eccl.* 5:21). The Sanhedrist Joseph, who buried Jesus, stemmed from Arimathaea

(Mark 15:43), today Rentis. Possibly Jesus already had sympathizers in Lydda and Joppa where messianic communities were firmly established before the evangelization of Peter (Acts 9:32–43). For Luke the cities in the Coastal Plain were the first step on the way of the gospel to Rome in the west.

RAINER RIESNER

Further reading

Arav, R. and R. A. Freund. *Bethsaida I/II*, Kirksville, MO: Thomas Jefferson University, 1995/1999.
Baldi, D. *Enchiridion Locorum Sanctorum*, third edition, Jerusalem: Franciscan Printing, 1982.
Bauckham, R. (ed.) *The Book of Acts in Its Palestinian Setting*, Grand Rapids, MI: Eerdmans, 1995.
Ben-Dov, M. *Historical Atlas of Jerusalem*, New York: Continuum, 2002.
Böhm, M. *Samarien und die Samaritai bei Lukas*, Tübingen: Mohr Siebeck, 1999.
Bösen, W. *Galiläa als Lebensraum und Wirkungsfeld Jesu*, Freiburg: Herder, 1998.
Chancey, M. A. *The Myth of a Gentile Galilee*, Cambridge: Cambridge University Press, 2002.
Crossan, J. D. and J. L. Reed. *Excavating Jesus*, San Francisco, CA: Harper, 2001.
Dalman, G. *Sacred Sites and Ways*, New York: Macmillan, 1935.
Davies, W. D. *The Gospel and the Land: Early Christianity and Jewish Territorial Doctrine*, Berkeley, CA: University of California Press, 1974.
Edwards, D. R. and C. T. McCollough. *Archaeology and the Galilee in the Graeco-Roman and Byzantine Periods*, Atlanta, GA: Scholars Press, 1997.
Fassbeck, G., S. Fortner, A. Rottloff, and J. Zangenberg. *Leben am See Gennesaret*, Mainz: Zabern, 2003.
Fleckenstein, K. H., M. Louhivuori, and R. Riesner. *Emmaus in Judäa*. Giessen: Brunnen, 2003.
Freyne, S., *Galilee and Gospel*, Tübingen: Mohr Siebeck, 2000.
Keel, O., Küchler, M. and Uehlinger, C. *Orte und Landschaften der Bibel I/II/IV*, Göttingen: Vandenhoeck & Ruprecht, 1982/1984/2006.
Kopp, C. *The Holy Places of the Gospels*, New York: Herder, 1963.
Levine, L. I. *Jerusalem: Portrait of the City in the Second Temple Period*, Philadelphia, PA: Jewish Publication Society, 2002.
Loffreda, S. *Recovering Capernaum*, second edition, Jerusalem: Franciscan Printing, 1993.
Möller, C. and Schmitt, G. *Siedlungen Palästinas nach Flavius Josephus*, Wiesbaden: Harrassowitz, 1976.
Nun, M. *Der See Genezareth und die Evangelien*, Giessen: Brunnen, 2001.
Pixner, B., *Wege des Messias und Stätten der Urkirche*, third edition, Giessen: Brunnen, 1996.
Richardson, P. *Building Jewish in the Roman East*, Waco, TX: Baylor University, 2004.
Riesner, R. *Bethanien jenseits des Jordan: Topographie und Theologie im Johannes-Evangelium*, Giessen: Brunnen, 2002.
Schnabel, E. J. *Early Christian Mission I: Jesus and the Twelve*, Downers Grove, IL: InterVarsity Press, 2004.

Schürer, E. *The History of the Jewish People in the Age of Jesus Christ II*, revised G. Vermes, F. Millar, and M. Black, Edinburgh: T. & T. Clark, 1979.

Tsafrir, Y., L. Di Segni, and J. Green. *Tabula Imperii Romani: Iudaea and Palaestina. Maps and Gazetteer*, Jerusalem: Israel Society of Sciences and Humanities, 1994.

Wilson, J. F. *Caesarea Philippi: Banias, the Lost City of Pan*, New York: Tauris, 2004.

GERASA

In the Gospels of Mark (5:1), Matthew (8:28), and Luke (8:26), the account of Jesus' encounter with two demoniacs in the "country of the Gerasenes" is set forth. Jesus exorcises these demons and they enter into a herd of pigs that rush down a steep bank and plunge into the Sea of Galilee and drown. There are problems with this account both in terms of textual variants for the term "Gerasenes" and for the actual location of this event. Many translations (including the NRSV) read the text in Matthew as "Gadarenes" while Mark and Luke continue to be read as "Gerasenes." In either case, the archaeological sites and the elements of the story are at odds. Gerasa is identified with modern Jerash, located some 37 miles from the Sea of Galilee, and Gadara is identified with Um Qeis, 5 miles from the sea. The actual site of the event is more likely to be associated with Gergesa (modern El Kursi), located on the east side of the Sea of Galilee. The excavations of Gergesa have uncovered a church and monastic complex built in the fifth and sixth centuries that appear to have been located to mark the spot of the miracle. Even though Gerasa is not likely to have been the location of the exorcism, it is nonetheless an interesting place in its own right. Moreover, as a city of the Decapolis Gerasa should be taken into account in appreciating the multiple references to Jesus's travels into foreign or pagan territories. Gerasa is a fine example of the social, cultural, religious, and architectural experience that such a journey may have entailed.

The link between Gerasa and the Gerasenes and modern Jerash is well established based on the references in Josephus and inscriptions found at the site. The city appears to have been founded shortly after the conquest of the area by Alexander the Great. During the period of the Seleucid rule the city was known as Antiochia ad Chrysorhoam (Antioch on the Chrysorhoas River). It was overtaken by Alexander Jannaeus in 85 BCE and incorporated into the Hasmonean kingdom. In 63 BCE, the city came into the possession of the Romans and Pompey assigned it to the Decapolis, a group of ten cities in the Jordan River valley and nearby.

Josephus relates that the city was attacked and overtaken by Jews during the first revolt against Rome (*Jewish Wars* 2.18.1) and then retaken by Vespasian. The city flourished in the second and third centuries when it was home to a population of approximately 15,000. It was well situated on the profitable spice and perfume north–south trade route between Mesopotamia, Palmyra, Damascus, and southern Arabia. It also benefited from being on a branch of the *Via Triana Nova* that linked it with Pella and on routes that led into Galilee and Judea. The political instabilities that wracked the Roman Empire in the third and fourth centuries dramatically impacted Gerasa's fortunes. The archaeological excavations have shown that, beginning in the fourth century, copious building efforts were replaced by dismantling of structures and there was very limited new construction until the advent of church building in the fifth century. In the eighth century, the city was severely damaged by a series of earthquakes and essentially abandoned. As there were only sparse building efforts in the vicinity in the modern period, the city was left virtually untouched and thus presents a wonderful opportunity to encounter a mid-size Roman provincial city.

The excavations of the site were carried out initially (1925) by a team organized by the British Mandatory Government. The excavations were continued (1931–34) by teams affiliated with Yale University and the British School of Archaeology in Jerusalem, as well as the American School of Oriental Research. The excavations continued in 1975 under the direction of a team from the University of Turin. In 1982, the Jerash Archaeological Project, composed of teams from a number of countries, was formed to oversee the ongoing work of unearthing this magnificent city.

The excavations have recovered a city that covered the banks of the Chrysorhoas River, which runs north–south through the middle of the city. The eastern bank of the river was home to the residential area. This area has not been excavated as the modern city of Jerash was built over these ruins and prevents exploration. The part of the city that was constructed on the west bank was laid out following the typical Roman urban plan (i.e. the Hippodamian plan) that imposed a grid of north–south, east–west streets on the topography. The principal north–south street, the *Cardo Maximus*, has as its southern point of origin the Oval Forum. This forum is a striking example of public architecture forming a large stone plaza (66 m x 99 m) that is framed on two sides by Ionic colonnades. A stroll down the streets will bring one into contact with a number of well-preserved typical Roman urban structures. The city was home to two theaters, two public bath complexes and two very impressive temples. Near the south gate is the Temple of Zeus, originally constructed in the Hellenistic period and renovated in the first century CE. In the center of the city is the large and richly decorated Temple of Artemis. This sanctuary, built to honor the patroness of the city, is one of the best preserved and most striking examples of sanctuary structures of the early Roman period. It was built in the second century CE and rests on a porticoed platform (121 m x 161 m) at the finale of a processional way that begins in the eastern sector of the city. The temple itself is enclosed by columns (6 x 11) built in the Corinthian order.

In the Byzantine period, the city was thoroughly Christianized. Chapels, baths for parishioners as well as a number of churches were added to the city landscape. The oldest church, called the Cathedral, was built just at the beginning of the fifth century near the Temple of Artemis. By the end of the sixth century, at least eight other churches had been built in Gerasa, including the "Synagogue Church" that has the remains of a synagogue below its foundation.

C. THOMAS MCCOLLOUGH

Further reading

Appelbaum, S. and A. Segal. "Gerasa," in E. Stern, A. Lewinson-Gilboa, and J. Aviram (eds) *New Encyclopedia of Archaeological Excavations in the Holy Land*, New York: Simon & Schuster, 1993, Vol. 2, pp. 470–79.

Aubin, Melissa. "Jerash," in E. M. Meyers (ed.) *Oxford Encyclopedia of Archaeology in the Near East*, 5 vols, Oxford: Oxford University Press, 1997.

Browning, Ian. *Jerash and the Decapolis*, London: Chatto and Windus, 1982.

GETHSEMANE

According to the Gospels of Matthew and Mark, Gethsemane is the site of Jesus' struggle in prayer with God regarding how his death might fit into God's salvific plan, and subsequently of his betrayal by Judas and his arrest (Matt 26:36; Mark 14:32). The word is a transliteration of the Hebrew/Aramaic *gat-šěmānî*, "oil press," and refers to an olive grove (and more specifically to a cave housing an olive press) on the slope of the Mount of Olives (Matt 26:30; Mark 14:26). Luke, who avoids Hebrew or Aramaic names, locates the incident on the Mount of Olives (22:39). John locates the arrest of Jesus in a garden across the Kidron Valley (18:1–2) but locates a version of

Jesus' prayer elsewhere in the narrative (12:27–29). All four gospels thus refer generally to the same location. Heb 5:7–10 bears witness to the Gethsemane tradition, but without reference to any narrative context or geographical location.

Scholars have questioned the historicity of the episode, drawing particular attention to the implausibility of extracting from his sleeping disciples eyewitness testimony to Jesus' prayer. Some have posited that the scene originated in reflection on the OT (e.g. Pss 22:20; 31:9–10, 22; 42:5–6, 11; 43:5; 69:1–2), or derives from early martyrological literature. Others have downplayed these problems, drawing attention to the presence of the "young man" in Mark 14:51–52 or to the large numbers of pilgrims present for Passover (e.g. Saunderson), and to the telling disjunction between the martyrs (who gladly and heroically embrace death) and Jesus (who is in anguish in the face of death). Additionally, no particular theological significance can be attached to the name of the location, "Gethsemane," and the use of "Abba" in Mark 14:36 is characteristic of Jesus when addressing God. All of this supports the conclusion that the episode is rooted in historical reminiscence.

Three other considerations speak strongly in favor of the historical character of the Gethsemane tradition. First, the failure of Jesus' disciples in this scene is scandalous enough that it is unlikely to have been created apart from some firm basis in history. Second, the criterion of multiple attestation ensures that the scene is rooted in early tradition. Although the episode in Matthew's Gospel is almost certainly dependent only on the Markan account, Luke's draws on another tradition (Green 53–58). Analyses are divided over the degree to which Mark's account rests on a pre-Markan passion tradition, but most agree that the prayer of Jesus in John's Gospel is not dependent on the other Gospels, and that Heb 5:7–10 represents yet another tradition. This means that the tradition of Jesus' anguished prayer in the face of death can be traced backward along four independent lines of tradition.

Third, it is highly unlikely that Jesus' followers would have created the memory of a scene that, theologically, was so problematic. Ancient and medieval theologians struggled with the christological problems that surface in this episode: If Jesus were Son of God, why did he appear to be so weak, require divine intervention, question the will of God, and succumb to his emotions (Madigan)? Although the earliest Christians may not have stumbled over these potentially later christological concerns, related obstacles would have been present. Thus, Jesus would have appeared as weak, lacking resolve, when compared with the heroes of the Maccabean martyr tales – male, female, young, and old, who faced death with courage, ready to give a noble example of dying for one's faith (e.g. 2 Macc 6:18–20, 24–28; cf. Heb 11:35–38). Indeed, in the second century, one of Christianity's most renowned opponents identifies the problem: "Why does he mourn, and lament, and pray to escape the fear of death, expressing himself in terms like these: 'O Father, if it be possible, let this cup pass from Me?'" (Origen, *C. Cels.* 2.24). Does this not evacuate claims regarding Jesus' divinity of all credibility? Similarly, modern translations reflect the absence of Luke 22:43–44 – Jesus was strengthened in his praying by an angel – from much of the manuscript tradition, either excluding these verses altogether or placing them in brackets. Likely original, these verses were quickly excised by scribes who found the consequent portrait of Jesus all too human; thus, an ancient marginal notation observed, "The one who was adored and glorified with reverent fear and trembling by all the heavenly powers did not require the strengthening of an angel!" Already in the NT itself, we see how troublesome the picture of Jesus in Gethsemane could be. Note that the agitation and distress attributed to Jesus in Mark 14:33 has in Luke's Gospel at least partially been shifted to the disciples (Luke 22:45). More significantly, in the Gospel of John, Jesus does not actually pray that God might remove the cup of suffering; rather, he seems to wonder aloud whether he should voice such a prayer, before coming quickly to the conclusion that he should not (John 12:27).

In the life of Jesus, this is a signal moment, with numerous motifs converging in one scene. These include the importance of prayer in Jesus' life, not least in the face of calamity; his unique relationship with God, marked by his addressing God as "Abba"; the perfect humanity of Jesus, expressed in the juxtaposition of his struggle in the face of death and this expression of unwavering obedience to God; the centrality of Jesus' death to God's salvific purpose; and Jesus' exemplary performance in the face of adversity presented as a model for his followers. In its most pristine form in the gospel tradition, here the faithfulness of Jesus Christ is on display.

JOEL B. GREEN

Further reading

Brown, Raymond E. *The Death of the Messiah – From Gethsemane to the Grave: A Commentary on the Passion Narratives in the Four Gospels*, 2 vols, ABRL, New York: Doubleday, 1994, Vol. 1, pp. 146–234.

Green, Joel B. *The Death of Jesus: Tradition and Interpretation in the Passion Narrative*, WUNT 2:33, Tübingen: Mohr Siebeck, 1988.

Madigan, Kevin. "Ancient and High-Medieval Interpretations of Jesus in Gethsemane: Some Reflections on Tradition and Continuity in Christian Thought," *HTR* 88 (1995) 157–73.

Murphy-O'Connor, Jerome. "What Really Happened at Gethsemane?," *BR* 2 (1998) 28–39, 52.

Saunderson, Barbara. "Gethsemane: The Missing Witness," *Bib* 70 (1989) 224–33.

Taylor, Joan E. "The Garden of Gethsemane – Not the Place of Jesus' Arrest," *BAR* 21:4 (1995) 26–35, 62.

GOD

The religion of Judaism into which Jesus was born was unswervingly monotheistic, as classically affirmed by Deut 6:4, which Jews recited three times daily: "Hear, O Israel, the Lord thy God is one." (Jesus himself refers to this passage in Matt 12:29–30.) Common references within Jewish writings to God's angelic retinue and celestial opponents can scarcely challenge this monotheistic viewpoint: God alone has existed from eternity, is all powerful, and dwells far above the heavens. Monotheism is perhaps the most cardinal tenet for the Judaism of Jesus' day, in spite of the occasional expansion of "god" terminology to include a vicegerent or heavenly redeemer. Angels, demons, and other celestial beings depend for their existence upon God. Humans and other moral agents have been given free will, but no mere creature can ever foil God's plan, although apocalyptic writings often portray God's enemies as possessing considerable freedom. This understanding of God's eternality, power, and transcendence can be sharply contrasted with the classical Greek understanding of the gods, in which the gods, though "immortal," came into being at a set time, are subject to fate (*moira*), and often are hardly any more transcendent than humans. They did not create the world (which existed from eternity), and they are even in need of sustenance (in the form of ambrosia and nectar). To some degree, the differences between the Greek and the Jewish conceptions of divinity can be summed up under their respective attitudes toward anthropomorphic descriptions of God/the gods. While the Greeks used anthropomorphic language as a matter of course, Jews shunned its use, even to the point of disposing of anthropomorphic expressions when translating the Hebrew Bible into Greek. The flight from anthropomorphism does not, however, stretch all the way to modern sensitivities regarding gender: No biblical figure thought of God in gender-neutral terms, and the most historically accurate way to discuss the God of the historical Jesus is through masculine pronouns.

The historical Jesus' understanding of God of course reflects the biblical (OT and NT) understanding of God. To come to terms with that understanding, we not only must reflect on that tradition's distance from classical Greek conceptions, but, perhaps more insistently, we also must get our minds around the fact that the God of the Bible differs in many ways from the God of the Western (Christian) theological tradition, and even more so from the God rendered by some dominant trends in current Anglo-American theology. A number of attributes of God that are considered axiomatic in present-day theological discussion are hardly so for the biblical writers. For example, despite the oft-repeated claim that God dwells outside of "space and time," the God of the Bible, in spite of all his transcendence, experiences time in much the same way as everyone else. Although the God of the Bible has existed from eternity, there is no thought, in the Bible, of God's transcendence of time, much less of time being a "thing" whose transcendence is conceptually afforded. The Bible does not explain how God knows future events, but it is doubtful that it thinks of God as dwelling or stepping outside of time in order to peer at the future. (For an OT example of God's genuine surprise at how events transpire, see Jer 32:35.) A further qualification of theology's contribution to the issues covered below concerns the nature of the divine fatherhood: The Bible knows nothing of the hypostatic or "economic" issues surrounding the Church's attempts to explain the respective places of Father and Son within the Christian doctrine of the Trinity. These elements of speculative theology are best left out of any account of the historical Jesus' understanding of God.

Continuity with the God of the Old Testament

Despite an age-old conceit of portraying the God of the OT as a God of wrath and the God of the NT as a God of grace (an active conceit already in the second century CE), the God that first-century Galileans encountered in Jesus' message was anticipated in the OT writings in nearly every detail. That is not to say, however, that the emphases in Jesus' theology were identical with those of most scriptural exegetes of his day, or even of the OT writings themselves. In that respect, we are met with both continuity and discontinuity (see below). Many of the principal emphases in Jesus' portrayal of God are also emphasized in the OT writings that the New Testament quotes the most: Isaiah and Psalms. (While it is sometimes debated whether Jesus quoted from the Bible, most scholars today believe that many of the quotations attributed to him were probably his.)

As Veli-Matti Kärkkäinen notes in *The Doctrine of God*, "nowhere does the New Testament begin from scratch or reinvent the view of God." The understanding of God that we find in Jesus' teaching, and in the New Testament more generally, is largely continuous with what we find in the Old Testament. There are, however, some different emphases as well as a few points of discontinuity. As for the latter, it is worth noting that the God of the (Hebrew) Old Testament is a *named* God (*Yahweh*, *El*, etc.), while neither Jesus nor the New Testament ever refers to God by a name. (The single possible exception is in Rev 19:1–6's use of "alleluia" [*hallelu-yah* = "praise Yah"], but that is a matter of a rote formula in a language different from the surface text, rather than a conscious reference to a divine name.) The elimination of divine names was not a new development with the New Testament, but rather the continuation of a program that left its mark on the Septuagint, where various designations of God were rendered by *theos* or *kyrios*. In the Judaism of Jesus' day, the name of God was considered too holy to be pronounced. Even the term "God" was sometimes avoided in favor of terms like "Lord" or "the Most High," or even by more distant circumlocutions like "Heaven" or "the Name." This development widened the gulf between the God of the Greek Old Testament and the gods of the Romans, who, as R. M. Ogilvie notes in *The Romans and Their Gods in the Age of Augustus*, "like dogs, will only answer to their names." With respect to the historical Jesus, it is difficult to know whether he used the circumlocutions attributed to him (e.g. "Power" [Matt 26:64 || Mark 14:62 || Luke 22:69], "Heaven" [Luke 15:7, 18, 21]), or whether those circumlocutions are elements of an evangelist's own style (cf. Matthew's "kingdom of heaven").

It is important to stress the point, not least because Jesus stressed it, that God is *good*. In fact, Jesus disowned the address "good teacher" because "no one is good except God" (Mark 10:18). (This in fact is what Jesus does in this passage, although interpreters like to think that Jesus is claiming divinity in a backhanded way.) In keeping with his goodness, God is a provider and a healer. God cares for the lilies and the birds, and his care and provision for humanity outstretches what the lilies and birds receive. (See below.) Thus Jesus taught his disciples not to worry, but to have faith. Just as an earthly father gives good things to his children, so (all the more) does God give good things to his children – those things, in this case, being either general "good things" that his children ask for (Matt 7:11) or the "Holy Spirit" in particular (Luke 11:13). God even blesses the wicked. He "makes his sun rise on the evil and on the good, and sends rain on the just and on the unjust" (Matt 5:45). God's goodness is reflected in his patience and his readiness to forgive (Luke 15:7, 10). Jesus taught that these traits of God are to be emulated by his disciples.

The mutual compatibility of apocalyptic and wisdom conceptions of God

Almost all would agree that some embellishments in the direction of ecclesiastical doctrine have crept into the gospels. The question is one of degree and, more immediately, of whether those embellishments affect the record of Jesus' teachings about God. One fusing of horizons within the accounts of Jesus' teaching that is sometimes touted as a source-critical seam is found within the coinherence of apocalyptic and wisdom elements within a single body of teaching. Both the general mood and content of apocalyptic writing tend to support an understanding of God that in some respects *competes* with that of wisdom writing: The God of apocalyptic is a vengeful figure, while the God of wisdom tradition is a beneficent provider, a bestower of life, and an altogether more transcendent figure. The God of apocalyptic moves on a timetable, while the God of wisdom provides the daily upkeep for an ongoing universe. It is flatly wrong, however, to deny the miscibility of the apocalyptic and wisdom conceptions of God. Although some scholars consider these two streams of thought to be too mutually incompatible for both to represent the teaching of the historical Jesus, it must be said that structuralism is a poor substitute for historical research. Few minds prior to the twentieth century would have argued (or *worked*) along those lines, and there is nothing within the mutual aspect of these streams of thought that suggests that they cannot be held together (just as they manifestly are for the evangelists). Understandably, there has been a backlash against the various attempts to separate the apocalyptic and wisdom strains of the gospel tradition (esp. Q) into distinct beds of tradition.

That is not to say, however, that the gospel traditions are to be accepted *in toto* as representing the historical Jesus' understanding of God. As we shall see, some aspects of Jesus' understanding of

God as "Father" stem from post-Jesuan developments, although the core of the theme is from Jesus.

Continuity with other Second Temple Jewish movements

Reconstructions of the historical Jesus have often emphasized elements of Jesus' (supposed) uniqueness over commonalities with other Jewish figures or streams of thought and piety, sometimes to the point of making those elements constitutive of Jesus' self-understanding. With respect to fundamental questions about God's character (among other things), it would be very wrong to cast the understandings of his contemporaries in terms strictly oppositional to his teaching. An extreme take on this procedure has a way of making Jesus seem like the only Technicolor character in a black-and-white world. While this way of setting the scene was once characteristic of a great deal of scholarship, it has now thankfully been pushed to the margins, although a less over-the-top variety of this procedure can still be found in the few continuing applications of the so-called criterion of dissimilarity. It should not be supposed that Jesus' teaching on God was totally revolutionary, although (as with many religious geniuses) it may have had elements of uniqueness.

There are five aspects of Jesus' teaching about God that any discussion must include: God's boundless love, God as "Father," God as judge, God as king, and God as the God of all creation.

God's boundless love

The formulation "God is love" begins, as far as we know, with the writer of 1 John, but it perfectly expresses a central aspect of Jesus' teaching. God's love for his creation knows no bounds. In the Sermon on the Mount, God's love is expressed through his provision and the personalness of his attention to his creatures. Jesus expressed this most memorably in the Sermon on the Mount:

> Look at the birds of the air; they neither sow nor reap nor gather into barns, and yet your heavenly Father feeds them. Are you not of more value than they? ... Consider the lilies of the field, how they grow; they neither toil nor spin, yet I tell you, even Solomon in all his glory was not clothed like one of these.
>
> (Matt 6:26 29)

As T. W. Manson suggested in *The Teaching of Jesus*, "God clothes the lilies of the field and God feeds the birds, one might almost say, because God is fond of beautiful flowers and fond of birds." Thus the doctrine of God's love is combined with the doctrine of God's rule over nature, yet we should not lose sight of the fact that the lilies and the birds are used as a point of comparison for God's love and care for his people. Jesus also expressed the depth of God's love in an unforgettable way through the story of the Prodigal Son (Luke 15:11–32), in which the father ran to embrace the son who wasted his living.

God as "Father"

One of the most prominent features of Jesus' teaching in the gospels is found in his repeated references to God as "Father." Jesus did not invent this point of view: The Old Testament was already aware of God's paternal standing and nature (see Deut 32:6; Ps 103:13; Prov 3:12; Jer 3:19; Hos 11). Although Ps 2:7 does not contain the word for "Father," it represents a particularly important use of the divine fatherhood motif, as it uses it in a way that could easily be taken as messianic: "You are my Son; today I have begotten you." While Jesus did not introduce this way of speaking about God, he apparently did emphasize it to a degree found nowhere in the Old Testament. The more usual OT understanding of God's fatherhood apparently has to do with the birth of Israel's nationhood (Deut 32:6; Isa 63:16; Mal 2:10). Although this understanding is often expressed in the terminology of creation (God is Father because God created), it is probably the creation of the nation that these passages have in view. That "creation" is the exodus under Moses, in which God calls his "son" out of Egypt (Exod 4:22–23). It is also worth noting that God was also called "Father" in Stoicism and Neoplatonism, but the impact on the New Testament from that direction is minimal at best.

Taken as a whole, Jesus' references to God as "Father," as we have them, cannot be reduced to a single field of meaning. According to one set of passages, the fatherhood of God conveys Jesus' messianic sonship, while another set conveys God's relation to Israel. Owing to the impact of William Wrede's views on the so-called "messianic secret" in Mark, it became unfashionable, at the end of the nineteenth century, to attribute messianic ambitions to the historical Jesus. Recent scholarship, however, has found the idea of the historical Jesus' messianic consciousness much more credible on historical grounds. This development has increased scholarly appreciation for the possibility that Jesus used "Father" as a sign of his own messianic self-awareness. Regardless of how one relates Jesus to a messianic consciousness, however, it hardly guarantees that scenario, as it is equally possible that Jesus spoke in terms of messianic self-awareness but that the messianic use of "Father" was added by the Church. This leaves scholarship with two competing understandings of "Father" ("my Father" versus "your Father"), but it is possible that Jesus used both conceptions in different contexts. It should be noted that Jesus did *not* teach the idea of God's universal fatherhood in the classical liberal sense of "the fatherhood of God and the brotherhood of man" (Adolf Harnack). When Jesus used "Father" in a broader sense, he used it only in reference to God's fatherhood of his people, defined more narrowly by Jesus in terms of those who obey him.

Each of the evangelists appears to be partial to one or the other of these views, but the tradition as a whole is mixed. Indeed, in an article on "The Doctrine of the Divine Fatherhood in the Gospels," H. F. D. Sparks was able to arrive at a homogeneous view of divine fatherhood in Mark only by dismissing the originality of some probably original verses. In this way, he could say that "God, according to St Mark, is Father of Jesus only; and He is Father of Jesus because Jesus is Messiah." As it stands, Mark's text is not patient of such a totalizing view, although the *weight* of the material is situated as Sparks has represented it. Accounts that posit a change in Jesus' practice at a set time in his ministry (e.g. at Peter's confession at Caesarea Philippi) seem to adopt the wrong approach. In terms of the regularity of the fatherhood terminology, however, we *are* dealing with a development of sorts: Mark contains only four references to God as "Father," while Matthew has thirty, and John has more than 120. This suggests that the idea of God's fatherhood found fertile soil in Christian thinking about God, and turned this originally limited spray of color into a vivid field of wildflowers. In spite of the secondariness of many of these references, however, it is almost certain that Jesus himself used this same language, but in a much more restrained manner than either Matthew or John would have us think. (Although the rabbinic-sounding expression "Father who is in heaven" is typically Matthean [appearing in Matthew twelve times], it also appears in Mark 11:25, and may well have been used by Jesus.)

Jesus' references to God as "*my* Father" recall the sort of personal, familial address of God found among a select group of Jewish wonder workers. The earliest of these figures, Honi the Circle-drawer, framed his prayers as if he were "a member of [God's] household," and the Rabbis compared his prayer technique and his ability to receive what he asked for with the hubris and position of a spoiled son. According to rabbinic tradition, another wonder worker, Hanina b. Dosa, was addressed by a heavenly voice as "my son." If anything, however, Jesus' self-aware relationship with the Father was even higher than that of Honi or Hanina.

One of the more significant aspects of Jesus' teaching on the divine fatherhood is found in his reference to God as "Abba," a name that modern writers sometimes wrongly equate with "Daddy." (As a term of endearment, it was used by adults as much as by children.) Joachim Jeremias famously argued, in *The Central Message of the New Testament*, that it "would have been irreverent and therefore unthinkable" to address God as "Abba," but others have pointed to how little we really know of the prayer habits of Jewish charismatic figures.

God as judge

We have already seen that the God of apocalyptic and the God of wisdom can represent two sides of the same coin, and so we find that the God who loves and cares for his creation is also a God who judges the world. The triple tradition includes an apocalyptic discourse (Matthew 24; Mark 13; Luke 21) in which the Romans seize Jerusalem, but God vindicates himself in the end. God's judgment of individuals on the last day is a recurring theme in Jesus' teaching, and the subject of some of the parables. God will not reward on the basis of outward appearances and mechanical observance, but according to the condition of the heart. The task of judging is to some degree turned over to the Son of Man, but the initiative is clearly God's.

Although both Hebrew and Jewish piety sometimes posit that God's judgment is tempered by his subjects' ignorance of what God requires of them (this esp. applies to the Gentiles), all creation is subject to God's commands and will one day answer for its actions and inaction. In Jesus' teaching, the Jews' responsibility is highlighted more along moral and moral-halakhic lines than along ritual-halakhic lines, and there is a notable tendency to subordinate the latter to the former. There is no indication within the Synoptic Gospels that Jesus ever advocated outright breaking of the Law, although there is a difference of opinion among scholars as to whether this holds true for the Fourth Gospel as well. Undoubtedly the degree to which Jesus seems to soft-pedal ritual halakha is

partly a trick of the light, reflecting the attitudes of the Evangelists' generation rather than that of Jesus himself. In this respect, Jesus' halakhic commentary should be read in the same way as the OT prophets. When Jesus speaks of God's judgment, therefore, he primarily has in mind judgment upon moral breaches among God's own people, but he does not therewith discount judgment upon other areas of laxness. Undoubtedly a principal target of Jesus' critique was the assumption that the Law can be adequately fulfilled strictly along juridical lines, in a way that allowed loopholes to get the better of underlying moral commitments. A major focus of Jesus' teaching is that true religion, like the religion of James 1:27, is one whose mechanism of halakhic decision-making has as much to do with heartstrings as with strict legal reasoning.

In spite of Jesus' teaching regarding God's nearness and the depth of his involvement, Jesus did not tear down the ritual demarcations of purity and impurity, or of the holy and the profane. Jesus' designs upon ritual halakha were driven by a heightening of moral obligations, a heightening that sometimes held ritual concerns in abeyance, but he never intended to retire the ritual categories as such. Thus the God of the Old Testament retains his holiness in Jesus' teaching, and the ritual apparatus designed to protect humans from that holiness remains firmly in place. Jesus' call to religious and moral integrity does not amount to a sacralization of the secular, and the Bible in general provides no purchase for the claim that "once there was no secular" (John Milbank).

God as king

As with other major aspects of Jesus' understanding of God, that of God's kingship continues a theme found already in the Old Testament, in which God is proclaimed sometimes as king of Israel (Exod 15:18; Num 23:21; Isa 43:15) and sometimes as king of the whole earth (2 Kgs 19:15; Ps 29:10; Isa 6:5; cf. Pss 29:10; 96:10).

Jesus' understanding of God as king is found almost exclusively from the parables. (Among other things, that means that this aspect of Jesus' teaching is virtually missing from the Fourth Gospel, which has no parables.) There are, in fact, two ways in which the parables might express God's kingship, but they are not equally secure in the likelihood that Jesus spoke in those terms or in the likelihood that they mean to speak of God in real terms. The more secure aspect from Jesus' parable instruction is found in its explicit references to the kingdom of God. In spite of how regular the formula "The kingdom of God is like ... "/"Kingdom of Heaven is like ... " appears to be, it is in all respects likely that Jesus taught in these very terms, or in something very similar.

From the predominance of this terminology, a few things can be safely inferred about the kingship of God. Of what is God king? In most instances, God appears to be thought of as king *of Israel*, but God is also king of the world, with Israel awaiting the glorious day when the world wakes up and recognizes God's kingship. Formulaic prayers addressing God as king, or acknowledging the advance of his kingdom, were common in contemporary Judaism. Jesus' use of kingdom of God language thus invokes a common set of ideas. No matter how cryptic the term "kingdom of God" sometimes seems to us, it was certainly rather clear to the original audience for Jesus' parables.

A second way in which the parables contribute to the idea of God's kingship has somewhat less going for it in terms of its usefulness for historical Jesus studies: two Matthean parables (the Parable of the Ungrateful Servant [Matt 18:23–35] and the Parable of the Banquet [Matt 22:1 14]) cast a king as a *dramatis persona*, a casting that understandably is often thought to refer to God, especially as it is congruent with the point of each of these parables for the "king" to stand for God. The problems with this are twofold: (1) the casting of a king within a parable might be a reflection of Matthew's style rather than of Jesus' own coinage (Luke's version of the Parable of the Banquet [14:16 24] does not mention a "king"); and (2) the "king parable" is a distinct genre (not only in the Synoptic Gospels but also in other works), in which the point of involving a king has little to do with the object lesson of the story. In Matthew's Gospel, moreover, the *Messiah* is called a "king" (5:35 [?]; 25:34, 40; cf. Luke 19:38; 23:2–3, 37–38), and it is eminently possible that the king in Matthew's two king parables is really the Messiah. And if kings in parables regularly stood for God, then we might have expected the owner of the vineyard in the Parable of the Vineyard (Matt 21:33 41; Mark 12:1–12; Luke 20:9–19) to be a king.

God as the God of all creation

We have already seen that the idea of God as Father has little to do with the idea of God as creator of the universe. The latter notion, nevertheless, was just as central within Jesus' teaching and in the Judaism of his day. By Jesus' day, the idea of YHWH as a territorial God – an idea that

surfaces several places in the Old Testament – had largely disappeared from view. The idea of a geographically centralized cultus, if ever connected to the idea of a territorial God, had lost that connection by Jesus' day: The Jerusalem Temple, as the navel of the world, was the Temple of the universal God. The God of the Bible is a universal ruler. This follows first and foremost from the confession of God as *creator* of the universe. Eternality belongs to God alone – all competing powers have real power only as allotted to them by God (who created them), and moral power only as it has been awarded them by the straying heart and mind of humankind. God holds all the cards.

According to Jesus' teaching, "heaven ... is the throne of God, ... the earth ... is his footstool, [and] Jerusalem ... is the city of the great King" (Matt 5:34–35). Jesus' remonstrations against the corruption of the Temple administration should be seen as adding to (rather than subtracting from) his regard for the Temple's role as a "house of prayer." The point of Jesus' cleansing the Temple courts from an abusive commercial system was to uphold the Temple's role as a "house of prayer," a role reflected in apocalyptic writings. Whether Jesus included Isaiah's words "for all the nations" is a matter of debate, as Mark includes the words while Matthew and Luke (in a so-called "minor agreement" against Mark) do not.

The theme of God's universal rule of course opens onto God's relation to the Gentiles. The gospels highlight a few instances in which Jesus ministers to those outside the people of Israel. Although the strains of Jesus' being sent to the "lost sheep of the house of Israel" (Matt 15:24; cf. the disciples' sending in 10:6) come out clearly in these instances, one can see that Jesus is more open to sharing God's blessings with "the stranger dwelling in the midst" than some of his contemporaries would have been. The Evangelists appear to key on the agreement between Jesus' *reduced* ethnocentrism and the Church's disavowal of any sort of ethnocentrism, and they have arranged their narratives so as to showcase these accounts. Yet even if the gospels inflate the amount of Jesus' ministry to the Gentiles, there can be little doubt that Jesus' understanding of God was significantly shaped by the theme of God's universal rule.

JOHN C. POIRIER

Further reading

Argyle, A. W. *God in the New Testament*, Philadelphia, PA: Lippincott, 1966.

Barr, James. "Abba Isn't 'Daddy'," *JTS* 39.1 (1988) 28–47.

Coppens, J. (ed.) *La notion biblique de Dieu: Le Dieu de la Bible et le Dieu des philosophes*, Gembloux: J. Duculot, 1976.

Dodd, C. H. *The Bible and the Greeks*, London: Hodder & Stoughton, 1954.

Flusser, David. *Jesus*, Jerusalem: Magnes, 1997.

Jeremias, Joachim. *The Central Message of the New Testament*, London: SCM Press, 1965.

Kärkkäinen, Veli-Matti. *The Doctrine of God: A Global Introduction*, Grand Rapids, MI: Baker Academic, 2004.

Manson, T. W. *The Teaching of Jesus: Studies of Its Form and Content*, second edition, Cambridge: Cambridge University Press, 1935.

Milbank, J. *Theology and Social Theory: Beyond Secular Reason*, Oxford: Blackmelly 1993.

Ogilvie, R. M. *The Romans and Their Gods in the Age of Augustus*, Ancient Culture and Society, New York: W. W. Norton, 1969.

Sparks, H. F. D. "The Doctrine of the Divine Fatherhood in the Gospels," in D. E. Nineham, *Studies in the Gospels: Essays in Memory of R. H. Lightfoot*, Oxford: Blackwell, 1967, pp. 241–62.

Stauffer, Ethelbert. "θεός κτλ.," in Gerhard Kittel (ed.) *Theological Dictionary of the New Testament*, Grand Rapids, MI: Eerdmans, 1964–76, Vol. 3, pp. 65–119.

GOGUEL, MAURICE

Goguel (1880–1955) wrote several books on the historical Jesus. He first published *Jésus de Nazareth: mythe ou histoire?* It intended to refute the mythical interpretation of the gospels that was represented in France by Paul-Louis Couchoud. Then he wrote *La Vie de Jésus*, the first volume of a trilogy entitled *Jésus et les origines du Christianisme*. This work, largely amplified, was republished in 1950 with another title, *Jésus*. Goguel considered it a new book. He also wrote books about John the Baptist (1928), faith in the resurrection of Jesus in early Christianity (1933) and a great number of articles and reviews dealing with the gospels and the historical Jesus.

Positions advocated

Goguel defended resolutely an historical-critical approach of the historical Jesus and deviated from Bultmann on this point. He criticized him for neglecting the biographical element and for preferring a personal and existential experience of history. But he also made a point of dissociating the question of the historical Jesus and the theological and religious problem of Christ. The first is valid for everyone and relates to judgments of facts, whereas the second only concerns believers and is based on value judgments. In his quest he attached great importance to a basic criterion for distinguishing between the teaching attributed to

Jesus and the views adopted by the early Church. He also emphasized the importance of a criterion that was related to the very original and typical form of the words of Jesus, which were by no means Greek but Semitic.

In fact, he wished to make the historical figure of Jesus psychologically understandable. To achieve this goal, he stressed the so-called crises of Jesus' ministry and intended to explain them psychologically. He thought that these crises were caused on the one hand by the experiences Jesus had, and on the other hand by reactions aroused by his teaching. Goguel was convinced that thanks to these crises the historian can understand the facts in depth and elaborate a synthesis. For him, such a synthesis was inevitably hypothetical but remained essential.

According to Goguel, the first significant event is Jesus' meeting with John the Baptist, at the end of 26 CE or at the beginning of 27 CE. But Jesus does not stay with him for a long time, for they part during the spring of 27 CE. From that day on, John considered Jesus as a disloyal disciple. Then follows the Galilean period that, in Goguel's view, runs until September 27 CE, and which he divides into two phases. During the first, Jesus has a relative success around Capernaum, in spite of the distrust of the religious authorities who could not stand his laxity towards the ritual regulations. During the second phase the opposition becomes clearer, mostly because of Herod Antipas, who tried to treat Jesus in the same way as John. According to Goguel, the story of the feeding of the crowd reflects a turning point. The crowd wishes to make Jesus its king and to force him to be a political Messiah, but because of Jesus' refusal the crowd turns away from him. Jesus, however, is comforted by a core of faithful disciples who expressed him their loyalty at Caesarea Philippi. He definitively leaves Galilee to go to Jerusalem. Meanwhile his thoughts develop. At the beginning Jesus was convinced that the role of the Messiah was to lead the glorious establishment of the kingdom of God, but he did not desire this title because he wanted to confine himself to a prophetic role. However, since his departure to Jerusalem he is convinced that the Messiah has to face opposition and rejection. He is now conscious of being the Son of Man and, for this reason, having the vocation of being a suffering Messiah. According to Goguel, Jesus goes to Jerusalem for the Feast of Tabernacles, not to die there yet being ready to die, and being especially determined to continue his preaching. It is inevitable that his preaching provokes a powerful reaction, for which reason the authorities decide to get rid of him. He stays in the holy city until December, before seeking refuge in Perea, since he has been compromised by his preaching relating to the Temple. On 14 Nisan, on the eve of Passover in 28 CE, he returns to Jerusalem and is killed there.

For Goguel, the proclamation of the kingdom of God by Jesus was eschatological, and was based on his expectation of the re-establishment of God's sovereignty on earth. Jesus' messianic conscience was real but discreet. To some extent his messianic conscience was a compensation of his ideals for reality.

Goguel was convinced that the problem of the historical Jesus and the issues about Christian origins are inseparable because no fact can be fully understood apart from the developments it generates. But he added that the faith of the primitive Church did not depend on Jesus' life but on the conviction of his resurrection that demonstrated his messianity.

How his work has been critically assessed

Of all French-speaking authors Goguel is certainly the one who devoted the most time and energy to the question of the historical Jesus. In his lifetime, his work was abundantly quoted and commented. Since he did not pledge allegiance to any school – although he can be linked to the symbolo-fideism of the School of Paris – he marked out an original path. However, he never really renewed his own approach, nor integrated the contribution of form-criticism or of the great discoveries, like the texts of Qumran. Thus he never departed from an historicism and a psychologism that may appear somewhat outdated today.

CHRISTIAN GRAPPE

Further reading

Baird, William. *History of New Testament Research. Volume Two. From Jonathan Edwards to Rudolf Bultmann*, Minneapolis, MN: Fortress Press, 2003, pp. 442–51.

Cuvillier, Elian. "Maurice Goguel (1880–1955)," *Bulletin de la Société de l'Histoire du Protestantisme Français* 149 (2003) 549–67.

Goguel, Maurice. *Jésus de Nazareth: mythe ou histoire?*, Paris: Payot, 1925 (ET: *Jesus the Nazarene: Myth or History?*, trans. Frederik Stevens, New York: Appleton, 1926).

—— *La Vie de Jésus*, Paris: Payot, 1932 (ET: *The Life of Jesus*, trans. Olive Wyon, New York: Macmillan, 1933).

—— *Jésus*, Paris: Payot, 1950

Johns, Alan H. *Independence and Exegesis: The Study of Early Christianity in the Work of Alfred Loisy (1857–1940), Charles Guignebert (1857–1939) and Maurice Goguel (1880–1955)*, Tübingen, Mohr Siebeck, 1983.

Reymond, Bernard. "L'Ecole de Paris," *ETR* 52 (1977) 371–83.

GOSPEL AS GENRE

A proper understanding of genre is crucial for the interpretation of any text or communication. Communication theory considers the relationship of transmitter, communication and receiver, or encoder, message and decoder. In written works, this becomes author or producer(s), text, and audience or reader(s). Immediately the importance of discerning the right kind of communication becomes clear: if it is being transmitted in Morse code but the receiver can only understand semaphore, there will be problems in communication. Both parties must use the same code or language, and so correct interpretation depends on a correct identification of the kind of communication or genre. One does not listen to a fairy story in the same way as to a news broadcast; each has its own conventions, expectations and rules.

Therefore genre is a key convention guiding both composition and interpretation. It forms a 'contract' or agreement, often unspoken or unwritten, or even unconscious, between authors and readers, whereby authors write according to a set of expectations and readers interpret the work using the same conventions. Genre is identified through a wide range of 'generic features' which may be signalled in advance through a preface; however, they are also embedded within the work's formal and structural composition (often called 'external features') and its content, style, mood and character ('internal features'). Taken together, such generic features communicate the 'family resemblance' of a group of works and thus enable us to identify the genre of a given text and interpret it accordingly.

Gospel genre in history and scholarship

For much of the ancient and mediaeval periods, the gospels, like the rest of the Bible, were interpreted on several levels: the literal meaning provided facts, while an allegorical interpretation applied the text to the story of redemption; moral approaches gave instructions for behaviour and an anagogical reading related it to the reader's spiritual pilgrimage. The Reformers rejected all levels of reading except for the literal, and on this basis the gospels were interpreted as history telling the story of Jesus, even sometimes being seen as biographies. They were used to produce romantic 'lives' such as Ernest Renan's *Life of Jesus* (1863). However, during the nineteenth century, biographies began to explain the character of a great person by considering his or her upbringing, formative years, schooling, psychological development and so on; furthermore, the subject would be set within the context of the main events of their time. With their relatively shorter length and narrower focus, the gospels began to look unlike such biographies.

Form critics and uniqueness

Therefore, scholars like Karl Ludwig Schmidt (1923) and Rudolf Bultmann (1921) rejected any notion that the gospels were biographies: the gospels have no interest in Jesus' human personality, appearance or character, nor do they tell us anything about the rest of his life, other than his brief public ministry of preaching, teaching and healing, with an extended concentration on his death. Instead, the gospels were seen as popular folk literature, collections of short stories (*pericopae*) handed down orally. Far from being biographies of Jesus, the gospels were considered 'unique' forms of literature, *sui generis* (see Bultmann 371–74). For Bultmann and Schmidt, this unique genre had theological implications about God's unique revelation of his Word in Jesus Christ.

Furthermore, such development of 'form-critical' approaches to the gospels meant that they were no longer read as whole narratives. Instead, the concentration on each individual *pericope* moved the focus for interpretation to the passage's *Sitz im Leben* in the early church. Meanwhile, the author was regarded as little more than a mere stenographer, recording the stories at the end of the oral tunnel, rather than an historian or writer with literary intentions. The quest for the historical Jesus concentrated instead on peeling back the layers in the *pericopae* to reveal any authentic sayings of Jesus on the one hand, and the history of the early Christian churches on the other.

Redaction critics and gospel communities

This historical search required careful study of how Matthew and Luke edited Mark, which revealed something of their theology, purposes and methods as each them acted as an 'editor', or *Redaktor* in German. The classic redaction studies were undertaken by Bornkamm (1948) on Matthew's revision of Mark for use within the new religious community of the Church and Conzelmann (1954) on Luke's understanding of the events of Jesus taking place 'in the middle of time' between Israel and the Church. Such redaction-critical approaches led to the development of theories about the communities which produced the gospels. The gospels were seen as 'community' documents, within which

the history of the community is overlaid upon the story of Jesus, giving a 'two-tier' approach to reading them. Therefore, interpretation began to focus upon the development of such groups like the Matthean community (through the work of K. Stendahl) or the Johannine community (see for example the writings of R. E. Brown and J. L. Martyn).

However, the fact that redaction critics saw the writers of the gospels as individual theologians with particular purposes brought back questions about authorial intention and literary aspirations. The development of new literary approaches to the gospels viewed them as conscious writers or artists, and attention began to be given to their techniques of composition and narrative skills such as plot, irony and characterization, through the work of D. Rhoads and D. Michie, J. D. Kingsbury and R. C. Tannehill.

Gospel genre as biography

Such literary analyses made it possible again to consider the question of the genre of the gospels and their place within the context of first century literature. Stanton (1974) was the first to raise the possibility of biographical material within the gospels once more, and later work by Talbert (1978) and Aune (1987) began to go against the current scholarly consensus and treat the gospels as ancient biographies. However, these approaches needed more undergirding in genre theory and classical literature if they were to succeed in changing the assumed paradigm.

Burridge's comparison of the gospels with ancient 'lives', originally published in 1992, identified a range of key 'generic features' which distinguished ancient biography from neighbouring genres in Graeco-Roman literature. Like such works, the gospels are continuous prose narratives of the length of a single scroll, comprising stories, anecdotes, sayings and speeches. Their concentration on Jesus' public ministry from his baptism to death, and on his teaching and great deeds is not very different from the content of other ancient biographies. The concentration on the last week of Jesus' life, his death and the resurrection reflects the amount of space given to the subject's death and subsequent events in works by Plutarch, Tacitus, Nepos and Philostratus. Verbal analysis demonstrates that Jesus is the subject of a quarter of the verbs in Mark's gospel, with a further fifth spoken by him in his teaching and parables. About half of the verbs in the other gospels either have Jesus as the subject or are on his lips. Thus, as in the focus in other ancient biographies upon their subject's teachings and activities, Jesus' deeds and words are of vital importance for the evangelists' portraits of Jesus. Therefore these marked similarities of form and content demonstrate that the gospels have both the external and internal generic features of ancient biographies.

This biographical understanding of the gospel genre has been subsequently confirmed in similarly detailed work by Frickenschmidt (1997) and has now become the accepted scholarly consensus. It has been queried by Collins (1995), who similarly rejects the unique, form-critical approach but prefers to see Mark more like historical monograph. Comparisons by Wills (1997) and Vines (2002) of gospels with early novels, especially of Jewish origin, have not gained great acceptance. Increasingly, gospel scholars and commentators now take the biographical genre of the gospels as their starting point, while the debate has moved on to the implications of this, both for their interpretation and the quest for the historical Jesus (see Burridge 2004: 252–88).

Implications for the historical Jesus

Given the centrality of genre for the interpretation of texts, then the presumed genre of the gospels has many consequences for how they are read. Before we can read or interpret them, we have to discover what kind of books they might be and how they compare with other texts from the same time period and location. Thus if Bultmann and the form critics were correct that the gospels were unique, then we would have no means of knowing how to interpret them, nor how to use them in the quest for the historical Jesus. Equally, if we consider them to be something like legend, then they would give us no assistance in our historical search. On the other hand, some people treat them as though they are history in the modern sense and think they can simply read from the surface meaning of the text to an accurate account. The biographical approach to the gospel genre occupies a mediating position between these extremes, as the gospels are be treated historically like other ancient biographies. Such ancient lives have some degree of interpretation about their subjects, but without the latitude permitted for, say, encomium. While accounts could be written to attack or defend someone, as in the many biographies of Socrates and Cato, there still had to be recognizable continuity with the historical person.

A christological hermeneutic

First, since the gospels are portraits of a person, they must be interpreted with a biographical focus

upon their subject, Jesus of Nazareth. Given that space is limited to a single scroll – ranging from Mark's 11,250 words to Luke's 19,500 – every story, *pericope* or passage has to contribute to the overall picture of Jesus according to each Evangelist. Thus Christology becomes central to the interpretation of the gospels. Each Evangelist builds up their account of Jesus through the selection, redaction and ordering of their material. The key question for the interpretation of any verse or section is what this tells us about Jesus and the writer's understanding of him, rather than the concern of form- and redaction-critical approaches for the history of the early church or the first communities. Thus the motif of the failure of the disciples to understand Jesus in Mark is not to be interpreted in terms of polemic against differing groups and leaders with 'traditions in conflict' inside the early church (see Weeden). Instead it is part of Mark's portrayal of Jesus as hard to understand and tough to follow – and therefore readers should not be surprised to find the Christian life difficult sometimes. Therefore, interpretation of the gospels requires a thorough understanding of the Christology of each of the Evangelists, while each section must be exegeted in the context of its place in the developing narrative as a whole. Burridge (1994/2005) has attempted to describe the particular Christology of each gospel narrative through the traditional gospel symbols as found in Irenaeus' *Against the Heresies*, III.11:8–9. Thus he uses the lion to describe Mark's enigmatic 'beast of conflict', while Matthew's account shows the human face of the Teacher of Israel who is rejected; the image of the ox reflects Luke's narrative of the burden-bearing Saviour and the high-flying, all-seeing eagle symbolizes John's account of the divine incarnation in Jesus.

Unity and diversity

The fact that the early church fathers chose to keep four separate accounts in the canon has caused some difficulties, both for early apologetics against pagan critics who noted the diversity of the portraits, and for modern readers. How can we reconstruct the historical Jesus from such different accounts? The decision not to follow Marcion's choice of using only one gospel or Tatian's so-called 'harmony of the gospels' in the *Diatessaron* demonstrates that the four gospels were recognized as coherent single accounts of Jesus, yet which belong together. In the historical search for Jesus, the existence of these separate yet parallel accounts has been vital as a way of reconstructing the development of the traditions about Jesus and attempting to trace it back to its authentic 'kernel'. The biographical approach can build upon redaction-critical analyses to enable scholars to understand and allow for each Evangelist's literary, theological and historical portrait of Jesus. Morgan (1979) sees the four canonical portraits as a 'stimulus' to produce more 'faith images of Jesus', as well as acting as a 'control' upon them. Stanton (1997) and Hengel (2000) have provoked renewed interest in the idea of the 'fourfold gospel' and its implications for their interpretation. It may even be that the early church's preservation of four gospels together may have stimulated the development of the codex in preference to the use of single scrolls.

Reconstructing the gospels' settings

Furthermore, the biographical genre of the gospels has implications for attempts to reconstruct their function and social setting. This is different from that of other genres, such as letters to particular groups, like Paul's churches. As already noted, form-critical approaches stressed the gospels' *Sitz im Leben*, while redaction criticism led to the development of theories about the communities within which and for which the gospels were produced, some of which were very specific. Further study of the way ancient lives functioned across a wide range of social levels in the ancient world cautions against too limited a view of the gospels' audiences. This has led Bauckham (1998) to argue that such 'community' approaches rested upon a genre mistake and treated the gospels like letters to specific churches; instead, ancient biographies were written for broader audiences – and the gospels were also intended for such wider circulation around the early churches. Equally, the gospels may have been read aloud in large sections, or even in their entirety, at meetings or in worship at the Eucharist in a manner similar to the public reading of lives at social gatherings or mealtimes in Graeco-Roman society. Study of the production of ancient biographies may provide an historical clue to the gospels' 'performance'. The previous scholarly consensus about the uniqueness of the gospels' genre saw them as a communication produced 'by committees, for communities, about theological ideas'. Burridge has argued instead that their biographical genre means that they must be interpreted as 'by people, for people, about a person' (Burridge 1998: 115, 144). As biographies, they are composed by a single person, the Evangelist, with a clear understanding of Jesus which he wishes to portray to a wide range of possible readers. Thus

once again, genre is the key to interpretation – and the biographical genre of the gospels has implications for the historical reconstruction of their social function, setting and delivery.

Therefore the study of genre in general, and of the gospels in particular, has played a pivotal role in historical studies both of Jesus and of the early Christian communities. From originally being read as stories of Jesus, through the period of the form-critics when they were seen as unique, the gospels are now again viewed as a type of ancient biography. Therefore they should be interpreted accordingly in the search for the historical Jesus.

RICHARD A. BURRIDGE

Further reading

Aune, David E. *The New Testament in Its Literary Environment*, Philadelphia, PA: Westminster, 1987.

Bauckham, Richard (ed.) *The Gospels for All Christians: Rethinking the Gospel Audiences*, Grand Rapids, MI: Eerdmans/T. & T. Clark, 1998.

Bornkamm, G. "The Stilling of the Storm in Matthew," in G. Bornkamm, G. Barth, and H. J. Held (eds) *Tradition and Interpretation in Matthew*, London: SCM Press, 1963, pp. 52–57 [ET; original 1948].

Brown, Raymond E. *The Community of the Beloved Disciple*, London: Geoffrey Chapman, 1979.

Bultmann, Rudolf. *Die Geschichte der synoptischen Tradition*. ET: *The History of the Synoptic Tradition*, revised edition with supplement, trans. John Marsh, Oxford: Blackwell, 1972 [1921].

Burridge, Richard A. *What are the Gospels? A Comparison with Graeco-Roman Biography*, SNTS MS 70, Cambridge: Cambridge University Press, 1992; revised and updated edition, Grand Rapids, MI: Eerdmans, 2004.

—— *Four Gospels, One Jesus? A Symbolic Reading*, London: SPCK; Grand Rapids, MI 1994: Eerdmans; revised and updated edition, 2005.

—— "About People, by People, for People: Gospel Genre and Audiences," in R. Bauckham (ed.) *The Gospels for All Christians*, Grand Rapids, MI: Eerdmans, 1998, pp. 113–45.

Collins, Adela Yarbro. "Genre and the Gospels," *JR* 75.2 (1995) 239–46.

Conzelmann, H. *Die Mitte der Zeit: Studien zur Theologie des Lukas*; ET: *Theology of St Luke*, trans. G. Buswell, London: Faber & Faber, 1960 [1954].

Frickenschmidt, Dirk. *Evangelium als Biographie: Die vier Evangelien im Rahmen antiker Erzählkunst*, Tübingen: Francke Verlag, 1997.

Hengel, Martin. *The Four Gospels and the One Gospel of Jesus Christ: An Investigation of the Collection and Origin of the Canonical Gospels*, London: SCM Press, 2000.

Kingsbury, Jack Dean. *Matthew as Story*, second edition, Philadelphia, PA: Fortress Press, 1988.

Martyn, J. L. *History and Theology in the Fourth Gospel*, Nashville, TN: Abingdon, 1979.

Morgan, Robert. "The Hermeneutical Significance of Four Gospels," *Interpretation* 33:4 (1979) 376–88.

Renan, Ernest. *Life of Jesus*, London: Kegan Paul, 1893 [ET; original 1893].

Rhoads, David and Donald Michie. *Mark as Story: An Introduction to the Narrative of a Gospel*, Philadelphia, PA: Fortress Press, 1982.

Schmidt, Karl Ludwig. "Die Stellung der Evangelien in der allgemeinen Literaturgeschichte," in Hans Schmidt (ed.) *Eucharisterion: Studien zur Religion und Literatur des Alten und Neuen Testaments*, Göttingen: Vandenhoeck & Ruprecht, 1923, Vol. 2, = *FRLANT*, NF 19:2, 50–134. ET: *The Place of the Gospels in the General History of Literature*, trans. Byron R. McCane, Columbia, SC: University of South Carolina Press, 2002, with an introduction by John Riches.

Stanton, Graham N. *Jesus of Nazareth in New Testament Preaching*, SNTS MS 27, Cambridge: Cambridge University Press, 1974.

—— "The Fourfold Gospel," *NTS* 43 (1997) 347–66.

—— *Jesus and Gospel*, Cambridge: Cambridge University Press, 2004.

Stendahl, Krister. *The School of St Matthew*, Philadelphia, PA: Fortress Press, 1968.

Talbert, Charles H. *What is a Gospel? The Genre of the Canonical Gospels*, Philadelphia, PA: Fortress Press; London: SPCK, 1978.

Tannehill, Robert C. *The Narrative Unity of Luke–Acts: A Literary Interpretation*, 2 vols, Philadelphia, PA and Minneapolis, MN: Fortress Press, 1986/1990.

Vines, Michael E. *The Problem of the Markan Genre: The Gospel of Mark and the Jewish Novel*, Atlanta, GA: SBL, 2002.

Weeden, Theodore J. *Mark: Traditions in Conflict*, Philadelphia, PA: Fortress Press, 1971.

Wills, Lawrence M. *The Quest of the Historical Gospel: Mark, John and the Origins of the Gospel Genre*, London: Routledge, 1997.

GOSPEL OF JOHN

Among NT scholars, the Gospel of John has been both esteemed as a valid source for the historical Jesus and vilified as a later re-forging of the portrait of Jesus. Both views can be seen today. Scholars who attempt a critical reconstruction of Jesus' life must choose whether to anchor this portrait only in the synoptics or whether to include John at any level. In the well-known Jesus Seminar, when John's historicity was weighed, scholars reached a remarkably negative verdict: Only three sayings of Jesus *in the entire gospel* bore a remote link to the historical Jesus. The balance of Jesus' sayings (the seminar argued) are the theological creation of the evangelist. Less severe, but perhaps more to the mainstream, C. K. Barrett's famous 1978 commentary concluded, "it was not John's intention to write a work of scientific history. Such works were extremely rare in antiquity ... John's interests were theological rather than chronological." Barrett believes that John used Mark as a source and when he did so "he did not hesitate to repress, revise, rewrite or rearrange" Mark's material.

In the earliest centuries of the church, John's gospel was deeply valued as stemming from an eyewitness, the "beloved disciple," which most assumed to be John, the son of Zebedee and apostle. This was a gospel that reached spiritual heights unmatched by other writers, penetrating the meaning of Jesus' life in ways the synoptics could not. Not without reason, by the second century Clement of Alexandria was calling it the "spiritual gospel" and soon it was represented in illuminated manuscripts with an eagle.

However, at the same time, Christians committed to a Gnostic view of Jesus likewise valued this gospel. The first commentary on John was written by the Gnostic Heracleon (*c.* 170) and this gave orthodox Christians pause. The letters of John, however, provided a clear refutation of any Christology that might deny an orthodox treatment of Jesus (such as a genuine incarnation). And together with the gospel, the letters were welcomed into the NT.

What makes John different?

Scholars from the beginning recognized that John's gospel was different. In most cases, John was seen as a helpful supplement to the synoptic story. But with the birth of critical NT scholarship (in the early 1800s), scholars listed so many substantive differences from the other gospels that they began to question its origin, its authorship, even its authority as a reliable historical source for Jesus.

Blomberg (1987, 2001) lists five distinctives that set John apart: First, John's *selection of material* is unique. Missing are Jesus' baptism, the calling of the Twelve, exorcisms, parables, the Transfiguration, and the Lord's Supper. John also includes stories found nowhere else such as the miracle of water and wine at Cana, Lazarus' resurrection, the foot-washing, and Jesus' numerous visits to Jerusalem. Second, John has a distinct *theological approach*. Jesus' divinity is in high relief (while in Mark, for instance, Jesus urges secrecy). Jesus makes explicit claims about his relation to God and even uses the poignant Jewish title for God ("I AM") as a suggestive title for Christ (8:58). Moreover, Jesus' chief theme here is eternal life while in the synoptics Jesus speaks frequently about the kingdom of God.

Third, John has a *distinct chronology*. John refers to three Passovers (2:13; 6:4; 13:1) and thus implies that Jesus' ministry lasted three years instead of one. But in addition, events are not found in the same order as in the synoptics: note the setting of Jesus' anointing in Bethany (12:1; cf. Mark 14:3) and the day of the crucifixion (19:14; cf. Mark 15:25). In the synoptics Jesus cleanses the temple at the end of his ministry (Mark 11:12–19) while in John it is this event that begins it (John 2:13–22). Fourth, scholars point to *historical discrepancies*. Did Lazarus' raising (John 11) inspire Jesus' arrest – or was it the temple cleansing? Does the language of excommunication in John 9 reflect a later era not known to Jesus? Fifth, John employs a distinct *literary style*. That is, the language of Jesus is indistinguishable from the language of the narrator in this gospel (or even the epistles). It almost seems as if the gospel has reframed and reshaped Jesus' style. Rather than short sayings, as in the synoptics, John's Jesus gives lengthy speeches. No pithy succinct arguments in John; rather, Jesus uses long discourse. In the upper room Jesus speaks for over 100 verses, while in the synoptics little is spoken outside the words of institution (which John fails to record). Jesus' vocabulary is different as well and it is filled with theological meaning: Jesus does not work "miracles" (Gk. *dunamis*) in John, rather his acts of power are "signs" (Gk. *semeion*) that unveil his identity.

The cumulative effect of this evidence has raised a whole host of new questions about the gospel. And for some scholars, confidence in John's historicity has been lost. Is this a gospel that knew and understood the Jesus tradition handed down through the synoptics? While the synoptics share a great deal of common material, over 90 percent of this gospel is unique to John (according to one scholar). But if John knew the synoptic tradition, why did he depart from and in some cases seemingly contradict it? On the other hand, if John wrote independently of the synoptics, what were his sources? Was John's gospel a later Christian project that reforged the historical Jesus into something new?

Authorship

If the historical character of John's gospel has been questioned, the same is true of its authorship. The gospel is anonymous but no doubt the key to its writer is the mysterious "Beloved Disciple" (or "disciple whom Jesus loved") mentioned in the gospel's second half (13:23; 19:26; 20:2; 21:7, 20). This is crucial because he is a witness at the cross, and at the end of the gospel we are told that it is his eyewitness testimony that stands behind the book. "This is the disciple that is bearing witness to these things and who has written these things and we know that his testimony is true" (21:24).

Scholars have nominated a number of names for this person. Lazarus is commonly suggested – note that this is the only character in the gospel whom Jesus explicitly "loved" (11:36). Recently Charlesworth (1995) nominated Thomas as author. Others have argued that "the Beloved Disciple" was a literary device, a model disciple or a symbol of what it means to follow Jesus. Still others think that we cannot know his identity, but that certainly it is a later Christian who has built the gospel with a view to his own experiences.

The traditional – and altogether defensible – answer has been John the apostle. When we note the central role the Beloved Disciple plays with Jesus (even in the upper room) and when we consider his regular comparison with Peter (20:1–10; 21:4–8), we begin to hear echoes of the synoptic role for John. Perhaps we can summarize as follows: the Beloved Disciple seems to be one of the Twelve who worked in close connection with Peter but whose name is absent. The logic of John 21 gives us a provocative hint: The context of the fishing scene shows that the disciples present are Peter, Thomas, Nathanael, and the "two sons of Zebedee." One of these is no doubt the Beloved Disciple (21:20). And since James the other son of Zebedee was martyred (Acts 12:2), this suggests John as the only remaining character who wrote the gospel.

But if authorship plays a role in assessing historical reliability, we must hold a flexible view of what it means in antiquity to "author" a text. Such writing may have taken time, passed through a period of oral tradition, even been compiled by a community (Brown). The Fourth Gospel ends with Peter enquiring about the Beloved Disciple's survival till the glorious return of Jesus (21:21) – which Jesus rebukes and the narrator corrects (21:22–23). This likely means that the Beloved Disciple – the source of the Jesus stories here – has died, that his disciples have put the finishing touches to his gospel material (21:24, "and *we know* that his testimony is true") and that they have venerated him with the endearing title "Beloved."

These disciple-editors wrote with confidence, claiming that their source for Jesus' life was an eyewitness (21:24). And if he was not John, he certainly knows Judaism intimately, he also knows Palestine well, and he comes from the inner circle surrounding Jesus.

New confidence in John

The beginning of the twentieth century saw numerous scholars argue that the gospel did not possess true historical credibility and that it was a wholesale Hellenizing of the Jesus tradition. For this reason readers of books about John need to be alert to the assumptions commentators bring to their work. But by mid-century, a change was in the air. In 1959, a British scholar named J. A. T. Robinson published an essay describing a shift in how the academy was viewing the Fourth Gospel. Robinson was no conservative, but this question so intrigued him that he continued to pursue scholarship's negative assumptions about the dates of the NT material (1976) and he ended his life writing his most intriguing book of all (1985). In a volume outrageously entitled *The Priority of John*, he argued that John held material that was as early as any synoptic story and that it was trustworthy. He even speculated that most of this gospel's material predated the devastating Jewish War of AD 66–70.

By mid-century scholars were looking at the gospel with new eyes. The discovery of the Dead Sea Scrolls in the 1940s urged them to acknowledge that Jews in the era before the war of AD 70 were using Hellenistic dualism (light/dark, above/below) exactly like John. Hence John's more "Hellenistic" style did not disqualify this gospel as late. Moreover, scholars well versed in Judaism began to understand that John's thinking betrayed a profound understanding of Jewish metaphor and argument one would not expect to find from a Hellenistic gospel. But the real crux was here: simply because a gospel departed from the Synoptic Tradition did not mean that its independent material was inauthentic. The well-known Cambridge NT scholar C. H. Dodd took up this question and in 1963 published his famous and lengthy analysis, concluding that "behind the Fourth Gospel lies an ancient tradition independent of the other gospels, and meriting serious consideration as a contribution to our knowledge of the historical facts concerning Jesus Christ." Dodd began by testing John's passion story against the synoptic version, found John to be an independent credible witness, and urged the plausibility of locating it in Palestine before the Jewish war. He wrote that although the data was different than the synoptics, "it deserved to be treated with respect." From here Dodd looked at John's treatment of Jesus' public ministry and sayings and again came away critical of the skepticism that had come against the gospel.

In 1959 Robinson referred to this shift as a "new look" on the Fourth Gospel. And he was correct. For the last fifty years scholars have returned to this gospel with a keen interest in historical sources. For some this has been an investigation into a "discourse source" (Jesus' teachings) or a "signs source" (Jesus' miraculous deeds) in the gospel. But where there has been openness to overturning the conventional wisdom, the Fourth Gospel has been deemed more historically reliable than ever thought possible. This has not simply been an effort among conservatives (Morris, Carson, Blomberg) but has now become an interest among many from critical theological perspectives (Smith, Fortna, Smalley). To simply dismiss the gospel of John as historically suspect is now passé.

Historical soundings in John

In order to understand the nature of John's historical interest, we need to approach the problem of John and history from a variety of angles. And we need to examine not only John's links to the Synoptic Tradition, but also those materials where he makes important historical departures.

The Synoptic Gospels

There are numerous places where John has direct parallels with the Synoptic Gospels. In most cases, John may present his version of the story with a distinct nuance, but nevertheless the core of the story remains the same. For example, John begins his gospel (John 1) using John the Baptist as the one who introduces Jesus to the public and fulfills Isaiah 40:3 ("one crying in the wilderness"). The water baptism of the Baptist is also contrasted with the Spirit-baptism of Jesus, who is also anointed by the Spirit at his baptism. Each of these are elements that one can easily find in both the synoptics and John. But the list is longer. One can profitably compare the story of Jesus feeding the 5,000 and walking on the water (John 6), as well as Jesus' anointing in Bethany (John 12) and the story of Jesus' arrest, trial, crucifixion, and resurrection (John 19–21).

There are other Johannine stories that do not have parallels but they have a distinctive "synoptic flavor." The phrase, "take up your bed and walk" appears not only as the climax of the healing of the paralytic in Mark 2:11, but it is the healing command of Jesus in John 5:8. Giving sight to the blind, raising a dead person, healing a paralyzed man, breaking and debating the Sabbath, even having hostile debates with the Jewish leadership – these were characteristic of Jesus' synoptic ministry but also appear in John. Likewise Jesus exhibits a style of teaching that echoes the synoptics. In most cases, the framework of the teaching is different; but still, there are clear links. Spiritual rebirth must precede entering the kingdom of God (John 3:3; Mark 10:15); Jesus refers to himself having a father/son relation with God (John 17:2; Matt 11:25–27); prophets have little honor in their own home (John 4:44; Mark 6:4); etc. Even though

John does not record any parables, still, Jesus' use of imagery points to similar images: shepherds and sheep, light, vines, persecution and flight, etc. Characteristic of the synoptic Jesus is his skill at storytelling. But John's Jesus likewise uses metaphor and story comfortably (the vineyard, the good shepherd) and even enacts metaphor in his activity at Jewish festivals (bread at Passover; water at Tabernacles). In the synoptics Jesus opens many sayings with "amen" (truly) – this same pattern is in John but it is doubled, "amen, amen."

All of this suggests that the gospel of John has a connection to the Jesus tradition which we know in the synoptics. And it explains why some scholars have argued that John may have known the synoptics and worked to supplement them. But perhaps this evidence leads a different direction. Scholars have wondered if John is not writing with another intent: perhaps John is thinking that his reader *knows Mark* already (Bauckham). One test of this view is in the parenthetical remark the gospel offers in 3:24, "for John had not yet been thrown into prison." This refers to John the Baptist introduced in chapter 1. But on its own John 3:24 makes no sense (the gospel has not referred to the Baptist's arrest!) unless we postulate that the gospel's readers know more about the story than John's gospel provides. Perhaps they have read Mark 1:14, "Now after John was arrested, Jesus came into Galilee ... " The Fourth Evangelist is then giving his reader a tip as to the placement of his third chapter in relation to Mark's chronology.

Another example of this is in 11:1–2. At the scene with Lazarus, Mary is introduced as the woman "who anointed the Lord with perfume." It is an awkward comment because John does not record this event of anointing till the next chapter (12:1–8). Therefore this parenthetical remark implies that John's reader must know Mary, know already what she did – and the source for this may have been a Synoptic Gospel. Then there are characters in the gospel whose identification is only obvious if one had read, say, Mark. Andrew is "Simon Peter's brother" (1:40) but we don't know Peter yet from the pages of the gospel of John. We read about "the twelve" in 6:67–71 but this term would only have meaning with a wider synoptic context. Judas Iscariot is introduced as betrayer (6:71), yet we don't know this about him until far later. Pilate is likewise introduced as if he is already known (18:29).

John may have known the synoptic tradition or he may be assuming that his readers know it. But at least his work shows a fundamental continuity with much more of the Synoptic Tradition than we expect.

Independent Johannine material

Of course, there are elements in the gospel of John which are independent of the synoptics and so different that many scholars would view them as historically problematic. Only John records such narratives as Jesus' conversation with Nicodemus (John 3) and the Samaritan woman (John 4). He alone tells us about the healing of paralyzed and blind men (John 5, 9). John has the raising of Lazarus (John 11) and the foot-washing (John 13) as well as Jesus' extensive upper room discourse (John 13:31 – 16:33). And rather than the difficult prayer in the garden before his arrest, John has Jesus praying at length and with confidence for twenty-six verses (John 17). Of course, the timeless question has been this: when John departs from the synoptic tradition, is his contribution reliable? Three test cases are helpful. And each demonstrates historical solutions that are plausible but too easily overlooked.

The wine miracle at Cana (2:1–11)

Stories about changing water into wine were well known in antiquity. Each year at Andros (an island in the southern Aegean) a spring from the temple of Bacchus-Dionysus ran with wine, but if the wine was taken out of sight of the temple it returned to water. Similar stories were told from ancient Teos, Elis, and Haliartus in Greece. It has not been uncommon to hear NT scholars say that John simply appropriated the Dionysus story for Jesus.

When C. H. Dodd (1963) tested the historicity of John, this story was important to him. Yet in it he found dramatic departures from the Greek legends and items that linked the Johannine story to the Jesus tradition: (1) that Jesus would contribute to a convivial occasion is a constant synoptic theme (Matt 11:19; Luke 7:34); (2) Jesus' exchange with his mother suggests family tension known elsewhere too (Mark 3:32–35; Luke 2:48–50); (3) the theme here is not wine but inauguration: Jesus' coming has birthed the true celebration; this idea is presupposed behind every synoptic gospel; (4) three synoptic parables use wedding feast imagery (Matt 22:1–14; 25:1–13; Luke 12:35–36); (5) the episode ends with the poignant remark, "you have kept the best wine till now," which has a distinctive synoptic ring that often ends conflict stories or parables but also evokes the same idea in the gospels: the ministry of Christ inaugurates the kingdom of God till now unseen in Judaism.

Dodd concluded that John 2:1–11 likely originated in a parable that was later historicized (much as scholars have suggested about the Lazarus story (John 11; Luke 16:19–21)). But Dodd urged that this view was only conjecture and even if the Dionysus legend contributed to the story, the heart of the episode stemmed from "the common tradition" of the historical Jesus.

The temple cleansing (2:13–22)

The synoptic story records the temple cleansing at the end of Jesus' ministry (Mark 11) and implies that it was the catalyst for Jesus' arrest. John records it at the beginning (John 2) and places the Lazarus story at the end as a catalyst for conflict. Scholars question: if there was one temple cleansing (and the two accounts have many parallels, implying they record the same event), we have to wonder when it happened. Other scholars have suggested that it happened twice, thus preserving a comfortable harmony between John and Mark.

But there may be another possibility. John's gospel may have a thematic outline more committed to a literary-theological development than to chronology. That is, John's stories may be *historical* while not necessarily being *chronological*. We see this freedom to move stories in the Synoptic Gospels and here we may have the same phenomenon. John has placed the temple cleansing in chapter 2 in order to contrast it with other Jewish institutions now made obsolete in his coming (e.g. water purification vessels at Cana). Therefore a chronological discrepancy in John does not invalidate its claim to be recording an episode that was important and historical.

The day of crucifixion (19:14)

In Judaism's Passover celebration, the day prior to Passover was a preparation day, commonly numbered as the fourteenth day in the Jewish month of Nisan. Here is where lambs were slaughtered for the feast that began at sundown which then began Nisan 15, the Passover. According to the synoptics, Nisan 14 ran through Thursday dusk and then Jesus' final meal was Nisan 15, a Passover meal, Thursday evening. However, John 13:1, 29; 18:28; 19:14, 31 each refer to the day of crucifixion as "the day of Preparation," which implies that it was Nisan 14 when he died – and it follows then that the Lord's Supper Thursday night was not a Passover meal. Scholars have argued that one gospel tradition must be right and the other wrong or that rival calendars made both accounts true.

But another creative look at the problem discloses a valuable solution. Many things in the Johannine account of the meal Thursday night imply it is Passover (e.g. levitical purity, 13:10). But if that is true – if John accepts the synoptic dating – how do we understand 19:31? "Preparation" (Gk. *paraskeue*) was used in Judaism only with reference to preparation for *the Sabbath*, not Passover. This term refers to the modern "Friday," meaning, the day when one prepared for the coming of Sabbath. Hence, according to John, Jesus was crucified on "Passover Friday," or the day in Passover when Judaism readied for Sabbath.

Such solutions as these three will be debated by scholars. But today they are acknowledged as reasonable explanations for notorious historical tensions that previous generations too glibly dismissed as holding no answer.

John and Judaism

Interpreters of the Fourth Gospel must regularly make a cultural/historical decision: is the formative milieu of the gospel to be found in Judaism (perhaps early Palestinian Judaism) or in the pagan world of Hellenism? Of course, we understand that Jews living in the Diaspora could have held as strictly to law and tradition as anyone in Jerusalem. And we understand that Judaism even in Jerusalem was deeply hellenized. But here our question is different: Does John betray a theological framework that assumes a deeply rooted commitment to the OT and Judaism or is it in the process of innovation?

Recent work on the gospel indicates that John's claim to a Jewish cultural-theological framework can be seen between the lines of the gospel. For instance, some have studied the simple form of John's Greek and found there strong hints of Aramaic. Some have even wondered if the gospel's stories originated in Aramaic. The gospel is also filled with parenthetical remarks, telling us that Messiah means Christ, that a rabbi is a teacher, and that the Sea of Galilee is also the Sea of Tiberius (1:38, 41; 6:1). And if we did not know that Jews and Samaritans did not talk, John explains it (4:9). These notes indicate that John is standing between two cultures, that he is bridging his readers from their Hellenism to his own native Judaism. He explains customs, geography, and attitudes of Jews living in Judea.

When an author makes a citation to a source and he/she thinks that the audience will miss it, the citation must be made explicitly (such as Matthew's use of the OT). John not only cites the OT in this manner (19:36) but he does something else. When author and reader are steeped in a *shared theological tradition*, the citation becomes an allusion with all its subtlety. This is the Johannine style: John alludes to the OT and assumes his readers will understand. Hence John 1:1–2 is nothing other than an overture to Genesis 1, "in the beginning was the word." In John 3:14 we don't need to be told about Moses and the serpent if we know Num 21 well.

Moreover, the gospel of John reflects a knowledge and use of Jewish thought that is stunning. For instance, when Jesus is charged with breaking the Sabbath in John 5, his defense follows not only the Jewish rules for witnesses, but it plays on a subtle Jewish argument for God's capacity to "break" his own Sabbath when unique needs arose. By holding this argument for himself – John lets this theme in the narrative ring with clarity – Jesus is claiming the same divine privilege for himself. Perhaps the most overt investment in Jewish culture is John's use of the annual Jewish festivals of Passover, Tabernacles and Hanukkah. The narrative is built to show us the Jewish expectation and tradition, Jesus' abundant provision, the new obsolescence of the ritual, and an application to Christ's identity. Thus in John 6, Jesus appears at Passover (recalling Moses), gives bread abundantly (recalling God's provision of manna), walks on water (recalling the sea miracle in Egypt), and shows that he himself is the "bread of life" that has come down like manna. If you eat it, you will live – but without it, you die in the wilderness.

If John's gospel presumes an authorial world deeply indebted to Judaism, if the interpretative keys to the gospels are found in the OT and rabbinic thought, we are a far cry from a formative setting in Hellenism. If the gospel's setting is early and Jewish, this discovery contributes to the likelihood that its sources may have been linked to the original Jesus tradition located in Palestine.

John, incarnation and history

The starting point for the scandal of the Fourth Gospel in the Hellenistic world was its absolute commitment to history. John would not compromise the notion that God had done something in Christ in history. Hellenism – especially those trajectories that led to Gnosticism – had a cavalier attitude toward the world and its events. Its dualistic instincts were happy with a Christ who bore a divine presence into the world and perhaps revealed the secrets of heaven; but to hold to such a divine claim and to hold that God *also* became "flesh" in the incarnation (1:14) was unexpected. John's Christology never lets the reader assume that Jesus lacks humanity. Jesus thirsts, he hungers, he weeps, he dies.

This is valuable because it means that when John wrote, his theological reflexes did not incline him to generate stories presenting theological ideals that did not happen in time. In other words, John's incarnational theology made him predisposed to a commitment to history, to "flesh," to real characters in whom divine events were transpiring.

But John has another commitment. Again and again the gospel refers to "truth" (John 4:24; 8:32; 14:17), affirming the trustworthiness of its account. Moreover, it refers as well to the importance of "witness," anchoring the validity of its story in a person (the Beloved Disciple) who had "seen" and "touched" and "heard" this reality:

> that which was from the beginning, which we have heard, which we have seen with our own eyes, which we have looked upon and touched with our hands, concerning the word of life – the life was made manifest, we saw it and testify to it, and proclaim to you this eternal life.
>
> (1 John 1:1–2)

A foundational commitment in the gospel of John is a commitment to what happened, that God acts in history, and that faith can make good use of the record found in this gospel.

Conclusion

Scholars will continue to dispute the historical value of the Fourth Gospel. For some (Casey) it is axiomatic that the gospel departed from the received historical tradition and, from the vantage of a faith found after Easter, built a portrait of Jesus that is inspiring but fanciful. But others firmly disagree (Meier 1991; Moloney). For them, the gospel makes a substantive and reliable contribution to the historical Jesus and merits careful study and respect.

GARY M. BURGE

Further reading

Note commentaries by Barrett (1978), Bernard (1928), Beasley-Murray (1987), Brown (1966–70), Bultmann (ET 1971), Burge (2000), Carson (1991), Haenchen (ET 1984), Keener (2003), Kostenberger (2004), Lindars (1972), Morris (1995), Schnackenburg (1979), and Witherington (1995).

Ashton, John. *Understanding the Fourth. Gospel*, Oxford: Clarendon, 1991.
Barton, Stephen. "The Believer, the Historian, and the Fourth Gospel," *Theology* 96 (1993) 289–302.

Bauckham, Richard. "John for Readers of Mark," in R. Bauckham (ed.) *The Gospels for All Christians. Rethinking the Gospel Audiences*, Grand Rapids, MI: Eerdmans, 1998, pp. 147–72.

Blomberg, Craig. *The Historical Reliability of the Gospels*, Leicester: InterVarsity Press, 1987.

—— *The Historical Reliability of John's Gospel*, Leicester: InterVarsity Press, 2001.

Brodie, Thomas. *The Quest for the Origin of John's Gospel: A Source Oriented Approach*, New York: Oxford University Press, 1993.

Brown, Raymond E. *The Community of the Beloved Disciple*, New York: Paulist Press, 1979.

Burge, Gary M. *Interpreting the Gospel of John*, Grand Rapids, MI: Baker, 1992.

Casey, Maurice. *Is John's Gospel True?* New York: Routledge, 1996.

Cassidy, Richard. *John's Gospel in New Perspective*, Maryknoll, NY: Orbis, 1992.

Charlesworth, James. *The Beloved Disciple. Whose Witness Validates the Gospel of John?* Valley Forge, PA: Trinity, 1995.

Coakley, James. "The Anointing at Bethany and the Priority of John," *JBL* 107 (1988) 461–82.

Culpepper, R. Alan. *The Johannine School*, Missoula, MT: Scholars Press, 1975.

Dodd, C. H. *The Interpretation of the Fourth Gospel*. Cambridge: Cambridge University Press, 1954.

—— *Historical Tradition in the Fourth Gospel*, Cambridge: Cambridge University Press, 1963.

Dunn, J. D. G. "Let John be John," in P. Stuhlmacher (ed.) *Das Evangelium und die Evangelien*, Tübingen: Mohr, 1983.

Dvorak, James D. "The Relationship between John and the Synoptics," *JETS* 41, (1998) 201–13.

Flanagan, N. "The Gospel of John as Drama," *TBT* 19 (1981) 264–70.

Fortna, Robert and Tom Thatcher (eds) *Jesus in Johannine Tradition*, Louisville, KY: Westminster, 2001.

Harvey, A. E. *Jesus on Trial: A Study of the Fourth Gospel*, Atlanta, GA: John Knox, 1977.

Hengel, M. *The Johannine Question*, London: SPCK, 1989.

Higgins, Angus J. B. *The Historicity of the Fourth Gospel*, London: Lutterworth, 1960.

Meier, J. P. *A Marginal Jew. Rethinking the Historical Jesus*, 3 vols, New York: Doubleday, 2001.

Moloney, Francis J. "The Fourth Gospel and the Jesus of History," *NTS* 46 (2000) 42–58.

Moody Smith, D. "Historical Issues and the Problem of John and the Synoptics," in M. C. deBoer (ed.) *From Jesus to John*, Sheffield: JSOT, 1993, pp. 252–67.

Morris, Leon. *Studies in the Fourth Gospel*, Grand Rapids, MI: Eerdmans, 1969.

Mussner, Franz. *The Historical Jesus in the Gospel of St John*, New York: Herder & Herder, 1967.

Painter, John. *The Quest for the Messiah. The History, Literature, and Theology of the Johannine Community*, Nashville, TN: Abingdon, 1993.

Robinson, J. A. T. "The New Look on the Fourth Gospel," *TU* 73 (1959) 338–50.

—— *Redating the New Testament*, London: SCM Press, 1976.

—— *The Priority of John*, ed. J. F. Coakley, London: SCM Press, 1985.

Smalley, Stephen. *John: Evangelist and Interpreter*, Exeter: Paternoster, 1978.

Thompson, Marianne. "The Historical Jesus and the Johannine Christ," in R. A. Culpepper and C. Black (eds) *Exploring the Gospel of John*, Louisville, KY: Westminster/John Knox, 1996, pp. 21–42.

GOSPEL OF LUKE

Luke offers the most extensive account of the life of Jesus preserved in our New Testament. It is more than 70 percent longer than Mark and more than 30 percent longer than John. It is even a little longer than Matthew (about 7 percent). It covers less ground than Matthew, but what it covers it treats in greater detail and in particular it gives more space to the infancy of Jesus and more space to the post-resurrection materials. What is more, something like 33 to 42 percent of the Gospel (judgments vary) is made of material that is not paralleled in any of the other gospels. For example: without Luke there would be no visit of Gabriel to Mary; without Luke there would be no meeting of the risen Jesus with the disciples on the road to Emmaus; without Luke we would not have the parable of the Prodigal Son or the parable of the Good Samaritan.

The Lukan Jesus

The Jesus of the Gospel of Luke is clearly the same Jesus as in Matthew and Mark, the other most closely related gospels (forming as a set the three so-called Synoptic Gospels), but nonetheless special emphases emerge.

The Lukan Jesus manifests a deep interest in people in their social relationships. In parables unique to Luke there are people showing kindness to others, ignoring the needs of others, prodded into action by persistent requests. In one story Jesus offers a touching scene of a father-and-son reconciliation, complete with a resentful and alienated older brother (15:11–32). In one way or another mercy is a recurring theme of the Lukan Jesus' parables (7:41–43; 10:29–37; 13:6–9; 15:3–7, 8–10, 11–32; 18:9–14). There is a warm humanity about the Lukan Jesus that shows through in his stories and in his own actions, but this is not to be confused with sentimentality (e.g. 12:13–15; 13:1–5, 6–9; 17:7–10),

Not unrelated to the interest in social relations is the concern for outcasts, sinners and Samaritans, which marks the Lukan Jesus. Samaritans do not feature at all in Mark and are only mentioned to be excluded in Matthew (10:5). Luke's first introduction of Samaritans does not seem auspicious: 'they did not receive [Jesus]' (9:58), but Jesus rebukes the angry response of his disciples (v. 55). And soon after, he tells one of parables in which a Samaritan plays the hero's role (10:29–37). Finally, as if to balance the negative response of the Samaritan village, we hear of an occasion of healing in which a Samaritan is the only one of the ten lepers healed who comes back to give thanks to Jesus (17:16). Jesus' association with sinners is marked in Luke first with his equivalent to Mark 2:15–17, where Jesus eats with and plays the doctor to sinners (Luke 5:29–32). But Luke also carries the theme forward by identifying the woman who anointed Jesus' feet as a sinner and having Simon the Pharisee underline the identification (7:37, 40). Then Jesus is in company with sinners again in 15:1 and there is complaint about this in 15:2, which forms the backdrop for the teaching about joy in heaven over the repentance of the sinner in vv. 7, 10. In 18:13–14 it is the one who self-identifies as a sinner who goes home from the Temple upright in the sight of God. Finally, in 19:7 Jesus' association with sinners is marked one last time in the grumbling of the onlookers that Jesus is going off to be a guest of a sinner. The offence taken at Jesus' association with sinners points to their social exclusion, as does the link established between tax collectors and sinners (5:29, 30; 7:34; 15:1). These and other outcasts are particular objects of Jesus' care and compassion. Each of the Synoptic Gospels has a version of the cleansing of the leper found in Luke 5:12–16 (Mark 1:40–45; Matt 8:2–4), and for Matthew it is significant that the kingdom mission involves the cleansing of lepers (10:8; 11:5). Luke agrees (7:22), but did not use either of his mission charges to reinforce this point. Instead, he has a 'mass healing' of lepers (ten to be exact – 17:12–19) and he gets the idea of healing of lepers into his story for the very first episode he reports of Jesus' ministry (4:27).

Luke brings into focus Jesus' respect for women and his readiness to engage with them. Only Luke tells us that Jesus and his band were provided for financially out of the wealth of a number of women (Luke 8:2–3). Quite a bit of the distinctive Lukan material has Jesus engaging with or speaking about women (engaging with: 7:11–17, 36–50; 8:1–3; 10:38–42; 11:27–28; 13:10–17; 23:27–31; and just possibly 24:13–35; speaking about: 15:8–10; 17:35; 18:1–8). (Luke has further upped the profile of women in his Gospel by including at the beginning of his story Infancy materials in which Elizabeth, Mary and Anna play significant roles.)

Both Mark and Matthew link repentance language with John the Baptist (Mark 1:4; Matt 3:8, 11). They both indicate that Jesus carried forward the challenge to repent, but offer little along these lines (Mark 1:15; 6:12; Matt 4:17; 11:20–21; 12:41). Luke reproduces the material found in Mark and Matthew, but he adds much more. The Lukan Jesus calls sinners *to repentance* (5:32). Others will perish like the Galileans who fell foul of Pilate or those on whom the tower of Siloam fell, unless they repent (13:1–5). There is joy in heaven over the repentant sinner (15:7, 10). The doomed rich man seeks an opportunity for his brothers to repent (16:30). Repentance is the key to restoration in 17:3–4. And the challenge to repentance is part of the message entrusted by the risen Jesus to his disciples (24:47).

The Lukan Jesus is particularly interested in issues of wealth and poverty, and is concerned to unmask the power of wealth to blind people to the central issues of life and of responding to God. These interests are well enough rooted in the material Luke shares with the other Synoptic Gospels (so: Mark 1:18, 20; 10:21, 25; 12:41–44; 14:11; Matt 5:40, 42; 6:24, 25–33; 8:20), but Luke has considerably more. The theme is already introduced in the Magnificat, where Mary extols God as the one who feeds the hungry and sends the rich away empty (Luke 1:53); and Luke's John the Baptist gives concrete teaching about the use of material things (3:11, 13, 14). 'Good news to the poor' comes in Jesus' first recorded act of ministry (4:18; echoed in 7:22 [paralleled in Matt 11:6]). The unparalleled woes in Luke 6:24–26 start with 'woe to you who are rich', set in parallel to the 'blessed are you who are poor' at the head of the Lukan beatitudes (v. 20). As well, Luke has distinctly the parables of the rich fool (12:16–21) and the rich man and Lazarus (16:19–26), and he applies the challenge of the parable of the dishonest steward (16:1–8), also distinctive to Luke, to the use of money, by means of the attached verses (vv. 9–13). Distinctive as well is the advice to invite the poor to one's dinners rather than one's rich neighbours (14:13). The Zacchaeus story is only in Luke, and Zacchaeus is treated as exemplary in his giving away of half of what he owns to the poor (19:8). The challenge to the 'little flock' in 12:32–34 is to sell one's possessions and give to the poor, and gain a treasure in heaven. The direction in 11:41 is to give alms as an expression of what is inside (my rendering). In 14:33 there is the stark, 'every one of you who does not give up all his goods cannot be my disciple.' The Lukan Jesus probably thinks rather of becoming disencumbered than of deliberate total self-impoverishment (as he saw it, preoccupation with property and wealth has a disastrous effect on the possibility of coming to terms with the discipleship demands of Jesus). But given the deceptiveness of riches, poverty is to be seen as much safer than wealth.

If we may bundle them together, the Lukan Jesus has a special interest in joy, prayer and the Holy Spirit. Mark has only two references to joy or rejoicing, one of the parables, and that turns out to be a still-born joy (4:16), and one in connection with the happiness of the chief priests at having the offer from Judas to betray Jesus (14:11). Both Matthew and Luke repeat Mark's parable reference, but also find many more occasions to speak of joy or rejoicing in fully positive contexts. On the lips of Jesus Matthew has four extra references in parables (13:44; 25:21, 23; 18:13) and one in a teaching context (5:12), and also notes the joy of the Magi at reaching their destination (2:10) and of the women at the news of Jesus' resurrection (28:8). Luke picks up both Mark's references to joy/rejoicing, but has two extra references in parables (15:7, 10) and two in a teaching context (6:23; 10:20), and has Jesus rejoicing in 10:21. On several occasions Luke marks the joyful response of people to Jesus or to what was happening in connection with him (10:17; 13:17; 19:6, 37), and the idea that Jesus is a bringer of joy is underlined by the role of joy and rejoicing in the Infancy materials (1:14, 47; 2:10) and in the post-resurrection context (24:41, 52). Luke also has the rather bitter-sweet reference to Herod's joy at his unexpected opportunity to see Jesus (23:8).

It is widely recognised that the Lukan Jesus is notably the praying Jesus. The Markan Jesus is reported as praying on three occasions: as he begins his itinerant ministry (1:35), after the feeding of the 5,000 and the sending off of the disciples across the lake of Galilee (6:46) and in the Garden of Gethsemane (14:32, 35, 39). In Matthew the first of these is lost and the second and the third retained, and Matthew has the children brought for prayer with laying on of hands (19:13). Luke has Mark's first generalised into a regular pattern (5:16); he loses Mark's second, with the loss of the disciple's boat journey; and repeats Mark's final set. But beyond this he has Jesus at prayer at key points in his ministry: in connection with the descent of the Spirit and the coming of the voice of affirmation from heaven (3:21); in connection with the choice of the twelve to be apostles (6:12); in connection with drawing from Peter his christological confession (9:18); in connection with his dazzling transfiguration on the mountain (9:28–29); and finally as the background for the disciples' request to be taught how to pray (11:1).

The fundamental significance of the Holy Spirit for Jesus is marked in each of the Synoptic Gospels.

Each of them have John the Baptist anticipate a baptising-with-the-Spirit role for the coming one (Mark 1:8; Matt 3:11; Luke 3:16); each reports the descent of the Spirit upon Jesus at his baptism (Mark 1:10; Matt 3:16; Luke 3:22); each points to the initiative of the Spirit in Jesus' move into the wilderness to be tempted by Satan (Mark 1:12; Matt 4:1; Luke 4:1). Beyond these shared foundations Mark has Jesus speak three times about the Spirit: once about the role of the Spirit in the past (David spoke by the Holy Spirit – Mark 12:36); once about the role of the Spirit in the future (the Holy Spirit will speak through Christians who are brought to trial – 12:36); and once implying a role for the Spirit in the ministry of Jesus (blasphemy against the Holy Spirit cannot be forgiven – 3:29). Matthew matches these (Matt 22:43; 10:20; 12:31–32), but goes beyond them in two respects. First, for him, a role for the Spirit in Jesus' ministry is not just left to be implied. Matthew identifies him as the servant upon whom God has placed his Spirit (12:18) and the Matthean Jesus says he casts out demons by the Spirit of God (12:28). The risen Matthean Jesus in the baptismal formula at the end of the gospel (28:19) points to the persistence beyond his own ministry of this role of the Spirit. As well, Matthew takes the link between Jesus and the Spirit back to the moment of his human origins: Mary's virginal conception is enabled by the Holy Spirit (1:18, 20). In his own way Luke has most of this in his Gospel, but since he has the luxury of a second volume to come, he can keep back a little for later. Of the extra Markan developments Luke matches two (12:12, 10), but defers mention of the role of the Spirit in David's speech for Acts (Acts 1:16). For Luke, as for Matthew, the role of the Spirit in Jesus' ministry is not just left to be implied. At the beginning of his ministry, Luke marks Jesus as one 'filled with the power of the Spirit' (4:14), and picks up on this in 5:17 in connection with healing with 'the power of the Lord was with him to heal'. For Luke too Jesus casts out demons by the Spirit, though he is content with the indirect language 'finger of God' instead of 'Spirit of God' (11:20). Luke has Jesus use words from Isaiah to say 'the Spirit of the Lord is upon me' (4:18). Luke anticipates not so much a continuation into the life of the church of the role of the Spirit in Jesus' ministry as an expanded role for the Spirit. The baptising in the Spirit of 3:16 becomes the promised power from on high in 24:49 (cf. Acts 1:4–5), which reaches its fulfilment in Acts 2:1–4. It is not entirely clear whether the gift of the Spirit to be sought in Luke 11:13 must await the period of post-ascension fulfilment, but a more coherent understanding of Luke emerges if we take it this way. Just as Matthew has, Luke takes the link between Jesus and the Spirit back to the moment of his human origins (1:35). Distinctive to Luke is the renewed activity of the Spirit in the period immediately before the birth of Jesus: Elizabeth (1:41); Zechariah (1:67); Simeon (2:25–27). Luke gives a rather more inward look with his suggestion in 10:21 that Jesus 'rejoiced in the Holy Spirit', which seems to mean that the Holy Spirit motivated or empowered Jesus' own rejoicing.

Each of the synoptics makes use of salvation language in connection with what Jesus is doing. In the case of Mark and Matthew the use is of the verb and often the sense hovers between being made well or rescued and being saved in some larger sense (e.g. Mark 5:28, 34; Matt 8:25); the one seems to stand symbolically for the other. But often enough the larger sense is directly intended (e.g. Mark 8:35; 10:26; 13:13, 20; Matt 1:21; 10:22; 16:25; 19:25; 24:13, 22). Luke has the same materials and adds new instances (e.g. Luke 19:11, 'The Son of Man came to seek and to save the lost'). But the Lukan distinctive is to make use of the nouns 'saviour' and 'salvation' to make the link between Jesus and God's saving purposes. Zechariah speaks of the unborn Jesus as 'the horn of salvation for us in the house of [God's] servant David' and anticipates 'salvation from our enemies and from the hand of all who hate us' (1:69, 71). In this connection, John the Baptist is to prepare people for a 'knowledge of salvation … by the forgiveness of their sins' (v. 76). The angel of the Lord says to the shepherds, 'to you is born this day in the city of David a Saviour' (2:11). Holding the infant Jesus in his arms Simeon says, 'my eyes have seen your salvation' (v. 30). Luke continues the quotation from Isaiah linked with the ministry of Jesus to include 'all flesh shall see the salvation of God' (3:6). And finally the Lukan Jesus says, 'Today salvation has come to this house, because he too is a son of Abraham' (19:9).

Other distinctives could be added, but these suffice to indicate the main contribution to the Gospel image of Jesus that the Lukan materials make.

Evaluating the historical worth

Evaluating the historical worth of the Lukan materials involves many different considerations, and these have been differently assessed and their respective importance differently weighted by scholars. Often the considerations interlock in ways that make it impossible to treat them entirely

separately. Here I can do no more than sketch the main lines of argumentation and indicate the range of views.

The continuing discussion here will assume that the Gospel and Acts are written by the same author. Though some have puzzled over why there are some striking differences between the two works, this is the overwhelming consensus of scholarship. Once we are confident that the two works come from the same author, the larger question of the relationship between the two works is a hermeneutical question, of vital importance in its own right, but one that takes us beyond the scope of this present discussion.

A first line of inquiry in connection with evaluating historical reliability is into the question of the authorship of this Gospel. The consensus view is that the traditional attribution to Luke, sometime companion of Paul, is to be treated with suspicion, mostly on the basis of the perceived differences between the Paul of Acts and the Paul of the epistles (but also on the basis of questions about Luke's historical reliability – see further below). Certainly Luke's theology is not notably Pauline, and he has a way of rendering the theology of each of his chief characters so that, for the most part, a single theology emerges. But in its strongest form the claim that the Paul of Acts and the Paul of the epistles are irreconcilable is too much under the influence of a German Lutheran reading of Paul to inspire confidence. As Pauline studies has moved on from being so dominated by a Lutheran theology of grace it has become increasingly clear that features from the Lukan rendering of Paul can actually illuminate the apostle's thinking and help to bring into visibility aspects that have tended otherwise to remain invisible. Something must stand behind the uniform church tradition that the author was Luke, the sometime companion of Paul, and since Luke is otherwise a figure with little visibility, it seems better to conclude that the tradition is historical than that it is only a speculation on the basis of the 'we' passages of Acts (16:10–17; 20:5–15; 21:1–18; 27:1–28:16) and Col 4:14 and 1 Tim 4:11.

Though scholarship has occasionally argued for a second-century date for the third Evangelist's writings (especially Acts), if Luke is the author then the Gospel (with Acts) is to be anchored firmly in the first century, and Luke's acquaintance with his topic is to be traced back to around the middle of the first century. The 'we' passages in Acts have been mentioned above. These have often been explained away as a particular narrative technique – perhaps a novelistic technique – or as an indication that the author has drawn upon a diary of another. Nobody doubts, however, that the 'we' passages would most naturally mark the presence of the author in his own story. Those who insist on a different explanation do so because they believe on other grounds that attribution of the work to a sometime companion of Paul is not credible – a matter which has been commented on above. In Acts the 'we' references begin with material set in Troas. They continue to link Luke with Paul during a period of ministry around the Aegean Sea. They suggest, further, that Luke travels with Paul to Jerusalem, and then travels with him to Rome, when Paul is a prisoner. So a good framework is in place for Luke to be well informed about the events about which he writes, not with the immediacy of eye-witness participation, but through contact with those who were eye-witnesses, and with fellow Christians for whom these matters were of vital importance.

Luke opens his Gospel with a preface (Luke 1:1–4) in which he offers something of a statement of intention and a rationale for what he has written. He offers as his central credential for writing his claim to have engaged in careful investigation. Three of his other statements in the preface help to add further definition to what such investigation may have entailed and what was its goal.

The starting point is the role of those who were eye-witnesses from the beginning, of what Luke writes about. Luke says that they became servants of the message that was generated by the events – an interesting idea in its own right; and it is clear that he, as part of the 'us' that is the church, is acknowledging his dependence on the initial eye-witness testimony of these people. But that he talks about investigation indicates that he does not want his reader to think that all he is doing is repeating what he has heard. What the investigation might have involved we can only imagine, but Luke is conjuring up an image of himself as one who has checked things out carefully.

Beyond the deposit created by this body of witness, Luke indicates that he is also aware that a number of others (he says many) have aspired to do what he is doing: to set out in a narrative the things that had been accomplished; their writings are a precedent for his (just as the transmission of the message by the original eye-witnesses is offered as a precedent in another way). He does not say, or even imply, that he actually made use of any of the works of these earlier writers, but on other grounds most scholars are confident he did.

Finally, Luke suggests some degree of contrast between the pre-existing state of knowledge of Theophilus and what is now being offered. Theophilus has heard reports; now he can gain confidence about the truth. It is unclear whether Theophilus' previous information is simply of limited scope or precision, or whether it is being considered erroneous in some way, or whether Theophilus is understood to have been hearing conflicting accounts and was in need of help in finding his way through the confusion.

It is sometimes suggested that Luke is taking a critical stance in relation to the writings of his predecessors, but since he appeals to their existence to justify his own writing this is unlikely. Only in the very restricted sense of not being immediately tailored to the specific needs of a Theophilus does Luke find inadequacy in the work of his predecessors.

Luke offers Theophilus a well-ordered account, which probably means an account which makes use of an ordering principle that sets the parts in logical relation to a coherently understood whole. That is, Luke is offering an interpreted account of the events, concerned to bring out what he and other Christians considered their intrinsic significance, but which he was well aware were being taken quite differently by those who stood opposed to this new religious movement.

There is an obvious studied secularity to the preface. The only specifically religious notion that betrays its presence is the idea that events have happened which generate a message (noted above). Otherwise each word is carefully chosen for its neutrality. Luke is not trying to fool anybody about the religious nature of the document to follow (we drop almost immediately into a Jewish worship atmosphere after the four verses of the prologue), but he is making a claim to be doing more than expressing his own faith. I have argued elsewhere that Luke is self-conscious about the role of historical evidence in commending Christianity to a degree not evident in the work of the other evangelists. Not that he thinks Christianity can be proved in this way – he is careful to record cases of people being impacted by important Christian events, but not coming to faith (Luke 4:22; Acts 6:15), but he does consider that there are publicly visible events that offer a challenge and cry out to be probed for their significance.

Luke's preface has been compared with those to historical works and with those to scientific treatises of the period. It certainly represents a claim to be taken seriously as an investigator, able to inform with a high degree of reliability. Luke was clearly taken seriously in just this way by his first readers, and his work was valued and preserved; and eventually it made its way into the canon of

Christian scripture. It is fair enough that scholars have at times considered that Luke was optimistic about his own capabilities; but suggestions that he felt free to make materials up to serve as vehicles for commending his own religious convictions smack of unwarranted scepticism. So often critical scholarship has assumed that if we cannot *prove* that early Christians did not make something up then we must *assume* that they did make it up. But to claim this in relation to one who has written Luke 1:1–4 is to impugn Luke's integrity in a manner that is hardly in accord with his evident religious values. For Christians like Luke, a knowledge of what Jesus had said and done was a sacred trust to be passed on and not simply a pretext for religious propaganda. They were not necessarily narrow literalists, and were at time capable of embellishing and perhaps even of producing symbolic narratives, but only in a manner and to a degree that they could see as consonant with their primary goal of passing on the sacred trust.

A striking feature of Luke's writing is the inclusion of so much detailed circumstantial information about the larger political and social context for the events he reports. This is particularly the case for Acts, but it is also evident at certain points in the Gospel. The first thing Luke does is to locate the opening scene of his story 'in the days of King Herod of Judea' (Luke 1:5); and in the same verse Zechariah is not simply a priest, but a priest of the order of Abijah. In 2:1–4 Luke explains the presence of Joseph and Mary in Bethlehem in terms of a registration decree of the Emperor Augustus, and he draws a link with Quirinius as governor of Syria. And when Luke begins the main body of his story in 3:1 he provides a sixfold synchronism, anchoring the events he is to narrate into the political realities in Palestine (Tiberius Caesar, Pontius Pilate, Herod, Philip, Lysanius, Annas, Caiaphas). Luke's general care with these matters is widely recognised and has contributed to his reputation for historical reliability. There are, however, a number of places where scholars have questioned Luke's accuracy about various items. In the case of the Gospel the main issues have to do with the registration and the juxtaposition of Annas and Caiaphas as occupants of the (single) high-priestly role.

There was no 'world census' of the kind that Luke's words have been taken to imply. But Luke's words may intend no more than to express simply the fact that the census in Palestine took place as part of the coordinated empire-wide policy of Augustus. A census by Rome in the territory of Herod the Great

seems politically unlikely, but perhaps not a census conducted by Herod at the instigation of his Roman overlords: his was a client kingdom. Quirinius was probably not governor of Syria during the reign of Herod, but Luke's language is awkward here, and it is quite possible that he means that the registration happened before that in the time of Quirinius as governor, and that he says it like this because the registration under Quirinius in AD 6 marked a major crisis in Jewish life, as Jewish Palestine was being fully incorporated into the Roman Empire. Caiaphas was actually high priest for the main period of Luke's story (he was high priest from AD 18 to 36), but Annas, his father-in-law, had been high priest from AD 6 to 18. The political control of the high-priestly office and the subsequent appointment of a new high priest in place of a still living office-holder were contrary to the OT law, and it is clear that in practice Annas still retained much of the power and prestige of the high-priestly office after his demotion. Is there anything wrong with Luke seeing it as Annas and Caiaphas sharing the role? The various difficulties in Acts invite a range of comparable considerations. If the Jewish writers Josephus and Philo are always more reliable than Luke, then Luke is sometimes wrong. But it is clear that Josephus and Philo make their own mistakes. We may at times need to correct Josephus in the light of Luke. There is no scholarly consensus at all about how to handle the small number of cases in which Luke is at variance with what has otherwise been reported in ancient courses or construed by modern historians. But even if we were unable, for the most part, to find in favour of Luke, there still remains an impressive array of accurate circumstantial information in Luke's writings.

One final matter is worth commenting on. Luke is sometimes accused of getting timings and sequences wrong. And indeed he does get them 'wrong'. But this is not necessarily a mark of defective knowledge, at least not in every case. Except in broad outline it is unlikely that anybody, eye-witnesses included, retained a knowledge of the specific sequence of the events reported in the Gospels. To a greater or lesser degree all the Gospels have a schematic approach to how they sequence the events, and Luke is no exception. The sequencing in Acts is rather less arbitrary, given the nature of the events he is dealing with, but here too Luke's overall schematic proves more important to him at times than chronological sequencing. At times he is being tidy in relation to his thematic developments, rather than strictly accurate in chronological sequencing. A harmless and rather obvious example of such schematisation in the Gospel is in 3:20 where Luke finishes his account of John the Baptist's public ministry before he introduces the adult Jesus, to begin his account of Jesus' ministry. On the face of it Luke has John absent from the baptism of Jesus!

Conclusion

Elsewhere I have examined the complex pattern of overlap and connection that the distinctive Lukan material has with other Gospel tradition, in order to show that this extra material has a claim to historicity that is comparable to that for the Markan material and that shared between Matthew and Luke. Here the concern has been to consider at a more general level the historical reliability of the third Gospel. There is considerable variation in the level of historical reliability attributed by scholars to the writing of the third Evangelist, but in relation to the various ways in which we may probe the question of his likely reliability he acquits himself well, even if not perfectly. It is an interpreted Jesus to whom we are introduced, but he has been interpreted by one for whom 'the facts' were fundamental.

JOHN NOLLAND

Further reading

Alexander, L. *The Preface to Luke's Gospel: Literary Convention and Social Context in Luke 1.1–4 and Acts 1.1*, Cambridge: Cambridge University Press, 1993.
Barrett, C. K. *Luke the Historian in Recent Study*, London: Epworth, 1961.
Bock. D. L. *Luke*, BECNT, Grand Rapids, MI: Baker Books, 1994–96.
Bovon, F. *Luke: A Commentary on the Gospel of Luke*, trans. C. M. Thomas, Minneapolis, MN: Fortress Press, 2002.
Fitzmyer, J. A. *The Gospel according to Luke*, AB 28, 28A, Garden City, NJ: Doubleday, 1981–85.
Green, J. B. *The Gospel of Luke*, NICNT, Grand Rapids, MI: Eerdmans, 1997.
Green, J. B. and M. C. McKeever. *Luke–Acts and New Testament Historiography*, Grand Rapids, MI: Baker Books, 1994.
Jervell, J. *Luke and the People of God: A New Look at Luke–Acts*, Minneapolis, MN: Augsburg, 1972.
Marshall, I. H. *Luke: Historian and Theologian*, Exeter: Paternoster, 1988.
Nolland, J. *Luke*, WBC 35, Dallas, TX: Word, 1989–93.
—— "Jesus Tradition in Lukes and Acts," in T. Holmén and S. E. Porter (eds) *The Handbook of the Study of the Historical Jesus*, Leiden: Brill, forthcoming.
Rothschild, C. K. *Luke–Acts and the Rhetoric of History: An Investigation of Early Christian Historiography*, Tübingen: Mohr Siebeck, 2004.
Shellard, B. *New Light on Luke: Its Purpose, Sources and Literary Context*, London: Sheffield Academic Press, 2002.
Verheyden, J. (ed.) *The Unity of Luke–Acts*, Leuven: Leuven University Press/Peeters, 1999.
Vielhauer, P. "On the 'Paulinism' of Acts," in L. E. Keck and J. L. Martyn (eds) *Studies in Luke–Acts*, London: SPCK, 1968, pp. 33–50.

GOSPEL OF MARK

Mark's Gospel has received widespread attention from historical Jesus scholars because it has repeatedly been deemed as the earliest gospel and our best source for reconstructing the sayings and deeds of Jesus. While it may be our best source, it is at the same time our biggest problem, for Mark is not a history of Jesus as we might understand history today. It is a narrative covering approximately one year of Jesus' life which blends history, politics, social and legal concerns with theology, written from the perspective of Christian faith to an audience sharing in that faith. Mark's portrayal of Jesus is a complicated interconnected web of Jesus material, early Christian oral tradition (along with possibly some textual tradition), and the Evangelist's redaction. Where one ends and the others begin has consumed the scholarly community since the eighteenth century. And the debate about which material goes back to Jesus shows no sign of compromise. On the story level, Jesus is portrayed as a misunderstood, secretive, and suffering messianic figure who announces the kingdom of God and attempts to enact it through the gathering of disciples, healings, exorcisms, legal and prophetic teaching, confrontations with the religious establishment, and prediction of restoration and resurrection (Hatina 90–135). Historical Jesus scholars, however, have used Mark to validate numerous reconstructions of Jesus, such as an eschatological prophet, a subversive wisdom teacher, a wandering cynic, and a nonviolent revolutionary.

The aim of this article is to describe the issues associated with Mark as a source for historical Jesus research. The topics covered include (1) Markan priority; (2) Mark and extracanonical gospels (3) dating and provenance; (4) authorship; (5) Markan genre and ancient historiography; (6) orality and collective memory.

Markan priority

Every evaluation of Mark as a source for studying the historical Jesus must take into consideration the literary relationship among the Synoptic Gospels, which is called the Synoptic Problem. The material that overlaps Matthew, Mark and Luke, in contrast to John, is so extensive in both content and order that early Christian interpreters concluded the these three gospels must be dependent on each other – that is, that one was written first and used as a source by the other two. In the earliest account discussing the relationship of the gospels, Clement of Alexandria (d. 215), quoted by Eusebius (*Hist. eccl.* 6.14.5–7), claims that Matthew and Luke are earlier than Mark (*Hypotyposeis* 6). The most influential view throughout much of Christian history was that of Augustine of Hippo (d. 430), who after an exhaustive comparative study of the Gospels concluded that Matthew wrote first, Mark condensed Matthew, and Luke edited Matthew and Mark (*Cons.* 1.2.4). In 1783 J. J. Griesbach retained Matthean priority, but argued that Mark was an abridgment of both Matthew and Luke. The so-called "Griesbach Hypothesis" endured as the dominant position for almost a century. Matthean priority began to be challenged in the early part of the nineteenth century by a handful of German scholars, such as C. G. Wilke (1826), C. H. Weisse (1838), and K. Lachmann (1835), who argued that Matthew and Luke offered independent revisions of Mark. But it was the work of H. J. Holtzmann (1863) that proved most influential, not only for establishing Markan priority as a major theory but for opening the door for another document (eventually called Q for *Quelle*) used by Matthew and Luke – the so-called "Two Source Hypothesis." In 1924, B. H. Streeter's *The Four Gospels: A Study of Origins* was responsible for establishing Markan priority as a scholarly consensus on the Synoptic Problem. The result has been nothing short of watershed in how historians have come to understand Christian origins and the life of Jesus. A more recent development of Markan priority is the so-called "Farrer Hypothesis," named after A. M. Farrer, who argued that Mark was Matthew's sole source and that the Q hypothesis is unnecessary if Luke's Gospel could be explained as a revision of Mark and Matthew. Farrer's view has been substantially developed in recent years by Michael Goulder and Mark Goodacre. The only significant challenge to Markan priority in contemporary scholarship has been the work of William Farmer and his followers, who have advocated a return to the Griesbach Hypothesis. To date, however, the vast majority of gospel scholars assume Markan priority in one form or another.

The major reasons in support of Markan priority, which should be taken in a cumulative manner, include the following.

1 *The argument from length.* Of Mark's 11,025 words, only 132 have no parallel in the other Synoptic Gospels. In terms of percentage, 97 percent of Mark is duplicated in Matthew and 88 percent is duplicated in Luke. When the comparison is turned around, less than 60 percent of Matthew is duplicated in Mark, and only 40 percent is found in Luke (Stein 48). If Mark is an abridgment, one is forced to explain why so much theological material, which Mark could have used for his purposes, was omitted. Moreover, some of Mark's material that parallels Matthew and Luke is not abridged at all, but is expanded.

2 *The argument from literary style.* In parallel material, Mark's writing style is often inferior to that of Matthew and Luke. Mark uses colloquialisms (e.g. Mark 2:4; Matt 9:2; Luke 5:18), incorrect grammar (e.g. Mark 5:9–10; Luke 8:30–31) and verbal usage (e.g. Mark 11:2; Matt 21:2; Luke 19:30) which are corrected or polished up by the other Evangelists. Mark uses Aramaic expressions which are omitted in the Matthean and Lukan parallels (e.g. *Boanerges* in Mark 3:17). And Mark uses redundant expressions on several occasions which are omitted in Matthew and Luke (e.g. Mark 1:32; Matt 8:16; Luke 4:40). Some have counted up to 200 redundancies in Mark.

3 *The argument from propriety or potential embarrassment.* On several occasions Mark portrays both Jesus and the disciples in ways that are undignified, unflattering, or at potential variance with early Christian belief. His portrayals may well have been misunderstood or may have been embarrassing to later Christian interpreters like the authors of Matthew and Luke, who saw the need to alter Mark. For example, in contrast to Matthean and Lukan parallels, Mark's disciples continually lack understanding (e.g. Mark 4:13; Matt 13:18; Luke 8:11) and faith (e.g. Mark 4:40; Matt 8:26; Luke 8:25). And Mark's portrayal of Jesus includes limitations to power (e.g. Mark 6:5–6; Matt 13:58) and a need for him to be baptized for the forgiveness of sins (Mark 1:4, 9–11; Matt 3:13–17; Luke 3:21–22).

4 *The argument from Matthean–Lukan divergence.* Where there is no Markan parallel, Matthew and Luke diverge the most. While Matthew and Luke share some common sayings (Q) which do not appear in Mark, they rarely appear in the same contexts. For example, the saying about serving two masters is verbatim, but in Matthew it is found in the Sermon on the Mount (6:24), and in Luke it

appears much later in the context of parables (16:13). Larger units which do not appear in Mark are significantly different, such as the Christmas story and the post-Easter accounts.

5 *The argument from Matthean–Lukan redaction.* This argument is potentially far-reaching and can incorporate some of the others, but what is often intended is to show how Matthew's and/or Luke's editing has on occasion created a difficulty due to the omission of significant material from Mark. For example, in Mark 10:35–37 James and John ask Jesus that they might sit at his right hand in his glory. In Matthew's account (20:20–21), it is the mother of James and John who asks. But in both accounts Jesus responds in the plural ("You [pl.] do not know what you [pl.] are asking") which strongly suggests that Matthew relies on Mark. Another useful way of applying this argument is in relation to clear Matthean and Lukan corrections of Mark's references to scripture. For example, Mark's (1:2–3) opening conflated quotation (Exod 23:20; Mal 3:1; Isa 40:3), introduced as being "written by Isaiah the prophet," is corrected by both Matthew (3:3) and Luke (3:4), who only quote from Isaiah. Another example is Matthew (12:3–4) and Luke's (6:3–4) omission of Mark's incorrect reference to Abiathar as high priest when David entered the "house of God" (2:25–26).

The arguments for Markan priority are, of course, broader and much more detailed than this sketch. What begins to emerge, however, even in this summary is that the Synoptic differences and similarities are best explained by postulating that the Mark is the earliest gospel.

Mark and extracanonical gospels

Although most historical Jesus scholars agree that Mark is the earliest Synoptic Gospel, a few – such as J. D. Crossan, H. Koester, and R. D. Cameron – have argued that Mark is antedated by some extracanonical (or so-called apocryphal) gospels, which in some cases contain material that was used by the four Evangelists. Most often discussed are Papyrus Egerton 2, which consists of five small codex fragments that resemble the synoptics and John, the *Gospel of Thomas*, which contains a list of 114 sayings of Jesus, the *Gospel of Peter*, which abruptly begins its synoptic-like narrative with Jesus' trial, and the *Gospel of the Hebrews*, which was originally a syncretistic Jewish-Christian Matthew-like

narrative, but today survives as a few quotations in early church writings. The parallels between Mark and extracanonical gospels are extensive and the debate over their chronological order and relationship is not resolved. The implication for historical Jesus research is that the earliest layer of sources, and possibly the most reliable, may or may not contain Mark. And if Mark is dependent on some of these sources, its value as a historical source becomes more limited. A helpful list of parallels between Mark and extracanonical sources is provided by Evans (xxxii–xxxiv).

Much of the debate about the relationship between Mark and extracanonical sources has focused on the *Gospel of Thomas* and the *Gospel of Peter*. Beginning with the former, the arguments for dependence or independence are rooted in Thomas' wording and structure of sayings. Individual parallel sayings are carefully analyzed to see which may be earlier, which may convey signs of redaction, and which may be coincidentally drawn from a common oral tradition. For example, Crossan (1971) argues that *Gos. Thom.* §65–66 preserves the earliest version of the parable of the Vineyard Tenants (Mark 12:1–11) because its abbreviated form and wording is much closer to that of a parable than that of Mark's allegorizing of the parable in which Christological and scriptural concerns emerge, whereas others, such as J.–M. Sevrin and B. Dehandschutter, argue that *Gos. Thom.*'s version is best explained as an edited abridgement of Luke's version (20:9–18) which contains less allegorizing and limits allusions to scripture (omitting Ps 118:23 and most of Isa 5:1–2). Proponents of *Gos. Thom.*'s dependence on the Synoptics must explain why *Gos. Thom.* differs in wording, structure of sayings, shift in genre, and omission of key events like the passion (which incidentally occurs in other early Christian Gnostic writings). However, proponents of *Gos. Thom.*'s independence are faced with at least three difficulties: (1) on four occasions the order of sayings in *Gos. Thom.* approximates that of the canonical Gospels (see the list in Cameron 537); (2) *Gos. Thom.* contains material that is distinctive to Matthew ("M"), Luke ("L"), and John; and (3) features of Matthean and Lukan redaction are found in *Gos. Thom.* For example, in some cases where *Gos. Thom.* approximates the triple tradition (parallel sayings in the Synoptics) the wording is closest to Matthew (e.g. Matt 15:11 = *Gos. Thom.* §34b; Matt 12:50 = *Gos. Thom.* §99) (Evans xli).

Scholarly discussion on the relationship between the *Gospel of Peter* and Mark (and the NT Gospels), which has received some attention since the end of the nineteenth century, was given new impetus in both popular and academic settings with the 1988 publication of Crossan's *The Cross that Spoke*, in which parts of the passion and resurrection narrative (the so-called *Cross Gospel*) are deemed to be early and used as the only source by Mark (xii–xiv). Following in the reasoning of Gardner-Smith, Denker, and most notably Koester that *Gos. Pet.* contains early independent traditions, Crossan has advanced the discussion by isolating the Gospel's redactional strata and constructing a theory explaining the development of the tradition from its earliest strata to its incorporation in the canonical Gospels. Crossan's claim that the *Cross Gospel* constitutes the basis for the passion accounts in the NT Gospels has received widespread criticism. Many scholars have reiterated and added to the work of Léon Vaganay, whose meticulous comparative analysis concluded that the author of *Gos. Pet.* was familiar with the canonical Gospels (e.g. Green, Meier). The line of reasoning is usually twofold. First, wording in the canonical Gospels which is also found in *Gos. Pet.* is deemed to be earlier. One example is the comparison of Mark 15:34 and *Gos. Pet.* 5:19. The former reads, "Jesus cried out with a loud voice ... 'My God, my God, why have you forsaken me?'" whereas the latter reads, "And the Lord called out and cried, 'My power, O power, you have forsaken me.'" It is argued that *Gos. Pet.*'s use of "Lord" (which is common along with "Son of God") in place of Mark's "Jesus" implies an elevated Christology, and the use of "My power ... " reflects Gnosticism. Second, if Mark is dependent on the *Cross Gospel*, it is perplexing that the passion account is followed but the resurrection account is omitted (Evans xxxvii–xxxviii).

Dating and provenance

Although there are sporadic attempts to date Mark in the 40s CE, the vast majority of Markan scholars argue for a date just before or just after the destruction of Jerusalem and the Temple in 70 CE. The crux of the debate is the prophetic material concerning the destruction of the Temple in 13:1–2 and the warning of the "abomination of desolation" in 13:14. Scholars are divided whether these predictions and warnings constitute actual predictions or recollections of the recent past in the form of predictions (so-called "*post-eventu* prophecy"). Those who advocate a post-70 dating often regard the events of Mark 13 – such as wars, rumors of wars, false prophets, the abomination, famine, persecution, and fleeing to the mountains – as

being too accurate in the life of Israel and the early church to be regarded as genuine predictions. Others who advocate a pre-70 dating point out that the situation during the war would not have even required special prophetic powers. The warning of the abomination of desolation, as Marcus argues, well fits the occupation of the Temple by the Zealots under the leadership of Eleazar in 67–68 (Marcus, 1999:38) and the events described throughout Mark 13 are thought to be too general. It is also pointed out that the huge fire that caused the Temple to collapse, recorded in Jewish and Roman histories (Josephus *J.W.* 6.250–87; Dio Cassius, *History* 66.6), is surprisingly missed if Mark wrote after the fact. Moreover, some have argued that since there were other Jewish public protestors and prophets who criticized the establishment throughout Israel's history and even in the first century, like Jesus ben Ananias (Josephus *J.W.* 6.300–6), it is not improbable that Jesus himself would have engaged in similar prophetic criticism. Even if making a firm decision on the dating of Mark is next to impossible, we can say that Mark is written in close proximity to the Temple's destruction which would have conjured up all sorts of eschatological fervor.

Mark 13 has also figured very prominently in recent discussions of provenance. The traditional position that Mark was written in Rome just after Peter's death during the Neronian persecution (Eusebius *Hist. eccl.* 3.39.15; *1 Clem.* 5:4–7; Ign. *Romans* 4:2–3; Irenaeus *Haer.* 3.3.2) still receives support (e.g. Hengel 29), but is under considerable fire. Mark's Latinisms (e.g. 12:42; 15:16) are no longer being limited to the western part of the empire and the references to persecution are more often being interpreted in light of the events connected with the revolt by Palestinian Jews against the Romans, rather than Roman persecutions of Christians. This is not say that Christian witness is of no concern in Mark 13. Exhortation to persevere before governors and kings (13:10) and warning of persecution and hatred of those who identify with Christ (13:12–13) can just as well be explained in the eastern part of the empire, even Palestine. When a broader survey of early Christian persecution is taken, the offending party is usually not Rome, but Jewish authorities, mobs, and client kings (Marcus 1999: 34). For example, Josephus records that James, the brother of Jesus, was killed by a Jewish mob (*Ant.* 20.200). And Luke records that Agrippa I was responsible for the execution of James the son of Zebedee and the imprisonment of Peter (Acts 12:1–5). Mark 13 seems to reflect a similar situation, which would explain the warning in 13:9 of being tried and beaten in synagogues.

Although there are no extant texts that record the persecution of Christians during the war, Josephus' description of the mock trials held in Jerusalem by the Zealots between 68–70 CE (*J.W.* 4.335–44; cf. 13:9) and references to the persecution of Christians by the Jewish leadership during the Bar Kokhba war in 132–5 CE suggest that it is a likely scenario for the Markan community. From a narrative perspective, the primary target of the political and religious hostility in Mark's story is not the Romans, but the Jewish establishment.

Mark's preoccupation with the moral decline of the Temple establishment, the events associated with the war, and its temporal proximity to it strongly points to a provenance that is much closer to the events than Rome. In the recent past several scholars have argued that Mark was composed in Galilee given its important function in the Gospel (e.g. Marxsen, Kelber), especially Jesus' prediction that he will meet the disciples there after he is raised from the dead (14:28). More recently, the Roman province of Syria has received considerable attention. Joel Marcus, for example, is hesitant to situate Mark in Galilee because it was predominantly Jewish and would have been at war in the late 60s. Syria, claims Marcus, is a much better option because it can accommodate much more of Mark's content, such as the proximity of the war, Jesus' interaction with Gentiles, freedom from the law, explanation of Aramaic terms and Jewish customs, and persecution from both Jewish and Gentiles fronts (1992; 1999: 35–36).

Authorship

Like the other synoptics, Mark's Gospel is anonymous. Whether it was originally so is, however, difficult to know. Nevertheless, we can be fairly certain that it was written by someone named Mark. Early extant manuscripts attach a title ("According to Mark" or "the Gospel According to Mark") at the end or at the beginning of the Gospel. And early Christian tradition unanimously attributes authorship to him. According to Eusebius (*Hist. eccl.* 3.39.15), Papias, relying on an elder named John, claims that:

> Mark, who became Peter's interpreter, accurately wrote, though not in order, as many of the things said and done by the Lord as he had noted. For he neither heard the Lord nor followed him, but afterwards, as I said, he followed Peter who composed his teachings in anecdotes and not as a complete work of the Lord's sayings. So Mark made no mistake in writing some things just as he had noted them. For he was careful of this one thing, to leave nothing he had heard out and to say nothing falsely.

There is no reason to think that Mark, which was one of the most common names in the ancient Mediterranean, was attributed pseudonymously, for he seemed to play a minor role in the early church. The difficulty is ascertaining the identity of Mark. Scholars debate whether he is John Mark of Jerusalem, associate of Paul (Acts 12:12, 25; 13:5, 13; 15:36–41; 2 Tim 4:11), and the one who may well be assumed by Papias as an associate of Peter (e.g. Hengel 45–53; Gundry 1026–45), or another person simply named Mark who was not native to Palestine. Many scholars have opted for the latter option due to the Gospel's lack of understanding of Jewish laws (1:40–45; 2:23–28; 7:1–23), incorrect Palestinian geography (5:1–2, 12–13; 7:31), and concern for Gentiles (7:24–28:10) (e.g. Marcus, 1999: 17–21).

Papias' claim that Mark was dependent on Peter has obvious potential historical implications not only for the identity of the author (i.e. John Mark), but for the Gospel as a reliable source for the modern study of Jesus. However, most scholars are skeptical about Mark's dependence on Peter chiefly because some of the language ("made no mistake in writing," "careful," "left nothing out," "nothing falsely") strongly suggests apologetic attempts to vindicate the trustworthiness of the Gospel in the face of opposition. It has often been observed that Mark's compositional features, such as sandwiching techniques, multiple traditional milieus (e.g. two feedings), and development of traditional units point to a complexity that surpasses preaching notes or the recollections (Guelich xxvii) of a single person, though it is possible that some of Peter's oral history may have been subtly incorporated into Mark (Byrskog 288–92). Nevertheless, even proponents of the reliability of Papias' claim have to admit to other sources since there are several accounts in Mark's story where Peter is either absent or is cast as a type instead of an actual person recalling his experiences (Hengel 51).

Markan genre and ancient historiography

The identity of Mark's genre is of crucial importance if the Gospel is to be used as a source for reconstructing the historical Jesus. Since there are no exact parallels among Greco-Roman and Jewish writings, several options have been proposed. We shall discuss three of them. First, during the rise of form-criticism in the early part of the twentieth century, many began to view Mark as a *sui generis* (unique) writing, which constituted in a sense the creation of a new genre. Scholars like Rudolf Bultmann argued that Mark is a passion narrative with an extended introduction and is to be viewed as the expansion and preservation of the kerygma (preaching) of the early church which focused on the death and resurrection of Jesus (Bultmann 374). According to this view, Mark is a kind of anthology of stories and oral traditions about the life and teachings of Jesus. Since Mark was viewed more as the preservation of preaching developed within the creativity of early church, as opposed to history, its value as a source for reconstructing Jesus was minimized. While some Markan scholars still advocate that Mark is a unique genre, much more emphasis tends to be placed on the interconnection of theology and history in a more or less unified narrative – as opposed to simply a collection of early Christian traditions – that is viewed much more optimistically as a source for reconstructing Jesus. Most contemporary historical Jesus scholars fall into this category, referring to Mark as a new genre which contains elements of other genres, such as biography (e.g. Evans lxv). Crossan avoids the designation "genre" altogether, and instead refers to Mark as a type of gospel, which is an intentionally vague term that incorporates both form and content (Crossan, 1998: 31).

Second, several scholars have compared Mark to Greco-Roman biographies, such as Plutarch, *Lives of the Noble Greeks and Romans*; Philostratus, *Apollonius of Tyana*; Tacitus, *Agricola*; Suetonius, *Lives of the Twelve Caesars*. Richard Burridge, building on previous studies (e.g. Talbert, Aune), has provided one of the most extensive treatments comparing the canonical gospels to Greco-Roman biographies ("Lives"). Casting his net widely to include Greek, Hellenistic and Roman biography, Burridge understands these ancient writings in a threefold manner: (1) they are writings which naturally emerge within a group that has been formed around the teachings or leadership of a charismatic leader; (2) their main purpose and function is found in the context of didactic or philosophical polemic; and (3) they are flexible, allowing for adaptation and growth (80–81). Burridge admits that on some levels the gospels fall short of an exact parallel with any one biography – for they tell us nothing of Jesus' home life, how he spent his youth, his personality traits or physical appearance – but he concludes that there seems to be no other literature prior to the gospels that we can point to with more precision.

If Mark is taken to be a form of ancient biography, historians must be mindful of at least four characteristics that have implications for reconstruction. First, ancient biographers were interested in portraying their main characters as relatively constant throughout their lives, which is a major shift from modern biographers who emphasize change. Events and experiences were chosen not for a lesson in history, but to demonstrate the exemplary traits and the consistency of character through difficult obstacles. Ancient audiences would pay close attention to how characters not only acted and reacted to challenges, sometimes through impressive deeds, but how they carefully articulated their verbal responses. Great persons were believed to be born great, and they became models for others to imitate. Second, ancient biographers attempted to entertain their readers and often promoted a virtue and philosophy of their subject which posed a challenge to mainstream society. Third, biographies of "holy men" or divine philosophers attributed divine qualities in varying degrees to their subjects. Some were characterized as sons of god, which implied divine parentage (e.g. like Apollonius of Tyana and Pythagoras), whereas others were deemed godlike (e.g. Plotinus) because they were gifted beyond ordinary men, despite their human parentage (Cox 30–44). Fourth, although ancient biographers wrote with historical intentions, a certain amount of fiction and exaggeration was commonplace. Data collection and verification of evidence cannot be compared to today's standards. Speeches and deeds, for example, followed consistent forms and were freely adapted to situations that would enhance the subject's traits and character, which was molded to an established model. As Cox summarizes, "From its inception, biography was marked by its encomiastic tendencies to exaggerate a person's achievements and virtues, carefully selecting traits and deeds that lent themselves to idealization" (15). This may be why biographies for the ancient Greeks and Romans did not fall within the five major categories of historical writing (genealogy or mythography, ethnography, history, horography or local history, and chronography) (Fornara 1–3). By the Imperial age, Plutarch (*Pomp.* 8) makes a clear distinction between history and biography. Whereas history recalls the chronological account of the life, biography provides a systematic treatment of character (Cox 12–13). During this period, the lives of the emperors gained popularity as means of not only promoting Caesar, but retelling and explaining events on a grander scale (Momigliano 99). In light of the function of these Roman biographies, Mark can be viewed as an alternative explanation on even a grander scale. Potter claims that "Ultimately, the most powerful of these alternative narratives was that offered in the Christian gospels, and they in turn reshaped the world in which they were read" (9).

If Mark was considered to be a biography by the early Christians – while it would not have been considered to be history in the Greco-Roman sense (Momigliano 12) – it is not easy to determine which typecast would have emerged as dominant. Mark's portrayal of Jesus could be compared to that of the divine philosopher who likewise performed miracles, gathered disciples, demonstrated devotion and purity, challenged the establishment, and shared their knowledge of god. Another option is that the portrayal, as Evans argues, could be regarded as a subversive "apologetic that boldly challenges the emperor's claim to divinity and his demand for the absolute loyalty of his subjects" (xi). A further option still is that Jesus is portrayed as the "prophet-king" in the pattern of Philo's presentation of Moses in *On the Life of Moses*. Or in the end Mark may have been woven together as some kind of biographical amalgam (Aune, Robbins).

Third, Mark's genre has been compared to Jewish novels. According to Michael Vines, Mark is a narrative in which God's intervention in human affairs is at the centre of the plot in much the same way as God is depicted in Esther, Susanna, and Daniel 1–6. Vines, relying on the principles of Mikhail Bakhtin's poetics, argues that genre needs to be distinguished from the form of a writing or its compositional features. Instead, genre, or "inner form," focuses on the presentation of various combinations such as time (past, present, or future) and space (foreign or local) which create meanings, ideology, moods, and discourse. Like Jewish novels, Vines argues that Mark creates a world open to divine intervention, even though the direct intervention usually does not occur, but is instead mediated through emissaries of God. One of the difficulties with Vines' proposal is that it is a generalization with little detailed exegetical support from Markan texts. Nevertheless, his careful examination of genre and critique of prior proposals require attention from historians. No historical Jesus studies, to my knowledge, have yet seriously interacted with Vines' proposal.

Implications of genre have been sorely lacking in discussions of the sources by Jesus scholars. What is common is that Mark is viewed as an integration of pre-Easter and post-Easter material. Reconstructions vary depending on where one places the emphasis and how one tries to bridge the chasm. In using a narrative like Mark which is written from the perspective of faith to an audience sharing in that faith, the historian must begin with a critical examination of the sources, which should include genre, and an open method (not just criteria of authenticity) which organizes texts and interpretation. Approaches based on "hypothesis and verification" models like that of N. T. Wright (87–88), which do not first critically examine sources and traditions, such as the literary and historical characteristics of Mark, but simply begin with a historicized theological/metanarrative hypothesis – and then try to verify it from whatever can be gleaned from the synoptics – have a difficult task of evaluating what constitutes legitimate textual evidence (Crossan, 1998: 98–101). A case in point is Steven Bryan's critique of Wright's use of ancient sources in support of Jesus' restoration agenda (Bryan 4–5, 11–20).

Orality and collective memory

If Mark is regarded as the earliest gospel, historical Jesus scholars will need to incorporate sociological and anthropological studies of collective memory in oral culture to better appreciate that the Jesus of Mark is more the Jesus of oral memory than the Jesus of factual history. Walter Ong's *Orality and Literacy* has served as a standard introduction to the psychodynamics of oral culture. As it pertains to historical Jesus research, the question of the meaning of history and how history was perceived in highly oral cultures comes to the forefront. Ong argues that the function of memory in oral cultures is oriented toward contemporary relevance. That is, analytical thought patterns are not exhibited, but instead memory functions in practical, situational patterns (52–53). The events remembered may well have a high degree of historicity (i.e. an event that occurred, was committed to memory, and was eventually synthesized into a memorable pattern of speech so as to preserve it), but they are not ultimately preserved for their own sake in an exact manner. If, as Joanna Dewey argues, Mark was intended to be an oral performance, perhaps even repeated in varying forms prior to its composition, then the general principles of oral compositions may be helpful for historical purposes, which include (1) Jesus may be patterned after heroic figures which share common characteristics; (2) the most repeated teachings of Jesus are historically rooted; (3) much of Jesus' life was irrelevant (and thus lost) to the Gospel audiences; and (4) easily remembered forms such as parables and aphorisms may have been accurately preserved.

With regard to collective memory, the work of sociologist Maurice Halbwachs has been foundational in recent years for a handful of NT scholars (e.g. Kirk and Thatcher). One of Halbwach's key observations on the function of memory within religious frameworks, which is reiterated in more recent studies of social memory, is that recollections of the past are assimilated within the frameworks of the present. But the past is not completely lost to the present. While the past is continually (re)shaped and (re)collected so as to have meaning in the present, the present is continually informed and guided by the past, especially if the tradition is older, is adopted by a large number of adherents, and is widespread (183). Since collective memory is operative in the compositional history of Mark, the implications for historical Jesus research are only recently being realized. One of these implications is the loss of Jesus' (Galilean) Jewishness and his adherence to purity laws as he is remembered within diaspora Jewish Christian and Gentile Christian communities.

THOMAS R. HATINA

Further reading

Aune, D. E. "The Problem of the Genre of the Gospels: A Critique of C. H. Talbert's *What is a Gospel?*," in R. T. France and D. Wenham (eds) *Studies of History and Tradition*, Gospel Perspectives 2, Sheffield: JSOT Press, 1981, pp. 9–60.

Bryan, S. M. "Jesus and Israel's Traditions of Judgment and Restoration," SNTSMS 117, Cambridge: Cambridge University Press, 2002.

Bultmann, R. *The History of the Synoptic Tradition*, revised edition, Oxford: Blackwell, 1972.

Burridge, R. A. "What are the Gospels? A Comparison with Graeco-Roman Biography," SNTSMS 70, Cambridge: Cambridge University Press, 1992.

Byrskog, S. *Story as History – History as Story: The Gospel Tradition in the Context of Ancient Oral History*, Leiden: Brill, 2002.

Cameron, R. "Thomas, Gospel of," in G. Kittel (ed.) *ABD* Vol. VI, New York: Doubleday (1992), pp. 535–40.

Collins, A. Y. *The Beginning of the Gospel: Probings of Mark in Context*, Minneapolis MN: Fortress Press, 1992, pp. 1–38.

Cox, P. *Biography in Late Antiquity: A Quest for the Holy Man*, Berkeley, CA: University of California Press, 1983.

Crossan, J. D. "The Parable of the Wicked Husbandmen," *JBL* 90 (1971) 451–65.

—— *The Cross That Spoke: The Origins of the Passion Narrative*, San Francisco, CA: Harper & Row, 1988.

—— *The Birth of Christianity: Discovering What Happened in the Years Immediately After the Execution of Jesus*, New York: HarperCollins, 1998.

Dehandschutter, B. "La parabole des vignerons homicides (Mc., XII, 1–12) et l'Évangile selon Thomas," in M. Sabbe (ed.) *L'Évangile selon Marc: Tradition et redaction*, BETL 34, Leuven: Leuven University Press, 1974, pp. 203–19.

Denker, J. *Die theologiegeschichtliche Stellung des Petrusevangeliums*, Europäische Hochschulschriften 23/35, Frankfurt: Lang, 1975.

Dewey, J. "The Gospel of Mark as an Oral-Aural Event: Implications for Interpretation," in E. McKnight and E. S. Malbon (eds) *The New Literary Criticism and the New Testament*, Valley Forge, PA: Trinity Press International, 1994, pp. 145–63.

Evans, C. A. *Mark 8:27–16:20*, WBC 34B, Nashville, TN: Thomas Nelson, 2001.

Farrer, A. M. "On Dispensing with Q," in D. E. Nineham (ed.) *Studies in the Gospels: Essays in Memory of R. H. Lightfoot*, Oxford: Basil Blackwell, 1955, pp. 55–88.

Fornara, C. W. *The Nature of History in Ancient Greece and Rome*, Berkeley, CA: University of California Press, 1983.

Gardner-Smith, P. "The Gospel of Peter," *JTS* 27 (1925–26) 255–71.

Goodacre, M. "The Synoptic Problem: A Way Through the Maze," The Biblical Seminar 80, London: Sheffield Academic Press, 2001.

Goulder, M. D. "Luke: A New Paradigm," JSNTSup 20, Sheffield: Sheffield Academic Press, 1989.

Green, J. B. "The Gospel of Peter: Source for a Pre-Canonical Passion Narrative?," *ZNW* 78 (1987) 293–301.

Guelich, R. A. *Mark 1–8:26*, WBC 34A, Dallas, TX: Word, 1989.

Gundry, R. H. *Mark: A Commentary on His Apology for the Cross*, Grand Rapids, MI: Eerdmans, 1992.

Halbwachs, M. *On Collective Memory*, ed. and trans. L. A. Coser, Chicago, IL: University of Chicago Press, 1992.

Hatina, T. R. *In Search of a Context: The Function of Scripture in Mark's Narrative*, JSNTSup 232, SSEJC 8, London: Sheffield Academic Press, 2002.

Hengel, M. *Studies in the Gospel of Mark*, trans. J. Bowden, Philadelphia, PA: Fortress Press, 1985.

Kelber, W. H. *The Oral and the Written Gospel*, Philadelphia, PA: Fortress Press, 1983.

Kirk, A. and T. Thatcher (eds) *Memory, Tradition, and Text: Uses of the Past in Early Christianity*, Semeia 52, Atlanta, GA: Society of Biblical Literature, 2005.

Koester, H. "Apocryphal and Canonical Gospels," *HTR* 73 (1980) 105–30.

Marcus, J. "The Jewish War and the *Sitz im Leben* of Mark," *JBL* 111 (1992) 441–62.

—— *Mark 1–8*, AB 27, New York: Doubleday, 1999.

Marxsen, W. *Mark the Evangelist*, Nashville, TN: Abingdon, 1969.

Meier, J. P. *A Marginal Jew: Rethinking the Historical Jesus. Volume One: The Roots of the Problem and the Person*, AB Reference Library, New York: Doubleday, 1994, pp. 116–18.

Momigliano, A. *The Development of Greek Biography*, revised edition, Cambridge, MA: Harvard University Press, 1993.

Potter, D. S. *Literary Texts and the Roman Historian*, Approaching the Ancient World, London: Routledge, 1999.

Robbins, V. *Jesus the Teacher: A Social-Rhetorical Interpretation of Mark*, Philadelphia, PA: Fortress Press, 1984.

Sevrin, J.-M. "Un groupement de trois paraboles contre les richesses dans l'Évangile selon Thomas," in J. Delorme (ed.) *Les Paraboles évangeliques: Perspectives nouvelles*, Paris: Cerf, 1989, pp. 425–39.

Streeter, B. H. *The Four Gospels: A Study of Origins*, London: Macmillan, 1924.

Talbert, C. H. *What is a Gospel? The Genre of the Canonical Gospels*, Philadelphia, PA: Fortress Press, 1977.

Vaganay, L. *L'évangile de Pierre*, EBib, Paris: Gabalda, 1930.

Vines, M. E. *The Problem of Markan Genre: The Gospel of Mark and the Jewish Novel*, Academia Biblical 3, Atlanta, GA: Society of Biblical Literature, 2002.

Wright, N. T. *Jesus and the Victory of God*, Christian Origins and the Question of God 2, Minneapolis, MN: Fortress Press, 1996.

GOSPEL OF MATTHEW

Matthew among the gospels

Without question the gospel of Matthew has been the most influential among the four canonical gospels for the vast majority of the history of the Christian church. The first gospel stood at the head of the list of the canonical gospels at least since the Muratorian Canon (*c.* 180, though perhaps much later), Irenaeus, and Origin. Among the reasons for Matthew's primacy in earliest Christianity is surely its relationship of nascent Christianity with early Judaism. More than the other gospels, Matthew's immediately addresses the question of whether Christianity was a sect of its parent religion or a religious order of its own. Such was a primary concern of earliest Christianity. Indeed, Matthew's gospel was widely held to have been written originally in a Semitic (Aramaic? Hebrew?) language rather than Greek, and for nearly 1,700 years the church has held to Irenaeus's statement (*Adv. Haer.* III.1.1; cf. Eusebius, *Hist. eccl.* III 39.16–24) that Matthew's gospel was written first. Other fathers concurred: Clement of Alexandria (preserved in Eusebius, *Hist. eccl.* V 8.2–4), Origen, Eusebius, Jerome and Augustine, though Matthean priority has almost completely fallen out of favor among modern scholars.

Authorship

As is the case with all four canonical gospels, Matthew is, strictly speaking, anonymous. Yet for internal evidence we can employ Narrative Criticism to profile the "implied author"; that is, the textual manifestation, or "literary version" of the real historical person who wrote the first gospel (Kingsbury: 31). He is the author's "literary version of himself, a second self, which the reader comes to know through the process of reading the story of the narrative" (Kingsbury: 31). Internal evidence indicates that the implied author is deeply concerned with the Jewish scriptures (see below), discipleship, the church, and ethics to name but a few subjects. While this in itself does little to identify

the individual (or individuals) responsible for the first gospel, a text of Matthew's gospel was first attributed to that apostle by name by Apollinarius of Hierapolis (*c.* 175 CE). There is no evidence that Matthew's gospel ever circulated *without* the title "According to Matthew" (κατὰ Μαθθαῖον) (Hengel 1985: 64–84), nor is there evidence that it was ever attributed to another person. Yet it has also been argued (Bacon 28–29) that this need not imply authorship but rather conformity to a type. Nevertheless, the church has uniformly taken it in the authorship sense at least since Papias. Papias, bishop of Hierapolis in Asia Minor (*c.* AD 140) is known only by reference found in Eusebius (*Hist. eccl.* III 39.14–16). Papias indicates that Matthew συνετάξατο (compiled? collected? composed? organized?) his τὰ λόγια (gospel? oracles? sayings?) in Ἑβραΐδι διαλέκτῳ (Hebrew language? Aramaic language? Semitic style?). Naturally, the mere fifteen words attributed to Papias have been the subject of some discussion. Even less helpful is that the quotation is found in the writings of Eusebius, who does not look kindly on him and dismisses the claim that Papias knew the apostles (*Hist. eccl.* III 39.1–7). Subsequent scholarship, seemingly dependent on the Papias tradition, widely accepted authorship by Matthew the apostle in an original Semitic language (Hebrew or Aramaic). Naturally, this Matthew is identified one of the Twelve (Matt 10:2–4; Mark 3:16–19; Luke 6:13–16; Acts 1:13), the tax-collector from Capernaum (Matt 9:9; 10:3), though Mark (2:14) and Luke (5:27) know the man as Levi. Stendahl argued that the Gospel was not the product of an individual but a Matthean "school" (Stendahl 1968: 30–35).

Date: internal evidence: destruction of the temple?

Scholars have looked in two distinct directions for dating Matthew's Gospel. First is internal evidence from the Gospel itself. What clues does the text provide to otherwise known historical events by which we can date the Gospel? Typically scholars look to the destruction of Jerusalem at the hand of the Romans in 70 CE. The focal point in Matthew's Gospel is 22:7 where, in the parable of the Wedding Feast, the king "sent his armies and destroyed those murderers and set their city on fire." Though placed in the prophetic voice of Jesus, many presume it to be an *ex eventu* prophecy referring to the already elapsed destruction of Jerusalem. However, as Evans has illustrated (1992), Jesus was not alone in positing such a fate for the holy city. Moreover, political and civil unrest was in such a state as to make the climate ripe for conflict, and the temple would be a natural target for Roman overlords seeking to smite Jewish ambitions of independence.

Date: external evidence: relationship to Mark and Q

The second source to consider in dating Matthew's gospel is its relationship to its sources. Since his literary sources, naturally, must predate Matthew's Gospel, and since scholars are widely agreed that Matthew makes primary use of Mark and Q, dating the latter two sources can provide a *terminus a quo* for the Matthean gospel. For much of the twentieth century, many scholars have held a firm date for Mark around 65 CE. Presuming Matthew has made use of Mark, scholars conjecture that sufficient time would have had to elapse to allow Mark to gain circulation and come into sufficient use by the church to have been used by the author of Matthew. This would place the Gospel sometime after 70 CE, with some suggesting around 80 or 90 to be more likely.

Interpretation: redaction criticism

The advancement of Markan priority and the Two Source hypothesis has had profound effects in elucidating the theology of the first Evangelist. If Matthew used Mark as a source, for example, what is Matthew's motivation in, at times, *altering* his source(s)? That is, he has selected, adapted, and arranged material from his sources for his own particular reasons. This has given rise to the recognition of the Evangelist as a theologian. The theological motivations for altering sources is known as redaction criticism. So important is this to Matthean studies, Graham Stanton asserts, that studying the first gospel without it "is rather like trying to play a violin or cello with one's left hand tied behind one's back: rather limited results are still possible, but that is all that can be said" (Stanton 1985: 1896). Pioneering work in redaction criticism in Matthew was undertaken by Günther Bornkamm. In his 1948 essay, "The Stilling of the Storm in Matthew," coupled with his "End-expectation and Church in Matthew's Gospel," Bornkamm employed redaction criticism as a means not to elicit the underlying tradition of the Gospel, but to analyze how the first Evangelist has selected, adapted, and arranged material from his (Markan) source. The object, then, became to elicit Matthew's *theological* motivations for the editorial adjustments he made.

Since then, France indicates, "the spotlight has moved away from history to theology" (France 23).

Interpretation: narrative criticism

The marriage of modern literary theory and gospels studies birthed narrative criticism. Pioneered by the work of Rhoads and Michie, narrative criticism seeks to employ modern literary techniques to analyze how a gospel author tells his story. The task was undertaken in Matthean studies by Jack Dean Kingsbury (Kingsbury). By paying attention to various aspects of modern literary theory and applying them to the first gospel, Kingsbury sought to explore the story of Matthew. With a plot driven largely by conflict – between both Jesus and the Jewish leaders and Jesus and his disciples – the story is formed by a combination of three components: events, characters, and settings. Story is what is told – the life of Jesus – while the discourse is "how" the story is told. This involves an implied author (the textual manifestation of the flesh-and-blood Evangelist), as well as the implied reader, who is an imaginary, idealized figure who responds to the gospel story at each point as intended by the story-teller, the implied author, who portrays his own evaluative point of view throughout the gospel. Narrative critics of the first gospel have isolated turning points in the narrative to outline its structure. Drawing on the statements "from that time Jesus began to ... " (4:17; 16:21), they have noted the story contains a beginning phase presenting Jesus the Messiah (1:1–4:16), a middle phase which portrays the ministry of Jesus to Israel and Israel's repudiation of him (4:17–16:20), and an ending phase narrating the journey of Jesus to Jerusalem and his suffering, death, and resurrection (16:21–28:20) (Kingsbury).

Theology

Redaction criticism, among other methods, has helped to elucidate Matthew's particular theology. These are only a small handful of the theological distinctives offered by the first Evangelist.

Fulfillment

Many have recognized Matthew's preoccupation with πληρόω to govern his appropriation of his sources and thus his theology. This is particularly the case in light of 5.17. "Do not think that I came to abolish the Law or the Prophets; I did not come to abolish, but to fulfill" (NAS). While the meaning of "fulfill" here is much discussed, it is probably best to recognize it in terms of the following context. That is, it is the antitheses in the Sermon on the Mount that could lead to the accusation that Jesus is "abolishing" the Law and Prophets. Therefore, "fulfillment" must be read within the context of what Jesus is teaching in these antitheses, specifically, to "enable God's people to live out the Law more effectively" (Nolland 2005: 219). Jesus, then, provides "a new depth of insight into what the Law requires over against what he (Matthew) considered to be a general superficiality, a foreshortened perspective, in the reading of the Law" (Nolland 2005: 219). Yet Matthew's concern that the life and work of Jesus, in some sense, "fulfills" something in the Old Testament goes well beyond the use of fulfillment language. While it is true that the so-called "formula quotations", where something happened in Jesus' life "to fulfill what had been spoken by the prophet, saying ... " (1:22–23; 2:15; 2:17–18; 2:23; 4:14–16; 8:17; 12:17–21; 13:35; 21:4–5; 27:9–10), occupy central roles in the first gospel (Stendahl 97–127, 183–127; Strecker 1971: 49–85; Gundry 1967: 89–127), identifying the text-form from which the citation is drawn has defied broad categorization and is best taken on a case-by-case basis (Beaton 14–43). Moreover, while "formula quotations" are surely a clue to Matthew's appropriation of OT texts to the life and ministry of Jesus, they are only the tip of the proverbial iceberg. For scholars have widely recognized that fulfillment in Matthew's Gospel also extends to a typological nature, specifically identifying Jesus as the "new Moses" (Allison) and, perhaps, the embodiment of Israel herself (Matt 2:15, citing Hos 11:1). For all its complications, surely what is clear is that Matthew saw the OT (Law and Prophets) as holding a prophetic function pointing to Jesus.

Christology

Matthew's distinctive Christology has first been analyzed with respect to christological titles, especially "Son of God" (Kingsbury). This title occurs in the very first verse of the Gospel, and is often found on the lips of those in need of deliverance from hardships (illnesses, etc.) with the inauguration of the Messianic era (cf. 9:27) of the Davidic Messiah. "Son of Man" is another christological title that has stirred extensive discussion. Occurring some sixty-nine times in the synoptics alone, the title seems to draw from the picture of "one like a son of man" in Daniel 7:13–14, and appropriated as a messianic figure. Yet Matthew employs the title with an additional component of suffering

and dying (Matt 16:21–23; 17:9–12, 22), frequently misunderstood by the disciples. Other scholars have argued that one must move beyond mere christological titles for a portrait of Matthean Christology (Hill, Verseput, France). For example, while "Son of God" is often used to connote filial obedience on the part of Jesus to the Father, that obedience may be demonstrated in the first gospel without employing the title (Verseput). Similarly, other scholars approach Matthean Christology along the lines of thematic trends, such as the Davidic covenant motif in Matthew 1–2 (Nolan) to identify Matthew's Jesus as the Davidic Messiah.

Ecclesiology

"Church" (ἐκκλησία) only occurs twice in Matthew (16:18; 18:17), but that it occurs in no other gospel has caused scholars to posit an inordinate emphasis upon its role in the first gospel. Matthew 16:18 seems to indicate the continuity of Jesus' group of disciples into a messianic community, in some way, distinct from others. Within this community lies a certain degree of authority to enact necessary discipline (18:15–18) in broad fashion. Details are wanting. What is clear is that the ethical standards Matthew underscores are integral to discipleship and go back to Jesus himself.

Critical issues

"History of effects" (Wirkungsgeschichte)

A unique aspect of Matthew's Gospel has been addressed almost single-handedly in the writings of Ulrich Luz. Throughout each of his three volumes of commentaries on Matthew (in English, four volumes in German) and more succinctly in his *Matthew in History: Interpretation, Influence, and Effects*, Luz mines the history of interpretation not as a means of antiquarian interest in itself, but as a means of interpreting and applying pericopae in modern situations. It presumes to point readers past the limitations of a historical-critical hermeneutic and demonstrate the richness of the insights that can be gleaned from the variety of influences and effects that the text has had in the history of its interpretation.

Relationship with Judaism

Much discussion has been posited on whether Matthew saw himself still within the confines of the diversity of Judaism in the first century or, in some sense, distinct from it. Traditionally, scholars such as Origen and Eusebius contended that Matthew was the first gospel written for and to a Jewish readership. This has largely been the preferred view even into the twentieth century (Schlatter). This view is not widely held today, since the wide acceptance of Markan priority toward the end of the nineteenth century. Kilpatrick (106) suggested that the phrase "their synagogue(s)" (συναγωγὴ αὐτῶν) indicates a dispute within Judaism. Bornkamm (22, n. 1) affirmed this conclusion, adding that the Temple tax pericope (17:24–27) underscores Matthew's understanding of his enduring attachment to Judaism. Stanton (1992: 114) opts that Matthew was written "in the wake of a recent painful parting from Judaism." He bases this (124) on the observation that "nearly every pericope of the gospel reflects rivalry between 'church' and 'synagogue'." Employing exemplary redaction criticism of key passages, Stanton uses Matthean redactional polemics against the Pharisees to underscore the division. However, for Matthew the Pharisees are surely not exemplary Israel, and one must not conflate separation from (hypocritical) Jewish leaders with separation from Judaism itself. Indeed, Matthew is known to have profoundly conservative views with respect to the Law (5:17). Moreover, his careful redaction of Markan texts indicates that he is not as anti-temple as many would think (Gurtner 2006). For Matthew seems to affirm the role of the Temple as a place of offering sacrifices (5:23–24; 8:4) and being a "house of prayer" (21:13). Negative utterances against it in the first gospel are careful polemics against its mismanagement, and discussion of its impending destruction is displayed in a Jeremiah-like lament (23:37–39). It seems plausible, then, that though Matthew would affirm a Judaism starkly different from that practiced by the Jewish leaders of the first century, he would very much see himself in continuity with Judaism as espoused in our Old Testament.

Roman Empire

Warren Carter (2001) has proposed that one give serious consideration to the social realities of life in the Roman Empire in the first century and Matthew's response to them. By analyzing the "networks of power" in first-century Roman politics and how they affected social life in first-century Mediterranean regions, Carter establishes a backdrop against which the first gospel can be placed, including "theological" claims made by the Empire that create conflict with those of Jesus. Matthew's portrayal of Jesus is set against the backdrop of

the imperial presence where they present conflict. Specifically, the kingdom of God, the presence of God in Jesus are taken as direct affronts to the Roman imperial pretensions and claims. For example, the sins from which Jesus will save his people are oppressive political, social, or economic in nature. Furthermore, Matthean citations of OT texts are taken to borrow the oppressive setting from that context as well. For example, Carter contends that Matthew's use of Isaiah 7–9 in 1:23 and 4:15–16 evokes the oppressive context in which Judah is oppressed by Assyria to posit a political interpretation of "Galilee of the Gentiles." Also, the paying of taxes (Matt 17:24–27) is a demonstration of God's authority even over Roman taxation.

Historical Jesus

In a sense, Matthew's gospel is itself a case-study in Historical Jesus methodologies. Its use of sources – Mark, Q, and M – have made it a battleground for proposing and challenging criteria of authenticity in Historical Jesus studies. For example, the coherence principle – which asserts that material that coheres or is consistent with material established as authentic by other means – has been used to recognized Jesus' statement to "repent, for the kingdom of heaven is near" (4:17) as authentic. As an eschatological teaching, it coheres with Mark 1:15. Yet it also coheres with a demand for repentance (Mark 8:35; 10:23b, 25; Luke 9:60a, 62; Matt 7:13–14) and the demand for a new way of thinking (Mark 7:15; 10:15; Luke 14:11; 16:15; Matt 5:39b–41; 44–48; Bultmann; Perrin). Likewise, Jesus' reply to Caiaphas (Matt 19:28) coheres with other dominical tradition based on the imagery of Daniel 7 (e.g. Mark 10:37–40; Matt 19:28// Luke 22:28–30; Evans 1991). Another criteria for authenticity argues that where a gospel text reflects a Semitic or Palestinian feature there is a higher likelihood for authenticity. While not all agree with the validity of this criteria, evidence is sometimes cited in the so-called "divine passives" used as a circumlocution in avoidance of uttering the divine name of God (5:3–10; 6:9; 13:11). Also evident are Semitic poetic devices (11:5–6), and Semitic wordplays, like "straining out a gnat" (*qalma*) and "swallowing a camel" (*gamla*; 23:24), or simply Semitic terms such as "*bar*" for "son" (16:17).

The criterion of "multiple forms" (Dodd 1937) is also found in Matthew. As Dodd defines it, this criterion suggests that if sayings of Jesus are found in two or more forms of gospel traditions, such as sayings, parables, etc., then they likely represent an early tradition and may well be authentic. In Matthew, we find Jesus' teachings on the kingdom of God (5:17; 9:37–38; 13:16–17; cf. Mark 2:18–20; 4:26–29; Luke 11:14–22; John 4:35) and Jesus' mercy to sinners (11:19; cf. Mark 2:15–17; Luke 15:2) fitting into this category. More difficult to discern is material that is contrary to editorial tradition. For example, while Matthew's Gospel claims to endorse the enduring value of the Law (5:17–20), he later suggests that it ends with John the Baptist (11:13; Moule; Calvert 1971).

Matthew's Gospel is also valuable for Historical Jesus studies in that it presents a fair amount of material that meets criteria employed by important Historical Jesus scholars across the spectrum of the discipline. First is the criterion of dissimilarity, claiming that material is regarded as having a high probability of authenticity if it is dissimilar or distinct from tendencies in early Judaism or the early church (Bultmann). Matthew's description of the violent entry of the kingdom (11:12) would fit into such a category, as would Jesus' call of people to discipleship (8:21–22; Hengel 1981). Also, the criteria of multiple attestation, affirming that sayings found in two or more early and independent traditions (Mark, Q, M, and L) have a higher likelihood to authenticity, can bear fruit in Matthew. F. C. Burkitt (1906) identified thirty-one such sayings, including the saying on the evil generation in Mark (8:12//Matt 16:4) and Q (Matt 12:39b//Luke 11:29b); the Lamp saying in Mark 4:21 (//Luke 8:16) and Q (Matt 5:15//Luke 11:33); the saying on what is hidden in Mark (4:22//Luke 8:17), Q (Matt 10:26b//Luke 12:2) and Thomas (5b).

Questions arise regarding whether additional information about the historical Jesus can be recovered within Matthean redaction, and particularly within that material which is unique to his gospel; the so-called "M" tradition. Frequently this is identified as Matthew's unique discourse material, located by source (e.g. Streeter, Kilpatrick, Manson) as a written source from around 60–65 CE and polemical in nature towards scribes and Pharisees. It was held by Streeter to include parables, such as that of the laborers in the vineyard (20:1–16), the hidden treasure and the pearl (13:44–46), but excluding the infancy narratives (Matt 1–2). Some have seen it as generally less reliable than Mark, Q, and L for authenticity. Indeed, some have seen it as a Jewish-Christian corruption of authentic teachings of Jesus, as it represents Jerusalem Christianity associated with James the brother of Jesus (Streeter 232). However, this assessment may be inordinately anachronistic, for much of its material is affirmed by other criteria. For instance, M material is said

to include its community's inclination to observing the Law (5:17–20; cf. 23:2–3), which Moule has identified as contrary to other Matthean editorial activity and therefore likely authentic.

In some matters M material, particularly that which is christological in orientation, seems to suspiciously cohere with the rest of the Gospel. In it, Jesus is presented as the authoritative interpreter of the Law (5:21–48; Davies 387–89) with the authority of God (6:1–8, 16–18; 18:19; cf. 11:28–30), and whose revelation is the measure by which God will judge the M community (5:17–20; cf. 25:31–46). The M Jesus is the founder of the end-time church community (16:18–29; cf. 18:17; 23:8–10), commissioned to a mission to Israel (10:5–7). Some redaction is more explicit. Some scholars see in M material the teachings of the Baptist (e.g. 3:7 par. Luke 3:7) clearly put into the mouth of Jesus (12:34; 23:33; Manson 1957: 25). However, that some material coheres with other Matthean material can tell us that it cannot be established as authentic using the same criteria that can be used with other material. That is, because the criterion of coherence cannot be allocated positively, it does not follow that it need be applied negatively and therefore necessarily exclude material that it cannot, by definition, demonstrate as authentic. Therefore Matthew potentially contributes a substantial amount of material to our knowledge of the historical Jesus.

DANIEL M. GURTNER

Further reading

Allison, Dale C. *The New Moses: A Matthean Typology*, Edinburgh: T. & T. Clark, 1993.

Bacon, B. W. *Studies in Matthew*, London: Constable, 1930.

Beaton, Richard. *Isaiah's Christ in Matthew's Gospel*, SNTSMS 123, Cambridge: Cambridge University Press, 2003.

Bornkamm, Günther, Barth, G. and Held, H. J. *Tradition and Interpretation in Matthew*, ET, London: SCM Press, 1963.

Brooks, S. H. "Matthew's Community: The Evidence of His Special Sayings Material," JSNTSup 16, Sheffield: JSOT, 1987.

Bultmann, Rudolf. *The History of the Synoptic Tradition*, ET. Oxford: Blackwell, 1963.

Burkitt, F. C. *The Gospel History and Its Transmission*, Edinburgh: T. & T. Clark, 1906.

Calvert, D. G. A. "An Examination of the Criteria for Distinguishing the Authentic Words of Jesus," *NTS* 18 (1971–72) 209–19.

Carter, Warren. *Matthew and Empire: Initial Explorations*, Harrisburg, PA: Trinity Press International, 2001.

Davies, W. D. *The Setting of the Sermon on the Mount*, Cambridge: Cambridge University, 1964.

Dodd, C. H. *History and the Gospel*, New York: Scribner's, 1937

Evans, Craig A. "In What Sense 'Blasphemy'? Jesus before Caiaphas in Mark 14:61–64," *SBLSP* 30 (1991) 215–34.

—— "Predictions of the Destruction of the Herodian Temple in the Pseudepigrapha, Qumran Scrolls, and Related Texts," *JSP* 10 (1992) 89–147.

France, R. T. *Matthew: Evangelist and Teacher*, Downers Grove, IL: InterVarsity Press, 1989.

Gundry, Robert H. *The Use of the Old Testament in St Matthew's Gospel, with special reference to the Messianic Hope*, Leiden: Brill, 1967.

—— *Matthew: A Commentary on his Literary and Theological Art*, Grand Rapids, MI: Eerdmans, 1982.

Gurtner, Daniel M. "Matthew's Temple and the 'Parting of the Ways'," in John Nolland and Daniel M. Gurtner (eds) *Built upon the Rock: Studies in the Gospel of Matthew*, Grand Rapids, MI: Eerdmans, 2006.

Hengel, Martin. *The Charismatic Leader and His Followers*, trans. J. Greig, Edinburgh: T. & T. Clark, 1981.

—— *Studies in the Gospel of Mark*, ET, London: SCM Press, 1985.

Hill, David. "Son and Servant: An Essay in Matthean Christology," *JSNT* 6 (1980) 2–16.

Kilpatrick, G. D. *The Origins of the Gospel According to St. Matthew*, Oxford: Clarendon, 1946.

Kingsbury, Jack Dean. *Matthew as Story*, second edition, Philadelphia, PA: Fortress Press, 1988.

Levine, A. J. *The Social and Ethnic Dimensions of Matthean Salvation History: "Go nowhere among the Gentiles" (Matt 10:5b)*, Lewiston, NY: Edwin Mellen, 1988.

Luz, Ulrich. *Matthew in History: Interpretation, Influence, and Effects*, Minneapolis, MN: Fortress Press, 1994.

—— *The Theology of the Gospel of Matthew*, Cambridge: Cambridge University Press, 1995.

Manson, T. W. *The Sayings of Jesus*, London: SCM Press, 1957.

Moule, C. F. D. *The Phenomenon of the New Testament*, London: SCM Press, 1967.

Nolan, B. M. *The Royal Son of God*, Göttingen: Vandenhoeck & Ruprecht, 1979.

Nolland, John. *The Gospel of Matthew*, NIGTC. Grand Rapids, MI: Eerdmans, 2005.

—— "Matthew and Anti-Semitism," in John Nolland and Daniel M. Gurtner (eds) *Built upon the Rock: Studies in the Gospel of Matthew*, Grand Rapids, MI: Eerdmans, 2006.

Perrin, Norman. *What is Redaction Criticism?* Philadelphia, PA: Fortress Press, 1969.

Rhoads, David, Joanna Dewey, and Donald Michie. *Mark as Story: An Introduction to the Narrative of a Gospel*, Minneapolis, MA: Fortress Press, 1999.

Schlatter, A. *Der Evangelist Matthäus: Seine Sprache, sein Ziel, seine Selbständigkeit*, Stuttgart: Calwer Verlag, 1929.

Stanton, Graham N. "The Origin and Purpose of Matthew's Gospel: Matthean Scholarship from 1945 to 1980," in W. Hasse (ed.) *Aufstieg und Niedergang der römischen Welt* 25/3, Berlin: de Gruyter, 1985, pp. 1889–951.

—— *A Gospel for a New People: Studies in Matthew*, Louisville, KY: WJK, 1992.

Stendahl, Kirster. *The School of St Matthew*, Philadelphia, PA: Fortress Press, 1968.

Stonehouse, Ned B. *Origins of the Synoptic Gospels*, Grand Rapids, MI: Eerdmans, 1963.

Strecker, Georg. *Der Weg der Gerechtigkeit: Untersuchung zur Theologie des Matthäus*, third edition, Göttingen: Vandenhoeck & Ruprecht, 1971.

Streeter, B. H. *The Four Gospels*, London: Macmillan, 1930.

Verseput, Donald. "The Role and Meaning of the 'Son of God' Title in Matthew's Gospel," *NTS* 33 (1987) 532–56.

GOSPELS, EXTRA-NEW TESTAMENT

In today's scholarly and popular press the most frequently mentioned writings outside of the New Testament Gospels are the *Gospel of Thomas*, the *Gospel of Peter*, Egerton Papyrus 2 (or *Egerton Gospel*), the *Secret Gospel of Mark*, and the *Gospel of Mary*. There are several other gospels, some of which survive only in part, either as papyrus fragments or as quotations in later writings. (For survey, bibliography, and English translation of most of these texts, see Elliott.)

Some scholars and popular writers have argued that a few of these extra-canonical writings contain traditions about Jesus that are early, independent, and perhaps even superior to what we have in the New Testament Gospels of Matthew, Mark, Luke, and John. This position, however, is highly debatable.

Most of the attention will be given to those writings that are early and have been put forward as important for understanding Jesus better: *Gospel of Thomas*, *Gospel of Peter*, *Egerton Papyrus 2*, other papyrus fragments of unknown gospels, Jewish Christian gospels, *Gospel of the Egyptians*, birth and infancy gospels, *Gospel of Nicodemus*, *Gnostic Gospels*, and *Secret Gospel of Mark*.

Gospel of Thomas

The Coptic version of the *Gospel of Thomas* was discovered in late 1945 in Nag Hammadi, Egypt. It is the second tractate in what is now identified as the second of thirteen leather-bound codices, dating to the second half of the fourth century. *Thomas* begins, "These are the secret words that the living Jesus spoke and Judas, even Thomas, wrote," and ends with, "the Gospel according to Thomas." Third- and fourth-century church fathers had mentioned a Gospel that went by the name of the apostle Thomas. It is very probable that the discovery at Nag Hammadi is this writing.

When the new discovery was read and translated (and was found to contain a Prologue and 114 sayings, or logia, mostly attributed to Jesus), scholars realized that parts of the *Gospel of Thomas* had in fact been found a half-century earlier, in the 1890s, in a different part of Egypt, in a place called Oxyrhynchus. Three Greek papyrus fragments published at the turn of the century, numbered 1, 654, and 655, contain about 20 percent of the *Gospel of Thomas*, at least as compared with the

Coptic version. The Greek fragments range in date from early to late third century.

The *Gospel of Thomas* is an esoteric writing, purporting to record the secret (or "hidden") teachings of Jesus, teachings reserved for those qualified to hear these teachings. A few scholars argue that the *Gospel of Thomas* contains primitive, pre-Synoptic tradition. A few have even suggested that an early version of *Thomas* may have existed in the middle of the first century. This is theoretically possible, but there are numerous difficulties that attend efforts to cull from this collection of logia, or sayings, material that can with confidence be judged primitive, independent of the New Testament Gospels, and even authentic.

The following factors suggest that *Thomas* is late, not early: (1) *Thomas* knows more than half of the New Testament writings; (2) *Thomas* contains Gospel materials that scholars regard as late (such as M, L, and John); (3) *Thomas* is familiar with later editing in the gospels (such as Matthean and Lukan redaction of Mark); (4) *Thomas* shows familiarity with traditions distinctive to Eastern, Syrian Christianity, traditions that did not emerge earlier than the middle of the second century. Indeed, as Nicholas Perrin has argued, *Thomas* was probably written in Syriac and then later in Egypt was translated into Greek and Coptic. At many points the readings of *Thomas* agree with Syriac tradition, including Tatian's *Diatessaron*, which was composed *c.* 175 (Perrin).

Gospel of Peter

Church historian Eusebius of Caesarea (*c.* 260–340) mentions a gospel attributed to Peter, which Serapion, bishop of Antioch (in office 199–211), eventually condemned (*Hist. eccl.* 6.12.3–6). In the winter of 1886–87, during excavations at Akhmîm in Egypt, a codex was found in the coffin of a Christian monk. The manuscript comprises a fragment of a gospel, fragments of Greek *Enoch*, the *Apocalypse of Peter*, and, written on the inside of the back cover of the codex, an account of the martyrdom of St Julian. The gospel fragment bears no name or hint of a title, for neither the beginning nor the conclusion of the work has survived. Because the apostle Peter appears in the text, narrating in the first person (v. 60: "But I, Simon Peter"), because it seemed to have a docetic orientation (that is, where the physical reality of Jesus appears to be discounted), and because the gospel fragment was in the company of the *Apocalypse of Peter*, it was widely assumed that the fragment belonged to the *Gospel of Peter* mentioned by Eusebius.

Critical assessments of the newly published gospel fragment diverged widely, with some scholars claiming that the fragment was independent of the New Testament Gospels and others claiming that the fragment is dependent on the New Testament Gospels. Throughout this debate no one seriously asked if the Akhmîm Fragment really was part of the second-century *Gospel of Peter*. It was simply assumed that it was.

In the 1970s and 1980s two more Greek fragments from Egypt were published, P.Oxy. 2949 and P.Oxy. 4009 (see below), which with varying degrees of confidence were identified as belonging to the *Gospel of Peter*. Indeed, one of the fragments was thought to overlap with part of the Akhmîm Fragment. The publication of these fragments renewed interest in the gospel, because it was felt that the identity of the Akhmîm Fragment as the late second-century *Gospel of Peter* was confirmed. Indeed, it has also been suggested that the Fayyum Fragment (see below), is yet another early fragment of the *Gospel of Peter*.

In recent years, Helmut Koester and a circle of colleagues and students have given new life to the view that the Akhmîm Fragment is independent of the gospels. According to Koester, the *Gospel of Peter* is probably independent of the canonical gospels (Koester 230). Koester's student Ron Cameron agrees, concluding that this gospel is independent of the canonical gospels, may even predate them, and "may have served as a source for their respective authors" (Cameron 78). This position has been worked out in detail by John Dominic Crossan, who accepts the identification of the Akhmîm Fragment with Serapion's *Gospel of Peter*. In a lengthy study Crossan argued that the *Gospel of Peter*, though admittedly in its final stages influenced by the New Testament Gospel tradition, preserves a very old tradition, on which all four of the canonical gospels' passion accounts are based. This old tradition is identified as the *Cross Gospel* (Crossan 1988: 404). Nevertheless, there are serious problems with this hypothesis.

It is difficult to conclude that this material, no matter how deftly pruned and reconstructed, could possibly constitute the earliest layer of tradition on which the passion narratives of the New Testament Gospels are dependent. Scholars a generation or two ago found no independent traditions in the Akhmîm Gospel fragment. Recently, other scholars have reached similar conclusions. John Meier describes the fragment as a second-century "pastiche of traditions from the canonical Gospels, recycled through the memory and lively imagination of Christians who have heard the Gospels read and preached upon many a time" (Meier 117–18). D. Moody Smith's rhetorical question only underscores the problematical dimension of Crossan's hypothesis: "[I]s it thinkable that the tradition began with the legendary, the mythological, the anti-Jewish, and indeed the fantastic, and moved in the direction of the historically restrained and sober?" (Smith 150). Indeed, it does seem unlikely. Finally, Charles Quarles has called attention to the coherence between the Akhmîm Fragment's description of the emergence from the tomb with similar fantastic descriptions from the third and fourth centuries (Quarles). All of this argues against an early dating for this document.

But more pressing is the question that asks if the existing ninth-century Akhmîm Gospel fragment *really is* a fragment of the second century *Gospel of Peter* condemned by Bishop Serapion in the early third century. The extant Akhmîm Fragment does not identify itself, nor do we have a patristic quotation of the *Gospel of Peter* with which we can make comparison and possibly settle the questions. Nor is the Akhmîm Gospel fragment Docetic, as many asserted shortly after its publication. If the fragment is not Docetic, then the proposed identification of the fragment with the *Gospel of Peter* is weakened still further. After all, the one thing that Bishop Serapion emphasized was that the *Gospel of Peter* was used by Docetists to advance their doctrines. And finally, as Paul Foster has shown, the connection between the Akhmîm Gospel fragment and the small papyrus fragments that may date as early as 200–250 is quite tenuous (Foster). Thus, we have no solid evidence that allows us with any confidence to link the extant Akhmîm Gospel fragment with a second-century text, be that the *Gospel of Peter* mentioned by Bishop Serapion or some other writing from the late second century. Given its fantastic features and coherence with late traditions, it is not advisable to make use of this gospel fragment for Jesus research.

Egerton Papyrus 2

Papyrus Egerton 2 was found somewhere in Egypt and fell into the hands of scholars in 1934, shortly after which it was published. It consists of three leaves, with writing on both sides of the leaves. The first leaf appears to preserve portions of two stories. In the first, Jesus is accused of breaking the law and is threatened with stoning. In the second, Jesus heals the leper. The second leaf appears to preserve two stories. The first is a version of the question put to Jesus about paying tax. The second appears

to be an apocryphal miracle story of sowing seed, which then brings forth abundant fruit. The third leaf preserves tiny fragments of two more stories, one which tells of Jesus threatened with stoning. These stories parallel the Johannine and Synoptic Gospels. Papyrus Köln 255, discovered sometime later, constitutes a related fragment of the text.

Crossan's analysis of these fragments leads him to conclude that Papyrus Egerton 2 represents a tradition that predates the canonical gospels. He thinks that the Synoptic Gospels are probably dependent on Egerton 2 and that Egerton 2 "gives important evidence of a stage in the transmission prior to the separation" of the Synoptic and Johannine traditions (Crossan 1992: 49). Helmut Koester agrees with Crossan's second point, saying that in Papyrus Egerton 2 we find "pre-Johannine and pre-synoptic characteristics of language [which] still existed side by side" (Koester 207). He thinks it unlikely, against other scholars, that the author of this papyrus could have been acquainted with the canonical gospels and "would have deliberately composed [it] by selecting sentences" from them (Koester 215).

Theoretically Crossan and Koester could be correct in this assessment. There are, however, some serious questions that must be raised. *First*, several times editorial improvements introduced by Matthew and Luke appear in Egerton 2 (e.g. compare Egerton 2 line 32 with Mark 1:40; Matt 8:2; Luke 5:12; or Egerton 2 lines 39–41 with Mark 1:44; Matt 8:4; Luke 17:14). There are other indications that the Egerton Papyrus is posterior to the canonical gospels. The plural "kings" is probably secondary to the singular "Caesar" that is found in the Synoptics (and in *Gos. Thom.* §100). The flattery, "what you do bears witness beyond all the prophets," may reflect John 1:34, 45 and is again reminiscent of later pious Christian embellishment that tended to exaggerate the respect that Jesus' contemporaries showed him (see the examples in *Gos. Heb.* §2 and Josephus, *Ant.* 18.64).

Koester's doubts about someone "selecting sentences" from the New Testament Gospels is without force, for this is the very thing that Justin Martyr and his disciple Tatian did. Sometime in the 150s Justin Martyr composed a *Harmony* of the Synoptic Gospels and a few years later Tatian composed a harmony (i.e. the *Diatessaron*) of all four New Testament Gospels. If Justin Martyr and Tatian, writing in the second century, can compose their respective harmonies through the selection of sentences and phrases from this gospel and that Gospel, why could not the author of the Egerton Papyrus do the same thing? Indeed, it is probable that this is the very thing that he did do.

Other papyrus fragments of unknown gospels

There are several papyrus fragments, some of which may have been part of gospels no longer known to us. These include P.Oxy. 210, a small fragment containing a version of Jesus' teaching on two types of trees; P.Oxy. 840, which contains an angry exchange between Jesus and a Pharisaic priest in the temple court; P.Oxy. 1081, a small Gnostic fragment, in which Jesus teaches his disciples; P.Oxy. 1224, which preserves exchanges between Jesus and "scribes, Pharisees, and priests"; P.Oxy. 2949, which mentions Pilate and the request to bury Jesus; P.Oxy. 4009, which preserves a version of Jesus' warning about wolves that attack the sheep; P.Oxy. 4010, which preserves a version of the Lord's Prayer, the Fayyum Fragment (or P. Vindob. G 2325), which preserves Jesus' allusion to the prophecy of the stricken shepherd; Strasbourg Coptic Fragment, which contains a version of Jesus' passion prayer and warning to his disciples; P.Cairo 10735, which relates the angelic warning to Joseph to flee with Mary and the infant to Egypt; P.Berlin 11710, which preserves a version of the exchange between Jesus and Nathanael; and P.Merton 51, which may be a homily based on Luke 6:7. P.Egerton 3 could also be mentioned, but it is probably a treatise or commentary of some sort. Of these fragments P.Oxy. 840 is the most important (Kruger).

Jewish-Christian gospels

Traditionally three lost writings have been identified as the *Gospel according to the Hebrews*, the *Gospel of the Nazareans*, and the *Gospel of the Ebionites*. These lost gospels are preserved in patristic quotations and the marginal notes of certain texts of Matthew. It is assumed that one or more of these lost gospels come from an Aramaic or Hebrew version of the Gospel of Matthew (cf. Papias, Frag. §3, *apud* Eusebius, *Hist. eccl.* 3.39.16). Possibly related is the Hebrew Matthew preserved in a lengthy, polemical treatise composed in the fourteenth century by Shem Tob ben Isaac (a.k.a. Ibn Shaprut).

The quotations and traditions provided by Origen roughly correspond to what has been called the *Gospel according to the Hebrews*, the quotations and traditions provided by Jerome roughly correspond to what has been called the *Gospel of the Nazareans*, and the quotations and traditions provided by Epiphanius correspond to what has been called the *Gospel of the Ebionites*.

In general, the Jewish Gospel exhibits four major characteristics: (1) wrestling with the validity and interpretation of the Law, both written and oral; (2) the restoration of Israel; (3) enhancement of the status of James the brother of Jesus; and (4) Christology. In the case of the latter, adoptionism appears to be the basic understanding. But from a Judaic perspective, this is not *low* Christology; it is *true* Christology. The Christology of the Jewish Gospels is sometimes enhanced through the witness of Scripture, whether explicit of implicit.

Gospel of the Egyptians

The *Gospel of the Egyptians* was in circulation among gentile Christians in Egypt. Clement of Alexandria is our primary source, though this gospel is also mentioned by Hippolytus and Epiphanius. *Egyptians* relates a conversation between Jesus and Salome which in some respects coheres with Gnostic emphases. In fact, some of the material in *Egyptians* also appears in the *Gospel of Thomas*.

Birth and infancy gospels

Beginning in the second century and continuing on into the Middle Ages several works were produced in an effort to satisfy curiosity about the early lives of the holy family. The most important of these works include: the *Protevangelium of James*, which tells the story of Mary's miraculous birth, dedication to the Temple, and betrothal to Joseph; the Coptic *History of Joseph*, which tells the story of the youth of Joseph; the *Infancy Gospel of Thomas*, which is preserved in several languages, including two major Greek recensions, and which tells several tales about Jesus' infancy, childhood, and adolescence; and the Latin *Infancy Gospel of Matthew*, which combined and supplemented the tales found the *Protevangelium of James* and the *Infancy Gospel of Thomas*. None of this material reaches back to the early first century.

Gospel of Nicodemus

The *Gospel of Nicodemus* constitutes the combination of the *Acts of Pilate* and the *Descent of Christ into Hell* (or the *Descensus ad Inferos*). The *Acts* offers a dramatic retelling of the trial and crucifixion of Jesus, complete with a report to the Sanhedrin relating to the resurrection. The *Descent* provides a detailed account of the harrowing of Hell by Jesus and the resurrection of the righteous. *Nicodemus* is fifth-century, but some of the traditions in *Acts* and *Descent* reach back to the second and third centuries.

Gnostic Gospels

There are several Gnostic Gospels, among them the *Gospel of Philip* and the *Gospel of Mary*, in which the status of Mary Magdalene is enhanced. In these Gospels Jesus is said to have loved Mary, even to have kissed her. The point is that Jesus showed Mary the same respect, perhaps more, as he showed the male disciples. Therefore, Mary's teaching is just as authoritative. The assertions of *Philip* and *Mary* do not imply that Jesus and Mary were lovers, as has been asserted in recent pseudo-scholarship. Typical of the Gnostic Gospels is the setting in which a luminous Jesus appears and imparts to his disciples special knowledge about the origin and nature of the world and how to escape its error and eventual doom.

Secret Gospel of Mark

In 1961 Morton Smith announced at the annual meeting of the Society of Biblical Literature that while cataloguing books in the Mar Saba Monastery, in the wilderness of Judea, he found a lost letter of Clement of Alexandria, in which are two quotations of a secret or mystical version of the Gospel of Mark. Twelve years later Smith published the text, along with detailed commentary. Almost immediately some suspected the discovery was a hoax. Recent publication of life-sized color photographs made it possible to submit the handwriting to analysis. Experts have pronounced the text a modern forgery. Stephen Carlson, who also observed the presence of certain Greek letters of the alphabet (such as *tau* and *lambda*) in the Clementine letter that match Smith's distinctive style of writing Greek, has concluded that the text was penned by Smith himself (Carlson). The evidence that Carlson has marshaled is substantial and seems to bear out his conclusion. A few scholars, however, still maintain that both the Clementine letter and the version of Mark to which it makes reference are genuine.

As interesting as the extra-New Testament Gospels are and as helpful as they may be for understanding better the diversity of traditions in the second century and later, on the basis of what is currently known it is not wise to depend on them for supplementing our knowledge of the historical Jesus.

CRAIG A. EVANS

Further reading

Cameron, R. (ed.) *The Other Gospels: Non-Canonical Gospel Texts*, Philadelphia, PA: Westminster, 1982.
Carlson, S. C. *The Gospel Hoax: Morton Smith's Invention of Secret Mark*, Waco, TX: Baylor University Press, 2005.
Crossan, J. D. *The Cross that Spoke: The Origins of the Passion Narrative*, San Francisco, CA: Harper & Row, 1988.
—— *Four Other Gospels: Shadows on the Contours of Canon*, Sonoma, CA: Polebridge, 1992 [1985].
Elliott, J. K. *The Apocryphal New Testament: A Collection of Apocryphal Christian Literature in an English Translation based on M. R. James*, Oxford: Clarendon Press, 1993.
Foster, P. "Are There any Early Fragments of the So-Called Gospel of Peter?," *NTS* 52 (2006) 1–28.
Koester, H. *Ancient Christian Gospels: Their History and Development*, London: SCM Press; Philadelphia, PA: Trinity Press International, 1990.
Kruger, M. J. *The Gospel of the Savior: An Analysis of P. Oxy. 840 and its Place in the Gospel Traditions of Early Christianity*, Texts and Editions for New Testament Study 1, Leiden: Brill, 2005.
Meier, J. P. *A Marginal Jew: Rethinking the Historical Jesus. Volume One: The Roots of the Problem and the Person*, ABRL, New York: Doubleday, 1991.
Perrin, N. *Thomas and Tatian: The Relationship between the Gospel of Thomas and the Diatessaron*, Academia Biblica 5, Atlanta, GA: Society of Biblical Literature, 2002.
Quarles, C. L. "The Gospel of Peter: Does It Contain a Precanonical Resurrection Narrative?," in Robert B. Stewart (ed.) *The Resurrection of Jesus: John Dominic Crossan and N. T. Wright in Dialogue*, Minneapolis, MN: Fortress Press, 2006, pp. 106–20.
Smith, D. M. "The Problem of John and the Synoptics in Light of the Relation between Apocryphal and Canonical Gospels," in A. Denaux (ed.) *John and the Synoptics*, BETL 101, Leuven: Peeters and Leuven University Press, 1992, pp. 147–62.

GREAT COMMANDMENT

The Great Commandment is a set of two commandments contained in the pericope of the same name. While the first of the two is referenced as "great," it is presented as inseparable from the second. The implication is that one must do the second in order to fulfil the first and that the second is not fulfilled until the first is achieved. This coupling of the two in the pre-eminent commandment has been understood since the earliest Christian traditions and is received as such by modern scholars, as well.

In the New Testament, the commands are detailed by Jesus when answering a scribe in Mark 12:28–34. The other synoptic versions have the precise commandments coming in dialogue with either one of the Pharisees (Matt 22:34–40) or a religious lawyer (Luke 10:25–28).

Where Matthew and Mark have the commandment on the lips of Jesus, Luke depicts Jesus teaching the lawyer with a leading question in Socratic fashion. In any of the three versions, the role of the inquirer is as one who holds a position secured by his religious knowledge. The precise nature of that position is not critical to the fundamental meaning of the pericope. What matters is that the inquirer was expected to be an expert in religious matters, and Jesus is seen to teach even him. As Bultmann has observed, the scene described may be that of a meeting on the street (*Streitgespräch*), but the interaction is most certainly that of a teacher and a pupil (*Schulgespräch*).

The Jewish origins of the commandments

Love of God

As is well known, the exhortation "Hear, O Israel" and the ensuing commands to love God are the opening lines from the twice-daily recited prayer, the *Shema*, itself a recitation of Deuteronomy 6:4–9. It is to be noted that only Mark includes the *Shema* itself. The other two synoptic writers include only Deuteronomy 6:5 and that in disparate forms.

The Hebrew text presents three vehicles by which love to God is to be individually expressed: heart, soul, and might. The Septuagintal rendering keeps the order but substitutes "power" for "might".

Where Deuteronomy incorporates three nouns into the commandment, however, Mark has four: heart, soul, mind, and strength. Matthew has three: heart, soul, and mind. And Luke resonates with Mark's four but in a different order: heart, soul, strength, and mind. Assuming Markan priority for the synoptic Jesus tradition, it is important to note that Jesus introduces the mind into the commandment and makes more palatable both the "might" of the Hebrew and the "power" of the Greek by rendering them as "strength."

Love of others

The love of one's neighbour is cited from Leviticus 19:18. In its original context, the commandment, in both Hebrew and the Greek translation, is for love of one's countrymen as one's neighbour. As E. F. Scott notes, Jesus removes these ethnic trappings by implying that anyone in need is one's neighbour:

> A man who is plainly in need of your help is by that fact your neighbour. His trouble gives him a claim upon you that you are not at liberty to disown. Your help must be rendered spontaneously without any enquiries as to who he is and whether he deserves your help.

The generalisation of one's neighbour to all of humankind, however, was not new at the time of Jesus. Rather, it is attested in several parts of

Second Temple Jewish literature, as France has noted. As early as 150 BCE, during the Maccabean Period, the Testament of Issachar pseudepigraphically records the patriarch's exhortation to his children: "Love the Lord and your neighbour" (5.2). In the last chapter of the testament, Issachar is depicted as generalising love of one's neighbour to all of humankind: "I acted in piety and truth all my days. The Lord I loved with all my strength; likewise, I loved every human being as I loved my children" (*T. Iss.* 7.6).

Similar parallels may be found in the *Testament of Daniel* 5.3 and at least three passages in Philo (*Spec.* 2.63, *Decal.* 20.154; 108–10, and *Abr.* 208). In addition to its other parallels with Jesus' message, *Jubilees* contains a further resonance with the commandment to love God and others in 36:3–8 (see also Jubilee, sin, and forgiveness).

In Luke, consequently, the lawyer is shown to draw on a common Jewish understanding of the question but is implied at the same time to fail in its fulfilment. While the substance of his answer is safely niched in the contemporary Jewish religious understanding, the precise teaching is not. None of the parallels evince scriptural support for what had clearly become a widespread understanding of piety and religion. Perhaps the closest is in *Sipra Leviticus* 19:18, where R. Akiba characterises the text as a summative principle (כלל) of the Torah but without giving it the primacy that Jesus does.

The Hellenistic origins of the coupling

Despite the various Jewish sources which combine love towards God and humankind as the whole of religious devotion, the coupling of piety and righteousness has long been understood as having Hellenistic origins. The myriad of commandments and ordinances detailed in the Mosaic Law and further expounded in the rest of the Hebrew Bible confound attempts to find a singular thread. Gerhardsson has noted that the Hellenistic literature, and the writings of Hellenistic Jews in particular, frequently divides the obligations of the faithful into piety (εὐσέβεια) and righteousness (δικαιοσύνη).

The Hellenistic origins of the summary are further underscored by the relative devaluation of offerings and sacrifices in Mark and the diminished need to account for the whole of the Law and the Prophets in Matthew. As Judea in general, and Jerusalem in particular, relied heavily on the Temple cult for both economic and religious stature (see Roads and commerce in Galilee and Judea), it was in the interest of the Judaeans to emphasise the *whole* law and to resist any diminishment of one part for another.

The newness of Jesus' teaching

Although the commandments themselves are part of the oldest Jewish traditions and the coupling of piety and righteousness is Hellenistic in origin, Jesus' teaching unites the two for the first time. Where not even the rabbinic literature has the coupling of these two commandments, Jesus is shown in Matthew and Mark as summarising the two complementary ideas as commandments in the Law. What is more, he introduces the two commandments in a new fashion, as a whole, and with the understanding of the two as complementary parts of the answer.

As France has noted (480), the two complements are united by the command to love and represent the two halves of the Decalogue: love God and neighbour. In a previous encounter with the rich young man (Luke uses "ruler"), Jesus offers rules for self-examination from the second table of the Decalogue (Mark 10:19; Matt 19:18; Luke 18:20). Here, however, a more general rule is requested, and Jesus presents the first tablet as being complemented in the second and, likewise, the second as baseless without the first.

As a summary of obedience

In Mark and Luke, the Great Commandment is presented respectively as the pre-eminent commandment and as the way to inheriting eternal life. One is therefore not surprised to find other authors present it as the sum of all commands. James 2:8 references the command "Love your neighbour as yourself" to be the "Royal Law." This understanding is echoed in Romans 13:9 and Galatians 5:14. Indeed, this is the understanding often perceived in the Matthean version of the Commandment: "In these two commandments rest all the Law and the Prophets."

Role in the early Church

While the precise commands are presented as summative of all divine commands, the purpose of this narrative, the import of those commands and their relation to the life of the Church differ between the gospels. The spectrum of understanding in this regard spans from an almost creedal confession to an early hermeneutical paradigm to an exhortation simply to obey the commandment.

Victor P. Furnish has observed that the Markan version of the Great Commandment is for apologetic purposes and is intended for use in evangelistic preaching. The missionary import is to present the message succinctly: There is One God, you must love God and your neighbour, and obedience to God's command of love is more important than ritual.

Matthew, on the other hand, presumes the character of God, excluding the *Shema*. Furnish has noted that the two parts represent the summation of the Hebrew Bible as it stood at this time. In rabbinic understanding, a commandment is said to hang on another if the first is able to be derived from the second. Matthew's presentation thus indicates the view that the Law and the Prophets in their entirety can be derived from the bipartite Great Commandment.

Gerhardsson has further observed that the Matthean version builds on the Markan and is intended to present a program of exegesis for the Matthean community. Instead of Hillel's seven *middoth*, or principles of exegesis, the Christian exegete is given two. Just as all of the commandments are able to be derived from the two, so they are only understood correctly in relation to those two. The two commandments thus become an early Christian paradigm for interpretation of the Jewish Scriptures.

Gerhardsson has observed that the expansions on the Torah in the Sermon on the Mount (5:17–48) develop from an application of this hermeneutic to the Torah. In addition to this, he has noted that Matthew's reduction of Mark's four-fold love of God to three (heart, soul, and mind), is hermeneutical in purpose. This is poignantly illustrated in the Matthean and Markan interpretations of the Parable of the Sower (Matt 13:18–23 and Mark 4:13–20) where Matthew's use of heart, soul, and mind corresponds to the three-fold return from the good soil in contrast to each of the failed attempts. Each return corresponds to the failure of the seed to bear fruit as a result of hardness of heart, seeking to save one's soul, or being mentally overcome by the desires and worries of the world.

In contrast, the Lucan version is exhortatory in purpose, as Furnish has argued. The Great Commandment is put on the lips of the lawyer as if to say that everyone knows what ought to be done. And to this reply Jesus answers in the affirmative: "You have answered rightly. Do this and you will live." The contestation is not about what should be done but on whether the lawyer is doing it. This then leads into the Parable of the Good Samaritan.

Authenticity

In his work on the Synoptic Gospels, Bultmann alleged that the gospel writers assigned the commandment to Jesus and doubted that it was born of even the faintest memory of Jesus' teachings. Fuller has also expressed doubt over the authenticity of the Great Commandment passages. Given the diversity in the textual versions of the commandment itself, the variety in the dynamics under which the commandment is given, and the sundry purposes for which the narrative has been redacted, one may readily opt to join them in that sentiment. However, other considerations mitigate against these three.

Jesus would have been asked frequently to summarise the 613 commandments of the Torah (365 negative, 248 positive). Rabbis often were, and gave a variety of answers. The fact that love of God and neighbour was well known as a summary is shown in the aforementioned Jewish parallels. The disciples may be expected to have heard this same essential teaching at least three different times in the years they spent with Jesus.

Given the several times the teaching would have been given and the number of other sources that resonate with its essential message, one would expect to find other sources that share this combination. Throughout early Second Temple Jewish literature, however, nowhere else can one find the coupling of the two Torah commandments as one.

The Great Commandment also resonates strongly with the central message of Jesus. As noted above with respect to Matthew's hermeneutical programme, Jesus' teaching was certainly in agreement with the present commandment. This is also shown in his parables and his teachings on forgiveness.

Further, the deuteronomic command to "love the Lord your God" is not cited in the New Testament outside of the Great Commandment. Rather, when the complementary command to love one's neighbour is cited, it presumes a love of God.

While the pervasiveness of this understanding does not prove the summary's origin with Jesus, it certainly suggests a very early source for the coupling. There is no substantial reason to dispute that the summary originated with Jesus and was then subject to variation and interpretation in the handing down of both oral and written traditions. Bultmann later relented from his position and assumed the authenticity of the teaching in his *Theology of the New Testament*.

ALBERT LUKASZEWSKI

Further reading

Allison, D. C., Jr. "Mark 12.28–31," in C. A. Evans and W. R. Stegner (eds) *The Gospels and the Scriptures of Israel*, JSNTSup 104, Sheffield: Sheffield Academic Press, 1994, pp. 270–78.
Bultmann, R. *History of the Synoptic Tradition*, Göttingen: Vandenhoeck & Ruprecht, 1963 [1921].
—— *Theology of the New Testament*, trans. Kenrick Grobel, London: SCM Press, 1952 [Mohr Siebeck, 1948].
Derrett, J. D. M. "'Love thy neighbour as a man like thyself'?," *ExpTim* 83 (1971) 55–56.
France, R. T. *The Gospel of Mark: A Commentary on the Greek Text*, Grand Rapids, MI, and Carlisle: W. B. Eerdmans and Paternoster Press, 2002.
Fuller, R. H. "The Double Commandment of Love: A Test Case for the Criteria of Authenticity," in *Essays on the Love Commandment*, trans. R. H. and I. Fuller, Philadelphia, PA: Fortress Press, 1978.
Furnish, V. P. *The Love Command in the New Testament*, New York: Abingdon Press, 1972.
Gerhardsson, B. "The Hermeneutic Program in Matthew 22:37–40," in *Jews, Greeks and Christians: Religious Cultures in Late Antiquity*, Leiden: Brill, 1976, pp. 129–50.
Gould, E. P. *A Critical and Exegetical Commentary on the Gospel According to St Mark*, New York: Charles Scribner's Sons, 1922.
Schottroff, L. "Non-Violence and the Love of One's Enemies," in *Essays on the Love Commandment*, trans. R. H. and I. Fuller, Philadelphia, PA: Fortress Press, 1978.
Scott, E. F. *The Ethical Teaching of Jesus*, New York: Macmillan, 1923.

GRECO-ROMAN CULTURE IN ISRAEL

One of the distinguishing characteristics of the "Third Quest" phase of Historical Jesus research is the increased attention to Jesus and Judaism in their Greco-Roman context. Scholars now recognize that by the time of Jesus, Palestine had been influenced by Greek culture for centuries. As Martin Hengel has influentially argued, all Judaism was Hellenistic Judaism (1974, 1989, 2001). Only a few decades before Jesus, the area had come under Roman domination and had thus begun to experience Roman culture, which itself had also been deeply influenced by the Greeks. Thus, in early first-century CE Palestine, Hellenistic, Roman, and local cultures mingled with and mutually influenced each other, just as they did throughout the eastern Mediterranean. Recent Historical Jesus scholarship has devoted particular attention to Greco-Roman culture in Galilee, Jesus' home region (Chancey 2005, Crossan and Reed).

Yet if scholars agree about the existence of such interaction in the early first century CE, they disagree about its extent, implications, and specific manifestations. Some have suggested, for example, that Greek was widely spoken, even among the masses, while others have argued that usage of Greek remained limited to the circles of the elites. One finds varying views in the scholarly literature on how common Greco-Roman architecture, art, and inscriptions were, as well as on how influential Greco-Roman education and philosophy were. Most scholars would grant, however, that the influence of Greco-Roman culture grew over time, and for this reason, a chronological overview is helpful.

The Hellenistic period (332–63 BCE)

Even before Alexander's conquest of Palestine, some cities, particularly those on the coast, were importing Greek pottery and other goods. The designs on Persian coins as well as those struck by local cities often imitated those on Greek coins. A few cities, such as Dor, were constructed on a grid plan, with streets intersecting at right angles.

Greek influence became far more noticeable in Alexander's wake, however. Under his successors, the Ptolemies and the Seleucids, new cities were founded and many cities took Greek names. The coastal city of Acco became Ptolemais, for example, and Beth Shean became Scythopolis. At some communities, Hellenistic-style fortifications, buildings with courtyards lined with Greek columns, and grid-based construction plans appeared. The amount of Greek imports, Greek-style coinage, and Greek inscriptions increased. Evidence for Ptolemaic and Seleucid governance includes a few inscriptions and the Zenon papyri, a group of mid-third-century BCE economic documents based on a Ptolemaic official's journey through the region.

Yet these developments should be kept in perspective. They were not spread evenly throughout Palestine; Galilee, in particular, has yielded less evidence of Hellenistic culture in this era than some other regions. Some forms of Hellenistic architecture, like theaters and hippodromes, do not appear to have been introduced, and even the archetypical Hellenistic building, the gymnasium, appears to have been absent until one was controversially built in Jerusalem c. 175 BCE. Likewise, while the increase in the number of inscriptions is notable, epigraphic evidence from this period is not as ample as is sometimes thought (Chancey 2005).

After Jews won their freedom from Seleucid rule in the Maccabean Revolt (c. 164 BCE), the new dynasty of Jewish kings, the Hasmoneans, embraced many aspects of Hellenistic culture – the taking of Greek political titles and personal names; the minting of coins, some with Greek inscriptions; the hiring of mercenaries; and the construction of Greek-style monuments (Gruen). Some also built Greek-style palaces for their personal use. Hellenistic culture was most visible at the Hasmonean capital, Jerusalem. Elsewhere in Hasmonean territory,

however, there is little reason to think that Hellenistic architecture and civic planning became widespread. The number of imported foreign goods diminished considerably, and, aside from coins, inscriptions do not yet appear to have been a common part of public or private life (Berlin).

From the advent of Rome to the First Revolt (63 BCE–70 CE)

In 63 BCE, the Roman general Pompey and his army arrived in Palestine, beginning a new era in the region's history. Though the Romans initially allowed the continuation of Hasmonean rule, they eventually deposed the dynasty and installed a new king, Herod the Great (40–37 BCE). Herod was an enthusiastic proponent of Roman culture (Richardson, Roller). His new city of Sebaste, built on the site of the ancient city of Samaria, was named in honor of the Roman emperor and contained a temple to Augustus and the goddess Roma, a stadium, streets aligned on a grid, and perhaps a Roman-style forum. His next foundation, Caesarea Maritima, was even more impressive, with an imperial temple, orthogonal planning, a theater, amphitheater, agoras, a palace, an aqueduct, and a technologically advanced harbor. Herod made use of Roman construction techniques to an extent unprecedented for the region. He celebrated the creation of this city by instituting a series of quinquennial games that included animal shows, gladiatorial combat, and musical and athletic competitions. In terms of architecture and civic planning, the new city was one of the most visible displays of Roman culture in the eastern Mediterranean. Its development continued long after the death of Herod himself.

In Jerusalem, Herod built a palace and a theater, and he constructed an amphitheater nearby. The most notable of his building projects there, however, was his renovation of the Jewish Temple. He doubled the size of the temple precinct, making it the largest such complex in the Mediterranean world. Around the temple building itself, he erected porticoes of marble columns. With four rows of 162 columns, the southernmost of these porticoes was larger than most basilical structures in the Roman world. Now, even the temple complex itself incorporated Roman architecture.

Other members of the Herodian dynasty also embraced Greco-Roman culture, such as Herod's son Antipas, who inherited Galilee and Perea. Antipas, client king (or, officially, "tetrarch") of Galilee during the time of Jesus, rebuilt the city of Sepphoris as Autocratoris. *Autocrator* is the Greek translation of the Latin imperial title *Imperator*, and so the city's name honored the emperor. Antipas's next major construction effort also honored the emperor: the city of Tiberias, constructed *c*. 20 CE on the shore of the Sea of Galilee.

Both of Antipas's cities reflected Greco-Roman influence to a degree unprecedented for Galilee. At Sepphoris, at least some cities were organized on a grid pattern, and a basilical building was constructed (Nagy *et al.*). Though some scholars have suggested that Jesus may have visited the Roman-style theater there, perhaps watching classical comedies or tragedies or learning the Greek word *hypocrite*, which literally means "actor," others have argued that archaeological evidence demonstrates that the building was not constructed until the late first or early second century CE. Less is known of early first-century Tiberias, since the presence of the modern city of the same name hinders excavation, but inscriptions attest to the use of a Greek title for market officials (*agoranomoi*). At the time of the first revolt, according to Josephus (*Life* 64, 169, 279, 284, 296; *J.W.* 2.639), the city had a *boule* (city council) and *dekaprotoi* (ten leading officials), positions that probably go back to its foundation, as well as a stadium, a form of Hellenistic sports architecture (*Life* 92, 331; *J.W.* 2.618, 3.539–42). Greco-Roman influence was also evident elsewhere in Galilee, such as at Magdala-Taricheae, which had a hippodrome (*J.W.* 2.599, *Life* 132–33). Overall, however, the amount of first-century CE evidence for Greco-Roman culture is considerably less than that from later centuries, and some have argued that scholars have at times exaggerated the extent of Greco-Roman cultural influence in the first century on the basis of later finds (Chancey 2005 and 2002).

Sepphoris was less than 4 miles from Jesus' home village, Nazareth, and anyone traveling around the vicinity of the Sea of Galilee, as Jesus did, would have had some familiarity with Tiberias. As for these cities' possible influence on Jesus, scholars have hypothesized a range of possibilities: his interaction with a diverse population may have contributed to his open-minded and accepting disposition; he might have encountered wandering Greco-Roman popular philosophers, such as Cynics; he resented the cities because of their function as Herodian power centers, their role in the economic and political exploitation of the Galilean countryside, and/or their association with Roman imperial power. The gospels, however, record no visits of Jesus to or explicit comments about either city, leaving his exact attitudes towards them a matter of speculation.

Greco-Roman culture was also manifest to varying degrees in the architecture, inscriptions, and civic organization of cities elsewhere in and near Palestine. Several cities of the Decapolis, for example, were quite close to Galilee, such as Scythopolis (on Galilee's southeastern border) and Hippos (across the Sea of Galilee from Tiberias). The gospels preserve traditions of Jesus' visit to the territory (if not the city itself) of Gerasa or Gadara, also both Decapolis cities (Mark 5:1–20; Matt 8:28–34; Luke 8:26–39), as well as to the territories of Caesarea Philippi (Mark 8:27; Matthew 16:13) and of Tyre and Sidon (Mark 7:24; Matt 15:21). Yet, as with Galilee, much of the evidence for Greco-Roman influence in these cities dates to the centuries after Jesus.

Palestine after 70 CE

The cultural shifts Palestine went through in the century after Jesus were enormous. With the deployment of the X Fretensis legion in Jerusalem following the first Jewish revolt (66–70 CE) and the stationing of the VI Ferrata legion in the Jezreel valley *c*. 120 CE, Palestine was exposed to Roman influence on a new scale (Chancey 2005). No Roman roads had yet been built in Jesus' day, but now they criss-crossed the land, lined with milestones with Latin and Greek inscriptions. Roman urban architecture became far more common, with numerous cities adopting orthogonal planning and constructing basilicas, theaters, bathhouses, stadiums, aqueducts, and temples. The synagogues built in the third, fourth, and following centuries incorporated aspects of Roman architecture, such as columns and, in some cases, a basilical design. The number of inscriptions multiplied exponentially, with Greek, Latin, Aramaic, and Hebrew represented. In contrast to earlier centuries, mosaics often depicted living things; an early third-century CE work at Sepphoris, for example, shows a symposium (a dinner with ample alcohol) attended by Dionysus, the god of wine, and the hero Hercules. Statues of gods, the emperor, and other figures became a more visible part of civic life, though less in predominantly Jewish Galilee than elsewhere. The designs on locally struck coinage became more and more similar to those issued elsewhere in the Empire, so that even the predominantly Jewish cities of Sepphoris and Tiberias minted coins with busts of the emperor and depictions of deities and pagan temples. Rabbinic sources attest to influence from Greco-Roman law, philosophy, ethics, education, and other spheres of culture (Schäfer 1998 and 2002; Schäfer and Hezser 2000).

The languages of Palestine

The widespread oral and written use of Aramaic in the Jewish parts of first-century CE Palestine is undisputed. The written use of Hebrew is also well documented, though the extent of its oral use is harder to gauge. Recent scholarship, however, has drawn attention to the possible use of Greek, with some suggesting that it was quite common (Hengel 1974, 1989, 2001). Such arguments are usually based on the presence of Greek inscriptions and manuscripts and the use of Greek personal names. Since Palestine's linguistic milieu strongly reflected Greco-Roman influence, some have argued, it is likely that Jesus knew at least some Greek. This possibility raises the chances that the canonical gospels might preserve some of the actual words of Jesus, rather than merely Greek translations of Aramaic sayings.

There is no doubt that the number of inscriptions in Palestine increased in the Greco-Roman era. Coinage provides the most obvious example of this phenomenon. In the early Hellenistic period, Ptolemaic and Seleucid coins were used, along with coins produced by cities like Tyre, Sidon, and Ptolemais – all with Greek inscriptions. When the Hasmoneans rose to power, they, too, minted coins. Though the earlier kings limited themselves to Semitic legends on their coins, the later ones employed Greek, as well. By the first century CE, Greek was the numismatic norm in Palestine as it was in most of the eastern Mediterranean, appearing on the issues of client kings, procurators, cities, and imperial mints.

Other epigraphic evidence also reflects the use of Greek. Perhaps the best-known category is that of ossuary inscriptions. Of the ossuaries discovered in the vicinity of Jerusalem, approximately 39 percent had Greek or, in a few cases, Latin inscriptions (Hengel 1989, 2001). Other well-known first-century Greek inscriptions include an imperial prohibition of tomb robbing in Galilee, a synagogue inscription from Jerusalem (the "Theodotus" inscription), and a warning to Gentiles not to proceed into restricted areas in the Jerusalem temple.

Coins aside, however, inscriptions (of whatever language) appear to have been considerably more common in Palestine in the second and following centuries CE than in the first century (Chancey 2005). Similarly, most Greek manuscripts found in the Judean desert post-date the first revolt. The extent to which inscriptions and manuscripts reflect the oral use of Greek is also a matter of debate. Furthermore, our evidence, both epigraphic and documentary, is heavily weighted toward the elites, not the commoners. Though some first-century Jews in Palestine held Greek names – including Jesus' disciples Philip, Andrew, and possibly Thaddaeus and Bartholomew – whether the use of such names indicates any additional facility in the Greek language is unclear; what is quite certain is that both Greek and Latin names were more frequent in the subsequent centuries. In light of the complexity of the evidence, the likelihood that Jesus spoke Greek may have been overstated.

Greco-Roman philosophy

Whether Jesus was influenced by Greco-Roman philosophy has also been contested. Some scholars associated with the Jesus Seminar have compared Jesus to a Cynic philosopher, arguing that Jesus and the Cynics had distinctive characteristics in common, including itinerancy, the use of pointed aphorisms, a rejection of social mores, and a renouncement of material possessions and family ties. The argument has sometimes been framed as one of influence (e.g. Jesus was influenced by Cynics). Indeed, Hengel has demonstrated that the cities of the southern Levant (e.g. Ashkelon, Gadara, Gerasa, Sidon, Tyre) produced several philosophers over the centuries (1974). No evidence for Cynics in first-century CE Palestine, however, has yet been discovered, and cases for a Cynic presence in Galilee have sometimes relied on anachronistic depictions of the overall evidence for Greco-Roman culture in Galilee, with a heavy dependence on post-first-century archaeological finds. More often, arguments about Jesus and Cynics have been stated not in the form of influence but rather as an analogy (e.g. a comparison of Jesus to Cynics illuminates aspects of his ministry, regardless of whether he ever encountered Cynics themselves). Other scholars have questioned the usefulness of both forms of the Cynic thesis, arguing that it de-emphasizes the distinctively Jewish ethos of Jesus' message and ministry.

MARK A. CHANCEY

Further reading

Ball, Warwick. *Rome in the East: The Transformation of an Empire*, London and New York: Routledge, 2000.

Berlin, Andrea M. "Between Large Forces: Palestine in the Hellenistic Period," *BA* 60:1 (1997) 2–57.

Chancey, Mark A. *The Myth of a Gentile Galilee*, Cambridge: Cambridge University Press, 2002.

—— *Greco-Roman Culture and the Galilee of Jesus*, Cambridge: Cambridge University Press, 2005.

Chancey, Mark and Adam Porter. "The Archaeology of Roman Palestine," *Near Eastern Archaeology* 64 (2001) 164–203.

Collins, John J. and Gregory E. Sterling (eds) *Hellenism in the Land of Israel*, Notre Dame, IN: University of Notre Dame Press, 2001.

Crossan, John Dominic and Jonathan L. Reed. *Excavating Jesus: Beneath the Stones, Behind the Texts*, San Francisco, CA: HarperSanFrancisco, 2001.

Fine, Steven. *Art and Judaism in the Greco-Roman World: Toward a New Jewish Archaeology*, Cambridge: Cambridge University Press, 2005.

Gruen, Erich S. *Heritage and Hellenism: The Reinvention of Jewish Tradition*, Berkeley, CA: University of California Press, 1998

Hengel, Martin. *Judaism and Hellenism*, trans. John Bowden, 2 vols, Philadelphia, PA: Fortress Press, 1974.

—— *The 'Hellenization' of Judaea in the First Century after Christ*, trans. John Bowden. London: SCM Press, Philadelphia, PA: Trinity Press International, 1989.

—— "Judaism and Hellenism Revisited," in John J. Collins and Gregory E. Sterling (eds) *Hellenism in the Land of Israel*, Notre Dame, IN: University of Notre Dame Press, 2001, pp. 6–37.

Levine, Lee I. *Judaism and Hellenism in Antiquity: Conflict or Confluence?* Peabody, MA: Hendrickson, 1998.

Millar, Fergus. *The Roman Near East: 31 BC – 337 CE*, Cambridge, MA, and London: Harvard University Press, 1993.

Nagy, Rebecca Martin, Carol L. Meyers, Eric M. Meyers, and Zeev Weiss (eds) *Sepphoris in Galilee: Crosscurrents of Culture*, Winona Lake, IN: Eisenbrauns, 1996.

Richardson, Peter. *Herod: King of the Jews and Friend of the Romans*, Columbia, SC: University of South Carolina Press, 1996.

Roller, Duane W. *The Building Program of Herod the Great*, Berkeley, CA: University of California Press, 1998.

Schäfer, Peter (ed.) *The Talmud Yerushalmi and Graeco-Roman Culture*, Vols 1 and 3, Tübingen: Mohr Siebeck, 1998, 2002.

Schäfer, Peter and Catherine Hezser (eds) *The Talmud Yerushalmi and Graeco-Roman Culture*, Vol. 3, Tübingen: Mohr Siebeck, 2000.

H

HARNACK, ADOLF VON

Carl Gustav Adolf von Harnack was born in 1851 in Germany, in Dorpat (now Tartu in Estonia) in the Russian province of Livonia. He was the second of five children. His father (Theodosius) was professor of theology and homiletics at the Lutheran University there. When Adolf was six years old, his mother (Marie Ewers) died at the age of twenty-nine after the birth of her fifth child. His mother's short life had a profound impact on Adolf; his father sacrificed to raise the family alone until he remarried in 1864, a fact that Adolf never forgot (A. von Zahn-Harnack 11–29).

The young Harnack's spiritual and intellectual foundation for life was laid during this period. He was raised in a deeply pious Lutheran home, which stressed the importance of the mind. He distinguished himself in school, particularly in his secondary education at Dorpat. Shortly before graduation, he wrote to a friend that he was interested in Christianity not just for its claims but for its impact on history; moreover, he believed that the main problems of humanity could be solved by religion – a critically appropriated religion (von Zahn-Harnack 39–40). As Rumscheidt (1989: 11) observes, this letter seems to have charted a course – a lifelong interest in history and Christianity, and a desire to filter its contents through a critical sieve, keeping that which remained while discarding the rest.

This course continued at the University of Dorpat where Harnack began studies in 1869. Moritz von Engelhardt, a professor there who had

a profound spiritual and intellectual influence on Harnack, developed in his avid pupil a strong interest in textual criticism and the importance of studying original sources (von Zahn-Harnack 49, 54–55). In a prize-winning essay on Marcion (Harnack 1990: i), the young Harnack developed a life-long first love for the ancient heretic of the church, who had rejected the Old Testament and reduced the gospel to non-judgmental redeeming love. These two characteristics were to have a profound influence on Harnack's understanding of Christianity.

Harnack pursued graduate studies at the University of Leipzig in 1872 where he managed to earn his doctorate with a provocative thesis entitled, "*Zur Quellenkritik der Geschichte des Gnostizismus*" ("Source Criticism and the History of Gnosticism"). A year later this work became the first of a multitude of publications during his lifetime, amounting to over 1,600 books, monographs, critical editions, essays and reviews (Lotz 198–99).

In 1874 Harnack began to lecture at the university and in 1876 was promoted to professor of church history. He moved to the University of Giessen and taught there from 1879 to 1885. It was during this period that his plans to write a history of Christian dogma began to take shape, eventually to be published as the *Lehrbuch der Dogmengeschichte* (1886–89, *History of Dogma*). Harnack wanted to illuminate dogma with history, essentially to show how an original pristine Christianity, which stressed the Fatherhood of God and the value of the individual soul, had been encrusted with layers of tradition and Greek philosophy ("a Greek spirit on the soil of the Gospel"). Consequently a "fanciful Christ" of the Church's faith had replaced the real Christ of history. The publication of the first volume of this work occurred in 1886 and stirred up a controversy with ecclesiastical authorities. But according to his biographer, Agnes von Zahn-Harnack (143–44), the greatest blow to Harnack was his father's disapproval of the book. Since his son had denied the bodily resurrection of Christ, his father called into question his Christian faith.

Harnack moved to Marburg in 1886 and lectured there for two years before being appointed to the University of Berlin. He taught here for the next thirty-three years, and formally retired in 1921, after which he was emeritus professor until shortly before his death in 1930. These years were obviously the most productive of Harnack's life and he was awarded many national and international honors.

In an important work on canon, *Das Neue Testament um das Jahr 200* (1889, *The Origin of the New Testament*), Harnack argued that the New Testament came into being alongside the Old Testament as a result of responses to the Marcionite and Montanist heresies. The former led to the creation of the canon and the latter inspired its closing. Thus the New Testament was a conscious creation with a deliberate design produced by the Church of Rome around 200 CE.

Controversy continued to follow Harnack. In 1892, seeking to make the Apostles' Creed more palatable to modern thought, he attempted to modify it with the use of historical criticism. At the turn of the millennium his liberal views were widely disseminated when he gave an immensely popular series of lectures on the essential meaning of Christianity, which communicated the relevance of the Christian faith for a new era. The lectures were later published as *Das Wesen des Christentums* (1900, *What is Christianity?*)

The gospel according to Harnack had three basic points: (1) the kingdom of God and its coming; (2) God the Father and the infinite value of the human soul; (3) the higher righteousness and the commandment of love (*What is Christianity?* 51). Consequently the only aim was that each individual find the living God as a personal source of peace and joy (191). This was the gospel stripped down to its essentials. Miracles – unpalatable to the modern mind – were discarded as the relics of a bygone age. Similarly eschatological ideas, judgment, apocalyptic, doctrinal formulations and much Old Testament influence could be eliminated as unnecessary husks encasing the kernel of the gospel:

> The Gospel is not a theoretical system of doctrine or philosophy of the universe; it is doctrine only in so far as it proclaims the reality of God the Father. It is a glad message assuring us of life eternal, and telling us what the things and forces with which we have to do are worth.
>
> (146)

Rather than the Sermon on the Mount being a revolutionary social program, it was simply a message to individuals; the gospel was not really concerned with mundane and material matters but with people's individual souls (116). Even the parables of Jesus with their emphasis on the kingdom became interpreted in a privatized, individualistic way: reading and studying the parables led to the conclusion that

> the kingdom of God comes by coming to the individual, by entering into his soul and laying hold of it. True the kingdom of God is the rule of God; but it is the rule of the holy God in the hearts of individuals; *it is God himself in his power.*
>
> (56)

This was not really Christianity but, as Rumscheidt has observed (1989: 41), an attempt to make Christianity acceptable to the bourgeoisie – *Kulturprotestantismus.*

That Harnack's classic expression of liberal theology was spiritually impotent can be shown by the presence of his signature on the German declaration of war in 1914. This was one of the reasons that led Karl Barth, who studied under Harnack, to rethink Christianity entirely.

After World War I, Harnack returned to his old first love, Marcion, and in *Marcion: Das Evangelium vom fremden Gott* (1921, *Marcion: The Gospel of the Alien God*) tried to show his relevance for understanding the Church. He argued that Marcion's teachings had produced counter reactions in the Church, leading not only to the formation of a New Testament canon but New Testament theology and the importance of soteriology (1990:130–31). He further argued that Marcion's New Testament God of redeeming love, and not wrath and justice, was more relevant than ever. Since the Old Testament was so offensive to modern sensibilities, the Church needed to reject it:

> Those who are most profoundly acquainted with the soul of the people, as that soul resides today in those who hold ecclesiastical Christianity in contempt, assure us that only the proclamation of hopeful, non-judgmental love now has any prospect of being heard.
>
> (1990: 143)

To continue to keep the Old Testament as canon "is the consequence of religious and ecclesiastical paralysis" (1990: 134). Unfortunately this would only contribute to the rising anti-Semitic spirit of the time, which led eventually to the unthinkable horrors of the Holocaust.

Harnack died in 1930, three years before Hitler rose to power. His theology with its stress on the individual's relationship with God and a rejection of the Old Testament helped contribute to the German Church's dismal failure to be a prophetic voice during this turbulent period.

STEPHEN G. DEMPSTER

Further reading

Harnack, A. von *The Origin of the New Testament and the Most Important Consequences of the New Creation*, trans. J. R. Wilkinson, London: Williams and Norgate, 1925.
—— *What is Christianity?* trans. T. Saunders, New York: Harper & Row, 1957.
—— *Marcion: The Gospel of the Alien God*, trans. J. H. Seely and L. D. Bierma, Durham, NC: Labyrinth Press, 1990.
Lotz, D. "Harnack, Adolf von," in M. Eliade (ed.) *Encyclopedia of Religion*, Vol. 6, New York: Macmillan, 1987, pp. 198–99.
Macquarrie, J. "Harnack, Carl Gustav Adolf von," in P. Evans (ed.) *Encyclopedia of Philosophy*, Vol. 3, New York: Macmillan, 1967, pp. 414–15.
Rumscheidt, M. *Adolf von Harnack: Liberal Theology at its Height*, London: Collins, 1989.
Zahn-Harnack, A. von. *Adolf von Harnack*, Berlin: Hans Bott Verlag, 1936.

HEAVEN AND HELL

The Synoptic Gospels record Jesus saying little about "heaven" or "hell" as places of future reward and punishment. Rather, Jesus' eschatology focuses primarily on the resurrection of the dead (see Mark 12:18–27//Matt 22:23–33//Luke 20:27) and the kingdom of God (see Mark. 1:15; 34; 4:11, 26, 30; 9:1, 46; 10:14–15; 23–25), or, as Matthew refers to it, the Kingdom of the heavens (see Matt 3:2; 4:8; 53, 10, 19–20; 6:10, 33; 8:11; 10:7; 11:11–12; 13:11–52; 18:1–4). When heaven is spoken of, it is primarily as the abode of God and angels (Matt 7:11; 18:10; Mark 11:25; Luke 10:20–21; 15:7; 18:22). The one exception is the parable of the Rich Man and Lazarus (Luke 16:19–31), which reflects a conventional understanding of Hades and paradise.

Afterlife in the Hebrew Bible and Judaism

The Hebrew Bible does not know of a personal afterlife. All people, good and bad, descend into the nether world, known as Sheol. It is a place devoid of praise to God (Ps 6:5; Isa 25:18; 38:11) and wisdom (Eccl 9:5, 10). Skepticism about the afterlife is also reflected in Ben Sira. In Hellenistic Judaism (Wis 5:1–5; 9:15) and apocalypticism, however, belief in an afterlife and a judgment of the dead emerged (see Collins: 362–63).

Following the Babylonian Exile, early apocalyptic writings, especially the Book of the Watchers (*1 En.* 1–36); the Parables of Enoch (*1 En.* 37–71), and the Testament of Abraham, provide some of the best examples of belief in both heaven and hell within early Judaism. The Book of the Watchers, in particular, presents a vivid portrayal of both, beginning with a vision of the heavenly throne (*1 En.* 14:1–7), which is followed by an otherworldly journey (*1 En.* 14:8–25:7). In the process, Enoch sees not only the heavenly luminaries and the tree of life (*1 En.* 23–34), but also the punishment of the fallen stars of heaven (*1 En.* 21–22).

Yet, despite reports of otherworldly journeys, in Palestinian Judaism the afterlife would be understood in terms of the resurrection of the dead (see Dan 12:2). This teaching is reflected in the stories of the Eleazar and the seven brothers in 2 Macc 6–7, where resurrected bodies await God's faithful servants. The NT representation of Pharisaic teaching confirms their belief in the resurrection (Acts 23:8). Josephus, however, inaccurately describes the Pharisees as accepting the Platonic concept of the immortality of the soul as he attempted to make Jewish beliefs comprehensible to a Greco-Roman audience (Elledge; see *B.J.* 2.162–63; *Ant.* 18.13–14).

Afterlife in the teachings of Jesus

Jesus' teaching on the afterlife is indebted to the apocalyptic tradition. He likely accepted the reality of rewards and punishments, as well as an interim state, such as that described in 1 En. Jesus' understanding may be summarized by examining the terms he is recorded as using to describe hell, his parable of the Rich Man and Lazarus, and his brief references to the heavenly abode of God and angels.

Hell

In the gospels, Jesus often refers to hell by the term Gehenna, or the Hinnom Valley, the place where Manasseh sacrificed infants to Moloch (2 Chr 33:6). In the first century, it was Jerusalem's garbage dump, notorious for its fires and noxious fumes (see Jeremias 1964a). This local color adds credence to the likelihood that either Jesus or the earliest church employed the term as a designation for the place of torment. As applied to the afterlife, Gehenna is the place where those who disregard Jesus' teachings will be consigned (Matt 5:23, 29).

It is a realm of unquenchable fire, to be avoided at all costs, even at the price of bodily mutilation (Matt 5:29–30; 18:8–9//Mark 9:43–49).

In contrast to Gehenna, Hades had a long history in the Greco-Roman world as the abode of the dead. Yet, in the parable of the Rich Man and Lazarus, Hades is a place of torment and fire (Luke 16:23–24). The rich man is consigned there, but is able to converse with Abraham, despite his inability to cross over to the land of the blessed (Luke 16:26). In short, the parable portrays both Hades and paradise as constituting different portions of the underworld, previously known as Sheol, where the wicked are in torment and the blessed are comforted.

Heaven

In contrast to Hades and Gehenna are paradise and the heavenly home of God. In the parable of the Rich Man and Lazarus, Lazarus receives comfort in the lap of Abraham as contrasted to the rich man's torment. Abraham's role as forerunner into the land of the blessed is documented in the *Apocalypse of Abraham*. In Luke 16:22, 23–31, however, he serves both as the one who comforts Lazarus and the interlocutor with the rich man. The description of the different fates of the two men employed conventional ideas reminiscent of Jewish apocalypticism, an Egyptian story, and the wider Greco-Roman environment (see Hock). Yet, despite the conventionality of the parable, there is no reason to doubt that the basic storyline derives from Jesus. Rather, on the grounds of coherence, it is reasonable that Jesus utilized traditional imagery to warn his listeners about the eternal hazards of neglecting the poor.

Jesus also describes heaven as the realm of God and angels, where the divine throne rests (Matt 5:34; 23:22). It is the place where the Son of man will be seated in glory, and where the disciples will sit on twelve thrones ruling over the tribes of Israel (Matt 19:28). In heaven, angels behold the face of the Father (Matt 18:10), and it is where they rejoice over those who repent (Luke 15:7). It is, ultimately, the place from which the Son of Man will come in glory and judgment (Mark 8:38; 14:62). All of these themes cohere with expectations found in first-century Judaism.

Conclusions

Jesus' conception of the afterlife undoubtedly corresponded to the thought of his age, particularly as represented in apocalyptic literature. While his main focus was on the future resurrection of the dead, it is also likely he spoke occasionally of an intermediate state, although it is unclear whether that state was a part of heaven or of the underworld. Jesus shared the understanding of the Jewish apocalyptic writers, such as the author of *1 En.* 14, who viewed heaven primarily as the abode of God's throne. In the same way, he undoubtedly accepted a belief in a place of torment, symbolized by the fires and stench of the Hinnom Valley.

RUSSELL MORTON

Further reading

Collins, John J. *Seers, Sibyls and Sages in Hellenistic-Roman Judaism*, Boston, MA: Brill, 2001.

Dunn, J. D. G. *Jesus Remembered*, Vol. 2, Christianity in the Making 1, Grand Rapids, MI: Eerdmans, 2003.

Elledge, C. D. *Life After Death in Early Judaism: The Evidence of Josephus*, WUNT 2:208, Tübingen: Mohr Siebeck. 2006.

Fitzmyer, Joseph A. *Luke the Theologian: Aspects of His Teaching*, New York: Paulist Press, 1989.

Himmelfarb, Martha. *Tours of Hell: An Apocalyptic Form in Jewish and Christian Literature*, Philadelphia, PA: University of Pennsylvania Press. 1983.

——— *Ascent to Heaven in Jewish and Christian Apocalypses*, New York: Oxford University Press, 1993.

Hock, Ronald F. "Lazarus and Micyllus: Greco-Roman Backgrounds to Luke 16:19–31," *CBQ* 106 (1987) 447–63.

Hultgren, Arand J. *The Parables of Jesus: A Commentary*, Grand Rapids, MI: Eerdmans, 2002.

Isaac, E. (trans.) "1 (Ethoiopic Apocalypse of) Enoch," in James H. Charlesworth (ed.) *The Old Testament Pseudepigrapha*, Vol. 1, Garden City, NY: Doubleday, 1983, pp. 5–89.

Jeremias, Joachim. "ᾅδης," in Gerhard Kittel (ed.) *Theological Dictionary of the New Testament*, Vol. 1, trans. Geoffrey W. Bromiley, Grand Rapids, MI: Eerdmans, 1964a, pp. 148–49.

———"γέεννα," in Gerhard Kittel (ed.) *Theological Dictionary of the New Testament*, Vol. 1, trans. Geoffrey W. Bromiley, Grand Rapids, MI: Eerdmans, 1964b, pp. 657–58.

Rowland, Christopher. *The Open Heaven: A Study of Apocalyptic in Judaism and Early Christianity*, New York: Crossroad, 1982.

Traub, Hellmut and Gerhard von Rad. "οὐρανός, κτλ.," in Gerhard Kittel (ed.) *Theological Dictionary of the New Testament*, Vol. 5, trans. Geoffrey W. Bromiley, Grand Rapids, MI: Eerdman, 1967, pp. 497–543.

Wright, N. T. *The Resurrection of the Son of God*, Christian Origins and the Question of God 3, Minneapolis, MN: Fortress Press, 2003.

HEROD ANTIPAS

The well-known king Herod the Great ruled as king of the Jews from 37 to 4 BC. Of his ten wives, Malthace, a Samaritan, gave birth to Archelaus, ethnarch of Samaria, Judea, and Idumea (4 BC–AD 6) and Herod Antipas, tetrarch of Galilee and Perea

(4 BC-AD 39). The latter figures more prominently in the Bible than the other Herods because his territories were those in which John the Baptist and Jesus conducted most of their ministries.

Antipas' early life

Herod Antipas was born in approximately 20 BC. It is probable that he followed the path of his brothers by going to Rome for his education, gaining knowledge of Hellenism and Roman politics, after which he returned to Israel shortly before his father's death in 4 BC.

Antipas' realm

After some debate over Herod the Great's will it was decided that Herod Antipas would rule as tetrarch over Galilee and Perea. Upon assuming this role he restored order and rebuilt that which had been destroyed by a revolt at the feast of Pentecost in 4 BC while the brothers were in Rome disputing Herod the Great's will.

Following in the footsteps of his father, Antipas founded cities. Around AD 8–10 he rebuilt Sepphoris and made it his capital city until he built Tiberias. Joseph, Mary's husband, living only 6.4 km (4 miles) SSW of Sepphoris, may have used his carpentry skills to help with this effort (Matt 13:55; Mark 6:3). In Perea, Antipas rebuilt a second city called Livias (or Julias) in honor of Augustus' wife Livia, completing it around AD 13 (Josephus *Ant.* 18.2.1:27). Although the Herodian family built a total of twelve cities, Tiberias was the first city in Jewish history to be founded following the municipal model of the Greek *polis*. Antipas had difficulty in populating this newly founded city because while building they struck a cemetery which the Jews considered an unclean area. He enticed them to move there by offering them free houses and lands as well as exemption from taxes for the first few years. The city, named in honor of Emperor Tiberius, was completed around AD 25 and served as his capital (Josephus *Ant.* 18.2.3:36–38).

Antipas' reign

Antipas and Archelaus

An important event early in Antipas' rule occurred in AD 6 when a delegation of Jews and Samaritans, his brother Philip the tetrarch (over Gaulanitis, Auranitis, Batanea, Trachonitis, Paneas, and Iturea), and he went to Rome to bring about the downfall of his brother Archelaus (Josephus *Ant.* 17.13.2:342). Although Antipas did not gain Archelaus' territory, nor the coveted title *king,* he did gain the dynastic title *Herod* (cf. Josephus *J. W.* 2.9.1:167; *Ant.* 18.2.1:27) which was of significance to his subjects and to the political and social circles of the Roman world.

Antipas and John the Baptist

Herod Antipas is most known for his imprisonment and beheading of John the Baptist (Matt 14:3–12; Mark 6:17–29; Luke 3:19–20; Josephus *Ant.* 18.5.2:116–19). He had been married to the daughter of the Nabatean king Aretas IV. This probably had been arranged by Augustus, who was known for instigating marriages between various rulers for the sake of peace in the empire. In this instance, it would have had the potential for peace between the Jews and the Arabs. Further, Aretas' territory served as a buffer between Rome and Parthia. This arranged marriage must have occurred before Augustus' death in AD 14. When Antipas traveled to Rome c. AD 29, he visited his brother Herod (Philip) who apparently lived in one of the coastal cities of Israel. While there he fell in love with Herodias, his brother's wife, as well as his own niece. She agreed to marry Antipas when he returned from Rome provided that he divorce his wife (Josephus *Ant.* 18.5.1:109–10). When Antipas' first wife learned of the plan she fled to her father, Aretas IV. The resulting divorce was not only a personal insult but also the breach of a political alliance and eventually resulted in retaliation against Antipas.

After Antipas married Herodias, he incarcerated John the Baptist for boldly criticizing him for marrying his brother's wife. The Mosaic Law prohibited this with the exception of a levirate marriage (Lev 18:16; 20:21) which was for the purpose of producing children for a deceased childless brother (Deut 25:5; Mark 12:19). However, Antipas' brother had a child by Herodias named Salome and, even more blatantly, Antipas' brother was still alive.

The identification of Herodias' first husband is problematic, for the gospels name him Philip (Matt 14:3; Mark 6:17) whereas Josephus lists him as Herod, the son of Herod the Great and Mariamne II, daughter of Simon the high priest (Josephus *Ant.* 18.5.1:109). Since the Herodian family is hopelessly confusing, many think that the gospel writers had confused this Herod with Philip the tetrarch, who later married Herodias' daughter, Salome. However plausible this may seem at first sight, it is indefensible for several reasons.

First, the gospels would be guilty of three historical errors, namely, (1) confusing this Herod with his half-brother Philip the tetrarch; (2) making Philip the tetrarch the husband of Herodias instead of the husband of her daughter Salome; and (3) making Salome the daughter of Philip the tetrarch who, according to Josephus, was childless. These errors would seem to be incredible in light of the Evangelists' familiarity with historical details. Furthermore, the early Christian community included people like Joanna, wife of Chuza, Antipas' financial minister (Luke 8:3), and Manaen, a close friend of Antipas (Acts 13:1), who would have known such details and could have prevented such historical blunders.

Second, the gospels speak of a daughter born to Herodias before she was married to Antipas (Matt 14:6, 8–11; Mark 6:22, 24–26, 28) which harmonizes precisely with Josephus' reference to Herod having a daughter named Salome (Josephus *Ant.* 18.5.4:136). There are too many factors involved for this to be mere coincidence and consequently it is improbable that the Evangelists confused the Philips.

Third, the argument by some that Herod the Great would not have had two sons with the same name is untenable, because although the two sons had the same father they had different mothers. Furthermore, Herod the Great had two sons named Antipas/Antipater and two sons named Herod, all of whom had different mothers.

Fourth, it is very likely that Herodias' first husband was called both Herod and Philip or Herod Philip. Although some argue that double names were not in use at that time, no one disputes that the Herod of Acts 12:1, 6, 11, 19–21 is the Agrippa of Josephus. Certainly double names were used of emperors like Caesar Augustus.

Fifth, if the Evangelists intended that Herodias' former husband was actually Philip the tetrarch, why did they not call him by that title as they did Herod Antipas (Matt 14:1)?

Sixth, it must be remembered that a name is only a means of identification. Josephus called him by his family name (Josephus *J.W.* 1.28.4:562; *Ant.* 18.5.4:136) but the biblical narratives may have designated him Philip (Matt 14:3; Mark 6:17) because in Galilee he may have been known by that name rather than the dynastic title "Herod" used first by Archelaus (Dio Cassius 55.27.6; as seen on coins, see Madden 91–95) and later by Antipas (Josephus *J.W.* 2.9.1:167; Matt 14:1, 3, 6; Mark 6:14, 16, 17, 18, 20, 21, 22; Luke 3:1, 19; 9:7, 9; 13:31; 23:7, 8, 11, 12, 15; Acts 4:27; 13:1). Thus, it seems that Josephus called

him by his family name or dynastic title while the Evangelists called him by his proper name or the name known in Galilee. Consequently, it can be concluded that the different accounts are speaking of one and the same person.

In conclusion, it seems most reasonable to consider that Philip in the gospels and the Herod in Josephus are the same person. To suggest otherwise would be to create inextricable confusion.

John the Baptist's imprisonment was not enough for Herodias. At an appropriate time, most likely Antipas' birthday party at Machaerus in Perea, Herodias arranged for the elimination of John. There her daughter danced before the dignitaries who served Antipas. Overwhelmed by her dance, he promised under oath to give her anything up to half of his kingdom. Advised by her mother, Salome asked for John the Baptist's head on a platter. Although Antipas regretted making such a promise, he had to fulfill the oath because it had been witnessed by the presence of his guests. John was beheaded c. AD 31 or 32.

Antipas and Jesus

Herod Antipas' relationship to Jesus is seen in three episodes. The first is when Antipas heard of Jesus' ministry and ironically thought that John the Baptist had been resurrected (Matt 14:1–2; Mark 6:14–16; Luke 9:7–9). In such circumstances he urgently wanted to see Jesus, but Jesus withdrew from his territories. Antipas, for fear that he might once again anger his people, did not force the issue.

The second episode was Jesus' final journey to Jerusalem. He had been warned by some of the Pharisees that he should leave Antipas' territories because Antipas wanted to kill him (Luke 13:31–33). Jesus replied "Go tell that fox" that he would continue casting out demons and healing in his domain for a short time. Furthermore, Jesus stated that he was not destined to be killed in Antipas' territories but in Jerusalem, where other prophets had been killed. The cowardly fox could not influence the Lion of Judah!

The third episode was during Jesus' trial by Antipas in AD 33 (Luke 23:6–12). Since this incident is not mentioned in the other gospels, some think it is legendary. However, Luke had a keen interest in the Herods and since Theophilus, the recipient of his letter (Luke 1:3; Acts 1:1), was probably a Roman official, it would be understandable for Luke to include this pericope showing the relationship between the Herods and the prefects of Judea and in particular the reconciliation between Antipas and Pilate (Luke 23:12). Since the incident results in no progress in the trial it is readily understood why the other gospel writers omitted it. Some suggest that the source for this story is in Acts 4:25–26 (which quotes Ps 2:1–2) but, when one examines the data, it seems that the opposite is true. Others think that the origin of this pericope was the *Gospel of Peter* but upon close examination it provides no real parallel with Luke's account of Antipas' trial of Jesus. In fact, the *Gospel of Peter* makes Antipas responsible for Jesus' death, whereas there is nothing of this in Luke.

To further elaborate on this event, Pilate, upon learning that Jesus was from Antipas' domain of Galilee, sent Jesus to Antipas, who was in Jerusalem for the Passover. According to Roman law Pilate was not obligated to do this. However, he was anxious to extricate himself from an awkward situation. Whereas the Jews were insisting on crucifying Jesus, Pilate felt that he was innocent. Furthermore, it was a ploy to improve his relationship with Antipas which had been strained on the occasion of the Galilean massacre (Luke 13:1) and also because Antipas (along with three others among the Herods) had reported to Tiberius the stir Pilate had caused among the Jews when he brought votive shields into Jerusalem. In the latter case, Tiberius had ordered Pilate to remove them immediately (Philo, *Legat.* 299–304). This incident probably occurred at the Feast of Tabernacles, October AD 32. Therefore, Pilate did not want to make another wrong move causing Antipas to report him again to Tiberius. Although the center of controversy among the Jews, Jesus was neutral ground as far as Pilate's and Antipas' relationship with each other was concerned. Hence, rather than taking a course of action which might again align Antipas and the Jews, Pilate wisely had handed Jesus over to Antipas, possibly hoping that Antipas would make a wrong move against either the Roman government or the Jews, or both. Antipas accepted the courtesy gesture but wisely chose not to presume on it and put himself in a precarious position. Therefore, after mocking Jesus, he sent him back to Pilate without comment, consequently effecting reconciliation between the two leaders from that day forward (Luke 23:12). As mentioned above, some scholars think this pericope is legendary, in part because there is no progress in the trial. However, understanding the historical situation, one sees that while there was no progress in the trial of Jesus there was progress in the reconciliation of the two leaders who had the potential to destroy one another.

Antipas and exile

In AD 36 Aretas attacked and defeated Antipas to avenge Antipas' abandonment of his daughter for Herodias. The Jews saw his defeat as a divine retribution for his killing of John the Baptist (Josephus *Ant.* 18.5.1 2:116–19). Tiberius did order Vitellius, governor of Syria, to help Antipas against Aretas, but before this could be accomplished, Tiberius died (16 March 37), and Vitellius withheld his aid until he received orders from the new emperor, Caligula (Josephus *Ant.* 18.5.3:120–24).

Upon his accession, Caligula gave his friend Agrippa I, brother of Herodias, the land of Philip the tetrarch as well as the tetrarchy of Lysanius, with the title *king* (Josephus *Ant.* 18.6.10:225–39). Later (*c.* August of 38) Agrippa went to Israel to see his acquisition. Upon his appearance in the land, his sister Herodias became intensely jealous because he had obtained the much coveted title *king*, which her husband had failed to obtain although he had ruled well and faithfully since 4 BC. As a result she convinced Antipas to go to Rome to seek the same title. Finally, in AD 39 Antipas and Herodias went to Rome, but meanwhile Agrippa dispatched one of his freedmen to Rome to bring accusations against Antipas. This resulted in Antipas' and Herodias' exile to Lugdunum Convenarum, now Saint-Bertrand de Comminges, in the foothills of the Pyrenees in southern France. Although Caligula discovered that Herodias was the sister of Agrippa I and excused her from the exile, she chose to follow her husband. As a result, Agrippa I gained Antipas' territories of Galilee and Perea (Josephus *Ant.* 18.7.1–2:240–55; *J.W.* 2.9.6:181–83).

HAROLD W. HOEHNER

Further reading

Bruce, F. F. "Herod Antipas, Tetrarch of Galilee and Peraea," *ALUOS* 5 (1963–65) 6–23.
Harlow, Victor E. *The Destroyer of Jesus: The Story of Herod Antipas, Tetrarch of Galilee*, Oklahoma City, OK: Modern Publishers, 1953.
Hoehner, Harold W. "Herod Antipas," in Matthew Black (ed.) *SNTSMS*, Vol. 17, Cambridge: Cambridge University Press, 1972; reprint, Grand Rapids, MI: Zondervan, 1980.
Jensen, Morten Hørning. *Herod Antipas in Galilee: The Literary and Archaeological Sources on the Reign of Herod Antipas and Its Socio-Economic Impact on Galilee*, WUNT, ed. Jörg Frey, Vol. 215, Tübingen: Mohr Siebeck, 2006.
Jones, A. H. M. *The Herods of Judaea*, Oxford: Clarendon Press, 1938.
Josephus. *Works*, trans. H. St J. Thackeray, Ralph Marcus, Allen Wikgren, and Louis H. Feldman, 9 vols, LCL,

Cambridge, MA: Harvard University Press; London: William Heinemann, 1926–65.

Madden, Frederic W. *History of Jewish Coinage and of Money in the Old and New Testament*, New York: Ktav, 1967.

Parker, Pierson. "Herod Antipas and the Death of Jesus," in E. P. Sanders (ed.) *Jesus, the Gospels, and the Church. Essays in Honor of William R. Farmer*, Macon, GA: Mercer University Press, 1987, pp. 197–208.

Perowne, Stewart. *The Later Herods: The Political Background of the New Testament*, London: Hodder and Stoughton, 1958.

Richardson, Peter. *Herod: King of the Jews and Friend of the Romans. Studies on Personalities of the New Testament*, ed. D. Moody Smith, Columbia, SC: University of South Carolina Press, 1996.

Schofield, Guy. *The Crime before Calvary: Herodias, Herod Antipas, and Pontius Pilate: A New Interpretation*, London: George G. Harrap, 1960.

Schürer, Emil. *The History of the Jewish People in the Age of Jesus Christ (175 BC AD 135)*, trans. Paul Winter, ed. and revised as a new English version Geza Vermes, Fergus Millar, and Matthew Black, Edinburgh: T. & T. Clark, 1973, Vol. 1, pp. 340–53.

HISTORICAL CRITICISM (OR GOSPELS AS SOURCES)

Matthew, Mark, and Luke are the three so-called *Synoptic Gospels* because they have close parallels in wording and in structure. The fourth canonical gospel, the *Gospel of John*, differs significantly in its portrait of Jesus, although it also tells the story of Jesus from his encounter with John the Baptist up to Jesus' death and resurrection. The differences between all of the canonical gospels, especially between the Synoptics and the Gospel of John, have been observed since the early church. Nevertheless, they have been accepted almost without question because of their assumed apostolic authorship (cf. Merkel).

The importance of historical criticism of the gospels lies in the meaning of these writings as sources for the teaching and the activity of Jesus. Their significance as sources is attributed to their origin and to their age. This was especially believed to be so in the observation of overlaps and parallels between the Synoptic writings. These observations advanced discussion concerning the authenticity of the Gospels as apostolic writings.

History

At the beginning the term "gospel" referred to oral proclamation of Jesus as God's son and as Christ who died for the people and rose from the dead (cf., e.g., Rom 1:3–4; 1 Cor 15:2–4). Later on, written documents collecting words and narratives about Jesus came into being and some of them narrated a story that contains something like a life of Jesus, mainly focusing on his proclamation, his miracles, and his death in more or less chronological order. Other texts also called "gospel" were produced in a narrative form, and still others in a form of sayings, collections or dialogue texts (cf., e.g., the presentation of Koester). In a much debated process of canonization (cf., e.g., Metzger; Lips) only four narrative gospels attributed to apostles or their disciples and therefore based on an assumed knowledge of eye-witnesses received a canonical acceptance and became part of the Christian New Testament canon: Matthew, Mark, Luke, and John.

At the risk of simplification, one can say that historical criticism of the gospels started as soon as more than one gospel became available to Christian communities. The number and differences between the gospels were positively explained by reference to their assumed apostolic authorship. According to Irenaeus there are four gospels just as there are four directions of the wind (*Haer.* 3.11.8) and the different gospels resemble the character of their different authors (*Haer.* 3.1.1 = Euseb., *Hist. eccl.* 5.8.4; for more information on the discussion and use of the four Gospels in the early church, see, e.g., Heckel: 266–355). The Gospel of John received critical scrutiny due to its special character and due to its early use in Gnostics groups (see, e.g., Nagel); the group of so-called *alogi* ("those who refuse the Logos") doubted the apostolic character of John (Epiphanius, *Panarion* 51–52; cf., e.g., Streeter: 436–42), but the early objection against John did not succeed. As not becoming part of the canonical collection and because of the relatively late finding of some of the extra-canonical gospel texts (although some of them are mentioned by church fathers and fragments who quoted some of these texts, many of the texts in debate became accessible in the middle of the twentieth century), the canonical gospels played a more important role as sources for the quest of Jesus in research. Early on the canonical gospels were harmonized, blending together the different versions of Jesus' deeds and words, thereby establishing the genre of "Gospel harmonies" (starting with Justin Martyr's *Harmony* and his pupil Tatian's *Diatessaron*; cf. Wünsch), later followed by critical use of mainly the Synoptic Gospels and their sources as the basis for reconstructing a life of Jesus and his proclamation.

The meaning of the gospels *as* sources lies in their supposed origin and age. That importance was called into question when a discussion on their authenticity as apostolic writings started. During the Enlightenment and the critical investigations thereafter they lost authority as sources for a reconstruction of the life of Jesus, because their apostolic authorship was called into question and accordingly their value as memories of eye-witnesses (for an overview cf. Kloppenborg Verbin 271–328). On the one hand, conservative exegetes tried to defend apostolic authorship and therefore eye-witness testimony. Defending the apostolic authorship of the gospels and their literary integrity sometimes was little more than part of a dogmatic approach intended to save the reliability of knowledge about Jesus. On the other hand, a search for older and more reliable sources began, supported by historical positivism supposing that the most original sources represented the historical events as they really happened. The research for the oldest tradition behind the gospels was also led by the interest in obtaining the most original information about Jesus by any reconstructed source. The literary parallels between the Synoptic Gospels led into research for their literary interrelation. Starting with the philological approach of humanism and questioning the medieval dogma of the inspiration of scripture, a more critical research focusing on the literary relationship of the gospels to each other emerged.

Four main approaches need to be introduced here: (1) the *UrGospel Hypothesis* (*Urevangeliumshypothese*) that relates the parallels of the Synoptic Gospels to a common Hebrew or Aramaic document that narrates the life of Jesus used by all of them (e.g. Johann Gottfried Eichhorn [1752–1827] 1820: 161–67; Gotthold Ephraim Lessing [1729–1784] 1778); (2) *Tradition Hypothesis* (*Traditionshypothese*): the parallels between the gospels are explained by reference to common *oral* gospel (e.g. Johann Gottfried Herder [1744–1803] 1797: 303–22; Johann Carl Ludwig Gieseler [1792–1854] 1818); (3) different documents that may be ascribed to eye-witnesses as sources for the Synoptic Gospels are assumed in a so-called *Fragment Theory* (*Fragmentenhypothese*) as proposed by Friedrich Schleiermacher ([1768–1834] 1817); (4) most influential until recent discussion have been the different kinds of *utilization theories* (*Benutzungshypothese*), assuming that the Synoptic authors used the other Synoptic Gospel(s) as their sources sometimes combined with another source. Of some importance are the following:

(a) The Augustinian model assumed a usage of a Gospel by the subsequent one in accordance with the canonical sequence: Matthew is used by Mark, and Luke was aware of Matthew and Mark in writing his Gospel (revised by, e.g., Butler; Wenham).

(b) Connected with the name of Johann Jakob Griesbach is the theory that Matthew is used by Luke and that Matthew and Luke are epitomized by Mark. This theory was named the Griesbach Hypothesis or the Two-Gospel Hypothesis.

(c) A major and most important step in discussion of the literary dependence of the Synoptic Gospels is the proposal to take the shortest text as point of departure: Mark. Mark as the earliest Gospel was interpreted as the source for Matthew and Luke (arguing against the Griesbach Hypothesis: Karl Konrad Friedrich Wilhelm Lachmann [1793–1851] 1835 and Christian Gottlob Wilke [1786–1854] 1838). The parallels in wording and partly in structure between Matthew and Luke brought the suggestion that both authors used another written source, later called "Q" (on the abbreviation, see Neirynck 683–90). The basic foundation of the so-called Two-Document Hypothesis was laid by Christian Hermann Weisse ([1801–66] 1838), by Heinrich Julius Holtzmann (1863) and later by Paul Wernle (1899; see also Schmid 1930). The Two-Document Hypothesis became most influential and seems to be the best tool to explain parallels and differences between the Synoptic Gospels, even if the thesis is not universally accepted.

Recent discussion

Securing reliable information about Jesus remains a task of modern gospel criticism. The situation has changed insofar as other early written sources and/or (oral) Jesus traditions were taken into consideration, including a more severe historical evaluation of the Gospel of John as well. Moreover, critical hermeneutical discussions have referred to the limits of historical knowledge. The discussion about the literary relationship within the Synoptic Gospels is still alive, too. Three source-critical models to explain the relationship are most popular: the Neo-Griesbach/Two-Gospel Hypothesis, the Farrer–Goulder Hypothesis, and the Two-Document Hypothesis.

(a) The Farrer–Goulder Hypothesis, named after Austin Farrer and Michael Goulder, is the most rejected hypothesis, mainly used in Great Britain (cf., e.g., Goodacre). This approach defends the hypothesis that Luke used both Mark and Matthew as his sources and that Matthew used only Mark as source and not Q; this is the reason why John Kloppenborg calls this hypothesis the "Mark-without-Q Hypothesis" (213), which is misleading and takes the Two-Document Hypothesis as foil for the naming. According to Goulder, Matthew reworked Mark as a lectionary book for community's purposes and thus *created* the non-Markan material.

(b) Since the publication of Farmer's *The Synoptic Problem* (1964), the Two-Gospel Hypothesis has been improved by analytical case studies that try to clarify the outline of Mark's use of his sources, Matthew, and Luke. This approach receives some support and acceptance mainly in North America and Great Britain (cf., e.g., Dungan, Longstaff, Orchard, Peabody). One of the most substantial problems of the Two-Gospel Hypothesis is still the technique of conflation applied by Mark; Mark needs to change from the usage of one source to the other, even within one pericope (an important critique of Mark's conflation is made by Tuckett 1983: 41–51) and although Mark's approach is to shorten his sources he sometimes presents material from both sources, even if they are in conflict with one another. Derrenbacker has clearly shown that such a composition technique is unparalleled within ancient use of sources that normally followed the wording of one source at a time (2005: 156–62).

(c) The *Two-Document Hypothesis* is the most frequently used theory to explain the relationship of the Synoptic Gospels. However, there are some aspects that may require additional explanations. Most prominent is the problem of the so-called "minor agreements" (cf., e.g., Strecker 1993; outline of the texts: Neirynck 1991). "Minor agreements" are those verbal agreements between the Gospel of Matthew and the Gospel of Luke that appear within contexts where Mark is used as source. Some scholars explain these agreements as independent redaction work (Neirynck 1991) or with the theory of Deutero-Mark, a revised version of canonical Mark, used by Matthew and Luke (e.g. Ennulat 1994). There are also surprising differences in those passages mostly taken from the supposed source Q; see, e.g., the Sermon on the Mount (Matt 5:3–7:27)/Plain (Luke 6:20b–49). Some scholars explain these differences by assuming different versions of Q used by Matthew and Luke (see, e.g., Sato 47–62; Luz; Schnelle 227; for the sermon on the Mount/Plain, see Betz, who assumed that the different versions of Q incorporated these different texts of the sermon). Such an idea is accordance with ancient writing techniques but, of course, it adds another hypothesis to a still debated theory.

In any event, within this theory Mark and Q and the special material used by Matthew and Luke are regarded as those texts that provide information for the reconstruction of the life of Jesus (cf., e.g., Meier 41–44; see also Dunn 143–61).

(d) New and recent models: the problem of the literary relationship of the Synoptic Gospels is still debated, and that reminds us that we are simply dealing with theories that heuristically explain observations on texts and need further to be discussed, although to my judgment the Two-Document Hypothesis is that theory which best explains most of the textual observations. Among those scholars who try to refine the answers for the synoptic problems and therefore also for the problem of the sources for a reconstruction of the life of Jesus, Martin Hengel is a prominent exegete. He accepts the priority of Mark but allows a use of Mark *and* Matthew by Luke (174). According to Hengel, Q is not an entire written source document, but contains different sources (177–78) so that Q might be taken more as a traditional layer than a source (e.g. Schröter 2003: 38; Pearson 2004) or its use interpreted under influence of oral tradition (Dunn 224–38). The theory of the priority of Mark is revised by Albert Fuchs and his disciples. He tries to explain the minor agreements between Matthew and Luke by accepting Deutero-Mark with such an extended text that the hypothesis of Q becomes superfluous; Fuchs accepts three stages of development: Mark; Deutero-Mark, Matthew, and Luke.

(e) The question of the gospels and their sources as base for a reconstruction of the life and teaching of Jesus became a much broader-based approach in recent research. The Gospel of John as well as its traditions and extra-canonical gospel texts were recognized as possible sources that may contain reliable information mainly to reconstruct the teaching of Jesus (see, e.g., Crossan).

Generally speaking, Friedrich Schleiermacher was the main example within scholarship who took the Gospel of John as a source for reconstructing the life of Jesus (1845: 315–16, 340). Already Clement of Alexandria called John a spiritual gospel, whereas the synoptics were more concerned with the earthly presence of Jesus (Eusebius, *Hist. eccl.* 6.14.7). That view is upheld and the Fourth Gospel is recognized as a witness for a more developed kind of early-Christian high Christology. Although the Gospel of John itself became part of source criticism, any attempt to reconstruct a pre-gospel source to obtain reliable information to reconstruct a life of Jesus was a mere exception (see, however, Wendt 1900, 1901). There is some change in recent research. Some scholars try to reconstruct a *Grundschrift* ("foundational writing") that is as early as the Gospel of Mark (Anderson 2001) or estimate that John is used by Luke (e.g. Matson; Shellard). From such theories, the historical question arose anew (e.g. Anderson 185). Nevertheless, such overall source theories are highly hypothetical and in recent Johannine scholarship there is more emphasis on reading the Gospel of John as a literary entity, with the possible exception of John 21 (cf., e.g., the reviews by Scholtissek 1998, 2001). Some information, provided by the Fourth Evangelist, was discussed in historical terms, especially the length of Jesus' mission including the number of his stays in Jerusalem and the date of his crucifixion, so that some more readiness could be observed to use single-sayings traditions or narrative traditions for getting access to information about historical Jesus (e.g. Moloney; see Smith 1993 on method). Nevertheless, John will only play a limited role in reconstructing historical Jesus, especially with regard to the still debated question concerning how John relates to the synoptics (cf., e.g., Neirynck 1977, 1992; Smith 2001; Labahn and Lang). If one or more synoptics have to be regarded as a direct literary source or an indirect, orally transmitted one (cf. the theory of *secondary orality*; cf. Labahn 1999: 195ff.; 2006: 141–42), only a little material may be detected that should be discussed for providing historical information. However, as a creative interpreter of Jesus tradition and in his christologically elaborated story, the fourth Evangelist preserves historical *memories* of Jesus: e.g. his openness to women (cf. John 4).

Already at the end of the nineteenth century scholars had become more seriously aware of Jesus traditions outside the canonical gospels. Focus was first directed to the so-called *agrapha* (the "unwritten" words) of Jesus that were collected and viewed as a possible sources for Jesus' teaching. The findings of papyri of extra-canonical gospel texts (e.g. P. Egerton 2, P.Oxy. 1, 654, 655, and the texts from the Nag Hammadi Library) led to a growing interest in these texts and their meaning for the reconstruction of historical Jesus. Again this interest was accompanied by literary-historical reconstructions of hypothetically older traditions that might even be older than Q or Mark itself. A masterful overview of such texts is given by Koester (1990), although his confidence in his literary method, in the age of texts and reconstructed sources, and in the meaning of that material compared to the synoptics has been debated for good reasons. One now must reckon with the probability that Morton Smith's *Secret Gospel of Mark* (which Koester takes seriously) is a hoax. As a most recent example of a new discovery, one may refer to the Gospel of Judas. Its editors think this new gospel may provide new understanding of historical Jesus and his disciple Judas Iscariot (Kasser *et al.*). However, this gospel does not really contain any dramatic new information about Jesus but rather the memory of Jesus advanced by a second-century Gnostic sect (see, e.g. Robinson 183). Agrapha and extra-canonical texts have to be considered and discussed in understanding the historical Jesus. The *Gospel of Thomas* is especially useful when taken into consideration, not as a more valuable tradition about Jesus compared to the Synoptic Gospels, but in dialogue with the canonical texts and their different portraits of Jesus.

Assessment

The third quest for the historical Jesus, although by no means a uniform enterprise, uses the Synoptic Gospels and their portraits of Jesus with more confidence as sources for historical reconstructions than in the critical approach of the early twentieth century. The Gospel of John and non-canonical texts are also considered and evaluated, sometimes with more confidence in historical reliability compared to the Synoptics.

However, since Albert Schweitzer's summary of life of Jesus research, it needs to be remembered that every retelling of the life of Jesus in modern times remains an individual concern of each exegete formed by one's own presuppositions (see Gadamer 1975). Not only modern historians but also the old narrators of Jesus in the canonical and non-canonical gospel texts present a construction of past events (cf., e.g., Schröter 2002) that is formed by their actual beliefs and aims at a better understanding of their presence and their future. Historical positivism in reconstructing history is no longer possible. However, the words and deeds of Jesus deeply impressed his followers and were seriously imprinted in their memories, so that they were present in their retelling of Jesus' teaching and his deeds. Therefore, the answer to historical positivism is not agnosticism, but serious reading of the different sources in dialogue with critical scholarship alongside methodological awareness of the constructive character of historical investigation. Such an approach leads to responsibility constructed ideas about the life and teaching of Jesus, based on the memory about Jesus, mainly but not exclusively presented in the Synoptic Gospels.

MICHAEL LABAHN

Further reading

On historical criticism (or gospels as sources)

Anderson, Paul N. "John and Mark: The Bi-Optic Gospels," in Robert T. Fortna and Tom Thatcher (eds) *Jesus in Johannine Tradition*, Louisville, KY: Westminster John Knox Press, 2001, pp. 175–88.

Betz, Hans Dieter. *The Sermon on the Mount: A Commentary on the Sermon on the Mount, including the Sermon on the Plain (Matthew 5:3–7:27 and Luke 6:20–49)*, Hermeneia, Minneapolis, MN: Fortress Press, 1995.

Butler, Basil C. *The Originality of St Matthew: A Critique of the Two-Document Hypothesis*, Cambridge: Cambridge University Press, 1951.

Crossan, John D. *The Historical Jesus. The Life of a Mediterranean Jewish Peasant*, San Francisco, CA: HarperCollins, 1992.

Darrenbacker, R. A. *Ancient Compositional Practises and the Synoptic Problem*, BETL 186; Leuven: Leuven University Press, 2005.

Dunn, James D. G. *Jesus Remembered*, Christianity in the Making 1, Grand Rapids, MI and Cambridge: Eerdmans, 2003.

Eichhorn, Johann Gottfried. *Einleitung in das Neue Testament*, Vol. I, second edition, Leipzig: Weidmann, 1820.

Ennulat, Andreas. *Die "minor agreements": Untersuchungen zu einer offenen Frage des synoptischen Problems*, WUNT II/62, Tübingen: Mohr Siebeck, 1994.

Farmer, William R. *The Synoptic Problem: A Critical Analysis*, New York: Macmillan, 1964.

—— "The Two-Gospel Hypothesis. The Statement of the Hypothesis," in David L. Dungan (ed.) *The Interrelations of the Gospels*, BETL 95, Leuven: Peeters, 1990, pp. 125–56.

Farrer, Austin M. "On Dispensing with Q," in Dennis E. Nineham (ed.) *Studies in the Gospels: Essays in the Memory of R. H. Lightfoot*, Oxford: Basil Blackwell, 1955, pp. 55–88.

Fuchs, Albert. *Spuren von Deuteromarkus*, 4 vols, SNTU. NF 1–4, Münster: LIT Verlag, 2004.

Gadamer, Hans-Georg. *Truth and Method*, New York: Continuum, 1975.

Gieseler, Johann Carl Ludwig. *Historisch-kritischer Versuch über die Entstehung und die frühesten Schicksale der schriftlichen Evangelien*, Leipzig: Engelmann, 1818.

Goodacre, Mark S. *Goulder and the Gospels. An Examination of a New Paradigm*, JSNTSup 133, Sheffield: JSOT Press, 1996.

—— *The Case Against Q. Studies in Markan Priority and the Synoptic Problem*, Harrisburg, PA: Trinity Press International, 2002.

Goodacre, Mark S. and Nicholas Perrin (eds) *Questioning Q: A Multidimensional Critique*, Downers Grove, IL: InterVarsity Press, 2004.

Goulder, Michael D. *Midrash and Lection in Matthew*, The Speaker's Lectures in Biblical Studies 1969–71, London: SPCK, 1974.

—— *Luke: A New Paradigm*, 2 vols, JSNTSup 20, Sheffield: JSOT Press, 1989.

—— "Sections and Lections in Matthew," *JSNT* 76 (1999) 79–96.

Griesbach, Johan Jakob, *Commentatio qua Marci Evangelium totum e Matthaei et Lucae commentariis deceptum esse monstratur I–II*, Jena: J. C. G. Goepferdt, 1789–90; reprinted in *Opuscula academica* [ed. Johann Philipp Gabler; vol. II; Jena: Frommann, 1825], pp. 358–425); ET by Bernard Orchard, "A Demonstration that Mark was Written after Matthew and Luke," in B. Orchard and T. R. W. Longstaff (eds) *Synoptic and Text-Critical Studies 1776–1976*, SNTSMS 34, Cambridge: Cambridge University Press, 1978, pp. 103–35.

Hawkins, John C. *Horae Synopticae – Contributions to the Study of the Synoptic Problem*, Oxford: Clarendon Press, 1899.

Heckel, Theo K. *Vom Evangelium des Markus zum viergestaltigen Evangelium*, WUNT 120; Tübingen: Mohr Siebeck, 1999.

Hengel, Martin. *The Four Gospels and the One Gospel of Jesus Christ. An Investigation of the Collection and Origin of the Canonical Gospels*, Harrisburg, PA: Trinity Press, 2000.

Herder, Johann Gottfried. *Von Gottes Sohn, der Welt Heiland. Nach Johannes Evangelium. Nebst einer Regel der Zusammenstimmung unsrer Evangelien aus ihrer Entstehung und Ordnung*, Christliche Schriften 3, Riga: Hartknoch, 1797 [1796].

Holtzmann, Heinrich Julius. *Die synoptischen Evangelien. Ihr Ursprung und ihr geschichtlicher Charakter*, Leipzig: Engelmann, 1863.

Kasser, Rodolphe, Marvin Meyer, and Gregor Wurst. *The Gospel of Judas: The Manuscript with Interpretative Commentary*, Washington, DC: National Geographic Society, 2006.

Kloppenborg, John S. "On Dispensing with Q? Goodacre on the Relation of Luke to Matthew," *NTS* 49 (2003) 210–36.

Kloppenborg Verbin, John S. *Excavating Q: The History and Setting of the Sayings Gospel*, Minnespolis, MN: Fortress Press, 2000.

Koester, Helmut. *Ancient Christian Gospels: Their History and Development*, London: SCM Press, 1990.

Labahn, Michael. *Jesus als Lebensspender: Untersuchungen zu einer Geschichte der johanneischen Tradition anhand ihrer Wundergeschichten*, BZNW 98, Berlin, New York: de Gruyter, 1999.

—— "Fishing for Meaning. The Miraculous Catch of Fish in John 21," in Michael Labahn, Lietaert Peerbolte, and Bert Jan (eds) *Wonders Never Cease: The Purpose of Narrating Miracle Stories in the New Testament and Its Religious Environment*, ECSO = LNTS 288, London: T. & T. Clark, 2006, pp. 125–45.

Labahn, Michael and Manfred Lang. "Johannes und die Synoptiker. Positionen und Impulse seit 1990," in Jörg Frey and Udo Schnelle (eds) *Kontexte des Johannesevangeliums: Das vierte Evangelium in religions- und traditionsgeschichtlicher Perspektive*, WUNT 175, Tübingen: Mohr Siebeck, 2004, pp. 443–515.

Lachmann, Karl Konrad Friedrich Wilhelm. "De ordine narrationum in evangeliis synopticis," *TSK* 8 (1835) 570–90.

Lessing, Gotthold Ephraim. "Neue Hypothese über die Evangelisten als bloss menschliche Geschichtsschreiber betrachtet," in *Theologischer Nachlass*, Berlin: Voß, 1784, pp. 42–75 [1778]; ET by Henry Chadwick, "New Hypothesis Concerning the Evangelists Regarded as Merely Human Historians," in Gotthold Ephraim Lessing, *Theological Writings*, Library of Modern Religious Thought, London: A. & C. Black, 1956, pp. 65–81.

Lips, Hermann von. *Der neutestamentliche Kanon: Seine Geschichte und Bedeutung*, Zürcher Grundrisse zur Bibel; Zürich: Theologischer Verlag, 2004.

Luz, Ulrich. "Matthäus und Q," in Rudolf Hoppe and Ulrich Busse (eds) *Von Jesus zum Christus. Christologische Studien: Festgabe für Paul Hoffmann*, BZNW 93, Berlin and New York: de Gruyter, 1998, pp. 201–15.

Matson, Mark A. *In Dialogue with Another Gospel? The Influence of the Fourth Gospel on the Passion Narrative of the Gospel of Luke*, SBLDS 178, Atlanta, GA: Society of Biblical Literature, 2001.

Meier, John P. *A Marginal Jew. Rethinking the Historical Jesus I: The Roots of the Problem and the Person*, ABRL, New York: Doubleday, 1991.

Merkel, Helmut. *Die Widersprüche zwischen den Evangelien. Ihre polemische und apologetische Behandlung in der Alten Kirche bis zu Augustin*, WUNT 13, Tübingen: Mohr Siebeck, 1971.

Metzger, Bruce M. *The Canon of the New Testament: Its Origin, Development, and Significance*, Oxford: Clarendon, 1987.

Moloney, Francis J. "The Fourth Gospel and the Jesus of History," *NTS* 46 (2000) 42–58.

Nagel, Titus. *Die Rezeption des Johannesevangeliums im 2. Jahrhundert. Studien zur vorirenäischen Aneignung und Auslegung des vierten Evangeliums in christlicher und christlich-gnostischer Literatur*, Arbeiten zur Bibel und ihrer Geschichte 2, Leipzig: Evangelische Verlagsanstalt, 2000.

Neirynck, Frans. "John and the Synoptics," in M. de Jonge (ed.) *L'Évangile de Jean. Sources, rédaction, théologie*, BETL 44, Leuven: Peeters, 1977, pp. 73–95.

—— *Evangelica*, ed. F. van Segbroeck, BETL 60, Leuven: Peeters, 1982.

—— *The Minor Agreements in a Horizontal-Line Synopsis*, SNTA 15, Leuven: Peeters, 1991.

—— "John and the Synoptics: 1975–1990," in Albert Denaux (ed.) *John and the Synoptics*, BETL 101, Leuven: Peeters, 1992, pp. 3–62.

Orchard, B. *Matthew, Luke, and Mark*, Manchester: Koinonis Press, 1976.

Peabody, David B. and Philip L. Shuler. "Narrative Outline of the Composition of Luke According to the Two-Gospel Hypothesis," *SBLSP* 34 (1995) 636–87.

Peabody, David B., Lamar, Cope, and McNicol, Allan J. (eds) *One Gospel from Two: Mark's Use of Matthew and Luke*. Harrisburg, PA: Trinity Press International, 2002.

Pearson, Birger A. "A Q Community in Galilee?" *NTS* 50 (2004) 476–94.

Robinson, James M. *The Secrets of Judas: The Story of the Misunderstood Disciple and his Lost Gospel*, New York: HarperSanFrancisco, 2006.

Sato, Migaku. *Q und Prophetie. Studien zur Gattungs- und Traditionsgeschichte der Quelle Q* (WUNT II/29); Tübingen: Mohr Siebeck, 1988).

Schleiermacher, Friedrich, *Ueber die Schriften des Lukas ein kritischer Versuch. Erster Theil*, Berlin: Reimer, 1817; reprinted in *Exegetische Schriften*, Kritische Gesamtausgabe I/8, Berlin–New York: de Gruyter 2001, pp. 1–180; ET: *Luke: A Critical Study*, trans. with an Introduction by Connop Thirlwall, with further essays, emendations and other apparatus by Terrence N. Tice, Schleiermacher Studies and Translations 13, Lewistone: Edwin Mellen, 1993.

—— *Einleitung ins neue Testament*, mit einer Vorrede von Friedrich Lücke, ed. Georg Wolde; Friedrich Schleiermacher's literarischer Nachlaß 3 = Friedrich Schleiermacher's sämmtlicher Werke, Abt. 1/8, Berlin: Reimer, 1845.

Schmid, Josef. *Matthäus und Lukas. Eine Untersuchung des Verhältnisses ihrer Evangelien*, BibS(F) 23, 2/4, Freiburg im Breisgau: Herder, 1930.

Schnelle, Udo. *Einleitung in das Neue Testament*, UTB 1830, fifth edition, Göttingen: Vandenhoeck & Ruprecht, 2005.

Scholtissek, Klaus. "Johannine Studies: A Survey of Recent Research with Special Regard to German Contributions," *CR:BS* 6 (1998) 227–59, and 9 (2001) 277–305.

Schröter, Jens. "Von der Historizität der Evangelien: Ein Beitrag zur gegenwärtigen Diskussion um den historischen Jesus," in Jens Schroter and Ralph Brucker (eds) *Der historische Jesus. Tendenzen und Perspektiven der gegenwärtigen Forschung*, BZNW 114, Berlin–New York: de Gruyter, 2002, pp. 163–212.

—— "Die Bedeutung der Q-Überlieferungen für die Interpretation der frühen Jesustradition," *ZNW* 94 (2003) 38–67.

Shellard, Barbara. *New Light on Luke. Its Purpose, Sources and Literary Context*, JSNTSup 215, Sheffield: Sheffield Academic Press, 2002.

Smith, D. Moody. "Historical Issues and the Problem of John and the Synoptics," in M. C. de Boer (ed.) *From Jesus to John. Essays on Jesus and New Testament Christology*, FSM de Jonge, JSNTSup 84, Sheffield: JSOT Press, 1993, pp. 252–67.

—— *John Among the Gospels. The Relationship in Twentieth Century Research*, second edition, Columbia, SC: University of South Carolina Press, 2001.

Strecker, Georg (ed.) *Minor Agreements*, Göttinger theologische Arbeiten 50, Göttingen: Vandenhoeck & Ruprecht, 1993.

Streeter, B. H. *The Four Gospels. A Study of Origins Treating the Manuscript Tradition, Sources, Authorship, and Dates*, fourth impression, revised, London: Macmillan, 1930.

Tuckett, Christopher M. *The Revival of the Griesbach Hypothesis*, MSSNTS 44, Cambridge: Cambridge University Press, 1983.

Weisse, Christian Hermann. *Die evangelische Geschichte kritisch und philosophisch bearbeitet*, 2 vols, Leipzig: Breitkopf & Härtel 1838.

Wendt, Hans Heinrich. *Das Johannesevangelium. Eine Untersuchung seiner Entstehung und seines geschichtlichen Wertes*, Göttingen: Vandenhoeck & Ruprecht, 1900.

—— *Die Lehre Jesu*, second edition, Göttingen: Vandenhoeck & Ruprecht, 1901, pp. 33–44.

Wenham, John. *Redating Matthew, Mark and Luke: A Fresh Assault on the Synoptic Problem*, Downers Grove, IL: InterVarsity Press, 1992.

Wernle, Paul. *Die synoptische Frage*, Freiburg im Breisgau: Mohr, 1899.

Wilke, Christian Gottlob. *Der Urevangelist, oder exegetisch-kritische Untersuchung über das Verwandtschaftsverhältnis der drei ersten Evangelien*, Dresden and Leipzig: Fleischer, 1838.

Wünsch, Dietrich. "Evangelienharmonie," *TRE* 10 (1982) 626–36.

Studies on the history of historical criticism

Dungan, David Laird. *A History of the Synoptic Problem: The Canon, the Text, the Composition, and the Interpretation of the Gospels*, ABRL; New York: Doubleday, 1999.

Kloppenborg Verbin, John. *Excavating Q: The History and Setting of the Sayings Gospel*, Minneapolis, MN: Fortress Press, 2000.

—— "On Dispensing with Q?: Goodacre on the Relation of Luke to Matthew," *NTS* 49 (2003) 210–36.

Longstaff, Thomas Richmond Willis and A. Thomas Page. *The Synoptic Problem. A Bibliography 1716–1988*, New Gospel Studies 4; Macon, GA: Mercer University Press, 1988.

Schmithals, Walter. *Einleitung in die drei ersten Evangelien*, de Gruyter Lehrbuch; Berlin and New York: de Gruyter, 1985.

Stoldt, Hans-Herbert. *Geschichte und Kritik der Markushypothese*, revised edition, Monographien und Studienbücher 2, Giessen–Basel: Brunnen-Verlag, 1986.

Tuckett, Christopher M. "Synoptic Problem," *ABD* 6 (1992) 263–70.

HISTORIOGRAPHY

Any discussion of historiography in relationship to the NT must be set in the context of the Greco-Roman tradition of historiography and history writing, yet there was also a Jewish historiographic tradition which calls for consideration. The question of historiography in NT writings needs to take account of both these traditions. Can any of the NT writings be called "history"? If so, in what sense?

"History" is of course used in more than one sense, as the previous paragraph has already suggested. Most historians, both in the past and in the present, have paid lip service to the question of truth. That still begs the question: what sort of truth? Is it a truth that involves the mechanical recording of a mass of technical details? Or is it a matter of underlying causes that have led to the visible effects? Are these causes the natural ones of the world order or are they divine causes – the manifestation of the deity – the actions of the gods? For some writers, the important goal was always *Heilsgeschichte* – "salvation history" – to which details of what happened were always of secondary importance. True becomes "poetic truth" or "theological truth", in which the message goes far beyond the question of specific events and the minutiae of "what actually happened".

Unlike the ancient Near East where the question of history writing is still disputed, the development of historical writing among the Greeks, and after them the Romans, is well documented. What might be called the beginnings of historiography can be traced in the myths of origin found in such writers as Hesiod who had attempted to synthesize traditional myths into some sort of coherent system. In the fifth century BCE a writer such as Hellanicus of Lesbos used the traditional mythological genealogies to develop a historical chronological system. It is Hecataeus of Miletus (flourished *c.* 500 BCE), however, about whom we first know anything extensive. We have indications that he championed the principle so important to subsequent Greek historians, that of *autopsy*, and some of his comments show a critical spirit of mind. Unfortunately, none of his writings is preserved intact, and all we have are quotes and excerpts.

Herodotus (*c.* 480–420 BCE) remains the "father of history" – the first one whose actual historical account is extant. In his writing we can see the historian at work and make explicit deductions about the process of critical historiography. Herodotus contains all sorts of material, to the point that some would see him as more of a travel writer than a historian. But a number of points arise from study of his work that show a critical spirit. First, for example, he critiques the standard story of the Trojan War and gives reasons why another version is more likely to be correct (2.118–20). He points to a tradition (obtained from the Egyptian priests, he says) at some variance with that found in the Homeric poems, a rather bold criticism since the Homeric poems had a quasi-canonical status in the Greek world. He also questions stories that he has heard but records them nevertheless, such as the position of the sun in the circumnavigation of Africa (4.42). In this he does not differ in kind from a modern historian who collects data and then attempts to evaluate it critically. Second, we have a fair amount of indirect evidence that Herodotus used good sources for important aspects of his history. Although he does not always name his informants, the ability to choose and interrogate good sources is part of the critical historical work. Third, Herodotus's qualitative advance over his predecessors can be seen by comparing him with Hellanicus of Lesbos, whose attempts to bring some chronological order into the heroic traditions look primitive beside Herodotus, yet Hellanicus is a contemporary of Herodotus and actually wrote some of his works after the great historian.

Herodotus was quickly followed by Thucydides (*c.* 460–400 BCE), whose methodological innovations still meet the standards of modern historical research. Thucydides tells us about some of the criteria he applied in his work (1.20–22). First, he was critical of tradition and traditional stories and accounts. Second, he advocated the collection of a variety of eye-witness and other accounts and their careful interrogation. Third, he argued that a critical judgment must be made on the various accounts to select the one that appears to be most credible according to common-sense criteria. Fourth, he used a chronological framework which dates all events to within six months, establishing a proper framework for events and their relationship with each other.

Thucydides was by common consent (even among ancient writers) the pinnacle of history writers in antiquity, and his successors did not rise to quite the same heights. Xenophon, who continued his history of the Peloponnesian War, was not of the same calibre. Yet Xenophon wrote an important account (the *Anabasis*) of his own adventures in Persia during the 401 BCE attempt by Cyrus the Younger to take the throne. On the other hand, most modern scholars consider the *Cyropaedia*, which ostensibly gives a life of Cyrus the founder of the Persian empire, as unreliable on the whole and to be used only cautiously and critically for information about Persian history. The anonymous writer known as the Oxyrhynchus Historian is thought to give a quite accurate portrayal of a few years of the Peloponnesian War; unfortunately, the author of this work is unidentified, and the principles on which it was written have yet to be determined.

Polybius (*c.* 200–120 BCE) perhaps holds second place in the ranks of ancient historians after Thucydides. He was an important historian who wrote not only about contemporary events that he witnessed himself but also about Roman history from the First Punic War, more than a century before his own time. Some centuries later, at the end of the fourth century CE, the Roman historian Ammianus Marcellinus produced work of similar quality, while Livy and Tacitus were not far behind. Of particular interest, because of his being a younger contemporary with some of the NT writers as well as the intrinsic interest about what he says, is Lucian of Samosata (*c.* 120–? CE). As a satirist he was scathing about deceptions by public figures and those he regarded as charlatans, but he also wrote a serious, if witty, work about the principles of historical composition, called "How to Write History".

This is not to suggest that all Greek "historians" from Herodotus on are examples of critical historians. On the contrary, many of them fall well short of even minimum standards as exemplified in Herodotus and Thucydides. Perhaps the nadir to Thucydides' zenith is Ctesias of Cnidus. He wrote about the same time as Xenophon and is thus a successor of the great historians. After being captured by the Persians and serving for seventeen years as the personal physician of Artaxerxes II, he should have been in a good position to report on many aspects of the Persian court and Persian history at first hand. Instead, he compiled a farrago of legends, inventions and gossip that was already denounced in antiquity. This is not to say that genuine historical data cannot be found in his account, but he shows little interest in distinguishing the historical from the romantic.

The Jewish historiographical tradition can boast such important works as the Deuteronomistic History and 1 and 2 Maccabees. Yet the Jewish writings almost always had as their first concern the actions of the deity. They definitely had an "antiquarian interest", but their main concern is not history but theology or ideology. Their history was primarily salvation history and, whatever the concern about relating past events, ultimately had a theological aim. What seems at first an exception is the one main Jewish historian preserved from antiquity, Flavius Josephus (37–*c.* 100 CE). He was well aware of the Greco-Roman historiographical tradition and has clearly modelled some aspects of his work on Dionysius of Halicarnassus and even Thucydides. In many ways, Josephus is typical of Hellenistic historians, but in some ways he continues the Jewish historiographic tradition in taking "providence" and the intervention of God as central themes of his work. A. Momigliano (18–20) expressed well the difference between the two sorts of historiography:

> Each Greek historian is of course different from the others, but all Greek historians deal with a limited subject which they consider important, and all are concerned with the reliability of the evidence they are going to use. Greek historians never claim to tell all the facts of history from the origins of the world, and never believe that they can tell their tale without *historia*, without research ... The point, however, is that he had to claim to be a trustworthy researcher in order to be respectable.

> Thus to the Hebrew historian historiography soon became a narration of events from the beginning of the world such as no Greek historian ever conceived. The criteria of reliability were also different. Jews have always been supremely concerned with truth. The Hebrew God is the God of Truth ... Consequently reliability in Jewish terms coincides with the truthfulness of the transmitters and with the ultimate truth of

God in whom the transmitters believe ... What Josephus seems to have missed is that the Greeks had criteria by which to judge the relative merits of various versions which the Jewish historians had not ... In Hebrew historiography the collective memory about past events could never be verified according to objective criteria. If priests forged records ... the Hebrew historian did not posses the critical instrument to discover the forgery. In so far as modern historiography is a critical one, it is a Greek, not a Jewish, product.

The one NT work that seems to aspire to history-writing according to the standards of the time is the writings of Luke. It is evident that the gospels and the Acts of the Apostles have theological aims and in that sense fit into the Jewish historiographical tradition, but can any of these be called "history" as such? The gospel of Luke and the Acts may once have been a single work; in any case, there is a strong consensus that both were written by the same person. The gospel of Luke is a gospel and would fall into a different genre (the genre biography), but the Acts of the Apostles shows various outward signs associated with history-writing of the time, and it has often been argued that Acts shares a number of points with Greco-Roman historiography. For example, the dedication of the gospel to Theophilus (Luke 1:3; Acts 1:1) is often seen as a clear connection with Greek history writing, though it has recently been pointed out that this has more in common with contemporary "scientific" or technical manuals. Luke also does not focus on political issues. Above all, his main concern is how the divine plan is being worked out in events.

Examples of Luke's accurate knowledge of some obscure data can be found listed in many commentaries, such as his knowing that Philippi was a "colony" (Acts 16:12) or that the city officials of Thessalonica were correctly referred to as *politarchai* (17:6) or that Sergius Paulus and Gallio were "proconsuls" (13:7; 18;12: *anthupatos*). Yet the argument that the "we" passages show that he was a companion to Paul has now been overtaken by other explanations, especially that this was a narrative device. It has long been argued that Luke's Paul has significant differences from the Paul of the epistles. Luke also called Agrippa I "Herod" (Acts 12:1), when it is almost certain that Agrippa's name was Marcus Julius Agrippa (Grabbe 1992: 430). Luke's Paul seems unaware that Berenice is not just the sister of Agrippa II but also a queen in her own right (26:2, 19, 27), since he fails to give her the correct address.

Perhaps the best example to illustrate Luke's weaknesses as a historian is found in Luke 2:1–3 (Grabbe 1992: 384–85). This was an important event in the history of Judah because the country was being transformed from a semi-independent "friendly kingdom" into a Roman province in 6 CE after the exile of Archelaus. A census was required so that the Roman taxes could be collected, which had not been necessary before because Rome did not tax a "friendly king". This was a unique event, with the census being required by the context. As expected, the census was carried out by Quirinius the governor of Syria and Coponius the governor of Judah. Luke unfortunately is unaware of the context of the census and has apparently simply appropriated the event for his purposes, without understanding its purpose or timing. He has therefore made the census empire-wide (no such census was ever carried out in the Roman empire) and pre-dated it to the time of Herod the Great, at which time it would have made no sense and would have been impossible to carry out, since the Romans would not have interfered with the internal affairs of a "friendly king" like Herod. Thus, as a historical source the book of Acts is a mixed bag. If it is meant to be history, this does not guarantee its accuracy. On the other hand, if it is something other than history, it still contains historical data that can be gleaned by the use of the proper critical tools.

These differences from Greco-Roman histories have led some to look for other literary categories for Acts. A genre related to historiography is biography. We have several sorts of biography in antiquity. One well known from Egypt is the autobiographical tomb inscription (e.g. Wenamun; the "Travels of Sinuhe"), but we have something similar in the "Nehemiah Memorial" (essentially Nehemiah 1–6, 13) in which the subject gives an account of his life or defends himself. The gospels were of course a sort of biography, but some have suggested that Acts falls into the same category: it is in some sense a biography of the early church, though the second part constitutes a biography of the apostle Paul. Others have seen Acts as a new genre, an apologetic history. Above all, Acts seems to combine elements of the Greco-Roman and the Jewish traditions of historiography.

LESTER L. GRABBE

Further reading

Drews, Robert. *The Greek Accounts of Eastern History*, Center for Hellenic Studies, Cambridge, MA: Harvard University Press, 1973.

Grabbe, Lester L. *Judaism from Cyrus to Hadrian: Vol. I: Persian and Greek Periods; Vol. II: Roman Period,*

Minneapolis, MN: Fortress Press; London: SCM Press, 1992.

—— "Who Were the First Real Historians? On the Origins of Critical Historiography," in Lester L. Grabbe (ed.) *Did Moses Speak Attic? Jewish Historiography and Scripture in the Hellenistic Period*, JSOTSup 317 = European Seminar in Historical Methodology 3, Sheffield: Sheffield Academic Press, 2001, pp. 156–81.

Marguerat, Daniel. *The First Christian Historian: Writing the "Acts of the Apostles"*, SNTSM 121, Cambridge: Cambridge University Press, 2002.

Momigliano, Arnaldo. *The Classical Foundations of Modern Historiography* (with a foreword by Riccardo Di Donato), Sather Classical Lectures 54, Berkeley and Los Angeles, CA: University of California, 1990.

Witherington, Ben III (ed.) *History, Literature, and Society in the Book of Acts*, Cambridge: Cambridge University Press, 1996.

HOLTZMANN, HEINRICH JULIUS

Heinrich Julius Holtzmann (1832–1910) was born in Karlsruhe as son of a Protestant pastor. He began the study of theology in Heidelberg in 1850, interrupted by a short stay in Berlin (1851–52) coming under the influence of Wilhelm Vatke. With the historical study *"De corpore et sanguine Christi quae statuta fuerint in ecclesia examinantur"* Holtzmann received his lic. theol. in 1858 and he began to teach in 1859 at the practical institute (Predigerseminar) of Heidelberg. In 1861 he became *Extraordinarius* for New Testament at the theological faculty. In 1865 he became full professor and, finally, he received a call at the Kaiser-Wilhelm University of Straßburg where he spent the greater part of his academic career as professor at the newly founded university of Straßburg (1874–1904) teaching New Testament as well as dogmatics and church history. During his time in Heidelberg he was a liberal member of the parliament of Baden (1867–71). With his appointment at Strasburg he had to promise to abstain from any ecclesiastical political engagement.

Holtzmann was the teacher of Albert Schweitzer. He impressively covered the whole field of contemporary theology, including systematic theology, and philosophy, preaching, ethics, and even Christian arts by studies he published himself or that he edited.

For gospel studies his book *Die synoptischen Evangelien* of 1863 was ground-breaking. The discussion about the literary relationship of the Synoptic Gospels received broad acceptance.

In dialogue with the preceding discussion, but in contrast to the results of the Tübingen school (Ferdinand Christian Baur) and Johann Jakob Griesbach, Holtzmann took up insights by Karl Lachmann, Christian Gottlob Wilke, and Christian Hermann Weiße regarding the priority of Mark and a source common to Matthew and Luke, which he called "L." Holtzmann refined these arguments and helped to establish the *Two Document Hypothesis*. According to his model, it is not canonical Mark that forms the first common source of Matthew and Luke but a so-called *Urmarkus* ("early Mark"), which he calls source "A," that is also used by canonical Mark. This source, which shows a more primitive style of narration and language, may have drawn on the memories of Peter recorded by John Mark. According to Holtzmann, both sources contain reliable information about the historical Jesus.

Regarding method, Holtzmann stresses a stylistic analysis to prove how his hypothesis works and to explain exegetical observations. In his introduction to the New Testament he finally identifies source "A" with canonical Mark (1892: 350; 1907b) and he accepts knowledge or perhaps use of Matthew through Luke, which replaces the assumption of *Urmarcus* without denying "L" (cf. 1892: 350). Before being incorporated into written sources, there is a longer period of oral transmission of Jesus traditions influenced by theological reflections about Jesus (1901: 20–21, 25–29).

Some scholars recently have suggested that the success of Holtzmann's Synoptic source hypothesis was related to political or theological schools-related influences (e.g. Reicke 1987). One cannot deny that the overall political situation may have been amenable to that theory. It is misleading, however, to explain the far-reaching consensus as simply the result of political pressures.

Historically, Holtzmann is not in opposition to Baur. Rather, he tried to develop further what he regarding as the enduring points of his research (cf. Merk 519–20 with reference to unpublished letters of Holtzmann). The basic arguments regarding the synoptic source theory adopted by Holtzmann were already developed and well founded before this. Further, Holtzmann's model was not simply copied by later exegetes but the hypothesis was still in debate and developed further by himself and other scholars in different circumstances. To this day it is still regarded as the most plausible model – with some adjustments in view of recent analysis by different scholars. It is important to observe within the history of gospel criticism that Holtzmann placed the role of oral tradition convincingly within a model of literary dependence.

Holtzmann's efforts regarding gospel criticism served a special aim. According to *Die Synoptischen Evangelien* the sayings source "L" and the narrative source "A" ("Urmarcus") functioned as reliable sources for a reconstruction of the life of Jesus including a reconstruction of the psychological interpretation of the human development of Jesus (1863: 468; for his reconstruction cf. 468–96) and even after abandoning the assumption of source "A" Holtzmann developed a picture of the life and message of Jesus optimistically based on these sources. (He does not place the Gospel of John among the reliable sources for reconstructing a life of Jesus, because he thinks it is a late writing under Hellenistic-philosophic influence.)

According to Holtzmann the teaching of Jesus is the basis of any Christian thinking (1867). Therefore, his famous New Testament theology starts with the religious ideas of Jesus who is presented as a religious genius (1911/I: 173). Paul was called a secondary founder of Christianity ("*sekundäre[r] ... Religionsstifter*": 1897/II: 203), for Jesus' teaching is the presupposition and basis of the theological thinking of Paul (1911/II: 229–36): "*Ohne diesen Größeren (sc. Jesus; M.L.) hinter sich verliert selbst Pls an Verständlichkeit und löst sich gerade der Mittelpunkt seines Denkens in Nebelmassen auf ...*" (1911/II: 236).

Holtzmann's interpretation of that kingdom is close to the liberal interpretation of Jesus and his message in so far as he does not accept an eschatological interpretation of Jesus' concept of the kingdom of God. Jesus' idea of God is understood as an ethical one and religion and ethics form a close relationship in this context. God is portrayed by Jesus as "love." A central role in Holtzmann's portrait of Jesus plays, struggling with William Wrede, that Jesus understands himself as (suffering) messiah, which means that he accepts the authenticity of sayings like Mark 8:31 and 12:35–37, which are crucial for Jesus' understanding of messianism in the title "son of man" (1907a).

Holtzmann was able to develop his general assumptions of gospel criticism based on the genuine exegetical analysis. That means his academic work is not monolithic but shows vivid interest in newer discussions and a development of his position. His recent meaning lies in his role of establishing the Two Document Hypothesis and in showing that it is a theory still needing adjustments to explain the agreements and disagreements between the Synoptic Gospels in order and in wording. That we may also today find interpretations of a non-eschatological Jesus, however, does not show the ongoing value of Holtzmann's portrait of a liberal Jesus, but should remind us about necessary criticism of such an interpretation. Also, Holtzmann's positivistic trust in historical reliability of early sources needs to be questioned.

Nevertheless, regarding his value for New Testament exegesis and especially for source criticism, Holtzmann is rightly judged by William Baird as the one who brings the earlier efforts into a "critical consensus" (Baird).

MICHAEL LABAHN

Further reading

Baird, William. *History of New Testament Research II: From Jonathan Edwards to Rudolf Bultmann*, Minneapolis, MN: Fortress Press, 2003, pp. 111–22.

Bauer, Walter. "Heinrich Julius Holtzmann, ein Lebensbild," in *Aufsätze und kleine Schriften*, ed. Georg Strecker, Tübingen: Mohr Siebeck, 1967, pp. 285–341.

Holtzmann, Heinrich Julius. *Die synoptischen Evangelien. Ihr Ursprung und ihr geschichtlicher Charakter*, Leipzig: Engelmann, 1863.

—— *Judenthum und Christenthum im Zeitalter der apokryphischen und neutestamentlichen Literatur*, Vol. 2 of Georg Weber, *Geschichte des Volkes Israel und der Entstehung des Christentums*, Leipzig: Engelmann, 1867.

—— *Lehrbuch der Historisch-Kritischen Einleitung in das Neue Testament*, Sammlung theologischer Lehrbücher, Freiburg: Mohr, 1885; third edition 1892.

—— *Hand-Commentar zum Neuen Testament. Erster Band: Die Synoptiker – Die Apostelgeschichte*, Freiburg: Mohr, 1889; second edition 1892; third, largely revised, edition 1901.

—— *Das messianische Bewusstsein Jesu. Ein Beitrag zur Leben-Jesu-Forschung*, Tübingen: Mohr, 1907a.

—— "Die Marcus-Kontroverse in ihrer heutigen Gestalt," in *ARW* 10 (1907b) 18–40, 161–200.

—— *Lehrbuch der neutestamentlichen Theologie*. Vol I and II, Sammlung theologischer Lehrbücher, Freiburg: Mohr, 1897; second edition, ed. Adolf Jülicher and Walter Bauer; Tübingen: Mohr, 1911.

Kloppenborg, John S. "Holtzmann's Life of Jesus according to the 'A' Source," *Journal for the Study of the Historical Jesus* 4 (2006) 75–108, 203–23.

Kümmel, Werner Georg. *Das Neue Testament. Geschichte der Erforschung seiner Probleme*, second edition, OA III/3, Freiburg and München: Alber, 1970, pp. 185–91.

Merk, Otto. "Holtzmann, Heinrich Julius," *TRE* 15 (1986) 519–22.

Peabody, David Barrett. "H. J. Holtzmann and his European Colleagues: Aspects of the Nineteenth-Century European Discussion of Gospel Origins," in Henning Graf Reventlow and William Farmer (eds) *Biblical Studies and the Shifting of Paradigms 1850–1914*, JSOTSup 192, Sheffield: Sheffield Academic Press, 1995, pp. 50–131.

Reicke, Bo. "From Strauss to Holtzmann and Meijboom. Synoptic Theories Advanced During the Consolidation of Germany, 1830–70," *NT* 29 (1987) 1–21.

Reventlow, Henning Graf. "Conditions and Presuppositions of Biblical Criticism in Germany in the Period of the Second Empire and Before: The Case of Heinrich Julius Holtzmann," Henning Graf Reventlow and William Farmer (eds) *Biblical Studies and the Shifting of Paradigms 1850–1914*, JSOTSup 192, Sheffield: Sheffield Academic Press, 1995, pp. 272–90.

—— *Epochen der Bibelauslegung IV: Von der Aufklärung bis zum 20. Jahrhundert*, München: Beck, 2001, pp. 295–302.

Rollmann, Hans, "Holtzmann, von Hügel and Modernism," *DReV* 97 (1979), 128–43, 221–44.

Strecker, Georg. "Holtzmann, Heinrich Julius," *DBI* 1 (1999) 516–17.

HOLY SPIRIT

The presence of the Holy Spirit in the life of Jesus is attested by all four canonical gospels and appears in every alleged source (Q, Mark, so-called L and M material, and in both the narrative and farewell discourses of the Fourth Gospel). This material deals both with the Holy Spirit in the experience of Jesus and the relationship of the Holy Spirit to Jesus' followers.

The experience of Jesus

A later summation from the book of Acts offers a salient précis of Jesus' experience of the Holy Spirit: "how God anointed Jesus of Nazareth with the Holy Spirit and with power; how he went about doing good and healing all who were oppressed by the devil, for God was with him" (Acts 10:38). The canonical gospels align neatly with this summary, which identifies three principal points of reference for the Holy Spirit in Jesus' public ministry: anointing (his baptism, testing, and early preaching); doing good; and exorcisms.

Anointing

Despite several differences, the Synoptic Gospels, and the fourth gospel in several respects, are unified in identifying the presence of the Holy Spirit with the initiatory experiences of Jesus: (a) John the Baptist predicts or recognizes that Jesus will baptize with the Holy Spirit (Mark 1:8; John 1:34); this prediction in Luke and Matthew has an added note of judgment through the addition of "and fire" – Jesus will baptize "with the Holy Spirit and fire" (Matt 3:11/Luke 3:16; see Isa 4:4); (b) the Holy Spirit descends upon Jesus like a dove (in bodily form, according to Luke) during or after his water baptism by John the Baptist (Mark 1:10–11/ Matt 3:16–17/Luke 3:21–22/John 1:29–34); (c) the Holy Spirit accompanies Jesus in the wilderness during a time of testing (Mark 1:12–13/Matt 4:1–11/Luke 4:1–13). In Mark, the Spirit drives Jesus out violently to live peaceably among the animals, perhaps in contrast to the primeval pair, who were driven out of Eden into a world of enmity with beasts. Matthew and Luke's reference to forty days of testing recalls Israel's emergence from Egypt and their forty years of wilderness wandering. This may account for Luke's description of Jesus as "led by the Spirit in the wilderness," rather than being driven by the Spirit into the wilderness (Luke 4:2; see Isa 63:7–14). Further, in Luke's Gospel, Jesus enters this period of testing full of the Spirit (4:1); he returns filled with the Spirit, and he teaches in the synagogues of Galilee (4:14), where he claims the Spirit in his work of preaching good news to the poor (4:18–19).

Doing good

The words at Jesus' baptism, "my beloved," offer a subtle reminiscence of the Isaianic servant (Isa 42:1). Luke continues this appeal to the later oracles of Isaiah with Jesus' first public sermon, in which Jesus lays explicit claim to such an anointing with a quotation of Isaiah 61:1–2: "The Spirit of the Lord is upon me, because he has anointed me to bring good news to the poor." The text continues with release to prisoners, sight for the blind, freedom for the oppressed (see Isa 58:6), and proclamation of God's favorable year.

Matthew too connects the baptism of Jesus with the public doing of good, though in a typically Matthean manner. After a summary statement about Jesus' curing all of the sick, Matthew concludes with the characteristic formula, "This was to fulfill what had been spoken through the prophet Isaiah," and a quotation from Isa 42:1–4, 9, which begins, "Here is my servant, whom I have chosen, my beloved, with whom my soul is well pleased. I will put my Spirit upon him." (See also Jesus' response to John the Baptist's messengers in Matt 11:2–6; Luke 7:18–23.) Both Matthew and Luke, then, in part through allusions to the so-called servant passages of Isaiah, draw a taut association between the anointing of Jesus by the Holy Spirit at his baptism and his ongoing vocation of doing good.

Exorcisms

Jesus' doing good extends beyond preaching and healing. In a context rife with polemic, Jesus exorcises a demon in a mute (and blind, according to Matt 12:22) man. Some are amazed; others accuse him of alignment with Beelzebul, the ruler of demons. Jesus responds that a house divided cannot stand, that Satan cannot disarm himself. Then, in Matt 12:28, he continues, "But if it is by the Spirit of God that I cast out demons, then the kingdom of God has come to you." Luke's version, surprisingly in light of his interest in the Spirit, reads, "But if it is by the finger of God that I cast out the demons … " (Luke 11:20). The occurrence of the word "finger" rather than "Spirit" of God draws the reader directly to the confrontation brought about by the plagues in Exod 8:15 (MT): "And the magicians said to Pharaoh, 'This is the finger of God!'" This suits Luke's New Exodus theme perfectly.

In Mark and Matthew's Gospels, the puzzling statement that blasphemy against the Holy Spirit comprises the unpardonable sin occurs directly after this confrontation (Mark 3:28–30; Matt 12:31–32). The implication is that the Jewish leaders who accuse Jesus of being aligned with Satan blaspheme the Holy Spirit. Luke, in contrast, places the word about blasphemy in another context altogether that has to do with testimony under constraint rather than Jesus' ministry of exorcism (12:8–12).

The experience of believers

Not during Jesus' lifetime

In contrast to the pivotal role the Holy Spirit plays in Jesus' initiation, his doing good, and his authority to exorcise, far less in the gospels serves to explain the function of the Holy Spirit in the life of believers. Jesus' followers, in fact, do not receive the Holy Spirit during his lifetime. Although the period prior to his birth is, according to the birth narratives, a flurry of Spirit-induced activity (Luke 1:15, 17, 41–42, 67; 2:25, 27, 28–35, 36–38 [Anna a prophet]; Matt 1:18, 20), only after his resurrection are Jesus' followers said to receive the Holy Spirit, and this in a variety of ways. Mark's longer ending does not mention the Holy Spirit, but Jesus predicts signs that suggest the Spirit's presence, including new tongues, picking up snakes and drinking poison unharmed, and healing the sick (Mark 16:17–18). In Matthew's final lines, Jesus commands his disciples to baptize in the name of the Father, Son, and Holy Spirit (Matt 28:16–20).

In Luke's Gospel, even when the disciples return from a remarkable mission during which the seventy exercised authority over snakes, scorpions, Satan, and spirits, the Holy Spirit is associated not with their fabulous feats but with Jesus' response of rejoicing: "At that same hour Jesus rejoiced in the Holy Spirit and said, 'I thank you, Father ... '" (Luke 10:17–21; similarly 1:41–42; 1:67; 2:28–35). It becomes clear that Jesus' followers must wait for power from on high (24:49), and this occurs in Acts (1:4–8; 2:1–13).

In the Fourth Gospel, Jesus talks to Nicodemus about the Spirit and new birth (3:5–8), to the Samaritan woman about living water that wells up

(4:10–14; see 7:37–39), and to the disciples about his own words as spirit and life (6:63). Yet in a narrative aside, the author notes, "Now he said this about the Spirit, which believers in him were to receive; for as yet there was no Spirit, because Jesus was not yet glorified" (7:39). Not prior to but after the resurrection does Jesus enter a locked room and "breathe into" (see Gen 2:7; 1 Kgs 17:17–24; Ezek 37:1–10) his disciples, with the words, "Receive the Holy Spirit" (20:19–23).

Public witness

The principal promise of the Holy Spirit in the gospels concerns public testimony. Mark's single promise of the Holy Spirit to believers occurs in a context in which Jesus predicts that families will be splintered by betrayal, in which only the one who endures will be saved (13:12–13). In this highly charged context, Jesus says, "When they bring you to trial and hand you over, do not worry beforehand about what you are to say; for it is not you who speak, but the Holy Spirit" (13:11). This is not a vague promise of joyful inspiration or an offer of liberation from suffering; it is rather a promise to a desperate, persecuted and betrayed people who stand before governors and kings in the service of the gospel (13:9–10); they may not survive, but they can endure faithfully to the end.

Matthew preserves a similar saying: "for it is not you who speak, but the Spirit of your Father speaking through you" (10:20). This is the true father, in contrast to the father who betrays his own child to the authorities (10:21).

Luke ties the knot of testimony under persecution even more tightly by setting this promise directly after the word about blasphemy against the Holy Spirit. It is not the Jewish leaders who own the potential to blaspheme, as in the gospels of Mark and Matthew; it is believers brought before the authorities who will be pressed to blaspheme in this way (12:8–10). For those who do not, there is no need to worry: "do not worry about how you are to defend yourselves or what you are to say; for the Holy Spirit will teach you at that very hour what you ought to say" (12:11–12).

The Paraclete

As in the Synoptic Gospels, Jesus in the Fourth Gospel also promises that the Spirit of Truth will testify on his behalf alongside, or perhaps through, the testimony of the disciples (15:25–26). In Jesus' absence, it will convict the world concerning sin, justice, and judgment (16:7–11).

In addition to this public function, the Spirit in the Fourth Gospel will, as "another Paraclete," engage in extensive teaching in Jesus' stead. Like Jesus, it will instruct and guide believers, in whom it will dwell (14:15–17). Its principal vocation will consist of teaching in continuity with Jesus: reminding believers of all that he said (14:25–26); teaching them "many things" that the disciples could not bear to hear during that final night (16:12); and guiding them into truth, presumably into a deeper understanding about Jesus' life and teachings than they had during his lifetime (16:13–15; see 2:22, 12:16, and 20:9 for examples of post-resurrection understanding).

Prayer

Luke associates the Holy Spirit with prayer and praise. Elizabeth and Zechariah praise God when they are filled with the Holy Spirit (1:41–42, 67). Jesus receives the Spirit at his baptism while he is praying (3:21). When the seventy return from their mission, he rejoices in the Holy Spirit and addresses God in prayer (10:21). In instructions about prayer, Jesus asks, "[H]ow much more will the heavenly Father give the Holy Spirit to those who ask him?" (11:13). This association of the Spirit and prayer characterizes only Luke's gospel; in Matthew's version of this saying (7:11), by contrast, believers are promised "good things," but not the Spirit. This Lucan promise of the Spirit is fulfilled, not during Jesus' own lifetime but after his resurrection – and then in good measure – when believers are filled with the Holy Spirit and begin to praise God's powerful acts (Acts 2:1–13; see 10:44–48).

JOHN R. LEVISON

Further reading

Barrett, C. K. *The Holy Spirit and the Gospel Tradition,* second edition, London: SPCK, 1966.
Bennema, Cornelis. *The Power of Saving Wisdom: An Investigation of Spirit and Wisdom in Relation to the Soteriology of the Fourth Gospel,* Tübingen: Mohr Siebeck, 2002.
Brown, Tricia Gates. *Spirit in the Writings of John: Johannine Pneumatology in Social-Scientific Perspective,* London, New York: T. & T. Clark, 2003.
Dunn, James D. G. *Jesus and the Spirit: A Study of the Religious and Charismatic Experience of Jesus and the First Christians as Reflected in the New Testament,* London: SCM Press, 1975; Grand Rapids, MI: Eerdmans, 1997.
Menzies, Robert P. *The Development of Early Christian Pneumatology with special reference to Luke–Acts,* Sheffield: JSOT, 1991.
Montague, George T. *The Holy Spirit: Growth of a Biblical Tradition,* Peabody, MA: Hendrickson, 1976.
Turner, M. M. B. *Power from on High: The Spirit in Israel's Restoration and Witness in Luke–Acts,* Sheffield: Sheffield Academic Press, 1996.
—— *The Holy Spirit and Spiritual Gifts in the New Testament Church and Today,* Peabody, MA: Hendrickson, 1996.

HOUSEHOLDS, JEWISH

The immediate problem that any discussion of Jewish households in first-century Palestine faces is the paucity of sources. To date we have no literary sources from rural villagers. The literary sources which we do have (e.g. Josephus, Philo, rabbinic literature) express the concerns and perspectives of the priestly, scribal, and elite classes; and in some cases, such as with the Mishnah (finalized at the beginning of the third century) they primarily attest to social life well after the destruction of the Temple. However, given the high degree of continuity over generations in agrarian peasant society, the use of rabbinic sources and later archaeological finds may be of great use if they are critically assessed (Horsley 197–98). The archaeological evidence is more direct, including discoveries of village and house foundations and domestic artifacts like pottery and cooking utensils (Crossan and Reed), but it is limited. In order to advance the reconstructions of early Jewish households, social historians interpret the sparse selection of sources in light of social models of current comparable peasant cultures (Hanson and Oakman 3–17). By "peasant" most social historians mean a subsistence economic stratum, which in the case of Roman Palestine would have consisted of approximately 90 percent of the population. Historical Jesus scholars are not only reliant on social reconstruction of ancient peasant life in Roman Palestine by historians and archaeologists, but have themselves played an important role in advancing research. Being raised in the small agricultural village of Nazareth, Jesus was a product of and interacted with members of rural, agrarian peasant Jewish households. Four main features of these households are summarized in this entry: the family unit, language and education, economic life, and religious life.

The family unit

The most basic social unit in a traditional agrarian society such as first-century Palestine was the patriarchal family which consisted of a husband, his wife and children, the husband's parents, and brothers' families. Domestic and public actions were governed by kinship within a political system rooted in inherited laws (e.g. Pharisaic, Sadducean) (Hanson and Oakman). Sons generally stayed at home after marriage. Virtually everyone married at least once. Women were usually married by their late teens. Men were slightly older. Within village households, roles and divisions of labor were established on both the domestic and public levels, but not as rigorously defined as those within urban upper-class families (Helly and Reverby). Men attended to most of the work in the fields (except at harvest when all family members participated), worked in trades, trained their sons, interacted with other household heads, and made important family decisions. Women looked after meal preparations, laundry and "working in wool," cleaning, and raising of the children (*m. Ned.* 7:8; *m. Ketub.* 5:5).

The household was instrumental in forming social identity among the members of a transgenerational family. Individual life, as it might be perceived in our modern Western culture, is inappropriate since roles, relations, rights, and vocations all stem from within household kinship. Women were subordinate to either their husbands or their fathers. The eldest son became the head of the family and bore the responsibility to ancestors and descendents (Horsley 196). On a broader scale, one's identity within the family, along with the reputation of the household, had a significant impact on membership within the larger community where shame and honor were determining factors. In villages, public and private distinctions would have been much more difficult to maintain in contrast to modern Western life. Families would have interacted with each other on a daily basis, especially in the production process, sharing common facilities such as wine and olive presses, grain grinders, threshing floors, pottery wheels, places for tanning hides (*m. Git* 5:9); and borrowing and lending of livestock, tools, and labor. Numerous controversial issues must have arisen from these interactions, even litigation, given the Mishnah's many citations on the fairness of the exchange of goods and services (e.g. *m. B. Qam.* 1:1; Horsley 201, 204–6). Judging from excavated family land plots, there is no indication of significant economic variation among villagers.

On a more basic level, the household unit was vital for survival which required a collaborated effort in the cycle of production, consumption, and reproduction. Perpetuation of the family unit through marriage ensured the inheritance and continued maintenance of the family land. But inheritance was not equally distributed. According to biblical law codes (Deut 21:17), the eldest son

would inherit twice that of any brother. The privileged status, along with the elevated responsibilities, of the first-born son in ancient Mediterranean culture provides an important exegetical background for the parable of the Prodigal Son (Luke 15:11–32) and the parable of the Wicked Tenants (Mark 12:1–11) and several christological images and titles in the New Testament, such as "son of God."

Daughters, by contrast, were valued less than sons (Sir 22:3; 42:9–14). Several rabbinic texts speak of an elevated rejoicing at the birth of a son in contrast to the birth of a daughter (*m. Ber.* 9:3; Safrai, "Home," 750–69). In dire economic situations when families had to provide a debt-slave, daughters were the first to go, since sons were needed to maintain the family line (*m. Ketub.* 4:6). According to marriage contracts, a daughter's value was primarily based on her potential fertility. A dowry would have been an economic liability, especially since its size displayed a family's honor (Hanson and Oakman 37–42). By twelve and a half, when the father no longer had dominion over his daughter (*m. Nid.* 5:7), she would be passed on through an arranged marriage to the husband, who would maintain patriarchal control. All of her economic assets, such as an inheritance, were transferred to the discretion of the husband (*m. Ketub.* 6:1). The wife's sexuality was under the control of the husband primarily for the perpetuation of the family line (Horsley 200). According to the Mishnah, the exclusion of women from several community cultic practices implies their confinement to domestic chores wherein they would developed social interaction with other women in the village, especially those with whom they shared a common oven, well, storage shed, or toilet facilities. Courtyards, which contained some of these amenities, would have served as a common meeting area and a group dining facility on special occasions (Safrai, "Home," 729–35). Some scholars have argued that the exclusion of women from public socio-religious life increased after the destruction of the Temple, when purity practices were no longer centralized in the priesthood but extended more broadly to social contexts where gender interaction could lead to cultic "pollution" (Wegner). At the same time this view must be tempered by a recognition that generations of families in autonomous villages outside the proximity of the Temple cult, such as in Galilee, would have lived according to local socio-religious practices that were developed over generations and not necessarily controlled by "official" practices. There is evidence from the Diaspora that women even participated in leadership roles in local assemblies (Brooten). The functional structure of the traditional Jewish patriarchal household wherein women were subordinate to the male head of the family, and often appear as chattels to modern Westerners, must be contextualized within ancient Mediterranean standards of respect, honor, and shame (Lamphere).

Language and education

Jewish households in first-century Palestine were probably bilingual to some extent, having a knowledge of Greek and Aramaic or Hebrew. It is, however, very difficult to say which of these languages were dominant. The epigraphic and literary evidence is not conclusive. For example, ossuaries from Judea, which are very personal family items, have been found with inscriptions in Aramaic, Hebrew, and in combination with Greek. One is even trilingual (Hebrew, Aramaic, and Greek), which is comparable to the *titulus* on Jesus' cross (which includes Latin). The evidence from the Dead Sea Scrolls is also difficult to assess. While most of the scrolls are in Hebrew, some are written in Aramaic and others in Greek.

It is doubtful that most Jewish peasants would have been literate, beyond perhaps an ability to write their names, numbers, receipts, and contracts for common transactions. Torah may have been taught to young boys in some capacity, though not in established schools as we might perceive; but there is little evidence that such education would have included reading and writing (*contra* S. Safrai). Josephus claims that the law required children to read and learn Torah (*Ag. Ap.* 2.204), but he gives no indication that this practice was carried out throughout the villages of Palestine. Many Jesus scholars apply to Palestine the conclusions of William Harris' broad study of ancient literacy that approximately 90 percent of the rural population would have been illiterate.

Being illiterate, however, should not be confused with being "unlearned" with respect to family and national history, tradition, and the Scriptures. Orality and memory figured very prominently in preserving Jewish identity. Walter Ong has argued that the function of memory in oral cultures is oriented toward contemporary relevance. That is, analytical thought patterns are not exhibited, but instead memory functions in practical, situational patterns (52–53). The events remembered may have had a high degree of historicity (i.e. an event that occurred, was committed to memory, and was eventually synthesized into a memorable pattern of speech so as to preserve it), but they were not ultimately preserved for their own sake in an exact manner. With regard to collective memory, the work of sociologist Maurice Halbwachs has been foundational in recent years for a handful of New Testament scholars (e.g. Kirk and Thatcher). One of Halbwach's key observations on the function of memory within religious frameworks, which is reiterated in more recent studies of social memory, is that recollections of the past are assimilated within the frameworks of the present. But the past is not completely lost to the present. While the past is continually (re)shaped and (re)collected so as to have meaning in the present, the present is continually informed and guided by the past, especially if the tradition is older, is adopted by a large number of adherents, and is widespread (183).

Economics

The economy in the Roman empire cannot be compared to today's Western economy which is market driven, sustained by a strong middle class, suited to mass transport of all goods, oriented toward fair remuneration for labor, accepting of organized labor, and not agriculturally based. By contrast, ancient economy, which was preeminently agricultural, can be summarized as being based not on markets as we understand them but on scarcity. Although some have attempted to argue that the economy of Roman Palestine was market driven beyond the village sphere (Z. Safrai), to date there is no supporting archaeological evidence (Goodman); and the ancient texts which speak of *agorai* ("marketplaces") may simply be referring to local "squares." The high cost of land transportation restricted trade to valuable commodities such as wine and oil. Transport by sea was cheaper and allowed for trade of high-volume goods such as grain, but this was limited to regions having seaports. In first-century Palestine, where most of the land was agriculturally usable (Josephus *Ag. Ap.* 1.12) and the vast majority of the population consisted of peasants (small farm owners and day laborers, not to be equated with the absolutely poor) working the land and living on a low subsistence level, production was geared toward immediate consumption and allowed for very little if any surplus or disposable income. According to Josephus, the agrarian life was nowhere more concentrated than in Galilee. Despite numerical and spatial exaggerations, Josephus' description of Galilee, in contrast to commercial cities on the coast, is noteworthy. He writes,

For the land is everywhere so rich in soil and pasturage and produces such variety of trees, that even the most indolent are tempted by these facilities to devote themselves to agriculture. In fact every inch of the soil has been cultivated by the inhabitants; there is not a parcel of waste land. The towns, too, are thickly distributed, and even the villages, thanks to the fertility of the soil, are all so densely populated that the smallest of them contains about fifteen thousand inhabitants.

(*J.W.* 3.42–43)

Basic staples of life such as food and clothing were met within the family household and through a reciprocal exchange of goods. During harvest a reciprocal exchange of workers would have been expected. For peasant families, their plots of inherited land were their greatest possession, providing for their families' sustenance and some degree of dignity in a society where the farmer was deemed by the educated as a necessary simpleton who had no impact on the cultural and political landscape (Sir 38:24–34). All too often, however, when the production yield could not sustain the family and forced it into a debt which could not be repaid, the land was taken over by creditors (some of whom were wealthy Sadducees) who exploited the former landowners as tenant farmers. Fear of drought was so prevalent that an entire tractate in the Mishnah, *Taanith*, ("Days of Fasting") was devoted to religious rituals that would ensure rain.

Jewish families who leased farms would have contracted to pay rent or a percentage of the crop yield to the landowner (Stegemann 44–45). The elite class, which comprised about 5 percent of the population, were often distinguished by their accumulated real estate holdings, as oppose to money or gold (Cicero *Off.* 1.150–51), and would have endorsed an economy based on redistribution where goods generated by working peasants were administered and distributed by institutional structure (like temples, taxation, large lease/landowners). Redistribution established and stabilized great power and wealth among the upper class in urban centers (Stegemann 35–37).

Some Jewish families maintained businesses which produced specialized goods (e.g. pottery, bricks, tiles) or provided specialized services (e.g. woodworkers, masons, smiths). Many of the craftsmen and service providers (e.g. wool weavers, barbers, doctors) would have had their shops attached to their homes, contributing to the village economy beyond simply a local central marketplace (Horsley 203). As a woodworker (or a worker of hard materials) Jesus and his brothers probably had a shop attached to their house, but during prosperous times under Tiberius they may have also been employed at Sepphoris, about an hour's walk from Nazareth. Although money was used more in cities where consumption surpassed production, village economies which were primarily based on bartering still needed to incorporate currency to pay taxes and debts.

Excessive taxation was a major burden for poor rural families. Payment was often difficult and at times resulted in indebted slavery, cruel punishments, and shame (Plutarch, *Luc.* 20). The misery resulting from indebtedness even led some to commit suicide (Philo, *Legat.* 3.159ff.). Herod's lavish building programs were certainly a sign of prosperity after several decades of war in the region, but they also led to a fiscal imbalance which brought about considerably arduous taxation and erosion of land, making it difficult for many free small farmers to economically sustain themselves. The decline from free farmers to leaseholders to day laborers and even beggars was not unusual during the Herodian dynasty. During the time of Jesus it is difficult to say whether free small farmers or tenant farmers constituted the majority of the peasant class (Stegemann 111–12). Jesus' parables, analogies, and even temple action would have been thoroughly at home in this agriculturally driven economy which incorporated the tensions between reciprocal and redistributive systems of exchange.

Religion

Religion was embedded in the social fabric of antiquity. Diverse religious beliefs and practices and their syncretism were commonplace, especially in the Diaspora where Hellenistic and Roman religions were prevalent; but Palestine was not immune to pagan cults as is evident, for example, in the building of a temple for the emperor cult adjacent to the shrine of Pan at the source of the Jordan River. Jewish people in the Diaspora would have rubbed shoulders in the marketplaces with various mystery cults (e.g. the mysteries of Isis, Dionysus, and Mithras), an array of astrology, magic and soothsaying, the cult of emperors and rulers, and a variety of philosophies, each espousing its version of the good life. There is also evidence to suggest that some contact with Gnosticism is plausible even in the first century CE (Klauck). Religious pluralism was a constant challenge to the distinctiveness of Judaism, which defined itself on monotheism, election, and the divine allocation of land. In a largely pluralistic and polytheistic socio-religious context of the ancient Mediterranean, monotheism was especially repugnant because it was perceived as intolerant and godless. Unlike the Seleucids, the Roman administration allowed the Jewish people to practice their faith and maintain their Torah-oriented legal system (overseen by the Sanhedrin), so long as it did not threaten the collective peace and the collection of taxes.

Everyday life for pious Jewish families was governed by religious customs which functioned as identity markers that distinguished them from Gentiles. These customs, which were grounded in Torah, included circumcision, observance of feast days, Sabbath, dietary regulations, fasts, purity, and the offering of daily prayers and blessings prior to meals (Safrai, "Religion")

Before its destruction in 70 CE, the Jewish temple in Jerusalem was the centre of Jewish identity for both local and diaspora Jews who supported its institution through distance taxation and occasional pilgrimages, such as on Passover. In addition to it being the cultic centre where worship and a variety of sacrifices were performed (e.g. annually on the Day of Atonement, daily, private, festal), the temple occupied an important educational, social, economic, and political function. It served as the repository of scrolls, money, and gold. Since the high priest functioned as a political authority, the temple can be viewed in modern terms as the highest ethnic government building.

In addition to the temple, Jewish families participated in local synagogues which should be understood foremost as "assemblies" or "congregations" and not as elaborate buildings used specifically for religious purposes (Goodman 84). If synagogues were buildings during Jesus' day (e.g. Foerster), as opposed to open-air gatherings (e.g. Horsley), they would have functioned as community centers for meals and celebrations, lodging for pilgrims, political meeting rooms (much like city halls), and storage facilities for the community's goods, in addition to functioning as venues for worship and the teaching of Torah (Josephus *Life* 276–77; *Ant.* 14.235; Stegemann 141). One of the difficulties in reconstructing the quantity and specific religious functions of synagogues in the first century is that in addition to the term *synagoge*, Josephus more often uses the term *proseuche* to refer to a kind of prayer (house), which has led some to argue that the former may have been more civic than religious (Oster). In Tiberias the *proseuche* is described by Josephus as a "great hall" able to accommodate a large crowd (*Life* 277–80). In the Synoptic Tradition, it is only associated with the Temple (Mark 11:17). Outside Jerusalem, Jesus never visits a *proseuche*, but he makes several visits to a *synagoge*.

The exact relationship between these terms (and the Mishnah's *bet ha-kenesset*) and the places they represent still require further research. Whatever the exact terminology may turn out to be for such meeting places, there is no doubt that civic and religious assemblies in a common location (be it a building or open-air area) figured prominently in the life of Jewish households in and outside of Palestine, and provided an ideal setting for a wandering rabbi looking for audiences. If synagogues were Pharisaic institutions in Palestine before the Jewish war, as is sometimes suggested (Gutmann), they would have provided fertile ground for conflicts between Jesus and the Pharisees who would have competed for adherents within the same social sphere. However, it is important to note that most of the conflicts between Jesus and the scribes and Pharisees in the Synoptic Tradition do not occur specifically in synagogue contexts.

THOMAS R. HATINA

Further reading

Archer, Leonie J. *Her Price is Beyond Rubies: The Jewish Woman in Graeco-Roman Palestine*, JSOTSup 60, Sheffield: JSOT Press, 1990.

Brooten, Bernadette J. *Women Leaders in the Ancient Synagogues*, BJS 36, Chico, CA: Scholars Press, 1982.

Crossan, John Dominic and Jonathan L. Reed. *Excavating Jesus: Beneath the Stones, Behind the Texts*, New York: HarperCollins, 2002.

Foerster, Gideon. "The Ancient Synagogues of the Galilee," in Lee I. Levine (ed.) *The Galilee in Late Antiquity*, New York: Jewish Theological Seminary of America, 1992, pp. 289–319.

Goodman, Martin. *State and Society in Roman Galilee, AD 132–212*, Totowa, NJ: Rowman & Allanheld, 1983.

Gutmann, Joseph. "Synagogue Origins: Theories and Facts," in Joseph Gutmann (ed.) *Ancient Synagogues: The State of Research*, Brown Judaic Studies 22, Chico, CA: Scholars Press, 1981, pp. 1–6.

Halbwachs, Maurice. *On Collective Memory*, ed. and trans. L. A. Coser. Chicago, IL: University of Chicago Press, 1992.

Hanson, K. C. and Douglas E. Oakman. *Palestine in the Time of Jesus: Social Structures and Social Conflicts*, Minneapolis, MN: Fortress Press, 1998.

Harris, William V. *Ancient Literacy*, Cambridge: Cambridge University Press, 1989.

Helly, D. O. and S. M. Reverby. *Gendered Domains: Rethinking Public and Private in Women's History*, Ithaca, NY: Cornell University Press, 1992.

Horsley, Richard A. *Galilee: History, Politics, People*, Valley Forge, PA: Trinity Press International, 1995.

Kirk, Alan and Tom Thatcher (eds) *Memory, Tradition, and Text: Uses of the Past in Early Christianity*, Semeia 52, Atlanta, GA: Society of Biblical Literature, 2005.

Klauck, Hans-Jose. *The Religious Context of Early Christianity: A Guide to Graeco-Roman Religions*, trans. B. McNeil, Studies of the New Testament and Its World, Edinburgh: T. & T. Clark, 2000.

Lamphere, Rosaldo and Louise Lamphere (eds) *Women, Culture, and Society,* Stanford, CA: Stanford University Press, 1974.

Ong, Walter J. *Orality and Literacy: The Technologizing of the Word,* London: Routledge, 1988.

Oster, Richard E. "Supposed Anachronism in Luke–Acts' Use of *Synagoge,*" *NTS* 39 (1993) 178–208.

Peskowitz, Miriam. "'Family/ies' in Antiquity: Evidence from Tannaitic Literature and Roman Galilean Architecture," in Shaye J. D. Cohen (ed.) *The Jewish Family in Antiquity,* Atlanta, GA: Scholars Press, 1993, pp. 9–36.

Safrai, S. "Home and Family," in S. Safrai and M. Stern (ed.) *The Jewish People in the First Century,* CRINT 1/2, Philadelphia, PA: Fortress Press, 1976, pp. 728–92.

—— "Religion in Everyday Life," S. Safrai and M. Stern (ed.) *The Jewish People in the First Century,* CRINT 1/2, Philadelphia, PA: Fortress Press, 1976, pp. 793–833.

—— "Education and the Study of the Torah," S. Safrai and M. Stern (ed.) *The Jewish People in the First Century,* CRINT 1/2, Philadelphia, PA: Fortress Press, 1976, pp. 945–70.

Safrai, Ze'ev. *The Economy of Roman Palestine,* London: Routledge, 1994.

Stegemann, Ekkehard W. and Wolfgang Stegemann. *The Jesus Movement: A Social History of Its First Century,* Trans. O. C. Dean, Jr, Minneapolis, MN: Fortress Press, 1999.

Wegner, Judith Romney. *Chattel or Person? The Status of Women in the Mishnah,* Oxford: Oxford University Press, 1988.

I

INSCRIPTIONS AND PAPYRI

Inscriptions

The term "inscription" embraces any writing which was intended to be durable or permanent, and the study of such writing is known as epigraphy. Most inscriptions were written on stone, but they can also be found on wall-plaster, metal or terracotta, or picked out in mosaics. The study of the writing on coins is a separate discipline (numismatics). Inscriptions can be of a public or private nature: public ones intended to be read by as many people as possible, or private ones which would, for example, be visible only to the people who entered a tomb. They could be inscribed by professional stone-cutters, or by amateurs such as bereaved relatives. In Judaea and Galilee in the first century CE, Aramaic and Greek were the normal languages for inscriptions; Latin was used occasionally by the Roman authorities (and was more common at Caesarea Maritima), and there are some examples of Hebrew, as far as it can be distinguished from Aramaic. A few inscriptions refer to people connected with Jesus' life, but their main value in the study of the historical Jesus is to provide insights into the society in which he lived. There are not many identifiable Jewish inscriptions from the Diaspora which can be dated to the first century CE or earlier, since the use of clearly Jewish symbols such as the menorah only began later; however, there is evidence from inscriptions of a first-century Jewish presence in Italy, Greece, Caria, Phrygia, Lycia, Egypt and elsewhere.

The destruction of the Temple in 70 CE eradicated most of the inscriptions which the building must have contained. A warning sign has survived in two copies of a Greek version (*Corpus Inscriptionum Judaicarum* (CIJ) 2.1400); it is also mentioned by Josephus in his description of the Temple, and he says it was in Greek and Latin (but does not mention Hebrew or Aramaic; *War* 5.194). It threatens death to any foreigner who enters "the enclosure around the sanctuary", and seems to imply that the Roman government allowed this power to the Temple authorities. There is also evidence that donors other than Herod the Great contributed to the rebuilding of the Temple during Herod's reign. A very fragmentary inscription records a contribution to the paving of the Temple by someone from Rhodes in Herod's twentieth year (Williams III.17). An epitaph written on an ossuary from Jerusalem commemorates the sons of "Nicanor the Alexandrian who made the gates" (Williams III.16), and he can probably be identified with the donor of the Gate of Nicanor which is mentioned in rabbinic sources as being made of Corinthian bronze.

Herod the Great is named in building inscriptions and on statue bases from a number of places which enjoyed his benefactions, including Athens and the Aegean island of Syros (*Inscriptiones Judaicae Orientis* (IJudO) 1.Ach38–9, 74). A statue base with his name comes from the temple of the Syrian god Baalshamim at Seeia in Auranitis (*Inscriptions Grecques et Latines de la Syrie* 2364). A text from Beirut shows that his great-grand-children Berenice and Agrippa II restored one of his buildings (*Année Épigraphique* 1928: no. 82). The inscriptions show that Herod's official Greek titles included "friend of the emperor/the Romans," "benefactor" and "pious" (but not "great"); these terms were used by many other rulers on the fringes of the Roman Empire. Thirteen Latin inscriptions on wine jars found at Masada show that "King Herod the Jew" was importing wine from Italy in 19 BCE (Cotton and Geiger nos 804–16). Herod's sons who ruled as tetrarchs are mentioned in inscriptions with their regnal years. A lead weight from Tiberias refers to the thirty-fourth year of Antipas (29/30 CE; Kokkinos: 223 n. 100), and an inscription in Nabataean or Aramaic is dated to the thirty-third year of Philip (28/9 CE; Kokkinos: 239). There was a statue of Antipas on the island of Delos (IJudO 1.Ach69).

Pontius Pilate is named once in an inscription. A fragmentary Latin text from Caesarea Maritima, found in reuse in the theatre there (Lehmann and Holum no. 43), contains the name *[Po]ntius Pilatus* with his official title, *praefectus Iudaeae* (Tacitus incorrectly calls him *procurator*). His *praenomen*, the first part of his name which would have been written in the inscription as one letter, e.g. M. for Marcus, has been lost. The inscription seems to refer to a Tiberieum, presumably a building in honour of the Emperor Tiberius (although "Tiberian games" has also been suggested). The lettering is relatively small, written on a limestone block which appears to have been part of a wall. The building was probably not a temple, since a more monumental inscription would be required and Tiberius did not encourage emperor-worship anyway; a lighthouse at the entrance to the harbour is a more likely possibility.

In Jerusalem in the early first century CE, the normal funerary rite was secondary burial: the body was placed in a tomb and left until the flesh decayed, when the bones were collected and placed in a stone or terracotta container now known as an ossuary. The name of the deceased was often inscribed on the ossuary, usually in rough, amateur lettering. Ossuaries of family members are often found together in one tomb, and some ossuaries contained more than one individual. One which was excavated in the Peace Forest at Jerusalem in 1990 (Reich) is inscribed in Aramaic "Joseph son of Caiapha", and contained the remains of a man aged about sixty as well as five other individuals. It was extremely ornate, and the name is likely to be that of the High Priest Caiaphas of the Gospels, in office 18–36 CE, whom Josephus refers to as "Joseph who was also called Caiaphas" (*Ant.* 18.4.3). The ossuary of "Theodotus, freedman of

Queen Agrippina" (Rahmani no. 789) commemorates an ex-slave of the wife of the Emperor Claudius and mother of Nero. He was buried in an elaborate family tomb at Jericho. The inscription does not indicate how he came to be enslaved, but does imply that his connection with Agrippina was seen positively. There has been great controversy about an ossuary with an Aramaic inscription which reads "James son of Joseph, brother of Jesus." If genuine, it could be the epitaph of James "the Just" (but need not be, as all three names are common ones). The inscription, or at least the last part of it, has been declared by a committee set up by the Israel Antiquities Authority to be a forgery on both scientific and palaeographical grounds, but the arguments used against it have themselves been subjected to considerable attack. The ossuary came to public light through the antiquities market, and there is no reliable evidence about its provenance.

A marble slab (*Supplementum Epigraphicum Graecum* 8.13) which was acquired by the archaeologist Wilhelm Froehner in 1876 and sent to Paris, where it is now in the Cabinet des Médailles, contains the Greek text of an imperial edict or rescript punishing tomb-violators with death. It is obviously translated from Latin but does not represent normal Roman law. It is usually known at the Edict of Nazareth, but the association with Nazareth depends on information from the antiquities market in the 1870s. The lettering suggests that it belongs to the first century CE. The inscription is often dated to the time of Claudius (although it has also been attributed on stylistic grounds to Nero), and if Nazareth was its original location it must date from after Galilee came under direct Roman rule in 44 CE. Some scholars have understood it as being aimed specifically at the followers of Jesus. References to the "cults (rendered) to humans" and to treating the offence as one against the gods are consistent with charges which were later levelled against the Christians, and the potentially retrospective nature of the edict could be associated with measures against Jesus' disciples, although these points do not prove that this was the edict's original intention. Another suggestion is that it was a response to an incident at Passover, 8 CE, when some Samaritans scattered remains of the dead in the Temple. The small lettering and lack of imperial titulature suggest that the inscription is not an official proclamation but a copy made for private purposes, presumably to deter violation of a specific tomb.

Dedications from synagogues form one of the largest categories of Jewish inscriptions, but most belong to a much later period. An inscription found in situ can help to identify a building as a synagogue, but first-century synagogue inscriptions have normally been found out of context. The inscription from the "synagogue of Theodotus" (Williams III.2) was found at the bottom of a cistern in Jerusalem in 1913. A dating to before 70 CE has been generally, although not universally, accepted. The inscription gives some insight into the workings of a synagogue in Jesus' time. The building had been established by Theodotus' ancestors and others, but was rebuilt by Theodotus himself, who is described as "priest and *archisynagogos*", and the son and grandson of *archisynagogoi*. The synagogue was for "the reading of the law and the teaching of the commandments", and included guest accommodation for people coming from abroad, i.e. pilgrims to Jerusalem. *Archisynagogos* is the main term used in the gospels for a synagogue leader; *archon* is an alternative. An inscription dated to 55 CE from Berenice in Cyrenaica (modern Benghazi in Libya; Williams I.107) contains a list of people who contributed to the repair of the synagogue, headed by ten men with the title *archon*, and also including two female donors. Another inscription from Berenice (Williams V.36) also mentions "the *archons* and *politeuma* of the Jews" and honours a benefactor, D. Valerius Dionysus, with exemption from duties, an honorific olive crown and woollen fillet, and ritual naming at meetings. The *politeuma* indicates an autonomous community within the city.

The gospels use the Greek term *synagogē* for the building in which the Jewish community met. Inscriptions show that *proseuchē* ("place of prayer") was the normal term used by the Jews themselves in the first century CE, with *synagogē*, a common term in non-Jewish usage to indicate some sort of association, referring to the community rather than the building. In some manumission inscriptions from the Bosporan Kingdom on the north coast of the Black Sea, dated to the first century CE (Levinskaya 229–42), both terms are used: the building is the venue of the slave's manumission, or the beneficiary of the ex-slave's future services, and the community acts as guarantor.

In Egypt before Roman rule, synagogue buildings often contained inscriptions with dedications to members of the Ptolemaic dynasty. These served to express the Jews' loyalty to their secular rulers, but avoided the divine titulature which the Ptolemies normally used. At Rome, there were synagogues of the Augustesians and Agrippesians (Williams 230); although the evidence for their existence is much later, they were presumably named in honour of the Emperor Augustus and his son-in-law Marcus Agrippa. There is no evidence for a synagogue of the Herodians at Rome, contrary to what is sometimes claimed; this results from a misunderstanding of a fragmentary inscription with the name Herodion (*Jewish Inscriptions of Western Europe* 2.292).

Inscriptions also provide evidence for a Jewish community at Leontopolis in the southern part of the Nile Delta, where a number of epitaphs are dated to the reign of Augustus. Josephus refers to the establishment there of the "Temple of Onias", which existed from the second century BCE until Vespasian closed it in 74 CE. The epitaphs show the existence of a very Hellenized community which wrote in Greek and composed Greek verse, even referring to "Hades" and "Fate", although it retained a tendency to use typically Jewish names such as Judas and Jacob.

Miracle cures in the pagan world, part of the background to Jesus's miraculous healings in Jewish settings, are also recorded in inscriptions. The best evidence is from Asclepius' cult centre at Epidaurus. A series of large stelae informed visitors of the miracles which the god had performed there. Although these inscriptions were composed in the fourth or third century BCE, they could still be seen until the second century CE. The methods and ideology of the healing at Epidaurus were completely different from Jesus' cures, but some of the medical problems were the same: paralysis, blindness and dumbness.

Papyri

Papyrus was the principal material in the ancient world for writing and was not intended to last indefinitely. Papyrology is the study of writing on papyrus and other temporary materials, including potsherds (ostraca) and parchment. Some papyri and other documents have been found in the Judaean Desert, at Masada (from the time of the Jewish Revolt, 66–73 CE), and at sites such as Dura and Bostra, but the vast majority (apart from those with biblical and other religious texts; the Dead Sea Scrolls form a separate discipline) come from Egypt. They provide great insight into life in an eastern province of the Roman Empire, but their function in the study of the historical Jesus is mainly illustrative. Judaea was not necessarily governed in the same way as Egypt, so the detailed knowledge of, for example, Egypt's taxation system under Roman rule which has been build up from papyri may not be entirely applicable to Judaea. The Zenon archive of papyri provides some information about Judaea under Ptolemaic rule in the third century BCE, but it survived precisely because the region was ruled from Egypt then, and there is no equivalent from the first century CE. Greek was the normal language for papyri recording official business in Egypt.

The procedure followed for the census in Egypt can be reconstructed from papyrological evidence, and contrasted with references in the gospels. It followed a regular fourteen-year cycle. The concept of a legal domicile for individuals developed in Egypt in the first century CE, as a measure against the avoidance of fiscal obligations. Reintegration edicts were regularly issued which told people to return to their domiciles unless they had a valid reason for remaining where they were. However, such measures are not normally associated with the census, and there is no evidence that they were ever used outside Egypt. An edict of 104 CE (Hunt and Edgar 2.108) requires people to return "to their own hearths" for the census, and is aimed specifically at those from the countryside who are in the cities and neglecting "the cultivation which concerns them"; such people can only be allowed to remain by special permission. In Egypt, household heads made census declarations at their place of residence, not at all the procedure described by Luke. A significant number of census returns have survived on papyrus, listing household members and their ages, and these have been the basis for demographic studies of the population of Roman Egypt. There is also a census reference in an inscription. The epitaph of Q. Aemilius Secundus (CIL 3.6687) records details of his military career including being "sent against the Ituraeans on Mount Lebanon" and "on the orders of Quirinius" taking a census in the city of Apamea. This evidently refers to a census in the province of Syria, and does not need to be connected to one in Judaea or Galilee.

DAVID NOY

Further reading

Boffo, Laura. *Iscrizioni Greche e Latine per lo studio della Bibbia*, Brescia: Paideia, 1994.

Cotton, Hannah and Joseph Geiger. *Masada II: the Latin and Greek Documents*, Jerusalem: IES, 1989.

Horbury, William and David Noy. *Jewish Inscriptions of Graeco-Roman Egypt*, Cambridge: Cambridge University Press, 1992.

Hunt, A. S. and C. C. Edgar. *Select Papyri*, 2 vols, London: Heinemann, 1932–34.

Kokkinos, Nikos. *The Herodian Dynasty: Origins, Role in Society and Eclipse*, Supp. Ser. 30, Sheffield: Journal for the Study of the Pseudepigrapha, 1998.

Lehmann, C. M. and Holum, K. G. *The Greek and Latin Inscriptions of Caesarea Maritima*, Boston, MA: ASOR, 2000.

Levinskaya, Irina. *The Book of Acts in its First Century Setting vol. 5: Diaspora Setting*, Grand Rapids, MI: Eerdmans, 1996.

LiDonnici, Lynn. *The Epidaurian Miracle Inscriptions*, Atlanta, GA: Scholars Press, 1995.

Rahmani, L. Y. *A Catalogue of Jewish Ossuaries in the Collections of the State of Israel*, Jerusalem: IAA/IASH, 1994.

Reich, Ronny. "Ossuary Inscriptions from the Caiaphas Tomb," *Jerusalem Perspective* 4.5–6 (1991) 13–21.

Tcherikover, V., A. Fuchs, M. Stern, and D. A. Lewis. *Corpus Papyrorum Judaicarum*, 3 vols, Cambridge, MA: Magnes Press, 1957–64.

Williams, Margaret. *The Jews among the Greeks and Romans. A Diaspora Sourcebook*, London: Duckworth, 1998.

INTERPRETATION OF SCRIPTURE

The approaches to the interpretation of Scripture among Second Temple Jews and Jesus in particular vary widely. These include translations and paraphrases, "rewritten Bible" and interpretation of Scripture. This article covers major examples in each of these areas.

Translations and paraphrases

Translations and paraphrases served at least two purposes. First, these versions provided a means for hearing Scripture by those who were no longer fluent in Hebrew. Second, "Translation became part of the attempt to make scripture meaningful to the present," and thus retain within Israel the immediacy of God (Bowker 8).

Septuagint

All translations are to some degree interpretation, and the Septuagint exemplifies this. While the Septuagint rendering of the Torah is quite literal generally, there are exceptions and the translations of other books, such as Isaiah, are interpretations, based upon the Hebrew texts we know. For example, Isa 40:5 in Hebrew says that all flesh will see the glory of God, while the Septuagint interprets this as "all flesh shall see the salvation of God." The translators sought to explain difficult Hebrew words and phrases and removed anthropomorphisms. At other times, there are changes that affect the meaning significantly. In Gen 2:2, according to the Hebrew text, God rested on the seventh day. In order to show that God did not do any work on the seventh day, thus promoting Sabbath-keeping, the Septuagint "translates" Gen 2:2 to say that God rested from his works on the sixth day.

Targums

During the Second Temple period, Aramaic paraphrases of the Hebrew Scriptures began to appear, known as Targums. Targums provide a version of the Scriptures of Israel in a language better known to late Second Temple audiences than Hebrew. The Targums are more blatant than the Septuagint in offering interpretations through their paraphrases of the Scriptures, though like the Septuagint there is a spectrum, with *Targum Onqelos* staying closer to the Hebrew text than other Targums. For example, while the Hebrew text of Isa 53:4 says that the servant "carried our sicknesses and bore our sorrows," the *Targum of Isaiah* says that the Messiah will pray for the people. How much this is a reaction against Christian use of Isaiah 53 is difficult to determine, but it does show the large degree of freedom exercised by Targumists in paraphrasing the Hebrew text and, in the process, offering Jewish interpretations of the Hebrew text. The Targums often sought to solve puzzles in the Hebrew text. While the Hebrew says in 1 Sam 13:1 that Saul was one year old when he became king, the Targum says that Saul was like a one-year old who has no sin when he became king. Like the LXX, the Targums sought to make the Scriptures meaningful in the present.

Rewritten Bible

Multiple texts roughly contemporary with Jesus of Nazareth exhibit revised versions of parts of the biblical narrative, and are called "rewritten Bible." They retold the biblical history, sometimes omitting material, sometimes adding material. Each shows an interpretation of the biblical historical accounts. The aim of such texts is generally not to replace the biblical text but to supplement it, filling in gaps and solving problems of interpretation. Most, except for Josephus' *Jewish Antiquities*, assume knowledge of the biblical text (cf. *Jub.* 6:22, where explicit reference to the Scriptures is made).

Jubilees

Jubilees, a work found among the Dead Sea Scrolls, contains a rewritten version of Genesis 1 through Exodus 19. It is noteworthy for providing a basis to the Qumran community for a different calendar than the calendar apparently used by the Jerusalem priesthood. Jubilees freely omits and adds material. The names of many women are added to the account. *Jubilees* states that it was revealed by God to Enoch that the calendar should be solar based, as a year is always 364 days long. Laws given to Moses in Exodus are seen being given to the patriarchs earlier. The patriarchs are made to look more positive. Levi is shown as a priest already and Abraham's lie about his wife is omitted.

Jubilees reads the account of the giving of the Law on the fifteenth of the third month to mean that the Festival of Weeks celebrates the giving of the law and the Qumran community renewed the covenant annually on this day. Jubilees changes the biblical narrative in order to solve problems and provide more information. As such, the narrative is itself exegesis. *Jubilees* interprets the biblical narrative to stress eschatology, much like other Jewish literature of the period, e.g. 1 *Enoch*, which has Enoch seeing visions of the end times and the eschatological Son of Man of Daniel 7:13–14.

Pseudo-Philo

Pseudo-Philo provides an account of biblical history from Adam through the death of Saul in a work entitled *Biblical Antiquities*. While there are quotations of the biblical material, in general Pseudo-Philo paraphrases, omits material, summarizes or adds material that has no counterpart in the biblical text. These additions include speeches, prayers, and conversations among the characters in the narrative. Pseudo-Philo seeks to clarify and actualize the biblical text. Pseudo-Philo shows many predictions, usually by God, and their fulfillment in his narrative, as part of his stress on divine causality. He also offers evaluations on the behavior of characters in the narrative, which the biblical text often does not do. Pseudo-Philo adds material to show moral causality. God declares that Samson must be punished for his sins, and he will be blind because he sinned with his eyes. Pseudo-Philo's rewriting of the biblical narrative also focuses heavily upon women, usually honoring them in some way. Pseudo-Philo as a narrative is not *per se* an interpretation of Scripture but shows themes important to Jews of this period by the way he rewrites biblical history. This work takes passages out of context to illuminate other passages. For example, in Ps-Philo 9:5–6, reference is made to the incident with Tamar in Genesis 38 but she does not seduce Judah.

Josephus

Josephus in the first century also produced a rewritten version of biblical history. Unlike Pseudo-Philo's, it covers all of biblical history, is about five times as long and covers Genesis through 1 Maccabees. Perhaps more important is that Josephus interprets Scripture for apologetic reasons, answering charges of opponents such as Apion and making Judaism more appealing to a pagan audience. While Josephus promises at the beginning of his work to write an account that follows the biblical narrative precisely, he often diverges from the biblical narrative, seemingly for his apologetic purpose of making Judaism more palatable and appealing to his Roman captors. The amount of material given to individuals such as Abraham, Samson and Solomon suggests that Josephus is putting these people forth as "heroes" with many of the traits expected in a Greek rhetorical *encomium* such as courage (Feldman 84–85). In this way, Josephus commends these Israelites to his pagan audience.

Interpretive approaches

Many interpretive approaches were employed by Second Temple Jews, some specific to a particular interpreter, others common to several authors.

Pesher

The term *pesher* as a type of interpretation of the Scriptures of Israel comes from various texts found among the Dead Sea Scrolls called *pesharim*. These texts are commentaries generally on a particular book such as the *Pesher on Habakkuk* (1QpHab) or various biblical texts brought together to support one theme (4QFlor). This text quotes a passage from Habakkuk and says "this means," using the Hebrew world *pesher*. *Pesher* is marked by the mapping of the biblical text to a historical reality. The pesharim are noteworthy for making the prophetic biblical texts predictive of the time of the Qumran community, which is construed generally as in "the end of days." For example, the *Kittim of Habakkuk*, which probably refers to the Babylonians, is interpreted by the pesher method as the Romans. The pesher interpretations are based upon revelations given to the Teacher of Righteousness by God.

Allegory

In an allegorical interpretation, events or individuals are used as symbols for other events or entities. Philo is the most well known for employing allegorical interpretation at length. Philo's exposition of the Law of Moses contains frequent allegorical elements. Jesus told allegorical parables,

such as the one concerning Israel's prophets, himself, and the leaders of Israel (Luke 20:9–19). Paul speaks about Christian freedom and bondage to the Law through an allegorical use of Hagar, Sarah, Sinai, and the Jerusalem above (Gal 4:21–31). The later rabbinic literature also employs allegory, as do Christian writers such as Origen.

Argument

Scripture was interpreted so that it could support arguments. In Acts 2, a series of texts are used in a sequence that leads up to Ps 110:1. This psalm is interpreted to apply to Jesus as a justification of his exaltation to God's right hand, from which he has poured out the promised Holy Spirit. Early Christians used Psalm 110 to argue that Jesus is the Messiah. The *T. Job* 33.3 alludes to Ps 110:1 to show the vindication of Job the righteous sufferer. The Temple Scroll, which resembles to some degree "rewritten Bible" also offers interpretations of biblical texts using analogical reasoning that is similar to later rabbinic Midrash: 4QMMT, for example, speaks of inappropriate types of marriage based upon mixing of inappropriate species through "metaphorical example." Scriptural narratives were also used implicitly, such as Paul's use of the Exodus theme of God's redemption from bondage in Romans or the story of Melchizedek in Hebrews 7 in which Jesus is cast as a priest in the order of Melchizedek, to argue for matters of Christian belief.

Midrash

Midrash, which gets its name from the Hebrew word *darash*, "interpret," refers to a particular approach to interpreting the Scriptures. It is best known from rabbinic midrashic material dating from the fifth century CE. Midrash lays great stress upon individual words or phrases in developing elaborate interpretations. There are a number of "rules" employed for midrashic interpretations, and "Two sets of rules were particularly respected, the seven rules (or *middoth*) of Hillel, and the extension of them in the thirteen *middoth* of Ishmael" (Bowker 315). While there may be some similarities to the approaches found in Second Temple literature, including the New Testament, it is anachronistic to label material prior to the Bar Kochba revolt of 135 CE as midrash. Furthermore, since rabbinic midrash followed specific principles, which earlier literature may not have followed, applying this term to earlier writings, such as the scriptural interpretations of Jesus creates difficulty, which "lies in its simultaneous imprecision and authoritative mysteriousness: the label *midrash* tends to bring the interpretive process to a halt, as though it had explained something..." (Hays 13–14).

Interpreters

There are several important interpreters of Scripture in the Second Temple period. Here the approaches of a few interpreters, particularly Jesus, are described.

Jesus

Jesus as presented in the canonical Gospels employs and interprets the Scriptures of Israel in several different ways through citations, allusions, and intertextual echoes.

Jesus in some cases gives a deeper or expanded meaning to a scriptural text. After Jesus states in the Sermon on the Mount that he has not come to abolish but fulfill the Law, Jesus offers a novel interpretation of Exod 20:13. He asserts that looking at a woman lustfully equates to committing adultery.

Jesus creates composite quotations of Scripture and applies them to himself. At the synagogue in Nazareth, Jesus cites Isaiah, combining Isa 58:6 and 61:1–2a and applies this to himself in describing his purpose for coming.

Jesus interprets scriptural texts as applying to his contemporaries, while they seem to refer to earlier generations. For example, in Mark 7:6–7, Jesus applied Isa 29:13 to the Pharisees and scribes because of the way these groups used, developed, and followed tradition and therefore neglected the commandment of God.

Jesus reads some biblical passages in the light of other texts, making some primary and others secondary. In Matt 19:7–9, Jesus explains that the commandment that allows divorce (Deut 24:1–4) should be understood in light of Gen 2:24, which implies that divorce in some cases equates to adultery.

Jesus uses the Scriptures by analogy to justify his own action. If it is justifiable for David and his men to eat the consecrated bread of the Tabernacle, then the Son of Man, someone greater than David, can bend the rules for the sake of people (Luke 6:3–5).

Jesus reads the Scriptures prophetically, noting at points that his experience actualizes them (Luke 24:44–49) or that the Scriptures are in some fashion "fulfilled" by himself (Luke 22:69) or others (Mark 14:27).

Like other interpreters, the gospel writers present Jesus' use of the Scriptures for their own purposes,

such as Luke, who uses the Scriptures of Israel ecclesiologically, as well as using the Scriptures of Israel in narrative contexts apart from the words of Jesus, such as Matthew's application of Hos 11:2 to Jesus returning from Egypt to Judea (Matt 2:15).

Philo

Philo's interpretation of Scripture was based upon an effort to combine Judaism with Platonism. Philo's works seem to show both an effort to present a religious philosophy with the aid of the Scriptures, and an effort at biblical exegesis through philosophy. For Plato, a law-book needed a *proem*, and Philo used the creation of the world in Genesis in this way to show that the Law of Moses is natural law. Yet, in Philo's allegorical commentary on the Law of Moses, its nature as a legal code is largely irrelevant and he treats it as a philosophical treatise. Philo used allegory to show the real, eternal meaning behind biblical words and individuals.

Josephus

Josephus not only wrote the *Antiquities of the Jews*, described above, but several other works, such as the *Jewish War*, which concerns the war with Rome of 66–70 CE and *Against Apion*, which challenges Apion's incorrect interpretation of the Jews. Unlike most of the other works and interpreters discussed here, Josephus' main audience seems to be Gentiles, which affects his biblical interpretation. For example, while the scriptural texts may show God working providentially, Josephus speaks of Fate. In all these works Josephus claims great accuracy and, following the model of Greek historiography, writes "apologetic historiography," using the past to legitimate Jews and their customs. His works are written primarily during his time at Rome as a prisoner, and he casts his writings in ways that will be more acceptable to the Romans. For example, Josephus shows how many important characters in Israel's history "possess the four cardinal virtues of wisdom, courage, temperance, and justice, plus the virtue of piety" (Feldman 96). Josephus did not interpret Scripture explicitly but implicitly by rewriting and modifying it or incorporating it into his narratives and arguments.

Apocrypha and Pseudepigrapha

The Apocrypha and Pseudepigrapha are full of biblical citations, allusions, intertextual echoes and episodes. The framework of scriptural stories is used as the basis for narratives, such as the use in 4 Ezra of the destruction of Jerusalem by the Babylonians to describe its destruction by the Romans (*4 Ezra* 3:1–2). Though not precisely interpretation, Jacob's blessing of his sons and lamentation after his death (Gen 49–50) gave rise to many testaments, such as the *Testament of Job* and the *Testament of Moses*. Scripture was sometimes "interpreted" by whole books being written that provide additional information on a person (often little known), often having the individual prophesy about the end times, e.g. *1 Enoch*, going far beyond the little known about Enoch from Gen 5:18–24. There are also texts that interpret biblical texts by expanding them to provide significantly more information, such as the nature of the garden in the *Life of Adam and Eve*. Scriptural elements are more implicit in the Apocrypha than in the Pseudepigrapha and are used more to make the text like its biblical models in genre and style.

Conclusion

The Second Temple period produced a wide variety of approaches to interpreting Scripture, from pesher to allegory. Much of it was focused on legitimating Judaism in general (Josephus), or one particular movement within Judaism (pesher at Qumran). Jesus and to a lesser extent the writers of the Qumran writings related to the Dead Sea Scrolls interpret the Scriptures to apply to themselves as individuals, which is not as common. Much of the interpretation of Scripture in this period sought to speak to Israel's situation of oppression under foreign powers, such as 2 Maccabees and offer hope for deliverance, such as *1 Enoch*.

KENNETH D. LITWAK

Further reading

Berrin, Shani. "Qumran Pesharim," in Matthias Henze (ed.) *Biblical Interpretation at Qumran*, Grand Rapids, MI: Eerdmans, 2005, pp. 110–33.

Bowker, John. *The Targums and Rabbinic Literature: An Introduction to Jewish Interpretations of Scripture*, Cambridge: Cambridge University Press, 1969.

Evans, Craig A. and James Sanders (eds) *Early Christian Interpretation of the Scriptures of Israel: Investigations and Proposals*, JSNTSup 148, Sheffield: Sheffield Academic Press, 1997.

Feldman, Louis J. *Josephus's Interpretation of the Bible*, Berkeley, CA: University of California Press, 1998.

France, R. T. *Jesus and the Old Testament*, Grand Rapids, MI: Baker Book House, 1982.

Hays, Richard B. *Echoes of Scripture in the Letters of Paul*, New Haven, CT: Yale University Press, 1989.

Juel, Donald. *Messianic Exegesis: Christological Interpretation of the Old Testament in Early Christianity*, Philadelphia, PA: Fortress Press, 1988.

Kimball, Charles A. *Jesus' Exposition of the Old Testament in Luke's Gospel*, JSNTSup 94. Sheffield: JSOT Press, 1994.

Le Deaut, R. *The Message of the New Testament and the Aramaic Bible (Targum)*, Rome: Biblical Institute Press, 1982.

Litwak, Kenneth D. *Echoes of Scripture in Luke–Acts: Telling the Story of God's People*, JSNTSup 282, London: T. & T. Clark, 2005.

Mulder, Martin Jan. *Mikra: Text, Translation, Reading and Interpretation of the Hebrew Bible in Ancient Judaism and Early Christianity*, Peabody, MA: Hendrickson, 2004.

Murphy, Frederick J. *Pseudo-Philo: Rewriting the Bible*, Oxford: Oxford University Press, 1993.

INTERPRETATION OF THE GOSPELS

The interpretation of the New Testament Gospels has undergone dramatic shifts in the last century. New ideas about the genre of the Gospels, their sources, and the way the material has been transmitted, edited, and presented as literature have engaged the attention of an ever increasing number of scholars.

Genre of the Gospels

It was conventional in the pre-critical era to regard the New Testament Gospels as biographies or apostolic memoirs (e.g. Justin Martyr, *1 Apol.* 66). Traditional beliefs about the authorship of the Gospels accommodated and encouraged this view. It was assumed that Matthew and John were written by the apostles of those names, and that the apostle Peter stood behind the Gospel of Mark. Similarly, Luke's presumed association with Paul lent a measure of apostolicity to the third Gospel.

The nineteenth-century (or "old") quest of the historical Jesus assumed that the Gospels were biographies, in a sense not too different from the modern understanding of biography. It was assumed that the material in the Gospels was in chronological order and that the development of Jesus' thinking could be deduced. This flawed understanding lies behind such diverse conclusions as that of H. J. Holtzmann (1863), who found a Jesus concerned with ethics and the internalizing of religion, and that of Albert Schweitzer (1906; English translation 1910), who found a Jesus convinced that divine judgment was unfolding and that human history was about to end.

With the emergence of the history of religions school of thought, the Gospels have been studied over against the Greco-Roman literature of late antiquity. A variety of genres have been suggested for the Gospels, including Greco-Roman aretalogy,

Greek tragedy, Greek comedy, tragi-comedy, origin myth, Greek romance, and Greco-Roman biography. Following K. L. Schmidt's lead, Rudolf Bultmann concluded that the Gospels, whose genre was a literary *novum*, should be defined as "expanded cult legends," based on the kerygma of Christ (1972: 371). The view that the Gospels were not biographies became a near consensus for half a century.

Recent work has returned to viewing the Gospels' genre as biography, but not in the uncritical understanding that characterized much of the nineteenth-century quest. Charles Talbert's study (1977) reopened the question, arguing that scholars had misunderstood Greco-Roman biography and so had failed to see the close parallels with the Gospel of Mark. Talbert shows that Greco-Roman biographies often contain mythical elements and sometimes perform cultic functions, very much as we see in the Gospels. Recently Richard Burridge (1992) has joined Talbert, providing a great deal more stylistic and literary critical data. Although Burridge disagrees with aspects of Talbert's analysis, he does conclude that the Gospels are indeed a species of the Greco-Roman biography. Scholars today are sharply divided over questions of the best background, in the light of which Jesus and the Gospels should be interpreted, with some urging comparison with Hellenistic sources and others urging comparison with Jewish sources. Nevertheless, ongoing archaeology in Israel, the publication of all of the Dead Sea Scrolls and related texts from Jewish late antiquity, and important advances in critical study of targumic and rabbinic literature recommend viewing Jesus and the Gospels in the light of Jewish patterns and exemplars.

Criticism of the Synoptic Gospels

Criticism of the Synoptic Gospels has advanced relatively rapidly and is marked by three important developments. Each development entails a method and a clearly defined goal.

Source criticism

Influenced by source criticism of the Pentateuch, scholars began the search for the sources of the Gospels. Since Augustine, it had been assumed that Matthew was the first Gospel written and that Mark was an abbreviation of it. In the 1760s and 1780s H. Owen and J. J. Griesbach argued that Matthew was first Gospel to be composed, that Luke made use of Matthew, and that Mark was written last, making

use of both Matthew and Luke. This view remained dominant until 1863, when Holtzmann concluded that Mark was written first and that Matthew and Luke wrote later, making use of Mark (or an earlier version of Mark) and a source of sayings (later to be called "Q," usually understood as the abbreviation for *Quelle*, "source"). Markan priority slowly gained ground, winning further adherents thanks to work by J. C. Hawkins (1898), William Sanday (ed., 1911), and B. H. Streeter (1924). Although this consensus has been challenged by William Farmer (1964) and a few students and colleagues, Markan priority has continued to be the dominant view. Advances in form and redaction criticism have lent additional support to the majority opinion (Tuckett 1983).

Source criticism of the Gospels has grown much more complicated in recent years thanks to the discovery and/or reassessment of several extra-canonical gospels. Four in particular have garnered a great deal of attention, with some scholars claiming their antiquity and independence from the canonical gospels. Some think the passion narrative of the *Gospel of Peter* predates the Synoptic Tradition. This is doubtful, however, for this narrative is replete with Mattheanisms and indications of composition in the second century. Others have claimed that the Egerton Papyrus 2 dates back to the 40s or 50s, before the bifurcation of Johannine and Synoptic traditions. But this view is highly problematic; it is much more likely that the Egerton Gospel represents a second-century pastiche in which Johannine and synoptic materials have been conflated from memory (as seen, for example, in Justin Martyr's conflated quotations of dominical tradition). Still others think that the *Secret Gospel of Mark*, mentioned and briefly quoted in a long lost letter by Clement of Alexander, preserves older tradition. But again, this is very doubtful. Not only has this Clementine letter not received proper critical scrutiny (and may even be a modern forgery), the testimony of Clement, who evinces astonishing credulity in matters of apostolic origins of this writing and that, should be viewed with skepticism. And finally, many scholars think that the *Gospel of Thomas* contains significant amounts of independent and in some cases possibly authentic material. But this document quotes or alludes to one half of the writings that make up the New Testament, exhibits secondary Mattheanisms and Lukanisms, and coheres with esoteric and ascetic tendencies that reflect eastern Christianity of the second century. Moreover, *Thomas* may also exhibit points of contact with Tatian's *Diatessaron*. These features point to the second century, not the first. *Thomas* may contain a few instances of independent material, but researchers should proceed with due caution.

Form criticism

Form criticism of the Gospels began with Julius Welhausen at the turn of the century and received its definitive statements in the work of K. L. Schmidt and Martin Dibelius in 1919 and in the work of Rudolf Bultmann and Vincent Taylor in 1921 and 1935, respectively. Form critics concluded that the tradition that makes up the Gospels circulated in small units (or what are called pericopes), which the Evangelists later collected, stitched together, and presented as continuous narratives. Only the Passion Narrative is believed to have circulated early on as a continuous narrative. By identifying the form and function of these units of tradition, form critics have had some success in inferring information about life in the early communities (*Sitz im Leben*). It was concluded that much of the material was edited and contextualized in the early church, though how much was actually created by these communities is debated (Bultmann thought much of it was; Taylor thought little of it was). Scholars remain divided over this question today, though the radical skepticism of Bultmann has fallen out of vogue.

Redaction criticism

In the 1950s form criticism was eclipsed by a new method that emphasized the contribution made by the Evangelists themselves. The distinction now was between inherited tradition and the editing (or redaction) of the Evangelists (in contrast to form criticism, which distinguished material created by the early church from material that originated with Jesus himself). Hans Conzelmann and Günther Bornkam, two prominent students of Bultmann, and Willi Marxsen offered important and lasting contributions to the new approach.

Hans Conzelmann (1954; English translation 1961) attempted to show that the Lukan evangelist, embarrassed by delay of the Parousia, muted ideas of eschatological imminence. He does this by structuring salvation history in three phases: (1) the Period of Israel, understood to be from creation to the imprisonment of John the Baptist (cf. Luke 16:16); (2) the Period of Jesus, understood to be from the baptism of Jesus until his post-Easter ascension (cf. Luke 22:35–37); and (3) the Period of the Church, understood to be from the ascension of Jesus until the Parousia (cf. Luke 4:21; Acts 1:6).

Günther Bornkamm and two of his students (1960; English translation 1963) showed to what extent the Matthean Gospel is thoroughly Jewish, focusing on fulfillment of prophecy, fidelity to the Law (with emphasis on the Love Command), and issues surrounding what constitutes righteousness.

Willi Marxsen (1956) attempted to discover the Markan evangelist's situation and theology. By probing the meaning of *euangelion* and offering a detailed study of the Parable of the Sower (Mark 4), Marxsen concluded that Mark successfully checked the gnosticizing tendency of the tradition by combining the Pauline kerygma and the Synoptic tradition.

In the decades since the publication of these seminal studies it has become apparent that the work of Conzelmann and Bornkamm was more successful than that of Marxsen. This is due, in no small way, to the simple fact that we have the sources of Matthew and Luke (i.e. Mark and Q). Therefore, through comparative analysis, we can observe in what ways the Matthean and Lukan evangelists edited, expurgated, and supplemented their sources. From this editing work (or redaction) we are able to infer the theological emphases of the respective evangelists. In the case of the Gospel of Mark, however, we are in no such position. Redaction critical study of Mark, from Marxsen and beyond, has been hampered by problems of subjectivity, in attempting to distinguish tradition (what the Markan evangelist inherited) from redaction (what the Markan evangelist contributed). For this reason, many Gospel scholars have experimented with new critical methods, emphasizing the literary wholeness of the Gospels, especially so in the case of Mark.

New forms of literary criticism

Largely in reaction to form criticism and redaction criticism, with their preoccupation with sources and reconstruction of hypothetical circumstances and experiences of the early Christian community, NT interpreters began focusing more carefully on the narrative strategies of the completed Gospels. Some focused on formal structures (structuralism, narrative criticism), imagined responses of readers (reader response, rhetorical criticism), and various perspectives (feminist, womanist, liberationist, and so forth). Most of these approaches have validity and have succeeded in alerting interpreters to dimensions in the Gospel narratives that modern readers may well overlook. At the very least, the new forms of literary criticism have forced interpreters to be more self-aware and to recognize the unconscious tendency to superimpose on the Gospels modern understandings of life.

However, many of these new forms of literary criticism have been criticized for minimizing, even ignoring the gains made in historical study, linguistics, comparative literature (such as the Dead Sea Scrolls, pseudepigrapha, and early rabbinic and targumic literature), archaeology, and geography. While it is surely correct to take a given Gospel on its own terms (e.g. not reading Matthew or Luke into Mark), it is not appropriate to read a given Gospel in isolation. Moreover, the practitioners of the new literary criticism sometimes read modern political and social issues into the Gospels, thus foisting upon these first-century writings issues and strategies that are quite foreign and anachronistic (see McKnight 121–37).

The positive contribution of the new literary criticism lies in making modern exegetes more aware of the purpose and goals of the respective Evangelists, to appreciate what each tried to accomplish. In short, this has been the goal of exegesis all along, though sometimes forgotten or obscured. The purpose of the Evangelist will be understood when the Gospel is studied in full context, which entails historical study, comparative literary study, and archaeological and geographical study. When the Evangelist's purpose is understood, the materials from which the historical Jesus may emerge are more clearly identified.

Criticism of the fourth Gospel

Criticism of the Fourth Gospel differs significantly from criticism of the Synoptic Gospels. This is because the style and contents of the Fourth Gospel are quite different and because its relationship to the Synoptic Gospels is uncertain. Moreover, opinion is much divided over the religious and social context in which the Fourth Gospel took shape.

Source criticism

Opinion over the literary relationship of the Fourth Gospel is sharply divided, with some scholars contending the fourth evangelist made use of one or more of the Synoptic Gospels, others contending that the fourth evangelist made no use of the Synoptic Tradition, and still others contending for a middle position, in which it is suggested that the fourth evangelist may have made use of sources (e.g. a Passion source) also utilized by the Synoptic evangelists. It is not clear at this time which view, if any, dominates the discussion.

Rudolf Bultmann (1941; English translation 1971) argued that the fourth Gospel was composed from a Signs source, a Gnostic Discourse source, and a Passion source, and was later edited by an ecclesiastical redactor. Although something of a classic, this imaginative reconstruction today is followed by almost no one. Besides piling hypotheses upon hypotheses, Bultmann's approached suffers from anachronistic use of sources that post-date the Fourth Gospel by several centuries.

Although divided over the question of John's literary dependence on the Synoptic Gospels, if any, a near consensus has emerged with regard to the probable existence of a Signs source (or Signs Gospel) that emerged in the Johannine community and later was expanded and supplemented with a Passion narrative and a series of discourses.

Tradition criticism

Another area of dispute in Johannine research concerns tradition and context. In the light of what background should the Fourth Gospel be studied? From the second century until the twentieth century it was supposed that in one way or another the Gospel was occasioned by an early form of Gnosticism. In the nineteenth century B. F. Westcott, following the lead of patristic authorities, argued that the theology and character of the Fourth Gospel were best explained as an attempt on the part of the Evangelist to combat Gnosticism with its own vocabulary, particularly as seen in the dualistic terminology (esp. light vs darkness) and the affirmation that the "Word became flesh" (1:14). The latter was understood as a refutation of Gnosticizing docetism, in which the humanity of Jesus was denied.

Bultmann turned the Gnostic interpretation of the Fourth Gospel on its head with his novel hypothesis that the Evangelist was a former Gnostic, who made use of Gnostic materials in the composition of his work. Almost no one follows this line of interpretation today. Increasingly the Fourth Gospel has come to be understood in the context of the synagogue, in which Jewish wisdom traditions are utilized in the formulation of Christology and Jewish scripture and exegetical traditions are invoked for apologetic and evangelistic purposes.

Interpretation of the Gospels

Interpretation of the Gospels today has been influenced by the significant increase of relevant primary literature that has comes to light in recent years. New social and literary studies, informed by ongoing archaeological work, have resulted in better nuanced and contextualized results. A few of the most important developments are summarized here. Fuller treatments can be found in the entries on the individual Gospels.

Mark

The meaning of the "messianic secrecy" theme in Mark, if one exists at all, continues to be debated (ed. Tuckett). The function of scripture in Mark is another important item of debate. But recent interpretation appears to be more focused on the Evangelist's use of literary and political traditions current in the Roman Empire of this period. For example, Dennis MacDonald has recently argued that the Markan evangelist has told the Jesus story in the light of the Homeric tradition (MacDonald). There may well be allusions here and there to the Homeric tradition, but the evidence is insufficient to sustain this hypothesis.

One is advised to take fully into account the Gospel's incipit: "The beginning of the good news of Jesus Christ, [the Son of God]" (1:1). Even without the words "Son of God," the allusion to the Roman imperial cult of the divine emperor is quite evident. The climactic utterance of the centurion – presumably Roman – at the moment of Jesus' death, "Truly this man was the Son of God" (15:39), confirms this point. If Mark was composed during or near the end of the first great Jewish revolt (66–70 CE), the political and social point that the Evangelist was trying to make seems clear: Julius Caesar and his successors, who with the death of Nero in 68 are no more, have egregiously failed to bring "good news" to the world, and so hardly can be regarded as sons of God. The Markan Evangelist urges the Roman public to consider Jesus Christ as the true Son of God, whose life and death were marked with stunning evidence of divinity. It is in him that the world will find authentic good news.

Matthew

The Matthean evangelist reorients his Markan source toward the persecution the Christian community is experiencing in the synagogue that views Jesus as antinomian and as a failed messianic claimant. The Evangelist alters the incipit to read: "The book of the genealogy of Jesus Christ, the son of David, the son of Abraham" (1:1). In doing this, the Evangelist underscores the Judaic heritage of Jesus (Sim). He is the "son of Abraham" (i.e. a true Jew) and he is the "son of David" (i.e. the

rightful messianic heir). The genealogy is constructed in such a way as to root the line of Jesus in Israel's rise, fall, and rise again. Besides the three fourteen-generations scheme (which through gematria refers to "David," i.e. $dvd = 4 + 6 + 4$), there are present in the genealogy five women (including Mary), whose presence in the messianic line attests to God's remarkable activity in Israel's history. Five prophecies are said to be fulfilled in the Infancy narrative proper. Jesus' teaching is presented in five major teaching blocks (i.e. chs 5–7, 10, 13, 18, and 24–25). King Herod's murder of the infants and the flight to Egypt leave little doubt that the evangelist has presented Jesus in Mosaic colors.

This is necessary, if he is to persuade a very skeptical synagogue that Jesus has not broken the Law, but has fulfilled it (cf. 5:17–20 and the five antitheses in 5:21–48). The Evangelist's concern with "righteousness" is seen in many places (Przybylski). The Gospel concludes with the risen Jesus affirming his "authority in heaven and on earth" and commanding his apostles to "make disciples of all the nations" (28:18–20). The language of the Great Commission is reminiscent of Daniel 7, in which the "Son of Man" figure is given authority, so that all nations will serve him. In Matthew's presentation, Jesus has fulfilled important facets of Jewish expectations. As the risen, glorified son of David and Son of God, he now directs his faithful followers to bring the Gentiles to obedience, to obey the Jewish Law as he himself taught it.

Luke

The theology of Luke is somewhat more complex, not least because the Evangelist produced two volumes, with the second (i.e. Acts) treating important figures and developments in the early church. Major emphases of the Evangelist are readily apparent. Proper use of one's material resources (3:10–14; 8:1–3; 19:1–10), compassion for the poor (14:12–14, 15–24), readiness to forgive (6:37; 7:42–48; 23:34), openness to outsiders (4:16–30; 7:36–50), and commitment to worldwide evangelism (3:6; 24:47) are among the Evangelist's principal concerns. The Lukan Evangelist is particularly concerned with election theology, with teaching on who are justified before God and who are not. Several parables found only in Luke speak to this theme. The parable of the Good Samaritan (10:30–39) teaches that the one who shows mercy fulfills the law. The parable of the Prodigal Son (15:11–32) shows that repentance – no matter how serious the sin – makes restoration with God possible, and should make it possible with humans as well. The parable of the Rich Man (16:19–31) shows that wealth and poverty are not trustworthy indicators of who are elect and who are not.

John

The Fourth Gospel develops a remarkable scriptural apologetic, in the face of a hostile synagogue that has expelled Christians. The Gospel's Prologue treats creation (1:1–5) and covenant (1:14–18), declaring that Jesus is none other than God's Word made flesh (vv. 1, 14). The first part of the Prologue interacts with Genesis 1 and Jewish interpretive traditions concerning the pre-creation presence and activities of God's word and/or wisdom. The last part of the Prologue interacts with the Exodus story of the giving of the Law at Sinai, particularly chs 33–34, where the covenant is given a second time, because God is "full of grace and truth" (John 1:14, alluding to Exod 34:6), and ch. 40, where the glory of the Lord fills the tabernacle, or tent (Gk. *skene*), made of skin. The story of Exodus adumbrated the story of Jesus, where God's glory – in the plain sight of the people of Israel – took up residence in a tent of skin.

As impressive as the Prologue may be, it alone would never persuade a doubting synagogue. The principal problem lay in the shameful execution of Jesus. This is the very point Trypho makes (c. early to mid-second century), when he demands of Christians to show where in the Scriptures the Messiah is to die such a shameful death (Justin Martyr, *Dialogue with Trypho* 89 and 91). Evidently at the end of the first century the fourth Evangelist faced the same question. A scriptural apologetic is mounted, in which several scriptures are cited, from chs 1–19. But in the first half of the Gospel (i.e. 1:23–12:16) scripture is never introduced as fulfilled. A variety of formulas are employed (e.g. "he said," "as it is written"). But at the mid-point of the Gospel (12:37–43), where readers are told that despite the many signs that Jesus performed, the people were not believing in him, the Evangelist consistently introduces scripture "in order that it be fulfilled" (cf. 12:38–19:37). It is in the rejection and execution of Jesus that, unwittingly, the Jewish people themselves play a part in the fulfillment of scripture and in the "lifting up" (lit. on a cross), or "exalting" (in the figurative sense of the word) of their Messiah Jesus.

Q

Q is a hypothetical source that most scholars think was utilized by the evangelists Matthew and Luke, in their respective revisions of Mark. Because Q is usually interpreted apart from the context in which it is found in the Gospels of Matthew and Luke, scholars have explored a variety of imaginative social and religious settings. Because the focus of the Q material is largely ethical, some scholars have tried to interpret Q in reference to Cynicism. However, most are not persuaded. Perhaps one of the most egregious errors in this approach is in the assumption that what is not in Q was either not known to the imagined "Q community" or had been rejected. Accordingly, because there is no Passion, it is asserted by some that the Q people had no interest in the death and resurrection of Jesus.

Recently, J. D. G. Dunn has made a powerful case for viewing Q as a very early compilation of the teaching of Jesus. It lacks a Passion Narrative because it is Jesus' pre-Passion teaching. The lack of Passion material argues not for a Passion-ignorant or Passion-rejecting Cynic community but for careful preserved authentic material that reaches back to the pre-Passion and pre-Easter Jesus.

CRAIG A. EVANS

Further reading

General studies

Bultmann, R. *The History of the Synoptic Tradition*, Oxford: Blackwell, 1972 [1921].

Burridge, R. A. *What Are the Gospels? A Comparison with Graeco-Roman Biography*, SNTSMS 70, Cambridge: Cambridge University Press, 1992.

Farmer, W. R., *The Synoptic Problem: A Critical Analysis*, New York: Macmillan, 1964.

Hawkins, J. C. *Horae Synopticae: Contributions to the Study of the Synoptic Problem*, Oxford: Clarendon, 1898.

Holtzmann, H. J. *Die synoptischen Evangelien: Ihr Ursprung und geschichtlicher Charakter*, Leipzig: Engelmann, 1863.

McKnight, S. *Interpreting the Synoptic Gospels*, Guides to New Testament Exegesis 2, Grand Rapids, MI: Baker, 1988.

Sanday, W. (ed.) *Oxford Studies in the Synoptic Problem*, Oxford: Clarendon, 1911.

Sanders, E. P. and M. Davies. *Studying the Synoptic Gospels*, London: SCM Press; Philadelphia, PA: Trinity Press International, 1989.

Schweitzer, A. *Von Reimarus zu Wrede: Eine Geschichte des Leben-Jesu-Forschung*, Tübingen: Mohr Siebeck, 1906; ET: *The Quest of the Historical Jesus*, New York: Macmillan, 1968.

Stanton, G. N. *The Gospels and Jesus*, Oxford: Oxford University Press, 1989.

Talbert, C. H. *What is a Gospel? The Genre of the Canonical Gospels*, Philadelphia, PA: Fortress Press, 1977.

Tuckett, C. M. *The Revival of the Griesbach Hypothesis: An Analysis and Appraisal*, Cambridge and New York: Cambridge University Press, 1983.

Studies and commentaries on Mark

Evans, C. M. *Mark 8:27–16:20*, WBC 34B. Nashville, TN: Thomas Nelson, 2001.

France, R. T. *The Gospel of Mark*, NIGTC; Grand Rapids, MI: Eerdmans; Carlisle: Paternoster, 2002.

Guelich, R. A. *Mark 1–8:26*, WBC 34A. Dallas, TX: Word, 1989.

MacDonald, D. R. *The Homeric Epics and the Gospel of Mark*, New Haven, CT: Yale University Press, 2000.

Martin, R. P. *Mark: Evangelist and Theologian*, Grand Rapids, MI: Zondervan, 1972.

Marxsen, W. *Mark the Evangelist*, Nashville, TN: Abingdon, 1969 [1956].

Pesch, R. *Das Markusevangelium*, HTKNT 2:1–2, Freiburg: Herder, 1977, 1991.

Tuckett, C. M. (ed.) *The Messianic Secret*, IRT 1; London: SPCK; Philadelphia, PA: Fortress Press, 1983.

Studies and commentaries on Matthew

Bornkamm, G., G. Barth, and Held, H. J. *Tradition and Interpretation in Matthew*, Philadelphia, PA: Westminster, 1963 [1960].

Davies, W. D. and Allison, D. C., Jr. *A Critical and Exegetical Commentary on the Gospel according to Saint Matthew*, ICC, Edinburgh: T. & T. Clark, 1988–97.

Gundry, R. H. *Matthew: A Commentary on His Handbook for a Mixed Church under Persecution*, Grand Rapids, MI: Eerdmans, 1994.

Hagner, D. A. *Matthew*, WBC 33, Dallas, TX: Word, 1993–95.

Przybylski, B. *Righteousness in Matthew and His World of Thought*, SNTSMS 41, Cambridge: Cambridge University Press, 1980.

Sim, D. C. *The Gospel of Matthew and Christian Judaism: The History and Social Setting of the Matthean Community*, Edinburgh: T. & T. Clark, 1998.

Stanton, G. N. *A Gospel for a New People: Studies in Matthew*, Edinburgh: T. & T. Clark, 1992; Louisville, KY: Westminster/John Knox, 1993.

Studies and commentaries on Luke

Conzelmann, H. *The Theology of St Luke*, New York: Harper & Row, 1961 [1954].

Fitzmyer, J. A. *The Gospel According to Luke*, AB 28, 28A, Garden City, NJ: Doubleday, 1981–85.

—— *Luke the Theologian: Some Aspects of His Teaching*, New York: Paulist, 1989.

Green, J. B. *The Gospel of Luke*, NIC-NT, Grand Rapids, MI: Eerdmans, 1997.

Jervell, J. *Luke and the People of God: A New Look at Luke-Acts*, Minneapolis, MN: Augsburg, 1972.

Marshall, I. H. *The Gospel of Luke*, NIGTC, Grand Rapids, MI: Eerdmans, 1978.

Nolland, J. *Luke 1–9:20*, WBC 35, Dallas, TX: Word, 1989–93.

Studies and commentaries on John

Brown, R. E. *The Gospel According to John*, AB 29, 29A, Garden City, NJ: Doubleday, 1966–70.

Bultmann, R. *The Gospel of John: A Commentary*, Philadelphia, PA: Westminster Press, 1971 [1941].

Dodd, C. H. *Historical Tradition in the Fourth Gospel*, Cambridge: Cambridge University Press, 1963.

—— *The Interpretation of the Fourth Gospel*, Cambridge: Cambridge University Press, 1953.

Hengel, M. *The Johannine Question*, Philadelphia, PA: Trinity Press International, 1989.

Lindars, B. *The Gospel of John*, NCB; Grand Rapids, MI: Eerdmans, 1986.

Schnackenburg, R. *The Gospel According to St John*, New York: Crossroad, 1980–82 [1965–75].

Studies and commentaries on Q

Allison, D. C., Jr. *The Jesus Tradition in Q*, Harrisburg, PA: Trinity Press International, 1997.

Dunn, J. D. G. *Jesus Remembered*, Christianity in the Making 1, Grand Rapids, MI: Eerdmans, 2003.

Kloppenborg Verbin, J. S. *Excavating Q: The History and Setting of the Sayings Gospel*, Edinburgh: T. & T. Clark, 2000.

Lührmann, D. *Die Redaktion der Logienquelle*, WMANT 33, Neukirchen-Vluyn: Neukirchener Verlag, 1969.

Robinson, J. M., P. Hoffmann, and J. S. Kloppenborg (eds) *The Critical Edition of Q*, Hermeneia, Minneapolis, MN: Fortress Press; Leuven: Peeters, 2000.

Tuckett, C. M. *Q and the History of Early Christianity: Studies on Q*, Edinburgh: T. & T. Clark, 1996.

ISAIAH

Sometimes the gospels as they stand (despite the fact they are written in Greek and usually refer to the Hebrew Scriptures in the Greek version called the Septuagint) have Jesus cite a form of Scripture that is closer to the Targum than to any other extant source. Particular attention has been devoted to the Targumic version of Isaiah, because (1) Isaiah is the biblical book of greatest prominence within the gospels, and (2) the roots of the Isaiah Targum have been shown to go back to the first century.

Targum Isaiah 6:9, 10 is an especially famous example, and it helps to explain Mark 4:11, 12. The Targum also (unlike the Masoretic Text and the Septuagint) refers to people not being "forgiven" (rather than not being "healed"). The statement in Mark could be taken to mean that Jesus told parables with the express purpose that (*hina*) people might see and not perceive, hear and not understand, lest they turn and be forgiven. The relevant clause in the Targum refers to people who behave *in such a way* "so that" (*d* in Aramaic) they see and do not perceive, hear and do not understand, lest they repent and they be forgiven. It appears that Jesus was characterizing people in the Targumic manner, as he characterizes his own fate similarly in Mark with a clause employing *hina* (cf. 9:12); he was not acting in order to be misunderstood (cf. also Mark 8:17–18).

The final verse of the book of Isaiah in the Targum identifies who will suffer – and specifies where they will suffer – at the end of time, when it says "the wicked shall be judged in *Gehinnam* until the righteous will say concerning them, We have seen enough" (66:24). "Gehenna" is just what Jesus associates with the statement that "their worm will not die and their fire will not be quenched" (Mark 9:48, and see vv. 44, 46 in many manuscripts), which is taken from the same verse of Isaiah. In the Targum, the first part of the phrase reads, "their *breaths* will not die." Rabbi Aqiba also is said to have associated Gehenna with the end of the book of Isaiah (in the Mishnah, see 'Eduyoth 2:10). Aqiba, however, refers to punishment in Gehenna having a limit, of twelve months; for Jesus, as in the Isaiah Targum, part of the threat of Gehenna was that its limit could not be determined in advance. Targumic *Gehinnam* and New Testament Gehenna correspond well.

A second type of affinity between Jesus and the Isaiah Targum does not involve the sharing of explicit wording, but it does presuppose a comparable understanding of the same passage that the Targum and the New Testament share. An example is Jesus' parable of the vineyard in Matt 21:33–46; Mark 12:1–12; Luke 20:9–19. After he has told his story of the abuse suffered by those the owner sends to acquire his share of the vintage, the Synoptic Gospels agree that the opposition to Jesus among the Jewish authorities hardened to the point that they wanted to seize him. When the symbolism of the vineyard in the Isaiah Targum 5:1–7 is considered, the opposition to Jesus becomes easily explicable. There, the vine is a primary symbol of the Temple, so that the tenants of Jesus' parable are readily identified with the leadership of the Temple. They knew he was telling the parable against them.

A third type of affinity concerns characteristically Targumic phrases appearing within the New Testament. The best example is the central category of Jesus' theology: the kingdom of God, which also appears in the form "kingdom of the LORD" in the Targumim (see *Targum Isaiah* 24:23; 31:4; 40:9; 52:7). The first usage in the Isaiah Targum (24:23) associates the theologoumenon of the kingdom of God with God's self-revelation on Mount Zion, where his appearing is to occasion a feast for all nations (see 25:6–8). The association of the kingdom with a festal image is comparable to Jesus' promise in Matt 8:11; Luke 13:28–29, that many will come from the ends of the earth to feast with Abraham, Isaac, and Jacob in the kingdom of God.

"With *the* measure you *were measuring with they will measure you*" appears in the Isaiah Targum 27:8 and, of course, a saying of Jesus' is strikingly similar (Matt 7:2; Mark 4:24). The fact is, however, that the measure in the Isaiah Targum is applied to a single figure, the oppressor of Jacob, rather than to a general group, as in Jesus' saying. A similar aphorism, crafted in the third person, was common in rabbinic literature (see, for example, *Sotah* 8b and Gen 38:25 in Pseudo-Jonathan), so it should be taken that we have here a proverb in Aramaic which Jesus and a *meturgeman* of Isaiah both just happened to use. This is an instance in which, despite close verbal agreement, no case for dependence can be made one way or the other.

Other usages from the Isaiah Targum may be mentioned under the category of comparisons of the third type. The phrase "mammon of deceit" in the Isaiah Targum is certainly not unique within rabbinic or Judaic usage, but the Isaiah Targum (5:23; 33:15) provides an analogy with Jesus' usage in the parable of the unjust steward (Luke 16:9), because in all those cases bribery is at issue. "The people inquire of their idols, the living from the dead," is a turn of phrase that is an obvious rebuke in the Targum (8:19), but its concluding expression may be echoed in the pointed question to the women at the tomb of Jesus (Luke 24:5). Obviously, these are matters of turns of phrase rather than content, but they remain striking. The Isaiah Targum speaks of "the righteous, who desire teaching as a hungry person desires bread, and the words of the law, which they desire as a thirsty person desires water" (32:6). That interpretation of hunger and thirst is reminiscent of the Matthean Jesus, who blesses those who hunger and thirst after righteousness (see Matthew 5:6). This comparison does not extend to the Lukan Jesus (compare Luke 6:21), which raises the possibility that the present wording in Matthew was shaped during the course of transmission along the lines of Targumic interpretation. Similarly, the Targum's association of the image of those who are lame with sinners and exiles might illuminate Matt 21:14–15 (see Isa 35:6).

BRUCE CHILTON

Further reading

Ådna, Jostein. "Der Gottesknecht als triumphierender and interzessorischer Messias. Die Rezeption von Jes 53 im Targum Jonathan untersucht mit besonderer Berücksichtigung des Messiasbildes," in Bernd Janowski and Peter Stuhlmacher (eds) *Die leidende Gottesknecht. Jesaja 53 und seine Wirkungsgeschichte*, FAT 14, Tübingen: Mohr, 1996, pp. 129–58.

ISAIAH

Chilton, B. D. *A Galilean Rabbi and his Bible. Jesus' Use of the Interpreted Scripture of His Time*, Good News Studies 8, Wilmington: Glazier, 1986; also published with the subtitle *Jesus' Own Interpretation of Isaiah*, London: SPCK, 1984.

—— *Targumic Approaches to the Gospels. Essays in the Mutual Definition of Judaism and Christianity*, Studies in Judaism, Lanham and London: University Press of America, 1986.

Evans, C. A. *To See and Not Perceive. Isaiah 6.9–10 in Early Jewish and Christian Interpretation*, JSOTSup 64, Sheffield: Sheffield Academic Press, 1989.

—— "A Note on 2 Samuel 5:8 and Jesus' Ministry to the 'Maimed, Halt, and Blind'," *JSP* 15 (1997) 79–82.

McNamara, Martin. *Targum and Testament. Aramaic Paraphrases of the Hebrew Bible: A Light on the New Testament*, Grand Rapids, MI: Eerdmans, 1972.

J

JAMES AND JOHN, SONS OF ZEBEDEE

A little-known secret in historical Jesus scholarship is the possibility that James and John, sons of Zebedee, were also sons of Salome, who may have been sister to Mary, mother of Jesus. Thus, two of the apostles were cousins of Jesus. Most historical Jesus scholars have discounted such possibilities, but recent attention to social connections has raised the possibility again (see Bauckham 1990 and the speculative web of Tabor 2006).

James the son of Zebedee

Each brother is of the Twelve (Matt 10:2 pars.) and summoned to follow Jesus while fishing with his father (Mark 1:16–20). It is likely that James was the elder of the two. James is mentioned to be in the presence of Jesus when Peter's mother was healed (Mark 1:29), at the raising of Jairus' daughter (5:37), at the transfiguration of Jesus (9:2), at the eschatological discourse (13:3), and when Jesus was in agony in Gethsemane (14:33). It is remotely possible James was at the Cana incident (John 2:1–11). He witnessed the resurrected Jesus (John 21:2–7).

Both seemed to be tempestuous and competitive by temperament. John questioned the legitimacy of an exorcist who was not in the "inner circle," to which Jesus uttered the thoroughly suggestive "whoever is not against us is for us" (Mark 9:38–40). Luke's Gospel (9:51–56) informs us that James and John, after finding little response to the kingdom

among the Samaritans, asked Jesus if it might not be time to "command fire to come down from heaven and consume them?" Both approach Jesus to ask, rather manipulatively, if each might be given a seat in the kingdom next to Jesus, to which Jesus replied with astonishment and reprimand about the need to be servants (Mark 10:35–45). On top of this, Mark's Gospel (3:17) tells us that their nickname was "sons of thunder" (*boanerges*). Whatever one makes of the specifics of these events historically, the fact remains that we have here a singularly consistent temperament sketch of the brothers as well as information that would have conflicted with their reputation and status in the earliest Christian churches.

The request of the brothers in Mark 10:35–45, Matthew tells us, was precipitated by their mother (20:20–21) – even though Jesus' answer addresses the sons (20:22). This request undoubtedly emerged from dynastic hopes on the part of the family of Jesus. Jesus' response, that connection to Jesus would mean drinking his cup, came true – James was beheaded under Herod Agrippa I (Acts 12:2). A later (probably legendary) account, now found in Eusebius, claims the accuser of James came to faith and died along with James (*Hist. eccl.* 2.9).

John the son of Zebedee

John was a disciple of the Baptist (John 1:35), and was possibly present at Cana (2:1–11). John was summoned to be an apostle while fishing with his brother and father (Mark 1:16–20). John was along with his brother James in the listed events mentioned above. In addition, he was one who was sent to ready the place for the last Passover (Luke 22:8). At the last supper, John reclined next to Jesus (John 13:23–25). After this event, John fled but eventually found a way to watch the proceedings against Jesus (Matt 26:56; John 18:15) and eventually stood with Mary and other women at the crucifixion of Jesus (19:26–27). Jesus committed his mother to John for care (19:25–27; cf. Eusebius, *Hist. eccl.* 2.2). He was informed of the resurrection (20:2–3). John is singled out by Peter about his fate, but Jesus responds to Peter that such concerns are no business of Peter's (21:20–23), and John becomes connected with the verity of the witness of the beloved disciple (21:24). John is connected with Peter in the Temple when they were going to afternoon prayers (Acts 3:1) when Peter healed a crippled beggar and spoke of the resurrection (3:3–26). John was arrested with Peter (Acts 4:3); when questioned, Peter speaks for them about the resurrection (4:8–22), and after the release John returns to the believers (4:23). John also visited Samaria (8:14–15). John seems to have remained a leader in Jerusalem, for Paul consulted with him (Gal 2:9). John is traditionally the author of 1–3 John and the Revelation (cf. 1:4, 9). Early Christian traditions about John abound: he resided in Ephesus (which could be the "elder" John instead of the "apostle" John).

Issues

It is not possible to resolve historical questions in this entry, but these observations can be made. First, the connection of John and James to Jesus via Mary through Salome is credible if somewhat speculative (see Bauckham for a denial of this connection), though all of this brings onto the near horizon the prickly nettles pertaining to Jesus' "brothers and sister," and the debates about them with Helvidius, Jerome, and Epiphanius. I think the stronger case can be made for Helvidius, in spite of Jerome's influence in the history of the Church. Here is the evidence:

At the scene of the crucifixion are women (Mark 15:40–41).

Women at the scene of the crucifixion

Mark	Matthew	John
Mary Magdalene	Mary Magdalene	Mary Magdalene
Mary of James and Joses	Mary of James and Joses	Mary (Jesus' mother)
Salome	Mother of sons of Zebedee	Sister of Mary

It is possible that Salome, the mother of the sons of Zebedee, and the sister of Mary are the

same. I find the report credible. If this is the case, Salome was the sister of Mary and married Zebedee. They had at least two sons, James and John, who were cousins of Jesus and his apostles. But, there are other explanations for this data, not the least of which was that the name was common enough for there to have been plenty of others (Bauckham: 9–13), and many today believe that the sons of Zebedee are not relatives of Jesus.

Is the "beloved disciple" the apostle John? Traditionally, yes. But the American scholar J. H. Charlesworth (1995) has mounted a robust defense of Thomas as the beloved disciple, along with a fair-minded description of the traditional view (197–213). Did the apostle John need an appendix, what many consider John 21, to verify his authority? Does the temperament of John in the synoptics match that in the Fourth Gospel? Most importantly, why is the apostle John not mentioned? In addition, why would an apostle call himself the "beloved disciple"? Most today are not persuaded by the traditional answer, even if some of the arguments against the tradition are not as insightful as others.

SCOT MCKNIGHT

Further reading

Bauckham, R. *Jude and the Relatives of Jesus in the Early Church*, Edinburgh: T. & T. Clark, 1990.
Charlesworth, J. *The Beloved Disciple: Whose Witness Validates the Gospel of John?* Valley Forge, PA: Trinity Press International, 1995.
Tabor, J. D. *The Jesus Dynasty: The Hidden History of Jesus, His Royal Family, and the Birth of Christianity*, New York: Simon & Schuster, 2006.

JEREMIAH

Matthew is the only evangelist to refer to Jeremiah by name, although other New Testament writers also cite or allude to his writings. At a key moment of christological definition, Jesus asks his disciples, "Who do people say that I am?" Mark reports their answer as, "John the Baptist; and others, Elijah; and still others, one of the prophets" (Mark 8:28). Matthew, however, inserts the name "Jeremiah" (Matt 16:14). Proposed explanations for this addition see Jeremiah as a premier or representative prophet; one who gives aid in time of need (2 Macc 15:13–16); one who, despite being martyred, was not ultimately subject to death (*Liv. Pro.* 2:19), or whose return heralds the end of time (cf. *5 Ezra* 2:18, Sir 49:10); as a messianic forerunner (cf. 2 Macc 2:1–12; 15:12–16), a prophet of destruction, or a prime example of rejection and unjust suffering. The key question is whether the perceived similarity is merely an opinion to be rejected, or an accurate reflection of Matthean Christology. A clearer indication of Matthew's intent may be found in two of his fourteen fulfillment quotations that appeal specifically to this prophet. In Matthew 2:17–18, Jeremiah's report of Rachel weeping for her children (Jer 31[38]:15) is said to anticipate Herod's slaughter of the infant boys of Bethlehem, while Matthew 27:9–10 comments on the fate of Judas by quoting a mixed text that combines Zechariah 11:12–13 with one or more of Jeremiah 18:1–2, 19:1–3, and 32[39]:6–9, and possibly Lamentations 4:2. These are unique among Matthew's fulfillment citations: both link Scripture with death or mortal opposition to the Messiah on the part of Israel's leaders, and both employ distinct fulfillment formulae that seek to avoid attributing such evils to divine providence. Thus, just as the Evangelist suggests lines of continuity and contrast between Jesus and Noah, Abraham, Moses, Elijah, David, and Jonah, using each as foils for his own portrait of the Messiah, so Matthew's references to Jeremiah serve to color Jesus in distinctly somber tones. Jesus thus fits the typical pattern of suffering and redemption exemplified by many rejected prophets – a motif that is especially prominent in Q tradition.

According to Q ("Jerusalem ... killing the prophets and stoning those sent to her," Matt 23:37// Luke 13:34), Jesus himself probably reflected on the example of Jeremiah, since contemporary tradition understood the prophet to have suffered death by stoning (*Liv. Pro.* 2:1, *Paraleipomena Jeremiou* 9:21–32; cf. Heb 11:37). Certainly he echoes Jeremiah's judgment against the sins of Israel (Mark 11:17 and parallels: "You have made [the Temple] a 'den of robbers'," citing Jer 7:11) and, like Jeremiah, is closely identified with the destruction both of the city and of its Temple in particular (Mark 13:2, 14:58, 15:29; cf. Luke 19:41–44, 21:24, etc.). Likewise the language of Matthew 15:3 ("Every plant that my heavenly Father has not planted will be uprooted") warns of judgment in language that strongly recalls the terms of Jeremiah's prophetic call (Jer 1:10), while the enigmatic episode of Jesus cursing the fruitless fig tree (Mark 11:12–14 and parallels) repeats the terms in which earlier prophets had denounced unfaithful leaders of God's people (especially Jer 8:13 and Mic 7:1).

At least for Matthew, writing in the aftermath of the first Jewish War, Jesus is indeed a Jeremiah-like prophet of doom. Much as Sirach 49:6–7 explains the first destruction of Jerusalem as a consequence of Jeremiah's martyrdom, so the shedding of Jesus' "innocent blood" seems to account for more recent disaster (compare, e.g., Matt 23:34–36; 27:4, 24–25, etc., with Jeremiah 19:3–4; cf. *Targum Lamentations* 4:12–13). Seeking to explain the two greatest tragedies ever to have befallen God's chosen people – the death of the Messiah and the destruction of the Sanctuary – Matthew sees in these events not only divine judgment, but also the assurance of restoration. For Jeremiah is equally the prophet of the "new covenant" (Jer 31:31–34), a motif likewise adopted at Qumran (e.g. *Damascus Document* 6:19, 8:21, 19:34, 20:12). Paul discusses the "new covenant" in 2 Corinthians 3:6 (cf. Rom 11:27); similarly, recitations of Jeremiah's prophecy in the letter to the Hebrews, once in full (Heb 8:8–13) and once in part (Heb 10:16–17), are the longest citations of Scripture in the New Testament (cf. Heb 9:15, 12:24). For the ministry of Jesus, the most significant reference to this theme appears in the words of institution at the Last Supper. Jesus' words of blessing occur in two different forms, one common to Mark and Matt (Mark 14:24//Matthew 26:28), the other represented by Luke and Paul (Luke 22:20//1 Cor 11:25), with the latter specifying that the wine represents the blood of a *new* covenant. Lest the allusion seem unclear, Matthew adds the phrase "for the forgiveness of sins" (from Jeremiah 31:34). Thus – both in the words of Jesus himself and in the Church's theological reflection on them – at the heart of Jesus' messianic self-offering lies the fulfillment of Jeremiah's prophecies and the promise of covenant renewal for God's people.

Both positive and negative characterizations of Jeremiah on the part of early Christians are broadly consistent with contemporary opinion. While Jeremiah's suffering and rejection are central themes of the book associated with his name, additions to canonical Jeremiah in the Septuagint (specifically, 1 Bar and the *Epistle of Jeremiah*) indicate ongoing development of traditions about the prophet, while numerous biblical and apocryphal texts from Qumran – especially concerning Jeremiah as a prophet to exiles – indicate his broader importance for the self-understanding of that community. Josephus, writing at about the same time as the Evangelists, expressly compares himself to Jeremiah, whose warnings of imminent catastrophe were (like his own) ignored by the inhabitants of Jerusalem, and comments that Jeremiah even foretold the destruction of the city by the Romans (*J. W.* 5.391–93; *Ant.* 10.79). Slightly later works such as *Second*

Baruch and the *Paraleipomena Jeremiou* indicate that contemporary Jews also looked to Jeremiah and his circle to help interpret the fall of Jerusalem and find hope for God's eventual restoration of his people.

MICHAEL P. KNOWLES

Further reading

Carmignac, Jean. "Pourquoi Jérémie est-il mentionné en Matthieu 16:14?," in G. Jeremias, H. W. Kuhn, and H. Stegemann (eds) *Tradition und Glaube: Das Fruhe Christentum in seiner Umwelt (Festgabe K. G. Kuhn)*, Göttingen: Vandenhoeck & Ruprecht, 1971, pp. 283–98.

Curtis, A. H. W. and T. Römer (eds) *The Book of Jeremiah and its Reception/Le livre de Jérémie et sa réception*, Bibliotheca ephemeridum theologicarum lovaniensium 128, Leuven: Leuven University Press/Peeters, 1997.

Knowles, Michael P. *Jeremiah in Matthew's Gospel: The Rejected Prophet Motif in Matthaean Redaction*, JSNTSup 68, Sheffield: JSOT Press, 1993.

Lehne, Susanne. *The New Covenant in Hebrews*, JSNTSup 44, Sheffield: JSOT Press, 1990.

Lundblom, Jack R. "New Covenant," ABD, 4 (1992) New York: Doubleday, 1088–94.

Menken, Maarten J. J. "The References to Jeremiah in the Gospel According to Matthew," *ETL* 60 (1984) 5–24.

—— "The Quotation from Jeremiah 31(38):15 in Matthew 2:18: A Study of Matthew's Scriptural Text," in S. Moyise (ed.) *The Old Testament in the New Testament: Essays in Honor of J. L. North*, JSNTSup 189, Sheffield: Sheffield Academic Press, 2000, pp. 106–25.

—— "The Old Testament Quotation in Matthew 27:9–10: Textual Form and Context," *Biblica* 83:3 (2002) 305–28.

Quesnel, Michel. "Les citations de Jérémie dans l'Évangile selon saint Matthieu," *ESTBib* 47 (1989) 513–27.

Vouga, François. "La Seconde Passion de Jérémie," *LumVie* 32, nr 165 (1983) 71–82.

Winkle, Ross E. "The Jeremiah Model for Jesus in the Temple," *AUSS* 24 (1986) 155–72.

Wolff, Christian. *Jeremia im Frühjudentum und Urchristentum*, TU 118, Berlin: Akademie Verlag, 1976.

JEREMIAS, JOACHIM

Joachim Jeremias (1900–79) was born and raised in Dresden as son of a Lutheran, who for five years was provost of Jerusalem. This city may have fostered his interest in Palestinian language and archaeology, providing him with the opportunity to gain familiarity with the landscape of Palestine. He studied theology and oriental languages in Tübingen and Leipzig, where he received his PhD, first as docent in Riga, 1928, as *extraordinarius* in Berlin and then as a full professor in Greifswald in 1929. It was here from 1935 to 1968 that he spent the longest part of his teaching career. As a member of the Confessing Church who opposed the Nazi regime, Jeremias earned the moral reputation that permitted him to participate in the reconstruction process of the University of Göttingen after

World War II. During that time many of his famous works on Jesus and Palestine were written and, often thoroughly, revised versions were published. His scientific research was often also published in shorter writings intended for laity, so that he kept theology and church in a dialogue.

In accordance with other scholars of the second or new quest for Jesus, Jeremias challenged Rudolf Bultmann's distinction between history and faith. Jeremias shared the basic assumption of the new movement that faith was interested in historical facts. Paul's message of the cross was an important aspect of Christian theology, which, however, should not be over-estimated with regard to the incarnation of the word (1961: 17; cf. John 1:14). In Jesus' words and deeds, God was present in human history. Even the kerygma, insofar as it proclaimed that God's reconciliation with the world, pointed to historical interest of Christian faith. In contrast to Bultmann, any New Testament theology therefore had to start with Jesus and his proclamation (1979). Christian faith originated not in the events of cross and resurrection but in the appearance of Jesus both in his words and in his deeds. From the following basic assumptions it became clear why Jeremias with some right challenged any uncritical use of the popular criterion of double dissimilarity (1979: 14).

Within Jeremias' approach, we can find a couple of reasons why he was so optimistic that the quest for the historical Jesus could be answered with some confidence. First of all, Jeremias found the process of transmission of the Jesus tradition essentially reliable. His view of the process of transmission and the activity of the later Christian community is in a good manner mirrored in the title of the Festschrift to his seventieth birthday: *Der Ruf Jesu und die Antwort der Gemeinde* (= "The Call of Jesus and the Answer of the Community") (E. Lohse [ed.], Göttingen: Vandenhoeck & Ruprecht, 1970, the title is based on a formulation of Jeremias himself; 1961: 24). The witness of faith is, by spirit, the answer of Christian communities to the call of Jesus Christ who is God's offer of salvation. Although that call is embedded in the community's answer, it deserves priority (1979: 295). According to Jeremias, inauthenticity, not authenticity of the Jesus tradition has to be proved (1979: 46).

He further established a linguistic principle in the search for Jesus. In light of the fact that Jewish people spoke Aramaic during the time of Jesus, traces of Aramaic style and language in the gospel tradition derived from Jesus (1979: 39–46; use of parables, riddles, kingdom of God, amen, abba).

So, the main goal of Jeremias' research was the quest for the *ipsissima vox* ("the very voice") of the historical Jesus and the *Sitz im Leben* ("life setting") in proclaiming the kingdom of God. This (reconstructed) *vox* ("voice") is the leading authority for Christian theological thinking. That this assumption is not only theologically problematic but also methodologically questionable needs to be mentioned here. With what certainty can modern scholars reconstruct a "voice" in a different language that has already gone through a process of oral transmission before being reshaped into a written text?

In his search for the authentic Jesus tradition Jeremias also searched the *agrapha*, that is, sayings that are attributed to Jesus but cannot be found in the canonical gospels (1963). This matter has reached new levels of complexity as scholars of the Third Quest continue to debate the value of the apocryphal Gospels themselves.

Jeremias was aware that reconstructing the *ipsissima vox* of Jesus placed Jesus within the Jewish *Volksreligion* ("people's religion") of his time. Therefore, Jeremias was not only interested in texts but also in archaeology as a mirror of religious beliefs. To understand Jesus it is important to know the historical, economic and social circumstances of Jerusalem to the time of Jesus, analyzing the whole range of archaeology and texts, mostly rabbinic sources. In the third edition of his *Jerusalem zur Zeit Jesu* (English translation: *Jerusalem in the Time of Jesus*) he also incorporated findings from Qumran.

It was one of the most important contributions of Jeremias and a still important task of the quest for Jesus to place Jesus and his appearance within the context of first-century Judaism. One may say that the diversity of Judaism was higher, and even included the influence of Hellenism, as Jeremias stated, and that Rabbinic Judaism did not play such a central role in analyzing Jesus' appearance as supposed by Jeremias. The sometimes uncritical use of rabbinic texts in reconstructing temporary Judaism is sharply criticized by Sanders (1991). Moreover, from a methodological-critical point of view, Jeremias underestimated each scholar's own part within the process of constructing past events.

Important for Jeremias' understanding of Jesus was his famous volume on the parables. The proclamation of Jesus could be reconstructed by analyzing his parables and probing for the authentic voice of Jesus and attributing them to their original place within the proclamation of Jesus. The focus of Jesus' parables is on the kingdom of God that is already in the course of realization. As a specific marker, Jesus called God "abba" which showed his basic confidence toward God ("*vertrauensvoll und geborgen*;" 1979: 73) using a word of intimacy normally used in a familial context. Using such a word from a profane sphere for religious purposes indicated the uniqueness of Jesus (1979: 67–73).

According to Jeremias, Jesus predicted his own death (Mark 8:31–33) and attributed meaning to his death by claiming himself to be the suffering servant in reference to Isaiah 53 (1979: 272–84). Not only within the words of Jesus but also within the tradition on his deeds, Jeremias found reliable historical information. According to Jeremias the last supper originally was a Passover meal that Jesus, fasting himself as a sign for the nearness of the end of time, celebrated with his disciples as his last meal. Jeremias pointed to parallels with the Jewish Passover meal and by his claim that the Greek text can be traced back to an Aramaic original. That meant that early Christianity's message of the redemptive death of Jesus was grounded in his own words. For a sharply divergent assessment of Jeremias' work, see the essays by Meyer and Sanders (1991).

Although Jeremias stressed the continuity between the proclamation of Jesus and the later Christian community, he did not overlook the fact that such a presentation was a theological reworking of tradition by the Evangelists. In his 1980 work, *Die Sprache des Lukasevangeliums* (= "The Language of the Gospel of Luke") he differentiated between tradition for which he accepted a Lukan *Sonderquelle* (= "special source") and redaction in the Gospel of Luke (1979: 48–49), producing a work that is still helpful.

MICHAEL LABAHN

Further reading

Braus, R. J. "Jesus as Founder of the Church according to Joachim Jeremias," dissertation, Rome, 1970.
Heyer, Cees J. Den. *Der Mann aus Nazaret. Bilanz der Jesusforschung*, Düsseldorf: Patmos, 1998, pp. 99–105.
Jeremias, Joachim. *Jerusalem zur Zeit Jesu. Kulturgeschichtliche Untersuchung zur neutestamentlichen Zeitgeschichte*, Leipzig, Göttingen: Pfeiffer, 1923–37; third edition Göttingen: Vandenhoeck & Ruprecht, 1962; ET: *Jerusalem in the Time of Jesus: An Investigation into Economic and Social Conditions during the New Testament Period*, London: SCM Press, 1969.
—— *Die Abendmahlsworte Jesu*, Göttingen: Vandenhoeck & Ruprecht, 1935; fourth edition 1967; ET: *The Eucharistic Words of Jesus*, Oxford: Basil Blackwell, 1955; London: SCM Press, 1966; Philadelphia, PA: Fortress Press, 1977.
—— *Die Gleichnisse Jesu*, AThANT 11, Zürich: Zwingli, 1947; second edition, Göttingen: Vandenhoeck &

Ruprecht, 1952; eleventh edition, 1998; ET: *The Parables of Jesus*, revised and enlarged edition, New York: Charles Scribner's Sons, 1963.

—— *Unbekannte Jesusworte*, AThANT 16, Zürich: Zwingli, 1951; third edition with Otfried Hofius; Gütersloh: Mohn, 1963; ET: *Unknown Sayings of Jesus*, London: SPCK, 1957.

—— *Heiligengräber in Jesu Umwelt. Eine Untersuchung zur Volksreligion der Zeit Jesu*, Göttingen: Vandenhoeck & Ruprecht, 1958.

—— *Das Problem des historischen Jesus*, Calwer Hefte 32, Stuttgart: Calwer Verlag, 1960; ET: *The Problem of the Historical Jesus*, Facet Books Biblical Series 13, Philadelphia, PA: Fortress Press, 1964.

—— "Der gegenwärtige Stand der Debatte um das Problem des historischen Jesus," in Helmut Ristow and Karl Matthiae (eds) *Der historische Jesus und der kerygmatische Christus*, second edition, Berlin: Evangelische Verlagsanstalt, 1961; pp. 12–25.

—— *Abba. Studien zur neutestamentlichen Theologie und Zeitgeschichte*, Göttingen: Vandenhoeck & Ruprecht, 1966.

—— *Neutestamentliche Theologie 1: Die Verkündigung Jesu*, Gütersloh: Mohn, 1971; third edition 1979; ET: *New Testament Theology: Part 1: The Proclamation of Jesus*, London: SCM Press, 1971.

—— *Die Sprache des Lukasevangeliums: Redaktion und Tradition im Nicht-Markusstoff des dritten Evangeliums*, KEK Sonderband, Göttingen: Vandenhoeck & Ruprecht, 1980.

Jeremias, Jörg. "Jeremias, Joachim," *Biograpisch-Bibliographisches Kirchenlexikon* III. Nordhausen: Verlag Traugott Bautz, 1992, cols. 51–53.

Lanza, Sergio. "Il problema del Gesù storico nel pensiero di Joachim Jeremias: una ricerca metodologica," dissertation, Pontificia Universitas Lateranensis, Rome, 1983.

Lohse, Eduard. "Die Vollmacht des Menschensohnes. Nachruf auf Joachim Jeremias," in Eduard Lohse (ed.) *Die Vielfalt des Neuen Testaments. Exegetische Studien zur Theologie des Neuen Testaments*, Göttingen: Vandenhoeck & Ruprecht, 1982, pp. 215–20.

—— "Jeremias, Joachim," *DBI* 1 (1999) 576–77.

Meyer, Ben F. "A Caricature of Joachim Jeremias and His Work." *JBL* 110 (1991) 451–62.

Oldenhage, Tania. *Parables for Our Time: Rereading New Testament Scholarship After the Holocaust*, AAR Cultural Criticism Series, Oxford: Oxford University Press, 2002, pp. 39–69.

Perrin, Norman. *Jesus and the Language of the Kingdom. Symbol and Metaphor in New Testament Interpretation*. London: SCM Press, 1976, pp. 91–107.

Sanders, E. P. "Defending the Indefensible." *JBL* 110 (1991) 463–77.

Sider, John W. "Rediscovering the Parables: The Logic of the Jeremias Tradition," *JBL* 102 (1983) 61–83.

Vander Broeck, R. "Jeremias, Joachim," in Donald K. McKim (ed.) *Major Biblical Interpreters*, Downers Grove, IL: InterVarsity Press, 1998, pp. 495–500.

JERICHO

"The City of Palm Trees," the Hebrew word "Yirecho" may come from the noun "moon," "Yareach" or from the noun "month," "Yerach." Aside from this, the meaning of the word is lost to us.

Geographically, Jericho was a town just northwest of the Dead Sea. The town in the New Testament era was just southwest of the mound upon which the OT city was located and surrounded the Hasmonean and Herodian palace complex, close to Wadi Qelt, situated only 20 km from Jerusalem. In modern times the site is known in Arabic as Tulul Abu el-Alayiq in order to differentiate it from the site of the OT location of Jericho at Tell es-Sultan. Jericho functioned as an agricultural center and a winter resort for Jerusalem's aristocracy during the New Testament period. It was ideally situated for both of these functions.

In the New Testament the word occurs only in Matt 20:29; Mark 10:46; Luke 10:30, 18:35, 19:1 in relation to the historical Jesus (and in Hebrews, but that lies outside our interest).

The context of Matthew 20:29 is Jesus' journey up to Jerusalem. On the way, he announces again his impending suffering and death. At precisely that point in the narrative, the mother of James and John, the sons of Zebedee, approaches Jesus and requests of him that her sons receive places of honor and importance in the coming kingdom. Jesus replies that such is not his to give. At hearing this, the ten are indignant and complain about the affront. Jesus calms them by reminding them that they are not to act as the gentile lords do. At this juncture in the narrative Matthew informs us that "as they were leaving Jericho, a large crowd followed him." Does this suggest that the discussion about lordship among the disciples took place in or near Jericho? That certainly seems to be the implication. The question of "rulership" certainly would fit the scene since Jericho was something of a "winter retreat" for the wealthy of Jerusalem and may well have triggered the "earthly" wishes of the disciples as they looked around at all the wealth and power on display there.

Jesus journeys along a bit outside of Jericho, on his way to Jerusalem, and he is confronted by two blind men who hail him as the "Son of David," requesting mercy of him as the "Davidic Messiah." The crowd reacts quite negatively, urging their silence, but Jesus stops in his tracks and asks what he can do for them. Their request is simple enough – they want to see. Moved with pity, he grants that request and continues his journey towards Jerusalem.

The Markan context of 10:46 is essentially the same as the Matthean, with a few details slightly different in the telling. Mark sets the stage for the encounter in Jericho with the same information as Matthew – the disciples, along with Jesus, are on their way to Jerusalem because Jesus must go there to suffer and to be killed, and then to be raised on the third day. Mark notes that the disciples were afraid (10:32). As they journeyed along, James and John themselves (and not through their mother) approach Jesus with a request for power. Since they don't know what they are asking, Jesus rejects their request and informs them that his disciples are not to be like the rulers of the world. After all, the Son of Man himself did not come to be ministered to but to minister to others. As they depart Jericho, one blind man cries out for Jesus' help, and Mark names him: Bartimaeus. Rebuked, he continues. Begging may have been quite lucrative in the area around Jericho since the wealthy were frequently there, but it was no substitute for sightedness. Jesus heals him in spite of the attempt of the many who rebuked the blind man, urging him to silence. Once healed, Bartimaeus follows Jesus, at least to his next destination, Bethphage.

Luke seems far more interested in Jericho than do either Mark or Matthew. Luke tells of encounters there on three occasions: in Luke 10:30, 18:35, and 19:1. In 10:30–37, Jesus tells the famed parable of the Good Samaritan, who finds a man injured beside the road on the way to Jericho. Jericho again appears in the text as a destination for the well-to-do. This man was sufficiently well off to be robbed. It is pure speculation, of course, as to what his status was socio-economically, but both he and the Samaritan were of means, as the story indicates that the Samaritan could afford the cost of care at the inn and the injured man's clothes were worthy of theft.

The second Lukan mention of Jericho, in 18:35, is the same setting as Matthew and Mark's, i.e. the healing of the blind man. This telling leads to the third use of Jericho in the Gospel. Luke 19:1–10 tells the story of Zacchaeus, a resident of Jericho itself. Luke, interestingly, makes use of a phrase that indicates that Jesus was simply passing through town (with no intention of lingering) when he happens upon the "tax collector in the tree." Once more, the locale makes perfect sense, as one would expect a wealthy man to have a residence in the city of Jericho. Luke describes Zacchaeus as not simply a tax collector, though, but as a "chief tax collector." The story unfolds with Jesus being extended an invitation to dinner, which he accepts, and concerning which the disgruntled complain since, for the Pharisees, eating with a tax collector was equivalent to collaborating with the enemy. Zacchaeus, though, has found salvation and his life has been changed accordingly.

Jericho, in the life of Jesus, was a place of healing and redemption. The wealthy there treated him, apparently, with due respect and consideration.

JIM WEST

Further reading

Arensburg, B. and P. Smith. "The Jewish Population of Jericho 100 BC–70 AD," *PEQ* 115 (1983) 133–39.

Bar-Nathan, R. "Qumran and the Hasmonaean and Herodian Winter Palaces of Jericho: The Implication of the Pottery Finds on the Interpretation of the Settlement at Qumran," in Katharina Galor, Jean-Baptiste Humbert, and Jürgen Zangenberg (eds), *Qumran, the Site of the Dead Sea Scrolls*, Studies on the Texts of the Desert of Judah 57, Leiden: Brill, 2006, pp. 263–77.

Begg, C. T. "The Fall of Jericho According to Josephus," *ESTBib* 63:2–3 (2005) 323–40.

JERUSALEM

The name Jerusalem (*Yerushalayim*) perhaps has been built on the verb *yarah*, which means "to lay a foundation," and "Shalem," a name of one of the Canaanite gods, meaning "Shalem laid the foundation." But this reading is not certain. The etymology of the word has never been satisfactorily explained. Most curious is the "dual" ending of the word. Literally in English it is "Jerusalems." The Greek New Testament also uses the "dual" or "plural" ending. Most likely this implies that Jerusalem was located on a number of hills by the time the city obtained its present name. In the New Testament, and in the life of the historical Jesus, this is certainly the case.

Jerusalem is located in the central highlands of Judea, situated on a limestone plateau 800 m above sea level. When Herod died Judea (and therefore Jerusalem) became a province of Rome, ruled by Roman prefects who made their residence in Caesarea. Indeed, so far as the Romans were concerned, it was Caesarea that was the capital of the province. This left the day-to-day affairs of government in the city to the Sanhedrin and the High Priest. The most famous of these Roman prefects was Pontius Pilate (26–36 CE), who figures prominently in the story of the execution of Jesus.

Jesus and Jerusalem

The gospels mention Jerusalem in sixty-six verses: thirteen in John, thirty in Luke, eleven in Mark, and twelve in Matthew. The fact that nearly half the occurrences come in Luke is not surprising, given the fact that he is, of all the gospel writers, most interested in the geography of events. Curiously, while Matthew and Mark distribute their references to Jerusalem evenly throughout their gospels, and Luke makes nearly constant reference to it, John only mentions it through chapter 12. The remainder of his Gospel does not use the word again. Here are the passages where Jerusalem occurs in the Synoptics: in Matthew: 2:1, 2:3, 3:5, 4:25,

5:35, 15:1, 16:21, 20:17, 20:18, 21:1, 21:10, and 23:37; in Mark: 1:5, 3:8, 3:22, 7:1, 10:32, 10:33, 11:1, 11:11, 11:15, 11:27, and 15:41; in Luke: 2:22, 2:25, 2:38, 2:41, 2:43, 2:45, 4:9, 5:17, 6:17, 9:31, 9:53, 10:30, 13:4, 13:22, 13:33, 17:11, 18:31, 19:11, 19:28, 21:20, 21:24, 23:7, 23:28, 24:13, 24:18, 24:33, 24:47, 24:52–53; in John: 1:19, 2:13, 2:23, 4:20, 4:21, 4:45, 5:1, 5:2, 7:25, 10:22, 11:18, 11:55, and 12:12.

In what follows an overview of the usage of the word "Jerusalem" in each of the gospels will be offered. The interested reader is encouraged to make use of the materials listed in the bibliography at the conclusion of this entry.

Jerusalem in Matthew's Gospel

The first appearance of Jerusalem in Matthew's Gospel is with the arrival of the wise men from the east. In connection with their arrival and departure Matthew mentions the city as the location where they discovered the place where the Born King of the Jews was to be found. Next we find all those in Jerusalem going to hear John the Baptist as he preaches in the wilderness. In chapter 4, Jesus' ministry is described as having adherents from all around Palestine, including followers from Jerusalem. In the Sermon on the Mount, Jesus mentions Jerusalem as the place by which persons must not swear. Matthew doesn't mention Jerusalem again until the fifteenth chapter where Pharisees send their disciples to enquire of Jesus concerning his fidelity and the fidelity of his disciples to purity laws. In the sixteenth chapter Jesus begins to announce his death, and from this point on in the Gospel Jerusalem is the place to which he must go to die. Jerusalem, formerly the place from which followers have come, now becomes the dread final destination of its soon-to-be executed Lord, who would love to gather her children together but who is rejected without cause.

It is interesting to note that the events described in chapter 15 seem to be the turning point of Jesus' disposition towards Jerusalem, and Jerusalem's disposition towards Jesus. When the disciples of the Pharisees accuse Jesus of behaving improperly in regard to the laws of purity it seems that Jesus recognizes that his relationship with the city, and its relationship to him, has turned a corner. Now, in the Gospel, the city becomes the place of rejection and death whereas formerly it was the source of interested followers and enquirers.

Jerusalem in Mark's Gospel

We first encounter Jerusalem in Mark's Gospel as the place where many are leaving in order to hear John the Baptist as he calls for national repentance and renewal. And, as in Matthew, Mark too suggests that large crowds of followers from all around Palestine followed Jesus during the early days of his ministry. But unlike Matthew, Mark observes that the first opponents of Jesus from Jerusalem do not accuse him of failing to adhere to purity laws: they accuse him of having Beelzebub. In the third chapter of his work, Mark notes that "scribes came down from Jerusalem and said, he has Beelzebub, and by the prince of the devils he casts out devils." It is not until the seventh chapter that Jerusalem is again mentioned, and this time the issue of purity is the cause of discontent among the Pharisees from the capital. By the time Jerusalem is mentioned again, Jesus is heading there to be executed and to be raised from the dead (ch. 10). The "Triumphal Entry" is next on the Jerusalem itinerary of Jesus and a quick perusal of the Temple precincts before he leaves once again at nightfall (ch. 11). At the conclusion of the eleventh chapter Jesus is asked by his opponents as to his authorization for doing and saying the things he has, once more suggesting that for Mark, as for Matthew, Jerusalem has become the center of opposition to Jesus' ministry. The final mention of Jerusalem in Mark's telling of the tale is the note that many of the women standing near the cross at Jesus' execution had come from Galilee and had come to Jerusalem with him (ch. 15).

Mark's interest in Jerusalem, like Matthew's, is to demonstrate that while early in his ministry people there were willing to follow him, as time went on the city turned on him and its representatives opposed him both as a tool of Beelzebub and as a representative of a lifestyle that was impure.

Jerusalem in Luke's Gospel

It has already been noted that nearly half of the occurrences of "Jerusalem" in the Synoptic Gospels come from Luke. Thirty times the Evangelist mentions the city; more than even Matthew or John.

Luke's first mention of Jerusalem is in the Infancy narrative concerning the appearance of Jesus at the Temple and the visits of Simeon and Anna. Both recognize Jesus as the anointed one of the Lord, the promised one whose coming now means that Simeon can depart this life having seen God's finest work. Jerusalem itself would be redeemed by this newborn lad (2:38). When next Jerusalem appears in the Gospel it is in connection with the visit of the twelve-year-old Jesus who, with his parents, is in the city for the festival. In the well-known account of 2:41ff, Jesus is missed when his family makes their way back to Nazareth and when his parents return, after they have searched for him for three days they find him in the Temple debating with the leaders of the people. In both of these accounts from the early life of Jesus, which have no parallel in the other gospels, Jerusalem figures as the place where redemption is first announced and the knowledge of the Anointed One is first demonstrated.

The city figures in the temptation narrative of chapter 4 as the place Jesus is urged to hurl himself from the pinnacle of the Temple in order to demonstrate to the crowds that he is under divine protection. Luke seems to be suggesting that Jerusalem is, in the life of Jesus, a place of temptation. So he seems to absent himself from the city until the final week of his life. Jerusalem appears again in chapter 5 as the source of Jesus' opponents (5:17) and in 6:17 as the place from which curious crowds come to him in a mountainous place to be healed after the selection of the twelve disciples.

Jerusalem is absent from the Gospel until the ninth chapter (v. 31) when, at his transfiguration, he discusses with Moses and Elijah the events about to take place in Jerusalem. In the same chapter the famed "Journey to Jerusalem" begins (v. 53), when Jesus sets his face towards the city that, once the place Jesus was recognized as the Anointed One, will become the place of his death and resurrection.

From this place forward in the Gospel, Jerusalem plays only a negative role. In the parable of the Good Samaritan, Jerusalem is the home of a priest and a Levite who have no concern for an injured and wounded man. Those two men "are going down" from Jerusalem to Jericho, where, as we have seen, they will "vacation." In 13:4, the inhabitants of Jerusalem are compared to those killed when the tower of Siloam fell, and thus those inhabitants are standing in danger of punishment. In 13:22 we find mentioned, once more, Jerusalem as the final destination of Jesus as he continues his journey towards death at the hands of his enemies, and 13:33–34 lists Jerusalem again as a place where those who serve God are not honored, but killed. And Jesus urges the city to accept him, to allow him to gather them together for protection and security in face of the impending wrath of God.

Luke's mentions of Jerusalem in chapters 17, 18, 19 all serve to remind the reader that Jesus is going there to be executed and to be raised from the dead. Chapter 21 offers Jesus' eschatological message that the inhabitants of Jerusalem are facing imminent destruction and those in her vicinity should flee her before God's vengeance is poured out. Jerusalem will be destroyed and will, in fact, become gentile territory.

Jerusalem naturally figures prominently in Luke's telling of the final days of Jesus' life, for we next encounter the city as the place where Jesus stands trial before Herod and before Pilate (23:7). At the conclusion of his trial he is led out to the place of execution where he announces to the "daughters of Jerusalem" that they need not weep for him, but for themselves (23:28). Those women would have been better off if they had never borne children.

After the trial and execution of Jesus, Luke leaves off mention of the city until he relates the story of the disciples on the road to Emmaus. Emmaus is described as being "threescore furlongs" from Jerusalem and the disciples are on their way there after the distressing death and amazing resurrection of their master (24:13). Jesus appears in their midst and discusses with them the events of the last few days. They are surprised that he alone of all the inhabitants of Jerusalem isn't familiar with what has happened there. After having spent the day with their Lord, yet not knowing him, he is finally revealed in the breaking of the bread and those disciples make way back to Jerusalem to relate what has happened to them. While they tell their story Jesus himself appears in their midst and commissions them to preach the gospel, beginning at Jerusalem (24:47).

Luke's Gospel closes as it opens in terms of mention of Jerusalem: those who believe are there worshiping Jesus as the expected Messiah (24:52–53). Luke's "theology" of Jerusalem is that it is, first and last, the place where Jesus is made known as the Messiah. There at his birth and there after his resurrection he is worshiped as the Christ. Jerusalem may well have been responsible for rejecting him, and would ultimately pay the price of destruction for it, but in the meanwhile, Jerusalem was the place where Jesus was adored.

Jerusalem in John's Gospel

Jerusalem first makes an appearance in the Gospel of John when it reports that "Jews from Jerusalem sent priests to ask John the Baptist if he were the Christ" which he denied (1:19). So, already in the Gospel of John, Jerusalem is the place from which enquirers come. When next we find Jerusalem the subject of John's discourse, it is in connection with the cleansing of the Temple (2:13–14). After that event John suggests that many in Jerusalem believed in him because they had seen the signs which he had done. In the fourth chapter in his discussions with the Samaritan woman, she raises the question of the proper place of worship, and naturally names Jerusalem, to which Jesus replies, "those who worship God, worship him in spirit and in truth" – or, it's not where one worships that matters but how. When Jesus returned to Galilee many who had seen what he had done and heard what he had taught in Jerusalem "believed in him" (4:39). In chapter 5, John tells the story of the cleansing of the sick man at the pool of Bethesda, which being in Jerusalem gives him opportunity to mention that city. Again, then, it seems that so far as John is concerned to this point, Jerusalem is a place where Jesus is believed and a place which is receptive to his teachings and healings.

John 7 is a turning point in the author's presentation: here, for the first time, we have an indication that some in the city, namely the leadership, have plans to kill Jesus because, evidently, they know him to be the Christ (7:25). Yet in John 10 (v. 24) more enquirers come to Jesus to ask him directly if he is the Christ (as they had earlier asked John the Baptist). In the story of Lazarus' raising Jerusalem is mentioned in connection to its proximity to Bethany (11:18) and, as in the Synoptic Gospels, in 11:55 Jerusalem is mentioned as the final destination of Jesus who is going there to face execution. The final mention of Jerusalem in John is at 12:12 as prelude to the triumphal entry. From that point on, Jerusalem is not mentioned again in John.

John first mentions Jerusalem in connection with "seekers" and his final mention of the city is in connection with the triumphal entry of the one they were "seeking." Throughout John, Jerusalem functions as the place where those who see and hear Jesus respond positively to him and his message with the singular exception of the "Jewish leadership" who seek to kill him – which they do.

Jerusalem is the most important city of the Bible, being mentioned over 760 times in its pages. In the life of the Historical Jesus it plays a monumental role. It is, most importantly from a theological perspective, the place where Jesus dies and rises again.

JIM WEST

Further reading

Avigad, N. and H. Geva. "Jerusalem, the Jewish Quarter of the Old City, 1981–82," *IEJ* 32 (1982) 158–59.

Bahat, D. *The Illustrated Atlas of Jerusalem*, New York: Simon & Schuster, 1990.

Brodie, T. L. "The Departure for Jerusalem (Luke 9:51–56) as a Rhetorical Imitation of Elijah's Departure for the Jordan (2 Kgs 1:1–2:6)," *Biblica* 70 (1989) 96–109.

Geva, H. (ed.) *Ancient Jerusalem Revealed*, Jerusalem: Israel Exploration Society, 1994.

Giblin, C. H. *The Destruction of Jerusalem according to Luke's Gospel*, AnBib 105, Rome: Pontifical Biblical Institute Press, 1985.

Hengel, M. "Jerusalem als Jüdische und Hellenistische Stadt," in B. Funck (ed.) *Hellenismus*, Tübingen: Mohr Siebeck, 1997, pp. 269–306.

Jeremias, J. *Jerusalem in the Time of Jesus*, Philadelphia, PA: Fortress Press, 1969.

Segal, P. "The Penalty of the Warning Inscription from the Temple of Jerusalem," *IEJ* 39 (1989) 79–84.

JESUS' SELF-UNDERSTANDING

One of the most vexing and most vigorously debated questions concerning the historical Jesus is how Jesus understood himself and his mission. A key issue lurking behind this important question is whether the post-resurrection Church departed from the historical Jesus in its high Christology and Christ-centered gospel, and thus fundamentally misunderstood and misrepresented the message and purpose of Jesus. It cannot be denied that the gospels are documents of faith and that to a considerable extent they portray Jesus with obvious hindsight. The identity of Jesus is perceived with much more clarity after the resurrection, and this inevitably affects the gospel accounts to some degree – though to what degree is debatable. It is thus improbable that we will find *absolute correspondence* between the Christ of the apostolic witness and the historical Jesus. Nevertheless, despite the frequent claims made recently by those who would pit history against faith, the evidence examined below will argue for a significant and substantial *continuity* between Jesus in the Synoptic Gospels and the witness of the earliest church.

The historical question

While the reliability of the content of the Synoptic Gospels is obviously an issue for practically everything considered under the rubric of the historical Jesus, it is nowhere more problematic than it is when we deal with the question of how Jesus understood himself. Even if we could count on the reliability of the material we have, we must face the fact that for our question the evidence is necessarily indirect, and more indirect than usual. The gospels provide us no window into the inner life of Jesus; although biography-like, they are not biographies in the usual sense of the word. The gospels, as we will see, present a figure who is of a unique, transcendent significance, yet one who is paradoxically fully a human being. In the gospel accounts Jesus does not expose himself to us in such a way as to enable us to penetrate into his consciousness. We have no access to what he was thinking about himself and his mission except indirectly through what he says and does, and in his reaction to what others say of him, i.e. in the words and deeds that have been recorded for us in the gynoptics. But the authors of the Synoptics indicate no concern with Jesus' own thinking about himself, or with any possible development in his thinking along this line. Indeed, in that culture individual identity was defined primarily in relationship with others, and thus it is intrinsically unlikely that Jesus would make direct statements about his identity (see Witherington). This does not mean that Jesus had no view of himself. Rather, the data of the gospels fit well the socio-cultural situation of Jesus. This also provides an explanation for the oft-noted objection that Jesus makes no (or very few) claims for himself. Self-testimony carried little weight (cf. John 5:31; 8:13f.). All of the above considerations make the question of Jesus' self-consciousness especially difficult.

In the investigation that follows, the Gospel of Mark and Q provide the most reliable material and are thus given priority. The special material of Matthew and Luke, however, is not necessarily to be treated as without historical value. The Fourth Gospel is also not without historical value, but although it would seem the most promising so far as penetrating the self-consciousness of Jesus is concerned, it must be left out of consideration here because of the evident degree of interpretation the author has allowed himself under the inspiration of the Spirit.

The focus of the gospel tradition

It is not uncommonly said these days that the message of Jesus was not about himself. This is true, of course. The message of Jesus was about the dawning of the kingdom of God and not a self-proclamation. Jesus does not draw attention to himself directly. At the same time, however, what must not be missed is the vital connection between the coming of the kingdom and the person of Jesus. This relationship means that the proclamation of the former inevitably involves a statement about the latter.

Although the resurrection of Jesus clearly serves as a prime catalyst for christological thinking, and from it the development of Christology receives its major impetus, the resurrection is not the beginning of Christology. Rather, Christology begins

with the appearance of Jesus. Throughout his ministry, down to and including the crucifixion itself, we are confronted with implicit – and sometimes even explicit – Christology. It is a fact that according to the synoptics Jesus probes the subject of his own identity quite directly in his famous question "Who do people say that I am?" and then, specifically to his disciples, "Who do you say that I am?".

Jesus apparently expects the correct answer to this question to be a matter of induction. On the basis of what they have heard him say and seen him do, they are expected to draw the appropriate conclusion. In a similar way, our approach here must be inductive. No single element can bear the entire weight of the argument. Rather, what is decisive is the total picture arrived at through the combination of various individual elements. And although the emphasis is more on function and event than ontology (see Cullmann), there is no part of the Synoptic Tradition that is non-christological (see especially the old, but still useful works of Hoskyns and Davey, and James Denney).

The evidence of the titles

Although the indirect evidence is perhaps more persuasive, an examination of the titles applied to Jesus provides a convenient starting point. It is the whole story of Jesus that is important, and in the end the titles function only as "summary abbreviations of the claim contained in the story," namely "the claim to authority which indicates the pre-understanding in which the individual parts of the story of Jesus are preserved" (G. Theissen and S. Merz 513).

Prophet

Jesus is described as a prophet at several points in the synoptics (Mark 6:15 [par.]; 8:28 [par.]; cf. 14:65 [par.]; Matt 21:11, 46; Luke 7:16, cf. 7:39). This was apparently the most widespread conclusion held concerning Jesus by his contemporaries, probably reflecting the unusual authority he exhibited in his teaching, his proclamation of the kingdom, and his dramatic deeds of power. The temporarily disillusioned Emmaus disciples summarize the widespread view of Jesus as one "who was a prophet mighty in deed and word before God and all the people" (Luke 24:19). Jesus accepts the designation in his statement, following his rejection in Nazareth, that "A prophet is not without honor, except in his own country, and among his own kin, and in his own house" (Mark

6:4 [par.]). Similarly, in contemplating his own death, Jesus asserts "Nevertheless, I must go on my way today and tomorrow and the day following; for it cannot be that a prophet should perish away from Jerusalem" (Luke 13:33). In this prophetic capacity Jesus knew that he was speaking and acting on behalf of God in his announcement concerning the dawning of the kingdom. In the Synoptic Tradition this is not yet the idea of *the* prophet, i.e. the eschatological figure who brings the end of the age, as in John 6:14. Many NT scholars conclude that the most appropriate description of the historical Jesus is that he was an eschatological prophet. This concept merges with the next titles, Messiah and Son of David.

Messiah and Son of David

The sense of the word "Messiah" is more than simply an "anointed one," but *the* anointed one who would bring the promised the age of salvation expected and hoped for by Israel. There is widespread agreement that although Jesus did not explicitly assert that he was the Messiah, he at least accepted the identification of himself as such. No one doubts the historical veracity of the titulus above the crucified Jesus that read "King of the Jews." The claim of kingship is a messianic claim, and Jesus was put to death for his allegedly messianic pretensions, construed politically by the Romans.

Important synoptic evidence indicates that Jesus was willing to accept acclamation as Messiah from others. The classic passage here is the confession at Caesarea Philippi (Mark 8:27–30 [par.]). The question concerning the identity of Jesus is interesting in itself for our purposes. Jesus poses the question not so much to gain information as to elicit the appropriate response from the disciples. The assumption is that Jesus thinks of himself in terms of the messianic category. All three synoptic accounts present "the Christ" as the answer, with expansions in Luke (9:20), "of God," and Matthew (16:16), "the Son of the living God." In the Markan and Lukan accounts, the so-called messianic secret motif follows immediately after the confession (in Matthew it is delayed until 16:20). Here Jesus exhorts the disciples not to spread this idea of his messianic identity to others. Jesus urges the secrecy not because he regards the confession as wrong or questionable, but rather because of the mistaken popular expectations concerning the Messiah (cf. John 6:15). Immediately after the confession in Matthew, by contrast, an elated Jesus applauds Peter's confession, certifying its truthfulness

with the words, "Blessed are you Simon Bar-Jona! For flesh and blood has not revealed this to you, but my Father who is in heaven" (Matt 16:17).

Another striking instance where Jesus encourages acclamation as Messiah is in the triumphal entry into Jerusalem (Mark 11:1–11 [par.]). Here, to be sure, the title "Messiah" does not occur. But we have the equivalent in the references to David and the coming kingdom. So as to come like the promised savior king of Zech 9:9, whose dominion will be "to the ends of the earth," Jesus carefully arranges to enter Jerusalem humbly on a donkey. The predictable response of the crowd is enthusiastically shouted out in words drawn from Ps 118:25f.: "Hosanna! [Matt adds: "to the son of David"] Blessed is he who comes in the name of the Lord! Blessed is the kingdom of our father David that is coming! Hosanna in the highest" (Mark 11:9f.). The Lukan parallel reads: "Blessed is the King who comes in the name of the Lord! Peace in heaven and glory in the highest!" Luke (alone) continues with the note that the Pharisees were offended by this messianic acclamation and excitement concerning deliverance, and asked Jesus to rebuke his disciples. Far from retreating from the affirmation, Jesus responds: "I tell you, if these were silent the very stones would cry out" (Luke 19:40). The following words in Luke are also significant: Jesus weeps over Jerusalem and says "Would that even today you knew the things that make for peace! But now they are hid from your eyes. [Judgment is coming upon Jerusalem] because you did not know the time of your visitation" (Luke 19: 41, 44). These words probably may be taken as historically authentic since they are coherent with abundant material that indicates Jesus saw his ministry as of pivotal importance in the dawning of the eschatological kingdom (see later).

The only place in the whole of the Synoptic Tradition where Jesus directly asserts his identity as Messiah is in the answer he gives to the High Priest in Mark 14:62. There, being asked "Are you the Christ, the Son of the Blessed?" he responds with the direct "I am" (cf. "You have said so," Matt 26:64; cf. Luke 22:67f.). The historical worth of this report is usually challenged, but the affirmative answer (and the words about the Son of Man coming in power) is very consonant with the charge "king of the Jews," for which Jesus was crucified. Earlier in the narrative Jesus implicitly affirms his messianic identity in the answer he gives to the question of John the Baptist about whether he was "the coming one" (Matt 11:2-6).

Consistent with this material is further – albeit indirect – evidence that Jesus thought of himself as

Messiah. Particularly illuminating here is the evidence that Jesus identified John the Baptist as functioning in the role of Elijah. According to Malachi (3:1; 4:5f.), Elijah is to return and prepare the way for eschatological judgment. Even though this particular work of the coming Messiah is exactly what Jesus has not (at this point) come to do (cf. Matt 13:24–30, 36–43; 13:47–50), Jesus nevertheless says of John the Baptist that he was more than a prophet: he was the one of whom Malachi spoke (Matt 11:10/Luke 7:27). A great premium is put upon this identification in Matthew, who records Jesus as saying "For all the prophets and the law prophesied until John; and if you are willing to accept it, he is Elijah who is to come" (Matt 11:13f.). Along the same line, note should be taken of Mark 9:13, "But I tell you that Elijah has come, and they did to him whatever they pleased, as it is written of him" (cf. Matt 17:12f.). It is clear from this material that Jesus regarded himself as the key figure mentioned by the Malachi prophecy, probably to be understood as the Messiah. Similarly, when Jesus refers to rebuilding of the Temple (O. Betz) in his answer to the high priest, he identifies himself as the Messiah, Son of David (cf. 4Q174).

It was widely believed that the Messiah was to be the Son of David mentioned in 2 Sam 7:8–17, whose promised kingdom would "be established forever" (cf. *Pss. Sol.* 17:21; cf. Ezek 34:23). Jesus is frequently addressed as "Son of David" in the Synoptic Gospels. The blind Bartimaeus of Mark 10:46–52 par.; cf. Matt 9:27 twice uses the title Son of David in his pleading that Jesus would restore his sight. So, too, the Canaanite woman of Matt 15:22 beseeches Jesus for her demon-possessed daughter with the words "Son of David." And after Jesus has healed the blind and dumb demoniac the crowd asks in amazement, "Can this be the Son of David?" (Matt 12:23). The remarkable ability to demonstrate power over sickness and evil turned the people's thoughts to the promised royal deliverer who would bring the age of perfection. Again it is others, rather than Jesus himself, who seemed willing to make use of the title of the promised Son of David. But Jesus does not protest the reference.

The equation of Son of David and Messiah is plainly assumed in the question Jesus asks: "How can the scribes say that the Christ is the son of David?" (Mark 12:35 [Matt 22:42; Luke 20:41]). Jesus asks the question not to dispute that the Messiah is the Son of David but to raise the puzzle caused by Ps 110:1 where, as the author of the psalm, David calls his son "lord" (Hebr. *adonai*), the one who is invited to sit at the right hand of

Yahweh until his enemies are made his footstool. If we may take this passage as historical it is of considerable importance to our subject, for Jesus speaks here not of another person (although this has been claimed by some), but of himself as the Son of David. If that is correct, then this passage indicates that Jesus thought of himself not simply as a descendant of David, however extraordinary, but also as David's lord, destined to sit at God's right hand. It is worth noting here that although Jesus is often addressed with the title "Lord" (*kyrios*), this does not contribute to our discussion. By the time of the gospel writers the word is understood as a divine title, during the ministry of Jesus it is merely an honorific address, meaning something like "Sir."

It is the extent and weight of this material that has encouraged the majority of NT scholars to conclude that although he did not use the titles in referring to himself, Jesus probably regarded himself as the Messiah, the Son of David (see, e.g., Hengel, Stuhlmacher). But here we must face what may well be the greatest surprise of the gospels, namely the fact that Jesus radically redefines the role the Messiah was expected to fulfill. If he comes as Messiah, as the tradition claims, he comes not as a triumphant king who brings eschatological judgment upon the enemies of God but, on the contrary, as a servant who suffers and dies for the redemption of his people. As a further quandary, for the time being he brings the messianic kingdom in a real but mysterious form, and not as the overwhelming force that was expected.

Son of Man

Among the titles applied to Jesus in the gospels, none is more challenging and disputed than "Son of Man." The number and character of the problems associated with this phrase can seem insurmountable and have called forth a huge discussion. Not only the meaning of the phrase, but also its historical authenticity has been much questioned. At the same time, ironically, according to the gospels it is the one expression that Jesus used repeatedly of himself. In the gospels there is no reference to Jesus as Son of Man by anyone other than Jesus. In the mouth of Jesus the words can be used on occasion quite innocently as a circumlocution for "I" (cf. Matt 16:13 with Mark 8:27/Luke 9:18), although this is hardly always the case (*pace* Vermes). It can also be understood in the generic sense of "man," most often a specific man, i.e. the man Jesus (cf. the frequent use of "son of man" to refer to the prophet in Ezekiel).

Perhaps Jesus favored using the phrase to refer to himself exactly because of its inherent ambiguity. It appears not to have been a well-known expression at the time, and certainly in itself did not necessarily have a messianic connotation. The only contemporary historical background for the phrase that we know of is in the Similitudes of Enoch (= *1 Enoch* 37–71), *4 Ezra* (= *2 Esdras*) 13 and Dan 7:13f. The dating of the Similitudes is a difficult question. Many scholars regard this section of *1 Enoch* as much later than the rest of the book, especially since it is lacking among the Aramaic fragments of Enoch found at Qumran. The current consensus dates the Similitudes somewhere in the middle of the first century. Though it seems rather unlikely, we must reckon at least with the possibility of Christian influence. The Son of Man in the Similitudes is a glorious apocalyptic figure, apparently a composite of Dan 7:13f., the suffering servant of Isa 42–53 (he is repeatedly called "the Elect One"), and the Davidic king of 2 Sam 7 and the messianic psalms (he is called Messiah in *1 Enoch* 48:10; 52:4) – the very combination we are familiar with from the NT.

Similarly, in *4 Ezra* 13 Son of Man becomes a messianic title, and is furthermore described as God's Son. This material is probably from the end of the first century and is dependent on Dan 7:13f. It is a separate document of the Enoch collection; it dates from the end of the first century, much later than our gospels, and therefore could possibly reflect Christian understanding of the phrase.

For all the difficulty of determining the source and meaning of Son of Man, and despite the variety of ideas connected with it (humanity, suffering, future triumphant appearance), it does seem to take on the character of a title within the gospels. Although disputed by some, the most important background for Son of Man as used in the gospels is Dan 7:13f. Although the phrase in Daniel is not strictly a title, and indeed is a corporate idea that refers in context to the saints of the Most High (7:27), eventually in the materials mentioned above it becomes a title and is understood to refer to an individual. Thus in the gospels Jesus identifies with *the* Son of Man when he quotes Dan 7:13 in reference to himself (Mark 13:26 [parr.]; 14:26 [par.]; cf. Matt 25:31). If Jesus self-consciously did use Son of Man in the Danielic sense as an apocalyptic, messianic title referring to himself, he must have thought of himself as the one to whom "dominion and glory and kingdom" will be given, the one whom "all peoples, nations, and languages" will serve, and whose "dominion is an everlasting dominion which shall not pass away,"

whose kingdom "shall not be destroyed" (Dan 7:14). These motifs cohere well with the titles of Son of David and Messiah. The orientation here is of course future, but the implications for the present are also momentous.

Against the idea that none of the Son of Man sayings in the gospels are historically authentic, but are to be understood as the creation of the early Christian community, is the lapidary fact that the title occurs nowhere else in the NT except for Acts 7:56. For whatever reason, this title simply was not an expression that the early church found useful or meaningful in terms of its own confession of faith. Given further its difficulty and ambiguity, it seems extremely unlikely that it would have so pervasively been put into the mouth of Jesus.

Son of God

This clearly elastic term is applied to angels, to the people of Israel, to kings, to righteous men, the disciples of Jesus, and so forth. Here, however, "Son of God" is being used in the unique sense, *the* Son of God, referring to one who is unlike any other, one with a special relationship with God enjoyed by no one else. That unique sonship is of course evident too in the absolute use of "Son" without a modifier. Did Jesus have a unique filial consciousness?

Jesus' use of the term *abba*, an Aramaic word of an intimate character for "father," has been the focus of much discussion. The word occurs only once in the Synoptics, in Jesus' Gethsemane prayer (Mark 14:36), where it receives the translation *pater*, "Father." The perceived distinctiveness of the Aramaic *abba* is evident by its preservation and use in Paul (Gal 4:6 and Rom 8:15). The strong claim of Joachim Jeremias that Jesus' addressing God in prayer as *abba* was unparalleled in first-century Judaism is now regarded by most scholars as a considerable overstatement. Jews did address God using the same root *ab*, as "my Father" and "our Father." But Jeremias was correct when he emphasized that the striking word *abba* captured the essence of Jesus' special relationship to his Father. Jesus never includes himself with others in referring to God as "our" Father, but refers instead to "my" Father, indicating the special, intimate and unshared character of his sonship.

Jesus is called the Son of God at several points in the gospel narratives. Prominent at the baptism of Jesus and the transfiguration is the voice "from heaven" repeating the words: "You are my beloved Son; with you I am well pleased" (Mark 1:11 [par. in third person]) and "This is my beloved Son

[Luke my Chosen]" (Mark 9:7 [parr.]). A striking aspect of the synoptics is that Satan and the demons seem immediately to know the identity of Jesus. Thus Satan assumes that Jesus is the Son of God according to Matt 4:3, 6, [par.]. (The "if" of the first class condition assumes the reality referred to and is readily translatable as "since;" cf. the statement of the sarcastic taunters in Matt 27:40.) The "unclean spirits" of Mark 3:11 cry out "You are the Son of God," and in another instance a demon cries out "What have you to do with me, Jesus, Son of the Most High God?" (Mark. 5:7 [parr.; Matt has simply "Son of God"]). The direct question of the High Priest to Jesus is "Are you the Christ, the Son of the Blessed?" (Mark 14:62; par. Matt 26:63 "Are you the Christ, the Son of God?" cf. Luke 22:70, "Are you the Son of God?"). To these questions, asked in unbelief, Jesus responds in Mark with the simple "I am," and in Matthew and Luke the more indirect affirmation "You have said so/You say that I am." An additional Matthean verse (27:43) records the crowd's witness that "He said 'I am the Son of God.'" At the end of the crucifixion scene, the Roman centurion confesses, "Truly this man was the Son of God" (hardly to be understood as "a Son of God," despite the lack of the definite article before Son in the Greek), Mark 15:39 [par.].

From the disciples, two passages are pertinent. In Matt 14:33, in response to the stilling of the storm, the disciples confess, "Truly you are the Son of God" (the definite article is again lacking). In Matthew's account of the confession at Caesarea Philippi, Peter identifies Jesus as the Messiah, "the Son of the living God" (16:16).

According to the synoptics, at several points Jesus implies that he is the Son of God. In the parable of the wicked tenants, the owner of the vineyard in a last attempt to obtain fruit sends his "beloved son" (Mark 12:6 [par.; Matt lacks the adjective]), who is put to death "outside the vineyard" (Mark 12:8 [par.]). In a remarkable statement concerning the time of the final judgment, Jesus says, "But of that day or that hour no one knows, not even the angels in heaven, nor the Son, but only the Father" (Mark 13:32 [par.]).

It is possible that Jesus thought of himself in terms of divine wisdom, but the evidence is perhaps too slight to be convincing (cf. the Q passage, Matt 11:19 = Luke 7:35; cf. the similarity between how Jesus speaks in Matt 11:27–30 and how wisdom speaks in Sir 6:28; 24:19; 51:23, 26–27; Mark 6:2).

Without question, the most impressive passage is the Q material (Matt 11:27 = Luke 10:22, with very slight differences) sometimes referred to as a Johannine bolt in the synoptics. In a prayer that twice addresses God as Father, Jesus is reported as saying, "All things have been delivered to me by my Father; and no one knows the Son except the Father, and no one knows the Father, except the Son and any one to whom the Son chooses to reveal him." Here intimacy of knowledge presupposes intimacy of relationship – an intimacy that by its nature is exclusive. Much debated is the question of the historical authenticity of this material. In their commentary on Matthew, Allison and Davies, for example, find themselves unable to decide one way or the other. This passage, however, is consonant with such a large portion of the Synoptic tradition concerning Jesus discussed here, that there seems little reason to reject it outright, unless for *a priori* reasons one feels compelled to reject the tradition *in toto*.

The titles we have examined compose a coherent pattern and present a cumulative argument that Jesus was conscious of his uniqueness. In his own person and role, Jesus fuses these various titles together. No single title is adequate. Before attempting to draw specific conclusions concerning the content of Jesus' self-understanding, we must look at the much larger body of material that presents indirect, but powerful, evidence concerning the identity of Jesus as he may have understood it. This material, which concerns the mission of Jesus in terms of what he said and did, presents a consistent pattern and coheres itself remarkably with what we have seen concerning the titles.

The evidence of the words and deeds of Jesus

As Hoskyns and Davey demonstrated, there is no strand of the gospels that is not christological. Given the account of the mission of Jesus – what he said and did – it is most unlikely that he had no concept of his own role and identity. How exactly that should be articulated is not as clear as it might be, but that the acts and words of Jesus are closely intertwined with his person cannot be challenged.

The kingdom of God

The Synoptic Gospels present the burden of Jesus' message in terms of the dawning of the kingdom of God. Everything Jesus says and does is related to this. At a minimum Jesus understood himself to be the Agent (cf. *shaliach*, one sent by God as his representative for a special purpose) of that kingdom. On this the tradition is overwhelming. At the beginning of Mark, Jesus comes "preaching the gospel of

God, and saying, 'The time is fulfilled, and the kingdom of God is at hand; repent, and believe in the gospel'" (Mark 1:15). A Q passage represents Jesus as saying, "But if it is by the Spirit of God that I cast out demons, then the kingdom of God has come upon you" (Matt 12:28 = Luke 11:20, "by the finger of God"). The healings and exorcisms done by Jesus are manifestations of the dawning reality of the kingdom. The attack on illness and demons amounts to a head-on confrontation of apocalyptic significance. Upon the exuberant return of the seventy from their mission, Jesus remarks, "I saw Satan fall like lightning from heaven" (Luke 10:18). The kingdom is mediated by Jesus himself. Luke 17:21 records Jesus as saying, "behold, the kingdom of God is in your midst (*entos hymon estin*)." Early in Luke's narrative Jesus in the synagogue at Nazareth reads from Isaiah 61:1f., a passage of messianic/eschatological promise, and then he applies it to his own ministry, saying, "Today this scripture has been fulfilled in your hearing" (Luke 4:21). In a Q passage Jesus answers John the Baptist's question about whether he was "the coming one." Jesus points out his deeds, appealing to a number of scriptures, such as Isaiah 26; 35; and again, Isaiah 61:1, as being realized in and through his ministry. (At Qumran, the messianic apocalypse 4Q521 articulates a similar complex of expectations.) Indeed, the way in which Jesus quotes or alludes to OT passages as being fulfilled in himself also points to a self-consciousness of his unique identity (France). Although contrary to popular expectation, judgment remains a future event, but with Jesus himself as returning judge (Mark 13:26 par.; Matt 24:50f.; 25:31–46).

The authority of Jesus

In his teaching and his deeds of power Jesus had an authority that constantly astonished the people. Mark notes from the beginning that when Jesus taught in the synagogue in Capernaum "they were astonished at his teaching, for he taught them as one who had authority, and not as the scribes" (1:22; cf. Luke 4:32). In Mark 2:23–3:6 Jesus shows an unhesitating, sovereign authority in determining the meaning of the sabbath commandment. After his exposition of righteousness in the Sermon on the Mount, the crowds responded with the same astonishment (Matt 7:28f.). There the authority of Jesus is evident in his authoritative interpretation of the Torah. His repeated "But I say to you" stands in sharp contrast to traditional interpretation. Although Jesus in some respects is like a prophet, he never uses the typical prophetic formula

"Thus says the Lord." His authority is of a personal kind, as we can also see from his unparalleled use of "Amen" introducing many of his Synoptic sayings. The number and character of the I-sayings of Jesus in the synoptics point to a unique authority. There is furthermore a sense in which the parables contain self-revelation of Jesus, alternately as son, savior, servant, and Lord (Vincent).

So, too, this unparalleled authority and supernatural power are seen in what Jesus does: in his exorcism of demons, his frequent healings of various maladies and, if it be allowed, his raising of the dead (Mark 5:41f., par.; Luke 7:11–17; cf. "the dead are raised up" in the Q passage, Matt 11:4; Luke 7:22). These deeds are of course closely related to the proclamation of the dawning of the kingdom. Jesus has bound Satan, the strong man, and plunders his house (Mark 3:27 par.; cf. Luke 11:22). The so-called nature miracles should also be mentioned here – e.g. the feeding of the multitude, the calming of the storm – although many would question their historicity.

Jesus displays a remarkable authority in a variety of other ways too. It is evident, for example, in Jesus' relationship with others (Witherington) and especially in his free association with sinners. Notable too is Jesus' forgiveness of sins, an action which caused the authorities to regard Jesus as blasphemous (Mark 2:1–12 par.). Finally we may mention the cleansing of the Temple (Mark 11:15–19 par.) as a demonstration of the authority of Jesus. The chief priests, scribes and elders put the question directly to Jesus: "By what authority are you doing these things, or who gave you this authority to do them?" (Mark 11:28, par.).

It is clear that these actions cannot have been performed without Jesus having had some inner sense of his own personal calling and role in God's overarching purposes. His deeds, like his words, point to something and someone unique in the history of God's dealing with his people (cf. Jesus' words concerning something greater than Jonah, Solomon, or the Temple: Matt 12:6, 41f.).

Jesus' demands concerning himself

Jesus is of central importance to the eschatological turning point announced in the kingdom. In the dawning of this new reality, he alone determines the relations between God and humanity. According to a Q passage, he puts himself in an unparalleled meditating position. "So every one who acknowledges me before others, I also will acknowledge before my Father who is in heaven; but whoever denies me before others, I also will deny before my Father who is in heaven" (Matt 10:32f.; Luke 12:8f. "The Son of Man will acknowledge before the angels of God ... will be denied before the angels of God"). This pivotal position points to a unique self-consciousness, even something close to the idea of incarnation (Fuller, "Clue").

The very fact that Jesus sovereignly calls disciples to leave all and to follow him rather than pointing them to God or to Torah obedience also suggests a unique self-consciousness (Hengel, 1981).

> He who loves father or mother more than me is not worthy of me; and he who loves son or daughter more than me is not worthy of me; and he who does not take his cross and follow me is not worthy of me. He who finds his life will lose it, and he who loses his life for my sake will find it.
>
> (Matt 10:37–39; cf. Luke 14:26f.)

Matthew continues with more words that indicate a unique self-consciousness in Jesus. "He who receives you receives me, and he who receives me receives him who sent me" (Matt 10:40; cf. Luke 10:16). Mark has equivalent material:

> If anyone would come after me, let him deny himself and take up his cross and follow me. For whoever would save his life will lose it; and whoever loses his life for my sake and the gospel's will save it ... For whoever is ashamed of me and of my words in this adulterous and sinful generation, of him will the Son of Man also be ashamed, when he comes in the glory of this Father with the holy angels.
>
> (Mark 8:34–38)

The aims of Jesus and his self-consciousness

It is abundantly evident from the Synoptic Gospels that Jesus came to proclaim the present dawning of the kingdom of God. This happens in and through his person and ministry, and more significantly through his death. Thus Jesus comes also to die. According to a threefold Synoptic tradition, each found in all three synoptics, Jesus foretold his imminent death and resurrection (Mark 8:31 parr.; 9:31 par.; 10:33f. par.; cf. Evans). Much debate surrounds the question of how Jesus understood the meaning of his death. Was it the death only of a prophet, or of a martyr, or the death of the servant of Isaiah 53? Of great importance here is the record that Jesus foretold his own death as the way of salvation (Taylor). In two Markan passages, both with parallels in Matthew, we have evidence of this. "For the Son of Man also came not to be served but to serve, and to give his life as a ransom for many" (Mark 10:45; Matt 20:28). This suggests

that Jesus thought of himself in terms of the servant of Isaiah 53. At the last supper, Jesus refers to the cup with the words, "This is my blood of the covenant, which is poured out for many" (Mark 14:24; Matt 26:28, adding the words "for the forgiveness of sins"). Jesus thus comes not merely to proclaim the kingdom but to establish it through his death. The cross is the means of the restoration of God's Rule or kingdom and the realization of salvation. It is true that in the synoptics we do not have as much here to help us to make this connection as we might like and therefore must rely on the post-resurrection interpretation we find in other parts of the NT. But this understanding of the death of Jesus is fully consonant with the data surveyed above. We note finally that it was the self-claims of Jesus – whether explicitly or implicitly – that led to his crucifixion.

Consciousness of uniqueness

It is very difficult, not to say impossible, to conclude that the historical Jesus was not conscious of his uniqueness. How precisely he would have directly articulated that consciousness is difficult to determine. He knew himself to have been sent by God. At a minimum he knew that he was sent by God – as a *shaliach* (representative or agent) – in a capacity and role unique in the history of salvation. Both the verb "sent" (Mark 9:37; 12:6 par.; Matt 10:40, par.; Luke 4:18; cf. 13:34; and John *passim*) and "came" (e.g. Mark 2:17 par.; Matt 10:34f.) can have this connotation. Note the parallel, "for this I came" in Mark 1:38 and "for this I was sent" in Luke 4:43. The statement in Luke 19:10 and Matthew 15:24 where Jesus says that he came (Matt: "was sent") to seek and save the lost (Matt: "to the lost sheep of the house of Israel") alludes clearly to the role of the promised shepherd king of Ezekiel 34:16, 23f.; 37:24 (cf. Jer 3:15; 23:4). In Zechariah 13:7 the shepherd, "the man who stands next to me" is stricken and the sheep scattered. Jesus applies the prophecy to himself in Mark 14:27 par.

Jesus very probably knew himself to be God's eschatological Messiah – not of the type that was popularly expected, but one sent to save his people through his sacrificial death (Stuhlmacher), probably with the both images in his mind: that of the servant of Isaiah 53 and the shepherd of Zechariah 13:7. He chose the Twelve as the nucleus of a new messianic eschatological community, meant not merely to be the restoration of Israel but one inclusive of the Gentiles. Jesus must have understood himself as fulfilling the promise of the Abrahamic covenant, and the goal of God's saving purpose.

As with the Christology of the NT, so too with the self-understanding of Jesus, the emphasis in the NT is upon function rather than ontology. This fact in itself enhances the probability that our material is historically reliable. The difference between the content of the synoptics over against the more reflective Gospel of John, the fantasies of the NT Apocrypha and the carefully crafted Nicene creed is striking.

The data are complex and Jesus cannot easily be fitted into any single category available to us. As much as Jesus can be seen as being like contemporary figures, there can be no question from what we have seen above that he is without analogy. Other construals can hardly make sense of the synoptic data. Though we cannot ultimately penetrate his self-consciousness, Jesus cannot have thought of himself as merely a teacher or healer, or even prophet.

DONALD A. HAGNER

Further reading

Allison, D. C. Allison, Jr and Davies, W. D. *A Critical and Exegetical Commentary on the Gospel According to Saint Matthew*, ICC, 3 vols, Edinburgh: T. & T. Clark, 1991–97.

Betz, O. *What Do We Know About Jesus?* Philadelphia, PA: Westminster, 1968.

Brown, Raymond E. *An Introduction to New Testament Christology*, New York: Paulist, 1994, pp. 17–102.

Cullmann, O. *The Christology of the New Testament*, revised edition, Philadelphia, PA: Westminster, 1963.

Denney, James. *Jesus and the Gospel: Christianity Justified in the Mind of Christ*, London: Hodder and Stoughton, 1908.

Dunn, J. D. G. "Messianic Ideas and their Influence on the Jesus of History," in J. H. Charlesworth (ed.) *The Messiah: Developments in Earliest Judaism and Christianity*, Minneapolis, MN: Fortress Press, 1992, pp. 365–81.

—— *Jesus Remembered*, Grand Rapids, MI and Cambridge: Eerdmans, 2003.

Dunn, J. D. G. and Scot McKnight. *The Historical Jesus in Recent Research*, Studies for Biblical and Theological Study 10, Winona Lake, IN: Eisenbrauns, 2005.

Evans, Craig A. "Did Jesus Predict his Death and Resurrection?," in S. E. Porter, M. A. Hayes and D. Tombs (eds) *Resurrection*, JSNTSS 186, Sheffield: Sheffield Academic Press, 1999, pp. 82–97.

Forsyth, P. T. *The Person and Place of Jesus Christ*, Eugene and Pasadena, CA: Wipf & Stock, 1996 (reprint of 1909 original).

France, R. T. *Jesus and the Old Testament*, Downers Grove, IL: InterVarsity Press, 1971.

Fuller, R. H. *The Foundations of New Testament Christology*, London: Collins, 1965, pp. 102–41.

—— "The Clue to Jesus' Self-Understanding," in Robert Kahl (ed.) *Christ and Christianity: Studies in the Formation of Christology*, Valley Forge, PA: Trinity Press International, 1994, pp. 37–46.

Harvey, A. E. *Jesus and the Constraints of History*, London: Duckworth, 1982.

Hengel, Martin. *The Son of God: The Origin of Christology and the History of Jewish–Hellenistic Religion*, Philadelphia, PA: Fortress Press, 1976.

—— *The Charismatic Leader and His Followers*, New York: Crossroad, 1981.

—— *Studies in Early Christology*, Edinburgh: T. & T. Clark, 1995.

Hoskyns, E. C. and N. Davey *The Riddle of the New Testament*, London: Faber & Faber, 1931.

Hunter, A. M. *The Work and Words of Jesus*, London: SCM Press, 1950.

—— "Critic's Crux: Matthew 11.25–30," in *Teaching and Preaching the New Testament*, Philadelphia, PA: Westminster, 1963, pp. 41–50.

Hurtado, Larry W. *Lord Jesus Christ. Devotion to Jesus in Earliest Christianity*, Grand Rapids, MI and Cambridge: Eerdmans, 2003.

Jonge, Marinus de. *God's Final Envoy: Early Christology and Jesus' View of His Mission*, Grand Rapids, MI and Cambridge: Eerdmans, 1998.

Lee, Aquila H. I. *From Messiah to Preexistent Son: Jesus' Self-Consciousness and Early Christian Exegesis of Messianic Psalms*, Tübingen: Mohr Siebeck, 2005.

Leivestad, Ragnar. *Jesus in His Own Perspective: An Examination of His Sayings, Actions, and Eschatological Titles*, trans. David E. Aune, Minneapolis, MN: Augsburg, 1987.

Marshall, I. H. "The Divine Sonship of Jesus," *Int.* 21 (1967) 89–103.

—— *The Origins of New Testament Christology*, Downers Grove, IL: InterVarsity Press, 1990, pp. 43–62.

Meyer, Ben F. *The Aims of Jesus*, London: SCM Press, 1979.

Pokorný, Petr. *The Genesis of Christology: Foundations for a Theology of the New Testament*, trans. M. Lefébure, Edinburgh: T. & T. Clark, 1987, pp. 38–62.

Riesenfeld, Harald. "Observations on the Question of the Self-Consciousness of Jesus," SEÅ 25 (1960) 21–36.

Robinson, J. A. T. "The Last Tabu? The Self-Consciousness of Jesus," in *Twelve More New Testament Studies*, London: SCM Press, 1984, pp. 155–70; reprinted in J. D. G. Dunn and S. McKnight (eds) *The Historical Jesus in Recent Research*, Winona Lake, IN: Eisenbrauns, 2005, pp. 553–66.

Sanders, E. P. *Jesus and Judaism*, Philadelphia, PA: Fortress Press, 1985.

Stuhlmacher, Peter. "The Messianic Son of Man: Jesus' Claim to Deity," in J. D. G. Dunn and S. McKnight (eds) *The Historical Jesus in Recent Research*, Winona Lake, IN: Eisenbrauns, 2005, pp. 325–44.

Taylor, Vincent. *The Cross of Christ*, London: Macmillan, 1956, pp. 11–23.

Theissen, G. Theissen and Merz, A., *The Historical Jesus: A Comprehensive Guide*, Minneapolis, MN: Fortress, 1998.

Tuckett, Christopher. *Christology and the New Testament: Jesus and his Earliest Followers*, Louisville, KY: Westminster John Knox, 2001, pp. 202–33.

Vermes G. *Jesus the Jew: A Historian's Reading of the Gospels*, London: Collins; Philadelphia. PA: Fortress, 1973.

Vincent, J. J. "The Parables of Jesus as Self-Revelation," *SE* I (1959) 79–99.

Vos, Geerhardus. *The Self-Disclosure of Jesus. The Modern Debate About the Messianic Consciousness*, Grand Rapids, MI: Eerdmans, 1954.

Warfield, B. B. *The Lord of Glory: A Study of the Designations of our Lord in the New Testament with Especial*

Reference to his Deity, Vestavia Hills, AL: Solid Ground, 2006 [1907].

Witherington, Ben. *The Christology of Jesus*, Minneapolis. MN: Fortress Press, 1990.

Wright, N. T. *Jesus and the Victory of God*, Minneapolis, MN: Fortress Press, 1996, pp. 475–653.

—— "Jesus' Self-Understanding," in Stephen T. Davis, Daniel Kendall, and Gerald O'Collins (eds) *The Incarnation: An Interdisciplinary Symposium on the Incarnation of the Son of God*, Oxford: Oxford University Press, 2002, pp. 47–61.

JESUS SEMINAR

Founded in 1985 by Robert W. Funk after years of careful preparation, the Jesus Seminar of North America has drawn widespread public attention – as well as scholarly praise and criticism – for its pronouncements regarding the authenticity of the gospels, and notoriety for its unconventional portraits of the historical Jesus.

The Seminar created a perennial media sensation by determining the authenticity or inauthenticity of the sayings of Jesus by vote: each of its members cast colored beads into a basket. A red bead indicated belief that the saying in question was authentic and accurately represented what Jesus said; a pink bead indicated belief that the saying was authentic but only approximated what Jesus said; a gray bead indicated substantial doubt, while a black bead indicated judgment that the saying in question certainly did not originate with Jesus. The Seminar has concluded in aggregate (see R. W. Funk and R. W. Hoover) that approximately 18 percent of the sayings (presented in red or pink in published form) originated with Jesus. A similar conclusion was reached with regard to the acts of Jesus (see R. W. Funk, 1998).

Angered by his sudden termination in 1980 as manager of Scholars Press, the publishing arm of the Society of Biblical Literature, Funk founded the Jesus Seminar as well the Westar Institute, an organization designed to rally support for the Seminar, to publish its work and associated writings, and to engage in programs of public education. Funk set himself three ambitious and clearly articulated goals, in each of them aiming to show the direction he felt the SBL should have taken: (1) to change the character of scholarly discourse concerning the New Testament in order to make findings clearer; (2) to bring the findings of scholarship to public attention; and (3) to help scholars develop a durable connection with a wide readership outside the professional guild. Hundreds of scholars were invited to join as Fellows, based upon their established place in the discipline of critical study of the New Testament; initially some three hundred did so.

Funk enhanced the impact of the Seminar's meetings, especially in the early years, by convening them in different cities, and preparing the ground for each session in the local as well as national press. His selection of particular issues, topics, and texts was always focused, pertinent, and presented with advance notice to colleagues as well as preliminary papers so as to facilitate discussion. Fellows became skilled at relating their often specialized qualifications in fields as diverse as Aramaic studies and rhetorical criticism to precisely formulated, common-sense questions, as they publicly debated propositions with one another and engaged with journalists and others interested in the work of the Seminar. Administratively, Funk's direction was impassioned, energetic, and virtually faultless in its execution. (In this regard, the contribution of his wife, Charlene Matejovsky, merits particular mention.) In its three principal aims, the Jesus Seminar succeeded, and has made an enduring contribution to the interpretation of the gospels in the United States. Its results and intellectual orientation are doubtful; its impact is not.

Despite its overall and undeniable success, the Seminar's membership shrank within a few years to approximately eighty more or less active members. This shrinkage of the total number of Fellows, together with a sporadic attendance at meetings that result in changing interpretative principles from season to season and year to year, signals one of the Seminar's most persistent flaws. Although its founding ethos stressed the importance of open public debate among professional participants, publicity prior to meetings often set up findings well in advance of discussion, with results that distorted not only the conduct of the Seminar but the public understanding of the gospels and their study in the United States. For example, Fellows were known to deny to the press that Jesus had ever prayed; he was portrayed as a Cynic philosopher despite evidence to the contrary that was always overwhelming; and Galilee – in a bizarre throwback to the position of Walter Grundmann during the Third Reich – was portrayed as an urban, non-Jewish environment. These positions were obvious mistakes from the moment they were framed, yet the Jesus Seminar not only tolerated them, but also seemed to endorse them. To this day, they impede a critical understanding of Jesus, and they bring scholarship into disrepute.

As media profiling increasingly shaped the findings and the conduct of meetings, many scholars originally interested in the Jesus Seminar ceased attending, or repudiated the effort as a whole. Those who held to an apocalyptic rather than a philosophical portrait of Jesus were among the earliest casualties of tactics by Fellows that sometimes involved vilification, lobbying, and tactical voting so as to eliminate points of view from consideration. Although experts in the field of ancient Judaism were occasionally consulted, the Seminar did not bring that dimension of Jesus' identity into its findings on a consistent basis.

Most of all, however, scholars who expressed positions that endorsed or were sympathetic to Christian faith felt excluded from the Seminar. Funk made much of his having left behind a Fundamentalist background, and jousting with Fundamentalism became an explicit theme in his choice of topics, his portrayal of the Seminar's findings, and his invitation of speakers. As frequently happens in "academic" circles, general attacks on Fundamentalism (especially when "Fundamentalism" is not defined, but is treated as a cultural class apart) became so routine and so broad as to include anyone who professed faith in Christ. On at least one occasion, an invited speaker was disinvited when Funk determined that his position had become too religious. Inevitably, these attitudes and practices gave some meetings the feel of revival meetings for secular humanism. Lubricated by the vineyards of California, where the Seminar became increasingly centered, meetings became interesting religious events in their own terms, down to a proposal that Fellows might put their minds to redrafting the Nicene Creed.

Although its forays into congregational identity may interest historians of contemporary religion, the Seminar's critical acumen suffered as a result of them. Attention to the appendices of published volumes of proceedings will show that the results as presented in different colors of type (red, pink, gray, and black) were made to seem more coherent than the discussions they allegedly represent. Even if no account is taken of the changing constituencies of meetings, and of the fact that Funk sometimes demanded re-votes on questions (so that they resembled push-polls), the Jesus Seminar's findings were more critical and lively than its reputation and the front pages of its own publications might suggest.

The conclusions of the Seminar have frequently been exaggerated and sometimes misrepresented in the popular press. That has produced further misunderstanding in popular literature (whether supportive or critical), as well as in scholarly discussion. Among attempts to set the record straight, one should consult R. W. Funk (1996) and R. J. Miller (1999). At times, mundane findings of literary criticism – such as that the nativity stories in Matthew and Luke differ, and appear to be later additions within the Synoptic Tradition – have been portrayed as innovative threats to traditional faith concocted by the Jesus Seminar.

As a result, a principal point of confusion remains: the extent to which the Seminar's assumptions and findings reflect mainstream scholarship. Members of the Seminar rightly insist that many of their views are unexceptional, even if they are not known by most churchgoers or admitted by the average seminary-trained pastor. These views include acceptance of Markan priority, the existence of the Sayings source (commonly called "Q"), and the use of these sources by Matthew and Luke. Conventional also is the Seminar's insistence that the Jesus tradition has been edited, often reflecting beliefs and issues in the life of the early church. Speculation about various layers of tradition in Q, including inferences about various communities that edited and contributed to these layers, may seem less conventional and less convincing, but such discussion is not the exclusive preserve of the Seminar.

In this regard, Funk's increasingly vocal opposition to Fundamentalism proved productive. He sometimes arranged for Fellows to speak to local Christian congregations in association with meetings; some sessions were actually hosted by churches. Membership of the Seminar has proven to be a recommendation for Fellows in some settings. Yet Funk's own aversion to belief inhibited him from letting the Seminar enter into critical discussion of theological implications of scholarly engagement with the text of the New Testament. As a result, what might have emerged as a fourth achievement of his work, a contribution to religious discourse in the United States, was never accomplished. Worse, his aversion to positions involving faith, or produced by scholars who were or are also believers, inclined the Seminar to undermine its critical credibility by embracing or tolerating specious views that had only their challenge of Christian faith to recommend them.

That explains why the Seminar has held views that mainstream scholarship regards as dubious. These views include a high regard for the antiquity and independence of the extracanonical gospels, such as the *Gospel of Thomas*, the Egerton Papyrus, and the now discredited *"Secret" Gospel of Mark* (for a convenient collection of these and other texts, with brief introductions, see R. J. Miller, 1992; J. D. Crossan, 1985; second edition,

1992). Also problematic is the tendency to situate Jesus at the very margins of Jewish Palestine and the Jewish faith. Jesus is seen as uninterested in Israel's scriptures, in Israel's redemption, in eschatology, and in messianism. It is assumed that these interests, well attested in the gospels themselves, reflect emphases in the early church. How so much discontinuity emerged in such a short time is not convincingly explained. In the opinion of many scholars, the Jesus Seminar reveals inadequate interest and expertise in archaeology, Judaica, and the Dead Sea Scrolls, and a programmatic aversion to appreciating why Jesus' followers saw him in messianic terms. In embracing the term "sage" as his preferred designation for Jesus, Funk apparently believed he had refuted the roles of eschatology, messianism, and Judaism in Jesus' identity, when in fact he only revealed how much of the evidence he had willfully ignored.

Critics of the Jesus Seminar have sometimes not appreciated that a diversity of opinion is to be found among its members. J. D. Crossan's theological views are unexceptional, almost orthodox, yet his solution of the Synoptic Problem is idiosyncratic and unconvincing. He argues that the extracanonical *Gospel of Peter* preserves a "Cross Gospel" (dubbed by some of his colleagues in the Seminar as "The Crossan Gospel") that predates the four canonical gospels and served as their principal source for the Passion Narrative (1988); that the Markan evangelist made direct use of the Egerton Papyrus; and that Secret Mark predates canonical Mark. His tendency to compare Jesus with Cynicism (1991) has also been roundly criticized. M. J. Borg (1987), on the other hand, holds to the conventional solution of the Synoptic Problem and tries to situate Jesus more generally in a Jewish milieu on the basis of interaction with the secondary literature, but thinks Jesus is best viewed not as a prophet or messiah but as a holy man, who may with profit be compared to Buddha.

In their differing ways, Crossan and Borg represent why, in its own terms, the Jesus Seminar did not fulfill its promise. From its earliest meetings, the Fellows recognized a principle established by Norman Perrin, that historical inquiry in regard to Jesus can only be pursued by tracing the development of traditions that refer back to Jesus in the gospels. The gospels refer back to Jesus as their generative point of origin, but there is no "historical Jesus" in the sense of a person whose deeds and character are accessible by means of verifiable public evidence. Expectations of that positivist kind have been disappointed for more than a century, and for the most part history is no longer defined in that reductionist way by scholars in the humanities in any case. The voting procedure of the Jesus Seminar, however, encouraged the false impression that the texts of the New Testament are either verbatim reports or secondary interpretations or some hybrid between the two, without acknowledging that the gospels and their sources were designed to convey perspectives of faith rather than atomistic data of history.

Only the literarily historical Jesus is a fact of reading. We cannot understand the documents unless we identify the Jesus they believe they are referring to. That Jesus, of course, is an object of their belief. He becomes historical for us in the literary sense when we discover that we must suppose facts about Jesus (for example, his teaching of the kingdom with an eschatological meaning) in order to explain the generation of a given text. For that reason, Jesus is a figure of critical history to the extent, and only to the extent, that he permits us to explain how certain sources and texts arose in their mutual relations and in their literary and cultural milieus. Yet the Jesus Seminar did not give much attention to the Greek text of the New Testament, its efforts of translation tending toward generalization and fashionable expression, and the issue of sources between Jesus and the text of the gospels was ignored for the most part, except for repetitive emphasis on the source called "Q" and sporadic consideration of non-canonical texts as alleged conduits of pre-canonical tradition.

Literary comparison of the New Testament with other texts of its time and its surrounding cultures by itself does not, of course, solve "the problem of the historical Jesus," but it can proceed in a way which does not exacerbate it, and which may be productive for further analysis. Finally, the "historical Jesus" is a variable in the overall equation of how the New Testament arose; for that reason, comparative study with other literatures may be expected to provide that variable with more specific value than is possible in positivistic assertions about Jesus. That next stage of comparison, historical rather than literary, involves inference on the basis of the sources that refer to Jesus, a logical terrain from which the Jesus Seminar excluded itself, because it did not attend sufficiently to how the gospels developed

BRUCE CHILTON
CRAIG A. EVANS

Further reading

Bonilla, M. "The Jesus Seminar, its Methodology and Philosophy: A Challenge to Catholic Biblical Theology." *ScEs* 54 (2002) 313–35.

Borg, M. J. *Jesus: A New Vision*, San Francisco, CA: Harper & Row, 1987.

Crossan, J. D. *Four Other Gospels: Shadows on the Contours of Canon*, New York: Harper & Row, 1985; repr. Sonoma: Polebridge, 1992.

—— *The Cross that Spoke: The Origins of the Passion Narrative*, San Francisco, CA: Harper & Row, 1988.

—— *The Historical Jesus: The Life of a Mediterranean Jewish Peasant*, San Francisco, CA: HarperCollins, 1991.

Funk, R. W. *Honest to Jesus: Jesus for a New Millennium*, San Francisco, CA: HarperCollins, 1996.

—— (ed.) *The Acts of Jesus: What Did Jesus Really Do? The Search for the Authentic Deeds of Jesus*, San Francisco, CA: HarperCollins, 1998.

Funk, R. W. and R. W. Hoover (eds) *The Five Gospels: The Search for the Authentic Words of Jesus*, Sonoma: Polebridge Press; New York: Macmillan, 1993.

Miller, R. J. (ed.) *The Complete Gospels*, Sonoma: Polebridge, 1992.

—— *The Jesus Seminar and its Critics*, Sonoma, CA: Polebridge, 1999.

Veitch, J. "The Jesus Seminar: What it is and What it isn't and Why it Matters," *The Journal of Higher Criticism* 6 (1999) 186–209.

Wright, N. T. "Five Gospels but no Gospel: Jesus and the Seminar," in B. D. Chilton and C. A. Evans (eds) *Authenticating the Activities of Jesus*, NTTS 28/2, Leiden: Brill, 1999, pp. 83–120.

JEWISH (FALSE) PROPHETS IN LATE ANTIQUITY

In dealing with prophets in Late Antiquity, several issues need to be recognized. The term "prophet" is our term; although it comes from Greek *prophētēs*, Greek also had other terms (such as *mantis* "mantic, ecstatic") and the Semitic languages used *nāvī'* "prophet", *rō'eh* "seer", *ḥōzeh* "seer", and so on. Thus, when we talk about "prophets", we are dealing with our concept – prophets are what we say they are. A second issue concerns "true" versus "false" prophets. These are relative terms: what one group thinks is a true prophet might be thought a false prophet by another. A good example is Jesus, who was accepted by some and rejected by many others. Thus, if we label a historical figure as a "false prophet", this is our value judgment – our bias. Naturally, the ancient sources also have their own biases and often make judgments as well, but we are hardly bound to follow these. It seems better to describe those that seem to be prophetic figures and leave the question of whether to consider them false or not to the individual reader.

It has often been suggested that prophecy died out in the post-exilic period, but the evidence is that the tradition of prophets continued, since we find references to prophetic figures periodically in the literature even if the information is sometimes minimal. For example, although Josephus claims that the "exact succession of the prophets" had ceased after the time of Artaxerxes (probably Artaxerxes I [465–424 BCE]: *Ag. Ap.* 1.8:40–41), he also claims that John Hyrcanus, the high priest and Hasmonean ruler (135–104 BCE), had the gift of prophecy (*J.W.* 1.2.8:68–69; *Ant.* 13.10.7:299). Similarly, 1 Macc 9:27 appears explicit in stating the view that prophecy had ceased: "So there was great distress in Israel, such as had not been since the time that prophets ceased to appear among them." According to this, prophets ceased sometime in the past and are no longer extant; however, other passages allow for a future return of prophets. In 1 Macc 4:44–46 the question of what to do with the altar polluted by Antiochus Epiphanes is discussed. They decided to tear it down and store the stones away in a place on the Temple Mount "until a prophet should come to tell what to do with them." The context would suggest that although there was no prophet currently available, it was still possible for one to come along in the future. The passage does not really argue for the cessation of prophecy but only that acceptable prophets were not necessarily common. A similar idea occurs a bit later in the book: "The Jews and their priests have resolved that Simon should be their leader and high priest forever, until a trustworthy prophet should arise" (1 Macc 14:41).

Josephus refers to a number of individuals as "false prophets" (*J.W.* 2.13.5:261–63; 6.5.2:285–87; 7.11.1–3:437–50; *Ant.* 8.9.1:236–42; 20.5.1:97; 20.8.6:169; 20.8.10:188; *Life* 76:424–25). This shows that he regarded them as having the persona of a prophet, but he took a quite negative view of any Jews who upset the social order. He clearly regarded them as false prophets and labelled them as such. Josephus only gives a couple of examples, but he gives the impression that this was only the tip of the iceberg.

One of these was an "impostor" named Theudas who Josephus says was called a "prophet" (*Ant.* 20.5.1:97; *J.W.* 2.13.5:259–60). This individual acquired a large following (400 according to Acts 5:36) and took them to the Jordan, promising that the river would part before them. The Roman procurator Fadus evidently thought that this was a potential problem and sent a unit of cavalry to disperse the followers and bring back Theudas's head. Exactly what Theudas taught or hoped to accomplish is not stated. Another individual, referred to simply as "a man from Egypt", is said to be self-designated as a "prophet" (*Ant.* 20.8.6:169; *Ag. Ap.* 1.35:312), though Josephus calls him "the Egyptian false prophet" (*J.W.*

2.13.5:261–63). He is said to have led 30,000 as far as the Mount of Olives with the aim of causing the walls of Jerusalem to fall down miraculously, overthrowing the Roman garrison, and setting himself up as ruler of the people. Felix set his soldiers on them, but the Egyptian himself managed to escape.

One group noted for their ability at prophecy were the Essenes. According to Josephus, some Essenes could make predictions because in their youth they were educated in holy books, purifications, and sayings of the prophets (*J.W.* 2.8.12:159). First, we find Judas the Essene who is referred to as a "seer" (*mantis* in Greek), but his predictions do not look different from those who are elsewhere labelled "prophet". He had a reputation that his predictions had never been wrong (*J.W.* 1.3.5:78–80; *Ant.* 13.11.2:311–13). But then he had made a prediction that Antigonus the Hasmonean would be assassinated at Strato's Tower (Caesarea) at a particular time. Yet shortly before the predicted time Antigonus was in Jerusalem, which was seventy miles or so away. Shortly afterward, though, Antigonus was killed in a tunnel to the temple at a spot known as "Strato's Tower", and Judas thus proved to be a true prophet after all. Another Essene Manaemus predicted to Herod as a boy that he would become "king of the Jews" (*Ant.* 15.10.5:373–79). After he achieved this office, Herod held the Essenes in honour. Finally, Simon the Essene correctly interpreted Archelaus's dream (*Ant.* 17.13.3:346–48).

Other individual teachers are mentioned a number of times by Josephus. For example, there was an Onias noted for his ability to make rain at the time the Romans extended their hegemony over Palestine (*Ant.* 14.2.1:22–24). He was called on to put a curse on the Hasmonean rebel Aristobulus who was being besieged in Jerusalem. When Onias refused but prayed that God would protect the priests in the siege, he was stoned to death. This sounds very similar to the story of Honi the Circle-drawer who is known from rabbinic literature as an individual who could make rain by symbolic action (*m. Taan.* 3.8). Although the description of him is legendary, a development in the tradition can be discerned: he does not fit the early rabbinic image of the sage and was thus evidently something of an embarrassment. The Tannaitic sources generally downplay miracle working, unlike the Babylonian Talmud which shows no sign of suppressing such claims. It has been argued that Honi has been "rabbinized" but his charismatic origins still shine through. The rabbinic tradition thus appears to be related to Onias the rain-maker mentioned by Josephus. Onias/Honi is not called a prophet, but like Elijah he has control of the weather.

There are fairly obvious indications that Josephus regarded himself as a prophet; however, at no time does he use the Greek word *prophētēs* of himself. How are we to understand his self-image? First, he is clear that he is able to foretell the future and claims to have a reputation for foretelling the future correctly, though this is in some way associated with the written prophecies (*J.W.* 3.8.3:351–53). Perhaps his most important prediction – vital for his treatment as a prisoner – is that Vespasian would become the emperor of Rome (*J.W.* 3.8.9:399–408). Josephus goes on to assert that Vespasian investigated his reputation as a prophet and found that the latter had correctly foretold when the city of Jotapata would be taken by the Romans and also that the Romans would capture him alive. According to the Jewish historian, this made Vespasian begin to put some store in Josephus's predictions about his becoming emperor. In another passage Josephus even asserts about himself that he is a messenger sent on a mission by God (*J.W.* 3.8.9:400).

The question is, then, why Josephus does not refer to himself specifically as a "prophet"? There are probably two reasons for this. Probably the less important reason is that he identifies himself as a priest and claims to obtain at least part of his skill through this fact. The other reason is more subtle but also likely to be more important: a blatant claim to be a prophet might cause a reaction. His own claims about his abilities show no concessions to modesty, so this is unlikely to be the reason; on the contrary, it would be preferable that others acclaim him as a prophet rather than doing it himself. Also, some people were suspicious of prophets, and it would be safer to work on the principle that "the wise would understand" without his having to spell it out.

Some of the comments given above hint at another view of prophecy: that it encompasses "inspired" interpretation of God's Word. As noted, Josephus says that the Essenes could make predictions because in their youth they were educated in holy books (*J.W.* 2.8.12:159). Similarly, Josephus associates his own ability to foretell the future with the written prophecies (*J.W.* 3.8.3:351–53):

suddenly there came back into his mind those nightly dreams, in which God had foretold to him the impending fate of the Jews and the destinies of the Roman sovereigns. He was an interpreter of dreams and skilled in divining the meaning of ambiguous utterances of the Deity; a priest himself and of priestly descent, he was not ignorant of the prophecies in the sacred books. At that hour he was inspired to read their meaning, and, recalling the dreadful images of his recent dreams, he offered up a silent prayer to God.

[Translation from the Loeb Classical Library edition]

Philo is another who expounds a concept of inspired interpretation. In *Moses* (2.264–65, 268–69):

Moses, when he heard of this [that the manna from heaven was doubled on the sixth day and did not evaporate] and also actually saw it, was awestruck and, guided by what was not so much surmise as God-sent inspiration, made announcement of the sabbath. I need hardly say that the conjectures of this kind are closely akin to prophecies ... After this, he uttered a third prophetic saying of truly marvellous import. He declared that on the sabbath the air would not yield the accustomed food ... but on the morrow some of the weaker-minded set out to gather the food but were disappointed and returned baffled, reproaching themselves for their disbelief and hailing the prophet as a true seer, an interpreter of God, and alone gifted with foreknowledge of the hidden future.

[Translation from the Loeb Classical Library edition]

Philo sees himself as understanding scripture by means of inspiration (*Cherubim* 27):

But there is a higher thought than these. It comes from a voice in my own soul, which oftentimes is god-possessed and divines where it does not know. This thought I will record in words if I can. The voice told me ...

This concept is best known, though, from the Qumran scrolls. The *Habakkuk Commentary* makes a statement about the interpretation of prophetic literature which suggests prophetic inspiration in interpreting the written Scriptures (1QpHab 7:3–5):

And God spoke to Habakkuk to write down the things coming upon the last generation, but the culmination of the age he did not make known to him, as it says, "That the one reading it may run" (Hab 2:2). Its interpretation concerns the Teacher of Righteousness, to whom God made known all the mysteries of the words of his servants, the prophets.

The Teacher was inspired to interpret prophecies of Habakkuk even though the prophet himself did not understand them. The implication is that interpretation was not just a matter of interpretative rules or techniques; on the contrary, interpretation was a matter of inspiration by the same spirit which had inspired the original prophetic writer.

What this brief survey has done is indicate the complexity of the question of prophecy. Prophecy was not confined to a narrow period or section of society in ancient Israel but was believed by many to have continued in a variety of forms in Judaism until the fall of Jerusalem (and probably beyond). Various individuals thought of themselves as prophets or were proclaimed as prophets in circumstances rejected by the majority of the people, but that was hardly different from most of the prophets of the Hebrew Bible. Few prophetic figures were accepted by the majority of the people – indeed, most were probably not even known by many – but there were exceptions. Some individuals gained a large following temporarily but went on to become discredited. Others continued to have a loyal following even when they had been killed or otherwise removed from the scene. Prophecy included a variety of forms, apparently encompassing inspired interpretation of prophetic writings, as well as oral prophetic sayings.

Prophets appear to have been particularly prevalent in the fraught times leading up to the fall of Jerusalem in 70 CE. At least, this is the impression that Josephus and other sources give us. Perhaps the most poignant example came in the very last throes of the siege of Jerusalem (*J. W.* 6.5.2:281–87). Even as the Romans were breaking through the defences and the temple had been set on fire, a group of 6,000 – many women and children – had gathered in one portico of the temple. They had done so because a "false prophet" had commanded them to assemble in the temple court and await their deliverance. Instead, they were killed by fire and Roman soldiers. According to Josephus this was only one of "many prophets" at this time calling on the people to be patient and trust in God. Such a message was hardly unique to "false prophets" but had been a prophetic theme from the early days of Israel.

LESTER L. GRABBE

Further reading

Feldman, Louis H. "Prophets and Prophecy in Josephus," in Michael H. Floyd and Robert D. Haak (eds) *Prophets, Prophecy, and Prophetic Texts in Second Temple Judaism*, LHBOTS 427, New York and London: T. & T. Clark International, 2006, pp. 210–39.

Grabbe, Lester L. *Priests, Prophets, Diviners, Sages: A Socio-historical Study of Religious Specialists in Ancient Israel*, Valley Forge, PA: Trinity Press International, 1995.

—— "Poets, Scribes, or Preachers? The Reality of Prophecy in the Second Temple Period," in Lester L. Grabbe and Robert D. Haak (eds) *Knowing the End from the Beginning: The Prophetic, the Apocalyptic, and their Relationships*, JSPSup 46, London and New York: T. & T. Clark International, 2003, pp. 192–215.

—— "Thus Spake the Prophet Josephus ... : The Jewish Historian on Prophets and Prophecy," in Michael H. Floyd and Robert D. Haak (eds) *Prophets, Prophecy, and Prophetic Texts in Second Temple Judaism*, LHBOTS 427, New York and London: T. & T. Clark International, 2006, pp. 240–47.

Gray, Rebecca. *Prophetic Figures in Late Second Temple Jewish Palestine: The Evidence from Josephus*, Oxford: Clarendon, 1993.

Horsley, Richard A., with John S. Hanson. *Bandits, Prophets, and Messiahs: Popular Movements at the Time of Jesus*, with new preface, Harrisburg, PA: Trinity Press International, 1999 [1985].

JOHN THE BAPTIST

Josephus and the New Testament, when read as both supplementing and correcting each other, provide a serviceable profile of John the Baptist. For Josephus (*Ant.* 18:116–19), the gospels (Mark 1:1–8; Matt 3:1–12; Luke 3:1–17, John 1:19–28) and Acts (19:1–7) John practiced immersion and supplied that ritual with theory. Josephus' treatment of John invites comparison with his presentation of Bannus, the ascetic sage with whom Josephus claims to have lived and studied for three years (*Life* 10–12). Bannus is both wise and pure, and his frequent ablutions in cold water are a part of the pattern of his wisdom.

Several features distinguish John from Bannus within Josephus' presentation. A large following is attributed to John, while Bannus is a solitary figure. Relatedly, there is a self-consciously public dimension involved in John's preaching, which leads to his execution at the hands of Herod Antipas, who fears John might lead an insurrection (however one reads the textual evidence in *Ant.* 18:118). John does not simply make ablution a personal practice, but also urges the activity upon those who come to him. In a word, John makes immersion a public program, which both earns him his sobriquet and distinguishes him from Bannus.

The symbolism of bathing is not transparently revolutionary, and John does not much look much like the false prophets Josephus describes elsewhere. John can scarcely be compared with what Josephus said they did: one scaled Mount Gerizim to find the vessels deposited by Moses (*Ant.* 18:85–87), Theudas waited at the Jordan for the waters to part (*Ant.* 20:97, 98), the Egyptian marched from the Mount of Olives so that he might conquer Jerusalem (*J.W.* 2:261–63). If there is an act in the gospels that approximates to such prophetic fanaticism, it is Jesus' entry into Jerusalem and his occupation of the Temple, an enactment of the eschatological prophecy of Zechariah. When Jesus is called a prophet in that context (Matt 21:11, 46), there is some affinity with the sort of usage that Josephus presupposes (cf. also Philo, *Spec. Laws* 1:315).

The practice of regular ablutions at Qumran shows that Bannus, John the Baptist, and the Pharisees were in no sense unique, or even unusual, in their insistence upon such practices. Yet the entire direction of Essene practice, the interest in the actual control of worship in the Temple, appears unlike John's. The argument is sometimes mounted that, because John preached a baptism of repentance for the forgiveness of sins, he consciously challenged the efficacy of sacrificial forgiveness, and therefore the Temple. Such assertions invoke a supposed dualism between moral and cultic atonement that has no place in the critical discussion of early Judaism, and they in no way suffice to establish that John deliberately opposed worship in the Temple.

The motif of his preaching "a baptism of repentance for the release of sins" may in any case represent the anachronistic assignment to John of an element of the language of catechesis within early Christianity. The phrase appears in Mark 1:4; Luke 3:3 (cf. 1:77) in relation to John, but "for release of sins" appears in manifestly Christian contexts at Matt 26:28; Luke 24:47; Acts 2:38; 5:31; 10:42; 13:38; 26:18; Col 1:14. Josephus observed that John's baptism was not understood to seek pardon for sins, but to purify the body (*Ant.* 18:117), adding the platonic note that the soul had already been cleansed by righteousness.

The motif of John's priesthood, an addition in Luke (through Zech 1:5, 8–23) motivated by the strong association between the Temple and the Spirit in both the Third Gospel and Acts, does not appear historical. John's status as a prophet similarly derives from the tradition of Christian apologetics (indeed, from Jesus himself, to judge from Matt 11:9; Luke 7:26), but John's activity and program within the terms of reference of Judaism made him a purifier or immerser. He was certainly not a routine figure, because his take on purity was both distinctive and controversial, but Josephus shows us that John cut a recognizable profile as a practitioner and teacher.

"Q" reflects an interest in the comparison between John and Elijah in particular. Within "Q," Malachi is cited after the presentation of John's question from prison, whether Jesus is "the one who is coming" (Matt 11:2–6, 10/Luke 7:18–23, 27). The identification of John as Elijah by means of Malachi 3 (cited with deviations from conventional texts, as is the citation in "Q") is also represented within Markan tradition specifically (1:2), an "overlapping" with "Q," as B. H. Streeter showed. By putting John the place of Elijah, Jesus implicitly compared himself to Elisha, who aspired to a double portion of has master's spirit (2 Kgs 2:9). His allusiveness in regard to John's identity and his own is intimated in Matt 17:10–13.

Whatever is made of this "overlapping" with "Q," Mark proceeds to cohere with the triple tradition as a whole in offering a citation of Isaiah 40 and a portrayal of John as a prophet in the wilderness (Mark 1:4–6; Matt 3:1–6 cf. Luke 3:4–6). The point of John's preaching is of the one who is stronger than he, whose baptism of judgment is to follow John's baptism with water (Matt 3:11/Mark 1:7, 8/Luke 3:16). When the scene in which Jesus is baptized follows (Matt 3:13–17/Mark 1:9–11/Luke 3:21, 22), there can be no doubt but that he fulfills John's reference to a figure greater than he. But it is equally plain that the pointing of John's preaching and activity towards Jesus is achieved by a shaping of its contextual presentation, and the probability is high that the conviction, derived from Jesus, that John was a messianic prophet in the manner of Malachi 3 and Isaiah 40 reshaped whatever meaning John and his followers originally attached to what he did and said. John 1:21 may just preserve an awareness of such distortion, by presenting the Baptist as denying he is Elijah or "the prophet."

Essene practice, together with Pharisaic, Sadducean, and Bannus' practice, does suggest by analogy a likely feature of John's baptism which contemporary discussion has obscured. It is routinely claimed that John preached "conversionary repentance" (Robert Webb's phrase) by means of baptism, an act once for all that was not repeatable nor to be repeated. That is a fine description of how baptism as portrayed in the Epistle to the Hebrews 6:1–8, and such a theology came to predominate within catholic Christianity. But ablutions in Judaism were characteristically repeatable, and even Hebrews must argue against the proposition that one might be baptized afresh. Only the attribution to John of a later, catholic theology of baptism can justify the characterization of his baptism as symbol of a definitive, unrepeatable "conversion."

If John's baptism was not in the interests of "conversion," or permanent purification, or opposition to atonement by means of cultic sacrifice, what was its purpose? Josephus in *Ant.* 18:117 asserts that John's baptism was to serve as a ritual of purity following a return to righteousness. Righteousness and bathing together made one pure. Josephus makes a nearly or actually dualistic distinction between the righteousness which effects purification of the soul and the baptism which symbolizes the consequent purification of the body, and that is consistent with his portrayal of others

with whom he expresses sympathy, the Essenes, the Pharisees, and Bannus. But his description also comports well with the gospels' presentation in terms of repentance and the promise of the Spirit of God.

John practiced his baptism in natural sources of water. It is sometimes taken that his purpose was to use literally moving water, but that is not specified in any source, and the waters of the Jordan or a pool in Peraea or an oasis in the valley of the Jordan would not necessarily be flowing. Water from a spring was equated with the category of naturally collected water by the first century. John's use of "living" water did not imply the especial corruption of what was thereby purified, as is sometimes supposed: corpse contamination, after all, was dealt with by means of the still water of the ashes of the red heifer, not living water (cf. Num 19 and Parah 5:1–8:11). John's baptism made no statement as to the nature of what was to be purified: his activity took that as being self-evident. John's baptism was, however, an implicit claim that there was no advantage in the pools of Qumran, the double-vatted *miqvaoth* of the Pharisees, or the private baths of aristocratic groups such as the Sadducees. He enacted what amounted to generic purification, in contrast to the deliberate artifice involved in several other movements, sectarian and non-sectarian. In that sense, his purpose was deliberately anti-sectarian.

John's baptism was driven by an eschatological expectation of divine judgment: a baptism of divine Spirit. The anticipation of imminent judgment would supply a suitable motivation for John's activity and help to account for his appropriation within early Christianity. Particularly, Jesus' defense of his own authority in terms of John's baptism shows that John's teaching of the Spirit inspired Jesus (Matt 21:23–27/Mark 11:27–33/Luke 20:1–8). John's practice of repeated immersion as the realization of forgiveness and the promise of God's Spirit, precedented by the book of Ezekiel (36:22–27) most prominently, was the characteristic feature of his public activity.

A reading of Josephus suggests that John need no longer be dated within the synoptic chronology, whose usage as a catechetical instrument – for preparing candidates for baptism within a year or so – compresses events within implausible frames of time. Rather, John was put to death *c.* 21 CE, during a period when Herod Antipas was emboldened by his recent foundation of Tiberias as well as his marriage to the ever-ambitious Herodias, once his brother's wife. That suggests that John affected Jesus more deeply than a passing visit from Galilee to Judea for baptism would indicate. Jesus would have known John during his adolescence, and the purifier's perspective on repentance and Spirit proved to be a formative influence.

Josephus' famous report about John in *Ant.* 18:116–19 is a flashback, related to explain the opinion among "some Jews" that the defeat of Antipas' army at the hands of Aretas, the king of Nabatea, was divine retribution for his treatment of John. What Josephus does not say, but the gospels attest (Mark 6:14–29; Matt 14:1–12; Luke 3:19–20), is that John had criticized Antipas for marrying Herodias, who had been married to his brother Philip. Josephus' account dovetails with the gospels, in that he gives the details of Antipas' abortive divorce from Aretas' daughter in order to marry Herodias (18:109–12). But Josephus also explains that this was merely the initial source of the enmity, which was later exacerbated by a border dispute that preceded the outbreak of hostilities (18:113).

No delay of time is indicated in the compressed narrative between the divorce and John's death and the start of the war, but mounting tension is indicated. It is also noteworthy that Josephus blames the defeat on the betrayal by some of Philip's troops, who had joined his army (18:114). So: the delay is long enough for tension to have mounted with Aretas, and for Antipas – however unwisely – to believe that his brother's troops would loyally fight for him. Philip died in 34 CE (see 18:106), and this defeat is usually placed *c.* 36. The death of Philip would have provided ample motivation for the soldiers to join Antipas, and a delay of some fifteen years from the divorce would perhaps account for Antipas' acceptance of their services. Commentators routinely argued, following Josephus, that the brother whose wife Antipas stole was not the tetrarch Philip, but another brother. The behavior of the troops (and of Antipas) as described by Josephus supports the gospels' identification, rather than what Josephus proposes.

Whenever Antipas made his decision, it was a bold move. It involved him in breaking with Aretas, and it inflamed Jewish opinion, bringing not only John's censure (as the gospels attest), but even that of Josephus (*Ant.* 18:110). Nor was there any mystery about the likely Jewish reaction against the marriage; after all, Archelaus had run afoul of popular opinion when he married the wife of a *dead* brother (*Ant.* 17:340–41). Antipas is usually credited with more sensitivity to the demands of the Torah than that, and it is doubtful he acted out of simple passion. Still, it was a rash act, and to this extent the suggestion by Christiane

Saulnier that the divorce and the new marriage were over and done with by the early twenties is plausible.

Josephus largely supports Saulnier, and even permits a somewhat more specific dating. Prior to dealing with Vitellius (from *Ant.* 18:88), and therefore flashing back to Antipas' various trials, Josephus has last spoken of Antipas in connection with the establishment of Tiberias in 19 CE (*Ant.* 18:36–38). Here, too, Josephus criticizes Antipas, because the city was partially established on the site of tombs, and he complains elsewhere that the palace there incorporated idolatrous representations of animals, which Josephus himself undertook to destroy (*Life* 64–69). Why, then, do we see Antipas in such an uncharacteristically trenchant philo-Roman mode, flouting commandments of the Torah in a way that could only have alienated his subjects? At the opening of his section on Tiberias, Josephus provides an answer: Antipas had advanced considerably within the circle of Tiberius' friendship (*Ant.* 18:36). Having been educated in Rome, his contacts with the city were no doubt good, but it is unlikely that this advance was accomplished without an actual visit. Was this the visit Josephus refers to in connection with Herodias in *Ant.* 18:110–11?

There is good reason to think so. After all, his tenure came to an abrupt end when, prodded by the same Herodias, Antipas made the trip to Rome in 39 CE to plead for the title of king (*Ant.* 18:240–56). Indeed, Gaius is said to have personally exiled her along with her husband for her ambition. Josephus opines that exile served Antipas right for his attention to the nattering of his wife. But her ploy was consistent with her marriage in the first place, and with the foundation of Tiberias, as part of a policy of establishing Antipas as a Herodian king on a good footing in Rome. She underestimated the cunning of Herod Agrippa, her own brother, but her influence was part of a strategic desire. That same desire had worked earlier, when her husband had returned from Rome to marry her, and the no doubt happy couple was ensconced in Tiberias. At that time, it only remained to see to the death of John (*c.* 21 CE) to make her happiness complete.

John the Baptist's role within the Synoptic Gospels, on the other hand, is both catechetical and christological. He points the way forward to believers' baptism after the manner of Jesus, who is greater than John. That is the case both in the apostolic catechesis of the triple tradition which conveys the scene of Jesus' own baptism in association with John's movement, and in the assertion in the Sayings source that the least in the kingdom is greater than John the Baptist (Matt 11:11b/Luke 7:28b). John's preaching of repentance in the mishnaic source conventionally known as "Q" is replete with warnings and encouragements for potential converts: Jewish opponents are a brood of vipers (Matt 3:7/Luke 3:7), what matters is producing fruits worthy of repentance rather than genetic kinship with Abraham (Matt 3:9/Luke 3:8), and the urgency of the imperative to repent is as keen as an ax laid at the root of a tree (Matt 3:10/ Luke 3:9). Whatever may or may not be reflected of John's preaching here, it is evidently cast within the needs of Christian catechesis and addressed to sympathetic hearers who are assumed to be at the margins of Judaism. Likewise, the advice to relatively prosperous converts in Luke 3:10–14 – presumably from the Lukan version of "Q" – is redolent of a social setting more reminiscent of Lukan Antioch than of the Baptist's Peraea: charitable giving by revenue agents and soldiers is not likely to have been the burden of the historical John's message. Yet the wellspring of this prophetic portrait of John, Jesus' characterization of his dead teacher, was fed by John's own teaching on repentance and Spirit as the practical content of an immersion that realized the promise of Ezekiel.

BRUCE CHILTON

Further reading

Chilton, Bruce. *Jesus' Baptism and Jesus' Healing. His Personal Practice of Spirituality*, Harrisburg, PA: Trinity Press International, 1998.
Hoehner, Harold W. *Herod Antipas*, Grand Rapids, MI: Zondervan, 1980.
Saulnier, Christiane. "Herode Antipas et Jean le Baptiste. Quelques remarques sur les confusions chronologiques de Flavius Josèphe," *RB* 91 (1984) 362–76.
Streeter, Burnett Hillman. *The Four Gospels. A Study of Origins*, London: Macmillan, 1924.
Taylor, Joan. *The Immerser: John the Baptist within Second Temple Judaism*, Grand Rapids, MI and Cambridge: Eerdmans, 1997.
Webb, Robert. *John the Baptizer and Prophet. A Socio-Historical Study*, JSNTSup 65, Sheffield: Sheffield Academic Press, 1991.
Wink, Walter. *John the Baptist in the Gospel Tradition*, SNTSMS 7, Cambridge: Cambridge University Press, 1968.

JONAH

Jonah is the prophet whose story is told in the Book of Jonah. Although that book is presumably fictional, Jonah himself appears to have been an historical figure. In 2 Kgs 4:25 he is spoken of as "Jonah son of Amittai, the prophet, who was from Gathhepher."

Three sayings attributed to Jesus mention Jonah: Matt 12:39–40 = Luke 11:29–30 (no sign will be given to Jesus' generation except "the sign of the prophet Jonah"); Matt 12:41 = Luke 11:32 (the people of Nineveh, who repented at Jonah's preaching, will arise and condemn Jesus' generation, which has not repented, despite the presence of something greater than Jonah); and Matt 16:4 (only the sign of Jonah will be given to "an evil and adulterous generation"). The last verse appears to be Matthew's redactional doublet of the saying in Matt 12:39–40 = Luke 11:29–30. As for the two logia that belong to both Matthew and Luke, those who believe in the two-source theory typically assign them to the Sayings source (Q). Both are, furthermore, widely credited to Jesus himself.

The saying about the Ninevites repenting at the preaching of Jonah depends directly upon the canonical story of Jonah, and it posits hearers who know, because they are familiar with the Tanak, who Jonah was and what he proclaimed, for to say that something or someone here is "greater than Jonah" is without meaning unless Jonah is a known entity. There are also verbal recollections. "The people of Nineveh" (ἄνδρες Νινευῖται) is lifted from Jonah 3:5 (LXX: οἱ ἄνδρες Νινευή). "Repented" is appropriate because the verb, μετανοέω, appears three times in LXX Jonah, in 3:9, 10; and 4:2. And "at the proclamation (κήρυγμα) of Jonah" also echoes LXX Jonah, which uses the verb, κηρύσσω, fully five times (1:2; 3:2, 4, 5, 7). Moreover, Jesus' saying takes for granted the great wickedness of the Ninevites, which is part of the plot of Jonah (cf. 1:2; 3:8).

The assertion that the Ninevites "will be raised at the judgment with this generation and will condemn it" almost certainly refers to the resurrection. The future tenses, the use of "at the judgment," the natural meaning of "will be raised" when followed by "at the judgment," the eschatological associations of "this generation" elsewhere in the Jesus tradition, the conventional idea that the last generation will be especially wicked (cf. 1QpHab 2:5–10; 2 Tim 3:1–5; *Sib. Or.* 4:152–61; *m. Sota* 9:15), and the gathering together of people from different times and places all tend to the same conclusion.

The saying about no sign being given except that of the prophet Jonah is usually thought to have originated separately from Matt 12:41 = Luke 11:32. As for its original meaning, opinion diverges. According to the *Lives of the Prophets*, which may derive from a first century CE Jewish composition, Jonah "gave a sign to Jews and to all the land: when they should see a stone crying aloud in distress, the end would be at hand; and when they should see all the Gentiles gathered in Jerusalem, the city would be razed to its foundation" (*L. Proph. Jonah* 8). This would seem to provide the closest ancient parallel to the synoptics' "sign of Jonah." It is, however, very difficult to imagine that a crying stone can have had anything to do with Jesus' reference to the sign of Jonah.

Until recently, exegetes, following Matt 12:40 ("so will the Son of man be three days and nights in the heart of the earth"), identified the sign of Jonah with Jesus' deliverance from death. But Luke has something different and more ambiguous ("so will the Son of man be to this generation"), and the last part of Matt 12:40 is now roundly reckoned editorial. This has made it possible to suggest that Matthew's interpretation does not correspond to Jesus' intention. Some recent scholars have identified the sign of Jonah with Jesus himself or with his proclamation or ministry, or with the eschatological return of the Son of Man, or with the destruction of Jerusalem. A few have urged that "Jonah" ('Ιωνᾶς) is a corruption of "John" ('Ιωάννης), and that Jesus was referring to John the Baptist.

In Mark 8:11–12, the parallel to Matt 12:38–42 and Luke 11:29–32, Jesus says nothing about Jonah, only that no sign will be given. It is unlikely that we here have two different stories or sayings from the life of Jesus, although some have thought so. Either the Markan tradition eliminated the reference to Jonah or the tradition common to Matthew and Luke added it. Whatever the truth, and whatever the precise meaning of the sign of Jonah, the saying in Matthew and Luke amounts to refusal, for Jesus performs no specific miracle for his audience. So the disagreement with Mark is more verbal than functional.

Beyond the few explicit references to Jonah in the synoptics, there is also one story that draws upon the Book of Jonah: Mark 4:35–41, with its parallels in Matt 8:23–27 and Luke 8:22–25. Both Jonah and Jesus depart by boat. Then the sea rages while both Jonah and Jesus sleep. Other passengers become badly frightened. Then the storm is miraculously stilled and, in response, people marvel. In addition to the similarity in plots, the synoptics contain some verbal reminiscences of Jonah (cf. Matt 8:24 with Hebrew Jonah 1:4; Mark 4:41 with LXX Jonah 1:16; Luke 8:22–23 with LXX Jonah 1:3–4). Perhaps the story in the gospels implicitly exalts Jesus by contrasting him with Jonah: unlike the latter, Jesus had command over the roaring waves.

DALE C. ALLISON, JR

Further reading

Chow, S. *The Sign of Jonah Reconsidered*, Stockholm: Almqvist & Wiksell, 1995.

Edwards, R. A. *The Sign of Jonah in the Theology of the Evangelists and Q*, London: SCM Press, 1971.

Landes, G. M. "Matthew 12:40 as an Interpretation of 'The Sign of Jonah' against its Biblical Background," in C. L. Meyers and M. O'Connor (eds) *The Word of the Lord Shall Go Forth*, Winona Lake, MI: Eisenbrauns, 1983, pp. 665–84.

JUBILEE, SIN, AND FORGIVENESS

The concepts of Jubilee, sin, and forgiveness were central themes in Jesus' ministry. While the latter two are obviously related deeply, they find their greatest prominence in the Jubilee as the central thread of Jesus' ministry.

Jubilee

Etymology

The word translated "Jubilee" (יובל) is of uncertain etymology. It is related, but not based upon, the Semitic root for the word "ram" (Koehler and Baumgartner). This is attested in Punic, but Exodus 19:13 also sees the phrase "blow the ram's horn" using the same form as "Jubilee."

As a pre-Christian concept

The institution of the Jubilee Year is an ancient one. While it was formalized for the Israelites in Leviticus 25, the seven-fold pattern of seven years is thought to have existed for centuries prior to the Mosaic tradition. The forces behind its conception are rooted in the agrarian culture of the area.

In the Ancient Near East, many religious frameworks held cosmic battles as being manifest in the annual cycles of the seasons. In Ugarit, Baal and Mot engaged every spring and autumn. Every spring Baal died, and Mot reigned through the sterile summer. Every autumn, Mot died for Baal to rule through the fertile winter. Similarly, the Akkadian *Descent of Ishtar* details the annual death of Ishtar, the goddess of fertility, her descent to the netherworld, and her subsequent rising again.

In the course of time, seven-year famines were known and analogously attributed to these cosmic events. So both the Akkadian *Epic of Gilgamesh* and the Atrahasis Epic attest to seven-year famines born from the death of heroes, as does the Ugaritic Aqhat. Similarly seven years of fertility arise in the Akkadian literature as Baal kills Mot seven years

JUBILEE, SIN, AND FORGIVENESS

in succession, but Mot, the god of death, eventually rises to fight Baal again. David's words about Saul and Jonathan in 2 Samuel 1:21 may call for a seven-year famine in parallel to the epics of Gilgamesh, Atrahasis and Aqhat (Gordon).

With the concern being that overuse of the land would lead to famine, the seventh or sabbatical year of rest for the land arose and is formalized in Leviticus 25:4–5. No farming or vine dressing was allowed; the natural yield of the ground was expected to be sufficiently plentiful for one's sustenance.

In this milieu, the Jubilee Year is a *prima facie* extension of the sabbatical year. Occurring every seven sabbatical years, it is defined by analogy with the sabbatical year, no husbandry was allowed. However, as formalized in Lev 25:8–12, two other economic stipulations went into effect: equitable distribution of wealth by providing liberty for those who were sold into slavery for their debt; and inalienability of property by the restoration of land that was sold out of economic hardship.

Implicit in the first ordinance is the understanding that debt is a form of imprisonment, and, in the Torah, God would have the people of Israel be free.

The second ordinance emphasized God as the ultimate owner of the land. All are therefore tenants and sojourners. The Lord is the master and gives to all according to his will. Therefore, all human business transactions are temporal. By implication, private property is abrogated.

The latter ordinance is unique to the Torah, but the former stipulation is resonant of another Ancient Near Eastern practice. As in the case of the Babylonian kings Hammurapi, Urnammu and Lipit-Ishtar, the first full year of a new king's reign saw the issuance of a *mišarum* (Finkelstein). This act consisted largely of debt remission for a limited time. In its Babylonian context, the remission came with a protocol by which the remission was to be affected. In practice, this practice was based on the king's goodwill and was not necessarily applicable to the entirety of society. Therefore, it largely served to better the king's image without upsetting the prevailing socio-economic system.

Questions about practice

While the history of the sabbatical year and the Jubilee Year as an institution are quite old, there is debate over whether the latter ever happened. No explicit, historical record of a Jubilee Year being observed has been found. While Isaiah 37:30 may be read as suggesting a Jubilee Year, this evidence is inconclusive. The lack of an overt reference suggests

that it may simply allude to an invasion or similar catastrophe.

Further, as mentioned above, although other Ancient Near Eastern cultures are known to have practised a national remission of debt, the extent of this remission is unclear. A national remission of all debt would indeed upset the balance of the entire socio-economic structure. It seems likely that the Babylonian practice of remission was restricted to portions of the economy and for a limited time only (Finkelstein).

In Judaism prior to Jesus

At the time of the Neo-Babylonian Empire (*c.* 626–539 BCE), Isaiah 61:2 alludes to the Jubilee Year as a divine unit of time that is separate from the time of liberation (BHS; all translations are those of the author):

> The spirit of the Lord God is upon me
> because the Lord has anointed me
> to bring glad tidings to the poor,
> He has sent me
> to bind the broken hearted
> to proclaim liberty for the captives
> and release for the prisoners,
> To proclaim the year of the Lord's favour
> and the day of vengeance of our God,
> To comfort all who mourn.

The two unique ordinances of the Jubilee were here distinguished but still joined in reference.

By the Second Temple Period, the Jubilee concept has divided into two concepts, one a present ethic and the other an eschatological anticipation and affirmation. The present focus is primarily on liberation for the captives as a mission from God. Restoration of the land has been absorbed into the eschatological conception of the Lord's favour. The earth remains the Lord's, but it will revert to God at the end of time instead of every fifty years. Forgiveness of debts has become non-usurious financial transactions. These concepts are particularly manifest in two precursors to Jesus' ministry.

The *Book of Jubilees* is a work of the second century BCE that offers a retelling of the patriarchal stories from Genesis 1 to Exodus 19. The original name for the work is likely to have been *The Book of the Division of the Times* (per the Prologue and *Jub.* 1:4 in Hebrew and Ethiopic). The history is retold in segments of fifty years divided into seven, the various events being packaged in sabbatical years and, ultimately, into Jubilee Years as a form of quasi-dispensationalism. An elevation of the

344

Jubilee Year is thus implicit in this structure and the aforementioned lack of observing Leviticus 25:8–12. In this writing, the Jubilee Year had apparently become a metric of the divine timetable; it is not designed for human observation but is used to measure time from God's perspective.

John the Baptist, Jesus' cousin and precursor, also preached a message consonant with the ethical stipulation of the Jubilee Year. In preaching a baptism of repentance, Luke portrays him as calling for general charity toward the unfortunate – sharing one's shirt and food – but then instructing tax collectors and soldiers against oppressing people with their authority and power, respectively (Luke 3.10–14). This, following his rebuke of the multitudes (Matt: Pharisees and Sadducees), serves to underscore the force of the ethic and its strangeness to his audience.

Jesus and the kingdom of God

The early Christian concept of the Jubilee as the basis of Jesus' ministry is clearly expressed by Luke when Jesus goes to the synagogue. In Luke 4:18–19, Jesus reads Isa 61:1–2 and thus affirms the ethic of forgiveness and the expected Jubilee Year of the Lord. The text of Jesus' reading, as cited by Luke, is from the Septuagint:

The Spirit of the Lord is upon me,
by whom he has anointed me,
To bring good news to the poor
he has sent me,
To proclaim release for the captives
and sight for the blind,
To send out the broken in forgiveness
to proclaim the favourable year of the Lord.

Although scholars are agreed that Jubilary language is implicit in Isa 61:1–2 and therefore in the "Nazareth manifesto" of Luke 4:16–30, what Jesus meant by that language has been debated. Some have posited that Jesus' reading was a call for a literal observance of the Jubilee Year as mandated in Leviticus 25 (Yoder). Others see the use of a prophetic text over a legal one to indicate the expected response to the kingdom of God.

After the work of Sloan, it is now widely recognized that the central thread connecting Jesus' reading with Isaiah's proclamation and the Jubilee ordinances of Leviticus 25 is the term "release" (Gk. ἄφεσις; lit.: "forgiveness"). In the Hebrew Bible and the Septuagint, the term is essentially a legal one. It was used to represent the release from the obligations of office or debt or, in the case of

divorce, marriage. Consequently, Jesus' reading and subsequent statement could only have been understood by his hearers and Luke's audience as representing the socio-economic re-enfranchisement of the poor, the sinful and the criminal. All debts are cancelled, and all are on equal footing. As Ringe has noted: "[These] traditions ... point to an actual change of circumstance for those who suffer, and thus to a change in the power relationship between oppressor and oppressed" (Ringe 95).

It was Jesus' reading about this anticipated change in the power relationship that, Luke records, caused "all of the eyes in the synagogue to fix on him" (Luke 4:20). Then, as he sits down, his expansion of this passage causes wonder at first (4:22) and then anger as he notes the miracles which God performed among the Gentiles to the exclusion of the Jews (4:25–27).

This change in the power dynamics of socio-economic relationships consequently forms the bedrock of Jesus' ministry as reflected in the gospels and in Luke particularly. It consistently forms the backdrop to the friction between Jesus and those in seats of power or authority. Not only did Jesus call for charity to the poor as part of their re-enfranchisement, but he also called for giving up one's riches for their sakes (Matt 5:40–42; Luke 6:30; 16:19–31) and for the sake of the kingdom of God (Matt 19:16–30; Mark 10:17–31; Luke 18:18–30). The fact that Jesus calls the rich man to give up everything in the present, not merely in the future, underscores the in-breaking nature of the kingdom and the inaugurated eschatology of the synoptic traditions (so Ladd 111). This integral part of the Jubilee, the recognition of God as the ultimate owner of the land and all things, is also reflected in the orthopraxy of the earliest church communities (Acts 2:44, 4:34–37, 5:1–11).

Jubilee motifs are found throughout both Matthean and Lucan versions of the gospels, particularly in Q and the materials unique to Matthew (M) and to Luke (L). A few examples will serve to illustrate this: the healing of the paralytic (Matt 9:1–8; Mark 2:1–12; Luke 5:17–26), the Beatitudes (Matt 5:2–12; Luke 6:20–23), Jesus' summary of his ministry (Matt 11:2–6; Luke 7:22–23), the woman with the ointment (Matt 26:6–13; Mark 14:3–9; Luke 7:36–50; John 12:1–8), the healing of the woman with the haemorrhage (Matt 9:18–26; Mark 5:25–34; Luke 8:40–56), the healing of the deaf mute and others (Matt 15:29–31; Mark 7:31–37), the story of Jesus and Zacclaeus (Luke 19:1–10), the Parable of the Great Banquet (Luke 14:12–24), the Parable of the Lost Sheep (Matt 18:10–14; Luke 15:4–7), teaching about the brother who sins

(Matt 18:15–20), the Parable of the Unforgiving Servant (Matt 18:21–35), and the Parable of the Prodigal Son (Luke 15:11–32).

Sin

Implicit in the liberation of the Jubilee Year as proclaimed by Jesus is the concept of sin. As reflected in the formalized gospels, the concept of sin cannot be divorced from the socio-linguistic milieu and Jewishness of early Christianity. While Jesus may have been reared in "Galilee of the Gentiles" (Isa 9:1), his was plainly a religious family with conservative practices (e.g. presenting their child in the Temple). Therefore, one should not expect to find Hellenistic concepts of Jewish religious terms in his teaching.

Word choice and usage

Within the gospels and Acts, six terms are used to designate various kinds of sin. Each is also used in the Septuagint to represent a range of Hebrew and Aramaic words for sin. The two most common are as follows:

hamartia (Gk. ἁμαρτία; cognates meaning "sin, sinners, to sin"; occurs 173 times in the New Testament, forty-one times in the gospels and eight times in Acts): the most general term for sin and the most frequent in the gospels and the New Testament writings on the whole. In the Septuagint, it is used to represent a wide range of words for wrongdoing.

ponēros (Gk. πονηρός; "evil"; occurs seventy-eight times in the NT, thirty-nine times in the gospels and eight times in Acts). While the Greek word is almost a direct equivalent of English "evil", the word is used in the Septuagint to represent a broad range of words, some of which overlap with *hamartia* (above).

The following are used in the minority of occurrences:

adikia (Gk. ἀδικία; "unrighteousness"; used twenty-five times in the New Testament, five times in the gospels, twice in Acts).

ofeiletēs (Gk. ὀφειλέτης; "debtor"; occurs nine times in the New Testament, three times in the gospels, and none in Acts).

Paraptōma (Gk. παράπτωμα; "trespass"; occurs nineteen times in the New Testament, three times in the gospels, sixteen times in the Pauline literature).

kakia (Gk. κακία; "wickedness", related to κακος for "bad"; occurs eleven times in the New Testament, but only once in the gospels and once in Acts).

Consequently, the references to religious waywardness in the traditions about Jesus are general ones. Of the eighty-nine times that synonyms for "sin" occur in the gospels and Acts, eighty occurrences reference either sin in general terms or evil in some form. If more specific terms were used in either a Hebrew or an Aramaic ancestor of the present tradition, the precision is lost to history. Further, given that adikia (ἀδικία) occurs within the gospels and only in Luke–Acts and John, it appears to be a later development in the Jesus tradition. Similarly, kakia (κακία) occurs only in Matthew's Sermon on the Mount.

Semitic backgrounds in the Gospels

Black observed correctly that the conception of wrongdoing in the Lord's Prayer was that of indebtedness (ὀφείλημα), not sin per se (ἁμαρτία, so Luke) or trespass (παράπτωμα, so Origen). The understanding of sin as debt resonates with the Hebrew *chob* (חוב) and Aramaic *chobah* (חובא), both meaning "debt", and is also attested in the Samaritan liturgy. This conception of sin naturally underscores the Jubilary nature of Jesus' teaching and is likely to be liturgical in origin (1967: 140).

It is worth noting in juxtaposition to Pauline theology that the concept of sin as "trespass" (παράπτωμα) plays a minor role in the Greek of the gospel traditions. Similarly, sin as a formal "transgression" does not appear in the formalized gospel traditions at all but occurs most often in the Pauline letters and twice in Hebrews (2:2; 9:15).

Forgiveness

Word choice and usage

Within the New Testament, there are only three terms used explicitly to convey forgiveness: *aphiēmi* "to forgive" (Gk. ἀφίημι), *aphesis* "forgiveness" (Gk. ἄφεσις) and *apoluō* "to loose from (obligation)" (Gk. ἀπολύω).

In the teaching of Jesus

Like that of sin, Jesus' concept of forgiveness was also rooted in the Jewish tradition of which he was a part. Much of New Testament scholarship has failed until recently to perceive or describe rightly the pious sense of forgiveness in Second Temple

Jewish practices, confusing it for what is portrayed in the New Testament as rigid religious formalism.

In fact, the concept of forgiveness played a central and heartfelt role in the practices of many Second Temple Jewish groups. In the pseudepigraphal story of Joseph and Aseneth, the latter, an Egyptian woman and a former pagan, says that, because God will forgive her every sin, she may speak freely with him (11:18). The Qumran community similarly maintained that salvation is by God's mercy, that true justice is only found with God and that, by his goodness, "he will forgive all of [their] iniquities" (1QS 11:11–14). The first-century pseudepigraphon the Prayer of Manasseh reflects the heartfelt plea of the son of Hezekiah for forgiveness based upon God's grace and mercy (11–14). Later in the same period, the *Amidah*, prayed daily at morning, noon and evening, focused on love, mercy and repentance (Sanders 1992: 448). Finally, the prayer of the high priest at Yom Kippur depicts the highest religious representative taking personal responsibility for the sins of the people (*m. Yoma* 3:8).

Forgiveness was different from reconciliation or atonement and was normally based upon repentance by the sinner. Forgiveness for the Jews of Jesus' time was, as it is today, a relational dynamic which leads to reconciliation. This was naturally a part of the earliest disciples' understanding as Christianity was a branch of Judaism. Within Jesus' teaching, the relational aspect of forgiveness was heavily emphasized. Starting in the Lord's Prayer, Jesus stressed that one's own forgiveness is related to one's forgiveness of others (Matt 6:12; Luke 11:4). And this forgiveness was to be had and given without limit (Matt 18:22; Luke 17:3–4).

Implicit in forgiveness is the concept of binding and loosing. The Johannine Jesus tradition depicts the disciples as receiving the power to forgive and to withhold forgiveness (John 20:23). Similarly, in Matthew, Jesus give the power to bind and loose (Matt 16:19). While this power probably refers to permission and prohibition in the first instance, binding and loosing are implied.

The unforgivable sin

In Mark 3:28–30 (Matt 12:31–32; Luke 12:10), however, Jesus presents the only offence for which forgiveness cannot be had: blasphemy against the Holy Spirit. This inclusion of an unforgivable sin within Jesus' religious framework is not without parallel. Jubilees 15:33–34 predicts the faithlessness of some, particularly the sons of Beliar. They are to leave their sons uncircumcised, "just as they were born". In this regard, "there is therefore for them no forgiveness or pardon" (15:34).

What exactly constitutes blasphemy in Jesus' pronouncement is unclear. Mark and Luke label it ambiguously as blaspheming, but Matthew describes it as speaking "against the Holy Spirit" (12:32). This seems to be a summarization of the reason used by Mark for Jesus' making this pronouncement: "[T]hey said, 'He has an unclean spirit'" (3:30).

Other commentators have read the unpardonable sin to be the rejection of the Holy Spirit. What this means is equally ambiguous. It should be noted that, while the blasphemy is portrayed only once in the present texts – "they said" – the actual sin may not be a single act but a life spent in rejection of the Holy Spirit as unclean (Redlich 1937: 167).

ALBERT LUKASZEWSKI

Further reading

Black, M. *An Aramaic Approach to the Gospels and Acts*, Peabody: Hendrickson, 1967.

Bultmann, R. *Theology of the New Testament*, Vol. 1, trans. Kendrick Grobel, London: SCM Press, 1952; Tübingen: Mohr, 1948.

Charlesworth, James H. (ed.) *The Old Testament Pseudepigrapha*, Vol. 2, ABRL, New York: Doubleday, 1985.

Danby, Herbert. *The Mishnah*, Oxford: Oxford University Press, 1933.

Finkelstein, J. J. "Ammisaduqa's Edict and the Babylonian 'Law Codes'," *JCS* 15.3 (1961), 91–104.

Garnet, P. *Salvation and Atonement in the Qumran Scrolls*, Tübingen: Mohr, 1977.

Gordon, C. H. "Sabbatical Cycle or Seasonal Pattern?" *Orientalia* 22 (n.d.) 79–81.

Hatch, E. and H. A. Redpath. *A Concordance to the Septuagint*, Grand Rapids, MI: Baker Books, 1998.

Jastrow, M. *A Dictionary of the Targumim, the Talmud Babli and Yerushalmi, and the Midrashic Literature*, New York: Judaica Press, 1996.

Jeremias, J. *The Parables of Jesus*, second edition, New York: Charles Scribner's Sons, 1972.

Koehler, L. and W. Baumgartner. *The Hebrew and Aramaic Lexicon of the Old Testament*, trans. M. E. J. Richardson, CD-ROM edition, Leiden: Brill, 1994–2000.

Ladd, G. E. *The Presence of the Future*, revised edition, Grand Rapids, MI: Eerdmans, 1974.

Perrin, N. *Rediscovering the Teaching of Jesus*, London: SCM Press, 1967.

Redlinch, E. B. *The Forgiveness of Sins*, Edinburgh: T. & T. Clarke, 1937.

Ringe, S. *Jesus, Liberation, and the Biblical Jubilee: Images for Ethics and Christology*, Philadelphia, PA: Fortress Press, 1985.

Sanders, E. P. *Paul and Palestinian Judaism*, Minneapolis, MN: Fortress Press, 1977.

—— *Jesus and Judaism*, Philadelphia, PA: Fortress Press, 1985.

—— *Judaism: Practice and Belief, 63 BCE–66 CE*, London and Philadelphia, PA: SCM Press/TPI, 1992.

Sokoloff, M. *A Dictionary of Jewish Palestinian Aramaic*, second edition, Ramat-Gan/Baltimore, MD and London: Bar Ilan University Press/Johns Hopkins University Press, 2002.

Yoder, J. *The Politics of Jesus*, Grand Rapids, MI: Eerdmans, 1972.

JUDAS ISCARIOT

Often designated as "one of the Twelve" (Matt 26:14, 47; Mark 14:10, 43; Luke 22:3, 47; John 6:71; 12:4; cf. Acts 1:17), Judas Iscariot assists the Jewish authorities in their arrest of Jesus. He appears last in lists of the twelve disciples (Matt 10:4; Mark 3:19; Luke 6:16), although this likely indicates his later ignominy rather than his original importance. Evidently Judas held a position of some significance among the group as treasurer (John 12:6; 13:29).

The name "Judas Iscariot"

In the New Testament, at least eight people are called Judas. Twenty-two times the name refers to Judas Iscariot. The name Judas is a Greek form of the Hebrew name Judah. Its original meaning is unknown, but it clearly pays tribute to the fourth son of Jacob. The designation "Iscariot" (Matt 10:4; 26:14; Mark 3:19; 14:10; Luke 6:16; 22:3; John 6:71; 12:4; 13:2, 26; 14:22) distinguishes Judas from others so named (e.g. Matt 13:55; Mark 6:3), especially from the other apostle named Judas (Luke 6:16; John 14:22; Acts 1:13). Three times Judas is identified as son of Simon, also called Iscariot (John 6:71; 13:2, 26).

Most theories about the derivation of Iscariot reflect the action of Judas in handing Jesus over to the authorities. The term may mean "assassin," if Iscariot is related to the Greek word *sikarios* (Acts 21:38). Josephus (*Ant.* 20.186; *J.W.* 2.254–57) uses the Latin term *sicarii* for Jewish revolutionaries known for carrying a short dagger or *sicarius*. The term may derive from a Hebrew root meaning "deceive," suggesting that Iscariot means "false one" or "liar." Or the term may derive from another Hebrew root meaning "deliver," denoting Judas's act of delivering Jesus to the authorities.

However, the most common explanation for Iscariot sees the term as a designation for the place of his birth. This understanding appeals to a supposed Hebrew phrase *îš Qěrîyôt* meaning "man of Kerioth." A variant reading in a fifth-century manuscript adds "from Kerioth" (John 6:71; 12:4, 13:2, 26; 14:22) and thus offers ancient support for the idea. Two possible identifications of the town include Kerioth of Moab, east of the Jordan (Jer 48:24; Amos 2:2), or Kerioth-hezron of southern Judah (Josh 15:25). If Judas hails from either place, he alone among the Twelve comes from outside Galilee. Nonetheless, the meaning of Iscariot remains in doubt (Brown 1413–16).

The act of Judas

The primary word used to describe the act of Judas is *paradidōmi*. More than one-third of its occurrences in the New Testament refer to Judas. In these instances, it is translated as "betray" and thus has perpetuated the pervasive tradition of Judas as betrayer. However, the use of παραδιδόμι elsewhere in classical and biblical literature does not corroborate a negative connotation for the word (Klassen: 41–61). Generally, the word means to deliver a person into the control of another. For example, the word also expresses the actions of the chief priests (Matt 27:2; Mark 15:1; Luke 24:20; John 18:30) and Pilate (Matt 27:36; Mark 15:15; Luke 23:25; John 19:16). Theologically, the word in its Pauline usage implicates both God and Jesus in the delivery of Jesus unto death (Rom 4:25; 8:32; 1 Cor 11:27; Gal 2:20; Eph 5:2, 25). Thus, for Judas *paradidōmi* signifies that he hands Jesus over to the Jewish authorities, an act accomplished by serving as a guide (*hodēgos*) for those who arrested Jesus (Acts 1:16).

The Synoptic Gospels recount how Judas contracted with the chief priests to deliver Jesus over to them (Matt 26:14–16; Mark 14:10; Luke 22:3–6). All three indicate that the chief priests agreed to pay Judas for his assistance. Only Matthew includes Judas's request for payment and specifies the amount paid to him, thirty pieces of silver – an amount that alludes to Zechariah 11:12 and anticipates the narrative of Judas's suicide in Matthew 27:3–10. During their narration of the Last Supper, the Synoptic Gospels include Jesus' prediction that one of his disciples would turn him over, but each differs in its description of the means by which this one is identified (Matt 26:22–24; Mark 14:18–21; Luke 22:21–23). More developed is John's account, in which Jesus identified Judas by giving him a piece of bread (John 13:21–27).

According to all four gospels, Judas led a large group from the chief priests to arrest Jesus in the garden of Gethsemane (Matt 26:47–50; Mark 14:43–46; Luke 22:47–48; John 18:2–5). Matthew and Mark indicate that Judas identified Jesus to them with the prearranged signal of a kiss, while Luke says that Jesus asked if Judas would kiss him. John omits any reference to a kiss from Judas, since this would conflict with the notion of power attributed to Jesus in the Fourth Gospel (cf. John 13:2–3). Rather, Judas merely stood with those coming to arrest Jesus, perhaps falling to the ground when Jesus revealed himself to them (John 18:5–6).

The traditions about Judas

According to two biblical traditions (Matt 27:3–10 and Acts 1:16–20; cf. Papias, *Frag.* 3), Judas died a sudden, violent death with some connection to acreage known as the "Field of Blood." The two traditions differ, however, regarding the manner of Judas's death (suicide by hanging or falling and bursting open), the purchase of the field (by the chief priests or by Judas), and the event's fulfillment of the Old Testament (Zech 11:12–13 and Jer 19:1–13, or Pss 69:26; 109:8). Even if the details of Judas's death are not ascertainable, both accounts depict it in a fashion similar to other death narratives deemed as divine punishment (e.g. 2 Sam 17:23; 2 Macc 9:5–10).

The gospels offer various interpretations of the act of Judas. Luke calls Judas a "traitor" (6:16) and intimates that Judas was prompted by satanic impulse (22:3). John implies a lesser motive of greed (John 12:6; cf. Matt 26:14–16) and accentuates the influence of Satan more than Luke does (John 13:2, 27, 30; 17:20; cf. *Acts Pet.* 8). Subsequent contemplations of how one so close to Jesus could hand him over tend toward a vilification of Judas (Paffenroth: 17–57), who epitomized the avarice and treachery of the Jews (Chrysostom, *Hom. Act.* 3). Intriguingly, other representations counter the condemnation of Judas (Paffenroth: 59–177). Most notable is the *Gospel of Judas* (Kasser), mentioned by Irenaeus in 180 CE (*Haer.* 1.31.1). According to this gnostic document, Judas alone understood the message of Jesus and did as he instructed, so that the divine being Christ might escape the human body of Jesus. Because of his obedient act, Judas was rejected and transcended the Twelve, standing beyond their number as "the thirteenth" (*Gos. Jud.* 46). While such later interpretations move beyond the historicity of the so-called betrayal, the early church would hardly have invented the incident of Judas handing Jesus over.

CLAY ALAN HAM

Further reading

Brown, Raymond B. *The Death of the Messiah*, 2 vols, New York: Doubleday, 1994.

Kasser, Rodolphe, Marvin Meyer, and Gregor Wurst (eds) *The Gospel of Judas*, Washington, DC: National Geographic, 2006.

Klassen, William. *Judas: Betrayer or Friend of Jesus?*, Minneapolis, MN: Fortress Press, 1996.

Paffenroth, Kim. *Judas: Images of the Lost Disciple*, Louisville, KY: Westminster John Knox, 2001.

Wright, N. T. *Judas and the Gospel of Jesus*, Grand Rapids, MI: Baker, 2006.

JUDGEMENT

Judgement is a main theme in the preaching of Jesus. It is not only the precondition for the final coming of salvation but also the necessary consequence of salvation rejected or despised. It is inextricably bound up with the coming and establishment of the reign of God. In view of that reign Jesus calls for a repentance that consists in turning to him and doing what he teaches. The refusal of that repentance and the rejection of God's reign brings with it a self-chosen exclusion from salvation. So the main intention of the teaching of judgement is warning. It is a menace only for demons (cf. Mark 3:27; Matt 12:28//Luke 11:20; Luke 10:18).

A quantitative overview shows the following results: In Q judgement sayings and parables comprise 35 per cent of the oral discourse, in Mark 22 per cent, in Matthew's special material 64 per cent, and in Luke's special material 28 per cent. Most conspicuous is the percentage in Matthew's special material, which indicates a particular interest on the side of the Evangelist for the theme of final judgement. In any case, more than a quarter of the traditional discourse material of Jesus is concerned with this item. And it is by no means absent in the Gospel of John (cf. John 3:16–21; 5:22–29; 9:39; 12:46–48).

Nevertheless, there are scholars and theologians who think that Jesus was not eschatological and suppose that even if he proclaims the eschatological reign of God he did not speak of God's judgement. Preaching which stresses judgement, they fear, will obscure the message of God's love and convey a distorted picture of a God who punishes. Jesus message was good news, not grim news. Threatening had no part in his preaching, they think.

But how can we reject a quarter of the sayings and parables of Jesus and claim that they were invented and added by post-eastern theologians? There are enough logia and parables on the subject of judgement which will turn out authentic even to the strictest rules of historical criticism. In the last analysis, one will find that the Evangelists only enlarged and developed themes and subjects they found in the received authentic traditions of Jesus. A survey of such traditions will substantiate the point.

In the double saying about the Queen of the South and the Ninevites (Matt 12:41–42//Luke 11:31–32) Jesus proclaims to 'this generation', that is, the whole nation of his contemporaries, the sentence that will be theirs at the last judgement, if they do not repent and listen to his message. In the judgement scene here intimated Jesus envisions traditional elements of early Jewish conceptions of judgement: it is conceived as a forensic trial; it presumes the general resurrection of the dead; witnesses arise and give testimony (cf. Dan 7:9–10; Wis 4:20–25:14; *1 En.* 90:20–26). 'This generation' is provocatively contrasted with 'good' Gentiles. The saying is clearly intended as a warning to Israel: this will come to pass if they don't repent. If even Gentiles like the Queen of the South came 'to listen to the wisdom of Solomon' (1 Kgs 5:14), and the Ninevites repented at the preaching of Jonah, how much more ought 'this generation' to listen to him, with whom there is more than Solomon's wisdom or Jonah's preaching. That is a direct but open christological claim in a saying with all claims to authenticity.

The motives of 'judgement' and 'repentance' reappear in the woe over the Galilean cities (Matt 11:21–14//Luke 10:13–15). This saying sounds like a condemnation more than a warning, though having seen the miracles of Jesus Chorazin and Bethsaida didn't repent. Therefore 'at the [day of] judgement it will be more tolerable for Tyre and Sidon' than for them. Here the miracles of Jesus are supposed to be proofs and real symbols of the present reign of God as in other sayings as well. They should serve as signals calling for repentance. Otherwise judgement is sure to come. As in the former saying, we find a provocative contrast between God's unfaithful people and the Gentiles. This contrast turns up again in the saying about the table companions of Abraham, Isaac, and Jacob in the reign of God (Matt 8:11–12//Luke 13:28–29). It presents to the eyes of Israel ('the children of the reign') a horrible vision: the patriarchs alone with Gentiles at the eschatological banquet on Mount Zion, while they themselves are 'thrown outside', probably into the valley of Hinnom, i.e. hell. This is not a prediction but a serious warning: do not let it come to that. Whereas judgement in this case is a form of exclusion, we once again find a judgement court in the saying about acknowledgment and denial (Luke 12:8–9//Matt 10:32–33). Here it is 'the Son of Man' who as conclusive witness determines the judge's

(that is God's) decision. The mention of angels is a reference to the judgement scene of Dan 7:9–10. The sole criterion for judgement is the acknowledgment of Jesus before others.

Among the parables of judgement, perhaps the most instructive is the one of the Unmerciful Servant (Matt 18:23–34). It first speaks of God's willingness to forgive even the greatest guilt ('debt' and 'guilt' are in Hebrew meanings of the same word; cf. 'and forgive us our debts' in the Our Father), then of the consequences that one has to draw from that forgiveness, and finally of the punishment that anyone must expect who fails to draw the consequences of received forgiveness. In the first scene we have a depiction of justification by God's grace, in the second of how one can lose this grace, in the third of what will follow. There are many more texts to be considered for a complete picture of Jesus' teaching of judgement, e.g. Matt 7:1–2//Luke 6:37–38; Matt 7:24–27//Luke 6:47–49; Matt 19:28//Luke 22:28–30; Matt 24:37–39//Luke 17:26–29; Matt 25,14–30//Luke 19:11–27; Mark 9:43–48; Mark 10:25; 14:62; Matt 13:24–30, 47–50; Luke 13:2–5, 6–9; Luke 16:1–7. 19–31.

In Jesus' concept of judgement there are many points of correspondence with the concept of judgement in the teaching of John the Baptist (cf. Matt 3:7–12//Luke 3:7–9, 16–17). Both of them stand within a broad Jewish tradition coming from the post-exilic prophets and their concept of 'the day of the LORD' (cf. e.g. Zeph 1:7–2:3). But while the Baptist wanted to gather the 'remnant', Jesus never gave up gathering the whole of Israel. And while the Baptist understood repentance as a return to the Torah, Jesus saw it as a turning to himself and to doing what he said. Whether the Baptist's awaited Stronger One refers to God himself or to the Messiah, the answer given by Jesus to his question from prison (Matt 11:2–6//Luke 7:18–23) is clear and, in all probability, authentic.

MARIUS REISER

Further reading

Reiser, M. *Jesus and Judgement: The Eschatological Proclamation in Its Jewish Context*, trans. Linda M. Maloney, Minneapolis, MN: Fortress Press, 1997.

K

KÄHLER, MARTIN

Martin Kähler (1835–1912) was born in Neuhausen near Königsberg. He first studied law, but soon changed his focus of study to theology. After school, he moved to Heidelberg, then to Halle (influenced by August Tholuck) and later to Tübingen where he became acquainted with Johann Tobias Beck, one of the opponents of Ferdinand Christian Baur. After his habilitation in 1860 in Halle, he became *extraordinarius* for New Testament and Systematic Theology in Bonn in 1864 and in 1867 in Halle where he finally received a full professorship in 1879. His studies combined both fields of research connected with his professorship as a biblical theologian, although his emphasis was in the systematic theology of his time, based in biblical themes.

With regard to Jesus and gospel studies, Kähler became famous for two theses which became very influential even in academic circles that did not accept his overall biblical approach. The first thesis had a negative effect on the theological estimation of historical Jesus studies, especially for the dialectical theological approaches like that of Rudolf Bultmann or Karl Barth, both of whom opposed the liberal life-of-Jesus research that Kähler criticized as being on the wrong track ("Holzweg;" 1953: 18). In his short book *Der sogenannte historische Jesus und der geschichtliche, biblische Christus* (English translation: *The So-Called Historical Jesus and the Historic Biblical Christ*), originating from a lecture given in 1892, Kähler criticized the scholarly portraits of the historical Jesus as mere invention of the modern human spirit (1953: 29–30).

He argued that the gospels are not biographies about Jesus, but instead texts that reflect the beliefs about Jesus. By pointing out that the gospels were not sources of high historical value, Kähler underlined the kerygmatic character of the gospel narratives inviting people to faith. Within historical research their reconstructed historical Jesus hides the "real Christ" who is the character that is important for Christian faith and who is witnessed by the New Testament writings: "*Der wirkliche Christus is der gepredigte Christus … der Jesus, dessen Bild wir uns einprägen, weil wir daraufhin mit ihm umgehen wollen und umgehen, als mit dem erhöhten Lebendigen*" (= "The real Christ is the proclaimed Christ … the Jesus, whose image we impress on ourselves, because we both would and do commune with him, as the exalted Living One"; 1953: 44–45). With the cross as the center of proclamation, Kähler targeted the soteriological meaning of Christ; cross and resurrection form the centre of Christology (e.g. 1885; 1911).

The gospel presents a true picture to the reader of Jesus' personality. Kähler used the term *unerfindbar* ("uninventable"; 1896 [in the second edition of his 1892 paper]: 79; cf. the term "incomparable" [*unvergleichlich*, in his first edition; 1953: 33 with n. 2]).

Kähler differentiated between *geschichtlich* ("historic") – something that became effective (*wirksam*) during history – and *historisch* ("historical"), that is, issues that are reconstructed by historical-critical method. *Geschichtlich* is Jesus only in so far as he is defined as the resurrected Christ as he was believed to be, the founder of communities of faith and one that effected salvation. According to Kähler, the historical meaning of the Bible lay in its effectiveness (cf. 1902): what is effected by the Bible has to be the subject of interpretation of Bible not the history or pre-history of its writings (1896: 70–71).

Kähler's second influential thesis considers the composition and theology of the gospel writings. In fact, a dictum of Kähler's became axiomatic in gospel criticism, especially with reference to the gospel of Mark. According to that dictum, the gospels are Passion Narratives with extended introductions (1953: 59–60 n. 1). That idea supports the central place of the cross in the Christology of Mark and, although not undisputed and with characteristic Johannine color, also in John. This thesis contradicts again a biographical interpretation of the gospel that seeks aspects of psychological development in the gospel text (1953: 24). Kähler's criticism does not answer form-critical questions, such as how far the gospels may relate to ancient biographical genre, but he opposes life-of-Jesus research that thinks it can reconstruct a psychological logical portrait of Jesus from the New Testament sources.

Interpreting past events is a process of ascribing meaning to something that became past. By doing so, the historian also seeks for meaning and orientation of that past event for present and future. The approach is a constructive one and therefore hypothetical and subjective as criticized by Kähler. Nevertheless, like the communities of the gospel writers, it is also important for contemporary theology to provide information concerning the meaning of past events in the life of Jesus. It is necessary because the believed Christ is not a mythic figure but a historical one who preached, healed, and was put to death on the cross.

The second or new quest for Jesus, defined and propelled forward by scholars like Ernst Käsemann or Günther Bornkamm, has had again to learn the theological meaning of historical analysis of Jesus and find a new rationale for the quest. Kähler's theologically negative judgment with respect to historical approaches is reminiscent of the difference between past event and interpretation. This difference, however, should not lead to the abandonment of historical research with regard to Jesus, for critical faith asks for the meaning of that figure and needs information about how the historical Jesus became the Christ in early and later confessions.

MICHAEL LABAHN

Further reading

Braaten, Carl Edward. "Christ, Faith, and History: An Inquiry into the Meaning of Martin Kähler's Distinction Between the Historical Jesus and the Biblical Christ Developed in its Past and Present Contexts," dissertation, Harvard University, Cambridge, MA, 1959.

Broadhead, Edwin K. "What are the Gospels? Questioning Martin Kähler," Pacifica 7:2 (1994) 145–59.

Kähler, Martin. Die Versöhnung durch Christum in ihrer Bedeutung für das christliche Glauben und Leben. Erläuterung zu Thesen, Erlangen: Deichert, 1885.

—— Der sogenannte historische Jesus und der geschichtliche, biblische Christus, Leipzig: Deichert, 1892; second edition 1896; Theologische Bibliothek 2; new edition ed. Ernst Wolf, München: Kaiser, 1953; ET: The So-called Historical Jesus and the Historic Biblical Christ, Philadelphia, PA: Fortress Press, 1970.

—— Jesus und das Alte Testament. Erläuterungen zu Thesen Leipzig: Deichert, 1896.

—— "Biblische Theologie," RE 3 (1897) 192–200.

—— Geschichte der Bibel in ihrer Wirkung auf die Kirche, Halle: Buchdruck des Waisenhauses, 1902.

—— Das Kreuz: Grund und Maß für die Christologie, Beiträge zur Förderung christlicher Theologie 1/15,1, Gütersloh: Bertelsmann, 1911.

Knauß, Karl. "Kähler, Martin" Biograpisch-Bibliographisches Kirchenlexikon III, Nordhausen: Verlag Traugott Bautz, 1992, cols 925–30.

Link, Hans Georg. Geschichte Jesu und Bild Christi. Die Entwicklung der Christologie Martin Kählers in Auseinandersetzung mit der Leben-Jesu-Theologie und der Ritschl-Schule, Neukirchen-Vluyn: Neukirchener Verlag, 1975.

Leipold, Heinrich. Offenbarung und Geschichte als Problem des Verstehens: Eine Untersuchung zur Theologie Martin Kählers, Gütersloh: Gütersloher Verlagshaus Mohn, 1962.

McGrath, Alister E. "Justification and Christology: the Axiomatic Correlation Between the Historical Jesus and the Proclaimed Christ," ModTh 1 (1984) 45–54.

Müller, Norbert. "Das Denken Martin Kählers als Beitrag zur Diskussion um eine bibl. Theologie'," EvTh 48 (1988) 346–59.

Nüssel, Friederike. "Kähler, Martin," RGG 4 (2001) 734–35.

Roloff, Jürgen. Das Kerygma und der irdische Jesus. Historische Motive in den Jesus-Erzählungen der Evangelien, Göttingen: Vandenhoeck & Ruprecht, 1970, pp. 9–13.

Schmid, Johannes H. Erkenntnis des geschichtlichen Christus bei Martin Kähler und bei Adolf Schlatter, Theologische Zeitschrift: Sonderband 5; Basel, Reinhardt. 1978.

KÄSEMANN, ERNST

Ernst Käsemann (1906–98) was born in Dahlhausen near Bochum. He studied theology at Bonn (under Erik Peterson), Marburg (under Rudolf Bultmann) and Tübingen. He received his doctorate in 1931, having written a dissertation entitled Leib und Leib Christi (= "Body and Body of Christ"; cf. BHTh 9; Tübingen: Mohr Siebeck, 1933) under the direction of Bultmann. As pastor in a Lutheran congregation in Gelsenkirchen-Rotthausen, he was arrested by the German regime for an interpretation of Isa 26:13. During his imprisonment he outlined his habilitation on Hebrews that appeared under the title *Das wandernde Gottesvolk* (FRLANT, 55; Göttingen, Vandenhoeck & Ruprecht, 1939; second edition 1957; English translation: *The Wandering People of God*, Minneapolis: Augsburg, 1984). His confrontation with the state and the style that his academic work displayed demonstrated the roles of freedom and policy in his theological thinking and exegesis. His scholarly work reflected the social, philosophical, and political situation in which he found himself.

During World War II, Käsemann was drafted for military service. After the war he held academic teaching posts. His first was in Mainz (1946–51). In 1951 he became full professor in Göttingen and in 1959 he moved to Tübingen where he taught until his retirement in 1971. On 24 May 1977, his daughter was murdered in jail by Argentina's military junta.

Käsemann was influential in different fields of New Testament research, principally in Paul, in the Gospel of John, and in the development and the role of New Testament canon. These fields of research benefit from his sharp and pointed style in monographs and his well-known commentary on Paul (*An die Römer* [HNT, 8b; Tübingen: Mohr Siebeck, 1973; fourth edition 1980]; English translation: *Commentary on Romans*, London: SCM Press, 1980), to mention only one of his prominent works.

Käsemann challenged assumptions of his teacher Bultmann in different fields of New Testament exegesis. Perhaps one of the most important fields was that of the quest for the historical Jesus, in which he became one of the fathers of the second or new quest for Jesus. It was on this topic that he presented his famous paper on "*Das Problem des historischen Jesus*" in 1953 (published in 1954). In his programmatic and ground-breaking essay he argued for two essential points: (1) there is an important meaning of historical knowledge for Christian faith; and (2) reliable information can be taken from the early Jesus tradition: there are passages in the Synoptic Tradition that any historian has to accept as authentic if he or she really worked historically ("*es ... Stücke in der synoptischen Überlieferung gibt, welche der Historiker als authentisch einfach anzuerkennen hat, wenn er Historiker bleiben will*"; 1960: 213). The last assumption is strengthened by the results of form criticism. In accordance with the results of the approach of Bultmann, he found traditions that

are at a certain range historically reliable because they can be separated from kerygmatic or historicizing tendencies in the transmission of the Jesus tradition (1964: 52). Combined with the quest for their theological meaning these results lead directly to approaching the problem of the historical Jesus in new ways. The first assumption is due to the fact that early Christianity identified the risen Christ with the earthly Jesus, even though the portrait of the earthly Jesus is absorbed by the kerygmatic Christ (1960: 191). The event of Easter functions as a bridge between Jesus and the later kerygma, in both some kind of continuity (Käsemann can use the term "kerygma *in nuce*"; e.g. 1964: 55) and discontinuity (1964: 46, 57): "*Der irdische Jesus mußte den gepredigten Christus davor schützen, sich in die Projektion eines eschatologischen Selbstverständnisses aufzulösen und zum Gegenstand einer religiösen Ideologie zu werden*" (= "The earthly Jesus had to guard the proclaimed Christ from dissolving into the projection of an eschatological self-consciousness and becoming the object of a religious ideology"; cf. 1964: 67).

Käsemann clearly acknowledged the necessity of criteria for historical work on Jesus. The most important criterion was that of double dissimilarity (1960: 205): as heuristic elements of reconstruction only those elements can be assigned to the historical Jesus that cannot be found in Judaism and in early Christianity (1960: 205). Käsemann clearly faced the problems of such a criterion for he is well aware that the historical Jesus had much in common with contemporary Judaism. His investigation convinced him that besides the parables of Jesus, no clear *formal* criterion for the quest for Jesus was available (1960: 204), and therefore he also sharply opposed other approaches of the New Quest, especially that of Joachim Jeremias, as *Sackgassen* ("dead ends") leading back to the positivistic positions of the nineteenth century (1964: 41). Important for the position of Käsemann was that he questioned the theological meaning and the role ascribed to the historical Jesus by Jeremias, who proposed that the transmission of the early community related as an answer to the call of Jesus. In contrast to Jeremias, he emphasized the meaning of Easter for "Easter evokes that proclamation into that the Jesus tradition is embedded" (1964: 34).

Jesus' teachings were according to Käsemann not apocalyptic, for his expectation of the kingdom of God did not entail a datable end of world and could not be put into religious historical categories (1964: 109). It was within the context of existential philosophy that Käsemann found the answer to the debate about Jesus' eschatology in the immediacy of God calling people into daily service. All life took place immediately in front of God (1964: 109–10, 118–19). It was the experience of Easter that drove the early community into apocalyptic interpretation and to expect the return of Jesus as heavenly Son of Man (1964: 117). For the early Christian community and their interpretation of Jesus and the world, apocalyptic became the "mother of theology" (1964: 100, 130). Käsemann reached this hypothesis in the study *"Anfänge christlicher Theologie"* (= "Beginnings of Christian Theology") based on form-critical insights into texts of Matthew that he interpreted as a writing in Jewish-Christian tradition for gentile Christianity. This study, which may be added to the redaction-critical studies, explained how far and in which way the Gospel of Matthew formed as an apocalyptic theology a "beginning of Christian theology."

In his proclamation and in the first, second, and fourth antitheses (cf. Matt 5:21–26, 27–30, 38–42) Jesus claimed an authority that was comparable with that of the Messiah, although Käsemann did not suggest that Jesus considered himself to be the Messiah; it was the message and not the person that was the central focus of Jesus' preaching (1960: 206, 211).

Within the theological perspective of Käsemann, Jesus became meaningful for political engagement and for a general call for freedom. We see this especially in Käsemann's *Jesus Means Freedom* (Philadelphia, PA: Fortress Press, 1970; English translation of *Der Ruf der Freiheit*, Tübingen: Mohr Siebeck, 1968, fifth edition 1972: Käsemann hints at the freeing power of Jesus' resurrection as he reminds the readers of Jesus' preaching of the freedom of childhood in God; 53, cf. 1960: 212). Käsemann's approach investigated the social and political consequences of exegetical theology in their quest for Jesus (cf. 2005: 128–29). His call was to leave the ivory tower of detailed exegetical discussion and to accept the creative theological power of early Christianity.

MICHAEL LABAHN

Further reading

Close, William J. "The Theological Relevance of History: The Role, Logic, and Propriety of Historical Understanding in Theological Reflection, Considered in the Context of the Debate on the Historical Jesus between Rudolf Bultmann and Ernst Käsemann," dissertation, University of Basel, 1972.

Gisel, Pierre. *Verité et histoire: la théologie dans la modernité, Ernst Käsemann*, Vol. 2, revised and corrected edition, Paris: Beauchesne, 1983.

Harrisville, Roy A. and Walter Sundberg. *The Bible in Modern Culture. Theology and Historical-Critical Method from Spinoza to Käsemann*, Grand Rapids, MI: Eerdmans, 1995, pp. 238–59.

Käsemann, Ernst. *Exegetische Versuchungen und Besinnungen*, 2 vols, Göttingen: Vandenhoeck & Ruprecht, 1960–64, Vol. 1, pp. 187–214, "Das Problem des historischen Jesus" [originally published in 1954]; Vol. 2, pp. 31–68, "Sackgassen im Streit um den historischen Jesus"; pp. 82–104, "Die Anfänge christlicher Theologie" [originally published in 1960]; pp. 105–31, "Zum Thema urchristlicher Apokalyptik" [originally published in 1962]; ET: *Essays on Theological Themes.* London: SCM Press, 1964.

—— *In der Nachfolge des Gekreuzigten Nazareners. Aufsätze und Vorträge aus dem Nachlass*, ed. Rudolf Landau in co-operation with Wolfgang Kraus, Tübingen: Mohr Siebeck, 2005.

Martin, Ralph P. "Käsemann, Ernst," in Donald K. McKim (ed.) *Major Biblical Interpreters*, Downers Grove, IL: InterVarsity Press, 1998, pp. 500–5.

Osborn, E. F. "Historical Critical Exegesis – Käsemann's Contribution," *ABR* 19 (1971) 17–35.

—— "Käsemann, Ernst," *Dictionary of Biblical Interpretation* 2 (1999) 14–16.

Schlosser, Jacques. "Le débat de Käsemann et Bultmann à propos du Jésus de l'histoire," *RSR* 87 (1999) 373–95.

Ulrichs, Karl Friedrich. "Käsemann, Ernst," *Biograpisch-Bibliographisches Kirchenlexikon* XVIII, Nordhausen: Verlag Traugott Bautz, 2001, cols 775–78.

KINGDOM OF GOD

The central category used by Jesus to express his mission and vision for what God was doing through him for Israel. Summarily put, kingdom refers to the society in which God is king and in which God's will is established for all. In the sweep of earliest Christianity, kingdom of God bears strongest resemblance to the Pauline and Johannine concepts of the church and the community's fellowship. It is inconsistent with Jesus' use of the term "kingdom" to interpret kingdom as either religious experience or the Reformation's terms for salvation. Kingdom is concrete, real, and social in Jewish thinking at the time of Jesus.

Kingdom of God: the expression

The term "kingdom" is found on no fewer than eighty-five separable occasions, omitting genuine parallels, in the Synoptic Gospels. Outside the Synoptics, the term *basileia* is found in John's Gospel (3x), Acts (8x), Paul's letters (13x), Hebrews (3x), once in each James and 2 Peter, and the Apocalypse (8x).

In the synoptics, the term is used in various forms: the "kingdom of God" (Mark 1:15), its Aramaic/Hebrew equivalent "the kingdom of heavens" (Matt 4:17), "my kingdom" (Luke 22:30), "his kingdom" (Luke 12:31), "the kingdom of our father David" (Mark 11:10), "the kingdom of my Father" (Matt 26:29), "the kingdom of their father" (Matt 13:43), "the kingdoms of this world" (Matt 4:8), "the kingdoms of this earth" (Luke 4:5), and "your kingdom" (Matt 6:10).

Expressions about the kingdom that pertain to *futurity* are mostly restricted to the period following the confession of Peter, though this is rarely recognized by those discussing kingdom of God. The preposition *in* (Gk. *en* or *eis*) focuses attention on both *place* and *futurity* (see Mark 9:47; 10:15; 14:25; Q: Matt 8:11 par. Luke 13:29; Matt 5:19, 20; 7:21; Luke 13:28; 22:16, 30; 23:42). There are only a few references in the synoptics that do not seem to fit this general conclusion (cf. Mark 10:23–25; Matt 11:11; 21:31).

Meaning of "kingdom of God"

The kingdom of God came into full view with the work of Johannes Weiss (1985 = 1892) and Albert Schweitzer (1901). What these two scholars, especially as brought into greater emphasis by Schweitzer (1906), concluded was the awareness that Jesus' message about the imminent arrival of the kingdom of God emerged from Jewish apocalypticism (Allison 1998). The work of Weiss especially broke the stranglehold of Liberalism on the historical Jesus and turned him loose in order to be set more firmly in a first-century Jewish context. For such scholars, and a modern proponent of such is E. P. Sanders (1983), the kingdom of God was an earthly "state of affairs," in some sense temporally imminent, and shaped everything about the message and ministry of Jesus.

Not all agreed with the Weiss–Schweitzer theory of a consistently futuristic or imminent earthly kingdom of God. C. H. Dodd (1936), on the other side of the English Channel, argued in fact that kingdom of God was a linguistic device, the husk around the inner core. The inner core, according to Dodd, was the ultimate, the eternal order, or the transcendent reality. Hence, "kingdom of God" was accommodating language of the day to express a far deeper and more eternal reality: God's presence. There were hints of classical Platonism in Dodd at times, but his general point was well taken.

What these two viewpoints assume is that specific texts can be rendered in a specific way. A critical text shaping the entire discussion is Mark 1:15: "The time is fulfilled, and the kingdom of God *has come near*; repent, and believe in the good news." The verb behind "has come near" is the Greek word *engiken*, and on this the above two viewpoints differed sharply. For the Weiss–Schweitzer line of thinking, "has come near" meant "is about to arrive and the cataclysm of God will alter life on earth dramatically." For Dodd, "has come near" meant "has already arrived in the person, ministry, and activity of Jesus himself." For the first, the Eschaton is imminent; for the second, the Eschaton has in fact already arrived. To support this Schweitzer can appeal to the text that many Christians recite daily: "May your kingdom come!" (Matt 6:10). On the other hand, Dodd can appeal to Matthew 12:28: "But it is by the Spirit [Luke: "finger"] of God that I cast out demons, then the kingdom of God has [already!] come to you." Following Dodd, Joachim Jeremias (1971) argued that the kingdom of God was " in the process of realizing itself." A modern proponent of Dodd's view, though with many variations, emendations and corrections, is N. T. Wright (1996). In fact, Wright's contribution to kingdom thinking is a good bridge to the next view, that of inaugurated eschatology.

If Schweitzer advocated consistent eschatology and Dodd a kind of "already realized" eschatology on the part of Jesus, then the task of synthesizing the two – along with the texts each can appeal to so persuasively – was left to the German scholar, Werner Georg Kümmel (1957, = 1946), to the English scholar R. H. Fuller (1954), and to the American scholar G. E. Ladd (1974, = 1964). In essence, the argument was simple: the kingdom was neither entirely future nor entirely present, but both present *and* future. Such simplistic syntheses, however, rarely meet realities. Each of these scholars – from Schweitzer to Ladd – operated with a both/and hermeneutic of a future and presence for the kingdom of God in Jesus' own thinking. The issue was to the degree of emphasis.

Where then are we today? It depends on where one is in the larger spectrum of Jesus studies: some still emphasize the Schweitzer line, others the Dodd line, while yet others work at a synthesis. With the advent of more Jewish material in contemporary Jesus studies, what seems to have disappeared from historical Jesus discussions about the kingdom of God is the old Protestant liberal line that the kingdom of God could be reduced to one's relationship with God, or the divine, or to spirituality. In fact, across the spectrum today – from S. Freyne (2004) and J. D. G. Dunn (2003) back to R. A. Horsley (1987) and E. P. Sanders (1983) – is the notion that "kingdom of God" was a description of an earthly, social reality wherein Israel as a nation was restored (Bryan). The kingdom of

God, then, is the society in which God is king and in which society God's will is manifestly present and which, to one degree or another, anticipates the future Eschaton (McKnight 1999). Or, as Theissen and Merz appropriately reduce the issues of the kingdom of God to this central question: "How does the one and only God establish his will in this world?" (277).

Themes

To facilitate description, the following discussion breaks down what Jesus said about the kingdom into its present and future dimensions. As long as one understands that the lines between the two are fluid because the long-awaited kingdom has in some sense broken through into history in Jesus himself, one can still use this simple breakdown with some degree of accuracy.

Furthermore, each theme addressed below is embedded in the ancient Jewish world, and thus to exploit Jesus' message of the kingdom one must come to terms with Jewish messianism, kingdom expectations, eschatology, and judgment (see Beasley-Murray 3–68).

Present

The kingdom begins with a declaration by Jesus that it has in some sense arrived (Mark 1:15). Jesus' declaration brings forth a variety of responses (4:1–9) even if at times violent (Matt 11:11–13). For Jesus, the declaration of the kingdom is a revelation both about what God is doing (Matt 13:16–17) and what that same God is doing through his own person and work (Luke 17:20–21). The declaration of the kingdom's presence finds expression in the miracles Jesus does (Matt 11:2–6; 12:28). That kingdom's declaration is that there is both a continuity and discontinuity with Israel's story: that is, it is the same but not just the same (Mark 2:18–22; Matt 13:51–52). The discontinuity means there is a change in kinship (Mark 3:31–35), space (Mark 14:12–26), and time (Mark 2:27).

Kingdom evokes for many the grand and glorious, but Jesus sabotaged such an idea with an emphatic focus on the inauspicious nature of the present kingdom of God. The kingdom had inauspicious beginnings – like a mustard seed (Mark 4:30–32), it was comprised of inauspicious people – like children (10:14–15) and tax collectors (Luke 19:1–10), it was led by an inauspicious person – Jesus (Luke 17:20–21), and yet this inauspiciousness would someday turn into a grand and glorious display (Matt 13:24–30, 36–43).

The rather boilerplate operation of the kingdom, however, needs to be balanced by the occasional sudden displays of power. Jesus states in no uncertain terms, in a text that bears dramatic resemblance to the expectation of the Messiah in the Qumran community, that what he is doing in Israel is what Isaiah foretold (cf. Matt 11:2–6 with Isa 29:18–19; 35:5–6; 61:1; see also 4Q521; Evans 53–250): Jesus' comment that the "blind receive their sight, the lame walk, the lepers are cleansed, the deaf hear, and the dead are raised" – not to forget that "the poor have the good news brought to them" – evince the power now at work through him. In addition, one must observe the powerful impact of Jesus led to the use of power against him in the name of Herod Antipas (Matt 11:12–13). What kind of power did Jesus show? The power to exorcise unclean spirits – exorcism (Mark 1:127).

If the kingdom of God is declared as present, simultaneously visible inauspiciously but with occasional flashes of power, how then does one enter the kingdom of God? A good place to begin to answer this question is with the so-called "entrance sayings." They illustrate not only a "form" of Jesus' teachings, but the *ad hoc* content of his teachings. Instead of giving a systemic approach to "how one enters," Jesus instances answers to such a question and we find then several answers: one must have surpassing righteousness (Matt 5:20), one must do God's will (7:21), one must be converted and become a child (18:3), one must perform radical surgery to separate from sin (18:8–9), one must discard riches (19:23–24), or one must separate from the Pharisees and scribes (23:13). Without engaging here a full discussion of the ethics of Jesus, we should at least observe that Jesus called for repentance and faith (Mark 1:15), perseverance (Matt 10:22), and righteousness (5:17–20). More centrally, however, Jesus summoned his followers to love God and love others (Mark 12:28–32). At times, Jesus made even sterner demands on those who would enter into the kingdom of God (Luke 9:57–62; Matt 19:10–12). This is not a grocery list of things to do, nor a new list of commandments, but instead particular instances of the kinds of things Jesus said one was to do if one chose to follow him in order to enter into the kingdom of God in the here and now.

Future

The emphasis of Jesus, especially according to Luke's Gospel, was on the future arrival of the kingdom. Anyone who taught his followers to repeat daily, in a prayer that adapted the traditional Jewish prayer called the Kaddish, "May your kingdom come!" certainly didn't think the kingdom had completely arrived just yet.

Herein lies one of the major issues of historical Jesus scholarship: To what degree was Jesus' vision of the kingdom tied into apocalypticism's belief that the kingdom was imminent? And, following this question, was Jesus mistaken? To answer these questions we have to examine what Jesus did say, and not all would agree that each of these sayings is authentic, though most might agree that the general theme was utilized by the historical Jesus.

First, the future kingdom Jesus expected grew out of Jewish soil and his vision was that old Jewish vision (cf. Mark 11:10; Luke 19:11; 23:42), and it is worth reminding ourselves that the acts of the Messiah in Matt 11:2–6 evince such a continuity with typical Israelite expectation. Second, those who will enter the future kingdom are those who are presently entering the kingdom Jesus declares (Matt 4:23; 13:19; 24:14; Luke 4:43; 8:1; 9:11; 22:29–30). Because the disciples were charged with extending Jesus' vision of the kingdom to others, those who responded to them would also enter that future kingdom (Matt 10:7; cf. 16:19; Luke 9:60; 10:9, 11).

Third, the future kingdom will begin with a judgment, which seems to be enacted by Jesus himself (cf. Matt 20:21), which is universal (25:31–46), and which separates people into judgment and salvation (25:46). That final kingdom is characterized by the Father's final approval and by the metaphor of table fellowship (Matt 13:43; 25:34; Luke 12:32; also Mark 14:25). The final kingdom, it goes without saying, will be magnificent and glorious (Matt 13:39, 49; Mark 9:1).

What then of Jesus' expectation? The first thing that needs to be said is that several texts shape the entire discussion, and they should be printed here.

> And he said to them, "Truly I tell you, there are some standing here who will not taste death until they see that the kingdom of God has come with power.
>
> (Mark 9:1)

> When they persecute you in one town, flee to the next; for truly I tell you, you will not have gone through all the towns of Israel before the Son of Man comes.
>
> (Matt 10:23)

> As they were listening to this, he went on to tell a parable, because he was near Jerusalem, and because they supposed that the kingdom of God was to appear immediately.
>
> (Luke 19:11)

> Truly I tell you, this generation will not pass away until all these things have taken place. Heaven and earth will pass away, but my words will not pass away.
>
> (Mark 13:30–31)

In some theological traditions, which shape both what one knows and how one is to "make such knowledge," such texts are either ignored or explained in such a way that one's faith is unchallenged. On the other hand, some Historical Jesus scholars find such traditions to be unworthy of intellectual freedom. What postmodernity has clearly taught is that there is not a group of free thinkers who have broken free of blind faith, but that each of us is shaped by our context, and it could be as much the context of the so-called "free thinkers" who are shaped by a tradition to find what they already believe (McKnight 2005: 3–6).

We begin with this: Jesus admits that he does not know exactly when the kingdom of God, or the Eschaton, will be consummated. Mark 13:32: "But about that day or hour no one knows, neither the angels in heaven, nor the Son, but only the Father." Second, Jesus clearly believes something big will happen within a generation – which means at some level his own eschatology has within it a sense of immanency. In light of Mark 13:24–27, it can be said with a fair degree of confidence that Jesus used apocalyptic images for the destruction of Jerusalem in 70 CE (Wright 339–68) as the singular event that was imminent. What Jesus expected beyond that day can only be guessed. Did he think that everything would be consummated at that time? Of course, the evidence can be read that way, but can we believe the gospel writers would write something that they thought made Jesus look wrong? Did he capture the destruction of Jerusalem in language, so typical for Jewish prophecy and apocalypticism, that connected the next big event in history with the final event in history? Probably so. Where many have been led by such considerations is that Jesus was not wrong, but that he was, like all Jewish prophets, limited in his knowledge to what the Father made known to him.

While such considerations are distracting to some, the study of prophetic language has shown that what Jesus did with his predictions was to capture the imminent work of God in real history with images that were drawn from the prophetic scriptures and which were pulled together into a new mix that evoked readiness and warning on the part of those who heard Jesus. Maybe, after all, C. H. Dodd was onto something, and just maybe the work of G. B. Caird (243–71) as brought up to date by N. T. Wright, has pointed the way forward:

apocalyptic language is not a snapshot of what *will* exactly happen but a Monet-like impression of the fact that God *will* work and *does* work.

SCOT MCKNIGHT

Further reading

Allison, D. *Jesus of Nazareth: Millenarian Prophet*, Minneapolis, MN: Fortress Press, 1998.

Beasley-Murray, G. *Jesus and the kingdom of God*, Grand Rapids, MI: Eerdmans, 1986.

Bryan, S. M. *Jesus and Israel's Traditions of Judgement and Restoration*, Cambridge: Cambridge University Press, 2002.

Caird, G. B. *The Language and Imagery of the Bible*, Louisville, KY: WJKP, 1980.

Dodd, C. H. *The Parables of the Kingdom*, London: Nisbet, 1936.

Dunn, J. D. G. *Jesus Remembered*, Grand Rapids, MI: Eerdmans, 2003.

Evans, C. A. *Jesus and His Contemporaries: Comparative Studies*, Leiden: Brill, 1995.

Freyne, S. *Jesus, A Jewish Galilean*, London: T. & T. Clark, 2004.

Fuller, R. H. *The Mission and Achievement of Jesus*, London: SCM Press, 1954.

Horsley, R. A. *Jesus and the Spiral of Violence*, San Francisco, CA: Harper & Row, 1987.

Jeremias, J. *New Testament Theology: The Proclamation of Jesus*, New York: Charles Scribner's Sons, 1971.

Kümmel, W. G. *Promise and Fulfillment: The Eschatological Message of Jesus*, London: SCM Press, 1957 [1946].

Ladd, G. E. *The Presence of the Future*, Grand Rapids, MI: Eerdmans, 1974 [1964].

McKnight, S. *A New Vision for Israel*, Grand Rapids, MI: Eerdmans, 1999.

—— *Jesus and His Death: Historiography, the Historical Jesus, and Atonement Theory*, Waco, TX: Baylor University Press, 2005.

Sanders, E. P. *Jesus and Judaism*, Philadelphia, PA: Fortress Press, 1983.

Schweitzer, A. *The Mystery of the kingdom of God: The Secret of Jesus' Messiahship and Passion*, New York: Schocken, 1964 [1901].

—— *The Quest for the Historical Jesus: A Critical Study of Its Progress from Reimarus to Wrede*, Minneapolis, MN: Fortress Press, 2001 [1906].

Theissen, G. and Merz, A. *The Historical Jesus*. Minneapolis, MN: Fortress Press, 1998.

Weiss, J. *Jesus' Proclamation of the kingdom of God*, Chico, CA: Scholars Press, 1985 [1892].

Wright, N. T. *Jesus and the Victory of God*, Minneapolis, MN: Fortress Press, 1996.

KLAUSNER, JOSEPH

Joseph Gedaliah Klausner (1874–1958) was a Jewish literary critic, historian, and Zionist as well as a professor of modern Jewish language and literature at the Hebrew University in Jerusalem from 1925. His significance for the study of the historical Jesus is mainly related to his book *Jesus of Nazareth: His Life, Times, and Teaching* (published in English in 1925; Hebrew original 1922), to a lesser extent to his other books translated into English (see bibliography).

Klausner's book was the first scholarly presentation of Jesus in the Hebrew language, written for a Jewish public. For this reason it attracted attention both in Jewish and Christian circles even if there was little new and sensational in the book. Nevertheless it became a milestone because it made Jewish study of Jesus a "kosher" subject (Sandmel 2004: 464). The fact that the author was well versed both in the Jewish sources and in the critical research of the life of Jesus made his book appealing also to non-Jewish readers. Soon it was translated into several European languages, and for decades it was regarded as the most important Jewish book on Jesus.

The main source of knowledge for the life and teaching of Jesus is, according to Klausner, the canonical gospels. The references to Jesus in Talmud are of little historical value, but some early traditions prove his existence. Among the gospels, Mark is the most important, composed near the time of the destruction of the Temple, based on written Aramaic (or Hebrew) sources. The Evangelists wrote for religious, not biographical or historical reasons. Thus it is difficult to know the chronological order of the events. Nevertheless Klausner uses the narrative structure of the synoptic gospel as basis for his biographical sketch of the life of Jesus.

Jesus in his Galilean context

Klausner's Jewish approach is apparent in his lengthy treatment of the political, economic and religious conditions of the times of Jesus. In Klausner's opinion these conditions were determined for Jesus and his teaching. The oppressive and cruel government of Herod and the Romans had created "unbalanced" men. They were either fanatic freedom fighters who joined the Zealots, or they were despairing visionaries and mystics "who abandoned interest in temporal things to dream of a future life, a life based on the ethics of the Prophets and the messianic idea ... It was from these circles of the 'meek' that Jesus and his new teaching sprang" (1925: 173).

Jesus had some points of resemblance with the Essenes, but it was first and foremost the Pharisees who influenced his teaching. Jesus conducted himself like a scribe or Pharisee and was regarded as such by the people. He differed, however, from the scribes and Pharisees in that he used parables instead of Scriptural exposition. Another notable feature was his miracles, which he himself understood as a sign of the Messianic age. These made him very popular among the simple people of Galilee, among whom there were many with mental afflictions. Klausner accepts that Jesus did miracles, especially in the cases when he cured nervous cases and hysterical women. This was possible through "Jesus's amazing, hypnotic personal influence" (1925: 270). Some of Jesus' miracles are brushed aside as hallucinations of simple, oriental people or explained as natural phenomena. When Jesus sometimes denied doing miracles, the explanation is that they not always were successful and therefore he was afraid to attempt them too often.

Jesus the Messiah

Klausner depicts Jesus as "a great and imaginative dreamer" who thought of himself as the Messiah. At his baptism – the most decisive moment in his life – Jesus's imagination led him to think that "the Shekinah shed his light upon him" (1925: 252), and he came to believe that he was the hoped-for Messiah.

Jesus had an "exaggerated sense of nearness to God" (1925: 378), which misled him to stress his own teaching in opposition to Moses and the prophets. In his excessive emphasis on the words "my heavenly Father" we find the germ to Paul's teaching of Jesus as the Son of God and the later doctrine of the Trinity. Because the Sanhedrin (mainly composed of Sadducees) saw Jesus as a troublemaker claiming to be the Messiah, they delivered him to the Roman governor who was responsible for his crucifixion. The story about the empty tomb came into existence because Joseph of Arimathea secretly removed the body and buried it in an unknown grave. The belief in the resurrection is not, however, based on a deception. "The women and disciples actually saw Jesus after his crucifixion – in a vision which appeared to them, enthusiastic to the point of madness and credulous to the point of blindness, as a complete reality" (1943: 256).

On the whole, Klausner portrays Jesus as a devout, Law-observant Jew. Klausner detects, however, a kernel to the abrogation of the ceremonial laws in Jesus's teaching, especially when he permitted foods forbidden by the Law of Moses (cf. Mark 7:17–23). "*Ex nihilo nihil fit:* had not Jesus's teaching contained a kernel of opposition to Judaism, Paul could never *in the name of Jesus* have set aside the ceremonial laws, and broken through the barriers of national Judaism" (1925: 369).

The main strength of Jesus lay in his ethical teaching. His ethics was not original; everything he taught can be found in the Old Testament or in the rabbinic literature. The only distinctive feature was his one-sided emphasis on individual ethics. Jesus showed no interest in social ethics and civil legislation. Jesus' lack of interest in family life, private property and civil justice was a consequence of his misapprehension of the nearness of the kingdom of God. Klausner criticizes the ethics of Jesus for being impossible in practice and for not embracing the whole of life and therefore not serving the Jewish nation. Jesus' ethics is an ideal ethics for the days of the Messiah, and one day his ethics may be regarded as "one of the choicest treasures in the literature of Israel for all time" (1925: 414).

Reactions to Klausner's work

Klausner's book on Jesus has been criticized for an uncritical approach both to rabbinic literature and the gospels. His reconstruction of the political and cultural conditions is questionable on many points. Klausner argues, for instance, for a sharp distinction between the "pure" Palestinian Judaism and the Hellenistic Judaism of the Diaspora influenced by paganism. This dichotomy cannot be upheld (cf. Kümmel 171–72); neither can his picture of the rural Galilee and its simple-minded inhabitants. Another embarrassing feature in Klausner's book is his tendency to offer psychological interpretations both of individuals and groups; they are highly questionable from a methodological point of view and seldom convincing.

Klausner stresses his objective attitude to the material, but fails to live up to the ideal. For one thing it is very evident that his evaluation of Jesus is controlled by his nationalistic/Zionistic view of Judaism. Besides, he explicitly says that the aim of his book "is not only to give the life of Jesus but also to explain why his teaching has not proved acceptable to the nation from which he sprang" (1925: 361). "For Klausner, rewriting the story of Jesus in Hebrew for the Jewish people is, in the final analysis, the act of a devoted Jewish nationalist who utilizes the methods of the critical study of religion to serve his people" (Sandmel 2002: 116).

REIDAR HVALVIK

Further reading

Klausner, J. *Jesus of Nazareth: His Life, Times, and Teaching*, New York: Macmillan, 1925.
—— *From Jesus to Paul*, New York: Macmillan, 1943.
—— *The Messianic Idea in Israel from Its Beginning to the Completion of the Mishnah*, New York: Macmillan, 1955.

Hagner, D. A. *The Jewish Reclamation of Jesus: An Analysis and Critique of the Modern Jewish Study of Jesus*, Grand Rapids, MI: Zondervan, 1984.

Kling, J. *Joseph Klausner*, New York: Thomas Yoseloff, 1970.

Kümmel, W. G. "Jesus und Paulus: Zu Joseph Klausners Darstellung des Urchristentums," in *Heilsgeschehen und Geschichte: Gesammelte Aufsätze 1933–1964*. Marburg: Elwert, 1965, pp. 439–56.

Lindeskog, G. *Die Jesusfrage im neuzeitlichen Judentum: Ein Beitrag zur Geschichte der Leben-Jesu-Forschung*, Uppsala: n.p., 1938; second edition Darmstadt: Wissenschaftliche Buchgesellschaft, 1973.

Sandmel, D. F. "Into the Fray: Joseph Klausner's Approach to Judaism and Christianity in the Greco-Roman World," dissertation, University of Pennsylvania, 2002.

—— "Joseph Klausner, Israel, and Jesus," *CurTM* 31:6 (2004) 456–64.

L

LANGUAGE CRITICISM

There have been four significant stages in language criticism with regard to the study of the historical Jesus. The history of discussion of language criticism is closely tied to the issues of both the language or languages that Jesus spoke and the language of the New Testament. While these four periods of language criticism are somewhat successive, they also have an element of contiguity that will become obvious in the presentation.

Aramaic emphasis

Nineteenth-century biblical scholarship rejected the notion that the language of the New Testament was a specially inspired form of Greek. Discussion of the language of Jesus, according to Schweitzer (*Historical Jesus*, 269–78, who claims to follow A. Meyer), went back to the sixteenth century. At that time, Joseph Scaliger, on the basis of a Syriac translation of the Bible and comparison with the Targums, was able to distinguish between Syriac and Aramaic, something previous scholarship had not done. Further work through the subsequent centuries was able to distinguish dialects of Aramaic. There was also recognition of the linguistic complexity of early Christianity, with there being advocates for Hebrew and Greek (and even Latin!) as the language of the Jews of the time. In the late nineteenth century, several grammars of Aramaic by Emil Kautzsch and Gustaf Dalman – were written that had an important influence in confirming Aramaic as the major language of the Jews

of the time of Jesus in Palestine – although many if not most scholars recognized that, at the time, Aramaic, Greek and Hebrew were all used. As a result, there were a number of attempts to retrovert the language of the New Testament into Hebrew and Aramaic. Franz Delitzsch translated the New Testament back into Hebrew. A number of scholars retroverted parts or particular grammatical patterns of the New Testament back into Aramaic, including Eberhard Nestle, Julius Wellhausen, Arnold Meyer, Friedrich Blass, Gustaf Dalman, Charles Torrey, and C. F. Burney. Some of these scholars did this for the sake of gaining understanding of the underlying Aramaic usage on the basis of perceived linguistic oddities in the Greek of the New Testament, while others, such as Nestle, Burney, and Torrey, were intent upon trying to establish an Aramaic source behind the gospels. These early and enthusiastic attempts at retroversion were criticized both then and later, even when various Semitic language hypotheses were revived (see below). For example, Hans Lietzmann had proposed that the term "son of man" in its original Aramaic meant simply "man," but this was rejected by Dalman, who argued that it was biblical language that reflected Daniel 7:13 (256–57). Later, many of the Semitic revivalists also criticized the excesses of this Aramaic emphasis. Matthew Black (6–7), for example, criticizes the use of the Aramaic of the Targums as the source language of comparison, the use of the primarily Alexandrian rather than the Western Greek text for collation, and, especially, the weight given to supposed errors in translation of the original Aramaic into Greek. Even for such material as the parables, Black contends that the "translation" is "not literal but literary," and hence the original cannot be reconstructed (Black 274).

Papyri appreciation

The discovery of the Greek documentary papyri in the late nineteenth century brought to the fore numerous Greek texts that had no literary pretensions but seemed to reflect the language of common people caught in the course of their everyday communication. Adolf Deissmann saw in these papyrus documents linguistic parallels to the Greek of the New Testament. This led to a response to the Aramaic emphasis that had been building in the nineteenth century. Among others, three scholars stand out for their work on the Greek of the time. Deissmann was one of the first to promote the papyri as important for understanding the Greek of the New Testament. He emphasized the Greek of the New Testament as similar to that of the popular Greek found in the Egyptian papyri. Deissmann, to be fair, accepted that portions of the material in the gospels were translated from Aramaic into Greek, but he doubted whether one could reconstruct the Aramaic *Vorlage* (as one could do with the Septuagint). Instead, Deissmann argued that most Jews of the time knew Greek, many as a first language. Therefore, he argued for examination of the Greek of the New Testament first before proceeding to evaluation of its Semitic elements. The observations and approach of Deissmann were applied more widely to the grammar and lexis of the Greek of the New Testament by James Hope Moulton and by Albert Thumb. Such findings served to reinforce the findings of those who argued that Greek was a possible language of Jesus. They contended that a number of the features of the language of Jesus in Greek in the New Testament may not have been instances of translation from Aramaic into Greek but of the vernacular in use at the time. Besides those numerous scholars who have recognized the multilingual environment of Palestine of the first century (e.g. T. K. Abbott, Schweitzer, George Milligan, J. Sevenster, Saul Lieberman, etc.), scholars such as A. Roberts, William Sanday, and Dalman in the earlier period, and later such scholars as Gustav Bardy, A. W. Argyle, and Nigel Turner, among others, argued that Jesus spoke Greek. Establishing that Greek was widely used in the Greco-Roman world, including in Palestine, however, is a far remove from establishing that Jesus used Greek in particular instances.

Semitic revival

The major advocates for study of the Greek of the New Testament in the light of the papyri and other documentary evidence were taken from the scholarly scene fairly quickly. This fact, combined with advances in Semitic language studies, including appreciation of the Qumran discoveries and advances in Targumic studies, led to a Semitic revival. It was during this time that the Semitic language criterion became a significant criterion for authenticity in study of the historical Jesus. Joachim Jeremias, who built upon the research by Burney (see above), was probably the first to use the Semitic or Aramaic language criterion widely in attempting to establish the authentic sayings of Jesus (see Porter 2000: 89–99). The method that he utilized in such works as his *Parables of Jesus, The Eucharistic Words of Jesus, Jerusalem in the Time of Jesus*, and his *New Testament Theology*, among others, was actually more encompassing than simply examining linguistic phenomena. Jeremias and others believed that there were a number of Palestinian environmental features noted in the gospels that indicate an origin of a particular tradition in Palestine itself. Scholars typically cite such environmental indicators as reference to customs, practices, geography or beliefs thought characteristic of Palestine in the first century, and supposedly known only by one who had firsthand familiarity with that particular place or location. The linguistic criterion functions similarly. Scholars note particular linguistic phenomena in the Greek usage of the New Testament that they believe are to be traced back to a Semitic, and, in most instances, an Aramaic original statement. There have been recent advocates of Hebrew as a language of the Jews of the time, and of Jesus (e.g. H. Birkeland), but the vast majority of scholars concentrate upon Aramaic. There has been discussion of what form of Aramaic was in use at the time. As Stuckenbruck recounts ("Approach"), the three major proposals have been the Targumic Aramaic of Onqelos (argued by Dalman), the Aramaic of the Cairo Geniza and Qumran Aramaic (argued by Paul Kahle), and Palestinian Aramaic (argued by Joseph Fitzmyer). This Aramaic language criterion has been used by numerous scholars. Some of the best known are T. W. Manson, Matthew Black, Fitzmyer, James D. G. Dunn, among many others.

There are several factors that make the Semitic revival different from the previous Aramaic emphasis. One is the milieu used for comparison. The earliest advocates of the Aramaic background of the New Testament examined it in terms of the New Testament as a Greek document and in terms of a Greek milieu. This later period has tended to downplay the multilingual nature of first-century Palestine and concentrate upon the Semitic background, including treatment of Jesus as virtually a unilingual Aramaic language user. A second factor is the development of more explicit criteria for linguistic comparison to determine the degree of Semitic influence. Thus, rather than simply listing Aramaic features as does Meyer, Black and others are more explicit in analyzing the possibilities in Aramaic regarding an individual phenomenon.

There have been two further developments with regard to the Semitic revival that are also worth noting. One is the work of Maurice Casey (1998). Casey contends that the Aramaic found in the Dead Sea Scrolls and that of the Targums provides a sufficient linguistic basis for establishing the kind of Aramaic in use in Palestine in the first century, to the point of being able to reconstruct the Aramaic substrata at several places in the Gospel of Mark (e.g. 9:11–13; 2:23–3:6; 10:35–45; 14:12–26). Casey believes that on the basis of our current knowledge we can essentially overcome the shortcomings of Meyer and Black, and he attempts to correct them by using the Aramaic of the Dead Sea Scrolls and other sources – even though he uses essentially the same method of retroversion based upon supposed translational difficulties in the Greek text. A second development is Chilton's and Evans's development of further criteria for determining whether Jesus' words reflect an Aramaic Targumic source. Chilton posits dictional – places where there is significant verbal similarity – and thematic coherence (1984). To these two, Evans adds exegetical coherence, which means that Jesus understands a passage in the same way as the Aramaic translators or interpreters (see Black: "Introduction," xv–xvii). These new criteria are designed to show that earlier interpretive traditions reflected in the later Targums also had an influence upon the words that Jesus used.

Despite the widespread use of this form of language criticism, there has been repeated criticism of the Aramaic language criterion in study of the New Testament. Lincoln Hurst ("Neglected Role") has made a number of telling points against such theories. These include the failure to recognize that the polysemous nature of words in languages – and their discontinuous mapping of various semantic fields within languages – makes iconicity between lexical items in two different languages virtually impossible. Thus, even if one were convinced that the Greek text is a translation of Aramaic,

attempting to establish the Aramaic is highly problematic. A second factor is failure to recognize and take into account diachronic linguistic development. This affects the chronological state of each language being compared and fails to recognize that change in language does not occur uniformly across phenomena (and certainly across languages). A related factor is that there are various linguistic levels (or styles) of any given language that must be taken into account, including in translation. Third is the varied nature and purposes of translations, even in the ancient world (as witnessed by the Septuagint). Ancient translation theory has not been sufficiently taken into account in attempts at retroversion. As a result of these and related criticisms, opinion is mixed regarding the use of an Aramaic language criterion in historical Jesus research. Some wish to use it to reinforce and confirm other criteria, while others treat it as of dubious worth and at best a secondary criterion (see Meier 178–80). Even those who, like Chilton, believe in its use admit to its limitations in establishing material independent of the Jesus tradition. The issue of establishing material by means of language criteria that are distinct to Jesus seems to assume a greater knowledge than is currently available, both with regard to the use of language at the time and with regard to the rate at which supposed Semitic elements increase or decrease in frequency in the tradition.

Linguistic evaluation

Much language criticism of the New Testament continues to be done reflecting the criteria of the Aramaic revival (see above for proponents). However, there have been several recent developments that prompt further linguistic evaluation of the New Testament, in particular the language of Jesus. One is the development of further linguistic criteria for evaluation of the ancient languages involved. Another is continued analysis of the Greek and Semitic language evidence from the ancient world, including further recognition of the multilingual milieu of first-century Palestine (e.g. Robert Gundry, Moisés Silva, Gerald Mussies, Martin Hengel, Sean Freyne, Eric Meyers and James Strange, Tessa Rajak, Bo Reicke, Greg Horsley, Peter van der Horst, among others). A number of scholars – such as G. R. Selby, Fitzmyer, Philip Hughes, Hans Dieter Betz, John Meier, Willem Vorster, Evans, and Ben Witherington, among others – are willing to admit the probability that Jesus spoke Greek on occasion. As a result, if it is possible Jesus spoke in Greek, then it should be possible to identify places where he possibly did speak Greek. Three new criteria of language criticism have recently been put forward to help in this effort (see Porter 2000, part II; Porter 2003).

Greek language and its context

The first is the criterion of Greek language and its context. This is a criterion of probability. This criterion analyzes units that contain actions and words of Jesus and others in the light of the multilingual context of first-century Palestine, including Galilee. An attempt is made to determine whether the units exemplify a plausible Greek-language-based correlation between the participants and their language or actions to determine if Jesus did speak Greek on a particular occasion. This criterion bases its correlation on three areas – (1) the participants and their background; (2) the events depicted; and (3) the context and theme of discussion – to determine whether in a particular instance Greek words of Jesus are recorded. On the basis of this criterion, eight possible passages where Jesus may have spoken Greek have been identified (in ascending order of probability):

Luke 17:11–19: Jesus' conversation with the healed leper (possibility);
John 4:4–26: Jesus' conversation with the Samaritan woman (some probability);
Mark 2:13–14//Matt 9:9//Luke 5:27–28: Jesus' calling of Levi or Matthew (reasonable probability);
Mark 12:13–17//Matt 22:16–22//Luke 20:20–26: Jesus' conversation with the Pharisees and Herodians (reasonable probability);
Mark 8:27–30//Matt 16:13–20//Luke 9:18–21: Jesus' conversation with his disciples (reasonably high probability);
Mark 7:25–30//Matt 15:21–28: Jesus' conversation with the Syrophoenician or Canaanite woman (reasonably high probability);
Matthew 8:5–13//John 4:46–54: Jesus' conversation with the centurion (reasonably high probability);
Mark 15:2–5//Matt 27:11–14; Luke 23:2–4//John 18:29–38: Jesus' conversation with Pilate (reasonably high probability).

So far, this criterion has elicited the most response in terms of recognition of it as a valid attempt to develop new language criteria in the light of the historical issues involved (see McKnight 45; Bird; response in Porter; cf. Dunn 82–83, who notes all three criteria).

Greek textual variance

The second new language criterion is that of Greek textual variance. Systematic study of Greek text-critical issues has been relatively neglected in discussion of the language of Jesus, because of the influence of the Aramaic language hypothesis (see above), but has been revived in recent discussion (see Porter and O'Donnell 1998a; 1998). This criterion attempts to move beyond the question of whether a given episode may record the tenor of Jesus' words and asks whether we may have the actual words themselves, and it uses variants in the textual tradition to determine this. This criterion requires multiple traditions or multiple forms that can be shown to be independent of each other, and argues that the level of variation in the traditions increases as the traditions are further removed from the common source. Of the passages noted above, four qualify for further analysis:

Mark 12:13–17//Matt 22:16–22//Luke 20:20–26: Jesus' conversation with the Pharisees and Herodians (content but no actual words);
Mark 8:27–30//Matt 16:13–20//Luke 9:18–21: Jesus' conversation with his disciples (probably some actual words);
Mark 7:25–30//Matt 15:21–28: Jesus' conversation with the Syrophoenician or Canaanite woman (probably some actual words);
Mark 15:2–5//Matt 27:11–14; Luke 23:2–4//John 18:29–38: Jesus' conversation with Pilate (probably actual words).

Discourse features

The third criterion is that of discourse features. To utilize this criterion, a linguistically based discourse model is applied to analysis of an extended body of material, in this instance Mark 13:5–37, the single largest discourse in Mark's Gospel. This criterion examines the elements of the register of the discourse: the mode of discourse and its textual function, the tenor of discourse and its interpersonal function, and the field of discourse and its informational function. This analysis isolates the particular discourse and compares it to features of the larger gospel in which it is embedded. The conclusions for this particular passage are that – if it is taken as a unity (an assumption of the method for the sake of performing the analysis) – the evidence points to the discourse in Mark 13 as an earlier unitary tradition that has been placed within the gospel, with minimal changes made to adapt it to the style of the gospel itself.

Conclusion

Rather than becoming simpler, the field of language criticism of the gospels, and in particular the language of Jesus, is becoming more complex. The areas of complexity include: recognition of the multilingualism of the first-century Mediterranean world; greater appreciation of the range and type of sources available for analysis; utilization of increasingly sophisticated linguistic methods that take into consideration the particular problems related to the study of ancient languages; greater utilization of linguistic insights regarding factors in a multilingual environment, such as prestige language; and increasing refinements in the general field of historical Jesus studies. With development and refinement of various forms of language criticism, there is potential for greater insight into the language of the Gospels and of Jesus.

STANLEY E. PORTER

Further reading

Bird, M. F. "The Criterion of Greek Language and Context: A Response to Stanley E. Porter," *Journal for the Study of the Historical Jesus* 4:1 (2006) 55–67.

Black, M. *An Aramaic Approach to the Gospels and Acts*, third edition with Introduction "An Aramaic Approach Thirty Years Later" by C. A. Evans, Peabody, MA: Hendrickson, 1998 [1946/1967].

Casey, M. *Aramaic Sources of Mark's Gospel*, Cambridge: Cambridge University Press, 1998.

Chilton, B. D. *A Galilean Rabbi and his Bible: Jesus' Use of the Interpreted Scripture of his Time*, Wilmington, DE: Michael Glazier, 1984.

Dalman, G. *The Words of Jesus Considered in the Light of Post-Biblical Jewish Writings and the Aramaic Language*, trans. D. M. Kay; Edinburgh: T. & T. Clark, 1909 [1898].

Dunn, J. D. G. *Jesus Remembered*, Grand Rapids, MI: Eerdmans, 2003.

Hurst, L. D. "The Neglected Role of Semantics in the Search for the Aramaic Words of Jesus," *JSNT* 28 (1986) 63–80.

McKnight, S. *Jesus and his Death: Historiography, the Historical Jesus, and Atonement Theory*, Waco, TX: Baylor University Press, 2005.

Meier, J. P. *A Marginal Jew*, I, New York: Doubleday, 1991.

Porter, S. E. *The Criteria for Authenticity in Historical-Jesus Research: Previous Discussion and New Proposals*, Sheffield: Sheffield Academic Press, 2000.

—— "Luke 17.11–19 and the Criteria for Authenticity Revisited," *Journal for the Study of the Historical Jesus* 1:2 (2003) 201–24.

—— "The Criterion of Greek Language and its Context: A Further Response," *Journal for the Study of the Historical Jesus* 4:1 (2006) 69–74.

Porter, S. E. and M. B. O'Donnell. "The Implications of Textual Variants for Authenticating the Activities of Jesus," in B. Chilton and C. A. Evans (eds) *Authenticating the Activities of Jesus*, Leiden: Brill, 1998a, pp. 121–51.

—— "The Implications of Textual Variants for Authenticating the Words of Jesus," in B. Chilton and C. A. Evans (eds) *Authenticating the Words of Jesus*, Leiden: Brill, 1998b, pp. 97–133.

Schweitzer, A. *The Quest of the Historical Jesus: A Critical Study of its Progress from Reimarus to Wrede*, trans. W. Montgomery; London: A. & C. Black, 1910 [1906].

Stuckenbruck, L. T. "An Approach to the New Testament through Aramaic Sources: The Recent Methodological Debate," *JSP* 8 (1991) 3–29.

LAST SUPPER, WORDS OF INSTITUTION

Jesus' Last Supper as a Passover meal

According to the Synoptic Gospels, Jesus' Last Supper was a Passover meal (Mark 14:12; Matt 26:17; Luke 22:7). The Gospel of John has been construed as placing Jesus' Last Supper on the day before Passover, but this is unnecessary. The ambiguity of Passover terminology allows the possibility of interpreting the reference to "eating the Passover" (φάγωσιν τὸ πάσχα) in John 18:28 as referring to eating the festival meal offered on Nisan 15, the first day of the feast, a requirement for all participants (see *m. Hag.* 1:3; *m. Pesah.* 6:3). In addition, the phrase παρασκευὴ τοῦ πάσχα in John 19:14 does not necessarily mean the "eve of Passover" (Nisan 14), but could be translated as Friday of Passover (week).

Because they are highly selective, the accounts of Jesus' Last Supper are not recognizable as a Passover meal. (Even Jesus' Last Supper in John shows no signs of being a Passover meal.) For this reason, knowledge of how a typical Passover meal in the first century would have proceeded is necessary in order to reconstruct Jesus' Last Supper. Information about Passover comes primarily from early rabbinic sources (*Mishnah, Tosefta, Mekilta, Sifre* [Numbers and Deuteronomy], *Sifra, Exodus Rabba, Genesis Rabba* and Targums). These can be supplemented by a few pre-destruction texts (New Testament, Septuagint, Josephus' works, *Book of Jubilees, Temple Scroll* and Philo's writings). On the assumption that early rabbinic sources preserve reliable historical material, a typical, pre-destruction Passover meal consisted of four courses structured around four cups of wine. In the evening of Nisan 15, a Passover habura meets together. (A new day begins at sunset.) The pouring of the first cup of wine followed by a blessing over it begins the first course of appetizers consisting of at least salad ("bitter herbs"), salad dressing and wine. The second course is begun by the pouring and blessing of a second cup, at which time the habura reclines together. The meal consists of at least unleavened bread, salad, salad dressing, fruit puree (*charoset*) and the Passover lamb. Following the blessing over the second cup comes the recitation of the Passover haggada and possibly the singing of the first part of the hallel. The paterfamilias then takes some of the unleavened bread, breaks it, says a blessing over it and distributes it. This signals the beginning of the main course. In order to bring the main course to an end, the paterfamilias takes a third cup of wine, called the cup of blessing, and says a blessing over it. No dessert course follows, however. At some point a fourth cup of wine is poured and a blessing is said over it, bringing Passover to a close. The second part of the hallel is sung.

Passover commemorates Israel's Exodus from Egypt, the realization of the covenant made with Abraham. The blood of the original Passover lambs is interpreted as redemptive. In the *Mekilta*, the "blood of the covenant" in Zech 9:11 is identified with the blood of the original Passover offerings, along with the blood of circumcision (Pisha 5:11–14; see *Tg.* on Zech 9:11). The same is true of the twofold blood in Ezek 16:6 (*Mek*. Pisha 5:1–10). Similarly, *Exod R.* 12:22 (17:3) and 12:43 (19:5) affirm that God protected the Israelites' first-born in Egypt because of the two kinds of blood – circumcision and Passover. *Tg. Ps-J.* on Exod 12:5 also interprets the blood of the Passover lambs and of circumcision as the means of Israel's redemption from Egypt. Finally, R. Meir is quoted as teaching that the redemptive benefit of the blood of the original Passover lambs was the expiation of sin (*Exod R.* 12:1 [15:12]).

At some point in the development of Jewish haggada, the Binding of Isaac is brought into relation to Passover. The blood of the Passover lambs is viewed as efficacious as a result of Abraham's prior willingness to sacrifice Isaac and Isaac's willingness to be sacrificed (*Frg. Tg.* on Gen 22; *Mek*. Pisha 7:78–82, 11:92–96). The same idea occurs in the poem of the four (Passover) nights in the Palestinian Targums, where it is specified that the binding of Isaac took place on Passover night.

In the LXX, *Mekilta*, and the Targumic material, there is evidence that, for its first-century participants, Passover anticipates the hope of a redemption analogous to the Exodus on the same date in the future. LXX Jer 31:8 (38:8) places the restoration of Israel – and by implication the establishment of the new covenant – on Passover. In the *Mekilta*, Nisan 15 is the designated time of redemption (*Mek*. Pisha 14:113–21). According to the poem of the four (Passover) nights, on the first Passover

night the world was created, and the Lord revealed himself to Abraham on the second Passover night. The third night saw the Exodus of the Israelites, in fulfillment of the promise to Abraham. The fourth night, the time of Israel's eschatological redemption, is yet to come. That Passover is the time of eschatological redemption is also found in *Exod R.* 12:1 (15:11).

Literary and tradition-historical analysis

There are four sources for a historical reconstruction of Jesus' Last Supper. Paul cites a version of the words of institution (1 Cor 11:23–26). Matthew, Mark, and Luke also have versions of the words of institution (Matt 26:26–29; Mark 14:22–25; Luke 22:15–20), situating them within the context of Jesus' last Passover meal (Matt 26:17–30; Mark 14:12–26; Luke 22:7–23). It is probable that Matthew is literarily dependent upon Mark. The question of the literary relation of Luke to Mark and 1 Cor 11:23–26 is more controversial. (The longer text of Luke, inclusive of Luke 22:19b–20, should be taken as more original.) It is probable that Luke 22:7–14 is literarily dependent on Mark 14:12–17. Luke 22:15–18, however, is likely an independent account with tradition-historical parallels to Mark 14:22–25. Luke 22:19a has numerous parallels to Mark 14:22a, but Luke 22:19b–20 is closer to 1 Cor 11:23–25. It is probable that Luke 22:19–20 is part of a liturgical tradition that is literarily independent of the forms of the tradition found in Mark 14:22–24 and 1 Cor 11:23–25. In addition, Luke seems to intend that 22:15–18 and 22:19–20 be read as a single chronological sequence and not as two versions of the same event. Finally, the Lukan announcement of the betrayal (22:21–23) is likely literarily independent of Mark 14:18b–21. In short, there are three literarily independent accounts of Jesus' Last Supper: Mark, Luke and 1 Cor.

The Markan and Lukan accounts of Jesus' Last Supper shows signs of being literarily composite. Mark seems to consist of traditions that once circulated orally and independently of one another, and are now connected by means of Markan redactional links: 14:12–16; 14:17–21; 14:22–24; 14:25. Likewise, Luke probably combines a portion of his Markan source (Luke 22:7–14||Mark 14:12–17) with non-Markan traditions (22:15–18; 22:19–20; 22:21–23). This accounts for the historical sketchiness of the narratives.

It is difficult to determine which of the three versions of the words of institution is closest to the hypothetical Aramaic original. There are three versions of the word over the bread: "This is my body" (τοῦτό ἐστιν τὸ σῶμά μου) (Mark 14:22); "This is my body given for you" (τοῦτό ἐστιν τὸ σῶμά μου τὸ ὑπὲρ ὑμῶν διδόμενον) (Luke 22:19); and "This is my body for you" (τοῦτό ἐστιν τὸ σῶμα τὸ ὑπὲρ ὑμῶν) (1 Cor 11:24). It would seem that the absence of the *hyper*-phrase in Mark is less original. If the two words of interpretation were separated from each other by an entire course, the simple identification of Jesus' σῶμα with the bread without further explanation would be unintelligible on its own. But if in the development of the eucharistic liturgy the meal framework was eliminated and the two words of interpretation were drawn together, it is understandable how the *hyper*-phrase could either become redundant and disappear or be moved to the word over the cup.

The versions of the word over the cup differ more widely: "This is my blood of the covenant shed for many" (τοῦτό ἐστιν τὸ αἷμά μου τῆς διθήκης τὸ ἐκχυννόμενον ὑπὲρ πολλῶν) (Mark 14:24); "This cup (is) the new covenant in my blood which (is) shed for you" (τοῦτο τὸ ποτήριον ἡ καινὴ διαθήκη ἐν τῷ αἷματί μου, τὸ ὑπὲρ ὑμῶν ἐκχυννόμενον) (Luke 22:20); and "This cup is the new covenant in my blood" (τοῦτο τὸ ποτήριον ἡ καινὴ διαθήκη ἐστιν ἐν τῷ ἐμῷ αἷματι) (1 Cor 11:25). The version of the word over the cup closest to the hypothetical Aramaic original is probably "This is the new covenant in my blood." What tips the balance in favor of the originality of the Lukan/Pauline version of the word over the cup is the parallelism exhibited in the Markan words of institution ("This is my body"/"This is my blood"), an indication of liturgical influence and, therefore, tradition-historical lateness. Moreover, Mark 14:24 cannot easily be translated into Aramaic. Luke has ἐν τῷ αἷματί μου as opposed to the Pauline ἐν τῷ ἐμῷ αἷματι. Of the two the Pauline is better Greek and is typical of the Lukan redactional style, whereas the Lukan form reflects the Semitic pronominal suffix. One is hard pressed to explain why Luke would make such a change. In addition, Luke's version does not have the copula ἐστιν, which again is both Semitic and non-Lukan. The Lukan participial phrase "which (is) shed for you" (τὸ ὑπὲρ ὑμῶν ἐκχυννόμενον) is likely less original. Luke's version of the word over the cup appears to be composite: there is a syntactical incongruity between the nominative τὸ ἐκχυννόμενον and its antecedent in the dative τῷ αἷματί μου. The ability of the Lukan version to tolerate the syntactical error of mismatched cases could be the result of liturgical use. In addition, the parallelism of the Lukan *hyper*-phrases is probably another indication of liturgical influence on Luke's version of the word over the cup.

Historical reconstruction

The events described in the gospels can be situated in the framework of a Passover meal. Contrary to what seems to be the usual practice at a festival meal, the first course is eaten in a reclining position (Mark 14:18; Luke 22:14). Before the start of the meal, Jesus tells his disciples that he will not eat the Passover again until it finds fulfillment in the kingdom of God (Luke 22:15–16; Mark 14:25). The Passover meal is a prefiguration of the messianic meal, to be held when the kingdom of God has come to completion. Jesus as the paterfamilias takes the first cup, and says a blessing over it. He then commands his disciples to take the cup and to divide its contents among themselves (Luke 22:17). Probably during the first course, Jesus announces his betrayal (Mark 14:20–21; Luke 22:21–23; John 13:24–30).

Next the second cup is mixed and the main course is brought out. Jesus says a blessing over the second cup. The Passover haggada is then recited, and the first part of the hallel is probably sung. Jesus next says the blessing over the bread, breaks it, distributes it and unexpectedly interprets it with reference to himself: "This is my body (given) for you." After the meal is complete, Jesus takes the third cup, the cup of blessing, gives thanks for the meal, passes the cup around, and again unexpectedly interprets it symbolically: "This cup is the new covenant in my blood." Jesus interprets the cup, or more precisely the red wine in the cup, as metaphorical of the blood that he is about to shed. One could paraphrase Jesus' words over the cup as follows: "The red wine in this cup represents the blood that I will shed in my death in order that the new covenant be established." After the third cup, presumably the fourth cup is poured and drunk, although there is no indication of this in the Last Supper narratives. The second part of the hallel is sung (Mark 14:26).

The separation of the words over the bread and the cup by the entire main course makes it probable that Jesus intends each word to make a self-contained point. His words over the bread "This is my body (given) for you" are said at the beginning of the meal. Taken by itself, it is a self-contained statement about the meaning of his impending death as vicarious. But when placed against a paschal background, Jesus' meaning can be further elucidated. Probably he is interpreting himself as the eschatological Passover lamb that will bring about expiation for eschatological Israel. Jesus sees his own death as typologically fulfilling the original Passover sacrifices as their eschatological counterpart, as giving them their true salvation-historical meaning. The tradition of the Binding of Isaac would make Jesus' communication of his own understanding of his death as the fulfillment or the antitype of the original Passover sacrifices relatively simple. It is just a matter of replacing Isaac with himself and making a few necessary salvation-historical alterations.

At the conclusion of the Passover meal, Jesus takes the third cup, the cup of blessing, and says about its contents that it is the new covenant in his blood, meaning that the new covenant is coming to realization through his death. The major reference to the new covenant in the Old Testament is Jer 31:31. The prophet speaks of a time in the future when God will make a new covenant with Israel and Judah. The new covenant is an eschatological idea. The covenant that Yahweh made with the generation of the exodus is contrasted with the covenant that he will make with the generation of the eschaton. By referring to the new covenant, Jesus is claiming that the time foretold by Jeremiah has come. Since he proclaimed the kingdom of God, it is not surprising to find Jesus speaking about the Jeremian new covenant: The idea of the new covenant is a correlate to Jesus' message of the kingdom of God. The new covenant, however, is not only a correlate of Jesus' concept of the kingdom of God, but also of the Second-Temple Jewish understanding of the Passover. The annual celebration of the Passover is an eschatologically charged festival, since Passover is the day of Israel's final redemption, expressed in Jer 31:31 as the making of a new covenant with the people. Jesus seems to have made this connection between new covenant and Passover. He understands his last Passover as the day of Israel's eschatological redemption, the day on which the new covenant will be established, when the kingdom of God is realized. This will be through his death.

Jesus' words over the bread situated at the beginning of the main course and his words over the cup situated at its completion form a climactic parallelism. The words over the bread establish that Jesus, as the eschatological paschal sacrifice, will die a vicarious and expiatory death. The words over the cup build upon this proposition, adding that his death will be the means by which the Jeremian new covenant will be realized. Each member of the parallelism is understandable in itself, but the second member furthers the meaning of the first.

Objections to the authenticity of the words of institution considered

The words of institution have never been a strong candidate for authenticity. The foremost argument against their authenticity is that they do not meet the criterion of dissimilarity. The criterion of dissimilarity is, however, a very coarse methodological sieve. It is more credible that the early church's stress on Jesus' expiatory death was the result of Jesus' own understanding of his death in such terms. Another major objection to the historicity of the words of institution is that they do not meet the criterion of coherence. The hypothesis that Jesus understands his death as an expiation for sin is supposed to run counter to his message of the kingdom of God. What is not taken into account is the decisive shift in the orientation of Jesus' ministry as a reaction to the resistance and ultimate rejection that he experienced. The words of institution represent an expression of how Jesus comes to understand his role as the messenger of the kingdom in light of his rejection.

BARRY D. SMITH

Further reading

Dalman, Gustaf. *Jesus-Jeshua. Studies in the Gospels*, London: SPCK, 1929.

Füglister, Notker. *Die Heilsbedeutung des Pascha*, SANT 5, Munich: Kösel Verlag, 1963.

Jeremias, Joachim. *The Eucharistic Words of Jesus*, third edition, London: SCM Press, 1966.

Kodell, Jerome. *The Eucharist in the New Testament*, Zaccheus Studies; Wilmington, DE: Michael Glazier; Collegeville, MN: Liturgical Press, 1988.

Le Déault, Roger. *La Nuit Pascale*, AnBib 22, Rome: Institut biblique pontifical, 1963.

Leon-Dufour, Xavier. *Sharing the Eucharistic Bread: The Witness of the New Testament*, New York: Paulist Press, 1986.

Marshall, Howard. *Last Supper and Lord's Supper*, Exeter: Paternoster, 1980.

Neuenzeit, Paul. *Das Herrenmahl. Studien zur paulinischen Eucharistieauffasung*, SANT 1, Munich: Kösel Verlag, 1960.

Patsch, Hermann. *Abendmahl und historischer Jesus*, CTM 1, Stuttgart: Calwer Verlag, 1972.

Pesch, Rudolf. *Das Abendmahl und Jesu Todesverständnis*, QD 80, Freiberg: Herder, 1978.

Schürmann, Heinz. *Der Paschamahlbericht. Lk 22, (7–14) 15–18*, NTAbh 19, Munster: Aschendorff, 1968.

—— *Der Einsetzungsbericht. Lk 22, 19–20*, NTAbh 20, third edition, Munster: Aschendorff, 1970.

Smith, Barry D. *Jesus' Last Passover Meal*, Lewiston, NY: Edwin Mellen, 1993.

Walther, Georg. *Jesus, das Passalamm des Neuen Bundes*, Gütersloh: Bertelsmann, 1959.

LAW (SABBATH, PURITY, COMMANDMENTS)

Love of God (Deuteronomy 6:5) and love of neighbor (Leviticus 19:18) were basic principles embedded in the Torah. Jesus discovered that the two were indivisible: love of God *was* love of neighbor, and vice versa. Jesus taught that the love one owed God was exactly what one owed one's neighbor (Mark 12:28–34; Matt 22:34–40; Luke 10:25–28).

Basic to this teaching was the conviction that every person was made in God's own image and likeness, because God created everyone in that way (Gen 1:26–27). In his concentration on the "one like a person" or "the son of man," Jesus incorporated the Danielic insight that humanity is represented before God's Throne. But then Jesus pursued this insight further: every person possessed the angelic likeness of the "one like a person" and mirrored some of the divine truth. God's Throne was there, shining through the eyes of a neighbor, even if that neighbor hated you (Matt 5:43–48; Luke 6:27–36). That is the basis of Jesus' distinctive and challenging ethics of love in the midst of persecution – a love that reaches out past the fear of reprisal from the agents of Rome, an Antipas, a Pilate, or a Caiaphas. Of all the teachings of Jesus, none is more straightforward, and none more challenging. Evil is to be overcome by means of what is usually called non-resistance.

Matthew states the principle of Jesus' teaching, that we are to love in the way that God does (Matt 5:43–48; see Luke 6:36). The fundamental quality of that teaching within Christianity is unquestionable (see Romans 13:8–10). But in the teaching about turning the other cheek, giving the cloak, going the extra mile, offering the money, everything comes down to particular conditions that prevailed during the Roman occupation of the Near East. The fact that this formulation only appears in Matthew (written around 80 CE) has given rise to the legitimate question whether it should be attributed to Jesus in its present form. The imagery corresponds to the conditions of the Roman occupation in an urban area, where a soldier of the Empire might well demand provisions and service and money, and all with the threat of force. But even if we acknowledge (as seems only reasonable) that Matthew has pitched Jesus' policy in the idiom of its own experience, the policy itself should be attributed to Jesus.

Why should what is usually called non-resistance to evil be recommended? It needs to be stressed that non-resistance is not the same as acquiescence. The injustice that is done is never accepted as if it were just. The acts of turning the other cheek, giving the cloak, going the additional mile, offering the money, are all designed to be excessive, so that the fact of the injustice of what is demanded is underlined. Indeed, it is not really accurate to call

the behavior "non-resistance." The point is for the person who makes demands that are unjust to realize they are unjust. Just that policy served Christians and their faith well during the centuries of persecution under the Roman Empire. It was effective because it brought about an awareness within the Empire, even among the enemies of Christianity, that the policy of violent persecution was unjust (and, for that matter, ineffective). Rather than a teaching of non-resistance, this is a version of the advice of how to retaliate. Instead of an eye for an eye, it suggests a cheek after a cheek. This is not non-resistance; it is exemplary response. That is, it is a form of retaliation: not to harm, but to show another way.

In portraying this teaching as the informing principles of the Torah and the Prophets, Jesus' method is reminiscent of Hillel's, his older contemporary. The Babylonian Talmud tells the story that Hillel was once approached by a man who wanted to convert to Judaism; he wished to be taught the Torah quickly, while he stood on one foot. Hillel told him: "That which you hate, do not do to your neighbor. That is the whole Torah, while everything else is commentary: go and learn it!" (see Shabbath 31a). It is true that the source that reports Hillel's position is much more recent than the gospels, but that only underscores the observation that the search for informing principles of the Torah, as characterized by Jesus' teaching, is typically Judaic. The centrality of the commandment to love one's neighbor is also asserted by Aqiba, the famous rabbi of the second century (Sifra, Leviticus 19:18). Differences of emphasis are detectable and important, but the fact remains that Jesus does not appear to have been exceptional in locating love at the center of the divine commandments. Any rabbi, a teacher in a city or a local village, might have come up with some such principle, although the expressions of the principle attributed to Jesus are especially apt, and involve a characteristic insistence that the commandments to love subsume all commandments (and in Matthew, all prophecies). In any case, the practical wisdom of consideration of one's neighbors is also endorsed in Tob 4:15 and Sir 31:15 (cf. Matt 7:12).

From the perspective of his understanding of the principles animating the Law and the Prophets, Jesus' contention that "The Sabbath happened for humanity and not humanity for the Sabbath" (Mark 2:27) is understandable. Yet precisely that stance is also represented in rabbinic literature, both in so many words (see *Mekilta, Shabbata* 1 to Exod 31:14; Yoma 85b in the Babylonian Talmud, cf. also 2 Macc 5:19) and in practical case after practical case in the Mishnaic tractate Shabbat. For these reasons, it is simply implausible, as W. L. Lane said, to insist there is anything "specifically 'un-Jewish' about Jesus' pronouncement on the Sabbath." The impression to the contrary is generated by the gospels' tendency of introducing the "Pharisees" in metonymy to Judaism as a whole, and then portraying Jesus as separate from Judaism.

Jesus' disputants in regard to the Sabbath stood closer to the Essenes than to the Pharisees, and he may have had the Pharisees in mind. He took it as a matter of course that a person would save an animal from a pit on the Sabbath (Matt 12:11; Luke 14:5, cf. 13:15). But 4Qhalakah A 2:5–7 teaches just the opposite of that, much as the *Manual of Discipline* from its outset insists that enemies are to be hated. No wonder Jesus made trenchant allusion to the Essenes (see Luke 16:8, where Jesus refers to "sons of light"): in his view, you could learn more from a corrupt manager (so Luke 16:1–8).

Jesus did disagree with the Pharisees of the time in regard to purity. Just as John had mastered the technique of achieving purity by immersion in living water, the Pharisees had evolved a complex metaphysics around the purity of meals. Special attention was paid to how food was kept in the home: covered vessels of clay protected moist produce such as olives from the uncleanness of a lizard that might touch the rim of the vessel or the impurity that radiated from a funeral cortege. Pharisees also judged whether purification by immersing one's hands and vessels prior to meals had been observed.

Jesus celebrated his trademark holy feasts widely, and these meals sometimes came to the attention of the Pharisees, who rightly doubted whether Jesus in fact observed their understanding of purity. Conflict with Jesus often resulted (Luke 11:37–40). Jesus is vociferous in this confrontation, typical of the kind of opposition he encountered in an ordinarily pious Pharisee, because he insisted that purity in Galilee already existed, and opposed the Pharisaic assumption that purity had to be achieved. His object was not to make Israelites clean, but to use their cleanness to invoke the presence of God in their meals. Pharisaism was a movement for towns and cities, such as Capernaum and Magdala, where the threat of impurity had to be countered daily. Jesus' practice was for areas accustomed to keeping their distance from urban corruption, and he disputed the logic of trying to clean outside with water what had already been tainted inside with *mammon*.

His stance reflected a teaching in the Mishnah. Rabbi Hillel (50 BCE–10 CE) had argued that the inside of a vessel, whether pure or impure, determined the purity or impurity of the whole vessel (in the Mishnah, see Kelim 25:6). In his criticism of the Pharisees, Jesus adhered to Hillel's principle: cleanness proceeds from within to without and purifies the whole. But if that is the case with cups, then all the more so with Israelites who are pure by their intention and the way they work the land. In extending Hillel's teaching in this way, Jesus was invoking the principle of the prophet Haggai, who had once declared that just as uncleanness is contagious, so God's spirit would one day make Israel clean by its holy contagion (Hag 2:4–5, 10–19).

It is what is *within* that makes a person pure. His well-known aphorism conveys just this insight (Mark 7:15, see also Matt 15:11). Washing did not make the produce of rural Galilee any purer than it already was. Against the Pharisees, Jesus asserted that purity was a matter of the totality of one's being. One was either clean or unclean; for Jesus, there was no vacillation. The Pharisees' policy of compromise with defilement, skillfully crafted to deal with the complexities of urban pluralism, found no resonance in his peasant's mind.

In the cleansing of the "leper," one of the most dramatic and telling stories in the gospels, Jesus pressed his program of purity into action. Jesus was dealing with a man with *tsara'at* (in Hebrew and Aramaic), which refers to an "outbreak" of the skin. It is clear that "outbreak" is not the disease we call leprosy; the book of Leviticus stipulates that walls and cloth – as well as people – may also contract, and be freed of, *tsara'at* (see Lev 13–14). The term was rendered *lepra* in the Greek version of the Hebrew Bible: in Greek, *lepra* refers to a scaly or scabby condition of the skin, and the term was picked up in English for the specific, irreversible complaint clinically known as Hansen's disease, which we call "leprosy." That modern definition has nothing to do with the story's reference to a range of ailments that probably included eczema, psoriasis, and shingles.

In the gospels (Matt 8:1–4; Mark 1:40–45; Luke 5:12–16), a person with an "outbreak" approaches Jesus in an unnamed village in Galilee and asserts that Jesus is able to "cleanse" him. "Outbreak" in humans (as distinct from cloth and houses) was signaled by broken flesh (Lev 13:14–15), or even a change in the pigmentation of the skin and accompanying hair. Unbroken flesh and consistent pigmentation signaled a return to cleanness (vv. 12, 13). The fundamental concern was broken flesh: that brought proximity to blood, to which no human correctly has access. Sufferers from an outbreak were banned from contact with the community during the period of their condition (vv. 45, 46).

Leviticus decrees that a priest must declare a person suffering from an outbreak clean: that is, ready to make the twofold offering prescribed before rejoining the community. The first offering is a local sacrifice, which may take place wherever there is running water. The priest (not in the Temple but simply a priest who lives in the village) twists the neck off a bird and lets the blood spurt into an earthen vessel. This vessel is held over a stream and the priest dips a living bird, which has a scarlet cord wrapped around its neck with a pouch that contains cedar bark shavings and a piece of hyssop, in the dead bird's blood. He then sprinkles the patient with the living bird, and releases it (14:1–7). That first sacrifice symbolically releases the person from impurity. After that purification, the person immerses and shaves all his hair (cf. vv. 8–9), and then offers two male lambs, an ewe, cereal, and oil in the Temple. These actions bring the sufferer back into the sacrificial community of Israel (14:10–20). Release from the condition and re-integration within the communal body were the portals one passed through to rejoin one's people, one's family.

But Jesus proved no more patient with the priestly program of purity than he was with the Pharisees' pronouncements. He skipped half the procedure set out in Leviticus. He told the outbreak-sufferer he did not need to see a local priest, and could proceed directly to the Temple and offer sacrifice. Jesus did not personally take over any specifically sacrificial function, but he did pronounce on matters of purity. The Pharisees saw that Jesus abrogated their principles about how purity should be achieved and maintained (see the tractate Negaim in the Mishnah, especially 14:1–13).

Jesus knew he was breaking barriers. He had been called out by the "leper," challenged to act out his principle of purification (Mark 1:40). Jesus agreed, but then scolded the man and told him not to publicize what had happened (Mark 1:41–44). Jesus knew his actions would arouse the ire of the Pharisees and many Jews with a traditional understanding of purity.

Just as Jesus applied a principle articulated by Hillel regarding immersion in a radical way, so his willingness to rule on the status of skin represents a remarkable revision of Pharisaic tradition. Pharisees debated in minute detail the cleanness and uncleanness of changes of skin color, bulges, raw flesh. A tractate of the Mishnah (*Negaim* 1:1–10:10) advises when to let the skin heal by itself and when

to remove a spot by cutting it. Pharisees instructed priests (whom they constantly sought to influence) on how to declare on issues of purity; they advised on the removal of suspicious growths by minor surgery; and they counseled the blemished on how long to wait after surgery before visiting a priest to be pronounced clean. But the cleansing of Jesus presupposes that purity is not a status to be attained prior to sacrifice, but a power which one's offering releases. He had usurped the priests role.

Christian theology and scholarship have persistently overlooked Jesus' distinctive approach to the entire issue of purity. They have denied that Jesus was concerned with purity and rejected any consideration that his actions stem from his insights into what was clean or unclean. Such views are uninformed and misleading. At a later stage, obviously, primitive Christianity *did* eschew many facets of Jewish ritual practice, but only when it had become a predominantly non-Jewish, Hellenistic movement. Purity was Jesus' fundamental commitment, the lens through which he viewed the world, and by means of which his distinctive attitude toward the Law becomes apparent.

BRUCE CHILTON

Further reading

Booth, Roger P. *Jesus and the Laws of Purity: Tradition History and Legal History in Mark 7*, JSNTSup 13, Sheffield: JSOT, 1986.

Chilton, Bruce. *The Temple of Jesus. His Sacrificial Program Within a Cultural History of Sacrifice*, University Park, PA: Pennsylvania State University Press, 1992.

Chilton, Bruce and J. I. H. McDonald. *Jesus and the Ethics of the Kingdom*, BFT, London: SPCK, 1987, and Grand Rapids, MI: Eerdmans, 1988.

Kazen, Thomas. *Jesus and Purity Halakhah. Was Jesus Indifferent to Impurity?*, ConBNT 38, Stockholm: Almqvist & Wiksell, 2002

Klawans, Jonathan. *Purity, Sacrifice, and Temple. Symbolism and Supersessionism in the Study of Ancient Judaism*, New York: Oxford University Press, 2006.

Lane, William L. *The Gospel According to Mark*, London: Marshall, Morgan & Scott, 1974.

Malina, Bruce J. *The New Testament World. Insights from Cultural Anthropology*, Louisville, KY: Westminster/John Knox, 2001.

Neusner, Jacob. *Purity in Rabbinic Judaism. A Systematic Account, the Sources, Media, Effects and Removal of Uncleanness*, Atlanta, GA: Scholars, 1994.

LITERARY CRITICISM, NEW FORMS OF

In the study of the Gospels, source, form, tradition and redaction criticism look at the historical background of the text: where it came from, what its earlier forms where, and how and why the traditions were edited together in the form in which we have the gospel today. These, however, all focus on the authorship and transmission of the tradition, an approach which, while still fruitful, has tended to beg the question of the present meaning of the received literary form of the text. It is this issue that a series of newer literary critical disciplines have addressed, all of which take their clues from other parts of the university curriculum, in particular the study of literature and the social sciences. What they have in common is that (1) they generally take the text as it stands rather than discuss the process by which the text came to its present condition and (2) they generally bracket issues of the historical behind the text, instead looking at issues of meaning in the text or the world constructed by the text.

There are two general types of literary criticism. In the first type, following to a degree on Aristotle's *Poetics*, form is viewed as the key to content and meaning and so the larger aspects of style are looked at. This is indeed the case with structuralism and discourse analysis. In the other type, following to a degree on Aristotle's *Rhetoric*, content can be separated from form, leading to a closer reading of the text. This is the case with narrative criticism and (socio-) rhetorical criticism. A further development has been that of post-structuralism, especially deconstruction and reader-response criticism, where the text itself is less the source of meaning than the reader upon which it has an influence. While in practice these various types blend into one another, we will take these up below in the order above.

Structuralism

Originally derived from the thought of Ferdinand de Saussure, Claude Lévi-Strauss, and Roland Barthes, among others, and applied to folk tales, the basic premise of structuralism is that the language is greater than the act of speaking/writing and thus imposes a structure upon (in our case) the document. The elements of language achieve meaning, not by some relationship to what they signify, which is arbitrary, but by contrasts, combinations and oppositions to one another. As a result, one can analyze the meanings in a text in total isolation from history or the development of the language over time.

If language is a product of a culture and the individual speech act participates in the overall language, then by using these deep structures of language one can break a speech act down into oppositions of actions and these will in turn lead

to the theme that will express the convictions of the author. While this explanation is obviously a simplification of structuralism, the structuralist ideal is that one can thus come to a relatively objective interpretation of the text, one that is linguistically determined. This methodology has been most accessibly applied to the gospels by Daniel Patte, who significantly focuses on the Fourth Gospel, for that, of course, has the long discourses that such an analysis requires.

The application of another form of structuralism to narrative has been developed by A. J. Greimas, who again works with oppositions, but in his case he also works with what for him are the functions of *actants* in narratives. The six actants themselves are:

Sender --------- Object --------- Receiver
                        |
Helper --------- Subject --------- Opponent

Naturally, since these are actants and not characters in the narrative, a given character can shift their actant role as the narrative develops. Furthermore, the actants do not need to be personal, so the helper could be a thing as well as a character. Since we are talking about deep structures of language, the actual narrative progression may well look the same whether one is analyzing "Little Red Riding-Hood" or a gospel narrative. On the other hand, this analysis has the advantage of making complex narrative sequences clear. Its application to the gospel narrative has been popularized by the work of N. T. Wright (1992, 1996), for whom the basic paradigm looks something like this:

God ----------------- Good order ----------------- World
                           |
                           |
Law/Holy Spirit ----- Israel/Jesus/church ----- Evil spiritual forces

While this has the advantage of clarity, it will raise the question as whether one can determine what the text actually refers to.

Discourse analysis

Discourse analysis is related to structuralism in that it also falls under the general heading of semiology, although it is more focused on the surface structure of the text than is structuralism. Thus a text may be analyzed to show its time indicators, its personal, social, temporal, locational, and discourse deixis of its utterances, its various sequences, or its internal structure. In each case one is looking for words and grammatical structures that indicate the boundaries and structures of the discourse. In other words, one is working in the field of pragmatics, or applied semantics. The goal is a relatively objective description of the text (whether speech or narrative) that makes its reference and development clear. Again, this is distinct from any relationship of the narrative to external reality, for discourse analysis takes place entirely within the world of the literary text (indeed, it defines what a text is in distinction to a collection of sentences). While first applied to gospel texts to aid in the translation of such texts into non-European receptor languages, it has come to be viewed as a means of getting at the meaning in the text that the Western world had assumed in ignorance of discourse structure that it had understood.

Narrative criticism

Narrative criticism, which developed from the study of modern fiction and Russian folk tales, is another form of text-centered criticism that looks at the text in its present final form abstracted from historical references. That is, it looks at the text as a tale. Thus it presents the text as revealing an implied author whose relationship to the actual author is not a topic of this type of critical thought. Likewise there is an implied reader, who is discernable in the narrative structures of the text but may or may not be identical to the actual readers for whom the text was written. This may be obvious, as in the case of the formal address in Luke 1:1–4 (which certainly indicates the implied reader, but may or may not indicate an actual patron) or unstated, as in the case of Matthew, where the implied reader might be described in part as a law-observant Jew who is probably already a member of the Jesus movement. This approach avoids some of the issues raised by redaction criticism by looking at the gospel itself and not comparing it with other gospels (and thus not focusing on the differences from other forms of a pericope) and it also avoids some of the issues of form criticism by looking at the plot of the work as a whole and thus not just the individual stories, each with individual transmission history. Instead, narrative criticism is interested in the sequence of stories in a given gospel with their narrative time, developing conflicts (and resolutions) and the like. This plot analysis brings out the author's point of view, which is further developed by an examination of characterization (especially examining which characters the reader is expected to empathize or

sympathize with or show antipathy toward) and setting. Robert Tannehill and Meir Sternberg are good examples of this approach.

Rhetorical and socio-rhetorical criticism

If narrative criticism looks at the point of view of the text, then rhetorical criticism looks at the intended effect of the text on the reader. "Intended" is the key word here, for the gospels developed in a context where rhetoric was part of any decent education; clearly the author of any text had had such an education. Thus it is reasonable to look in the text for rhetorical structures as defined by Greco-Roman rhetoricians and to view them as conscious structures. While this could be applied to the gospels as a whole (given that ancient texts were more performed orally than read privately), it was originally applied to specific speeches within the gospels, e.g. viewing the Sermon on the Mount as deliberative rhetoric that uses various rhetorical devices (e.g. the approach of G. A. Kennedy).

When rhetorical criticism is applied to more than the rhetorical analysis of speeches, the social setting of the writers and implied readers must be taken into account. Thus one comes to socio-rhetorical criticism. A writer such as Vernon K. Robbins, for example, divides his analysis into five sections, starting with inner texture (which is basically narrative criticism), moving on to intertexture (how it interacts with written and other materials in the world around it), social and cultural texture (its use of topics from the culture), ideological texture (which is close to various types of reader-response criticisms), and sacred texture. While there is a recognition that the text is located in a culture and thus historical in that sense (indeed, without this social location one could not apply this critical methodology effectively, since one needs to identify the assumptions that the author has taken over from his or her social world), this criticism remains text-focused in that it is the devices and cultural assumptions of the author that are being investigated, not either the history of the materials that he or she uses or the historical reference made by those materials. A project that is the result of such a critical stance is the commentary project of Ben Witherington III, although his conclusions are far more traditional than those of Robbins.

Deconstruction and reader-response approaches

Given that texts are cultural artifacts and thus dependent upon cultural settings and given that no one can reproduce the cultural setting of a text, even of a modern text (in that no one will have the same set of assumptions and values as the author), can one say that a text has a meaning, or at least a fixed reading? Deconstruction is post-structuralist in that it turns structuralist tools against their own results and thus questions whether there is an objective deep structure to the text to be discovered. Whether it uses structuralist tools or the tools of narrative and other forms of criticism, it does so playfully, since it is convinced that texts are polyvalent and one can deconstruct any given interpretation, even that presented by the critic (as S. D. Moore freely admits). The reader cannot get beyond his or her own subjectivity and thus their interpretation of the text will be dependent upon their own ideology; it is not something given by the author. In one sense a deconstructionist approach could lead to non-interpretation of a text, since one cannot find any absolute meaning in it. Most of those who have applied such approaches to the New Testament, however, do so with more confidence of finding something meaningful, but only in the sense of meaningful to them (and presumably, they hope, to those who read their writings). At their best such approaches are playful reminders of the subjective captivity of the human reader and the relativity of human interpretation.

Although not necessarily directly informed by deconstruction/post-structuralism, reader-response approaches are its logical implication, so long as they do not take themselves too seriously. The point is that texts, once released to the public, take on a life of their own. The author is no longer around to interpret the text, but the author has left "gaps" in the text where the reader must fill in information and assumptions from their cultural background. Given that the reader does not share the identical background with the author, the reader will fill in this information from his or her own cultural and ideological position. The reader does, however, share a relatively common set of assumptions with a group of his or her contemporaries; together these form a reading community for whom the text takes on meaning in a particular way. One could, of course, be part of a community that tries to read the text from the perspective of an ancient reader; such a response might not differ significantly from rhetorical or narrative forms of criticism. But it would also not be an interpretation for the world in which the reading community lives. Usually, then, one reads the text consciously or unconsciously from a particular ideological perspective. Indeed, one may see the ideological perspective as a prerequisite for

interpretation. Thus one may read a text consciously from a Marxist or feminist or African-American perspective, in which case one may "hear" different details in the text (or "under the text," if one's encounter with the text leads one to view it as having suppressed voices, such as those of women or the poor) than if one had been coming at the text from a different perspective. One may agree that this is not the ideological perspective of the author, but that the author has released the text into the world and it has taken on a life of its own. When taken earnestly, such an approach assumes that its ideology is *the* way to understand the text in the present context. If taken less earnestly, such approaches show the variety of meanings that can be seen in a text and are part of the enrichment of its various textures.

PETER H. DAVIDS

Further reading

Alter, Robert. *The Art of Biblical Narrative*, New York: Basic Books, 1981.

Barthes, Roland. *Structural Analysis and Biblical Exegesis: Interpretational Essays*, Pittsburgh Theological Monograph Series 3, Pittsburgh, PA: Pickwick Press, 1974.

Barton, John (ed.) *The Cambridge Companion to Biblical Interpretation*, Cambridge: Cambridge University Press, 1998.

Calloud, Jean. *Structural Analysis of Narrative*, Missoula, MT: Scholars Press, 1976.

Cotterell, Peter and Turner, Max. *Linguistics and Biblical Interpretation*, Downers Grove, IL: InterVarsity Press, 1989.

Elliott, John H. *What is Social-Scientific Criticism?*, Minneapolis, MN: Fortress Press, 1993.

Forenza, Elizabeth Schüssler (ed.) *Searching the Scriptures, vol 2: A Feminist Commentary*, New York: Crossroad, 1994.

Kennedy, George A. *New Testament Interpretation through Rhetorical Criticism*, Chapel Hill, NC: University of North Carolina Press, 1984.

Kingsbury, Jack D. *Matthew as Story*, Philadelphia, PA: Fortress Press, 1986.

McKnight, Edgar V. *Postmodern Use of the Bible: The Emergence of Reader-Oriented Criticism*, Nashville, TN: Abingdon, 1988.

McKnight, Scot. "Literary Criticism," in *Interpreting the Synoptic Gospels*, Grand Rapids, MI: Baker, 1988.

Marguerat, Daniel, Yvan Bourquin, and Marcel Durrer. *How to Read Bible Stories*, London: SCM Press, 1999.

Moore, Stephen D. *Literary Criticism and the Gospels*, New Haven, CT: Yale University, 1989.

—— *Poststructuralism and the New Testament*, Minneapolis, MN: Fortress Press, 1994.

Powell, Mark A. *What is Narrative Criticism?*, Philadelphia, PA: Fortress Press, 1991.

Patte, Daniel M. *What is Structural Exegesis?*, Philadelphia, PA: Fortress Press, 1976.

—— *Structural Exegesis for New Testament Critics*, Philadelphia, PA: Fortress Press, 1990.

Patte, Daniel M. and Aline Patte. *Structural Exegesis: From Theory to Practice*, Philadelphia, PA: Fortress Press, 1978.

Rhoads, David M. and Donald Michie. *Mark as Story: An Introduction to the Narrative of a Gospel*, Philadelphia, PA: Fortress Press, 1982.

Robbins, Vernon K. *Exploring the Texture of Texts*, Valley Forge, PA: Trinity Press International, 1996.

Spencer, Richard A. (ed.) *Orientation by Disorientation: Studies in Literary Criticism and Biblical Literary Criticism*, Pittsburg, PA: Pickwick, 1980.

Sternberg, Meir. *The Poetics of Biblical Narrative: Ideological Literature and the Drama of Reading*, Bloomington, IN: Indiana University, 1985.

Tannehill, Robert C. *The Narrative Unity of Luke-Acts: A Literary Interpretation I: The Gospel According to Luke*, Philadelphia, PA: Fortress Press, 1986.

Witherington, Ben, III. *John's Wisdom*, Louisville, KY: Westminster John Knox Press, 1995.

Wright, N. T. *The New Testament and the People of God*, Minneapolis, MN: Fortress Press, 1992.

—— *Jesus and the Victory of God*, Minneapolis, MN: Fortress Press, 1996.

LORD

Old Testament evidence

The two Hebrew equivalents for the word "Lord" are *Baal* and *Adôn*. Both words indicate "possession and ownership" and being the "master" of individuals or property. The former is rarely used for God in the Old Testament because of its associations with a Canaanite storm deity later in the history of Israel (cf. 1 Hos 2:18 [Eng. 2:16]; cf. 1 Chr. 12:6). The latter word (*Adôn*) was used instead; it frequently signifies the Lord as Master, while its antonym is "servant." Thus it was appropriate to call Joseph, the Master or *Adôn* of Egypt since he was appointed by Pharaoh with all the requisite powers to enforce the Pharaoh's will (Gen 45:9). Similarly Abraham was the Master of Eleazer, his servant (Gen 24:27). On a much larger scale God is recognized to be the great *Adôn*, the Lord of the whole earth (Jos 3:11, 13; Mic 4:13).

Many times in the Old Testament, this word occurs in a unique form as *Adōnai*, the *ai* ending indicating a first-person singular suffix for a plural noun (lit. "my lords"), or a form of an archaic case ending. In the former case, it would suggest a plural of intensity, signifying the fullness of lordship or absolute lordship. Tradents responsible for copying the Hebrew Bible (Masoretes) lengthened the final vowel to distinguish it as a sacred title, simply indicating (divine) "Lord." This divine title designates God as the one who has ultimate authority and power.

The Septuagint

When the Jews in Alexandria needed a translation of the Hebrew Bible for their largely Greek-speaking community, the Septuagint was produced (250–150 BCE). The translators could have used a number of options to translate the Hebrew word used most often for Lord (*Adôn*). The main options were *kyrios* and *despotēs*. But the latter term was generally avoided. It was used about sixty times and half of its usages were translations of *Adôn/Adōnai* when there exists a Hebrew original. It was probably avoided since it often had negative connotations associated with power exercised arbitrarily and sometimes oppressively. *Kyrios* was the translation of choice for *Adôn/Adōnai*, virtually being used as an equivalent since it stressed more the idea of legal authority. It is used over 9,000 times in the Septuagint and it can be used of a human master (Gen 24:54) or one to whom social deference is given (Gen 33:13), as well as a title for God. It may be going too far to suggest that when it designates divinity it means "God's legitimate, unrestricted and invisible power of disposal over all things" (Foerster 1082) but this points in the right direction. Perhaps for this reason it was pressed into service as a substitute for the divine name YHWH (יהוה) which occurs over 6,000 times in the Old Testament.

However, there is uncertainty here. Early Jewish tradition refused to pronounce the divine name for fear of sacrilege. Consequently pious Jews were to read *Adōnai* in its place. Perhaps it was for this reason that *kyrios* is found in the Septuagint. On the other hand it may be the other way around: the word *kyrios* influenced the substitution of *Adōnai* for YHWH. But this probably was not the case.

There is also some evidence that early Greek manuscripts did not have *kyrios* for YHWH but either transcribed the Hebrew or a Greek equivalent for the divine name. Some scholars suggest that Christian scribes transmitting the Greek manuscripts of the Septuagint would have later substituted *kyrios* for the divine name (Jellicoe 271 ff.; Shaw). Some of the Greek manuscripts in question, however, are revisions toward the Hebrew and therefore cannot count as evidence for an original Septuagint. Studying the translation technique of the Greek Pentateuch, Pietersma has made a convincing case for the originality of *kyrios* as a substitute for YHWH. In his view, this best explains the way the Greek noun is declined in this text and how it is used with conjunctions, and other words.

One of the examples Pietersma (94) uses shows clearly the meaning of the title *kyrios* when used of

God. In the story of the liberation of Israel from Egypt, God indicates to Pharaoh the purpose of the plagues of judgment. The Hebrew text reads: "in order that you may know that I am YHWH in the midst of the earth" (8:18). The Septuagint, however, reads "in order that you may know that I am Lord (*Kyrios*), the Lord (*Kyrios*) of the whole earth" (8:22). Here *kyrios* means the Creator and Ruler of the entire earth and therefore the one to whom Pharaoh must submit.

The evidence of the New Testament would support the early use of *kyrios* as a substitute for the ineffable name, since when it cites the Old Testament in its Septuagint form, *kyrios* is found where the Hebrew text has YHWH (e.g. Isa 40:3; Mark 1:3). Foerster's comment is apt:

> The God to whom the Canon bears witness is called "Lord" because He is there shown to be the exclusive holder of power over the cosmos and all men, the Creator of the world and the Master of life and death.
>
> (1062)

The New Testament

In the New Testament, the word *kyrios* is used 717 times, 485 times in Luke/Acts and Paul's letters (68 percent). Of these Paul uses the term over 200 times.

Secular usage

Kyrios is used in secular contexts to indicate the owner of money (Matt 25:18), animals, a vineyard, an estate, and slaves. Jesus is reminded by the Canaanite woman that dogs eat the crumbs which fall from their owners' tables (Matt 15:27). The wicked servant buries the money given to him by his lord (Matt 25:18). The owner of a vineyard pays wages as he sees fit (Matt 20:8). The lord of a house leaves his servants in charge while away on a journey (Mark 13:35). The owners of slaves are regarded as their lords (Acts 16:15; Eph 6:5–9; Col 3:22–24:1).

Jesus uses the term in a natural way when he states that no one is able to serve two masters (Matt 6:24). The servant submits to a lord and the lord commands a servant. This is also found in the sayings in the gospels that a servant is not above his lord, and that a servant knows the will of his lord (Matt 10:24–25). Those who call Jesus their Lord are obligated to obey him since they are his servants. If they do not obey him, they are impostors, and he is not their master (cf. Matt 7:21–22).

When a military officer recognizes a parallel between himself and Jesus, he is able to persuade him to heal his servant from a distance (Matt 8:8–13). The officer is able to see the analogy between his authority in the military realm and the authority of Jesus in the spiritual sphere.

The word for Lord can also be used as a simple address of social deference such as the English term "Mr" or "Sir." This is clearly the case when the Samaritan woman addresses Jesus as Lord; she is using the term *kyrios* as a term of respect (John 4:15). Similarly when the Philippian jailer addresses Paul and Silas as "Lords," he is recognizing their spiritual authority (Acts 16:31).

Sacred usage

God

In the same way, this word denoting authority and ownership can be transferred to God who is the Lord of the universe. Jesus describes God as the Lord of the eschatological harvest of converts (Matt 9:38). He prays to God as his Father, "the Lord of heaven and earth" (Matt 11:25) as does Paul at Athens when he describes the identity of the unknown God as "the God who made the world and everything in it; this One, being the Lord of heaven and earth, does not live in temples made with human hands" (Act. 17:24). As indicated before, the New Testament, probably basing itself on the Septuagint, used the word *kyrios* for the Hebrew divine name when citing the Old Testament. This usage stands in continuity with the use of the word in the Old Testament as a title for God, stressing the Creator's omnipotent power revealed in history and the divine dominion (Bietenhard 514).

Jesus (pre-resurrection)

In the New Testament *kyrios* is rarely used as a divine title for the pre-resurrection Jesus, but there are significant exceptions. Probably Luke understands Jesus' birth this way, when he describes the infant as a "savior who is Christ the Lord" (Luke 2:11). Jesus describes himself as the Lord of the Sabbath, meaning that he has the power to exercise authority over the Sabbath (Matt 12:8). Jesus also uses the title "Lord" of the Messiah in a text in which he alludes to himself (Mark 12:35–37). Pslm 110 is cited to indicate that the Messiah is far superior to a Davidic descendant, since David himself called him *kyrios*, and this *kyrios* was to be appointed as ruler at God's right hand.

Usually, however, when the title Lord is ascribed to Jesus in the gospels, it is the normal title of respect given to an important figure. When the disciples cry out in a turbulent sea, "Lord, save us, we perish!" (Matt 8:25), they have no idea that he has such divine power to calm the storm. Similarly, when the blind man asks for healing, he refers to Jesus as "Lord" (Matt 20:31–33), an honorific title. Frequently in the gospels, Jesus is addressed in such a manner with the vocative "Lord" (Matt 8:2; Mark 10:51; John 6:68). Probably the reason why the divine title is not used of Jesus before the resurrection was to avoid anachronism. Before the resurrection the disciples did not really know who Jesus really was, and the gospels reflect this.

Jesus (post-resurrection)

There is a critical theological development that takes place with the resurrection of Jesus, which is quite remarkable. Something stupendous has happened. In a statement in which the Gospel of John reaches a climax (Cullman 232), doubting Thomas addresses the resurrected Jesus with the exclamation, "My Lord and my God" (John 20:28). The Great Commission to evangelize all nations is predicated on the basis of his new Lordship: "All authority in heaven and earth" (Matt 28:18) has been given to Jesus and "the one who has authority is Lord" (Foerster 1089). In Acts, Jesus is virtually immediately addressed as "the Lord Jesus" (Acts 1:21 cf. 7:59, 8:16, 11:20, 15:11) or the "Lord Jesus Christ" (Acts 11:17, 18:26, 20:21, 28:31). To a potential gentile convert, Jesus is described as the "Lord of all peoples" (Acts 10:36). As Peter makes clear in an early sermon, God has exalted him to be Lord and Christ (Acts 2:36). Consequently the Old Testament text par. excellence which is used to describe the resurrected Jesus's new status is Psalm 110 (Acts 2:34–35, 5:31, 7:55; 1 Cor 15:25; Eph 1:20; Heb 1:13; 1 Pet 3:22). By virtue of his resurrection and ascension Jesus has become Lord of the universe, reigning at God's right hand. To sit at God's right hand is not a passive activity. As Metzger (127) observes,

> this is metaphorical language for divine omnipotence. Where is it? Everywhere. To sit, therefore, at the right hand of God does not mean that Christ is resting; it affirms that he is reigning as king, wielding the powers of divine omnipotence.

Thus while Jesus preached the message of the kingdom of God in the gospels, *he now becomes the object of the apostolic preaching*. As Schillebeeckx (545) puts it:

> Jesus, who had announced the imminent rule of God, had not, despite the contradiction of his rejection and death, been wrong. With him who during his life had identified himself with God's cause, the coming rule of God, God has now identified himself by raising him from the dead; Jesus Christ is himself that rule of God. Unintentionally, therefore, though Jesus preached not himself but the rule and lordship of God, it was "himself" that he had proclaimed: the Proclaimer is the One proclaimed.

(See also Marshall 2004: 160.)

The title as applied to Jesus is ubiquitous in Paul's letters. In the salutations and benedictions Jesus of Nazareth has become the "Lord Jesus Christ" or the "Lord Jesus," and Paul is his bond-slave (1 Cor 1:2–3, 16:22–23; 2 Cor 1:2, 13:13; Gal 1:3, 6:18, etc.). The fact that the term is used repeatedly in Paul as a title for Jesus does not suggest that there is a foreign element which has been introduced into a Jewish religion. Rather, it is clear that Paul has inherited an early Christian confession about Jesus and reworked everything he has understood theologically in the light of his profound Damascus Road experience and the significance of the resurrection. As Dunn (1998: 239) remarks, the resurrection became "the key term which redefined all his language, the paradigmatic event by which all reality was to be conjugated."

But the resurrection itself had registered a powerful impact on the early Christian tradition inherited by Paul. He incorporates an early Christian benediction in its pristine Aramaic form in a letter to Greek-speaking Christians. In line with its Greek equivalent (Rev 22:20), *Maranatha* was a prayer meaning: "Our Lord, Come!" (although it could possibly mean "Our Lord has come" or "Our Lord will come"). In its context this refers to Jesus, and it could not be predicated of a Jesus who was still in the tomb, nor could it derive from a Hellenistic setting. Another inherited tradition is found in Romans 10:9 when Paul states, "If you confess with your mouth that Jesus is Lord and believe in your heart that God raised him from the dead, you will be saved." The emphasis on public confession and personal faith suggests that Paul was drawing upon a baptismal initiation rite of the early church, which linked resurrection and conversion. Paul also appropriated an early hymn that outlines the significance of the death and resurrection of Jesus of Nazareth. Jesus the slave (*doulos*) became Jesus the Lord (*kyrios*). Unlike Adam, who was made in the image of God, Jesus did not grasp for power. Instead, he gave up his rights and became a servant, suffering even the humiliation of death on a cross. But this did not spell his end but rather a new beginning – to a position in which God has highly exalted him over all reality so that all of reality will someday respond with the confession that Jesus Christ is Lord to the glory of God the Father (Phil 2:6–11; cf. Eph 1:17–23). Thus Jesus's new status merits a change in name – he receives the name that is above every name – *Kyrios*! This confession that " 'Jesus is Lord' is the climactic expression of the universe's worship" (Dunn 1990: 50). The public confession of a new Christian becomes the public confession of the entire universe at the end of history. It is clear, then, that Paul's pervasive use of the term "Lord" was informed by the earliest Christian tradition, and because the term was a common one in Greek culture, it became extremely appropriate to use in his communication of the gospel to Gentiles.

If the early Christian confessions and Paul stressed that Christ was the Lord of Creation, it is equally clear that the resurrected Jesus was also the Lord of History. In the Apocalypse which closes the New Testament, Jesus Christ is introduced as "the firstborn from the dead and the ruler of the kings of the earth" (Rev 1:5). The central image of this book is a throne upon which sits God and a slain Lamb, covered with seven eyes and having seven horns, symbolizing the victory of Christ over death and his possession of omniscience and omnipotence (5:6). As he was the only one in heaven who was able to open a sealed book, indicating the meaning of history, he is the Lord of History (5:5–14). Consequently he will defeat all the forces of evil and bring history to its triumphant conclusion because "He is the Lord of Lords and King of Kings" (Rev 17:14). It is probably not coincidental that the titles of "Lord" and "God" given to Jesus in the Apocalypse reflect usage of the same expressions by a contemporary of the author, the Emperor Domitian, as Bietenhard suggests (518). The real Lord and God is Jesus; Domitian and the Roman emperors are simply imposters, whose true character can be seen in the image of a beast. Consequently Jesus is virtually on the same footing with God the Father, as already indicated in his being placed alongside Him in epistolary salutation and benediction formulas.

Thus it is clear "that the name of Kyrios implies a position equal to that of God" (Foerster 1089). In one passage in particular, Paul contrasts the many gods and lords in pagan religions with "the one God the Father from whom all things come and for whom we live and one Lord Jesus Christ through whom all things come and through whom we live" (1 Cor 8:6). This is an absolutely shocking statement to make for someone steeped in Jewish orthodoxy, but clearly for Paul there is no choice. Even the *Shema* (Deut 6:4), the highest creed of

Judaism, has to be revised in the light of the resurrection of Jesus of Nazareth! "Here the title 'one Lord' expanded the *Shema* to contain Jesus. Using the classic monotheistic text of Judaism, Paul recast his perception of God by introducing Jesus as 'Lord' and redefining Jewish monotheism to produce a christological monotheism" (Collins 137; Wright).

Implications

A high Christology is not a doctrine that was imposed by a later church but was there in latent form from the beginning in the first generation of Christians. The fact that many times texts from the Old Testament in which the divine name Yahweh is used can be claimed for Jesus in the New Testament demonstrates this further (e.g. Isa 45:23; Phil 2:11). The significance of the resurrection may at first sight suggest an adoptionist Christology in which an essentially good man became the Son of God, but the texts suggest otherwise. The resurrection opened the disciples' eyes to the real identity of Jesus (Luke 24:13–49), whose status was changed by the resurrection.

Jesus Christ's Lordship circumscribes the entire life of Christians. Their entrance into the faith is marked by a confession of his Lordship (Rom 10:9), which cannot be made by anyone apart from the presence of the Holy Spirit (1 Cor 12:3). Similarly when believers die, they die in the Lord (Rev 14:13) to be resurrected by their Lord who will someday finally defeat the last enemy, death (1 Cor 15). Between the poles of birth and death, the Lordship of Jesus revolutionizes everything, including ethics. Christians are urged to have the mind of their exalted Lord (Phil 2:5–11), who served the lowest of the low, to bring every thought captive to his Lordship (2 Cor 10:5); sexual purity is now the norm since their body as the temple of the Holy Spirit belongs to the Lord (2 Cor 6:16). Under the direction of their new Lord relations between genders, roles and races are revolutionized for all are now one in him (Gal 3:28; cf. Eph 5:21–26:9). There is thus a new attitude to everyone and everything. The individual learns that the way of service is the way to glory, humility to exaltation, the way of being a *doulos* leads to becoming a *kyrios* (cf. Mark 10:35–45).

It is interesting that in modern Western Christianity Christ is known more often as "Savior" than "Lord," but the title "Lord" is found many more times in the New Testament and any potential dichotomy between these two titles is absent from the Bible. In fact the titular combination of

"Savior and Lord" is found only four times and in each the title "Lord" occurs first: "our Lord and Savior Jesus Christ" (1 Pet 1:11, 2:20, 3:2, 18; cf. Phil 3:20). Clearly, to experience salvation meant to enter a new sphere of reality in which Christ was Lord. Old things are passed away and there is a new creation (2 Cor 5:17). The idea of serving two masters is out of the question (cf. Matt 6:24); Christ is Lord of the individual's life as well as that of the community of which he or she is a member. Lordship signifies an ethical Copernican revolution. The self has been displaced as the center of one's personal universe by the Lord of glory.

Christians are described by a variety of metaphors in the New Testament which presuppose the Lordship of Christ. They are members of Christ's body whose head is Jesus (1 Cor 12). They are members of the household of faith whose elder brother and firstborn is Jesus (Heb 1:4–6, 2:17). They are the sheep of the flock whose shepherd is Jesus (1 Pet 2:25). They are the bride of Christ (Eph 5:22–33; Rev 21:9). They are members of the new temple whose chief cornerstone is the Lord (1 Pet 2:7). But one of the most common ways to describe Christians is by the phrase "in the Lord," which occurs fifty times, forty-eight times in Paul's epistles. "The whole of life, both in the present and in the future, is determined by the fact of Christ which is expressed by this formula" (Bietenhard 517). One can be said to remain in the Lord (Acts 11:23), be persuaded in the Lord (Rom 14:14), be exhorted in the Lord (1 Thess 4:1), be received in the Lord (Rom 16:2), be greeted in the Lord (16:8), to labor in the Lord (16:12), to write in the Lord (16:22), to boast in the Lord (1 Cor 1:31), to have a child in the Lord (4:17), to experience a call in the Lord (7:22), to marry in the Lord (7:39), to have an opportunity for mission in the Lord (2 Cor 2:12), to be a prisoner in the Lord (Eph 4:1), to witness in the Lord (4:17), to honor one's parents in the Lord (6:1), to be strengthened for spiritual battle in the Lord (6:10), to stand in the Lord (Phil 4:1), to rejoice in the Lord (Phil 4:4), to benefit others in the Lord (Phlm 20), and even to die in the Lord (Rev 14:13). In fact all of life is to be lived in the Lord, i.e. in the sphere of God's all-encompassing Lordship in Jesus Christ. No one lives to himself anymore, nor does one die to herself any longer. "Whether we live or die, we belong to the Lord" (Rom 14:8).

That Christ has been exalted to Lord means that humanity has been raised to a new dignity, which had been lost at the Fall. Originally created to have dominion over the creation, human beings became subject to sin and death and evil powers.

But now with Christ's death and resurrection these powers have been defeated and this lost human lordship has been restored and raised to a new unsurpassed level (Dempster). As Dunn (1998: 254) observes, "It is a lordship which fulfills God's purpose in making humankind."

As the Bible began with notes of dominion and lordship, and the loss of that lordship and dominion, it is probably no accident that it ends on the note of Lordship once again, a restored Lordship, a new heavens and a new earth in which righteousness will find a home, over which God and his people will rule. But this awaits complete fulfillment and thus there is the prayer: Come *Lord* Jesus! (Rev 22:20).

STEPHEN G. DEMPSTER

Further reading

Bietenhard, H. "Lord, Master," *DNTT* 2 (1976) 508–20.

Collins, G. *Christology: A Biblical, Historical and Systematic Study of Jesus*, Oxford: Oxford University Press, 1995.

Cullman, O. *The Christology of the New Testament*, trans. S. Guthrie and C. Hall, Philadelphia, PA: Westminster Press, 1963.

Dempster, S. G. *Dominion and Dynasty: A Theology of the Hebrew Bible*, Leicester: Apollos, 2003.

Dunn, J. D. G. *Unity and Diversity in the New Testament: An Enquiry into the Character of Earliest Christianity*, London, SCM Press, 1990.

—— *The Theology of Paul the Apostle*, Grand Rapids, MI: Eerdmans, 1998.

Eissfeldt, O. "אדון *'ādôn*" *TDOT* 1 (1977) 59–72.

Foerster, W. and G. Quell. *"kyrios,"* *TDNT* 3 (1998) 1039–98.

Jellicoe, S. *The Septuagint and Modern Study*, Oxford: Oxford University Press, 1968.

Jenni, E. "אדון *'ādôn*, lord," *TLOT* 1 (1997) 23–31.

Marshall, I. H. *The Origins of New Testament Christology*, Downers Grove, IL: InterVarsity Press, 1990.

—— *New Testament Theology: Many Witnesses, One Gospel*, Downers Grove, IL: InterVarsity Press, 2004.

Metzger, B. M. "The Meaning of Christ's Ascension," in J. M. Myers, O. Reimherr, and H. N. Bream (eds) *Search the Scriptures: New Testament Studies in Honor of Raymond T. Stamm*, Leiden: E. J. Brill, 1969, pp. 118–28.

Pietersma, A. "*Kyrios* or Tetragram: A Renewed Quest for the Original Septuagint," in A. Pietersma and Claude Cox (eds) *De Septuaginta: Studies in Honour of John William Wevers on His Sixty-Fifth Birthday*, Mississauga, ON: Benben, 1984, pp. 85–102.

Ramsay, W. M. *The Christ of the Earliest Christians*, Richmond, PA: John Knox Press, 1959.

Rose, M. "Names of God in the OT," in D. N. Freedman (ed.) *Anchor Bible Dictionary Vol. 4*, New York: Doubleday (1992), pp. 1001–11.

Schillebeeckx, E. *Jesus: An Experiment in Christology*, trans. H. Hoskins, New York: Crossroad, 1981.

Shaw, F. "The Earliest Non-mystical Jewish Use of IAW," PhD dissertation, University of Cincinnati, 2002.

Sobrino, J. *Christology at the Crossroads: A Latin American Approach*, Maryknoll, NY: Orbis, 1984.

Stauffer, E. *New Testament Theology*, trans. J. Marsh, London: SCM Press, 1955.

Witherington, B., III. *The Christology of Jesus*, Minneapolis, MN: Fortress Press, 1990.

—— "Lord," in J. Green, S. McKnight, and I. H. Marshall (eds) *Dictionary of Jesus and the Gospels*, Leicester: InterVarsity Press, 1992, pp. 484–92.

Wright, N. T. "Monotheism, Christology and Ethics: 1 Corinthians 8," in *The Climax of the Covenant: Christ and the Law in Pauline Theology*, Minneapolis, MN: Fortress Press, 1991, pp. 120–36.

LOVE

The broad theme of love (Gk. *agape, filia, splanchnon*, etc., and *cognates*) manifests itself in several ways in the Jesus tradition. I shall first address the different appearances of the theme individually, then consider them together trying to evaluate the theme as an element of the mission and message of the historical Jesus.

The commands to love: The Great Commandment (Mark 12:28–34)

The question about the correct order of priority of God's commandments arose, for example, in situations where two (or more) commandments appeared to collide. The duties considered weightier were then given precedence. Performing the due temple service, for instance, overrode the prohibition to work on the Sabbath day (*m. 'Erub.* 10:11–15; cf. Matt 12:5). Devoting certain assets to the Temple, again, could oblige a man to refrain from giving his wife her sustenance (*Hypoth.* 7.5), perhaps even from honoring his father and mother (cf. Mark 7:10–12; *m. Ned.* 9.1; see *m. Ned.* 1). According to Mark 12:28–34, Jesus presents Deut 6:4–5 (love of God) and Lev 19:18 (love of neighbor)as commandments which, inseparable from each other, take priority over all others. Logically, then, the scribe who had asked Jesus about the issue concludes that these outweigh even the temple service (Mark 12.33; cf. Matt 22.40). More specifically on Mark 12.28–34 → Great Commandment.

The commands to love: "Love your enemies!"

Jesus' command to love one's enemies in Matt 5.44–45/Luke 6:27–28, 35 has evoked much scholarly discussion. Corresponding views have been located in the Hellenistic world, especially in Cynic and Stoic thought (Epictetus, *Diss.* 3.22.53–55; cf. also Seneca, *Ben.* 4.26.1). In the Old Testament, too, scholars have pointed out how one is ordered to help one's enemy (Exod 23:4; but cf. Deut 22:1);

and later Jewish accounts also come close to the command (cf. *Jub.* 20:1–2; *T. Iss.* 7:6). Still, the tradition in Matt 5:44–45/Luke 6:27–28, 35 does feature some rather distinct aspects.

The command to love one's enemies is "a utopian standard" (Zeitlin xxv). In comparable contemporary thoughts, the goodness to be shown to the enemy consists of individual and concrete things which tend to demand what is realistic, what can reasonably be required. Likewise, the aim of the goodness is often to persuade the enemy to repent and/or to create conditions for getting along. In contrast, Jesus' command to love one's enemies holds no utilitarian motive. It proffers no realistic model for peaceful co-existence, no counsel on how to remain calm and composed when faced with the evil of this world, nor does it try to play down the discrepancy between the bad and the good in the sense "we are all brothers." The command is realistic about the evil of the world and the people one can call enemies. But it is plainly unrealistic about loving those people in that world. There is no consideration of how its wisdom could be lived up to, how life could continue under its guidance (cf. Sir 12:10–18).

Furthermore, the command to love one's enemies obscures the commandment to love one's neighbor in Lev 19:18. In the thinking induced by the Torah commandment, love is seen as the force that strengthens the inner bond of the covenant people. Hate in particular is not commanded to be shown to enemies (see, however, 1QS 1:9, 10; cf. also 1QS 1:4). Yet it is clear that to outsiders an attitude quite different from love is demanded. As love of one's neighbor ties the people together, some attitude separating the people from those outside should be adopted. The other way around, while hating the neighbor is generally considered a violation of the Torah commandment, loving the enemy constitutes an irrational idea. It means stretching the boundaries of friendship and alliance to those who markedly do not belong within them: love, strengthening the inner bond of the people, is to be pursued vis-à-vis the enemy, the one against whom the people is strengthened. This oxymoron of the command to love one's enemies utterly confuses the logic the Torah commandment relies on. It probably does not directly oppose the commandment but seizes its inherent idea and turns it inside out. That a redefinition of the concept of neighbor is called for here is an obvious but, in the end, insufficient observation. So far "to love" has guided the understanding of "neighbor" and vice versa. Now both need to be comprehended in a new way.

The Samaritan's love

Closely related to the above point is the parable of the Good Samaritan in Luke 10.30–35. Irrespective of the question whether we in the Samaritan's compassionate love (cf. especially Luke 10.33) should see a deliberate reference to Jesus' own behavior, the parable naturally proposes to disclose his understanding of the issue. Indeed, given the mutual enmity between the Jews and the Samaritans, the concrete act of love depicted by the parable can well be perceived as an example of the love of one's enemies commanded by Jesus. However, the Lukan context offers the parable as an explication of the commandment to love one's neighbor (see Luke 10:29, 36–37; compare Luke 10:25–28 with Mark 12:28–34).

God as a loving father

Jesus describes God as a father who knows the troubles and cares, comes to aid, has compassion and forgives (Matt 6:25–32/Luke 12:22–30; Matt 7:7–8/Luke 11:9–10; Matt 10:29–30/Luke 12:6–7; Matt 6:8; 18:19–20; Luke 6:36; cf. Matt 5:48). God is *Abba*, "dad," who implicitly loves his children. This conviction plays an important role in Jesus' parables as well (e.g. Matt 7:9–11/Luke 11:11–13; Matt 18:12–13/Luke 15:4–7; Luke 15:11–32). On the other hand, God the father is also the one who makes his sun rise both on the evil and the good, thus warranting love of one's enemies (Matt 5:45/Luke 6:35).

Jesus' love of people in general

Compassionate, merciful love towards the distressed in general represents a major characteristic even of Jesus' own behavior. The gospels establish it as the motive behind Jesus' healings and other miracles (Mark 1:41; 8:2–9; Matt 14:14; 20:34; Luke 7:13), even his teaching activity (Mark 6:34; Matt 9:35–38; Mark 10:21).

Jesus' love of (or friendship with) outcasts

As a distinct instance of the previous point, Jesus' friendship with sinners should be mentioned. Jesus accepted the company of tax collectors and other outcasts and was on account of this called "a friend of sinners" (see Mark 2:15–17; Luke 19:1–10; Matt 11:18–19/Luke 7:33–35), a label which he apparently approved. We can probably consider this a further example of the love of one's enemies, for sinners were regarded as enemies of God and,

as such, as enemies of those, too, who sided with God (Ps 37:20; 68:2–4; 139:19–22).

The exclusiveness of love

The Q-passage Matt 6:24/Luke 16:13 underlines the danger of "mammon" service (Gk. *mamonas*, "money," "wealth," "property") by posing an either–or relation between this and the service of God. The stress on the impossibility of having both also seeks to highlight that a heart truly devoted to God must be undivided, a fact that could appropriately be illuminated by speaking about love. When one truly loves something, one's devotion is complete and exclusive. This point is also pursued by the provoking Luke 14:26, where love is not mentioned but is probably implied. Allegiance to Jesus requires that one can cut him- or herself loose even from the closest relatives. One must (be prepared to?) hate them so that one can join Jesus in a proper way, namely with complete, undivided devotion (= loving him). This kind of extreme devotedness harks back to the example of the Levites described in Exod 32:26–29 (see also Deut 33:9). Understood as a Semitic hyperbole, "to hate" being rendered "to love less" (cf. Matt 10:37), the point here is altered with the effect that the exclusiveness of love no more comes to expression.

Miscellaneous sayings about love

Love growing cold because of lawlessness (Matt 24:12); great love shown as a result of many sins being forgiven (Luke 7:47); neglecting justice and love of God (Luke 11:42; but cf. Matt 23:23).

Some Johannine traditions

Jesus' love of his followers (e.g. John 11:36; 13:1; 15:9; 15:13; 17:23); the followers' love of Jesus (e.g. John 14:15–24; 15:10; 16:27; 21:15–17); the followers' mutual love (e.g. John 13:34–35; 15:12–17).

Taken, then, together, what can these traditions tell us about love as a theme of the mission and message of the historical Jesus? First of all, we should observe the peculiar tension encountered between the Great Commandment (esp. Mark 12:28–34) and the command to love one's enemies. The latter dissolves the thinking built on by the commandment to love one's neighbor in Lev 19:18, while the former seems to affirm just that. Commanding the love of one's enemies, Jesus presupposes a new understanding not only of neighbor but also of love, but in the appeal to the

Torah passage as forming part of the Great Commandment he seems to advocate the traditional notion. The Great Commandment has many times been described as the very center and the distinctive feature of Jesus' teaching. However, love of one's enemies has actually a firmer foothold in the Jesus tradition. Besides the Q-logion Matt 5:44–45/Luke 6:27–28, 35, the idea of enemy love can be detected in the parable of the Good Samaritan. It is probably operative in Jesus' friendship with sinners, too. At the same time, no particular interest in the idea can be discerned in subsequent early Christian ethics and theology, a fact which also supports its authenticity. Therefore, sustaining the authenticity of the Great Commandment as well would at least require postulating it an original historical context which problematizes the traditional conception of neighbor love. In fact, this could be something along the lines of what we have in Luke 10:25–37 (although according to Luke, Jesus never himself put forward the Great Commandment).

Further, the motifs accounted in the three sections above on God's and Jesus' love are strongly attested to in the tradition (→ exorcisms and healings; sinners) and can be considered historical. In their light it is difficult to avoid the conclusion that by showing love to all kinds of people Jesus intended to express or emulate God's fatherly love as he understood it. This is evident especially with respect to enemy love, which is said to be based on God's equal goodness towards both evil and good people. Seeing in Jesus' love of sinners (regarded as God's enemies) a concretization of this understanding, a close correlation between love and forgiveness also becomes visible. In reality, then, the tradition would support enemy love as a center of Jesus' teaching and doing. Scholarship has also established the command to love one's enemies, not so much the Great Commandment (cf. some parallels in *T. Iss.* 5:1–2; 7:6; *T. Dan* 5:3; *Spec. Laws* 2.63), as a truly distinct, indeed, even unique form of wisdom. Due to its "utopian" character, this love would best be viewed within the framework of Jesus' eschatological proclamation about the kingdom of God.

As it happens, the exclusiveness of love appears now surprisingly unconnected with the thinking reviewed so far. How could one hate one's father and mother, etc., if one should love one's neighbor, indeed even one's enemies? How could one's allegiance to God/Jesus be liable to being compromised by one's other relationships if loving God and loving the neighbor should be understood as commandments inseparable from each other? On the other hand, that Jesus placed considerable weight on following himself urgently and leaving behind both one's family and possessions is well rooted in the tradition (e.g. Matt 8:19–22/Luke 9:57–62). Therefore it is probably best not to dismiss the motif focused on in the exclusiveness of love as inauthentic but to regard it as belonging to a context within Jesus' mission different from that represented by the other material reviewed here. The purpose of the sayings addressed in the exclusiveness of love was not to teach about the concept of love, but the concept became involved *ad hoc*. This can hold true with respect to some instances mentioned in miscellaneous sayings as well.

Finally, we cannot ascertain the historicity of the individual Johannine sayings. Secondary is at least the reflection which sees in the "new commandment" to love one another, given to the disciples (John 13:34; see also 15:12, 17), a reshaping of the Torah commandment of neighbor love (cf. 1 John 4:20–25:2). In general, however, there is no reason why we should not believe that Jesus loved his disciples, that they loved him, and that he presupposed that they would also love each other.

Tom Holmén

Further reading

Furnish, V. P. *The Love Command in the New Testament*, London: SCM Press, 1973.

Holmén, T. *Jesus and Jewish Covenant Thinking*, Leiden: Brill, 2001.

Meisinger, H. *Liebesgebot und Altruismusforschung: Ein exegetischer Beitrag zum Dialog zwischen Theologie und Naturwissenschaft*, Göttingen: Vandenhoeck & Ruprecht, 1996.

Nissen, J. "The Distinctive Character of the New Testament Love Command in Relation to Hellenistic Judaism: Historical and Hermeneutical Reflections," in P. Borgen and S. Giversen (eds) *The New Testament and Hellenistic Judaism*, Aarhus: Aarhus University Press, 1995, pp. 123–50.

Piper, J. *'Love Your Enemies': Jesus' Love Command in the Synoptic Gospels and the Early Christian Paraenesis*, Cambridge: Cambridge University Press, 1979.

Swartley, W. M. (ed.) *The Love of Enemy and Nonretaliation in the New Testament*, Louisville, KY: Westminster/John Knox Press, 1992.

Zeitlin, S. "Prolegomenon," in G. Friedlander (ed.) *The Jewish Sources of the Sermon on the Mount*, New York: KTAV, 1969, pp. ix–xxxiii.

M

MAGIC, SORCERY

"Magic" is generally defined as the manipulation of supernatural forces for specific means, in contrast to "religion" which relies on appeals to God or gods. "Sorcery" is understood as "black magic" involving attempts to harm individuals as opposed to "white magic" which is used to defend against such curses. As religious and magical elements are often intermixed and as "magic" is often a pejorative term used by groups to marginalize social deviants (Segal 349–51), some scholars (Aune 1513–15; cf. Hull, Remus) deny that there are any objective differences. Though there is not always a clear-cut distinction, it certainly is the case that there is usually a contrast between what a religious community approves as a valid custom (e.g. Jewish phylactery) and popular but questionable magical practices (cf. Lange 435).

Magic in the New Testament world

Belief in magic was widespread in the biblical world (Yamauchi 1983). In Samaria Peter encountered Simon who "practiced sorcery" (NIV, Acts 8:9), and on Cyprus Paul rebuked a Jewish "sorcerer" named Bar-Jesus (NIV, Acts 13:6). Those converted by Paul at Ephesus made a bonfire of their magical scrolls (Acts 19:17–19). Paul rebuked the Galatians of being "bewitched" (NIV, Gal 3:1; Gk. *ebaskanen*). The New Testament condemns those who use drugs for nefarious purposes (Gal 5:20; Rev 9:21; 21:8; 22:15), passages which use Greek words related to *pharmakon* and which are translated as references to magic, sorcery or witchcraft (see C. Brown and J. S. Wright).

Accusations against Jesus in the first century

Jesus did not use magical formulae to effect his miracles or exorcisms (Twelftree 157–64). The closest instance in the gospel traditions to a magical cure is the case of the woman with an incurable flow of blood who was healed by touching Jesus' garment (Mark 5:24b–34; Matt 9:20–22; Luke 8:42b–48), but the Evangelists emphasize that it was her "faith" that healed her and not simply her touch (Bromley 86–102).

Though Jesus is not explicitly accused as a *magos* "magician" in the gospels, the charges that he exorcised demons by Beelzebul (Matt 12:24; Mark 3:22; Luke 11:15) and that he was a "deceiver" (Matt 27:63; Gk. *planos*) have persuaded some scholars (Smith, Stanton, Welch; cf. Samain) that Jesus was in effect accused of being a magician.

Accusations against Jesus in the second century

The early Christian apologist Justin Martyr (c. 160 CE) rebuts the claim of those who dismissed Jesus' miracles as magic (*Dial.* 69.7) "For they even dared to say that he was a magician and a deceiver of the people [Gk. *magos kai laoplanos*]."

The anti-Christian critic Celsus, as cited by Origen in his *Contra Celsum* 1.6, alleges that "it was by magic that he [Jesus] was able to do the miracles which he appeared to have done," having learned magic in Egypt. Celsus (*Cels.* 6.39) also declared that Christians "use some sort of magic and sorcery and invoke demons with barbarous names."

Origen responded that unlike sorcerers Jesus called his followers to lives of moral transformation. Other church fathers stressed the point that Jesus performed miracles without the use of magical materials. According to Arnobius (*Adv. Nat.* I.44), "But it is agreed that Christ did all He did without any paraphernalia, without the observance of any ritual or formula but only through the power of His name."

Later accusations against Jesus

The accusations of Celsus, who may have derived them from Jewish sources, are echoed in the Babylonian Talmud (*b. Sanh.* 43a), where we read: "On the eve of Passover Yeshu was hanged. For forty days before the execution took place, a herald went forth and cried, 'He is going forth to be stoned because he has practiced sorcery and enticed and led Israel astray.'" Another passage (*b. Sanh.* 107b) reads: "And a Master has said, 'Jesus the Nazarene practiced magic and led Israel astray.'" The medieval Jewish work, *The Toledoth Yeshu* (ninth century CE) speaks of Jesus's healing by the use of a magical incantation.

Recent depictions of Jesus as a magician

J. M. Hull holds that Jesus was depicted particularly in Mark and Luke as using magical means in his miracles, even though he does not believe that Jesus thought of himself as a magician. Hull's premise seems to be that exorcisms were unavoidably magical in nature.

David Aune, operating with a sociological definition of magic, agrees with Hull in stressing the similarity between Jesus's exorcisms and magic.

Partly with the support of the copy of a letter of Clement of Alexandria (150–211 CE), which he discovered in the Mar Saba Monastery, Morton Smith interprets a passage from an alleged Secret Mark to maintain that not only was Jesus accused of magic, he was indeed a magician, who initiated his followers with a homoerotic ritual. He interprets the Eucharist on the basis of erotic magical texts, and cites parallels from the *Life of Apollonius of Tyana* to argue his case. There are some striking parallels to Jesus's command, "Come out of him" (Mark 1:25 and Luke 4:35) in the *Greek Magical Papyri* (IV.1243 ff. and 3013 ff.). But these parallels, it should be noted, come from the third and fourth centuries CE. Smith concedes that the gospels do not depict Jesus as a magician, but ascribes this lack of evidence as the result of a "cover-up."

Smith's provocative thesis has been criticized in numerous reviews and in works on miracles and exorcisms by Howard Clark Kee and Graham Twelftree. Kee, who argues that we can distinguish between magic and miracle, notes that Jesus' miracles were not just acts of compassion but were signs revealing the coming of the kingdom of God prophesied in the Old Testament. Twelftree, while conceding that Jesus used formulae similar to that used by contemporary exorcists, maintains that unlike them Jesus did not use any mechanical devices, offer explicit prayers, call upon any other source of authority, or use any "powerful name."

EDWIN M. YAMAUCHI

Further reading

Aune, D. E. "Magic in Early Christianity," *ANRW* 2.23.2 (1980) 1507–57.
Bromley, D. H. "Jesus: Magician or Miracle Worker?" online; available at www.annarborvineyard.org/media/pdf/DHB.Thesis.pdf.
Brown, C. and J. S. Wright. "Magic, Sorcery, Magi," *NIDNTT* 2 (1975) 552–62.
Hull, J. M. *Hellenistic Magic and the Synoptic Tradition*, London: SCM Press, 1974.
Kee, H. C. *Miracle in the Early Christian World*, New Haven, CT: Yale University Press, 1983.
Lange, A. "The Essene Position on Magic and Divination," in M. Bernstein, F. G. Martinez, and J. Kampen, *Legal Texts and Legal Issues*, Leiden: Brill, 1997, pp. 77–435.
Remus, H. *Pagan-Christian Conflict over Miracles in the Second Century*, Cambridge, MA: Philadelphia Patristic Foundation, 1983.
Samain, P. "L'accusation de magie contre le Christ dans les Evangiles," *ETL* 15 (1938) 449–90.
Segal, A. F. "Hellenistic Magic: Some Questions of Definition," in R. van den Broek and M. J. Vermaseren (eds) *Studies in Gnosticism and Hellenistic Religions*, EPRO 91, Leiden: Brill, 1981, pp. 349–75.
Smith, M. *Jesus the Magician*, San Francisco, CA: Harper & Row, 1978.
Stanton, G. N. "Jesus of Nazareth: A Magician and False Prophet who Deceived God's People?," in J. B. Green and M. Turner (eds) *Jesus of Nazareth: Lord and Christ*, Grand Rapids, MI: Eerdmans, 1994, pp. 164–80.
Twelftree, G. H. *Jesus the Exorcist*, Tübingen: J. C. B. Mohr, 1993; Peabody, MA: Hendrickson, 1993.
Welch, J. W. "Law, Magic, Miracles and the Trial of Jesus," in J. H. Charlesworth (ed.) *Jesus and Archaeology*, Grand Rapids, MI: Eerdmans, 2006, pp. 349–83.
Yamauchi, E. M. "Magic in the Biblical World," *TynBul* 34 (1983) 169–200.
—— "Magic or Miracle? Diseases, Demons and Exorcisms," in D. Wenham and C. Blomberg (eds) *Gospel Perspectives VI: The Miracles of Jesus*, Sheffield: JSOT Press, 1986, pp. 89–183.

MANSON, THOMAS WALTER

T. W. Manson, (1893–1958), Rylands Professor of Biblical Criticism and Exegesis in Manchester from

1936 until his death, belonged within the tradition of gospel criticism typical of the UK in the first half of the twentieth century. His first and most influential book, *The Teaching of Jesus* (1931), was written at a time when the priority of Mark and the four-documentary hypothesis were regarded as having been established beyond reasonable doubt, and when Mark's Gospel was still generally assumed to be a biographical sketch of Jesus' ministry. Working on these presuppositions, Manson understood Peter's confession at Caesarea Philippi to be the great turning-point of Jesus' life, and assumed that Jesus' teaching belonged to the various periods of his ministry and was addressed to the various audiences indicated by Mark, and that it should be interpreted accordingly.

This first book shows no awareness of the work of the German form-critics, whose writings were largely unknown outside Germany at the time. Unlike Bultmann, the foremost form-critic, Manson believed that historical enquiry into the life and teaching of Jesus was essential for Christian faith. Nevertheless, he acknowledged the difficulty of discovering the *ipsissima verba* of Jesus, and – supposing this to be possible – of comprehending them. In order to understand Jesus' teaching it was, he believed, essential to explore its roots in Judaism. For this, Manson was able to draw on his expertise in biblical and rabbinical Hebrew and Aramaic and his knowledge of the Jewish scriptures.

In *The Teaching of Jesus*, Manson explored the central themes of Jesus' teaching, and over half the book is devoted to that of "God as King". In Germany, two diametrically opposed views had been suggested: one thought of God's kingdom as something that arrived by a process of evolution, and understood Jesus to be teaching ideals after which men and women should strive, while the other believed that the kingdom was a supernatural realm, and concluded that Jesus was proclaiming the imminent end of the present world-order. In Manson's view, both interpretations were wrong. The kingdom was independent of space and time: it was essentially a personal relationship between God and individuals, and it was pointless to ask whether it was present or future, since God's sovereignty is an eternal fact, is manifested in the present life of the people of God, and will finally be consummated at the end of time.

Manson's understanding of God's kingship was based on his study of Jewish thought, and he demonstrates how these three aspects of the kingdom are rooted in the Old Testament, and are reflected in the Pseudepigrapha and rabbinical writings. Since he understood God's kingdom to be manifested on earth in the lives of those who acknowledge God to be their king, he saw Jesus as calling men and women to live in obedience to God. It is in this context that Manson introduced his interpretation of the phrase "the Son of man". He argued that its use by Jesus was based on Dan 7:13, where it was used as a symbol for "the saints of the Most High", and so stood for "the manifestation of the kingdom of God on earth in a people wholly devoted to their heavenly king" (*Teaching*, p. 227). Jesus invited his disciples to share the role of the Son of Man: hence the close link between the "passion predictions" and the demands he makes of his followers, e.g. Mark 8:34; 10:32–40; 14:26–31. In the event, however, it was Jesus alone who suffered. Unlike those scholars on the continent who were arguing (on the basis of I Enoch 37–71) that the Son of Man was an eschatological Redeemer, whose arrival was expected by first-century Jews, and that the only authentic "Son of Man" sayings were those which referred to future vindication, Manson saw no problem in attributing these sayings, as well as those about suffering, to Jesus. Manson's interpretation of the phrase gained little support on the continent but was influential in the English-speaking world, especially Great Britain, where it was advocated by C. F. D. Moule, M. D. Hooker and G. B. Caird.

In an essay published in 1942 entitled "Is it Possible to Write a Life of Christ?" Manson indicated the difficulties involved in such a project: the paucity of the material, and doubts concerning its authenticity and arrangement. Though acknowledging the work of the form critics, he is sceptical about their conclusions regarding the reliability of the evidence, commenting dryly that the fact that a story has a "*Sitz im Leben der alten Kirche*" does not automatically mean that it cannot have a "*Sitz im Leben* Jesus" (p. 249). Yet even though he believed that there was a great deal of material that went back in essentials to eyewitnesses and to Jesus himself, he conceded that there was insufficient evidence to write a continuous account of Jesus' ministry. To understand Jesus, he must be seen in his historical context, and that means in relation both to Judaism and to the Church.

Following this essay, Manson delivered a series of lectures in the 1940s under the general heading "Materials for a Life of Jesus". Less sure than he had been about the reliability of the Markan framework (questioning, e.g., the dating of the Entry into Jerusalem), he nevertheless concludes that some of it, like the tradition itself, may go back to Peter. In a lecture delivered in 1949 entitled "The

Quest of the Historical Jesus – Continued" he reaffirmed his conviction that the gospels provided reliable material for an outline of the ministry which fitted into contemporary Jewish faith and life, made sense in the context of Roman imperial policy, and provided an adequate explanation of the existence of the Church. It was this outline that he attempted to produce in his final book, *The Servant Messiah.*

Manson's work was characterized by careful exegesis of the text, as well as by original insights. Developments in the second half of the twentieth century meant a move away from the traditional assumption of the historicity of the material. But Manson's real contribution lay in his emphasis on Jesus' Jewish context. The next generation of scholars were to ignore his insights, believing that in order to discover the authentic core of Jesus' teaching, it was necessary to apply the criterion of "dissimilarity", so *isolating* Jesus from both Judaism and the Church. More recently, however, it has been increasingly recognized (by E. P. Sanders, among others) that it is impossible to comprehend Jesus unless he is seen in his Jewish context.

MORNA D. HOOKER

Further reading

Caird, G. B. *New Testament Theology,* ed. L. D. Hurst, Oxford: Clarendon Press, 1994.
Hooker, M. D. *The Son of Man in Mark,* London: SPCK; Montreal: McGill, 1967.
—— "Is the Son of Man Problem Really Insoluble?," in Ernest Best and R. McL. Wilson (eds) *Text and Interpretation: Studies in the New Testament presented to Matthew Black,* Cambridge: Cambridge University Press, 1979, pp. 155–68.
Manson, T. W. *The Teaching of Jesus,* Cambridge: Cambridge University Press, 1931.
—— *The Sayings of Jesus,* London: SCM Press, 1949 (first published as Part II of *The Mission and Message of Jesus,* 1937).
—— "Is it Possible to Write a Life of Christ?," *ExpTim* 53 (1942) 248–51.
—— *The Servant Messiah,* Cambridge: Cambridge University Press, 1953.
—— *Studies in the Gospels and Epistles,* ed. Matthew Black, Manchester: Manchester University Press, 1962.
Moule, C. F. D. *The Origin of Christology,* Cambridge: Cambridge University Press, 1977.
Sanders, E. P. *Jesus and Judaism,* London: SCM Press, 1985.
—— *The Historical Figure of Jesus,* London: Penguin, 1993.

MARTYRS AND MARTYRDOM IN JEWISH LATE ANTIQUITY

The term "martyr" is usually used to describe a person who chooses to accept death rather than violate his or her allegiance to a higher cause; in religious environments, this generally means refusing to compromise his or her performance of his or her obligations to God and the values or behaviors prescribed by God as delineated by his or her particular religious tradition. The word, which also appears in legal contexts in Greco-Roman society to describe someone who bears testimony relevant to a case, highlights the public nature of this renunciation of life for the sake of piety, and hence the "testimony" that the witness bears (increasingly in forensic settings where the martyrs are put on trial) to the supreme value of fidelity to God.

Early Jewish martyrs and the significance of their deaths

Although the figure of the martyr would be far more common and more broadly celebrated in Christian literature and experience, the roots of the Western tradition of the religious martyr are to be sought in Second Temple Judaism. While there are examples of martyrs earlier in Jewish literature (see below), the martyr rises to prominence for the first time in texts written in the shadow of the Hellenizing Reform and Maccabean Revolution. The Jerusalem elites, led first by the high priest Jason and then his usurper, Menelaus, sought to re-found Jerusalem as a Greek city with a Greek constitution, initiatives that were welcomed by the Seleucid king, Antiochus IV, who saw this as a means toward a more unified kingdom (and welcomed the additional funds being promised for the privileges). Local in-fighting between Jason, Menelaus, and other parties led Antiochus to support harsh, repressive measures against continued observance of the Judeans' ancestral customs, which were no doubt cited (rightly) as a rallying point for resistance.

Despite these measures, Jews were remembered to have resisted by persevering in their ancestral ways and distinctive practices, even though this directly resulted in their deaths. The author of 1 Maccabees mentions that those who preserved copies of Torah were put to death, and tells briefly of the execution, together with their infants, of Jewish mothers who had circumcised their babies. He also relates that many "chose to die rather than to be defiled by food or to profane the holy covenant" (1 Macc 1:60–64). No particular value, however, is attached to their deaths, which were merely a consequence of their fidelity.

The author of 2 Maccabees, however, a text generally held to be written in the late second or early first century BCE, offers dramatically expanded narration of those who refused to eat defiling foods as a sign of their acquiescence to apostasy, telling in detail of the martyrdoms of the aged priest Eleazar, seven brothers, and the mother of the seven (6:18–7:42). The author sets these martyrdoms within an interpretative frame. On the one hand, he presents their torments, in keeping with the Deuteronomistic view of Israel's rising and falling fortune, as a manifestation of God's chastisement of Israel, which has been unfaithful to the covenant, particularly in the persons of its Hellenizing high priest and aristocracy. It is a sign of God's mercy to punish God's people before their sins have reached the point of no return (2 Macc 6:12–17). The seventh brother, the final martyr to receive the author's detailed attention, voices a more nuanced hope in this context, however, namely that God would "soon show mercy" toward the rest of the nation (2 Macc 7:37), and, indeed, that their deaths would "bring an end to the wrath of the Almighty" against the nation (2 Macc 7:38). The martyrs offers their lives, thus, to hasten the "reconciliation" with God that they expect would follow the period of chastisement (2 Macc 7:33). It is noteworthy in this regard that the martyrs die out of a *refusal* to break God's laws (2 Macc 6:19–20, 30; 7:2), not as a consequence of their own participation in apostasy (i.e. as a punishment that justly falls on them as individual transgressors). While they suffer "justly" as part of the disobedient nation, they are also in a position to offer their lives to God out of innocence and obedience as a plea that God would act favorably toward the disobedient nation. Within the narrative frame, the author suggests that God has accepted the martyrs' plea, for in the immediately following scene Judas and his armies enjoy their initial successes, "for the wrath of the Lord had turned to mercy" (2 Macc 8:5). The martyrs thus stand in the tradition of Moses and David who, as it is related in *Mek. Pisha* 1.103–13, offered their lives on behalf of a disobedient nation that had provoked God's wrath (as cited in Eduard Lohse, *Märtyrer und Gottesknecht*).

Such reflection on the significance of the voluntary death of righteous, obedient martyrs would certainly have been available to Jesus. This is not to suggest that the actual martyrs (the historicity of these narratives being rather problematic) had viewed their deaths this way, but only that the author of 2 Maccabees joins the interpretation to the paradigm in such a way that future martyrs could think of their own deaths in these terms. The martyrs in 2 Maccabees also give frequent and prominent expression to the expectation of vindication by God through resurrection (2 Macc 7:9,

11, 14, 23, 29, 36) or, in other texts (such as *4 Macc.* and Wis 1–5), to some other form of life beyond death, suggesting that this was an integral part of this paradigm, even as it appears to be an integral part of the passion predictions.

Eleazar, the seven brothers, and their mother are the focal examples in 4 Maccabees, a text that uses them as the climactic proof that "devout reason," that is to say the rational faculty that has been trained by following the Jewish Torah, can master the passions (*4 Macc.* 1:1, 7–9) and thus achieve the moral ideal of the Greco-Roman sages. Fourth Maccabees is a Jewish text written in Greek somewhere between Syrian Antioch and Cilicia, sometime in the mid to late first century CE. While this text is too far removed in time and geography to be said to have exerted any influence upon the historical Jesus, it is valuable as a witness to Jewish reflection on the significance of the death of the righteous martyr as a parallel, and perhaps mutually informing, development to early Christian interpretations of the significance of the death of Jesus.

The author of 4 Maccabees attests to a much more highly developed theology of the efficacy of the death of the righteous person than its source, 2 Maccabees. Both remain appeals to God for "mercy" (2 Macc 7:37; *4 Macc.* 6:28), and both view reconciliation – and, therefore, God's saving intervention in the affairs of the nation – as the result of these deaths (2 Macc 7:33, 38; 8:5; *4 Macc.* 17:22b). In two passages, the author of 4 Maccabees uses much more explicitly sacrificial and cultic imagery to describe the efficacy of the martyrs' death. On the basis of his voluntary obedience to the point of death, Eleazar prays: "Be merciful to your people, and let our punishment suffice for them. Make my blood their purification, and take my life in exchange (*antipsychon*) for theirs" (6:28–29). After the martyrdoms of all nine figures, the author describes their achievement in cultic terms:

> the tyrant was punished, and the homeland purified – they having become, as it were, a ransom (*antipsychon*) for the sin of our nation. And through the blood of those devout ones and their death as a propitiatory sacrifice (*hilastērion*), divine Providence preserved Israel that previously had been mistreated.
>
> (17:21–22)

The author twice uses the language of "cleansing" or "purification" to speak of the political results of the resistance spawned by the martyrs' dedication (1.11; 17:21), by which he means the expulsion of Antiochus and his forces.

The connection between the violent shedding of blood (6:29; 17:22) and the exchange of a life for the life of another (*antipsychon*) resonates with the fundamental principle undergirding the Levitical sacrificial system, namely that the blood of sacrificial victims was provided by God for the sake of making atonement between God and God's people: "as life, it is blood that atones for a life" (ἀντὶ τῆς ψυχῆς; Lev 17:11). Moreover, the term ἱλαστήριον (16:13) is related to the verb used throughout the Septuagint for "propitiate," "atone," or "reconcile," and is itself used to describe the cover of the ark of the covenant, the place where atonement is made on Israel's behalf. While a human sacrifice is nowhere prescribed by Torah, in the absence of a functioning sacrificial system (as was the case during the period of these martyrs) the voluntary self-sacrifice of a righteous person is seen to function as would a sin offering (and can come to be regarded as a superior one, as in Heb 9:11–14 reflecting on the death of Jesus). The martyrs' deaths have two important results: God now acts favorably toward God's people to deliver them; covenant obedience among God's people is revived (17:22; 18:4).

This introduction to the development of Jewish martyrology would be incomplete without looking at several prominent precursors. Fourth Maccabees explicitly connects the martyrs' predicament with the stories of Isaac, Daniel, and the three youths in Assyria (*4 Macc.* 16:16–23; 18:10–19), who are seen as important prototypes of the martyrs. Second Temple Period developments of the tradition of the binding of Isaac emphasized his voluntary consent to die in obedience to God's command (*Tg. Neof.* 22:10; Josephus, *Ant.* 1.232; Pseudo-Philo *L.A.B.* 32.2–3). More significantly, Isaac's near-sacrifice is believed to have beneficial effects for the people of Israel in their relationship with God. The merits of this obedient death result in the election of Israel (Pseudo-Philo, *L.A.B.* 18.5), are recalled before God in the Levitical sacrifices (*Lev Rab.* on Lev 1:5, 10; *Tg. Neof.* Lev 22:27), prefigure the Passover sacrifices (*Jub.* 17:15), and remain in God's memory to assure the favorable hearing of the prayers of Israel when in distress (*Targum Neofiti* Gen 22:14).

The tales in Daniel 3 and 6 gained currency in the Antiochene persecution, when the visions of Daniel were composed. The story of the three youths who braved the fiery furnace rather than yield to the king's command to bow down before an idol anticipates the forensic situation in which the martyrs would find themselves. The developments of this tale in Greek Daniel move in the direction of interpreting the obedient death of the righteous as an act that reconciles the people to God. In the Prayer of Azariah, Azariah prays that

the willing, obedient deaths of himself and his two companions would be accepted by God and have the effect of properly offered burnt offerings, and that their sacrifice would have an expiatory effect for the sins of the people that led to gentile domination in the first place. Up to the point of their miraculous deliverance Daniel 3 is essentially a martyr text.

The emphasis in these texts falls upon the obedience of the martyr as effective for the relationship between God and God's people, not the shedding of blood *per se*. Sacrificial imagery is interpretive. As such, martyr ideology is a development of the covenant theology of Deuteronomy, according to which the people's return to obedience effects the reversal of the covenant curses (Deut 30:1–5), using the imagery of the Levitical sacrificial system (both because it provides a means for describing reconciliation with God and because of the similarities between the ritual violence of sacrifice and the fate of Jewish martyrs). The signal difference is that, now, it is the *representative* obedience of the martyrs that brings a return of covenant blessings to the larger, disobedient nation.

One other background deserves mention here, and that is the development of the tradition of the deaths of the prophets. The earliest witness to this tradition appears to be Neh 9:26. Describing the period of the divided monarchy, the author writes that the people "cast Your law behind their backs and killed Your prophets who had rebuked them so that they might return to You." While the historical books, together with the prophetic books, of the Hebrew Bible give ample attention to the witness of these prophets, they are rather lacking in regard to details concerning their violent deaths (save for the stoning of Zechariah, 2 Chr 24:17–22). The *Lives of the Prophets* provides a bridge between the scriptural tradition of the prophets as obedient witnesses to God's covenant and the traditions of the prophets as martyrs (attested as a "given" of Jewish cultural knowledge in Matt 23:29–36//Luke 11:47–51; Acts 7:52). Expanding the biblical tradition, the *Lives of the Prophets* tells of the deaths of Isaiah (*Liv. Pro.* 1.1), Jeremiah (*Vit. Proph.* 2.1), Ezekiel (*Liv. Pro.* 3.1–2), Micah (*Liv. Pro.* 6.1–2), Amos (*Liv. Pro.* 7.1–3), and Zechariah (*Liv. Pro.* 23.1) on account of their bearing witness to the word of the Lord, confronting the covenant infidelity of Israel and her rulers. Another text, the *Martyrdom of Isaiah*, a work that in its present form has clearly been heavily edited by Christian scribes, describes the persecution and martyrdom of Isaiah in detail, fully combining the prophetic and martyrological traditions. This is not to say that *every* prophet was remembered to have died a martyr's death on account of their witness to the righteous demands of God's covenant (within the *Lives of the Prophets*, the majority still die peacefully), only that the traditions about the deaths of prophets about which the Jewish Scriptures are silent have multiplied significantly by the time of Jesus, who is thus well poised to regard himself standing in line with this tradition (perhaps even as the climax of this tradition, as the parable of the Wicked Tenants suggests).

Examples of Jewish martyrs from the Maccabean period on could be multiplied. In 1 Macc 2:29–38, large numbers of Jews are reported to have refused to defend themselves when attacked on the Sabbath, so as not to violate the Sabbath. Philo relates in his *In Flaccum* how, during the anti-Jewish riots in Alexandria, many Jews repeated the bravery of the martyrs celebrated in 2 Macc 6–7, refusing to deny their way of life by eating pork to escape physical abuse and even lynching. The figure of Razis (2 Macc 14:37–46) is often identified as a martyr (committing suicide so as to avoid the degradation of torture), as are the literary characters of Taxo and his sons, who commit to fast for three days and depart to a cave in the desert to die rather than participate in apostasy (*T. Mos.* 9.1–7). Only in the latter case is there some minor interpretative significance ascribed to the death of the martyr (Taxo hopes to provoke God to avenge the deaths of his faithful ones by voluntarily adding to their number), aside from seeing in their deaths a testimony to their own steadfastness and virtue.

Jewish martyrology and early Christian interpretations of Jesus' death

The recovery of Jesus' understanding of his own ministry is vexed by numerous points, from the question of the authenticity of key sayings and traditions to the question of the adequacy of the materials deemed authentic to provide a sufficient basis for discerning how Jesus understood his own impending death. The background of the martyrological tradition, including the deaths of the prophets, provides adequate ground for suggesting that Jesus foresaw that this prophetic witness would lead to his death if he persisted, and that Jesus embraced this end as an act that would bring benefit to others in their experience of God's favor.

The Jesus tradition strongly attests Jesus' expectation that his ministry would end in a violent death at the hands of those whom he opposed,

from the celebrated triple "passion predictions" (Mark 8:31//Matt 16:21//Luke 9:22; Mark 9:31//Matt 17:22//Luke 9:44; Mark 10:33–34//Matt 20:18–19//Luke 18:31–33) to less fully developed expressions of this sense of impending martyrdom (Mark 9:12//Matt 17:12; Mark 10:38//Matt 20:22; Mark 10:45//Matt 20:28; Matt 26:2; Mark 14:22//Matt 26:26–28//Luke 22:19), not to mention Johannine attestations to the same. According to Sydney Page, the historicity of the claim that Jesus expected to die a violent (martyr's) death is virtually assured by the number of sayings to that effect in the Jesus tradition (attested in multiple streams of tradition, in multiple forms, and often obliquely or subtly, the last point suggesting authenticity because secondary commentary would tend to be more explicit), though it remains likely that many of the discrete sayings underwent development in the history of transmission.

The tradition of the deaths of the prophets provides added plausibility to this claim, a tradition made poignantly pertinent by the arrest and execution of Jesus' cousin and, perhaps, mentor, John the Baptist, who clearly identified himself with the prophetic tradition. Jesus' predictions of his death need not be doubted on the basis of the reluctance of historians to believe that the future can be foreseen: Jesus had ample precedent for expecting his own demise without any recourse to the prophetic gift.

The Q tradition particularly gives prominence to Jesus' consciousness of standing in the tradition of the prophets. Jesus assumes that the line of prophets constituted a line of martyrs from Abel to Zechariah (Matt 23:29–36//Luke 11:47–51), and that his followers' fates would continue that trend. Q shows Jesus preparing his followers for such resistance to their prophetic witness (Luke 12:4–5//Matt 10:28), and denouncing Jerusalem chiefly for its murder of the prophets who witnessed to the city's disloyalty to the covenant and called for repentance (Luke 13:34//Matt 23:37). In a saying peculiar to Luke in this context (Luke 13:33), Jesus intimates that he goes to Jerusalem to meet the same end: "the next day I must be on my way, because it is not possible for a prophet to be killed outside of Jerusalem." The Parable of the Wicked Tenants, of course, places Jesus at the pinnacle of this tradition of martyred prophets (Mark 12:1–12//Matt 21:33–44//Luke 20:9–19). In Matthew's presentation of Jesus' activity in Jerusalem, Jesus' contemporaries popularly regard him as a prophet (21:11, 46), and so give evidence that they found Jesus' activity congenial to the paradigm of the prophet who confronted the powers that be at great risk to himself, and would continue to use the paradigm of the martyred prophet after the crucifixion to make sense of the outcome (as in Luke 24:19–20), and even after the experience of the resurrected Jesus (as in Acts 2–3, where the paradigm of the "Prophet like Moses," whom the people handed over to be killed, remains prominent).

A more vexed question concerns whether or not Jesus ascribed value to his death in terms of having beneficial effects on the relationship between God and other people. Within the Jesus tradition, two texts principally attest to this possibility. The first is Mark 10:45 (//Matt 20:28), where Jesus says: "The Son of Man came not to be served but to serve, and to give his life as a ransom for many." The second is found in the context of the Last Supper (Mark 14:22–24//Matt 26:26–28//Luke 22:19–20). The recovery of the original wording is a matter of considerable debate, but there is general agreement that, in the "cup word," Jesus spoke of his blood being "poured out for many" and described the cup as "the blood of the covenant." The fracturing and distributing of the bread as "my body" is also performative of the interpretation of his death as undertaken on behalf of others.

The interpretation of the deaths of the Maccabean martyrs in 2 Macc 7:37–38; 8:5 as a beneficial death for others within the framework of God's covenant provides a significant precedent to the interpretation of the death of Jesus, and may well have informed his own understanding of his impending death. It was a tradition available to Jesus in his time and location, and likely to have received regular attention in the annual celebration of Hanukkah. It was also a living, growing tradition, as the developments in 4 Maccabees show. Indeed, Jesus' statements about his own death are a rather remarkable development of the same tradition in the same direction, as one observes in the statements placed on Eleazar's lips in *4 Macc.* 6:28–29 and offered by the author in *4 Macc.* 17:21–22 about the martyrs' deaths. The ransom saying attributed to Jesus (Mark 10:45//Matt 20:28) resonates linguistically and conceptually with the interpretation of the martyrs' deaths as an *antipsychon*, a "life given in exchange for others," in *4 Macc.* 6:29; 17:22: "The Son of Man came . . . to give his life a ransom for many" (δοῦναι τὴν ψυχὴν αὐτοῦ λύτρον ἀντὶ πολλῶν). Moreover, Jesus' emphasis on his "blood poured out" for others in the cup word at the Last Supper resonates with Eleazar's prayer that his blood, shed in obedience to God, should effect the purification of his fellow Jews (and the restoration of the covenant relationship between God and the nation; *4 Macc.* 6:28–29).

At this point, however, it becomes necessary to consider another "martyrological" tradition in the Hebrew Bible, namely the Suffering Servant of Isaiah 52:13–53:12. Scholars have generally insisted that the Jesus traditions about a death on behalf of others must be derived *either* from the Maccabean martyrs *or* from the Servant Song of Isaiah. The fact that both are able to marshal so much evidence in favor of their position strongly suggests that we should look to the *blending* of these two traditions behind the early church's interpretation of Jesus' death, perhaps beginning with Jesus himself (who is also commonly credited with blending the figures of the Danielic Son of Man and the Isaianic Suffering Servant in Mark 10:45, a blend also observed in such texts as 11QMelch and the *Parables of Enoch*).

The Suffering Servant song, though perhaps originally meant to speak of the redemptive effects of Israel's sufferings on behalf of the Gentiles, or the suffering of a remnant within Israel on behalf of the sinful nation as a whole, could be read in a new light in the wake of the martyrdoms celebrated from the Maccabean period, and might indeed have fueled the author of 4 Maccabees' reflection on the significance of those deaths. The servant becomes now a particular righteous person whose sufferings and death become (by the servant's own self-offering, 53:10b, and by God's action, 53:6b) the functional equivalent of an offering for the sins of the nation. The servant's mutilation and torment (Isa 52:14 and 53:3), his voluntary offering of himself having atoning efficacy (Isa 53:4–6, 8, 10, 12b), the narrator's affirmation that the death had this effect (Isa 53:10b–11), and the concluding celebration of the servant's virtue and achievement (Isa 53:12a) all parallel the author of 4 Maccabees' treatment of the Jewish martyrs.

In the case of the Jesus tradition, the phrase "for many" in the two sayings in which Jesus interprets his own death as an act bringing benefit to others (placed at two critical junctures in the Markan narrative, Mark 10:45; 14:22) echoes the prominence of the "many" who benefit from the servant's sufferings in Isa 53:11–12. His intent to "give his life" (Mark 10:45) could be heard as an abbreviated paraphrase of Isa 53:10 ("when you make his life an offering for sin"). The "ransom saying" concerning the "Son of Man who came . . . to serve and give his life as a ransom for many" (Mark 10:45//Matt 20:28) can be regarded as an appropriate summary of the career of the servant of Isa 53:4–12 who offered his life as a substitute for the many.

Moreover, other sayings attributed to Jesus regarding his own suffering point to the paradigm of Isaiah 53, e.g. the assumption that the Scriptures speak about the Son of Man "suffering many things and being treated with contempt" (Mark 9:12), which, as Rikk Watts observes, resonates conceptually and even linguistically with the terms "suffer" in Isa 53:3, 4, 10 and "treat with contempt" in the non-Septuagintal Greek versions of Isa 53:3. The paradigm of the Maccabean martyrs, especially as developed in the trajectory leading from 2 Maccabees toward 4 Maccabees, reinforces the reading of Isaiah 53 as the divine appointment of a righteous individual's death to be suffered on behalf of the people.

The words of Jesus at the Last Supper continue to be informed by the paradigm of the Suffering Servant, as observed above. These words, however, move explicitly sacrificial and cultic imagery to the foreground in the interpretation of Jesus' death. As Jeremias observed in his book, *The Eucharistic Words of Jesus*, the separate attention given to the "body" and the "blood" in the words and acts at the Last Supper in itself recalls the Levitical sacrifices, in which blood is separated from the sacrificial animal's body and poured out as a separate act from the ritual handling of the flesh ("body") of the victim.

While sacrificial imagery is not foreign to Isaiah 53 (the phrase "poured out for many," suggestive of the sacrificial disposition of the blood of the victim, echoes Isa 53:12, and the servant's life is made by God "an offering for sin," Isa 53:10), Jewish martyrological texts are much more explicit about the death of a righteous person functioning as a propitiatory or expiatory sacrifice, as in the Prayer of Azariah and most explicitly in 4 Maccabees, down to the mention of the martyrs' "blood" as a purificatory agent (6:29) and their deaths as "propitiatory offerings" (17:22). In the Jesus tradition, Jesus appears to combine the image of the sacrifice of atonement (blood "poured out for many," resonating with the restorative effects of the deaths of the martyrs and the Suffering Servant on the divine–human relationship injured by transgressions of the covenant) and the sacrifice of covenant inauguration (the "blood of the covenant," specifically recontextualizing a phrase from Exod 24:8, the original covenant-inauguration rite). Stuhlmacher has observed how these two rites are already blended in *Targum Onqelos* and *Targum Yerushalmi* I Exod 24:8, where the "blood of the covenant" is sprinkled on the altar "to make atonement for the people."

To what extent these texts represent Jesus' self-understanding in regard to his own death depends on one's assessment of their authenticity. A significant number of scholars, however, affirm the authenticity of these sayings (allowing for the problem of recovering the Aramaic original) and are prepared to see in them a genuine reflection of Jesus' own approach to his death. This approach, then, would be deeply influenced by the tradition of Jewish martyrology (both the deaths of the prophets and the obedient deaths of the martyrs who gave their lives for the sake of securing divine benefits for the nation), understood within the framework of covenant renewal (or even inauguration).

Jesus' contemporaries, however, at least those who were favorably disposed toward him and his ministry, were certainly poised to interpret his death in terms of these traditions, as seen throughout the literary reflections on his death left by his followers. Many of these followers, moreover, understood themselves to continue in that tradition, anticipating that their calling involved not only "serving" as the Servant of the Lord came to serve, but also "giving their lives" in obedient witness to God as did Jesus (compare Mark 10:38–39 with 10:45).

This understanding extended to the establishment of the new covenant promised by Jeremiah (31:31–34), seen from the additions to the words of institution in Luke ("the *new* covenant in my blood," Luke 22:19; "poured out *for the forgiveness of sins*," Matt 26:28). This emphasis on the "forgiveness of sins," the hallmark of Jeremiah's "new covenant," appears also in the naming of Jesus (Matt 1:18), Jesus' first declaration about the purpose of his mission ("to forgive sins," Matt 9:2, 6//Mark 2:5, 10//Luke 5:20, 24), and the proclamation of forgiveness in Jesus' name after his passion (Luke 24:46–47; John 20:23), reaching its pinnacle, of course, in the central argumentative section of the *Epistle to the Hebrews* (8:1–10:18).

Early Christian literature outside the gospels shows just how fruitful – and pervasive – the interpretation of Jesus' death in line with the martyrological tradition was among Jesus' contemporaries and the succeeding generation. The martyrs themselves are used as moral examples (Heb 11:35b), and the example of Jesus, "who endured a cross, despising shame" (Heb 12:2), is portrayed in martyrological language, recalling Eleazar's bold stance as he "endured the pains and scorned the compulsions" (*4 Macc.* 6:9). These early Christian authors often use language to interpret the significance of Jesus' violent death similar to the language used by the author of 4 Maccabees to interpret the violent deaths of the martyrs. Just as Eleazar's blood was seen to have purificatory efficacy (*4 Macc.* 6:29; 17:22), so Jesus' blood is said to be a purifying or atoning agent (Rom 3:25; 5:10; Eph 1:7; Heb 9:12–14; 13:12; 1 Pet 1:2, 19; 1 John 1:7; Rev 7:14). Like the Maccabean martyrs, Jesus is set forward as a "propitiatory sacrifice," an offering that propitiates the Deity who has been alienated by human sinfulness (*hilastērion*, *4 Macc.* 17:22; Rom 3:25). Although the word *antipsychon* recedes before terms more explicitly connected with "ransoming" (*antilytron*), the notion of Jesus' life being given in exchange for others remains prominent under this new term (1 Tim 2:6; see also Rom 3:24; Tit 2:14; 1 Pet 1:19) or in terms of dying "on behalf of" others (*hyper*, Rom 5:6, 8; Gal 2:20; Eph 5:2; 1 Thess 5:10; 1 Tim 2:6; Tit 2:14), often specifically "on account of the sins" of "many" or "all" (*hyper hamartiōn*, 1 Cor 15:3; Gal 1:4), so that these sins are "passed over" by God (Rom 3:25), resonating with the deaths of the martyrs "as a ransom for the sins of the nation" (*4 Macc.* 17:21).

This "reconciliation" between God and God's people ("his own servants"), and the turning away of God's "wrath," was promoted by the martyrs' deaths in 2 Maccabees (7:33, 37–38; 8:5); "reconciliation" becomes a key term describing the results of Jesus' death for the divine–human relationship (Rom 5:10–11; 2 Cor 5:18–20), which also involves the removal of people from the sphere of God's "wrath" (Rom 5:9). The sacrificial language never obscures the fact that it was Jesus' *obedience* unto death, like the obedience of the martyrs (*4 Macc.* 6:27–28), that was the essential component for God's acceptance of his offering as an act that would reconcile God's self to sinful people (Phil 2:5–11; Rom 5:19). The scope of that reconciliation, of course, is seen to be much broader in the case of early Christian reflection on the death of Jesus, transcending ethnic boundaries (2 Cor 5:14; Rom 3:29–30; 5:1).

In both the paradigm of the martyrs and the case of Jesus, reconciliation between God and the disobedient people is only one facet of the achievement of those who were obedient unto death. Just as the exemplary deaths of the martyrs revived covenant obedience among the people (*4 Macc.* 18:1–2, 4), the death of Jesus also results in a return to obedience among the community of the reconciled (Rom 8:2–4, 7–8). These two components together constitute the restoration of "peace" (*eirēnē*) in both early Christian writings and 4 Maccabees. It is highly probably that 4 Maccabees was written later than many of the New Testament documents. Nevertheless, the conceptual and linguistic parallelism between early Christian reflection

on Jesus' death and early Jewish reflection on the deaths of martyrs suggests strongly that the developments in the Jewish martyrological tradition reflected in the former deeply informed the latter.

DAVID A. DESILVA

Further reading

Barrett, C. K. "Mark 10.45: A Ransom for Many," in *New Testament Essays*, London: SPCK, 1972, pp. 20–26.

Daly, Robert J. "The Soteriological Significance of the Sacrifice of Isaac," *CBQ* 39: (1988) 45–75.

Davies, W. D. and D. C. Allison, Jr. *The Gospel According to Saint Matthew. Volume III*, Edinburgh: T. & T. Clark, 1997.

de Jonge, Marinus. *Jesus, the Servant Messiah*, New Haven, CT: Yale University Press, 1991.

deSilva, David A. *Introducing the Apocrypha: Message, Context, and Significance*, Grand Rapids, MI: Baker Academic, 2002.

—— *4 Maccabees: Introduction and Commentary on the Text of Codex Sinaiticus*, Septuagint Commentary Series, Leiden: Brill, 2006.

Droge, A. J. and J. D. Tabor. *A Noble Death: Suicide and Martyrdom among Christians and Jews in Antiquity*, San Francisco, CA: Harper, 1992.

Dunn, J. D. G. *Jesus Remembered*, Grand Rapids, MI: Eerdmans, 2003.

Evans, C. A. *Mark 8:27–16:20*, WBC 34B, Nashville, TN: Thomas Nelson, 2001.

Frend, W. H. C. *Martyrdom and Persecution in the Early Church: A Study of Conflict from the Maccabees to Donatus*, New York: New York University Press, 1967.

Hooker, M. D. "Did the Use of Isaiah 53 to Interpret His Mission Begin with Jesus?," in W. H. Bellinger and W. R. Farmer (eds) *Jesus and the Suffering Servant*, Harrisburg, PA: Trinity Press International, 1998, pp. 70–87.

Jeremias, Joachim. *The Eucharistic Words of Jesus*, New York: Charles Scribner's Sons, 1966.

Lohse, Eduard. *Märtyrer und Gottesknecht: Untersuchungen zur urchristlichen Verkündigung vom Sühntod Jesu Christi*, Göttingen: Vandenhoeck & Ruprecht, 1963.

Luz, Ulrich. "Matthew 21–28," *Hermeneia*, Minneapolis, MN: Fortress Press, 1989.

Moulder, W. J. "The Old Testament Background and the Interpretation of Mark X.45," *NTS* 24 (1977) 120–27.

O'Hagan, A. "The Martyr in the Fourth Book of Maccabees," *SBFLA* 24 (1974) 94–120.

Page, S. H. T. "The Authenticity of the Ransom Logion (Mark 10:45b)," in R. T. France and David Wenham (eds) *Gospel Perspectives: Studies of History and Tradition in the Four Gospels. Volume 1*, Sheffield: JSOT Press, 1980, pp. 137–61.

Seeley, D. *The Noble Death. Graeco-Roman Martyrology and Paul's Concept of Salvation*, JSNTSS 28, Sheffield: Sheffield Academic Press, 1990.

Stuhlmacher, Peter. "Jesus' Readiness to Suffer and His Understanding of His Death." in J. D. G. Dunn and Scot McKnight (eds) *The Historical Jesus in Recent Research*, Winona Lake, IN: Eisenbrauns, 2005, pp. 392–412.

Taylor, Vincent. "The Origin of the Markan Passion-Sayings," *NTS* 1 (1954–55) 159–67.

van Henten, J. W. *The Maccabean Martyrs as Saviors of the Jewish People: A Study of 2 & 4 Maccabees*, Leiden: Brill, 1997.

van Henten, J. W. and Friedrich Avemarie. *Martyrdom and Noble Death: Selected texts from Graeco-Roman, Jewish and Christian Antiquity*, London and New York: Routledge, 2002.

Watts, R. E. "Jesus' Death, Isaiah 53, and Mark 10:45: A Crux Revisited." in W. H. Bellinger and W. R. Farmer (eds) *Jesus and the Suffering Servant*, Harrisburg, PA: Trinity Press International, 1998, pp. 125–51.

Williams, S. K. *Jesus' Death as Saving Event: The Background and Origin of a Concept*, HTRDS 2, Missoula, MN: Scholars Press, 1975.

MARY MAGDALENE

Mary Magdalene was a disciple of Jesus from the town of Magdala in Galilee. She was neither a prostitute nor Jesus' wife, but with other women she supported Jesus materially and accompanied him for part of his ministry. In the gospel tradition she is remembered as being a prominent female disciple of Jesus and one of the first witnesses to the resurrection. In non-canonical traditions she is regarded as a symbolic representative of those who have been enlightened by *gnosis*.

The name "Mary Magdalene" betrays very little information about her. The name "Mary" from the Hebrew *Miriam* was popular in Palestine in the first century and in the gospels alone there are four other women named "Mary": Mary the mother of Jesus (Mark 6:3; Matt 1:16–18; Luke 1:27; Acts 1:14), Mary of Bethany (Luke 10:39–42; John 11:1–2; 12:3), Mary the mother of James and Joses (Mark 15:40, 47; 16:1; Matt 27:56, 61; 28:1), and Mary wife of Cleopas (John 19:25). The mother of John Mark is also named Mary (Acts 12:12) and Paul mentions an unspecified Mary at the end of Romans (Rom 16:6). Magdala (known also as *Taricheae*, e.g. Josephus *Ant.* 20.159, *J.W.* 2.252) was a prominent town on the west side of the Sea of Galilee with a thriving agricultural and textile industry. The presence of a hippodrome (Josephus *J.W.* 2.599) indicates the influence of Hellenism. The area was famous for its pickled fish (Strabo, *Geog.* 16.2.45) and large tower (*Migdal Nûnnaya* means "tower of fish" in *b. Pesah.* 46a).

In Luke 8:2–3, Mary Magdalene is designated as one "from whom seven demons had gone out" suggesting she was once exorcised by Jesus (cf. Mark 16:9). She is also named alongside Joanna and Susanna as women who provided support for Jesus in his itinerant ministry. These women were essentially patrons of Jesus and financially supported him in his work in Galilee. One can only speculate from this whether Mary Magdalene was wealthy, or whether or not she was married at some point. If she was perceived as a demoniac then it would probably have impacted her marital status in some way, either by prevention of marriage or as a cause of divorce (Bauckham 134) and effectively made her a social outcast for a time. In Mark 15:40–41, Mary Magdalene is named beside other women as those who "used to follow him and provided for him when he was in Galilee" which suggests that Mary Magdalene was part of the larger retinue of Jesus' disciples.

The gospels also indicate that Mary Magdalene was a witness to Jesus' crucifixion (Mark 15:40; Matt 27:55–56; Luke 23:49; John 19:25), she observed his burial in the tomb (Mark 15:47; Matt 27:61; Luke 23:55), she was one of the first witnesses to the empty tomb and to the angels (Mark 16:1–8; Matt 28:1–8; Luke 24:1–8; John 20:1), his resurrection (Mark 16:9; Matt 28:9–10; John 20:11–18), she was also among first to worship him (Matt 28:9), and the first to proclaim the resurrection (John 20:18).

In Western Church tradition Mary Magdalene is erroneously identified with the sinful woman of Luke 7:36–50, the woman caught in adultery in John 8:1–11, and even Mary of Bethany in John 11–12. It is ironic that one sexual fiction about Mary Magdalene – that she was a reformed prostitute – has been replaced by a different sexual fiction, namely that she was Jesus' wife and bore him children (e.g. Dan Brown's *The Da Vinci Code*). For the most part the Christian tradition did not venerate Mary Magdalene because of her marital status or focus on her sexual history, but rather she was remembered as a faithful disciple of Jesus and a witness to his resurrection.

Mary Magdalene emerges as a central character in several non-canonical writings. The Ethiopic version of the *Epistula Apostolorum* (re-)tells the story of Mary's encounter with the risen Jesus and the disciples' disbelief of her testimony. The *Gospel of Peter* refers to her as a "woman disciple of the Lord" who did not weep at Jesus' tomb for fear of the Jews (*Gos. Pet.* 12.50). In the *Gospel of Thomas* Mary asks Jesus a question about his disciples, which leads to an extended response about preparedness (*Gos. Thom.* 21). In the final saying, Peter asks Jesus to send Mary Magdalene away and Jesus retorts with an enigmatic remark about salvation through androgyny (*Gos. Thom.* 114). In *The Dialogue of the Saviour* Mary Magdalene is portrayed as the exemplary Gnostic who surpasses Judas and Matthew in her understanding (*Dial. Sav.* 53). In *Pistis Sophia* Mary Magdalene has a superior knowledge to the disciples and is called the pleroma of pleromas and the completion of completions (*P.S.* 19). In the *Gospel of Phillip* Mary Magdalene is called Jesus' "companion" (*Gos. Phil.* 59, 63), she is identified as the one whom Jesus would often "kiss", and the disciples complain that Jesus loved her "more than all of us" (*Gos. Phil.* 63–64). But "kissing" here is symbolic for the imparting of mystical knowledge and not for physical intimacy (see *Gos. Phil.* 59). In the *Sophia of Jesus Christ* Mary asks Jesus a number of questions about the disciples and the source of superhuman knowledge. Finally, the *Gospel of Mary* concerns the secret revelations that Jesus gave to Mary Magdalene. These traditions are mostly gnosticized fictions and have little or no claim to being genuine historical reminiscences of the historical Jesus or the historical Mary Magdalene. The significance of Mary Magdalene for the Christian tradition is best understood from another angle.

> I should emphasize that even though Christianity is based ultimately on the life and ministry of Jesus, it is much more than that. Traditional Christianity is the belief that he died for the sins of the world and was raised from the dead. Technically speaking, Christianity could not begin until someone proclaimed Jesus was raised from the dead. It appears that the first to do so was Mary Magdalene. If so … Mary really is the one who started Christianity. There could scarcely be a more significant woman for the history of Western civilization – or man, for that matter – who is at the same time less known than Mary Magdalene.
>
> (Ehrman 331)

MICHAEL F. BIRD

Further reading

Bauckham, Richard. *Gospel Women: Studies of the Named Women in the Gospels*, Grand Rapids, MI: Eerdmans, 2002.

Bellevie, Lesa. *The Complete Idiot's Guide to Mary Magdalene*, New York: Alpha, 2005.

Brock, Ann Graham. *Mary Magdalene, The First Apostle: The Struggle for Authority*, HTS 51, Cambridge, MA: Harvard University Press, 2003.

Chilton, Bruce D. *Mary Magdalene: A Biography*, New York: Doubleday, 2005.

Collins, Raymond F. "Mary (Person)," *ABD* 4 (1992) 579–81.

Ehrman, Bart D. *Peter, Paul and Mary Magdalene: The Followers of Jesus in History and Legend*, Oxford: Oxford University Press, 2006.

Lahr, Jane. *Searching for Mary Magdalene: A Journey Through Art and Literature*, New York: Welcome Books, 2006.

Meyer, Marvin M. and Esther de Broer. *The Gospels of Mary: The Secret Tradition of Mary Magdalene, the Companion of Jesus*, San Francisco, CA: HarperCollins, 2004.

Schaberg, Jane and Melanie Johnson-DeBaufre. *Mary Magdalene Understood*, London: T. & T. Clark Continuum, 2006.

Witherington, Ben. *Women in the Ministry of Jesus: A Study of Jesus' Attitudes to Women and their Roles as Reflected in his Earthly Life*, Cambridge: Cambridge University Press, 1984.

MARY, MOTHER OF JESUS

The name "Mary" derives from Miriam (Moses' sister) and was an extremely common name in Jesus' day. Jesus' mother can be distinguished from Mary Magdalene and Mary the wife of Clopas, both present with Jesus' mother in John 19:25; Mary the mother of James and Joses (Mark 15:40, 47; 16:1, possibly Jesus' mother or Mary of Clopas); and Mary the sister of Martha.

Matthew focuses on Joseph in Matthew 1–2 while Mary remains in the background. When she is found to be pregnant before the marriage is consummated, Joseph's initial desire to divorce her (righteously and quietly) is reversed by divine intervention. Matthew notes that a virgin birth fulfills Isaiah 7:14 (LXX). Joseph takes her to his home but avoids sexual contact. Such abstinence was widely celebrated as exemplary ethical behavior and need not imply post-partum abstinence (Allison 163–72). In Matthew 2, Mary celebrates Jesus' birth with pagan magicians, then experiences oppression, fleeing Herod's wrath and living as a refugee until resettling in Galilee. The remainder of the evidence in Matthew and Mark includes a list of Jesus' brothers and mention of sisters (Mark 6:3; Matthew 13:55). It is not explicitly stated that they are full brothers and thus offspring of Mary and Joseph, but this is a more than reasonable supposition. Jesus is sometimes identified as the son of Mary, not Joseph (Mark 6:1–4; Matthew 13:55–57; but contrast Luke 4:22 and John 1:45, 6:42).

Mary's portrait in Luke is more detailed. Mary has relatives who are Levites, though the precise relationship between the Galilean Mary and her Judean "relative" Elizabeth (1:36), the mother of John the Baptist, is unclear. Luke portrays a righteous, faithful family. Joseph and Mary performed "everything according to the Law of the Lord" including circumcision and purification rites (2:21–39, quoting 39) after Jesus' birth, and participated in yearly festival pilgrimages (2:41). Efforts to reconcile Jesus' disparate genealogies sometimes tie the genealogy in Luke 3 to Mary, but this is far-fetched. Some have seen in Luke 2:52 an offhand reference to Mary as a source for later stories about Jesus, particularly family experiences in his early years. The song attributed to Mary (1:46–55, the Magnificat) is controversial; some doubt Mary's ability to produce such a song. It may not have been composed on the spot, yet it is reasonable to see a young peasant girl celebrating her religion, especially given the tradition of Jewish women involved in bringing about or celebrating God's work in Israel's history and relying on his promises of redemption (e.g. Miriam and Deborah, who both sing; cf. 2 Maccabees 7, Esther, Judith). In particular, the Magnificat evokes the expectation of God's "Coming Age" of fulfilled promises, restoration, and the reversal of fortunes which would have been common among those in her Jewish context (McKnight).

John contains only two references to Jesus' (unnamed) mother, both unique to John. She instigates Jesus' mission (2:1–12) and is at the cross (19:25–27) at its fulfillment. Data in the New Testament from outside the gospels is even scarcer. Jesus is merely said to be "born of a woman" (Galatians 4:4), but Mary herself is not important as a personality. Some have seen a reference to Mary in Revelation 12, but again this is unclear.

Mary remains relatively unimportant in most early Christian literature. The *Infancy Gospel of Thomas* (11; 14; 19) is typical, including scant references to Mary as a backdrop to Jesus' early life. On some occasions, it is difficult to say which "Mary" is in view, as in the *Gospel of Thomas* (21, 114), although in general Gnostic texts feature Magdalene (Jones). The fullest treatment of Mary is found in the second-century *Protevangelium of James*, which heavily influenced early Christian theology and literature before and after being labeled heretical in the sixth century. This three-part story begins by describing Mary's parents, Joachim and Anna, who overcome infertility with divine help. In the second part, Joseph is portrayed as a widower with children in need of a godly wife, and Mary – whose adolescence will threaten Temple purity – becomes Joseph's responsibility. The third section relates the birth stories, relying on the canonical gospels and other traditions. Mary's virginity is again confirmed, this time postpartum (19–20). Much post-canonical material on Mary supports a theological agenda, whether that of Gnosticism, with its interest in denying the humanity of Jesus; or more orthodox interest in celebrating Mary and her sexual purity before or after Jesus' birth, as defense against Jewish and later pagan critics (Schaberg 138–68). Such material sheds little light on Jesus, although belief in the virgin birth appears to be early and universal.

Apart from her debated role in Jesus' birth, Mary and Jesus' siblings are a foil for Jesus'

teaching on the "family" of disciples, whose "fictive kinship" ties may even replace those of natural kin (Matt 12:46–50; Mark 3:31–35; Luke 8:19–21) – a shocking, even scandalous teaching. Luke even deflects "blessing" of Mary in favor of the blessing that comes from discipleship (Luke 8:19–21, 11:27–28). The presence of Jesus' relatives in the early church (Bauckham) proves that the redefinition did not always exclude the nuclear family, provided they were disciples or otherwise predisposed to dwell peaceably with believing relatives (compare Luke 14:25–26; 18:20; 1 Cor 7:12–16; 1 Tim 5:8). John 19:25–27 expresses the redefinition differently, employing Mary positively. This passage reflects the commitment among early Christians to care for widows in particular and the family of believers generally, in keeping with the pattern of fictive kinship instituted by Jesus, and suggests the continued presence of Mary among the disciples (Acts 1:14).

A mother in early Judaism could have a profound influence on her children (2 Macc 7), even one as poor as Mary likely was. According to some, Mary mothered early leaders of the Jerusalem church. If Jesus and the author of James are both sons of Mary, and if the song ascribed to Mary in Luke 1 accurately reflects this young Jewish peasant girl's theology and hopes, it is not surprising that her sons stress the great economic reversal in their service of a God who "lifted up the humble and filled the hungry, but sent the rich away empty" (Luke 1:52–53).

JASON B. HOOD

Further reading

Allison, D. C. *Studies in Matthew: Interpretation Past and Present*, Grand Rapids, MI: Baker Academic, 2005.

Bauckham, Richard. *Jude and the Relatives of Jesus in the Early Church*, Edinburgh: T. & T. Clark, 1990.

Brown, Raymond. *The Birth of the Messiah: A Commentary on the Infancy Narratives in the Gospels of Matthew and Luke*, second edition, ABRL, New York: Doubleday, 1993.

Jones, F. Stanley (ed.) *Which Mary? The Marys of Early Christian Tradition*, SBLSymS 19, Atlanta, GA: SBL, 2002.

McKnight, Scot. *The Real Mary*, Brewster, MA: Paraclete Press, 2006.

Schaberg, Jane. *The Illegitimacy of Jesus: A Feminist Theological Interpretation of the Infancy Narratives*, Twentieth Anniversary Expanded Edition, Sheffield: Sheffield Phoenix, 2006.

MASTER/RABBI

In the gospels Jesus is addressed as "rabbi," a Greek transliteration of the Aramaic title for a teacher, more than by any other designation (Matt

26:25, 49; Mark 9:5; 10:51; 11:21; 14:45; John 1:38, 49; 3:2; 4:31; 6:25; 9:2; 11:8). The term meant "my great one" or "my master," and was the normal means of referring to a teacher, as in the case of the disciples (or *talmidim*) of John the Baptist, who call him "rabbi" in John 3:26. When Greek words are factored in that render the term "rabbi" – namely "master" and "teacher" – and when it is recollected that "lord" might also correspond to "rabbi" on occasion, the numerical preponderance of this title is nothing short of overwhelming. Moreover, Jesus is addressed as "rabbi" not only by his disciples, but also and explicitly by those on the margins of his movement (Mark 10:51; John 6:25), and he is known as such even among those potentially or actually opposed to him (John 3:2, cf. Mark 12:14). As judged by the depth and breadth of these references, as well as their number, the best historical designation for Jesus is clearly "rabbi."

Despite the clear import of these simple facts, verifiable with the help of a concordance and recourse to a critical edition of the Greek Gospels, scholars such as Casimir Bernas have routinely objected that Jesus was not a rabbi but a prophet. Jesus was indeed hailed as a prophet, especially near the climax of his confrontations with the religious authorities in Jerusalem, but never as persistently or as widely as he was called rabbi. In any case, the one address by no means excludes the other (or addresses such as "God's son" and "son of man"). A desire for an instantly unique Christology, easily dissociable from Judaism, has resulted in the sidelining of some of the most historically reliable data in the New Testament.

That the term "rabbi" was current in Jesus' time is plain from Daniel 2:48; 4:6; 5:11 and Mishnah Avoth 1:6, 16, as well as from the inscriptional evidence discussed by J. P. Kane. (In earlier Hebrew texts a "Rab" was a high officer; 2 Kgs 18:17.) But being called "rabbi" did not involve an institutional qualification until a much later period, well after the destruction of the Temple, although it seems clear that during the first century a Jewish teacher in Galilee whose wisdom was valued would be called "rabbi."

Pharisaism instances how local rabbis, in this case within urban environments, might crystallize into a movement. The Pharisees are portrayed by Josephus as being critical of the Hasmonean priesthood. Their expression was at first political (Josephus, *Ant.* 13:288–98), and could extend to violent action, as in the demand that the counselors who advised Alexander Jannaeus to kill some of their sympathizers should themselves be executed (Josephus, *J.W.* 1:110–14). At base,

however, the orientation of the Pharisees was towards the achievement and maintenance of purity. The purity they strived for had fundamentally to do with making offerings, people, and priests fit for the cult of sacrifice in the Temple. For that reason, the issues of the personnel of the priesthood, the sorts of animals and goods that might be brought and by whom, and their permitted proximity to all sources of uncleanness, were vitally important.

By the dawn of the Common Era, the Pharisees found a distinguished teacher in the person of Hillel, who is justly famous for the dictum, uttered some twenty years before Jesus, "That which you hate, do not do to your fellow; that is the whole Torah, while all the rest is commentary thereon" (*b. Shab.* 31a). The similarity to Jesus' teaching (see Matt 7:12; Luke 6:31, and the discussion in this volume under Law (Sabbath, purity, commandments)) is striking, but it can also be misleading. Hillel in the tale is talking to an impatient proselyte, who wished to learn the Torah while standing on one foot; his impatience had just won him a cuff with a measuring rod from Shammai, the rabbi with whom Hillel is typically contrasted in rabbinic literature. Obviously, Hillel has no desire to reduce the Torah on the grounds of principle, and he goes to tell the proselyte, "Go and learn it." In other words, the Gentile learns that the revelation to Moses is the expression of the best ethics, and that for that reason the whole should be mastered.

In any case, Hillel was understood among the Pharisees to have come to prominence for adjudicating quite a distinct issue: whether the Passover could be offered on the Sabbath. Hillel first offers a Scriptural argument for accepting the practice: since other forms of priestly service are permitted, so is the slaying of the lamb. His hearers are unimpressed, until he simply states that he learned the position in Babylon, from Shemaiah and Abtalion, distinguished predecessors in the movement. Their authority is sufficient to displace the current leaders of Pharisaic opinion, the sons of Bathyra (cf. *t. Pesah.* 4:13, 14; *y. Pesah.* 6:1; *y. Shabb.* 19:1; *b. Pesah.* 66a, b).

This story is redolent of Pharisaic concern with cultic questions. Hillel is also said to have convinced another teacher, Baba ben Buta, to provide cultically correct beasts in great numbers for slaughter, with the stipulation (against the school of Shammai) that the offerer lay hands on the victim immediately prior to the killing (cf. *t. Hag.* 2:11; *y. Hag.* 2:3; *y. Besa* 2:4; *b. Besa* 20a, b). To conform to this teaching, Baba ben Buta mounted a demonstration in the Temple.

Hillel embodied the Pharisaic principle that the "chains" of their oral tradition were normative for purity. Such chains were understood to have been developed from Moses to Ezra, after that by "the men of the great congregation," and then by teachers who were generally invoked as "pairs" (*m. Avot* 1:1–18). The last "pair" was Hillel and Shammai, from which point the Pharisees acknowledged that division increased in Israel (*b. Sotah* 47b; *b. Sanh.* 88b; *t. Sotah* 14:9; *t. Hag.* 2:9; *t. Sanh.* 7:1; *y. Hag.* 2:2; *y. Sanh.* 1:4). The notion of primeval unity disturbed by recent faction is probably mythical, but it is plain that the Pharisees developed their oral tradition by means of a structured understanding of the past, as well as by mnemonic techniques.

The term "Pharisee" is probably an outsiders' name for adherents of the movement, meaning "separatist" or "purist;" participants in the movement appear to have referred to their ancient predecessors (after Ezra) as "the sages" or "the wise," and to their more recent predecessors and contemporaries as "teachers" (cf. *rab* in *m. Aboth* 1:6, 16; *sophistes* in Josephus). Like the Pharisees, Jesus also showed a characteristic interest in purity, one that put him at odds with Pharisaic teaching in his time (see Mark 7:15) and a dispute concerning appropriate sacrifice in the Temple cost him his life. This explains why in the Gospels Jesus typically enters into disputes with Pharisees (Matt 9:10–13, 14–17; 12:1–8, 9–14; 15:1–26; 16:1–12; 19:3–12; 22:15–22; Mark 2:15–17, 18–22, 23–28; 3:1–6; 7:1–23; 8:11–21; 10:2–12; 12:13–17; Luke 5:29–32, 33–39; 6:1–5, 6–11; 11:37–12:1; 15:1, 2). These disputes with the Pharisees typically center upon issues of purity (Matt 9:10–13/Mark 2:15–17/Luke 5:29–32; Matt 15:1–26/Mark 7:1–23; Matt 16:5–12/Mark 8:14–21/Luke 12:1; 15:1, 2), fasting (Matt 9:14–17/Mark 2:18–22/Luke 5:33–39), keeping the sabbath (Matt 12:1–8, 9–14/Mark 2:23–28; 3:1–6/Luke 6:1–5, 6–11), tithing (Matt 23:23/Luke 11:42, cf. Matt 17:24–27; 22:15–22/Mark 12:13–17/Luke 20:20–26), and the interpretation of scripture (Matt 19:3–12/Mark 10:2–12/Luke 16:18), all of which are characteristic of Pharisaic concerns. The most natural inference is that, as a rabbi from rural Galilee, Jesus' concerns intersected with the Pharisees', but that he frequently differed with them in approach.

When scholars have expressed reservations in respect of that finding, they have had in mind the distortion of identifying Jesus with the Rabbinic movement after 70 CE, which was more systematized than before that time, and which amounted to the normative authority within Judaism. Unfortunately,

anxiety in respect of that anachronism can result in the far greater error of bracketing Jesus within "sectarian" Judaism (as if "orthodoxy" existed in early, pluralized Judaism prior to the Rabbinic Period), or – worse still – of placing him within no Judaism at all.

Until 70 CE, Pharisaic teaching was targeted the conduct of the cult in the Temple, but its influence was limited. Nonetheless, Pharisees seem to have succeeded reasonably well in town, even in Galilee, where they urged local populations to maintain the sort of purity which would permit them to participate rightly in the cult. Josephus' fellow in the armed resistance against Rome and arch-rival, John of Gischala, may well have been representing Pharisaic interests when he arranged for Jews in Syria to purchase oil exclusively from Galilean sources (*J.W.* 2:591–94). In any case, it does appear plain that some Pharisees supported the revolt of 66–70 CE, while others did not. But while many priests and Essenes perished in the war with the Romans and the internecine strife of the revolt, and while the aristocracy of scribes and elders in Jerusalem was discredited and decimated, the Pharisees survived the war better than any other single group. They were well accepted locally, had long ago accommodated marginal influence, and survived with their personnel and their traditions comparatively intact.

Rabbinic literature itself personifies the survival of the movement in a story concerning Rabbi Yochanan ben Zakkai. According to the story, Yochanan had himself borne out of Jerusalem on the pretense he was dead and hailed the Roman general Vespasian as king; on his ascent to imperial power, Vespasian granted Yohanan his wish of settlement in the town of Yavneh, the group of Rabbi Gamaliel, and medical attention for Rabbi Zadok (cf. *b. Gittin* 56a, b). In that Josephus claims similarly to have flattered Vespasian (*J.W.* 2:399–408), and to have seen in his coming the fulfillment of messianic prophecy (*J.W.* 6:310–15), the tale is to be used with caution, but it remains expressive of the Rabbinic ethos.

With the foundation of academies such as the one at Yavneh after 70 CE, one may speak of the transition of Pharisaism to Rabbinic Judaism. The Rabbis (with an initial capital), who directly contributed to rabbinic literature and to the Judaism which is framed by that literature, belonged to a movement much changed from the popular Puritanism of the Pharisees. The sort of leadership that a Yochanan ben Zakkai might offer became suddenly attractive, in the absence of priestly, Essene, or scribal alternatives. The target of the tradition's application became correspondingly wider, as the Pharisaic/Rabbinic program was applied, not simply to issues of purity and sacrifice, but to worship generally, ethics, and daily living. To Yochanan is attributed the view that the world, which had been sustained by the Temple, the law, and deeds of faithful love, now was to be supported only by the last two of the three (*Abot R. Nat.* 4). Moreover, he adjudicated, on the basis of his tradition, how feasts might be kept in the gathering for reading, prayer and discussion which was called a "congregation" or "synagogue" (*kenesset*, also applied to buildings erected for the purpose of such gatherings; cf. *m. Sukk.* 3:12; m. *Rosh Hash.* 4:1, 3, 4). Such developments have nothing to do, of course, with the way in which Jesus was addressed as "rabbi."

In the wake of 70 CE and the Roman confiscation of the tax formerly paid for the Temple, neither Jerusalem nor its environs was amenable to the maintenance of a hub of the movement, and even Yavneh was eclipsed during the second century by centers in prosperous Galilee, such as Usha and Beth She'arim. Later, metropolitan cities such as Sepphoris and Tiberias were the foci of leadership. The health of the movement required a shift from the highly personal authority of the Pharisees to an ideal of learned consensus.

Just that shift is reflected in a Talmudic story concerning a great teacher, Rabbi Eliezer ben Hyrcanus. The story has it that, against a majority of his colleagues, Eliezer held that a ceramic stove, once polluted, might be reassembled, provided the tiles were separated by sand. The majority taught that the result would be unclean; such materials should never be used again. Eliezer's correctness was demonstrated by a tree which was uprooted at his behest, by a stream which ran backwards at his command, by a building he similarly demolished, and by a voice from heaven. Despite all that, the majority held that its decision was binding – and God approved the result (*b. B. Mes.* 59a, b). As institutional authority emerged, even Eliezer's personal authority clearly diminished; the Rabbis of the second century were to stress a rational, consensual achievement of purity, and the Talmud confirmed that orientation.

The historic concern for the Temple as the actual focus of purity nonetheless resulted in a final and disastrous attempt – encouraged by some Rabbis – to free and restore the holy site. The most prominent rabbinic supporter of that attempt was a student of Eliezer's renowned for his expertise in the tradition, Aqiba. Aqiba supported the claims of Simeon bar Kosibah to be the new prince of Israel, acting in conjunction with a priest named Eleazar. Simeon's supporters referred to him as Bar Kokhba, "son of a star," projecting onto him the messianic expectations of Num 24:17, while his detractors came to know him as Bar Koziba, "son of a lie." His initial success and military acumen is attested in letters he sent his commanders during his revolt and regime, which lasted from 132 CE until 135 CE. The response of the Roman Empire was even more definitive than it had been in 70 CE. The remnants of the Temple were taken apart, and new shrines were built in the city; Jerusalem itself was now called Aelia Capitolina, Jews were denied entry, and Judea came to be designated Syria Palaestina.

The Rabbis survived by disowning the aspirations embodied by Aqiba, but keeping much of his teaching. "Aqiba, grass will grow out of your jaw, before the son of David comes" (*y. Ta'an.* 4:7; *Lamentations Rabbah* 2.2.4); that is to say, the Messiah is to be of David, not of popular choosing, and his time cannot be pressed. But the greatness of the Rabbinic response to national defeat, and their consequent redefinition of Judaism, consisted less in their formulation of a particular teaching regarding messianism (which emerges in any case from time to time in many forms of Judaism) than in their textual constitution of a form of thought, discipline, and life: the Mishnah. By that time, of course, Christians had long before moved into a different position, maintaining in their master's name that, just as the Messiah was the one true guide, so only that teacher could truly be called "rabbi" (Matt 23:8, 10).

BRUCE CHILTON

Further reading

Bernas, Casimir. "Review of *A Galilean Rabbi and His Bible*," *TS* 46 (1985) 129–30.

Chilton, Bruce. *A Galilean Rabbi and His Bible. Jesus' Use of the Interpreted Scripture of His Time*, Wilmington: Glazier, 1984; also published with the subtitle *Jesus' Own Interpretation of Isaiah*; London: SPCK, 1984.

—— *Rabbi Jesus. An Intimate Biography*, New York: Doubleday, 2000.

Finkel, Asher. *The Pharisees and the Teacher of Nazareth*, Arbeiten zur Geschichte des Spätjudentums und Urchristentums 4, Leiden: Brill, 1964.

Kane, J. P. "Ossuary Inscriptions of Jerusalem," *JSS* 23 (1978) 268–82.

Levine, L. I. *The Rabbinic Class of Roman Palestine in Late Antiquity*, New York: Jewish Theological Seminary, 1989.

Neusner, J. N. *The Pharisees. Rabbinic Perspectives*, Hoboken, NJ: KTAV, 1973.

—— *Torah. From Scroll to Symbol in Formative Judaism*, The Foundations of Judaism, Philadelphia, PA: Fortress Press, 1985.

Schürer, E. *A History of the Jewish People in the Age of Jesus Christ*, ed. G. Vermes, F. Millar, and M. Goodman, Edinburgh: T. & T. Clark, 1973–87.

MESSIAH/CHRIST

Although one of the main thoughts of the New Testament is that Jesus of Nazareth is the 'Messiah', one must differentiate between christological, eschatological, and messianic concepts and expectations. Of the 529 times the word χριστός, apparently the Greek equivalent of the Hebrew מְשִׁיחַ, is used in the New Testament, Paul refers to the various forms of it 379 times, 1 Peter twenty-two times, Acts twenty-five times, the Johannine writings nineteen times, Matthew seventeen times, Mark seven times, Luke twelve times, and the rest of the New Testament forty-eight times. In all of these cases it is important to be aware of the fact that 'Christ' does not necessarily have to mean 'messiah' according to the definition used (see Messianism and messianic figures in Second Temple Judaism).

The belief in Jesus as the Messiah or Christ developed after the death and resurrection of Jesus of Nazareth, without which he might have experienced the same fate as the 'messiah-pretenders' criticized by Josephus. For his followers it meant that Jesus' messiah-ship and his resurrection were intrinsically connected with each other. Although the connection between Jesus' resurrection and his messiah-ship thus form the centre of the Christian faith, it is not possible to access the pre-Easter meaning of Jesus' life. However, through the documents of early Christianity, we can get closer to how others may have perceived Jesus as Messiah or Christ.

Paul

In most of the Pauline Epistles, as well as in those epistles ascribed to him, we find primarily christological, i.e. realized-messianic, instead of eschatological or future-messianic, sayings. This is the case in, for instance, Gal 3:13 and 4:4–5, in (the non-Pauline) Eph 4:8–10 (with a quotation of Ps 68:19), in Phil 1:6, 10 and in (the non-Pauline) Col 3:1, in 1 Cor 3:19–23 (with quotations from Job 5:13 and Ps 94:11); 4:1; 10:4; 2 Cor 1:21–22 and 5:10; and Rom 1:1–4. Passages with explicit eschatological or future messianic conceptions are 1 Thess 4:16 and 5:23; (non-Pauline) 2 Thess 2:1, 14, 16; 1 Cor 15:22–24; 2 Cor 5:10 and Rom 15:12.

First and Second Thessalonians

As far as future expectations are concerned the First – as well as the Second (non-Pauline) – Epistle to the Thessalonians is to be situated between the latter-day expectations of the disciples of Jesus and the Christology of the early post-Easter church. In 1 Thessalonians, the oldest epistle of Paul and of the New Testament as well, the author expects and describes in detail the Parousia of the Lord, but does not speak of a delay of his coming yet, as the Synoptic Gospels would thematize it several decades later. In 1 Thess 1:9–10, Paul refers to a (probably oral) latter-day expectation of primitive Christianity by saying that

> they themselves have shown of us what manner of entering in we had unto you, and how you turned to God from idols to serve the living and true God; and to wait for his Son from heaven, whom he raised from the dead, even Jesus, which delivered us from the wrath to come.

And in 1 Thessalonians one also finds an (either oral or written) transmitted 'Word of the Lord', from whose contents it can be deduced that Paul, and with him at least a portion of the primitive church, lived with the hope of the return of the Lord and the raising of the dead.

An important function of this immediate latter-day expectation obviously lies in motivating the early Christians to persevere and in comforting them in a time of distress, and only secondarily in theorizing about the exact contents of this early Christian hope. In 1 Thess 4:13–17 the coming of the Lord is connected with the rising of the dead, not in order to thematize the coming of the Lord itself, but to stress the Lord's power over life and death. This hope was an acute one, as its fulfilment was expected to occur while some of the audience were still alive. At the same time, the problem of a delayed Parousia seems to emerge in 1 Thess 4:13–17, as the question some of the community members have asked Paul is: what exactly is the relation between those who have died and those who have yet to die, as regards the Lord's return, since the Lord had not yet come during the lives of those who already have died?

1 Corinthians 15

In the fifteenth chapter of the First Epistle to the Corinthians written in the mid-50s of the first century, Paul discusses the question of the resurrection. The meaning of the resurrection is an eschatological one and points not only to the restoration of the Jewish nation, but to the restoration of the whole creation. This Paul attempts to illustrate by way of a comparison between Adam, through whom death has come into this world, and Christ, through whom the resurrection of the dead will come (1 Cor 15:20–28). Christ's reign refers to 'all enemies' including 'death' (based on Ps 8:7). The resurrection of Christ – as the firstfruit – and his reign over all also imply that in the face of the coming end the community of Christ should live without sin (1 Cor 15:29–34). In other words, Paul's eschatological consciousness leads to an emphasis on a presently oriented moral behaviour. Two further questions need to be elucidated here: first, the question of Christ's precise function at the end of days; second, the question of its relation to apocalypticism (see Apocalyptic).

Christ's eschatological role becomes important at the time of his expected return. The connection between Jesus' earthly life and his Parousia as Lord is made here with the concept of the 'rising of the dead', a concept which is rare in the Hebrew Bible but can be found in, for instance, Dan 12:1–3. Just as faith in Jesus Christ leads to a new creation, the resurrection of the dead at the end of days will bring the restoration of creation. Before this will happen, however, judgement will have to take place and the powers of this world will be destroyed. Afterwards the Son (1 Cor 15:28) will give the reign to God the Father and will also be subjected to him. The Parousia in Paul's eschatology is, therefore, connected with the latter-day judgement in a theocentric and christocentric way.

Furthermore, in 1 Cor 15:35–49 Paul has clear ideas about how the resurrection of the dead at the end of days will look, as he distinguishes it from other contemporary apocalyptic conceptions: the resurrection is to be understood as 'spiritual' (cf. 1 Cor 15:50). All that is natural will disappear. The spiritual, however, will remain: a kernel of a human being (1 Cor 15:37), an image of the heavenly being (1 Cor 15:49). What has been sowed on earth will not return, but on the contrary, will be raised and appear as its opposite (1 Cor 15:42–44).

Paul may originally have been dependent on contemporary apocalyptic conceptions, but he undoubtedly incorporates and transforms them into his own theocentric and christocentric interpretation of world history in light of Jesus Christ.

Romans 5:1–5

Romans 5:1–5 belongs to the narrower context of the passage Rom 5:1–11 and to the wider context of Rom 5–8. In Rom 5–8 Paul treats the 'reality of God's righteousness' from several points of view – being of importance for preaching the gospel and for the Church – after which in Rom 9–11 he speaks about the relation between Law and gospel and between Church and Israel. In Rom 5:1–11 he

speaks about the certainty of salvation and in Rom 5:12–21 he gives a typology between Adam and Christ, followed in Rom 6 by exhortations on baptism, in Rom 7 on the relation between Law, sin, and faith, and in Rom 8 on a life in the Spirit. From this wider context one can conclude that, according to Paul's view of history, at its beginning Adam represents 'the image of him who will come' and at its end Christ represents the second Adam (Rom 5:12–21). Paul defines the present as a situation that is characterized by sin, law, and grace of God.

Even if implicitly we are dealing here with an eschatological and dualistic view of history, in which one even finds a periodization of history (Adam to Moses, Moses to Christ, Christ to the end of days), typical of the contemporary Jewish apocalypses, Paul does not portray his worldview in world-political periods, but applies his 'theology of history' only to the three 'periods' relevant for the history of salvation: from Adam to Moses, from Moses to Christ, and from Christ to his Parousia. In other words, he offers a purely christological view of (salvation) history.

Furthermore, although the consequences that Paul draws from this worldview may have their origin in Jewish apocalypticism, he relates it only to the situation in which the Christians find themselves. In Pauline theology, one cannot separate Christology, eschatology, pneumatology, and ecclesiology, as they are intrinsically interrelated. Finally, in contrast to the apocalyptic ideas found in the Revelation of John and the Synoptic Apocalypse, Paul does not aim at world-political issues, but only at the life and teaching (catechesis) of the Christian community and its individual members.

Romans 11:1–10

The present is defined for Paul by the new life 'in Christ'. However, this raises a special hermeneutical problem in the case of the new 'people of God' in relation to Israel, whose children are now those who are in Christ (whether Jew or 'heathen'). Paul treats this problem in Romans 9–11. If we look here only at the relation to the Jews, from Rom 11:1–10 one may conclude that Israel has been and still is the chosen people. However, those Jews who have not accepted Christ, which Paul calls their 'fall', enabled the Gentiles to receive salvation as well, because if the root (Israel) is holy, also its branches (Gentiles) are holy (Rom 11:11–16). Israel is the righteous olive tree with its natural branches, and the 'Gentiles' are the wild branches; and this should be a warning for them (Rom 11:17–24).

Whereas in Christ the salvation of the world has begun, at the end also the whole of Israel will be saved, as is written in Isa 59:20 and Jer 31:33, and quoted in Rom 11:26–27 (see also Rom 11:25–32): 'There shall come out of Zion the Deliverer, and shall turn away ungodliness from Jacob: For this is my covenant unto them', after which Paul adds: 'when I shall take away their sins [Isa 27:9]'. How this will take place is only known to God (thus Isa 40:13 and Job 41:3 in Rom 11:33–36). For Paul, Christ is the new Adam, the first of the new order of creation, who brought to an end the diabolic circle of sin and law, for both Jews and Gentiles.

The power of Pauline thinking lies in the image that those who believe in Christ are already saved. Here it may be significant that Paul expected the end of days and the Parousia of the Lord within his own time. This in its turn may have led to the fact that one does not find a great tension between theocentrism and christocentrism in Paul's eschatology, as well as the fact that there is no discrepancy between the Christ who is the risen Lord and the Christ who will return, as for Paul all four conceptions form a unity.

Sayings source Q

When looking at passages in Sayings source Q, the second earliest witness of early Christian reflections on Messiah and Christ after the letters of Paul, Q 3:16 speaks of a 'messianic' in terms of a royal or priestly latter-day saviour, whereas the passages Q 6:22; 11:30; 12:8 and 17:24, 26, 30 mention a 'Son of Man' (see Son of man).

In Q 3:16 John the Baptist says to the people that not he but Jesus is the Messiah, as Jesus will baptize them with the Holy Spirit and with fire. John's baptism with water is the preparation of the baptism by the 'One who is stronger', namely Jesus, whose baptism with fire is clearly associated with the fire in the latter-day judgement (see Judgement), where the chaff is said to be burned with 'unquenchable fire'. In Q 3:16–17 we are therefore dealing with an apocalyptic and dualistic future expectation, in which the wicked will be punished and the righteous will be rewarded and in which the 'One who is stronger than I' will execute judgement. It is obvious that Jesus is meant here as the executer of the final judgement, who is more than only the announcer of the final judgement as he is characterized as the one who is 'more than his predecessors'.

Whereas in Q 6:22 all those who follow the 'Son of Man' are praised, in Q 11:30 the 'Sign of Jonah' is given for the Son of Man, and Q 12:8 reads: 'Whosoever shall confess me before men, him shall

the Son of Man also confess before the angels of God.' The first saying belongs to the Beatitudes of Q 6:20b–23 and stands in connection with 6:24–26 (woes); 6:27–35 (love of enemies); 6:36–42 (non-retaliation) and 6:43–49 (parable of the tree and the house). The passage stresses that one should persevere 'now' (and love his enemies but not judge), as the reward will be given 'later' (in heaven), which will come to be as surely (6:23) as one knows the tree by its fruits (6:43–49). In this connection of ethics and eschatology there is the implication of a latter-day judgement, although the figure of a latter-day judge is lacking, probably due to the fact that 6:22 refers to a 'present' situation, in which Jesus' disciples are obviously reproached, and not to a future situation.

Q 11:29 as well as the logion Q 11:30 belong to the passage Q 11:29b–32, where we find two 'signs': the sign of Jonah and the sign of the queen of the South. Jonah warned the Ninevites for the destruction of their city (Jon 3:5), so the sign in 11:30 may have been understood as a warning. The queen of the South came to listen to the wisdom of King Solomon, but in the coming judgement she will speak the judgement of death upon 'this generation'. Q 11:30, therefore, may contain an eschatological and apocalyptic announcement of woe and judgement. The phrases 'more than Solomon' and the 'more than Jonah' refer to Jesus as the last and final prophet (in the line of the earlier prophets) who has come to warn of the end of days and the coming judgement.

In Q 17:24, 26, 30 the apocalyptic signs before the coming of the 'Son of Man' are revealed: it will be as the lightning in heaven, as in the days of Noah and of Lot, when the 'Son of Man' comes. The passage seems to suggest that the community of Q, unlike the later communities of the Synoptic Apocalypse, lived with the immediate expectation of the coming of Jesus, that is, his Parousia as the 'Son of Man', unless these are later editorial additions. The apocalyptic conception of an equivalent between primordial time (time of Noah) and end time (Son of Man) glimmers through. We are dealing here with a 'salvation historical comparison', a prophetic announcement of woes that probably reflects a saying of Jesus that has been adapted by a later redactor.

Synoptic Gospels

Mark

The Gospel of Mark, written in the eastern part of the Roman Empire around 70 CE, forms together with Q the second source for the Gospels of Luke and Matthew. It contains designations about Jesus as 'Son of God' (Mark 3:11; 5:7 and 13:32), as 'Anointed' (Mark 1:1; 8:29; 12:35; 13:21 and 15:32), as 'Son of David' (Mark 12:35), as 'King of Israel' (Mark 15:32) and as 'Son of Man' (Mark 13:26). All of these expressions are connected with each other in Mark 14:61–62.

The Gospel of Mark thus designates Jesus with several other biblical epithets, such as 'Anointed', in addition to 'Son of Man' in Q. In all of this, Mark's Jesus is first of all the 'Son of God' and the 'Son of Man'. As most of the sayings about Jesus' life and work in Mark are to be understood as christological ones, that is as 'realized messianology', there are few messianic expectations in Mark's Gospel with a clear eschatological focus, notably the Synoptic Apocalypse in Mark 13:5–37 par.

The Synoptic Apocalypse Mark 13:5–27

In a tradition-historical study of Mark 13 and other Jewish apocalypses by L. Hartman, the development of the basic 'eschatological discourse' of the Apocalypse of Mark is described as follows. The 'nucleus', Mark 13:5b–8; 12–16; 19–22 and 24–27, can be seen as a *midrash* on Daniel, in which one pole of the apocalyptic and eschatological field consists of the activity of 'Antichrist', viz. the 'I am', the abomination of desolation and the false prophets giving 'signs and wonders', and the other pole . . . consists of a description of the Parousia of the Son of Man, in order to gather the faithful into the eternal kingdom.

At a later stage sayings of Jesus and logia concerning persecutions (Mark 13:9 and 11), pointing to the experiences of the early church, have been added to this 'nucleus'. At a final stage the *topos* of the Parousia has been connected with a reflection on the fall of Jerusalem (Mark 13:1–4 and 28–32), whereas Mark 13:10 clearly reflects the mission of the early church.

Whereas in the *Vorlage* of Mark 13 one can point to the influence of Jewish apocalypticism, one should also see differences, especially in the emphasis on the theophany of Jesus the 'Son of Man'. In this respect it should be noted that Mark 13, as well as Q, formulates the expectation of the coming of the 'Son of Man' rather than of a priestly or royal end-time liberator, an expression found only in Q, the Synoptic Gospels and *1 Enoch*.

The Matthaean redaction of the Apocalypse

In the Gospel of Matthew Jesus is designated as 'Anointed' (Matt 1:1; 23:10 and 27:17); as 'Son of David' (Matt 1:1); as 'Son of Abraham' (Matt 1:1); as 'King of the Jews' and as 'Prince' and 'Shepherd' (Matt 2:5–6); as 'the One who is coming' (Matt 11:3); as 'Christ' (Matt 16:6 and 26:63); as 'Son of God' (Matt 16:16 and 26:63), and as 'Son of Man' (Matt 24:27, 30, 37, 39 and 26:64). Biblical 'messianic' passages are also referred to, such as Mic 5:3; 2 Sam 5:2 and 1 Chr 11:2 in Matt 2:6; Isa 29:18 and 35:5 in Matt 11:5. However, within the catechetical framework of the whole of Matthew's Gospel, Jesus is portrayed as the Davidic king-messiah.

In the Matthaean Apocalypse Matt 24:5–41, as in Mark 13, the Parousia of the 'Son of Man' plays the major role. The Apocalypse, at the end of the first century, shows its life-setting in its adaptation of the Markan material. The verses with warnings against persecutions as well as against seductions by false messiahs are considerably enlarged (Matt 24:9b–14:24–28); the same goes for the verses speaking about the coming of the 'Son of Man' (Matt 24:30–31). In these additions the catechesis of the community is emphasized, as Hartman states:

> Also the Matthaean form of the eschatological discourse is obviously, so to speak, addressed to the Church. It came into existence in connection with the needs of Church teaching and so came to be a comprehensive teaching tract on the end and on the demands which the prospect of the end made on Christians. It is 'a pure Parousia discourse'.

In the Matthaean context the messianic sayings about Jesus, in which not only his royalty but also his humility (Matt 11 and 12) are stressed, should therefore be understood as apologetical, as D. Verseput states:

> The expected messianic King, the very rumour of whom stirred rulers, was intended by God from of old to be a lowly messenger of salvation, preaching to the poor and delivering the afflicted. Thus, although the kingship of Jesus was an undeniable right, in the purpose of God it was not yet a reality. His enthronement must await his return.

The Lukan redaction of the Apocalypse

In the Gospel of Luke, which can be characterized by a certain historicization and de-eschatologization of the life of Jesus, one finds the expressions 'Son of God' (Luke 1:32 and 22:70); 'Chosen' (Luke 23:35); 'Saviour' (Luke 2:11); 'Anointed (of God)' (Luke 2:11; 9:21; 23:35 and 24:26); 'Son of David' (Luke 1:32 and 20:41–44); 'Anointed King' (Luke 23:2); 'Christ' (Luke 20:41); and 'Son of Man' (Luke 21:27, 36).

In the Lukan Apocalypse, Luke 21:5–36, it is stressed that, contrary to the Markan Apocalypse, what has been prophesied has now been fulfilled. Luke stresses this in a number of verses: vv. 21–22 ('flee from the city and from Judaea, because these are the days of vengeance, that it may be fulfilled what has been written'), v. 24 (Jerusalem and its inhabitants will fall, until the time for the nations has been fulfilled), vv. 25–26 (signs will happen, people will fear for what will come), v. 28 (when this all begins, liberation is near), as well as vv. 34–36 (be awake and flee for what will happen before the Son of Man). These verses are mainly connected with the destruction of Jerusalem and they are an example of an *ex eventu* prophecy. The hermeneutic basis for Luke can thus be described with the notion 'prophecy and fulfilment', even when it is the fulfilment of something negative. The time of the redaction of the Apocalypse can be dated shortly after the fall of Jerusalem, so that the siege and destruction of the city are understood by Luke as the fulfilment of what has been written. The (therefore?) postponed expectation of the Parousia is connected with the fall of the city.

Revelation

In the Revelation of John a great number of expressions for one and the same latter-day figure are found: the 'Lamb', the 'Son of Man', the 'Word of God', and 'Christ'. Rome and a time of persecutions form the background of a process of conceptualization of both the author and his readers. The first-century Jewish expectation of a 'Son of Man', who will come to conquer Rome, to judge and to rule, has been the starting point. The messiah concept in the book of Revelation has strong military, royal, and juridical aspects, but in the end is only adapted to and seen through the lens of Jesus Christ. Christ will come to judge and punish the rulers of the world, gather the saints, and then become ruler himself.

Conclusion: Messiah/Christ from Paul, to Q, the Synoptic Gospels and Revelation

If one would try to summarize the latter-day events expected by early Christianity, beginning with Paul and continuing with Q, the Synoptic Gospels and Revelation, one may be able to portray it as follows, even if this involves a certain harmonization:

- First there will be a time of uproar, rumours, and seduction.
- An angel will appear.
- The voice of a trumpet of God will be heard.
- Christ will return from heaven.
- Next will come the resurrection of the dead.
- Those who have been raised from the dead will be brought into heaven.
- At the end, Christ will execute the final judgement.
- All enemies of this world, including death and the Antichrist, will be destroyed.
- Finally, the restoration of the whole creation can take place.

Paul's central aim is to portray an end-time scene in which Christology and eschatology are in harmony with each other, as his thinking seems to aim at the eschatological unification of all believers with Christ, when God is all in all and the restoration of the whole universe will take place. This is the Christian hope and everything else is to be subjected to it. In this theology of history Christ has become a 'mediatory' figure, a pre-existent figure sent and glorified by God and connected with angelological and sapiential traditions.

Wherever in Paul's theology one finds apocalyptic structures, the decisive difference between the view of history and the end of days in contemporary apocalypses and that of Paul is found not only in the lack of a cosmic theory of crises, as for instance in 1 Cor 15:20–28, but also and foremost in Paul's hermeneutics. Whereas the apocalypses interpret history from a moment that is still in the future (no matter whether an actual situation caused the view), Paul's criterion for interpreting history is found in an event already having taken place in the death and resurrection of Christ, as well as in the salvation of those believing in the risen Christ, even if the salvation of the whole of creation is still at hand.

When we ask how the messianic expectations connected with Jesus the Messiah or Christ may have further developed in relation with their historical context after Paul, i.e. from the 60s to the end of the first century CE, first in Q and later in the Synoptic Apocalypses, two observations can be made. First, Jesus is portrayed in several ways, and in an antithesis to the persecutions, false messiahs, and false prophets, namely as the promised 'Anointed', 'Son of Man', and so on. The decisive historical situation is found in the political confusion in Palestine in the time during and after the First Jewish War. Evidently influenced by an apologetic interest, Q and the Synoptics have criticized the messianic traditions of their Jewish contemporaries. Second, one can also speak of an inner-Christian development in the further growth of messianic expectations, as the postponement of the expected Parousia may have resulted in new ways of reflecting upon the meaning of Jesus as Messiah.

Matthew portrays Jesus as a Davidic king-messiah, whereas Mark still speaks of a Son of Man. Luke stresses the biblical origin of the Messiah with his scheme of prophecy and fulfilment. In all three gospels we find a great number of biblical as well as Hellenistic expressions, with which Jesus' life on earth and his expected return are described. All authors put Jesus into antithesis with the persecutions, false anointed ones, and false prophets. It seems that in this process of conceptualization a discussion with both Jewish apocalyptic material and Hellenistic ideas has taken place.

When looking back at the whole development of messiah concepts and its connection with Jesus within the New Testament canon, asking whether an originally Jewish messianic expectation later may have been 'Hellenized' might be the wrong question. Instead one should perhaps ask whether the expression 'Christ', originating from a Jewish-Hellenistic community, and represented by Paul, has been used as the name and title of someone sanctified by God, namely Jesus, especially after his death and resurrection, and whether the expression 'Christ' afterwards has been reinterpreted in the Synoptic Apocalypse as a 'messianic' and 'apocalyptic' figure, namely in a discussion with contemporary Jewish messianic expectations and biblical and messianic epithets, interpreted within a specific political situation.

In the observations made so far, we have to state that Paul almost exclusively speaks of 'Christ', and Q of a 'Prophet' and 'Son of Man', but that the gospels two and more decades later begin to enlarge the combinations of expressions and messianic *epitheta* used for Jesus, for instance with the expression 'Son of David' and 'King-Messiah', and that emphasis is laid on his return as the mighty end-time Judge and Son of Man.

This concept is further enlarged in the book of Revelation within the context of the Roman Empire. Formulated as an hypothesis: the earthly Prophet Jesus, who had announced the coming of the kingdom of God, in Q also called the 'Son of Man', and was designated by Paul as the Saviour of the nations, sanctified by God and given the title 'Christ', for some time had also been seen as the Jewish Messiah, especially in the gospels, but in the last third of the first century, in conflict with the politics of the Roman Empire, he took on more and more the role of a universal Ruler, who would return as latter-day Judge and Son of Man.

GERBERN S. OEGEMA

Further reading

Bultmann, R. *The History of the Synoptic Tradition*, trans. John Marsh, New York: Harper & Row, 1963.

Charlesworth, J. H. *Jesus within Judaism: New Light from Exciting Archeological Discoveries*, London: SPCK, 1989.

Hartman, L. *Prophecy Interpreted: The Formation of Some Jewish Apocalyptic Texts and of the Eschatological Discourse Mark 13 par.*, Lund: Gleerup, 1966.

Hengel, M. *The Son of God: The Origin of Christology and the History of Jewish-Hellenistic Religion*, trans. John Bowden, Philadelphia, PA: Fortress Press, 1976.

Holleman, J. *Resurrection and Parousia: A Traditio-Historical Study of Paul's Eschatology in I Corinthians 15*, Leiden: Brill, 1996.

Jonge, M. de. *Christology in Context: The Earliest Christian Response to Jesus*, Philadelphia, PA: Westminster Press, 1988.

—— *Jesus: The Servant-Messiah*, New Haven, CT: Yale University Press, 1990.

Juel, D. *Messianic Exegesis: Christological Interpretation of the Old Testament in Early Christianity*, Philadelphia, PA: Fortress Press, 1988.

Kaestli, J.-D. *L'eschatologie dans l'oeuvre de Luc: Ses caracteristiques et sa place dans le développement du Christianisme primitif*, Geneva: Labor et Fides, 1969.

Karrer, M. *Der Gesalbte: Die Grundlagen des Christustitels*, Gottingen: Vandenhoeck & Ruprecht, 1991.

Kloppenborg, J. *The Formation of Q*, Philadelphia, PA: Fortress Press, 1987.

Kreitzer, L. J. *Jesus and God in Paul's Eschatology*, JSNTSup 19, Sheffield: JSOT Press, 1987.

Lambrecht, J. *Die Redaktion der Markus-Apokalypse: Literarische Analyse und Strukturuntersuchung*, Rome: Pontifical Biblical Institute, 1967.

Mack, B. L. *A Myth of Innocence: Mark and Christian Origins*, Philadelphia, PA: Fortress Press, 1988.

Oegema, G. S. *The Anointed and his People: Messianic Expectations from the Maccabees to Bar Kochba*, Sheffield: Sheffield Academic Press, 1998.

Schade, H.-H. *Apokalyptische Christologie bei Paulus: Studien zum Zusammenhang von Christologie und Eschatologie in den Paulusbriefen*, Gottingen: Vandenhoeck & Ruprecht, 1981.

Verseput, D. *The Rejection of the Humble Messianic King: A Study of the Composition of Matthew 11–12*, New York: Peter Lang, 1986.

MESSIANIC SECRET

Messianic Secret is the term used by William Wrede (1971 [1901]) to describe a complex of motifs in Mark's Gospel that include (1) Jesus' commands to demons to be silent and not make him known – commands that come after the demons have declared his identity; (2) his commands to his disciples to "tell no one" about his identity as the Christ, or about the Transfiguration vision, until after his resurrection; (3) his performance of miracles "privately" or secretly, and commands to those he had healed not to make him known – commands that often were disobeyed;

(4) the chronic failure of the disciples to understand either his identity or destiny; and (5) the purpose the Markan Jesus attributed to his parables: that is, of concealing (rather than revealing) the "secret of the kingdom" (Mark 4:11–12).

Wrede understood these motifs as elements in Mark's redaction of Jesus traditions available to him. (Accepting the view that Mark was the first of the Synoptic Gospels, Wrede declared that Matthew and Luke merely reproduced and rearranged the material they took over from Mark without understanding or reproducing the Messianic Secret.) The Messianic Secret was properly to be investigated as an aspect of Mark's literary composition and the theology it expressed, rather than as a feature of the historical Jesus' activity. This marked a departure from earlier discussions which had read Jesus' commands to silence as evidence that the historical Jesus had sought to wean his followers from political and nationalist understandings of messiahship. Wrede observed that Mark never provides any explicit teaching in which Jesus modified the concept of Messiah.

In Wrede's view, Mark created the Messianic Secret motif in order to integrate fundamentally unmessianic traditions about the earthly Jesus into the early Christian proclamation of Jesus as the exalted Lord. Mark's purpose was apologetic: he took up earlier traditions, according to which Jesus had not identified himself as Messiah but had become Messiah only at his resurrection, and modified them to represent the earthly Jesus as simultaneously revealing and concealing his messianic identity. Wrede acknowledged that Mark had not carried through this compositional technique thoroughly: Jesus' efforts to remain secret appear to be thwarted within the narrative by his ever-increasing reputation with "the crowd."

Following Wrede, many interpreters of the Messianic Secret have accepted his view that the secrecy motif is Mark's literary creation, imposed on earlier traditions for Mark's own theological ends, rather than historical reminiscence. (James D. G. Dunn is a prominent contemporary advocate of the view that the secrecy motif goes back to Jesus' own understanding of messiahship.)

Wrede's description of the purpose behind Mark's composition has not found wide acceptance, however, because it could not explain why Jesus' efforts to keep his identity a secret were unsuccessful. In Jesus' commands to silence after performing miracles, Martin Dibelius recognized a pattern of "secret epiphanies," which (like Wrede) he attributed to Mark's apologetic purpose; but Dibelius explained these as serving to explain why

Jesus had been rejected and crucified by some of his contemporaries. Others regard such "apologetic" explanations as unconvincing because Jesus' identity is not completely concealed in Mark. Offering what has come to be called an "epiphanic" explanation, H. J. Ebeling regarded Jesus' thwarted attempts to remain secret as merely a literary foil for a more fundamental theme in the Gospel, the manifestation of Jesus as Son of God. Ulrich Luz distinguished the function of commands to those who had been healed from commands to demons and Jesus' disciples not to reveal his identity: the latter commands, which are not disobeyed, are meant to show that Jesus' true identity could be understood only in light of the cross. Heikki Räisänen argued that only the latter commands expressed a genuine secrecy motif springing from Mark's christological convictions; other motifs that Wrede had treated together in fact had different and varied explanations. T. J. Weeden regarded Mark's purpose as a christological polemic aimed, not against Jewish nationalist ideas about the Messiah, but against a "divine man" Christology alive in the early Hellenistic church which regarded Jesus as Son of God by virtue of his miraculous powers.

The last view relies on the negative portrayal of the disciples in Mark, who are repeatedly described as "hard of heart," and regards Mark's disciples as representing a Christian group in Mark's own day whose christological views Mark considers inadequate. Clearly the Markan portrayal of the disciples is of particular importance for the interpretation of the Messianic Secret. As Nils Dahl observes, the disciples constitute an "inner circle" who receive special revelations, yet remain incapable of understanding those revelations. Dahl contrasted Mark with the Epistle of Barnabas, where Jesus' disciples are judged in retrospect as "sinful beyond measure" (5:9): Mark's purpose, in Dahl's view, remained paraenetic, exhorting Christians to remain aware of how great was the mystery revealed to them.

On the other hand, James M. Robinson observed that similar negative portrayals of the original disciples and the idea that Jesus could be rightly understood only after Easter, and only by a chosen few, are regular features in the later Gnostic Christian writings. While some interpretations of the Messianic Secret give priority to the motif either of concealment ("apologetic" explanations) or of revelation ("epiphanic" explanations), the key to the Messianic Secret may lie in recognizing that both concealment and revelation occur simultaneously as the effect of Jesus' presence, words, and works. This double effect is clearest in the way the disciples are portrayed as "insiders" to whom the secret of the kingdom is given, often privately (4:11, 34; 7:17), yet at the same time they remain "hard of heart" and incapable of understanding (4:13; 6:52; 7:18; 8:17–21). Mark clearly expects his implied readers not to suffer this double effect: that is, they are to be more perceptive than the original disciples. Comparison of this aspect of Mark's narrative with the distance from the original disciples effected, for example, in the Letter of Barnabas and later Gnostic writings awaits further exploration along the lines suggested by Robinson.

NEIL ELLIOTT

Further reading

Blevins, James L. *The Messianic Secret in Markan Research, 1901–1976*, Washington, DC: University Press of America, 1981.

Dahl, Nils. "The Purpose of Mark's Gospel," in *Jesus in the Memory of the Early Church*, Minneapolis, MN: Augsburg, 1976, pp. 55–60.

Dibelius, Martin. *From Tradition to Gospel*, trans. B. L. Woolf, New York: Charles Scribner's Sons, 1934.

Dunn, James D. G. "The Messianic Secret in Mark," *TynBu* 21 (1970) 92–117; reprinted in C. Tuckett (ed.) *The Messianic Secret*, IRT I, Philadelphia, PA: Fortress Press, 1983, pp. 116–31.

Ebeling, H. J. *Das Evangelium nach Markus*, Göttingen: Vandenhoeck & Ruprecht, 1949.

Elliott, Neil. "The Silence of the Messiah: The Function of 'Messianic Secret' Motifs Across the Synoptics," in Kent Richards (ed.) *SBLSP 1993*, Missoula, MT: Scholars Press, 1993.

Luz, Ulrich. "The Secrecy Motif and the Markan Christology," *ZNW* 56 (1965) 9–30; reprinted in C. Tuckett (ed.) *The Messianic Secret*, IRT I, Philadelphia, PA: Fortress Press, 1983, pp. 75–96.

Räisänen, Heikki. *The Messianic Secret in Mark's Gospel*, trans. Christopher Tuckett, London: T. & T. Clark. 1986.

Robinson, James M. "Gnosticism and the New Testament," in B. Aland (ed.) *Gnosis. Festschrift for Hans Jonas*, Göttingen: Vandenhoeck & Ruprecht, 1978, pp. 125–43.

Tuckett, Christopher (ed.) *The Messianic Secret*, IRT I, Philadelphia, PA: Fortress Press, 1983.

Weeden, T. J. *Mark–Traditions in Conflict*, Philadelphia, PA: Fortress Press, 1971.

Wrede, William. *The Messianic Secret*, trans. J. C. G. Greig, London: James Clarke, 1971.

MESSIANISM AND MESSIANIC FIGURES IN SECOND TEMPLE JUDAISM

Messianism

Messianism is the systematic overview (not the doctrine) of messianic texts, messianic expectations, Messiah concepts and messianic figures according to literary, historical and hermeneutic criteria. A messianic text is a text from the Hebrew Bible or the early Jewish and Christian tradition, in which the coming of a Davidic priest and/or king is expected, who has been promised to Israel, who is filled with the Holy Spirit and who will free the people of God from the nations of the world at the end of time and rule over them with justice and peace. Thus, a Messiah is a priestly, royal or otherwise characterized figure, which will play a liberating role at the end of days.

Messianic texts can be studied from several angles: (1) biblical or traditional: which 'traditional', that is, biblical or early Jewish material has been used in a certain text? (2) hermeneutical or exegetical: how has this material been interpreted in a 'messianic' way, that is, been referred to a Messiah? (3) political: to which political situation has a 'messianic' interpretation been referred and in which political context does it have to be understood? (4) social: in which socio-economic context has a 'messianic' interpretation taken place and how is it to be understood? and (5) religious: what was the religious life-setting of the 'messianic' interpretation and how can the theology or ideology of the 'messianic' interpretation of a certain writing be described?

Messianic concepts and figures can also be arranged by historical periods, notably by the following periods: (a) up to the time of the Maccabees; (b) from Judas Maccabeus to Pompeius; (c) from Pompeius to Titus and Vespasian; (d) from Titus and Vespasian to Bar Kochbah; and (e) after Bar Kochbah. In every period one can furthermore observe the activities of historical figures who by their contemporaries were seen as messianic figures. In addition, messianic concepts and future expectations also reveal aspects of their immediate historical circumstances.

Messianic figures and Messiah concepts

Apart from Isaiah (Cyrus), Haggai and Zachariah (Serubbabel and Joshua), Philo (Claudius), the Qumran writings (Teacher of Righteousness), the New Testament (Jesus of Nazareth), the Bar Kochbah letters and rabbinic literature (Bar Kochbah), it is especially Josephus who speaks of historical figures being seen as Messiahs or Messiah pretenders.

In the case of Josephus, the rebels against Rome, whom he often portrays as freedom fighters with royal aspirations – yes, even Messianic figures – he mainly criticizes as robbers and murderers in the end. To be mentioned here are the following Messiah pretenders: Simon, Anthronges, Menachem, Simon bar Giora, as well as Judas, the Galilaean, the founder of the Zealot movement. Against the background of his critique of the Jewish attitude before and during the First Jewish War (66–73 CE) and his conviction that fate had decided that Rome would win, he criticizes the messianic expectations of his people, especially the interpretations of Num 24:17, as in his view Num 24:17 had prophesied Vespasian's installation as Imperator on Jewish soil. And with this, in fact, Josephus considered Vespasian himself to be a Messiah appointed by God.

Historical developments from the Maccabees to Bar Kochbah

Messianic concepts up to the time of Judas Maccabaeus

When looking at the period up to the Maccabees, one can state that although messianic expectations are found in earlier times, namely in various passages of the Hebrew Bible, e.g. in some of the Psalms and in Zechariah, in the Septuagint as well as in *Ben Sira*, the conceptualization of eschatological figures reaches a first climax in the book of Daniel.

Although the end-time liberator in Daniel is not called a Messiah, he is set in the literary framework of an apocalypse with a periodized and eschatologized portrayal of history, one of the main genres in which Messiah figures are found. Surprisingly enough, however, it is not the concept of the Messiah itself (as righteous king or priest of the latter days) that is found here, but instead a figure not found in any of the other biblical books: the 'One like a Man' in Daniel 7:13. This multivalent figure is to be associated with the various connotations of the expression *brns*, for example a political and religious 'attorney' or 'deputy', who in Daniel 7 may well be symbolizing 'representation of (Divine) authority on earth', an interpretation that would also fit with a second meaning of the 'One like a Man', namely that of angelic being or *archon*.

Messianic concepts from Judas Maccabaeus to Pompeius

In the Maccabaean and Hasmonaean period, i.e. from the second half of the second century BCE onwards, in the Essene writings found in Qumran, 1QS, 1QSa (1Q28a), 1QSb (1Q28b), 4QTestim (4Q175) and CD, one finds a surprising number of multi-dimensional and multivalent eschatological figures. In addition, the Teacher of Righteousness and founder of the community was also connected with eschatological and messianic expectations.

For the time after 100 BCE, the eschatological figure(s) hoped for are often conceptualized as prophets and more often as priests and/or kings, and the expression "until the Coming of a Prophet" is often used. This expression reminds us of Num 24:17, Hag 2:20–23; Zech 4:11–14; *T. Jud.* 21:1–5, and other biblical, contemporary and later 'parallels', for example 1 Macc 4:46.

Part of the explanation of this diversity of messianic expectations in the Qumran writings lies in the diverse and conflict-ridden political situation during Maccabaean and Hasmonaean times. However, in the centre of everyone's interest stood the offices of the priesthood and kingdom: 'until a reliable Prophet would rise' (1 Maccabees) or 'until the coming of the Anointed from Aaron and Israel' (*Damascus Document*). Simon, son of Judas Maccabaeus, was the first to be called 'High Priest, Strategian and Leader of the Jews'. His son John Hyrcan took over the title in 135/134 BCE and established close connections with the Sadducees. We are thus able to observe that the idea that kingdom and priesthood could be united in one person had actually been put into political practice and at the same time had been formulated in some of the messianic expectations of the time.

Understood in this way, a criticism of the Hasmonaean priest-kings is clearly found in the messianic expectations found in the Qumran writings 1QS, 1QSa (1Q28a), 1 QSb (1 Q28b), 4QTestim (4Q175) and CD. Here, the latter-day figures are mostly portrayed as priest, king, prophet, or *strategos*, and often even as a combination of more than one of these figures, especially of king and priest. The Hasmonaean leaders had done the same, they were priest, *strategos* and king; John Hyrcan had even combined all three offices in one person.

Messianic figures from Pompeius to Titus and Vespasian

In the first known writing of the Pharisaic movement, the *Psalms of Solomon*, one finds a consistent Messiah concept with a clear life-setting (*Pss. Sol.* 17–18). In the older Psalms a Davidic king-Messiah is expected, in the younger Psalms a latter-day liberator is conceptualized as leader and teacher of Israel. In both cases the Messiah is subordinated to God's dominion.

In the balance of power in Palestine during the first century BCE (especially after 63 BCE), the

Romans under the leadership of Pompeius had taken over control of Palestine, the Idumaeans were installed instead of the Hasmonaeans as vassal kings and the Pharisees become more and more influential. It is therefore understandable that in the messianic expectations of the *Psalms of Solomon* only the royal dominion over Palestine is criticized and that it was important to stress that the power (or its procuration) of God's government remained in Davidic hands.

An interesting parallel to *Pss. Sol.* 17–18 is found in the Damascus Document *CD*, which partly can also be dated in the time from Pompeius to Caesar. In *CD* 7:14–21 Amos 5:26; 9:11 and Num 24.17 are interpreted in such a way that the biblical verses refer to both a Prince of the Congregation and a Teacher of Torah. In particular, Num 24:17, a verse which is normally used for a king-Messiah, is stressed here exegetically to emphasize the role of the Teacher of Torah.

With the change of the balance of power in the following decades, also the messianic expectations would change, which is especially the case in 1QM, 4QPatr, 4QTestim and 4QpIsa of the Herodian period.

In the *War Scroll*, 1QM 11 Num 24:17 is not interpreted in a messianic way as in previous interpretations, but is now applied to God's role in the latter-day battle, which is modelled on a biblical pattern and which leads to the final judgement. The text of 1QM 11, written in the second half of the first century CE, shows a remarkable parallel with Philo's *De praemiis et poenis* 95, in which Num 24:17 has been interpreted in the same way, namely not in a messianic but in a more theocentric and eschatological way. Also for Philo, God – and not the Messiah – is the decisive factor in the war between Israel and its enemies.

However, most of the Qumran writings of this period offer different concepts: they expect a Messiah with strong royal and military aspects, as this kind of intervening was especially needed in a situation of changing balance of power. The fragmentary writings 4Q525 5:1–5 (*Pesher on Gen* 49:10: a Davidide will keep the Torah) and 4QFlor (4Q174) (*Pesher on Amos* 9:11 and 2 Sam 7:14, etc.: the Davidic King Messiah will erect the Torah in Israel after a latter-day battle) stress exactly this kind of messianic concept.

More difficult to interpret is another writing from approximately the same period, namely *1 Enoch* 37–71. In the 'Parables of Enoch' the expressions 'Messiah', 'Son of Man', 'Chosen' and 'Just One' are on the one hand different names and concepts, but on the other hand they do have to be

identified with one and the same latter-day figure. His functions are mainly those of a latter-day 'judge', his attributes are those of a righteous 'king' and his task at the end of days is to gather together the people of God.

Also the 'Son of Man' (*1 En.* 46:3–5 *et al.*) has been reinterpreted as a latter-day liberator with royal and military characteristics. An abundance of biblical material (Dan 7; Isa 11 and 24) has been used here. In the eschatological battle this complex figure will judge the mighty ones and reward the righteous. To date this figure and the writing itself, however, has shown to be extremely difficult, as there is still uncertainty about the historical context of the parables, as well as the life-setting.

In the partly contemporary and partly later Synoptic Apocalypse(s) one finds yet other Messiah concepts. Matthew portrays Jesus as a Davidic king-Messiah, whereas Mark speaks of a Son of Man. Luke stresses the biblical origin of the Messiah with his scheme of prophecy and fulfilment. In all three gospels we find a great number of biblical as well as Hellenistic expressions, with which Jesus' life on earth and his expected return are described. Jesus is put by all authors in antithesis with the persecutions, false anointed and false prophets and it seems that in this process of conceptualization an interaction between both Jewish apocalyptic material and Hellenistic ideas has taken place.

When looking at the development of Messiah concepts in the New Testament canon, one may want to ask whether the expression 'Christ', originating from a Hellenistic-Jewish community, and explained by Paul and in Q as based on a religious experience, may have been used as the name and title of someone 'sanctified' by God, namely Jesus of Nazareth after his death and resurrection, and whether this expression of 'Christ' at a later stage has been reinterpreted in a different way. This process of reinterpretation in the Synoptic Apocalypses may very well have taken place within the context of a discussion with contemporary Jewish messianic expectations and messianic epithets and thus have led to a certain degree of 'Judaization', a connotation which it originally may not have had.

Messianic figures from Titus and Vespasian to Bar Kochbah

During the period between the First and Second Jewish Wars the Messiah is most often conceptualized as a combination of a Son of Man, judge and king (who will gather the people of God), especially in the *Apocalypses of Abraham, Baruch, Ezra*, John and in *Sibylline Oracle 5*. In

2 Baruch and in *4 Ezra* the Roman Empire and the order of its emperors play a dominant role in the view of history and influence the conceptualization of Messiah figures.

In *2 Baruch* 35–41, Ezekiel 17 and Daniel 7 the interpretation is such that the latter-day liberator is expected at the end of a periodized history to judge and destroy the remaining rulers of the nations, to gather the remnant of the people of God and to rule for ever. The latter-day figure in *2 Bar.* 70–73 has received more direct military and juridical functions. He will judge the nations who have ruled over Israel, and deliver them to the sword.

In *4 Ezra* 11–12 the vision of Daniel 7 is enlarged, actualized and applied to Rome. The latter-day liberator, who has been kept by God until the end of days, is portrayed as a lion and can thus be understood as a Davidic king-Messiah. Additionally it is said that he will judge the kings and free the remnant of the people of God. In ch. 13 the Messiah is portrayed as the 'One like a Man', who with the fire of his will kills those who make war with him. He will restore the creation and gather the nine-and-a-half tribes.

In the book of Revelation a great number of expressions for one and the same latter-day figure is found: the Lamb, the Son of Man, the Word of God and Christ. Rome and a time of persecutions form the background of both the author and his readers. The Messiah concept has strong military, royal and juridical aspects and is then adapted to Christ: Christ will come to rule and to gather the saints.

In *Apocalypse of Abraham* 29 a latter-day liberator is expected, who will play the role of a righteous judge in the twelfth period of the age of wickedness. He is also called the 'Chosen' and will gather the people of God. Abraham's rejection of idolatry is exemplary for the fate of the just in the latter day.

Finally, *Sibylline Oracle* 5 should also be mentioned here. Whereas *Sibylline Oracle* 3 hails a Ptolemy as latter-day liberator, *Sib. Or.* 5:414 and 526 expect a Man from the sky to oppose the historical figure of Nero. He is portrayed as a warrior-king, judge and Son of Man (the latter based on Isa 11:1–5 and Dan 7:13).

Conclusion

Every messianic text is unique in the way it interprets biblical or traditional material and refers it to a specific Messiah concept, often in an interaction with history.

GERBERN S. OEGEMA

Further reading

Charlesworth, C. H. (ed.) *The Messiah. Developments in Earliest Judaism and Christianity*, Minneapolis, MN: Fortress Press, 1992.

Collins, J. J. *The Sceptre and the Star: The Messiahs of the Dead Sea Scrolls and Other Ancient Literature*, New York: Doubleday, 1995.

Gruenwald, I., Shaked, S. and Stroumsa, G. G. (eds) *Messiah and Christos: Studies in the Jewish Origins of Christianity. Presented to David Flusser on the Occasion of his Seventy-Fifth Birthday*, Tübingen: J. C. B. Mohr [Paul Siebeck], 1992.

Neusner, J., Green, W. S. and Frerichs, E. (eds) *Judaisms and their Messiahs at the Turn of the Christian Era*, Cambridge: Cambridge University Press, 1987.

Oegema, G. S. *The Anointed and His People*, JSJSup 95, Sheffield: Sheffield Academic Press, 1998.

Stegemann, E. (ed.) *Messias-Vorstellungen bei Juden und Christen*, Stuttgart: W. Kohlhammer, 1993.

METAPHOR AND SIMILE

Both metaphors and similes establish unexpected and memorable correspondences between two entities that are simultaneously alike and different. Their impact resides in the tension between likeness and *"unlikeness."* They function at both emotional and cognitive levels, surprising the audience and setting up new models for perceiving and processing reality, thereby extending meaning. Similes are more explicit than metaphors, using "like" or "as" to establish the connection. While some metaphors do primarily involve simple transposition of words, the processes of inventing and recognizing resemblances in the framework of whole sentences are more dynamic. There is a sense in which all language is metaphorical; verbal characters represent phenomena in our experiential spheres, and language represents thought. Metaphorical concepts shape how we think about our worlds, and how we express those thoughts. Many gospel metaphors established associations already lodged in the culture of the Hebrew Bible.

Similes

When the Evangelists posed similes, it was a means to express the inexpressible. The events that unfolded particularly in regard to the instances when heaven and earth converged, such as the baptism and Transfiguration, created associations between the terrestrial and celestial spheres. At the baptism, the Spirit descended like a dove (Matt 3:16 and parallels), reminiscent of the metaphorical action in the creation narrative of the Spirit "hovering" over the face of the waters (Gen 1:2). At the Transfiguration, the face of Jesus shone like the sun and His clothes were white as light (Matt 17:2). After the resurrection, the appearance of angel is likened to lightning, his clothing was white as snow, but the guards became like dead men (Matt 28:3–4).

Many of the brief similes in Jesus' teaching gave His audiences memorable perspectives on human character. The person who hears the words of Jesus and either obeys them or does not, is like one who builds his house on rock or sand respectively (Matt 7:24–27; Luke 6:47–49). The people of that generation were like petulant children in market places (Matt 11:16–17; Luke 7:31–32). The Twelve whom He sent out would be as vulnerable as sheep among wolves, and He admonished them to be shrewd as snakes and innocent as doves (Matt 10:16; cf. Luke 10:3). Jesus likened the hypocritical scribes and Pharisees to whitewashed tombs (Matt 23:27). A number of the similes focus on the kingdom of heaven, employing tiny illustrative vignettes to illustrate the nature of the kingdom.

Metaphors

Both John the Baptist and Jesus found ample resources for metaphor in the natural environment. They excoriated evil people as a brood of vipers (Matt 3:7; 12:34; 23:33). Features of the pastoral milieu embedded in the Old Testament shaped Jesus' portrayal of His relationship to His people amidst the threats of an evil world; they were a "little flock" (Luke 12:32) and the lost sheep of Israel (Matt 10:6), in need of a shepherd (John 10:2–16). False prophets were wolves in sheep's clothing (Matt 7:15). He called the teaching of the Pharisees leaven (Matt 16:6–12; Mark 8:15; Luke 12:1), illustrative of the pervasive and spreading effects of their instruction. In John 15, Jesus wove together the extended metaphors of the vine, the gardener, branches, and fruit (cf. Isa 5:1–7).

Metaphorical actions transformed static images into dramatic scenes. John the Baptist challenged his unbelieving audience to produce fruit, declaring that God could raise up children of Abraham from stones, warning that the ax was at the root of the tree (Matt 3:8–10; Luke 3:8–9), further prophesying that Jesus would come and baptize with the Holy Spirit and with fire (Matt 3:11; Luke 3:16), as His fork was in His hand to winnow (Matt 3:12; Luke 3:17)! Jesus' exhortation not to throw pearls to swine (Matt 7:6) was an arresting warning against inappropriately placing the treasure of the truth in the presence of those who would sully it. Jesus declared that it was easier for a camel to go through the eye of a needle than for a rich man to enter the kingdom of heaven (Matt 19:24; Luke 18:25).

Following Jesus is depicted as putting one's hand to the plow (Luke 9:62); and obedience as taking His "yoke" (Matt 11:29–30), both arduous tasks. Jesus repeatedly admonished His disciples to take up the cross and follow Him (Matt 10:38; 16:24; Mark 8:34; Luke 9:23; 14:27). Discipleship is a costly enterprise (Luke 14:28–33), emphasized in Jesus's challenge to His disciples to drink the cup He would drink and be baptized with the same baptism that He would undergo (Mark 10:38–39). The metaphor of the cup of God's wrath (Jer 25:15) infused Jesus' prayer in the Garden of Gethsemane (Matt 26:39–44; Luke 22:42).

In the face of His impending death, Jesus likened the anguish of the disciples to the pain of a woman giving birth who forgets it when the child is born (John 16:21–22). Death warranted its own set of metaphors, some designed to soften its terrible impact.

"Lazarus has fallen asleep, but I will wake him" (John 11:11). Jesus spoke of "tasting" death (Luke 9:27) and addressed the value of His own impending death with the image of a kernel of wheat that only bears fruit when it falls to the ground and dies (John 12:24).

Jesus declared that they would see the angels of God ascending and descending on the Son of Man (John 1:51). Son of God and Son of Man were titles of filial relationship, binding divinity and humanity into the Person of Christ. When Jesus spoke of destroying and rebuilding the Temple in three days, John the Evangelist explicitly made the connection with the Body of Christ (John 2:19–21). John the Baptist declared that Jesus is the Lamb of God (John 1:29–36), the perfect Sacrifice.

Calling Jesus the Word (John 1:1) is a metaphor that speaks forcefully of revelation, culminating in the Word made Flesh (John 1:14), born into the world. Light came into the world, both at creation and at the incarnation (John 3:19), and to be children of light *we* must be born again (John 3:3–8). The I AM proclamations drew the divine covenant name, Yahweh, into dynamic relationship with Jesus Himself, shocking His audience. He said, "I AM the bread of life" (John 6), "the light of the world" (John 8:12; 9:5; 12:35–36, 46), the "good shepherd" (John 10:11–15), "the resurrection and the life" (John 11:25–26), and "the way, the truth, and the life" (John 14:6).

ELAINE A. PHILLIPS

Further reading

Cobern, Camden M. "Metaphor," in James Hastings (ed.) *A Dictionary of Christ and the Gospels*, New York: Charles Scribner's Sons, 1908.

Ricoeur, Paul. *Interpretation Theory: Discourse and Surplus of Meaning*, Fort Worth, TX: Texas Christian University Press, 1976.

—— *The Rule of Metaphor: Multi-disciplinary studies of the creation of meaning in language*, trans. Robert Czerny, Toronto: University of Toronto Press, 1977.

Ryken, Leland. *Words of Delight: A Literary Introduction to the Bible*, second edition, Grand Rapids, MI: Baker, 1992.

Thiselton, Anthony. *New Horizons in Hermeneutics*, Grand Rapids, MI: Zondervan, 1992.

Vanhoozer, Kevin. *Is There a Meaning in this Text?: The Bible, the Reader, and the Morality of Literary Knowledge*, Grand Rapids, MI: Zondervan, 1999.

MEYER, BEN F.

Benjamin Franklin Meyer (1927–95) studied at the University of Santa Clara in California, the Biblical Institute in Rome, and the Gregorian University. He served as assistant professor of religion at the Graduate Theological Union in Berkeley from 1965 to 1968; from 1969 until his retirement in 1992, he taught in the Department of Religious Studies at McMaster University. Principally a theologian, whose thought reflects the influence of Bernard Lonergan, Meyer shaped current critical study of Jesus with a single, seminal book.

The Aims of Jesus (London: SCM Press, 1979) signaled a fresh and vital engagement with Judaism by scholars of the New Testament. Meyer focused upon the texts of the gospels in the first instance, with a critical capacity to allow for the tendencies of development that developed from the time of Jesus. In his exegetical focus as well as in his sensitivity to literary development, Meyer presaged the work of the next decades, the most intense and critical discussion of Jesus since the previous century. At the same time, Meyer never lost sight of the catalytic place of eschatology within the Judaic milieu of Jesus, and of the principal terms of reference within the Judaism of Jesus' period. Meyer's book is an enduring monument of its own insight and of what was to come, as important in its time as Weiss's *Die Predigt Jesu* was in the nineteenth century.

The principal insight that Meyer offers is that Jesus is only to be understood within the medium of Judaism, but that the movement of which the New Testament is the greatest monument itself represents an understanding of Jesus. Where Geza Vermes sketched a version of early Judaism within which he attempted to categorize Jesus, Meyer located Jesus within Judaism, but then allowed of the distinctive character and logic of his movement. Vermes's Jesus is a charismatic miracleworker whose teaching was incidental; Meyer's

Jesus is galvanized by a particular and specifiable purpose that his teaching expresses and his actions effect. The focus of Jesus' aims, according to Meyer, was the restoration of Israel (p. 221): "In sum, once the theme of national restoration in its full eschatological sweep is grasped as the concrete meaning of the reign of God, Jesus' career begins to become intelligible as a unity."

Even the number of the apostles who are commissioned to preach and heal is not a coincidental rounding in Meyer's analysis, but corresponds to the paradigm of the tribes of Israel (pp. 153–54). Jesus and his followers were motivated by the hope of the restoration and extension of the people of God, in that for them (p. 223) "the religious factor should become absolutely decisive for the self-definition of Israel."

Meyer's analysis was not, and did not pretend to be, entirely original. Joachim Jeremias, in *Jesu Verheissung für die Völker*, had already called attention to the symmetry between the prophetic and rabbinic expectation of the eschatological extension of Israel, and the radical claims attributed to Jesus. In the view of Jeremias those attributions are correct, while Meyer is more cautious in his assessments of authenticity. Meyer's book would merit continued attention if its only contribution was to re-tool Jeremias's analysis for a new day. But its genuine originality is more profound. Meyer was not trapped, as Jeremias ultimately was, by the programmatic assumption that the gospels are reliable as history. Rather, Meyer freely allowed that the gospels are tendentious, but he went on to argue convincingly that the positions ultimately attributed to Jesus are most easily explicable on the supposition that the theology of restoration in fact reflected Jesus' aim.

Meyer elegantly rectified an anomaly within the critical study of Jesus. The anomaly had been that, while scholars of the New Testament generally stressed the importance of developing tendencies within the corpus, the old encyclopedic comparisons with Judaism were inclined to accept assertions in the gospels at face value. Since the Synoptic Gospels in their received forms are the products of communities in the Hellenistic world that lived in tension with Jewish institutions, it is all too easy to read a Jesus off the page who triumphantly transcends Judaism.

Instead, Meyer showed how Jesus needs to be located critically within Judaism, and then allowed his individual motivation, by following Lonergan's principle that historical narrative must refer at every step to evidence, but never mistake that for mere data. While the objects of natural science are inert, history concerns events with meaning and value from first to last. The necessary medium of history, whether we mean history as events or history as narratives, is meaning. Only what is meaningful is remembered as history; only an account of its meaning can be related as history. Arguments concerning the relation of histories to realities considered more "objective" – such as sociology or economics – may or may not be fruitful, but the association of history's beginning and end with meaning is apparent.

Meyer showed how the religious meanings of Scriptures within the contexts and phases of their developments might be defined in relation to Jesus, providing an account of how meanings developed with Jesus as their point of origin. He in no way denied contradictions, major gaps in understanding, and cultural contexts that seem out of place in respect of our own, but he also identified rich resources within the gospels for the description of God and his ways which are resonant with our experience. Jesus in his analysis became a figure of critical inference and at the same time a source of continuing challenge – a truly historical figure once again.

BRUCE CHILTON

Further reading

Lonergan, Bernard J. F. *Method in Theology*, New York: Herder and Herder, 1972.
Martens, John W. "Introduction to Ben F. Meyer's 'Election Historical Thinking in Romans 9–11, and Ourselves'," *Logos* 7:4 (Fall 2004) 150–70.
Meyer, Ben F. *The Aims of Jesus*, London: SCM Press, 1979.
—— *Critical Realism and the New Testament*, Alison Park, PA: Pickwick Publications, 1989.
—— *Reality and Illusion in New Testament Scholarship: A Primer in Critical Realist Hermeneutics*, Collegeville, PA: Liturgical Press, 1994.
Westerholm, Stephen. "Passages: Benjamin Franklin Meyer," *Studies in Religion/Sciences Religieuses* 24:4 (1995) 491–93.

MIDRASH AND RABBINIC RULES OF INTERPRETATION

The Hebrew noun *midrash* is derived from the verb *darash*, which means to "search (for an answer)." Midrash accordingly means "inquiry," "examination," or "commentary." The word often refers to rabbinic interpretation, with respect to both method and form. Scholars therefore refer to midrashic interpretation and rabbinic midrashim. However, in recent years midrash has been discussed against the broader background of ancient

biblical interpretation and textual transmission in general. It has become increasingly apparent that portions of the NT itself reflect aspects of midrash. Indeed, there has been considerable interest recently in the question to what extent Jesus and the Evangelists may have employed midrashic exegesis.

Semantic development

The verb *darash* occurs in a variety of contexts in the OT meaning "to seek," "to inquire," or "to investigate." Scripture speaks of seeking God's will (2 Chr 17:4; 22:9; 30:19; Ps 119:10), making inquiry of God through prophetic oracle (1 Sam 9:9; 1 Kgs 22:8; 2 Kgs 3:11; Jer 21:2), or investigating a matter (Deut 13:14; 19:18; Judg 6:29; cf. 1QS 6:24; 8:26). The nominal form, *midrash*, occurs in the OT twice meaning "story," "book," and possibly "commentary" (2 Chr 13:22; 24:27, cf. RSV). In later usage there is a shift from seeking God's will through prophetic oracle to seeking God's will through study of scripture. In later traditions we are told that Ezra the scribe "set his heart to search the Law of the Lord" (Ezra 7:10). Other texts convey similar meanings: "Great are the works of the Lord, studied by all who have pleasure in them" (Ps 111:2); "I have sought thy precepts" (Ps 119:45; cf. vv. 94, 155); "Observe and seek out all the commandments of the Lord" (1 Chr 28:8). Although this "searching" of God's Law should not in these passages be understood as exegesis in a strict sense, it is only a small step to the later explicit exegetical reference of midrash: "This is the study [*midrash*] of the Law" (1QS 8:15); "The interpretation [*midrash*] of 'Blessed is the man ... '" (4QFlor 1:14; cf. Ps 1:1). Indeed, the Teacher of Righteousness is called the "searcher of the Law" (CD 6:7). Philo urges his readers to join him in searching (*ereunan* = *darash*) Scripture (*Worse* 57; 141; *Cherubim* 14). In rabbinic writings midrash becomes standard and its practice as an exegetical method was consciously considered.

Rabbinic midrash

In the writings of the rabbis, midrash attains its most sophisticated and self-conscious form. In "searching" the sacred text the rabbis attempted to update scriptural teaching to make it relevant to new circumstances and issues. This approach was felt to be legitimate because scripture was understood as divine in character and therefore could yield many meanings and many applications: "'Is not my word like a hammer that breaks the rock in pieces?' [Jer 23:29]. As the hammer causes numerous sparks to flash forth, so is a verse of Scripture capable of many interpretations" (*b. Sanh.* 34a; cf. *'Abot* 5:22). There are different approaches to midrash.

Halakah/haggadah

Rabbinic midrash falls into two basic categories. These categories are distinguished not by method, but by objectives. Halakah (from *halak*, "to walk") refers to a legal ruling (plural: *halakoth*). Hence, halakic midrash is in reference to legal interpretation. The purpose of *halakoth* was to build an oral "fence" around written Torah, making violation of it (written Torah) less likely (*'Abot* 1:1; 3:14). Haggadah (lit. "telling," from the root *nagad*, "to draw") refers to the interpretation of narrative and is usually understood as homiletical or non-legal interpretation (plural: *haggadoth*). Best known is the Passover Haggadah (cf. *b. Pesah.* 115b, 116b). Haggadic midrash was much more imaginative in its attempts to fill in the gaps in scripture and to explain away apparent discrepancies, difficulties, and unanswered questions. Legal rulings were not to be derived from haggadic interpretation (cf. *y. Pe'ah* 2:6).

Rabbinic periods

The rabbis of the pre-Mishnaic period (50 BCE–200 CE) are referred to as the Tannaim (i.e. the "repeaters"), while the rabbis of the later period ("early": 200–500 CE; "late": 500 CE–1500 CE) are called the Amoraim (i.e. the "sayers"). Obviously the Tannaitic traditions are of the greatest value for NT interpretation.

Rabbinic literature

The legal corpus, in which halakic concerns predominate, is made up of Mishnah (lit. "repetition" or "[memorizable] paragraph"; *c.* 200 CE), Tosefta (lit. "supplement [to Mishnah]"; *c.* 300 CE), and Talmud (lit. "learning"; Palestinian [or Jerusalem]: *c.* 500 CE; Babylonian: *c.* 600 CE; note that the word for "disciple" is *talmid*, i.e. "one who learns"). Many of the *halakoth* found in the Mishnah date back in one form or another to the time of Jesus (e.g. compare Mark 2:16 and *m. Demai* 2:3 concerning being the guest of a non-observant Jew; Mark 3:1–6 and *m. Šhabb.* 14:3–4; 22:6 concerning healing on the Sabbath; Mark 7:3–13 and *m. Ned.* 1:3 concerning *qorban*). It was believed that the Oral Law ultimately derives from Moses: "Many

rulings were transmitted to Moses on Sinai [and] ... all of them are embodied in Mishnah" (*y. Pesa.* 2:6).

Many of the non-legal works are called midrashim ("commentaries"). From the Tannaitic period we have *Mekilta de Rabbi Ishmael* (on Exodus), *Sipre Numbers*, *Sipre Deuteronomy*, and *Sipra Leviticus*. From the early Amoraic period we have *Midrash Rabbah* (on the Pentateuch and the Five Scrolls), *Midrash on the Psalms*; *Pesiqta Rabbati*, *Pesiqta de Rab Kahana*, *Seder Eliyahu Rabbah*, and *Midrash Tanhiuma*. Tannaitic tradition is often found in these writings as well (and when it is, it is called *baraita*).

Forms of midrash

J. Neusner (1987) classifies midrash as three "types": (1) paraphrase (e.g. the LXX and targums), midrash of the synagogue and of diaspora Judaism; (2) prophecy (e.g. Qumran and Matthew), midrash of eschatologically oriented Judaism; and (3) parable (e.g. Philo and the rabbis), midrash of the academies. Midrash operates at two levels: obvious and subtle. M. Gertner (268) describes these levels as "overt" and "covert" midrash. To be preferred, however, is E. Ellis's use of the words "explicit" and "implicit" (1988: 703–9). Interpretive paraphrase, as in the LXX, the Targum, or even echoing older scriptural traditions in later scriptural texts, is covert or implicit, while citing scripture (i.e. the lemma) and then interpreting it (i.e. the midrash or pesher) is overt or explicit. The rabbinic writings, the pesharim of Qumran, and many passages of the NT (as seen particularly in Matthew, John, and Paul) afford examples of explicit interpretation. The retelling of biblical history, as seen in *Jubilees*, 1QapGen (*Genesis Apocryphon*), Pseudo-Philo's *Biblical Antiquities*, Josephus' *Jewish Antiquities*, and the targums, represents implicit interpretation. The very manner in which the biblical narrative is retold in these writings brings to light new insights and new teachings. Its purpose is, in effect, to update scripture. Matthean and Lukan rewriting of Mark may at places parallel this kind of midrashic paraphrase (see later).

Jesus and the exegetical rules of Hillel

Seven rules of exegesis, or *middot* ("measurements"), are attributed to Hillel (cf. *t. Sanh.* 7.11). These rules probably took their formal shape after Hillel's time, though it is possible some of them do in fact derive from the famous sage. Most of these rules are contextual, and are frequently driven by the desire to resolve apparent contradictions in scripture, or to create rulings not otherwise covered by scripture.

Tradition holds that these rules were expanded to thirteen by Ishmael, a rabbi of the second century (cf. *Beraita deRabbi Ishmael* §1 in Prologue to *Sifra*). Rabbi Eliezer ben Yose the Galilean is credited with further expanding these rules, particularly as they relate to the interpretation of narrative. He is probably the author of the tractate *Thirty-Two Rules for Interpreting the Torah* (also called the *Baraita of Thirty-Two Rules*, cf. beginning of *Midrash Mishnat R. Eliezer* and beginning of *Midrash ha-Gadol* on Genesis). Unlike the seven *middot* of Hillel the Elder, many of these later rules are contrived and atomistic (e.g. finding significance in the numerical value of the letters themselves) and have little or nothing to do with the literary or historical context of the scriptural passage under consideration. Most of these thirty-two rules, rules which made it possible to enjoy the "savory dishes of wisdom" (*'Abot* 3:19), were applied to homiletical midrash, not legal.

Many of the rules associated with Hillel can be seen in Jesus' teaching. They are as follows.

Qal wa-homer *(lit. "light and heavy")*

According to this rule, what is true or applicable in a "light" (or less important) instance is surely true or applicable in a "heavy" (or more important) instance. Such a principle is at work when Jesus assures his disciples (cf. Matt 6:26 = Luke 12:24) that because God cares for the birds (= light), as taught in scripture (cf. Ps 147:9; *Pss. Sol.* 5:8–19), they can be sure that he cares for them (= heavy). A similar saying is attributed to Rabbi Simeon ben Eleazar:

> Have you ever seen a wild animal or a bird practicing a trade? – yet they have their sustenance without care and were not created for anything else but to serve me? But I was created to serve my Maker. How much more then ought not I to have my sustenance without care?
>
> (*m. Qidd.* 4:14)

Other dominical examples come to mind: "If God so clothes the grass of the field ... " (Matt 6:30 = Luke 12:28; cf. *Mek.* on Exod 16:4 [*Vayassa'* §3]: "He who has what he will eat today and says, 'What shall I eat tomorrow,' behold, this man lacks faith"); "If you then, who are evil, know how to give good gifts to your children ... " (Matt 7:11 = Luke 11:13; cf. *y. Sheb.* 9.1: "Rabbi Simeon ben Yohai ... said: 'A bird apart from heaven will not perish, how much less (the) son of (the) man!'").

Gezera shawa *(lit. "an equivalent regulation")*

According to this rule, one passage may be explained by another, if similar words or phrases are present. Hillel taught that because the word *mo'ado* ("its appointed time") is used of the daily sacrifice (Num 28:2) and of Passover (Num 9:2), one may infer that what applies to the one applies to the other (*b. Pesah.* 66a). When Jesus took action in the Temple precincts, he quoted phrases from Isa 56:7 and Jer 7:11: "Is it not written, 'My house shall be called a house of prayer for all the nations'? But you have made it a 'cave of robbers'" (Mark 11:17). Reference to "house" in Isaiah 56 and Jeremiah 7 suggested the linkage of the passages.

Binyan 'ab mikkatub 'ehad *(lit. "constructing a father [i.e. principal rule] from one [passage]")*

From *yimmase'* ("he is found"), the rabbis deduced that two or three witnesses are always required, since this command precedes a series of examples in Deuteronomy 17 (*Sipre Deut* §148 [on Deut 17:2]). In another place the rabbis taught that people who are to be put to death for the various offenses described in Lev 20:10–21 should be stoned, because the phrase *demehem bam* ("their blood [be] upon them") that appears in these verses (vv. 11, 13, 16) also appears in a verse (v. 27) that describes an offense for which stoning is specifically commanded (*Sipra Lev* §209 [on Lev 20:13–16]). Jesus's defense of the resurrection evidently presupposed this rule. Since God is not the God of the dead, but of the living, the revelation at the burning bush, "I am the God of Abraham" (Exod 3:14–15), implies that Abraham is to be resurrected. From this one text and its inference one may further infer, as Jesus did (Mark 12:26), the truth of the general resurrection.

Binyan 'ab mishshene ketubim *(lit. "constructing a father [i.e. principal rule] from two writings [or passages]")*

This *midda* functions as the one above, except that it constructs its general principle from two passages. For a rabbinic example of this rule of interpretation, see *Mek.* on Exod 21:26–27 (*Neziqin* §9), where on the basis of the two commands to compensate a slave for having lost either an eye or a tooth, one may infer that for any irreplaceable loss a slave must be set free. When Paul argues that as an apostle of Christ he deserves his food (1 Cor 9:1–14), he appeals to the general principle that the treading ox must be allowed to eat of the grain

(Deut 25:4) and to Scripture's specific command that the priests receive a share of the burnt offering (Deut 18:1–8; cf. 1 Cor 9:13). This teaching, he says, he received from Christ: "The Lord commanded that those who proclaim the gospel should get their living by the gospel" (1 Cor 9:14).

Kelal upherat upherat ukelal *(lit. "general and particular, and particular and general")*

This *midda* is based on the assumption that general principles can be inferred from specific statements in scripture, or that specific principles can be inferred from general statements. Hillel's summary of the whole Torah (cited above) reflects this principle. Rabbi Ishmael is credited with explaining the principle as follows: "Anything which is included in the general statement and which is specified in order to teach (something) teaches not only about itself but also teaches about everything in the general statement" (*Baraita R. Ishmael* §1; cf. the explanations in *Num. Rab.* 3.7 [on Num 3:15]; and *Num. Rab.* 10.9 [on Num 6:4]). Commenting on Lev 19:18, Aqiba is reported to have said: "That is the greatest principle in the Law" (*Sipra Lev.* §200 [on Lev 19:15–19]). When Jesus replies that the greatest commandment is to love the Lord with all one's heart (Deut 6:4–5) and to love one's neighbor as one's self (Lev 19:18), he has summed up in one "general" commandment all of the "particular" commandments (Mark 12:28–34).

Kayyose bo bemaqom ʻaher *(lit. "to which something [is] similar in another place [or passage]")*

This *midda* is similar to the principle of *gezera shawa*, excepting that whereas the latter is limited to a common word or phrase, the former takes into account similar ideas or events, as well as common vocabulary. The principle is well illustrated in a Tannaitic discussion of the dividing of the sea. According to Rabbi Shemaiah, God declares: "The faith with which their father Abraham believed in Me is reason enough that I should divide the sea for them, as it is written: 'And he believed in the Lord' [Gen 15:6]." To this Rabbi Abtalyon adds: "The faith with which they believed in Me is reason enough that I should divide the sea for them, as it is written: 'And the people believed' [Exod 4:31]" (*Mek.* on Exod 14:15 [*Beshallah* §4]; cf. *Exod Rab.* 23.5 [on Exod 15:1]). The faith of Abraham led to the dividing of the animal pieces; so it was that the faith of Israel led to the dividing of the sea.

The principle seems to have been employed by Jesus as well. If the "son of man" (or Messiah) is to sit on one of the thrones set up before the Ancient of Days (Dan 7:9, which is apparently how Rabbi Aqiba interpreted Daniel's plural reference to "thrones," cf. *b. Hag.* 14a; *b. Sanh.* 38b; *Midr. Tanh.* on Lev 19:1–2 [*Qedoshim* §1]), and if Messiah is to sit at God's right hand (Ps 110:1), it may be inferred that when the Son of Man comes with the clouds (Dan 7:13–14), he will be seated at the right hand of God and will judge his enemies. This is evidently what Jesus implied in his reply to Caiaphas (Mark 14:62).

Dabar halamed me'inyano *(lit. "a word of instruction from [its] context [or subject]")*

According to this *midda*, the meaning of a given passage may be clarified from its context. Rabbi Aqiba explained it accordingly: "Every Scripture passage that is close to another must be interpreted with respect to it" (*Sipre Deut.* §131 [on Deut 16:4]). The validity of this principle is plainly evident. Hillel invoked this principle to explain the meaning of the priestly declaration of "clean" (*Sipra Lev.* §140 [on 13:32–37]; cf. *m. Neg.* 3:1).

This rule is exemplified in Jesus' teaching against divorce (Matt 19:3–8 = Mark 10:2–9). Although it is true that Moses allowed divorce (Deut 24:1–3), it is also true that God never intended the marriage union to be broken, as implied in Gen 1:27 ("male and female he created them") and 2:24 ("a man ... shall cleave to his wife, and they shall become one flesh"). Jesus has interpreted the marriage union (Gen 2:24) in terms of the creation of man and woman (Gen 1:27), thus linking the institution of marriage to creation itself. The future tenses of Gen 2:24 ("shall leave," "shall cleave," "shall become") connote the sense of command, as do, for example, the future tenses of the Decalogue. This imperative sense overrides the concessive and permissive sense of Moses' law in Deut 24:1–3.

CRAIG A. EVANS

Further reading

Carson, D. A. and H. G. M. Williamson (eds) *It is Written: Scripture Citing Scripture*, Cambridge: Cambridge University Press, 1988, pp. 99–140.

Chilton, B. D. *A Galilean Rabbi and His Bible*, Wilmington, DE: Glazier, 1984.

——— *Targumic Approaches to the Gospels*, Studies in Judaism, Lanham and New York: University Press of America, 1986.

Deaut, R. le. "Apropos a Definition of Midrash." *Int* 25 (1971) 259–82.

Downing, F. G. "Redaction Criticism: Josephus' *Ant.* and the Synoptic Gospels," *JSNT* 8 (1980) 46–65; 9 (1980) 29–48.

Ellis, E. E. "Midrash, Targum and NT Quotations," in E. E. Ellis and M. Wilcox (eds) *Neotestamentica et Semitica*, Edinburgh: T. & T. Clark, 1969, pp. 61–69.

—— "Biblical Interpretation in the NT Church," in J. Mulder (ed.) *Mikra*, Philadelphia, PA: Fortress Press; Assen: Van Gorcum, 1988, pp. 691–725.

Evans, C. A. (ed.) *From Prophecy to Testament: The Function of the Old Testament in the New*, Peabody, MA: Hendrickson, 2004.

—— (ed.) *Of Scribes and Sages: Early Jewish Interpretation and Transmission of Scripture*, 2 vols, LSTS 50–51, SSEJC 9–10, London and New York: T. & T. Clark, 2004.

France, R. T. and D Wenham (eds) *Studies in Midrash and Historiography*, Gospel Perspectives 3, Sheffield: JSOT, 1983.

Gerhardsson, B. *The Origins of the Gospel Traditions*, Philadelphia, PA: Fortress Press, 1979.

Gertner, M. "Midrashim in the NT," *JSS* 7 (1962) 267–92.

Juel, D. *Messianic Exegesis*, Philadelphia, PA: Fortress Press, 1988.

Kugel, J. and R. Greer. *Early Biblical Interpretation*, Philadelphia, PA: Westminster, 1986.

Lieberman, S. *Hellenism in Jewish Palestine*, second edition, New York: Jewish Theological Seminary of America, 1962, pp. 47–82.

McNeil, B. "Midrash in Luke?," *HeyJ* 19 (1978) 399–404.

Miller, M. P. "Targum, Midrash, and the Use of the OT in the NT," *JSJ* 2 (1971) 29–82.

—— "Midrash," *IDBSup* (1976) 593–97.

Neusner, J. *Midrash in Context: Exegesis in Formative Judaism*, Philadelphia, PA: Fortress Press, 1983.

—— *What is Midrash?* GBS, Philadelphia, PA: Fortress Press, 1987.

Patte, D. *Early Jewish Hermeneutic in Palestine*, SBLDS 22, Missoula, MT: Scholars Press, 1975.

Porton, G. "Defining Midrash," in J. Neusner (ed.) *The Study of Ancient Judaism*, New York: KTAV, 1981.

—— *Understanding Rabbinic Midrash*, Hoboken, NJ: KTAV, 1985.

Riesner, R. *Jesus als Lehrer. Ein Untersuchung zum Ursprung der Evangelien-Überlieferung*, Tübingen: Mohr Siebeck, 1981; third edition 1988.

Vermes, G. "Bible and Midrash: Early OT Exegesis," in P. R. Ackroyd and C. F. Evans (eds) *The Cambridge History of the Bible*, Cambridge: Cambridge University Press, 1970, pp. 199–231.

MIRACLE STORY

Defining the miraculous as that which is extraordinary and caused by a god, the traditions about Jesus in the gospels contain many stories with miraculous elements (e.g. Mark 15:38; Luke 1:20, 64) as well as stories of miracles associated with (e.g. Mark 9:2–13) and conducted by him (e.g. Mark 3:1–6). In that miracle stories were taken to have meaning and point beyond themselves (Klein 50), the stories of Jesus conducting miracles are of

particular interest in assessing how he was understood. The Synoptic Gospel writers distinguish between exorcisms and other kinds of healing (e.g. Matt 8:16; Mark 1:32–34); the Fourth Gospel relates miracle stories that conveyed the grand, even cosmic, scale and other-worldly context of Jesus' ministry. The so-called nature miracle stories stand out in all the gospels: only the disciples are reported as being aware of them, their support in the sayings of Jesus is limited or non-existent, the summaries of Jesus' miraculous activity do not mention them, and Old Testament motifs, as well as beliefs and practices of the early church, pervade them.

Gospel miracle stories

Of all the activities ascribed to Jesus, conducting miracles dominates Mark, the earliest gospel. Depending how they are counted, there are seventeen stories (1:21–28, 29–31, 40–45; 2:1–12; 3:1–6; 4:35–41; 5:1–20, 22–43; 6:35–44, 47–52; 7:24–30, 31–37; 8:1–10, 22–26; 9:14–29; 10:46–52; 11:12–14 and 20–24), as well as summary reports of, healings (1:32–34, 39) so that 168 of the 666 verses (about 25 percent) up to Mark 16:8 are related to Jesus being a miracle worker. In turn, of the thirteen stories of healing in Mark, four are of exorcism (1:21–28; 5:1–20; 7:24–30; 9:14–29) making it the most numerous category of healing story in Mark. In the Fourth Gospel, the seven stories (2:1–11; 4:46–54; 5:1–9; 6:1–14, 16–21; 9:1–7; 11:1–44) account for only 100 verses out of the 523 up to the end of chapter 11 (about 19 percent). Nevertheless, more obviously than in the Synoptic Gospels, even though fewer in number, the Fourth Gospel miracle stories (called signs) pervade the Johannine narrative and are intended to have God as their source and to reveal him at work in Jesus (e.g. John 2:11). Being written up on such a grand scale and including a number of miracles of nature, the historical reliability of the stories in the Fourth Gospel is often questioned (Twelftree 1999).

Miracle stories in context

From the evidence we have, there is no other figure in the period who has as many miracle stories associated with him (Kahl). Moreover, Jesus is the first figure in history for whom the conducting of miracles was very soon taken to be fundamental in understanding both his identity and mission (e.g. Matt 11:2–6; 12:28). Somewhat later, writing in the early third century CE, Philostratus tells only nine miracle stories to enhance the reputation of the first century CE wandering sage Apollonius of Tyana (*Life* 1.4; 4.10, 13 [cf. 5.18], 20, 25, 45; 6.27, 43; 8.38). For example, a young lad's loud and coarse laughter is said to interrupt him while speaking:

Then Apollonius looked up at him and said: 'It is not yourself that perpetrates this insult, but the demon who drives you on without your knowing it' ... Now when Apollonius gazed on him, the ghost in him began to utter cries of fear and rage ... and the ghost swore that he would leave the young man alone and never take possession of any man again.

(4.20)

The story goes on to relate the devil causing a statue to fall as proof of leaving the lad, as well as the ensuing hubbub in the crowd. Also, in a story reminiscent of one about Jesus, Apollonius is said to have stopped a funeral procession for a newly married girl:

"Put down the bier, for I will stay the tears that you are shedding for this maiden" ... [T]ouching her and whispering in secret some spell over her, at once woke up the maiden from her seeming death; and the girl spoke out loud, and returned to her father's house.

(*Life* 4.45; cf. Luke 7:11–17)

Nearer the time of Jesus, Josephus tells a story of Eleazar, a Jew who conducted exorcisms by putting a ring to the nose of the sufferer and, as the person smelled the roots in it, drew out the demon (Josephus *Ant.* 8.45–49). However, in this story Solomon is being honored through the use of his incantations; the identity of Eleazar the healer is not important. In the Talmud, Hanina ben Dosa is said to heal at a distance the son of Gamaliel, as well as the son of Johanan ben Zakkai, through praying (*y. Ber.* 5.5; *b. Ber.* 34b). Hanina is also said to take Rabbi Johanan by the hand and raise him from his sick bed (*b. Ber.* 5b). However, the point of relating these stories is to illustrate propositions rather than contribute to the biography and reputation of a healer.

Interpreting the gospel miracle stories

In seeking rational explanations, Karl F. Bahrdt (1741–92) is among the first to apply a non-supernatural interpretation to the miracle stories. For example, in the case of Jesus walking on the sea he said that we can imagine that there was a piece of timber in the water near the shore. Jesus stepped onto it and, finding it bore his weight, approached the boat on it. Only limited knowledge caused the disciples to assume a miracle had taken place (*Briefe über die Bibel im volkston*, 1782).

Reacting against the antiquated systems of supernaturalism and naturalism, *The Life of Jesus* (1834) by D. F. Strauss (1808–74) marks a watershed in the study of the miracle stories. His starting point is the tension between the great number of miracle stories in the gospels over against the epistles, where the miracle stories of Jesus appear to be unknown. Strauss' radical solution was to say that the miracles are mythical elements in the sources, having no rightful place in history. Some of the miracle stories are, in his view, *pure* myths in the sense that they, like the healing of the blind, have no historical foundation. Other miracle stories are *historical* myths in that they have a historical core that has provided the seed out of which the story grew. An example would be the story of Peter's miraculous catch of fish (Luke 5:1–11) growing out of the statement of Jesus about his followers being called to be fishers of men (Mark 1:17). Strauss put an end to miracle as a matter of historical belief so that the miracle stories became of little interest to many students of the historical Jesus.

The discussion on myth was kept alive well into the twentieth century through the work of Rudolf Bultmann (1884–1976), who argued that the world view of the New Testament was mythical ("New Testament and Mythology," 1941). In relation to the miracles, interest in the subject of myth died down late in the twentieth century not only because of the renewed confidence in historically reliable data in the gospels, but also because of the failure of Bultmann's program to assign the origins of the miracle stories of Jesus to sources outside Christian tradition. To appreciate Bultmann's treatment of miracle in the life of the historical Jesus we need to note two other streams of research in late nineteenth- and early twentieth-century study: the history of religions school and the supposed figure of a "divine man."

Stimulated by the sensational archeological and papyrological discoveries of the late nineteenth century, an important point established by the *Religionsgeschichtliche Schule* (History of Religion School) was that the reported miracles of Jesus in the gospels are similar to the stories reported of other miracle workers of the period (see above). However, just which traditions the miracles of Jesus were like and what that analogy may mean was a matter of debate. Paul Fiebig (1876–1949) championed the closeness of Jesus to the rabbis. Adolf Schlatter (1852–1938) held to the superiority of Jesus over the rabbis who, he said, used magic. Schlatter also argued that it was not possible to find a miracle-free gospel among the early traditions about Jesus, and the attempt to distance miracle stories from the tradition was to distance the historian from the real events. Such conservative approaches (also, e.g., William Sanday, 1843–1920, and Arthur C. Headlam, 1862–1947) were out of step with the prevailing theological and philosophical climate and, until early in the twenty-first century, remained in the shadow of the work of Bultmann. In any case, what was less contended by the vast majority of New Testament scholars was that the miracle stories were no longer the center of attention for understanding the story of Jesus, not only because of the argued centrality of the *kerygma* (a position brought to the English-speaking world by C. H. Dodd), but also because the miracle stories were considered secondary to the gospel tradition. Representative of this position, and highly influential in himself, was Adolf von Harnack (1851–1930) for whom, as well as the liberal tradition he came to represent, the essence of Christianity was not to be found in the miracles but in the religious experience of Jesus and in his teaching about God the Father and the infinite value of the human soul.

One of the products of the History of Religion School was that a general conception of a *theios anthrōpos* (divine human) began to prevail. According to this view, a person of a higher nature combines within himself personal holiness, the profoundest knowledge, vision, and the power to work miracles. Notably, the concept was used by Bultmann and Martin Dibelius (1883–1947) to explain the Hellenistic origin of miracle stories in the gospels, Bultmann saying that in Mark Jesus is a *theios anthrōpos*. Although this theory was adapted, by the late twentieth century it was being called into question, along with its value for understanding the gospel miracle stories, and continued attempts to use the *theios anēr* (divine man) concept to interpret the miracle stories of Jesus have not been widely accepted. The diverse miracle workers – giving rise to different kinds of miracle stories, whose divinity was expressed with a range of terms equally diverse – were rarely called *theios anēr* (Blackburn 1991).

Interest in miracles stories in the ancient world generated by the History of Religion School – along with the concept of a divine man – provided foundational material for Bultmann and other form critics. Also, the deep skepticism fueled by phenomenalism, positivism, and empiricism established an intellectual climate for the way form critics of the early twentieth century approached the miracle tradition, so that confidence that the earliest strata of the New Testament documents

could take us back to Jesus had been undermined. In his introduction to *Jesus* (1926), Bultmann said that he thought we could know almost nothing about the life and personality of Jesus. Even though he thought that most of the miracle stories in the gospels were legendary or had legendary embellishments, those deeds done by Jesus which were then considered miracles, such as healing the sick and casting out demons, Bultmann attributed to natural causes (pp. 124–27). On the nature miracles Bultmann concluded that "Hellenistic miracle stories offer such a wealth of parallels to the Synoptics, particularly in style, as to create a prejudice in favor of supposing that the Synoptic miracle stories grew out up on Hellenistic ground" (p. 240). The significance of these views is that Bultmann both encapsulates the implications of the work of Strauss and the History of Religion School and articulates a position on the miracles of Jesus that continues to be important for many presently writing on the miracle stories.

Dibelius was more conservative than other critics in his assessment of the miracles of Jesus, saying they are "not something that was imposed on his portrait later on; from the beginning they formed an essential part of the tradition about him" (*Jesus*, 1963: 73). However, he also said that these reports are not medically or scientifically critical. In Jesus' healing activity "we have to do with psychically conditioned maladies which are healed by means of an impact upon the psychical life of the patient. And this impact is effected frequently by means of a command which brings about a psychical reaction" (76). Dibelius says that in shock therapy and the curative effects of fear or anger, such curative approaches are also known to us. In the case of epiphanies – the Transfiguration, the feeding of the multitude, perhaps the walking on the water, and certainly the raisings from the dead – the exalted Lord of the community is being depicted (77). Dibelius thought that in the cases of the stories of the miraculous feedings and the raising of the dead, as well as the healing of the Gadarene demoniac, the changing of water into wine and the story of the coin in the mouth of a fish, we may have examples of the Christians appropriating to themselves and transferring to their Savior not only foreign motives but also whole stories of foreign origin (79). In Dibelius' mind, the significance of the miracles is that they stand in the service of his whole message about the kingdom of God. That is, ignoring the import of Matt 12:28/Luke 11:20, the miracles are "not the Kingdom but *signs* of this Kingdom" (81). Nevertheless, with this as his perspective, Dibelius declares that it is not possible to separate Jesus' message and Jesus' deeds from his person.

By the middle of the twentieth century, the miracle stories hardly featured in assessments of the historical Jesus (e.g. G. Bornkamm, *Jesus of Nazareth*, 1960). Indeed, in some studies of Jesus the miracles remain marginalized, as in, for example, E. P. Sanders, *Jesus and Judaism* (1985) and N. T. Wright, *Jesus and the Victory of God* (1996). However, because of the failure to show that the miracle stories generally originated outside the Jesus tradition, the increased confidence in the historical reliability of the gospel traditions, the mounting material and increased knowledge of the milieu in which Jesus lived, the use of more sensitive and sophisticated historical and social-scientific methods, and caution in judging what is historically not possible, the miracle stories are attracting attention in the assessment of the historical Jesus.

Geza Vermes proposed that Jesus is to be understood as the preeminent example of the early *hasidim* or holy men who were known for their miracle working (*Jesus the Jew*, 1973). However, Vermes has been censored particularly for an uncritical use of material that is too late to help understand first-century miracle stories, for not taking into account that the *hasidim* were not the only miracle workers operating in the time of Jesus, and that, unlike his contemporaries, Jesus gave a particular significance to his miracle working. In *Jesus the Magician* (1978), Morton Smith (1915–91) argued that Jesus was a magician. However, because of unresolved discussions on what material can be used to understand the first-century debates between Jesus and his critics and on how magic is to be defined, it is not yet agreed whether or not Jesus was considered by some of his audience to be a magician. The most detailed and thorough recent treatment of the miracle stories in relation to the historical Jesus has been provided by John P. Meier in *A Marginal Jew: Rethinking the Historical Jesus* (1991–2001). He concludes that some miracle stories, such as the healing of Bartimaeus, have a historical foundation in an event in which witnesses believed Jesus restored sight to a blind person. Other stories, such as the feeding of the multitude, may have a symbolic base, in this case a meal Jesus shared with a large crowd, a meal perhaps only later taken to be miraculous. He also concludes that, with the exception of the feeding of the multitude, all the so-called nature miracles appear to have been created by the early church. In *The Historical Jesus: The Life of a Mediterranean Jewish Peasant* (1991), J. D. Crossan also regards the miracle stories of healing and exorcism as critical in understanding Jesus' work and message about the kingdom. But the miracle stories reflect not the coming of God's reign but Jesus' response to a colonial people under political and religious pressure. Also, notably, as in the case of stories of Jesus cleansing lepers, Crossan interprets the miracles not as cures but as stories of refusals to accept the associated ritual uncleanness and social ostracism involved.

Despite the often positive assessment of the historicity of the miracle stories of healing and especially exorcism, the same is not true of the so-called nature miracle stories. Many treatments of these stories argue that they are apparitions or pure invention, as in the case of raisings from the dead, echoing the experience of the post-Easter church (e.g. G. Lüdemann, *The Great Deception*, 1999) or are no more than elaborations of a symbolic base as in, for example, a shared meal giving rise to stories of miraculous feedings (Meier). Rational explanations have also remained current (e.g. E. P. Sanders, *The Historical Figure of Jesus*, 1993). So long as the nature miracles remain in what has been called a "historical suspense account" the historical Jesus will remain fundamentally different from the Jesus of the gospels.

GRAHAM H. TWELFTREE

Further reading

Blackburn, B. L. *Theios Aner and the Markan Miracle Traditions*, Tübingen: Mohr Siebeck, 1991.
—— "The Miracles of Jesus," in Bruce Chilton and Craig A. Evans (eds) *Studying the Historical Jesus: Evaluations of the State of Current Research*, Leiden: Brill, 1994, pp. 353–94.
Brown, C. *Miracles and the Critical Mind*, Grand Rapids, MI: Eerdmans, 1984.
Brown, R. E. "The Gospel Miracles," in his *New Testament Essays*, Ramsey, NJ: Paulist, 1965, pp. 169–91.
Bultmann, R. *History of the Synoptic Tradition*, Oxford: Blackwell, 1963 [1921].
Dibelius, M. *From Tradition to Gospel*, Cambridge and London: Clarke, 1971 [1919].
Fridrichsen, A. *The Problem of Miracle in Primitive Christianity*, Minneapolis, MN: Augsburg, 1972 [1925].
Fuller, R. H. *Interpreting the Miracles*, London: SCM Press, 1963.
Funk, R. W. and The Jesus Seminar. *The Acts of Jesus: What Did Jesus Really Do? The Search for the Authentic Deeds of Jesus*, New York: HarperCollins, 1998.
Grant, R. M. *Miracle and Natural Law in Graeco-Roman and Early Christian Thought*, Amsterdam: North Holland, 1952.
Harvey, A. E. *Jesus and the Constraints of History*, London: Duckworth, 1982.
Hooker, M. D. *The Signs of a Prophet: The Prophetic Actions of Jesus*, London: SCM Press, 1997.
Hull, J. M. *Hellenistic Magic and the Synoptic Tradition*, London: SCM Press, 1974.

Kahl, W. *New Testament Miracle Stories in their Religious-Historical Setting: A Religionsgeschichtliche Comparison from a Structural Perspective*, Göttingen: Vandenhoeck & Ruprecht, 1994.

Kee, H. C. *Miracle in the Early Christian World: A Study in Sociohistorical Method*, New Haven, CT and London: Yale University Press, 1983.

—— *Medicine, Miracle and Magic in New Testament Times*, Cambridge: Cambridge University Press, 1986.

Keller, E. and M.-L. Keller. *Miracles in Dispute: A Continuing Debate*, London: SCM Press, 1969.

Klein, G. "Wunderglaube und Neues Testament," in *Ärgernisse. Konfrontationen mit dem Neuen Testament*, Munich: Kösel, 1970, pp. 13–57.

Loos, H. van der. *The Miracles of Jesus*, Leiden: Brill, 1965.

Meier, J. P. *A Marginal Jew: Rethinking the Historical Jesus*, Vol. 2: *Mentor, Message, and Miracles*, New York: Doubleday, 1994.

Richardson, A. *The Miracle Stories of the Gospels*, London: SCM Press, 1941.

Theissen, G. *Miracle Stories of the Early Christian Tradition*, Edinburgh: T. & T. Clark, 1983.

Twelftree, G. H. *Jesus the Miracle Worker: A Historical & Theological Study*, Downers Grove, IL: InterVarsity Press, 1999.

—— "The History of Miracles in the History of Jesus," in S. McKnight and G. Osborne (eds) *The Face of New Testament Studies: A Survey of Recent Research*, Grand Rapids, MI: Baker; Leicester and InterVarsity Press, 2004, pp. 191–208.

Wenham, D. and C. Blomberg (ed.) *Gospel Perspectives 6: The Miracles of Jesus*, Sheffield: JSOT, 1986.

MOSES

That Moses is a foundational figure in the religion and political self-understanding of Israel is common knowledge. What is of particular interest to Historical Jesus scholars is the re-appropriation of Moses and his promise of another prophet like himself in Deut 18:15–18 in early Judaism and Christianity. In the Deuteronomic narrative, Moses' prediction is most likely intended to refer to Joshua, and possibly a succession of prophets (Deut 34:9; Sir 46:1), but the narrative ends with a curious denial: "and a prophet like Moses did not arise again in Israel ... and none like him for all his mighty power and all the great deeds which Moses did in the sight of Israel" (Deut 34:10–12). The unfulfilled promise has left the door wide open for variety of post-biblical interpretations. Rabbinic typological interpretations, which are not the focus of this entry, are particularly diverse in assigning an eschatological function to the Prophet (see Jeremias).

Early Jewish appropriation

In the early Jewish period, the figure of Moses as the divine lawgiver and prophetic spokesman for God played an important role for individuals and groups who sought to legitimize their authority over and against rival parties. Identification with Moses took on various forms (Hafemann). We shall address three of these which would have circulated in the late Second Temple period and may have influenced Jesus' self-understanding and later interpretations of him and his mission: (1) self-proclaimed interpreters of Moses; (2) expectation of an eschatological prophet like Moses; and (3) Moses *redivivus*.

First, within the context of the rivalry of Jewish groups, each sought supremacy over the other. Josephus, for example, regards the Pharisees as the most accurate interpreters of the Mosaic Law (*J.W.* 2.162). Some later Rabbis claim – some of which possibly reflects sentiments that extend back to the Pharisees – that prophecy given by the Holy Spirit had ceased in Israel since the last of the canonical prophets (e.g. *t. Sot.* 13:2). The claim probably reflects an attempt to legitimize these Rabbis' status as successors of Moses and the prophets over and against rival groups, and thereby they may be attempting to ensure that no inspired "prophet" claiming to be a spokesman for divine revelation would usurp their authority. Some have argued that after the destruction of the Temple, the claim of cessation of the Holy Spirit was intended to undermine Christian authority. The view that prophecy given by the holy spirit had ceased does not, however, appear to have been widespread since contrary views are expressed in some late Second Temple literature, such as CD 7, *4 Ezra* 14, *1 Enoch* 91 (Aune 104).

Second, the prediction of a prophet like Moses in Deut 18:15–18 was influential for some Jewish groups in their formulation of an awaited eschatological prophet at the end of the age when God would come to restore the righteous (Poirier). The earliest eschatological interpretations of the Prophet in Deut 18:15–18 are found in the Qumran Scrolls. For example, in 1QS 9:10–11, the community is told to continue in their religious instruction "until the coming of the Prophet and the Anointed of Aaron and Israel." And in 4QTestim. 1–20, which likewise refers to Deut 18, the awaited eschatological prophet is clearly linked with Moses. Although some Qumran scholars have linked the Prophet with the Teacher of Righteousness (van der Woude), most today do not view the Teacher's role as stemming from the sect's interpretation of Deuteronomy 18. While prophetic and royal features were combined in Hellenistic Jewish traditions about Moses, the prophet, like Moses, did not appear to be interpreted messianically in

Palestinian Judaism (Meeks, Aune). Expectations of an eschatological prophet which were more directly connected with other biblical figures may have also been influenced, though indirectly, by the Moses story. Elijah is particularly significant because, due to the long-standing tradition that he did not die but was taken into heaven (2 Kgs 2:9–12; Sir 48:9; 1 Macc 2:58; *1 En.* 89:52), it was believed even by early Jewish followers of Jesus (Mark 9:11–13) that he would reappear before the coming of Yahweh and/or his messiah(s). It is possible that expectations of Elijah's return as they are found in Malachi 3 (and picked up by the Evangelists) may have been influenced by Deut 18:15–18 (Aune 125).

Third, others identified with Moses more directly by taking on his role and promising their followers miracles in the wilderness and deliverance from Rome (Hengel 16–27). Within the larger context of socio-political crises, the expectation of a Moses *redivivus* or promise of another prophet like Moses in Deut 18:15–20 may have provided the impetus for the rise of such charismatic figures. Josephus, our best source, who clearly portrays Moses as a paragon of the cardinal virtues (Feldman) refers to (1) the Samarian prophet who assured his followers that on their arrival at Mount Gerizim they would be shown the sacred vessels of Moses (*Ant.* 18:85–87); (2) Theudas, who promised his followers that he would part the Jordan River (*Ant.* 20:97–98; Acts 5:36); (3) the Egyptian prophet who promised his followers that the walls of Jerusalem would collapse (*Ant.* 20:168–72; Acts 21:38); and (4) an anonymous "imposter" who promised salvation to anyone who would follow him into the wilderness (*Ant.* 20:188). There may be a parallel in Philo's portrayal of Moses who on occasion functions as the image of the divine king, resembling the emperors Gaius Caligula (Borgen, Scott).

Early Christian appropriation

In the New Testament, Moses is mentioned more than any other biblical figure. References to Moses and the events associated with him, like the giving of the Law and the exodus, serve a variety of functions (Lierman). Yet at the same time, they all share a common aim in establishing that Moses prefigures Christ within the continuity of salvation history spanning from Israel to the followers of Jesus (O'Toole). Points of contact between Moses and Jesus in the New Testament convey that each endorses the other, but Moses always takes the subordinate position as one who either foreshadows, predicts, validates, or typifies Christ. Moreover, while Moses is the most central figure

for salvation history in later Judaism, since Torah is viewed as the main revelation of God, he is not the controlling figure for early Christology, but one of several influences. Jeremias' comprehensive treatment of Moses in the New Testament, wherein he is mentioned some eighty times, is still very helpful. Jeremias places the references to Moses under three categories. First, Moses is primarily viewed as a messenger and servant of God (Acts 7), who mediates the divine Law and the prophesies of Christ, and models the posture of faith (Hebrews). Second, in John 5:45 Moses is given an eschatological function as a chief witness against the "Jews." And third, Moses serves as a theological comparison for interpreting the Baptist and especially Jesus. The accounts of Moses as a theological prototype, however, are not uniform. In some texts, Jesus is a type of Moses who reveals God's will and brings to fulfillment the new Law (Matt 5–7); whereas in others the typology is developed differently, such as in 2 Corinthians 3 where Moses represents the inferior old covenant which is contrasted with Jesus who clearly reveals the "glory of the Lord" (Jer 864–73), or in Mark 7 where the dietary laws are abolished. Varied accounts have led to diverse positions on Jesus' approach to the Law, such as abrogation, exposition, replacement, radicalization, and addition (Moo). The broadest use of Moses typology in the New Testament is found in John's Gospel where Jesus surpasses Moses in, for example, revealing "grace and truth" (1:17), ascending to heaven (3:13), giving the true "bread of life" (6:32–40), offering the true Passover lamb (19:13, 32–34), and taking on the role of the true shepherd (10:11, 14) and the Prophet like Moses (6:14; 7:40) (Harstine, Boismard, Meeks).

Jesus' appropriation

To date, there has been very little historical work published on Jesus' appropriation of Moses or the Moses typologies that preceded him. Whether Jesus identified himself with Moses or the Moses tradition is dependent on the method of historical enquiry. If on the one hand, the historian begins from a form-critical perspective which (1) views the Gospels (and Q) as repositories of sayings which circulated orally and somehow retained their textual form and meaning as opposed to viewing them as windows into a social process, (2) appeals to individual memory and disregards social memory which regards tradition as a vital component for effective communication, and (3) attempts to isolate unique sayings of Jesus apart from his early Jewish culture and later Christian interpretations, then the allusions in Mark and elsewhere to Moses, the exodus, and Mosaic covenantal patterns must be relegated to later Christian interpretation and not to Jesus. This approach is advocated by Crossan (78–79) and some other members of the Jesus Seminar. Crossan is particularly intent on situating Jesus and his teaching within a cosmopolitan Galilee which had limited connections with Israelite tradition. The problem, apart from the lack of consideration given to advancements made in the function of social memory in historical study, is that Crossan's reconstructed data in which he finds "total newness" contains allusions to Israelite and early Jewish traditions – such as "finger of God" as a reference to the exodus and legal discussions regarding adultery and the tribute to Caesar which echo Mosaic covenantal law (Horsley 68–70).

On the other hand, if the historian begins with the social-scientific assumption that effective communication by social critics like Jesus can only occur within the bounds of a social group's tradition, which is its identity and memory, then Jesus' references and allusions to Moses and the Mosaic covenant in Mark and Q fall well within the historical data. The difficulty for traditional form-critical Jesus scholars is that while Mark and Q may accurately reflect Jesus as one who engaged in debates with legal authorities and subverted their interpretations of Torah, and effectively established himself as a legal authority, recognition of the function of social memory within a primarily oral culture wherein discourse is characterized by multiple speech acts varying in meaning frustrates the search to uncover the original words of Jesus (Kelber 238). Nevertheless, it allows us to discern the "shared meanings" of his teaching and actions in the broader (oral and peasant) cultural patterns of his day. For Horsley, the Mosaic covenant within the mission of the restoration of Israel is not only the principal framework for the organization of sayings and dialogues in Q (e.g. 6:20–49) and Mark (e.g. 7:1–13; 10; 14:17–25), but the framework of self-understanding for those communities where the sayings and gospel stories were being performed (74–78).

Appealing to social memory theory has more potential for bridging the frustrating chasm between Jesus and the gospels, and oral and literary history. One of the outstanding issues to resolve, however, is demonstrating how the supposed underlying Mosaic renewal covenant pattern in Q and the story of Mark correspond to their use of explicit scripture quotations taken from non-"Mosaic" texts. After all, many patterns have been proposed

for Mark's story (Hatina 8–48). If Jesus did identify himself with the expected Mosaic prophet, he would have understood his mission as an eschatological deliverer who would religiously prepare Israel for the Day of Yahweh, which would have entailed suffering in behalf of the nation, a definitive interpretation of Torah, intercession with God for Israel, miracles as demonstrations of his authority, and the prediction of judgment and salvation (Teeple, Aune, 126).

THOMAS R. HATINA

Further reading

Aune, D. F., *Prophecy in Early Christianity and the Ancient Mediteranean World*, Grand Rapids, MI: Eerdmans, 1983.
Borgen, P. "Moses, Jesus, and the Roman Emperor: Observations in Philo's Writings and the Revelation of John," *NovT* 38 (1996) 145–59.
Boismard, M.-É., *Moses or Jesus: Ann Essay in Johannine Christology*, Leuven: Peeters; Minneapolis, MN: Fortress, 1983.
Crossan, J. D. *The Historical Jesus: The Life of a Mediterranean Jewish Peasant*, New York: HarperCollins, 1992.
Feldman, L. H. "Josephus' Portrait of Moses: Part Three," *JQR* 83 (1993) 301–30.
Hafemann, S. J. "Moses in the Apocrypha and Pseudepigrapha: A Survey," *JSP* 7 (1990) 79–104.
Harstine, S. *Moses as a Character in the Fourth Gospel: A Study of Ancient Reading Techniques*, JSNTSup 229, London: Sheffield Academic Press, 2002.
Hatina, T. R. *In Search of a Context: The Function of Scripture in Mark's Narrative*, JSNTSup 232, SSEJC 8, London: Sheffield Academic Press, 2002.
Hegel, M., *Studies in the Gospel of Mark*, Philadelphia, PA: Fortress, 1985.
Horsley, R. A. "Prominent Patterns in the Social Memory of Jesus and Friends," in A. Kirk and T. Thatcher (eds) *Memory, Tradition, and Text: Uses of the Past in Early Christianity*, Semeia Studies 52, Atlanta, GA: Society of Biblical Literature, 2005, pp. 57–78.
Kelber, W. H. "The Works of Memory: Christian Origins as MnemoHistory—A Response," in A. Kirk and T. Thatcher (eds) *Memory, Tradition, and Text: Uses of the Past in Early Christianity*, SemeiaST 52, Atlanta, GA: Society of Biblical Literature, 2005, pp. 221–48.
Lierman, J. *The New Testament Moses: Christian Perceptions of Moses and Israel in the Setting of Jewish Religion*, WUNT II.173, Tübingen: Mohr Siebeck, 2004.
Meeks, W. A. *The Prophet-King: Moses Traditions and the Johannine Christology*, NovTSup 14, Leiden: Brill, 1967.
Moo, D. J. "Jesus and the Authority of the Mosaic Law," *JSNT* 20 (1984) 3–49.
O'Toole, R., *The Unity of Luke's Theology*, Wilmington, DE: Glazier, 1984.
Poirier, J. C. "The Endtime Return of Elijah and Moses at Qumran," *DSD* 10 (2003) 221–42.
Scott, I. W. "Is Philo's Moses a Divine Man?," *SPhilo Annual* 14 (2002) 87–111.
Teeple, H. M. *The Mosaic Eschatological Prophet*, JBL Monograph Series 10, Philadelphia, PA: Society of Biblical Literature, 1957.
van der Woude, A. S. *Die messianischen Vorstellungen der Gemeinde von Qumrán*, SSN 3, Assen: van Gorcum, 1957.

N

NAZARETH

The village of Nazareth lies some 3.5 miles southeast of Sepphoris, a major city in Galilee, rivaled only by Tiberias, on the shore of Lake Gennesaret (or the Sea of Galilee). Nazareth is situated on a rocky ridge, at an altitude of about 1,300 ft, about 20 miles from the Mediterranean and about 15 miles from the lake. Archaeologists estimate that the village in the time of Jesus occupied some 60 acres (Strange: 1050).

The derivation and meaning of the name "Nazareth" is uncertain. Some think is it is related to *netser* ("branch"; cf. Isa 11:1), or *nezer* ("separated," "consecrated"), or *natsar* ("to guard," "watch"). The village's location, on high ground, overlooking the Netofa Valley that runs east to west between Sepphoris and Cana, lends support to the last suggested meaning.

Nazareth is not mentioned in our early sources. It goes unmentioned in Old Testament literature, in Josephus, and in the Talmud. Pseudo-scholarship has suggested that the village did not exist in the time of Jesus, but excavations have shown that it most certainly did. The absence of early references indicates the insignificance and smallness of the village, as reflected in the unflattering question "Can anything good come out of Nazareth?" (John 1:46). The only reason the village is mentioned at all is because of its famous resident, Jesus.

Ongoing archaeological work in Nazareth has revealed surprising evidence of stone masonry and viticulture. Although the extent of archaeological investigation thus far is quite limited (owing to the fact that modern Nazareth is a large, inhabited city), all indications at present suggest that Nazareth of late antiquity – in close proximity to a major highway linking Caesarea Maritima in the west to Tiberias in the east – was an active and productive centre, whose inhabitants would in all probability have had no need to seek employment in outlying areas. Portraits of Nazareth as a sleepy, isolated village are the stuff of pious imagination and hagiography, not critical study. (For archaeological reports, see Bagatti; Finegan: 27–33; Reed: 131–32; Crossan and Reed: 31–41; Chancey: 83–85).

This reassessment is supported by the discovery of an inscription that refers to the priestly family of Pises (cf. 1 Chr 24:15, where the family name is given as Happizzez), which relocated to Nazareth after the destruction of Jerusalem in 70 CE (see Avi-Yonah). The very interesting "Nazareth Inscription" (*SEG* VIII 13), which records Caesar's decree against grave robbery and vandalism, though discovered in Nazareth, is in fact of unknown provenance. In all probability it had not been set up in or near Nazareth.

Lake Gennesaret, some 13 miles in length (north to south) and 3 to 7 miles wide, is situated about 700 ft below sea level. In the time of Jesus the lake supported (and still supports) a thriving fishing industry (cf. Strabo, *Geog.* 16.2; Pliny, *Nat.* 5.15; Josephus, *J.W.* 3.506–8; Mark 1:16–20 par.; Luke 5:1–10; John 21:1–11). A network of roads encouraged a modicum of commerce, especially in the case of pottery, whose production was limited to areas that possessed sufficient amounts of appropriate clay. Most of the pottery in use in Galilee was produced at Kefar Shikhin, near Sepphoris, and Kefar Hananyah, situated near the center of Galilee.

These archaeological and geographical considerations are consistent with literary sources, whose data suggest that most economic activity in Israel in this period of time was agrarian, centered on the production of food, and domestic, based largely on the labor of the family. Most families owned small parcels of land, which produced vegetables, grain, grapes, and olives. Some facilities, such as presses and mills, were shared by clusters of families or by whole villages. There was some commercial farming, supported by landless peasants and laborers. Most families produced their own clothing, shoes, and furniture, though there was trade and some men and women were artisans and tradesmen. Jesus himself was called a "carpenter" (or "builder"; Gk. *tekton*) or "son of a carpenter" (Mark 6:3; Matt 13:55). There were also professionals and retainers, such as priests, physicians, scribes, stewards, and collectors (at various ranks) of tolls and taxes. There were also persons who filled various offices of authority. These included magistrates, judges, and various Roman officers, including the governor (who in Jesus' time served at the rank of *praefectus*) and centurions.

Archaeologists and interpreters have suggested that Sepphoris probably influenced nearby Nazareth (e.g. Rousseau and Arav 1995: 214). This was probably the case. At least one scholar has put forth the novel suggestion that Sepphoris was largely a gentile city, in which Greek philosophy and lifestyle flourished, including Cynicism. It has been further suggested that Jesus of Nazareth came under Cynic influence.

However, the archaeological data do not bear out this interpretation, especially in reference to Sepphoris. Among the faunal remains that date before 70 CE archaeologists have found virtually no pig bones, which is inexplicable if we are to imagine the presence of a significant non-Jewish population. In contrast, after 70 CE and after a sizeable growth in the non-Jewish population, pig bones come to represent 30 per cent of the faunal remains. Over 100 fragments of stone vessels have been unearthed thus far, again pointing to a Jewish population concerned with ritual purity (cf. John 2:6). Consistent with this concern is the presence of many *miqvaoth*, or ritual bathing pools. Coins minted at Sepphoris during this period do not depict the image of the Roman emperor or pagan deities (as was common in the coinage of this time). In contrast, in the second century coins were minted at Sepphoris bearing the images of the emperors Trajan (98–117 CE) and Antoninus Pius (138–61 CE), and the deities Tyche and the Capitoline triad. Indeed, in the reign of Antoninus Pius the city adopts the name Diocaesarea, in honor of Zeus (Dio) and the Roman emperor (Caesar).

The discovery at Sepphoris of a Hebrew ostracon and several lamp fragments bearing the image of the menorah (the seven-branched candelabra) and dating from the first century CE, along with the absence of structures typically present in a Greco-Roman city (such as pagan temples, gymnasium, odeum, nymphaeum, or shrines and statues), lead to the firm conclusion that Sepphoris in Jesus' day was a thoroughly Jewish city. Finally, the distribution of Jewish and non-Jewish pottery in Galilee lends additional support to this conclusion. Whereas non-Jews purchased Jewish pottery, the Jews of Galilee did not purchase and make use of pottery manufactured by non-Jews. Accordingly, Jewish pottery that dates prior to 70 CE is found in Jewish and non-Jewish sectors in and around Galilee, while non-Jewish pottery is limited to the non-Jewish sectors. These patterns of distribution strongly suggest that the Jewish people of Galilee were scrupulous in their observance of Jewish purity laws (Finegan 28–29; Chancey 2002: 69–83).

Accordingly, the Nazareth in which Jesus grew up was in all probability a thoroughly Jewish village, in which was present a small synagogue (Finegan 33; Rousseau and Arav 214), in which the villagers met regularly for prayer, readings of scripture, and socialization.

Jesus is known as "Jesus of Nazareth" (Matt 21:11: ὁ ἀπὸ Ναζαρέθ), or "Nazarene" (Mark 1:24: Ναζαρηνός), or "Nazoraean" (Matt 2:23: Ναζωραῖος). All of these forms signify one who is "from Nazareth."

There is one notable account of Jesus' visit to Nazareth (Mark 6:1–6; Luke 4:16–30). We are told that Jesus is "the carpenter, the son of Mary" (Mark 6:3). The qualifier "son of Mary," instead of "son of Joseph," is interesting and may well hint at questions regarding his paternity. His brothers are mentioned by name: "James and Joses and Judas and Simon." James becomes leader in the church (cf. Acts 15; letter of James), as well as Judas (cf. letter of Jude). Nothing solid is known of Joses and Simon.

The indignant crowd also asks: "Are not his sisters here with us?" Jesus' former neighbors and acquaintances evidently were not impressed. They wondered at his wisdom and at the mighty works done by his hands (Mark 6:2) and so took offense (6:3). Jesus retorted: "A prophet is not without honor, except in his own country, and among his own kin, and in his own house" (6:4). Jesus seems to have had in mind his own family (cf. Mark 3:20–35). Evidently, the villagers, including family members, think Jesus has become pretentious (Johnson: 33).

The longer version in Luke's Gospel suggests that the inhabitants of Nazareth took offense because Jesus intended to extend the messianic good news of Isa 61:1–2 to Gentiles (Luke 4:23, "Doubtless you will quote to me this proverb, 'Physician, heal yourself; what we have heard you did at Capernaum, do here also in your own country'").

CRAIG A. EVANS

Further reading

Albright, W. F. "The Names 'Nazareth' and 'Nazoreans'," *JBL* 65 (1946) 397–401.

Avi-Yonah, M. "A List of Priestly Courses from Caesarea," *IEJ* 12 (1962) 137–39.

Bagatti, B. *Excavations in Nazareth*, Vol. 1, Studium Biblicum Franciscanum 17, Jerusalem: Franciscan Printing Press, 1969.

Chancey, M. A. *The Myth of a Gentile Galilee*, SNTSMS 118, Cambridge: Cambridge University Press, 2002, pp. 69–85.

Crossan, J. D. and J. L. Reed. *Excavating Jesus: Beneath the Stones, Behind the Texts*, San Francisco, CA: HarperCollins, 2001, pp. 31–41.

Finegan, J. *The Archeology of the New Testament*, Princeton, NJ: Princeton University Press, 1969, pp. 27–33.

Horsley, R. A. *Archaeology, History, and Society in Galilee: The Social Context of Jesus and the Rabbis*, Valley Forge, PA: Trinity Press International, 1996, pp. 108–12.

Johnson, S. E. *Jesus and His Towns*, GNS 29, Wilmington, NC: Glazier, 1989, pp. 26–37.

Kelso, J. *An Archaeologist Looks at the Gospels*, Waco, TX: Word, 1969, pp. 36–48.

Meyers, E. M. and J. F. Strange. *Archaeology, the Rabbis, and Early Christianity*, London: SCM Press, 1981, pp. 56–57.

Reed, J. L. *Archaeology and the Galilean Jesus: A Re-examination of the Evidence*, Harrisburg, PA: Trinity Press International, 2000, pp. 131–32.

Rousseau, J. J. and R. Arav. *Jesus and His World: An Archaeological and Cultural Dictionary*, Minneapolis, MN: Fortress Press, 1995, pp. 214–16.

Sanders, J. A. "Ναζωραῖος in Matthew 2.23," in C. A. Evans and W. R. Stegner (eds) *The Gospels and the Scriptures of Israel*, JSNTSup 104, SSEJC 3, Sheffield: Sheffield Academic Press, 1994, pp. 116–28.

Strange, J. F. "Nazareth," in D. N. Freedman (ed.) *The Anchor Bible Dictionary*, 6 vols, New York: Doubleday, 1992, Vol. 4, pp. 1050–51.

OATHS AND SWEARING

An oath is a solemn attestation that is meant to confirm the truth and seriousness of a human statement of declaration or promise. The religious nature of an oath becomes especially obvious if a person includes a formula like "with God's help".

Oaths in ancient Judaism

Oath taking was very common in the Hellenistic-Roman world. It happened in all forms of legal treaties, contracts and agreements as well as in everyday speech. Philo mentions people, who "from a bad habit incessantly and inconsiderately swear upon every occasion" (*Decal.* 92), which profanes the divine name (*Spec.* 4.40; *Decal.* 93–95). In any case, he argues, even truthful oath taking would only be the second best possibility because "by the mere fact of swearing at all, the swearer shows that there is some suspicion of his not being trustworthy" (*Decal.* 84; cf. *Spec.* 2.1–8).

Josephus reports that the Essenes avoid any swearing (Josephus *B.J.* 2.135; cf. Philo *Prob.* 84). As one can observe from the Qumran-Essenes this view is based on their pious aversion to using the name of God (CD 15:1–5; 1QS 6:27; cf. Josephus *B.J.* 2.139, 142). However, upon entry to their community an oath was required (CD 15:1–6; 1QS 5:8–11) and, in any case, they did not object to oath taking in general (CD 9:8–12; 16:7–12).

In order to prevent any profaning of the divine name (Exod 20:7) Philo recommends so-called substitute oaths (*Spec.* 2.3–5). These formulas try to employ the authority of "heaven" and "earth" (Matt 5:34–35; cf. *m. úebu* 4:13; Philo *Spec.* 2.5), "Jerusalem" (Matt 5:35; cf. *m. Ned.* 1:3; *t. Ned.* 1:3) or one's head (Matt 5:36; cf. 1 Chr. 12:19 MT; *m. Sanh.* 3.2).

In ancient Judaism the terms "oath" and "vow" were often used synonymously. However, later rabbinic literature pays considerable attention to the description of different kinds of oaths and vows (cf. *m. úebu* re oaths and *m. Ned.* re vows).

Jesus' abolition of oaths

Reservations against swearing are quite common in antiquity (cf. e.g. Sophocles *Oed. col.* 650; Epictetus *Ench.* 33.5). However, Jesus may be the first who rejected oath taking altogether. After summarizing the OT teaching not to swear falsely but to carry out the vows one has made to the Lord (Matt 5:33 cf. Exod 20:7; Lev 19:12; Num 30:3–15; Deut 23:21–23) Jesus rejects any swearing of oaths unconditionally (Matt 5:34). This radicalization in the fourth antithesis of the Sermon on the Mount does not even allow substitute oaths because such evasions ultimately involve God as well. Positively speaking, Jesus' command can be interpreted to instruct his followers to abstain from any double standard of truthfulness. A "yes" shall imply nothing but a "yes" and a "no" nothing but a "no" (Matt 5:37). Thus there is only one unified and undivided truth, which cannot possibly be qualified. To interpret the "yes, yes" and "no, no" as another type of substitute oath would miss the point of Jesus' argument (see, however, such a substitute oath mentioned in *2 En.* 49:1–2; *b. Sebu.* 36a).

Another discussion of substitute oaths follows in Matt 23:16–22, where some formulas – "by the sanctuary" or "by the gold of the sanctuary", "by the altar" or "by the gift that is on the altar", "by heaven" or "by the throne of God and by the one who is seated upon it" – are all without exception judged to be valid oaths. Since there is no general rejection of oaths in this context some scholars believe that this line of reasoning contradicts Jesus' earlier statement (Matt 5:34). However, it is also possible to understand this discussion concerning the validity of substitute oaths as a more academic type of dispute with Jesus' opponents. After all, the argument is in favour of a general validity of oath formulas, not about allowing some oaths and forbidding others. Thus it opposes the popular usage of substitute oaths as a supposed solution against the danger of desecrating the divine name by oath taking. Therefore, it is not necessary to interpret this argument as a correction of Jesus' earlier statement in Matt 5:34–37. Consequently, when the high priest adjures Jesus "by the living God" to tell if he is "the Christ, the Son of God", the accused answers with a simple "you have said so" (Matt 26:64; cf. Mark 14:61–62) and thus refrains from any swearing.

Nevertheless, there are a number of instances in the NT where actual oaths and vows are referred to or even quoted. Negative examples include Peter's swearing that he did not know Jesus (Mark 14:71 par. Matt 26:72, 74), Herod's vow that led to the beheading of John the Baptist (Mark 6:23 par. Matt 14:7) and an oath of Jewish opponents to kill Paul (Acts 23:12). As in Matt 5:33 perjury is also rejected in 1 Tim 1:10 (cf. *Did.* 2:3). Other statements like Jas 5:12 and possibly 2 Cor 1:17 quote or at least allude to Jesus' position. Other texts, however, come close to oaths and vows, as when the apostle Paul calls on "God as witness" against him (2 Cor 1:23; cf. Rom 1:9; Phil 1:8; 1 Thess 2:5) or when he adjures the Thessalonians "by the Lord" (1 Thess 5:27). The seer John even sees an angel swearing "by him who lives for ever and ever" (Rev 10:6).

Finally, some NT texts refer to the oaths, which God swore to Abraham (Luke 1:72–73; Heb 6:13) and his heirs (Heb 6:17; cf. Philo *Abr.* 273), to King David (Acts 2:30) and against Israel in the wilderness (Heb 3:11, 18; 4:3; cf. Ps 95:7–11). Even Jesus' installation "as a priest forever" is said to have been confirmed with an oath (Heb 7:20–22). Unhesitatingly, the author of Hebrews refers to the general practice of oath taking (Heb 6:16),

which indicates that he perhaps did not know about Jesus' strong opposition to oath taking in general.

Although the early church adopted almost entirely the argument of Matt 5:33–37, later development, especially since the Constantinian turn, moved towards the establishment of a "Christian" oath over pagan formulas. During the Middle Ages the Cathars and the Waldenses, and since the Reformation the Anabaptists and later on the Quakers, have refused to take oaths, appealing to Jesus' rejection of them.

CARSTEN CLAUSSEN

Further reading

Betz, H. D. *The Sermon on the Mount: A Commentary on the Sermon on the Mount, including the Sermon on the Plain (Matthew 5:3–7:27 and Luke 6:20–49)*, Hermeneia, Minneapolis, MN: Fortress Press, 1995, pp. 259–74.

Bonhoeffer, D. *The Cost of Discipleship*, New York: Touchstone, 1995, pp. 135–39.

Davies, W. D. and D. C. Allison. *The Gospel According to Saint Matthew: Vol. I: Introduction and Commentary on Matthew I–VII*, ICC 1, Edinburgh: T. & T. Clark, 1988, pp. 533–8.

Garland, D. E. "Oaths and Swearing," in Joel B. Green, Scot McKnight, and I. Howard Marshall (eds) *Dictionary of Jesus and the Gospels*, Downers Grove, IL: InterVarsity Press, 1992, pp. 577–78.

Guelich, R. A. *The Sermon on the Mount: A Foundation for Understanding*, Dallas, TX: Word, 1982, pp. 211–19.

Lieberman, S. *Greek in Jewish Palestine*, New York: Jewish Theological Seminary of America, 1942, pp. 115–43.

Link, H.-G. "Swear, Oath," *NIDNTT* 3 (1975) 737–43.

Luz, U. *Matthew 1–7: A Commentary*, Minneapolis, MN: Augsburg Fortress, 1989, pp. 310–22.

Schneider, J. "ὀμνύω," *TDNT* 5 (1967) 176–85.

—— "ὅρκος κτλ.," *TDNT* 5 (1967) 457–67.

Vahrenhorst, M. "'Ihr sollt überhaupt nicht schwören': Matthäus im halachischen Diskurs," WMANT 95, Neukirchen-Vluyn: Neukirchener Verlag, 2002.

OBDURACY, HARDNESS OF HEART

Ancient Hebrew uses a number of synonyms to describe the "hardening" of the "heart," including כבד ("to make heavy," Exod 9:34; 1QM 11.8 להל חם//להכבד, "to make heavy [the heart of] our enemies"//"to make war against our enemies"); חזק ("to make firm/hard/stubborn," Exod 4:21; 1QM 16:13–14 חזק את לבבם, "he will harden/ make firm their hearts"); קשה ("to make hard," Exod 7:3; 1QM 14:7 לבב קושי, "hard heart"); שמן ("to make fat/dull," Isa 6:10; 4Q424 frag 3:6 לב שמן, "dull mind"); and קשח ("to harden/make stubborn," Isa 63:17). LXX usually translates these terms with σκληρύνω ("to harden") or παχύνω ("to make dull").

Biblical writers universally presume that the decision to harden one's heart against God is both futile and dangerous (e.g. "Who has hardened himself against him and prospered?" Job 9:4). But when the deity himself decides to harden the hearts of human individuals this invariably generates various degrees of theodical concern. Philosopher-theologians tend to explain this behavior as part of a "biblical doctrine of reprobation." That is, Yahweh's decision to harden Pharaoh's heart (Exod 4–14) cannot and should not be interpreted apart from his parallel decision to "love Jacob and hate Esau" (Mal 1:2–3; Feenstra, Griffin 35). Among others, the Apostle Paul defends this behavior as an example of divine sovereignty, not caprice (Rom 9:15; Philo, *Fug.* 124; Wakefield 69).

Biblical scholars, however, tend to see rather complex histories behind these so-called "reprobation" texts. A few interpret the character of "Pharaoh" as an eponym for "Egypt" (Cranfield 230–35), but most source critics view the plagues narrative (Exod 4–14) as the product of a multi-staged development in which an early tradent (Yahwist?) portrays Pharaoh making his own heart "heavy" (כבד) in his futile attempt to understand Moses' demands (Exod 8:11[15], 28[32]; 9:34; cf. 1 Sam 6:6). Later tradents (elohist? priestly?) reformulate the tradition to make Yahweh the "hardening agent" in Israel's "war" against Egypt (קשה/חזק) (Exod 4:21; 7:3; 9:12; 10:20, 27; 11:10; 14:4, 8, 17; cf. Deut 2:30; 11:20; Wilson; Niditch 144). Whether one sees Yahweh hardening Pharaoh's heart as Israel's "Divine Warrior" or Egypt's "Divine Judge" cannot easily be determined (Good 399–400).

Similarly complex histories lie behind the "lying spirit" text in *Kings* (רוח שקר, 1 Kgs 22:23; Hirth; de Vries 128–29) and the "strong delusion" text in *Thessalonians* (ἐνέργειαν πλάνης, 2 Thess 2:11; Moore 126–30; McGinn 44). Yet the OT text generating by far the greatest impact on the NT is Yahweh's warning to Isaiah about the negative response he should expect to prophetic preaching (Isa 6:9–10). This programmatic text – intertextually reflected in Deut 29:4 – warns Isaiah that genuinely prophetic preaching will always make hearts "dull" (שמן; lit. "fat"), ears "heavy" (כבד), and eyes "blind" (שעע; lit. "sealed up/pasted together"). Observing this response firsthand, the earliest Christians imagine it as a fulfillment of this prophecy. Thus Luke seizes on this passage to explain both Roman (Acts 28:27) as well as Jewish resistance to the Gospel message ("Oh, how foolish you are! How slow of heart [τῇ καρδίᾳ] to believe all that the prophets have declared," Luke 24:25).

Each of the four Evangelists cites this same "principle" to explain (a) why Jesus so heavily relies on parables in his preaching (Matt 13:15); (b) why those hostile to God still misunderstand the "mysteries of the kingdom" (Mark 4:10–12; Luke 8:9–10); and (c) why miraculous signs cannot in and of themselves create belief in hardened hearts (John 12:39–40; on Isa 6:9–10 in the sospels, see Evans). Without citing Isaiah explicitly, several NT tradents allude to this "hardening" principle as a recurring motif: (a) Jesus grieves over the "hardness of their hearts" when his hearers demand that Sabbath observance be prioritized over salvific healing (Mark 3:5); and (b) the writer of the letter to the Hebrews, responding to Israel's behavior (Ps 95:7–11), warns his audience to "take care, brothers and sisters, lest there be in any of you an evil, unbelieving heart" (Heb 3:12).

MICHAEL S. MOORE

Further reading

Cranfield, C. E. B. *Romans: A Shorter Commentary*, Grand Rapids, MI: Eerdmans, 1985.

Evans, C. A. *To See and Not Perceive: Isaiah 6.9–10 in Early Jewish and Christian Interpretation*, JSOTSup 64, Sheffield: JSOT Press, 1989.

Feenstra, R. J. "Reprobation," in E. Craig (ed.) *Routledge Encyclopedia of Philosophy*, London: Routledge, 1998.

Good, R. M. "The Just War in Ancient Israel," *JBL* 104 (1985) 385–400.

Griffin, D. R. *God, Power, and Evil: A Process Theodicy*, Louisville, KY: Westminster/John Knox Press, 2004.

Hirth, V. "'Der Geist' in I Reg 22," *ZAW* 101 (1989) 113–14.

McGinn, B. *Antichrist: Two Thousand Years of the Human Fascination with Evil*, San Francisco, CA: HarperSanFrancisco, 1994.

Moore, M. S. *Faith Under Pressure: A Study of Biblical Leaders in Conflict*, Siloam Springs, AR: Leafwood, 2003.

Niditch, S. *War in the Hebrew Bible: A Study in the Ethics of Violence*, New York: Oxford University Press, 1993.

Vries, S. J. de. *Prophet Against Prophet*, Grand Rapids, MI: Eerdmans, 1978.

Wakefield, A. H. "Romans 9–11: The Sovereignty of God and the Status of Israel," *RevExp* 100 (2003) 65–80.

Wilson, R. R. "The Hardening of Pharaoh's Heart," *CBQ* 41 (1979) 18–36.

OLD TESTAMENT SCRIPTURES

For Jews of the first century CE, the appeal to tradition – in oral or written form – was among the strongest possible "proofs" in support of a given belief or practice. Thus it is not surprising that references to "scripture" are frequent throughout the New Testament to buttress the claim that Jesus as Messiah fulfilled prophecies recorded long before his time.

This article looks at the extent, division, and wording of what would have constituted "scripture" within the Jewish community of Jesus' day. The term "Old Testament" or "Hebrew Bible" would not have been used at that time, and it would be equally anachronistic to speak of a canon of sacred writ. Nonetheless, it is possible to determine, in at least broad contours, what constituted authoritative written material in the early to mid first century CE.

Contents of scripture

A canon might be defined as the definitive list of inspired, authoritative books that constitute the recognized and accepted body of sacred scripture for a given religious group. This collection of books is closed or fixed in so far as the group is concerned. Because of its unique status, canonical material is typically cited in a unique way ("So it is written" or "As the prophets foretold," for example).

It is difficult to pinpoint the precise time at which the process of canonization commenced. Conservative researchers would locate what might be called a canonical consciousness as early as Moses himself (see, for example, Deuteronomy 32) and Joshua (see especially chapter 8). More broadly, there is agreement that certain material was viewed as authoritative at the time of Josiah in the late seventh century CE (see "the scroll of the Teaching" in 1 Kgs 22) and during the activities of Ezra and Nehemiah in the fifth century BCE (Nehemiah chapter 8, with its "scroll of the Teaching of Moses," is particularly instructive in this regard).

The second book of Maccabees (part of the Roman Catholic and Orthodox Christian Bible), dating to the second century BCE, also ascribes to Nehemiah a decisive role in the gathering of sacred texts and the founding of a library. Interestingly enough, Second Maccabees attributes similar activities to the contemporary Jewish hero Judah Maccabee (or Judas Maccabeus). It is therefore quite possible that at several points in pre-Christian times, leaders of the Jewish community took steps to recognize; that is, canonize, materials. Such actions would have resulted in a definitive; that is, closed, list for the intended audience, but in no way precluded later communities and their leaders from recognizing a larger number of books as canonical.

From the early second century CE onward, Rabbinic Judaism has spoken of a canon consisting of twenty-four books. These are the same books, although in a different order and with a different

enumeration, as those found in the Protestant Old Testament. Almost all of these books are cited as authoritative in one or another New Testament passage; sometimes, the citation includes the name of the book, although more often the name is lacking. From this we can conclude that, roughly speaking, first-century CE Jews (from among whom Jesus and his earliest followers derived) had a strong sense, one might even speak of a consensus, that they had access to divinely inspired written materials that they could cite on occasion as "proof texts."

In this belief, Jesus and his followers were not alone. It is clear that a similar perspective animated the lives and writings of those, probably Essenes, who inhabited Qumran and produced the Dead Sea Scrolls. Although the results of these two groups' reliance on "scripture" differed, their approaches were quite similar. Thus it is noteworthy that the prophets, especially Isaiah, and the Pslter (possibly consisting of more than 150 psalms at Qumran) played large, even decisive roles in determining beliefs and practices for both groups. At Qumran, only the book of Esther, among those viewed as canonical by Christians and later Jews, is not found or definitely referred to. Although New Testament writers do not cite as many books as did the authors of the Scrolls, nonetheless all of the books of the Torah (or the Pentateuch, the Five Books of Moses) and of the Prophets are referenced in some way.

Division and ordering of scripture

In order to advance our discussion, we need to point out that traditionally the books of the Hebrew Bible/Old Testament have been divided into three sections or categories by Jews: The Torah, the Prophets or Nevi'im (which include Joshua, Judg, Samuel, and Kgs [but not Ruth], as well as Isaiah, Jeremiah, Ezekiel, and the twelve Minor Prophets [but not Lamentations or Daniel]), and the Writings or Ketuvim (the remainder of "scripture"). An acronym formed from the three terms in Hebrew yields Tanak (also Tanakh or Tanach) as a term preferred by Jews for the Old Testament; however, this term is not ancient and would not have been used or known in Jesus' day.

From a period slightly later than Judah Maccabee (see above), we have what might well be the first clear reference to this tripartite division. In the introduction to the book of Ben Sirach (as with Maccabees, this forms part of the Catholic and Orthodox Bible), the grandson of the author, writing around 130 BCE, speaks of "the law, the prophets, and the other books of our ancestors." The first two phrases accord well with the first two divisions of traditional Judaism. However, "the other books of our ancestors" (elsewhere, "the others that followed them") is vague.

This vagueness about the contents of the third "part" of scripture continues in other Jewish writings. Thus, for example, in one of the earliest documents from Qumran (MMT; it is, like Ben Sirach from the latter half of the second century BCE), we find reference to "the book of Moses and the books of the prophets and the writings of David, along with the events/chronicles of ages past." The "writings of David" would appear to be a specific reference to Psalms, thus corroborating their importance throughout Judaism of this period. "Events" or "chronicles" are, on the other hand, impossible to identify with equal precision. Similar language appears in the works of the Jewish philosopher Philo, who lived and wrote in Alexandria, Egypt, during the first decades of the common era; that is, at the very time Jesus was active in Palestine. In describing a contemplative Jewish sect, the Therapeutae, he refers to their use of "laws and oracles delivered through the mouth of prophets, and psalms and other books [or: anything else] by which knowledge and piety may be increased and perfected."

The evidence from the New Testament concerning Jesus' statements is consistent with the findings presented just above. Throughout the gospels, Jesus is portrayed as referring to the Law and the Prophets in a way that makes it clear that his audience understood, and accepted the uniqueness of, the books Jesus was citing or alluding to. When it comes to what later become known as the "Writings," we must rely on a passage such as Luke 24:44 for information about Jesus' thinking: "the Law of Moses and the Prophets and the Psalms" contain "things written about him [that] must be fulfilled." Other portions of the Writings, but not all of the books, are cited as authoritative elsewhere in the New Testament.

The result of this investigation thus far is the recognition that within many (but by no means all) Jewish communities of the pre-Christian and early common eras, the Torah and the Prophets and the Psalms were accepted as Sacred Writ. Other books appear to have the same status, but it was not until later in the first century and early second century CE that the contents of this third section were finally settled on. Even then, there was apparently ongoing debate for some time about some of the Writings, and their order varied for an even longer period.

The text of scripture

Our definition of canon, given above, describes it in terms of "the definitive list of inspired, authoritative books." The word "books" was deliberately chosen; canons enshrine specific books, but not the text of those books. Thus, it is possible for one version of a canonized book to differ from others in overall length, order of chapters and verses, and the wording of individual verses. This situation can be referred to as textual fluidity.

Textual fluidity is not simply a scholarly construct; rather, it accurately describes the state and status of Scripture at the time of Jesus and before (the fall of the Jerusalem Temple in 70 CE appears to have inaugurated an intense, and largely successful, effort to stabilize or fix the text). The biblical scrolls from Qumran reflect this circumstance well: for many books of the Bible (for example, Samuel and Jeremiah) several versions circulated within the community at the same time. From all available evidence, there were few, if any efforts to standardize the text over the two centuries or so that the Essenes occupied Qumran.

Although this may strike modern readers as odd, impractical, confusing, or even impious, it was, as will be noted below, a situation that characterized Judaism at large through the first half of the first century CE. Moreover, it is not without a parallel in today's society; after all, traditional Jews and Christians would affirm that they are all reading the same book of Jeremiah, for example, but in fact the texts of the translations generally used vary widely from the formal (ArtScroll for Jews, New American Standard Version for Christians, for example) to the functional/dynamic or even periphrastic (as in the New Jewish Version or *The Message*).

Although the Dead Sea Scrolls provide the first extensive ancient evidence of textual fluidity in Hebrew, this phenomenon was already well known among scholars of the Septuagint, the Greek translation of the Old Testament that was initiated in Alexandria, Egypt, in the first half of the third century BCE. While it is not possible to provide an assessment that would cover all of the Septuagint translators, it is surely the case that many of them endeavored to translate quite literally the Hebrew text that lay before them. And that Hebrew text often differed from the traditional Masoretic text that lies behind most translations today.

The reasons for these differences in the Hebrew are numerous; generalizations must be avoided, as each case needs to be investigated and interpreted on its own. But the upshot is that we have at least two (and in the case of the Torah, with the Samaritan Pentateuch, three) textual traditions circulating before and during the time of Jesus and that each of them was regarded or could be regarded as valid in its own right.

The extent of these differences varies widely from book to book and even within the same book. Jeremiah in the Septuagint (and in Hebrew texts from Qumran that reflect the Hebrew behind the Septuagint) is one seventh shorter than the Masoretic Text (also found at Qumran). Books like Proverbs do not exhibit such variation in terms of length, but the wording of individual chapters and verses often varies widely.

In the scholarly literature, it used to be commonly asserted that New Testament quotations and citations from scripture regularly followed the Septuagint. Since both the Septuagint and the New Testament are in Greek, this would seem to make a good deal of sense. And indeed there are a number of places where the Septuagint and the New Testament agree against the Masoretic Text.

But the truth, that is the whole truth, of the matter is not so simple. Even when the Septuagint and the New Testament happen to agree, this agreement need not be the result of the New Testament writer's direct knowledge or use of the Septuagint. After all, he may have simply hit upon the same Greek wording as the Septuagint translator on the basis of a similar underlying Hebrew. This option gains in scholarly acceptance when it is recalled that the Dead Sea Scrolls do contain in Hebrew what until their discovery had been termed distinctive Septuagint readings.

Moreover, we see in many New Testament citations a text that is similar to the Septuagint, but nonetheless distinct. This could occur when the New Testament writer used a later version of the Septuagint (we know that the Septuagint was repeatedly revised from at least the first century BCE on) or when he adapted scripture (from Hebrew or Greek) to its new context in a gospel or Epistle. Further, the New Testament writer may have worked from memory rather than from a written source, at least on occasion.

To fill out this picture, we need to note two further phenomena. The first, like the Septuagint and its development, took place before the time of Jesus; the second, afterwards. In addition to translation from Greek to Hebrew, translation from Aramaic to Hebrew also occurred. This phenomenon, at least in oral form, may go back to the time of Ezra and Nehemiah, when Aramaic became the dominant language of Judaea. Full-blown written Aramaic versions, called Targumim,

do not develop until after the time of Jesus, but at Qumran Targumim, including a lengthy one of Job, are found. This opens up the possibility that some New Testament citations of Scripture are based not on Hebrew or Greek, but on Aramaic.

No matter how and when the books of the New Testament were first composed, all knowledge of them up until the fifteenth century (with the invention of the printing press) is almost entirely dependent on manuscript copies: that is, scribal copies individually made by hand. Scribes, being human (perhaps all too human), were susceptible to conscious and subconscious, accidental and purposeful alterations of the texts they "copied." Scriptural texts were not immune. We are fortunate that textual critics have labored long and hard to arrive at the earliest recoverable form of each book of the New Testament, including scriptural citations. But this is not the same as saying that we have recovered the original form of any book of the New Testament or that such an original form contained the *ipsissima verba* (that is, the very words) of Jesus, Paul, or anyone else.

In short, there remain many unanswered and probably unanswerable questions about "Old Testament Scripture" at the time of Jesus and the writing of the New Testament. But surely all is not lost: It can be confidently affirmed that the notion of canon (but not the terminology itself) was deeply embedded in first-century Judaism; that this canon consisted of all of the books presently constituted in the first two parts (Torah and Prophets) of Tanak and some (but not all) of Ketuvim, especially Psalms; and that Jesus and those who wrote of him and about him were creatively at ease with the concept of textual fluidity.

LEONARD GREENSPOON

Further reading

Abegg, Martin, Jr, Peter W. Flint, and Eugene Ulrich (eds) *The Dead Sea Scrolls Bible*, San Francisco, CA: HarperCollins, 1999.

Evans, Craig A. "The Scriptures of Jesus and His Earliest Followers", in Lee Martin McDonald and James A. Sanders (eds) *The Canon Debate*, Peabody, MA: Hendrickson, 2002, pp. 185–95.

Greenspoon, Leonard. "Hebrew into Greek: Interpretation In, By, and Of the Septuagint," in Alan Hauser and Duane F. Watson (eds) *History of Biblical Interpretation*, Grand Rapids, MI: Eerdmans, 2003, Vol. 1, pp. 80–113.

—— "Jewish Translations of the Bible," in Adele Berlin and Marc Zvi Brettler (eds) *The Jewish Study Bible*, New York: Oxford University Press, 2003.

Helmer, Christine and Christof Landsmesser (eds) *One Scripture or Many? Canon from Biblical, Theological and Philosophical Perspectives*, Oxford: Oxford University Press, 2004.

Hengel, Martin. *The Septuagint as Christian Scripture: Its Prehistory and the Problem of Its Canon*, Grand Rapids, MI: Baker, 2004.

Herbert, Edward D. and Emanuel Tov (eds) *The Bible as Book: The Hebrew Bible and the Judaean Desert Discoveries*, New Castle, DE: Oak Knoll, 2002.

Lim, Timothy H. *Holy Scripture in the Qumran Commentaries and Pauline Letters*, Oxford: Oxford University Press, 1997.

McLay, R. Timothy. *The Use of the Septuagint in New Testament Research*, Grand Rapids, MI: Eerdmans, 2003.

Nickelsburg, George W. E. *Jewish Literature between the Bible and the Mishnah*, second edition, Minneapolis, MN: Fortress Press, 2005.

Schiffman, Lawrence H. *Reclaiming the Dead Sea Scrolls: The History of Judaism, the Background of Christianity, the Lost Library of Qumran*, Philadelphia, PA: Jewish Publication Society, 1994.

Sundberg, Alfred C., Jr. *The Old Testament of the Early Church*, Cambridge, MA: Harvard University Press, 1964.

Tov, Emanuel. *Textual Criticism of the Hebrew Bible*, second revised edition, Minneapolis, MN: Fortress Press, 2001.

Ulrich, Eugene. "Qumran and the Canon of the Old Testament," in J.-M. Auwers and H. J. de Jonge (eds) *The Biblical Canons*, Leuven: University Press, 2003, pp. 57–80.

VanderKam, James C. *The Dead Sea Scrolls Today*, Grand Rapids, MI: Eerdmans, 1994.

OSSUARY OF JAMES

In the summer of 2002 Old Testament scholar and epigrapher Andre Lemaire chanced upon an ossuary (or bone box) in Israel in private hands, inscribed with the words "Jacob [or James], son of Joseph, brother of Jesus." Lemaire consulted with Hershel Shanks of the Biblical Archaeology Society and the *Biblical Archaeology Review*. The ossuary was examined by members of the Israel Geological Survey, who concluded that the ossuary and the Aramaic inscription dated to late antiquity, probably the first century BC or first century AD, a period in which a great many limestone ossuaries were produced. The remarkable discovery was announced in October of that year, with publications quickly following (Lemaire; Shanks and Witherington; for a catalogue of Jewish ossuaries from late antiquity, see Rahmani; for interpretation of the significance of ossuaries, see Meyers).

The ossuary was exhibited by the Royal Ontario Museum in Toronto, Canada, in connection with the 2002 annual meeting of the Society of Biblical Literature (SBL). The Museum staff examined the ossuary and inscription. Their examination, which was facilitated in an inadvertent manner by the accidental breaking of the ossuary, agreed with the earlier findings of the Israel Geological Survey. However, certain individuals associated with the Israel Antiquity Authority (IAA) expressed the view – even before examining the ossuary – that all or part of the inscription (though not the ossuary itself) was of modern origin.

The IAA studied the ossuary in the winter of 2003. In the IAA report of June 2003 geochemist Yuval Goren declared the inscription a forgery, based on the alleged presence of an inauthentic patina. Goren's technical explanation of the false patina – how it was produced and how it was applied – has been widely disputed. Moreover, German geochemist Wolfgang Krumbein has observed that the spurious patina, seen in the photographs of the inscription published by Goren, is not present in the photographs taken by the Royal Ontario Museum. Indeed, in a photograph dating to 1976 one can see all of the disputed inscription. This troubling discrepancy raises serious questions about the integrity of the IAA's report. At the 2006 annual Biblical Archaeology Society SBL Fest in Washington DC, respected Israeli archaeologist Gabriel Barkay publicly stated that in his opinion the James Ossuary inscription is indeed authentic. Like Lemaire and Barkay, other leading paleographers such as Israel's Ada Yardeni have also pronounced the inscription ancient. The matter is still before the court in Israel.

If the James ossuary inscription is authentic and if this ossuary is indeed the ossuary of James, the brother of Jesus, what might we learn? It seems we might gain at least four things, all four of which contribute significantly to understanding better the world in which James lived and in which the early Christian movement grew.

1 Because the ossuary inscription is in Aramaic, we may infer that James and family probably spoke Aramaic, which scholars have long recognized as Jesus' first language. The James ossuary lends an important measure of support to this hypothesis. Of course, one could object and say that all we know is that the inscriber of the ossuary spoke Aramaic; not necessarily James. But given the personal, family-oriented reality of *ossilegium*, it is wiser to assume that the language used in the inscription is the language of the family and, therefore, of the deceased.

2 James, originally of Galilee, continued to live in or near Jerusalem. We are left with this impression in the New Testament (particularly the book of Acts and Paul's letter to the churches of Galatia) and in later Christian history and tradition. After all, if James' family and home were still in Galilee, then we should not have expected his ossuary to be found in

Jerusalem. Its discovery in Jerusalem shows that in all probability his home had become Jerusalem. Therefore, when his bones were gathered and placed in an ossuary, the ossuary remained in Jerusalem, in the family tomb.

3 The James ossuary may also suggest that James probably died in or near Jerusalem, as early Church traditions maintain. If the ossuary was discovered in a burial vault near the Temple Mount, perhaps in the Kidron Valley, as has been conjectured, this may offer a measure of support to the tradition that James was closely associated with the Temple, even if at odds with the powerful priestly family of Annas (a.k.a. Hanin). Of course, this suggestion is at best tenuous, but the discovery of the ossuary of James in the general vicinity of the Temple Mount does lend a small measure of support to Christian tradition and to the brief report of James' death found in Josephus (*Ant.* 20.9.1:200–203).

4 And finally, secondary burial, according to Jewish burial custom, implies that James, though a follower of Jesus and part of a movement that was beginning to drift away from its Jewish heritage, continued to live as a Jew, and so was buried as a Jew. The Christianity of James, we may infer, was not understood as something separate from or opposed to Jewish faith. This observation is completely in accord with a critical reading of the traditions about James found in the New Testament, especially in the unvarnished account we have in Paul, in his letter to the churches of Galatia. There we are told that even a major figure like Peter was cowed by the arrival in Antioch of "men from James," with the result that the apostle no longer ate with Gentiles (Gal 2:11–14). It is clear from the context that Peter withdrew from Gentiles because the men from James were Torah-observant and evidently expected Peter and other Jewish believers (such as Barnabas) to be Torah-observant also.

If the James ossuary is indeed the ossuary of James, the brother of Jesus, we are in possession of a truly significant artifact that confirms and clarifies several important aspects of the life and impact of James, an important leader in the early Christian movement, who has by and large been overlooked and whose contribution has been minimized.

CRAIG A. EVANS

Further reading

Evans, C. A. *Jesus and the Ossuaries*, Waco, TX: Baylor University Press, 2003.
—— "Jesus and the Ossuaries," *BBR* 13 (2003) 21–46.
Lemaire, A. "Burial Box of James the Brother of Jesus," *BAR* 28/6 (2002) 24–33, 70.
Magness, J. "Ossuaries and the Burials of Jesus and James," *JBL* 124 (2005) 121–54.
Meyers, E. M. *Jewish Ossuaries: Reburial and Rebirth*, BibOr 24; Rome: Pontifical Biblical Institute Press, 1971.
Rahmani, L. Y. *A Catalogue of Jewish Ossuaries in the Collections of the State of Israel*, Jerusalem: The Israel Antiquities Authority, 1994.
Shanks, H., and Witherington, B. III. *The Brother of Jesus*, San Francisco, CA: HarperCollins, 2003.

P

PARABLE AND PROVERB

It is beyond dispute that the historical Jesus spoke in parables. Beyond this fact, however, there is little agreement. Part of the problem arises from the lack of precision in the word itself. The term parable is a transliteration of the Greek *parabolē*, which may be translated literally as "set beside." In literature, *parabolē* has a broad range of meanings, including: (1) a comparison or illustration (Aristotle, *Pol.* 2.5; *Rhet.* 1393a; Quintillian 5.11.23) including similes and metaphors; (2) a proverb or similitude (Plato, *Phaed.* 82e; 85e; 87b); or, (3) a short, illustrative story (as in the gospels).

In the LXX, *parabolē* is usually used to translate the Hebrew *mashal*, a word that can be translated in a variety of ways, including: a proverb, parable, or by-word. For example, the Hebrew title for Proverbs is *Mishelai*, from *mashal*. In the OT, story parables are rare. Some of the closest parallels to Jesus' use of parables are: Jotham's tale of the trees in Judg 9:7–15; Nathan's story of the rich man stealing the poor man's ewe lamb in 2 Sam 12:1–15; the song of the vineyard of Isa 5:1–2; and the useless vine of Ezek 15:1–5.

Parables are more common in the rabbinic literature. The rabbinic parables in general, however, are from a later period than the time of Jesus. Furthermore, they function exegetically, to demonstrate a point in interpretation of scripture (see McArthur and Johnson, Young).

Jesus' parables are recorded in four sources: the Synoptic Gospels and the Coptic *Gospel of Thomas*. Ten parables of the Synoptic Tradition are paralleled in the *Gospel of Thomas*. These are: the Sower (*Gos. Thom.* 9//Mark 4:3–8//Matt 13:3–8// Luke 8:5–8); the Mustard Seed (*Gos. Thom.* 20// Mark 4:30–32//Matt 13:31–32//Luke 13:18–19); the Wheat and the Weeds (*Gos. Thom.* 57//Matt 13:24–30); the Rich Fool (*Gos. Thom.* 63//Luke 12:16–21); the Banquet (*Gos. Thom.* 64// Matt 22:1–10// Luke 14:16–24); the Wicked Tenants (*Gos. Thom.* 65//Mark 12:1–12//Matt 21:33–46// Luke 20:9–19); the Pearl of Great Price (*Gos. Thom.* 76//Matt 13:45–46); the Leaven (*Gos. Thom.* 107//Matt 13:33//Luke 13:20–21); the Lost Sheep (*Gos. Thom.* 107//Matt 18:12–14//Luke 15:4–7); and the Treasure in the Field (*Gos. Thom.* 109//Matt 13:44). In addition, four parables in the *Gospel of Thomas* are unparalleled in the Synoptic Gospels. These are: the Wise Fisherman (*Gos. Thom.* 8); the Disciples as Children (*Gos. Thom.* 21); the Woman with the Jar (*Gos. Thom.* 97); and the Assassin (*Gos. Thom.* 98) (Hultgren 2000).

Scholars disagree on whether the parables common to the synoptics and the *Gospel of Thomas* represent independent versions of the parables, the author of Thomas' knowledge of a version of the Q source common to Matthew and Luke, or Thomas' dependence upon the canonical gospels. There is also no unanimity on whether the parables of the *Gospel of Thomas* provide a more or less accurate representation of the words of the historical Jesus. Jeremias (second edition, 1972), for example, held that the simpler forms of many of the parables in the *Gospel of Thomas* indicate that they are more authentic versions of Jesus' sayings. Yet a comparison of the narratives of Matthew and Mark demonstrates that the later

Matthean form can be shorter and more abrupt (cf. Mark 5:21–43 and Matt 9:18–26). There is no "rule" that shorter, less elaborate forms of a story are necessarily earlier. The opposite is often the case. Thus, priority is to be discerned from context and tendency, not form. Nevertheless, the *Gospel of Thomas* remains a valuable resource for the study of the historical Jesus as storyteller primarily because of its inclusion of four unparalleled parables.

The Gospel of John contains no parables. Rather, the Johannine Jesus employs "figures of speech" (*paroimia*), such as those recorded in John 10:1–16; 16:21–22. While superficially similar to parables, the *paroimia* function as illustrative devices for Jesus' speech rather than as parables proper.

Jesus' parables

The parables of Jesus include the following types: aphorisms and similitudes, story parables; example stories; and parables with allegorical elements.

Aphorisms and similitudes

The aphorisms and similitudes are similar to proverbial statements. They are short pithy observations about life. One example is Luke 4:23, where the statement "Physician, heal yourself" is introduced as a "parable." Likewise, Jesus' assertion that it is not those who are well but the sick who need a physician (Mark 2:17//Matt 9:12//Luke 5:31) represents an example of an aphorism functioning as a parable. Finally, the observations that no one will sew a patch of new cloth on an old garment (Mark 2:21//Matt 9:16//Luke 5:36) or put new wine into old wineskins (Mark 2:22//Matt 9:17//Luke 5:37–38) are aphoristic comparisons falling under the general, imprecise rubric of parable. These types of sayings are among the closest to the Hebrew understanding of *mashalim*, or proverbs, such as those found in the Wisdom tradition.

Similitudes, as the name implies, are similes. Examples include the parables of the Seed Growing by Itself (Mark 4:26–29), the Mustard Seed (Mark 4:30–32//Matt 13:31–32//Luke 13:18–19), and the Leaven (Matt 13:33). Similitudes are often introduced by a phrase such as "the kingdom of God/heaven is like … " and in the gospel tradition serve as illustrations of the nature of Jesus' teaching about God's reign.

Story parables

Story parables are constructed in the past tense, and could be introduced by phrase "once upon a time." A series of examples is found in Luke 15, containing the parable of the Lost Sheep (15:3–7), the Lost Coin (15:8–10), and the Prodigal Son (15:11–32). In each of these instances, the stories appear true to life, yet contain shocking elements. For example, would a shepherd leave ninety-nine sheep in the wilderness to look for a single lost sheep? In *Gos. Thom.* 107 the shepherd's behavior is explained by the fact that the lost sheep was more valuable than all the others.

The parable of the Prodigal Son contains numerous shocking elements. First, the father accedes to the younger son's demand, even though the latter assumes the role of the rebellious child (see Deut 21:18–21). The father's yearning for the son, and his greeting, are also out of character. Heads of household in first-century Palestine would normally neither run nor display extravagant affection in public (Luke 15:20).

The parable of the Workers in the Vineyard (Matt 20:1–18) also combines the realistic setting of the harvest with the shocking behavior of its principal player. In this case, the generous owner gave the daily wage to those who worked only one hour (20:8–10). His response to the seemingly justified complaints of those who labored all day (20:13–15) would not be convincing in a real-world situation, leaving the owner hard pressed to hire anyone to work in the vineyard the following year.

Yet the unrealistic elements are important. By including such surprising features in the context of apparently mundane stories the parables make their points through shock. They demonstrate that the values of the God are not the same as those of humans. God's love is extravagant. Whereas humans cry for retribution, God acts mercifully. It is this mercy that the followers of Jesus are especially encouraged to emulate in some of the example stories.

Example stories

Since the time of Jülicher (1888–99) four parables have been categorized as "example stories." All of these occur in Luke, and are: the Good Samaritan (10:25–37); the Rich Fool (12:16–20); the Rich Man and Lazarus (16:19–31); and, the Pharisee and the Tax Collector (18:9–14). The purpose of an example story is to indicate types of behavior, to be either emulated or avoided.

The most famous example story is the parable of the Good Samaritan (Luke 10:25–37). The parable is set in the context of a dispute between Jesus and a legal expert on the greatest commandment (10:25–28). When Jesus answers from Deut

6:5 and Lev 19:18 that the two great commands are to love God and to love one's neighbor (10:27), the legal expert replies with the inquiry of "Who is my neighbor?" This question reflects a real concern about the definition of "neighbor" in first-century Palestine. Was the neighbor any Israelite (Lev 19:17–18), or the faithful remnant of Israel (1QS 1.10)? In the course of the story, the focus changes from the question "Who is my neighbor?" to "What does it mean to be a neighbor?" (Luke 10:36). Again, the point is made through shock. Not only was the one who acted like a "neighbor" neither the priest nor the Levite; he was a despised Samaritan, whose mercy transcended expectations (Luke 10:33–35). Jesus' concluding inquiry, "Which of these three ... was a neighbor?" places the onus upon all who hear or read the parable. They are left with the uncomfortable self-question, "When am I a neighbor?"

Parables with allegorical elements

Allegories are tales where each of the story's elements has a symbolic meaning. Parables with allegorical features include: the Wicked Tenants (Mark 12:1–12//Matt 21:33–46; Luke 20:9–19); the Ten Virgins (Matt 25:1–13) and the Sheep and the Goats (Matt 25:31–46). Two parables have allegorical interpretations: the Sower (Mark 4:3–9, 13–20; Matt 13:1–9, 18–23; Luke 8:4–8, 11–15) and the Wheat and the Weeds (Matt 13:24–30, 36–43).

In the Wicked Tenants, the owner is undoubtedly God, the servants the prophets and the son Jesus. The tenants represent Jesus' opponents. In the Ten Virgins, the young women await the wedding feast of the bridegroom, an image the church would later ascribe to Christ's Parousia (see Rev 19:9–10). In the Sheep and the Goats, the differing fates of true and false disciples are described.

Critical interpreters have been wary of allegorical elements or interpretations of parables, often understanding these features as inauthentic additions by the Church and foreign to the setting of the historical Jesus (see Jülicher 1886–99); Dodd revised edition 1961; Jeremias second edition 1972). For example, the delay of the bridegroom in the Ten Virgins is understood as representing the church's concern about the delay of the Parousia. Although the parable was interpreted in this manner by the Church, the warning could, nevertheless, fit within Jesus' ministry as a warning against complacency about God's impending eschatological judgment (see Hab 2:2–3).

More problematic is the parable of the Sheep and the Goats, which corresponds closely to Matthew's concern about true and false disciples (cf. Matt 7:21–23). The allegorical interpretations of the Sower and the Wheat and the Weeds also demonstrate features of the Church's later reflection. The interpretations do not seem to correspond to the primary points of the parables, and are missing from the versions of the parables found in the *Gospel of Thomas*.

Interpreting the parables

Throughout most of the history of the Christian church, Jesus' parables were understood as complex allegories. One of the best examples is the exegesis of the Good Samaritan. This parable was understood not as an example of what it is to be a neighbor, but as a complex outline of salvation history (Augustine, *Quaest. ev.* 2.19).

Jülicher (1886–99) is credited with liberating parable exegesis from allegory. Jülicher's contribution was to demonstrate that parables were not allegories, but pithy sayings meant to make a single point. Allegorical features, along with the Markan theory as to why Jesus spoke in parables (Mark 4:10–12) were relegated to the work of the later church and considered foreign to the "mind of Jesus." Jesus' stories, by contrast, were simple maxims of eternal religious truth, congenial to the liberal religious spirit of Jülicher's day.

Dodd (second edition 1961) built upon the work of Jülicher, recognizing that parables make a single point. For Dodd, however, the focus of Jesus' parables was not an "eternal religious truth," but the presence of the kingdom of God. The kingdom of God was interpreted in terms of "realized eschatology," by which Dodd understood that the kingdom was initiated through Jesus' own preaching.

A more satisfactory conclusion was that of J. Jeremias (second edition 1972). Jeremias concluded that many of Jesus' parables functioned as warnings for his hearers. These parables pointed to an impending eschatological crisis. As the prophets of the Hebrew Bible, Jesus warns his audience of the "Day of the Lord," which is a day of judgment. The hearers are in danger of being caught unaware (Amos 5:18–20). Thus, Jesus was calling people to repentance. If they did not, that day would come upon them unexpectedly, like the "thief in the night" (cf. 1 Thess 5:2).

More recently, parables have been understood metaphorically (Crossan; Funk; Scott). Based on the work of literary theorists, the hypothesis is that unlike allegories, which have external referents, parables are metaphors, in that they create their

own literary world and give no information. As
metaphors, parables are disturbing, breaking down
previous expectations. They do not function as
transmitters of information. Rather, they evoke
emotions and questions. This theory, while intriguing and aesthetically pleasing, fails to note the
role of parables as instructional aids. As such, the
hearers would undoubtedly have understood that
the stories did not exist in a vacuum, but alluded
to situations in the real world.

Finally, Blomberg (1990) and Drury (1985) take
us full circle. Both note that the term parable is
imprecise in the ancient world. Blomberg, in particular, considered the creative activity of the
Church to be a less significant factor in the transmission of parables than did Jülicher, Dodd or
Jeremias. While abandoning the complex allegories
of earlier exegesis, Blomberg has concluded that
allegorical features by themselves are not indications of inauthenticty. Rather, parables may make
more than one point. One example is the parable
of the Prodigal Son, in which each of three characters illustrates a different type of individual. The
father represents the character of God. The prodigal is the repentant sinner. The older brother is the
resentful religious establishment.

Conclusion

Parables represent a wide spectrum of gospel literature. They contain both wisdom and prophetic
elements. Aphorisms and similitudes, in particular,
bear striking resemblance to proverbs. On the
other hand, several of the story parables not only
contain wisdom features, but utilize shocking
details to show the difference between God's values
and those of humans. Likewise, example stories,
such as the Good Samaritan, demonstrate the
other characteristic of prophetic discourse: a concern
for how to live and act as the people of God in the
present.

With regard to interpretation, Jülicher, Dodd,
and Jeremias may have been too simplistic in their
understanding of how parables made only one
single point in all cases. Yet Blomberg errs in
seeing some parables having multiple points. A
more accurate conclusion is that some parables
make one point in the context of complex stories.
The parable of the Prodigal Son, for example, is an
illustration of the extravagant love of God, which
far exceeds that which one could expect from any
human father. The parables of the Workers in the
Field (Matt 20:18) illustrates a similar concern
through its portrayal of a gracious landowner
acting as no real-world employer could be expected

to do. In both cases, one point is made *through* the
interactions and responses of several people.

RUSSELL MORTON

Further reading

Blomberg, Craig L. *Interpreting the Parables*, Downers Grove, IL: InterVarsity Press, 1990.
Borsch, Frederick Houk. *Many Things in Parables*, Philadelphia, PA: Fortress 1988.
Crossan, John Dominic. *In Parables*, New York: Harper & Row, 1973.
Dodd, C. H. *The Parables of the Kingdom*, revised edition, New York: Charles Scribner's Sons, 1961.
Donahue, John R. *The Gospel in Parable*, Philadelphia, PA: Fortress, 1988.
Drury, John. *The Parables in the Gospel*, New York: Crossroad, 1985.
Funk, Robert. *Parables as Presence*, Philadelphia, PA: Fortress, 1982.
Hedrick, Charles W. *Parables as Poetic Fictions*, Peabody, MA: Hendrickson, 1994.
Hendrickx, Herman. *The Parables of Jesus*, San Francisco, CA: Harper & Row, 1986.
Herzog, William R., II. *Parables as Subversive Speech*, Louisville, KY: Westminster/John Knox Press, 1998.
Hultgren, Arland J. *The Parables of Jesus*, Grand Rapids, MI: Eerdmans, 2000.
Jeremias, Joachim. *The Parables of Jesus*, second revised edition, New York: Charles Scribner's Sons, 1972.
Jülicher, Adolf. *Gleichnisreden Jesu*, Tübingen: J. C. B. Mohr [Paul Siebeck], 1886–99.
Linnemann, Eta. *Jesus of the Parables: Introduction and Exposition*, New York: Harper & Row, 1966.
Longenecker, Richard N. (ed.) *The Challenge of Jesus' Parables*, Grand Rapids, MI: Eerdmans, 2000.
McArthur, Harvey K. and Robert M. Johnson. *They also Taught in Parables*, Grand Rapids, MI: Academie Books, 1990.
Perkins, Pheme. *Hearing the Parables of Jesus*, New York: Paulist Press, 1981.
Scott, Brandon B. *Hear Then the Parable*, Minneapolis, MN: Fortress, 1989.
Stein, Robert H. *An Introduction to the Parables of Jesus*, Philadelphia, PA: Westminster Press, 1981.
Stern, David. *Parables in Midrash: Narrative and Exegesis in Rabbinic Literature*, Cambridge, MA: Harvard University Press, 1991.
Wenham, David. *The Parables of Jesus*, Downers Grove, IL: InterVarsity Press, 1989.
Westermann, Claus. *The Parables of Jesus in the Light of the Old Testament*, Minneapolis, MN: Fortress, 1990.
Young, Brad. *The Parables: Jewish Tradition and Christian Interpretation*, Peabody, MA: Hendrickson, 1998.

PAROUSIA

Jesus taught that the kingdom of God was both a
present and future reality. The future aspect would
include an act of judgement against the Temple
and its leadership and such an event constitutes
the vindication of the Son of Man. At the same
time, the cataclysmic destruction of the Temple

marks the acceleration of the eschatological scenario towards the final dénouement and the consummation of God's purposes.

Parousia in the early church

A survey of materials demonstrates a relatively widespread and uniform hope for Jesus' return in the NT. Linguistically the phrase, "the second coming" is not found in the NT but it is signified by other terms:

1 *Parousia*, which means literally "presence after absence" or "arrival." In the Hellenistic world the word often referred to the arrival of a ruler in a city as inscriptions from Asia Minor and Egypt demonstrate (Deissmann 368–72). *Parousia* can be used in a non-eschatological sense in the NT (1 Cor 16:17; 2 Cor 7:6–7; 10:10; Phil 1:26; 2:12) or to refer to Christ's second advent (1 Cor 15:23; 1 Thess 2:19; 3:13; 4:15; 5:23; 2 Thess 2:1, 8; Jas 5:7; 2 Pet 1:16; 3:4, 12; 1 John 2:28).
2 *Epiphaneia*, which means "manifestation" or "appearance." It is used of the incarnation (2 Tim 1:10) and of Christ's return (2 Thess 2:8; 1 Tim 6:14; 2 Tim 4:1, 8; Tit 2:13; cf. *phaneroō* in Col 3:4).
3 *Apocalypsis*, which is translatable as "revelation" or "revealing" and signifies a form of divine disclosure (1 Cor 1:7; 2 Thess 1:7; 1 Pet 1:7, 13; 4:13).
4 *Day of the Lord*: this phrase is taken up from the OT (cf. Amos 5:18, 20; Obad 15; Zeph 1:7, 14; Zech 12:4) and is linked to Christ's advent in several places (1 Cor 1:8; 5:5; 2 Cor 1:14; Phil 1:6, 10; 2:16; 1 Thess 5:2; 2 Thess 2:2).
5 In Revelation the culmination of the narrative is the coming of Christ from the "open heaven" (Rev 19:11–21).

Belief in Christ's return fostered several pastoral problems in the early church. In 1 Corinthians 7 the "present crisis" (7:26 = persecution [Acts 18:1–18] and world-wide famine [Acts 11:28; Suetonius, *Claud.* 18.2; Tacitus, *Ann.* 12.43; Dio Cassius, *Hist.* 60.11]) and the fact that "time is short" (7:29 = *parousia* [cf. 1 Pet 4:7; Jas 5:8; Rev 22:7, 12, 20]) gave way to the Corinthians' questions about virgins and marriage which Paul answers. In 1 Corinthians 15, Paul attends to the problem of a lack of eschatological orientation in Corinth that either denied a future resurrection or had questions about the nature of a future resurrection body. In response, Paul places Christian resurrection in

relation to the consummation of God's plan of salvation. In 1 Thessalonians Paul addresses the problem of those who have already died in relation to the *parousia* (1 Thess 4:13–18). In 2 Thessalonians Paul warns against believing in false oracles or reports that the Day of the Lord has already happened (2 Thess 2:2, cf. 2 Tim 2:18); he argues that the Day will not occur until the man of lawlessness is revealed (2 Thess 2:3–12) and exhorts against idleness caused by eschatological enthusiasm (2 Thess 3:6–15). The second book of Peter addresses the problem caused by the apparent delay of Christ's return (2 Pet 3:3–18) and the epilogue of the Gospel of John confronts the erroneous belief that the beloved disciple would not die prior to the *parousia* (John 21:20–23). The issue of delay was apparent elsewhere in the early church (see 1 Clement 23–27; 2 Clement 11–12; *Apocalypse of Peter* and Justin *Apol.* 1.28.2) but nowhere did it lead to a complete restructuring of eschatology (Erlemann 1995).

In the gospels the central thread of Jesus' teachings concerns the kingdom of God. The phrase *hē basileia tou theou* ("the kingdom of God") is probably equivalent to the "rule" or "reign of God" and looks forward to the climactic day when God would reveal his kingship for Israel in a dramatic way. Modern scholarship has debated whether Jesus' eschatology was strictly futuristic (J. Weiss, A. Schweitzer, D. C. Allison, B. Ehrman), present/realized (C. H. Dodd, J. A. T Robinson, T. F. Glasson, G. B. Caird, N. T. Wright, A. Perriman), or inaugurated, i.e. now but not yet (J. Jeremias, W. G. Kümmel, G. E. Ladd, G. R. Beasley-Murray). There is good reason to support the inaugurated eschatological perspective since Jesus could speak of the kingdom as both present (e.g. Mark 1:15; Luke 11:20/Matt 12:28; Luke 7:28/Matt 11:11; Luke 16:16/Matt 11:12; Mark 4:11–12; Luke 17:20–21) and future (e.g. Luke 11:2–4/Matt 6:9–13; Luke 13:28–29/Matt 8:11–12; Luke 12:32; Mark 9:1/Matt 16:28/Luke 9:27).

Even if one consents to this inaugurated scheme there are still sayings that depict the kingdom as being somehow "imminent" (Mark 9:1; Matt 10:23; Mark 13:30) which comports with Jesus' apocalyptic orientation. In this case, it is supposed that Jesus predicted the end of the world and was simply mistaken in that estimation. But unlike other apocalyptic seers Jesus did not set a time-table for the end (Allison 1998: 130; Witherington 1999: 261–62) and so the kingdom's final consummation was indeterminate. Moreover, the imminence of the kingdom must be understood in conjunction with other complexes in which Jesus entertains the possibility of the delay of the kingdom. The trial or testing (*peirasmos*) has not yet occurred (Luke 11:4/Matt 6:13), persecution implies a further period of activity (Mark 8:35–38/Matt 16:25–27/Luke 9:24–26; Matt 10:16–25; Luke 11:49–50), the parable of the unjust judge contemplates the prospect of postponement (Luke 18:7), Jesus' refusal to drink from the "fruit of the vine" until the kingdom comes in its fullness (Mark 14:25/Matt 26:29/Luke 22:18), and his apparent ignorance of the timing of the end (Mark 13:32/Matt 24:36) may also be indicative of an interval of some kind. Similarly, the parables of growth (Mark 4:1–32/Matt 13:1–32/Luke 13:18–19/*Gos. Thom.* 9, 20), the reference to time being cut short (Mark 13:20/Matt 24:22), and the parable of Ten Talents, in which the nobleman goes to a distant country to become king (Luke 19:11–27), may be taken to involve some notion of delay. The paradox between Jesus' proclamation of both the imminence and presence of the kingdom is resolved when it is realized that Jewish thinking could accommodate the arrival of the kingdom as extending over time, in and through a series of events that could invade the present (e.g. *Jub.* 23; *1 En.* 91:12–17). What is more, some of these purportedly imminent sayings can arguably be identified with events other than a "cosmic meltdown" including Jesus' death (Mark 9:1), the destruction of Jerusalem (Matt 10:23; Mark 13:30), or the enthronement of Jesus into heaven (Mark 14:62). Consequently, the reference to the kingdom's imminence does not necessarily entail the imminence of the entire eschatological scenario (Witherington 1999: 263–65).

Others have argued that the references to delay or postponement are secondary and are projected onto the lips of Jesus by the early church in order to adjust their beliefs to match up with failed expectations (esp. in studies on the eschatology of Luke–Acts, but see Ellis 117–19). Against this view:

1 References to delay are multiply-attested and are therefore probably authentic.
2 The tension created by an apparent delay was not unique to Christianity as many Jews had already wrestled with the problem of the apparent delay of God's saving intervention, e.g. 1QpHab 7.6–14 (Bauckham).
3 Balabanski (1997) has pointed out that if the early church was disappointed by the failure of Christ to return, such a disappointment is not reflected in the key texts. The intensity of

hope for Christ's return fluctuated in some contexts and there was no definite tendency towards diminished eschatological enthusiasm since Matthew actually intensifies rather than plays down Mark's eschatological material.

4 If the delay of the *parousia* was so detrimental to early Christian belief then one must wonder why the church of the second century did not find the predictions inherently embarrassing (Wright 1992: 342–43, 459–64).

The coming Son of Man

The Son of Man sayings are much debated in meaning and authenticity. The predictions of the Son of Man's coming in particular have been variously interpreted. Several scholars (e.g. R. Bultmann, E. P. Sanders) think that Jesus referred to a figure other than himself who was to come in the near future. Others understand the coming of the Son of Man to represent a significant stage in the ushering in of the kingdom and the vindication of Jesus (C. H. Dodd, G. B. Caird, N. T. Wright).

In support of this last view of the Son of Man as a cipher for the vindication of God's representative is that it appears to be a natural reading of Daniel 7 (Wright 1992: 280–99; 1996: 360–67). If the text is read not as the prediction of the cosmic return of an individual from heaven, but as part of the well-worn Jewish pattern of suffering–vindication situated in corporate terms, then the Son of Man's coming and enthronement can be understood as the vindication of the saints. When this interpretation is applied to the gospels the picture that emerges is that Jesus pronounced judgement against faithless Israel and the wicked Judean leadership and that this judgement would be manifested in the destruction of the Temple which would constitute the vindication of himself and his followers.

The Olivet discourse of Mark 13 (Matt 24:1–36; Luke 21:5–36) begins with Jesus' disciples admiring the adornments of the temple and Jesus responds that the great religious monument will be thrown down. The disciples ask what will be the sign that such things are about to happen and the subsequent speech is an exposition of that point, namely the destruction of the Temple. The content of vv. 5–23 concerns the tumultuous event leading up to the sacking of Jerusalem, including rumours of war, messianic pretenders, persecution by authorities, familial discord and the desecration of the Temple. The object of vv. 24–28 is the coming of the Son of Man. The accompanying language about the stars falling and so forth invests a socio-political disaster with cosmic imagery in order to underscore its catastrophic significance. Whether the "coming" of the Son of Man is from heaven to earth or from earth to heaven is ultimately of little significance; what really counts is the transfer of sovereignty, the display of judgement, and the enthronement of the Son of Man (Perriman 55, 61). It may be possible to take vv. 32–37 as referring to Jesus' *parousia* or to detect a merging of historical and eschatological events throughout the speech, but this is far from certain. The most obvious point of reference is that the entire speech refers to the destruction of Jerusalem which is a vindication of Jesus as the prophet who opposed the Temple. That is confirmed by the reference to the fig tree in v. 28, which links the Olivet discourse to the parabolic statement about the fig tree in Mark 11:12–23 that also intimated the destruction of the Temple. Another confirmation is the mention of "this generation" in v. 30, who are not those alive at the *parousia*, but those who will be alive when the destruction of the Temple takes place. The Olivet discourse then does not *directly* involve events beyond 70 CE (McKnight 130–39).

This perspective may shed new light on a whole range of complexes. In the so-called "Q Apocalypse" (Luke 17:22–37/Matt 24:26–28, 37–41) when judgement comes, as in the days of Noah and Lot, Jesus warns his audience to do all that they can to escape without hesitation. This may be a better description of refugees fleeing a city before they are taken in judgement rather than warning about a cosmic rapture. Jesus commissioned his disciples to be heralds of judgement, warning of the coming of the Son of Man and judgement in their own lifetime (Matt 10:23). Persistence is needed in the current climate like a widow badgering a corrupt judge because the Son of Man will soon vindicate his people, but will he find faith at that time (Luke 18:1–8)? Servants are expected to be awake and alert with lamps lit for when the master returns from a wedding banquet (Luke 12:35–38). Or maidens waiting for the bridegroom should have enough oil to keep their lamps glowing until he comes (Matt 25:1–13). The Son of Man will break into a house like a thief in the night (Luke 12:39–40/Matt 24:43–44; *Gos. Thom.* 21, 103). The faithful and wise steward who is about his business will be rewarded while the cruel steward will be beaten when the master returns (Luke 12:41–48/Matt 24:45–51). The nations are summoned by the Son of Man to effect judgement and the Jerusalemites are judged on the basis of

how they responded to the Son's emissaries (Matt 25:31–46; cf. links to the mission discourse in Matt 10:1–42 and par.). The early church did not completely abandon belief in a historical judgement for a purely eschatological one, as Paul maintained that the Judeans could face wrath because of their rejection of Christ (Rom 9:22) or for hindering Christ's envoys (1 Thess 2:15–16).

Several units, though often regarded as referring to Jesus' second coming, are better understood as a parabolic descriptions of Jesus' mission to go to Jerusalem to announce, embody, and enact the return of YHWH to Zion. Jesus reportedly weeps over Jerusalem, he longs to protect the people like a hen protects her chicks, but the inhabitants will be judged and the temple destroyed because they did not welcome the one who comes in the name of the Lord (Luke 13:34–35/Matt 23:37–39). When a rightful king returned from afar, his servants would be rewarded but his opponents would incur judgement (Luke 19:11–27/Matt 25:14–30/*Gos. Naz.* §3). In Luke 12:35–48, we have a cycle of stories that call for readiness and watchfulness about the coming of the Son of Man or Master. Yet these sayings are also linked to units that promise that the master will gird up his loins like a servant, recline with his subjects, and serve them (Luke 12:37; cf. Mark 10:45). In Luke's context these warnings are in proximity to sayings that Jesus has come to cast fire and bring division, and that he has a baptism to undergo, most probably referring to his death (Luke 12:49–51). Such material correlates more naturally with Jesus' ministry in Jerusalem than it does to his second coming. These stories borrow heavily from prophetic language and themes (Mal 3; Isa 40, 52) and signify that the day that YHWH becomes king and offers salvation to Israel is to be identified with Jesus' entry into Jerusalem as the new Davidic shepherd-king. This climactic moment would ferment division and be the catalyst for judgement (Wright 1996: 632–42).

Jesus and the *parousia*: final observations

Several pertinent observations can be made. First, the discourse of Mark 13 and the parables of Matthew 24–25 have as their primary referent the destruction of Jerusalem which constitutes the "coming of the Son of Man" and signifies judgement upon faithless Israel and the vindication of Jesus and his followers. Yet in many ways these enigmatic oracles allow or even demand application to a broader scenario that includes the judgement of the nations and restoration of creation. In fidelity to the narrative of Daniel 7, the judgement rendered against Jerusalem and the Judean leadership looks beyond the borders of Palestine and will eventually extend to the nations so that the pagan beasts like Rome get their just desserts at a future point (e.g. Rev 18). As Heinrich Holtzmann saw long ago, the destruction of Jerusalem itself marks the beginning of God's final judgement (cf. McKnight 145). The "Day of the Lord" and the "coming of the Son of Man" that bring judgement on Jerusalem remain a *typos* for a future judgement of the inhabited world and the salvation of the elect. As Jerusalem is the epicentre of the cosmos, what happens there must eventually spill over into the entire world. The reconstitution of a *New Israel* is for the purpose of projecting God's purposes into the world until the arrival of a *New Heavens* and a *New Earth* (e.g. Isa 66; Rev 21–22). The fact that Jesus spoke of a future resurrection implies that he did see beyond the portentous events of 70 CE (Mark 11:18–27/Matt 22:23–33/ Luke 20:27–39; Luke 14:14). Second, a prerequisite to the final eschatological dénouement is that the gospel must be preached to all nations (Mark 13:10; Matt 10:18; 24:14; 28:19–20; Luke 24:46–48; Acts 1:8) and although this can be partly attributed to the period prior to 70 CE (e.g. the success of the Pauline mission), ultimately this prediction calls for a more expansive fulfilment and a final consummation beyond that period. Third, if the coming of the Son of Man in the gospels refers to a transfer of authority from YHWH to Jesus (Perriman, then it arguably anticipates an on-going role in the exercise of that authority and, given the constraint of monotheism, looks forward to a time when that authority is returned to the Father (e.g. 1 Cor 15:24, 28). Fourth, according to Luke, the second coming is predicated on the ascension (Acts 1:11) and heralds a future completion of the Messiah's earthly work. Fifth, ironically the clearest mention of a second coming on the lips of Jesus occurs in the gospel touted as being the most uneschatological of the canonical gospels (John 14:3; 21:22). This shows that the Fourth Evangelist has not emptied his Jesus-story of apocalyptic motifs (although how these sayings relate to the historical Jesus will depend on what one thinks of John's tradition and theology). Sixth, if the Jesus tradition is employed in the "word of the Lord" in 1 Thess 4:15–17, this would support the view that Jesus was remembered as predicting a cataclysmic event that Paul believed would affect believers at a future juncture (cf. Mark 13:26–27; Matt 24:30–31). The prayerful cry of *maranatha* deriving from early Aramaic-speaking Christian circles (1 Cor 16:22; Rev 22:20; *Did.* 10:6) supposes something more than the destruction of Jerusalem and looks forward to Christ's return as well.

MICHAEL F. BIRD

Further reading

Allison, Dale C. *The End of Ages has Come*, Minneapolis, MN: Fortress, 1985.
—— *Jesus of Nazareth: Millenarian Prophet*, Minneapolis, MN: Fortress, 1998.
Balabanski, Victoria. *Eschatology in the Making: Mark, Matthew and the Didache*, SNTS 97, Cambridge: Cambridge University Press, 1997.
Bauckham, Richard. "The Delay of the Parousia," *TynBul* 31 (1980) 3–36.
Beasley-Murray, G. R. *Jesus and the Future*, London: Macmillan, 1954.
—— *Jesus and the kingdom of God*, Grand Rapids, MI: Eerdmans, 1986.
Carroll, John T. (ed.) *The Return of Jesus in Early Christianity*, Peabody, MA: Hendrickson, 2000.
Deissmann, A. *Light from the Ancient East*, London: Hodder & Stoughton; New York: George H. Doran, 1927; repr. Peabody, MA: Hendrickson, 1995.
Ellis, E. Earle. *Christ and the Future in New Testament*, Leiden: Brill, 2000.
Erlemann, K. *Naherwartungen und Parusieverzögerung im Neuen Testament: ein Beitrag zur Frage religiöser Zeiterfahrung*, Tübingen and Basel: Francke, 1995.
McKnight, Scot. *A New Vision for Israel: The Teaching of Jesus in National Context*, Grand Rapids, MI: Eerdmans, 1999.
Moore, A. L. *The Parousia in the New Testament*, Leiden: Brill, 1966.
Perriman, Andrew. *The Coming of the Son of Man*, Milton Keynes: Paternoster, 2005.
Wilson, Alistair. *When Will these Things Happen? A Study of Jesus as Judge in Matthew 21–25*, Carlisle: Paternoster, 2005.
Witherington, Ben. *Jesus, Paul and the End of the World: A Comparative Study in New Testament Eschatology*, Downers Grove, IL: InterVarsity Press, 1992.
—— *Jesus the Seer*, Peabody, MA: Hendrickson, 1999.
Wright, N. T. *The New Testament and the People of God*, COQG 1, London: SPCK, 1992.
—— *Jesus and the Victory of God*, COQG 2, London: SPCK, 1996.

PASSION PREDICTIONS

The passion predictions are multiply attested in the gospels: the predictions locate Jesus' death in the context of Jewish prophet–martyr traditions, they follow the Isaianic and Danielic patterns of suffering–vindication, and indicate that the historical Jesus saw his death as redemptive and functioning to absorb the messianic woes about to fall upon Israel.

Survey of materials

Three explicit passion predictions are given in the Synoptic Gospels:

First prediction	Mark 8:31	Luke 9:22	Matt 16:21
Second prediction	Mark 9:31	Luke 9:44	Matt 17:22–23
Third prediction	Mark 10:32–34	Luke 18:31–33	Matt 20:17–19

In the Markan framework these predictions function to change the tone and direction of Mark's narrative and propel Jesus towards the cross. Although Mark has obliquely intimated Jesus' fate earlier (e.g. Mark 2:18–20; 3:6; 6:6–31), prior to Mark 8:30 he portrays Jesus as the powerful Son of God who is sovereign over nature, illness and evil spirits. The thrice-repeated passion predictions in the second half of the story dramatically alter the mood of the gospel and identify Jesus as the suffering Son of Man whose dark fate is divinely ordained (Mark 8:31; 14:21). Luke and Matthew redact this material in their own ways. For Luke, the passion predictions are tied to his portrayal of Jesus as the rejected prophet (Luke 4:16–30; 9:51; 13:33) while Matthew situates the sayings in light of his emphasis on Jesus as the righteous Jewish martyr-king (Matt 16:15–19). Echoes of Dan 7:13, 25 and 12:2 are evident and the reference to resurrection may substantiate an allusion to Isa 53:11–12. It is impossible to tell for certain if these sayings were repeated by Jesus during his ministry or whether their repetition is part of the looming shadow of the cross that unfolds in the narrative due to the literary artistry of the Evangelists. The saying has been shaped by the tellers of the passion story after the events themselves (hence Mark's "after three days" is changed by Matthew and Luke to "on the third day"), but at its core we probably have a single saying, a Jesuanic *mashal* to the effect that "the man is to be handed over to sinful men and they will kill him and some time after he will rise".

The Fourth Gospel has its own set of predictions which merge the Johannine Jesus' death with his exaltation and glorification. John speaks of the "lifting up" of the Son of Man (John 3:14; 8:28; 12:32, 34) as well as his "glory" (John 12:23; 13:31; 17:5; 21:19) which are allusions to Jesus' death. These sayings represent traditional material being interpreted through a grid of incarnational Christology that attributes both soteriological and doxological significance to Jesus' death. Closer to the Synoptic Tradition is the logion in John 2:19–22 where Jesus predicts that the temple of his body will be torn down and raised within three days (cf. Mark 14:58; 15:29; Matt 26:61; *Gos. Thom.* 71; Acts 6:14).

There is a whole range of sayings that contain predictions of suffering and vindication.

1 *Parables.* The parable of the bridegroom (Mark 2:18–20) relates the taking away of the bridegroom to a climactic "day" which is probably a reference to the "Day of the Lord" (cf. Amos 5:18, 20; Obad 15; Zeph 1:7, 14; and esp. Zech 12:4). The parable of the Wicked Tenants (Mark 12:1–12), including the reference to Ps 118:22, interprets Jesus' death and vindication at the hands of the Jewish leadership in images reminiscent of the vineyard allegory of Isaiah 5. One can add here the enigmatic utterance that "the poor you will have always ... but you will not always have me" (Mark 14:7; Matt 26:11; John 12:8) that implies a premature death.

2 *Last Supper tradition.* That Jesus spent a final quasi-passover meal with his disciples prior to his execution is well attested (1 Cor 11:23–26; Mark 14:17–31; Luke 22:13–38; Matt 26:20–30), and at this meal Jesus probably intimated his coming death, its divinely ordained and scriptural character, and its sacrificial meaning, and spoke of the prospect of participating in the patriarchal feast in the kingdom of God in the future.

3 *Metaphors of suffering.* The Jesus tradition uses several metaphors to describe Jesus' grim fate. "Baptism" or being plunged into a flood has obvious connotations of judgement (Gens 6–7; Exod 14:16–31; Job 9:31; Pss 18:16–17; 32:6; 42:7–8; 69:1–2, 14–15; 124:4–5; 144:7; Isa 8:7–8; 43:2; Jonah 2:5). This imagery surfaces in Mark 10:38–39 and Luke 12:50 to the effect that Jesus must enter into the wake of God's judgement. In Luke's version the baptism saying is accompanied by a preceding reference to "fire" (Luke 12:49; cf. *Gos. Thom.* 10). It may be possible to correlate this mention of "fire" with the Baptist's prediction that the coming one would baptize with the Holy Spirit and with "fire" (Luke 3:16/Matt 3:11) so that Jesus saw his own role as a readiness to be baptized into the coming eschatological wrath. The "cup" metaphor is used in the gospels in connection to Jesus' forthcoming passion (Mark 10:38–39/ Matt 20:22–23; Mark 14:36/Matt 26:39/Luke 22:42; John 18:11). In the prophetic tradition "cup" could signify either Israel (Isa 51:17–23) or the nations (Jer 25:15–29) drinking the "dregs of God's wrath" (cf. Pss 11:6; 75:7–8; Ezek 23:31–34; Hab 2:16; Zech 12:2; 1QpHab 11.14–15; *Tg. Neof.* on Deut 32:1; *Pss. Sol.* 8.14; Rev 14:10; 16:19; *Mart. Isa* 5.13). Similar to the "cup" is the theme of the approaching "hour" of Jesus' suffering (Mark 14:35, 41; Matt 26:39, 45; Luke 22:53)

which becomes theologically significant in the Fourth Gospel (John 2:4; 7:30; 8:20; 12:23; 13:1; 16:4, 21, 25, 32; 17:1).

4 *Rejected-prophet sayings.* Jesus was seemingly aware of the prospect that he could experience rejection just like the ancient prophets (Luke 11:47–51/Matt 23:29–31, 34–35; Luke 13:34–35/Matt 23:37–39) and there is good reason to think that he did experience hostility at times (e.g. Mark 6:4/Matt 13:57; Luke 4:24; John 4:44). Such rejection appears to have given occasion to the "sign of Jonah" logion (Luke 11:29–30/Matt 12:39–40; 16:4) where the preaching and vindication of the Jonah-like prophet is a sign of judgement to his recalcitrant audience. Elsewhere Jesus depicts himself as destined to die in Jerusalem like the prophets before him (Luke 13:33). Jesus may have reckoned with himself being stoned as a false prophet (Luke 13:34/Matt 23:37; John 8:59; 10:31–36; 11:8). In the Lucan tradition Jesus is remembered as saying that he would be "numbered among the lawless" (Luke 22:37) and making further reference to the rejection of the Son of Man (Luke 17:25). The coming of Elijah would result in the suffering of the Son of Man (Mark 9:11–13/Matt 17:10–12). If Jesus did allow a woman to anoint him for burial (Mark 14:8/Matt 26:12) then he anticipated burial without anointing, or a criminal's burial.

5 *Ransom logion.* The logion in Mark 10:45/ Matt 20:28 depicts Jesus as saying that he will give his life as a ransom (*lytron*) for many, attributing redemptive significance to his death.

Religious background.

There were several streams of tradition that may have influenced both Jesus' formulation of his death and resurrection and also the transmission of the tradition in in the early church.

1 In Jewish traditions there was a familiar pattern of the righteous who suffer unjustly and are vindicated by God (Pss 22; 69; 34; 118; Isa 52–53; Dan 7, 12; Wis 2:10–24; 3:1–19; 5:1–23; *T. Mos.* 10.9).

2 The Hellenistic period witnessed the origin of martyrdom stories that narrated the death of Jewish heroes who paid for their faithfulness to the covenant with their lives (1 Macc 2:50; 6:44; 2 Macc 7:33–38; 1QS 5.6; 8.3–10).

3 The use of "Son of Man" as a self-designation by Jesus is disputed in authenticity, origin

and meaning; nonetheless, the explicit passion predictions in Mark 8:31, 9:31, 10:32–34 and par., show clear dependence on Daniel 7. One possible reading of Daniel 7 is that Jesus identified himself as the representative of Israel who suffers beneath the wrath of the pagan beasts but is ultimately vindicated and co-enthroned with God on behalf of Israel.

4 The significance of the Suffering Servant of Isaiah 52–53 for understanding both Jesus and the early church remains mooted in scholarship. Still, it represents a certain pool of tradition that was available to Jesus, Paul and the Evangelists to use in their reflection on the motifs of death, atonement and vindication. That Jesus merged the figures of Isaiah's Servant, Daniel's Son of Man and the Messiah in his own vocation continues to command supporters (e.g. Stuhlmacher 1.124, 127–30).

5 In the Greek tradition several philosophers paid with their lives for their subversive attitude or offensive behaviour (e.g. Socrates). Cynic philosophers were said to have prepared themselves especially for death (see Epictetus, 4.1.153; 4.8.30–32 on Diogenes). Greco-Roman authors often depicted philosophers and rulers as exhibiting great virtue in their premature demise and lauded them for exemplifying the "noble death" (Seeley). Although Jesus' view of his death was probably not influenced by these Hellenistic traditions, they may have influenced the transmission or reception of the passion predictions outside of Palestine.

Authenticity

These predictions are frequently regarded as *ex eventu* sayings that have been placed on the lips of Jesus by the early church (e.g. Bultmann 1.29). The fact remains that these materials are just so widely attested in various sources across the tradition that it is difficult to detect a better established motif in Jesus' teachings (see list of sources and materials in McKnight 79–81). Moreover, the predictions of death and resurrection are entirely comprehensible in a first-century Palestinian setting. Jesus knew the traditions of the rejected prophets from Israel's sacred traditions (Luke 11:47–51/Matt 23:29–31, 34–35; Luke 13:34–35/Matt 23:37–39) and he saw himself in this stream (Luke 13:33). This perspective contributed significantly to his self-understanding, his exercise of the prophetic vocation, and the realization that a premature death awaited him, as several logia make clear. It did not take a clairvoyant to realize that if Jesus kept proclaiming the kingdom of God and amassing large crowds of people in the process then, like John the Baptist before him, he would find himself facing capture and execution. Jesus' itinerant movements across socio-political borders were arguably intended to keep him beneath the radar of Herod Antipas' security apparatus. The fact that Roman authorities did not hold back from using crucifixion to destroy political agitators at the vaguest hint of a threat meant that death on a cross was not an empty metaphor (cf. Mark 8:34/Matt 16:24/Luke 9:23; Matt 10:38/Luke 14:27) but a stark possibility. To add to that hope for resurrection or to interpret such a death in sacrificial terms (as was done of the Maccabean martyrs, e.g. 2 Macc 7:9–14; *4 Macc.* 6:27–30) is no less plausible.

It has been proposed that Jesus did not talk of his own death until entering Jerusalem (Evans 86–91). What counts against this is that the passion predictions and forecasts of suffering–vindication are set in pre-Jerusalem episodes. That Jesus' passion predictions precede his final period of ministry in Jerusalem is probable given that John the Baptist's demise may have prompted Jesus to speak of his own fate fairly early on; Jesus' experience of rejection from crowds and confrontation with Pharisees and Judean leaders in Galilee could have triggered such enigmatic predictions, and the fact that Jesus appears to have "scripted" his ministry with an assortment of texts including Isa 40–55, Ps 8, 1 Kgs 19, Zech 14 and Dan 7–12 which all include suffering and vindication (see Wright 584–91; McKnight 2005: 190–205, 238).

If Jesus spoke of his death it is probable that he also spoke of his vindication (McKnight 229). Dan 7, Isa 53 and Ps 118 all follow rejection with *vindication* and it is likely that this fuelled Jesus' hope that God would vindicate him. In the gospels this vindication can take on a variety of forms including the destruction of the Jewish temple (Mark 13:1–2, 26), enthronement as God's vice-regent (Mark 14:62), feasting in the kingdom of God (Mark 14:25) and resurrection (Mark 8:31; 9:31; 10:32–34). Did Jesus think that he would be raised with other Jewish martyrs at the end of the age, or did he anticipate his own personal resurrection ahead of the eschaton? While it is possible that the idea of resurrection after "three days" was borrowed from Hos 6:2 in early Christian reflection on the passion story, this is unlikely for two reasons: (1) Hos 6:2 is not directly cited anywhere in the New Testament even though it is remarkably fitting for the Easter events; and (2) "third day" is most likely idiomatic for "a short while" as in John 16:16–19 (see on three days/nights Jonah 1:17;

Matt 12:40; Luke 2:46; 13:32–33; Acts 9:9). The resurrection predictions then are predictions for an individual resurrection ahead of the general resurrection. Such an expectation is at once dissimilar to Jewish hopes which located resurrection as a corporate event set to transpire at the eschaton (e.g. Dan 12:2; 2 Macc 7:23; John 5:28–29; 11:24; 1 Cor 15:51–52). Yet this expectation corresponds to beliefs that prophets of old could return *redivivus* (Mark 8:28/Matt 16:14/Luke 9:19; Mark 6:14/Matt 14:2/Luke 9:7; Luke 7:16). For Jesus to speak of his own resurrection some time after his death but prior to the general resurrection is conceivable and not necessarily a Christianization of the story.

Meaning of the passion predictions in the context of Jesus' ministry

Albert Schweitzer advocated that Jesus intended to force God's hand to launch the kingdom and in doing so he allowed the messianic woes to fall upon himself (Schweitzer 347–49). In other words Jesus forecast an eschatological crisis that he himself would experience as a parabolic foretaste of what was to come, but also to brunt its full devastating effect for those entrusted to his care, those who now form the reconstituted Israel (see Wright 577–84; 609–10; Dunn 808–9, 817–18; McKnight 83–84, 119, 339; Pitre 381–507). Jesus drinks the cup of wrath and undergoes a baptism of fiery judgement as the hour of despair comes upon him. What is more, in Jewish eschatological hopes the onset of the period of tribulation was the prerequisite to the final restoration of Israel. Thus, by connecting his death to the tribulation Jesus was intimating that his death would have a positive effect for the Jewish nation. The New Exodus would be preceded by a New Passover (see Pitre).

It is also possible to plot the genesis of a pre-Easter atonement theology. The citation of Zech 13:7 in Mark 14:27/Matt 26:31 probably combines the coming tribulation with a model of vicarious atonement somewhat akin to CD 19.7–10 where the "poor ones of the flock" escape the judgement because of the death of the shepherd [= Teacher of Righteousness at Qumran]. The ransom logion (Mark 10:45/Matt 20:28) interprets Jesus' death in terms of a new redemptive event, and regardless of whether or not Isaiah or Daniel stand behind this logion, both books include atonement as part of the result of the suffering–vindication pattern (Isa 53:10–12; Dan 9:24). At the Last Supper, Jesus proclaims that the cup symbolizes the "blood of the new covenant which is poured out on behalf of many" (Mark 14:24/Matt 26:28/Luke 22:20; 1 Cor 11:25) that has overtones of covenant sacrifice and sin offering (Exod 24:8; Isa 53:10–12). Taken together this saying implies that Jesus regarded his death as having atoning value in the sense of being vicarious and protecting (McKnight 339). Jesus' death is *inclusive* as he is one from Israel who takes the place of Israel, but his death is also *exclusive* in the sense that he suffers in their place so that Israel or the "many" do not have to. Finally, I conclude with the words of McKnight (238):

> Jesus, from the time of John's death, thought about his possible death. And what he seems to have thought about was that he would die prematurely, that it was part of God's plan, that he was like other martyrs and prophets and figures in the Tanakh, and, most especially, that his death would occur at the onset of the Final Ordeal. The connection Jesus makes in the passion predictions to the Son of man is similar: as the Son of man experienced (what can only be called) eschatological tribulation, so Jesus himself, as one like that Son of man, will also suffer the Final Ordeal. And, like that Son of man, Jesus will also be vindicated.

MICHAEL F. BIRD

Further reading

Balla, Peter. "What Did Jesus Think about His Approaching Death?" in Michael Labahn and Andreas Schmidt (eds) *Jesus, Mark and Q: The Teaching of Jesus and Its Earliest Records*, Sheffield: Sheffield Academic Press, 2001, pp. 239–58.

Bayer, H. F. *Jesus' Predictions of Vindication and Resurrection*, WUNT 2.20, Tübingen: Mohr Siebeck, 1986.

Bultmann, Rudolf. *Theology of the New Testament*, 2 vols, trans. K. Grobel, New York: Charles Scribner's Sons, 1952.

Dunn, James D. G. *Jesus Remembered: Christianity in the Making Volume 1*, Grand Rapids, MI: Eerdmans, 2003.

Evans, Craig A. "Did Jesus Predict His Death and Resurrection?," in Stanley E. Porter, Michael A. Hayes, and David Tombs (eds) *Resurrection*, JSNTSup 186, Sheffield: Sheffield Academic Press, 1999, pp. 82–97.

McKnight, Scot. *Jesus and His Death: Historiography, the Historical Jesus, and Atonement Theory*, Waco, TX: Baylor University Press, 2005.

Pitre, Brand. *Jesus, the Tribulation, and the End of the Exile*, WUNT 2.204, Tübingen: Mohr Siebeck, 2005.

Schweitzer, Albert. *The Quest for the Historical Jesus*, third edition, trans. W. Montgomery, London: Unwin, 1911.

Seeley, David. *The Noble Death*, JSNTSup 28, Sheffield: JSOT, 1990.

Stuhlmacher, Peter. *Biblische Theologie des Neuen Testaments*, Göttingen: Vandenhoeck & Ruprecht, 1992, pp. 16–29.

Wright, N. T. *Jesus and the Victory of God*, COQG 2, London: SPCK, 1996.

PAUL, JESUS TRADITION IN

In the NT letters attributed to Paul, the person and work of Christ are central. Paul's primary interests, as evidenced in his letters, are the cross and resurrection of Jesus (e.g. 1 Cor 1:18; 2:2; 15:3–8). Only a few references to the sayings and activities of Jesus prior to his crucifixion appear. In this regard the Pauline corpus is not unlike other NT letters, the Acts of the Apostles and the Apocalypse. These too contain few quotations of or allusions to Jesus' teachings and deeds during his earthly ministry. Primarily, the traditions associated with Jesus' preaching, healing and disciple-making are recorded in the gospels.

The centrality of the cross and resurrection plus the lack of known Jesus traditions in his letters have led interpreters to wide-ranging conclusions. First, some scholars think Paul had limited information regarding the earthly Jesus. Since he was not an eyewitness and since he had limited access to those who knew Christ, his letters could not contain much in regard to Jesus' sayings, miracles, activities, etc. Those who hold this position situate Paul outside the first circle of disciples and emphasize that Paul's access to the Jesus tradition came mainly through the Hellenistic communities. Second, others conclude that Paul had limited interest in the Jesus of history. Paul's own faith in Christ has been formed primarily through powerful religious experiences of the risen Lord (Gal 1:11–17; 2 Cor 3:18–4:5; 12:1–10; Phil 3:3–16; cf. Acts 9:1–9). Accordingly, Paul's focus lies in the crucified, exalted and coming Christ; what the earthly Jesus may have said or done holds limited relevance to him. Third, others point out that too much is read into Paul's silence on the Jesus tradition, especially in light of a similar silence in the other NT letters. They argue that the paucity of Jesus tradition in Paul's letters does not mean that he had no access to or only limited interest in the earthly Jesus. According to these interpreters, there are other, more plausible explanations for the few references. We do not know, for example, what Paul may or may not have preached during his initial mission to any given city. Likewise, we do not know whether he viewed the letter genre generally as an appropriate vehicle for transmitting the Jesus material. Given the extent of orality in Mediterranean culture, it may well be that leaders like Paul preferred to preach Jesus rather than write about him. Nevertheless, Paul's letters do contain traditional materials that provide insight into the gospel Paul preached and the churches he established.

Paul's access to the Jesus tradition

Paul's access to the Jesus tradition came from several sources. First, prior to his conversion-call to be the apostle to the Gentiles, Paul persecuted the followers of Jesus and fought to stop the movement (Gal 1:11–14). As one "zealous for the traditions of his fathers," Paul's persecution of Jesus' immediate followers had some basis in beliefs and practices that went back to Jesus himself. While Paul never explained his pre-conversion opposition to the Jesus movement, he did report that the idea of a crucified Messiah is offensive to the Jews (1 Cor 1:23). Claims to Christ's divinity and religious devotion directed to him may also have been construed as blasphemy. Second, Paul described his transformation in language of mystical revelations (e.g. Gal 1:15–17; 2 Cor 12:1–6). These revelations caused him to reevaluate his understanding of Jesus and to join the community he had previously tried to destroy. In connecting with Jesus' followers, the apostle entered into the stream of tradition and reinterpreted his past and present experience in light of the beliefs and values of the Christian community. He received teachings and then continued to transmit them to various churches in his letters. It is taken for granted that his missionary preaching would have also contained references to these early Jesus traditions. Finally, in a rare autobiographical moment Paul related an experience he had three years after his conversion-call. He traveled to Jerusalem to receive information from Peter (Gal 1:18), and for about fifteen days he had immediate, personal contact with one of the Twelve. In subsequent visits he subjected his gospel to the scrutiny of the "pillar apostles" in Jerusalem and received their approval to carry his gospel to the Gentiles (Gal 2:1–9).

Paul's use of the Jesus tradition

Scholars disagree regarding the extent of the Jesus tradition in Paul's letters. Some allow only a few examples. Others argue that hundreds of allusions to traditional materials show up in the authentic letters. Likely the truth lies somewhere in the middle. Paul was aware of traditions regarding Jesus' Jewishness (Gal 4:4), his royal lineage (Rom 1:3–4), and his brother James (Gal 1:19). Beyond these bare facts there are other traditional elements.

1 Corinthians 15:1–8

Employing the language of tradition (*paredōka* = "I delivered"; *parelabon* = "I received"), Paul passed on to the Corinthians the centrality of Christ's death and resurrection. Paul inherited this tradition from the earliest churches that had already assigned atoning significance ("for our

sins") to his crucifixion. Furthermore, these crucial events were understood by these early Jewish believers as being "according to the scriptures." Soon after the crucifixion the followers of Jesus searched the Hebrew Bible to comprehend these fateful events in God's saving history. They found that not only had these events not contradicted scripture but Jesus' death, burial and resurrection had formed a fitting climax to the covenant story. Paul also received accounts of resurrection appearances to Peter, James (the brother of Jesus) and "the Twelve." According to both intra- and extra-canonical gospels, these disciples figure prominently in the Jesus tradition. Furthermore, the centrality of the cross and resurrection parallel other early Christian writings including the gospels where Jesus' passion comprises the central act of the story.

1 Corinthians 11:23–26

The earliest account of "the Lord's supper" is recorded in Paul's correspondence with the Corinthians. Paul "received" (*parelabon*) from the Lord this account that finds a prominent place in the Synoptic Gospels (Mark 14:22–24; Matt 26:26–28; Luke 22:19–20). Since Paul used traditional language, we may rule out that he received this as a direct revelation. Instead we should likely understand this in two ways: (a) the account goes back to an event in the life of the earthly Jesus, and (b) his interpretation of the supper came "from the Lord" by means of revelation (11:26). The details of Paul's account of the supper correspond closely to the NT Gospels. Paul knew that it took place at night, that Jesus took bread, gave thanks to God, broke it and gave it to his disciples. The "words of institution" bear close verbal affinity with the gospels as well. The memorial atmosphere of the meal corresponds to the Lukan account.

Romans 8:15–17; Galatians 4:6–7

Paul's address to God as "Abba! Father!" likely originated with Jesus. The similarities in Romans and Galatians suggest that Paul was relying on traditional materials. Both passages indicate that the "Abba! Father!" (a) characterized Christian prayer; (b) indicated the Spirit's work; (c) demonstrated that believers possess a new status as "sons" and "heirs." The presence of this Aramaic address to God in Greek-speaking churches is evidence of both its antiquity and its authenticity within the Jesus tradition. "Abba" is not a common prayer-address at the time and so it likely reflects Jesus' own prayer practice and teaching.

Words of the Lord

Most scholars allow that some of Paul's ethical instructions depend on the sayings (*logia*) of Jesus. Whether Paul had access to oral traditions or a sayings collection, as scholars reconstruct in "Q," we do not know. Nevertheless, there are parallels between some of the *logia* found in the gospels and what we find in Paul's paraenesis. In 1 Cor 7:10, for example, Paul instructed the married not to separate and, if they did, not to marry. He indicated these teachings came from "the Lord" and he contrasted them with his own counsel (7:12). The words of the Lord for him carried authority beyond his own. Likely, Paul referred here to the dominical teaching later codified in Mark 10:11–12 (cf. Matt 5:32). Similarly, Paul recalled the Lord's command that permits financial support for those who preach the gospel. This command is similar to the *logia* in Luke 10:7: "for the worker is worthy of his wage."

Allusions to Jesus' sayings occur in Paul's letters without referring to them as words or commands of the Lord. For example, in writing of love's supremacy (1 Cor 13:2) Paul echoed Jesus' teaching that faith can move mountains (Matt 17:20). Paul instructed the Romans to bless and not curse those who persecute them (Rom 12:14). This has clear resonance with Jesus' teaching regarding love of enemies (Luke 6:27–28 and Matt 5:44). Paul's reference to the day of the Lord coming as a thief in the night (1 Thess 5:2, 4) may well have originated in Jesus' teachings regarding the unknown day and hour when the Son of Man returns (Matt 24:43; Luke 12:39). Later in that same letter Paul's admonition for the Thessalonians to live at peace with each other (1 Thess 5:13) finds a clear parallel in Jesus' call to "live in peace with one another" (Mark 9:50). Other, possible examples include:

Paul	Gospels
Rom 12:17, 21	Luke 6:27–36; Matt 5:38–48
Rom 13:7	Mark 12:13–17
Rom 13:8–10	Mark 12:18–34; Matt 22:34–40; Luke 10:25–28
Rom 14:14	Mark 7:15; Matt 15:11
1 Thess 5:3	Luke 12:39ff.; 21:34
1 Thess 5:6	Mark 13:37; Matt 24:42; Luke 21:34, 36

The kingdom of God

The gospel traditions portray Jesus as one who proclaims the presence and coming of "the kingdom of God" (alternatively, "the kingdom of heaven"). Outside the gospels, Paul employed kingdom language more than any other NT writer. The apostle described the kingdom as consisting of justice (righteousness), peace and joy in the Holy Spirit (Rom 14:17). He urged the Thessalonians to walk worthy of God who is calling them into his kingdom and glory (1 Thess 2:12). The gospel Paul preaches is, in fact, a word about the kingdom (1 Thess 2:9–13). He warned the Corinthians that the kingdom is more than fine words and rhetoric; it consists of power (1 Cor 4:20). The unrighteous and immoral, Paul wrote, will not "inherit" the kingdom (1 Cor 6:9; Gal 5:21; cf. Eph 5:5) neither will flesh and blood (1 Cor 15:50). The kingdom figures ultimately in Paul's understanding of the *eschaton*. Following the Parousia, the Son will deliver the kingdom over to God the Father after the subjection of all the powers to the Son so that "God may be all in all" (1 Cor 5:20–28). In Col 1:12–13 Paul gives thanks to God for delivering believers from the domain of darkness and transferring them into the kingdom of his beloved Son. For Paul, the rule of God is realized in the Lordship of Christ, who is the source of forgiveness and redemption. As in the gospels, there is an "already–not yet" aspect to Paul's teaching of the kingdom. Likely Paul's ideas about the kingdom draw from the Jesus tradition. Still the language of the kingdom is not as common in the letters as it is in the gospels. This has caused some scholars to question whether Paul's essential message is congruent with Jesus' teaching. Others find similarity in Paul's teaching of the Spirit. In the gospels God's rule is manifest through Jesus by the Spirit (Matt 12:28; cf. Luke 11:20). For Paul God's rule is manifest now in the Spirit of God whom he also calls "the Spirit of Christ" (Rom 8:9; 14:17). The Spirit's powerful presence constitutes a new reality or new creation (2 Cor 5:17) that for the apostle may well correlate with the presence of the kingdom (1 Cor 6:9–11; Gal 4:6–7).

The law of Christ

Many scholars believe that when Paul speaks of "the law of Christ" (Gal 6:2) he had in mind Jesus' teaching on the greatest commandment (Mark 12:28–34 and par.). The command to love God and love one's neighbor is derived initially from the Hebrew scriptures (Deut 6:6–8; Lev 19:18) and yet becomes "the law of Christ" through the weight of his teaching and example. Earlier in the letter Paul urged the Galatians to pursue freedom through service, acknowledging that the entire Law is fulfilled in loving one's neighbor (Gal 5:13–14; Lev

19:18; cf. Rom 13:8–10). Such service clearly includes bearing one another's burden. It follows that "the law of Christ" may refer to Christ's example as one who fulfills the law (Matt 5:17–20).

Imitation of Christ

In Paul's day the imitation of a worthy person was an important strategy in moral formation. On a number of occasions Paul appealed to the example of Christ and urged others to imitation. For example, he encouraged the Philippians to have the mind of Christ in humility and service (Phil 2:5–11). Elsewhere he instructed the Romans to put on the Lord Jesus Christ and avoid self-gratification (Rom 13:14). In the midst of Jewish–Gentile discord in the Roman church, Paul told them to welcome each other as Christ has welcomed them (Rom 15:7). The apostle even urged the Corinthians to imitate him since he imitated Christ (1 Cor 11:1). Admonitions to imitate Christ depend ultimately on having authentic traditions regarding Christ's life. The traditions about how Christ lived would have provided a script for imitation. When, for example, Paul taught the Romans to strive to please their neighbors, he appealed to Christ's example: "for Christ did not seek to please himself" (Rom 15:3). For Paul, Jesus' willingness to go to the cross may have been principally in view; however, this does not preclude other accounts wherein he gave himself for others.

The Twelve

The earliest historical reference to "the Twelve" is found in 1 Cor 15:3–8. Paul recounted the tradition that the risen Jesus appeared to an inner circle of disciples called "the twelve." He also recognized Peter's (Cephas') special role in the Jerusalem church (along with John; Gal 1:18; 2:9). This is consistent with the gospel tradition where (a) Jesus was concerned with restoring Israel (see, e.g., Matt 10:6; "go to the lost sheep of the house of Israel"); (b) he chose "the Twelve" by a prophetic act that reconstitutes Israel; and (c) he appointed Peter to a special leadership role in the new movement (e.g. Matt 16:13–20). Paul reflected similar priorities in his own ministry. Although the risen Christ appointed Paul to be the apostle to the Gentiles (Gal 1:16; 2:7–10), he took the gospel first to Jews (Rom 1:16). Furthermore, recent scholarly inquiry into the theology of Romans demonstrates that Rom 9–11 is crucial to the letter. In these chapters Paul was occupied with the relationship of Israel to the Gentiles now that the Messiah has come.

Employing the image of an olive tree, he portrayed God's inclusion of the nations into Israel through faith. He was even able to describe the church of believing Jews and Gentiles as "the Israel of God" (Gal 6:16).

In the Gentile mission the relationship of Jews to Gentiles at the common table constituted a fundamental problem. In Antioch Paul opposed Peter publicly for his hypocrisy when the latter withdrew from fellowship with the Gentiles. Paul's description of Gentiles as "sinners" (Gal 2:15) may well recall that opponents charged Jesus with being a friend of sinners (e.g. Mark 3:13–17; Luke 15). That Jesus is known to have welcomed sinners may have inspired Paul to welcome Gentiles and advocate mutual welcoming among his churches (Rom 14–15).

Conclusion

The centrality of the cross and resurrection plus the lack of Jesus tradition in Paul's letters has given risen to the Jesus–Paul debate, a question that has occupied scholarly interest since the nineteenth century. Essentially, the question may be expressed this way: what is the relationship between Jesus' message of the kingdom of God and Paul's gospel of the crucified and risen Christ? On one end of the spectrum, some affirm that Paul's gospel of the Son of God (e.g., Rom 1:3–4) represented a significant departure from Jesus' imminent announcement of the kingdom. From this perspective Paul was an innovator who introduced foreign elements into the Jesus movement. On the opposite end, others deny the claim and assert that Paul's gospel was a legitimate development of the kingdom message of Jesus. While not denying that differences did exist between them, these interpreters explain the differences as necessitated by (a) the demands of the gentile mission and (b) the new situation created by the cross and resurrection of Jesus. Consensus on the Jesus–Paul question is unlikely without the introduction of new methods into future research.

At one time it was scholarly commonplace to interpret 2 Cor 5:16 as evidence that Paul had little interest in the life of Jesus. It is now widely recognized that the phrase *kata sarka* ("according to the flesh") is an adverbial modifier, not a reference to the earthly life of the Messiah. Paul's point is to emphasize that the new creation inaugurated by the cross and resurrection has altered his perspective on everyone, especially the Messiah.

DAVID B. CAPES

Further reading

Allison, Dale C. "The Pauline Epistles and the Synoptic Gospels: The Pattern of the Parallels," *NTS* 28 (1982) 1–32.

Bultmann, Rudolph. "The Primitive Christian Kerygma and the Historical Jesus," in Carl E. Bratten and Roy A. Harrisville (eds) *The Historical Jesus and the Kerygmatic Christ: Essays on the New Question of the Historical Jesus*, New York: Abingdon, 1964.

Davies, W. D. *Paul and Rabbinic Judaism: Some Rabbinic Elements in Pauline Theology*, revised edition, Philadelphia, PA: Fortress, 1980.

Dungan, David L. *The Sayings of Jesus in the Churches of Paul*, Oxford: Blackwell, 1971.

Dunn, James D. G. *Jesus, Paul and the Law: Studies in Mark and Galatians*, Louisville, KY: Westminster John Knox, 1990.

Dunn, James D. G. "Jesus Tradition in Paul," in B. D. Chilton and C. A. Evans (eds) *Studying the Historical Jesus: Evaluations of the State of Current Research*, NTTS 19, Leiden: Brill, 1994, pp. 155–78.

—— *The Theology of Paul the Apostle*, Grand Rapids, MI: Eerdmans, 1998.

Ellis, E. Earle. *The Making of the New Testament Documents*, Leiden: Brill, 2002.

Furnish, Victor Paul. "The Jesus–Paul Debate: From Baur to Bultmann," *BJRL* 47 (1965) 343.

Hengel, Martin. *Between Jesus and Paul*, Philadelphia, PA: Fortress, 1983.

Machen, J. Gresham. *The Origin of Paul's Religion*, Grand Rapids, MI: Eerdmans, 1947.

Wedderburn, A. J. M. and C. Wolff (ed.) *Paul and Jesus*, JSNTSS 37, Sheffield: JSOT, 1989.

Wenham, David. *Paul: Follower of Jesus or Founder of Christianity?* Grand Rapids, MI: Eerdmans, 1995.

—— *Paul and Jesus: The True Story*, Grand Rapids, MI: Eerdmans, 2002.

Wrede, William. *Paul*, London: Philip Green, 1907.

PEACE

Although the Greek word *eirēnē* originally signified rest from the turmoil of war, in the centuries prior to Jesus it was also used to refer to inner peace or tranquility of the soul. Interpreters of Jesus' teaching concerning peace have at various times highlighted both of these themes. Those who penned the nineteenth-century "lives of Jesus" generally regarded Jesus as a moral teacher who sought to bring interior, spiritual peace; meanwhile, a parallel stream of interpretation persistently sought to demonstrate Jesus' political aspirations, sometimes even his affinity with the revolutionary Zealot movement (e.g. Brandon). Most contemporary scholars locate Jesus somewhere between these two extremes. A more precise interpretation of Jesus' peace stance requires an understanding of the Jewish concept of *shalom* that informed his life and teaching. Moreover, Jesus' ministry and its New Testament interpretation must be viewed against the backdrop of Jewish discontent with an imposed *Pax Romana*.

Shalom in the OT

The Hebrew word *shalom* has been interpreted variously as totality or wholeness (Pedersen), well-being (von Rad), harmony/fulfillment (Harris *et al.*), or even justice (cf. Isa 32:17–18; 59:8). All agree it is deeper and broader than both inner tranquility and absence of war. Its connection to *shillem* (requital, payment of compensation) suggests that it also involves "debts fully paid"/"no outstanding issues"/"nothing standing between persons or between a person and God." *Shalom* reigns, for individuals and communities, when all material, social and spiritual needs are met, when "there is no more debt" (Ott 10).

Israel's prophetic hope was that God would bring about full *shalom* – would meet all needs, arrange payment of all debts, create justice and wholeness. To confess "our God reigns" was construed as a "Gospel of *shalom*" (Isa 9:6–7; 52:7; Zech 9:9–10). Isaiah expressed the hope that God's faithful servant would "pay the debt" – would by his stripes make Israel whole (*shalom*).

Pax Romana

The beginning of the Common Era was a time of unprecedented peace and prosperity for the Roman Empire. The celebrated *Pax Romana*, associated in particular with the consolidation of Roman power under Caesar Augustus, provided safety and security for most of the known world. But the *Pax Romana* encompassed more than just politics; indeed, for the Romans this peace was a sign of the gods' favor and was therefore an affirmation of the legitimacy of imperial rule. In return for ushering in this era of peace, Augustus was praised as the savior of Rome and even a son of god (Wengst).

But not everyone experienced this as a golden age. In Palestine, far from the center of Roman power, many Jews saw the Romans not as peacemakers but as oppressors. Heavy taxation, occasional Roman disregard for Jewish religious scruples, and a lively tradition of nationalist resistance movements sparked the rise of messianism and social banditry (Horsley and Hanson). Clearly, the Palestinian Jesus movement must be located within the broad spectrum of groups seeking to restore and re-envision faithfulness to Israel's God in this insupportable political situation.

Jesus as peacemaker

Those scholars who view Jesus as an itinerant Cynic sage generally interpret his teaching as a deconstruction of, among other things, political pretension (e.g. Crossan). Jesus' insistence that "the kingdom of God is within [or among] you" (Luke 17:20–21; cf. *Gos. Thom.* 3, 113; John 18:36) can easily be read as evidence that the peace sought by Jesus was a spiritual reality that could not be institutionalized.

Others see Jesus' ministry as a direct challenge to Rome's imposed peace. Jesus' announcement, "I have not come to bring peace, but a sword" (Matt 10:34; Luke 12:51; cf. *Gos. Thom.* 16; Luke 22:36), is occasionally interpreted as a call to arms; more often, Jesus' disclaimer is read as a refutation of those who imagine that he will countenance a facile peace that does not involve *shalom*.

Finally, a number of scholars argue that peace functions in the ministry of Jesus as both end and means. Central to this argument is Jesus' command that his followers love their enemies (Matt 5:44; Luke 6:27; cf. Luke 10:25–37; see Klassen). Walter Wink's (1992) convincing exegesis of the injunction to "turn the other cheek" (Matt 5:39; 6:29) suggests that Jesus did not advocate passive submission but rather non-violent resistance toward oppressors (Swartley 102–25). Jesus' notorious table fellowship with tax collectors actualized such teaching and demonstrated the potential of enemy love to effect communities of peace.

Seen from this perspective, Jesus' crucifixion was the culmination of his ministry of peace. It is difficult to ascertain what Jesus himself believed about the significance of his death; nevertheless, the belief, well-attested in early Christianity, that the cross effects peace with God (Rom 5:1–12) and erases enmity among humans (Eph 2:14–18) certainly coheres with Jesus' message that, unlike the *Pax Romana*, true peace emerges not from violence but from the expression of divine love.

Peace and salvation in the NT

The New Testament writers present Jesus as the *shalom*-bringer. At Jesus' birth heaven's messengers announce "on earth peace" (Luke 2:14). Influenced by the LXX's frequent rendering of *shalom* with members of the *sōzō* and *eirēnē* word group, New Testament references to saving/salvation and peace often encompass the breadth of meaning in the OT Hebrew word *shalom*. Jesus' own words to those he restored to wholeness and community were, "Your faith has made you whole (*sesōken*), go in peace (*eirēnē*)" (Luke 8:48; Mark 5:34).

Thus Jesus' saving ministry includes preservation, rescue, restoration, wholeness, justice, debts paid. To follow Jesus is by definition to be peacemakers, engaged in holistic ministry that creates *shalom,* including crossing barriers of race, creed and social status, loving the enemy, and choosing non-violent responses to aggression even at personal cost (cf. Matt 5:9–10, 38–48).

Reflecting on the significance of the cross, the New Testament affirms that Jesus "is our peace" (Eph 2:14) – that through his life, death, and resurrection, *shalom* is possible in all its dimensions, not least of which is the mending of shattered relationships with God, with others in the believing community, and among the divided peoples of the earth.

RYAN SCHELLENBERG
TIMOTHY J. GEDDERT

Further reading

Brandon, S. G. F. *Jesus and the Zealots,* New York: Charles Scribner's Sons, 1967.

Crossan, John Dominic. "Jesus and Pacifism," in James W. Flanagan and Anita Weisbrod Robinson (eds) *No Famine in the Land: Studies in Honor of John L. McKenzie,* Missoula, MT: Scholars Press, 1975, pp. 195–208.

Harris, R. Laird, Gleason L. Archer, and Bruce K. Waltke (eds) *Theological Wordbook of the Old Testament,* Chicago, IL: Moody, 1980.

Horsley, Richard. *Jesus and the Spiral of Violence: Jewish Resistance in Roman Palestine,* San Francisco, CA: Harper & Row, 1987.

Horsley, Richard and John Hanson. *Bandits, Prophets, and Messiahs: Popular Movements at the Time of Jesus,* New York: Winston, 1985.

Klassen, William. *Love of Enemies: The Way to Peace,* Philadelphia, PA: Fortress Press, 1984.

Ott, Bernard, *God's Shalom Project,* Intercourse, PA: Good Books, 2004.

Pedersen, J. *Israel: Its Life and Culture,* vol. 1, London: Oxford University Press, 1926.

Rad, G. von, "εἰρήνη κτλ.," *TDNT* 2: 402–406.

Swartley, Willard M. (ed.) *The Love of Enemy and Non-retaliation in the New Testament,* Studies in Peace and Scripture, Louisville, KY: Westminster/John Knox, 1992.

Wengst, Klaus. *Pax Romana and the Peace of Christ,* trans. John Bowden, Philadelphia, PA: Fortress, 1987.

Wink, Walter. *Engaging the Powers: Discernment and Resistance in a World of Domination,* Minneapolis, MN: Fortress Press, 1992.

—— *Jesus and Nonviolence: A Third Way,* Philadelphia, PA: Fortress, 2003.

Yoder, John Howard. *The Politics of Jesus: Vicit Agnus Noster,* second edition, Grand Rapids, MI: Eerdmans, 1994.

Yoder, Perry B. and Willard M. Swartley (eds) *The Meaning of Peace: Biblical Studies,* second edition, Studies in Peace and Scripture, Elkhart, IN: Institute of Mennonite Studies, 2001.

PHARISEES

Pharisees were a group of Jewish religious figures who appear, frequently in situations of conflict with Jesus, on the pages of the gospels. Sanders (1985) suggests they numbered about 6,000 in the time of Jesus (cf. *Ant.* 13.10.6:298; 18.1.3:20; 17.2.4:42). Their origin has been the subject of some scholarly dispute, though they seem to have flourished only prior to the destruction of Jerusalem (70 CE). Many contend that their name derives from the Hebrew *pᵉrûšîm*, meaning "separated ones." The nature and origin of this label are uncertain. They may derive from a group affiliated with the Maccabean Revolt. That they were meticulous observers of the Law is well-known (*Life* 191:38; *J.W.* 1.5.2:110; cf. Acts 26:5; Phil 3:5). They came from all classes and professions, and as a group they seemed to hold some political sway (*J.W.* 2.8.14:162; 2.17.3:411; *Life* 20–23:5; Saldarini), though some have contended that Josephus exaggerates their authority (Neusner). Their interpretation of the Law was nearly codified in tradition (παράδοσιν) of binding legal material, for which they received criticism (*Ant.* 13.10.6:297; Mark 7:6–13; cf. 1QH 4:10), especially pertaining to tithing and ritual purity.

Josephus claims firsthand knowledge of the Pharisees, having been among them himself (*Life* 10.12:2; cf. Mason). Among other things, they held to the resurrection of the righteous (*J.W.* 2.8.14:163), the immortality of the soul (*Ant.* 18.1.3:14), and a limited view of fate (*Ant.* 13.5.9:172; cf. 18.1.3:13; *J.W.* 2.8.14:162–63). Their depiction in the NT is routinely negative, especially with respect to confrontations with Jesus. Noteworthy are the portrayals of Pharisees criticizing Jesus for associated with "tax collectors and sinners" (Mark 2:16–17; cf. Matt 21:31; Luke 7:37; 19:7). However, Sanders (1990) suggests that the Pharisees were actually more tolerant than frequently characterized, though Dunn finds this unlikely.

The gospels depict Pharisees as prideful and contemptuous (Matt 23:5–7; Luke 11:43; cf. *Ant.* 17.2.4:41), particularly in contrast to the piety of, for Luke, the poor and humble (Luke 7:37–50; 15:1–32; 18:9–14; 19:1–10). They are noted for their outward perfectionism but inward corruption (Matt 23:23, 25–26; Luke 18:9–12; cf. *Ant.* 17.2.4:41–45). Mark, though not noted for his knowledge of first-century Palestine, nonetheless depicts the Pharisees' dissatisfaction with Jesus (though cf. 12:28–34), and plot against him (3:6; cf. 7:1; 8:11; 12:13). They contest his association with sinners (2:16), transgression of traditions pertaining to fasting (2:18), the Sabbath (2:24; 3:2), purity (7:3, 5) and matters of divorce (10:2–9). Regardless, Mark pays strikingly little attention to Jesus' response to them (cf. 7:6–13).

Matthew clearly escalates Mark's record of conflict between Jesus and the Pharisees. They appear early in the narrative and are pivotal in their conflict with Jesus throughout. At the outset, John the Baptist calls the Pharisees and Sadducees a "brood of vipers" (Matt 3:7). As in Mark, the Pharisees question Jesus' disciples about Jesus' associates (9:11), his disciples' violation of the Sabbath (12:2), hand washings (15:1–2), and divorce (19:3), and plot to destroy Jesus (12:14). John's disciples recognize that those of the Pharisees fast, but Jesus' do not (Matt 9:14). The Pharisees also accuse Jesus of casting out demons "by the prince of demons" (9:34; 12:24). The Pharisees are often coupled with the scribes. For instance, Matthew's Jesus urges his disciples that their righteousness must surpass that of the scribes and Pharisees (5:20). It is the scribes and the Pharisees who want to see a sign from Jesus (12:38). They, along with the Sadducees, test Jesus by asking him for a sign from heaven (16:1), and question him about hand washing (15:1–2).

In Matthew, Jesus is said to have offended the Pharisees with his teaching on cleanliness regulations (15:12). He also warns his disciples about the "leaven" (16:6, 11) or "teaching" (16:12) of the Pharisees and Sadducees. He uses parables to speak directly against them (21:45). In Matthew, Pharisees seek to trap Jesus (22:15), and join with the Sadducees to do so (22:34). The tension then escalates. First Jesus questions them (22:41), then chastises them as hypocrites (23:2–3) who keep people out of the kingdom of heaven (23:13) and make their proselytes "twice as much a child of hell" as themselves (23:15). They neglect matters of the law (23:23) and, though they look good externally, they are internally, "full of extortion and rapacity" (23:25, RSV; cf. vv. 26, 29), "like whitewashed tombs" (23:27). Finally, they appear before Pilate to ensure Jesus' tomb is sealed to prevent the disciples from stealing his body (27:62). For Matthew, the inept leadership provided by the Pharisees, among others, bears the blame for the imminent destruction of Jerusalem (Matt 24).

In Luke's thought, for which we must consider Luke and Acts, the Pharisees are not so clearly characterized. Jesus heals in the presence of the Pharisees (Luke 5:17), and they question him with accusations of blasphemy (5:21). With Mark and Matthew, Luke's Jesus is criticized by the Pharisees for his association with tax collectors and sinners

(5:30; 7:39; cf. 15:2), Sabbath observance (6:2; cf. v. 7), and washing before dinner (11:38). In response, Jesus criticizes the Pharisees for their external cleanness but internal "extortion and wickedness" (11:39). This sets up a series of teachings against them pertaining, as in Matthew 23, largely to matters of hypocrisy (Luke 11:42, 43; 12:1; cf. 14:3). Luke alone contains an editorial comment that the Pharisees were "lovers of money" (16:14), and uses them negatively in an illustration in a parable (18:10, 11). It was Pharisees within the Church who insisted Gentiles be circumcised prior to becoming Christians (Acts 15:5). And those outside the Church still squabbled with Christians (Acts 23:7, 8).

For Luke, the Pharisees did not so much test Jesus as "press him hard, and ... provoke him to speak of many things" (11:53, RSV; cf. 19:39). Nevertheless, they are also portrayed in a more positive light. It was they who invited Jesus to eat at their house (7:36–37; 11:37; cf. 14:1). They were seeking the coming of the kingdom of God (17:20). It was Pharisees who warned Jesus to flee Herod (Luke 13:31). In Acts it was a Pharisee, Gamaliel, who was a voice of reason when assessing the fledgling church (Acts 5:34). Moreover, it was a Pharisee who suggested Paul was innocent of accusations against him (Acts 23:9). John presents the Jewish leaders very generally, with the Pharisees frequently functioning as representatives of the whole (3:1; 7:32, 45; 11:47, 57; 18:3), though, as in Luke, there are some who betray openness toward Jesus (3:1; 7:50–51).

DANIEL M. GURTNER

Further reading

Baumgarten, A. I. "The Name of the Pharisees," *JBL* 102 (1983): 411–28.
—— "The Pharisaic Paradosis," *HTR* 80 (1987) 63–77.
Cohen, J. D. "The Significance of Yavneh: Pharisees, Rabbis, and the End of Jewish Sectarianism," *HUCA* 55 (1984) 27–53.
Cook, D. E. "A Gospel Portrait of the Pharisees," *RevExp* 84 (1987) 221–33.
Dunn, J. D. G. *Jesus, Paul and the Law*, Louisville. KY: Westminster/John Knox, 1990.
Kampen, J. *The Hasideans and the Origin of Pharisaism*, Atlanta, GA: Scholars, 1988.
Mason, S. "Was Josephus a Pharisee? A Re-Examination of Life 10–12," *JJS* 40 (1989) 31–45.
—— *Flavius Josephus on the Pharisees*, Leiden: Brill, 2001.
Neusner, J. *From Politics to Piety*, Englewood Cliffs, NJ: Prentice-Hall, 1973.
Saldarini, A. J. *Pharisees, Scribes and Sadducees in Palestinian Society*, Wilmington, DE: Michael Glazier, 1988.
Sanders, E. P. *Jesus and Judaism*, Philadelphia, PA: Fortress, 1985.
—— *Jewish Law from Jesus to the Mishnah: Five Studies*, London: SCM Press, 1990
Schwartz, D. R. "Josephus and Nicolaus on the Pharisees," *JSJ* 14 (1983) 157–71.
Westerholm, S. *Jesus and Scribal Authority*, Lund: CWK Gleerup, 1978.

PIETY, JEWISH

Piety, cult and life-commitment

Cicero (106–43 BCE) defines *pietas* as "justice towards the gods" (*iustitia adversum deos*) (*Nat. d.* 1.116), by which he means that piety is the rendering of religious duty or propriety. In each of the three cultures, Roman, Greek and Jewish, piety was expressed in careful attention to matters of cult by ensuring that all aspects of the sacrificial ceremony were carried out according to custom. The god must be rightly invoked in the right place, the correct prayers intoned, and the priestly actions precisely performed. Priests and worshippers were required to observe ritual purity. Failure in any of these matters would render the sacrificial act null and void, and amounted to impiety with respect to the divinity.

But piety was also expressed in showing respect to one's parents and ancestors, and in dutifully performing one's obligations to the gods in the non-cultic (i.e. non-sacrificial) sphere of life. In early Judaism, for example, Tobit's exhortation on piety to Tobias in Tob 4:3–19 is expressed without reference to the cult. Early Christians also understood piety in terms of moral duty. Such a view is well expressed in James 1:27 where the writer defines "religion" (Gk. *thrēskeia*) that is acceptable to God as caring for widows and orphans in their affliction and keeping oneself undefiled by the world. In Judaism, especially after the destruction of the Temple in 70 CE, prayer was understood as a replacement for sacrificial worship. Before 70 CE, in the Qumran community, prayer effects atonement in the absence of cult (see the Community Rule [1QS] 9.4–5).

All Jews were expected to undertake the duties customarily associated with Jewish piety, namely male circumcision, the keeping of the food laws, the observance of the Sabbath, prayer, tithing and fasting on holy days. Circumcision, an ancient rite not wholly unique to Jews, recalled the establishment of a covenant between God and Abraham and his descendants by which he would become a mighty nation (Gen 17:1–10). Jewish food laws seem designed to underscore a distinct ethnic identity especially apparent where Jews lived in a minority among Greeks and Romans. The observance of the Sabbath was recalled in the Hebrew Bible as a commemoration of both the completion of the creative work of God (Exod 20:8–11) and the redemption from Egypt (Deut 5:12–15). Sabbath-keeping was a major identity-marker of Jews in their Greco-Roman social context, and is commented upon frequently, often pejoratively, by Greek and Roman writers. The prayer of the Pharisee in Luke 18:12 mentions fasting twice weekly and the tithing of income. The early Christian work known as the Didache counsels readers to fast on Wednesdays and Fridays in contradistinction to the custom of the Jews (whom the writer calls "hypocrites") who fast on Mondays and Thursdays (8.1). Luke 2:37 records the regular fasting and persistent prayer of the pious Anna in the Temple precincts. For the vast majority of Jews, the synagogue was the dominant feature of Jewish life, not only in Palestine but also throughout the Diaspora. It functioned as a focus for community life, and in particular for prayer, and for the reading, expounding and study of scripture.

Jerusalem and Jewish piety

Jewish worship, unlike that offered by Greeks and Romans, was strictly aniconic and monotheistic. Most Jews were irregular in their participation in the cult because sacrifice could only be offered in Jerusalem. Only those who lived in close proximity to the Temple could sacrifice regularly. A two-drachma Temple tax was collected from all adult male Jews throughout the empire and sent to the treasury for the support of the cult (see Josephus, *Ant.* 18.312; Matt 17:24). After the destruction of the Temple, the cult ceased to be observed in a literal fashion. Nevertheless, reflection and teaching centred on the sacrificial system as though it was still in operation continued to exercise a powerful influence on Judaism. This is evidenced by Josephus, *Ag. Ap.* 2.193–98 and *Ant.* 3.224–57, the tractates of the Mishnah, and other rabbinic writings, and in Christian writings in Heb 10:1–3, *1 Clem.* 41:2–3 and the *Epistle to Diognetus* 3. Jerusalem was also the place at which Jews marked the completion of a Nazirite vow of special consecration to God (Num 6; *m. Ker.* 2.1; and, perhaps, Acts 21:23–26). According to the Mishnaic tractate *Keritot* (2.1), Gentiles wishing to become proselytes were required to offer sacrifice in Jerusalem.

In addition to Jerusalem being the only authorized place for sacrifice, the city was also the focus for pilgrimage. Deuteronomy 16:1–17 commands all male Jews to present themselves at three major

festivals. These were (1) Passover (also called Unleavened Bread, which was originally a festival celebrating the beginning of the barley harvest) commemorating the exodus from Egypt in spring; (2) Pentecost (also called Weeks because it occurred seven weeks after the end of Passover) celebrating the end of the barley and wheat harvests in summer; and (3) Booths celebrating the harvest of grapes and other summer fruit in autumn. Tobit 1:6 depicts an ideal custom of participation in the festivals as required by the commandment. Josephus (see, for example, *J.W.* 2.223–27) and the New Testament (see Luke 2:41–51; Acts 2:1, 5–11; 8:27; 21:15–36) testify to the large numbers of Jews and proselytes, and even gentile God-fearers (synagogue adherents) (John 12:20; Josephus, *J.W.* 6.427), who made pilgrimages to Jerusalem. Luke's gospel reports that Jesus' family attended Passover annually (Luke 2:41).

Such occasions, according to Josephus, sometimes resulted in outbreaks of violence and demonstrations against an occupying power as happened at Pentecost in 4 BCE (Josephus, *J.W.* 2.42–44) when indignant pilgrims besieged a Roman force from the province of Syria after the death of Herod the Great. Josephus asserts that 1,100,000 died during the final siege of the city which began suddenly at Pentecost in 70 CE. Most of the dead were Jewish pilgrims from all over the empire (*J.W.* 6.420; cf. Tacitus, who reports that the besieged numbered 600,000 in *Hist.* 5.13). The Gospel of John records that Jesus undertook several pilgrimages or was in the city at festival times (John 2:13 [Passover]; 5:1 [unnamed festival]; 7:10 [Booths]; 10:22 [Hanukkah]; 12:12 [Passover]). Nevertheless, the opportunity to undertake a pilgrimage, especially for those living outside Judea and Galilee, was probably not often taken. Philo of Alexandria (c. 20 BCE–50 CE) made the pilgrimage at least once (see *Providence* 2.64) and refers to the multitudes undertaking the pilgrimage and the sense of fellowship engendered by this act of piety (*Spec. Laws* 1.69–70).

Mosaic law

The Law revealed to Moses defines Jewish cultural and religious identity. It contains food laws and rules for keeping the Sabbath, as well as prescriptions for circumcision, the avoidance of ritual impurity and the restoration of purity, and the rituals appropriate for holy days and festivals. The law defines the pious life. The beginning of this devotion can be traced to the work of Ezra the scribe, who, on an appointed day in the mid fifth century

BCE, undertook to read the law to the assembled people (see Neh 8:1–12). It was interpreted to the people in Aramaic (see 8:8). The next day there was a gathering of all the heads of the ancestral houses to study the law (8:13). Hereafter the reading and study of the law became defining features of a Jewish life-commitment, and were perpetuated from this time in the practice of the synagogue not just in Judea but wherever Jews were found in any number.

The period from Ezra passed quietly enough, with occasional threats to Judean political and religious stability posed by Alexander the Great and the later Ptolemies, heirs of Alexander's conquest of Egypt. The Ptolemaic dynasty exercised a largely benevolent hegemony over Judea. However, the ascendancy of the Greek Seleucid dynasty in Syria from about 200 BCE was to have major repercussions for the practice of Jewish piety. The incursion of Antiochus Epiphanes, king of Syria, into Judean politics in the years 167–164 BCE resulted in the outlawing of some of the chief marks of Jewish piety. Most notably, Antiochus imposed a ban on circumcision. Objectors were forced to eat "unclean" food and to sacrifice to Olympian Zeus, for whom the Jerusalem Temple was appropriated (2 Macc 6:2). These outrages prompted a resistance movement consisting of those seeking righteousness and justice. However, their decision not to take arms against the Greeks when attacked on the Sabbath led to their defeat (1 Macc 2:34–38). Another rebellion was instigated by the minor priestly family of Asmoneus, which was soon under the headship of Judas, called Maccabeus (the "Hammer"), and his brothers. These rebels were prepared to fight on the Sabbath (1 Macc 2:39–41) in defence of their lives and the ordinances of the law. Mighty warriors known as the Hasidim ("pious ones") rallied to their cause. While the precise relationship between the Hasidim and the Maccabean warriors is unclear, both groups were insistent upon the need to resist not only the ethnic Greeks but also those Jews ("sinners and renegades") who were prepared to accommodate themselves to the king's decrees against the law (see 1 Macc 2:44). The Maccabean warriors were ultimately victorious and directed the cleansing of the Temple (1 Macc 4:36–58). Jonathan and Simon, younger brothers of Judas Maccabeus, were the first of a succession of princely high priests, the Hasmoneans, who exercised rule down to the early years of the reign of Herod the Great (37 BCE–4 CE).

Maccabean resistance to religious innovation perceived as a threat to Jewish distinctiveness and pious practice served as an inspiration in later Judean history, especially in defence of the Temple. In 4 BCE, as Herod lay dying, two popular scribes, outraged by the erection of an image of a golden eagle over the great gate leading into the Temple in defiance (Josephus explains) of the second commandment (Exod 20:4), incited the populace to hack it down to avenge God's honour (Josephus, J.W. 1.648–53). Not surprisingly, the tradition of pious resistance is carried on into the period of direct Roman rule from 6 CE. In that year, Judas the Galilean raised a revolt on the premise that Jews ought not to pay tribute to the Romans because God, not mortals, was their master (Josephus, J.W. 2.118). The next sixty years were punctuated by revolts and demonstrations prompted in large part by perceptions of pious duty. In the context of the real possibility that Jews might suffer for their piety, 4 Maccabees was written to exhort the pious to continued vigilance with respect to the law and to count the blessings of a heavenly reward and the resurrected state above the pains of martyrdom. Despite considerable differences between Jewish groups of the Second Temple era, all are agreed that piety prescribes obedience to the law as a matter of supreme priority.

Essenes

Essenes lived in communities throughout Palestine, and numbered about 4,000 according to Philo and Josephus. It has been strongly argued that originally they broke away from the Jewish priestly establishment during the early years of the Hasmonean high priesthood to form a community with its centre at Qumran by the Dead Sea. According to the Cairo *Damascus Document* – an Essene writing, fragments of which have been found at Qumran – the schism was prompted by arguments about the correct interpretation of the Mosaic law, among which failure to distinguish between clean and unclean are prominent (CD 5.6–7; 12.1–2; cf. the *Habakkuk Pesher* [1QpHab] 12.3–9). Essenes were zealous in the rigor with which they applied the law, drawing a neat distinction between themselves and other Jews, the Temple establishment included, even branding the Pharisees as "seekers after smooth things". They also followed a solar calendar in distinction to the solar/lunar calendar of the Jerusalem Temple. The Qumran text known as "Some Observances of the Law" (MMT, 4Q394–99) is best understood as a communication from the leader of the Qumran community to the Jerusalem priestly establishment detailing purity regulations that were the subject of debate. Philo describes a contemplative, ascetic Egyptian group called the Therapeutae ("healers") with clear affinities to the Essenes.

Pharisees

Pious devotion to the law exemplified by the Hasidim and the Essenes is also evident in the group of laymen known as Pharisees. They sought to engage the wider Jewish population in a movement to reform Judaism by not only applying to themselves the prescriptions for ritual purity prescribed for the priests in the performance of their cultic duties, but also devoting themselves to the demands of the oral law as handed down by scholar sages (see Matt 15:2; Mark 7:3, 5). Josephus testifies to the Pharisees' strictness of their observance of the law (*J.W.* 1.110; 2.162; *Ant.* 17.41; *Life* 191) and to their commitment to the oral tradition. According to the mishnaic tractate *'Abot* 1.1, the two-fold law, the written deposit and oral tradition, derives from Moses and was transmitted in an unbroken chain to Joshua, the "elders", the prophets, the men of the Great Synagogue, and then to scholars who teach it to the Pharisees. The oral traditions were only consigned to writing in the Mishnah (c. 200 CE). The New Testament Gospels are well aware of the Pharisees' observance of the oral tradition of the interpretation of the law (Mark 7:1–7), as is Paul (Acts 22:3; Phil 3:5).

According to Josephus, the Pharisees were the most accurate interpreters of the law (*J.W.* 2.162). Jesus accepts that they "sit in the seat of Moses" (Matt 23:2). Paul affirms that as a Pharisee he was blameless with respect to the righteousness required by the law (Phil 3:6). Josephus testifies to the popularity of the Pharisees among the people, even to the extent that the Sadducees were prepared to regulate the exercise of their public activity in accordance with Pharisaic teaching (see, for example, *Ant.* 13.288). To the people, the life-commitment of the Pharisees represented a pious ideal.

Jesus and the Pharisees

The Pharisees appear in the gospels, often with the scribes who were the authoritative teachers of the Pharisaic movement. They challenge the authority of Jesus and criticize his lack of piety with respect to the law (see, for example, Matt 15:1–2; Mark 2:15–17, 23–28; 7:1–23; Luke 11:38). Jesus, as the agent of the in-breaking kingdom of God, claims the authority to forgive sins, assumes lordship over the Sabbath as Son of Man (Mark 2:28), and does

not observe Pharisaic strictures of ritual purity but rather blurs the precise boundaries between clean and unclean that the Pharisees marked out with respect to meals. Jesus promoted open commensality in contrast to the Pharisees' insistence on maintaining carefully delineated distinctions between observant and non-observant Jews as required by their interpretation of the law. For Jesus, the interpretation of the Mosaic code in the tradition of the "fathers" missed the point of what really defiled a person (see Matt 15:1–20; Mark 7:1–23; Luke 11:38–52). Moreover, Jesus is critical of the ostentatious piety of the Pharisees (Matt 6:1), and also of their scrupulous concern for the minutiae (Matt 23:23–26). Yet the scribes and Pharisees, Jesus affirms, rightly occupy the seat of Moses (Matt 23:2).

The sustained attack on the piety of the Pharisees recorded in Matthew 23 may reflect a bitter struggle between the later first-century Matthean church and the rabbis, heirs of the Pharisees in the post-70 CE era. Nevertheless, Jesus is not an iconoclast with respect to the fundamental aspects of Jewish piety. He is zealous for the integrity of the Temple (Matt 21:13; Mark 11:17; John 2:16), upholds the sanctity of the law (Matt 5:17–20), attends the synagogue, and nowhere undermines the distinction between Jew and non-Jew.

Sadducees

The Sadducees, an aristocratic Jewish group, both priestly and lay, of the early Jewish era, did not observe the oral law but rather appealed to the sole authority of the written prescriptions of the Pentateuch. For this reason they did not believe in the concept of the resurrection of the dead since that doctrine is not found in the Pentateuch. At the time of the arrest and trial of Jesus, the chief priests were unwilling to enter the praetorium, as though that act would defile them and thus render them ritually unfit to eat the Passover, where defilement imposes a one month's postponement of the festival (John 18:28; cf. Num 9:6–12).

MARK HARDING

Further reading

Chilton, Bruce and Jacob Neusner. *Judaism in the New Testament: Practices and Belief*, London and New York: Routledge, 1995.

Cohen, Shaye J. D. *The Beginnings of Jewishness: Boundaries, Varieties, Uncertainties*, Berkeley and Los Angeles, CA: University of California Press, 1999.

Crabbe, Lester L. *Judaic Religion in the Second Temple Period: Belief and Practice from the Exile to Yavneh*, London and New York: Routledge, 2000, especially Part II.

Feldman, Louis and Meyer Reinhold. *Jewish Life and Thought among Greeks and Romans: Primary Readings*, Minneapolis, MN: Fortress Press, 1996.

Fine, Steven. (ed.) *This Holy Place: On the Sanctity of the Synagogue during the Greco-Roman Period*, Notre Dame, IN: University of Notre Dame Press, 1997.

Jeremias, Joachim. *Jerusalem in the Time of Jesus*, Philadelphia, PA: Fortress Press, 1969.

Murphy, Frederick J. *The Religious World of Jesus: An Introduction to Second Temple Palestinian Judaism*, Nashville, TN: Abingdon, 1991.

Neusner, Jacob. *The Mishnah: Introduction and Reader*, Philadelphia, PA: Trinity Press International, 1992.

Nickelsburg, George W. E. and Michael E. Stone. *Faith and Piety in Early Judaism: Texts and Documents*, Philadelphia, PA: Fortress Press, 1983.

Riches, John. *The World of Jesus: First Century Judaism in Crisis*, Cambridge: Cambridge University Press, 1990.

Sanders, E. P. *Judaism: Practice and Belief 63 BCE 66 CE*, London and Philadelphia, PA: SCM/TPI, 1992.

PONTIUS PILATE

Pontius Pilate was the Roman prefect of Judaea from 26 to 37 CE. It was during his governorship that Jesus of Nazareth was crucified.

Pilate's background

Virtually nothing is known of Pilate before his arrival in Judaea. He belonged to the equestrian class (the lowest rung of the Roman nobility); enjoyed free birth and a certain level of wealth; and may have distinguished himself on the battlefield prior to his appointment (on the date of this, see Schwartz 1992, who favours 19 CE rather than the generally accepted 26). It is often claimed that Pilate owed his position to the influence of Sejanus, the allegedly anti-Semitic prefect of the Praetorian Guard and a man with considerable influence over the Emperor Tiberius. The evidence for Sejanus' anti-Semitism, however, is weak (Philo's *On the Embassy to Gaius* 159–60 is highly rhetorical; see also Eusebius, *Hist. eccl.* 2.5.5). Sejanus may have been Pilate's patron, but the suggestion that he (and therefore Pilate) was anti-Semitic seems unlikely. Given Tiberius' expulsion of Jews from Rome in 19 CE (Suetonius, *Tib.* 36.1; Tacitus, *Ann.* 2.85.5), though, it is possible that his reign may have witnessed a less compromising attitude towards Judaea than those of earlier emperors.

Responsibilities

Pilate's title, prefect or *eparchos* in Greek (on which see the Caesarea inscription, Vardaman 1962), denotes a military posting. By 26 CE, Judaea had been under direct Roman rule for only twenty years and as the fifth prefect Pilate's first duty was to maintain law and order in the small but often troublesome province. In this he had only auxiliary troops at his disposal, amounting to five infantry cohorts and one cavalry regiment; in times of emergency he called on the more powerful neighbouring Syrian legate, who commanded four legions. Like earlier prefects, Pilate established his headquarters and provincial capital in the coastal (and predominantly Gentile) city of Caesarea. Most of his auxiliaries would have been stationed here, though others were scattered throughout the province with a permanent garrison housed in the Antonia Fortress in Jerusalem. At times, particularly during feasts, Pilate visited the traditional capital of Jerusalem accompanied by additional troops. It was at festivals that tension was at its highest and rebellion most likely to break out, though ironically the presence of the Roman governor and his troops only served to increase resentment.

Pilate's other duties included overall judicial responsibility for the province and the supervision of tax-collection. Like some other Roman governors he also struck bronze coins. These contained symbols from the Roman cult but no human images; their use until the time of Agrippa I (41–4 CE) suggests they were not regarded as unduly offensive by the Jewish residents of the province (see Bond 1996). Previous prefects had also appointed Jewish high priests. Joseph Caiaphas, however, was appointed in 18/19 by Pilate's predecessor Gratus and remained in post until shortly after Pilate's departure. Perhaps the two men worked well together, or perhaps (as Schwartz 1992 suggests) the right to appoint high priests was transferred to the Syrian legate by Germanicus during his tour of the East in 17–19 CE.

Jewish sources

Apart from a brief reference to Pilate's execution of Jesus in Tacitus (*Ann.* 15.44), nearly all of our information concerning Pilate comes from two Jewish writers, Philo of Alexandria and Flavius Josephus.

Philo, a contemporary of Pilates, gives a detailed account of an incident in which Pilate set up gilded shields inside Herod's palace (his Jerusalem headquarters) in honour of the emperor. These shields bore inscriptions noting the name of both the dedicator (presumably Pilate) and the dedicatee (Tiberius). Presumably the offence was caused by Tiberius' full name (Tiberius Caesar Divi Augusti Filius Augustus) which included a reference to his adoptive father, the 'deified Augustus'. When the presence of the shields was widely known, the people appealed to four Herodian princes who were in Jerusalem (probably for a feast). They appealed unsuccessfully to Pilate, then wrote to Tiberius who furiously ordered that that shields be removed to the Temple of Augustus in Caesarea (*Embassy* 299–305).

Running through this account are several slurs on Pilate's character: Philo suggests that Pilate's intention in setting up the shields was to annoy the Jews (299), later he is said to be 'a man of inflexible, stubborn and cruel disposition' (301), and Philo lists 'his venality, his violence, his thefts, his assaults, his abusive behaviour, his frequent execution of untried prisoners, and his endless savage ferocity' (302). Philo's narrative, however, cannot be taken at face value. It is part of a letter, supposedly written by Agrippa I to Gaius Caligula, attempting to dissuade the emperor from setting up a statue of himself in the Jerusalem Temple. Philo's/Agrippa's point is to show how a small infringement of the law angered Tiberius. It suits the rhetoric of the piece to darken Pilate's character as much as possible in order to emphasise Tiberius' fine imperial qualities (which contrast starkly with those of Gaius). Furthermore, all of the slurs used against Pilate are used of 'bad governors' elsewhere in Philo (especially *Flaccus* 105), suggesting they are stock charges used against anyone of whom Philo disapproves. While it would have been difficult for Philo to write such an account if Pilate were generally known to have been a saint, the specifics must be treated with caution.

Pilate's offence here does not seem to have been great. The Roman headquarters was clearly the most appropriate place for the shields and Philo admits that they were inside and contained no images; presumably there were many other articles containing the emperor's official name in the building. Pilate's reluctance to remove the shields was presumably not because he worried an embassy would expose his crimes but because he feared Tiberius' reaction if he dismantled shields set up in his honour. This fear would be all the more founded if the incident took place in the uncertain years after Sejanus' execution in 31 CE, when no provincial governor would wish his loyalty to the emperor to be challenged.

Josephus, writing several decades later, adds a further three incidents (besides the much disputed *Testimonium Flavianum*, *Ant.* 18.63–64). The first, narrated in both *J.W.* 2.169–74 and *Ant.* 18.55–59 (with slight variations), seems to have occurred early in Pilate's governorship, perhaps during his first winter. Josephus says that under cover of darkness Pilate moved a detachment of troops whose standards contained images of the emperor into Jerusalem. Next day, when the Jerusalemites saw the images, they went to Caesarea and appealed en masse for their removal. Since a squadron's standards were inseparable from the squadron itself, the request was tantamount to a request for the removal of the squadron from Jerusalem. On the sixth day, Pilate summoned the people, threatening to kill them if they continued their protest. They, however, bared their throats, declaring themselves ready to die rather than transgress ancestral traditions. Pilate, overawed at their religious devotion, removed the detachment. (For an argument that this is the same incident as that of the shields, see Schwartz 1983).

Again, this incident needs to be treated with care. Josephus is anxious to stress the strength of Jewish devotion to ancestral traditions in both works, and the *Ant.* (which accuses Pilate of deliberately intending to 'subvert Jewish practices', 18.55) suggests that a contributory cause of the Jewish revolt of 66 CE was the deteriorating quality of Judaea's Roman governors. The incident probably shows a new prefect intent on inaugurating his governorship with a firm hand and reluctant to allow provincials to dictate which troops he should use in Jerusalem. There is a certain insensitivity here and a determination to be master in his own province, but Pilate's readiness eventually to back down suggests a dislike of excessive bloodshed and a willingness to co-operate in the interests of maintaining peace.

The second event narrated by Josephus, again in both *J.W.* 2.175–77 and *Ant.* 18.60–62, concerns the building of an aqueduct for Jerusalem using money from the temple treasury. The scheme was presumably a commendable undertaking, one which would have benefited the city (and the temple) enormously. The Mishnah allows the use of surplus money for 'all the city's needs' (*m. Shek* 4.2) and Pilate presumably had the permission of Caiaphas and the temple authorities to use the funds. Trouble, however, broke out when Pilate was in Jerusalem (perhaps for a feast) and a riot ensued during which many were killed by Pilate's troops or trampled to death in the resulting stampede. The precise cause of the trouble is uncertain: *Jewish War* suggests that Pilate began to drain the treasury, perhaps demanding more than the surplus; *Antiquities*, however, notes a problem with the 'operations that this involved' (18.60), suggesting that the difficulty revolved around the route taken by the aqueduct or the method of its construction (which perhaps compromised the water's purity). The precise date of this incident is unknown.

Josephus' third and final story, found only in *Ant.* 18.85–89, recounts the events leading to Pilate's dismissal from the province. A man claiming to be the Samaritan Messiah (the Taheb) persuaded large numbers of Samaritans to climb the sacred mountain of Gerizim where he promised to reveal certain vessels deposited by Moses. His followers took up arms and assembled in the nearby village of Tirathana, preparing to ascend the mountain. Before they were underway, however, Pilate blocked their route with a detachment of cavalry and heavy-armed infantry; many prisoners were taken and the leaders and influential men were executed. Afterwards, the Samaritan council complained to Vitellius, the legate of Syria, regarding Pilate's excessive force: it was not as rebels from Rome that they had gathered, they argued, but as 'refugees from the persecution of Pilate' (18.88). Again, it is important to see beyond Josephus' negative bias. Perhaps the prefect's treatment of Samaritans was heavy-handed, but it must also be noted that any provincial governor who did not take such an incident seriously would be failing in his duty.

Vitellius ordered Pilate to Rome to answer to the emperor. This is not necessarily an indication that the legate accepted the charges against him; Vitellius was Pilate's superior in the East, but only the emperor could try a provincial governor. Pilate 'hurried to Rome', but found on his arrival that Tiberius was dead (March 37), a detail that locates his departure from the province early in 37 CE.

Pilate in the gospels

Apart from a brief reference in 1 Tim 6:13, Pilate appears in the NT only in the gospels. Luke 13:1 alludes to some Galileans whose 'blood Pilate mingled with their sacrifices' and Mark 15:7 (followed by Luke 23:19) mentions 'the riot' during which Barabbas was arrested. Both incidents have sometimes been linked with the riot associated with the aqueduct, but with no certainty. Pilate's long tenure undoubtedly included many unknown incidents; minor riots and troublemakers were probably a common feature, particularly during festivals. The remaining references to Pilate in the gospels occur during the trial of Jesus.

All four gospels agree that Jesus was handed over to Pilate by the Jewish priestly leaders, though only John records the presence of Roman troops at Jesus' arrest, a detail which suggests prior Roman involvement (John 18:3). From this point, however, the gospels differ enormously in terms of the precise sequence of events, the details of Jesus' trial, and Pilate's attitude towards both Jesus and his Jewish opponents.

Mark's Pilate is often said to be a weakling, vainly attempting to release Jesus but forced, in the end, to send him to the cross (see Winter). Read in a first-century context, however, this seems unlikely: the governor's repeated references to Jesus as 'King of the Jews' or 'your King' seem calculated to test the crowd, to see whether they would stand up for a messianic leader, rather than serious attempts to free him. There is no doubt that Mark places primary responsibility for Jesus' death on the Jewish leaders, but Pilate is not exonerated. John too presents a harsh, mocking Pilate. The central scene of the trial narrative depicts Jesus' flogging and mockery, a mockery which continues until the final dramatic scene when it is only at the chief priests' acceptance that they have 'no king but Caesar' (John 19:15) that Pilate hands Jesus over to crucifixion (on Pilate in John, see Rensberger 1988; in the gospels generally, see Bond 1998).

Matthew, who follows Mark closely, is more interested in heightening Jewish responsibility than he is in Rome: alone of the Evangelists, he introduces Pilate's wife, who declares Jesus righteous; Pilate's washing of his hands (a ritual which follows Deut 21:6–9) and declaration of his own innocence; and the crowd's final acceptance of responsibility (27:25). Pilate for Matthew – and probably the other Evangelists too – represents the type of Roman governor before whom Christians may be forced to stand trial.

In contrast, Luke's Pilate is a weakling. Faced with three specific charges against the prisoner, he declines to take the case seriously and sends him to Antipas (who was also in Jerusalem for the feast). Three times Pilate declares Jesus innocent but lacks the resolve to release him when faced with opposition from the Jewish crowd. Luke is anxious to show that Jesus was innocent under Roman law; what sent him to the cross was a combination of the Jewish tradition of killing prophets (13:34, 24:19–20) and a weak Roman governor (a pattern which is repeated in relation to Christian missionaries throughout Acts).

Pilate's involvement in Jesus' trial

In view of the differences in the gospels' accounts of the Roman trial and their clearly theological and pastoral purposes, it is not surprising that doubts have sometimes been expressed over Pilate's involvement in Jesus' death (see in particular Crossan). Crucifixion was clearly a Roman punishment, but given the Passover setting, the high level of alert in the city, and Jesus' peasant status, it is argued that it would not have been necessary to go very far up the Roman chain of command to have him nailed to a cross. Jesus could have been arrested after the temple incident and crucified almost immediately without Pilate's personal involvement.

This is of course possible, but much depends on how we interpret the gospels. Although there is disagreement over details, all four agree that Jesus was handed over to Pilate at dawn, that the governor heard the prisoner (however briefly) and that as a result of this hearing Pilate gave the order to execute Jesus. Josephus also suggests the direct involvement of Pilate, though the authenticity of *Ant.* 18.64 is questionable. The story of Jesus ben Ananias in 62 CE, however, shows that a Roman governor could take a personal interest in a case: this man (who prophesied against the Temple) was arrested and tried by leading Jews, then handed over to the procurator Albinus, who decided that he was mad, had him flogged and released him (*J.W.* 6.300–9). Jesus of Nazareth was more dangerous than Jesus ben Ananias: he had a following and had already caused a disruption in the Temple. If Albinus could try a peasant prophet, it is not unlikely that Pilate did the same, particularly if he had heard reports about him for up to three years. Overall, then, there is no reason to doubt Pilate's personal involvement in sending Jesus to the cross.

HELEN K. BOND

Further reading

Bond, H. K. "The Coins of Pontius Pilate: Part of an Attempt to Provoke the People or to Integrate them into the Empire?," *JST* 27:3 (1996) 241–62.

Bond, H. K. *Pontius Pilate in History and Interpretation*, Cambridge: Cambridge University Press, 1998.

Crossan, J. D. *Who Killed Jesus? Exposing the Roots of Anti-Semitism in the Gospel Story of the Death of Jesus*, San Francisco, CA: Harper, 1996.

McGing, B. C. "Pontius Pilate and the Sources," *CBQ* 53.3 (1991) 416–38.

Rensberger, D. *Johannine Faith and Liberating Community*, Philadelphia, PA: Westminster, 1988.

Schürer, E. *The History of the Jewish People in the Age of Jesus Christ*, revised and ed. G. Vermes, F. Millar, and M. Goodman, Edinburgh: T. & T. Clark, 1973–87, Vol. 1.

Schwartz, D. R. "Josephus and Philo on Pontius Pilate," *The Jerusalem Cathedra* 3 (1983) 26–45.

—— "Pontius Pilate," *ABD* (1992) 5:395–401.

Smallwood, E. M. "The Date of the Dismissal of Pontius Pilate from Judaea," *JJS* 5 (1954) 12–21.

—— *The Jews Under Roman Rule: From Pompey to Diocletian*, Leiden: Brill, 1976.

Vardaman, E. J. "A New Inscription which Mentions Pilate as Prefect," *JBL* 81:1 (1962) 70–71.

Winter, P. *On the Trial of Jesus*, Berlin: Walter de Gruyter, 1961.

PRAETORIUM

By the first century CE, the Latin word *praetorium* – which originally referred to the tent of a praetor or general in an army camp – had come to include the official residence of a provincial governor. The related Greek word, *praitōrion*, is used in the New Testament (and translated as praetorium, palace, or judgement hall) to refer either to the Roman administrative headquarters in Caesarea (Acts 23:35) or, more frequently, to Pontius Pilate's headquarters in Jerusalem – the scene of the Roman trial of Jesus (Matt 27:27, Mark 15:16, John 18:28, 33, 19:9). After briefly discussing the praetorium in Caesarea, this article will focus on the location of the Jerusalem praetorium.

In 6 CE, following the deposition of Herod the Great's son Archelaus, Judaea became a Roman province. The Roman prefect made his headquarters in the predominantly Gentile coastal city of Caesarea. Acts 23.35 shows that by the time of Felix (52–60 CE), the praetorium was located in Herod's former palace, but it is likely that earlier Roman governors also made this impressive and luxurious building their own. Here they would have lived with their families and slaves; their entourage of secretaries, administrators, and advisors; and a body of auxiliary troops. When necessary, however, and particularly during festivals, the Roman governor and a detachment of soldiers would relocate to Jerusalem. The precise site of the Jerusalem praetorium is disputed, though there are two main contenders: the Antonia Fortress and Herod's palace.

The Antonia Fortress could perhaps be regarded as the "traditional" site of the praetorium and was still the favoured site in the early twentieth century. From Crusader times, the route of the Via Dolorosa started here and made its way to the Church of the Holy Sepulchre, the traditional location of Calvary. Situated in the northwest corner of the temple mount, the Antonia was a tall square or rectangular building, surrounded by steep walls and a moat, with a tower at each of its corners (for a fuller description, see Josephus, *J.W.* 5.238–47). Herod the Great completely rebuilt and expanded an earlier Hasmonaean fortress and named it after his patron, Mark Antony, some time before 31 BCE (when the latter was killed at the battle of Actium).

It was a large, spacious complex with porticoes and baths. According to Josephus "from its possession of all conveniences it seemed a town, from its magnificence, a palace" (*J. W.* 5.241). More importantly, however, its imposing site overlooking the Temple made it the perfect place to guard against insurrection. A cohort of troops was permanently garrisoned here (*J. W.* 5.244; Acts 21.32), and during pilgrimage festivals soldiers were posted on top of the fortress and on the roofs of the outermost temple court.

Today, little remains of the fortress and the site is occupied by the Omariyyeh School, the Convents of the Flagellation and Our Lady of Sion, and the Ecce Homo arch. Excavations by L. H. Vincent and M. Godelene of the École Biblique in 1931–7 under the Convent of Our Lady uncovered extensive water systems and a large limestone pavement on which was etched in one place what seems to be a large board game. Visitors are commonly told that this pavement is the *lithóstroton* (lit. pavement) on which, according to John 19:13, Pilate had his judgement seat; but more recent investigations suggest that both the pavement and the Ecce Homo arch in front of the convent date to the Hadrianic reconstruction of Jerusalem in 135 CE. There is thus no firm archaeological connection between the Antonia Fortress and Pilate's praetorium.

As the twentieth century progressed, scholarly attention shifted to Herod's palace in the Upper City, largely as a result of the investigations of P. Benoit. Herod's Jerusalem residence, as we might expect, was a feat of architectural achievement and luxury: "In extravagance and equipment no building surpassed it," wrote Josephus (for a fuller description of the banquet halls, cloisters and sumptuous building materials, see *J. W.* 5.176–81). As a royal palace, and the home of Herod's court, however, the complex also needed to be well defended. The city wall itself formed the western boundary while the inner wall was 45 ft high with towers at regular intervals. To the north, commanding the highest point of Jerusalem and a site of strategic importance overlooking the city, was a fortress with three towers named after people dear to Herod: Hippicus, Phasael and Mariamne (*J. W.* 5.160–73). Nothing remains of the palace, except for one foundation (probably that of Phasael's tower), now part of David's citadel.

All our literary information regarding the location of the Roman praetorium points to this second site. Describing an incident from the time of Pilate, Philo of Alexandria suggests that Herod's palace was the site of the praetorium (*Embassy* 299, 306). The procurator Florus, too, seems to

have resided here shortly before the Jewish revolt of 66 (*J. W.* 2.301–8). Furthermore, when Agrippa II visited the city in the 60s, he lived in the Hasmonaean palace (*Ant.* 20.189–95), suggesting that the Herodian palace had been commandeered by the Roman governors. As a palace and a fortress, Herod's residence would more than meet the demands of a visiting Roman governor and his troops (not to mention his wife if she accompanied him, see Matt 27:19). When the prefect was not in residence, the palace was probably occupied by a small detachment of troops and a body of slaves supervised by a steward. Responsibility for routine law and order in Jerusalem would revert to the Roman tribune and his troops in the Antonia Fortress.

In the late twentieth century, B. Pixner argued that the praetorium was located in the Hasmonaean palace in the upper Tyropoean Valley (the exact location is uncertain) and that Roman governors lived in Herod's palace while using the Hasmonaean palace as their administrative headquarters. This theory, however, has not won wide acceptance (see Benoit 1984). The likeliest location for the Roman praetorium in Jerusalem, and therefore the place where Jesus was tried by Pilate, remains Herod's palace in the Upper City.

HELEN K. BOND

Further reading

Benoit, P. "The Archaeological Reconstruction of the Antonia Fortress," in Y. Yadin (ed.) *Jerusalem Revealed*, New Haven, CT: Yale University Press and Israel Exploration Society, 1976, pp. 87–89.
—— "Le Prétoire de Pilate à l'époque Byzantine," *RB* 91 (1984) 161–77.
Finegan, J. *The Archeology of the New Testament*, revised edition, Princeton, NJ: Princeton University Press, 1992, pp. 246–59.
Pixner, B. "Was the Trial of Jesus in the Hasmonaean Palace?," in A. L. Eckhardt (ed.) *Jerusalem: City of Ages*, Lanham, MD: University Press of America, 1987, pp. 66–70.
Rousseau, J. J. and R. Arav *Jesus and His World: An Archaeological and Cultural Dictionary*, London: SCM, 1996, pp. 12–14, 151–52.
Vincent, L. H. "L'Antonia et le Prétoire," *RB* 42 (1933) 83–113.

PRAYER

Prayer might be broadly defined as address to God or the gods in prose or lyric form. The phenomenon must be considered to belong to the deepest and most immediate expressions of that sense of human contingency and dependency on the divine that is encountered in every religion. Invocation of the deity is a constituent of worship, in which prayer is offered in the context of an act of sacrifice in the temple precinct. Prayer is also ubiquitous in the non-sacrificial gatherings of the Jewish synagogue or Christian church which take the form of a meeting for the reading and expounding of scripture. Commonly, such prayer is offered in the form of petition, confession, complaint or praise. In Second Temple Judaism (c. 500 BCE–135 CE), prayer came to be regarded metaphorically as an atoning sacrifice, a service equivalent to or superior to that of the altar. Once the Temple had been destroyed by the Romans in 70 CE, this view of prayer became commonplace.

In the Second Temple era, the works brought together to form the Hebrew Bible and the Greek Old Testament (Septuagint), the Dead Sea corpus, the New Testament, and those conveniently gathered into the collection known as the Pseudepigrapha, all attest the centrality of prayer in the life of the pious. Among those with a sense of their religious obligation and duty, prayer was the chief verbal expression of dependence on God for all that is good in life. The confession of sins, both personal and communal, is frequently encountered, as is praise and adoration.

The Jewish context of the origin of Christianity explains the considerable affinities between Jewish and early Christian prayer. This is particularly noticeable in the early Christian use and development of Jewish doxologies, and in the composition of Eucharistic prayers based on the Jewish practice of offering a thanksgiving or blessing before meals, such prayer offered in praise of God for provision and sustenance.

Jesus and prayer

The New Testament Gospels reveal the centrality of prayer in the life and ministry of Jesus. This is evident across the gospel accounts, not only in the accepted Synoptic Gospel sources – Mark, Q, and the material unique to Matthew (M) and to Luke (L) – but also the Fourth Gospel. Jesus is presented in the gospels as a pious Jew for whom prayer is at the centre of his religious life-commitment.

The gospels frequently depict Jesus at prayer. He prays at his baptism (Luke 3:21). He withdraws to a desert place to pray (Mark 1:35; Luke 5:16; cf. Matt 14:23; Mark 6:46; Luke 9:28). He prays all night before choosing his disciples (Luke 6:12), such prayer exceeding attested Jewish practice of prayer three times daily, in the morning, afternoon and before retiring. He prays over children (Matt 19:13). In typical Jewish manner, he offers prayer

before meals (Mark 6:41 par.; Mark 14:22 par.). He affirms that the Temple is a house of prayer (Matt 21:13; Mark 11:17; Luke 19:46; cf. Isa 56:7). He prays in the Garden of Gethsemane on the night of his betrayal (Mark 14:32–42; Matt 26:39; Luke 22:44), the Lukan account underscoring the anguish of his prayer, though this verse is not present in some early manuscripts. At his trial, Jesus asserts that a prayer to his heavenly Father for deliverance would result in more than twelve legions of angels coming to rescue him (Matt 26:53). While the Fourth Gospel records Jesus at prayer less frequently, see John 6:11 and 11:41, the lengthy discourse of John 17 is in fact a prayer to God and constitutes the longest of the prayers attributed to him. A consistent and coherent picture emerges in the sources of Jesus as a person of prayer that demands acceptance as an assured historical datum. Heb 5:7, a witness early enough to be independent of the written gospels, agrees.

There are nine prayers of Jesus preserved in the gospels. These are (1) the Lord's Prayer (Matt 6:9–13; Luke 11:2–4); (2) the praise of the Father on the occasion of the disciples' return after their first mission (Matt 11:25–27); (3) the prayer at the tomb of Lazarus (John 11:41–42); (4) the prayer in the temple precincts (John 12:27–28a); (5) the so-called "high priestly" prayer of John 17; and (6) the prayer in Gethsemane (Matt 26:39, 42; Mark 14:36; Luke 22:42). Three prayers are prayed by Jesus on the cross. These are (7) the prayer for God's forgiveness of those crucifying him (Luke 23:34, though this verse does not appear in some early manuscripts); (8) the cry of dereliction (Matt 27:46; Mark 15:34); and (9) the prayer at the point of death (Luke 23:46).

Jesus' teaching on prayer is found in all gospel sources and is concentrated in Matt 6:5–15, 7:7–11; Luke 11:2–13 and 18:1–14, and more briefly elsewhere, such as Matt 5:44 (= Luke 6:28), Mark 11:22–24 (= Matt 21:21–22) and Mark 12:40 (= Luke 20:47). In Matt 6:5–8 Jesus counsels his disciples to pray in secret rather than ostentatiously in full public view (vv. 5–6). He urges simple and direct praying to the Father, not the heaping up of empty phrases as in the prayers of the Gentiles (v. 7), as though such prayers were designed to persuade the gods to answer. Rather, says Jesus, "your Father knows what you need before you ask him" (v. 8, NRSV). Jesus teaches that the Father is a generous giver, more willing to give than we are to pray (see Matt 7:7–11; Luke 11:9–13). Prayer for God's forgiveness will only be granted those who humble themselves. By contrast, the prayers of those who pride themselves on their moral achievement will not be heard (Luke 18:9–14). He condemns the long prayers of the scribes (Mark 12:40; Luke 20:47). He teaches that his disciples should pray for those who persecute and abuse them (Matt 5:44; Luke 6:28). Forgiveness of others is the ground upon which God will forgive the sins of the disciples (Matt 6:12, 14–15; Mark 11:25). Prayer will be answered, Jesus asserts in Mark 11:22–24 (= Matt 21:21–22), if the disciples pray in confidence that God will grant their requests and believe that they have already received that for which they ask. He proposes that certain demons can only be exorcised by prayer (Mark 9:29) and urges his disciples to pray in the face of trial (Matt 26:41; Mark 14:38; Luke 22:40; cf. Polycarp, *Phil.* 7:1–2).

Prayer is not only an integral expression of Jesus' life-commitment but also of his expectation of his disciples, as Matt 21:22, Mark 11:24 and Luke 18:1–8 make clear. In the book of Acts the disciples are depicted spending much time in prayer (Acts 1:14) and are present in the Temple at one of the customary hours of prayer (Acts 3:1). Luke also records that the disciples of John the Baptist and the Pharisees frequently fast and pray (see Luke 5:33).

God as Father in the prayers and teaching of Jesus

The gospel sources are agreed that Jesus addressed God as "Father." Mark 14:36 actually records Jesus' ascription of the Aramaic word *'abbā*, father, to God in prayer. This use of *'abbā* is unique in early Jewish usage. The Greek *patēr* ("father"; vocative *pater*) appears frequently in the gospel accounts, especially in Matthew (forty-two times) and John (109 times), but less so in Mark (five times) and Luke (fifteen times). In the Fourth Gospel the absolute, "(the) Father" (*ho patēr*) is frequently encountered. This usage extends to the *Gospel of Thomas* in which Jesus refers to God as "the Father" in twelve logia (for example, §40, §57, §69), and less commonly as "my Father" (four logia; for example, §61, §99) and the "living Father" (two logia; §3, §50). Also unique, thus far attested, is Jesus' consistent use of the term "Father" as an address to God. Only in the cry of dereliction (citing Ps 22:1) does Jesus not address God as Father. Indeed, Jesus teaches that "father" should be reserved for God alone and not ascribed to anyone on earth, because even polite and honorific usage compromises the singularity of God as Father (Matt 23:9). *'Abbā* of God also appears in Rom 8:15 and Gal 4:6 (*'abbā ho patēr*), and should

be taken as further evidence of the remembrance in the early church of a distinctive characteristic of the speech of Jesus about God.

Addressing God as father is by no means unique to Jesus, even if his use of the Aramaic *'abbā* is. God is ascribed as father – that is, as founder and sustainer – of the nation of Israel in the Hebrew Bible (Deut 32:6). But, in books emanating from Second Temple Judaism, the use of the term comes to denote a personal relationship between God, as Father, and individuals, a usage that Jesus so consistently underscores. This is apparent, for example, in Wis 2:16, Sir 23:1, 51:10 and 3 Macc 6:8.

"Father" expresses Jesus' confident sense of the filial dimension of his relationship to God which Christians continue to evoke, not least in the ubiquitous Lord's Prayer. Matt 11:25–27, with its discourse of the revelation of the "Father" to which the "son" is uniquely privy, is more amply mirrored in the Fourth Gospel in which Jesus regularly refers to God as "the Father" and to himself as "the son". This characteristic of Jesus' speech in the gospel accounts commends the view that he saw himself as the child or servant (*pais*) of God and thus the divinely appointed agent in the establishment of the kingdom, as implied in Matt 12:18 (citing Isa 42:1) and expressed explicitly in Acts 3:13; 4:27, 30.

The most distinctive teaching of Jesus relates to his theology of God as "Father". This imparts to Jesus' prayers and his teaching on the subject a compelling sense of the immediacy of God, the assurance of an intimate relationship with God that the disciples can in full confidence share, and a supreme conviction in unmediated access to God for all who come to him as Father. If Jesus calls God "my Father" he can also assure the disciples that God is both "your Father" (Matt 6:4, 6) and also "our Father" (Matt 6:8, 9, 14). This theology is the ground of Jesus' teaching that whatever the disciples ask in faith will be given. The heavenly Father longs to give good gifts to those who ask him (see Matt 7:7, 10, 11; Luke 11:9–13), even the bestowal of the Holy Spirit, the supreme eschatological gift. Not surprisingly, the Matthean Jesus teaches that whatever two or three ask in faith will come to pass (Matt 18:19). Elsewhere he makes the extravagant claim that prayer offered in full confidence will be granted, even a prayer that a mountain might be cast into the sea (see Matt 21:21–22; Mark 11:22–24). Such teaching serves to underscore the open-hearted, unlimited generosity of God whose gifts are available to all, even those who follow Jesus. The Fourth Gospel mirrors this teaching when Jesus teaches that whatever the disciples ask in his name the Father will give them (see John 14:13–14; 15:7, 16; 16:23, 24, 26). Martha recognizes that whatever Jesus asks of God, God will grant (John 11:22). Confidence in God as a loving, tender Father expressed in the Qumran *Hodayot* at 1QH 17.35–36 provides a close parallel to the teaching of Jesus, although his audience was by no means constituted by the conventionally pious:

> For thou art a father to all [the sons] of Thy truth, and as a woman who tenderly loves her babe, so dost Thou rejoice in them; and as a foster-father bearing a child in his lap so carest Thou for all Thy creatures.
>
> (trans. Vermes)

The Lord's Prayer

Jesus taught his disciples to pray, as did John the Baptist (Luke 11:1), offering an example of the kind of prayer that he endorses. The prayer is recorded in two forms: a longer version in Matt 6:9–13 and a shorter in Luke 11:2–4. The prayer also appears in the *Didache* 8:2, which reflects the Matthean version. There are echoes of the prayer in the mid second-century CE works *Apocryphon of James* 4.28–30 and *Gospel of the Nazarenes* fragment 5.

In effect, the Lord's Prayer summarizes Jesus' teaching about prayer. In common with the prayers of contemporary Judaism, the prayer affirms the transcendence of God and articulates a fervent hope for the coming of the Kingdom, such as is expressed in the *Qaddish* (the prayer before meals), the daily prayer called the *Amidah* (or the Eighteen Benedictions), and a saying preserved in the Mishnah (*Sota* 9.15) of the late first-century CE rabbi Eliezer the Great. The Lord's Prayer is a prayer for communal praying. It acknowledges the sanctity of the name of the heavenly Father, petitions him to advance his cause in the world as it is in heaven and requests daily sustenance, "daily bread". It is possible, however, that Jesus means "tomorrow's bread", that is, eschatological bread, the bread of heaven. Jesus also draws a causal relationship between divine forgiveness and preparedness on the part of those praying to forgive others (see also Matt 6:14–15). The prayer concludes by requesting that we not be brought to the time of apocalyptic trial (implied in the NRSV) but rescued from the evil one. The concluding doxology of later Christian liturgy does not appear in the earliest gospel manuscripts.

Jesus and prayer in the early non-canonical Gospels

The possibly early *Gospel of Thomas* and the non-canonical gospel traditions generally are not nearly as forthcoming as the New Testament gospels in their presentation of Jesus as a person of prayer and as a teacher about prayer. The *Gospel of Thomas* mentions prayer infrequently. Jesus gives no teaching that responds to the disciples' request of logium six as to how they should pray. In logium 104 Jesus replies to the disciples' exhortation to pray and fast with the words: "What is the sin that I have committed, or wherein have I been defeated? But when the bridegroom leaves the bridal chamber then let them fast and pray" (trans. Wilson). In logium fourteen Jesus affirms that the prayers of his disciples will only bring condemnation upon them (cf. *Apocryphon of James* 11.30–34). Only in logium seventy-three does Jesus exhort the disciples to pray, beseeching the Lord to send out labourers into the harvest. Logium seventy-four is a question posed by Jesus to "the Lord". The fragment of the *Gospel of Peter* that narrates the crucifixion and resurrection records a self-directed variant of the cry of dereliction at 5:19: "My power, O power, thou hast forsaken me."

Amen

The Hebrew particle *āmēn* is derived from the verb *'mn*, to be trustworthy, reliable or valid. Jesus is recorded using the term to preface confident, authoritative assertions in all the gospel sources, especially in Matthew (thirty-one times; for example 5:18, 26; 11:11; 24:2) and John (twenty-five verses). In the latter amen is always doubled for emphasis (as in 1:51; 3:3, 5, 11; 8:3) such that it probably reflects Jewish liturgical contexts represented in the Hebrew Bible by Nums 5:22; Pss 41:13; 72:19; 89:52; Neh 5:13. Amen appears less often in Mark (thirteen times; for example, 3:28; 8:12; 9:1) and infrequently in Luke (six times; for example, 4:24; 12:37). Jesus always follows his amen with the words "I say to you". As far as is known, this use of amen is unique to Jesus.

Amen expresses solemn assent or endorsement, a liturgical "so be it". As such it is an affirmation, binding, for example, the respondent to each of the terms of the covenant ratification ceremony in Deut 27:15–26. In prayers and doxologies, the term expresses a validation or endorsement of what has been spoken. It is used in this way, for example, at Jer 28:6. This use of amen is a mark of the way in which the first-century Jewish context has influenced the development of Christian prayer formulation, as at Rom 1:25; 9:5; 11:36; 15:33; 16:24, 27 and elsewhere in the New Testament (1 Cor, Eph, Phil, 1–2 Tim, Phlm, Heb, 1–2 Pet, Jude, Rev). Amen is frequently attested in the apostolic

Fathers (for example *1 Clem.* 20:12; 32:4; 38:4 *et al.*; *2 Clem.* 20:5; *Diogn.* 12:9; *Mart. Pol.* 14:3; 15:1; 21:1; 22:3; *Did.* 10:6). In Rev 3:14 God is termed "the Amen", the trustworthy One. This use of amen is not found in prayer or doxological contexts in the gospels, except in late manuscripts of Matt 6:13; 28:20; Luke 24:53; John 21:25 and in the conclusion of the late supplement to Mark 16 (vv. 9–20).

Amen persisted in the Greek- and Latin-speaking church. It belongs to a small group of words found in prayer contexts – the Hebrew terms "alleluia" and "hosanna", the Aramaic *'abbā* and the phrase *māranā thā* ("our Lord, come", 1 Cor 16:22; *Did.* 10:6) – that survived from their Jewish context.

MARK HARDING

Further reading

Charlesworth, James H. (ed.) *The Lord's Prayer and Other Prayer Texts From the Greco-Roman Era*, Valley Forge, PA: Trinity Press International, 1994.

Chazon, Esther G. "Hymns and Prayers in the Dead Sea Scrolls," in Peter W. Flint and James C. VanderKam (eds) *The Dead Sea Scrolls after Fifty Years: A Comprehensive Assessment Volume 1*, Leiden: Brill, 1998, pp. 244–70.

Crump, David M. *Jesus the Intercessor: Prayer and Theology in Luke–Acts*, WUNT 2.49, Tübingen: Mohr Siebeck, 1992.

Cullmann, Oscar. *Prayer in the New Testament*, London: SCM, 1995.

Hamman, A. *Prayer: The New Testament*, Chicago, IL: Franciscan Herald Press, 1971.

Jeremias, Joachim. *The Prayers of Jesus*, Philadelphia, PA: Fortress Press, 1978.

Karris, Robert J. *Prayer and the New Testament: Jesus and His Communities at Worship*, New York, Herder & Herder, 2000.

Kiley, Mark. (ed.) *Prayer from Alexander to Constantine: A Critical Anthology*, London and New York: Routledge, 1997.

Lochman, Jan Milič. *The Lord's Prayer*, Grand Rapids, MI: Eerdmans, 1990.

Longenecker, Richard N. (ed.) *Into God's Presence: Prayer in the New Testament*, Grand Rapids, MI: Eerdmans, 2001.

Miller, Patrick D. *They Cried to the Lord: The Form and Theology of Biblical Prayer*, Minneapolis, MN: Fortress, 1994.

Werline, Rodney A. *Penitential Prayer in Second Temple Judaism: The Development of a Religious Institution*, Atlanta, GA: Scholars Press, 1999.

Wright, N. T. *The Lord and his Prayer*, London: Triangle, 1996.

PROPHECY

The subject of prophecy impacts historical Jesus studies chiefly in two ways: (1) There is a question of the extent (if at all) to which Jesus applied to himself the prophetic texts that the Evangelists adduced in support of a theological understanding of the Christ event. Was Jesus conscious of answering to the prophecies of Isaiah, Zechariah, and other prophets (as well as Deuteronomy and Psalms)? (2) There is also a question of how (if at all) the historical Jesus answered to the description of a prophet. This raises a significant side issue. Besides possibly seeing himself as a prophet, did Jesus understand himself to be the eschatological (Mosaic) Prophet that many were expecting on the basis of Deut 18:15, 18? And how does John the Baptist answer to these categories?

Application of OT messianic prophecies

All four gospels present Jesus' ministry as a fulfillment of OT messianic prophecies. As C. H. Dodd notes, "the application of prophecy was probably the earliest form of Christian theological thought" (60). As the gospels were all written well after Paul's letters, it is hardly surprising that they should know formalized appeals to prophecy similar to those Paul knows. Matthew has by far the most references to the fulfillment of OT prophecies (1:22; 2:5, 15, 17, 23; 3:3; 4:14; 8:17; 12:17; 13:14, 35; 15:7; 21:4; 24:15; 26:56; 27:9; cf. Mark 1:2; 7:6; Luke 3:4; 4:21; 18:31; 24:25, 27, 44; John 1:23, 45; 6:45; 12:38), as well as the most unbelievably wooden rendering of that fulfillment (even to the point of depicting Jesus astride two beasts at the Triumphal Entry [Matt 21:1–7]). The multiplication of prophetic signposts in Matthew (as compared to Mark) shows their secondariness vis-à-vis the earliest gospel outline, so it is pertinent to ask whether the historical Jesus was conscious of fulfilling Scripture during his ministry, and especially through his suffering on the cross. Towards the end of the twentieth century, scholarship began to change its stance after several decades of skepticism regarding two key factors in that scenario. For a long time prior, most scholars had held that the historical Jesus had *none* of the messianic consciousness that the gospels depict him as having (with the so-called "messianic secret" functioning to conceal the seam of a secondarily added messianic consciousness). For even longer, scholars assumed Jesus to have been illiterate, certainly lacking the scribalist familiarity with Scripture that the gospels portray him as having. One can no longer speak of a consensus on these two questions. This means that the notion of a historical Jesus who viewed his own actions and fortunes in relation to Scripture is given a warmer reception today than it once was. It still holds that the invasiveness of the

Evangelists' hand is most transparent at precisely this point, but the question of whether Jesus envisioned his own mission in scriptural-prophetic terms is not reducible to questions of form and redaction criticism. The question still awaits a decisive treatment.

The prophetic spirit in contemporary Judaism

According to some Jewish writings from the period (or shortly thereafter), the prophetic spirit left Israel upon the deaths of Haggai, Zechariah, and Malachi, the last three of the OT prophets. This cessationist view was especially associated with Rabbinic Judaism, as it is at least partially an attempt to cordon off the unique authority of Torah and to provide for the brokering of "prophetic" power to interpret Torah by trained expositors (viz. the Rabbis). As far as we can tell, however, many (if not most) Jews of the period believed that the prophetic spirit still operated, even if only rarely. Certainly believing in contemporary prophecy did not imply that someone had an overly apocalyptic bent. Such a belief was simply too widespread to be confined to only one general orientation, although those who tried to quash apocalyptic idealism for the sake of relations with Rome naturally would have sought to marginalize or institutionalize any exercise of prophecy. With respect to the question of prophecy's cessation, there was also a "both/and" position, for which Josephus is a perfect example. He attested that the prophetic spirit had abandoned Israel at the death of the last canonical prophets, yet he *also* described ongoing feats of prophetic insight (including those worked by him [*Ant.* 14.174–75, 15.3–4]) and described the Pharisees as having access to divine foreknowledge (*Ant.* 17.41–44). This is perhaps best explained along the lines of a qualitative distinction between the "golden age" of the OT prophets and the poorer situation of a later day: Josephus apparently saw a qualitative difference between the prophetic unction enjoyed by the biblical prophets and that accessible to the prophets of his own day. It should also be noted that priests (like Josephus) were often thought to possess prophetic powers, by virtue of their mediatorial office. This was particularly so in the case of an officiating priest, or especially of the high priest, a view that allowed for openness to prophecy but which safely confined it to an institutional context. For Hecataeus of Abdera (see Diodorus of Sicily 40.2:5–6) and others, priests were given prophetic powers for the sake of delivering religious decrees. But priests were also sometimes regarded as diviners

of the future. In John 11:51, this power was specially relegated to the high priest, who operated in it, not only unwittingly, but also without respect to any moral ballast.

Jesus as prophet

What was the role of prophecy in Jesus' ministry? The evidence for the working of a prophetic unction within Jesus' own ministry is considerable, giving him supernatural insight, for instance, into the circumstances of those he encountered (as is regularly shown in the Fourth Gospel's depiction of Jesus) or into the impending doom of the Jewish nation at the hands of the Romans (as shown in the apocalyptic discourse of Matthew 24||Mark 13||Luke 21). Jesus' contemporaries often referred to him as a prophet (see Matt 21:46; Luke 7:16; 24:19; John 4:19; 9:17). When the Pharisee who invited Jesus to dinner saw him allow a sinful woman to wash his feet, his conclusion that Jesus could not be a prophet (Luke 7:39) was evidently an adjustment to what he had heard or believed. Jesus also referred to himself as a prophet. In Luke 13:33, he defended his plans to go to Jerusalem by remarking that "it is impossible for a prophet to be killed outside of Jerusalem." (The association of Jerusalem with killing prophets appears also to inform the association of the two witnesses' deaths with the streets of Jerusalem in Revelation 11.) When Jesus remarks that "prophets are not without honor, except in their hometown, and among their own kin, and in their own house" (Mark 6:4; slightly different in Matt 13:57; Luke 4:24), his words do not necessarily imply that he was claiming to be a prophet, yet that is apparently how the writer of the Fourth Gospel understood him (John 4:44).

As evidence for Historical Jesus studies, of course, this is all open to question, and its usefulness is subject to the application of some hotly debated methods and assumptions. If traditions of Jesus' prophetic ministry were edited in the early going, they likely would have been edited in the direction of the more spectacular predictions. It is commonly supposed that Jesus' predictions of the destruction of the Temple and his warnings to flee to the hill country were added to the tradition sometime after the events of 70 CE. Yet it would not be remarkable if Jesus predicted the fall of the Temple, since Josephus tells us that other prophetic figures in his day did exactly that. When Jesus' omniscience takes on more than prophetic dimensions (e.g. as often in the Fourth Gospel), it may be that his feats of insight have been modeled on those of Elijah and Elisha, whose abilities excelled those of other prophets.

Were Jesus' prophetic powers those of a prophet *simpliciter*, or did they point to his messianic identity? That a messiah should be specially endowed with prophetic powers is hardly surprising. Of the three major messianic models circulating in Jesus' day, at least two (the priestly and the prophetic) were closely identified with prophetic powers. It should also be noted that the Holy Spirit was thought of primarily in terms of a prophetic spirit, so that any reference to being anointed with the Spirit (as in Isa 61:1, quoted in Luke 4:18) would have been closely tied with some measure of prophetic ability.

Among the varieties of messianic expectation in Jesus' day was a belief in an eschatological Prophet answering to the description in Deut 18:15, 18. (This passage was not originally about an eschatological figure, but it was read that way in the first century.) Sometimes this figure was conceived in terms of a Moses *redivivus*, a conception that probably bears on the origins of Moses' appearance on the Mount of Transfiguration (Matt 17:3–4|| Mark 9:4–5||Luke 9:30, 33) and his (probable) appearance as one of the two witnesses in Revelation 11. There are several indications within the gospels that Jesus was sometimes thought of in terms of this endtime prophet. Although all three Synoptic Gospels refer to a blindfolded Jesus being told to prophesy the identity of those flogging him (Matt 26:68||Mark 14:65||Luke 22:64), Matthew adds the words "you Messiah!" apparently tying an ability to prophesy with a messianic claim (or vice versa). In John 6:14, the people respond to a sign wrought by Jesus by calling him "*the* Prophet," a title that had earlier in that gospel had been disowned by John the Baptist (1:21, 25). When the Pharisees declare that "no prophet is to arise from Galilee" (John 7:52), they seem to be referring to the expected Mosaic figure. (Indeed, some of the OT prophets *did* come from Galilee.) Luke 7:16 and John 9:17 are also possible references to a *messianic* prophet, although that is far from clear. A number of detailed studies have explored the possible indications of a Mosaic Christology in Matthew and John, but their importance for Historical Jesus studies is relatively slight.

Apart from this belief in *the* Prophet, the gospels also refer to a belief that Jesus was one of the "ancient prophets" risen from the dead (Matt 16:14; Mark 6:15; 8:28; Luke 9:8, 19). As far as we know, this belief was not widespread in the Judaism of Jesus' day. It may have been driven by an appreciation for the level of Jesus' prophetic abilities,

coupled with a supposed qualitative distinction between the prophetic unction of the OT prophets and that of postbiblical prophets. (See above.) It should be noted that this reference to the return of one of the OT prophets is probably not a restatement of the belief in *Moses'* return, as the more common belief (in spite of Deuteronomy 34) was that Moses had ascended to heaven without dying. (Indeed, "Jeremiah" is explicitly mentioned as one of these prophets whom the people speculated Jesus to be. The name of Jeremiah may have been evoked by Jesus' predictions about the destruction of the Temple, a message that recalled Jeremiah's prophecies.) It is perhaps significant that "Elijah" is presented as a choice over against these "ancient prophets." This may have less to do with the fact that Elijah did not die (and thus would not need to return "from the dead"), and more to do with the fact that, when Elijah was categorized in eschatological terms, he was more often designated a *priest* rather than a prophet (although the former title is not exclusive of the latter).

Other prophets

In this connection, it should be noted that Jesus is not the only person from his day to whom the gospels apply the title "prophet." John the Baptist, we are told, was widely regarded as a prophet – so much so that the authorities feared to deny him that title (Matt 21:26||Mark 11:32||Luke 20:6; cf. Matt 11:9||Luke 7:26; Matt 14:5; Luke 1:76). John's prophetic ministry was likely similar to that of Jesus, in spite of Jesus' own reference to some basic differences in behavior (Matt 11:18–19||Luke 7:33–34). Both John and Jesus were identified in terms of an Elijah *redivivus*, a fact that may shed light on the quality and public nature of their respective calls to preach and prophesy. In the Lukan Infancy narrative, two other figures are said to prophesy: Zechariah (1:67) and Anna (2:36). Aune notes, "An interesting feature of the overall structure of Luke–Acts is that the author describes a flurry of prophetic activity both *before* and *after* the appearance of Jesus, yet during Jesus' lifetime the author portrays only Jesus as a prophet" (1983: 155). In Matthew's Gospel, Jesus warns that "many" will (claim to) have prophesied in his name, yet be cast out as unworthy.

Jesus himself drew some connections between himself and the OT prophets. The most recurrent connection in Matthew and Luke, however, was one that his followers also shared: just like the prophets of old, Jesus' disciples would be *persecuted* for their witness. Jesus told his followers,

"Rejoice and be glad, for your reward is great in heaven, for in the same way they persecuted the prophets who were before you" (Matt 5:12; cf. Luke 6:23). Jesus warned the scribes and Pharisees that they were "descendants of those who murdered the prophets" (Matt 23:30; cf. 23:29–34||Luke 12:47–50). In keeping with the axiom that a prophet (such as himself) cannot be killed outside Jerusalem, he called Jerusalem "the city that kills the prophets and stones those who are sent to it" (Matt 23:37||Luke 13:34). In Luke 6:26, Jesus warns his disciples against the praise of evildoers ("hypocrites" being a distinctively Matthean term), "for that is what their ancestors [gave] to the false prophets." While the theme of persecution does not directly translate into prophetic categories, Jesus made the connection and through it conceived of his disciples' mission as in some respect continuous with that of the OT prophets.

JOHN C. POIRIER

Further reading

Aune, David E. *Prophecy in Early Christianity and the Ancient Mediterranean World*, Grand Rapids, MI: Eerdmans, 1983.

Boring, M. Eugene. *The Continuing Voice of Jesus: Christian Prophecy and the Gospel Tradition*, Louisville, KY: Westminster/John Knox, 1991.

Dodd, C. H. *History and the Gospel*, London: Nisbet, 1938.

Dunn, James D. G. *Jesus and the Spirit: A Study of the Religious and Charismatic Experience of Jesus and the First Christians as Reflected in the New Testament*, London: SCM, 1975.

Gray, Rebecca. *Prophetic Figures in Late Second Temple Jewish Palestine*, Oxford: Oxford University Press, 1993.

Meyer, Ben F. *The Aims of Jesus*, London: SCM, 1979.

Powery, Emerson B. *Jesus Reads Scripture: The Function of Jesus' Use of Scripture in the Synoptic Gospels*, BIS 63. Leiden: Brill, 2003.

Reiser, Marius. *Jesus and Judgment: The Eschatological Proclamation in Its Jewish Context*, Minneapolis, MN: Fortress Press, 1997.

Sanders, E. P. *Jesus and Judaism*, London: SCM, 1985.

Teeple, Howard M. *The Mosaic Eschatological Prophet*, SBLMS 10, Philadelphia, PA: Society of Biblical Literature, 1957.

Q

Q

Extent and nature of Q

'Q' (from *Quelle*, 'source') is a hypothetical document posited as a corollary to the conclusion that Matthew and Luke independently used Mark, and that they had no direct contact with one another. It is then necessary to posit a second common source in order to account for the approximately 4,000 words shared by Matthew and Luke, which they did not take over from Mark. In a significant amount of the 'Q' material Matthew and Luke exhibit high verbal agreement and more than one-third of the units occur in the same *relative* order in their gospels (even though they usually connect Q with different Markan contexts). These two features make it highly probable that Q was a written document rather than simply a body of oral tradition (Kloppenborg 1987: 72–80; 2000: 56–72). The consensus is that Q was composed in Greek, though probably on the basis of Greek and Aramaic oral traditions, and consisted largely of sayings collected into clusters or proto-speeches and *chreiai*, with a few introductory and transitional phrases, but no continuous narrative framework.

Galilee is normally suggested as the provenance of Q (Reed). Q's attention to basic issues of subsistence, local violence and conflict, and debt, and its negative representation of cities, judicial processes, rulers, and the priestly hierocracy suggest an origin in towns and villages of the lower Galilee, probably before the first revolt, but achieving its final form near the time of the revolt or even slightly after it.

In the early part of the twentieth century several reconstructions of Q in Greek were published, of which the most important and least idiosyncratic was Adolf von Harnack's, even though Harnack thought that Matthew best preserved the original order of Q, against what has come to be the modern consensus (generally) in favour of Luke. In the 1970s efforts were rekindled to reconstruct Q and to describe its literary organization and theology, with reconstructions appearing by Athanasius Polag (1979) and Wolfgang Schenk (1981) and synopses by Frans Neirynck (1988) and John S. Kloppenborg (1988). Renewed interest in Q highlighted the need for a critical text of Q to replace the private and often idiosyncratic reconstructions used in the past. The International Q Project (IQP) published in 2000 a 'critical edition' of Q (Robinson *et al.* 2000) along with a multi-volume database of reconstructions of Q from 1838 to the present (Robinson *et al.*).

The IQP text of Q contains approximately 4,000 words in 268 verses. Unbracketed verses are assigned in whole or in part to Q with a high probability, and others ([[ ]]) less so. The resultant text, in Lukan versification, includes: 3:2b–3, 7–9, 16b–17, [[21–22]]; 4:1–4, 9–12, 5–8, 13, 16; 6:20b–23, 27–28, 35cd, 29, [[Q/Matt 5:41]], 30, 31, 32, 34, 36, 37–38, 39–45, 46–49; 7:1b, 3, 6b–10, 18–19, 22–23, 24–28, [[29–30]], 31–35; 9:57–60; 10:2–16, 21–22, 23–24; 11:2–4, 9–13, 14–15, 17–20, [[21–22]], 23, 24–26, [[27–28]], 16, 29–32, 33–35, 39a, 42, 39b–41, 43–44, 46b, 52, 47–51; 12:2–12, 22–31, 33–34, 39–40,

Q

42b–46, [[49]], 51, 53, [[54–56]], 58–59; **13**:18–19, 20–21, 24–27, 29, 28, [[30]], 34–35; **14**:[[11]], 14:16–21, 23, 26–27; **17**:33; **14**:34–35; **15**:4–7, [[8–10]]; **16**:13, 16, 17, 18; **17**:1b–2, 3b–4, 6b, [[20–21]], 23–24, 37b, 26–27, 28–29, 30, 34–35; **19**:12–13, 14, 15b–24, 26; **22**:28, 30. A few other units of special Lukan material have sometimes been proposed as belonging to Q: Luke 6:24–26; 9:61–62; 11:5–8, 36; 12:13–14, 16–20. Less frequently, Matt 10:23; 11:28–30 are ascribed to Q.

Early views of Q and the historical Jesus

In spite of the fact that a common sayings source had been posited for Matthew and Luke as early as 1838, Q had little impact on the quest of the historical Jesus as long as Mark (or an *Urmarkus* closely related to Mark) was treated as a reliable biographical source. Confidence in Mark as a reliable source, however, began to erode with William Wrede's book on the messianic secret (1901), which argued that significant portions of Mark were a theological construction of the post-Easter church. Confidence was further diminished when Karl Ludwig Schmidt (1919) argued that the chronological and topographical frameworks of the gospels were artificial arrangements of smaller units of tradition. It was at this point that Q began to assume importance: in 1908 Harnack argued that Q was uncontaminated by editorializing and offered nearly complete access to the moral teachings of Jesus and suggested that Q 10:21–22 was the key to Jesus' self-understanding.

Harnack's high estimation of Q as a reliable access to the historical Jesus was in turn undermined by early developments in form criticism. Alfred Loisy (1907–8) and Julius Wellhausen (1911) challenged the historicity of several key Q sayings which Harnack had privileged, and Rudolf Bultmann's first article on Q urged that it was not unalloyed, but contained a mixture of early Christian traditions, bits of secular wisdom, and various "foreign influences" (1994 [1913]: 23). Q was more properly a source for the early church than it was for the historical Jesus. In the period between the world wars, Q was treated within the conceptual framework of form-criticism. From a literary point of view, Q was paraenetic or catechetical, and theologically it served as a supplement to the Easter kerygma.

The composition, genre and conceptual affinities of Q

It was only after the Second World War and the rise of redaction criticism that the literary, theological and historical assessments of Q were revised. Instead of treating Q as a supplement to the Easter kerygma, scholars came to regard Q as a document of theological interest in its own right and to represent a 'second sphere' of early Christian theologizing about Jesus. Instrumental in this reassessment was Heinz Eduard Tödt's study of the Son of Man sayings in the synoptic tradition (1965 [1959]), who argued that Q's representation of Jesus' proclamation of the kingdom amounted to a kerygma parallel to, but independent of, the Easter kerygma. James M. Robinson (1971) stressed that Q represented an independent stream of theologizing, focusing on the sapiential character of Q's Christology. As an instance of the genre *logoi sophōn* ('words of the sages'), Q tended to associate the speaker of the wise sayings (Jesus) with heavenly Sophia (wisdom) and ultimately displayed a gnosticizing proclivity, which was neutralized only when Q was recast with the framework of Mark's gospel. Helmut Koester likewise saw a gnosticizing tendency in Q, but located a decisive shift away from gnosticism within the redaction history of Q itself: Q's original depiction of Jesus as a wisdom teacher was modified by the insertion of apocalyptic Son of Man sayings (1965).

During the 1970s and 1980s most of the attention of scholars was devoted to the reconstruction of Q (above, 'Extent and nature of Q') and the discussion of its composition and conceptual location in the early Jesus movement. Several compositional issues have had (largely unintended) effects of the quest of the historical Jesus. Migaku Sato argued that Q's composition should be understood as a prophetic book which had undergone various 'unsystematic expansion' by such sayings as Q 11:2–4, 9–13; 11:33–35; 12:2–12; and 12:22–31, 33–34 (1988); Kloppenborg urged that the document developed in two main stages, from a smaller collection of instructional speeches (6:20b–49; 9:57–60, 61–62; 10:2–11, 16 [23–24?]; 11:2–4, 9–13; 12:2–7, 11–12, [13–14, 15–20?], 22–31, 33–34; 13:18–19, 20–21, 24; 14:26–27; 17:33; 14:34–35) to a larger collection of *chreiae* with significant prophetic elements, but ultimately moving in the direction of a *bios* (1987; 2000); Arland D. Jacobson detected a core of materials marked by the motif of the deuteronomistic view of history and of the prophets, later expanded by an 'enthusiastic' stage (Q 10:21–22; 11:2–4, 9–13; 17:6), and completed by the temptation story with its critical view of thaumaturgy (1992). Dale C. Allison suggests a three-stage development, from a small collection of sayings directed at itinerants (Q 9:57–11:13 [minus 10:13–15]; 12:2–32), expanded with the addition of community-directed paraenesis

(Q 12:33–22:30), and completed by the addition of Q 3:7–7:35 and 11:14–52, which gave the collection some of the features of a *bios* (1997). Alan Kirk by contrast argued that the whole of Q can be comprehended as a sapiential instruction, evincing the characteristics of a sub-type of Hellenistic Jewish instruction (1998).

In spite of differences in the assessment of the genre of Q, there is wide agreement that the editing of Q has been strongly influenced by deuteronomistic theology, which regarded the history of Israel as a repetitive cycle of sinfulness, prophetic calls to repentance, punishment by God, and renewed calls to repentance with threats of judgment (Jacobson). In this schema, the prophets are depicted as repentance preachers who are inevitably rejected, persecuted and even killed. Q opens with an oracle of coming judgment (Q 3:7–9, 16–17), it privileges repentance as a central theological category (3:8; 10:13; 11:32), and views the rejection of Jesus (and John) through the lens of the deuteronomistic theology of the sorry fate of the prophets (7:33–34; 11:47–51; 13:34–35). The story of Lot, invoked at several points (3:2b–3, 7–9; 10:12; 17:28–29, 34–35), further dramatizes Q's announcement of an imminent fiery judgment (Kloppenborg 1990).

Related to varying assessments of the compositional history and genre of Q, its conceptual orientation has been characterized variously. Sato acknowledges the presence of sapiential materials in Q, but stresses the ways they have been 'prophetized' (1995; similarly, Tuckett). Kirk, by contrast, tried to show that all of Q is comprehended as wisdom discourse (1998). Both Ronald A. Piper (1989) and John S. Kloppenborg (1987; 2000) emphasize that at one compositional level wisdom discourse (and the implicit characterization of Jesus as a wisdom teacher) is important, although Kloppenborg's model also allows for diachronic developments that incorporated prophetic sayings and apocalyptic sayings without, however, shifting Q (and its implicit characterization of Jesus) into either a collection of oracles or an apocalyptic tractate. The Jesus of Q never speaks with the *Botenformel* of prophecy or invokes visions, dreams or heavenly tours as a means of authorizing discourse. However, Q cannot be characterized as 'common wisdom'. On the contrary, like 4QInstruction its 'wisdom' is not common wisdom but that of an especially endowed teacher; it is definitive, saving wisdom (cf. Q 6:47–49; 10:16; 11:23, 31–32) and has esoteric aspects (10:21–22, 23–24), just as wisdom at Qumran (Kloppenborg 2007). In a significant departure from other conceptual

characterizations of Q, Leif E. Vaage (1994), Burton L. Mack (1993) and F. Gerald Downing (1992) contend that Q's intellectual posture is comparable to that of Graeco-Roman Cynics, although both Vaage and Mack are careful to argue that this does not imply direct genealogical connections between Cynics and Jesus (see Smith; Ebner). Downing compares Q with Cynicism in literary terms, arguing that based on an analysis of use of verbs of speaking, the allocation of space, topical organization, length and general character, that Q most closely resembles philosophical *bioi*, especially Cynic *bioi* such as Lucian's *Demonax*.

Q can be said to have a Christology, but lacks the terms Messiah (*Christos*), Son of David and King of Israel. The temptation account uses 'Son of God' twice, but the main designation of Jesus is 'son of Man', referring to Jesus (6:22; 7:34; 9:58; 11:30) and to a coming advocate or judge (12:8, 10, 40; 17:24, 26, 30) but never in relation to Jesus as a suffering figure. The Son of Man is treated in Q 7:33–35 as a child of heavenly Sophia, along with John the Baptist. The depiction of Sophia as sending (Q 11:49–51; cf. 13:34–35) and vindicating prophetic figures, including John and Jesus, has led to suggestions that Q has a Sophia Christology or sophialogy. Q 10:21–22 comes close to depicting Jesus ('the Son') in the same exclusive relation to God that Sophia in Second Temple wisdom literature enjoyed. In this regard, Q anticipates the most vigorous development of wisdom Christology evidenced in the Fourth Gospel.

Q and the historical Jesus

Since Harnack, Q has been used in scholarship on Jesus and in recent years it has become the special focus of attention, although most of the scholarship on Q in the 1970s and 1980s expressly warned against naively converting conclusions about Q's compositional history, genre and conceptual orientation into conclusions about the historical Jesus (Kloppenborg 1996). Nevertheless, the stratigraphic analysis of Q proposed by Kloppenborg (1987) was employed in John Dominic Crossan's book on Jesus in a larger effort to create a comprehensive stratigraphic analysis of the entire Jesus tradition and in this analysis, Q's 'sapiential stratum' *inter alia* was privileged. By contrast, John P. Meier (1994) treats Q as an essentially unedited 'grab bag' of sayings while Richard Horsley and Jonathan Draper (1999) hold that Q is a simple transcription of oral tradition, and can thus ignore not only editorial features in Q but also the issues of the composition of the document and its rhetorical construction of the implied speaker. Both the naive privileging of literary stratigraphy and the naive rejection of the compositional features of Q have led to Q continuing to be treated in a manner that was long ago rejected in respect to Mark and the later synoptic gospels (see Kosch 1992; Kloppenborg 1996). Nevertheless, careful attention to the ways in which the Jesus tradition was configured in Q at its various compositional levels, and careful comparison with the deployment of the Jesus tradition in other parallel documents (Mark; James; the *Gospel of Thomas*, for example), may allow for the construction of a 'map' of the Jesus tradition and controlled inferences, based on actual rhetorical deployments of Jesus' sayings in those documents, about the originating sense and discursive context of Jesus' sayings.

JOHN S. KLOPPENBORG

Further reading

Allison, Dale C. *The Jesus Tradition in Q*, Valley Forge, PA: Trinity Press International, 1997.

Bultmann, Rudolf K. "What the Saying Source Reveals about the Early Church," in John S. Kloppenborg (ed. and trans.) *The Shape of Q: Signal Essays on the Sayings Gospel*, Minneapolis, MN: Fortress Press, 1994 [1913], pp. 23–34.

Downing, F. Gerald. *Cynics and Christian Origins*, Edinburgh: T. & T. Clark, 1992.

Ebner, Martin. "Kynische Jesusinterpretation 'disciplined exaggeration'? Eine Anfrage," *BZ* 40 (1996) 93–100.

Harnack, Adolf von. *The Sayings of Jesus: The Second Source of St. Matthew and St. Luke*, New Testament Studies 2, London: Williams & Norgate; New York: G. P. Putnam's Sons, 1908 [1907].

Horsley, Richard A. and Jonathan A. Draper. *Whoever Hears You Hears Me: Prophets, Performance, and Tradition in Q*, Harrisburg, PA: Trinity Press International, 1999.

Jacobson, Arland D. *The First Gospel: An Introduction to Q*, FF Reference Series, Sonoma, CA: Polebridge, 1992.

Kirk, Alan. *The Composition of the Sayings Source: Genre, Synchrony, & Wisdom Redaction in Q*, NovTSup 91, Leiden and New York: Brill, 1998.

Kloppenborg, John S. *The Formation of Q: Trajectories in Ancient Wisdom Collections*, SAC, Philadelphia, PA: Fortress Press, 1987.

—— *Q Parallels: Synopsis, Critical Notes, and Concordance*, FF, New Testament. Sonoma, CA: Polebridge, 1988.

—— *Q-Reader*, Sonoma, CA: Polebridge Press, 1990.

—— "The Sayings Gospel Q and the Quest of the Historical Jesus," *HTR* 89 (1996) 307–44.

—— *Excavating Q: The History and Setting of the Sayings Gospel*, Minneapolis, MN: Fortress Press; Edinburgh: T. & T. Clark, 2000.

—— "Sagesse et prophétie dans les paroles de l'Evangile Q," in Daniel Marguerat (ed.) *La Source des paroles de Jésus aux origines du christianisme*, Genève: Labor et Fides, 2007, forthcoming.

Koester, Helmut. "ΓΝΩΜΑΙ ΔΙΑΦΟΡΟΙ: The Origin and Nature of Diversification in the History of Early Christianity," *HTR* 58 (1965) 279–318.

Kosch, Daniel. "Q und Jesus," *BZ* 36 (1992) 30–58.

Loisy, Alfred. *Les Évangiles synoptiques*, Ceffonds, Près Montier-en-Der: Chez l'auteur, 1907–8.

Mack, Burton L. *The Lost Gospel: The Book of Q and Christian Origins*, San Francisco, CA: HarperSanFrancisco, 1993.

Meier, John P. *A Marginal Jew: Rethinking the Historical Jesus. Volume II: Mentor, Message, and Miracles*, ABRL, New York: Doubleday, 1994.

Neirynck, Frans. *Q-Synopsis: The Double Tradition Passages in Greek*, SNTA 13, Leuven: Leuven University Press, 1988.

Piper, Ronald A. *Wisdom in the Q-Tradition: The Aphoristic Teaching of Jesus*, SNTSMS 61, Cambridge and New York: Cambridge University Press, 1989.

Polag, Athansius. *Fragmenta Q: Textheft zur Logienquelle*, Neukirchen-Vluyn: Neukirchener Verlag, 1979.

Reed, Jonathan L. *Archaeology and the Galilean Jesus: A Re-Examination of the Evidence*, Harrisburg, PA: Trinity Press International, 2000.

Robinson, James M. "LOGOI SOPHON: On the Gattung of Q," in James M. Robinson and Helmut Koester, *Trajectories through Early Christianity*, Philadelphia, PA: Fortress, 1971, pp. 71–113.

Robinson, James M., Paul Hoffmann, and John S. Kloppenborg (eds) *Documenta Q: Reconstructions of Q Through Two Centuries of Gospel Research*, Leuven: Uitgeverij Peeters, 1996–.

—— *The Critical Edition of Q: A Synopsis, Including the Gospels of Matthew and Luke, Mark and Thomas, with English, German and French Translations of Q and Thomas*, Hermeneia Supplements, Leuven: Uitgeverij Peeters; Minneapolis, MN: Fortress Press, 2000.

Sato, Migaku. *Q und Prophetie: Studien zur Gattungs- und Traditionsgeschichte der Quelle Q*, WUNT 2/29, Tübingen: J. C. B. Mohr [Paul Siebeck].

—— "Wisdom Statements in the Sphere of Prophecy," in Ronald A. Piper (ed.) *The Gospel Behind the Gospels: Current Studies on Q*, NovTSup 75, Leiden, New York, and Köln: Brill, 1995, pp. 139–58.

Schenk, Wolfgang. *Synopse zur Redenquelle der Evangelien: Q-Synopse und Rekonstruktion in deutscher Übersetzung*, Düsseldorf: Patmos, 1981.

Schmidt, Karl Ludwig. *Der Rahmen der Geschichte Jesu: Literarkritische Untersuchungen zur ältesten Jesus-Überlieferung*, Berlin: Trowitsch, 1919.

Smith, Jonathan Z. *Drudgery Divine: On the Comparison of Early Christianities and the Religions of Late Antiquity*, Chicago, IL: University of Chicago Press, 1990.

Tödt, Heinz Eduard. *The Son of Man in the Synoptic Tradition*, London: SCM, 1965 [1959].

Tuckett, Christopher M. *Q and the History of Early Christianity: Studies on Q*, Edinburgh: T. & T. Clark; Peabody, MA: Hendrickson, 1996.

Vaage, Leif E. *Galilean Upstarts: Jesus' First Followers According to Q*, Valley Forge, PA: Trinity Press International, 1994.

Wellhausen, Julius. *Einleitung in die drei ersten Evangelien*, 2 Aufl, Berlin: Georg Reimer, 1911.

Wrede, William. *Das Messiasgeheimnis in den Evangelien*, Göttingen: Vandenhoeck & Ruprecht, 1901.

QUEST OF THE HISTORICAL JESUS

The Quest of the Historical Jesus has its roots in Enlightenment rationalism and English Deism

(Baird). One of the guiding principles of the early quest is that Jesus' teaching was misunderstood by the early church, where the proclaimer of God's universal love became the proclaimed redeemer.

In the seventeenth and eighteenth centuries previously cited evidences of faith, such as proof from miracle and fulfilled prophecy, were questioned. The greatest evidences for any religion were rationality and moral virtue. One example is Thomas Woolston, who published *Six Discourses on the Miracles of Our Saviour* (1727–30). He concluded that miracles were fallacious and dishonored Christ's name (Baird 46). In Woolston and his contemporaries the ideological foundation was laid for other scholars to build upon.

From Reimarus to Schweitzer

Between 1774 and 1778, Gotthold Ephraim Lessing posthumously published seven portions of Hermann Samuel Reimarus's (1694–1768) *Apology for the Rational Worshipers of God* under the title *Fragments of an Unknown*. Lessing knew Reimarus while both lived in Heidelberg. Reimarus had not published his work fearing that its rationalism would not be tolerated (Baird 170; Schweitzer 14). In the seventh fragment, *Concerning the Intention of Jesus and His Teaching* (Reimarus), Reimarus stated that the evangelists' interpretations were inaccurate. Rather, Jesus was essentially a moral teacher whose instruction focused on love of God and neighbor and repression of evil desires. Jesus had no intention of introducing a new religion, although he saw himself as Israel's Messiah, and expected to reign as king. Instead he died forsaken by God. After Jesus' death the disciples invented the idea that he was God's suffering savior.

Reimarus rejected traditional Christian proofs of Jesus' status and authority, such as proof from miracle and proof from prophecy. An example of the rejection of proof from miracle was Reimarus's analysis of Matthew's account of Jesus' resurrection. He concluded that the resurrection narratives of the four gospels diverged so much that they were not credible. The apostles preached that Jesus was raised from the dead because they were men from the lower strata of society, who enjoyed new status as followers of Jesus. When Jesus died, they wished to cling to their newfound power. They did so by inventing not only the proclamation of the resurrection, but also the doctrine of Christ's return. Proof from prophecy was likewise excluded, since the exegetical method of the Evangelists misrepresented the original intention of the Hebrew Bible.

If Reimarus was skeptical about gospel miracles, Heinrich Eberhard Gottlob Paulus (1761–1851) rationalized them in his four-volume work that appeared in 1828. Although Paulus did not wish his views on miracles to be the center point of his work, it is still cited as one of the purest examples of rationalization (Baird 201). For Paulus, there were natural explanations for Jesus' miracles. The gospels' descriptions of Jesus raising people from the dead were actually reports of individuals who recovered from comas. The feeding of the multitude happened when the wealthy in Jesus' audience emulated his example of sharing. The resurrection was accomplished through a natural resuscitation of Jesus' body. Although Paulus's rationalism would be criticized by later scholars, beginning with D. F. Strauss, his method continued to appear in popular accounts of the life of Jesus (see Dunn 31–32). Yet, Paulus's main interest was not the explanation of Jesus' miracles, but in Jesus' teaching, especially Matthew's version of the Sermon on the Mount. "According to Paulus, the ethic of Jesus is primarily concerned with inner motivation and intention" (Baird 205). This emphasis also characterized other nineteenth-century lives of Jesus, such as Schleiermacher's.

Friedrich Daniel Ernst Schleiermacher (1768–1834) accepted Paulus's rationalism, but supplemented it with his own understanding of Jesus' religious consciousness. Schleiermacher's lectures on Jesus were not published until 1864, derived from students' notes. Although suspicious of miracles, he concluded that Jesus performed healings, although not "contrary to nature" (Schleiermacher 209). Likewise, the resurrection narratives actually resulted from Jesus' resuscitation from a trance-like state that occurred during his crucifixion. From the gospel accounts, especially John, Schleiermacher asserted that Jesus lived for a time among his disciples. Something occurred during Jesus' ascension, but we cannot ascertain the nature of the event (Schweitzer 64–65). But Schleiermacher was particularly interested in Jesus' self-understanding, especially as expressed in the Gospel of John. Schleiermacher's Jesus has a special God-consciousness, which was imparted to believers. Jesus continued to be present in the lives of believers as they experienced union with God (Baird 218).

David Friedrich Strauss (1808–74) delivered the crippling blow to Paulus's type of rationalism. Strauss, in two works on the life of Jesus, introduced the importance of myth to the study of the life of Jesus. Although initially influenced by Schleiermacher's idealism, Strauss came to reject

473

Schleiermacher's method (Strauss). Between 1835 and 1840 Strauss published four editions of his *Life of Jesus* (English Translation: 1892, representation 1972). Strauss's work combined the Hegelian dialectic with strict historical criteria to form a coherent method for determining historical events. Unhistorical legends were identified by form. Two reliable indicators of legendary narratives were: (1) if events could not have taken place as related; or, (2) if accounts were contradictory.

Strauss noted the gospel accounts of miracles were not reports of eyewitnesses, but were expanded in the same way as other mythological tales developed (Strauss). Other features of the gospels' portrayal of Jesus were also subject to legendary expansion. Strauss provided numerous explanations for how legendary features developed. The temptation narratives of Matt 4:1–11//Luke 4:1–13, for example, reflected Israel's history in its conflict between good and evil. Strauss was one of the first to recognize that the Johannine discourses were likely composed by the Fourth Evangelist. It is difficult to exaggerate the importance of Strauss's work. It laid the foundations for much of the later life of Jesus research. His seminal understanding of the eschatology of the Synoptic Gospels would later be elaborated by Weiss and Schweitzer.

Strauss's observations were made without utilizing what would become the two foundation stones for later investigators of the historical Jesus: the priority of Mark and Matthew, and Luke's utilization of a second source of Jesus' sayings, later known as Q. The hypothesis of Markan priority was first proposed by Christian Gottlob Wilke (1786–1854) in 1838. The theory that Matthew and Luke independently used a sayings source independent of Mark was first proposed in 1838 by Christian Hermann Weisse (1801–66). These two hypotheses would establish the framework for how nineteenth-century scholars utilized the Synoptic Gospels to derive historical information on Jesus. They theorized that, as the earliest sources, these two documents were least influenced by theology. In 1863 Heinrich Julius Holtzmann combined the hypothesis of Markan priority with liberal theology to produce a psychological interpretation of the life of Jesus (Schweitzer 1968: 204). Jesus' messianic consciousness underwent gradual development. Holtzmann rejected the possibility that Jesus expected the establishment of God's kingdom on earth, along with any expectation of a second advent (Kümme 152).

The most famous psychological evaluation of Jesus' life was Ernest Renan's (1823–92). Originally educated for the priesthood, Renan came to question his faith, and withdrew himself from ordination. He went on to become distinguished in Semitic studies at the University of Paris. In 1860–61, he pursued archaeological studies in Syria and the Near East, and was encouraged by his sister Henriette, to write a life of Jesus. She died at Byblos in 1861, and it is to her that Renan dedicated his book.

Renan's *Vie de Jésus* (1863) quickly became one of the most popular of the lives of Jesus, and was translated into most of the European languages, including English. Methodologically, Renan utilized not only canonical sources, but extra-canonical material such as *1 Enoch*, which he thought provided background for Jesus' enigmatic self-designation Son of man, as well as Josephus, Philo and the Talmud. His use of the gospel materials was cautious, since he found miraculous elements in them. While not saying miracles were impossible, Renan stated that none were verified in the modern period, so "we shall maintain then this principle of historical criticism – that a supernatural account cannot be admitted as such" (Renan xxvii). Of the gospel sources, Renan favored Mark for narrative, and the Sayings source behind Matthew for Jesus' words.

Renan's Jesus was a man in conflict with the religious establishment. Jesus opposed the religion of the Pharisees, which Renan understood as external and ritualistic. Jesus, on the other hand, proposed a religion of the heart, stripped of the superficial. Evidence for this proposal was provided by gospel accounts of Jesus' attitudes about Sabbath observance and his interactions with Samaritans and non-Jews. As time progressed, opposition from the Jewish establishment grew more intense, culminating in a plot to kill Jesus that led to his eventual execution. Renan's *Life of Jesus* was, ultimately, a triumph of historical imagination. It captivated audiences with its novelistic style, yet was unconvincing in its portrayal of the historical Jesus.

In contrast to the liberal psychological reconstruction of Jesus' messianic consciousness was Johannes Weiss's proposal (1892; English translation 1971). Weiss understood Jesus as an apocalyptic preacher of the imminent reign of God. Weiss agreed that any historical reconstruction of Jesus' life and message must derive from the synoptic Gospels. Where he disagreed with earlier writers was in his contention that the apocalyptic eschatology of the Synoptics derived not from the later church, but from the preaching of Jesus himself. Jesus understood himself as the eschatological Son of man of Daniel and *1 Enoch*. Thus, Jesus proclaimed in himself the coming of God's kingdom, although God alone would establish it. Jesus hoped to live to see the coming of God's reign, but eventually thought that it would not take place until after his death. Then God would destroy the world, and establish his kingdom, based in the land of Palestine. Jesus and his faithful followers would rule over this realm.

The confidence of Weiss and others in the Gospel of Mark as a main source for Jesus' preaching and biographical details of his life would be dealt a serious blow by William Wrede (1859–1906). In 1901, Wrede published a book, the English title of which is *The Messianic Secret in the Gospel* (English Translation: 1971). Wrede contended that Jesus did not make messianic claims during his lifetime. It was only after the resurrection experience that messianic status was attributed to Jesus by the Church. Yet, if Jesus did not understand himself as the Messiah, how is later attribution of messianic status to be explained? Wrede proposed that Mark solved the problem by inventing what Wrede called the "messianic secret." After the resurrection experience, the community attributed the messianic secret to Jesus to explain why he was not recognized as Messiah in his lifetime. Jesus' commands to secrecy (see Mark. 1:43; 5:43; 7:36–37; 9:9) reflect Mark's imposition of the theme of "messianic secret" upon the tradition. Thus, Mark cannot be understood as a simple report of what Jesus said and did, but has its own theological agenda. Wrede's conclusion demonstrated the weakness of earlier attempts to derive the historical Jesus from the Gospel of Mark, since Mark, like the other gospels, had a theological agenda.

The death knell of the first quest occurred when Albert Schweitzer (1875–1965) published *Von Reimarus zu Wrede* (1906), translated as *The Quest of the Historical Jesus* (1911, repr. 1968). Schweitzer analyzed the nineteenth-century quest, and concluded:

> [t]he Jesus of Nazareth who came forward publicly as the Messiah, who preached the ethic of the kingdom of God, who founded the kingdom of heaven on earth, and died to give His work its final consecration, never had any existence. He is the figure designed by rationalism, endowed with life by liberalism, and clothed by modern theology in historical garb.
>
> (Schweitzer 398)

The nineteenth-century quest failed in that it attempted to explain Jesus' self-consciousness, which was irretrievable. All that we can recover is Jesus' apocalyptic eschatology. The nineteenth-century authors of lives of Jesus attempted to understand him as a teacher of timeless truths.

Such a Jesus could not be an eschatological prophet from Galilee. Yet Schweitzer affirmed that Jesus is to be understood primarily in terms of eschatology. He cannot be not familiar to us, for he truly expected his ministry to initiate the kingdom of God on earth, and in this expectation he was wrong.

Bultmann to the "New Quest"

After Schweitzer, attempts to recover the historical Jesus, at least in Germany, were largely suspended. From the period before World War I to the 1950s, New Testament scholarship was more concerned with analyzing the development of Christian tradition within the context of Christian communities and the manifestation of Jesus' existential presence in the proclamation of the Church. In these efforts, no figure was more important that Rudolf Bultmann (1884–1976). For the study of the historical Jesus, perhaps Bultmann's major contribution was the publication of his 1921 work, translated as the *History of the Synoptic Tradition* (1963, rev. ed. 1968). Bultmann analyzed how the forms of the synoptic narratives were developed and transmitted. He identified the "life situation" of Synoptic Tradition less in terms of Jesus' life than in the life of the communities in which traditions existed and, in many cases were formed. Bultmann was skeptical of the possibility of writing a history of Jesus, whose personal consciousness was unavailable. This conclusion did not mean that scholars could not know certain aspects of Jesus' message. Bultmann agreed with Schweitzer that Jesus' message was essentially eschatological, although that aspect was already being toned down in John and Paul. Yet, "[h]istorical research can never lead to any result which could serve as a basis for faith, for *all its results have only relative validity*" (Bultmann 1969: 30, emphasis his).

Interest in the historical Jesus was reinvigorated in Germany on 20 October 1953, when Ernst Käsemann, one of Bultmann's students, presented a lecture, translated into English as "The Problem of the Historical Jesus" (1964). Käsemann noted that several features of the gospel tradition could be traced back to Jesus himself. First, Jesus was a person of great authority, who presented himself as a second Moses when he proclaimed "but I say to you" in the Sermon on the Mount (Matt 5:21–42). Jesus also asserted his authority in undermining Jewish concepts of purification in Mark 3:27// Matt 12:28. Käsemann concluded that with these assertions Jesus certainly saw himself as more than a prophet. The essence of Jesus' distinctiveness was to be found in his preaching, which included expectation of the imminent appearing of God's kingdom.

Käsemann's essay was followed in 1956 by Günther Bornkamm's book on Jesus (English Translation: 1960). Jesus was located in Jewish Palestine, as a practitioner of the Jewish religion. He shared Judaism's self-understanding that Israel was a unique people elected by God. Jesus was closely connected with John. Jesus was also a person of great sovereignty and authority, whose proclamation of the kingdom of God was not a vague concept for his hearers. Rather, it resonated with deeply held beliefs rooted in the Hebrew Bible. Yet Jesus' message was of a hidden kingdom (Mark 4:10–13). It was both present and future. Jesus' proclamation of the will of God was of a new righteousness, where the new and old could not be combined (Mark 2:21–22). Opposition to Jesus developed as a result of the entry into Jerusalem and Jesus' actions in the Temple, leading to Jesus' crucifixion and death. Jesus' messianic status was affirmed by the Church, but had its origins in Jesus' words and deeds. As with Käsemann, the historical core of the life of Jesus was to be found in the record of his preaching.

Joachim Jeremias was another important figure in this "New Quest." Unlike Käsemann and Bornkamm, Jeremias was not Bultmann's student. He attempted to discover, if not Jesus' *ipsissima verba* (true words), at least his *ipsissima vox* (true voice) from the gospel accounts (Jeremias 1971). Jeremias had particular confidence that the Aramaisms in the gospel tradition, which he attempted to translate back to Aramaic from Greek (Jeremias 1971), as well as Aramaic terms such as *abba* (Mark 14:36; cf. Matt 6:9//Luke 11:2), *amen, talitha cumi* (Mark 5:41), and *rabbi*, can be traced back to Jesus. Other features of Jesus' teaching that reflected Jesus' Palestinian Jewish environment were his teaching in parables, use of riddles, and proclamation of the eschatological day of crisis, which initiated God's kingdom. These conclusions did not mean that Jeremias accepted the gospel accounts at face value. Rather, he presented specific rules of how sayings, particularly parables, were elaborated in the later church, especially through the addition of allegorical elements (Jeremias 1972). These conclusions were thought to be confirmed by simpler versions of some of the parables in the *Gospel of Thomas*, such as the Parable of the Sower (cf. Mark 4:3–8 and *Gos. Thom.* 9). While Jeremias expressed confidence in discovering the *ipsissima vox* of Jesus, other scholars have questioned his method, pointing out that Aramaic terms or expressions may have derived not from Jesus, but from the earliest, Aramaic-speaking church.

Norman Perrin also expressed confidence in being able to recover an irreducible core of Jesus' teachings. Perrin is most famous for his utilization of what he understood as the "fundamental criterion for authenticity upon which all reconstructions of Jesus must be built," the criterion of dissimilarity (Perrin 38–39). A saying is authentic if it is dissimilar both to Second Temple Judaism and later Christianity. While this criterion has the effect of emphasizing the unique in Jesus' teaching at the expense of his Jewish heritage, Perrin's desire was to discover the irreducible minimum that could be attributed to Jesus. This core consisted of three parts: the parables, Jesus' preaching of the kingdom of God, and the Lord's Prayer.

Third Quest

The so-called Third Quest of the Historical Jesus represents not so much a single quest as the common interest of a number of researchers: to understand Jesus within the context of Second Temple Judaism. To accomplish this goal, various methodologies have been employed, including detailed study of Second Temple Judaism and cross-cultural anthropology, in an attempt better to understand Jesus' person and message.

One of the first scholars who sought to understand Jesus primarily as a Second Temple period Jew was Geza Vermes (1973). Unlike other writers who focused upon Jesus' teachings, Vermes gave serious attention to gospel accounts of Jesus' work as a healer. This portrayal fits well with what is known of Galilean Judaism and the occupation of the *hasidim* or "devout persons." In particular, Vermes pointed to later accounts of Honi the Circle-drawer. Wonder workers had a great popular appeal to the masses, but were later displaced in Judaism by rabbinic teaching. Likewise, titles ascribed to Jesus in the gospels place him squarely in the company of Jewish *hasidim*. It was only as Christianity moved outside of Palestine that Jesus was acclaimed as divine.

E. P. Sanders had also sought to place Jesus squarely within the context of Second Temple Judaism (Sanders 1985; 1993). Sanders focused primarily on the facts of Jesus' life and only secondarily upon the sayings. Sanders was suspicious of the criterion of double dissimilarity as biasing any study toward emphasizing uniqueness, rather than recognizing that Jesus' place within Judaism was the necessary starting point of any study.

Sanders understood Jesus as a Jewish prophet who expected God's impending restoration of Israel. Sanders asserted that the most secure starting point for study of the historical Jesus could be found in Jesus' "cleansing" of the Temple, which was an eschatological sign of God's judgment. This action carried with it the expectation that God would soon create a new temple. Likewise, the appointing of twelve disciples demonstrated the expectation of the restoration of the people of Israel. What was remarkable in Jesus' ministry was that, unlike other eschatological preachers, he envisaged a kingdom where sinners were welcome, without the requirement of repentance. This feature was demonstrated by Jesus' open table fellowship with outcasts.

In contrast to scholars who understood Jesus as an eschatological prophet, the findings of the Jesus Seminar and those most closely associated with it presented a very different picture. Founded in 1985 by Robert Funk, the Jesus Seminar was a gathering of scholars working together to strip the Jesus tradition of accretions added by the later Christian church and to isolate those elements that most certainly derived from Jesus. To accomplish this task, the Seminar did not restrict itself to the canonical gospels, but also mined non-canonical materials, especially the Coptic *Gospel of Thomas*, the *Gospel of Peter* and the hypothetical "Q" traditions of Matthew and Luke, for authentic Jesus material (see Funk *et al.* Funk and the Jesus Seminar). Particular attention was given to Q and the *Gospel of Thomas*. Sayings or narratives were differentiated by type, and then voted upon by committee. Members used colored marbles: red for sayings Jesus certainly said; pink for sayings Jesus likely said; gray for sayings that reflect something Jesus might have said; and black for things Jesus definitely did not say. The emerging picture was very different from Schweitzer's. Jesus was no longer a preacher who expected the impending end of the age. He no longer saw himself as the eschatological Son of Man, a conception attributed instead to the early church. Rather, Jesus was a teacher of non-eschatological wisdom.

Examples of these findings can be found in three representative members of the Jesus Seminar: Marcus Borg, Robert Funk, and John Dominic Crossan. For Borg, Jesus was the "spirit person" who preached the unmediated compassion of God. Unlike Pharisees and Essenes, Jesus had no place for the "politics of holiness" that isolated the people of God. Rather he preached God's graciousness to sinners (Borg 1987). Funk understood Jesus as "a comic savant," an irreverent gadfly,

analogous to Socrates, Mark Twain, or Will Rogers (Funk). The Jesus of Christian orthodoxy was a later creation. This traditional understanding has now run its course and needs to end. Finally, John Dominic Crossan provided a methodologically rigorous analysis of Jesus' life and message (Crossan 1991). He first classified sources under four different strata of tradition of decreasing reliability. In the process, he dated certain non-canonical sources, such as the *Gospel of Thomas* and the *Gospel of Peter*, earlier and as more reliable than did most scholars. The final result was a Jesus who both acts as a wonder worker in the tradition of Honi the Circle-drawer, and was a sage, in the Cynic tradition, who proclaimed "the brokerless kingdom of God."

One of the most energetic proponents of the hypothesis that Jesus was influenced by the Cynic tradition and acted as a Cynic philosopher has been Burton L. Mack (1988). Mack understood the environment of first-century Galilee as being predominately Hellenistic, or Greco-Roman, rather than Jewish sectarianism. It is, therefore, understandable for Jesus to have been a teacher in the Greco-Roman tradition most well known for its wandering teachers, the Cynics. Examples of Cynic influence upon Jesus included Jesus' unique sayings, in particular the parables, as indicative of the Cynic method of teaching. Likewise, Jesus' social criticisms were typical of Cynic teaching. The Greco-Roman environment also influenced Jesus' teaching on the kingdom of God, which was not apocalyptic, but more representative of opposition to prevailing cultural norms and expectations.

Although the Jesus Seminar and those associated with it have been effective in publishing their views, these theories have been met with some skepticism. Criticisms included critiques of the methodological assumptions of the practitioners and their mistaken historical conclusions. Among the former, reliance upon non-canonical writings, including the *Gospel of Thomas*, has been questioned. While it is possible that the *Gospel of Thomas* contains some traditions that derived from the historical Jesus, the work as a whole is understood by many scholars to reflect mostly a second-century environment. Likewise, the *Gospel of Peter* is dated by the majority of scholars not connected with the Jesus Seminar to the second century. Early dating of these documents has been perceived of as eccentric. Furthermore, many scholars have questioned the existence of an established Cynic tradition in Galilee in the time of Jesus. Thus, scholars not affiliated with the Jesus Seminar have provided their own reconstructions of the historical Jesus. Among these individuals are Elisabeth Schüssler-Fiorenza, Gerd Theissen, John Paul Meier, N. T. Wright and James D. G. Dunn.

Elisabeth Schüssler-Fiorenza has understood Jesus within the context of wisdom tradition. She has focused on Luke 7:35, where Jesus stated that wisdom was justified by her children (Schüssler-Fiorenza 1994). On the basis of this saying, Schüssler-Fiorenza understood that Jesus was a wisdom (Gk. *sophia*) prophet, who offered a kingdom to all people. This offer was distinctly counter to the prevailing patriarchy of the first century, and was manifested not only in preaching, but in actions. Jesus shared table fellowship with sinners. Jesus was, therefore, one of a succession of prophets of the gracious Sophia God, a succession continued by the Q community and actively articulated by women. This tradition was suppressed by later Christian confessional tradition represented by Paul (see 1 Cor 15:3–8).

Another reconstruction has been Gerd Theissen's. Theissen achieved fame for his sociological analysis of the early Jesus movement in Palestine (Theissen 1979; 1992). Theissen focused on the combination of Markan and Q material in Matt 10:5–42, as well as instruction in the early Syrian Christian document known as the *Teaching of the Twelve Disciples* or the *Didache* (*Did.* 11–13). He concluded that the early Jesus movement of Palestine and Syria was characterized by an ethic of "wandering radicalism." Wandering preachers without a home base would engage in preaching and healing ministry, following the example of Jesus (Theissen 1979). Theissen has also suggested his own criteria for determining authentic Jesus tradition in contrast to the criterion of dissimilarity (Theissen and Winter) In its place, Theissen recommended criteria of historical plausibility and coherence of sources. Plausibility explains what events likely led to certain historical effects. Coherence refers to elements that occur repeatedly. Theissen concluded that Jesus appeared as a wandering, homeless charismatic preacher of God's messianic kingdom and healer, whose teaching aroused opposition. After his death he was seen as alive by early followers, who then ascribed to him the messianic title.

John Paul Meier's *A Marginal Jew* (1991) now consists of three volumes, with a fourth volume in production. Meier's first volume was a prolegomenon, establishing method, sources and dealing with basic questions about Jesus' identity as a first-century Jew. In his second volume, Meier concerned himself with Jesus' relationship with John the Baptist, Jesus' message of the kingdom of God, and Jesus'

miracles. In volume three, Meier discussed Jesus' "companions and competitors." A fourth volume is intended, where Meier will discuss Jesus' teachings, including the parables. Meier has adopted strict criteria of evidence, with the canonical gospels having priority as sources. In contrast to many scholars, he has found elements of the Gospel of John useful for his historical reconstruction. Meier has emphasized, among other criteria, the criterion of embarrassment for determining if a saying derives from the Historical Jesus. For example, Mark 9:1, which is not fulfilled, is more likely to have been derived from Jesus than from the early church. On the basis of this and other evidence, Meier concludes, in contrast with the Jesus Seminar, that Jesus was, indeed, a preacher of God's imminent kingdom (Meier 2:248–51).

N. T. Wright also has also understood Jesus' message as the preaching of the eschatological kingdom of God. He rejected, however, the corollary that Jesus understood the world to come to an imminent end. History would continue, but in a new form. Instead of the end of history, Jesus' proclamation anticipated a new exodus, when God would return Israel from exile. The result of the return would be a renewal and fulfillment of the covenant promises of the Hebrew Bible (Wright).

Like Meier and Wright, James D. G. Dunn has also understood the kingdom of God to be central to Jesus' message. In Dunn's view, Jesus' message was: (1) that God is "king," and; (2) that in Jesus' actions of preaching and deeds, the divine reign was unfolding (Dunn 2003). Dunn's most important contribution, however, may have been his understanding of the influence of first-century orality upon the gospel tradition. Thus, the message of Jesus was not so much proclaimed by early preachers as it was performed by them. In this context, verbal variation between parallel accounts of the Synoptic Tradition occurred as individuals and communities publicly rehearsed Jesus' teaching, but in the process expressed it with different emphases and applications.

Conclusion

If the original Quest of the Historical Jesus was guided by Enlightenment rationalism and the New Quest may be characterized by a post-Bultmannian desire to discover the irreducible core of Jesus' teaching, the Third Quest has featured methodological plurality. This phenomenon is to be expected. Just as the previous quests were rooted in the ideological framework of their social location, so the Third Questers are, more than they may admit, driven by the impulses of postmodernism. The results are both exciting and unsettling. On the one hand, the different methods of the various practitioners have opened up new possibilities for understanding features of Jesus' life and teaching hitherto overlooked. On the other hand, lack of agreed-upon methodological restrictions may also result in ideology masquerading as research. The temptation of the original Quest of constructing a "historical Jesus" in the researcher's own image remains. It is hoped that the various reconstructions of the Third Quest will provide the grist for further reflection and methodological development as scholars develop a more accurate picture of Jesus in the context of first-century Palestine.

RUSSELL MORTON

Further reading

Baird, William. *The History of New Testament Research. Volume 1. From Deism to Tübingen.* Minneapolis, MN: Fortress Press, 1992.

Borg, Marcus. *Jesus A New Vision: Spirit, Culture and the Life of Discipleship*, San Francisco, CA: Harper & Row, 1987.

—— *Jesus in Contemporary Scholarship*, Valley Forge, PA: Trinity Press International, 1994.

Bornkamm, Günther. *Jesus of Nazareth*, New York. Harper, 1960.

Bultmann, Rudolf. *History of the Synoptic Tradition*, revised edition, New York: Harper and Row, 1968.

—— *Faith and Understanding*, New York: Harper & Row, 1969.

Crossan, John Dominic. *The Historical Jesus: The Life of A Mediterranean Jewish Peasant*, San Francisco, CA: Harper, 1991.

Dunn, James D. G. *Jesus Remembered*, Christianity in the Making 1, Grand Rapids, MI: Eerdmans, 2003.

Funk, Robert. *Honest to Jesus: Jesus for a New Millennium*, San Francisco, CA: HarperSanFrancisco, 1996.

Funk, Robert, and the Jesus Seminar. *The Acts of Jesus: The Search for the Authentic Deeds of Jesus*, San Francisco, CA: HarperSanFrancisco, 1998.

Funk, Robert, Roy Hoover, and the Jesus Seminar. *The Five Gospels: The Search for the Authentic Words of Jesus*, New York: Macmillan, 1993.

Holtzmann, Heinrich Julius. *Die synoptischen Evangelien: ihr Uhsprung und geschichtlicher Charakter*, Leipzig: W. Engelmann, 1863.

Jeremias, Joachim. *New Testament Theology: The Proclamation of Jesus*, New York: Charles Scribner's Sons, 1971.

—— *The Parables of Jesus*, second revised edition, New York: Charles Scribner's Sons, 1972.

Käsemann, Ernst. *Essays on New Testament Themes*, London: SCM Press, 1964.

Kümmel, Werner Georg. *New Testament: The History of the Investigation of its Problems*, Nashville, TN: Abingdon, 1972 [1970].

Mack, Burton. *A Myth of Innocence: Mark and Christian Origins*, Philadelphia, PA: Fortress, 1988.

Meier, John Paul. *A Marginal Jew: Rethinking the Historical Jesus*, 3 vols, with Vol. 4 forthcoming, New York: Doubleday, 1991–

Paulus, Heinrich Eberhard Gottlob. *Exegetisches Handbuch über die drei ersten Evangelien*, 3 vols, Heidelberg: C. F. Winter, 1830–33.

Perrin, Norman. *Rediscovering the Teaching of Jesus*, London: SCM Press, 1967.

Powell, Mark Allan. *Jesus as a Figure in History: How Modern Historians View the Man from Galilee*, Louisville, KY: Westminster/John Knox Press, 1998.

Reimarus, Hermann Samuel. *Fragments*, ed. Charles Talbert, Lives of Jesus Series, Philadelphia, PA: Fortress Press, 1970.

Renan, Ernest. *The Life of Jesus*, Cleveland, OH: World Publishing, 1941.

Sanders. E. P. *Jesus and Judaism*, Philadelphia, PA: Fortress Press, 1985.

—— *The Historical Figure of Jesus*, London; New York: Penguin, 1993.

Schleiermacher, F., *The Life of Jesus*, trans. S. M. Gilmour; ed., with Introduction by J. C. Verheyden, Philadelphia, PA: Fortress Press, 1975.

Schüssler-Fiorenza, Elisabeth. *Jesus: Sophia's Prophet. Miriam's Child: Critical Issues in Feminist Christology*, New York: Continuum, 1994.

Schweitzer, Albert. *Quest of the Historical Jesus*, New York: Macmillan, 1968 [1911].

Strauss, David Friedrich. *The Life of Jesus Critically Examined*, trans. G. Eliot, ed. P. C. Hodgson; Philadelphia, PA: Fortress Press, 1972 [1892].

Theissen, Gerd. *Sociology of Early Palestine*, Philadelphia, PA: Fortress Press, 1979.

—— *Social Reality and the Early Christians: Theology, Ethics and the World of the New Testament*, Minneapolis, MN: Fortress Press, 1992.

Theissen, Gerd and Annette Merz. *The Historical Figure of Jesus*, Minneapolis, MN: Fortress Press, 1998.

Theissen, Gerd and Dagmar Winter. *The Quest for the Plausible Jesus*, Louisville, KY: Westminster/John Knox Press, 2002.

Vermes, Geza. *Jesus the Jew: A Historians Reading of the Gospels*, Philadelphia, PA: Fortress Press, 1973.

Weiss, Johannes. *Jesus' Proclamation of the kingdom of God*, Lives of Jesus Series, Philadelphia, PA: Fortress Press, 1971.

Wrede, William. *The Messianic Secret*, London: James Clarke, 1971.

Wright, N. T. *Jesus and the Victory of God*, Christian Origins and the Question of God, Minneapolis, MN: Fortress Press, 1996.

R

RABBINIC ETHICS

Portrayed in Scripture as read by the Rabbinic sages of the first six centuries CE, rabbinic ethics (questions of right or wrong), rabbinic morality (questions of good or bad), and rabbinic theology form a coherent system and cannot be considered in separation from one another. As portrayed in the Mishnah, Talmuds, and Midrash-compilations, the native categories of rabbinic Judaism, halakhah, law, norms of behavior, and haggadah, lore, norms of belief (narrative, amplification of Scripture), join together to set forth as a cogent statement the rules of conduct and conviction that embody that system. The Rabbinic system translates into the design of holy Israel's social order the will of God as expressed in the Torah given by God to Moses at Mount Sinai.

Accordingly, ethics derives from the Torah and defines God's judgment for practical conduct between one person and another. Morality, originating in the same source, extends the domain of divine judgment to matters that bear upon relationships of a person to oneself. And theology, also embodied in rules of belief and behavior, shapes relationships between the individual within the community of Israel and God. These cover the three dimensions of conduct and character: between one person and another, between a person and his or her own conscience, and between a person and God.

The 613 commandments and their single purpose

Basic to rabbinic Judaism are the commandments (*mitzvot*), which encompass in action symbols rules of what is to be done and not done, the Judaic world view and way of life. The commandments are grouped. People speak of 613 commandments, the Ten Commandments, and commandments concerning particular topics, such as the Sabbath and its commandment to rest and cease from creative labor. The commandments, enumerated at 613, 365 matching the days of the solar year and 248 corresponding to the number of bones of the body, govern everyday life and transactions, both social and personal.

These commandments concern theological convictions, "You shall love the Lord your God with all your heart, with all your soul, and with all your might" (Deut 6:4). They encompass ethical obligations. They concern matters of ritual. Judaism knows no distinction between right and rite, between theology and law. Rather, it treats each as the realization of the other and its fulfillment. The entire way of life and world view embody Israel's covenant with God. At hand is a system of covenantal nomism.

What is the point of the covenant? The Torah not only commands Israel "you shall be holy, for I the Lord your God am holy" (Lev 19:2), it defines holiness through the performance of religious duties, which are many. At the same time the Torah offers general rules of sanctification of the community of Israel, for example, "You shall love your neighbor as yourself" (Lev 19:18). Accordingly the master-narrative of Judaism at its foundations describes in vast detail the rules for living in God's kingdom under the yoke of the Torah.

Through a myriad of details, it is, then, easy to lose sight of the purpose of the whole. Hence, as Moses did in Leviticus 19:2 and 19:18, so too the rabbinic sages made every effort at teaching the purpose of the laws of the Torah, finding the main point realized in the details. In a series of stories and sayings, they declared what they deemed to form the heart and soul, the center of the system as a whole.

"The righteous shall live by his faith"

Among many efforts at summarizing life under the law of the Torah, the most comprehensive is attributed to R. Simelai, in the following composition:

Talmud of Babylonia *Makkot* 23b–24a/3:16 II.1

R. Simelai expounded,

Six hundred and thirteen commandments were given to Moses, three hundred and sixty-five negative ones, corresponding to the number of the days of the solar year, and two hundred forty-eight positive commandments, corresponding to the parts of man's body.

David came and reduced them to eleven: "A Pslm of David: Lord, who shall sojourn in thy tabernacle, and who shall dwell in thy holy mountain? (i) He who walks uprightly and (ii) works righteousness and (iii) speaks truth in his heart and (iv) has no slander on his tongue and (v) does no evil to his fellow and (vi) does not take up a reproach against his neighbor, (vii) in whose eyes a vile person is despised but (viii) honors those who fear the Lord. (ix) He swears to his own hurt and changes not. (x) He does not lend on interest. (xi) He does not take a bribe against the innocent" (Ps 15).

Isaiah came and reduced them to six: "(i) He who walks righteously and (ii) speaks uprightly, (iii) he who despises the gain of oppressions, (iv) shakes his hand from holding bribes, (v) stops his ear from hearing of blood (vi) and shuts his eyes from looking upon evil, he shall dwell on high" (Isa 33:25–26).

Micah came and reduced them to three: "It has been told you, man, what is good, and what the Lord demands from you, (i) only to do justly and (ii) to love mercy, and (iii) to walk humbly before God" (Mic 6:8).

"only to do justly:" this refers to justice.

"to love mercy:" this refers to doing acts of loving kindness.

"to walk humbly before God:" this refers to accompanying a corpse to the grave and welcoming the bride.

And does this not yield a conclusion a fortiori: if matters that are not ordinarily done in private are referred to by

the Torah as "walking humbly before God," all the more so matters that ordinarily are done in private.

Isaiah again came and reduced them to two: "Thus says the Lord, (i) Keep justice and (ii) do righteousness" (Isa 56:1).

Amos came and reduced them to a single one, as it is said, "For thus says the Lord to the house of Israel. Seek Me and live."

Habakkuk further came and based them on one, as it is said, "But the righteous shall live by his faith" (Hab 2:4).

The Talmudic rabbis here try to define the point of the myriad of religious obligations of which the Torah is comprised. The way of life embodies the world view, and the world view explains the way of life. But at the heart of matters is the definition of the Israelite and his or her purpose in life. While many of the commandments concern matters we regard as ritual, fasting on the Day of Atonement, for example, the great sages insist that the heart of the matter concerns moral and ethical conduct. And these come to their climax in the attitude of the Israelite: faith in God, integrity in walking humbly with Him.

"What is hateful to you, to your fellow don't do." That's the entirety of the Torah; everything else is elaboration. So go, study!

Simelai's is only one such effort at summarizing the whole Torah in a few encompassing rules. The single most famous such statement of "the whole Torah" derives from Hillel, the first-century CE Pharisaic authority:

Talmud of Babylonia tractate *Shabbat* 30b–31a/2:5 I.12

There was another case of a Gentile who came before Shammai. He said to him, "Convert me on the stipulation that you teach me the entire Torah while I am standing on one foot." He drove him off with the building cubit that he had in his hand.

He came before Hillel: "Convert me."

He said to him, "'What is hateful to you, to your fellow don't do.' That's the entirety of the Torah; everything else is elaboration. So go, study."

This famous saying frequently is cited only in part, the part that amplifies Lev 19:18: "Love your neighbor as yourself." The climax about elaboration and Torah-study is left out. But, we see, Torah-study is integral to life under the law of the Torah, and ignorance is the enemy of piety. So we have to ask whether the Rabbinic sages address the question of which takes priority, study or action.

The final question concerning the Golden Rule is, how do the Rabbinic sages translate the commandment into concrete behavior? Here is their discussion of Lev 19:18, how they amplified the "Go, study," of Hillel's instruction.

Sifra CC:III.1, 4–7

1 A "You shall not hate your brother in your heart, [but reasoning, you shall reason with your neighbor, lest you bear sin because of him. You shall not take vengeance or bear any grudge against the sons of your own people, but you shall love your neighbor as yourself: I am the Lord]" (Lev 19:17–18).

B Might one suppose that one should not curse him, set him straight, or contradict him?

C Scripture says, "in your heart."

D I spoke only concerning hatred that is in the heart.

4 A "You shall not take vengeance [or bear any grudge]":

B To what extent is the force of vengeance?

C If one says to him, "Lend me your sickle," and the other did not do so.

D On the next day, the other says to him, "Lend me your spade."

E The one then replies, "I am not going to lend it to you, because you didn't lend me your sickle."

F In that context, it is said, "You shall not take vengeance."

5 A " . . . or bear any grudge":

B To what extent is the force of a grudge?

C If one says to him, "Lend me your spade," but he did not do so.

D The next day the other one says to him, "Lend me your sickle,"

E and the other replies, "I am not like you, for you didn't lend me your spade [but here, take the sickle]!"

F In that context, it is said, "or bear any grudge."

6 A "You shall not take vengeance or bear any grudge against the sons of your own people":

B "You may take vengeance and bear a grudge against others."

7 A " . . . but you shall love your neighbor as yourself: [I am the Lord]":

B. R. Aqiba says, "This is the encompassing principle of the Torah."

C. Ben Azzai says, "'This is the book of the generations of Adam' (Gen 5:1) is a still more encompassing principle."

The little debate at the end concludes the Halakhic, or practical, legal exposition with an Aggadic, or theoretical, theological debate.

The Ten Commandments

The Ten Commandments (Exod 20:1–17/Deut 5:6–21) are basic to Judaism and exhibit that insistence on the cogency of theology and law, ethics and ritual, right and rite that characterizes Judaism as a whole. At the centerpiece of the covenant, stand the Ten Commandments. For the Ten Commandments are not ten different things. They are one thing in ten forms: "I am the Lord your God . . . therefore, don't do this, and do that." The Ten Commandments are the details, the "I am the Lord your God" is the main thing. So the Ten Commandments outline a path to follow to make God "your God." And to leave that Egypt that "the Lord your God" helps you escape: slavery in one form or another.

How do the Ten Commandments define the Israelite's relationship with God? The very order of matters answers. God begins by announcing that Israel is to have only the Lord for God. Why start there? Because before one can agree to the details, one has to adopt the main point. God rules, and Israel accepts God's dominion. On the basis of that fact, all else follows.

The whole holds together if we look for points in common and correspondences. People familiar with the symbols of Judaism will know that the Ten Commandments are set forth in two groups of five, facing one another. So there are correspondences between the commandments. If you do one, the other follows. Violate one, the other is broken as well. When we recognize these correspondences between each set of five commandments and the complementary ones, we grasp the unity of rite and right, of ethics and ritual, in Rabbinic Judaism.

Mekilta attributed to R. Ishmael LIV:III.1 Bahodesh 8

How were the Ten Commandments set forth? There were five on one tablet, five on the other. On the one was written, "I am the Lord your God" and opposite it: "You shall not murder."

The Torah thus indicates that whoever sheds blood is regarded as though he had diminished the divine image.

The matter may be compared to the case of a mortal king who came into a town, and the people set up in his honor icons, and they made statues of him, and they minted coins in his honor.

After a while they overturned his icons, broke his statues, and invalidated his coins, so diminishing the image of the king.

Thus whoever sheds blood is regarded as though he had diminished the divine image, for it is said, "Whoever sheds man's blood . . . for in the image of God he made man" (Gen 9:6).

The whole of the Torah's picture of humankind is going to emerge in the Ten Commandments. We recall how the Torah insists that we are in God's image and likeness, and that means we look like God. Then murder diminishes God's image too.

So much for murder and God's image. Along these same lines, adultery represents a denial of God:

> On the one was written, "You shall have no other god."
> and opposite it: "You shall not commit adultery."
>
> The Torah thus indicates that whoever worships an idol is regarded as though he had committed adultery against the Omnipresent, for it is said, "You wife that commits adultery, that takes strangers instead of your husband" (Ezek 16:32); "And the Lord said to me, Go yet, love a woman beloved of her friend and an adulteress" (Hos 3:1).

Taking God's name in vain is the result of thievery. People often taken oaths, so Judaism notes, in connection with the claim that they have not taken someone else's property. Hence the correspondence:

> On the one was written, "You shall not take the name of the Lord your God in vain."
> and opposite it: "You shall not steal."
>
> The Torah thus indicates that whoever steals in the end will end up taking a false oath: "Will you steal, murder, commit adultery, and swear falsely?" (Jer 7:9); "Swearing and lying, killing and stealing, and committing adultery" (Hos 4:2).

What about the Sabbath? That is surely a commandment that has no counterpart, since it is (so it is seen by outsiders) a matter of pure "ritual," without ethical or moral implications. But the Sabbath stands for creation and celebrates God's creating the world. It is a concrete celebration of the theology of Creation. And in its concern for the workers' rights, it explains the ritual by appeal to ethics. There is nothing less narrowly ritualistic than the Sabbath, given its sense and meaning:

> On the one was written, "Remember the Sabbath day to keep it holy."
>
> and opposite it: "You shall not bear false witness."
>
> The Torah thus indicates that whoever violates the Sabbath is as though he had given testimony before the One who spoke and brought the world into being, indicating that he had not created his world in six days and not rested on the seventh, and whoever keeps the Sabbath day is as though he had given testimony before the One who spoke and brought the world into being, indicating that he had created his world in six days and rested on the seventh: "For you are my witnesses, says the Lord" (Isa 43:10).

Is there a reward and punishment contained within the correspondences? So our sages maintain:

> On the one was written, "Honor your father and your mother."
> and opposite it: "You shall not covet your neighbor's wife."
>
> The Torah thus indicates that whoever covets in the end will produce a son who curses his father and honors one who is not his father.
>
> Thus the Ten Commandments were given, five on this tablet, and five on that, the words of R. Hananiah b. Gamaliel.

What Hananiah has done is to discover many of the basic principles of Judaism, that is, of the Torah, in these Ten Commandments.

JACOB NEUSNER

Further reading

Bockmuehl, Markus. *Jewish Law in Gentile Churches. Halakhah and the Beginning of Christian Public Ethics*, Edinburgh: T. & T. Clark, 2000.

Cohen, Abraham. *Everyman's Talmud. The major teachings of the Rabbinic Sages*, New York: Schocken, 1995.

Heschel, Abraham J. *God in Search of Man. A Philosophy of Judaism*, Philadelphia, PA: Jewish Publication Society of America, 1955.

Kadushin, Max. *Worship and Ethics: A Study in Rabbinic Judaism*, Evanston, IL: Northwestern University Press, 1964.

Meyerowitz, Arthur. *Social Ethics of the Jews*, New York: Block, 1935.

Montefiore, É. G. and H. Loewe. *Rabbinic Anthology*, London: Macmillan, 1938.

Moore, George F. *Judaism. The Age of the Tannaim*, Cambridge, MA: Harvard University Press, 1927.

Neusner, Jacob. *The Theology of the Oral Torah. Revealing the Justice of God*, Kingston and Montreal: McGill-Queen's University Press, 1999; Ithaca, NY: Cornell University Press, 1999.

Sanders, Edward P. *Paul and Palestinian Judaism: A Comparison of Patterns of Religion*, Philadelphia, PA: Fortress Press, 1977.

—— *Judaism. Practice and Belief. 63 BCE–67 CE*, Philadelphia, PA: Trinity Press International. Paperback, 1992.

Schechter, Solomon. *Some Aspects of Rabbinic Theology*, New York: Schocken, 1965.

Schofer, Jonathan Wyn. *The Making of a Sage. A Study in Rabbinic Ethics*, Madison, WI: University of Wisconsin Press, 2004.

Urbach, Ephraim E. *The Sages. Their Beliefs and Opinions*, trans. Israel Abrahams, Jerusalem: Magnes Press of the Hebrew University, 1979.

RABBINIC LITERATURE

In the wake of 70 CE, neither Jerusalem nor its environs was amenable to the development of oral teaching among Pharisees and the other teachers (that is, rabbis) who focused on the living authority of the Torah. Even Yavneh was eclipsed during the second century by centers in prosperous Galilee, such as Usha and Beth She'arim. Later, metropolitan cities such as Sepphoris and Tiberias were the foci of leadership. There was at first nothing like a central leadership, or even a common policy, but rabbinic Judaism was constituted in the Pharisaic, priestly, and scribal quest for the purity of Israel despite the loss of the Temple. The health of the movement required a shift from the highly personal authority of the Pharisees to some notion of learned consensus. The Rabbis (capitalized to refer to contributors to the literature of Rabbinic Judaism) of the second century were to stress a rational, consensual achievement of purity, and by the time of the Talmud that was held to be a greater purity than charismatic authority could achieve.

Mishnah

Rabbis such as Aqiba during the second century had taught their own norms, which came to be known as *halakhoth*, and had their disciples learn them by heart. A disciple (*talmid*) might himself internalize what he learned (his teacher's Mishnah), and proceed to promulgate both it and his own *halakhoth*. But after the failure of Bar Kokhba, the Rabbis engaged in an extraordinary, synthetic effort, under Rabbi Judah ha-Nasi (or, "the Prince") to combine the *mishnayoth* commonly held to be worthy.

The Mishnah represents earlier traditions – some going back generations and even centuries – placed in a dialectical relationship; dialogue unfolds in an eternal present among positions in fact separated by time and/or geography. An invitation to dialectical reasoning concerning purity, unconstrained by history or chronology, is the principal contribution of Mishnah. The often uneven synthesis that results is presented in a definite plan of tractates, which typically address the topic of their title, arranged within orders (sedarim). Each order presupposes the agricultural activity the Rabbis came to see as normal for Israel. As Rabbis, they implied, we speak of the purity we may achieve for a Temple which should always have been, but we do so in the knowledge that the Israel we address and which supports us is more a collection of farms than a nation. Paradoxically, however, Rabbi Judah's move from Beth She'arim to Sepphoris signaled the emergence of rabbinic authority within cities, and in close association with Roman power.

The centralization accomplished under Rabbi Judah ranks with Ezra's reform among formative events in the history of Judaism. But where Ezra's program was located in a particular city (which could only be Jerusalem), Judah's was headquartered in one (whether Beth She'arim or Sepphoris), but located in the mind. The Mishnah that emerged offered a pattern of reflection that enabled any Rabbi anywhere to join in the reflection and the discipline of keeping or making Israel pure. Sanctity in that sense could become the project of the learned in any place.

The emergence of the Mishnah, of course, called into question its status as compared to Scripture, and the revolt under Bar Kokhba radically raised the issue of the status of those works which had promised the speedy rebuilding of the Temple after AD 70 (cf. 2 Esdras and the *Targum of Isaiah* at its earliest stage). The priestly canon, represented (although oddly counted) by Josephus (*Against Apion*, 1.39), had already called for the recognition of twenty-four books, and the Rabbis could both invoke the support of that group and control messianic yearnings by insisting that those who read books "outside" that canon would have no part in the world to come (*m. Sanh.* 10:1). Nonetheless, the issue of messianism was more accidental than systemic: it needed to be addressed by the Rabbis, and it was definitively addressed, but the crucial matter was the relationship between Scripture and Mishnah. That relationship required several centuries to resolve.

Midrash

Midrash may be said to be a category of thought and literature which seeks the resolution of Scripture with the teaching of the Rabbis. It is true – and frequently repeated – that the noun derives from the verb *darash*, which means to "inquire," but that fact is largely beside the point. Formally, any midrash will cite the scriptural locus under consideration, somewhat in the manner of the *pesherim* of Qumran, but typically exegesis is not the point of the exercise. Rather, the citation becomes an occasion to invoke the rabbinic teaching which may be associated with Scripture at that juncture. The relative autonomy of that teaching from any text is usually apparent in what are called the Tannaitic or Halakhic Midrashim. "Tannaitic" refers to the Tannaim ("repeaters," the Rabbis of the Mishnaic period, although the ascription to that period is traditional and open to serious question), while "Halakhic" refers to the substance of their teaching. Such documents include two midrashim on Exodus, each called the *Mekilta* (which means "measure"); one is ascribed to R. Ishmael and another to R. Simeon ben Yohai, both of whom lived during the second century. Leviticus receives similar treatment in *Sifra*, and Numbers and Deuteronomy in *Sifre*.

The influence of R. Ishmael is apparent in the attribution to him (as to Hillel during the first century) of "rules" (*middoth*) of interpretation. The rules represent the evolving grammar of the association of rabbinic teaching with Scripture. Formally, the *middoth* set out the patterns of similarity, analogy, and logical categorization which might permit scriptural patterns to be adduced in support of a given teaching or assertion. Their application may be observed within rabbinic discussion, but they are more in the nature of a description of the sort of inference involved in interpretation than they are the rigid program by which that association was effected. The clear impression conveyed by *Mekilta* (in both traditions), *Sifra*, and *Sifre* is that the biblical text is an occasion for the exposition of fundamentally Rabbinic ideas and modes of thought.

Tosefta

Despite the success of Rabbi Judah's bold experiment, the third century saw a crisis in the understanding of what might be done with the Mishnah. The crisis is visible in two dilemmas. The first dilemma concerned Scripture, as discussed above. The second was even more basic, in that it involved how the discussion occasioned by Mishnah was to be continued. The former question turned on the issue of the Rabbis' authority in respect of the past, as embodied in the canon; the latter question turned on the issue of their authority in respect of that of their successors. Mishnah developed a dialectic of eternal purity, but how was that dialectic and its findings, once it was consigned to writing, to be related to further rabbinic discussion?

Both dilemmas receive a tentative treatment in the Tosefta. The term means "addition," in that the corpus was seen as an addendum to the Mishnah in later centuries. In fact, however, the Tosefta seems intended more as a fresh Mishnah, which incorporates the work of later Rabbis, and brings their views into a pattern of discussion with those of the Tannaim. Nonetheless, the Tosefta is essentially conservative in its reliance upon the materials of Mishnah, and it does not promulgate the radical notion – adumbrated in *'Abot*, a tractate appended to the Mishnah around AD 250 – that, alongside the Torah written in Scripture, Moses received an oral Torah, which was passed on through the Prophets and Sages, and finally to the Rabbis. Tosefta represents a greater comprehensiveness in its supplementation of the Mishnah, but it points to the necessity of the daring it lacks, to elevate Rabbis not merely by including their teaching, but by permitting them to engage directly in dialogue with their illustrious predecessors in Scripture and memory.

Talmud

The relative comprehensiveness of the Tosefta did not assure its triumph. It did not supersede the Mishnah, nor did any subsequent work within the rabbinic tradition. The problem of how to address the present with the eternal truth of the tradition (and vice versa) was met by means of an innovation. The Rabbis, as expositors (Amoraim, as distinct from Tannaim), undertook to treat Mishnah as Scripture, that is, to generate a commentary on Mishnah which became known as Talmud (a noun which means "learning"). The "commentary" (as in the case of Midrash) is more a matter of using text as an occasion on which to associate teaching than it is an exposition or exegesis, but the Amoraim triumphantly accomplished what the Rabbis of the Tosefta did not: Mishnah was preserved, and at the same time its generative activity and logic was perpetuated in the present. The ideological advance which allowed of that accomplishment was the doctrine that Torah was known orally, not only in writing.

The Talmud of Jerusalem (c. 400 CE), or the Yerushalmi, was the last great product of rabbinic Judaism in Palestine (as it came to be called in the Roman period). Sociologically, it was difficult to maintain the sort of discipline of purity the Rabbis practiced, and wished others to practice, in a territory recently vanquished and urbanized by the Romans. The Hadrianic prohibition of circumcision may or may not have been a great impediment (depending upon time and place within the history of the Empire and how stringent that prohibition was intended to be), but the incursion of Roman institutions and culture, even at a local level, was a reality from the second century in a way it had not been earlier.

While progressive urbanization was not congenial to the maintenance of rabbinic power in Palestine, Babylonia during the third century saw the rise of the Sassanids and their form of Zoroastrianism, whose policy towards the practice of Judaism was relatively tolerant. The economic life of the Jews in Babylon, in largely autonomous towns and villages, supported by agriculture, was better suited to the rabbinic ethos than the increasing syncretism of the Roman Empire from the second century. Particularly, the Sassanids encouraged or tolerated (in varying degrees over time) the formation of the academies which were the dynamos of rabbinic discussion, in places such as Sura, Pumbeditha, and Nehardea.

The Rabbis of Babylon gave rabbinic Judaism its distinctive character, at least until the modern period, which was and is conveyed in their monument (probably completed during the sixth century or slightly later), the Babylonian Talmud, or the Babli. It is a more comprehensive and subtle treatment of the Mishnah than the Yerushalmi, often employing rich, narrative means which permit of the contemporization of the rabbinic ethos. Each Rabbi is here to some extent a Moses of his own, as when Moses himself is said to visit the academy of Aqiba, and to observe to God that the discussion is so complex, his own unworthiness is obvious (*b. Menah.* 29b). But the Rabbis are also respectful tradents, as when Rab Joseph of Pumbeditha, the blind master, acknowledges that, without the Targum, he would not understand Scripture (*b. Sanh.* 94b). Although the Talmud (and Babli, for practical purposes, is the Talmud) is vast, its very range is a succinct statement of its intent, to transform the whole of life with the light of the Torah as interpreted by the Rabbis.

Targumim and Midrash Rabbah

Their energy and their resources enabled the Rabbis of Babylon to see to the completion of the standard recension of the Targumim, renderings of Scripture in Aramaic, and to the publication of as definitive a form of the Midrash as was ever produced. Midrash *Rabbah* presents not only the biblical books used for festal and commemorative occasions (Esther, Ruth, Song of Songs, Ecclesiastes, Lamentations), but also the Pentateuch. The confidence of the Rabbis of Babylonia in their own ethos was so great that the comment upon Scripture might include explicit narrative concerning Rabbis, as well as exposition and discourse. Midrash Rabbah was likely completed during the eighth century, and it represents the confidence that Torah, whether in Scripture or Talmud, is fundamentally one. The Targumim also represent the attempt, in a variety of styles, to weave traditional or innovative understandings into the text of the Scripture by means of paraphrase and addition. The interweaving of Scripture and Rabbinic teaching is further represented in the homiletic Midrashim of a later period, the *Pesiqta Rabbati*, the *Pesiqta de-Rab Kahana*, and *Tanhuma*.

The Sefer Yesirah

The rabbinic period closes with the rise of Islam, and the subsequent reaction of the Geonim, the successors of the Rabbis who maintained and extended Rabbinic Judaism with a distinctively academic and sometimes rationalistic bent. Increasingly, their work took on a literary character, and a tendency towards philosophy and esoterism becomes manifest even as the rabbinic canon assumes a more and more axiomatic role. The Sefer Yesirah, or "book of formation," is a good representative or a work which is transitional between the Amoraim and the Geonim, and was perhaps composed during the seventh century. It builds upon a mystical tradition which reaches back at least until Yochanan ben Zakkai during the first century, according to which it is possible to see the chariot (the "Merkabah") of Ezek 1, and to know the structure of the creation. But where the Rabbis from the second century held that such experiments were a matter for private exposition (and then under tight controls, cf. *b. Shab.* 80b; *b. Hag.* 11b, 13a, 14b), the Sefer Yesirah commences a tradition of literary and rational esoterism, which is more typical of the Qabbala of the Middle Ages than of the mystical Judaism of the Rabbis. The dialectic of the Rabbis was rooted in the oral argument which produced their literature, and which their literature was designed to serve and extend; when the logic of literary discourse takes over from dialectical argument, the constitution of the Judaism which is reflected, even though tightly focused on rabbinic literature, takes on a different character.

Rabbinic literature and Jesus

The utility of the documents of rabbinic Judaism in assessing Jesus and the gospels is qualified by three critical considerations. First, the relatively late date of the literature must be taken into account, although the continuities between Rabbinic Judaism and Pharisaism during the first century rule out any global refusal to countenance analogies between the gospels and Rabbinica. Second, a recognition of the social and religious transformations involved in the emergence of rabbinic Judaism must alert the reader to the possibility of anachronistic attributions or to the presentation of early teachers as spokesmen of later theologies. And finally, the initial target of inquiry must be understood to be the recovery, not so much of particular events and sayings "paralleled" in the gospels, but of the milieu of early Judaism, reflected indirectly both in the gospels and in rabbinica, which was the matrix of the Christian faith.

Yet these cautions should not be construed to defend ignoring rabbinic literature in study of Jesus. Exegetes routinely refer to later Roman historians, such as Tacitus and Dio Cassius, to later Hellenistic authors, such as Philostratus and Athanaeus, to later Christian writers, such as Justin Martyr and Eusebius, and to later Gnostic sources, such as the "Trimorphic Protonnoia" and "On the Origin of the World," all in order to understand the New Testament better. These examples involve a time-lag after Jesus which is comparable to the delay in the production of the Mishnah, the Talmud, and the Targumim. In cases other than rabbinic literature, the principle of extrapolating backward from literary evidence is accepted; that principle should be applied consistently.

BRUCE CHILTON

Further reading

Epstein, I. *The Babylonian Talmud*, 35 vols, London: Soncino, 1935–48.

Hammer, R. *Sifre: A Tannaitic Commentary on the Book of Deuteronomy*, YJS 24, New Haven, CT and London: Yale University Press, 1986.

Lauterbach, J. Z. *Mekilta de-Rabbi Ishmael*, 3 vols, Philadelphia, PA: Jewish Publication Society of America, 1933–35 (repr. 1976).

Maccoby, H. *Early Rabbinic Writings*, Cambridge: Cambridge University Press, 1988.

Neusner, J. *The Tosefta: Translated from the Hebrew*, 6 vols, New York: KTAV, 1977–86.

——— *Judaism: The Evidence of the Mishnah*, Chicago, IL: University of Chicago Press, 1981.

——— *The Talmud of the Land of Israel*, 35 vols, Chicago, IL: University of Chicago Press, 1982–94.

——— *The Mishnah: A New Translation*, New Haven, CT: Yale University Press, 1988.

——— *Introduction to Rabbinic Literature*, ABRL, New York: Doubleday, 1994.

Strack, H. L., and Stemberger, G. *Introduction to the Talmud and Midrash*, Edinburgh: T. & T. Clark, 1991; Minneapolis, MN: Fortress Press, 1992).

RANSOM SAYING

The so-called ransom saying of Mark 10:45/Matt 20:28 is of great importance because it is one of two places where Jesus explicitly reveals how he understood his imminent death, i.e. that he did so in sacrificial terms (the other being the words of institution at the Last Supper). The passage has also been hotly disputed in terms of both its historical reliability and its background. Apart from the opening connective (Mark: "For also"; Matt: "Just as"), the logion is verbatim in both gospels: "the Son of Man came not to be served but to serve, and to give his life as a ransom for many (*lytron anti pollon*)."

The integrity of the passage

The questions are whether the last clause, the determinative one, is in fact to be understood as belonging originally with the first part of the sentence in Mark 10:45, and second, whether the verse itself belongs with the preceding verses, and hence in its present context. In both gospels the context has to do with service. The passage (Mark 10:35ff.; Matt 20:20ff.) grows out of the ambition of James and John to sit on either side of Jesus in his kingdom/glory. In the words just prior to our logion, Jesus says "whoever would be great among you must be your servant, and whoever would be first among you must be slave of all" (cf. Mark 9:35). Some scholars conclude that the final clause, "to give his life a ransom for many," does not fit well with what precedes and seems to be added by Mark from some other context. A cognate passage found in Luke 22:24–27 ends with the words "But I am among you as one who serves," thus providing an ethical model, but with no reference to the ransom. At the same time, because of the parallel idea of 1 Tim 2:5f., "For there is one God, and there is one mediator between God and men, the man Christ Jesus, who gave himself as a ransom for all," the question of authenticity arises. Scholars, depending on their predisposition, either regard Mark 10:45c as an example of Christian atonement theology retrojected into Mark, or regard the parallel in 1 Tim as dependent on the dominical logion in Mark.

A good case, however, can be made for concluding that the whole of Mark 10:45 circulated independently of its present context, with the second part of the verse providing a specific content to the service motif. This logion may then have been added by Mark to the verses about service that precede it in its present context (Stuhlmacher), and if this is so, then the passage may be taken as a unity as it is found in Mark. Although at first glance the introduction of the ransom motif may look foreign to the Markan context, the reference to the cup that Jesus must drink and the baptism with which he must be baptized (Mark 10:38f.) concerns the death of Jesus, and also raises the specter of martyrdom for the disciples. This combination of the motifs of service and death in the immediate context can well explain reference to, and the interpretation of, the death of Jesus found in 10:45.

Authenticity

Those who argue against the authenticity of the ransom logion put special weight upon the general lack of evidence that Jesus interpreted his death in terms of atonement. The noun *lytron* is found nowhere else in the teaching of Jesus. Such an explicit interpretation, it is alleged, reflects the theology of the church put into the mouth of Jesus. The very tense of the verb ("I came," *elthen*) seems retrospective and could be taken in a similar way.

To take up the last point first, the aorist verb does not necessarily reflect the perspective of the post-resurrection church. The aorist is the default tense in Koine Greek, and is often used when one views something as a whole; it does not necessarily view something as past. Here it functions in a summative manner, describing the purpose of Jesus. The verbs "come" and "send" are commonly used in this manner in the synoptics, and this therefore constitutes no convincing argument against these words being said by Jesus.

The noun *lytron* occurs in the whole of the NT only in Mark 10:45 and its Matthean parallel. The only parallels are the cognate verb *lytroun* found in Titus 2:14, and *antilytron* in 1 Tim 2:6. Furthermore, Mark's *anti pollon* occurs only here in the NT; Paul prefers the preposition *hyper* in speaking of the substitutionary work of Christ. This is not to deny that the thought of the verse is consonant with that of the early Christian community. But the precise language of our passage is not found elsewhere in the NT where the death of Jesus is understood as having atoning significance. Thus the actual language of the ransom saying does not support the conclusion that it reflects the theology of the Church.

It is very important to note that the ransom saying does not stand alone in the NT as an interpretation of the death of Jesus as an atoning sacrifice. It is true that when Jesus prophesies his death in the synoptics he nowhere gives it a sacrificial interpretation (by contrast, cf. John 10:11). At the Last Supper, however, Jesus interprets the cup and the wine as his body and blood, with the latter said to be "my blood of the covenant, which is poured out for many (*hyper pollon*)" (Mark 14:24; Matt 26:28: *peri pollon*, adding "for the forgiveness of sins"; Luke 22:19f.: *hyper hymon*, "for you," repeated in reference to both the bread and the cup). While this passage is a parallel to the

Markan logion, there is no linguistic reason to conclude that the latter is derived from the eucharistic material. Jeremias, who readily admits that the authenticity of the ransom saying is a difficult question, nevertheless notes the strong Semitic character of the words and concludes "Anyone who regards the nucleus of the eucharistic words as genuine will have no hesitation in deriving the substance of this *logion* from Jesus" (Jer 294). When compared to 1 Tim 2:6 (and Luke 22:24–27), the Greek of Mark 10:42–45 is Semitic and reflects a Palestinian background (thus Jeremias). It is thus more primitive and probably reflects earlier rather than later material.

If the ransom logion is the creation of the Church, furthermore, it seems odd that it would be so brief and undeveloped. One might well expect the interpretation of the death of Jesus to have been given a much fuller and more explicit treatment. A more plausible conclusion is that the Church's theology of the atoning death of Jesus derives at the beginning from this original saying of Jesus that eventually made its way into Mark's Gospel from the oral tradition..

Background

But can Jesus have thought of his death as sacrificial? If he did so, against what specific background was this interpretation made? Here again we encounter a much disputed topic. The opinion common for so long that the ransom saying depends on the suffering and dying Servant of Isa 52:13–53:12 has been strongly challenged by some who deny any specific connection altogether. Because the ransom saying begins with "the Son of Man," scholars have given much attention to Daniel as its background.

The main points in the argument against dependence upon Isaiah are the following (see Barrett, Hooker): (1) the key word of Mark 10:45, *lytron* ("ransom") does not appear in the LXX of Isa 53 and is never used in the LXX to translate *'asham* ("offering for sin"), the word that occurs in Isa 53:10; (2) the verbs "not to be served, but to serve" are from *diakonein*, a verb not found in Isa 53. In Isa 53 the verb "to serve" does not occur at all. Further, in the Servant Songs the noun *'bd*, "servant," is translated either by *pais* or *doulos* and not *diakonos*; (3) the clause "to give his life" has only the noun *psyche*, "life," in common between Isa 53:12 ("he poured out his soul to death") and Mark 10:45.

It has to be admitted that the case for direct dependence of Mark 10:45 on Isa 53, if we are speaking of verbatim agreement, is not very strong. On the other hand, it still is difficult to miss the similarity of the passages. The thought of the two passages runs along exactly the same lines. Especially striking is the presence of substitution and sacrifice in both passages. The servant of Isa 53 "was wounded for our transgressions, he was bruised for our iniquities" (v 5f.), "stricken for the transgression of my people" (v 8), and "he bore the sin of many" (v 12). Although the word *lytron* is not used, the idea of "ransom" is nevertheless obvious. And earlier in the Servant Songs the idea of ransom is explicit. Thus in Isa 43:3f.,

> For I am the Lord your God, the Holy One of Israel, your Savior. I give Egypt as your ransom [LXX: *allagma*, not *lytron*], Ethiopia and Seba in exchange for you. Because you are precious in my eyes, and honored, and I love you, I give men in return for you, peoples, in exchange for your life.

It can be argued that this passage is the background for Mark 10:45, but one need not let this passage displace Isa 53 as the primary background of the ransom saying (Stuhlmacher allows both, with the "primary accent" coming from Isa 43).

The fact that the *diakonein* root is not used in reference to the Servant in the Isaiah Servant Songs is not particularly significant. The discussion of service just prior to Mark 10:45 employs *diakonos* and *doulos* as synonyms. A variety of words can be used to express the idea. And to the phrase "to give his life," a parallel should be noted in the Hebrew of Isa 53:10: "when you make his soul [*nephesh*] an offering for sin" (Page).

Two other important points support a connection between Isa 53 and Mark 10:45. First is the distinctive use of *polloi* in the ransom saying, which may be a direct reflection of the "many" (*rabbim*; LXX: *polloi*) in Isa 53:12, "he bore the sin of many" (cf. Mark 14:24). This is the single direct linguistic agreement between the two passages. A final piece of evidence that Isa 53 served as a background to the death of Jesus is the quotation from Isa 53:11f. in Luke 22:37: "For I tell you that this scripture must be fulfilled in me, 'And he was reckoned with transgressors'; for what is written about me has its fulfillment." If we may trust Luke, here we have clear evidence that Jesus interpreted his death in terms of the suffering and dying Servant of Isa 53 (cf. too the quotation of Isa 53:4 in Matt 8:17).

Prompted by the initial reference to "the Son of Man," Barrett and Hooker find an alternate background for the ransom saying in Dan 7. They argue that the form of the saying, "came not to be served, but to serve," is meant to turn on its head the notion of the triumphant apocalyptic figure of Dan 7:13, of whom it is said "all peoples, nations, and languages should serve him." Martyrdom is an important theme in the book of Daniel, and before the Son of Man enters into his glory he undergoes suffering representatively, like the martyrs, on behalf of others, and hence as a "ransom for many." The redemption in view is the restoration of the people of God in accord with the vision of Dan 7.

This view may be plausible, but apart from the reference to the Son of Man, it rests no more on actual verbal correspondence than does the appeal to Isa 53. In both cases appeal must be made to the "sense" of the passage. That being the case, the suffering servant of Isa 53 retains its ability to explain Mark 10:45.

> The earthly Jesus himself understood his witness and his approaching death in the light of the tradition already given to him in Isaiah about the (vicariously suffering) Servant of God. He understood the suffering laid upon him as an event in which God's will was fulfilled.
>
> (Stuhlmacher 2004: 153)

Significance

If we may accept the authenticity of Mark 10:45/Matt 20:28, then together with the words of institution at the Last Supper, we have strong evidence of the way in which Jesus understood his death. We may conclude that the early church's exposition of the death of Jesus as a substitutionary, atoning sacrifice does not betray or depart from his intention. The ransom saying indicates instead that far from being an unfortunate accident of history, Jesus chooses to go to his death in order to accomplish redemption and so to fulfill the saving plan of God for the salvation of Israel and the world (*anti pollon*, "for many," is to be taken in an all-inclusive sense). In the first-century context of Hellenistic Palestine, the key word *lytron* would have connoted the manumission of slaves. The metaphor of slavery fits well the hopelessness of the human situation. Human beings enslaved by their transgressions have need of a redeemer. A passage that contains vivid ransom language is Ps 49:7–9:

> Truly no man can ransom himself, or give to God the price of his life, for the ransom of his life is costly and can never suffice that he should continue to live on for ever, and never see the Pit.

(LXX twice uses the verb *lytroun* in this passage). Jesus understood his mission as one of dying, like

Isaiah's Servant, vicariously for the expiation of the sins of the people. Even the explanation of the ransom saying as deriving from Dan 7, should one prefer it, points in the same direction: the Son of Man as one who goes to his death like a martyr, on behalf of the salvation of others, atoning for their sins.

DONALD A. HAGNER

Further reading

Barrett, C. K. "The Background of Mark 10:45," in A. J. B. Higgins (ed) *New Testament Essays. Studies in Memory of T. W. Manson*, Manchester: Manchester University Press, 1959, pp. 1–18.

France, R. T. "The Servant of the Lord in the Teaching of Jesus," *TynB* 19 (1968) 26–52.

—— *Jesus and the Old Testament: His Application of Old Testament Passages to Himself and His Mission*, London: Tyndale, 1971, pp. 116–21.

Hengel, M. *The Atonement: The Origins of the Doctrine in the New Testament*, trans. J. Bowker, Philadelphia, PA: Fortress Press, 1981.

Hooker, Morna D. *Jesus the Servant*, London: SPCK, 1959.

—— *The Son of Man in Mark: A Study of the Background of the Term "Son of Man" and its Use in St Mark's Gospel*, Montreal: McGill University Press, 1967.

Jeremias, Joachim. *New Testament Theology*, London: SCM Press, 1971.

Kim, Seyoon. "The Eucharistic Words of Jesus as the Words of 'the Son of Man'," in *The Son of Man as the Son of God*, Tübingen: Mohr Siebeck, 1983; Grand Rapids, MI: Eerdmans, 1985, pp. 38–73.

Lindars, Barnabas. "Salvation Proclaimed. VII. Mark 10:45: A Ransom for Many," *ExpT* 93 (1982) 292–95.

Page, Sydney H. T. "The Authenticity of the Ransom Logion (Mark 10:45b)," in R. T. France and D. Wenham (eds) *Gospel Perspectives*, Sheffield: JSOT, 1980, Vol. 1, pp. 137–61.

Stuhlmacher, P. "Vicariously Giving His Life for Many, Mark 10:45 (Matt 20:28)," in *Reconciliation, Law, and Righteousness: Essays in Biblical Theology*, trans. E. F. Kalin, Philadelphia, PA: Fortress Press, 1986.

—— "Isaiah 53 in the Gospels and Acts," in Bernd Janowski and Peter Stuhlmacher (eds) *The Suffering Servant: Isaiah 53 in Jewish and Christian Sources*, trans. Daniel P. Bailey, Grand Rapids, MI: Eerdmans, 2004.

Taylor, Vincent. "The Origin of the Markan Passion-sayings," in *New Testament Essays*, London: Epworth, 1970, pp. 60–71.

Wilcox, M. "On the Ransom-Saying in Mark 10:45c. Matt 20:28c," in H. Lichtenberger (ed.) *Geschichte–Tradition–Reflexion*, FS Martin Hengel, Tübingen: Mohr Siebeck, 1996, Vol. 3, pp. 173–86.

REDACTION CRITICISM

Redaction criticism is a free English rendering of *Redaktionsgeschichte*, "redaction history," a term popularized by Willi Marxsen in his seminal monograph *Der Evangelist Markus* (1956). In principle, redaction criticism may be practiced with any biblical book that seems to bear discernible traces of its author's adaptation of antecedent oral or literary traditions. Thus, the redaction critic may discern later additions and modifications within a Pentateuchal book (e.g. Exod 20:1–21), the Acts of the Apostles (see Haenchen 1971), or a Pauline letter (Phil 2:1–11). In practice, however, at least within the New Testament, redaction criticism has been most commonly applied in exegesis of the gospels. It is on these documents that this article is focused, (1) describing redaction criticism's operation, (2) surveying its origin and development in modern scholarship, (3) noting important redaction-critical studies, and (4) identifying the contributions and limitations of redaction criticism as an exegetical method.

The method in operation

A comparative analysis of different accounts of Jesus' baptism in the gospels (RSV) offers a simple exercise in redaction criticism (see Box 1)

Mark's version of this epiphany is the most straightforward. It may have been the earliest and a basis for the others. Luke's version evinces slight adjustments: couched in a relative clause, the narration of the baptism is made in passing, almost as though Luke wished not to detract from God's more detailed and dramatic intervention in Luke 1–2 (an Infancy narrative absent from Mark). Characteristically in Luke, prayer accompanies revelation (3:21; see also 1:10; 5:16; 6:12; 9:18, 28; 11:1; 18:1, 10; 22:39–45). Luke is the only Evangelist that describes the Holy Spirit's descent upon Jesus "in bodily form, as a dove" (3:22), which anticipates the Holy Spirit's manifestation at Pentecost by sensory means: a heavenly sound, a rush of wind, and "tongues as of fire" (Acts 2:1–2).

The changes in Matthew's description of Jesus' baptism are more obvious: (1) Matthew is more explicit about Jesus' intent to be baptized (3:13); (2) John the Baptist is reluctant to cooperate: Jesus ought to be baptizing him (3:14; see also 3:11–12); (3) John consents when assured by Jesus that "thus it is fitting for us to fulfill all righteousness" (3:15), an important theme in Matthew's Gospel (1:19; 5:20; 25:31–46); (4) unlike Mark and Luke, Matthew describes the voice from heaven as addressed, not to the baptized Jesus (3:16), but to an attending audience – "*This* is my beloved Son" (3:17) – thus heightening parallel acclamations at Jesus' transfiguration (17:5) and crucifixion (27:54).

Typically, John seems to presuppose knowledge of the other gospels while going his own way. John the Baptist (never so identified in this gospel) offers a secondhand account of Jesus' baptism, reporting a vision of the Spirit's dove-like descent from heaven and remaining on Jesus (1:32). Unlike Matthew, in this gospel John had not previously known Jesus until God revealed him (1:31, 33). In the Fourth Gospel Jesus' divine accreditation is directly conveyed to John (1:33), whose primary task is to bear witness to Jesus as "the Son of God" (1:34) while directing others to "the Lamb of God, who takes away the sins of the world" (1:29; see also 1:6–8, 35–37; 3:22–30).

Observing these various modifications of a similar story, most historians conclude (a) that John probably did baptize Jesus, (b) remembrance of which likely stimulated theological questions among early Christians. For example, both Matthew and John demonstrate a concern for properly correlating the Baptist with Jesus, clarifying that the latter was no disciple of the former but superior to him. Others may have wondered why Jesus availed himself of a ritual whose purpose was the remission of sins (Mark 1:4–5; Matt 3:7–10 = Luke 3:7–9; cf. 2 Cor 5:21; Heb 4:15). Matthew addresses that issue with a detailed rationale; Luke seems to dismiss it with nonchalance. The noncanonical *Gospel according to the Hebrews* attacks the matter

---

Box 1. Simple exercise in redaction criticism

Matt 3:13–17	*Mark 1:9–11*	*Luke 3:21–22*	*John 1:31–34*
[13]Then Jesus came from Galilee to the Jordan to John, to be baptized by him. [14]John would have prevented him, saying, "I need to be baptized by you, and do you come to me?" [15]But Jesus answered him, "Let it be so now; for thus it is fitting for us to fulfill all righteousness." Then he consented. [16]And when Jesus was baptized, he went up immediately from the water and behold, the heavens were opened and he saw the Spirit of God descending like a dove and alighting on him; [17]and lo, a voice from heaven, saying, "This is my beloved Son, with whom I am well pleased."	[9]In those days Jesus came from Nazareth of Galilee and was baptized by John in the Jordan. [10]And when he came up out of the water, immediately he saw the heavens opened and the Spirit descending upon him like a dove; [11]and a voice came from heaven, "Thou art my beloved Son; with thee I am well pleased."	[21]Now when all the people were baptized and when Jesus also had been baptized and was praying, the heaven was opened, [22]and the Holy Spirit descended upon him in bodily form, as a dove, and a voice came from heaven, "Thou art my beloved Son; with thee I am well pleased."	[31]"I myself did not know him; but for this I came baptizing with water, that he might be revealed to Israel." [32]And John bore witness, "I saw the Spirit descend as a dove from heaven, and it remained on him. [33]I myself did not know him; but he who sent me to baptize with water said to me, 'He on whom you see the Spirit descend and remain, this is he who baptizes with the Holy Spirit.' [34]And I have seen and borne witness that this is the Son of God."

head-on: When encouraged by his family to go to John for baptism, Jesus replies, "In what have I sinned that I should go and be baptized by him? Unless, perhaps, what I have just said is a sin of ignorance" (Jerome, *Against Pelagius* 3.2).

Origins and development

Modern anticipations of the redaction-critical perspective may be detected in the Wolfunbüttel *Fragments* (1774–78; English translation 1972) of Hermann Samuel Reimarus (1694–1768), who hypothesized creative, albeit duplicitous, alterations by the Evangelists of the earliest traditions about Jesus; in the more orthodox reflection of Martin Kähler (1835–1912), an early critic of the so-called "quest for the historical Jesus" (1896); and in the research of Julius Wellhausen (1844–1913) and William Wrede (1859–1906), who encouraged source critics to attend more closely to the Evangelists' theological biases (Wrede 1901; Wellhausen 1905). The nineteenth and twentieth centuries witnessed the flowering of source criticism as a means of addressing the synoptic problem, which assumes adaptations by one Evangelist of the others (Wilke 1838; Weisse 1856; Holtzmann 1863), and form criticism's attention to various genres among the gospels' preliterary traditions and their putative function in earliest Christianity's teaching and preaching (Schmidt 1919; Dibelius 1919; Bultmann 1921). The immediate impetus for redaction criticism was the form critics' tendency to atomize the gospels' pericopae, isolated from their narrative contexts, and to denigrate the Evangelists as "vehicles of tradition" but "only to the smallest extent authors" (Dibelius 1934: 3, 23), incapable of mastering their inherited traditions (Bultmann 1963: 350).

In three important ways Marxsen differentiated his approach to the gospels from that of his precursors: (1) a primary interest in "an individual, an author personality who pursues a definite goal with his work" and "the particular interest or point of view of the evangelist concerned"; (2) "the 'framework' [or] the itinerary and scenic links" within the narrative, as well as "textual transformations, to the extent we can recognize them"; (3) the "'third situation-in-life' [*Sitz im Leben*] ... the situation of the community in which the gospels arose," in contrast to "the 'first situation-in-life' located in the unique situation of Jesus' activity" and "the 'second situation-in-life' mediated by the situation of the primitive church" (1969: 18, 23–24). To those who had considered the Evangelists mere

"scissors-and-paste" editors, another redaction critic retorted, "[T]he 'scissors' were manipulated by a theological hand, and the 'paste' was impregnated with a particular theology" (Stein 1969: 46). To offset imbalances in previous scholarship, therefore, redaction criticism emerged as a way of reading the gospels that accented their character as unitary creations by Evangelists functioning as genuine authors and theologians.

Major redaction-critical studies

With that point of view ensconced, accompanied by temporary quiescence in quest of the Jesus of history (cf. Robinson), much gospel criticism from the mid-twentieth century refined the redaction-critical method and applied its insights to different aspects of all the gospels (Rohde). On the generally accepted assumption of Mark's chronological priority among the synoptics, Günther Bornkamm and his students undertook important studies of Matthew's understanding of the Church, the Law, and miracles (1960), while Hans Conzelmann offered a significant redaction-critical study of Lukan eschatology (1953). Mark and John presented special problems for redaction critics, because their sources, and thus any alterations made to them, could not be identified with comparable confidence. That, however, did not deter scholars from drawing redaction-critical conclusions on the basis of Mark's allegedly characteristic locutions (Turner 1923–27; Pryke; Peabody), his putative arrangement of earlier traditions (Lightfoot, Lohmeyer; Farrer), particularly the passion narrative (Dormeyer), and salient motifs like the much debated "messianic secret" (Tuckett). Careful attempts were made to identify a secure basis for Markan redaction criticism (Stein 1971; Perrin 1971). Redaction criticism of the Fourth Gospel was based on assumptions, drawn largely from Bultmann's influential commentary (1971), about the character of John's antecedent traditions (Fortna). More recently, some Johannine redaction critics have proceeded on the assumption of John's knowledge and use of one or more of the synoptics (see the discussion in Smith). Noncanonical gospels, such as that of *Thomas*, have also been analyzed by way of redaction criticism (Koester). Many of the twentieth century's major commentaries on the gospels were fundamentally redaction-critical in approach (Luz 1989–2005; Pesch 1976, 1977; Fitzmyer 1981, 1985), and redaction criticism still governs the investigation of important clusters of material in the gospels, such as the parables of Jesus (Hultgren).

Contributions and limitations

Basic in the formulation of redaction criticism have been three claims: the Evangelists' activity as authors and theologians, painting distinctive portraits of Jesus in response to important religious issues in their respective communities, and their gospels as literary entities to be interpreted holistically. Redaction criticism has typically found its hermeneutical center of gravity in the Evangelists, regarded as narrative theologians (Perrin 1976). By encouraging biblical scholars to consider the gospels' authors as creative theologians, redaction criticism has paved the way for more recent, literary-critical and canonical approaches to the gospels. Moreover, *Redaktionsgeschichte* virtually set the agenda for the full range of critical inquiry into the gospels during much of the twentieth century. Its premises and procedure have proved appropriable by the modern church, across all major denominations and a broad theological range, from conservative to liberal (e.g. the papal encyclical *Divino Afflante Spiritu*, Rome 1943: 97). Perhaps most important, redaction criticism's emphasis on the gospels' theological character resonates with the express intent of at least some of the Evangelists (Luke 1:4; John 20:31) and the tenor of the patristic church in its identification of orthodoxy (Eusebius *Hist. eccl.* 3.39.3).

Like every interpretive approach to scripture, redaction criticism has limitations, most of which have become evident across decades of its practice. Its concentration on the Evangelists as authors has created different kinds of problems, many of which – ironically – have obscured other important facets of the redaction-critical enterprise. Thus, its consideration of those ancient communities for which the gospels were written has at times assumed a truncated aspect, lacking the complexity and texture that only more nuanced social-scientific inquiries of the literature may be able to provide (Keck 1974; Theissen 1991). Some redaction critics have found the method's focus on the author too constraining; accordingly, they have broadened their study to account for other dimensions of the gospels' literary character, such as plot, discourse, characterizations, and the varied responses evoked in readers (Culpepper; Tannehill 1986, 1990; Kingsbury; Fowler 1991). Beyond the fact that redaction critics have often posed important questions that the method itself is not adequately equipped to answer, at times they have also been less than clear in their exegetical intentions: whether, for instance, they are more concerned with a gospel's overall composition than with strict distinctions between tradition and redaction. Especially in the case of Mark, on the assumption of that gospel's chronological priority, the exegetical results of even scrupulous redaction criticism have proved extraordinarily incoherent (Black 1986, 1989).

The significance of redaction criticism for historical reconstructions of Jesus remains somewhat equivocal. On the one hand, it has long served as, and remains, an important tool for historians in their attempt to distinguish probably authentic Jesus material from later interpretive accretions (invoking the so-called "criterion of dissimilarity"; see, e.g., Meier 1991, 2001). On the other hand, a hyper-skeptical adoption of redaction criticism can preclude the quest for the Jesus of history, if one holds that "the Gospels offer us primarily the primitive Christian kerygma, and ... [historical] criticism can only help us to arrive at corrections and modifications in the kerygma but never at a word or action of the earthly Jesus himself" (Käsemann 34–35; cf. Marxsen 1969: 23–24).

On balance, redaction criticism has proved to be an exceptionally important tool in twentieth-century investigation of the Gospels, absorbing the insights of previous methods of inquiry while laying foundations for new hermeneutical enterprises. It remains to be seen whether, in the twenty-first century, it will retain its integrity as a recognizable exegetical strategy, among others, or will gradually metamorphose into other approaches to the gospels' interpretation.

C. CLIFTON BLACK

Further reading

Black, C. C. "The Quest of Mark the Redactor: Why Has It Been Pursued, and What Has It Taught Us?" *JSNT* 33 (1986) 19–39.

—— *The Disciples According to Mark: Markan Redaction in Current Debate*, JSNTSup 27, Sheffield: Sheffield Academic Press, 1989.

Bornkamm, G., G. Barth, and H.-J. Held. *Überlieferung und Auslegung im Matthäusevangelium*, Neukirchen: Moers/Neukirchener, 1960.

—— *Tradition and Interpretation in Matthew*, Philadelphia, PA: Westminster, 1963.

Bultmann, R. *Die Geschichte der synoptischen Tradition*, Göttingen: Vandenhoeck & Ruprecht, 1921.

—— *The History of the Synoptic Tradition*, revised edition, New York: Harper & Row, 1963.

—— *The Gospel of John. A Commentary*, Philadelphia, PA: Westminster, 1971.

Conzelmann, H. *Die Mitte der Zeit*, Tübingen: Mohr Siebeck, 1953.

—— *The Theology of St. Luke*, New York: Harper & Row, 1961.

Culpepper, R. A. *Anatomy of the Fourth Gospel: A Study in Literary Design*, Philadelphia, PA: Fortress Press, 1983.

Dibelius, M. *Die Formgeschichte des Evangeliums*, Tübingen Mohr, 1919.
—— *From Tradition to Gospel*, New York: Charles Scribner's Sons, 1934.
Dormeyer, D. *Die Passion Jesu als Verhaltensmodell: Literarische und theologische Analyse der Traditions-und Redaktionsgeschichte der Markuspassion*, Münster: Aschendorff, 1974.
Farrer, A. M. *A Study in St Mark*, Westminster: Dacre, 1951.
Fitzmyer, J. A. *The Gospel According to Luke*, 2 vols, AB 28, 28A, Garden City, NY: Doubleday, 1981, 1985.
Fortna, R. T. *The Gospel of Signs: A Reconstruction of the Narrative Source Underlying the Fourth Gospel*, SNTSMS 11, Cambridge: Cambridge University Press, 1970.
Fowler, R. M. *Let the Reader Understand: Reader-Response Criticism and the Gospel of Mark*, Philadelphia, PA: Fortress Press, 1991.
Haenchen, E. *The Acts of the Apostles: A Commentary*, Philadelphia, PA: Westminster, 1971.
Holtzmann, H. J. *Die synoptischen Evangelien: Ihr Ursprung und geschichtlicher Charakter*, Leipzig: Engelmann, 1863.
Hultgren, A. J. *The Parables of Jesus: A Commentary*, Grand Rapids, MI and Cambridge: Eerdmans, 2000.
Kähler, M. *Der sogenannte historische Jesus und der geschichtliche, biblische Christus*, Leipzig: Deichert'sche Verlagsbuchhandlung, 1896.
—— *The So-Called Historical Jesus and the Historic Biblical Christ*, Philadelphia, PA: Fortress Press, 1964.
Käsemann, E. "The Problem of the Historical Jesus," *Essays on New Testament Themes*, London: SCM Press, 1964, pp. 34–55 [1950].
Keck, L. E. "On the Ethos of Early Christians," *JAAR* 42 (1974) 435–42.
Kingsbury, J. D. *Matthew as Story*, second edition, Philadelphia, PA: Fortress Press, 1988.
Koester, H. *Ancient Christian Gospels*, Philadelphia, PA: Trinity Press International, 1990.
Lightfoot, R. H. *History and Interpretation in the Gospels*, London: Hodder and Stoughton, 1935.
Lohmeyer, E. *Galiläa und Jerusalem*, Göttingen: Vandenhoeck & Ruprecht, 1936.
Luz, U. *Matthew 1–7. A Commentary*, Continental Commentaries, Minneapolis, MN: Augsburg, 1989.
—— *Matthew 8–20: A Commentary*, Hermeneia, Minneapolis, MN: Fortress Press, 2001.
—— *Matthew 21–28: A Commentary*, Hermeneia, Minneapolis, MN: Fortress Press, 2005.
Marxsen, W. *Der Evangelist Markus: Studien zur Redaktionsgeschichte des Evangeliums*, FRLANT NF 49, Göttingen: Vandenhoeck & Ruprecht, 1956.
—— *Mark the Evangelist: Studies on the Redaction History of the Gospel*, Nashville, TN and New York: Abingdon, 1969.
Meier, J. P. *A Marginal Jew: Rethinking the Historical Jesus*. Vol. 1: *The Roots of the Problem and the Person*. Vol. 2: *Mentor, Message, and Miracles*. Vol. 3: *Companions and Competitors*, New York: Doubleday, 1991, 1994, 2001.
Peabody, D. B. *Mark as Composer*, Macon, GA: Mercer University Press, 1987.
Perrin, N. "The Christology of Mark: A Study in Methodology," *JR* 51 (1971) 174–75.
—— *What Is Redaction Criticism?* Philadelphia, PA: Fortress Press, 1976.
Pesch, R. *Das Markusevangelium*, 2 vols, second revised edition, HTKNT 2, Freiburg: Herder, 1976, 1977.

Pryke, E. J. *Redactional Style in the Markan Gospel: A Study of Syntax and Vocabulary as Guides to Redaction in Mark*, SNTSMS 33, Cambridge: Cambridge University Press, 1978.
Reimarus, H. S. *Reimarus: Fragments*, LJS, ed. C. H. Talbert; Philadelphia, PA: Fortress Press, 1970.
Robinson, James M. *A New Quest of the Historical Jesus*, SBT 25, London: SCM Press, 1959.
Rohde, J. *Rediscovering the Teaching of the Evangelists*, NTL, Philadelphia, PA: Westminster, 1968.
Rome and the Study of Scripture: A Collection of Papal Enactments on the Study of Holy Scripture Together with the Decisions of the Biblical Commission, St Meinrad, IN: Abbey, 1943.
Schmidt, K. L. *Der Rahmen der Geschichte Jesu: Literarkritische Untersuchung zur ältesten Jesusüberlieferung*, Berlin: Trowitzsch, 1919.
Smith, D. M. *John Among the Gospels*, second edition, Columbia, SC: University of South Carolina Press, 2001.
Stein, R. H. "What is *Redaktionsgeschichte*?," *JBL* 88 (1969) 45–56.
—— "The Proper Methodology for Ascertaining a Markan Redaction History," *NovT* 13 (1971) 181–98.
Tannehill, R. C. *The Narrative Unity of Luke–Acts: A Literary Interpretation*, 2 vols, Philadelphia, PA: Fortress Press, 1986, 1990.
Theissen, G. *The Gospels in Context: Social and Political History in the Synoptic Tradition*, Minneapolis, MN: Fortress Press, 1991.
Tuckett, C. (ed.) *The Messianic Secret*, IRT 1, Philadelphia, PA and London: Fortress Press and SPCK, 1983.
Turner, C. H. "Markan Usage: Notes, Critical and Exegetical, on the Second Gospel," *JTS* o.s. 25 (1923): 377–86; 26 (1924): 12–20, 145–56, 225–40, 337–46; 27 (1925): 58–62; 28 (1926): 930, 349–62; 29 (1927): 257–89, 346–61.
Weisse, C. H. *Die Evangelienfrage in ihrem gegenwärtigen Stadium*, Leipzig: Breitkopf & Härtel, 1856.
Wellhausen, J. *Einleitung in die drei ersten Evangelien*, Berlin: Reimer, 1905.
Wilke, C. G. *Der Urevangelist: oder, Exegetische kritische Untersuchung über das Verwandtschaftverhältnis der drei ersten Evangelien*, Dresden and Leipzig: Fleischer, 1838.
Wrede, W. *Das Messiasgeheimnis in den Evangelien: zugleich ein Beitrag zum Verständnis des Markusevangelium*, Göttingen: Vandenhoeck & Ruprecht, 1901.
—— *The Messianic Secret*, Greenwood, SC: Attic, 1971.

REIMARUS, HERMANN SAMUEL

Hermann Samuel Reimarus (1694–1768) is often cited as the person who initiated the first "quest of the historical Jesus." Perhaps it is more accurate to say that Reimarus was one of the first people to ask truly critical questions about Jesus and the origins of Christianity and that his writings thrust a variety of historical questions about Jesus to the forefront of biblical scholarship.

A native of Hamburg, Germany, Reimarus lived during the German Enlightenment. He studied theology, classical philology, and philosophy at Jena (1714–16), and he continued his studies at

Wittenberg (1716–19) where he also taught as an adjunct professor (1719–23). In the meantime, while on study tours in England and Holland (1720–21), Reimarus encountered English Deism for the first time, which eventually transformed his thinking and his scholarship. In addition, from 1723 to 1727 Reimarus served as the schoolmaster at the city school in Wismar.

For much of Reimarus's career, however, he was a Professor of Hebrew and Oriental Languages at the Academic Gymnasium in Hamburg (1727–68). In this capacity, Reimarus taught philosophy, mathematics, and natural sciences while writing thirty-seven books on a variety of topics. For instance, he edited a collection of Dio Cassius's writings in 1750–52, wrote an important philosophical monograph on logic in 1756 (*The Doctrine of Reason*), and published a noteworthy piece on animal psychology in 1760 (*General Observations on the Behavior of Animals*). Yet, he is primarily known today for his religious works. For instance, he set forth a defense of natural theology in *The Principal Truths of Natural Religion* (1754). Here, Reimarus argues that human reason is a reliable path for acquiring knowledge about God.

It was his last work on natural religion, however, originally known as *Apology or Defense of the Rational Worshippers of God* that sparked the first "quest of the historical Jesus" and that gained Reimarus so much notoriety. Here Reimarus not only advocates on behalf of natural religion, but he also attacks traditional Christianity in the process. Reimarus wrote and revised this manuscript over a twenty-three-year period (1744–67) though he declined to publish it due to its controversial nature. Yet, after Reimarus's death in 1768, Gotthold Ephraim Lessing, the librarian at Wolfenbüttel, published seven anonymous excerpts from Reimarus's manuscript (1774–78). As a result, the excerpts became known as the Wolfenbüttel *Fragments of an Unknown Author*. Eventually, in 1814 Reimarus's son acknowledged that his father had penned the volatile words. Further portions of Reimarus's manuscript were then published by C. A. E. Schmidt (1787), W. Klose (1850–52), C. Voysey (1879), and C. H. Talbert (1970), but an exhaustive copy of Reimarus's manuscript was not published until 1972 (G. Alexander).

In the *Apology*, Reimarus first argues for the superiority of "natural" or "reasonable" religion over so-called "revealed" religion. In Part I, Reimarus makes the case for Deism over against orthodox Christianity, which Reimarus believes stifles love and virtue. While doing so, Reimarus subjects "revealed" Christianity to the logic of the philosopher

Christian Wolff (1679–1754), who claimed that true revelation must be both necessary and without contradiction. First, Reimarus begins with the Old Testament and questions the moral standing of the patriarchs and prophets through whom revelation had supposedly come. Then once he has documented the pervasive immorality of these men, he concludes that divine revelation cannot come through such imperfect vehicles. Furthermore, Reimarus rules all references to miracles out of bounds because reason calls all supernatural claims into question.

In Part 2, Reimarus moves on to the New Testament. Here, he questions the morals of the apostles and the veracity of biblical history. Consequently, Reimarus became the first scholar to differentiate Jesus' intentions, actions, and teachings from the intentions and later teachings of the apostles. In essence, he questions whether the Jesus of the gospels was the Jesus of history. While doing so, Reimarus argues that Jesus saw himself as a devout Jew who advocated an enlightened form of Jewish morality. Consequently, Jesus had no interest in rejecting the Law or presenting any new articles of faith. Then once he encountered opposition he began to proclaim himself as a Jewish messiah with the political goal of Jewish freedom. He was not a miracle worker and if he ever referred to himself as a "Son of God," he did not attribute divine status to such a title. Rather, Reimarus argues that the dejected apostles fraudulently conceived a plot to deceive people, win followers, and retain their influential positions. As a result, they stole Jesus' body after the crucifixion and claimed he had been resurrected. The contradictory accounts of Jesus' resurrection in the gospels confirm this act of fraud for Reimarus. The disciples then went on to claim that both the Hebrew Bible and Jesus had predicted his death and resurrection. Finally, they introduced into their accounts of Jesus the idea that Jesus would soon come again to establish his earthly kingdom.

After treating the New Testament, Reimarus goes on to provide a rational, as opposed to a supernatural, explanation of the spread of Christianity and the development of Christian doctrine, which eventually espoused the view that Jesus was God incarnate. Of course, Reimarus thought that natural religion based upon reason would correct the mistakes of orthodox Christianity, which had been founded on incorrect historical assertions and claims of revelation.

While later biblical scholars did not embrace Reimarus's views on apostolic fraud (e.g. David Friedrich Strauss and Albert Schweitzer), many embraced his questions about whether or not the gospels accurately depict the historical Jesus as opposed to a spiritualized Jesus set forth by his followers. They embraced Reimarus's belief that both realities had been merged in the gospels as we know them and that biblical scholars should seek to separate them. Scholars also embraced his efforts to recognize the differences among the four gospels and to ask what those inconsistencies might tell us. In many ways, the questions that Reimarus dared to ask have driven historical research of the gospels and Jesus for the last two hundred years.

ANDREW ARTERBURY

Further reading

Baird, William. *History of New Testament Research, 1: From Deism to Tübingen*, Minneapolis, MN: Fortress Press, 1992.
Brown, Colin. "Reimarus, Hermann Samuel (1694–1768)," in Donald K. McKim (ed.) *Historical Handbook of Major Biblical Interpreters*, Downers Grove, IL: InterVarsity Press, 1998, pp. 346–49.
de Jonge, H. J. "The Loss of Faith in the Historicity of the Gospels: H. S. R. (c. 1750) on John and the Synoptics," *BETL* 101 (1992) 409–21.
Kümmel, Werner Georg. *The New Testament: The History of the Investigation of Its Problems*, trans. S. McLean Gilmour and Howard C. Kee, Nashville, TN: Abingdon, 1972.
Reimarus, Hermann Samuel. *Apologie oder Schutzschrift für die vernünftigen Verehrer Gottes*, 2 vols, ed. Gerhard Alexander, Frankfurt: Suhrkamp, 1972.
Schweitzer, Albert. *The Quest of the Historical Jesus: A Critical Study of Its Progress from Reimarus to Wrede*, New York: Macmillan, 1968.
Talbert, Charles H. (ed.) *Reimarus: Fragments*, Philadelphia, PA: Fortress Press, 1970.

REPENTANCE

Repentance refers to a "turning away" from anything which hinders the trusting relationship to God and consequently to a "turning to" God as the one who deserves one's love and obedience. As repentance involves the change of direction of someone's life and thought, it is closely linked to concepts of contrition, penitence, and conversion.

Repentance in the OT and in ancient Judaism

The OT does not know a systematic concept of repentance. However, Isa 55:7 describes what it means: "Let the wicked forsake their way, and the unrighteous their thoughts; let them return (*éub*) to the Lord, that he may have mercy on them, and to our God, for he will abundantly pardon" (NRSV). Technical terms like the Hebrew *tešûbāh* only

appear in later rabbinic literature. The Greek *metanoia*, which appears frequently in the NT (22x), is almost entirely absent in the LXX (only Prov 14:15). However, the Hebrew verb *éub* occurs especially frequently in the prophetic literature. Thus Jeremiah pronounces God's judgment upon the people of Judah since "they did not turn from their ways" (NRSV Jer 15:7; cf. 3:21f.; 31:18f.) and Ezekiel speaks of God's call to repent and turn away from "idols, transgressions and abominations" (cf. Ezek 14:6; 18:30; 33:11). For Jeremiah repentance is the means for salvation (Jer 3:23; 4:1; 7:3–7). According to Ezekiel the consequence of repentance is life (Ezek 18:23, 27, 32; 33:9, 11). Within deuteronomistic history in general the call for the renewal of Israel while facing the Babylonian exile of Israel is of central importance (Deut 30:1–10; 1 Sam 7:3; 1 Kgs 8:33, 35; 2 Kgs 17:13).

Repentance may be accompanied by and signaled through weeping, fasting, rending garments and wearing sackcloth and ashes, uttering penitential prayers, observing certain days of repentance; and it may involve confession, restitution and offering sacrifices (Lev 5:1–6; Num 5:5–7; Ps 51; Joel 2:12f.; Hos 14:1–3). Communal and national repentance was enacted on the Day of Atonement (Exod 30:10; Lev 23:27–32, 25:9; Num 29:7–11), but penitent individuals could make offerings at the Temple in order to atone for transgressions at any time. However, the prophets heavily criticize rituals without change of heart (Jer 7). Metaphors like the call to "circumcise your heart" (Deut 30:6; Jer 4:4), "wash your heart" (Jer 4:14; cf. "new heart" in Ezek 18:31; 36:26), to become single-hearted (Jer 32:39; cf. the "whole heart" in *Jub.* 1:15,23; 1QHa 8:7) clearly indicate the importance of inward turning from sin and toward God's covenant. In Qumran those who enter the community are viewed as entering a "covenant of repentance" (CD B 19:16; cf. "covenant of mercy" in 1QS 1:8). Probably the Qumranites prayed penitential prayers daily (4Q504).

Repentance in the NT gospels

In the NT repentance is expressed by the three word-groups of μετανοέω, μεταμέλομαι and ἐπιστρέφω. The noun μετάνοια (22x) and the verb μετανοέω (34x) appear frequently in the Synoptic Gospels (together 24x) but never in John. The verb μεταμέλομαι is rare in the gospels (Matt 21:29, 32; 27:3) and its meaning is very similar to μετανοέω. ἐπιστρέφω, which is rendered "to (re-)turn," is especially frequent in Luke (7x: Luke 1:16f.; 2:39, etc.; cf. Acts 11x) but occurs also in Mark (4:12;

5:30; 8:33; 13:16) and Matthew (10:13; 12:44; 13:15; 24:18).

John the Baptist is pictured as "proclaiming a baptism of repentance for the forgiveness of sins" (NRSV Mark 1:4; Luke 3:3). He calls Israel to repent – "for the kingdom of heaven has come near" (Matt 3:2) – and thus to receive the baptism of repentance as preparation for the coming of the Messiah (Luke 3:4–14). His call for repentance involves the acknowledgment of sinfulness (Mark 1:5 par. Matt 3:6) and a commitment to "bear fruit worthy of repentance" (Matt 3:8 par. Luke 3:8; Luke 3:10–14).

The call for repentance is at the heart of Jesus' (Mark 1:15 par. Matt 4:17) and his disciples' ministry (Mark 6:12; Luke 24:47; cf. Acts 2:37–39; 3:19; 5:31; 11:18 etc.). As Jesus receives John's baptism of repentance (Mark 1:9–11 parr.) he links himself to the preaching of the Baptist. Jesus then continues and enlarges the call for repentance: "The time is fulfilled, and the kingdom of God has come near; repent, and believe in the good news" (NRSV Mark 1:15). He thus links his concept of repentance to the notion of fulfillment and to faith in the gospel. As a transformation of the whole person (Matt 18:3; Luke 14:33) repentance can be described in terms of conversion (cf. στρέφω in Matt 18:3). However, Jesus does not only call individuals to repent but also aims for a national and universal repentance of Israel (Matt 11:20–24 par. Luke 10:13–15; Luke 13:1–5; Matt 12:39–42 par. Luke 11:29–32).

Although all three synoptics mention repentance, the emphasis is slightly different in each of them. In Mark repentance mainly appears in a summary of Jesus' ministry (Mark 1:15; cf. 6:12). Q contains two sayings of Jesus where he criticizes those Galilean towns, which failed to repent (Matt 11:21 par. Luke 10:13) but praises the people of Niniveh for their repentance at the preaching of Jonah (Matt 12:41 par. Luke 11:32). Thus either people "repent" or "perish" (Luke 13:3,5; 15:24, 33), receive forgiveness, salvation and thereby enter the kingdom of God (Luke 7:36–50; 19:9; cf. Mark 9:45) or, if unrepentant, be placed under the judgment of God (Matt 11:20–24 par. Luke 10:12–16 Matt 12:39–42). Especially in Luke repentance is described as the dividing issue between life and death. This is exemplified in a number of stories: the incidents with the rich man (Mark 10:17–31 parr.) and Zacchaeus (Luke 19:8) and the parables of the Prodigal Son (Luke 15:17 cf. 15:7,10) and the tax collector (Luke 18:13). Through redacting the summary of Jesus' preaching to that of John the Baptist (Matt 4:17 cf. par. Mark 1:15; Matt

3:2) Matthew links them even more closely than Mark. To sum up, all three synoptic Gospels confirm in different ways that the emphasis on repentance is firmly rooted in the historical Jesus tradition.

CARSTEN CLAUSSEN

Further reading

Behm, J. and E. Würthwein. "μετανοέω, μετάνοια," TDNT IV (1974) 975–1008.

Dunn, J. D. G. *Jesus Remembered*, Christianity in the Making 1, Grand Rapids, MI: Eerdmans, 2003, pp. 498–500.

Goppelt, L. *Theology of the New Testament, Vol. 1: The Ministry of Jesus in Its Theological Significance*, Grand Rapids, MI: Eerdmans 1981, pp. 77–138.

Jeremias, J. *New Testament Theology, Vol. 1: The Proclamation of Jesus*, New York: Macmillan, 1971.

Lunde, J. "Repentance," in J. B. Green, S. McKnight, and I. H. Marshall (eds) *Dictionary of Jesus and the Gospels*, Downers Grove, IL: InterVarsity Press, 1992, pp. 669–73.

Nitzan, B. "Repentance in the Dead Sea Scrolls," in P. W. Flint and J. C. VanderKam (eds) *The Dead Sea Scrolls After Fifty Years. A Comprehensive Assessment*, Leiden: Brill, 1999, Vol. 2, pp. 145–70.

Werline, R. A. *Penitential Prayer in Second Temple Judaism: The Development of a Religious Institution*, SBL Early Judaism and Its Literature 13, Atlanta, GA: Scholars Press, 1998.

RESURRECTION OF JESUS

From the earliest days, Jesus' followers called others to belief in Jesus as Messiah with the claim that God had raised him from the dead. Paul's letters, our earliest written evidence for Christian beliefs, repeatedly use short formulaic phrases that refer to this conviction (see Rom 1:3–4; 4:24–25; 1 Cor 15:3–5; 2 Cor 5:15; Gal 1:1; Phil 3:10–11; 1 Thess 1:9–10). Resurrection was so central to the earliest Christian preaching that it was possible to consider it an epithet for God. God is the one who raised Jesus from the dead (Rom 4:24; Gal 1:1; Col 2:12) and does the same for the faithful, whether it be the suffering apostle (2 Cor 1:9) or the Christian, who has been buried and raised with Christ in baptism (Rom 6:3–4; Col 2:12; 3:1).

This evidence indicates that the earliest Christians were not engaged in simply preserving the wise teachings of Jesus as though he were a figure comparable to one of the prophets, a philosopher like Socrates or a religious innovator like Buddha or Mohammed. They insisted that the individual they had known as Jesus of Nazareth had passed through death into an extraordinary new life with God. Further, this exalted status was associated with the degrading death that Jesus had suffered on the cross (Phil 2:6–11). Even though many twenty-first-century Christians prefer to think of Jesus as a teacher of wisdom or a visionary social reformer who was executed because his ideas and popularity disturbed those in power (Borg; Crossan), the claim that God raised Jesus from the dead must be factored into an understanding of the historical figure.

There are four facets to this investigation: (1) what did the expression "resurrection from the dead" mean to Jews in the first century CE? (2) did the teachings of Jesus of Nazareth include resurrection for himself, for believers or for humanity generally? (3) what information do the gospel narratives provide? (4) what consequences did belief in Jesus's resurrection have in the lives of his followers?

Resurrection, immortality and eternal life in first-century Judaism

The Jewish Scriptures open with a tale about how humanity lost the possibility of immortality because Adam and Eve disobeyed God's command (Gen 3:1–24). Thereafter, death marked the termination of human life. The realm of the dead, Sheol, is a place devoid of God's presence according to the Psalmist (Pss 31:23; 49:10–20; 69:15; 71:20; 88:4–12). The fate of all, prominent and lowly, wicked and righteous, is the same once they die (Job 3:11–22). The discovery of literature from the surrounding nations in the ancient near east provided evidence that the Hebrew conception of death was shared by its neighbors. The *Epic of Gilgamesh* tells the tale of a hero's desperate search for immortality after witnessing the death of his companion. An arduous journey to the garden where the gods have installed the couple who survived the flood enables him to gain a plant of immortality. But on the homeward journey, Gilgamesh loses the plant to a snake, so he must reconcile himself to mortality.

The benefits which humans can expect from God (or the gods) in this view are a long and prosperous life, many descendants, and rescue from such threats as illness, famine or war. This ancient near eastern outlook has a lot in common with the depiction of Hades in the Homeric epics. It stands in sharp contrast to concept of an immortal soul, which carries personal identity beyond the death of the body and may be subject to judgment or reward in the afterlife as in Egyptian texts or Greek religious cults. Nor does it reflect the philosophical arguments for immortality of the soul familiar to students of Plato (Assmann; Cullmann; Segal). Experiences of national disaster associated with the Babylonian exile elicited images of the death and rebirth of God's people that would later be read as evidence for resurrection of individuals from death. Ezekiel's great vision of the valley of bones being endowed with flesh once again (Ezek 37:1–14) is an act of recreation in which God breathes life into them (Ezek 37:9, using the verb *nph* as in Gen 2:7). A warrior-king might boast that he would fill the enemy's land with corpses or warn a vassal that such a fate awaited those who broke their covenant. So Ezekiel's vision promises an end to Israel's punishment for her disloyalty to God.

However, both Christian and Jewish readers of the first century CE and later read this passage as the promise of resurrection for all the dead. Paintings in the synagogue of Dura-Europos on the upper Euphrates (third century CE) show a group standing praising God while winged psyches enter the dead bodies. The Rabbis and medieval Jewish commentators discuss both possibilities. Ezekiel was using the image as a parable for restoring the nation after exile. God also promises that all the Israelite dead will be raised at the end-time. The imagery has already found its way into Matthew's account of the crucifixion. As Jesus dies on the cross, a cohort of the righteous buried nearby come to life but must remain in their tombs until Jesus' resurrection. Then they too appear around Jerusalem (Matt 27:51–53).

Other prophetic oracles that promise life to those who lie in the dust of the earth also anticipate the new order of justice and peace that will follow upon God's judgment. Isaiah 26:19 contrasts a group who will experience this awakening to new life with another group (v. 14) whose memory is to be erased entirely. The Babylonian oppressor will be consigned to Sheol (as in Isa 14:8–20), while God's people will be restored to life. Taken as evidence for the eventual fate of the dead, these images present resurrection as reward, return to life for God's faithful people. The wicked or the oppressors remain in Sheol.

Although Sheol is clearly a dark, damp region under the earth, the locale in which the resurrected dead will experience new life is less clearly defined. The prophetic images focused on national restoration so the location is clearly the land itself, the holy city and/or the mountain on which God's temple rests. Returning to life in God's presence there requires complete restoration of the body which lies in the dust. Daniel 12:1–3 employs the language of Isa 26:19 to refer to the resurrection of individuals. However, the contrast between those who awake to everlasting life, and those to reproach and eternal disgrace is ambiguous. Where are the wicked awakened? A pseudepigraphal work also from the second century BCE (or earlier), *1 Enoch* 22:13, has a group of sinners to be judged who will not exit Sheol. Similarly the community rule of the Essene sect speaks of sinners being punished in a dark place where the fire is eternal (1 QS 2:4–9; 4:11–14). Daniel does not detail how or where the wicked are punished but may assume that its readers share a similar scenario.

The concluding verse distinguishes another group, "the wise," said to shine like the stars of heaven (Dan 12:3). This depiction could be an allusion to a form of heavenly existence distinct from that promised in verse 2. Since the stars are often equated with the angelic hosts, these figures who have taught others righteousness could be promised entry into the angelic assembly (compare *1 En.* 104:2–6). Matthew 22:30 also speaks of "being like the angels of heaven" in the resurrection. These images do not presume that the new life to which the righteous dead awaken requires restoration of the physical body dismembered by death. Although they are capable of appearing as physical, human beings, angels do not inhabit such bodies.

Unlike the ambiguous language of Dan 12:2–3, the martyrdom story of the mother and her seven sons in 2 Macc 7 highlights the physical aspects of the risen body. God's creative power can restore to the martyr life and bodily existence (2 Macc 7:9–11, 22–23). Only those faithful to God can hope for such a resurrection to life (2 Macc 7:14). The early sections of 1 En which refer to resurrection and to the punishment of the wicked dead were written before the Maccabean crisis addressed in Dan and 2 Macc. However, the apostasy of some and the persecution of Jews who remained loyal to their ancestral faith may have contributed to the popularity of these ideas. Thanks to Daniel and the Enoch books the ideas about resurrection and/or eternal life among the angelic hosts are well-known features of first-century CE Jewish apocalyptic. Whether as restoration to a bodily kind of life or as transformation to an angelic existence, resurrection to life is reward for the righteous. In some examples, an author imagines a kind of awakening for the wicked as well, so that they will experience the eternal shame and punishment that divine justice requires.

Since the images are quite fluid, scholars remain divided over whether or not particular texts are speaking about the resurrection of individuals or restoration of God's people. Some interpreters insist on confining the term "resurrection" to those texts which explicitly mention bodily restoration

and using a different category for those which speak of eternal life with God or likeness to angels. In any case, this set of images differs markedly from beliefs about an immortal soul or an immediate post-mortem sorting and dispatch to the place of punishment or reward. Resurrection of the dead is a new act of God's creative and saving power closely linked to the divine judgment that is to bring an end to sin, evil and death.

Did Jesus teach resurrection from the dead?

Prior to the rise of modern gospel criticism, the question of whether or not Jesus taught his followers to expect resurrection as part of his message about God's reign would have been a simple "yes." Predictions of his impending death in Jerusalem culminate in the promise of Jesus's own resurrection (Mark 8:31//Matt 16:21//Luke 9:22; Mark 9:31//Matt 17:22–23; Mark 10:33–34//Matt 20:18–19// Luke 18:31–33). The fact that the gospel narratives present the disciples as completely unable to comprehend Jesus' words and as taken completely off guard, not anticipating his reappearances on Easter in any way, did not raise questions about the historical veracity of these scenes. Modern interpreters recognize that ancient lives were expected to present an author's perspective on their subject. Gospels were composed to represent Jesus as Christians believed in him some forty years after his death. Consequently predictions of his shocking execution and his resurrection were reformulated after the fact. What Jesus, himself, may or may not have said on the issue cannot be recovered from these texts. Insofar as the rest of his teaching challenged the entrenched positions of religious and political authorities, it is probable that Jesus did make comments to his followers about dangers awaiting them in Jerusalem. Insofar as Jesus began his public ministry in the wake of John the Baptist's prophetic announcement that the time of God's judgment was at hand, it is also plausible to assume that Jesus and his audience shared the Jewish apocalyptic imagery that gave birth to beliefs about resurrection from the dead.

A second bit of gospel evidence depicts Jesus defending this belief in a general resurrection of the dead against opponents of the Sadducee party, which did not accept that view (Mark 12:18–27// Matt 22:23–33//Luke 20:27–38). Once again critical considerations rule out a naive reading of this scene. Mark has put together a series of controversy stories that may have circulated independently in the oral tradition in order to match Jesus against religious teachers in the temple. The malice of these opponents becomes evident from the outset. They know that the Baptist was from God but refused to believe his word (Mark 11:27–32). Jesus' own address to them opens with a parable that allegorically anticipates God's response to the execution of the son, rejection of Israel's leaders, and the gathering of a new people of God (Mark 12:1–12). It concludes with Jesus silencing the opposition on a christological point. David, speaking prophetically in the psalms, saw that the Messiah would not be a king from his line but Lord (Mark 12:35–37).

Jesus' answer to the assertion that belief in resurrection produces the absurdity of a woman married to a string of brothers patches together two different arguments. It presumes that resurrection can be defended both as an expression of God's power and as taught in Scripture. Lack of such teaching in the Torah and prophets would have been the reason that Sadducees objected to it. In the concise fashion of Jewish debates, neither argument is spelled out. The power of God must be associated with the idea of the resurrected dead as transformed, like angels. Hence, though bodily, resurrection no longer involves physical relationships such as marriage. The proof from Scripture relies upon the present tense of the verb in Exod 3:6, but the verb is not found in Mark's citation as it is not present in the Hebrew text. It does occur in the Greek translation of the Jewish Scriptures used by the New Testament authors. Matthew supplies it in his version (Matt 22:31). Not only is this point difficult to make on the basis of the Hebrew, it does not apply to resurrection from the dead as found in the Jewish sources, since it requires that the patriarchs be alive with God (like Enoch and Elijah), not among the dead. Therefore many exegetes see the influence of Christian views about the resurrection of Jesus in this story as well. Resurrection has been divorced from its place as part of the end-time scenario. Jesus is exalted above the angelic host and very much alive to his followers. Once again these interpretations do not make it improbable that Jesus spoke of resurrection from the dead in speaking about God's reign, but as in Jewish texts of the time, it may have been a minor note.

Finally a number of contemporary scholars do not think that Jesus's message had anything to do with the questions posed in Jewish apocalyptic texts. They understand Jesus as a populist teacher of wisdom and a charismatic healer. His teaching engaged the concrete issues and tensions of a rural peasantry that had little contact with the speculation characteristic of a literate, religious elite. The

case for this view of the historical Jesus often appeals to a complex hypothesis about the Jesus traditions shared by Matthew and Luke but not found in Mark (Q). Along with additional variants of those sayings and stories found in the second-century *Gospel of Thomas*, these selections are used to reconstruct a sayings collection that these scholars call the Q gospel. Then it becomes the subject of analysis leaving a primitive wisdom layer to which apocalyptic elements were added later. The primitive layer brings us back within a decade of Jesus's own ministry according to this view. This group of sayings has no passion and resurrection sayings or discussion of resurrection from the dead as the fate of the righteous.

Since the explicit evidence for Jesus' teaching about resurrection is so limited, it was probably not a characteristic feature of his preaching. The Evangelists treat those sayings which predict resurrection after the Passion as private instruction of the disciples. Resurrection from the dead was likely a conviction that Jesus and his disciples shared with some Jews but not others. As we have seen, a promise of bodily resurrection figured in stories of the Maccabean martyrs. Certainly Jesus' death could be perceived as an attack on God's righteous ones by the wicked. That might elicit the hope that he would be raised up like the martyrs or even given the astral glory of those who taught the people righteousness in Dan 12:3. However, such hopes could not be realized until God's final judgment. Therefore such reconstructions as have a weakened, comatose Jesus survive crucifixion (Wilson), which could happen, fail to explain why his followers spoke of Jesus as raised from the dead. Even they did not anticipate the events encapsulated in the brief creed of 1 Cor 15:3–5 (Gehrhardsson).

Gospel narratives about the resurrection of Jesus

Both the formula in 1 Cor 15:3–5 and Paul's references to his own experience of the risen Christ (Gal 1:16; 1 Cor 15:8) use the language of visionary revelation to refer to the event. If Paul's indirect reference to a heavenly ascent in 2 Cor 12:1–5 also speaks of that encounter with the Lord, then it differs from the image of resurrection of the dead in Jewish martyrdom texts and in the gospel narratives. The visionary language suggests a figure exalted to God's throne much in the manner of the Son of Man vision from Dan 7:14. The bodily resurrection from the dismemberment of martyrdom suggests return to a transformed creation. Some scholars insist that historians must limit speaking about the resurrection of Jesus to visions and revelations that Jesus' followers interpreted to mean that God had raised him from the dead (Lüdemann 1994; Marxsen 1970). From this perspective stories in the gospels which speak of encounters with the risen Jesus as an embodied figure reflect later Christian mythologizing of the story. Scholars who reject that hypothesis insist that the first-century Jew, Jesus of Nazareth, who died on a cross, was physically raised from death. His reappearance in the spatio-temporal world and encounters with his followers should be considered an historical event (Craig; Habermas and Flew).

Form-critical analyses of the resurrection narratives suggest a complicated development (Alsup; Brown; Fuller). The original ending of Mark's Gospel – or at least the ending known to both Matthew and Luke a decade or so later – had no appearance stories at all. An angel informed the women that Jesus had been raised and his disciples would see him again in Galilee as he had promised (Mark 16:7). The women flee terrified and say nothing about what had happened at the tomb (Mark 16:8). Mark's Christian audience presumably knew that such a Galilee appearance had occurred. But it is possible that neither the Evangelist nor his audience had any more information than the sort of formula or appearance list found in 1 Cor 15:3–7. Matthew's Gospel provides notices concerning two encounters with the risen Jesus. The women meet him as they are leaving the tomb. Jesus entrusts them with the same message for his followers that they had received from the angel (Matt 28:9–10). A variant of this tradition reappears in John's Gospel, where it has been expanded into a much more extensive narrative piece focused on Mary Magdalene (John 20:1–2, 11–18). Where Matthew's version has the women grasp his feet in a gesture of worship, John has an expanded warning not to touch or hang on to Jesus because he has to return to his Father. This expansion is governed by the Evangelist's view of the cross as exaltation, as the Son's return to the glory he had with the Father before the beginning of the world.

Matthew also has a concise narrative about Jesus' encounter with the Eleven on a mountain in Galilee (Matt 28:16–20). The tradition-history of the scene is complex. It appears to be of a piece with other appearance scenes in which Jesus commissions the disciples (Luke 24:36–49; John 20:21–23). However, it incorporates two distinctive elements: an affirmation that Jesus has been invested with divine authority (v. 18) and an ecclesial expansion on the command to evangelize the nations. A trinitarian

baptismal formula is specified, as is instruction in the teaching of Jesus (vv. 19–20a). Presumably the Evangelist expects his gospel to serve that purpose. Jesus' promise to remain with his followers until the end of the age (v. 20b) picks up on the name "Emmanuel" from Matthew's birth story (Matt 1:23). The earlier encounter with the women was sufficient to show Matthew's readers that Jesus had been raised out of the grave. This scenario places him on God's throne as sovereign over the nations.

These concise resurrection narratives point toward two functions of such traditions as they were handed on and reshaped by Christians: a commissioning to evangelize and a re-founding of the community of disciples. Paul presented his own vision of the Lord as a commissioning. God had intended him to take the gospel to non-Jews since his birth. Both community founding and commissioning are evident in the expanded resurrection stories to be found in Luke and John. The several meal gatherings at which the risen Lord appears or is revealed in the guise of a stranger (Luke 24:28–35, 36–49; John 20:10–23; 21:9–13) reflect both Jesus' earlier meals with his disciples and the later eucharistic meal of the Christian community. Luke also highlights the process by which Christians came to reinterpret the Scriptures as referring to Jesus' death and resurrection as necessary for God's messiah (Luke 24:25–27, 44–46). John employs the tradition of an appearance by the Sea of Galilee to rehabilitate and commission Peter as the one charged with caring for Jesus' flock (John 21:15–19).

The longer stories have incorporated other details addressed to those who might doubt the truth of the Christian proclamation. Matthew 28:17c says simply, "some doubted." Presumably they overcame that initial skepticism. Both Luke 24:37–43 and John 20:20, 24–28 take a more direct approach to doubt. Jesus exhibits the physical evidence that his body is the one which had suffered crucifixion. By eating with the disciples in Luke, he demonstrates that he is not an apparition or a shade from Hades. Matthew discusses a different type of doubt, polemics from the Jewish community of his own day. Allegations that the disciples had faked a resurrection of Jesus by removing his corpse from the tomb are really the cover-story put about by those assigned to guard Jesus's tomb (Matt 27:62–65; 28:11–15).

Suspicions of a body gone missing also figure in John's narrative. Because Jesus had been buried by outsiders, Mary Magdalene at first reports that "they" have done something with the body (John 20:2). She later asks the cemetery attendant (Jesus) to tell her where he put the body (v. 15). Since

those Jews who believed that there would be resurrection of the dead considered it part of the end-
time scenario, it could hardly serve to account for
a missing corpse. Although "was buried" is part of
the formula in 1 Cor 15:3–5, some exegetes even
doubt the historicity of the tradition that Jesus was
buried by a pious Jewish sympathizer. They appeal
to the common Roman practice of leaving bodies
to rot or tossing criminals in a common grave and
suggest that the burial stories arose to mitigate the
degrading death that Jesus suffered (Crossan).
However, both Jewish piety and influence with the
Roman prefect could have made Jesus' case an
exception to ordinary practice. In any case, the
Maccabean martyr traditions rely on God's creative power to reassemble bodies for the righteous
no matter what torturers did to them. Therefore
the resurrection of Jesus is not dependent upon the
ability of his followers to identify a tomb in which
he had been laid to rest.

The earliest resurrection testimony takes the
form of confessional statements that God raised
the crucified Jesus from the dead and that Jesus
appeared to a varied series of witnesses. Details
about those appearances are not consistent across
the various narratives some half-century later.
Mark and Matthew locate the appearance of Jesus
to the Eleven in Galilee, though Matthew does
recount a Jerusalem appearance to the women.
Luke insists that the disciples never leave Jerusalem. John's gospel reworks variants on all the
traditions: an appearance to Mary Magdalene near
the tomb; appearances to the disciples in Jerusalem, and an appearance in Galilee. The latter
occurs in connection with the disciples fishing
rather than with a mountain, as in Matthew. The
Evangelist or the final editor of the gospel has tried
to sort this material chronologically but leaves
Peter's return to fishing in Galilee unexplained.
The list of appearance stories that Paul mentions
in 1 Cor 15:3–10 includes several for which we have
no early narratives at all. Certainly for those Jews who
imagined resurrection as the re-embodiment of
faithful martyrs, an empty tomb would be the
logical conclusion of believing that God had raised
Jesus from the dead. Paul's explanation in 1 Cor
15:42–44 is more ambiguous. Does the sown
physical or material body, the corpse, have to disappear in order for the spiritual one to be created?
As far as believers are concerned, Paul is more
interested in reiterating the apocalyptic time-table.
Christ has been raised in anticipation of the end-
time resurrection of the faithful. Some scholars
insist that this apocalyptic scenario indicates that
Paul also expected the spiritual body to be a
transformed physical one (Wright), others that the
"physical" element in question is an astral body,
not flesh and blood (Martin). On that reading,
what Paul or other Jews who used the same categories thought happened to the corpse cannot be
determined.

The resurrection of Jesus and Christian life

The difference between a modern scientific understanding of the universe and of human biology
leads some theologians to insist that even if our
only witnesses for the resurrection of Jesus considered it to be an historical event, that designation
is a category mistake. The physical remains
decayed, as all bodies do. Whatever it means to
claim that Jesus continues to be alive with God,
that confession of faith refers to religious experiences of individual believers and the communities
to which they belong. The formulaic references to
the death and resurrection of Christ as the core
message are only part of the story. Jesus will be
God's agent in bringing the present age to its conclusion (1 Thess 1:10). Believers will be raised to
share in that triumph over death (1 Thess 4:13–18).
And in addition to such expectations derived from
Jewish apocalyptic hopes, Christians experienced
the power of resurrection.

Baptismal rites could be presented as dying and
rising with Christ (Rom 6:4; Col 3:1). The risen
Lord was present in the meal that Christians celebrated (Luke 24:30–31). In both suffering endured
for the gospel (Phil 3:10–11) and a renewed ethical
life (Col 3:1–15), believers participate in the power
of the resurrection. Sinners can appeal to the exalted Christ for forgiveness (1 John 2:1). Whatever
their status in this world, Christians belong to the
commonwealth that has the risen Lord as its head
(Phil 3:20–21). Since resurrection from the dead
was not a central theme of first-century Jewish
religion or even in the preserved teachings of Jesus,
its flowering in Christian circles must be rooted in
powerful communal experiences. The crucified
Jesus did not remain among the dead awaiting
God's vindication like the martyrs. Jesus lives –
a life that would not be possible without bodily
resurrection.

PHEME PERKINS

Further reading

General studies of resurrection and afterlife

Assmann, J. *Death and Salvation in Ancient Egypt*. Ithaca,
NY: Cornell University Press, 2005.

Bauckham, R. "Visiting the Places of the Dead in the Extra-canonical Apocalypses," *PIBA* 18 (1995) 78–93.

Cavallin, H. C. C. *Life After Death: Paul's Argument for the Resurrection of the Dead in 1 Cor 15. Part I. An Inquiry into the Jewish Background*, Lund: C. W. K. Gleenip, 1972–73.

Cullmann, O. *Immortality of the Soul or Resurrection of the Dead*, New York: Macmillan, 1958.

Davies, J. *Death, Burial and Rebirth in the Religions of Antiquity*, London: Routledge, 1999.

Nickelsburg, G. W. E. *Resurrection, Immortality and Eternal Life in Intertestamental Judaism*, HTS 26, Cambridge, MA: Harvard University Press, 1972.

Park, J. S. *Conception of Afterlife in Jewish Inscriptions with Special Reference to Pauline Literature*, WUNT 2/21, Tübingen: Mohr Siebeck, 2000.

Puech, E. *La Croyance des Esséniens en la vie future: immortalité, résurrection, vie éternelle? Histoire d'une croyance dans le Judaïsme ancien*, Paris: Cerf, 1993.

Segal, A. F. *Life after Death. A History of the Afterlife in the Religions of the West*, New York: Doubleday, 2004.

Setzer, C. *Resurrection of the Body in Early Judaism and Early Christianity: Doctrine, Community, and Self-Definition*, Leiden: Brill, 2004.

Resurrection and the historical Jesus

Alsup, J. *The Post-resurrection Appearance Stories of the Gospel Tradition: A History-of-Tradition Analysis with Text Synopsis*, Calwer Theological Monographien 5, Stuttgart: Calwer Verlag, 1975.

Borg, M. J. *Jesus: A New Vision. Spirit, Culture and the Life of Discipleship*, San Francisco, CA: HarperCollins, 1987.

Brown, R. *The Virginal Conception and Bodily Resurrection of Jesus*, New York: Paulist Press, 1973.

Bultmann, R. *History of the Synoptic Tradition*, New York: Charles Scribner's Sons, 1968.

Craig, W. L. *Assessing the New Testament Evidence for the Historicity of the Resurrection of Jesus*, Lewiston, NY: Mellen Press, 1989.

Crossan, J. D. *The Historical Jesus. The Life of a Mediterranean Jewish Peasant*, San Francisco, CA: HarperCollins, 1991.

Dibelius, M. *Jesus*, Philadelphia, PA: Fortress Press, 1949.

Fuller, R. *The Formation of the Resurrection Narratives*, Philadelphia, PA: Fortress Press, 1970.

Gerhardsson, B. "Evidence for Christ's Resurrection according to Paul, 1 Cor 15:1–11," in D. F. Aune, T. Seland, and J. H. Unrichsen (eds) *Neotestamentica et Philonica. Studies in Honor of Peder Borgen*, Leiden: Brill, 2003, pp. 73–91.

Habermas, G. *The Risen Jesus and Future Hope*, Lanham, MD: Rowman & Littlefield, 2003.

Habermas, G. and A. G. N. Flew. *Did Jesus Rise from the Dead?*, ed. T. L. Miethe, San Francisco, CA: HarperCollins, 1987.

Lüdemann, G. *What Really Happened to Jesus?*, Louisville, KY: Westminster John Knox, 1995.

—— *The Resurrection of Christ. A Historical Inquiry*, Amherst, NY: Prometheus Books, 2004.

Marxsen, W. *The Resurrection of Jesus*, trans. Margaret Kohl, London: SCM Press, 1970.

—— *Jesus and Easter: Did God Raise the Historical Jesus from the Dead?*, trans. V. Furnish, Nashville, TN: Abingdon, 1990.

Wilson, I. *Jesus, the Evidence*, London: Thames and Hudson, 1984.

Resurrection in the New Testament

Avemarie, F. and H. Lichtenberger (eds) *Auferstehung – Resurrection*, Tübingen: J. C. B. Mohr, 2001.

Bartsch, H. W. "Inhalt und Funktion des Urchristlichen Osterglaubens," *NTS* 26 (1980) 180–96.

Bieringer, R., V. Koperski, and B. Lataire (eds) *Resurrection in the New Testament. Festschrift für J. Lambrecht*, Leuven: Peeters, 2002.

Dhanis, E. (ed.) *Resurrexit: Actes du symposium international sur la Résurrection de Jésus*, Rome: Libreria Editrice Vaticana, 1974.

Dodd, C. H. *The Apostolic Preaching and Its Developments*, Grand Rapids, MI: Baker, reprint 1980 [1936].

Evans, C. F. *Resurrection and the New Testament*, London: SCM Press, 1968.

Grass, H. *Ostergeschehen und Osterberichte*, Göttingen: Vandenhoeck & Ruprecht, 1962.

Harris, M. *Raised Immortal: Resurrection and Immortality in the New Testament*, Grand Rapids, MI: Eerdmans, 1983.

Léon-Dufour, X. *Resurrection and the Message of Jesus*, trans. G. Chapman, New York: Holt, Rinehart and Winston, 1974.

Longenecker, R. (ed.) *Life in the Face of Death. The Resurrection Message of the New Testament*, Grand Rapids, MI: Eerdmans, 1998.

Lorenzen, T. *Resurrection and Discipleship*, Maryknoll, NY: Orbis, 1995.

Martin, D. *The Corinthian Body*, New Haven, CT: Yale University Press, 1995.

Müller, U. B. *Die Entstehung des Glaubens an die Auferstehung Jesu*, Stuttgart: Katholisches Bibelwerk, 1998.

Perkins, P. *Resurrection. New Testament Witness and Contemporary Reflection*, New York: Doubleday, 1984.

Pesch, R. *Biblischer Osterglaube*, Neukirchen-Vluyn: Neukirchener Verlag, 1999.

Porter, S. E., M. Attayes, and D. Tombs (eds) *Resurrection*, Sheffield: Sheffield Academic Press, 1999.

Riley, G. *Resurrection Reconsidered. Thomas and John in Controversy*, Minneapolis, MN: Fortress Press, 1995.

Wright, N. T. *The Resurrection of the Son of God*, Minneapolis, MN: Fortress Press, 2003.

Resurrection and Christian theology

Bultmann, R. *Theology of the New Testament*, New York: Charles Scribner's Sons, 1965.

Bynum, C. W. *The Resurrection of the Body in Western Christianity 200–1336*, New York: Columbia University, 1995.

Carnley, P. *The Structure of Resurrection Belief*, Oxford: Oxford University Press, 1987.

Durwell, R. X. *La Résurrection de Jesus, mystère du Salut*, Paris: Xavier Mappus, 1963.

Künneth, W. *The Theology of the Resurrection*, trans. J. W. Leitch, London: SCM Press, 1965 [Ger. 1951].

Lüdemann, G. *The Resurrection of Jesus. History, Experience, Theology*, Minneapolis, MN: Fortress Press, 1994.

Osborne, K. *The Resurrection of Jesus. New Considerations for Its Theological Interpretation*, Mahwah, NJ: Paulist Press, 1997.

Pannenberg, W. *Jesus, God and Man*, Philadelphia, PA: Westminster, 1968.

O'Collins, G. *Jesus Risen*, New York: Paulist Press, 1987.

Swinburne, R. *The Resurrection of God Incarnate*, Oxford: Oxford University Press, 2003.

Trumbower, J. A. *Rescue for the Dead. The Posthumous Salvation of Non-Christians in Early Christianity*, New York: Oxford University, 2001.

Wedderburn, A. J. M. *Beyond Resurrection*, London: SCM Press, 1999.

REWRITTEN SCRIPTURE

Rewritten Scripture (also rewritten Bible) refers to the practice, conscious or otherwise, of retelling or paraphrasing the text and stories of Scripture. Whereas it may not be inaccurate to describe the category of "rewritten Scripture" as a broad category in which targums, midrashim, and other forms of exegesis may be included, it is probably more accurate to think of rewritten Scripture as the earliest form of exegesis. This rewriting activity begins within the Bible itself. It has been described as "haggadah within Scripture" (S. Sandmel) and recently as "inner-biblical exegesis" (M. Fishbane). The Pseudepigrapha represent attempts at rewriting Scripture outside of the Bible itself, but still via the biblical story ("para-biblical rewriting"). One's exegesis is to some extent camouflaged within the biblical story itself.

In the time of Jesus Scripture was being retold or rewritten through its translation into other languages. By the first century various portions of Hebrew Scripture had been translated into Greek, Aramaic, and (probably) Latin (i.e. Old Latin, not the much later translation by Jerome, eventually known as the Vulgate). Fragments of Greek Scripture have been found at Qumran (i.e. cave 7) and at Nahal Hever (e.g. the Greek Minor Prophets Scroll). Fragments of Aramaic Scripture have also been found at Qumran (e.g. 4QtgLeviticus, 4QtgJob, and 11QtgJob). Aramaic Scripture would in time form what came to be called Targums, which we think took shape in the synagogue.

Discrete units of Scripture were also paraphrased within various works, sometimes as part of a midrash (an interpretive "searching" of Scripture for less obvious meaning). And in some cases whole biblical books were paraphrased. *Jubilees* and Pseudo-Philo's *Biblical Antiquities* are well-known examples, in which major portions of Torah are paraphrased. Qumran offers a number of examples. Perhaps best known among them are several manuscripts referred to as Reworked Pentateuch (4Q364–68).

As in the case of the so-called books of the Old Testament Pseudepigrapha, some of the Qumran Scrolls are creative extensions of the life or oracles of a given Old Testament worthy. Just as we have a Testament of Moses in the Pseudepigrapha, Qumran gives us apocrypha (or secret books) "of Moses" (i.e. 2Q20; 4Q375–77, 385a, 387a, 388a, 389–90). Qumran has provided us with a rewritten version of Joshua (i.e. 4Q47), what appears to be a rewritten version of Kgs (4Q382), and apocrypha of Jeremiah (4Q383–84, 385b, 387b, 389b), Ezekiel (4Q385–88, 391), and the Pslter (4Q381–82). Qumran offers us a secret "Book of Noah" (a.k.a. *Genesis Apocryphon*), which is an Aramaic paraphrase of patriarchal narratives, much focused on Abraham.

Even in the case of the relatively stabilized Hebrew text of Scripture there are what appear to be four versions. These include a proto-Masoretic text type, a text type that agrees with the Old Greek (e.g. 1–2 Samuel and Jeremiah), a text type that agrees with the Samaritan Pentateuch, and a fourth text type that had been unknown prior to the discovery of the Dead Sea Scrolls.

Appreciation of this textual diversity enables a more nuanced assessment of Jesus' use of Scripture and style of teaching. He freely adapts Scripture, sometimes following what appears to be the emerging Aramaic paraphrase. We see this in his paraphrase of Isa 6:9–10 in Mark 4:12 ("lest they should turn again, and be forgiven"), or in his allusion to Lev 18:5 in Luke 10:28 ("Do this, and you will live [in the world to come]"). Jesus' pithy saying in Matt 26:52 ("all who take the sword will perish by the sword") coheres with a distinctive reading preserved in *Tg. Isa* 50:11.

The Evangelists, particularly Matthew, make use of the Greek translation of Hebrew Scripture. In view of the evidence of the Scrolls, we should no longer assume that differences with the Masoretic Text indicate poor translation. We should assume that in many, perhaps most, cases the Greek reflects a slightly different Hebrew text.

Jesus uses Scripture as a point of departure for many of his parables. His parable of the Sower (Mark 9:3–9) draws on Jer 4:3 ("Break up your fallow ground, and sow not among thorns") and Isa 55:10–11 ("bring forth and sprout, giving seed to the sower and bread to the eater, so shall my word be that goes forth from my mouth"). His parable of the Good Samaritan (Luke 10:30–35) retells the story of the good Samaritans (2 Chr 28:8–15). The parable of the Wicked Vineyard Tenants makes use of Isaiah's famous Song of the Vineyard (Isa 5:1–7), but as understood in the Aramaic paraphrase (*Tg. Isa* 5:1–7; cf. 4Q500).

Jesus' creative, allusive, and experiential approach to Scripture coheres with the very personalized, allusive use of Scripture we see in the *Hymn Scroll* (1QH). His provocative, argumentative engagement with legal Scripture, as seen, for example, in the so-called antitheses of Matt 5:21–48, is scarcely more provocative than what we see in some of the Scrolls concerned with legal matters. And finally, Jesus' creative development of eschatological and apocalyptic utterances and discourses, whereby various prophetic Scriptures are woven together (in effect, an instance of "rewritten prophecy"), is analogous to several apocalypses found among the Dead Sea Scrolls.

CRAIG A. EVANS

Further reading

Alexander, P. S. "Retelling the Old Testament," in D. A. Carson and H. G. M. Williamson (eds) *It is Written: Scripture Citing Scripture. Essays in Honour of Barnabas Lindars*, Cambridge: Cambridge University Press, 1988, pp. 99–121.

Bernstein, M. "4Q252: From Re-Written Bible to Biblical Commentary," *JJS* 45 (1994) 1–27.

Brooke, G. J. "Parabiblical Prophetic Narratives," in P. W. Flint and J. C. VanderKam (eds) *The Dead Sea Scrolls after Fifty Years: A Comprehensive Assessment*, 2 vols, Leiden: Brill, 1998–99, Vol. 1, pp. 271–301.

—— "Rewritten Bible," in L. H. Schiffman and J. C. VanderKam (eds) *Encyclopedia of the Dead Sea Scrolls*, 2 vols, Oxford: Oxford University Press, 2000, pp. 777–81.

Charlesworth, J. H. "The Pseudepigrapha as Biblical Exegesis," in C. A. Evans and W. F. Stinespring (eds) *Early Jewish and Christian Exegesis: Studies in Memory of William Hugh Brownlee*, Homage 10; Atlanta, GA: Scholars Press, 1987, pp. 139–52.

Crawford, S. W. "Reworked Pentateuch," in L. H. Schiffman and J. C. VanderKam (eds) *Encyclopedia of the Dead Sea Scrolls*, 2 vols, Oxford: Oxford University Press, 2000, pp. 775–77.

Evans, C. A. "Luke and the Rewritten Bible: Aspects of Lukan Hagiography," in J. H. Charlesworth and C. A. Evans (eds) *The Pseudepigrapha and Early Biblical Interpretation*, JSPSup 14, SSEJC 2, Sheffield: JSOT Press, 1993, pp. 170–201.

France, R. T. *Jesus and the Old Testament: His Application of Old Testament Passages to Himself and His Mission*, London: Tyndale, 1971.

Nickelsburg, G. W. E. "The Bible Rewritten and Expanded," in M. E. Stone (ed.) *Jewish Writings of the Second Temple Period*, CRINT 2:2, Assen: Van Gorcum; Philadelphia, PA: Fortress Press, 1984, pp. 89–156.

RHETORIC

Rhetoric in the Greco-Roman culture of the first century CE was defined as the technique of words or the art of speech. In more practical terms, it was more narrowly defined as determining the most effective means of persuasion in each speech situation. The nature of Hellenistic society put great emphasis on public speaking, with the political assembly or council, law courts, and public ceremonies being key settings. In order to train a young person to function well in these contexts, a theory of oral discourse developed that was labeled rhetoric. Training in rhetoric was a required part of a child's education, though this education was primarily reserved for the wealthy or elite. It is highly debatable how much rhetoric influenced Jesus, his disciples, and his later followers.

The practice of rhetoric in the first-century CE

The practice of rhetoric in the first century CE was shaped by the theory developed in the rhetorical handbooks of the classical period, particularly those of Aristotle, Cicero and Quintilian. Rhetorical practice was set out according to five key elements: invention (identifying the subject of the speech, the stance the speaker will take, and the arguments to be used); arrangement (ordering the arguments and speech elements into the most effective order for the situation); style (developing or enhancing the argument and speech elements through their grammatical or figural presentation); memory (putting the speech to memory for effect and naturalness); and delivery (developing the use of voice and gestures when giving the speech). Rhetorical theory described three main types of speeches: judicial (trial before a jury or judge), deliberative (political debate in the assembly or council), and epideictic (public ceremonies or occasions). The three essential factors that governed the persuasiveness of a speech were ethos (the character of the speaker), pathos (the appeal to emotion), and logos (the content or ideas of the speech). The content or logos was regarded as the most important factor and content was often related to the use of proofs (*pisteis*). Proofs were not just logical arguments, but those social and cultural aspects of life which were shared by the speaker and audience to which the speaker might appeal. The pattern of argumentation or the arrangement of the speech was thought to consist of a standard six-part pattern: introduction (*exordium*), statement of the case (*narratio*), statement of the speaker's thesis (*partitio*), supporting arguments (*probatio*), refuting opposing arguments (*refutatio*), the conclusion (*peroratio*). However, the pattern varied depending on the type of speech and the exigencies of the speech context.

It is hard to determine how widespread the theoretical knowledge and practice of rhetoric was in the first century. From extant writings of this time, rhetoric played a key role among the free citizens and the wealthy of Hellenistic society. But this would comprise at most 10 percent of the population. In addition, most such writings came from the important political and cultural urban centers like Rome, Athens, Alexandria and Antioch. Rhetoric was most likely less pervasive in the provincial and rural parts of the empire. However, archaeological and other similar historical evidence reveal that many aspects of Hellenistic culture influenced all sectors of society in every place. As effective communication was important throughout the empire, people no doubt absorbed and imitated unwittingly many communication conventions that originated in rhetoric.

Rhetoric, that is persuasive argumentation, was not limited to classical Greco-Roman rhetorical theory. Jewish argumentation was a distinct form at the time of Jesus. One form was the practice of Halakah. This consisted of applying a statement of law given in the Bible or from oral tradition (midrash) to some aspect of daily life. This was an oral process in which the rabbis and students engaged in lecture, disputation and discussion. Effective argumentation was based on the ability to cite accepted authoritative writings and traditions and to speak clearly and concisely without figures and tropes. As the discussion was generally extempore based on question and debate, such discourse did not lend itself to the five elements of good speech as in classical rhetorical theory.

There is ongoing debate as to whether Christian discourse developed a distinctive rhetoric. Generally, the writers of the NT write to persuade to some degree. What then makes their writings persuasive, particularly with reference to the appeal to authority? G. A. Kennedy suggests that some Christian rhetoric is radical in that it asserts by proclamation without rational appeal, while some Christian rhetoric engages in rational or logical argument. Other scholars have noted that the Christian kerygma or tradition forms the foundation for argumentation. The distinctive nature of Christian rhetoric remains an open question.

The rhetoric of the gospels

Rhetoric in its classical form is not obviously present in the teaching and activities of Jesus as recorded in the gospels. However, in order to determine the degree to which rhetoric may have influenced Jesus and the gospel writers, the genre of the gospels and the forms of argumentation found within the gospels need evaluation as to their rhetorical nature.

Genre of the gospels

Determining the genre of the gospels in relation to ancient literary practice is greatly debated among biblical scholars. However, it is generally agreed that chronological narrative is a primary generic form for the gospel writings. The use of narrative was not a general topic of the rhetorical handbooks or theoreticians. Aristotle in *Poetica* did discuss the significance of characterization and plot, especially in tragedy, but not as a means of persuasion. The lack of any correlation between narrative and rhetoric is not surprising since rhetorical theory was primarily applied to speech.

David Aune and Richard Burridge have both done extensive comparative analysis of the gospels with contemporaneous literature of the first century CE. Both conclude that the gospels are most like Greco-Roman biography, *bios* or *vitae*, with influence from other Jewish and oriental literary forms. Ancient biography was a specific genre of historical literature with broad and flexible generic features. First-century examples include Nicolas of Damascus' *Life of Augustus*, Tacitus's *Vita*, and Philo's *Life of Moses*. Burridge (1997: 507–32) in particular attempts to analyze the gospels according to the five essential elements of rhetoric and finds that they are more like *bioi* than rhetorical speech. But the pervasiveness of rhetoric in shaping all manner of communication conventions suggests that there may be correlations between rhetoric and biography at a generic level yet to be discovered.

Forms of argumentation in the gospels

While the gospels at a generic level show little if any affinity with Greco-Roman rhetoric, at the level of smaller literary units which compose the gospels, rhetoric may be more influential. Ancient biography included many different generic elements or literary forms. The general narrative framework was amplified by anecdotes, maxims, speeches and documents. Traditional form criticism of the gospels has concluded that there are constituent oral forms which can be classified as based on either narrative or sayings. Narrative oral forms include miracle stories and pronouncement stories; sayings/oral forms include parables and aphorisms. These literary forms contribute to the arrangement and argument of the gospels.

Out of this array of constituent literary forms, pronouncement stories, anecdotes and aphorisms in particular offer potential instances where rhetoric may have played a significant role. Each of these forms appears to be related to the *chreia* (pl. *chreiai*), a literary form which formed the building blocks of ancient biography. A *chreia* is defined as a concise and pointed account of something said or done, attributed to some particular person. The *chreia* was used in oral and written communication in order to preserve and elaborate the words and deeds of important as well as ordinary people. *Chreiai* were a rhetorical means of preserving conventional wisdom. An example of a *chreia* is: "Being asked once how far the boundaries of Laconia extended, Agesilaus said, with a flourish of his spear, 'As far as this can reach'" (Plutarch, *Mor.* 210E.28).

The relationship and the importance of the *chreiai* in relation to rhetoric is established by the central role they played in teaching rhetoric in the first to fifth centuries CE. *Chreiai* formed one of the many types of rhetorical exercises included in the rhetorical textbooks of this period, called *Progymnasmata*. The oldest surviving *Progymnasmata* is by Aelius Theon of Alexandria (*c.* 50–100 CE). Exercises included the elaboration of a *chreia* both to demonstrate a grasp of the meaning of the *chreia* and to construct a fuller argument or entire speech based on the *chreia*.

Recent scholars such as Burton Mack and Vernon Robbins (1989), suggest that study of the *chreiai* demonstrate the manner in which the Jesus tradition was formed, transmitted and developed. As a particular example, they posit that pronouncement stories are elaborated *chreiai*. An example is Matt 19:13–15 which is then found in an elaborated form in Mark 10:13–16. All this assumes that the sayings and actions of Jesus were originally transmitted as *chreiai*, that the literary forms of the gospel tradition are directly related to *chreiai*, and that the gospel writers were familiar with the rhetorical practice related to *chreiai*, hence educated in rhetorical theory. These assumptions have not found universal acceptance among biblical scholars.

The potential significance of the *chreiai* tradition for relating the sayings and actions of Jesus in the gospels to the historical Jesus is interesting. Placing the sayings and actions of Jesus in a *chreia* form ensured that a perceived core would be preserved in any elaboration or embellishment. Elaboration of a *chreia* required isolating the central meaning and ensuring that any elaboration preserved that meaning. Such parameters may have helped preserve faithful transmission of the Jesus event.

Another form of argumentation based on ancient rhetorical theory that may illumine the argumentation of the Jesus tradition is the *enthymeme*.

The *enthymeme* is often defined as an argument constructed from a premise and conclusion with one premise unstated, a truncated syllogism. It is also described as a deductive proof. There remains a great deal of theoretical debate over defining an *enthymeme*. However, unpacking the sayings of Jesus as an *enthymeme* may illumine the manner and meaning of Jesus' argument or that of the Gospel writers. For example, the beatitude, "Blessed are the poor in spirit, for theirs is the kingdom of heaven" (Matt 5:3), has as its major premise "those who receive the kingdom of heaven are blessed," and as its minor premise "the poor in spirit will receive the kingdom of heaven." The effectiveness of the saying rhetorically depends on how it is persuasive. Is it persuasive because it is a shared or common perspective between the speaker and hearers or because the authority of the speaker makes the uncommon perspective of the minor premise valid?

Rhetoric and rhetorical criticism of the gospels

Rhetorical criticism is the attempt to analyze a text according to a theory of rhetoric. The practice of rhetorical criticism spans a variety of understandings of rhetoric from ancient classical Greco-Roman rhetoric to a modern understanding of rhetoric often called New Rhetoric. At the heart of all forms of rhetorical criticism is analyzing a text in order to assess and evaluate the modes and means of the argumentation and the effects of that argumentation in terms of its power to persuade. Rhetorical criticism of the gospels can help in understanding the presentation of Jesus in the gospels whatever rhetorical method or theory is used.

Many scholars are attempting to use the categories of Greco-Roman rhetoric to analyze the gospels or parts of the gospels. For instance, G. A. Kennedy analyzes Matthew's Gospel as whole: 1:1–17 is the introduction; 1:18–4.25 is the narration or statement of the case; 5:1–7:29, the Sermon on the Mount, is the proposition or the speaker's thesis; the remainder of the gospel functions as proof or supporting arguments. He also suggests that one can apply ancient rhetoric to smaller units, so he analyzes the Sermon on the Mount (Matt 5–7) as a form of deliberative rhetoric and St John's Farewell Discourse (John 13–17) as a form of epideictic rhetoric. As noted before, because of the narrative nature of the gospels and their genre as ancient biography, such rhetorical analysis can only be analogical to Greco-Roman rhetorical theory and is heuristic at best.

Another approach is to define rhetoric more in terms of literary artistry or narrative rhetoric. From this perspective the gospels are evaluated as a story that is constructed in order to influence its readers by employing a set of particular literary techniques and devices. Macro literary techniques such as narration, point of view, plot, characterization, and micro literary devices such as parallelism, repetitions, chiasm, intercalation, are evaluated as to how they make the story effective and communicate theological intentions. This approach, however, is rooted more in an aesthetics of the imagination than in a concept of argumentation or persuasion. However, this more fluid and less historical understanding of rhetoric is proving creative in interpreting the gospels.

A growing rhetorical theory of analysis is advocated by V. K. Robbins. His socio-rhetorical analyses of Mark and other gospel pericopes are complex sociological and ideological examinations of the ancient literary forms and patterns and of the ancient cultural traditions and influences imbedded in the gospels in order to determine how the gospel stories changed social attitudes and promoted new behavior. He suggests that Mark's Gospel represents effective rhetoric because it posits an image of Jesus as an extraordinary human teacher, an understanding of discipleship, and a learning cycle, all of which are compatible with the cultural ideological and communication norms of the Hellenistic world. It is the compatibility which makes it more persuasive and able to gain a hearing, but its pushing of the cultural boundaries which makes it transformative.

Rhetoric criticism is not limited to the application of ancient classical rhetorical theory to the gospels. Rhetorical theory can be related to literary theory and to social science in order to illumine the way the Jesus story in the gospels persuades the readers to share and adhere to the beliefs which underlie the telling of the Jesus event.

DENNIS STAMPS

Further reading

Aune, David E. *The New Testament in its Literary Environment*, Philadelphia, PA: Westminster Press, 1987.
Black, C. Clifton. *The Rhetoric of the Gospel: Theological Artistry in the Gospel and Acts*, St Louis, MO: Chalice Press, 2001.
Burridge, Richard A. *What are the Gospels? A Comparison with Graeco-Roman Biography*, Cambridge: Cambridge University Press, 1992.
—— "The Gospels and Acts," in Stanley E. Porter (ed.) *Handbook of Classical Rhetoric in the Hellenistic Period 330 BC–AD 400*, Leiden: Brill, 1997.

Classen, Carl J. *Rhetorical Criticism of the New Testament*, Leiden: Brill, 2002.
Henderson, Ian H. *Jesus, Rhetoric and Law*, Leiden: Brill, 1996.
Hock, Ronald F. and Eugene N. O'Neil (eds) *The Chreia in Ancient Rhetoric: Vol. 1. The Progymnasmata*, Atlanta, GA: Scholars Press, 1986.
Kennedy, George A. *Classical Rhetoric and Its Christian and Secular Tradition from Ancient to Modern Times*, Chapel Hill, NC: University of North Carolina Press, 1980.
—— *New Testament Interpretation through Rhetorical Criticism*, Chapel Hill, NC: University of North Carolina Press, 1984.
Mack, Burton L. *Rhetoric and the New Testament*, Minneapolis, MN: Fortress Press, 1990.
Mack, Burton L. and Vernon K. Robbins. *Patterns of Persuasion in the Gospels*, Sonoma, CA: Polebridge Press, 1989.
Robbins, Vernon K. *Jesus the Teacher: A Socio-Rhetorical Interpretation of Mark*, Philadelphia, PA: Fortress Press, 1984.
Watson, Duane F. and Alan J. Hauser (eds) *Rhetorical Criticism of the Bible: A Comprehensive Bibliography with Notes on History and Method*, Leiden: Brill, 1994.
Wilder, Amos N. *Early Christian Rhetoric: The Language of the Gospel*, London: SCM Press, 1964.

RIGHTEOUSNESS, JUSTICE

In the gospels, δικαιοσύνη, the Greek word translated as "righteousness" or sometimes "justice," reflects one use of the Hebrew צדק or צדקה. The Aramaic equivalent is קשוט or קשוטא, which is the word that Jesus probably used. As used by Jesus, the term "righteousness" refers to conformity to God's will, usually synonymous with obedience to the commandments. The person who is in conformity to God's will has righteousness as a result. In Jesus' teaching, righteousness characterizes the kingdom of God and is indispensable in order for a person to enter it.

Religious-historical background

The use of "righteousness" (צדק or צדקה) to mean conformity to God's will, usually synonymous with obedience to the commandments, occurs in the Hebrew Bible with some frequency (עשה צדקה) (see Gen 30:33; Deut 9:5; Jer 22:13; Ezek 3:20; 18:20; 33:12; Hos 10:12). Righteousness results from keeping the commandments (Deut 6:25). To conform to God's will is called "to do righteousness" (עשה צדקה) (Gen 18:19; Ps 106:3; Isa 56:1; 58:2; 64:5; Ezek 18:22). God loves righteousness, but hates its opposite, wickedness (רשע) (Ps 45:7; see Eccl 7:15). Reference is sometimes made to the way or path of righteousness in order to describe a life characterized by conformity to God's will (Prov 8:20; 16:31). The word "right-eousness" is often used in synthetic parallelism with "judgment" (מִשְׁפָּט) to mean the same as "righteousness" used alone (Gen 18:19; Prov 2:9; 21:3; Isa 5:16; Ps 106:3; 119:121; Prov 2:9; Jer 22:13; Ezek 18:5). Because they have "right-eousness," God delivers individual Israelites from the effects of his wrath on the nation (Ezek 14:14, 20). Likewise, in Proverbs having righteousness negatively delivers from danger and death and positively brings reward and life (10:2; 11:4–6; 11:18–19; 12:28). Since David walked in truth, righteousness and uprightness of heart, God shows him lovingkindness (חֶסֶד) (1 Kgs 3:6; see Prov 21:21). On account of his righteousness, the psalmist says that he beholds the face of Yahweh (Ps 17:15). Finally, a person can learn righteousness (לָמַד צֶדֶק) (Isa 26:10), pursue righteousness (רֹדֵף צֶדֶק) (Isa 51:1) and seek righteousness (בַּקֵּשׁ צֶדֶק) (Zeph 2:3).

In non-sectarian texts from the second-Temple period, the term "righteousness" also occurs with the meaning of conformity to God's will, usually synonymous with obedience to the command-ments. In some cases, however, the texts have sur-vived only in translation, so that it is not always certain what the original Hebrew or Aramaic was. Ben Sira says that it grieves him to see a man who turns from righteousness to sin (ἀπὸ δικαιοσύνης ἐπὶ ἁμαρτίαν) (26:28); these two terms refer to obedience and disobedience to the commandments respectively. In Sir 16:22 there is found the phrase "acts of right-eousness" (מַעֲשֵׂה צֶדֶק/ἔργα δικαιοσύνης), which is an objective genitive: doing righteous deeds. In 1 Macc 2:29, the author explains that many who were seeking righteousness and judgment (ζητοῦντες δικαιοσύνην καὶ κρίμα) went out to the wilderness in support of Mattathias; as in the Hebrew Bible, these two terms function as a hen-diadys, referring to obedience to the command-ments. There is also a reference to Simon's righteousness, which refers to his obedience to the commandments (14:35). In *Genesis Apocryphon* (1Q20), Enoch says that during his days on earth he "did righteousness" (קוּשְׁטָא ... דברת) (6:2; see 2:7, 10, 18; 2:5, 22; 19:25). *Aramaic Levi* contains the phrase "paths of righteousness" (אָרְחָת קֻשְׁטָא), referring to a life of obedience to the command-ments (4Q213 frags 3–4 9; see אָרְחָת קֻשְׁט) in 4Q213a frag. 1 1.12). Finally, in 11QTemple, the Israelites are told: "Righteousness, righteousness you are to pursue (צֶדֶק צֶדֶק תִּרְדּוֹף) in order that you might live and take possession of the land" (51.15). To pursue righteousness is to strive to con-form to the will of God by obeying the command-ments given through Moses (see also 51.13, 17).

In *1 Enoch*, when used in reference to human beings, the term "righteousness" refers to con-formity to God's will (see 12:4; 15:2; 39:6; 81:9; 82:4; 91:13). The opposite of "righteousness" is "great sin" (104:9). The patriarch Enoch encourag-es his children to "walk in righteousness" (91:4) and to "love righteousness and walk therein" (94:1). He also tells them, "Seek and choose for yourselves righteousness and an elect life" (94:4). Living in conformity to God's will is to be on the "paths of righteousness" (91:18–19; 94:1; 99:10). To have "died in righteousness" (102:4; 103:3–4) or "fallen asleep in righteousness" (49:3) is to have died with a record of obedience. Likewise, in the *Book of Jubilees*, "righteousness" refers to con-formity God's will (7:37; 10:17; 25:1; 30:20; 35:2; 35:13). A person who obeys the commandments is said to "do righteousness" (7:20; 20:2; 20:9; 30:20, 23; 36:3). The idiom "to walk in righteousness" (7:26) describes habitual obedience to the com-mandments and the related term "way of right-eousness" denotes a life of obedience (23:21, 26; 25:15). It should be noted, however, that in the original Hebrew of *Jub.* 21:21 it is said about sinful humanity that "there is no truth with them" (וְאֵין אֱמֶת אִתָּם) (4Q219 2.24), so that it is possible that other instances of "righteousness" could have originally been "truth," its functional equivalent. (In 4Q176 frags 19–20 1, the term "truth" probably stood in parallelism with "righteousness" [צְדָקָה].) In *Psalms of Solomon*, "righteousness" (δικαιοσύνη) is used to refer to obedience to the commandments (5:17; 8:6; 14:2; 17:26; 18:8; see 1:1–3). In *Ps Sol.* 9:5, it is explained that "the one who does right-eousness" (ὁ ποιῶν δικαιοσύνην) stores up life (see Lev 18:5). The biblical sounding phrase "to do righteousness and judgment" (ποιῶν δικαιοσύνην καὶ κρίμα) means the same as to do righteousness (17:19).

Among the Qumran sectarian writings, the term "righteousness" sometimes occurs, but not with the frequency of other similar terms, such as "truth." In the *Rule of the Community* is found the redun-dant phrase "to do truth, righteousness and judg-ment," the meaning of which is to obey the commandments properly interpreted (1.5; see 8.2). Habitual obedience to the commandments is called "service of righteousness" (עֲבוֹדַת צֶדֶק), which is probably a genitive of content: service (to God) consisting of righteousness (4.9). The phrase "judgments of righteousness" (מִשְׁפְּטֵי צֶדֶק) prob-ably refers to the commandments properly inter-preted (3.1; 4.4; see CD 20.30–31). The members of the community are called "sons of right-eousness" (בְּנֵי צֶדֶק), which is genitive of quality

(3.20, 22). In the *Damascus Document*, an appeal is made to those who "know righteousness" (צדק יודעי), which no doubt means those who know the commandments (CD 1.1). It is stressed that it was not on account of the Israelites' righteousness that they dispossessed the nations in the land, which means that God did not act because they had been obedient to the commandments (CD 8.14 / 19.27; see Deut 7:8; 9:5). In the *War Scroll*, because of their disobedience to the commandments, the enemies of the community are described as "the ones who hate righteousness" (משנאי צדק) (1QM 3.5–6). Conversely, those who obey God's commandments are called those who "serve him in righteousness" (משרתיו בצדק) (13.3). According to the *Thanksgiving Hymns*, righteousness does not belong to a human being, which implies that no one obeys the commandments completely (12.30). Reference is also made to the paths of righteousness (נתיבות צדקה) (15.14), which denotes a life characterized by obedience to the commandments properly interpreted. The same is meant by the phrase "the ways of righteousness" (צדק מדרכי) (4Q184 frag. 1 16). In the *Halakhic Letter* (4QMMT) the author affirms, "Thus, it will be reckoned to you as righteousness (לצדקה) when you do what is upright and good before God" (C 30–33). The word "righteousness" is used in this context to denote what a Jew possesses as a result of obedience to the commandments properly interpreted.

Jesus and righteousness

In some of Jesus' sayings, the term "righteousness" (δικαιοσύνη) occurs with the meaning of conformity to God's will, usually synonymous with obedience to the commandments. All but one of these sayings in the Synoptic Gospels are in Matthew. It is circular reasoning, however, to conclude that the author of Matthew is responsible for the creation of these sayings. Five of the seven sayings are found in the Sermon on the Mount, which suggests that the use of the term is characteristic of this collection of Jesus tradition. The term "righteousness" also occurs once in Luke and twice in John with the same meaning.

Matthew 3:15

In Matthew's account of Jesus' baptism, John the Baptist attempts to discourage Jesus from being baptized; he says that it is he who needs to be baptized by Jesus, not Jesus by him. Jesus' reply is, "Allow it for now, for thus it is fitting for us to do

this in order to fulfill all righteousness" (πληῶσαι πᾶσαν δικαιοσύνην). Used as such, "righteousness" means conformity to God's will, so that Jesus sees his submission to John's baptism as fulfilling God's requirement for him. In this case, righteousness refers to conformity to the special will of God, not to the commandments. The unanswered question is why Jesus' baptism at the hands of John is a requirement for him. Probably, Jesus undergoes baptism in order to identify himself vicariously with Israel, even though he himself does not need to repent and be forgiven.

The fact that there are minor agreements between Matthew and Luke against Mark suggests that Matthew and Luke had access to another version of Jesus' baptism and were influenced by this when redacting their Markan source. If there was another version of Jesus' baptism, it is possible that Matthew's dialogue between Jesus and John that serves to explain Jesus' request to receive John's baptism (Matt 3:14–15) derives from this non-Markan source. So, contrary to some commentators, it is not incontestable that the author of Matthew composed this dialogue himself with the apologetic aim of correcting what he considered to be a theological embarrassment in Mark: that Jesus needed forgiveness for sins.

"Righteousness" in the Sermon on the Mount

As indicated, five of Jesus' sayings in the Sermon on the Mount contain the term "righteousness." In four cases, it means conformity to God's will expressed in the commandments, and in the remaining saying it has a related meaning.

Matthew 5:6

In the fourth Matthean beatitude, Jesus says that a person is "blessed" or happy if he or she "thirsts and hungers after righteousness." Jesus is using the desire for water and food as a metaphor for the pursuit of obedience to the commandments, which is what "righteousness" means in this context (see Pss 42:2; 63:1;143:6; Isa 55:1; Amos 8:11–12; Sir 24:19–22; 1QH^a 12.10–12). The commandments are like the drink and food that a thirsty and hungry person ardently seeks. Using the same metaphor, Jesus compares the future reward of the one who pursues righteousness as being "filled" (divine passive). That filling no doubt is entrance into the kingdom of God in its future realization (see Matt 8:11–12 = Luke 13:28–29).

Many scholars argue that Matt 5:6 is a Matthean redaction created from the simpler Lukan version, "Blessed are those who hunger because they shall be filled" (6:21) (see *Gospel of Thomas* 69b). On this view, Matthew introduces his characteristic term "righteousness" to the original version as the object of the verb (and also adds another verb "to thirst") and thereby creates a metaphor from what was originally intended as literal. But only when one assumes that there was one original version of this beatitude, originating in the hypothetical Q-source, does this become necessary. It is conceivable that Jesus used two similar beatitudes on different occasions. The assumption that those who in the present suffer ("hunger") do so precisely because they are righteous unifies these two beatitudes.

Matthew 5:10

In the eighth Matthean beatitude, Jesus says that a person is "blessed" or happy when he or she experiences persecution "on account of righteousness" (ἕνεκεν δικαιοσύνης), because the kingdom of Heaven belongs to that person (Luke 6:22–23). (The phrase "because theirs is the Kingdom of Heaven" in Matt 5:3 and 5:10 forms an inclusion around the beatitudes.) What is meant is that those who are persecuted because of their obedience to the commandments in the present will be recompensed by being given a place in the kingdom of Heaven in its future realization. Before that time, it is possible for the application of retributive justice to be suspended, which leads to unjustified suffering (see Dan 11:33–35; 12:1–3; 2 Macc 7:9; *1 En.* 102:4–5; 103:3; *2 Bar.* 19:7; 30:1–2; 48:50; 51; 73–74; 1QS 4.18–20; 1QpHab 5.5–6; 8.1–3; 4Q416 frag. 2 1.5–6 = 4Q417 fr. 1, 10–12). Some scholars claim that the whole of Matt 5:10 is Matthean redaction, created in order to serve as an introduction to Matt 5:11, but the evidence for this conclusion is far from compelling.

Matthew 5:20

Jesus tells his disciples, "Unless your righteousness exceeds that of the scribes and Pharisees you will not enter the kingdom of heaven." The term "righteousness" in this saying refers to conformity to God's will expressed in the commandments. It is "your" righteousness in the sense that it belongs to a person insofar as he or she has habitually obeyed the commandments. The manner in which this righteousness exceeds that of the scribes and Pharisees – whose reputation for righteousness is unrivaled – is found in Jesus' intensification of the demands of the Law in the antitheses that follow

(Matt 5:21–48). Jesus' point is that a condition of entrance into the kingdom of heaven in its future realization is obedience to the commandments (see Matt 5:48 = Luke 6:36). To enter the kingdom in the present requires repentance, to which God graciously responds by forgiving past sins, but entrance into the future kingdom requires continued obedience to the commandments. Because of the presence of the term "righteousness" and other typically Matthean vocabulary, such as "the scribes and Pharisees," some commentators have concluded that the entire saying is a Matthean creation, designed to introduce the antitheses in Matt 5:21–47. Such a conclusion is unjustified, however, since the saying in Matt 5:20 is coherent with other of Jesus' sayings about obedience as a condition of entrance into the kingdom (Luke 6:46–49 = Matt 7:24–27; Matt 7:13–14; 7:20–21; 21:31; Luke 10:25–28).

Matthew 6:33

In Matt 6:33, Jesus says, "Seek first the kingdom of heaven and his righteousness and all these things will be added unto you." Jesus establishes a hierarchy of concerns, with the kingdom having priority over a person's material needs. God's righteousness is the totality of God's commandments; to seek the kingdom of heaven and God's righteousness is to resolve to be in the kingdom on the condition of obedience to the commandments. Of course, to seek the kingdom also requires the acceptance of its messenger and mediator, Jesus. If the one who seeks the kingdom of heaven has been disobedient up to that point, then seeking the kingdom will require repentance, turning from sin to obedience to the commandments. In this case, Jesus' directive would be another way of saying "Repent and believe the good news" (Mark 1:15).

Most exegetes claim that the author of Matthew is responsible for the interpolation of the phrase "and his righteousness" into his source, because of his interest in righteousness as a theme. Luke's version, "Seek his kingdom, and these things shall be added unto you" (12:31), is usually assumed to be more original, deriving from the hypothetical Q-source. But only when one assumes that there was originally only one version of this saying is such a hypothesis required. It is equally possible that the Matthean version of the tradition contained the phrase or that the author of Matthew knew both versions and preferred the fuller one. But even if the author did insert it, the phrase "and his righteousness" is simply explicative of what it means to seek the kingdom of heaven.

Matthew 6:1

Jesus instructs his disciples that they should be careful not to do their "righteousness" before human beings in order to be seen by them. From the context, "righteousness" means giving of alms to the poor, which Jesus says should be done secretly (see Tob 12:8).

Other occurrences of "righteousness"

There are two sayings in which the term "righteousness" occurs in relation to John the Baptist. In Matt 21:32, Jesus refers to John as coming in "the way of righteousness," by which he means that John's message was that people should repent and become obedient to God's will as expressed in the commandments. In the Song of Zachariah, it is said that God will bring it about that people will serve him "in holiness and righteousness all of our days" (1:75). The phrase "in holiness and righteousness" is a *hendiadys*, denoting conformity to God's will (see Wis 9:3).

The term "righteousness" δικαιοσύνη occurs in the Gospel of John in relation to the Spirit (Paraclete). Jesus says that the Spirit will convict the world concerning sin and righteousness (16:8–10). What is meant is that the Spirit will communicate to human beings what is displeasing to God (sin) and what is pleasing to God (righteousness). In this context, righteousness is the opposite of sin, and denotes conformity to God's will expressed in the commandments.

BARRY D. SMITH

Further reading

Davies, W. D. *The Setting of the Sermon on the Mount*, Cambridge: Cambridge University Press, 1964.

Dupont, Jacques. *Les Béatitudes*, vol. 3, *Les Évangélistes*, revised edition, Paris: Gabalda, 1973.

Przybylski, Benno. *Righteousness in Matthew and His World of Thought*, SNTSMS 41, Cambridge: Cambridge University Press, 1980.

Reumann, John, J. A. Fitzmyer, and L. A. Quinn. *Righteousness in the New Testament*, Philadelphia, PA: Fortress Press, 1982.

Streck, Georg. *Der Weg der Gerechtigkeit. Untersuchung zur Theologie des Matthäus*, FRLANT 82, third edition, Göttingen: Vanderhoeck & Ruprecht, 1971.

ROADS AND COMMERCE IN GALILEE AND JUDEA

Roads played a critical role in the economic and cultural development of Galilee and Judea. Whether used for conquest, commerce, or evangelisation, roads of various types framed the existence of Jesus and his contemporaries. Wherever roads reached, commerce typically followed to the same degree as the road's importance.

Most of the roads in Eretz Israel, a sub-region of Coele Syria (Gk. κοίλη Συρία), pre-existed Roman rule and were used and developed by its predecessors in the region, the Persians, Assyrians, and Babylonians. Some, like the King's Way, are attested in the earliest biblical traditions (e.g. Num 20:17–21). All, however, provided means of trade and ensured the strategic significance of the area for trade throughout the ancient Near East.

Roads

Four indicators are commonly used to date road development: geographical determinism, literary sources, archaeological evidence, and ancient milestones. Geographical determinism relies upon the tendency of the ancient Near East to remain relatively static, thus allowing one to use modern geographic conditions to project the conditions of an event from 2,000 years ago. Literary sources include not only scriptural texts and extra-scriptural writings but any of the several historic descriptions and itineraries used in ancient times as well as the records of subsequent pilgrimages and modern geographic studies. Naturally, archaeological evidence further clarifies the details of the ancient routes. Finally, milestones are used to date the development of the road. Using the script and composition of the stone, archaeologists are able to date paved parts of major roads. Where no milestones are found, however, the dating becomes less certain.

In general, roads in the ancient Near East conformed to the geographic characteristics of the land. Ancient, unpaved roads preceded Roman pavement throughout Eretz Israel. Most roads in Judea and Galilee were unpaved at the time of Jesus. Naturally roads that were paved may be considered to have been major roads, minor roads being those that did not manifest Roman technology.

Major roads

In the early first century, the major international trade routes naturally ran north to south. Significant arteries, however, existed to allow access to the interior of the region.

North–south

Throughout the region commonly called Israel, two major roads had been established from ancient times. These were based on trade routes which ran from Egypt and Arabia to the rest of the Levant while avoiding the Syrian wilderness and the Arabian Desert.

The oldest, and the only one that passed through the Land of Israel itself, was the "Way of the Sea," sometimes called the "Way of the Philistines" and, later in Latin, the Via Maris. It is known to have been used consistently since the Egyptian New Kingdom. The region of the road extended down the western coast from Antioch to Alexandria. Under Roman rule, it was paved and well maintained, thus linking the military garrisons at its respective end points. While running close to the sea between Antioch and Caesarea, the road moved inland as it progressed through Samaria and Judea, thus connecting Caesarea Maritima with Lydda and Jamnia, and then coming closer to the sea in order to connect Gaza and Raphia before entering Egypt. The inclusion of the route from Caesarea Maritima through Joppa, frequently recorded as the route of the Via Maris, was not developed until the time of Vespasian (c. 69–79 CE).

On the east side of the Jordan, along the eastern lowlands of the Transjordanian Plateau, was the King's Way. It reached from Resafa on the Euphrates and proceeded through Damascus, down to Aila (modern-day Elat) and the Gulf of Aqaba before crossing the Sinai and finally terminating in Egypt. After approximately 124 CE, the King's Way was called the Via Nova Traiana, a Latin phrase meaning "Trajan's New Road," because of the Roman emperor's refurbishment of it. From ancient times, it was used to convey goods from Egypt to and from Mesopotamia.

East–west

At the time of Jesus, there were four major arteries. None of these passed through Galilee.

In the north, an artery connected the Decapolian city of Scythopolis (Beth She'an) with the Via Nova. Running from the region of Hauran and the Transjordanian Plateau, through the Plain of Beth She'an, it turned at Scythopolis to pass along the southwestern border of the Decapolis, through Pella and Gerasa, meeting the highway again at Philadelphia. This last leg was not paved until Hadrian's rule (c. 129/130 CE).

In Judea, a major artery connected the Via Maris at Antipatris with Jerusalem, passing through Thimna, Gophna and Bethel. At Gophna, it connected Jerusalem's Damascus Gate with the mountainous way to Shechem (the modern Nablus Road, through Samaria. Other, shorter arteries

connected Lydda with Joffa and Ashkelon with the main part of the Via Maris. The former is known to have existed since the time of Solomon's building of the Temple as the port from which Lebanese timber was conveyed to Jerusalem (2 Chr 2:15, English Bible reference 2 Chr 2:16; and Ezra 3:7).

Minor roads

Galilee

Galilee (גליל, "the circle") in the time of Jesus was commonly regarded in the south as a hinterland, in the pejorative sense of the term. One recalls the scornful reference by Isaiah to "Galilee of the Gentiles" (9:1). Its distance from the Temple served to alienate its population from, and to foster a level of prejudice among, those in Judea. The reader may recall Nathanael's words of incredulity in the Fourth Gospel: "Can anything good come out of Nazareth?" (John 1:46).

The eastern borders of Galilee were formed by the Sea of Galilee, Lake Huleh, and the swampish region which connects them. The southern border of Galilee is the Valley of Jezreel and the Caesarea–Scythopolis road. Its western boundary is the Plain of Accho. In the north, Galilee was hedged in by the encroaching boundary of Phoenician Tyre. While Josephus leads one to believe the boundary was the city proper (J.W. 3:39), a boundary running west from Lake Huleh, between Kadasa and Gischala, is more likely (Freyne 117).

The geographical subparts of Galilee were referenced both by Josephus and by the Mishnah. Where the former notes only Upper and Lower Galilee, the latter draws the more specific characterisations in terms of Upper and Lower Galilee and "the Valley". The demarcation of Upper and Lower Galilee was at Kefar Hananya (14 km west of Chorazin), located at the tree-line of the sycamore north of the Beth Kerem Valley (700 m above sea level). This is virtually the same location as Bersabe of Jesus' time. The third category, the Valley, is the area closest to the eastern bodies of water, including the environs of Tiberias and Kadesh (modern Qadas). Josephus regularly refers to the latter location as part of Upper Galilee, but the Mishnah's demarcation places it in the Valley around Lake Semechonitis, modern Lake Huleh (Ant. 5:91; m. Sheb. 9:2).

Galilee differed substantially from Judea in that it had an abundant water supply, this aspect being illustrated most fully by the Sea of Galilee feeding the Dead Sea. It was extremely fertile, as it remains today. Consequently, Lower Galilee eventually became one of the major grain producers of the empire. Likewise, the hill countries of the Galilee produced wine and olives. These all were required throughout the Roman empire.

Given these agricultural dynamics, it is not surprising that the significant roads of Galilee served to connect the arable regions with the major trade centres. As Avi-Yonah (1950) and Sean Freyne (1980) have demonstrated, every significant road in Galilee served to connect with either Caesarea Maritima (Samaria), Acre (Phoenicia) or Damascus (greater Coele Syria). The major routes currently known are: Caesarea Maritima to Sepphoris, an extension of the Caesarea Maritima–Scythopolis road; Tiberias to Acre, passing through the Tir'an Valley; Tiberias to Damascus; and Tiberias to Bostra. The road from Tiberias to Bostra also intersects with the Damascus–Scythopolis–Philadelphia artery. In so doing, the road served to connect Galilee with the King's Way (later the Via Nova Traiana) at two points, thus fostering trade.

As all major routes led around and not through it, Galilee was an area commonly circumnavigated by any who travelled. However, the intersection of the Tiberias–Acre and Caesarea Maritima–Sepphoris roads and the arteries to Damascus and Scythopolis made for increased trade traffic between the Via Maris and the Via Nova Traiana. One is not surprised, therefore, to find a fortress at Sepphoris and a rival city in Tiberias.

Although the major trade route from the south came from Caesarea Maritima and connected with the Tiberias–Acre road at Sepphoris, a secondary road is known to have run southeast from Sepphoris to intersect the Legio–Scythopolis road (a subsection of the Caesarea Maritima–Scythopolis road) at Esdrelon. This route effectively turned Nazareth from a would-be terminus, a village on the outskirts of Sepphoris, to a more significant thoroughfare for trade to Scythopolis and Judea in the south.

Judea

In contrast to Galilee, Judea knew several arteries, almost all of which led to or around the greater area of Jerusalem. The paved roads that connected Ashkelon and Joppa with the Via Maris also served to convey trade goods to and from Judea.

Although the most developed road from Jerusalem at this time was to Antipatris (via Gophna and Timna), a critical network of roads ran from Joppa (modern Tel Aviv) to Jerusalem. The British Archaeology Report details several roads that were of secondary, but more than local, importance. A highway ran from Joppa to Lydda, thus connecting

with the Via Maris, and two highways from Lydda to Jerusalem, one passing through Emmaus and another through Beth Horon further north. In addition, the Emmaus–Beth Horon road connected the two arteries. Jesus' post-resurrection appearance would have occurred on the southern-most of these two roads (Luke 24:13).

It is noteworthy that all main roads to the Transjordan were in the north, the Jordan Valley in the south being too wide for most commercial passage in Jesus' time. The Jordanian transversal between Jericho and Bethsaida (or Julius, south of Abila) was not fully developed until Hadrian's rule (c. 117–38 CE). This adversely influenced the economic development of Judea and shielded it from the cultural influences to which Galilee was exposed.

A system of local roads is also known to have been circumjacent to the west of Jerusalem. The aforementioned artery from Beth Horon continued in a less developed form to Beth Gubrin where it joined a larger circuit that included Hebron and extended to En Gedi on the Dead Sea.

Commerce

Currency

For common trade, Roman currency was prevalent throughout the Land of Israel at the time of Jesus. Coinage was of two types. Silver coinage came from the imperial mints located in Antioch, Alexandria, or even Rome. Of this type, the common denomination was the denarius. A denarius was the accepted pay of a worker for one day (Matt 20:2-13). The shekel equivalent of a denarius was also the annual tax at the Jerusalem Temple, presumably including fees for money-changers (Matthew 22:19). Within Judea and Galilee, however, the bronze Herodian coins were more common. Minted in Jerusalem and Tiberias, these were meant, in effect, as common coinage for daily use. For Temple trade, Temple shekels were required. The annual tax for an adult male was a half-shekel (Exod 30:13; *Shekalim* 1:3) and was roughly equivalent to a silver didrachma (Matt 17:24).

Galilee

Galilean cities

SEPPHORIS

Josephus and the Mishnah both bear witness, and archaeology has confirmed, that Sepphoris was a major stronghold in Galilee (*m. Arak.* 9:6). The "strongest city of Galilee" (*J.W.* 2:510–11) was located not more than 5 km from Jesus' home town of Nazareth. Situated as it is at the end of a major artery, Caesarea Maritima, and less than 3 km from the Tiberias–Acre road, one is not surprised to find a major trade centre there. It was the most important centre in Galilee. For all the trade that passed from Acre or Caesarea Maritima to Tiberias, it all passed through Sepphoris first.

Being close to the Plain of Acre, the Plain of Esdrelon and the rest of the Jezreel Valley, Sepphoris benefited from trading in the three main agricultural products of the area: grain, olive oil and wine. The runoff from the rains and snow of the upper Galilee made the soil extremely fertile. Therefore, agricultural trade also included fruit, figs, dates and honey.

The relevance of Sepphoris for gaining a perspective on the early life of Jesus cannot be overestimated. At 5 km, the town was well within a day's journey from Nazareth.

TIBERIAS

Sepphoris' rival in Galilee was Tiberias. Located on the western shores of the Sea of Galilee, it was situated in the most fertile region of Galilee and benefited from fish trade on the Sea and the agricultural trade nearby. Simon, Andrew, James and John were either fishermen by trade or from fishing families (Matt 4:19, 21; Mark 1:17, 19).

Tiberias benefited from trade with the seaport in Acre and was the hub for trade between Galilee and the Transjordanian regions of the Decapolis, Gaulanitis and greater Coele Syria. While it was on one of the main routes around the Sea of Galilee from Damascus to Jerusalem, there is uncertainty over how much trade passed through it for this purpose. From Damascus, the greater artery passed from the Via Nova Traiana past Hippos to Scythopolis, itself also along the route of trade from Caesarea Maritima to the interior.

Because of the peculiar geographic formations of the area, Tiberias was known for its springs and attracted visitors to use them. Josephus attests that John of Gischala, his rival, used the ruse of an illness to visit the springs and raise opposition against the general-cum-historian (*J.W.* 2:614; see also *Life* 85).

Notable non-Galilean cities of influence

Situated furthest to the north, Galilee was subject to several Hellenising influences. These typically came via the cities with whom Galilee traded, many of which had been established at least since the Seleucids and the Ptolemies.

THE DECAPOLIS

As the major roads to the Transjordan were in the north of Eretz Israel, one is not surprised to find significant Transjordanian influence on Galilee from pre-Roman times. Philadelphia exerted influence since it was founded by Ptolemy II as Philoteria. Of particular influence was Scythopolis, the major thoroughfare for trade. Such influence was not always received well, and the two regions had a history of conflict even in Seleucid times (*J.W.* 2:458). Nonetheless, some of Jesus' earliest followers were from the Decapolis (Matt 5:25).

ACRE AND TYRE

Since being renamed Ptolemais in 261 BCE, Acre was a major source of Hellenistic influence and agitation towards the Jewish hinterland of Galilee. It was the closest port and therefore the most natural trading partner for Lower Galilee. However, even under the Seleucids, the textual evidence attests to significant and frequent hostilities between the two regions (1 Macc 5:15–22, 12:48–53; *J.W.* 2:67, 2:458; *Life* 213–14).

Tyre was a bustling seaport in Jesus' time. Ezekiel 27 notes that all of Eretz Israel traded its agricultural wealth with the city for its merchandise. This rendered Tyre heavily dependent on Eretz Israel – and particularly Galilee – for food (Acts 12:20).

Judea

Given the more extensive study of Jerusalem, the commercial aspects of Judea are more readily accessible than those of Galilee. Most of what is known about the region's economy is derived from its capital city. For each marketplace, there was a tax-collector. The seller stopped at the tax-collector's booth and paid duty to the tax-collector upon entering the market. He was then allowed to set up his trading stall. Matthew is called to be a disciple while attending his booth (Mark 2:14; Luke 5:27).

Local secular trade

AGRICULTURE

The area around Jerusalem was full of agriculture. Simon of Cyrene, presumably on pilgrimage from

Libya, is depicted in the gospels as having come "from the field" when he is forced to carry Jesus' cross (Mark 15:21; Luke 23:26). Given the road system around Jerusalem, he would have come from Libya by either the north or the west (most probably the latter). Also, the early church was comprised of landowners who had sold their property (Acts 4:34), thus suggesting agricultural estates in the environs of Jerusalem.

Throughout Judea, grain of various kinds was grown. Grain was of foremost importance and in times of famine was the first to wane. Pseudo-Aristeas notes crops of corn around Jerusalem, as well as olive groves and fields of pulse (112). Wheat was also common. Despite this, the limestone of the Judean mountains would not allow for much vegetation, and much of the grain used by Judea was imported from the Transjordan, Samaria and Galilee, as mentioned above. However, for the Temple, Judean grain was preferred, particularly from Machmas in the Judean foothills, west of Jericho, and Zanoah in the Shephelah, south of Beth Shemesh (*m. Men.* 8:1).

Second importance to grain was the growing of olives. One is reminded that Jesus' preferred place of teaching, meditation and prayer was the Mount of Olives, immediately east of Jerusalem (Matt 5:1; 21:1; 24:3; 26:30; Mark 11:1; 13:3; 14:26; Luke 19:37; 22:39; John 8:1). It was here that several oil presses were found, the most famous being at Gethsemane (John 18:1, 26; 19:41; 20:15). Olive trees were also cultivated south of Jerusalem.

Third, Judea cultivated grapes for wine. This was apparently for domestic use only and was not exported. Zechariah places the royal wine presses in the Valley of Kidron, southeast of the city (14:10). The Mishnah records five vineyards that provided wine to the Temple. The exact location within Judea is known for only two: Beth Rimma and Beth Luban (modern Bet Rima and al-Lubban, respectively). These are approximately 30 km northwest of Jerusalem and lie on either side of the Antipatris–Jerusalem artery. Keruthin is thought to have been north of Antipatris. The other pre-eminent vineyard, Hattulim, is thought to have been located in the wadi north of Jericho. Kefar Signah, the least of the five, is postulated to have been near Joppa.

Given the largely rocky terrain of Judea, it is unlikely that orchards would have been as prevalent as elsewhere in Coele Syria. Nonetheless, the presence of date trees is explicitly attested by several authors of antiquity and is corroborated when Jesus enters Jerusalem. John records the use of palm branches (John 12:13); Mark notes the use of fruit branches "cut from the fields" (Mark 11:8),

while Matthew records them as lining the southern road from Bethphage or Bethany to Jerusalem (Matthew 21:8). The fig tree that Jesus cursed was probably one among many that also lined the same road (Mark 11:13; Matthew 21:19). In the middle of the first century, Agrippa I built a wall around the northern part of Jerusalem (*J.W.* 5:146). One is confident that there were several gardens in this area as the entrance was called the Garden Gate. Even after the wall was built, and beyond the gardens not enclosed by Agrippa's wall, Titus came upon hedged-in gardens and groves of cultivated trees woven amidst rocky precipices when he arrived from Mount Scopus in the north (*J.W.* 5:106–8).

Josephus (*J.W.* 5:507) notes a village to the southwest of Jerusalem which was called "The House of Erebinthi" (Gk. Ἐρεβίνθων οἶκος; lit. "house of chickpeas"). Therefore, one may speak of chickpea cultivation in this area as well.

LIVESTOCK

Most large livestock consumed in Judea was predominantly from either the coastal plain between Joppa and Lydda or from the Judean hills. Chickens were also raised throughout Judea, as evinced by the cock crowing at Peter's denial (Mark 14:72 and parallels).

While the Mishnah makes explicit reference to the purchase of calves in Sharon, the coastal plain between Joppa and Lydda, it explicitly allows the purchase of eggs and chickens anywhere (*M.B.K.* 10:9). Within Jerusalem, there was at least one poulterers' market, although the reference may be to a more generic butcher's market; the two are often combined even today (*m. Erub.* 10:9).

Herdsmen were forbidden by religious practice (but not by Roman law) from selling kids, wool, milk or other animal products themselves. Rather, the woman of the household was expected to handle the sale (*M.B.K.* 10:9).

WOOD

Most of the wood grown in Judea was used for domestic firewood or for sacrificial purposes. Any commerce that arose around common wood sales was domestic only. Cedars from Lebanon, however, were imported for use in Temple structures and in the sacrificing of the heifer as detailed in the Mishnah (*m. Par.* 3.8–10).

PERFUMES AND RESINS

Perfumes and resins were among the chief products of Coele Syria. There is evidence that Jerusalem was not excluded in the production of such goods, but it was certainly dwarfed in importance by Arabia. Given Jerusalem's relative remoteness from major trade routes, Mary's application of nard from Nepal becomes even more costly (Matthew 26:6–13; Luke 7:37–38; and John 12:1–8).

TRADES AND CRAFTS

Based upon archaeological and textual evidence, trade in earthenware was prevalent throughout Judea. Within Jerusalem, however, proscriptions existed against using certain sources for clean pottery. If a piece of earthenware came from beyond Modeïn (27 km from Jerusalem, approximately 7 km east of Lydda), it was forbidden for use as a clean vessel (*m. Hag.* 3:5).

Archaeological evidence also attests to excellent stone and glass work. Avigad notes finding excellent stone vessels, furniture and architecture in Jerusalem. In the Jewish Quarter, archaeology has also unearthed the remnants of a glass factory which manufactured both glass bowls and small bottles.

According to the Mishnah, Judean women were known for their woollen goods (*M.B.K.* 10:9). Indeed, a wool-dealers' market is known to have existed in Jerusalem in the early first century (*m. Erub.* 10:9)

SALT

The gospel writers mention Jesus' reference to salt in several places (Matt 5:13–14; Mark 9:49–50; Luke 14:34). While there is no evidence of a salt market, one must expect that there was one as the average person could not readily gather salt for their daily needs.

SLAVES

The later rabbinic writings testify to the sale of slaves, both male and female and both Jew and Gentile, in Jerusalem (*Sife Leviticus* 25:42, *Sife Deuteronomy* 26). However, this testimony is not corroborated for Jesus' time.

Foreign secular trade

EXPORTS

Jeremias has noted rightly that the only Judean resource of sufficient abundance for export was olives. The Mount of Olives, east of Jerusalem, contained olive presses to extract oil from the olives grown there. Gethsemane (Gk. Γεθσημανί) was a garden located on the Mount; the name is derived from the Hebrew and Aramaic words for "oil press". The region south of Jerusalem also grew olives.

Based on archaeological and textual witnesses, however, the other products of Judea simply were not exportable. The plight of the other two major trade items of Judea illustrate this.

As noted above, grain production in Judea was not sufficient for the local populus and therefore was not an exportable commodity. As the primary use of Latin among Judean Jews in Jesus' time was for household servants who needed to read the writing on wine vats and similar extra-Judean goods, one may conclude that wine also was not an exported commodity.

IMPORTS

Although flour for the Temple was made from Judean grain, and wine and oil came from Judean grapes and olives, domestic agriculture could not satisfy the needs of the entire population. Therefore, these three staples were also imported from the Transjordan, Hauran (northeast of Scythopolis) and Galilee.

Despite the comparatively high volume of produce in Judea, one may also expect imports of fruits and vegetables to sustain pilgrims who came for the three annual feasts, the greatest number presumably coming to celebrate the Passover.

Spices and perfumes came from Arabia primarily via the Aila–Gaza road. Given the good political ties between the Nabateans and the Judeans during Jesus' time, it is possible that the aforementioned glass bottles were designed to hold Arabian perfumes.

Trade related to the Temple

GOODS

The Temple cultus and its related organisations were a major economic force in first-century Judea. The sacrificial animals required, the incense to be burned, the trade of pilgrims and the selling of the ceremonial by-products required enormous amounts of resources. Although it is an exaggeration, it is noteworthy that Josephus estimates over 255,000 lambs as being sacrificed for one Passover in Jerusalem (*J.W.* 6:424). If Pseudo-Aristeas (112) and the Babylonian Talmud (*b. Men.* 87a) are followed, the main forms of livestock in Judea were cattle, sheep, goats and doves. Sacrificial rams were brought from Transjordanian Moabitis (ancient Moab) in Arabia. The Mishnah cites that the need for sacrifices was so great that any livestock found between the Temple and Migdal-Eder, near Bethlehem (approximately 8.5 km away), were presumed to be destined for sacrifice: males for whole-offerings and females for peace-offerings. Thirty days prior to Passover, the same were destined to be Passover-offerings (*m. Shek.* 7:4).

From at least Maccabean times and until late in the second century CE, markets were available within the Temple for those who did not bring their animals to the Temple for sacrifice (Zechariah 14:21, *m. Shek.* 1:3). These traders are detailed by the gospel writers as selling doves, oxen and sheep (Matt 21.12; Mark 11:15; John 2:14). Incense for the Temple was brought from as far away as India. The gems for the high priest's breastplate were bought from abroad.

Although those near to Jerusalem were allowed to sustain themselves on the Second Tithe (one-tenth of all agricultural and animals in their fourth year), pilgrims who came from afar were required to convert their tithe into money. They were then required to spend this money in Jerusalem during their pilgrimage. More on the Second Tithe may be found in the Mishnah tractate *Ma'aser Sheni* ("The Second Tithe").

Given the large number of sacrifices regularly yielded by religious observances, the Temple had a drainage system for blood to flow outside of the city towards the Kidron Valley. Gardeners captured and bought the blood from the Temple for use as fertiliser; to take it without paying was sacrilege according to the Mishnah (*m. Yom.* 5:6).

The domestic wood used for the Temple included fig, pine, date, wild olive and walnut trees (*m. Tam.* 2:3). As such wood is not required of the one sacrificing, it was assumed to have been purchased from local orchards. The only wood expressly forbidden for ceremonial purposes was the olive tree and the grape vine.

SERVICES (MONEY CHANGING)

Although money changers are often associated with the Temple, they conducted currency exchanges of all types. The Mishnah notes that, within the month of Adar, the tables of money changers were set up from the middle of the month and in the Temple only from the 25th of the month. As Adar has twenty-nine days regularly and thirty in a leap year, the money changers conducted most of their business out of the Temple precinct (*m. Shek.* 1:3). Jesus' overturning of their tables may therefore be set at the end of the month (Matt 21:12; Mark 11:15; John 2:14–15).

For all monetary offerings, Temple currency was required. Pilgrims would be required to use a moneychanger to change their currency into the ritual denominations (*m. Shek.* 1:3).

Further to Temple matters, the Second Tithe was exchanged into local currency for spending (*m. Maas. Shen.*). The Mishnah contains debate among the Rabbis of Jesus' time over how this was to be done. If the pilgrim exchanged the money, laws governed how much he could exchange at a time. Alternatively, he could put his Second Tithe on deposit at a shop and draw on it gradually; in this case, the merchant would exchange the currency (*m. Eduy.* 1:9-10).

Brigandage

Negative forms of commerce were also prevalent in the time of Jesus. People throughout history have resorted to brigandage when they could not survive economically. Given its relative remoteness from the major north–south trade routes and the rocky terrain of the major inbound roads, Judea proved no exception.

As recently as the nineteenth century, the environs of Jerusalem knew whole villages of robbers (e.g. Abu Rosh to the northwest, Abu Dis to the southeast). Josephus records robberies in Beth Horon, on the road from Lydda to Jerusalem. The Mishnah alludes to those who have been robbed of their Second Tithe, potentially leaving the people of the town to pay it (*m. Shek.* 2:1). In Jesus' parable of the Good Samaritan, one of the four travellers on the road from Jericho was robbed and half-killed (Luke 10:30–37).

ALBERT LUKASZEWSKI

Further reading

Abel, F.M. "La Distance de Jérusalem à Emmaus," *RB* 34 (1925) 347–67.

Aharoni, Y. "The Roman Road to Aila (Elath)," *IEJ* 4 (1954) 9–16.

——— "Tamar and the Roads to Elath," *IEJ* 13 (1963) 30–42.

Avi-Yonah, Michael. "The Development of the Roman road System in Palestine," *IEJ* 1 (1950–51) 54–60.

——— "A New Dating of the Roman Road from Scythopolis to Neapolis," *IEJ* 16 (1966) 75–76.

Avigad, Nahman. *Discovering Jerusalem*, Jerusalem: Shikmona with IES, 1980.

Bahat, Dan with Chaim Rubinstein. *The Illustrated Atlas of Jerusalem*, trans. Shlomo Ketko, Jerusalem: Carta, 1996.

Beauvery, Robert. "La Route Romaine de Jérusalem à Jéricho," *RB* 64 (1955) 72–101.

Bimson, John J., and J. P. Kane. *New Bible Atlas*, Wheaton, IL: InterVarsity Press, 2000.

Chevallier, Raymond. *Roman Roads*, trans. N. H. Field, London: B. T. Batsford, 1976.

Cohen, R. "New Light on the Date of the Petra-Gaza Road," *BA* 45 (1982) 240–47.

Danby, Herbert. *The Mishnah*. Oxford: Oxford University Press, 1933.

Fischer, Moshe, B. Isaac, and I. Roll. *Roman Roads in Judaea II: The Jaffa-Jerusalem Roads*, BAR International Series No. 628, Oxford: Tempus Reparatum, 1996.

Freyne, Sean. *Galilee: From Alexander the Great to Hadrian, 323 BCE to 135 CE*, Edinburgh: T. & T. Clark, 1980.

Harel, M. "The Roman road at Ma'aleh 'Arabbim ('Scorpions' Ascent')," *IEJ* 9 (1959) 175–79.

Isaac, B. "Milestones in Judaea, From Vespasian to Constantine," *PEQ* 110 (1978) 47–60.

—— *Roman Roads in Judaea II: The Legio-Scythopolis Road*, BAR International Series No. 141, Oxford: BAR, 1982.

Jeremias, Joachim. *Jerusalem in the Time of Jesus*, Philadelphia, PA: Fortress Press, 1969.

Kallai, Z. "Remains of the Roman Road Along the Mevo-Beitar Highway," *IEJ* 15 (1965) 195–203.

Meshel, Z. "Was There A 'Via Maris'?," *IEJ* 23 (1973) 162–66.

Meshel, Z. and Y. Tsafrir. "The Nabatean Road From 'Avdat to Sha'ar-Ramon: Part 1," *PEQ* 106 (1974) 103–18.

—— "The Nabatean Road From 'Avdat to Sha'ar-Ramon (concluded): Part 2," *PEQ* 107 (1975) 3–21.

Meyers, Eric M. and James F. Strange. *Sepphoris*, Winona Lake, IN: Eisenbrauns, 1992.

Mittmann, Siegfried and Götz Schmitt. *Tübinger Bibelatlas*, Stuttgart: Deutsche Bibelgesellschaft, 2001.

Negev, A. "The Date of the Petra-Gaza Road," *PEQ* 88 (1956) 89–98.

Price, Jonathan. "The Jews and the Latin Language in the Roman Empire," in Menachem Mor, J. Pastor, A. Oppenheimer and D. R. Schwartz (eds) *Jews and Gentiles in the Holy Land*, Jerusalem: Yad Ben-Zvi Press, 2003, pp. 165–80.

Roll, I. and E. Ayalon. "Roman Roads in Western Samaria," *PEQ* 118 (1976) 113–34.

Saldarini, Anthony J. *Pharisees, Scribes, and Sadducees in Palestinian Society*, Grand Rapids, MI and Cambridge: Eerdmans, 2001; reprinted from Wilmington, DE: Michael Glazier, 1988.

Shishah Sidrey Mishnah, Jerusalem: Horev Publishing House, 1993.

Wilkinson, J. "The Way From Jerusalem to Jericho," *BA* 38:1 (1975) 10–24.

ROBINSON, JAMES M.

James McConkey Robinson (b. 1924) is the son of William Childs Robinson (Professor of Church History and Apologetics at Columbia Theological Seminary) and brother of William Childs Robinson Jr (who for many years taught New Testament at Perkins School of Theology and at Andover Newton Theological School). James Robinson earned graduate degrees at the University of Basel, where he wrote a dissertation in theology, under the direction of Karl Barth, and at Princeton Theological Seminary, where he wrote a dissertation in New Testament, under the direction of Otto Piper (see Robinson 1957). Most of Robinson's career was at Claremont, where for many years he was the Arthur Letts Jr Professor of Religion.

Robinson's contribution to Historical Jesus research falls into three categories: (1) reporting and analysis of the New Quest; (2) publication of the Nag Hammadi texts and the quest for the origins of Christology; and (3) reconstruction and interpretation of Q, the document most gospel scholars think was utilized by the Evangelists Matthew and Luke.

The New Quest

Robinson had the good fortune of attending Rudolf Bultmann's lectures, toward the end of the latter's career, and of becoming acquainted with several of Bultmann's leading pupils, who at this time were being appointed to some of the most influential chairs in theology and New Testament in Germany and elsewhere.

As it turned out, Robinson was well positioned to inform the English-speaking world of the emergence among Bultmann's pupils of a fresh round of debate concerning the relevance and relationship of the historical Jesus to the Christ of faith. This debate began with Ernst Käsemann's paper, "Das Problem des historischen Jesus" (English translation: "The Problem of the Historical Jesus") read at the 1953 annual gathering of the old Marburgers and published the following year. Probing essays by Ernst Fuchs and Günther Bornkamm, among others, generated what came to be called the New Quest of the Historical Jesus. Robinson himself prepared lectures, which formed the basis of a brief but incisive analysis of the discussion, which gave the new movement its name (Robinson 1959).

The deeply theological orientation of the New Quest was never in doubt, but just how historical were the assumptions and methods of those involved with it was another question entirely. Moreover, the tendency to link "authentic" tradition with existentialist relevance struck historians as odd. In reference to this way of thinking, Robinson explains:

> One may however observe that material regarded as wholly "unauthentic" in terms of positivistic historiography may not seem nearly as "unauthentic" in terms of modern historiography. For a saying which Jesus never spoke may well reflect accurately his historical significance, and in this sense be more "historical" than many irrelevant things Jesus actually said.
>
> (Robinson 1959: 99 n. 2)

For criticism of the misuse and misinterpretation of the views of historian R. G. Collingwood, see P. Merkley (1970). The New Quest lost momentum in the 1960s and faded from scholarly discussion in the 1970s. Subsequent and ongoing Jesus research, which is oriented more to history, sociology, and the Jewish world of late antiquity, rarely makes reference to this phase of critical study.

Nag Hammadi and the origins of Christology

Following the lead of Rudolf Bultmann, Hans Jonas, and others, Robinson believed that the origins of Christology could be extracted from critical study of certain Gnostic texts from late antiquity (Robinson 1971; 1982). This conviction led him to take an active role in securing, editing, translating, and publishing the contents of the Coptic Gnostic Nag Hammadi Codices (Robinson 1977). To accomplish this ambitious task, Robinson assembled an international team, which labored some twenty years.

What Robinson sought was evidence of a pre-Christian myth of a descending–ascending redeemer, which supplied a template for the development of Christology (as especially seen in Pauline and Johannine theology). Robinson believes that some of the Nag Hammadi materials offers such evidence. Few scholars accept this view (for early and trenchant criticism, see Talbert 1975–76), arguing instead that New Testament Christology is rooted in the teaching of the historical Jesus and enriched in Jewish interpretive traditions reflected in wisdom and mystical ideas.

Notwithstanding the apparent failure of this hypothesis, Robinson and some of his students continue to examine various Gnostic writings, most stemming from the second and third centuries, for evidence of Christian diversity as early as the second century. To this end, appeals are made to such writings as the *Gospel of Mary*, the *Gospel of Philip*, and the *Gospel of Thomas*. It is doubtful, however, that any of this material is early enough to bear the weight of the hypotheses that have been set forth.

Reconstruction and Interpretation of Q

Following the completion of his work in Nag Hammadi, Robinson returned to study of Q, the sayings collection that was utilized by the Evangelists Matthew and Luke. Robinson again assembled an international team, which in time was able to produce *The Critical Edition of Q* (2000). Robinson and team believe that Q contains the earliest

material from which a portrait of the historical Jesus may be produced. Q is understood as part of a wisdom trajectory, a trajectory shared by the *Gospel of Thomas*. Robinson contends that Q is an instance of the genre *logoi sophon* ("sayings of the wise"), which has been edited in the light of the later, inauthentic Son of Man tradition. The genre is preserved in a more primitive form in *Thomas*. At almost every point this theoretical construct is criticized and doubted by many, especially by those with expertise in Judaic tradition and pre-70 Jewish Palestine.

Robinson's contribution to historical Jesus research is varied and controversial. For his most recent statement, see *The Gospel of Jesus* (2005).

CRAIG A. EVANS

Further reading

Merkley, P. "New Quests for Old: One Historian's Observations on a Bad Bargain," *CJT* 16 (1970) 203–18.
Robinson, J. M. *The Problem of History in Mark*, SBT 21, London: SCM Press, 1957.
—— *A New Quest of the Historical Jesus*, SBT 25, London: SCM Press, 1959.
—— (ed.) *The Nag Hammadi Library*, Leiden: Brill; San Francisco, CA: Harper & Row, 1977.
—— "Jesus: From Easter to Valentinus (or the Apostles' Creed)," *JBL* 101 (1982) 5–37.
—— *The Gospel of Jesus: In Search of the Original Good News*, San Francisco, CA: HarperCollins, 2005.
Robinson, J. M., and H. Koester. *Trajectories through Early Christianity*, Philadelphia, PA: Fortress Press, 1971.
Robinson, J. M., P. Hoffmann, and J. S. Kloppenborg (eds) *The Critical Edition of Q*, Hermeneia; Minneapolis, MN: Fortress Press; Leuven: Peeters, 2000.
Talbert, C. H. "The Myth of a Descending–Ascending Redeemer in Mediterranean Antiquity," *NTS* 22 (1975–76) 418–40.

ROMAN GOVERNMENT IN ISRAEL

When the Church professes to believe in Jesus Christ, God's only Son, "our Lord" who "suffered under Pontius Pilate, [and] was crucified . . . ," it is an affirmation that Christology is intimately associated with circumstances in the life of the historical Jesus. The execution of Jesus was the judicial prerogative of the Roman government in Israel (Judea) at that time. A proper understanding of the political situation of the early Christian era is essential both for understanding the historical Jesus in his time and the appropriate interpretation and exegesis of the New Testament. Whether or not the imperial decree of Luke 2 or the saying "render unto Caesar" happen to be the topic of discussion, or whether the researcher is confronting the question "Why did Jesus die on a cross?"

the issue of the Roman government in Israel is significant. The intention of this article is to outline how Rome came to exercise governmental authority in Israel during the time of the historical Jesus. Although Alexander the Great's military supremacy and virtual empire emerged within about twelve or thirteen years (336–323 BCE), the power that was Rome was quite slow to develop. Indeed, the first century BCE began as a time of civil war and unrest in the Republic and the concept of a dictator, as one who might impose order and security, was becoming popular. The Roman general Sulla began this transition of authority (82 BCE) but retired to private life in 80 BCE. Following his death, Crassus and Pompey, the latter being married to Sulla's stepdaughter, came to power in Rome.

During the Maccabean/Hasmonean period of Jewish history (166–63 BCE) the nation enjoyed relative independence from foreign political domination. The last Hasmonean queen to rule was Salome Alexandra and she installed her son, Hyrcanus II, to be the high priest. When Salome died (67 BCE), her other son, Aristobulus, attempted to assume political power. Hyrcanus II, influenced or even manipulated by Antipater, then the governor of Idumea, sought to overthrow Aristobulus. The feuding brothers appealed for Roman intervention to settle the dispute. The Roman leader commissioned to resolve the conflict was Pompey who chose instead to make the nation subject to the authority of Rome. Eventually capturing Jerusalem, employing a "Sabbath-strategy" whereby the Jews were unwilling to resist the Roman advance, Pompey entered the Temple, even the Holy of Holies, and came to make Aristobulus an exiled prisoner. Hyrcanus II continued as the high priest and Antipater was given substantial authority to maintain control for the Romans. In 60 BCE Pompey, Crassus, and Julius Caesar formed a "triumvirate" to rule Rome. Antipater was shrewd and pragmatic and when Pompey and Julius Caesar became rivals (Crassus died in 53 BCE), Antipater supported Caesar and won his friendship. After Caesar's eventual triumph (Caesar defeated Pompey at the battle of Pharsalus in 48 BCE; Caesar became dictator in 47 BCE), Antipater was declared "governor" of the Jewish territory. Antipater later appointed his sons, Phasael and Herod, as rulers. A surviving son of Aristobulus, Antigonus, with the assistance of the Parthians, was able to win back the throne for the Hasmoneans and Herod escaped to Rome, where he was received by Antony and Octavius (Julius Caesar's adopted son who would later become the first

emperor, Augustus). The senate conferred on Herod the title "king of Judea" (40 BCE) and with the support of the Roman army Herod retook Jerusalem in 37 BCE. His administration is notorious for several reasons and many incidents could embellish his story (including the one in Matt 2) but perhaps his most noteworthy achievement, from the perspective of research into the life of the historical Jesus, is the remodeling and expansion of the Temple. The project was begun in 20 BCE and is significant for the exegesis and interpretation of several texts in the gospels (e.g. Mark 13:1–2; John 2:13–22).

Herod suffered a miserable death (4 BCE) and after a brief period of turmoil in the region the emperor (Augustus) chose to fulfill most of Herod's will. Archelaus, Herod's son, was designated as the ethnarch of Judea, Samaria, and Idumea. Herod Antipas, another son, became the tetrarch of Galilee (and the significance of his position is implied in Luke 23:6–12) and Perea. A third son, Philip, was appointed tetrarch of the areas north and east of the Sea of Galilee. Archelaus ruled for about ten years (4 BCE–6 CE) but the populace vehemently complained about his governance and his territory became a Roman province with a Roman procurator as the primary authority responsible to the emperor. A garrison of soldiers and the procurator's residence were to be in Caesarea. The first procurator of Judea was Coponius, but the most significant of the procurators was the fifth, Pontius Pilate, who served from 26 CE until 36 CE.

The actions of Pontius Pilate were not favorably recorded by writers of the first century CE. Josephus reports that at one time Pilate sent a number of troops into Jerusalem by night and the soldiers carried their ensigns, which were normally left behind. These ensigns bore the images of eagles and the emperor. They were particularly offensive to the Jews because of the law forbidding images, and when the people saw them they sent a delegation to Pilate in Caesarea asking that the ensigns be removed. Initially resorting to intimidation, Pilate was influenced by the Jews' willingness to die for their convictions (*Ant.* 18.3.1; *J.W.* 2.9.2–3). Josephus describes an incident where Pilate did not show restraint. In building an aqueduct into Jerusalem, Pilate used the money in the sacred treasury called "Korban." When a crowd of Jews protested this "misuse" of the funds used for the purchase of sacrificial animals, Pilate had his soldiers beat them (*Ant.* 18.3.2; *J.W.* 2.9.4). Finally, Philo records that Pilate had gold shields which were inscribed with his and Tiberius' names dedicated in Herod's palace in Jerusalem. Once again the Jews protested and threatened to send a petition to the emperor. Indeed, Tiberius himself ordered that the shields be removed to Caesarea (*Embassy* 38.299–305).

The principal responsibility of the procurator was to administer "justice" for the ultimate well-being of Rome. This entailed suppressing any possible insurrection. Second, the procurator was to help organize, maintain, and enforce the local system of revenue collection or tax gathering. Thus, the charges against Jesus that were brought to Pilate's attention (Luke 23:2) did not concern blasphemy or violation of the Sabbath laws and several traditions indicate Pilate's interest in the claim that Jesus was a king (Mark 15:2; 15:26; Luke 23:2; John 18:33; 19:3, 19:12–13). In this connection, it is likely that Barabbas had received a death sentence for anti-Roman violence (Mark 15:7).

Whether or not the Roman procurator alone had authority to administer capital punishment within first-century Judea is disputed. Some would argue that the evidence of John 18:31 is definitive, indicating that the Jews could not (legally) execute Jesus and that is why he was taken to Pilate. Others maintain that the stonings of Stephen (Acts 7) and of James (*Ant.* 20.9.1) and an inscription in the Temple threatening Gentiles with death if they should trespass (cited in Barrett 1989) certainly imply that the Jews of that time, independent of Roman jurisdiction, could administer the death penalty. This argument has able defenders on both sides and the issue remains undecided. Because of the brutality and inequality of the Roman practice of tax collection, individuals who professionally participated in the hated activity were regarded with contempt. Those Jews who actively opposed submission to foreign taxation came to be called "Zealots." It is one of the psychological oddities of the ministry of Jesus that disciples were apparently recruited from both groups and the issue of "rendering to Caesar" seemingly remained controversial in early Christianity (see Luke 23:2; Rom 13:6–7). Augustus was the emperor of the Roman Empire from 27 BCE until 14 CE and was hailed by many in the Empire as "a son of a god" (see e.g. Virgil, *Aen.* 6.7912). He was succeeded by Tiberius, Augustus' stepson (14–37 CE), who was fifty-six years old when he took the throne. Under Tiberius' rule the ministry of the historical Jesus took place (Luke 3:1). It was during Tiberius' reign that Pontius Pilate became procurator in Judea and it was Pilate who authorized the execution of Jesus (see Tacitus, *Ann.* 15.44). It is, however, one of the

strange ironies of history that Tacitus wrote, regarding first-century CE Israel, that "not much happened while Tiberius was emperor" (*Hist.* 5.9).

ROMAN GARRISON

Further reading

Barrett, C. K. *The New Testament Background: Writings from Ancient Greece and the Roman Empire that Illuminate Christian Origins*, revised edition, San Francisco, CA: HarperCollins, 1989.

Jones, A. H. M. *The Herods of Judaea*, Oxford: Clarendon Press, 1938.

—— *Studies in Roman Government and Law*, Oxford: Blackwell, 1960.

Josephus. *New Complete Works of Josephus*, trans. W. Whiston, Grand Rapids, MI: Kregel, 1999.

Koester, H. *Introduction to the New Testament. Volume 1: History, Culture and Religion of the Hellenistic Age*, Berlin and New York: de Gruyter, 1982.

Leon, H. J. *The Jews of Ancient Rome*, The Morris Loeb Series, Philadelphia, PA: Jewish Publication Society of America, 1960; revised with Introduction by C. Osiek, Peabody, MA: Hendrickson, 1995.

Sherwin-White, A. N. *Roman Society and Roman Law in the New Testament: The Sarum Lectures 1960–61*, Oxford: Oxford University Press, 1963; repr. Grand Rapids, MI: Baker, 1978, 1992.

Tacitus. *The Histories*, trans. K. Wellesley, New York: Penguin, 1998.

—— *The Annals of Imperial Rome*, trans. A. J. Church and W. J. Brodribb, Lawrence, KS: Neeland, 2005.

Virgil. *Aeneid*, trans. R. Fagles, New York: Viking, 2006.

ROMAN RULE IN PALESTINE

As Roman influence in Palestine underwent change and development through time, it had variable effects upon Jewish thinking and worldview. This article explores sources that describe the Roman presence and actions and consequent Jewish reactions, orientations and reflections for what they disclose.

The earliest Roman influence

Friends to tributaries

The Jewish people first experienced the Roman influence as a boon in 161 BCE when the Maccabees contracted and several times renewed a friendship alliance with them as a protection against their hostile neighbors (1 Macc 8; 12; 14:16f., 24; 15:15–24; Josephus, *Ant.* 12.10.6:414–19; 13.5.8:163–65; 13.9.2:259–66). By this means the Jewish priorities of Law observance, Temple worship, and national independence were helped. In the next century, the Jewish nation grew geographically and its religious influence was felt in the conquered territories. There was religious and political disagreement, however, in bringing high-priestly and kingly offices together and furnishing candidates who were descended from neither Zadok nor David.

In 65 BCE, rival Hasmonean claimants appealed to the Roman general Pompey for his support. He sided with Hyrcanus II against Aristobulus II, but this "win" was a great shock for Judaism. Pompey marched into Jerusalem in 63 BCE, slaughtered its defenders, desecrated the Temple, and enslaved Aristobulus II, his family and many others. Pompey installed Hyrcanus II and ordered the reestablishment of the cultus. The Jewish nation became a temple state, decimated and under tribute (Josephus *Ant.* 14.4.1–5:54–79; 14.5.4:14.6.1; *J.W.* 1.6.4–7.7:131–58; 1.8.6:171–74; 4Q183; 4Q322; 4Q324a fr. 2; 4Q324b fr. 1)

The dynastic squabbling and massive Roman intrusion are the subject of Jewish reflection in the Qumran *Commentary on Habakkuk* (1QpHab) and the *Psalms of Solomon*. According to the contemporizing interpretation of 1QpHab, the Chaldean invaders are the "Kittim," a cipher for the Romans (1QpHab *passim*). They have "entered the land by the advice of a family of criminals" (4:11 = Hyrcanus II) and are famed for bloodshed without respect for age or gender (6:10f.) and the imposition of an annual "yoke of their taxes" (6:1–8). In the universe of 1QpHab all this is a manifestation of the divine judgment upon those who have been unfaithful to the Law (5:3–8) and a test of faithfulness for those who obey the Law and the words of the Teacher of Righteousness (5:3–8; 7:11f.; 8:2f.).

Pss. Sol. 17:5–15 reflects a different perspective. It indicates that the nation, owing to its sins, has come to be governed and sorely oppressed by leaders who are themselves sinners – indicating Aristobulus I and his progeny who "laid waste the throne of David in tumultuous arrogance" (17:8). The Pslm avers that Pompey exposed "the rulers of the land unsparingly to derision" (17:14) and this too is part of how God "cast them down, and remove[d] their seed from the earth" (17:8). The actions of Pompey are one and all identified as the judgment of God upon the Jewish people "according to their deeds" (17:9). Pompey's service as divine agent does not exonerate him as he remains the "man that was an alien to our race" (17:9; cf. 17:15). He is the "sinner" of *Pss. Sol.* 2 who battered down fortified walls and ascended the altar (2:1) and was himself slain by God (2:30–35).

King makers

Following Pompey's defeat in 48 BCE, Caesar reconfirmed Hyrcanus II as high priest and made

him Jewish Ethnarch. He also made Hyrcanus' supporter, the Idumean Antipater II, administrator of Judea (Josephus *Ant.* 14.8.1–5:127–55, 10.2:191; *J.W.* 1.6.2:123; 1.9.3–10.4:187–203). In following years, Antipater's son Herod came to the ascendancy, but not without shrewd balancing, intrigue and danger. He survived the whipsaw swings from one Roman faction to another during the civil war and the rise and fall of Jewish support. He governed with competence and zeal for the Romans, surviving Jewish intrigues and escaping the Parthian invasion of 40 BCE. Fleeing to Rome, he received from Antony, Octavius and the Roman Senate the Jewish kingship (Josephus *Ant.* 14.14.3–5:377–89; *J.W.* 1.14.4:282–85). Herod returned to campaign against the Parthians and their nominee, becoming *de facto* monarch in 37 BCE (Josephus *Ant.* 14.15.8–16.2:439–80; *J.W.* 1.16.7–18.3:320–57; Dio Cassius 49.22; Plutarch *Anton.* 1.16.7). Herod won Octavius' confidence and the re-confirmation of his kingship after Antony's defeat at Actium in 31 BCE (Josephus *Ant.* 15.6.1–7:161–95; *J.W.* 1.20.1–2:386–92). Rome's involvements in the religious-political process had significantly altered the Jewish reality.

Indirect Roman presence and its effects

Herod

In keeping with Roman policy, Herod ruled with the honorific, "ally and friend of the Roman People" (*socius et amicus populi romani*). In Jerusalem and throughout the East, he was formally recognized as "friend of Caesar" (*philokaisaros*), "friend of the emperor" (*philosebastos*) and "friend of Romans" (*philoromaios*). He had earned the honor through loyalty and, in a sense, continued to purchase it. Herod does not appear to have paid tribute to Rome, but he gave large cash gifts and support to the Romans throughout his reign. He also demonstrated loyalty to Rome in various architectural ventures. Josephus remarks that

> one can mention no suitable spot within his realm, which he left destitute of some mark of homage to Caesar. And then, after filling his own territory with temples, he let the memorials of his esteem overflow into the province and erected in numerous cities monuments to Caesar.
>
> (Joseph *J.W.* 1.21.5:407; cf. ibid., 1.21.1–7:401–14)

Richardson is probably right to say that Herod was pious but not fully Torah-observant, as he had realistically to balance obligations to God, the emperor, and his family (2004: 238). Certainly there were self-preserving and self-perpetuating objectives in his Roman building, and genuine and obvious benefits and protections did accrue to Jews at home and abroad. But the significant cash flow to support and memorialize a relationship with Rome was not only a heavy financial burden. It was made heavier for Jews with stricter commitments to Torah-observance and aspirations for national independence.

A significant flashpoint occurred over the image of a golden eagle Herod had placed atop the great gate during the rebuilding of the Temple. It was offensive to most Jews, being an obvious violation of the second commandment (Exod 20:4) and also quite likely because it was doing double service as the symbol of Roman power (cf. Tacitus *Ann.* 2.17). Herod had been reproached by the teachers Judas and Matthias and their followers when it was set up but no immediate action was taken. Later, as Herod lay dying, the eagle was hacked down. The perpetrators and Matthias were caught. Declaring their loyalty to God and His Law as their motive, they were executed. Josephus intimates that sympathy with the martyrs was very strong, running even to the level of the Sanhedrin and its priestly leadership. The Sanhedrin barely escaped Herod's wrath, though the high priest was removed "as being partly to blame" (Josephus *Ant.* 17.6.2–4:149–67, 206–9; *J.W.* 1.33.2–4:648–55).

Archelaus

The transition to new arrangements in governance of Palestine following Herod's death in 4 BCE was bloody, drawing upon Herod's military and the entire Roman legionary and cavalry forces of Syria. It began when Herod's son Archelaus tried to ingratiate himself to the Jewish populace by hastily assenting to a number of requests. Emboldened, pleadings became demands as Passover was celebrated. Archelaus called for a military action for fear of an insurrection. Three thousand worshipers were killed and the festival was abandoned (Josephus *Ant.* 17.8.4–9.3:200–18; *J.W.* 2.1.1–3:1–13). Archelaus then went to Rome.

Quinctilius Varus, the legate of Syria, sent a legion into Jerusalem to combine with the royal forces in Archelaus' absence. It was not enough. At Pentecost, Jewish worshipers laid siege to the combined forces. Varus brought his two remaining legions and four regiments of cavalry into Palestine. The insurrection was put down. Varus crucified 2,000 of the worst offenders and imprisoned others. He then withdrew to Syria, leaving one legion quartered in Jerusalem until a nominated royal returned from Rome (Josephus *Ant.* 17.10.5–10:271–98; *J.W.* 2.4.1–3:56–65).

In Rome, different Jewish parties pressed their competing visions of the nation upon Augustus. He listened to Herodian royals compete for variations of the status quo, Archelaus anxious that he simply replace his father. A delegation of fifty Palestinian Jewish elites supported by 8,000 Jews living in Rome proposed a dissolution of the monarchy and the creation of a temple state administered by the high priest and annexed to Syria. This proposal conceded a Roman presence but asked that it be at distance (Josephus *Ant.* 17.11.1–2:299–314; *J.W.* 11.6.1–2:80–92). In Palestine, variations on the theme of a popular Jewish kingship without any Roman involvement were being violently played out by Judas ben Ezechias, Simon a servant of Herod, and the shepherd Athrongaeus and his brothers. Herodian relatives not named in the will also saw this time as an opportunity to thrust themselves before the people.

Augustus in the end honored the provisions of Herod's will, including the grant of Idumea, Judea and Samaria to Archelaus, but not the royal title (Josephus *Ant.* 17.11.4:317–20). Within ten years Archelaus' ethnarchy was so troubled that he was deposed and exiled (Josephus *Ant.* 17.13.2:342–44; *J.W.* 2.7.3:111). It became a Roman province directly governed by Roman prefects of equestrian rank in 6 CE.

Direct Roman presence and its effects

Rome was generally uninterested in socio-religious and economic reformist agendas, preferring rather to "under-govern" its subject populations as much as possible through existing local structures (Garnsey and Saller 1987: 20f.; cf. Josephus *J.W.* 6.6.2:333–34). However, the shift from the rule of Jewish client kings to Roman governors created shock waves. Millar puts it well: "To a very remarkable degree the entire structure of the governor's activity was determined by that of the dynasty which he had replaced." (1993: 45). Arguably, the areas of greatest impact were taxation, the high priesthood and maintenance of the sanctity of Jerusalem and its Temple.

Taxes

Augustus' first action following the creation of provincial Judea was to appoint Coponius praefect and charge the Syrian legate Quirinius with taking a census of persons and property for the purpose of levying tribute (Josephus *Ant.* 17.13.5:355;

18.1.1:1f.; cf. Millar 1993: 46 and Stern 1974 CRINT 1:372–73 on Luke 2:1). Though we do not know the exact weight of the tax, Syrian and Judean pleas for tax relief in 17 CE suggests it was heavy (Tacitus *Ann.* 2.42; cf. Schmidt 1992: 804f.). When superimposed upon Jewish religious dues, the total amounted to 30–40 percent of gross national income if modern guesstimates can be believed.

The census divided Jews. The high priest, as surrogate for the Romans, argued for compliance (Josephus *Ant.* 18.1.1:2–3). But he did so against a militant opposition led by Judas the Galilean and a Pharisee named Saddok who counseled many to refuse to enroll themselves. Their argument was founded upon an absolute theocratic conviction – "God alone is their leader and master" (Josephus *Ant.* 18.1.6:23; *J.W.* 2.8.1:118). Submission to the Roman authority was an encroachment upon the divine governance; to honor Rome in paying tribute and taking the oath of loyalty to the emperor was to dishonor the heavenly majesty. The novelty in their argument was the insistence that the demands of exclusivism and militancy were religious requirements. Judas argued thus: successful resistance would mean prosperity; failure and death would win honor and renown; and in any event, "Heaven would be their zealous helper" (Josephus *Ant.* 18.1.1:5) toward ultimate success. The resistance movement was as violent against collaborationist Jews as Romans.

Judas was killed by the Romans and his followers were scattered (Acts 5:37). But the trouble arising from heavy Roman taxation and the new terms of the debate continued. That Josephus calls Judas' view a "philosophy," refers to Judas as a "teacher," notes the militancy of later family members of Judas implying a dynasty of dissent, and blames it for the demise of the nation in 70 CE indicates it cast a long shadow.

Others held common cause with Judas and his like during Jesus' ministry (Luke 23:19; John 18:40; cf. Mark 15:27; Matt 27:38, 44) and the debate was brought directly to Jesus. When the Pharisees and Herodians asked Jesus, "Is it right to pay taxes to Caesar or not? Should we pay or shouldn't we?" (Mark 12:14f.; cf. Matt 22:17; Luke 20:22), they hoped he would make himself guilty of sedition and counseling others likewise (cf. Luke 23:2; Matt 26:55; Mark 14:48; Luke 22:52). Otherwise, he might be disqualified from his popularity as a Roman collaborationist and "friend of tax collectors" (Matt 11:19; Luke 7:34; cf. 19:7). Jesus called for a *denarius* of Tiberius, the coin in which the tribute was calculated and very likely paid (H. St J.

Hart 1984). His counsel to "Give to Caesar what is Caesar's and to God what is God's" (Mark 12:17; cf. Matt 22:21; Luke 20:25) astonished the questioners. Far from choosing between options, it indicated a duality of responsibility that lifted the theological discussion to an entirely new level, giving comfort to neither pacifist acquiescence nor violent revolution.

High priests

The high priesthood from of old was to be heritable from the line of Zadok (2 Sam 15), anointed by God, and for the lifetime of each candidate. Its removal from the Zadokite line, installment by investiture, and politicization through appointment at the royal pleasure removed it far from the ideal. Direct Roman rule steepened the decline in that Gentiles came to nominate and depose candidates to the sacred office directly. It did not help that the Romans also kept the high priestly vestments under seal in the Fortress Antonia as the kings had done. It was clearly coercive (Josephus *Ant.* 18.4.3:92; cf. 18.4.3:93–95; cf. Jeremias 1962; English translation 1967: 148).

The complexities of high-priestly qualification argue that the nomination process had to be cooperative, but the political initiative and priority were definitely Roman. When Quirinius deposed Joazar in 6 CE because he had been "overpowered by a popular faction" (Josephus *Ant.* 18.2.1:26) and when the Judean governor Valerius Gratus installed and then deposed four high priests in only three years from 15 to 18 CE (Josephus *Ant.* 18.2.2:33–35), these were obvious signs that the high priests' loyalties were too Jewish in Roman estimation. Alternately, the fact that Joseph Caiaphas (Luke 3:2) served from 18 to 36 CE through the final eight years of Gratus' governorship and the full ten years of Pontius Pilate's clearly indicates a man who could be counted on to serve strongly to Roman tastes (cf. John 19:12, 15).

The assessment of a significant damage to the high priesthood is noted in the events of the first major Roman intervention in 63 BCE. The document 1QpHab speaks of a "Wicked Priest" (1:13; 8:8–13; 8:16–19:16; 11:4–8; 11:12–12:10). Continued downward shifts in the high priesthood through the influence of the Herodian kings and the Romans only served to encourage a continued contemporizing reading of the earlier literature. That literature, broadly viewed, seems to anticipate God's provision of an anointed high priest who will prepare Jewish troops for a final battle of liberation against the Kittim and lead praise to God through its conduct (1QM 2:1; 15:4; 16:13; 18:5; 19:11). At the end of battle, he and his fellow priests will rejoice before God over the enemy dead (1QM 19:9–14) and order Israel's cleansing after victory (4Q285 frag. 2, 5). Called the anointed of Aaron, he will preside over an eschatological banquet according to 1QSa 2:11–22. Some Qumran documents also expect an anointed political figure who is quite consistently called not "king" but "prince," standing in a position subordinate to the anointed priest (1QSa 2:11–22) and taking direction from them (4Q161 frag. 8+9+10:22–29). This duality is also present in *Testaments of the Twelve Patriarchs* (*T. Reub.* 6:7–12; *T. Sim.* 7:1f.; *T. Levi* 8:11–16; *T. Iss.* 5:7), *Book of Jubilees* 31.9–21 and *Pss. Solomon* 17.

Jerusalem and the Temple

Herod the Great had done much to make Jerusalem internationally famous. The Temple especially was Herod's architectural set piece (Josephus *Ant.* 15.11.1–7:380–425; *J.W.* 1.21.1:401f.; 5.4.3–5.8:161–247; cf. Pliny *Nat.* 5.14). He had had to convince both official Judaism and a skeptical Rome of the merits of the Temple project (Richardson 1996: 249). For local Jews, diaspora Jews and Gentile god-fearers, the Temple became the destination of pilgrimage. Its fame and symbolic power could be measured in the numbers who swelled the city at the festivals and the wealth in the temple treasury. Even sectarian Jews (Josephus *Ant.* 18.1.5:19) and members of the imperial family sent offerings and Augustus had arranged for the perpetuation of the daily whole burnt offering at his own expense (Philo *Leg. Gai.* 36:291; 37:297; 39:317). The Jews would not worship Caesar, but they were not loathe to offer sacrifices and prayers on his behalf (Josephus *J.W.* 2.10.4:197; Philo *Leg. Gai.* 36:280).

Notwithstanding, the governors permanently garrisoned Jerusalem with a military cohort and cavalry contingent and quartered significant additional forces there from Caesarea at festivals to enforce the peace. When Jewish religious fervor was highest, the temple environs and city resembled an armed camp. The Roman presence was not only offensive, it created risks to the sanctity of the city and its temple.

In 26 CE, Pontius Pilate tested Jewish religious convictions by bringing forces into the city carrying military standards to which were affixed busts of the emperor (Josephus *Ant.* 18.3.1:55; cf. *J.W.* 2.9.2:169; Tacitus *Hist.* 2.89; 4.62). These reliefs violated the second commandment as graven

images and objects of Roman worship (Josephus *J.W.* 6.6.1:316). News of the sacrilege spread from city to countryside and protest was raised. Impervious, Pilate returned to Caesarea. A deputation followed him, continuing to plead over five days for the standards' removal. Surrounding them with armed forces, Pilate threatened to cut them down unless they acquiesced. He was shocked when they bared their necks, declaring that "they were ready rather to die than to transgress the law" (Josephus *J.W.* 2.9.3:174). He relented.

Another clash occurred when Pilate used funds from the Temple treasury to build an aqueduct to Jerusalem. Protest was raised as Pilate sat on his tribunal in Jerusalem. At a signal, troops who had been disguised and secreted in the crowd began to XXXX it with clubs. Protesters and bystanders were killed and maimed in the melee (Josephus *Ant.* 18.3.2:60–62; *J.W.* 2.9.4:175–77). The aqueduct venture must have been undertaken with official Jewish backing; perhaps through the high priest. Josephus would surely have mentioned if Pilate had violently stolen the funds (Josephus *Ant.* 20.9.7:220). Besides, the temple treasury referred to was the *Corbonas* (so Josephus) which could be used for such projects (*m. Shek.* 4.2). Why then was there protest? The upset may have come out of dissent and agitation from a faction within the Sanhedrin at such use and/or collaboration, or perhaps out of mounting fears that the *Corbonas* would be exhausted by the project (Josephus *J.W.* 2.9.4). In any event, the disagreement was sealed in Jewish blood.

Luke is very economical in his mention of another occasion regarding certain "Galileans whose blood Pilate had mixed with their sacrifices" (Luke 13:1). No reason for the action is noted, but given that the worshipers were cut down by troops while they attended the slaughter of their sacrifices, the time was Passover and the place the forecourt of the priests in the Temple. Jesus' interlocutors had fatalistically identified the slaughter as a divine punishment for some great sins committed by the victims. Jesus rejected the hypothesis, preferring rather to identify the Galileans' sudden and horrible death as a compelling example of the need for all to repent of their sins.

About the year 31 CE, Pilate again violated Jewish religious sensibilities during one of the festivals by setting up gilded shields honoring Tiberius in his Jerusalem residence (Philo *Leg. Gai.* 38:299–306). Sejanus, the praetorian prefect and Pilate's likely sponsor, had just been executed in Rome for treason. The gilded shields may have been both an expression of disassociation from

Sejanus and undivided loyalty to the emperor so he might avoid a similar fate. Pilate had apparently learned from the earlier standards incident: the shields were aniconic and placed inside his residence rather than in public. However, after the official honorific pattern, the shields probably identified Tiberius as "son of the divine Augustus" which would have caused Jewish offense. Josephus is silent as to how the presence of the shields came to be known, who organized the protest and who deputized Herod's sons to ask Pilate to remove them. The answer must certainly be the Jewish religious leaders. The royal deputation accused that Pilate's action was more a pretext to outrage the nation and overthrow the Jewish Law than to honor Tiberius. It insisted he produce imperial documents showing that this action was sanctioned. If he could not, Pilate should immediately remove them. This created a dilemma. If Pilate removed the shields he would assuage Jewish offense but offend the emperor. Pilate did nothing. When Tiberius was notified, his response was immediate and angry; he ordered that Pilate remove the shields to the temple of Augustus in Caesarea.

Pilate, high priests and the trial of Jesus

The intersection point between Rome and Judaism in the trial of Jesus is filled with strong antagonism, not unlike what has been noted above. The gospels represent the Jewish leaders as wanting to see Jesus executed. But they must bring him before the Roman governor because the power to capitally punish is his exclusive domain (John 18:31; cf. Josephus *Ant.* 18.1.1:2; *J.W.* 2.8.1:117–26). In all four gospels the focal charge brought against Jesus is that he has laid claim to the Jewish kingship (Mark 15:1; Matt 27:11; Luke 23:2f.; John 18:33; cf. Luke 23:2, 5 who adds insurrection and opposing the Roman tax). By Roman political reckoning, it was Caesar's pleasure to make or unmake kings; in the absence of a Jewish king, Caesar himself was the king of the Jews and no other. This logic was rehearsed to Pilate by the high priests (John 19:15). The gospels represent Pilate as having insight that the high priests' motive in preferring charges was envy (Mark 15:10; Matt 27:18) which may be consistent with the threat of a popular religious figure to a much less popular high priesthood entwined in religious politics and too near association with the Roman authority.

Pilate is not represented as cowed or indecisive in his interactions with the Jewish leadership. Rather, his questions and statements, and especially his use of the expressions "king of the Jews" and "your king," are filled with mockery and used for humiliating effect. This also appears to be the intent of the use of "king of the Jews" on the *titulus* fixed to the cross (Mark 15:26; Matt 27:37; Luke 23:38; esp. John 19:19–22). In John's Gospel Pilate does make an attempt to release Jesus on hearing that he has claimed to be a "Son of God" (John 19:7). But he is levered by the chief priests when they accuse that if he releases a royal pretender against the arrangements of the emperor, he is "no friend of Caesar" (John 19:12). If the gilded shields episode has been read rightly and predates Jesus' trial, Pilate would have been particularly sensitive to the risk of such an accusation. He authorizes the crucifixion.

BRIAN M. RAPSKE

Further reading

Applebaum, S. "Economic Life in Palestine," in S. Safrai. M. Stern, D. Flusser, and W. C. van Unnik (eds) *The Jewish People in the First Century*, CRINT 2, Assen: Van Gorcum, 1976, pp. 631–700.

Bammel, E. (ed.) *The Trial of Jesus*, London: SCM Press, 1970.

Bond, H. *Pontius Pilate in History and Interpretation*, SNTSMS 100, Cambridge: Cambridge University Press, 1998.

Bruce, F. F. "Render to Caesar," in E. Bammel and C. F. D. Moule (eds) *Jesus and the Politics of His Day*, Cambridge: Cambridge University Press, 1984, pp. 249–63.

Dyson, S. L. "Native Revolts in the Roman Empire," *Historia* 20 (1971) 239–74.

Garnsey, P. and R. Saller. *The Roman Empire: Economy, Society and Culture*, Berkeley and Los Angeles, CA: University of California Press, 1987.

Goodman, M. (ed.) *Jews in a Graeco-Roman World*, Oxford: Clarendon Press, 1998.

—— *The Ruling Class of Judaea: The Origins of the Jewish Revolt Against Rome AD 66–70*, Cambridge: Cambridge University Press, 1987.

Grant, M. *The Jews in the Roman World*, New York: Charles Scribner's Sons, 1973.

Hart, H. St J. "The Coin of 'Render Unto Caesar ... ' (A note on some aspects of Mark 12:13–17; Matt 22:15–22; Luke 20:20–26)," in E. Bammel and C. F. D. Moule (eds) *Jesus and the Politics of His Day*, Cambridge: Cambridge University Press, 1984, pp. 241–48.

Hoehner, H. W. "Herodian Dynasty," in C. A. Evans and S. E. Porter (eds) *Dictionary of New Testament Background*, Downers Grove, IL and Leicester: InterVarsity Press, 2000, pp. 485–94.

Horsley, R. and J. S. Hanson. *Bandits, Prophets, and Messiahs – Popular Movements at the Time of Jesus*, New Voices in Biblical Studies, San Francisco, CA: Harper & Row, 1985.

Jackson, B. S. "On the Problem of Roman Influence on the Halakah and Normative Self-Definition in Judaism," in E. P. Sanders, A. I. Baumgarten, and A. Mendelson (eds) *Jewish and Christian Self-Definition*, Philadelphia, PA: Fortress Press, 1981, pp. 157–203, 352–79.

Jeremias, J. *Jerusalem in the Time of Jesus*, trans. F. H. and C. H. Cave, London: SCM Press, 1969 [1962, 1967].

Jones, S. and S. Pearce (eds) *Jewish Local Patriotism and Self-Identification in the Graeco-Roman Period*, JSPSS 31, Sheffield: Sheffield Academic Press, 1998.

Millar, F. *The Roman Near East 31 BC–AD 337*, Cambridge and London: Harvard University Press, 1993.

Millar, F. and E. Segal (eds) *Caesar Augustus: Seven Aspects*, Oxford: Clarendon Press, 1984.

Neusner, J., E. S. Frerichs, P. Borgen, and R. Horsley (eds) *The Social World of Formative Christianity and Judaism: Essays in Tribute to Howard Clark Kee*, Philadelphia, PA: Fortress Press, 1988.

Rapske, B. M. "Roman Governors of Palestine," in C. A. Evans and S. E. Porter (eds) *Dictionary of New Testament Background*, Downers Grove, IL and Leicester: InterVarsity Press, 2000, pp. 978–84.

Rhoades, D. M. *Israel in Revolution: 6–74 CE. A Political History Based on the Writings of Josephus*, Philadelphia, PA: Fortress Press, 1976.

Richardson, P. *Herod: King of the Jews and Friend of the Romans*, Columbia, SC: University of South Carolina Press, 1996.

—— *Building Jewish in the Roman East*, Waco, TX: Baylor University Press, 2004.

Safrai, S. "Jewish Self-Government," in S. Safrai, M. Stern, D. Flusser, and W. C. van Unnik (eds) *The Jewish People in the First Century*, CRINT 1, Assen: Van Gorcum, 1974, pp. 377–419.

—— "The Temple," in S. Safrai, M. Stern, D. Flusser, and W. C. van Unnik (eds) *The Jewish People in the First Century*, CRINT 2, Assen: Van Gorcum, 1976, pp. 865–907.

Schmidt, T. E. "Taxes," in J. B. Green, S. McKnight, and I. H. Marshall (eds) *Dictionary of Jesus and the Gospels*, Downers Grove, IL and Leicester: InterVarsity Press, 1992, pp. 804–7.

Schwartz, S. *Imperialism and Jewish Society, 200 BCE to 640 CE, Jews, Christians and Muslims from the Ancient to the Modern World*, Princeton, NJ and Oxford: Princeton University Press, 2001.

Smallwood, E. M. *The Jews under Roman Rule: From Pompey to Diocletian*, Leiden: Brill, 1976.

Stern, M. "The Province of Judaea," in S. Safrai, M. Stern, D. Flusser, and W. C. van Unnik (eds) *The Jewish People in the First Century*, CRINT 1, Assen: Van Gorcum, 1974, pp. 308–76.

—— "The Reign of Herod and the Herodian Dynasty," in S. Safrai, M. Stern, D. Flusser, and W. C. van Unnik (eds) *The Jewish People in the First Century*, CRINT 1, Assen: Van Gorcum, 1974, pp. 216–307.

—— "Aspects of Jewish Society: The Priesthood and other Classes," in S. Safrai, M. Stern, D. Flusser, and W. C. van Unnik (eds) *The Jewish People in the First Century*, CRINT 2, Assen: Van Gorcum, 1976, pp. 561–630.

Winter, P. *On the Trial of Jesus*, ed. and rev. T. A. Burkill and G. Vermes, second edition, Berlin: Walter de Gruyter, 1974.

RULING PRIESTS

Within the gospels, priests appear locally, in adjudications of purity (Matt 8:1–4; Mark 1:40–45; Luke 5:12–16; 17:14). Their role is challenged by Jesus, who claims that he can declare clean in a matter that Leviticus expressly assigns to priests (cf. Lev 14:1-9). Jesus evidently understood purity in a way that brought him into conflict with a traditional, priestly interpretation of scripture, and the issue of purity also set him at odds with some Pharisees.

The Mishnah (*Taanit* 4:2) envisages a system in which priests, Levites, and Israelites gathered in local synagogues while their representatives were in Jerusalem. The priestly system of "courses" of service was the germ of such piety: it allowed for a substantial population of priests, which it divided into twenty-four courses. While a few priests from each group were chosen to officiate in Jerusalem during the week that the group was appointed to cover, the remainder gathered and read the appropriate lections in the villages of Judea and Galilee where they normally lived (1 Chr 24:1–19; Josephus, *Ant.* 7.365–67; cf. Luke 1:5–23; 10:31). The inclusion of the faithful in Israel generally in such meetings was a natural development, since meetings for prayer and instruction had long been a customary feature of Judaism in the Diaspora. The development of worship in synagogues as something of a replacement for worship in the Temple was therefore precedented prior to 70 CE.

References to high priests in the gospels portray their power as essentially circumscribed by the boundaries of Jerusalem, or they use Jerusalem as a base of power (cf. Matt 2:4; 16:21; 20:18; 21:15, 23, 45; 26:3, 14, 47, 51, 57, 58, 62, 63, 65; Mark 8:31; 10:33; 11:18, 27; 14:1, 10, 43, 47, 53, 54, 60, 61, 63, 66; 15:1, 3, 10, 11, 31, cf. 2:26; Luke 3:2; 9:22; 19:47; 20:1, 19; 22:2, 4, 50, 52, 54, 66; 23:4, 10, 13; 24:20; John 1:19; 7:32, 45; 11:47, 49, 51, 57; 12:10; 18:3, 10, 15, 16, 19, 22, 24, 26, 35; 19:6, 15, 21). Their close association with the execution of Jesus makes it plain that his activity in the Temple figured centrally in his condemnation before Pilate.

Although only one person served as high priest at any given time, the plural is used by Josephus (*Against Apion* 2.104) as well as in the gospels (Matt 2:4; 16:21; 20:18; 21:15, 23, 45; 26:3, 14, 47; Mark 8:31; 10:33; 11:18, 27; 14:1, 10, 43; 15:1, 3, 10, 11, 31; Luke 9:22; 19:47; 20:1, 19; 22:2, 4, 52, 66; 23:4, 10, 13; 24:20; John 7:32, 45; 11:47, 57; 12:10; 18:3, 35; 19:6, 15, 21) to refer to the families that regularly filled the office. Their violence in defense of their prerogatives was feared by many of the predecessors of the Rabbis (cf. Babylonian Talmud, *Pesahim* 57a). These Sadducees, as the New Testament calls them (that is, putative inheritors of Zadok) are typically portrayed in a doctrinally negative light, as not teaching the resurrection of the dead (cf. Josephus, *J.W.*

2.165; Matt 22:23; Mark 12:18; Luke 20:27; Acts 23:8), but the issue may have been one of emphasis: the Torah had stressed that correct worship in the Temple would bring with it material prosperity, and the elite priests attempted to realize that promise.

Jesus was not unique among rabbis in insisting on what he saw as the correct procedure for sacrifice against the high priests. Rabbi Hillel had taught that sacrificial animals should have hands laid on them by their owners, and then be given over to priests for slaughter. Worshipers offered their own property to express the direct link between God and Israel, and touching them was a statement of ownership. The followers of Rabbi Shammai, however, insisted that animals could be given directly to priests for slaughter, without the laying on of hands. The debate raged between the two rabbinic schools. The Talmud recounts an abrupt about-face by a wealthy Shammai disciple, who was so struck by the rectitude of Hillel's position that he had herders drive 3,000 sheep and goats into the Temple (see *b. Bezah* 20a-b; *t. Chagigah* 2.11; *y. Chagigah* 2.3 and *Bezah* 2.4). Anyone who wanted to could lay hands on the beasts before they were slaughtered. In effect, Hillel's occupation of the Temple was the complement of Jesus'.

Gamaliel's influence was so great he could enforce his teachings – even in the Temple – by means of his devoted disciples (his *talmidim*). When he gave in the annual shekel tax in the Temple, Gamaliel had a member of his household throw it right in front of the collector, to make sure his money went for public sacrifices (*m. Sheqalim* 3:3) rather than general maintenance. If the collector needed prompting to pick the shekel up and put it in the right container, a little gang of Pharisees loyal to the patriarch gathered, yelling out, "Take up, take up, take up!" It did not take long for the collector to get the point, and set aside Gamaliel's shekels for sacrifices alone. Gamaliel's followers also insisted on their own rules for determining when an animal should be excluded from sacrifice on the grounds of a blemish (*Bekhorot* 6:9).

The structure of a local council prevailed under Roman rule in Jerusalem, and the Greek term *sunedrion* was applied to it; it has become known as "the Sanhedrin," largely as a result of the Mishnah. The Mishnah, a document of the second century, cannot be taken as a sure guide of events and institutions during the first century, but it does seem clear, from the gospels, Josephus, with the Mishnah, that the council in Jerusalem was largely controlled by the high priests, but that elders or aristocrats of the city also participated, among whom were Pharisees (and, of course, some scribes, who may or may not have been priests, elders, or Pharisees). Whether there were actually seventy-one members of the Sanhedrin (as in rabbinic literature) cannot be known with certainty, and the extent of its capital jurisdiction is not known. But the Romans appear to have given the council the authority to execute perpetrators of blatant sacrilege (Josephus, *J.W.* 5.194; *Ant.* 15.417). The authority of the council of Jerusalem outside of the city followed the prestige of the city itself, and the acknowledged centrality of the Temple. But a ruling of the council there was not automatically binding upon those in the countryside and in other major cities; acceptance of a given teaching, precept by precept, was the path of influence. Pharisees also taught in and around the Temple, the focus of their discussion of purity, and the Pharisees in Jerusalem were the nucleus of the movement.

The Pharisees of the period before and after 70 were sufficiently flexible to accommodate an influx of priests and scribes into their ranks. The priestly interest of the Pharisaic movement, of course, was historically organic, and the references to priests in stories and teachings from the time of Yochanan (cf. Rabbi Yose the Priest, *m. 'Abot* 2:8) and well into the second century are striking. Moreover, the consolidation of the Rabbis' power after 70 CE, predicated as it was on local influence, could only be assured by means of the control of local adjudication, as well as worship and study. The tendency of scribes to align themselves with the Pharisees, together with priestly adherents and sympathizers with the movement, assured the emergence and the success of the Rabbis. At the same time, the triumph of Rabbinic authority assured the continuing influence of the priests in decisions regarding purity, in blessings, and in receipts of payment of redemption and of tithe, while scribal influence, in the production of written materials and the convocation of formal courts, is also striking. Nonetheless, the functional consolidation of the power of the old groups and factions was only achieved during the time of Rabbi Judah, with the emergence of a patriarchate recognized and supported by the Romans.

BRUCE CHILTON

Further reading

Chilton, B. *The Temple of Jesus: His Sacrificial Program within a Cultural History of Sacrifice*, University Park, PA: Penn State Press, 1992.
—— *Rabbi Paul. An Intellectual Biography*, New York: Doubleday, 2004.

Evans, C. A. "Jesus' Action in the Temple and Evidence of Corruption in the First-Century Temple," in D. J. Lull (ed.) *Society of Biblical Literature 1989 Seminar Papers*, SBLSP 28, Atlanta, GA: Scholars Press, 1989, pp. 522–39.

Goodman, M. *The Ruling Class of Judea. The Origins of the Jewish Revolt against Rome AD 66–70*, Cambridge: Cambridge University Press, 1987.

Mason, S. "Chief Priests, Sadducees, Pharisees and Sanhedrin in Acts," in R. Bauckham (ed.) *The Book of Acts in its Palestinian Setting*, The Book of Acts in its First Century Setting 4, Grand Rapids, MI: Eerdmans, 1995, pp. 115–77.

Neusner, J. "Sacrifice and Temple in Rabbinic Judaism," in J. Neusner, A. J. Avery-Peck, and W. S. Green (eds) *The Encyclopedia of Judaism*, New York: Continuum, 2005, pp. 1290–302.

Sanders, E. P. *Judaism. Practice and Belief 63 BCE–66 CE*, Philadelphia, PA: Trinity Press International, 1992.

S

SACRIFICE, TITHES, OFFERINGS

The English word "sacrifice," from the Latin noun *sacrificium* (*sacer*, "holy" + *facere*, "to make"), refers to any religious act designed to consecrate an object to God/the gods (Henninger 544). Whether this refers to the offering of food *to* the deity or to communal participation in a sacred meal *with* the deity, the Hebrew term and its cognates clearly refer to the custom of animal slaughter (Hebr. זבח "to slaughter," Akk. *zebû* "to slaughter," *zíbu* "food offering," Ug. *dbh* "to sacrifice," Aram. זבח "to slaughter," Arab. *dabaha*). The primary term for "sacrifice" in the NT (θυσία) comes from the old Attic verb θύω ("to swirl") and presumably refers to the swirling, odoriferous smoke of charred animal flesh. Evidently the Greeks believe that something in this "swirl" invokes the gods to bend their ears to human petitions. At a critical point in the siege of Troy, for example, Achilles encourages Patroclus "to sacrifice to the gods" (θεοῖσι δὲ θυσαῖ = *Iliad* 9.219). Cyrus, having learned in a dream that the gods plan to take his life, responds by "taking priestly victims (and) sacrificing them to Zeus" (λαβὼν ἱερεῖα ἔθυε Διΐ; Xenophon, *Cyr.* 8.7.3).

Anthropologically "sacrifice" connotes several related, overlapping functions (action, transcendence, exchange, ritual, transformation, solidarity, cosmology; Dunnill 80–81), but to most ancient writers it has primarily to do with the task of matching the appropriate ritualized response to a given sacral breach. The Hittite "Plague Prayers of Mursilis," for example, imagine sacrifice as a response to the sacral breach committed by Šuppiluliumas I (the king's father) and perpetuated by Muwattalis II (his brother; *ANET* 394–96). The prophetic corpus of the Hebrew Bible alludes to the problem of sacral breach in texts like 1 Sam 5:1–7:1 (the Ark crisis), 2 Sam 21:1–14 (Saul's bloodguilt), and 1 Kgs 16:29–18:45 (the Baal crisis; Hanson 22–25). The priestly texts of the OT, however, deal with a much broader set of possibilities, laying out several priestly antidotes in the opening chapters of Leviticus: עלה ("whole burnt offering"), קרבן ("grain offering"), שלמים ("peace offerings"), חטאת ("purity/sin offering"), and אשם ("restitution offering"). While these sacrifices can and do overlap in both form and function, most have historical cognates in other Near Eastern cultures (Moore 20–65) and serve distinguishable functions within the Israelite cult (Milgrom, Levine, Anderson, D. Wright).

Lucian of Samosata (120–80 CE) satirizes the institution of sacrifice in a humorous essay entitled, simply, "Concerning Sacrifices." Denouncing the institution as "silly" (ἀβελτερία) and mocking its participants as "dolts" (μάταιοι), Lucian challenges his contemporaries to question whether they truly believe the gods to be "so low and mean as to stand in need of men" (Lucian, p. 153). Do the gods become "angry when slighted"? Do they constantly hunger after "human flattery" through these practices? Instead of censuring sacrifice altogether, however, he suggests that "a Heraclitus or a Democritus" be found, "one to laugh at their ignorance, the other to weep over their folly" (p. 171). Like satirists everywhere, Lucian delights in criticizing the idiosyncrasies of his culture's most sacred institutions (Jemielity 21–49).

Desperation and satire, however, figure much less prominently in the writings of the NT. Although a few passages allude to examples of non-Hebraic "sacrifice" (Luke 13:1; Acts 14:13; 1 Cor 10:20), NT writers are more interested in Christology than literary criticism or anthropology. In fact, one of the great accomplishments of the NT is its redefinition of θυσία within categories established by "the apostle and high priest of our confession" (Heb 3:1), the one John the Baptist calls "the Lamb of God who takes away the sin of the world" (John 1:29). For the writer of Hebrews, the sacrifice of Christ is "more excellent" (διαφορώτερος, Heb 8:6) because (a) the Cross has the power to deal once and for all with the tragedy of sin (Heb 2:17; Rom 3:25; 1 John 2:2); (b) the Cross enables believers everywhere to administer the healing effects of Christ's sacrifice to one other (i.e. without relying on a centralized clerical bureaucracy; Heb 4:14–15:10; 1 Pet 2:5–8); and (c) the Cross "abolishes" (ἀναιρέω, Heb 10:9) any further need for sacrificing bulls and goats to propitiate God's wrath (Heb 8:6–13; 10:1–14). As Hebrews puts it, the sacrifice of Christ is sufficient "for all time" (εἰς τὸ διηνεκὲς, Heb 10:12).

Pauline theology moves beyond reflection on this mystery to practical application of it, re-imagining the life of discipleship as a replication of the Cross in the believer's daily life (Cousar 135–75). Describing himself as "crucified with Christ" (Gal 2:19), Paul preaches the Cross-centered life as the ultimate ideal upon which to model all aspects of the Faith, including missionary service (Phil 2:17), economic stewardship (4:17), marital love (Eph 5:2, 21–33), liturgical worship (Heb 13:15), and the intellectual life of the mind (Rom 12:1–2). For Paul, the Cross is the only place in Creation able to reveal the deepest and fullest meaning of "sacrifice." As Christ is "killed" (הרג) so "we are killed all day long" (θανατούμεθα ὅλην τὴν ἡμέραν); as Christ is "slaughtered" (טבח), so "we are reckoned like sheep for slaughter" (ἐλογίσθημεν ὡς πρόβατα σφαγῆς; Rom 8:36, citing Ps 44:22 LXX).

The gospels address the meaning of θυσία not in Pauline ethical categories, and certainly not in Attic literary categories, but as decaying ritual dangerously close to losing its connection to ethics altogether (Spohn 120–41). Jesus of Nazareth repeatedly addresses this danger because so many of the religious people in his environment restrict the meaning of "sacrifice" to (a) magical behavior independent of moral repentance (Luke 13:1), and/or (b) cultic behavior segregated from religious

obedience (Matt 9:13). Repeatedly he cites prophetic texts like Hos 6:6 to remind his listeners that God "desires steadfast love (חסד) over sacrifice (זבח; LXX θυσία), the knowledge (ידע) of God over burnt offerings" (Matt 9:13; 12:7). Sometimes they grasp the significance of this distinction (see Mark 12:33); sometimes they don't (Matt 12:24).

Yet several encounters sharply emphasize it. On one occasion Jesus watches several wealthy people drop large sums of money into the Temple "collection box" (γαζοφυλάκιον). His relationship to the wealthy, like that of all prophets, is ambivalent and complex (A. Wright), so when a poor widow queues up to drop everything she has into the same box (λεπτὰ δύο, KJV "mites") Jesus seizes on this incident to teach a lesson about the ultimate meaning of "sacrifice" (Mark 12:41–44//Luke 21:1–4). The act of giving to others cannot in and of itself be "sacrificial," he argues, nor can the amount of the gift be a determining factor. What makes an offering "sacrificial" lies solely in the heart of the offerer (Paul elaborates this point at length in 2 Cor 8–9). Givers who give out of socioeconomic poverty are thus much more likely to understand the meaning of this teaching than those who calibrate their giving based on relatively high levels of socioeconomic abundance.

On another occasion a young man asks Jesus, "What must I do to inherit eternal life?" (τί ποιήσας ζωὴν αἰώνιον κληρονομήσω, Luke 18:18). As Jesus begins reciting the Decalogue in response the young man suddenly interrupts, evidently to inform him of his spotless record in keeping the commandments. Genuinely touched by his zeal (according to Mark he "loved" him), Jesus points out that he "lacks" one thing (λείπω, v. 22; ὑστερέω, Mark 10:21; Matt 19:21 reads "if you would be perfect," τελέω). To inherit eternal life this young man needs to pull away from his possessions and give to the poor. Only by renouncing his "health and wealth" ideology will he learn how to ask deeper questions about the *purpose* of the commandments (Hellerman 162–64).

In each of these scenarios Jesus invites his listeners to look behind the cultic institution of "sacrifice" in order to redefine the term from a deeper perspective. In this he follows in the footsteps of the prophets. The OT prophets constantly warn their listeners that priestly institutions like "sacrifice" can easily atrophy into meaningless ritual (Mic 6:6–8; Hos 6:6; Ps 51:16–17). Prophetic theology is the only proven antithesis to this tendency toward atrophy. Whereas priests tend to look centripetally inward ("sanctification"), prophets tend to look centrifugally outward ("redemption").

When the Aaronids, for example, fall prey to priestly exclusivism in the wilderness, Moses calls them back to compassionate inclusiveness (e.g. in the statute permitting aliens and defiled worshipers to celebrate Passover with the rest of the congregation; Num 9:1–14).

Priestly ritual finds its deepest *raison d'être* in the notion that "defilement is lethally contagious" (Douglas 24, 41–57; Eliade 8–10; Otto; Gammie 9–44), yet ritual sacrifice, left to itself, more often than not becomes spiritually impotent. When this happens the result is the "defilement" of Torah (Matt 7:12; 22:40), which in turn triggers the wrath of the prophets, both OT (Janzen 55–86) and NT (Harvey 1–14). When sin drives its practitioners to violate the boundaries of the sacred, priestly ritual is the only way to repair the breach and restore the violator. NT writers enthusiastically endorse this OT priestly theology, but only on the condition that terms like "High Priest," "lamb" and "sacrifice" be re-imagined christologically under the shadow of the Cross. This theology of "sacrifice" sharply distinguishes the Nazarenes from other Second Temple sects (Flusser 190–91).

The Hebrew institution of tithing can be interpreted (a) as a levitical "tax" designed to supply the needs of the priesthood more or less automatically (Jagersma 127–28), or (b) as a symbol of the "gift-exchange" system rooted in the covenant between Yahweh and Israel (Herman 139). Whereas the first focuses on the legitimate needs of the priestly bureaucracy, the second focuses (a) on the concept of sacrifice as a "gift" (Gray), an ideology which sustains (b) anthropological parallels with other gift-exchange systems all over the world (Mauss). Because the Akkadian word *ešrû* does not always technically mean "one-tenth" (Dandamayev, 89–90), and because מעשר does not always technically mean "one-tenth" in the Bible (Mal 3:8–10; Baumgarten 246), in Philo (Ritter 117), in the rabbinic texts (Jaffee), and in the Qumran texts, it seems likely that מעשר can also denote, in addition to its technical numeric meaning, "a general term for any tax payable to the Temple or the clergy" (Baumgarten 246). Although (a) the Mishnah devotes an entire tractate to tithing (*m. Maaserot*), and (b) the phenomenon of tithing comes to expression in several Qumran texts (11Q19 60.9, 4QMMT 66, 4Q270 fr. 6.17, 3Q15 1.11; 9.6; 11.4,10, 15), and although (c) Christians are evidently aware of the practice (Matt 23:22; Heb 7:5–9), no evidence exists in the NT to prove that Christians practice tithing in the first century CE.

MICHAEL S. MOORE

Further reading

Anderson, G. *Sacrifices and Offerings in Ancient Israel: Studies in Their Social and Political Importance*, HSM 41. Atlanta: Scholars Press, 1987.

Baumgarten, J. "On the Non-literal Use of *ma'ăśēr/dekatē*," *JBL* 103 (1984) 245–61.

Cousar, C. B. *A Theology of the Cross: The Death of Jesus in the Pauline Letters*, Minneapolis, MN: Fortress Press, 1990.

Dandamayev, M. "Der Tempelzehnte im Babylonien während des 6.-4. Jh. v.u.Z," in R. Stiehl and H. E. Stier (eds) *Beiträge zur Alten Geschichte und deren Nachleben. Festschrift für Franz Altheim*, Berlin: W. de Gruyter, 1969, pp. 82–90.

Douglas, M. *Purity and Danger: An Analysis of the Concepts of Pollution and Taboo*, London: Routledge, 1966.

Dunnill, J. "Communicative Bodies and Economies of Grace: The Role of Sacrifice in the Christian Understanding of the Body," *JR* 83 (2003) 79–93.

Eliade, M. *The Sacred and the Profane*, trans. W. Trask, New York: Harcourt, Brace and World, 1959.

Flusser, D. "The Parable of the Unjust Steward: Jesus' Criticism of the Essenes," in J. H. Charlesworth (ed.) *Jesus and the Dead Sea Scrolls*, ABRL, New York: Doubleday, 1992, pp. 176–97.

Gammie, J. *Holiness in Israel*, Minneapolis, MN: Fortress Press, 1989.

Gray, G. B. *Sacrifice in the Old Testament: Its Theory and Practice*, New York: KTAV, 1971 (reprint of 1925 edition with a "Prolegomenon" by B. A. Levine).

Hanson, K. C. "When the King Crosses the Line: Royal Deviance and Restitution in Levantine Ideologies," *BTB* 26 (1996) 11–25.

Harvey, A. E. *Strenuous Commands: The Ethic of Jesus*, Philadelphia, PA: Trinity Press International, 1990.

Hellerman, J. "Wealth and Sacrifice in Early Christianity: Revisiting Mark's Presentation of Jesus' Encounter with the Rich Young Ruler," *TJ* 21 (2000) 143–64.

Henninger, J. "Sacrifice," *ER* 12 (1987) 544–56.

Herman, M. *Tithe as Gift: The Institution in the Pentateuch and in Light of Mauss' Prestation Theory*, San Francisco, CA: Mellen Research University Press, 1991.

Jaffee, M. S. *Mishnah's Theology of Tithing: A Study of Tractate Maaserot*, BJS 19, Chico, CA: Scholars Press, 1981.

Jagersma, H. "Tithing in the Old Testament," *OTS* 21 (1981) 116–28.

Janzen, W. *Old Testament Ethics: A Paradigmatic Approach*, Louisville, KY: Westminster/John Knox, 1994.

Jemielity, T. *Satire and the Hebrew Prophets*, Louisville, KY: Westminster/John Knox, 1992.

Levine, B. A. *In the Presence of the Lord*, Leiden: Brill, 1974.

Lucian. *Works, Vol. III*, trans. A. M. Harmon, LCL, Cambridge, MA: Harvard, 1921.

Mauss, M. *The Gift: Forms and Functions of Exchange in Archaic Societies*, London: Cohen and West, 1966 (trans. from 1925 French edition).

Milgrom, J. *Cult and Conscience: The Asham and the Priestly Doctrine of Repentance*, Leiden: Brill, 1976.

Moore, M. S. *The Balaam Traditions: Their Character and Development*, SBLDS 113, Atlanta, GA: Scholars Press, 1990.

Otto, R. *The Idea of the Holy*, Oxford: Oxford University, 1928 (trans. from 1917 German edition).

Ritter, B. *Philo und die Halacha*, Leipzig: Hinrichs, 1879.

Spohn, W. C. *Go and Do Likewise: Jesus and Ethics*, New York: Continuum, 1999.

Wright, A. "The Widow's Mites: Praise or Lament?," *CBQ* 44 (1982) 256–65.

Wright, D. *The Disposal of Impurity: Elimination Rites in the Bible and in Hittite and Mesopotamian Literature*, SBLDS 101, Atlanta, GA: Scholars Press, 1987.

SADDUCEES

The Sadducees are widely known in modern biblical studies, both because they occur in the NT and also because of rabbinic literature. What is often not realized is how little we know about the Sadducees. At the head of the difficulties is the fact that we have not a word from someone who claimed to be a Sadducee. All we know about them is at best from outsiders and often from those who were hostile to them. This bias has spilled over even into much modern scholarship. Thus, the Sadducees have tended to be the whipping boys of most writers, whether Jewish or Christian. In addition, the little information extant is very skimpy and tends to be overinterpreted by most who write on them.

We have three main sources: Josephus, the NT, and some scattered references in rabbinic literature. Josephus introduces the Sadducees into his narrative first during the reign of John Hyrcanus (*Ant.* 13.10.6:293–98). Hyrcanus, who Josephus claims was himself a Pharisee, fell out with them and sided with the Sadducees for the rest of his reign because of undiplomatic criticism by one of the Pharisees. Opposition to the Pharisees continued under Alexander Janneus, though nothing further is said about the Sadducees at this point, nor about them in the reign of Alexandra Salome when the Pharisees became the dominant influence in her government. Much later, just before the war with Rome, the high priest Ananus, who had James the brother of Jesus condemned, is said to have been one of the Sadducees (*Ant.* 20.9.1:199).

Otherwise, no other specific persons are said to be Sadducees; instead, Josephus makes some general statements that reflect anti-Sadducean and pro-Pharisaic bias, such as the following (*J.W.* 2.8.14:166):

> The Pharisees are affectionate to each other and cultivate harmonious relations with the community. The Sadducees, on the contrary, are, even among themselves, rather boorish in their behaviour, and in their intercourse with their peers are as rude as to aliens.

Most historians would quickly seize on a statement that "Methodists are affectionate to each other, but Presbyterians, on the contrary, are boorish and rude." Yet the number who have accepted this statement by Josephus without question is surprising.

In the NT, the Sadducees are represented as the dominant group on the Sanhedrin, even though there are also Pharisees present on it such as Gamaliel. Acts 5 (ostensibly about 33 CE) associates the Sadducees with the high priest: "But the high priest rose up and all who were with him, that is, the party of the Sadducees" (v. 17; also 4:1). According to the picture in Acts 23:6–10 (dated by the author to about 59 CE) the Sanhedrin seems more evenly divided; nevertheless, the Sadducees are able to enforce their will to keep Paul under arrest. They are also said not to believe in angels or the resurrection. The Sadducees are mentioned in the gospels as well, but without much specificity. They may be little more than ciphers to fill out the quota for "opponents of Jesus".

In recent years some have wanted to identify the Qumran group with the Sadducees. The Qumran document 4QMMT has been invoked, with the argument that the authors of this document were "Sadducean", but this seems doubtful (Grabbe 196). Qumran beliefs show little in common with the special beliefs of the Sadducees. In rabbinic literature "Sadducee" seems to be interchangeable with "Boethusian". This is often explained as a reference to the family of Boethus which provided a number of the high priests from the time of Herod on. If so, the association of Sadducees and Boethusians is explicable without assuming a precise identity. Here are some of their beliefs:

- They reckoned Pentecost as being the Sunday following the seventh weekly Sabbath after the wavesheaf day.
- They rejected the concept of the *eruv*, which was a means in rabbinic literature for extending the limits of a Sabbath day's journey.
- They may also have objected to the popular customs of pouring water and beating with willow branches at the Feast of Tabernacles.
- It is often asserted that they accepted only the Pentateuch as canonical, but it is not clear that the OT canon was closed at this time in any case. The Sadducees may well have accepted the Pentateuch, Prophets, and some of the Writings just as apparently many other Jews did.

Evaluation of the data we have is very difficult. The earliest references to the Sadducees (in Josephus) indicate that they are a political party with the Pharisees as their primary rivals, but no particular religious beliefs are indicated. Otherwise, they tend to be characterized by particular religious positions, but these have a rather miscellaneous character about them – they do not form a coherent set of beliefs: When we take account of the nature of our evidence, there is much uncertainty. The best we can do is attempt some sort of reasonable hypothesis. The most certain conclusion is that the group first appeared as a political entity (whatever its origin and other characteristics) and continued to exist in some form until after the fall of Jerusalem. Several bits of information suggest some sort of connection with the priestly establishment and the Temple, while Acts 5 makes them the high priestly party. Josephus states that they were to be identified with the upper socio-economic class. This is not confirmed in other sources, but it is compatible with an association with the priestly establishment and membership on the Sanhedrin. However, this is not to suggest that the two were co-extensive. Not all Sadducees were priests or perhaps even wealthy, nor were all priests or upper-class individuals Sadducees.

LESTER L. GRABBE

Further reading

Grabbe, Lester L. *Judaic Religion in the Second Temple Period: Belief and Practice from the Exile to Yavneh*, London/New York: Routledge, 2000, pp. 185–99.
LeMoyne, J. *Les Sadducéen*, EB, Paris: Leoffre, 1972.
Saldarini, Anthony J. *Pharisees, Scribes and Sadducees in Palestinian Society: A Sociological Approach*, Wilmington, DE: Glazier, Edinburgh, T. & T. Clark, 1988.

SALVATION

The term "salvation" refers to any kind of deliverance from danger, difficulty, failure or destruction. In the NT it is used for the rescue from danger, the healing from sickness or with reference to God's deliverance of humans from sin through the work of Jesus Christ as the σωτήρ (saviour). As salvation is obviously one of the key concepts which bind together the whole Bible this article needs to be confined to the word group and cannot develop the broader idea. However, it needs to be pointed out that the NT also uses a number of other terms to express salvation, like, e.g., "justification", "life", "reconciliation", "redemption", "resurrection", etc.

Salvation in the OT and in Ancient Judaism

Behind the LXX translation of the word group σώζω one usually finds *ysh'* (to deliver, save) and its derivates in the Hebrew Bible. It can mean all sorts of help (Exod 2:17; Josh 10:6), rescue or salvation either by humans, circumstances or through the intervention of God. Finally it refers to the deliverance from evil powers and in terms of the eschatological salvation in the final judgment (Isa 49:6; Jdt 8:17; Wis 16:6; 18:7; Sir 46:1; 1 Macc 5:62). This eschatological dimension of salvation becomes especially prominent in the later books of the OT and in Ancient Judaism. The LXX does not use the noun σωτήρ for the Messiah but it sometimes refers to humans who are empowered by God (Judg 3:9, 15; Neh 9:27). Mostly and especially in the Psalms it is used for "God, my/our saviour" (Pss 25:5; 27:1,9; 62:3,7; 79:9). In Qumran the word group is used to describe God's saving of the children of light in the final battle against the children of darkness (1QM 10:4,8; 11:3; CD B 20:20). When the children of light return from the battle victoriously, they shall write on their banners "God's salvation" (1QM 4:13).

Salvation in the NT gospels

In the NT the verb σώζω (to save) appears frequently in the gospels (Matt 15x; Mark 15x incl. Mark 16:16; Luke 17x; John 6x). It refers to the delivering from danger like that of drowning (Matt 8:25; 14:30) or from dying on the cross (Mark 15:30 par. Matt 27:40; Mark 15:31b parr. Matt 27:42b/Luke 23:35b; Matt 27:49; Luke 23:37,39) or in a general sense to Jesus saving others (Mark 15:31 parr. Matt 27:42a/Luke 23:35a).

The noun σωτηρία (salvation), which appears in the gospels altogether four times in Luke (1:69,71,77; 19:9), once in John (4:22) and in the secondary ending of Mark (16:8), is found on the lips of Jesus only when he proclaims salvation onto the house of Zachaeus (Luke 19:9) and in the dialogue with the woman of Samaria (John 4:22): "for salvation is from the Jews". It is especially frequent in OT quotations (Luke 1:69 cf. Acts 13:47).

In the NT gospels the term σωτήρ (saviour) is used only once for God (Luke 1:47 in the NT altogether 8x) and only twice for Christ (Luke 2:11; John 4:42; in the NT altogether 17x). However, already in his name "Jesus" (= "God saves") points to the interpretation that "he will save his people from their sins" (Matt 1:21).

When God is called the σωτήρ in the hymn of praise which is traditionally called the Magnificat, this is clearly motivated by OT usage (cf. Hab 3:18; 1 Sam 2:1–10). Shortly after this and still in the birth narratives Jesus is praised as a σωτήρ. This identifies Jesus with God's activity towards the salvation of Israel. Especially in the Psalms this title is used for God (Ps 24:5). However, in the LXX it can also refer to the saviours of Israel, which God raised (Judg 3:9,15). In Zechariah's Benedictus "horn of salvation" (Luke 1:69; cf. 2 Sam 22:3; Ps 18:2) is used to describe a Davidic ruler. By calling Jesus σωτήρ on one side he is put in line with David and the God of Israel. On the other side this puts him in contrast to the Roman emperor for whom this title was commonly used (Josephus *J.W.* 7:71). Such anti-imperial overtones are even more obvious in the story of the Samaritan woman meeting Jesus at the well (esp. John 4:39–42). There the pattern of going to meet him (4:40a), then inviting him into town (4:40b) and most of all calling him σωτέρ fits the way people embraced especially the emperor but also other rulers (cf. Josephus *J.W.* 3:459; 7:70–71; 4:112–13; 7:100–3). In Johannine circles the universal title "saviour of the world" (John 4:42) seems to have become a recognized designation for Jesus (cf. 1 John 4:14) where he is portrayed as identifying himself as not having come "to judge the world, but to *save* the world" (John 12:47).

Consequently the term σωτηρία is used for the messianic deliverance from the hand of the national enemies (Luke 1:69,71; cf. Ps 106:10). But it can also refer to the deliverance of the people from sin (Luke 1:77).

In the NT gospels saving and salvation have a number of different dimensions, which cannot always be separated from each other. However, the frequent use of the verb σώζω allows for a more systematic analysis of the physical, spiritual and eschatological dimensions of salvation.

The *physical* or *earthly* dimension features especially prominently in Luke. Here the Benedictus reflects the hope of God's covenant with Israel in saving his people from their enemies (Luke 1:68–79). This focus of hope remains on the redemption of Israel, as can be seen in the words of Cleopas and his companion on their way to Emmaus: "But we had hoped that he was the one to redeem Israel" (Luke 24:21; cf. Acts 1:6). However, Jesus then goes on to correct this inadequate understanding of salvation (Luke 24:25–27; cf. Acts 1:7–8). Not only in Luke's gospel, Jesus message calls on the wealthy to care for the poor, the crippled, the lame, and the blind (Luke 14:13; cf. 4:18; 7:22; 14:21). In light of the coming judgment this tending for the earthly needs of the people who are at a disadvantage conforms to the priorities of the kingdom (Matt 25:31–46). Such physical healing may even involve a halachik conflict between life and death regarding the Sabbath, or as Jesus puts it:

"Is it lawful to do good or to do harm on the sabbath, to save life or to kill?" (Mark 3:4 par. Luke 6:9).

While Jesus' miracles heal men and women physically they also symbolize the *spiritual* dimension of faith and of sins being forgiven. Thus the blind Bartimaeus and the woman who had been suffering from haemorrhage are being told: "Your faith has made you well (σώζω)" (Mark 10:52 cf. Mark 5:34; parr. Matt 9:22/Luke 8:48 cf. Luke 7:50). Sometimes the spiritual usage of σώζω is linked to earthly matters like giving all things to the poor, as, i.e., Jesus encourages a wealthy (young) man to do so (Mark 10:21 par. Matt 19:21/Luke 18:22). This is followed by Jesus' pointing to the spiritual dimension of such activity to the entering of the kingdom of God (Mark 10:23 parr. Matt 19:23/Luke 18:24) and the disciples' question: "Then who can be saved?" (Mark 10:26 par. Matt 19:25/Luke 18:26).

The *eschatological* dimension is obvious wherever σώζω refers to the entering into the kingdom of God (Mark 10:25f. par. Matt 19:24f./Luke 18:25f.; cf. Luke 13:23). The context of losing one's life is present where being "saved" appears in opposition to "perish". Thus his disciples when facing a severe storm call upon Jesus: "Lord, save us! We are perishing!" (Matt 8:25; Luke 19:10). Such an antithesis of losing or saving one's life can also have eschatological overtones, as when Jesus teaches his disciples: "For those who want to save (σώζω) their life will lose it, and those who lose their life for my sake, and for the sake of the gospel will save (σώζω) it" (Mark 8:35 par. Matt 16:25/Luke 9:24; cf. Mark 8:36 par.). The followers of Jesus are called to endure because: "the one who endures to the end will be saved" (Mark 13:13 par. Matt 24:13, 10:22; cf. Luke 21:19).

Although the concept of salvation is crucial for all four NT gospels it is nevertheless important to note the particular emphasis of each individual text. For *Mark* entering the kingdom of God is synonymous with being saved (Mark 10:24–26 par. Matt 19:23–25/Luke 18:24–26). However, as most occurrences of σώζω in Mark are basically about physical healing (Mark 3:4; 5:28,34; 6:56; 10:52), restoring or saving life (Mark 5:23; 15:30), theological overtones are less frequent. However, the eschatological endurance of Jesus' followers despite suffering and persecution (Mark 8:35; 13:13,20) or the ironic comment on the lips of the Jewish leaders that the crucified Jesus "saved others; he cannot save himself" (Mark 15:31) indicates that Mark was aware of the broader concept of salvation.

In *Matthew* the significance of saving and being saved are not spelled out in detail. However, at the Last Supper Matthew lets Jesus interpret his own death as a pouring out of his blood "for many *for the forgiveness of sins*" (Matt 26:28). Looking at the structure of Matthew as a whole, short references to the saving activity of Jesus seem to form a bracket. As already noted, Jesus' name is interpreted as the one who "will save his people from their sins" (Matt 1:21) at the beginning of the narrative when an angelic messenger informs Joseph about the special calling of Mary's child. This announcement is mirrored in the ironic summary on the lips of the Jewish authorities when Jesus is crucified: "He saved others" (Matt 27:42a), which also appears in the other Synoptic Gospels (Mark 15:31b; Luke 23:25b). Also for the disciples persecution is part of their expectation as is final salvation (Matt 10:22). However, the eschatological expectation that "if those days had not been cut short, no one would be saved" (Matt 24:22 par. Mark 13:20) reveals that the seriousness of such suffering is not to be underestimated.

The usage of the whole word group is especially broad in *Luke*. Here it refers to being saved when in danger (Luke 23:35, 37, 39 cf. Acts 27:20, 31) or even being restored to life after having died (Luke 8:50). It also denotes all sorts of physical healing (Luke 6:9; 8:48; 17:19; 18:42; 23:35) and the liberating activity of driving out demons (Luke 8:36). σώζω can refer to the forgiveness of sins (Luke 7:47f., 50 cf. John the Baptist in Luke 1:77 cf. 3:3). People experience being saved already in their present lifetime (Luke 7:50; 19:9). However, the ultimate objective of such saving activity is eternal life (Luke 9:24; 13:23; 18:26).

Although the word group σώζω is not very prominent in *John* the saving activity of Jesus is portrayed in a significant way. Also here salvation is a central aspect of Jesus' mission (John 3:17, 35–36; 4:22, 42; 5:21–24, 34; 6:40; 10:9; 12:47). But John's language puts much more emphasis on the term "life" (5:21; 10:10) than on "salvation". It is only on the lips of the Samaritans that Jesus is called saviour (John 4:42; cf. 3:17) and only in conversation with the Samaritan woman that σωτηρία appears on the lips of Jesus (John 4:22). While it is this same salvation that comes from the Jews, unlike in the Synoptic Gospels in John salvation is not confined to Israel but is for the "world" (John 3:17; 4:42).

Crucial for the understanding of salvation in the Synoptic Gospels is the concept of the kingdom of God (Mark 1:15; Luke 4:43; 8:1; cf. kingdom of heaven in Matt 4:17; kingdom in Matt 9:35).

Through Jesus' preaching and healing ministry the final saving intervention of God is initiated (Matt 4:23; 9:35). Salvation is presented as the human activity of entering the kingdom of God (Mark 10:23–26 parr. Matt 19:23–25/Luke 18:24–26) and as accepting it like a child (Mark 10:15 par. Luke 18:17). Another metaphor for being saved is "sitting at the table" in God's kingdom (Luke 13:23–30). In order to enter the kingdom of God Jesus calls his listeners to repentance and thus challenges them to change their life in a most radical way (Mark 8:34–39:1 parr. Matt 16:24–28/Luke 9:23–27; 10:17–31 parr. Matt 19:16–30/Luke 18:18–30): "The time is fulfilled, and the kingdom of God is at hand; repent, and believe in the gospel" (Mark 1:15). As a consequence, the wealthy are called to care for "the poor, the crippled, the lame, and the blind" (Luke 14:13).

So although the Evangelists have recognized that the mission of Jesus is about the various aspects of physical, spiritual and eschatological salvation, the language of the kingdom of God is definitely more prominent in the Synoptic Gospels, especially in Mark. Thus one needs to recognize that salvation is only an expression for what it means to enter the kingdom of God, which is the much wider and eventually universal concept. However, as the Evangelists present Jesus as the saviour for the first time, σωτήρ is linked to the title of the Messiah who brings God's salvation for his people Israel and to the world through healing, raising the dead, forgiving people's sins and granting them eternal life. As such, salvation is a comprehensive term for the benefits for humans by God's sovereign activity in and through Jesus, the Messiah.

CARSTEN CLAUSSEN

Further reading

Goppelt, L. *Theology of the New Testament, Vol. 1: The Ministry of Jesus in Its Theological Significance*, Grand Rapids, MI: Eerdmans 1981.

Green, M. *The Meaning of Salvation*, London: Hodder and Stoughton, 1965.

Ladd, G. E. *A Theology of the New Testament*, Guildford and London: Lutterworth Press, 1975, pp. 73–77.

Schneider, J. and C. Brown. "Redemption etc.," *NIDNTT* 3 (1992) 205–21.

SAMARITANS

The Samaritan community is a fluid social group characterized by adherence to its own version of the Mosaic Pentateuch (with points of comparison to DSS texts) and a conviction that Mt Gerizim is the appropriate place for religious ritual and worship. The sect has had a continuous existence since at least the second century BCE. The Samaritans of the first century CE participated in many rites and rituals very similar to their Jewish neighbors but held a theologically grounded philosophy of history that distinguished the Samaritan community from both their Jewish and Gentile neighbors. The Samaritans trace their history back to a schism led by Eli, during the period of the judges. In Samaritan tradition, Eli elevated himself and established a place of worship at Shiloh as a rival to the divinely ordained site at Shechem. A large number of Israelites followed Eli into error while "True Israel" (the Samaritans) maintained orthodoxy and worship on Mt Gerizim near the city of Shechem. A period of Divine Disfavor ensued that still continues, only to be reversed at the appearance of the *Taheb*, a prophet in the tradition of Moses, who will restore both the prominence of the "True Israelites" and a renewed condition of Divine Favor. The Samaritans have maintained their existence as a visible minority community to this day. At times, this minority status has been preserved through peaceful coexistence and cultural tolerance, as evidenced in both rabbinic and Samaritan sources. But at other times, the Samaritan minority has been the object of and participant in violent clashes with its near neighbors that have resulted in deep resentments and have, occasionally, threatened the very existence of the Samaritan community.

Samaritan and Jewish tensions

Both the Samaritan and the Jewish accounts of Samaritan origins reach beyond what is historically verifiable. What is historically certain, however, is that the Samaritan community existed as a distinct religious group by the middle of the second century BCE and that the sect lived in tension with their Jewish neighbors. The early second-century BCE writer of Ecclesiasticus, Ben Sira, provides a cryptic yet demeaning assessment of the Samaritans (Ecclesiasticus 50:25–26). Ben Sira's negative attitude toward the Samaritans is shared by others and with tragic consequences toward the middle part of the second century BCE. The Samaritans were excluded from participation in the Maccabean revolt (167–164 BCE), presumably because their religious expression was not part of the religious form the Maccabees sought to liberate. Later, after the Seleucids were expelled by the Maccabees, John Hyrcanus (134–104 BCE), the powerful high priest in Jerusalem, treated the Samaritans like Gentiles and, when opportunity arose, initiated a violent attack on the cities in Samaria, including the Samaritan communities at Shechem and Mt Gerizim. The sack of Shechem and Gerizim (completed by Hyrcanus' two sons, Aristobulus and Antigonus) left the worship site (the existence of a Samaritan temple on the site is debated) on Mt Gerizim in shambles and contributed to a Samaritan diaspora throughout the eastern Mediterranean basin.

A series of incidents involving open hostilities between the Samaritan and Jewish communities provides evidence to suggest that these tensions continued in the first century CE. During the reign of the Roman-appointed governor, Coponius (6–9 CE), a group of Samaritans infiltrated the grounds of the Jerusalem Temple and scattered human bones in the courtyard, thus seeking to make the site unclean and unfit for worship. While Pontius Pilate was procurator (26–36 CE), a group of Samaritans armed themselves and sought to take control of the ascent to Mt Gerizim. Pilate responded militarily by securing the route of ascent and in the process a number of Samaritan zealots were killed. This failed Samaritan attempt to control Mt Gerizim was certainly an act of religious enthusiasm but also functioned as a focal point for nationalistic, ethnic, and cultural identity. The Samaritan rejection of Jesus and his disciples expressed in Luke 9: 52–53 because "his face was set toward Jerusalem" speaks of an attitude similar to that which sparked an incident occurring in 52 CE. A party of Jewish pilgrims from Galilee, while on their way to Jerusalem, was ambushed and killed by a group of Samaritans. And just as the disciples of Jesus sought to retaliate against their Samaritan antagonists by calling down fire from heaven (Luke 9:54), the later attack on the Jewish pilgrims prompted a Jewish retaliation. An escalation in violence between the two groups was averted only by the military intervention of Agrippa. During the initial confusion attending the Jewish Revolt (66–70 CE), a second attempt was made by Samaritan zealots to seize the route of ascent to the top of Mt Gerizim. The initial success of the zealots was soon reversed when, in 67 CE, Vespasian responded against the Samaritan defenders with a force of 600 mounted troops and 3,000 foot soldiers. Even though the Samaritans had amassed a sizable fighting force of their own, the rebellion was soon defeated by the Romans. Soon afterward (probably 72–73 CE), and as a measure to prevent future Samaritan attempts at nationalistic rebellion, the Romans established the city of Neapolis on the site of ancient Shechem to further protect the route of ascent up Mt Gerizim from occupation by Samaritan zealots seeking to establish a center of political identity.

Certainly, it is impossible to conclude individual attitudes by this survey of group conflict, but this much seems certain – in the first century CE the Samaritan community existed as a minority group seeking to assert (sometimes violently) political, ethnic, and religious recognition from the Jewish majority that was always reluctant and sometimes hostile toward the Samaritan minority. A quite different attitude is evident in the New Testament.

Samaritans in the New Testament

Matthew

According to Matthew, the initial commission (10:5–6), by which Jesus sent out the disciples, indicates a concern only for the "lost sheep of the house of Israel," and does not include a Samaritan or Gentile audience. It would be wrong, however, to conclude an anti-Samaritan bias from this instruction, for the exclusivity is not maintained, even in Matthew, as is evident by the very inclusive expectation voiced in the Great Commission by which the book ends (28:18).

John

The story related in John 4 describing the conversation between Jesus and the Samaritan woman is notable in several respects. The parenthetical statement of verse 9 acknowledges that Jesus was breaking a social norm by sharing a drinking vessel with a Samaritan, let alone entering into a lengthy conversation with this woman stranger (v. 27). And when the Samaritan woman questions Jesus concerning the proper location of worship (Mt Gerizim or Jerusalem), one of the most contentious of differences between the Jewish and Samaritan communities is readily acknowledged. But this and other differences are brushed aside when Jesus replies to the woman that these places of worship are secondary to the Father's desire for worship that is in spirit and truth. Jesus bridged a second gulf separating the Samaritans and the Jewish community. The Samaritans expect the appearance of the *Taheb*, a divinely appointed prophet who, in the tradition of Moses, will restore the Samaritan community to an era of Divine Favor while the Jewish community seek a Messiah to restore the fortunes of the Davidic kingdom. The Samaritan woman questioned whether Jesus could possibly be the long-awaited prophet – the *Taheb*. Rather than correcting her expectation,

Jesus simply responded affirmatively and so welcomed Jew and Samaritan into a new vision of the Savior of the world. In fact, from John's notation in verses 40–41, Samaritans were among the very first to follow after Jesus. It may be that John 8:48 provides a tacit welcome of Samaritans into the community of faith. There, Jesus is insulted by being accused of having a demon and being a Samaritan. Jesus only denies having a demon.

Luke

The parable of the Good Samaritan in Luke 10:29–37 broke all the rules. In this well-known story, the Samaritan is held up for exemplary behavior, fulfilling the expectation established in Deuteronomy 6:4–5, while the priest and the Levite, religious experts from the Jewish community, fail miserably. Even the expert in the law, the one initially questioning Jesus, is advised to follow the example set by the Samaritan. By making a Samaritan the personification of an example to be followed, Jesus effectively turned things upside down, welcoming the marginalized minority in preference to the powerful of the majority.

Luke records a second incident that effectively extended a welcome to the Samaritan community. In 17:11–19 the story is told of the healing of ten lepers, one of whom was a Samaritan. While all ten were cleansed, only one, explicitly identified as a Samaritan and a foreigner, returned to offer thanks to Jesus and praise to God. Jesus responded to the man by saying that his faith made him whole.

Acts

Acts 7 has long held the interest of those seeking to understand the Samaritan influence in early Christianity. Stephen's speech incorporates a Samaritan text type of the Old Testament and his emphasis on Samaritan heroes as well as his modification of the Hebrew text in favor of Samaritan interests suggests that Stephen was at least quite familiar with the Samaritan community, if not a Samaritan himself. Acts 8:5–6 notes that Samaritan conversions to Jesus' followers were the result of Philip's influence. This account in Acts may be a reference to converts from the northern region of Samaria and not just those from the Samaritan sect. In any case, the group mentioned in Acts 8 seems to have had an aversion to the Jerusalem temple and so shared at least this one important characteristic with the Samaritan community.

Samaritan view of early Christianity

Samaritan literature also provides information concerning the interaction between the followers of Jesus and the Samaritan community. The story of the Samaritan community is contained in several chronicles that variously trace the community's existence from the time of Eli to the beginning of the twentieth century. Chronicle II has a fairly lengthy account of the early Christian movement. The Chronicle is able to name early disciples of Jesus, can outline Paul's career, and is familiar with at least some of the early Christian literature (using the same genealogy for Jesus as appears in Matt 1:3–16). Besides listing writings of Paul, Luke and the other gospel writers familiar in the New Testament, the Chronicle lists thirty-five other "gospel-books" that were used by the "kingdom of the Nazarenes." The Chronicle takes pains to describe Samaritan noninterference with the early Christian movement:

> Now Jesus the Nazarene did not consult the community of the Samaritan Israelites at any time in his life. He did not stand in their way, nor did they stand in his way. They did not impose upon him, nor he on them in any way.
>
> (Anderson and Giles 2005: 256)

TERRY GILES

Further reading

Anderson, R. T. and Terry Giles. *The Keepers: An Introduction to the History and Culture of the Samaritans*, Peabody, MA; Hendrickson Press, 2002.

—— *Tradition Kept: The Literature of the Samaritans*, Peabody, MA: Hendrickson Press, 2005.

Crown, Alan D. (ed.) *The Samaritans*, Tübingen: Mohr, 1989.

Crown, Alan and Lucy Davey (eds) *Essays in Honor of G. D. Sixdenier: New Samaritan Studies of the Société d'Études Samaritaines*, Sydney: University of Sydney, 1995.

Eshel, Esther and Hanan Eshel. "Dating the Samaritan Pentateuch's Compilation in Light of the Qumran Biblical Scrolls," in S. M. Paul, R. A. Kraft, L. A. Schiffman, and W. W. Fields (eds) *Emanuel: Studies in Hebrew Bible, Septuagint and Dead Sea Scrolls in Honor of Emanuel Tov*, Leiden: Brill, 2003, pp. 215–40.

Hall, Bruce. *Samaritan Religion from John Hyrcanus to Baba Rabbah: A Critical Examination of the Relevant Material in Contemporary Christian Literature, the Writings of Josephus, and the Mishnah*, Sydney: Mandelbaum, 1987.

Manns, F. and E. Alliata (eds) *Early Christianity in Context: Monuments and Documents*, Jerusalem: Franciscan Printing Press, 1993.

Morabito, V., A. D. Crown, and L. Davey (eds) *Samaritan Researches*, Sydney: Mandelbaum, 2000.

Tal, A. and M. Florentin (eds) *Proceedings of the First International Congress of the Société d'Etudes Samaritaines*, Tel Aviv: Chaim Rosenberg School for Jewish Studies, 1991.

SANDERS, ED PARISH

Ed Parish Sanders (1937–) is one of the most influential proponents of the thesis that the historical Jesus was a Jewish apocalyptic prophet. In addition to his research on Jesus, he has written extensively on the nature of early Judaism, the comparison of Paul's theology to that reflected in other Jewish texts, and critical problems posed by the gospels. After receiving his doctorate at Union Theological Seminary as a student of W. D. Davies, he held positions at McMaster University (1966–84), Oxford University (1984–90), and Duke University (1990–2005).

Sanders contextualizes Jesus within the world of Judaism, rather than contrasting him with it (1985, 1993a), as some previous scholars had done (e.g. Wilhelm Bousset, Rudolf Bultmann, and Günther Bornkamm). In emphasizing Jesus' Jewishness, Sanders is reacting against earlier studies that used Judaism as a foil for Jesus, depicting it as a religion of legalistic works–righteousness and him as a prophet proclaiming God's grace. Sanders argues vigorously that early Judaism believed in a gracious and merciful god. He suggests that most forms of Judaism can be understood within the framework of "common Judaism" and shared the same basic theological convictions, which he calls "covenantal nomism": God elected the people of Israel and gave them the Torah (Jewish law); Israel's covenant obligation was to abide by the Torah, which included provisions for atonement for transgression; fidelity to Torah kept one within the covenant; those who belonged to the covenant would be saved (1977, 1985, 1992, 1993a). He also believes that some scholars have exaggerated the extent of Greco-Roman culture in Galilee at the time of Jesus and have under-emphasized the importance of his Jewish context (1993b, 2002)

Many studies of the historical Jesus begin with an analysis of the various sayings of Jesus, sifting through them to determine which were actually uttered by Jesus and which reflect later traditions. Sanders's work in the canonical gospels (1969, 1989) made him somewhat skeptical of the possibility of ascertaining with certainty the "reliability" of individual Sayings. Instead, he focused first on what he regarded as "unassailable facts" about Jesus (that he preached in Galilee, was baptized by John the Baptist, was crucified by the Romans as a kingly pretender, etc.), only then turning to the sayings material. Some have noted that Sanders's lists of "unassailable facts" varied between his primary study, *Jesus and Judaism*, and his later popular-level treatment, *Jesus as a Figure in History* (Powell).

The most important of these facts, in Sanders's opinion, was Jesus' demonstration in the Temple. Rather than being a protest against the sacrificial cult, the commercialization of the Temple's operation, or priestly oppression or corruption, the action was a symbolic prophecy of the Temple's imminent destruction and replacement by an eschatological one. Sanders appeals to a variety of Jewish sources (e.g. Isaiah, *1 Enoch*, *Jubilees*, the *Psalms of Solomon*, the *Temple Scroll*, the *Sibylline Oracles*) to argue that expectations of a new Temple were widespread in Judaism. Sanders thinks that Jesus likely also preached about the Temple's destruction, a fact that later Christians tried to suppress (cf. Mark 15:29 and parallels and Acts 6:13). Jesus' action in the temple, viewed as provocative by both the temple authorities and the Romans, led to his arrest and execution.

Jesus' understanding of the kingdom of God included not only the establishment of a new temple, but also the restoration of the twelve tribes of Israel, symbolized in the selection of twelve disciples. The kingdom's arrival would be preceded by the coming Son of Man. Jesus believed that he himself would play a central role in the kingdom, though our sources do not allow us to understand exactly what he perceived that role to be. Sanders thus finds himself in general agreement with scholars like Bart D. Ehrman and Paula Fredriksen, and in continuity with a tradition of scholarship extending back to Albert Schweitzer and beyond.

One of the more controversial aspects of Sanders's reconstruction is his proposal that Jesus believed that unrepentant sinners would be included in the kingdom. Though the Gospel of Luke emphasizes the importance of repentance, Sanders posits, Jesus himself most likely did not. Preaching repentance, he points out, would not have been controversial. Jesus' association with "sinners and tax collectors," however, offended many of his contemporaries. Sanders also argues that while Jesus may have had distinctive understandings of the Torah, he was not opposed to it. Some scholars have suggested, however, that the idea that unrepentant sinners would be saved requires a rejection of the Torah's provisions for atonement and forgiveness (Powell).

Sanders argues that the canonical gospels exaggerate the amount of enmity between Jesus and the Pharisees. In his view, many of the conflict stories reflect tension between later Christians and Pharisees, not reminiscences of actual historical events; those that are authentic reflect intra-Jewish debates about Torah interpretation and practice. New Testament scholars have often overestimated the power and influence of the Pharisees. They have also misunderstood the purity laws. Impurity was not a sin; the purity laws regulated only access to the Temple. Thus, they were not widely viewed as oppressive. Sanders's critics have charged him with selective use of sources (Hengel and Deines), a charge he levels back at them.

Sanders differs considerably from some sectors of Historical Jesus research, such as that represented by the Jesus Seminar: his dismissal of the non-canonical gospels as a useful source for understanding the historical Jesus, emphasis on apocalypticism, defense of the authenticity of coming Son of Man sayings, rejection of the idea that Q material can be stratified into early and late layers, downplaying of the notion that Jesus was politically oriented or sought social reform, and insistence that Jesus' Galilee had not yet been extensively Hellenized. Even many scholars who disagree with his reconstruction of Jesus, however, have expressed appreciation for his desire to understand Jesus as a part of, rather than apart from, early Judaism.

MARK A. CHANCEY

Further reading

Ehrman, Bart D. *Jesus: Apocalyptic Prophet of the New Millennium*, New York: Oxford University Press, 1999.

Fredriksen, Paula. *Jesus of Nazareth: King of the Jews*, New York: Vintage Books, 1999.

Hengel, Martin and Roland Deines. "E. P. Sanders' 'Common Judaism', Jesus, and the Pharisees." *JTS* 46 (1995) 1–70.

Powell, Mark Allan. *Jesus as a Figure in History: How Modern Historians View the Man From Galilee*, Louisville, KY: Westminster John Knox Press, 1998.

Sanders, E. P., *The Tendencies of the Synoptic Tradition*, SNTSMS 9, Cambridge: Cambridge University Press, 1969.

—— *Paul and Palestinian Judaism*, Minneapolis, MN: Fortress Press, 1977.

—— *Jesus and Judaism*, Philadelphia, PA: Fortress Press, 1985.

—— *Judaism: Practice and Belief: 63 BCE–66 CE*, London: SCM Press; Philadelphia, PA: Trinity Press International, 1992.

—— *The Historical Figure of Jesus*, London: Allen Lane, Penguin, 1993a.

—— "Jesus in Historical Context," *ThTo* 50 (1993b) 429–48.

—— "Jesus' Galilee," in Ismo Dundergerg, Kari Syreeni, and Christopher Tuckett (eds) *Fair Play: Diversity and Conflicts in Early Christianity: Essays in Honour of Heikki Räisänen*, Leiden: Brill, 2002, pp. 3–41.

Sanders, E. P. and M. Davies. *Studying the Synoptic Gospels*, London: SCM Press; Philadelphia, PA: Trinity Press International, 1989.

Schweitzer, Albert. *The Quest of the Historical Jesus*, trans. W. Montgomery, New York: Macmillan, 1968.

SANHEDRIN

In the time of Jesus the term "Sanhedrin" was used for the supreme Jewish council in Jerusalem, as well as for the smaller bodies governing the Jewish communities throughout Palestine and the Diaspora (Josephus *Ant.* 14.89–91). The fragmentary nature of our sources and the changes in leadership bodies that took place over time limit what we can know about the Sanhedrin to the extent that almost every aspect of its nature and function is debated in a way that cannot be reflected within the scope of this article. The Mishnah, produced about 200 CE and probably reflecting the situation at Jamnia rather than in early first-century Jerusalem, says that there were two major courts in the city (*m. Sanh.* 1:6). However, according to Greek sources nearer the time of Jesus and therefore to be favored in helping understand the Sanhedrin in that period, there was a single governing body in Jerusalem (Josephus *Ant.* 14.167–80; *Life* 62). In the gospels, apart from Matthew 5:22, 10:17, and Mark 13:9, the Sanhedrin is mentioned as the body seeking to destroy Jesus. See Matthew 26:59; Mark 14:55; 15:1; John 11:47, and Luke 22:66 which also uses the word *presbyterion*.

Background

The roots of the Jerusalem Sanhedrin in the time of Jesus go back to the period of Ezra and Nehemiah. Joshua the high priest and the Davidic governor of Jerusalem, Zerubbabel, ruled the community together (Hag. 1:1) and the community was headed by a priestly nobility which formed an aristocratic council (Neh 2:16; 5:7). With the death of Zerubbabel the house of David came to an end and the high priest emerged as the head of the *gerousia* and Jewish state (1 Macc 12:6). In 47 BCE Caesar made the high priest and the Jerusalem council responsible for the affairs of the entire nation, even though regional councils (*synedria*) survived (Josephus *Ant.* 14.91, 192–95). With an increasing sense of its power, Herod was summoned to stand trial on capital sentences he had passed without the Sanhedrin's authority (Josephus *J.W.* 1.204–15). However, when Herod took Jerusalem in 37 BCE, he killed the entire membership of the Sanhedrin (Josephus *Ant.* 14.174, cf. 15.6). Under the Roman procurators (6–41 CE) the Sanhedrin's power increased again (Josephus *Ant.* 20.251) so that, in the gospels, the Sanhedrin is represented as the supreme court of justice (Mark 14:55). After the destruction of Jerusalem the Sanhedrin was reconstituted at Jamnia in the northwest of Judea (*m. Sota* 9:11; *m. Sanh.* 11:4) before moving to Galilee in 118 CE.

In the time of Jesus the Sanhedrin, increasingly influenced by the Pharisees (Josephus *Ant.* 13.408; 18.17), probably had seventy-one members (cf. Josephus *J.W.* 2.482; *m. Sanh.* 1:6). The chief priests (predominantly Sadducees, Acts 5:17; Josephus *Ant.* 20.199) were the key figures (Mark 14:53; Josephus *J.W.* 2.316–42) and the scribes (predominantly Pharisees, Josephus *J.W.* 2.411) who dominated the body were the second major component of the Sanhedrin (Acts 5:34; Josephus *Ant.* 18.17; *J.W.* 2.411). The term "elders" was used for a third group consisting of priests and lay members of the nobility (Luke 19:47; *J.W.* 2.410). There may also have been a distinct group of the ten foremost members (*Ant.* 20:194). The president was the high priest, often appointed arbitrarily by the Romans (*Ant.* 20.197–200, 247–51). Second in rank was the captain of the Temple (Josephus *Ant.* 20.131; Acts 4:1); Josephus mentions a secretary (*J.W.* 5.532). Members may have been co-opted (*m. Sanh.* 4:4; *Qidd.* 4:5) and were probably admitted through the laying on of hands (cf. Num 27:18–23).

Powers and procedures

When Augustus appointed a procurator for Judea in 6 CE, "with full powers, including the infliction of capital punishment" (Josephus *J.W.* 2.117), the Sanhedrin could no longer order and execute a capital sentence (John 18:31; *y. Sanh.* 18a; 24b; *b. Sanh.* 41a; *b. 'Abod. Zar.* 8b). The signs in the second court of the Temple, that "No foreigner is to enter within the forecourt and the balustrade around the sanctuary. Whoever is caught will have himself to blame for his subsequent death" (*CII*, 1400 n. 85), were likely to be warnings against being lynched (cf. Acts 6:8–8:2; John 10:31). In any case, taking the opportunity of convening the Sanhedrin before Albinus, the new procurator, had arrived, Ananus the high priest had James, the brother of Jesus, condemned to be stoned (*Ant.* 20.197–203). Whether or not the Sanhedrin was able to execute capital punishment, the Romans maintained the right to intervene when a political crime was suspected (Acts 22:30–38).

The Sanhedrin probably met in its own building on the western boundary of the Temple, perhaps next to the gymnasium (Josephus *J.W.* 5.144; 6.354). We have no record from the period of the proceedings of the Jerusalem Sanhedrin. If we rely on the Mishnah, members sat in a half-circle so they could see each other. Before them stood two scribes, one writing down what was said in favor and the other what was said against the accused. Before them sat three rows of students who could participate in non-capital trials (*m. Sanh.* 4:1–4). Non-capital trials began with either case, but capital trials were to begin with the case for acquittal. A majority of one was sufficient in non-capital trials to acquit the accused of a capital charge. A majority of two was required for a guilty verdict on a capital charge. Verdicts could be reversed but not from an acquittal to a conviction in a capital trial. Those participating in the case could speak for and against the accused in non-capital trials. In capital trials a speaker in favor of conviction could only change and argue in favor of the accused, not the reverse. In non-capital cases the daytime trial could be followed by reaching a verdict that same night. In capital cases the verdict for an acquittal could be reached that night but a verdict of conviction had to wait until the following day (*m. Sanh.* 4:1). This enabled members of the Sanhedrin to go off in pairs to eat a little (no wine was permitted) to discuss the case all night before meeting in court early next morning (*m. Sanh.* 5:5). Therefore, trials were not to be held on the days before a Sabbath or festival (*m. Sanh.* 4:1). In capital cases voting began with the most junior members standing, each giving their verdict (*m. Sanh.* 5:5).

Jesus and the Sanhedrin

Tension between the gospel accounts (see Matt 26:57, 59–68; 27:1–2; Mark 14:53, 55–65, 15:1; Luke 22:54, 63–23:1; John 18:13–15, 19–24, 28) – including the Fourth Gospel omitting mention of a session of the Sanhedrin, but having pertinent details dispersed throughout the gospel (John 1:51; 2:19; 10:24–25, 33, 36; 11:47–53) – has raised doubt that a Jewish trial of Jesus took place (e.g. Winter). Nevertheless, though it is generally agreed that Jesus faced the Sanhedrin, it is not clear if there was a preliminary hearing before Annas in the high priest's palace (Luke 22:52) where he was also struck (John 18:13, 19–24). Alternatively, there could have been two trials (Mark 14:53; 15:1) or, as is probably the majority view, there was only a single meeting of the Sanhedrin (Luke 22:66–23:1). If there was a single trial, it was probably held during the day (Luke 22:66; e.g. Catchpole), as most agree, rather than overnight (Matt 26:59–68; Mark 14:55–65) for trials were only held during the hours of daylight (cf. *m. Sanh.* 4:1).

GRAHAM H. TWELFTREE

Further reading

Bammel, E. (ed.) *The Trial of Jesus*, London: SCM Press, 1970.

Blinzler, J. *The Trial of Jesus*, Cork, Eire: Mercer, 1959.
Catchpole, D. R. *The Trial of Jesus*, SPB 18, Leiden: Brill, 1971.
Hoenig, S. B. *The Great Sanhedrin*, Philadelphia, PA: Dropsie College, 1953.
Lohse, E. "συνέδριον," *TDNT* VII (1972) 860–71.
Mantel, H. *Studies in the History of the Sanhedrin*, Cambridge: Harvard University Press, 1961.
Saldarini, A. J. *Pharisees, Scribes and Sadducees in Palestinian Society*, Grand Rapids, MI and Cambridge: Eerdmans, 1988.
Schürer, E. *The History of the Jewish People in the Age of Jesus Christ (175 BC–AD 135)*, revised and ed. G. Vermes and F. Millar, 3 vols, Edinburgh: T. & T. Clark, 1973–87, Vol. 2, pp. 199–226.
Sherwin-White, A. N. *Roman Law and Roman Society in the New Testament*, Oxford: Oxford University Press, 1963.
Winter, P. *On the Trial of Jesus*, Berlin: de Gruyter, 1974.

SCHILLEBEECKX, EDWARD

Edward Schillebeeckx is a Flemish Dominican, born in Antwerp 1914. He grew up in the outskirts of Brussels, and from 1958 to 1985 was full professor of systematic theology at the Catholic University of Nijmegen, Gelderland province, the Netherlands. He founded two journals, *Tijdschrift voor Theologie* in Dutch, and *Concilium*, published simultaneously in over six languages. He was also for a time editor of a journal of spiritual life. He is a product of the Flemish cultural movement within Belgium, and as a Dominican was trained in a sort of progressive Thomism linked with Louvain University and the French Dominican theological faculty, Le Saulchoir, located just outside Paris. Major influences on him were D. de Petter, Chenu and Congar. He served for many years as student master of Dominican seminarians and was known for his kindness.

Before the Second Vatican Council (1962–65), he taught especially the tractates on Christology and sacraments on the basis of the third part of Thomas Aquinas' *Summa Theologiae*, and was known for his books on sacraments (including marriage) and Mary. After the Council, he realized that faith in Christ was being threatened in the Netherlands and decided to do what he could to stem the tide. Although he was not trained as a biblical scholar, he plunged himself into modern biblical studies about the historical Jesus, New Testament Christology, and soteriology. The result of his efforts emerged in three large dense tomes, entitled in English: *Jesus, Christ, Church*. They were first published in Dutch and quickly translated into major Western languages, except French (English publication dates 1979, 1980, 1991 respectively). Of these three volumes, the first is the

SCHILLEBEECKX, EDWARD

most relevant to the historical Jesus, but it requires correction in one major point from the third volume. In the first two volumes Schillebeeckx had underinterpreted the theme of the kingdom of God. By the time he came to the third volume, he realized his mistake and made the kingdom the key to everything. Better late than never. Together the three volumes replace earlier efforts to write a theology of the New Testament, e.g. the works of Bultmann, Stauffer, Conzelmann, Kümmel, Meinertz, Schelkle, Lemonnyer-Cerfaux, Bonsirven, Ceuppens.

Schillebeeckx's *Jesus* book concentrates on the Synoptic Gospels. Schillebeeckx wants to write a narrative Christology, so he retells the gospel story in the light of modern scholarship. But three moments are not treated: the virginal conception, the temptation in the desert, the Transfiguration. The story begins as in Mark, with John the Baptist and the baptism of Jesus, goes on to Jesus' proclamation of the kingdom in parable and beatitude, and then presents the manner of Jesus' life: his miracles as evoking faith, his meals with sinners, his relationship to the Jewish law, his awareness of God as his father in a unique, absolute way. This filial consciousness of Jesus, as contrasted with a messianic consciousness, is the most likely source of Christology in the pre-Easter Jesus himself. (Here Schillebeeckx is closely dependant upon the Q text Luke 10:21–22.) The work goes on to the death of Jesus and gives three early interpretations of the death. The resurrection of Jesus is then discussed as a conversion experience of the disciples (pp. 320–97). This last point is one of the most controversial in the book and has provoked the most criticism (see below).

The book makes five major contributions.

1 Jesus' meals with his disciples and social outcasts (200–18) were moments of joy, freedom, divine forgiveness and acceptance. Often Jesus is the host, and the abundance is a sign of the end times (Amos 9:13). The meals become acted-out parables of the process of salvation.

2 Schillebeeckx integrates Helmut Koester's four early gospel types, which each contain a particular Christology and a social or community type. Schillebeeckx is the first major systematic theologian to recognize the fruitfulness of the four types for theology. The four gospel types with their characteristic titles and group categories are: (a) the apocalyptic; Son of Man; discontented rebels; (b) aretology, i.e. collection of miracle/healing stories of a "divine man"; Son of David; charismatic groups that pray for healing or deliverance, healing sanctuaries, hospitals; (c) the words of the wise or sayings collection, e.g. Q or the *Gospel of Thomas*; Jesus as Wisdom personified, or as prophet like Moses; a Christian school, monastery, Gnostic coterie; (d) the kerygma, a book based on the suffering, death and resurrection of Jesus as saving event, e.g. the *Gospel of Peter*; Christ, Messiah, Lord; Church (for all). The first three can easily become sectarian; the fourth gospel type, the kerygmatic, can integrate the others, as is the case in the four canonical gospels:

3 For Schillebeeckx, the Easter *appearances* of the risen Jesus are of primary significance in the matter of the resurrection. The empty tomb stories are secondary elaborations. For the disciples, Jesus' rising from the dead was also a conversion experience and an experience of forgiveness (for their desertion, their betrayal and, in the case of Paul, for his persecution of Christians). Cf. Acts 9,22,26. This view has been severely criticized, by R. H. Fuller and John Macquarrie, as if the resurrection were something that happened to the disciples and not to Jesus. For Schillebeeckx, what is *historically* certain is that the early disciples believed that Jesus had risen from the dead. Their faith is the basis of later Christian faith. Their faith was supported by Scripture, e.g. Isa 52:13; 53:10; Wis 2:17–3:4.

4 Schillebeeckx contributes a short section (pp. 576–82) on three different rhythms or rates of historical and cultural change: ephemeral, like changes in fashion; conjunctural, taking several centuries, and structural, taking millennia. This is useful to help understand the slow evolution of the concept of person, important for the next point.

5 In technical, dogmatic Christology, Schillebeeckx wants to revive a concept that was rejected in the fight with Nestorius (fifth century AD): *enhypostasis,* as opposed to *anhypostasis.* For Schillebeeckx, the gospels present us with a human person who has a unique relationship to the divine, and whom it is appropriate to address with divine titles. This fully human person exists *within* the divine person of the Son of God (*enhypostasis*). Schillebeeckx wants to go beyond the Byzantine theology of two natures in Christ, human and divine, but only one person and that person a divine one, so that Jesus was

546

not a human person (*anhypostasis*). Schillebeeckx affirms the full humanity of Christ, without denying his divinity. One of his reasons for this is that in the modern, evolved, sense of the word "person," the Jesus of the gospels is a full human person. To the modern reader this is self-evident. Schillebeeckx thinks that we must start with this understanding, and then go beyond it.

B. T. VIVIANO

Further reading

Bowden, J. S. *Edward Schillebeeckx: Portrait of a Theologian*, London: SCM Press, 1983.

Kennedy, Philip. *Schillebeeckx*, London: Chapman, 1993.

Macquarrie, John. *Jesus Christ in Modern Thought*, London: SCM Press, 1990.

Schillebeeckx, Edward. *Jesus: An Experiment in Christology*, New York: Seabury, 1979.

—— *Christ: The Experience of Jesus as Lord*, New York: Seabury, 1980.

—— *Interim Report on the Books Jesus and Christ*, New York: Crossroads, 1981.

—— *Church: The Human Story of God*, New York: Crossroad, 1991.

—— *I am a Happy Theologian: Conversations with Francesco Strazzari*, New York: Crossroads, 1994 (an informal autobiography).

SCHLEIERMACHER, FRIEDRICH

Friedrich Daniel Ernst Schleiermacher (1768–1834) was born in Breslau in a family of pastors, as son of a chaplain of the Prussian army in 1768. During his years in the *Paedagogicum* of Niesky (Oberlausitz: 1783–85) and in the theological institute of Barby (1785–87), he underwent an education in the tradition of Herrnhut, before – dissatisfied by pietistic thinking – going to Halle (1787–90) mainly studying philosophy and becoming influenced by the philosophy of Kant. After his second examination in 1790 he became a teacher in the house of Graf Dohna in Schlobitten (Prussia: 1790–93). In 1794 he was appointed pastor in Landsberg (Brandenburg) and in 1796–1802 preacher at the famous Berlin hospital Charité. Schleiermacher accepted the call to an associate professorship of theology to Halle in 1804. In 1806 the troops of Napoleon conquered Halle and the university was closed. He returned to Berlin in 1807 where he became a member of the commission for founding the new Berlin university, professor of theology (together with, c.g., W. M. L. de Wette), and the first dean of the theological faculty. He also worked as Reformed pastor and preached regularly at the Trinity Church.

As professor in Halle and in Berlin he continuously lectured on New Testament subjects. His lectures on *Introduction to the New Testament* and his lecture on *The Life of Jesus* were published after his death in the series of his collected works. His understanding of the New Testament and its exegesis has also to be taken from his encyclopedic, systematic and philosophical writings (especially his remarks on canonical criticism or on the role of the Old Testament in Christian faith) and of course from his preaching activity. Schleiermacher is not only famous as a theologian and philosopher but also contributed as a philologist – well known is his contribution to research in Plato with his important German translation of Plato's work.

The meaning – far too often overlooked – of Schleiermacher for Jesus and Gospel studies originates from his contribution to Gospel criticism and from his lectures on the life of Jesus. Of course, his contribution to the theory of hermeneutics as being relevant for any historical study should also not be overlooked.

To start with his contribution on Gospel criticism, Schleiermacher presents himself as an original thinker even in this regard. He disagrees with current conceptions like the Urgospel Hypothesis or the Mutual-Dependence Theory, considering a relatively late date for written records that he places not before the end of the Jewish War. Transmission of the Jesus tradition was first mostly oral ("*Und so wurde viel Einzelnes erzählt und vernommen, das meiste wohl ohne aufgeschrieben zu werden*"; 1817: 9) but soon increasingly became written records. Luke took up collections of material, possibly arranged according to formal categories ("*so sammelte vielleicht wol der eine nur Wundergeschichten, der andere nur Reden, einem dritten waren vielleicht anschließend die lezten Tage Christi wichtig oder auch die Auftritte der Auferstehung*"; 1817: 13) that stem from eyewitnesses and which Schleiermacher called inspired (1817: 14) and combined into a – modern spoken – narrative *plot*. Extensive collections used by Luke are the travel narrative, Luke 9:51–19:48, and the Passion and resurrection story, which seemed to be identically transmitted because of its dignity. Before his death, Schleiermacher returned to his source theory and suggested that Papias' reference to the Gospel of the apostle Matthew (Eusebius, *Hist. eccl.* 3.39.15–16) refers to a collection of sayings of Jesus, not used by Luke (1845: 251), containing the five great speeches of Matthews' Gospel (1832: 738 ff.).

We can see that ideas of Schleiermacher reappear in later studies, e.g. the conceptions of miracle collections in Mark or John, which are rightly questioned in recent studies. The Papias-based assumption of a collection of sayings reappears in the model of the Two-Document Hypothesis with some modification. Still important is especially that Schleiermacher acknowledges the creative role of the gospel writers in structuring their material, an insight for which we may call him a forerunner of redaction criticism (cf., e.g., DeVries 1998: 353), although he coins Luke, like the later father of redaction criticism, a collector who formed his story by selecting *"ächte und gute Stükke"* (1817: 219–20).

Although Schleiermacher contributed to the question of synoptic source criticism, which was at its start mainly a concern to receive sources for a historically reliable reconstruction of the life of Jesus, he chooses the Gospel of John as the main source for the historical Jesus in his 1864 post-humously published lectures on the life of Jesus (*Das Leben Jesu*). According to his *Introduction into New Testament*, the portrait of Jesus in the Gospel of John is more authentic (1845: 315–16, 340); therefore the Gospel of John, written by an eyewitness, is prior to the Synoptics (1845: 219–21) and more reliable in its chronology and order than the other gospels. Although eyewitness tradition could be detected in all gospels, Luke is in relation to John of secondary importance. This is a decision made on theological reasoning, for the Jesus portrait in John is more in accordance with the theological and christological thinking of Schleier-macher (Lange 1975; Moretto 1981).

Schleiermacher himself clearly acknowledged that a complete bibliography of Jesus could not be written: "it is undeniable that we cannot achieve *a connected presentation of the life of Jesus.* We must limit our task in accordance with the material at our disposal" (English translation 1975: 43; 1864: 44). The main goal of his studies in Jesus is to show Jesus as an example for communicating a perfect God-consciousness to his contemporaries and to the later church. That message constitutes Jesus' dignity (1864: 283; English translation 1975: 265). With regard to that message one can say that for Schleiermacher "the Jesus of history and the Christ of faith are one and the same" (Baird 220).

As an important forerunner of modern herme-neutics (his self-portrait as pioneer of that dis-cipline ought to be criticized; cf., e.g., Nowak 200), Schleiermacher influenced most theories of herme-neutics from his time on. He did not write a book on text interpretation but he repeated his lectures in Halle and in Berlin. Like some of his major exegetical contributions, his lectures on hermeneutics were also published after his death by a disciple. It was his famous student Friedrich Lücke who prepared the first edition of Schleiermacher's hermeneutic, which appeared in 1838 (on the problems and meaning of this edition cf., e.g., Virmond; Christophersen 117–20), followed up by more recent editions and translations. New Testament interpretation is part of the general hermeneutics, which is *separated* by Schleiermacher into a *grammatical* (analyzing lan-guage and style within its historical context) and a technical one, later called *psychological* (under-standing the author's intention), which do not inter-act. The New Testament's hermeneutic is a historical approach but Schleiermacher concedes that New Testament writings are the most original presentation of Christian God-consciousness. Hermeneutic in his view is more an "art of understanding" ("*Kunst des Verstehens*") dealing with communication than a science, with its final aim of understanding a speech better than even the author himself does.

It cannot be denied that Schleiermacher's con-tribution to New Testament scholarship is an ori-ginal one and therefore still readable, although his assumptions and proposals will not find many supporters in recent scholarship. However, it is interesting to see that, for instance, the contribu-tion of the Johannine Gospel to the historical research in Jesus has in recent years been newly evaluated. Nevertheless, the historical information of John is limited and will never reach the impor-tance it received in Schleiermacher's reconstruction of the life of Jesus.

MICHAEL LABAHN

Further reading

Baird, William. *History of New Testament Research I: From Deism to Tübingen*, Minneapolis, MN: Fortress Press, 1992, pp. 208–20.
Christophersen, Alf. *Friedrich Lücke (1791–1855)*, Theolo-gische Bibliothek Töpelmann 94, Berlin and New York: W. de Gruyter, 1999.
DeVries, Dawn. *Jesus Christ in the Preaching of Calvin and Schleiermacher*, Columbia Series in Reformed Theology, Louisville, KY: Westminster John Knox Press, 1996.
—— "Schleiermacher, Friedrich Daniel Ernst," Donald K. McKim (ed.) *Major Biblical Interpreters*, Downers Grove, IL: InterVarsity Press, 1998, pp. 350–55.
Lange, Dietz. *Historischer Jesus oder mythischer Christus: Untersuchungen zu dem Gegensatz zwischen Friedrich Schleiermacher und David Friedrich Strauss*, Gütersloh: Gütersloher Verlagshaus Mohn, 1975.
Moretto, Giovanni. "Angezogen und belehrt von Gott. Der Johanneismus in Schleiermachers 'Reden über die Reli-gion'," *ThZ* 37 (1981) 267–91.
Nowak, Kurt. *Schleiermacher. Leben, Werk und Wirkung*, UTB 2215, second edition, Göttingen: Vandenhoeck & Ruprecht, 2002.

Schleiermacher, Friedrich Daniel Ernst. *Einleitung ins neue Testament*, mit einer Vorrede von Friedrich Lücke, ed. Georg Wolde, Friedrich Schleiermacher's literarischer Nachlaß 3 = Friedrich Schleiermacher's sämmtliche Werke, Abt. 1/8, Berlin: Reimer, 1845.
—— *Das Leben Jesu. Vorlesungen an der Universität zu Berlin im Jahr 1832*, ed. Karl August Rütenik, Friedrich Schleiermacher's literarischer Nachlaß 1 = Friedrich Schleiermacher's sämmtliche Werke, Abt. 1/6, Berlin: Reimer, 1864; ET: *The Life of Jesus*, ed. Jack C. Verheyden, Lives of Jesus Series, Philadelphia, PA: Fortress Press, 1975.
—— *Hermeneutik und Kritik*, ed. and introduced by Manfred Frank, stw 211, Frankfurt: Suhrkamp, 1977; ET: *Hermeneutics and Criticism and Other Texts*, ed. Andrew Bowie, Cambridge: Cambridge University Press, 1998.
—— *Exegetische Schriften*, Kritische Gesamtausgabe, I/8; Berlin and New York: de Gruyter, 2001, pp. 1–180 ("Ueber die Schriften des Lukas ein kritischer Versuch. Erster Theil," first printed: Berlin: Reimer, 1817); ET: *Luke: A Critical Study*, trans. with an Introduction by Connop Thirlwall, with further essays, emendations and other apparatus by Terrence N. Tice, Schleiermacher Studies and Translations 13, Lewistone: Edwin Mellen, 1993, pp. 229–54; ("Ueber die Zeugnisse des Papias von unsern beiden ersten Evangelien," first printed in: *Theologische Studien und Kritiken* 5 (1832) 735–68).
Schmithals, Walter. *Einleitung in die drei ersten Evangelien*, de Gruyter Lehrbuch; Berlin and New York: de Gruyter, 1985, pp. 67–72.
Verheyden, Jack Clyde. "Christology and Historical Knowing: A Study Based on the Thought of Friedrich Schleiermacher and the New Quest of the Historical Jesus," dissertation, Harvard University, 1968.
Virmond, Wolfgang. "Neue Textgrundlagen zu Schleiermachers früher Hermeneutik. Prolegomena zur kritischen Edition," in Kurt-Victor Selge (ed.) *Internationaler Schleiermacher-Kongreß Berlin 1984*, Berlin and New York: de Gruyter, 1985, pp. 575–90.
Weisweiler, Hilger. "Schleiermachers Arbeiten zum Neuen Testament," unpublished dissertation, Bonn, 1972.

SCHMIDT, KARL LUDWIG

As a contemporary of Rudolf Bultmann and Martin Dibelius, Karl Ludwig Schmidt (1891–1956) belonged to a group of three German scholars whose work profoundly re-shaped the discipline of New Testament studies in general – and historical Jesus scholarship in particular – during the early twentieth century. It was the triumvirate of Bultmann, Dibelius, and Schmidt that brought the method of *Formgeschichte* into the mainstream of NT scholarship, and Schmidt's form-critical analysis of the gospels has made a lasting contribution to our knowledge of both the gospels and the historical Jesus. Two books in particular have had ongoing significance: *Der Rahmen der Geschichte Jesu* (The Framework of the Story of Jesus), published in 1919, and *Die Stellung der Evangelien in der allgemeinen Literaturgeschichte* (The Place of the Gospels in the General History of Literature), published in 1923.

Der Rahmen der Geschichte Jesu is a long and detailed monograph, initially presented to the theological faculty at Berlin as Schmidt's *Habilitationschrift*. Schmidt completed the first draft while recuperating in a German military infirmary during World War I after being wounded in battle. He had lost the use of his right hand, so he wrote out the draft longhand using only his left hand. The finished work employs form-critical methods to demonstrate that the gospels provide no reliable chronology or itinerary for the public ministry of Jesus. Exhaustive analyses of every pericope in the Gospel of Mark, carefully comparing each one on a word-by-word basis with its parallels in Matthew and Luke, establish that the Markan outline is just that – Markan, a construct of the earliest Evangelist. In case after case Schmidt proves that the stories about Jesus in the Gospel of Mark originally circulated orally with little or no reference to specific locations or settings. These oral stories were then collected and arranged by Mark, and later re-arranged by Matthew and Luke. As a result, the written gospels contain few if any traces of the original historical settings of the stories. Since neither the oral tradition nor the earliest Evangelist had much interest in such details, "only the ruined rubble of an itinerary can be recovered" (*Der Rahmen*, vi). Schmidt does not necessarily doubt that particular stories have historical roots, but he was convinced that the places and times in which they originally occurred can no longer be known.

Today the best scholarly work on the historical Jesus continues to operate on this basis. The second volume alone of John Meier's *A Marginal Jew*, for example, refers to Karl Ludwig Schmidt and *Der Rahmen* some twenty times. Yet because the book has not yet been published in English translation, its thesis has occasionally been overlooked. This problem was unfortunately embodied in the short-lived suggestion, expressed by Paul Hollenbach and also by John Dominic Crossan, that Jesus made a break with John the Baptist over apocalyptic eschatology. This assertion was based on the argument that the sayings about John the Baptist in Matt 11:7b–9 par. and Matt 11:11 par. reflect (respectively) Jesus' earlier positive view and later negative view of the Baptist. Of course, Schmidt's work in *Der Rahmen* had conclusively established that it is not possible for us to know the original chronological order of those sayings. Since we cannot know which saying came first, there is no basis in those sayings for the argument that Jesus and John had a parting of the ways. If Jesus made a break with John the Baptist over apocalyptic eschatology, the evidence for that break will have to be found elsewhere.

Schmidt's second important contribution to historical Jesus scholarship was *Die Stellung der Evangelien in der allgemeinen Literaturgeschichte*, originally published in 1923 as an essay in *Eucharisterion*, a Festschrift for Hermann Gunkel. As such it naturally celebrates the value of the form-critical method, which Gunkel had previously pioneered in the study of the Hebrew Bible. Perhaps for that reason *Die Stellung* does not feature the kind of close reading and exhaustive detail which characterize *Der Rahmen*. Instead it is a brief and breezy discussion of the literary genre of the gospels, in which Schmidt argues that the gospels have no literary parallels in the ancient world. Among all the literature from antiquity, he maintains, only the gospels are the written detritus of an oral tradition, the sociological product of the cultic life of a worshiping community, rather than the creative output of specific individual authors. The gospels are, he asserts, *Kleinliteratur* ("low literature") rather than *Hochliteratur* ("high literature"). As a result, generic parallels to the gospels cannot be found anywhere else in antiquity, but only in *Kleinliteratur* from other places and times, such as the early Christian *Apophthegmata Patrum* and the medieval German folk legends of Doktor Faustus.

As an expression of basic form-critical insights, the argument in *Die Stellung* rapidly gained wide acceptance, and continued to hold sway through much of the twentieth century, for it supported a general consensus among scholars of the time that the genre of the gospels was "unique" or *sui generis*. It is important to note in this regard that Schmidt never asserted (as is often suggested) that the genre of the gospels was utterly unique, with no parallels of any sort at any time. He argued only that the gospels had no generic parallels in antiquity. Over time, however, even this more modest claim has come in for criticism. In particular, Schmidt's rather rigid distinction between *Hochliteratur* and *Kleinliteratur* has been increasingly challenged, and with it the notion that the genre of the gospels was *sui generis* in antiquity. With the rise of redaction criticism, for example, the Evangelists were granted more influence over the finished product of the gospels, and more recently, it has become clear that the gospels can indeed be situated along a continuum of ancient biographical writings (cf. Burridge). As literary study of the gospels has continued to advance, Schmidt's form-critical category of *Kleinliteratur*

has seemed less adequate. Today it is recognized that while the gospels do rise from the oral tradition of worshiping communities, that fact does not exclude the possibility of using types of literary analyses which Schmidt would have thought appropriate only for *Hochliteratur*.

BYRON R. McCANE

Further reading

Burridge, R. *What Is A Gospel?*, New York: Cambridge, 1992.
Schmidt, K. L. *The Place of the Gospels in the General History of Literature*, trans. B. R. McCane, Columbia, SC: University of South Carolina, 2002.

SCHWEITZER, ALBERT

For a century Schweitzer's *Quest of the Historical Jesus* (German, 1906; English, 1910) has enjoyed the reputation of being the definitive history of research into the historical Jesus. This impression was reinforced by the publication of "The First Complete Edition" (2001) – despite the fact that it went no further than the 1913 German edition. Schweitzer's work was unquestionably a *tour de force*, made all the more remarkable by the circumstances of its author's life.

Formative years

Albert Schweitzer (1875–1965) was the eldest son of the Lutheran pastor of Kaysersberg, Upper Alsace, which had been ceded to Germany as a result of the Franco-Prussian War. Schweitzer grew up bilingual, and entered the University of Strassburg at the age of eighteen, where he studied theology and philosophy – a choice that left its mark on Schweitzer's subsequent thinking. In 1898 he took the first theological examination, but then turned to philosophy. His treatise on *Die Religionsphilosophie Kants* (1899) earned him a doctorate in philosophy at the age of twenty-four. The work was written in Paris where he also studied organ technique under Charles-Marie Widor and Marie Jaëll-Trautmann, whose work on *Touch* Schweitzer anonymously translated into German. At Widor's instigation he wrote in French a book on Bach (1905), which he later translated and enlarged in German. The book and Schweitzer's organ performances helped to fund his education. In the meantime, regulations at the Bibliothèque Nationale proved so cumbersome that Schweitzer concentrated on the primary sources of Kant's *Critique of Pure Reason* and *Religion within the Limits of Reason Alone*. An outcome was that

Schweitzer detected fundamental inconsistencies in Kant's philosophy of religion not previously noticed.

While correcting the proofs for the published version of his dissertation, Schweitzer resolved to take his Licentiate (university teaching qualification) in theology. In 1899 he was appointed Preacher at the Church of Saint Nicholas in Strassburg. By this time Schweitzer had already formed the elements of his eschatological interpretation of Jesus and the kingdom of God. He dated his discovery from his military service in the autumn of 1894 when he took his Greek New Testament in his knapsack on maneuvers.

During the summer Schweitzer had studied the commentary of his teacher, H. J. Holtzmann, with its claims that Mark was the oldest gospel and a major source of Matthew and Luke. He now noted features of Matt 10 and 11 that challenged this view. In his mission charge Jesus warned his disciples that they would undergo persecution, but the Son of Man would appear before they had gone through all the towns of Israel (10:23). Jesus was astonished at their return alive! Dissatisfied with Holtzmann's explanation that the mission charge was not a historical discourse, Schweitzer came to the conclusion that the kingdom would be a supernatural kingdom, which would replace the present world-order. This conviction was reinforced by Jesus' pronouncement that among those born of women none was greater than John. Nevertheless, the least in the kingdom of heaven was greater than John, who was the Elijah who would precede the coming One (11:12–13).

In his examinations Schweitzer kept these ideas to himself, but became increasingly convinced that Jesus' mission charge held the key to problems posed by life of Jesus research. Schweitzer spent the summer of 1899 in Berlin, reading philosophy and hearing among others the lectures of Harnack. This encounter led to their life-long friendship. For his Licentiate Schweitzer wrote a two-part dissertation on *The Problem of the Lord's Supper according to the Scholarly Research of the Nineteenth Century and the Historical Accounts* (1901). Part 1 dealt with *The Lord's Supper in Relation to the Life of Jesus and the History of the Early Church*. Part 2, *The Mystery of the kingdom of God: The Secret of Jesus' Messiahship and Passion*, explored events leading to the Last Supper.

The key to understanding the Last Supper was a point that Schweitzer had come across in the thesis he wrote for his first theological examination – Schleiermacher's observation that in both Matthew and Mark there is no command to repeat the meal.

Jesus declared that he would never again drink of the fruit of the vine until he drank it new in the kingdom of God (Mark 14:25; Matt 26:29). Schleiermacher did not press the point, but Schweitzer took it as a pointer that Jesus' death would inaugurate the eschatological kingdom.

The secret of Jesus' messiahship and passion took up Schweitzer's earlier idea that Jesus did not expect the disciples to return from their mission. When they returned unscathed, Jesus realized that he himself was called to initiate the messianic woes by going to Jerusalem and giving his life as a ransom for many (Mark 10:45). Building on Johannes Weiss's *Jesus' Proclamation of the kingdom of God* (1892), Schweitzer proposed an "eschatological–historical" solution.

On the same day that the twenty-six-year-old Schweitzer's work was published, the renowned Breslau scholar William Wrede published his account of *The Messianic Secret*. Both titles contained the word *Geheimnis*. Schweitzer's translator took it to mean "mystery." In Wrede's work it meant a "secret" which was bound up with Jesus' injunctions not to tell anyone that he was the Messiah, for there was no evidence that Jesus claimed to be the Messiah. Apparent evidence to the contrary was the work of the Christian community who had come to see Jesus as the Messiah in light of their resurrection faith. The scholarly world's acceptance of Wrede's solution at the expense of Schweitzer's set the latter on a course of self-vindication in a work entitled *Von Reimarus zu Wrede. Eine Geschichte der Leben-Jesu-Forschung.* In English it is known as *The Quest of the Historical Jesus: A Critical History of its Progress from Reimarus to Wrede.*

The course of the quest

Schweitzer delivered his inaugural lecture on the Logos doctrine in 1902. The following year he became Principal of the Collegium Wilhelmitanum. With Holtzmann's approval, in the summer term of 1905 Schweitzer lectured two hours weekly on research into the life of Jesus. His great book appeared the following year. Thanks to Eduard Reuss and other Strassburg scholars, the University Library was uniquely well stocked with books on the subject, together with an almost complete collection of the controversial writings surrounding Strauss and Renan.

Schweitzer traced the origin of the quest to Hermann Samuel Reimarus (1694–1768) whom he declared to be a bolt from the blue without predecessors or successors, and was the first to grasp that the thought-world of Jesus was eschatological. In view of its neglect of eschatology, the subsequent movement of the quest down to Johannes Weiss appeared "retrograde." Reimarus taught oriental languages in Hamburg, and was well known in the German Enlightenment for his learned writings. Privately he composed an *Apology or Defense for the Rational Worshippers of God*, which (as its title suggested) was a vindication of Deism. During his stay in Hamburg the dramatist Gotthold Ephraïm Lessing (1729–81) became acquainted with the Reimarus family, and obtained a copy of the manuscript. Later as librarian to the Duke of Brunswick, Lessing published extracts entitled *Fragments of an Unnamed Author*, supposedly found in the library at Wolfenbüttel. A pamphlet war ensued, affording Lessing occasion to air his own views. The most formidable reply came from the pen of the founder of "liberal theology," Johann Salamo Semler.

Schweitzer focused on the seventh and last *Fragment* entitled *The Intentions of Jesus and His Disciples*. Jesus was a Jewish reformer who had no desire to found a new religion. "Son of God" simply meant "God's Beloved." Jesus' fatal mistake was to embrace political messianism. He had come to think that the kingdom of God could be established by his own death, but his dying words "My God, my God, why have you forsaken me?" attest his disillusionment. The resurrection (critiqued in an earlier *Fragment*) was a fraud put out by the disciples.

Schweitzer identified three decisive confrontations that determined the outcome of the quest. The first was the choice between a "purely historical" and a "purely supernatural" Jesus. The issue was raised by David Friedrich Strauss in his *Life of Jesus Critically Examined* (1835). Strauss had obtained his doctorate at Tübingen under F. C. Baur and came to Berlin with the hope of pursuing further study with Hegel. But the latter's premature death deprived him of the opportunity. Having read notes on Schleiermacher's lectures on the life of Jesus, Strauss determined to write his own account. He scorned orthodoxy and Schleiermacher's attempt to restate it in terms of Jesus' God-consciousness. He despised the rationalism of H. E. G. Paulus who sought natural explanations for the miracle stories. Strauss proposed that the gospel narratives were shaped by the myth-making tendency to make Jesus the miraculous fulfiller of the OT. Schweitzer concluded that from now on the "purely historical" approach to Jesus must exclude the supernatural.

The second confrontation was over the question whether to follow the Synoptic Gospels or John.

Schweitzer followed the Tübingen School and Holtzmann in rejecting John in favor of the Synoptics, though he regretted Holtzmann's attempt to interpret the kingdom idealistically. To Schweitzer, the victory of Markan priority belonged not to the hypothesis pure and simple but to the hypothesis "psychologically interpreted by liberal theology." Schweitzer followed Baur in preferring Matthew.

The third confrontation was whether Jesus was "eschatological" or "non-eschatological." Liberal theology had opted for the latter, depicting Jesus as a teacher of higher morality and the kingdom as the spread of God's ethical lordship. Typical was Ernest Renan's best-selling *Life of Jesus* (1863) which Schweitzer described as a work of "imperishable charm," written by an author who had to perfume the NT "with sentimentality in order to feel himself at home in it." The liberal interpretation was undermined by Johannes Weiss's *Jesus' Proclamation of the kingdom of God*, which argued that for Jesus the kingdom was never inward and spiritual, but was an objective messianic kingdom whose advent was imminent.

Schweitzer's *Quest* left readers with the final choice: either the "thoroughgoing skepticism" of Wrede or Schweitzer's "thoroughgoing eschatology" (*konsequente Eschatologie*). In Schweitzer's mind, his own version of eschatology was more thoroughgoing than Weiss's, in that eschatology was not only the key to Jesus' teaching but also the key to his determination to go to Jerusalem in order to initiate the messianic woes that would inaugurate the kingdom.

Schweitzer's Jesus

It is ironic that Schweitzer presented the final choice as one between Wrede's "thoroughgoing skepticism" and his own "thoroughgoing eschatology," for both were forms of skepticism. Eschatology was the key to understanding Jesus, but it had no objective reality. Jesus the "imperious ruler" had "overthrown the Modern Jesus," but titles like Messiah, Son of Man, Son of God are "merely historical parables." No designation expresses what Jesus is today. He had tried to move the wheel of the world, and when it finally moved it crushed him.

The wheel rolls onward, and the mangled body of the one immeasurably great Man, who was strong enough to think of Himself as the spiritual ruler of mankind and to bend history to His purpose, is hanging upon it still. That is His victory and His reign.

(*Quest*, 371)

Schweitzer's Jesus was (to borrow a phrase from Kant) *a Jesus within the limits of reason alone.* As B. H. Streeter observed in *Foundations* (1912), Schweitzer's Jesus was Nietzsche's *Übermensch,* the "superman" in Galilean garb who willed to revalue the values of his time. Schweitzer had long been an admirer of Nietzsche, who in turn admired men of genius and strong individuality who allowed the greatness in them to have free play. Schweitzer saw his own philosophy of reverence for life as a superior version of Nietzsche's. Heroic individualism embodied supremely in Jesus proved to be the beacon that guided Schweitzer's career.

While still working on the closing chapters of the *Quest* Schweitzer embarked on a plan dating from 1896. Up to the age of thirty he felt justified in living for science and art in order to devote himself from then on "to the direct service of humanity." He was impelled by Jesus' saying: "Whosoever would save his life shall lose it, and who shall lose his life for my sake and the gospel's shall save it." In October 1905 Schweitzer resigned his position in order to enter medical school at the beginning of the winter term. His State Medical Examination in 1911 was followed by a year's hospital internship and thesis for his doctorate. He chose as his topic *The Psychiatric Study of Jesus,* defending Jesus against charges of paranoia, delusions of grandeur, and fanaticism. Schweitzer was prepared to admit that the charges might fit the Johannine Jesus, but the Synoptic Jesus could not be blamed for holding eschatological ideas that belonged to the common stock of late Jewish belief. In any case no clinical diagnosis could be made at this point in time. In 1913 Schweitzer and his wife left for French Equatorial Africa where he built a hospital at Lambaréné, which was moved to a fresh site in 1925. Schweitzer continued to write extensively. He was awarded the Nobel Peace Prize in 1952.

Assessment

At Oxford William Sanday brought the attention of English readers to Schweitzer. Among them was F. C. Burkitt of Cambridge, who arranged for his student W. Montgomery to translate Schweitzer's work into English. In entitling the book *The Quest of the Historical Jesus* Montgomery's bravura translation gave a name to a discipline that Schweitzer had thought of as merely attempts to write the life of Jesus. Reception of Schweitzer's *Quest* remains mixed. In 1913 the leading British authority on eschatology, R. H. Charles, complained that Schweitzer had no knowledge of primary sources and a poor grasp of secondary literature. The charge is echoed by T. F. Glasson who contends that the term "the apocalyptic view" should be dropped as meaningless and confusing. Schweitzer's "messianic woes" appears to be a synthetic concept, which fused together ideas taken from different contexts. Though itself not free from difficulties, C. H. Dodd's "realized eschatology" showed the limitations of Schweitzer's view.

Schweitzer paid no attention to genre or sources. On the one hand, his reading of Matthew has the air of being virtually pre-critical. On the other hand, "thoroughgoing eschatology" consigns Jesus' moral teaching to the status of an *interim ethic,* valid until the inauguration of the kingdom.

From the standpoint of objective history, Schweitzer's work raises questions. Unsuspecting readers would not guess Reimarus's debt to the English Deists whose work was well known in France and Germany. Schweitzer's account was based almost exclusively on German and French writers. His work, like the old quest generally, was characterized by scant interest in Judaism and Jewish scholarship. After 1913 Schweitzer stopped updating the *Quest,* leaving it like an object frozen in time, oblivious to further developments. Perhaps these limitations are best explained by the book's organizing principle. It was a study in self-vindication, which in the interests of accuracy might be properly entitled, as Paul Wernle suggested, *From Reimarus to Schweitzer.*

COLIN BROWN

Further reading

Brown, Colin. *Jesus in European Protestant Thought, 1768–1860,* Durham, NC: Labyrinth Press, 1985.
Dawes, Gregory W. (ed.) *The Historical Jesus Quest: Landmarks in the Search for the Jesus of History,* Louisville, KY: Westminster John Knox Press, 2000.
Glasson, T. Francis. "Schweitzer's Influence – Blessing or Bane?," in Bruce Chilton (ed.) *The kingdom of God,* Philadelphia, PA: Fortress Press, 1984, pp. 107–20.
Perrin, Norman. *The kingdom of God in the Teaching of Jesus,* London: SCM Press, 1963.
Schröter, Jens and Ralph Brucker (eds) *Der historische Jesus. Tendenzen und Perspektiven der gegenwärtigen Forschung,* Berlin: Walter de Gruyter, 2002.
Schweitzer, Albert. *The Lord's Supper in Relationship to the Life of Jesus and the History of the Early Church,* ed. John Reumann, Macon, GA: Mercer University Press, 1982 [1901].
—— *The Mystery of the kingdom of God: The Secret of Jesus's Messiahship and Passion.* London: A. & C. Black, 1914 [1901].
—— *The Quest of the Historical Jesus: A Critical Study of its Progress from Reimarus to Wrede,* Introduction by James M. Robinson, New York: Macmillan, 1968 [1906; English, 1910]

—— *The Quest of the Historical Jesus: First Complete Edition*, ed. John Bowden, Minneapolis, MN: Fortress Press, 2001 [1913].

—— *The Psychiatric Study of Jesus: Exposition and Criticism*, Boston, MA: Beacon Press, 1948 [1913].

—— *My Life and Thought*, London: A. & C. Black, 1933 [1931].

—— *The kingdom of God and Primitive Christianity*, London: A. & C. Black, 1968 [1967].

Theissen, Gerd and Dagmar Winter. *The Quest for the Plausible Jesus: The Question of Criteria*, Louisville, KY: Westminster John Knox Press, 2002 [1997].

Weaver, Walter P. *The Historical Jesus in the Twentieth Century, 1900–1950*, Harrisburg, PA: Trinity Press International, 1999.

Willis, Wendell (ed.) *The kingdom of God in 20th-Century Interpretation*, Peabody, MA: Hendrickson, 1987.

SCRIBES

The term "scribe" in a NT context generally makes one think of the "scribes and Pharisees" in the gospels. In fact, the scribe was a ubiquitous profession in the ancient world where ability to write with facility was possessed by only a relatively small portion of the population. The word "scribe" (*grammateus*) is widely used in Greek literature to mean "secretary, recorder, clerk" and those of similar function which involved writing, often in the context of a civic or public office. A parallel usage is found in Jewish literature. As ones with the skills to read and write, and trained in record keeping and document drafting, scribes were essential in society and the backbone of administration. We find references to scribes in many documents from the ancient Near East. Many references to scribes are found in the Hebrew Bible, such as David's scribes (2 Sam 8:17; 20:25); Solomon's scribe (1 Kgs 4:3); Shebna the scribe (2 Kgs 18:18, 37; 19:2); Shaphan the scribe (2 Kgs 22:3, 8–10, 12; 2 Chr 34:15, 18, 20). The book of Jeremiah speaks of the chamber of Gemariah son of Shaphan the scribe in the temple (36:10) and Elishama the scribe (36:12, 20, 21). Baruch the scribe plays a prominent role in the book.

Thus, when we think of a scribe in the ancient world, we would first think of the person whose duties had to do with record keeping, drafting of documents, and writing in a professional capacity. The main employers of scribes would have been the provincial administration and the temple (Grabbe 152–71). Scribes would have worked at various levels, however, all the way from high up in the administration where they advised and supported the governor and the main offices of the provincial administration, to posts in the treasury where records of payments and even lists of taxpayers were kept, to storage warehouses for taxes and tithes where they kept inventory of incoming produce and dispersals for approved purposes. We also know about temple scribes. For example, they are referred to in the decree of Antiochus III about 200 BCE (*Ant.* 12.3.3:142). The temple scribes would have had similar record-keeping duties, but in addition they would have had the responsibility of copying any sacred writings, manuals, instruction books, lists of regulations, priestly genealogies, and the like relating to the temple administration. Some scribes were quite powerful with a high office whereas others had rather mundane duties.

Occasionally, however, we find hints that the term could also be used of someone learned in the divine law and looked up to as an interpreter of scripture. Perhaps the most famous passage on the scribe is that of Ben Sira (38:24–39:11) in which he associates the scribe with studying the law of God. It is not clear, however, that Ben Sira was suggesting that everyone with scribal training was to be an expert in the Law. He has no doubt given us an idealized image; however, Ben Sira's close association with the Temple should be kept in mind. The use of the term "scribe" in Jewish literature after the time of Ben Sira follows basically the usage already outlined: normally, "scribe" refers to a professional: someone trained to write, copy, keep accounts, and otherwise carry out the functions we now associate with being a clerk or secretary. It is primarily from the NT that the issue of a religious entity called "the scribes" arises. In some NT texts "scribe" seems to have almost a sectarian meaning, as if "the scribes" were a religious group alongside the Sadducees, Pharisees and others. Thus, Mark 7:1–23 mentions both Pharisees and scribes together, as do Matthew 12:38, 23:2 and Luke 5:21. Is this a new and different identity for the "scribes"? Is there now a religious sect known as "the scribes"? The answer is not an easy one and needs to take into account recent study of the gospel writers, their knowledge and intent.

Several recent attempts at investigating the question have been made, with rather different conclusions (cf. Cook 71–73). Some seem to identify the scribes with the Pharisees; however, Josephus never associates the two. D. R. Schwartz (89–101) has noted that since the temple personnel were often drawn on for their scribal skills, the "scribes" of the gospels may in many cases be Levites. The key may lie in passages that some scholars have dismissed as secondary. The most likely reading of Mark 2:16 is "scribes of the Pharisees", which suggests that scribes were not a separate party but certain professionals among them. Acts 23:9 likewise speaks of "scribes of the

Pharisees' party". According to this explanation the term "scribe" applies to all those learned in the Law.

Scribes as such seem to be referred to in the pre-Markan tradition and in Q. If this is historical, it suggests that they were not to be identified with the Pharisees but constituted those learned in the Torah, regardless of their sectarian affiliation. This suggests that other parties (e.g. the Sadducees) also had their own scribes, perhaps individuals with special expertise in the law or legal interpretations of the sect in question. If so, this usage would be in line with that of Ben Sira in which the "ideal" of the scribe is not only one with professional knowledge and skills but also knowledge and understanding of God's law. Also, this explanation need not contradict D. R. Schwartz's argument, since some of the Levites may well have belonged to various of the sects extant at the time.

LESTER L. GRABBE

Further reading

Cook, M. J. *Mark's Treatment of the Jewish Leaders*, NovTSup 51, Leiden: Brill, 1978.

Grabbe, Lester L. *Priests, Prophets, Diviners, Sages: A Socio-historical Study of Religious Specialists in Ancient Israel*, Valley Forge, PA: Trinity Press International, 1995, ch. 6.

Schams, Christine. *Jewish Scribes in the Second-Temple Period*, JSOTSup 291, Sheffield: Sheffield Academic Press, 1998.

Schwartz, Daniel R. *Studies in the Jewish Background of Christianity*, WUNT 60, Tübingen: Mohr Siebeck, 1992.

SCRIPTURE IN TEACHING AND ACTIVITIES OF JESUS

According to the Synoptic Gospels (France 259–63), Jesus quotes or alludes to twenty-three of the thirty-six books of the Hebrew Bible (counting the books of Samuel, Kings, and Chronicles as three books, not six). Jesus alludes to or quotes all five books of Moses, the three major prophets (Isaiah, Jeremiah, and Ezekiel), eight of twelve minor prophets (i.e. Hosea, Joel, Amos, Jonah, Micah, Zephaniah, Zechariah, and Malachi), and five of the "writings" (i.e. Psalms, Proverbs, Job, Daniel, and Chronicles). In other words, Jesus quotes or alludes to *all* of the books of the Law, *most* of the Prophets, and *some* of the Writings. Superficially, then, the "canon" of Jesus is pretty much what it was for most religiously observant Jews of his time (Evans 2002).

Jesus appears to have been guided by scriptural traditions at important junctures in his teaching and activities (Chilton and Evans). These scriptures and how Jesus understood them must be taken into account, if Jesus himself is to be understood. Some of the most important of these include the following:

Proclamation of the kingdom (or rule) of God

At the very heart of Jesus' teaching was his proclamation of the kingdom (or rule) of God: "The time is fulfilled, and the kingdom of God is at hand; repent, and believe in the gospel" (Mark 1:15). In proclaiming the gospel or good news (*euaggelion*) of the rule of God (*basileia tou theou*) Jesus has alluded to the good news of the coming reign of God promised in the prophet Isaiah, especially as it was interpreted in the Aramaic tradition: "You who proclaim good news [*mbesoriyn*] to Jerusalem ... say ... 'The kingdom of your God [*malkuta' delohekon*] is revealed!'" (*Tg. Isa.* 40:9; cf. 52:7; 61:1–2; Chilton).

The importance of Isaiah for Jesus is seen in a number of places, including his Nazareth sermon (Luke 4:16–30) and his reply to the imprisoned John the Baptist (Matt 11:2–6; Luke 7:19–23). Jesus' interest in Isaiah is shared with his colleague John the Baptist, with whom Isa 40:3 ("In the wilderness prepare the way of the Lord") was associated.

Appointment of the Twelve

Jesus' interest in Isaiah and the good news of Israel's redemption is seen his appointment of twelve Apostles (i.e. those who are "sent out" as ambassadors or messengers). Part of the inspiration for the creation of the Twelve likely derived from Isa 61:1–2, which proclaims the anointing of God's messenger (or prophet, according to the Aramaic version), who has been "sent" to proclaim the good news to the oppressed. Jesus' reply to the imprisoned John alludes to this very passage: "Go and tell John what you hear and see: the blind receive their sight and the lame walk, lepers are cleansed and the deaf hear, and the dead are raised up, and the poor have good news preached to them" (Matt 11:4–5).

Self-understanding as the Son of Man

Several times Jesus refers to himself as the "Son of Man" (e.g. Mark 2:10, 28; 8:31; 9:9; 10:45; 14:62). These sayings form a typological unity founded upon Daniel 7 (and not *1 Enoch* 37–71 and *4 Ezra* 13, as is often assumed). It must be insisted that they do indeed derive from Jesus. There is little evidence that these sayings or the idiom "son of man" were of special interest to the early church, which preferred to speak of Jesus as Lord and Son of God. Hence the likelihood that they derive from Jesus.

Jesus probably saw himself as the fulfillment of the prophesied "son of man" of Daniel 7, who stands before God and with the saints, and, after initial opposition and defeat, overcomes and receives the promised kingdom. Jesus' sayings about rejection, suffering, and death (Mark 8:31; 9:31; 10:33; 14:21) reflect the first aspect (an aspect enriched by allusions to the Suffering Servant of Isaiah 53), while the sayings that speak of vindication (Mark 9:9; 13:26; 14:62) reflect the second. (More on the Passion sayings below.)

Jesus' combination of Dan 7:13–14 with Ps 110:1 ("Sit at my right hand") affirms both his divine authority and his royal status, at which he had hinted in the temple precincts (Mark 12:35–37: "How can the scribes say that the Christ is the son of David?"). The combination of these texts is accommodated by their shared language and imagery, in which thrones are envisioned and in which judgment upon God's enemies takes place. The negative reaction of the ruling priests and council should hardly occasion surprise.

Entry into Jerusalem

Jesus' entry into Jerusalem, mounted on a donkey, was a deliberate enactment of Zech 9:9 (cf. Mark 11:1–8), which may or may not have been recognized by the Markan Evangelist (though it certainly was by the Matthean and Johannine Evangelists). The prophecy of Zechariah comes into play elsewhere in the teachings and events of Passion Week (e.g. Zech 14:20–21 in Mark 1:16 and Zech 13:7 in Mark 14:27). At the time of the entrance the followers of Jesus allude to words and phrases from Pslm 118: "Hosanna! Blessed is he who comes in the name of the Lord! Blessed is the kingdom of our father David that is coming! Hosanna in the highest!" (Mark 11:9–10; cf. Ps 118:25–26). The appearance of the name David in this context once again betrays acquaintance with the Aramaic paraphrase of scripture, in which the story of David's selection by Samuel the priest as Israel's new king is blended with the pilgrim's greeting of Ps 118:19–27. Accordingly, Jesus concludes his juridical parable of the Wicked Vineyard Tenants with a citation of Ps 118:22–23 (Mark 12:1–11), which in the Aramaic speaks of David as Israel's worth king and ruler.

Action in the temple precincts

Jesus demonstrates in the temple precincts by disrupting the commercial trafficking in animals and monetary exchange (Mark 11:15–18 and parallels). In doing so he appeals to Isa 56:7 and Jer 7:11: "Is it not written, 'My house shall be called a house of prayer for all the nations'? But you have made it a den of robbers" (Mark 11:17). The words from Isaiah 56 are part of an oracle (Isa 56:1–8) that envisions a time when all the nations will seek the God of Israel at the Temple in Jerusalem. This oracle is itself related in some way to King Solomon's prayer of dedication of the Temple (cf. 1 Kgs 8:40–43). Not only has Jesus implied that under the leadership of the ruling priests the Temple has not fulfilled this glorious destiny, he also declares that it has become "a den of robbers." Here Jesus has quoted a phrase from Jer 7:11, part of a lengthy criticism of the Jerusalem temple establishment in the time of Jeremiah the prophet. Because of the nation's sin, particularly with reference to the corruption and injustice on the part of the political and religious leaders, Jeremiah foretold coming judgment. Jesus' allusion to this portion of prophetic scripture would have been very offensive to the aristocratic priesthood and would have been viewed as a threat (cf. Mark 14:58).

Passion predictions and related sayings

Although it has been fashionable to assign the Passion predictions (e.g. Mark 8:31; 9:31; 10:32–34) to the post-Easter Christian community, ongoing research has led many to conclude that Jesus himself spoke of his impending suffering (Bayer; Evans 1999). Jesus' sorrowful prayer in Gethsemane, where he begs God to take away the cup of suffering (Mark 14:34–36) is not the stuff of pious imagination, for this story stands in tension with the portrait of the assured Jesus, who moves forward in the knowledge and power of God. Jesus' prediction that he will be raised up "on the third day" (or "after three days") is almost certainly based on Hos 6:2 (Jer 1971: 226–29), though again as the scripture is interpretively paraphrased in the Aramaic: "*on the day of the resurrection of the dead he will raise us up*" (with the Aramaic innovations presented in italics). Jesus' teaching regarding his death develops further in the words of institution.

Words of institution

On the occasion of what would turn out to be his final meal with his disciples, Jesus commented in reference to the bread he distributed: "Take; this is my body" (Mark 14:22). He then distributed a cup of wine and said: "This is my blood of the covenant, which is poured out for many. Truly, I say to you, I shall not drink again of the fruit of the vine until that day when I drink it new in the kingdom of God" (Mark 14:24–25). Although it is disputed, it seems likely that Jesus has alluded to Exod 24:8, where Moses throws sacrificial blood on the people and says, "Behold the blood of the covenant"; Isa 53:12, where the Servant of the Lord pours out his soul to death; Jer 31:31, where God says through his prophet, "I will make a new covenant"; and Zech 9:11, where God says through another prophet, "Because of the blood of my covenant with you, I will set your captives free" (see Meyer).

The words of institution, viewed in the light of the scriptures just cited and in the light of martyrdom traditions (as in 2 Macc 6–7; Ps-Philo, *Bib. Ant.* 18:5; *T. Mos.* 9:6–10:1), indicate that Jesus understood his death as benefiting the people of God. Pouring out his blood, brought to mind by the blood-red color of the wine, would be the equivalent of the shedding of the blood that initiated the original covenant at Sinai, on the one hand, and the fulfillment of the promise of the new covenant declared in Jeremiah 31, on the other. Accordingly, the sacrificial interpretation of Jesus' death originated with Jesus himself (Bayer 29–53).

CRAIG A. EVANS

Further reading

Bayer, H. F. *Jesus' Predictions of Vindication and Resurrection: The Provenance, Meaning and Correlation of the Synoptic Predictions*, WUNT 2/20, Tübingen: Mohr Siebeck, 1986.

Chilton, B. D. *God in Strength: Jesus' Announcement of the Kingdom*, SNTU 1, Freistadt: Plöchl, 1979; repr. BibSem 8; Sheffield: JSOT Press, 1987.

Chilton, B. D. and C. A. Evans. "Jesus and Israel's Scriptures," in C. A. Evans and B. D. Chilton (eds) *Studying the Historical Jesus: Evaluations of the State of Current Research*, NTTS 19, Leiden: Brill, 1994, pp. 281–335.

Evans, C. A. "Did Jesus Predict His Death and Resurrection?," in S. E. Porter, M. A. Hayes, and D. Tombs (eds) *Resurrection*, JSNTSup 186, RILP 5, Sheffield: Sheffield Academic Press, 1999, pp. 82–97.

—— "The Scriptures of Jesus and His Earliest Followers," in L. M. McDonald and J. A. Sanders (eds) *The Canon Debate*, Peabody, MA: Hendrickson, 2002, pp. 185–95.

France, R. T. *Jesus and the Old Testament*, London: Tyndale, 1971.

Jeremias, J. "Die Drei-Tage-Worte der Evangelium," in G. Jeremias, H.-W. Kuhn, and H. Stegemann (eds) *Tradition und Glaube: Das frühe Christentum in seiner Umwelt*, Göttingen: Vandenhoeck & Ruprecht, 1971, pp. 221–29.

McKnight, S. "Jesus and Prophetic Actions," *BBR* 10 (2000) 197–232.

Meyer, B. F. "The Expiation Motif in the Eucharistic Words: A Key to the History of Jesus?," *Greg* 69 (1988) 461–87.

Moo, D. J. *The Old Testament in the Gospel Passion Narratives*, Sheffield: Almond Press, 1983.

SEA OF GALILEE

The Sea of Galilee and its surroundings

The Sea of Galilee is a small freshwater inland lake, 13 miles long (north to south) and 7.5 miles wide (21 by 12 kilometers). Today it serves as a main water reservoir for the State of Israel. The lake is a remnant of an ancient and much larger body of water that once filled the entire Jordan Valley termed the Lisan Lake. It receded, leaving the Jordan river system with the Hula swamps in the north, the Sea of Galilee and the Dead Sea in the south.

Throughout history the lake has been named after the largest cities on its shores, or after the most important geographical regions adjacent to it. In modern Hebrew it is still known by its most ancient name, *Kinneret* or *Yam Kinneret* (Sea of Kinneret), after the large Early Bronze–Iron Age site of Tell Kinnarot on its northwest shore. When this site was destroyed in 732 BCE by the Assyrian king Tiglat Pileser III, the lake became known as the Sea of Ginosar or Gennesaret (Luke 5:1; Josephus, *J.W.* 3:515) after the city and the valley of Ginosar. Following the founding of the city of Tiberias in 20 CE the lake also became known as the Sea of Tiberias (John 6:1; 21:1). The gospels prefer the name "Sea of Galilee" (Matt 4:18; 15:29; Mark 1:16; 7:31; John 6:1), which refers to the lake's proximity to the region of Galilee in northern Israel. The English name has retained the term "sea" rather than "lake" due to ancient Hebrew not differentiating between the two.

Many myths and legends grew up regarding the lake. The earliest of these may be the epic of Aqhat, discovered at Ugarit in Syria. An existent copy dates to the fourteenth century BCE. but the story itself may be much older.

The lake's economic importance derived first from the abundance of fish in its rich waters, which constituted an important source of protein, and, second, from its position as a vital nautical transport hub between the Galilee, the Golan Heights and the Jordan Valley.

After leaving Nazareth, Jesus moved to Capernaum on the Sea of Galilee's northwest coast, possibly residing in the home of Simon Peter (Matt 4:13; 8:14–16; Mark 2:1). Thus, Jesus' ministry took place for the most part around the lake.

In Jesus' time, Jewish settlements surrounded the lake except on its southeastern flank. There the pagan cities of Hippos (Susita) and Gadara (Gader) bordered its shore. It is not surprising, therefore, that Jesus and his disciples interacted in this region with swineherds with their droves of pigs, which would have been anathema in the Jewish areas (Matt 8:29–31; Mark 5:10–12).

Boats, fishing and seafaring on the Sea of Galilee play an important part in the gospels. Jesus chose his first disciples from among Galilean fishermen, making them "fishers of men" (Matt 4:19; Mark 1:17; Luke 5:10). At times Jesus spoke to groups from boats (Matt 13:1–3; Mark 3:9; 4:1). In one parable he compared heaven to a seine (*segena*) net (Matt 13:47–50), an association easily understood by the audiences from the local fishing communities who had come to hear him. Several miracles relate to fishing (Matt 17:24–27; Luke 5:1–11) and the gospels identify two specific vessels as belonging to Zebedee and Simon Peter (Mark 1:20; Luke 5:3). The fishing techniques described in the gospels continued in use on the lake till the mid-twentieth century.

Clearly an understanding of the lake's geography, seafaring and fishing can contribute significantly to a better comprehension of the gospel accounts.

The Galilee Boat (aka Kinneret Boat or "Jesus Boat")

When a drought caused the lake's water level to plummet in 1986, two brothers from Kibbutz Ginosar, Moshe and Yuval Lufan, discovered the outline of a boat buried in the lakebed that had been revealed by the receding waters. The Israel Department of Antiquities and Museums (IDAM, now the Israel Antiquities Authority, or IAA) received notification of the discovery and immediately carried out a limited probe excavation. This revealed a well-preserved hull and two artifacts – a cooking pot (casserole) and an oil lamp – both dating to the end of the first century BCE or the early first century CE.

Upon its discovery the boat became the focus of intense media attention, which raised concerns for the vessel's safety. This forced IDAM to immediately launch a full-scale excavation. At its conclusion the boat was packaged in a protective cocoon of fiberglass and polyurethane, floated out on the lake and successfully moved to the nearby Yigal Allon Museum at Kibbutz Ginosar. There it underwent extensive conservation, which was completed in 1995. The vessel is now exhibited in a specially designed hall dedicated to it in the museum.

The hull reveals a remarkable view of life on the lake during the time of Jesus. The boat is preserved to a length of 26.9 feet, a breadth of 7.5 feet and a height of 3.9 feet (8.2 by 2.3 by 1.2 meters). Although both the stem construction and the sternpost had been removed in antiquity, sufficient evidence survived to determine that the hull originally had a cutwater bow and a recurving stern, similar to the Migdal boat mosaic (see below).

Although iron nails (0.4 percent carbon content, equivalent to modern 1040 steel) held the frames to the planking and in some cases to the keel, the hull had been built in the ancient shell-based technique in which planks are edge-joined with pegged mortise-and-tenon joinery. In this construction technique the hull is built up by attaching the planks to the keel, the stem and sternposts and to each other, thus creating a shell before the frames are inserted. The planking, then, defines the strength and shape of the hull and the frames serve a secondary purpose. This form of ship construction has been used in the eastern Mediterranean at least since the fourteenth century BCE and was only gradually phased out during a lengthy period covering the latter part of the Roman and the beginning of the Byzantine periods. By the fifth century CE Mediterranean shipwrights had begun to build vessels in frame-base construction in which the keel, stempost and sternpost are first laid, and frames are then attached to them forming a skeleton to which the planking is fastened. Clearly, the Galilee Boat's builder learned his craft on the Mediterranean coast or had apprenticed under someone who had.

The boat is largely constructed of recycled timbers, which in at least some cases had been reused from older vessels. All the boat's timbers have been studied and their taxonomy identified. Most of the planks are Lebanese cedar (*Cedrus*), the sole timber used in the boat's construction that is not available locally: the majority of the frames are oak (*Quercus*). However, a total of twelve different types of timber used in the vessel's construction and repairs included the following: Allepo pine (*Pinus halepensis*), Atlantic Terebinth (*Pistachia atlantica*), Carob (*Ceratonia siliqua*), Christ thorn/Sidder (*Ziziphus spina-christi*), Hawthorn (*Crataegus*), Laurel (*Laurus*), Plane (*Platanus*), Redbud (*Cercis siliquastrum*), Sycamore (*Ficus Sycomorus*), and Willow (*Salix*). This hodge-podge of genera was not used for specific purposes: rather, it appears that the boat was built and repaired with any timbers that came to hand. Even the keel was made of three parts, each from a different type of wood. Some of the frames are little more than rough branches that still retain their bark and align poorly to the planking.

The wretched quality of many of the boat's timbers would have precluded their use on a contemporaneous Mediterranean vessel. One of the timbers comprising the keel has a row of mortise-and-tenon scars from use in a previous hull. The multiplicity of wood types evident in the hull, along with the evidence for the recycling of wood, indicates that either a situation of wood starvation existed, or that the boat's owner could not afford better timber for his vessel. Of the two possibilities, the latter is to be preferred as Josephus describes the Valley of Ginosar as being particularly rich and fertile (*J.W.* 3:516–18). Considering that a boat owner could employ men to crew his boat (Mark 1:20), he cannot be considered to be at the bottom of the economic pyramid of his day. This aspect of the boat alone speaks volumes about the pecuniary difficulties of the times recorded both in the gospels and by Josephus.

The boat could have moved under sail or oar and its size suggests a crew of five – four oarsmen and a helmsman/captain. This class is mirrored in an image of a boat (or a model of a boat?) in a first-century CE mosaic from nearby Migdal. The vessel faces left, carries two oars and a quarter rudder on its port side.

Although it is not possible to connect this hull with any specific persons or events, based on crew sizes one can demonstrate that the Galilee Boat is representative of the *class* of vessel used by Jesus' followers. Thus, when Jesus met James and John on the shores of the Sea of Galilee they were in the boat with their father and "the hired men" (Mark 1:20). Zebedee's boat, then, would have required a crew of at least five. And when, following the crucifixion, Simon Peter went fishing in his boat, he took with him six others, making a seven-man crew (John 21:2–3): when fishing, more men were required than just the basic crew. Similarly, when Josephus put together a sham war fleet at Migdal to prevent the city of Tiberias from going over to the Romans during the early part of the Jewish War, he placed crews of four rowers and a captain in each of the vessels (*Life* 163; *J.W.* 2:635, 641).

It is likely that, along with this large-size fishing vessel, a class of smaller vessels also existed contemporaneously with it on the lake. Evidence for this smaller type of boat is limited to Josephus' reported escape from a rabble of enraged citizens of Tiberias with only two bodyguards in a boat (*Life* 96; *J.W.* 2:619). Such a getaway would have

been difficult in a vessel the size of the Galilee Boat.

Christian art cherishes scenes of Jesus sailing with the twelve apostles but in the gospels he is recorded as being with his disciples rather than his apostles. As the persons participating in the voyages are not named specifically, and as Jesus had many more disciples than apostles (Acts 1:15), it is impossible to know how many persons actually took part in the recorded voyages. Josephus, however, in describing his sham fleet that he raised against Tiberias, indicates that this large-size boat could have held at least fifteen men (*Life* 164, 168; *J.W.* 2:639).

During its work life the boat would have served primarily for fishing, probably with the seine net for which it was best suited. The boat's owner could have added to his meager income by transporting people and supplies around the lake.

The Galilee Boat is similar in size to a class of fishing boat that existed on the lake into the twentieth century: the *arabiyeh* boat was designed for use with the seine net (*jarf* in Arabic) and had a large stern deck to facilitate the handling and spreading of this large and heavy net.

The evidence indicates that the boat ended its days in a boatyard on the outskirts of Migdal. Apparently after many years of service and after many repairs, the owner brought his weakened boat to the boatyard where it was stripped of all reusable timbers, including the stem assembly, the sternpost, the mast step and several of the frames.

The construction techniques exhibited by the hull, ceramics found in and around the boat and a series of radiocarbon tests carried out on the boat's timbers all indicate that the vessel saw service sometime in the first centuries BCE or CE, but probably was deposited prior to the destruction of Migdal by the Romans in 67 CE.

Battle of Migdal (*J.W.* 3:443–505, 522–42)

In reconquering the settlements surrounding the Sea of Galilee at the outset of the Jewish War in 67 CE, Vespasian first took the city of Tiberias, which surrendered without a fight. Jeshua ben Shaphat, the local leader of rebel forces in the city, escaped to Migdal, from where he led a waterborne commando assault on the legionary encampment located between the two cities. His men succeeded in destroying part of the Roman protective wall. When discovered, the Jews retreated in an orderly fashion to their boats and, anchoring them within bowshot from the shore, assailed the Roman defenders with arrows.

Soon Roman cavalry under Titus invested Migdal by swimming their horses around the fortifications that protected the city on its landside but not on its lakeside. As the Romans took the city, some of its defenders escaped in a fleet of boats. The next day Vespasian ordered vessels constructed for the pursuit of the refugees in the lake. Josephus terms Vespasian's craft *schedia* in Greek, a term that usually is translated as "rafts." From Josephus' description of the battle it is clear that these *sxedia* were not simple rafts, however. A more likely explanation is that Josephus is describing hastily built catamarans constructed from pairs of vessels like the Galilee Boat coupled by simple fighting platforms.

With these vessels ready, legionnaires and auxiliary archers embarked on them. The battle was lopsided and the Romans routed the Jews, forcing the remaining boats to shore where land-based soldiers awaited to kill those who tried to escape ashore. Josephus relates that in the aftermath of the battle the water was crimson with blood and the wrecks of boats and dead bodies crammed the shore.

A pyramidal iron arrowhead found inside the Galilee Boat is similar to fourteen arrowheads found at Gamla, which was the next city to be destroyed by Vespasian after Migdal. It is, therefore, likely that the arrowhead derives from the Battle of Migdal. This does not, however, indicate that this specific boat was involved in the conflict, as the arrowhead could have drifted into the vessel long after the latter had been deposited on the lakebed.

Other evidence for seafaring on the lake

Archaeology supplies additional information on maritime activity on the lake in antiquity. Numerous ancient stone anchors and net weights have been found in and around the lake. More enigmatic are *shfifons:* these are pierced stone monoliths, found mainly in the regions surrounding the southern half of the lake. These artifacts, which date to the Early Bronze Age, seem to represent stone anchors but are too large for actual use and were usually left unfinished at their lower extremity, indicating that they are designed to be partially buried.

During the time of Jesus the fishing settlements surrounding the lake had harbors. These follow a basic plan: a breakwater encloses a relatively small area, protecting it from wind and waves while a promenade on shore allows access to it. The harbors vary considerably based both on local meteorological conditions and on the fiscal capabilities of each settlement.

SHELLEY WACHSMANN

Further reading

Cohen, O. "Conservation of the Ancient Boat from the Sea of Galilee," *Atiqot* 50 (2005) 219–32.
Margalit, B. "Studia Ugaritica: II. Studies in *Krt* and *Aqht*," *Ugarit-Forschungen* 8 (1976) 137–92.
—— "The Geographical Setting of the AQHT Story and Its Ramifications," in G. D. Young (ed.) *Ugarit in Retrospect: Fifty Years of Ugarit and Ugaritic*, Winona Lake, IN: Eisenbrauns, 1981, pp. 131–58.
Nun, M. *The Sea of Galilee and its Fishermen in the New Testament*, Ein Gev: Kibbutz Ein Gev Tourist Department and the Kinnereth Sailing Co., 1989.
—— *Sea of Galilee: Newly Discovered Harbours From New Testament Days*, third revised edition, Ein Gev: Kibbutz Ein Gev Tourist Department and the Kinnereth Sailing Co., 1992.
—— *Ancient Stone Anchors and Net Sinkers from the Sea of Galilee*, Ein Gev: Kibbutz Ein Gev Tourist Department and the Kinnereth Sailing Co., 1993.
—— "Cast Your Net Upon the Waters: Fish and Fishermen in Jesus' Time," *BAR* 19:6 (1993) 46–56, 70.
Pitard, W. T. "The Reading of *KTU* 1.19: III:41: The Burial of Aqhat," *BASOR* 293 (1994) 31–38.
Rainey, A. F. and R. S. Notley. *The Sacred Bridge: Carta's Atlas of the Biblical World*, Jerusalem: Carta, 2006, pp. 351–60.
Reich, R. "A Note on the Roman Mosaic at Magdala on the Sea of Galilee," *Liber Annuus* 41 (1991) 455–58.
Wachsmann, S. "The Galilee Boat: 2,000-Year-Old Hull Recovered Intact," *BAR* 14:5 (1987) 95–103.
—— (ed.) *The Excavations of an Ancient Boat from the Sea of Galilee (Lake Kinneret)*, 'Atiqot 19, Jerusalem: Israel Antiquities Authority, 1990.
—— *The Sea of Galilee Boat: An Extraordinary 2000 Year Old Discovery*, New York: Plenum Press. 1995. (Reprinted in 2000 under the title *The Sea of Galilee Boat: A 2000 Year Old Discovery from the Sea of Legends*, Cambridge: Perseus Publishing.)
—— *Seagoing Ships and Seamanship in the Bronze Age Levant*, College Station and London, Texas A. & M. University Press and Chatham Press, 1998, pp. 262–65, 270–71.
Werker, E. "Identification of the Wood in the Ancient Boat from the Sea of Galilee," *Atiqot* 50, (2005) 233–36.

SERMON ON THE MOUNT

The Sermon on the Mount comprises a speech of about 107 verses attributed to Jesus (Matt 5–7). As presented in Matthew's Gospel, Jesus delivers it to his disciples on an unspecified mountain in Galilee (5:1–2), though within hearing distance of crowds (7:28–29). Throughout the Church's history, the Sermon has been regarded as a central collection of Jesus' teaching.

While only Matthew's Gospel includes the Sermon on the Mount, Luke's Gospel includes some of the same or similar material in a much shorter collection of twenty-nine verses (Luke 6:20–49). Jesus teaches this material from a "level place" (Luke 6:17), hence its common designation, the Sermon on the Plain.

Luke	Matthew
6:20a	5:1–2
6:20b–34	5:3–12
6:29–30	5:38–42
6:27–28, 31–36	5:43–48
6:37–43	7:1–5
6:31	7:12
6:34–35	7:16–20
6:46	7:21
6:47–49	7:24–27
7:1	7:28

Parts of Matthew's Sermon also appear elsewhere in Luke (compare, for example, Matt 5:13 and Luke 14:34–35; Matt 5:15 and Luke 8:16/11:33; Matt 5:18, 31–32 and Luke 16:17–18; Matt 5:25–26 and Luke 12:57–59; Matt 6:9–13 and Luke 11:2–4; Matt 6:19–21 and Luke 12:33–34; Matt 6:25–34 and Luke 12:22–32 etc.). Other parts of the Sermon appear only in Matthew with no parallels in any canonical gospel (for example, Matt 5:21–24, 27–28, 33–37; 6:1–8, 16–18).

This description identifies some of the complex issues to be addressed in determining the Sermon's contribution to the teaching of the historical Jesus. Both Matthew's Gospel and Luke's Gospel were probably written in the 80s or 90s of the first century CE, some fifty to sixty years after the crucifixion of Jesus. Understanding what happened to Jesus' teaching and traditions about Jesus in those fifty or so years in communities of his followers is crucial for assessing the Sermon's contribution to a historical reconstruction of Jesus' teaching. How much of Jesus' teaching was preserved? How much expansion, abbreviation, and revision took place through the decades? By understanding these processes, is it possible to identify the teaching of the historical Jesus in the Sermon on the Mount?

For example, is Matthew's presentation of the Sermon's setting authentic? Did Jesus speak the whole Sermon on one occasion and at one location, as Matthew presents it? An affirmative response seems unlikely given the existence of two versions of quite different length and content, the occurrence of Sermon material throughout Luke's Gospel outside chapter 6, and inclusion of material in Matthew's Sermon that has no parallel in the other gospels. These observations suggest that the origin of the Sermon's material is more complicated than Matthew's narrative scenario allows.

A second possibility suggests that Jesus spoke the material on different occasions and the writer of Matthew's Gospel, some fifty to sixty years later, collected it together. But this approach does not take account of what might have happened between the time of Jesus and the writing of the gospel, different versions of this material, and the absence of some of the Sermon's material from the other gospel accounts of Jesus' public activity.

A third possibility exists. Jesus spoke some of the material on various occasions and in various locations. It was remembered, collected, and added to by his followers and the gospel writer over the subsequent thirty to forty years to form the Sermon as we now read it. This third scenario is, in general terms, the most common way in which scholars understand the Sermon's origin and current form. But if we want to identify the teaching of the historical Jesus, this scenario requires us to separate later expansions and additions in the present form of the Sermon from material spoken by Jesus. Using various methods, scholars work back through the tradition, peeling back the layers, to identify the teaching of the historical Jesus and to explain the relationship between Jesus and the Sermon in its current form.

Origin and sources

The dominant view argues that the Sermon on the Mount is, finally, the construction of the writer of Matthew's Gospel (the identity of "Matthew" is not certain). This writer creatively edits or redacts a collection of teachings from Jesus that has been expanded over subsequent decades by Jesus' followers. This collection, known as Q (short for the German word *Quelle*, meaning "source"), has never been found but most scholars think it was a written collection of sayings of Jesus that had developed (perhaps in several versions) through the 40s and 50s CE. Q is regarded as the source for, and as comprising the material that is common to, Matthew and Luke but absent from Mark.

Scholars point to several factors in the material in Matthew's Sermon and in Luke's Gospel (whether the Sermon on the Plain or elsewhere in Luke) that suggest it originates from Q. They note word-for-word correspondence in parts of the two Sermons (compare, for example, Matt 7:3–5 and Luke 6:41–42; Matt 7:7–11 and Luke 11:9–13), the frequent common order in which the similar material appears (see the list in "Description" above), and literary and theological unities in this shared material. These factors suggest that Matthew and Luke used a common written source for (parts of) their respective Sermons.

There are, though, differences in this common material. Some of these differences can be explained as the editorial or redactional work of the writers of Matthew and Luke. Other differences in the common material that do not reflect their redactional activity suggest to some, though not all, scholars the existence of different versions of Q (QMt and QLk).

Discussions of the Sermon's opening nine beatitudes or statement of blessings ("Blessed are ... ") offer an example of this approach (Matt 5:3–12). Three of the first four beatitudes (Matt 5:3, 4, 6) parallel the three beatitudes in Luke 6:21b–22. Matthew's ninth beatitude ("blessed are you when people revile you" 5:11–12) parallels Luke's fourth ("Blessed are you when people hate you" Luke 6:22–23). These four beatitudes are commonly understood to belong to Q. But there are also differences between Matthew's and Luke's forms. Matthew 5:3 identifies the "poor in spirit" while Luke's blessing is on "the poor." Matthew uses the third person "theirs is the kingdom" and "they will be comforted/satisfied" while Luke employs the second person "yours is the kingdom" and "you shall. ... " The order of the beatitudes differs, as does some of their language (Matthew – poor, mourn, hunger; Luke – poor, hunger, weep). Matthew's beatitude on those who hunger includes distinctive Matthean language ("for righteousness"). Luke follows his four blessings with woes ("woe to you rich") that are not in Matthew. Matthew has another five beatitudes not in Luke, one of which seems to duplicate the beatitude of 5:11–12 (compare 5:10).

How might one explain these differences? One possibility is that, if the changes are consistent with the ways in which the gospel writers Matthew and Luke redact other material from Q, we could conclude that they have redacted this material also to suit their purposes. But if the changes are not consistent, another possibility exists, namely that Matthew and Luke use different forms of Q (identified as QMt and QLk) in which some or most of these differences already exist. Both possibilities, as well as a combination of both, have support from scholars. Identifying Q material and possible redactional activity helps to a significant degree in moving back through the tradition to the teaching of the historical Jesus but leaves open the difficult question of the relationship between Q and Jesus' teaching.

What might be the origin of the five beatitudes present in Matt 5:3–12 but absent from Luke (Matt 5:5 the meek, 5:7 the merciful, 5:8 the pure in heart, 5:9 the peace makers, 5:10 the persecuted)? One possibility is that the writer of Matthew, faithfully elaborating the teaching of Jesus, creates them and inserts them into Q material. One of the five (5:10) includes Matthew's common vocabulary ("righteousness" and "kingdom of the heavens"). It largely duplicates the content of the ninth beatitude (from Q) and its second line resembles the opening beatitude, suggesting it is a Matthean creation.

And the remaining four beatitudes (Matt 5:5, 7–9)? Some scholars think that they existed as part of a separate collection or source of either written or oral teaching material. This collection, known only by Matthew, is identified as "M." Other scholars think that they were part of the version of Q known to Matthew (QMt) but not to Luke. In support of either option is the observation that none of these four includes particular Matthean vocabulary (though the attention to "mercy" in 5:7 also appears in Matthew's addition of references to mercy in citing Hos 6:6 in 9:13 and 12:7), so they do not seem to be Matthean creations. In support of the theory that they belonged to QMt is the observation that three of the beatitudes incorporate themes and emphases present elsewhere in Q's Sermon (Matt 5:7 mercy and Luke 6:36; Matt 5:8 pure in heart and Luke 6:45; Matt 5:9 peacemakers and Luke 6:35). These links suggest to some that these beatitudes were included in QMt to signal important themes at the beginning of the Sermon. The remaining beatitude in 5:5 (the meek) quotes Psalm 37 and seems to elaborate the first beatitude, suggesting it may also originate in QMt.

This dominant approach suggests that at least one of the nine beatitudes originated with Matthew and not Jesus (5:10) and that at least one (5:5) was added in QMt. There also seems to be widespread agreement that four found in Q (5:3–4, 6, 11–12) originated with Jesus, at least in some form (e.g. were they second [Luke] or third person [Matthew] in form originally?). Scholars appeal to various factors or criteria for thinking these four are authentic to Jesus.

1 For some scholars, their belonging to Q (they are not sure that 5:7–9 did) suggests early material that probably derives from Jesus.
2 The content of these four is seen as cohering with emphases elsewhere in Jesus' teaching (on the "kingdom of God," special favor for those in socio-economically distressed situations, God's intervention to reverse present circumstances and effect eschatological salvation

or establish God's just and final purposes, conflict with socio-political power). Some suggest, on the basis of similarities in language, that Jesus formulated these beatitudes on the basis of Isa 61:1–3, a text that depicts God's salvific and eschatological intervention.

3 The combination of various features of the form of these beatitudes (beatitudes grouped together, "blessed" as first word, a definite article and adjective/participle to designate the sufferers, the *hoti* clause to express God's action) is somewhat rare in the numerous beatitudes of various Jewish writings.

4 The brief, pithy, and paradoxical style of three of these beatitudes (5:3–4, 6) is consonant with the memorable oral teaching of a wisdom teacher/eschatological prophet like Jesus. This factor counts for some against the authenticity of 5:11–12, at least in its present form, which may reflect subsequent experiences of Jesus' followers.

5 The absence of eschatological reversal from 5:7–9 also suggests to some that these beatitudes do not originate with Jesus, though others do not find this a definitive point because these beatitudes promise eschatological inclusion (experiencing God's mercy, seeing God, being children of God).

6 Some of the above factors (consonant content, form, style) could also be adduced to suggest 5:5 (the meek) originated with Jesus.

7 For those who see the beatitudes in 5:5, 7–9 as belonging to M material rather than Q, there is a further important factor. These three beatitudes cohere with the Q beatitudes in that they share the same content (God's saving intervention), employ the same form, and utilize the same style. A good case, then, could be made for the origin of several of these M beatitudes from Jesus. If this is so, both Q and M beatitudes would provide multiple attestation for the origin of most of the nine beatitudes, at least in some form, from Jesus.

This discussion of the Sermon's opening beatitudes illustrates some of the difficulties, possibilities, methods, and varied results in trying to peel back the layers of material in the Sermon to reconstruct the teaching of the historical Jesus. Issues of sources, redaction, and ecclesial circumstances as well as criteria of coherence, form, style, and multiple attestation play a role. So too do the assumptions and commitments of scholars. That is, having

eliminated signs of the redactional activity of gospel writers, scholars must decide the relationship between Jesus' teaching and Q or Jesus' teaching and M. This issue involves weighing various factors and determining degrees of continuity or discontinuity, careful preservation or editorial creativity, conservation or expansion in the transmission of material between Jesus' death and perhaps the 50s or so of the first century. These are difficult issues to adjudicate in an objective manner.

Building databases

Using the approaches outlined above, scholars work through the Sermon to determine what teaching might be attributed to the historical Jesus and what develops through the tradition and with subsequent redaction. Not surprisingly, results vary greatly and impact significantly understandings of the historical Jesus' teaching. It is true, though, that generally scholars claim significant continuity between the historical Jesus and the Sermon's content. That is, for many the Sermon generally offers a reliable collection of central aspects of Jesus' teaching.

Some scholars, though, have questioned this high level of confidence. Perhaps the most well-known challenge originates with a group known as the Jesus Seminar who published their findings through the 1980s and 1990s. The Seminar debated each saying using the criteria noted above, but especially emphasized features of oral speech such as brevity, repetition, provocativeness, and the memorability of a saying's unconventional, even shocking, content. They voted to classify each verse according to a system of color-coding. Red signified that Jesus *undoubtedly* made this statement or something like it. Pink also indicated a positive evaluation though with some hesitation (Jesus *probably* said something like this). Black indicated a clear negative evaluation (Jesus did not say this) while gray nuanced this negative verdict. Jesus did not say this, but it might contain ideas close to his.

The Seminar concluded that Jesus undoubtedly said very little of what is attributed to him in the Sermon. Only 5:39–42a (no violent resistance), three words in 5:44 ("Love your enemies"), and two words in 6:9b ("Our Father") are colored red. That is, out of 107 verses, the Seminar regarded only parts of six verses as undoubtedly originating from Jesus. Pink votes for all or parts of thirty-two further verses signified Jesus probably said something like this (5:3, 4, 6, 13bc, 14b–15, 25–26, 42b,

45b–46; 6:3, 9c, 10a, 11–12, 24, 25–30; 7:3–5, 7–11, 16b). That is, the Seminar decided that all or parts of thirty-eight of the Sermon's 107 verses undoubtedly or probably originated with Jesus. The remaining two-thirds of the Sermon, including well-known parts such as six of the beatitudes, much of 5:21–48 ("You have heard it said ... but/ and I say to you"), and the story of the two houses (7:24–27) did not originate with Jesus but derive from developing traditions and communities of his followers. Such a conclusion significantly impacts reconstructions of the teaching of the historical Jesus.

Another scholar who finds minimal content in the Sermon originating with Jesus is John Dominic Crossan. Crossan, frequently emphasizing multiple attestation as a key criterion and locating Jesus in the harsh imperial realities of first-century, Roman-controlled Galilee, concluded that at least parts of the following originated from Jesus: 5:3, 4, 6, 11, 13, 14a, 14b, 15, 23–24, 32, 34–35, 39–41, 44; 6:14, 19, 24, 25, 26, 28–29, 33; 7:7. On my count, Crossan includes (parts of) twenty-five of the Sermon's 107 verses in his database of authentic sayings originating from Jesus.

Conclusions that posit significant discontinuity between the Sermon's content and the historical Jesus are not typical of the general confidence that scholars have shown in being able to identify a considerably higher number of authentic teachings from Jesus. Continuity rather than discontinuity, preservation rather than addition, conservation rather than creativity have much more often dominated the quest for Jesus' teaching in the Sermon.

Alternative methods

It should also be noted that not all scholars employ the dominant approach outlined above based on the scrutiny of every verse and sources such as Q/QMt and M. For instance, Hans Dieter Betz, building on insights from discussions of the Sermon through the eighteenth to twentieth centuries, argues that the Sermon is not ultimately Matthew's creation but a pre-QMt composition (around 50 CE in Jerusalem for Jewish converts) that was later incorporated unchanged into Matthew's Gospel. Betz posits a similar composition process for Luke's Sermon (for Gentile converts). Betz sustains the pre-Q composition of the Sermons by highlighting the compositional, functional, and theological unity of each composition. Nor does he think redaction by the respective gospel writers can explain differences between the

two Sermons. He emphasizes significant differences between the Sermon and the rest of Matthew's Gospel to argue that it was not redacted by the gospel writer. Limitations of space prevent an adequate discussion of Betz's sophisticated approach here. Suffice it to note that while his approach has provoked much debate, it does not seem to have persuaded many. Betz, though, emphasizes throughout his insightful and rich commentary on the Sermons considerable continuity between the Sermons and the teaching of the historical Jesus.

Another scholar, James Dunn, also building on insights from previous work, has questioned other aspects of the dominant paradigm while emphasizing considerable continuity between the Sermon and the historical Jesus. Particularly troubling for Dunn is the over-emphasis on the literary nature of the dominant paradigm with its focus on written sources, its close attention to individual verses, and neglect of the oral transmission of traditions about Jesus. Dunn notes the problem of the variableness of levels of similarity between the two Sermons. While high levels of similarity between the third quarter of the Sermon (Matt 6:22–27:12) and various parallels in Luke (compare Luke 11:34–36; 16:13; 12:22–32; 6:37–42; 11:9–13; 6:31) might confirm the literary paradigm, much of the Sermon does not share these levels and casts doubt on theories of literary dependence and multiple versions of Q. Instead Dunn proposes that it is more convincing to explain this variableness on the basis of two different *oral* forms of the same tradition. He notes instances where, as is typical of oral material, the teaching is the same and carried by stable words and phrases while details or elaboration of the points differ significantly in ways appropriate to different situations (compare Matt 5:13 and Luke 14:34–35; 5:25–26 and Luke 12:57–59; 5:39b–42 and Luke 6:29–30; 6:19–21 and Luke 12:33–34; 7:13–14 and Luke 13:24; Matt 7:24–27 and 6:47–49). Dunn does not conclude that Q did not exist but rather emphasizes that it was a form of oral retelling of material and that communities of Jesus' followers transmitted traditions orally. Dunn focuses not on isolated individual texts but on the broad picture created by these traditions.

Interpretation

The sort of work described above provides the means whereby scholars seek to identify the likely teaching of the historical Jesus in the Sermon on the Mount. Once likely authentic material has been identified, a further task remains, namely that of interpretation. What does Jesus teach in the Sermon? What sort of figure does it show him to be? Interpreters across two millennia of the Church's history have answered these questions in various ways. I will note several dominant emphases from the last century.

One approach sees Jesus as an apocalyptic preacher who proclaims an "interim ethic" in the Sermon. The works of Johannes Weiss (1892) and Albert Schweitzer (1901) marked a turning point in studies of the historical Jesus. These scholars used a history-of-religions approach to locate Jesus in his first-century context rather than in the context of nineteenth-century culture and liberal philosophy. Focusing on Jesus' proclamation of the coming kingdom, Weiss and Schweitzer emphasized the eschatological center of Jesus' preaching in which he announced the imminent end of the world. Facing God's definitive intervention, Jesus proclaims the Sermon as an interim ethic. It comprised demands of repentance and moral renewal in preparation for the imminent kingdom. Weiss sees Jesus' demand for no vengeance (5:38–42) and for love of enemies (5:43–48) as examples of these interim demands that can be met with difficulty only in the short time of great stress and struggle before the end. On this analysis Jesus is an apocalyptic preacher expecting God's intervention at any moment and providing in the Sermon demands that must be fulfilled to encounter God's imminent kingdom. Jesus' Sermon has no relevance for long-term existence, since it is impossible to perform over the long haul.

Not many have found the notion of a short-term or "interim" ethic convincing. The issue of the Sermon's practicability has been, according to Robert Guelich, a recurring debate throughout the history of its interpretation. Attention, though, to Jesus' eschatological worldview and proclamation of God's kingdom, has proven, albeit in different ways, very important for recent discussions of the Sermon. We will return to these below.

Martin Dibelius also emphasized the eschatological nature of Jesus' ministry but rejected the Sermon's identity as an interim ethic. Dibelius distinguished between Jesus' proclamation and the Sermon as a later construction of the church and the gospels. For the latter, the Sermon was a rule of conduct or ethical instruction. But for the historical Jesus, his teaching that becomes the Sermon comprised the will of God that disregarded this world and offered signs of the coming kingdom of heaven. Dibelius did not think it could be performed. Rather, its hearing was meant to transform people for the coming kingdom so that they

lived appropriately before God. It was not intended to be a new ethic or law as it became in the later Sermon. Jesus did not set forth ethical demands that were to be, or even could be, obeyed in daily life. His teaching, turned into the Sermon, was the impracticable proclamation of an eschatological prophet anticipating the coming kingdom.

Hans Windisch developed a different approach. He located Jesus within what he understood to be the obedience ethic of the Old Testament and first-century Judaism. The Sermon set out a similar demand for ethical perfectionism that humans were to obey in order to enjoy life and God's favor. That is, the Sermon made demands that were practicable and were to be achieved in order to gain salvation. Windisch noted similarities between Jesus' teaching and that found in the Jewish Talmud such as forms of the golden rule found in Matt 7:12.

Dietrich Bonhoeffer emphasized the doing of Jesus' teaching. The Sermon was no short-term ethic and it was not impracticable. Bonhoeffer saw it as making demands that were to be lived in everyday life. But these demands were not a way to salvation. The Sermon's proclamation instructed Jesus' followers on the works that were to mark a life of faith. Bonhoeffer's emphasis on the radical and practicable demands of the Sermon for everyday Christian discipleship typifies a long line of similar radical-reformation or Anabaptist interpretations.

Joachim Jeremias advocated a somewhat similar approach. Employing his Lutheran framework of grace against works, Jeremias rejects Weiss and Schweitzer's interim-ethic approach, Windisch's obedience ethic, and the view of "Lutheran orthodoxy" that in the Sermon Jesus offered an impossible ideal to lead people to an awareness of sin, to despair, and to cry out for God's mercy. In Jeremias' view all three fail because they regarded the Sermon as law. These legalistic interpretations inadequately depict Jesus as an apocalypticist, a teacher of law, and a preacher of repentance. Instead Jeremias argues that in the Sermon, Jesus teaches Christians to live a way of life in contrast to their Jewish contemporaries (for example, 5:17–48). The Sermon is Jesus' catechetical instruction for post-baptismal living. It delineates God's will, "lived faith," the life of those who live on the basis of God's salvation. The Sermon follows the proclamation of the gospel, the gift of the kingdom or salvation in Jesus' ministry. It outlines a way of life that follows conversion. The Sermon does not provide a complete statement of this life but offers "symptoms, signs, examples," or visions of the sort of life of discipleship created by the in-breaking of

God's kingdom. This line of interpretation is developed in a number of commentaries on the Sermon.

Jeremias' ecclesial framing of his discussion in terms of catechesis and baptism is anachronistically problematic for reconstructions of the historical Jesus. So too is his use of doctrinal categories of law and grace to style first-century Judaism inappropriately as legalistic (rather than as covenantal or apocalyptic, for example) and to oppose Christian discipleship to it. But valuable as a counter to the future oriented eschatology of Weiss and Schweitzer is his emphasis on the presence of God's intervention and on the practicability of the Sermon.

An apocalyptic Jesus?

Many of the issues identified in this brief survey are current in numerous contemporary interpretations of the historical Jesus and of the Sermon. One crucial issue concerns the role of eschatology in Jesus' teaching. A brief discussion of two scholars, particularly their discussion of the Sermon's notion of God's kingdom, will highlight important differences.

The discussions surveyed above frequently emphasize God's imminent intervention, though there are significant differences over whether it is present or future or both. John Dominic Crossan emphasizes that Jesus is not an apocalyptic seer pointing to a future intervention and imminent end of the world (Crossan's definition of apocalyptic) but a Cynic-like sage (impacted by wisdom traditions) who announces and enacts God's sapiential kingdom or dominion in the present. This kingdom includes nobodies, takes care of human needs, opposes the patriarchal family, embodies radical egalitarianism, and counters imperial kingdoms. Crossan employs parts of the Sermon that he considers authentic to sustain this interpretation: the beatitudes of 5:3 ("the destitute"), 4 ("the sad"), 6 ("the hungry"), and 11 ("the abused and rejected"); parts of the Lord's prayer that emphasize care for human needs (6:11 daily bread; 6:12 forgiveness of debt; also 7:7–11, 12); criticism of wealth (6:19–20); teaching against male power exercised in divorce (5:31–32). Throughout, Crossan rejects a future-oriented, apocalyptic interpretation to emphasize the presence of God's kingdom.

In focusing on the "broad picture" of Jesus' teaching, James Dunn argues not only for the presence of the kingdom but also, contrary to Crossan and others such as Marcus Borg, for Jesus' expectation of its future coming. The future kingdom is imminent, is marked by eschatological reversal, is preceded by suffering, involves judgment and reward or vindication, and is certain to arrive after an interval that requires a certain way of life in the light of its coming. Dunn recognizes that in his expectation of a coming kingdom Jesus was wrong. Dunn finds numerous aspects of the Sermon that sustain the claim of a future kingdom: "your kingdom come" (6:10, along with 6:11–13a); eschatological reversal in the beatitudes of 5:3–6, 11–12 comprising restoration of land, social justice, world domination (?) and eternal life; expectations of suffering (6:13a; 5:11–12); judgment (5:25–26); vindication (5:3–6, including the eschatological banquet) and reward (6:1, 2, 5, 16); and an interval before its arrival (6:13). Dunn finds support for the presence of the kingdom in the gospel traditions in claims of the fulfillment of time and realizations of expectations, differences between John the Baptist and Jesus, and Jesus' exorcisms and parables. But significantly in contrast with Crossan, the only support *from the Sermon* that Dunn offers for a present kingdom concerns the petition in 6:10b ("your will be done") where Dunn entertains the possibility that the doing of God's will is a sign of the presence of God's kingdom.

Interestingly a similar situation occurs in John Meier's discussion of the present and future kingdom. From the Sermon, Meier discusses 6:10 ("your kingdom come") and the beatitudes as support for a future kingdom, but nothing *from the Sermon* in support of a present kingdom. According to Dunn's (and Meier's) analysis, it seems that the Sermon is more interested in a future kingdom; according to Crossan, a present kingdom. Such decisions about the relationship of the present and the future significantly impact interpretations of sections of the Sermon such as the beatitudes and the Lord's Prayer. It should, though, be noted that Dunn's subsequent discussion has some similarity to Crossan's in identifying various dimensions of the Sermon that shape lived discipleship in anticipation of the coming kingdom: blessing on the poor (5:3); loyalty to God (6:24); childlike trust (6:9, 25–33); prayer (6:9–13; 7:7–11); suffering (5:11–12); divorce (5:32); prohibitions against unjustified anger and murder (5:21–22), adultery and lust (5:27–28), false oaths and misleading speech (5:33–37), and retaliation (5:38–42); love for enemies (5:43–48; 7:12), and forgiveness (6:12, 14–15).

Closing observations

While this brief discussion of the work of Crossan and Dunn has focused on their presentations of the kingdom, four other important aspects of contemporary work on the Sermon can be noted briefly.

1 Consideration of the Sermon's meaning cannot be isolated from the wider discussion of Jesus' identity and overall public activity, including both his teachings and his actions. The Sermon has often been considered on its own as though it were an isolated text. Rather, the Sermon offers insight into one part of Jesus' teaching but it cannot be taken as the whole. It contributes to a comprehensive understanding of the historical Jesus.

2 Consideration of the Sermon's meaning cannot be isolated from understandings of the historical and geographical settings of Jesus' ministry. Traditionally this issue has been framed in religious terms of Jesus' relation to Judaism and, more specifically, to the law. Claims of fulfillment and antithetical teaching (5:17–48) have been common. Contemporary scholarship, though, has shown that the issue of locating Jesus' public activity is much broader, involving the diversities of first-century Judaisms and the realities of socio-political life under Roman rule. To determine material authentic to the historical Jesus in the Sermon and to interpret that material requires consideration of first-century Galilean and Judean life.

3 The practicability of Jesus' teaching in the Sermon and its importance for lived discipleship have been disputed. For those who affirm the Sermon's practicability, debate will continue as to what sort of culturally contextualized life and community it shapes among followers of Jesus.

4 While this article has focused appropriately on the Sermon in relation to the historical Jesus, it should not be forgotten that in its final form it comprises part of the Gospel of Matthew, where it is shaped by decades of traditioning and redactional activity, contributes to Matthew's engagement with post-70 Judaism and the fresh assertion of Roman imperial power in the destruction of Jerusalem and its Temple in 70 CE, and is contextualized by affirmations about the person and mission of Jesus (Matt 1–4).

WARREN CARTER

Further reading

Betz, Hans Dieter. *The Sermon on the Mount, Hermeneia,* Minneapolis, MN: Fortress Press, 1995.

Bonhoeffer, Dietrich. *The Cost of Discipleship,* New York: Macmillan, 1949.
Borg, Marcus. "An Orthodoxy Reconsidered: The 'End-of-the-World Jesus'," in L. D. Hurst and N. T. Wright (eds) *The Glory of Christ in the New Testament,* Oxford: Clarendon, 1987, pp. 207–17.
Carter, W Carter. *What Are They Saying about Matthew's Sermon on the Mount?,* New York: Paulist, 1994.
—— "Some Contemporary Scholarship on the Sermon on the Mount," *Currents in Research: Biblical Studies* 4 (1996) 183–215.
—— *Matthew and the Margins: A Socio-Political and Religious Reading,* JSNTSup 204, Sheffield: Academic Press, 2000
Crossan, John Dominic. *The Historical Jesus: The Life of a Mediterranean Peasant,* San Francisco, CA: Harper, 1991, pp. xiii–xxvi, 265–302.
Davies, William D. and Dale Allison. *A Critical and Exegetical Commentary on the Gospel According to Saint Matthew,* Vol. 1, Edinburgh: T. & T. Clark, 1988, pp. 429–731.
Dibelius, Martin. *The Sermon on the Mount,* New York: Charles Scribner's Sons, 1940.
Dunn, James D. G. *Jesus Remembered,* Grand Rapids, MI: Eerdmans, 2003, pp. 383–487.
Funk, Robert, Roy Hoover, and the Jesus Seminar. *The Five Gospels: What Did Jesus Really Say?* New York: Macmillan/Polebridge, 1993.
Guelich, Robert. *The Sermon on the Mount,* Dallas, TX: Word, 1982.
Jeremias, Joachim. *The Sermon on the Mount,* trans. Norman Perrin, Philadelphia, PA: Fortress Press, 1963.
Luz, Ulrich. *Matthew 1–7. A Commentary,* trans. W. C. Linss, Minneapolis, MN: Augsburg, 1989, pp. 209–460.
MacArthur, Harvey. *Understanding the Sermon on the Mount,* London: Epworth, 1961.
Meier, John P. *A Marginal Jew: Rethinking the Historical Jesus,* Vol. 2, New York: Doubleday, 1994, pp. 237–506.
Patte, Daniel. *The Challenge of Discipleship: A Critical Study of the Sermon on the Mount as Scripture,* Harrisburg, PA: Trinity Press International, 1999.
Schweitzer, Albert. *The Mystery of the kingdom of God,* London: Black, 1914.
Weiss, Johannes. *Die Predigt Jesu vom Reiche Gottes,* Göttingen: Vandenhoeck & Ruprecht, 1892; ET *Jesus' Proclamation of the kingdom of God,* trans. Richard Hyde Hiers and David Larrimore Holland, Chico, CA: Scholars Press, 1985.
Windisch, Hans. *Der Sinn der Bergpredigt,* Leipzig: J. C Hinrichs, 1929, 1937; ET *The Meaning of the Sermon the Mount,* trans. S. MacLean Gilmour, Philadelphia, PA: Westminster, 1951.

SERVANT OF THE LORD

The English term "servant" can be used to translate various Greek words, including *pais* ("child"; hence either "son/daughter" or "servant/slave"), *doulos* ("slave") and *diakonos* ("servant", "minister"). *Pais* occurs rarely in the New Testament as a way of referring to certain people as servants of God (or of the Lord), namely the people of Israel collectively (Luke 1:54) and King David (Luke 1:69; Acts 4:25).

The underlying Hebrew term *'ebed*, used scantily in the historical books for Isaac, Jacob, Moses, David and the prophets, is found more extensively in the prophetic writings for such people, including the Israelites collectively and kings and prophets. The New Testament usage thus places Jesus in the company of responsible and privileged figures who are referred to as the servants of Yahweh.

The Servant in Isaiah 40–55

Isaiah 40–55 contains numerous references to a figure designated by God (speaking through the prophet) as "my servant". In some passages the phrase might well be understood to be referring to an unnamed individual, but in others it certainly refers to Israel or a faithful group within Israel (Isa 41:8–9; 43:10; 44:1) and expresses the dignity and role of Israel as God's collective servant whom he is going to help and vindicate. The Servant is the express topic of four passages that used to be identified as originally separate compositions (the so-called "Servant songs"; Isa 42:1–9; 49:1–6; 50:4–11; 52:13–53:12) but are now generally understood to be inseparable from the stream of prophecy in which they occur. Unfortunately the interpretation of the statements made about this figure remains extremely controversial.

Some scholars take all the references to the Servant collectively, describing the humiliation of the people in exile and God's promise of their vindication and his call to service (cf. Isa 44:1, 21; 49:3). But an individual view is also possible, with reference to some past king, or the prophet himself, or a future figure (e.g. the "prophet like Moses"; cf. Hugenberger). In some passages this is unavoidable: when the Servant has a mission to Israel (Isa 49:5f.), either an individual or a group within Israel must be meant. The Servant is associated with the covenant (Isa 42:6) and a world-wide mission (Isa 49:5f.); he acts like a prophet but is treated with ignominy (Isa 50:4–11); he will be exalted, but first he suffers and bears the sin of others so that he may put other people right with God by bearing their punishment and by intercession (Isa 52:13–53:12). Whether this suffering was instead of the suffering of others (Hofius) or a sharing in their suffering (Hooker) is disputed.

The translators of the Hebrew Bible into Greek (LXX) inevitably tried to incorporate in their translation interpretation of the material for the benefit of their readers and they generally took the Servant passages collectively (thus in Isa 42:1 they expanded the text to read "Jacob my servant ... Israel my chosen one"). The translation of Isaiah 53 made the theme of the chapter the Lord's vindication of the Servant rather than his justification of sinners; the Servant's suffering is *not* due to the will of the Lord, and the Lord vindicates him by cutting short his sufferings and saving him from death; his death is *not* seen as a sacrifice for sins, and he bears sin, through "humiliating sufferings and denial of justice with which the people identify and which stopped short of death" (Sapp 186). Consequently, early Christian readers who were not familiar with the Hebrew text would not have seen here so easily the role model for Jesus.

By contrast the paraphrastic translation of the same chapter into Aramaic in the Targum clearly identifies the Servant as the Messiah, but then proceeds to rewrite the chapter to systematically eliminate any suggestion that he suffers!

In 1 En the Righteous and Elect One (the Son of Man) is described as the light of the Gentiles (1 En. 48:4; Isa 42:6), chosen and hidden before God (*1 En.* 48:6; Isa 49:2), and worshipped by kings (*1 En.* 55:4; Isa 49:7). Here phrases applied to the Servant in Isaiah (but not the actual term "Servant") are used.

Although the Messiah is called God's servant in *4 Ezra* 7:28f.; 13:32, 37, 52; 14:9; *2 Bar.* 70:9, there is no clear indication here to the specific Servant in Isa 40–55.

There was thus no unanimity in the various Jewish sources as to the identity of the Servant, to whether or not the Servant suffered, and (if he did) whether his sufferings had any kind of salvific or sacrificial function; certainly an individual interpretation, rather than a collective one, is found in some of the sources, and Hengel thinks that the possible existence of traditions of a suffering and atoning Messiah cannot be excluded.

The early Christian understanding of Jesus (and his messengers) as fulfilling the role of the Servant

The term *doulos* is used once by Paul to describe the earthly role of Jesus (Phil 2:7) and *pais* is used occasionally (Matt 12:18; Acts 3:13, 26; 4:27, 30), although it was never used on its own for referring to Jesus in the way that terms like "the Lord" or "the Son of Man" are used. While the references in Acts might be thought to be quite general (cf. the parallel description of David in Acts 4:25), the language of Acts 3:13 echoes Isa 52:13.

Alongside these references there is a greater number of places where texts about the Servant in Isa 40–55 are explicitly quoted or fairly clearly echoed. In Mark 1:11 the wording of the heavenly voice "with you I am well pleased", coupled with the reference to the descent of the Spirit, echoes Isaiah 42:1. Matthew, who likes to quote Old Testament texts that are fulfilled in Jesus, cites Isa 53:4 (Matt 8:17) and Isa 42:1–4 (Matt 12:17–21) with reference to his healing of ill people and more generally of his powerful proclamation of judgment and salvation. Luke records that Jesus cited Isa 53:12 with reference to his own death alongside criminals (Luke 22:37). Likewise John cites Isaiah 53:1 (John 12:38) and Luke tells us about how Philip preached about Jesus on the basis of Isa 53:7–8 to the Ethiopian eunuch (Acts 8:32–35).

The first book of Peter gives a description of the suffering and death of Jesus as both an exemplary figure and a Saviour, using phraseology from Isaiah 53 (1 Pet 2:22–25). What begins as the statement of an example to follow turns into a description of one who dies in order to take away sin and heal. There is a probable allusion in Heb 9:28 (Isa 53:12).

Paul cites Isaiah 49:6 but applies it not to Jesus but to the Church (Acts 13:47); similarly, his description of his own calling uses phraseology from Isa 42:6 (Acts 26:17f.) and Isa 49:1 (Gal 1:15). He also cites Isa 52:15 and 53:1 (Rom 15:21; 10:16), in both cases with reference to the proclamation and reception of the message about Jesus. Paul's use of these citations strengthens the case that in Rom 4:25 and 1 Cor 15:3–5 he is also alluding to Isaiah 53 with specific reference to the substitutionary death and resurrection of Jesus; the latter passage certainly cites early church tradition. There are possible allusions in 1 Cor 11:23; Rom 8:32, 34 (cf. Hofius).

These texts show that some early Christians were familiar with the material regarding the Servant and his mission in Isa 40–55. This is not at all surprising in view of the widespread use of Isaiah as a whole (cf. Watts), and especially of the imagery of the return from exile understood as a second exodus, by various New Testament writers. What may be surprising is the comparative sparsity of references that thematically and unambiguously interpret the work of Jesus in terms of the sacrificial suffering and death of the Servant. Nevertheless, there is clear evidence for an underlying shaping of the language by the Servant texts.

Did Jesus understand his role in the light of the Servant?

But when did this interpretation start? There is a long tradition of seeing it reflected in the sayings of Jesus himself, specifically in Mark 10:45; 14:24; Luke 22:37, with which may be linked Mark 1:11;

9:12; Luke 4:16–21. It has always been difficult to account for Jesus consciousness of his need to die on behalf of others and be raised in terms of the roles of the Messiah and Son of Man, and many scholars have argued that it was his association of the suffering Servant with these roles that created the new understanding of suffering messiahship. On the other hand, a strong body of scholarship has argued that the evidence for his use of the Servant role is weak and unpersuasive.

Some argue that we can know virtually nothing about whether he had a mind on this matter because the texts in question were created by the early church and are not authentic (or have been significantly edited by the early church). R. Bultmann is famous for asserting rhetorically that all predictions of Jesus' death must be inauthentic, presumably since nobody possesses supernatural foreknowledge. Others, who accept their authenticity, argue that they are better explained against a different background. Thus Hooker holds that the Son of Man in Daniel 7 is a suffering figure (as representing the persecuted saints in Dan 7:21, 25). She also argues that, where there are allusions to the Servant, these are related to his innocent suffering rather than to any vicarious, saving role. Moreover, the Servant was understood as a collective term for Israel rather than for their future ruler. A number of Psalms alluded to in the Gospels reflect the fate of the suffering righteous man of God (Pss 22, 69), a role fulfilled by Jesus. And there was a Jewish martyrological literature which understood the Maccabean martyrs to be dying to appease God because of the sins of the nation but did not draw on the motif of the suffering Servant to fortify this interpretation (2 Macc 7; 4 Macc 17; does this indicate that the authors recognised that the Servant was a specific individual and not a role description for martyrs?).

So the question is whether Jesus did use the Servant motif and, if so, how he understood it.

1 We should not be surprised that Jesus said little about the significance of his death to disciples whom it was hard to convince that he would be put to death, and that a fuller realisation of its meaning could not develop until afterwards.

2 There is a good case that, even apart from any possession of supernatural insight, Jesus must have realised that the course of events was leading to the likelihood of his being put to death (Jeremias, *TDNT* V:713–14).

3 The understanding of Jesus' role (both by himself and by his followers) was based on

several Old Testament models, and in view of the overlap of the imagery it is not always possible to identify with certainty which particular source was influential. Thus in Mark 8:31; 9:12, when Jesus talks about being rejected, the language could be seen as echoing Ps 118:22 (cf. Mark 12:10; Acts 4:11; 1 Peter 2:4, 7) or Isa 53:3 (for the latter see Watts).

4 A contested point is whether, when a New Testament author refers to a verse in the Old Testament, he and the readers would remember and think of associated material in the original context or would treat the text atomistically (so Hooker). Thus, when Philip spoke to the eunuch starting from Isa 53:7–8, would he have brought the rest of that chapter into his discussion and said something about the Servant's role in respect of the sins of the people, or would he have simply referred to him as an innocent victim? The wealth of allusion over the New Testament as a whole to nearly every verse in the passage strongly supports the former option, and there is plenty of similar evidence in respect of other Old Testament passages that were read as wholes and not simply as sources for verses taken out of context.

5 There is an explicit citation of Isa 53:12 in Luke 22:37. It has been argued that, although it is given as a saying of Jesus, it was placed on his lips by the evangelist (Nolland 1993: 1076–77; Dunn 811–12) and fits into the pattern of his other references to Jesus as the Servant in Acts; nevertheless, the citation differs from the LXX and fits in with the self-identification of Jesus as a person who consorts with sinners and is so regarded by the Jewish authorities (Green 774–76). In Luke 4:16–21 Jesus cites Isa 61:1–2, a passage that may be understood as a reference to the Servant in the earlier chapters since it uses the same kind of language (it is cited along with Isa 52:7 in 11Q13 [11QMelch]). Again the question of authenticity arises; it is strongly defended by Nolland 1989: 193.

6. The most important text is Mark 10:45 (par. Matt 20:28). This saying is absent from Luke who has a somewhat similar saying in Luke 22:25–27 where Jesus is compared more broadly to one who serves and the specific idea of laying down his life as a ransom for many is absent. It is unlikely, however, that the saying in Mark should be seen as a later revision of the one in Luke. It has a particularly

Semitic form as compared with the more idiomatic Greek form in 1 Tim 2:6 (cf. also Titus 2:14). Its authenticity is strongly defended (France; Page; Stuhlmacher). But is it an allusion to the Servant and what he does? The unusual use of "many" (Hebrew idiom for "all") gives a strong link with Isaiah, as do the notions of service (Isa 53:11) and of giving one's life (cf. Isa 53:12). The concept of doing something on behalf of them aptly sums up the thought of Isaiah 53, and Hofius has noted that the concept of an innocent person undergoing substitutionary suffering for the sins of others is found nowhere else in the Old Testament (Hofius 110–14). What is problematic is the use of "ransom" (*lytron*), to which the nearest term in Isaiah 53 is Heb *'asham*, a word that normally refers to a guilt offering (so LXX here: *peri hamartias*). France argues that the offering of a sacrifice functioned like a ransom to deliver the sinner from the penalty of their sin; Hofius holds that in Isaiah 53 the term does not refer to a sacrifice but to the payment that cancels out guilt (cf. R. Knierim, *THAT* I, 254). Another concomitant possibility is that Jesus' saying reflects Isaiah 43:3 MT, where God refers to the ransom that he will give for Israel (but hardly as the primary influence; cf. Watts, "Jesus' Death", 144–47). Nor should we overlook Ps 49:15 where the Psalmist contrasts the death and decay of the wicked, who are like sheep with death as their shepherd (Ps 49:14; cf. Isa 53:6) and cannot give to God a sufficient ransom to save them, with his own assurance that God will redeem him from the realm of the dead. Whatever the background, the concept of a substitutionary bearing of the consequences of sin by Jesus is firmly embedded in the saying.

There are also possible echoes of the chapter elsewhere in the gospels. The references to Jesus being "handed over" (Mark 9:31; 10:33) may reflect Isa 53:12 (cf. 43:4). The deliberate silence of Jesus before his judges is reminiscent of Isaiah 53:7. The difficult problem is knowing whether these apparent allusions were in the mind of Jesus or are the fruit of later reading that recognised the similarities between his career and that of the Servant.

The sayings of Jesus at the Last Supper may also allude to the role of the Servant. Discussion is difficult both because the authenticity of the sayings is questioned by some scholars and also by the fact that there are differences in the handing down of the wording in the gospels and in 1 Cor 11. In Mark 14:24 Jesus says: "This [sc. the wine in the cup] is my blood of the covenant which is poured out for many" (Matt 26:28 adds "for the forgiveness of sins"). But in 1 Cor 11:25 Jesus says: "This cup [Luke 22:20 adds "that is poured out for you"] is the new covenant in my blood." It is probably impossible to be certain about the original wording, but in both forms there is a reference to the covenant, which may pick up the link between the Servant and the covenant in Isa 42:6; the words "for many" link the saying with Mark 10:45 and with the use of the term in Isa 53:11–12, and, if "poured out" is original, it may echo Isa 53:12.

The evidence suggests that the concept of the suffering Servant who bears the sins of the many was an integral part of the self-understanding of Jesus.

I. HOWARD MARSHALL

Further reading

Barrett, C. Kingsley. "The Background of Mark 10:45," in A. J. B. Higgins (ed.) *New Testament Essays: Studies in Memory of T. W. Manson*, Manchester: Manchester University Press, 1959, pp. 1–18.

Bellinger, William. H., Jr, and William R. Farmer (eds) *Jesus and the Suffering Servant: Isaiah 53 and Christian Origins*, Harrisburg, PA: Trinity Press International, 1998.

Betz, Otto. "Jesus und Jesaja 53," in H. Lichtenberger (ed.) *Geschichte–Tradition–Reflexion: Festschrift für Martin Hengel zum 70. Geburtstag. Band III Frühes Christentum*, Tübingen: J. C. B. Mohr (Paul Siebeck), 1996, pp. 3–19.

—— "Jesus and Isaiah 53," in William H. Bellinger, Jr, and William R. Farmer (eds) *Jesus and the Suffering Servant: Isaiah 53 and Christian Origins*, Harrisburg: Trinity Press International, 1998, pp. 70–87 (N.B. this article gives the substance of the German one listed above).

Dunn, James D. G. *Jesus Remembered*, Grand Rapids, MI: Eerdmans, 2003, pp. 809–18.

France, Richard T. "The Servant of the Lord in the Teaching of Jesus," *TynBul* 19 (1968) 26–52.

—— *Jesus and the Old Testament*, London: Tyndale, 1971.

Green, Joel B. *The Gospel of Luke*, Grand Rapids, MI: Eerdmans, 1997.

—— "The Death of Jesus, God's Servant," in D. D. Sylva (ed.) *Reimaging the Death of the Lukan Jesus*, Frankfurt am Main: Anton Hain, 1990, pp. 1–28, 3.

Hegel, M. "Zur Wirkungsgeschichte von Jes 53 in vorchristlicher Zeit," in B. Janowski, ed., *Der Leidende Gottesknecht: Jesaja 53 und seine Wirkungsgeschichte*, Tübingen: Mohr Siebeck, 1996, 49–91.

Hofius, Otfried. "Das vierte Gottesknechtlied in den Briefen des Neuen Testaments," *New Testament Studies* 39 (1993) 414–37; reprinted in Bernd Janowski and Peter Stuhlmacher (eds) *Der leidende Gottesknecht: Jesaja 53 und seine Wirkungsgeschichte*, Tübingen: J. C. B. Mohr (Paul Siebeck), 1996, pp. 107–27.

Hooker, Morna D. *Jesus and the Servant: The Influence of the Servant Concept of Deutero-Isaiah in the New Testament*, London: SPCK, 1959.

Hugenberger, Gordon P. "The Servant of the Lord in the 'Servant Songs' of Isaiah; a Second Moses Figure," in Philip E. Satterthwaite, Richard S. Hess, and Gordon J. Wenham (eds) *The Lord's Anointed: Interpretation of Old Testament Messianic Texts*, Carlisle: Paternoster; Grand Rapids, MI: Baker, 1995, pp. 105–40.

Janowski, Bernd and Peter Stuhlmacher. *Der leidende Gottesknecht: Jesaja 53 und seine Wirkungsgeschichte*, Tübingen: J. C. B. Mohr (Paul Siebeck), 1996; ET *The Suffering Servant: Isaiah 53 in Jewish and Christian Source*, trans. Daniel P. Bailey, Grand Rapids, MI: Eerdmans, 2004.

Jeremias, Joachim. *New Testament Theology*, London: SCM Press, 1971.

Jeremias, Joachim and Walther Zimmerli. "παῖς θεοῦ κτλ.," *TDNT* V (1967) 654–717.

Moulder, William J. "The Old Testament Background and the Interpretation of Mark X.45," *NTS* 24 (1978) 120–27.

Nolland, John. *Luke 1:1–9:20*, Dallas, TX: Word, 1989.

—— *Luke 18:35–24:53*, Dallas, TX: Word, 1993.

Page, Sydney. "The Authenticity of the Ransom Logion (Mark 10:45b)," in R. T. France and D. Wenham (eds) *Gospel Perspectives 1: Studies of History and Tradition in the Four Gospels*, Sheffield: JSOT, 1980, pp. 137–61.

Sapp, David A. "The LXX, 1QIsa, and MT Versions of Isaiah 53 and the Christian Doctrine of Atonement," in William H. Bellinger, Jr, and William R. Farmer (eds) *Jesus and the Suffering Servant: Isaiah 53 and Christian Origins*, Harrisburg, PA: Trinity Press International, 1998, pp. 170–92.

Stuhlmacher, Peter. "Vicariously Giving His Life for Many, Mark 10:45 (Matt 20:28)," in *Reconciliation, Law and Righteousness: Essays in Biblical Theology*, Philadelphia, PA: Fortress Press, 1986, pp. 16–29.

—— "Jes 53 in den Evangelien und in der Apostelgeschichte," in Bernd Janowski and Peter Stuhlmacher (eds) *Der leidende Gottesknecht: Jesaja 53 und seine Wirkungsgeschichte*, Tübingen: J. C. B. Mohr (Paul Siebeck), 1996, pp. 93–105.

Watts, Rikki E. "Jesus' Death, Isaiah 53, and Mark 10:45: A Crux Revisited," in William H. Bellinger, Jr, and William R. Farmer (eds) *Jesus and the Suffering Servant: Isaiah 53 and Christian Origins*, Harrisburg, PA: Trinity Press International, 1998, pp. 125–51.

Wolff, Hans Walter. *Jesaja 53 im Urchristentum*, mit einer Einführung von Peter Stuhlmacher, Giessen: Brunnen, 1984.

SIMON, PETER

The Simon who came to be called Peter is not the principal subject of any of the gospels. But they refer to him frequently and coherently, and allusions to him – allowing for the tendencies of the sources – permit a profile to be inferred.

Simon and his (probably elder) brother Andrew came from the fishing town Bethsaida, as is plain from an incidental reference in John's Gospel (John 1:44). That reference and its context reflect the brothers' particular connection with Philip, who came from the same prosperous town, which Herod Philip later developed into a city. "Andrew," "Philip," and even "Simon" (when spelled *Simon* rather than *Sumeon*) are attested as names in Hellenistic Greek, suggesting that the disciples from Bethsaida were more acquainted with the global culture and language of their time than their colleagues from the other side of the Sea of Galilee.

The story of the healing of Peter's mother-in-law (Mark 1:29–31; Matt 8:14–15; Luke 4:38–39) shows that both Peter and his brother had moved to Capernaum, and were living with the family of Peter's wife, a natural arrangement in Galilee. Capernaum's Jews were poorer than Bethsaida's, but the static stock of housing throughout Jewish Galilee meant that marriage often involved men moving in with their in-laws. Jesus was able to establish himself as a rabbi in Capernaum because Simon and Andrew both (see Mark 1:29), presumably having married sisters, received him into their home in Capernaum.

The gospels portray Jesus as calling Peter and Andrew to become his disciples, along with two other brothers named James and John, while he was walking along the shore of the Sea of Galilee (Mark 1:16–20; Matt 4:18–22). A vignette that appears in Luke 5:1–11 portrays as present from the outset the dynamic that would mark Jesus' relationship with his prime disciple. Peter is obdurate, and Jesus pushes him. Peter relents, breaks through, shares Jesus' insight, repents and asks forgiveness for his human failures and doubts. Although the descriptions involved are schematic, they give a more accurate impression than the description in John of Andrew and Peter having been disciples of John the Baptist (John 1:35–51). The purpose of that claim appears to be to preserve their positions as having precedence over Philip and Nathanael, who had been the Baptist's disciples along with Jesus.

The healing of Peter's mother-in-law begins a sequence of passages in which he appears to be the origin of an oral source best preserved in Mark, which relates healings of Jesus in which Peter is named as witness (1:29–32, 35–45; 5: 22–24a, 35–43, cf. Papias' testimony concerning Mark's Gospel and its relationship to Peter in Eusebius, *Hist. eccl.* 3.39.15–16). An emphasis upon Jesus' healings also characterizes the summary message concerning Jesus' activity attributed to Peter in Acts 10:36–38. Moreover, the words of Peter quoted in the book of Acts identify Jesus as the one whom God "anointed with Holy Spirit and power" (Acts 10:38), a key theme within the gospels.

Because the forgiveness of sin featured centrally in Jesus' therapy of healing as he delivered it to his apostles, the promise of the keys of the kingdom of heaven (Matthew 16:17–19, cf. 18:15–18) is best understood within that context, rather than in the ecclesiastical terms that have mired the saying in controversy in the West. The time from which Simon would have been called Peter (that is, *Kepha'* in Aramaic) should accordingly be reckoned from when the apostles, with Peter in lead position, were delegated to heal and preach on Jesus' behalf (Mark 3:16; Matt 10:2; Luke 6:14). That activity involved adjudications of purity as the apostles moved into new environments within Israel, and the echo of Isa 22:22 (especially the Targumic form of Isa 22:22) in the promise of the keys corresponds to that necessity. That the "Rock" of forgiveness should be the owner of a boat which Jesus himself had used reflects an element of humor characteristic of other nicknames that Jesus assigned. The moment of Simon being called "Rock" by Jesus is moved forward to the beginning of Peter's discipleship in John 1:42, which accords with the general impression given in the gospels that the nickname Jesus assigned Simon had begun to be his primary designation during his lifetime, and increasingly as the gospels developed.

Peter's persistent position at the head of any listing of the disciples and apostles, together with his nickname, clearly makes him the most prominent of Jesus' disciples within the Synoptic presentation. For that reason, Jesus' rebuke of Peter as "Satan," where it concerns the necessity of Jesus' suffering as the anointed (Mark 8:27–33; Matt 16:13–23, cf. Luke 9:18–22), is all the more striking. The story of Jesus' Transfiguration follows (Mark 9:2–10; Matt 17:1–9; Luke 9:28–36), where Peter is the principal witness. Peter heads the list of the three premier apostles who were present at the Transfiguration and saw their rabbi transfigured with heavenly light, speaking with Moses and Elijah. Peter was evidently the principal source of this story, the teacher within Jesus' movement who passed it on and shaped its meaning within Christianity's oral tradition until it made its way to the written gospels. Peter's offer to build shelters or booths in the story reflects its Judaic background, and specifically an association with the festival of Sukkoth. Zechariah 14 had prophesied that at Sukkoth the Temple would become the definitive tabernacle, the place where Israel would be regenerated and sacrifice in the Temple would become a universal feast, open to all peoples who accepted the truth that had been initially revealed to Israel alone. The vision may seem to resolve the issue of Jesus' identity, but in fact Peter's denial of even knowing Jesus after the arrest (Mark 14:66–72; Matt 26:69–75; Luke 22:54–62), despite the disciple's brave claim to be prepared to suffer with his rabbi (Mark 14:26–31; Matt 26:30–35; Luke 22:31–34; John 13:36–38), is consistently attested with variation of emphasis and detail but with commonality of pattern. Yet the pattern does not diminish Peter's paradigmatic place.

The resurrection in fact enhanced Peter's role; Mary Magdalene and her companions are instructed by their vision of the young man at the tomb to tell Jesus' "disciples and Peter" to meet Jesus in Galilee (Mark 16:7). Because the best texts of Mark stop when they do, no actual resurrection appearance to Peter is recorded. Matthew also omits any special appearance to Peter; nonetheless, Peter is among the eleven disciples in Galilee who received their commission at the end of the gospel from the risen Jesus (Matt 28:16–20). Luke places all of its resurrection appearances in the vicinity of Jerusalem, although it does record the confession, already traditional in Luke's time, "The Lord has been raised, and has been seen by Simon" (Luke 24:34). Because he is called "Simon" rather than "Peter" here, it has been argued that the sobriquet and the promise of the keys should be seen in the context of the resurrection, but that surmise runs against the evidence of the gospels in aggregate. In any case, Luke 24:34 agrees with Paul's bare assertion, in the earliest written reference to Jesus' resurrection, that Cephas encountered the risen Jesus first (1 Cor 15:5), but Luke gives no more detail than Paul, and leaves the impression that Simon's vision took place in or near Jerusalem. John, at least, provides a Galilean narrative worthy of being in some kind of sequence with the vision of Mary Magdalene and her colleagues (John 21:1–19). The same Johannine narrative, with the multiple commands Jesus gives to Peter to feed the same sheep the good shepherd has given his life for (see John 10:1–18), provides the clearest indication in all the gospels that Peter is to take on responsibility for believers as a community.

After his experience of Jesus as risen from the dead, Peter made baptism – until his time strictly a ritual of immersion for the sake of purity within Judaism – into the moment of one's immersion in Spirit. His vision of Jesus, which took place in Galilee, pressed him to return to Jerusalem. This was where Jesus had promised that God – just as the Prophets predicted – would make the Temple there into a house of prayer for all the nations of the world (Mark 11:17), the fountain of Spirit for

all the earth. With Peter's guidance, other apostles returned to Jerusalem, and they joined with him in collective experiences of Jesus guiding the Spirit of God in their midst. During Jesus' life Peter had already emerged with the sons of Zebedee as one of three Galilean disciples most skilled in their rabbi's mystical practice. Peter's visionary accomplishment made him the first of them to see Jesus alive after his crucifixion and his experience included the conviction that the Spirit of God was being poured over those who believed in Jesus. For the group that remembered the Twelve gathering around Peter in Jerusalem, the timing of the coming of the Holy Spirit was unequivocal (Acts 2:1–4).

The stress that the full number of the Twelve (Matthias having replaced Judas; Acts 1:15–26) were together in a single place emphasizes that the gift of the Spirit pertains to Israel. Precisely at Pentecost, the Spirit is portrayed as descending on the twelve apostles, and they speak God's praises in the various languages of those assembled from the four points of the compass for that summer feast of harvest, both Jews and proselytes (Acts 2:5–12). The mention of proselytes (2:11) and the stress that those gathered came from "every nation under heaven" (2:5) clearly point ahead to the inclusion of non-Jews by means of baptism within Acts. But even Peter's explanation of the descent of the Spirit does that (Acts 2:14–37). He quotes from the prophet Joel to insist that "all flesh," not only historic Israel, is to receive of God's Spirit: the Twelve are its focus of radiation, not its limit, and Acts speaks of the baptism of some 3,000 people in response to Peter's invitation (Acts 2:37–41).

The outward radiance of the Spirit makes Pentecost the most notable feast (in calendrical terms) of Peter and his circle. The distinctively Christian take on Pentecost is echoed when Peter speaks in the house of Cornelius in Acts 10, and the Spirit falls upon those who are listening. Those there with Peter who were circumcised were astounded "that the gift of the Holy Spirit has been poured out even upon the nations" (10:44–45). The choice of the verb "to pour out" is no coincidence: it is resonant with the quotation of Joel in Acts 2:17. Indeed, those in Cornelius' house praise God "in tongues" (10:46) in a manner reminiscent of the apostles' prophecy at Pentecost. (The assumption here and in Acts 2 is that the Spirit makes people more articulate than they normally are. That is also the way Paul believes tongues are properly to be conceived, as opposed to those who see the gift of tongues as resulting in incoherence – see 1 Corinthians 14.) Peter directs that this non-Jewish household be baptized "in the name of Christ Jesus" (10:47–48).

That is just the direction Peter gave earlier to his sympathetic hearers at Pentecost (2:37–38). Probably in the case of his speech at Pentecost, and more definitely in the case of his speech in the house of Cornelius, Peter's directions were in Greek, and we should understand that immersion is not for the general purpose of purification; it is into Jesus' name, which has entered the Greek language (*Iesous*) as defining the aim of baptism. Christian baptism, immersion into the name of Jesus with reception of the Holy Spirit, was developed within the practice of the circle of Peter.

Taken together, the two passages do not suggest any real dispute as to whether the gift of the Spirit followed or preceded baptism into Jesus' name. The point is rather that belief in and baptism into him is connected directly to the outpouring of God's Spirit. The apparent disruption of the usual model in Acts 10 is intended to call attention to the artificiality (from the point of view of the emergent Petrine theology) of attempting to withhold baptism from those who believe (as Peter actually says in 10:47).

In Peter's speech at Pentecost, Jesus, having been exalted to the right hand of God, receives the promise of the Holy Spirit from the Father and pours it out on his followers (2:33). The Spirit that is poured out, then, comes directly from the majesty of God, from his rule over creation as a whole. This is the Spirit as it hovered over the waters at the beginning of creation (Genesis 1:2), and not as limited to Israel. Because the Spirit is of God, who creates people in the divine image, its presence marks God's own activity, in which all those who follow Jesus are to be included. The *Gospel according to Mary* portrays Mary Magdalene as first to achieve this visionary insight – just as she was first to learn of Jesus' resurrection – and to have conveyed it to Peter.

Jesus' own program had involved proclaiming God's kingdom on the authority of his possession of God's Spirit (see Matt 12:28). Now, as a consequence of the resurrection, Jesus had poured out that same Spirit upon those who would follow him. Baptism in the Spirit (see Acts 1:4–5) and baptism into the name of Jesus were one and the same thing for that reason. In the new environment of God's Spirit which the resurrection signaled, baptism was indeed, as Matthew 28:19 indicates, an activity and an experience which involved the Father (the source of one's identity), the Son (the agent of one's identity), and the Holy Spirit (the medium of one's identity).

When these followers of Jesus claimed in Jerusalem God had raised him from the dead, and that signs were done in his name Caiaphas wanted to ban them and their teaching from the vicinity of the Temple. He even arrested some of them, and kept them in the custody of his police (Acts 5:12–32). But Gamaliel the Pharisee resisted Caiaphas (Acts 5:34–42), arguing that no one could yet discern whether Jesus' followers were deluded or not. The Sanhedrin prevailed on Caiaphas to release Peter, James, and John, the triumvirate among Jesus' apostles. Gamaliel's opposition undermined the high priest's already waning power.

Despite resistance from the high priest, the disciples worshiped regularly with Peter in the Temple, and took meals together – which emerged as the practice of Eucharist – in their common home (Acts 2:42–47). Peter's group lived communally in Jerusalem like an extended, Galilean family. They also replicated the Galilean custom of living at home without money: their possessions were communal. They ate Eucharist together as a domestic meal, beginning with a patriarch's petition for divine blessing, spoken over the bread and invoking Jesus' visionary presence. Peter's group was ferocious when it came to the ideal of communal wealth. Once a man and his wife both claimed to have given the full value of a property they sold to the apostles, but in fact held some money back for themselves. Peter interrogated them one after the other (Acts 5:1–11). He accused them of lying to God, and supernatural violence broke out upon the man and his wife in turn. Assessing the accuracy of this account isn't at issue here. The point is that the story was told, insisting that lying about wealth in this commune brought the retribution of the Holy Spirit. The same Spirit that had descended on Jesus at his baptism was poured out on those who believed in his resurrection, and transformed the apostles in the Temple into prophets of the new, prophetic order. That order, that Spirit, included the power of death itself.

Indirectly familiar with Peter's teaching as a result of controversy about it in Jerusalem, Paul the persecutor embraced it as a result of his vision. His move after his conversion to consult Peter personally made eminent sense. When he visited Peter in 35 CE (Gal 1:18), his senior colleague was already developing the distinctive halakhic teaching, baptism into Jesus' name, and the distinctive theology, of a new release of Spirit through Jesus upon all flesh, that made his contribution to Jesus' movement and to the growth of the gospels fundamental. How his relationship with Paul developed, of course, would take us well beyond the scope of the study of Jesus in history. But it is well worth keeping in mind at all times during the study of Jesus that Peter's influence – and the influence of teachers like him in the primitive phase of Christianity – was greater than was the norm among a rabbi's disciples in Judaism. A rabbi was usually someone who had ordered his own teaching into a Mishnah for his disciples to memorize and repeat. Jesus, killed around the age of thirty, was taken from his followers before he could do that. So Peter was in a position to craft the disciples' memories within his own outline of faith. That is what he instilled in Paul (as Paul says, Gal 1:18) during just over two weeks of intense meeting.

BRUCE CHILTON

Further reading

Barrett, C. K. *The Acts of the Apostles I: The International Critical Commentary*, Edinburgh: T. & T. Clark, 1994.

Chilton, Bruce. *Targumic Approaches to the Gospels. Essays in the Mutual Definition of Judaism and Christianity*, Studies in Judaism, Lanham, MD and London: University Press of America, 1986, pp. 63–80.

—— "Shebna, Eliakim, and the Promise to Peter," in J. Neusner, P. Borgen, E. S. Frerichs, and R. Horsley (eds) *The Social World of Formative Christianity and Judaism*, Philadelphia, PA: Fortress Press, 1989, pp. 311–26.

—— *Redeeming Time. The Wisdom of Ancient Jewish and Christian Festal Calendars*, Peabody: Hendrickson, 2002.

Hartman, Lars. *"Into the Name of the Lord Jesus." Baptism in the Early Church*, Studies of the New Testament and its World, Edinburgh: T. & T. Clark, 1997.

Lapham, Fred. *Peter: The Myth, the Man and the Writings. A Study of Petrine Text and Tradition*, Journal for the Study of the New Testament Supplement 239, Edinburgh: T. & T. Clark. 2004.

Wiarda, Timothy. *Peter in the Gospels. Pattern, Personality and Relationship*, WUNT 2, Reihe 127, Tübingen: Mohr Siebeck, 2000.

SINNERS

The tradition names sinners and comparable people as Jesus' habitual company. Relating to this theme, the entry discusses following questions: the historicity of Jesus' company with sinners; the meaning of the designation "sinners"; and the implications of Jesus' company with sinners.

Historicity of Jesus' company with sinners

There is in scholarship a virtual consensus about the fact that Jesus accepted the company of sinners and the like. The acceptance is testified in both multiple forms (sayings, parables, narratives) and sources: Mark 2:15–17; Matt 11:18–19/Luke 7:33–35 (= Q); Luke 19:1–10 (= L^S). It can also be argued

to display dissimilarity to early Christian attitudes (cf. 1 Cor 5:11). Of individual traditions relevant here, good claims to authenticity have in particular Matt 11:18–19/Luke 7:33–35 where Jesus himself refers to a pejorative label attached to him because of his companionship with dubious people. A point seldom made but worth noting is that Jesus did associate with other kinds of people too. Naturally, he kept (sometimes exclusive) company with his disciples, and Luke even describes Jesus as visiting the homes of some Pharisees (Luke 7:36; 11:37; 14:1). Whatever one can make of these and similar instances, there is no reason to think that Jesus would have agreed to associate only with sinners (and his disciples), although it was understandably this company that stood out and caught the contemporary eye. As to Jesus, however, one should probably consider an in-principle openness to all kinds of people.

Meaning of the designation "sinners"

In Jewish literature the Hebr. *rasha'* ("wicked") and Gk. *hamartolos* ("sinner") basically serve to signify apostates and heinous, willful sinners who do wrong without conscience. Many times, however, the terms function as sheer devices of polemics and denunciation, one Jewish grouping judging the other. Important in this respect is that in the gospels the designation "sinners" (*hamartoloi*), characterizing a certain group of people with whom Jesus kept company, is used by all sides involved in the debates of Jesus' company: the evangelist (Mark 2:15), the Pharisees (Mark 2:16), Jesus himself (Mark 2:17), and people in general (Matt 11:19/Luke 7:34; cf. also Luke 19:7). Taken together, these instances (and the last instance even in itself) suggest that those so characterized were sinners in general respect: that is, they were regarded as sinners by Jews in general, not only by some particular interest group seeking to label Jesus and his company. To a similar conclusion point the mentions of tax collectors (*telonai*). Tax collectors (as well as prostitutes; see Matt 21:31–32; cf. even Luke 7:36–50) were despised by all Jews. That they are in the gospels regularly mentioned in combination with "sinners" (independently of each other: Mark 2:15–16; Matt 11:19/Luke 7:34; Luke 15:1; see also Luke 19:7) clearly implies that the latter characterization was not meant just as some special grouping's judgment of other people.

J. Jeremias in his later work sought to identify Jesus' dubious company with the common people (or "the people of the land") called sinners because of their suspected negligence of some, mainly

Pharisaic, purity and food regulations (Jeremias, 1971, 108–13). E. P. Sanders has successfully advocated the interpretation presented above (Sanders 174–211). In fact, the interpretation had earlier been sustained even by Jeremias himself (1931).

Implications of Jesus' company with sinners

Central to the implications of Jesus' company with sinners is the main form of this companionship: he shared table with them. In Jewish tradition, table fellowship was synonymous with fellowship in all aspects of life. It created a bond with mutual obligations between the people involved. The happy and joyful situation of dining together also easily attracted religious connotations. For instance, salvation was often pictured as a banquet where the Messiah or God himself is the host. From this banquet sinners and idolaters would be excluded to go hungry and thirsty (Isa 25:6–8; 65:13–14; *1 En.* 62:13–14; 1QSa. 2:11–22). Even in general the faithful were advised to keep apart from sinners (Ps 1; Sir 12; *Pss. Sol.* 3; *1 En.* 97:4; 1QS 5:1–2). Sharing table with them would constitute a capital breach against the advice.

What could have been Jesus' own and intended purpose(s) in associating with sinners and gathering at table with them? Scholarship has almost unanimously seen in the table fellowship Jesus' means of imparting the message about the kingdom of God. While the ascetic faster John the Baptist preached imminent judgment, Jesus' proclamation was mainly characterized by the joyful kingdom message. As for Jesus, then, fasting was simply impossible, just as it would have been impossible at a wedding banquet (see Mark 2:18–19; cf. Matt 11:18–19/Luke 7:33–35; see Isa 62:2–5; Jer 33:10–11 for a wedding as a picture for the time of salvation). Instead, sharing the table was a cheerful occasion suitable for the cheerful message. But table fellowship served well in conveying the message for another reason too: it called for mutual acceptance. That is, not only did Jesus accept those with whom he shared the table, those enjoying Jesus' company and the joyous message about the kingdom were also supposed to accept Jesus as the bearer of the kingdom (message).

For many outside observers, however, the impression Jesus left by associating this way with sinners would have appeared as harsh. Accepting freely the company of sinners Jesus made himself suspect of being one of them. If Jesus was instead understood to make the claim that these people could and should be seen as accepted members of society – even as legitimate heirs of the kingdom – another kind of disturbing thought would have been evoked: what use was there of all labor in trying to heed God's commandments and lead a life in agreement with his will? In other words, Jesus' behavior would have blurred the difference between righteous and sinners and frustrated covenant loyalty. Because Jesus made his appearance, among other things, as that of a religious teacher (with following), this behavior would have been experienced as not only outrageous but also alarming. Such sentiment of offence has left a clear trace in the tradition and was probably one factor among others to spur the leading religious figures to take action against Jesus.

Sanders rightly reasoned that had the sinners with whom Jesus associated been perceived as repentant ones, no serious offence would have emerged. However, his further conclusion that Jesus did not at all require repentance has often been deemed as unnecessarily hasty (see Allison; Chilton). Maybe acceptance of sinners was Jesus' peculiar way to encourage them to repent: that is, to return to God. In particular, maybe Jesus saw the reciprocal challenge of accepting him as something that would count as – or involve steps equivalent to – repentance. This would explain the fact that while Jesus in principle was open to all kinds of people, *en masse* only those who knew themselves as being in need of repentance joined him: they were prepared to accommodate to the requirement of accepting Jesus and what this entailed.

TOM HOLMÉN

Further reading

Allison, D. C. "Jesus and the Covenant: A Response to E. P. Sanders," *JSNT* 29 (1987) 57–78.

Blomberg, C. *Contagious Holiness: Jesus' Meals with Sinners*, Downers Grove, IL: InterVarsity Press, 2005.

Chilton, B. "Jesus and the Repentance of E. P. Sanders," *Tyndale Bulletin* 39 (1988) 1–18.

Cover, R. C. "Sin, Sinners," *ABD* 6 (1992) 31–40.

Dunn, J. D. G. "Pharisees, Sinners, and Jesus," in J. Neusner (ed.) *The Social World of Formative Christianity and Judaism*, Philadelphia, PA: Fortress Press, 1988, pp. 264–89.

Feeley-Harnik, G. *The Lord's Table: The Meaning of Food in Early Judaism and Christianity*, Washington, DC: Smithsonian Institution Press, 1994.

Holmén, T. *Jesus and Jewish Covenant Thinking*, Leiden: Brill, 2001.

Jeremias, J. "Zöllner und Sünder," *ZAW* 13 (1931) 293–300.

—— *New Testament Theology I: The Proclamation of Jesus*, London: SCM Press, 1971.

Koch, D.-A. "Jesu Tischgemeinschaft mit Zöllnern und Sündern," in D.-A. Koch, G. Sellin, and A. Lindemann,

Jesu Rede von Gott und ihre Nachgeschichte im frühen Christentum, Gütersloh: Mohn, 1989, pp. 57–73.
Sanders, E. P. *Jesus and Judaism*, London: SCM Press, 1985.

SLAVERY, SERVANTS

Slavery is shown in the gospels as being as much a part of the fabric of society as any other human relationship. Although many translators render the Greek term for 'slave' (*doulos*) as 'servant', there is no doubt that the word meant 'slave' in every sense. Slaves are mentioned regularly in Jesus' parables; the faithfulness and obedience of the good slave is set as a model for the believer (Luke 12:35–38) and the powers of the master over the slave are taken for granted (Luke 12:47–49).

Slaves were an accepted part of Jewish society, although in fairly limited numbers. This agricultural society depended largely on free, hired labour and the presence of slaves in any households but those of the wealthy would have been rare. The most common and indeed the only acceptable way for a Jew to become a slave to another Jew was through debt. Interest rates in the ancient Near East – despite laws curtailing or attempting to ban it – were penal and could lead to a crippling debt burden for farmers. The resulting bankruptcy usually led to the family being sold into slavery. Such debt bondage was classed with other debts and by law was supposed to be remitted after six years (Exod 21:2–4; Deut 15:12), although there is evidence that this law was widely ignored. The law also made provision for a slave who wished to have this temporary debt slavery made permanent (Exod 21:4–6 and Deut 16–17). Jewish law laid down strict rules about the treatment of slaves, especially those who were fellow countrymen (Lev 25:39–55). A slave was not to be seen as a possession, but as a member of the household with human rights and obligations. Harsh treatment of slaves was forbidden (Lev 25:43). Slaves were included in the injunction to rest on the Sabbath (Deut 5:12–15) and they had religious obligations to fulfil (Deut 16:11–15). The killing of a slave carried penalties (Exod 21:20–21) and a slave mutilated by the owner was entitled to freedom (Exod 21:26–27). Fugitive slaves could not be returned to their owner but must be taken into the household where they had sought refuge (Deut 23:15–16). By the time of Jesus, however, these more humane traditions were being rapidly superseded by those of the prevailing Roman culture, especially in urban contexts. There is evidence that by now there were Jewish slaves in Jewish households and that the privileges granted by their religion were not always observed.

In the slave-owning societies of Greece and Rome, hired labour was rarely made use of and was, indeed, regarded as in itself a form of slavery beneath the dignity of a free person. Slaves participated in every level of society and their lives differed widely depending on their situation. A domestic slave might be regarded as one of the family, and those used as tutors or secretaries were frequently better educated than their owners. On the other hand, slaves in the agricultural chain gangs of the great estates and those labouring in the mines lived lives of terrible hardship. The latter two types of slave are mentioned nowhere in the New Testament – it is likely that such slavery did not feature at all in the experience of Jesus and his contemporaries.

Although war had provided a major source of slaves in the form of captives in the past, by this time slaves were largely bred at home or purchased at the market place from traders who brought them in from all parts of the world. A good proportion of the traders' stock, however, especially those destined for prostitution, would originate as babies who had been abandoned by their parents at birth. This was an acceptable form of family planning in the Roman world, and anyone who cared to was entitled to pick up such a baby and keep it. In contrast to the Jewish tradition, the Roman law made it a serious offence to harbour a runaway slave, and such must be returned to their owner immediately.

Slaves at this time were not readily distinguished from free persons by race, education or clothing. Social mobility in and out of slavery was common in Roman culture, and slave careers might be as impressive as those of free persons. In Roman society at the time of Jesus, some slaves reached positions of great wealth and influence, as in the case of the emperor's slaves who were put in charge of the imperial administration. Further down the scale it was common for competent slaves to be entrusted with money (Matt 25:14–30; Luke 19:11–27), business dealings, and even farms or households (Matt 24:45–51; Luke 12:42–48).

The defining feature of all slaves, from the lowest to the most privileged, was the fact that in law they, unlike free persons, had no rights over their own bodies. In law at least, only slaves could be subject to physical punishment and to torture. Some towns even had professional torturers to enable masters to punish their slaves more conveniently (Matt 18:34). To be flogged was the punishment for slaves and crucifixion, burning alive and being fed to animals in the arena were considered the appropriate methods of execution. By this time, such abuses were beginning to be extended to the lower classes in general, but the association with slavery was still vivid.

There is no evidence whatsoever that any thought was taken on the part of philosophers, early Christians or even slaves themselves as to whether slavery itself could or should be abolished. The occasional philosopher might condemn it but only on the basis that it corrupted the owner to have too many slaves or to abuse them, and in those rare cases where slaves rose up in organised revolt, their intention was always to take the position of masters and in turn enslave others. Abolition of slavery itself had not begun to be thought of, and it would be several hundred years before even a few theologians would begin to suggest such a concept.

I. A. H. COMBES

Further reading

Bradley, K. R. *Slaves and Masters in the Roman Empire: A Study in Social Control*, New York, Oxford: Oxford University Press, 1987.

Buckland, W. W. *The Roman Law of Slavery: The Condition of the Slave in Private Law from Augustus to Justinian*, Cambridge: Cambridge University Press, 1970.

Chirirchigno, Gregory C. *Debt-Slavery in Israel and the Ancient Near East*, Sheffield: Sheffield Academic Press, 1993.

Glancy, Jennifer A. *Slavery in Early Christianity*, New York: Oxford University Press, 2002.

Martin, Dale B. "Slavery and the Ancient Jewish Family," in Shaye J. D. Cohen (ed.) *The Jewish Family in Antiquity*, Atlanta, GA: Scholars Press, 1989, pp. 113–29.

Mendelsohn, I. *Slavery in the Ancient Near East: A Comparative Study in Babylonian Assyria and Palestine from the Middle of the Third Millennium to the end of the First Millennium*, New York: Oxford University Press, 1949.

SOCIAL SCIENTIFIC CRITICISM

Social scientific criticism is a way of interpreting biblical documents in terms of the social system of the persons to whom writers originally directed their writings. Such interpretation is rooted in the premise that the meanings which people communicate through language and behavior always derive from their shared social system. Hence if one wishes to understand what a biblical writer said and meant to say to some original audience, one must necessarily bring an understanding of the writer's and audience's social system to one's reading of a given biblical document.

As a method in the toolkit of biblical interpreters, social scientific criticism emerged after a series of methods generally labeled with the final noun: "criticism," originating in German scholarship.

In the beginning there was historical criticism, then history of literary forms and literary criticism, followed by editorial or redactional criticism, source criticism, and rhetorical criticism (see Hochschild). Social scientific criticism presumes and is built on all of these approaches. What they all have in common is that scholars developed them to reduce anachronism and ethnocentrism in their biblical interpretation. They likewise presumed that biblical documents are documents written some two millennia ago by people in the Eastern Mediterranean. As written documents they have been composed in various literary genres, communicating through a range of literary forms or patterns, to make historically specific points. Many of those documents have been reworked by persons called "editors," who used a range of sources. What social scientific criticism adds to these approaches is an awareness of the fact that these ancient writings likewise derive from persons enculturated in social systems in culture areas rather fully removed from modern Euro-American culture areas. And since meanings derive from social systems, to understand these documents it is necessary to move from one's own social system into that of the ancient Eastern Mediterranean in order to hear and understand what those documents were intended to communicate and actually communicated to their initial audiences.

The present forms of social scientific criticism are rooted in sociolinguistics, cultural anthropology, social psychology, and macrosociology, all outfitted with historically sensitive cross-cultural, comparative components. The reason for this is that to understand any other social system, one must understand one's own social system reflexively (that is, its institutions, values and person types) and proceed by comparison with the social system under study. Social scientific criticism in its present forms developed from the perspectives of early twentieth-century social philosophers such as Karl Marx and Max Weber (and a number of others) who attempted to understand and explain various social systems in terms of common generalizations. As philosophers, they were little concerned with verifying their contentions with adequate empirical proof. The interest of these social philosophers was in the whole of society, including what they called middle and lower "classes." This interest spurred and supported the writing of "social" history, to understand the "social" question of the day ("social" here meant of or relating to the economically poor). This led a number of biblical scholars to refocus their study of historical narrative on ordinary people in the biblical period, and to adopt the questions and range of interests of social philosophers as well as that of a number of early sociologists concerned with social classes, class conflicts, family structures and religions of the past. The result was great interest in social history, meaning the story of ordinary people, the poor and non-elite "little people" who really formed the warp and woof of humanity, today as well as in the past.

Social history

This interest in social history led some biblical interpreters to adopt and apply pertinent socio-logical studies in their work. In biblical studies, the result was often called "sociological exegesis." The phrase was an offshoot of German, once more, in which the words "social" and "sociological" have the same general meaning (the same holds for French, Italian, and Spanish). The outcome was confusion in English since "social" means of or pertaining to humans in groups, while "socio-logical" means of or pertaining to sociology, the scientific study of human society, including both social organization and social action.

Furthermore, in US universities and colleges, sociology is the study of American society, while cultural anthropology is the comparative study of one's own society and some alien society. The basic problem with using US sociology for under-standing the past is that interpreting the story of biblical people through sociological lenses results in a story in which biblical people are described in terms of what they would have been like had they been US persons. This is often the trap into which social historians of the Bible fall. It is a sort of "what would Jesus (or Paul) and early Jesus group members do if they were Americans?" This is like-wise the problem ignored by sociologists such as Stark and Blasi (and his recent *Handbook*, 2002).

While historical criticism made one aware of anachronism, sociological exegesis did not elim-inate ethnocentrism or abstract anachronisms. It was the ethnocentric bias in the Teutonic "Geschichten" as well as in the social history rooted in the social philosophy of Max Weber that made the social context (*Sitz im Leben*) found in the New Testament look very much like that of the scholars describing it. For example, it never dawned on those insisting on Jesus as charismatic that the category might be overly Teutonic and irrelevant to the biblical periods. And people spoke of the religion of Jesus without a thought to the fact that religion (and economics) was embedded in the political and kinship institutions of the time.

Sociological exegesis

In the late 1970s a number of persons in the US (Gottwald; Scroggs; Elliott 1981), and Europe (Theissen; Holmberg; Aguirre) took up the social historian's focus and hit upon using contemporary sociology to describe and explain the social beha-viors and organizations described in the Bible. Some Europeans (Belo; Houtart) called this a materialistic approach to the Bible, even a Marxist approach. This approach was called "sociology" or "sociological exegesis."

At the same time, several biblical scholars who lived for extended periods in foreign cultures and learned cultural anthropology to make sense of their culture shock and cross-cultural under-standing found the "sociology" label inappropriate. The experience of these scholars was no different from that of people doing Bible translations in foreign countries, yet it seems that these translators never realized that the societies depicted in the Bible were as foreign and esoteric as the societies for whom they were translating (e.g. consider the missionary anthropologist Kraft). Rohrbaugh (1978) highlighted the problem with his book on reading the peasant Bible in an industrialized world.

Social scientific criticism

Malina introduced the label "social sciences" rather than "sociology" in a 1981 task group at the Catholic Biblical Association that he has convened annually since then. That same year his cultural anthropological introduction to the New Testa-ment appeared. Malina also introduced the task group members to the work of Carney (1975) who successfully attempted to interpret the Greco-Roman world with cross-cultural lenses and set out his comparisons in terms of sets of abstract con-ceptual relations called models. The label "social scientific criticism" was coined by Malina and Elliott after Malina pointed out the inadequacy of labeling what Elliott sought to do as "sociological exegesis." Elliott adopted the new label as the title of his book, *What is Social Scientific Criticism?* (1993).

Social scientific approaches employ a collection of appropriate cross-cultural generalizations and models from the social sciences to interpret the sources for the study of New Testament documents. What makes a social scientific generalization or model appropriate depends upon social scientific and historical judgment. The social scientific judg-ment of appropriateness relates to whether the behaviors in question conform to the social system of the Eastern Mediterranean cultural region, with its traditional values (e.g. gender roles, concern for honor) and social structures (e.g. kinship focus, endogamous marriage). The historical judgment of appropriateness relates to whether the generalizations and models can be shown to trace back to the first-century Eastern Mediterranean. To make such a historical judgment, the interpreter must remove the filters deriving from the historical developments called Technologism and Scientism, Romanticism (or post-Modernism), the Industrial Revolution, Sense of History, the Enlightenment, the Renaissance and Reformation, the Scientific Method, Scholasticism, Islam, Christendom, Jewishness (Rabbinic and Talmudic), Augustine, Constantine, Origen and the like. Each of these historical episodes introduced social features that obfuscate an understanding of the first-century Eastern Mediterranean.

The use of the social sciences in the historical enterprise of New Testament interpretation is evidenced by the exegetes' use of explicit, testable and systematic conceptualizations in place of the usual historical approaches typical of traditional social historical research rooted largely in the usually unwary adoption of implicit, arbitrary and unsystematic conceptualizations. Furthermore, and most significantly, social scientific approaches seek to set out the underlying social structures that provided the meanings articulated in the sources used in historical Jesus research (see Barraclough 1978).

After filtering out the accretions of social development evidenced both in his or her own society as well as in the modern Mediterranean, the investigator will seek the behaviors and values that have survived in the region through all historical vicissitudes to be quite useful. The historical leap from the Mediterranean present to the ancient Mediterranean is not unlike that of historians of ancient music (see the symposium edited by Kenyon; Shull). As a number of modern scholars have demonstrated, the Mediterranean is a culture area, remarkably stable in cultural values and percepts (Horden and Purcell). Murdock (1980), for example, produced a small book in which he took 186 societies and compared them in terms of similarities and differences relative to sickening. Thanks to his categorizations, he surfaced the main theories of illness common to various groupings of these various societies. This book is significant because one of Murdock's unexpected conclusions was to discover a theory of illness characteristic of and distinctive to the Circum-Mediterranean region, regardless of the particular histories of the distinctive ethnic or national groups: Trial and error showed, however, that if North Africa were detached from sub-Saharan Africa and the Near East from Asia, and if both were grouped with Europe to form a composite Circum-Mediterranean region, this would yield three regions reasonably comparable not only to one another but also to each American continent and the Insular Pacific. The experimental tabulation of the incidence of the major theories of illness in these ad hoc regions led to a serendipitous discovery: the theories actually showed some tendency toward segregation by region (1980: 42). Illness theories are replications of the interpretive themes of a culture, and common illness theories would point to common interpretive themes. Thus as regards illness perception, the Mediterranean is different, a difference Murdock traces back to antiquity.

Among social scientific topics thus far successfully applied to New Testament interpretation, we might mention, for example, kinship and the kin group over all other institutions, primacy of the ingroup, anti-language and anti-society, ancestrism, endogamy, patron–client relationship, giftgiving, the role and function of holy men, shame as sanction, concern for honor, agonism, coalitions, networks, violence and physical force in defense of honor, sexual organs as symbolizing honor, the primacy of honor over wealth, hospitality, almsgiving, fasting, small group development, embedded religion/economics, altered states of consciousness as normal and common human experiences, gender division of labor, cross-cultural healing patterns, folk healing, limited good, envy and the evil eye, social impact of astronomy, time perception, and collectivistic personality.

For the most part, social scientific research in biblical studies has been largely focused on the New Testament. And New Testament research has been concerned with interpreting the documents of the New Testament, not with the general storytelling of historians (an exception is Stegemann and Stegemann). This is perhaps why as yet there exists no full "life" of the historical Jesus based on social scientific interpretations. Yet the social scientific interpretative enterprise has produced works bearing upon exegetical and historical understanding of Jesus' career in such great quantity and of such superb quality that one can speak of social scientific approaches to New Testament interpretation in general and to Jesus research in particular (see Malina 2002).

By and large, the main contributors to original research employing social scientific methods are members of the Context Group (founded in 1983), an international gathering of scholars devoted to studying the New Testament in its historical and cultural environment. The members of the group include: Rafael Aguirre, S. Scott Bartchy, Carmen Bernabé, David Bossman, Pieter Craffert, Zeba Crook, Richard DeMaris, Adriana Destro, Craig DeVos, Dennis Duling, John H. Elliott, Philip Esler, Elisa Estevez, Carlos Gil, Santiago Guijarro, Anselm Hagedorn, K. C. Hanson, William Herzog, T. Raymond Hobbs, Stephan Joubert, Stuart Love, Bruce J. Malina, David May, Halvor Moxnes, Dietmar Neufeld, Jerome Neyrey, Douglas Oakman, Mauro Pesce, John Pilch, Ronald Piper, Richard Rohrbaugh, Torrey Seland, Gary Stansell, Wolfgang Stegemann, Christian Strecker, Walter Taylor, Andries Van Aarde, and Ritva Williams. References to their works can be readily accessed on Ebsco, ATLA, or NTAbstracts CD; and a large collection of bibliographical references may be found in Elliott (1993) and more recently in Pilch (2001) and Stegemann *et al.* (2002).

BRUCE J. MALINA

Further reading

Aguirre, Rafael. *Del movimiento de Jesús a la iglesia cristiana: ensayo de exégesis sociológica del cristianismo primitivo*, Bilbao: Desclée de Brouwer, 1987.

Barraclough, Geoffrey. *Main Trends in History*, New York: Holmes & Meier, 1978.

Belo, Fernando. *Lecture matérialiste de l'évangile de Marc: Récit-Practique-Idéologie*, Paris: Cerf, 1974; second revised edition 1975.

Blasi, Anthony J., Jean Duhaime, and Paul-André Turcotte (eds) *Handbook of Early Christianity: Social Science Approaches*, Walnut Creek, CA: AltaMira Press, 2002.

Carney, Thomas F. *The Shape of the Past: Models and Antiquity*, Lawrence, KS: Coronado Press, 1975.

Elliott, John Hall. *A Home for the Homeless: A Sociological Exegesis of 1 Peter, its Situation and Strategy*, Philadelphia, PA: Fortress Press, 1981.

—— *What Is Social-Scientific Criticism?*, Guides to Biblical Scholarship, New Testament Series, Minneapolis, MN: Fortress Press, 1993.

Gottwald, N. K. *The Tribes of Yahweh: A Sociology of the Religion of Liberated Israel, 1250–2050 BCE*, Maryknoll, NY: Orbis Books, 1979.

Hochschild, Ralph. *Sozialgeschichtliche Exegese: Entwicklung, Geschichte und Methodik einer neutestamentlichen Forschungsrichtung*. NTOA 42, Fribourg: Editions universitaires; Gottingen: Vandenhoeck & Ruprecht, 1999.

Holmberg, Bengt and Paul Power. *The Structure of Authority in the Primitive Church as Reflected in the Pauline Epistles*, Philadelphia, PA: Fortress Press, 1980.

Horden, Peregrine and Nicholas Purcell. *The Corrupting Sea: A Study of Mediterranean History*, Oxford: Blackwell, 2000.

Houtart, François. *Religion et modes de production précapitalistes*, Brussels: Editions de l'Université de Bruxelles, 1980

Kenyon, Nicholas (ed.) *Authenticity and Early Music: A Symposium*, Oxford: Oxford University Press, 1988.

Kraft, Charles H. *Christianity in Culture: A Study in Dynamic Biblical Theologizing in Cross-Cultural Perspective*, Maryknoll, NY: Orbis, 1979.

Malina, Bruce J. *The New Testament World: Insights from Cultural Anthropology*, third revised edition, Louisville, KY: Westminster/Knox, 2001 [1981].

—— "Social Scientific Method in Historical Jesus Research," in Wolfgang Stegemann, Bruce J. Malina, and Gerd Theissen (eds) *The Social Setting of Jesus and the Gospels*, Minneapolis, MN: Fortress Press, 2002, pp. 3–26.

Murdock, George P. *Theories of Illness: A World Survey*, Pittsburgh, PA: University of Pittsburgh, 1980.

Pilch, John J. (ed.) *Social Scientific Models for Interpreting the Bible: Essays by the Context Group in Honor of Bruce J. Malina, BibInt* 53, Leiden: Brill, 2001.

Rohrbaugh, Richard L. *The Biblical Interpreter: An Agrarian Bible in an Industrial Age*, Philadelphia, PA: Fortress Press, 1978.

Scrogg, R., "The Earliest Christian Communities as Sectarian Movement," in D. G. Horrell, ed., *Social-Scientific Approaches to New Testament Interpretation*, Edinburgh: T. & T. Clark, 1999.

Shull, Jonathan. "Locating the Past in the Present: Living Traditions and the Performance of Early Music," *Ethnomusicology Forum* 15 (2006) 87–111.

Stegemann, Ekkehard W. and Wolfgang Stegemann. *The Jesus Movement: A Social History of the First Century*, Minneapolis, MN: Fortress Press, 1999.

Stegemann, Wolfgang, Bruce J. Malina, and Gerd Theissen (eds) *The Social Setting of Jesus and the Gospels*, Minneapolis, MN: Fortress Press, 2002.

Theissen, Gerd. *Soziologie der Jesusbewegung: ein Beitrag zur Entstehungsgeschichte des Urchristentums*, München: Kaiser, 1977.

SOLOMON

Gospel references to Solomon

With just nine references, Solomon does not play a major role in the four canonical gospels. In evaluating the relationship of Solomon to the public activity of the historical Jesus, we can note that three of the nine references result from the gospel writers' redaction. Two of these occur in the opening genealogy of Matthew (1:6–7) that highlights Jesus' connection with David (1:1, 6, 17). This emphasis recalls the divine promise that David and his descendants will rule forever (2 Sam 7) in representing God's rule of justice and peace (e.g. Ps 72). Solomon is located in this context. A third reference in John 10:23 places Jesus at the feast of Dedication (Hanukkah) "in the temple, in the portico of Solomon." The reference continues John's temple theme in which Jesus replaces the destroyed temple post 70 CE. The link, though, with Hanukah and the unusual timing of the scene in winter may indicate a reliable historical memory.

While these three references are editorial, they may reflect remembrances of some association between Jesus and Solomon. The remaining references comprise sayings found in Q.

Solomon's glory: Matt 6:29/Luke 12:27b

This saying, "Yet I tell you, even Solomon in all his glory was not arrayed like one of these" belongs to a Q passage in the Sermon on the Mount (Matt 6:25–34). The passage (including Matthean redaction) emphasizes God's care that counters anxiety and exhorts human trust. Most interpreters see the passage's core originating with Jesus though there is debate about details. Most affirm 6:29 as originating from Jesus. Several linguistic features in 6:29 – "I say to you" and "who among you" (6:27) – reflect Jesus' speech, as does the extended parallelism between 6:26 and 6:28b–30 (compare Mark 9:43–47; Luke 11:31–32), the use of images from nature in 6:26 and 28, and the sustained emphasis on God's providential care.

The interesting question concerns the reference's meaning. Does Jesus argue from the lesser to the greater whereby Jesus presents the proverbially wealthy Solomon as a positive example of human achievement before acknowledging God's even greater accomplishment in clothing the flowers? Or does Jesus criticize Solomon as an anxious person by contrasting God's gracious and abundant provision with Solomon's untrusting exploitative and oppressive actions in securing excessive wealth? The latter view seems likely. The phrase "I tell you" in other Q sayings expresses Jesus' authority and introduces a contrast (Matt 3:9 and Luke 3:8; Matt 5:26 and Luke 12:59; Matt 5:44 and Luke 6:27, etc.). The one other reference to "glory" in Q material is negative denoting the exploitative power of empires in Satan's control (Matt 4:8 and Luke 4:6). Hebrew Bible traditions offer extensive critique of Solomon's exploitation and greed. Moses warns against the evil ways of kings in acquiring horses, numerous wives, and great wealth (Deut 17:16–17), all of which Solomon does (horses, 1 Kgs 4:26; 10:26–29; wives, 1 Kgs 11:1–8; wealth through forced labor [1 Kgs 4:6; 5:13–18], co-opted food and tribute [1 Kgs 4:7, 21–25, 27–28]). Jesus evokes the wealthy and powerful ruler Solomon to discredit him as one who lived contrary to God's just will and to enhance Jesus' own activity.

Greater than Solomon: Matt 12:42/Luke 11:31

From wealth to wisdom, from Solomon the rich ruler to the archetypal sage, this Q saying discredits Solomon's proverbial wisdom. While it is great enough to attract the Queen of Sheba (compare 1 Kgs 10:1–13), something greater – perhaps God's kingdom/empire – is present in Jesus though the present generation does not recognize it and will be condemned at the judgment. Is the saying authentic? The Jesus Seminar thinks not, because it considers expectations of future judgment to arise not from the historical Jesus but from the early church's disappointment with its failed mission. Those who understand Jesus proclaiming an eschatological message generally accept it as authentic. The emphasis on repentance, the use of unlikely heroes such as Jonah and a Gentile queen, the affirmation of the present as a time of salvation, its semitic diction, the argumentation of the saying, and the unparalleled symmetry with the preceding Jonah saying cohere with features of the historical Jesus' teaching and speech and suggest authenticity. Jesus evokes Solomon to assert his own superior role as a herald of God's kingdom.

Solomon: the miracle-working son of David

At a number of points, the gospels link Jesus with David (Mark 11:10) and/or identify him as Son of David (Matt 1:1). While kingly traditions inform some references, one scene in the common tradition (Mark 10:47–48; Matt 20:29–34; Luke 18:35–43) and one saying in a (largely) Q tradition (Matt 12:22–30 and Luke 11:14–15, 17–23, with Matthean redaction and material from Mark 3:22–27) link "Son of David" with Jesus' healings and exorcisms. Matthew's gospel adds references to Jesus as Son of David to healing and exorcism scenes (Matt 9:27; 12:23; 15:22). Significantly, literary traditions (*Wisdom of Solomon* 7:15–22; Josephus, *Ant.* 8.42–49; *Testament of Solomon*) and archeological traditions (Aramaic Incantation Bowl texts and amulets) present David's son, Solomon, as a miracle worker and exorcist.

Does this link between Solomon as son of David and Jesus as exorcists and healers originate with the historical Jesus? The healing of blind Bartimaeus points to this possibility (Mark 10:46–52). John Meier identifies several factors in Mark's scene that suggest authenticity. Rarely do Jesus' healings name the beneficiary (10:46). The scene includes two Aramaic words, the man's identification as Bartimaeus (10:46) and his address to Jesus as "Rabbouni" (10:51). The man's location in Jericho, a gathering place for pilgrims to Jerusalem, is at least realistic. And the story identifies Jesus as Son of David (10:47), an unlikely Markan redaction given the minimal role of the designation in the gospel. The Jesus Seminar colors much of the scene pink, indicating it probably occurred.

References to Solomon are not common in the gospels. Traditions, though, seem to link the historical Jesus with Solomon, contrasting him with an untrusting wealthy king and inferior wise man. Given these unfavorable comparisons, it seems that Jesus is also greater than Solomon as a healer and exorcist. The unfavorable comparisons enhance Jesus' authority and legitimacy as God's agent.

WARREN CARTER

Further reading

Carter, Warren. "'Solomon in All His Glory': Intertextuality and Matthew 6:29," *JSNT* 65 (1997) 3–25.
—— *Matthew and the Margins: A Sociopolitical and Religious Reading*, JSNTSup 204, Sheffield: Sheffield Academic Press, 2000.
Davies, William D. and Dale Allison. *A Critical and Exegetical Commentary on the Gospel According to Saint Matthew*, Vol. 1, Edinburgh: T. & T. Clark, 1988, pp. 645–63.
Duling, Dennis. "Solomon, Exorcism, and the Son of David," *Harvard Theological Review* 68 (1975) 235–52.
—— "The Eleazar Miracle and Solomon's Magical Wisdom in Flavius Josephus' *Antiquitates Judaicae* 8.42–49," *HTR* 78 (1985) 1–25.
—— "The Testament of Solomon: Retrospect and Prospect," *JSP* 2 (1988) 87–112.
Funk, Robert and the Jesus Seminar. *The Acts of Jesus: The Search for the Authentic Deeds of Jesus*, San Francisco, CA: HarperSanFrancisco and Polebridge, 1998, pp. 118–19.
Funk, Robert, Roy Hoover, and the Jesus Seminar. *The Five Gospels: What Did Jesus Really Say?* New York: Macmillan and Polebridge, 1993.
Graham, Helen. "A Solomonic Model of Peace," in Rasiah Sugirtharajah (ed.) *Voices from the Margin: Interpreting the Bible in the Third World*, London: SPCK, 1991.
Meier, John P. *A Marginal Jew: Rethinking the Historical Jesus*, Vol. 2, New York: Doubleday, 1994, pp. 404–23, 686–90.

SON OF DAVID

In the New Testament Gospels "son of David" is a messianic epithet. It occurs some seventeen (or eighteen) times (de Jonge; Lohse). A few times it is specifically applied to Jesus. Its precise contribution to Jesus' self-understanding and to subsequent Christology is somewhat ambiguous.

Old Testament and Judaic background

The messianic associations of the epithet "son of David" have their origin in the Hebrew Bible and in Judaic traditions that antedate Jesus and the early Christian movement. The covenant with David, whereby Israel's great king is promised a descendant who will sit on his throne forever (2 Sam 7:10–16; Ps 89:1–4, 19–37; 132:11–12), is the foundation on which Davidic messianism will grow (Pomykala). In these traditions David is the Lord's anointed (or *messiah*) par. excellence, whose future son will be called God's "son" (2 Sam 7:14 "I will be his father, and he shall be my son"; Ps 2:7 "You are my son") and will sit on God's throne (1 Chr 29:23 "Then Solomon sat on the throne of the Lord as king instead of David his father"), over God's kingdom (1 Chr 28:5 God "has chosen Solomon my son to sit upon the throne of the kingdom of the Lord over Israel").

The awaited messianic descendant is often referred to as the "Branch," an epithet that may have originated with Isaiah (cf. 11:1 "There shall come forth a shoot from the stump of Jesse, and a branch shall grow out of his roots"). It gains a firmer place in later messianic hopes (Jer 23:5 "Behold, the days are coming, says the Lord, when I will raise up for David a righteous Branch, and he shall reign as king"; 33:15 "In those days and at that time I will cause a righteous Branch to spring forth for David"; Zech 3:8 "Hear now ... behold, I will bring my servant the Branch"; 6:12 "Behold, the man whose name is the Branch"). David is also called "prince" (2 Sam 6:21; 7:8; 1 Chr 17:7), whose son Solomon is also called prince (1 Chr 29:22). This epithet also becomes part of Davidic messianism, as seen in the Prophets (Ezek 34:24; 37:25).

Davidic messianism flourished in the two centuries leading up to the time of Jesus. The epithet "prince" also appears in the Scrolls (1QSb 5:50; 1QM 5:1; 11Q5 28:11). Yeshua ben Sira speaks of David's "covenant of kings and a throne of glory in Israel" (Sir 47:11) and the hope of an everlasting "root" (47:22). The author of 1 Maccabees affirms that, "David, because he was merciful, inherited the throne of the kingdom for ever" (1 Macc 2:57).

The "Branch" epithet was a favorite in the Dead Sea Scrolls (4Q161 fr. 8 x 17; 4Q174 frs 1–2 i 12; 4Q252 5:3 "until the righteous Messiah, the Branch of David, has come;" 4Q285 fr. 7 lines 3–4 = 11Q14 fr. 1 lines 12–13 "the Branch of David will have him [the Roman Emperor] put to death"). *Psalms of Solomon* 17–18 gives expression to similar hopes:

> Behold, O Lord, and raise up to them their king, the son of David, at the time, in the which you choose, O God, that he may reign over Israel your servant. And gird him with strength, that he may shatter unrighteous rulers. And that he may purge Jerusalem from nations that trample [her] down to destruction.
>
> (17:21–22)

And he [shall be] a righteous king, taught of God, over them. And there shall be no unrighteousness in his days in their midst, for all shall be holy and their king the Lord's Messiah.

(17:32)

Passages such as these attest "a fairly vigorous and sustained hope of a royal messiah within several at least of the various subgroups of Israel at the time of Jesus, and that that hope was probably fairly widespread at a popular level" (Dunn 367; cf. Johnson; Schneider 1971). Addressing Jesus as "son of David" would have invoked much of this messianic expectation.

Historical Jesus

According to the genealogies of Jesus found in Matthew (1:1–17) and Luke (3:23–38), Jesus was a descendant of King David. Some critics have contended that tradition of this descent arose only later, in the aftermath of the early Church's proclamation of Jesus as Messiah. To herald Jesus as Israel's Messiah, so the argument goes, would require Davidic descent. Therefore, "Davidic" genealogies were created.

It is claimed further that there were no records of Davidic descent extant in the time of Jesus. Therefore, the genealogies found in Matthew and Luke are likely not genuine. This claim, however, is dubious. Eusebius reports that Vespasian (*Hist. eccl.* 3.12), Domitian (3.19–20), and Trajan (3.32.5–6) persecuted the family of David, so that no royal claimant might arise and challenge the authority of Rome. Not long ago an ossuary dating from the first century BCE was found in Jerusalem bearing the inscription: "of the house of David." According to early rabbinic literature, "the family of David" brought the wood-offering of the priests to the temple on the 20th of Tammuz (cf. *m. Ta'anith* 4:5; *t. Ta'anith* 3.5). Later rabbinic traditions claim that various rabbis (*b. Shab.* 56a), including Hillel himself (*y. Ta'anith* 4.2), were descendants of David. It is speculated that Josephus' remark that Rabbi Simeon ben Gamaliel (grandson or great-grandson of Hillel) came from "a very illustrious family" (Josephus, *Life* 191) alludes to Davidic ancestry. Given the Flavian dynasty's antipathy towards Jewish patriotic hopes in general and the Davidic dynasty in particular (as documented in Eusebius), we may understand Josephus' reluctance to be more specific than he is.

The evidence of recognized Davidic lineage in the time of Jesus is compelling. Early Christians knew of Jesus' Davidic descent, but apparently made little of it (cf. Paul's remarks in Rom 1:3–4). Indeed, Jesus himself challenges the adequacy of understanding the Messiah in terms of the epithet "son of David" (in Mark 12:35–37; see below). In short, New Testament Christology is founded on other, more important traditions than mere Davidic descent. Nevertheless, Davidic messianism, especially the specific epithet, "son of David," played an important role in the early understanding of Jesus. There are four passages that call for comment.

Mark 10:46–52

As Jesus passes through Jericho, accompanied by a large crowd, a blind beggar named Bartimaeus, or "son of Timaeus," cries out, asking for mercy. The crowd tries to silence him, but he continues to cry out, "Son of David, Jesus, have pity on me!" Jesus gives the blind man an audience and learns that he wishes to have his sight restored. Jesus heals him and then he follows Jesus on the way. The story is repeated by Matthew (20:29–34) and Luke (18:35–43), though in a more polished and economizing style. The story of the healing of the blind man, where Jesus is hailed as "son of David," prepares for the entrance narrative (11:1–11), where the crowd will speak of the "coming kingdom of our father David." It is the last healing episode recounted in the Gospel of Mark.

The epithet "son of David" may denote a Solomonic identity (*Pss. Sol.* 17:21), for several times in the Hebrew Bible Solomon is called "son of David" (1 Chr 29:22; 2 Chr 1:1; 13:6; 30:26; 35:3; Prov 1:1; 1 Esdr. 1:3; cf. 4Q397 fr. 14 xxi 16; 4Q398 fr. 11 xiii 1). And, of course, David's great son was famous for his healing powers and formulas for exorcism. In one incantation Solomon is addressed as the "son of David" and is petitioned for protection against sickness (Charlesworth 137). Indeed, the *Testament of Solomon*, which is largely devoted to traditions about Solomon and the demonic, testifies to the widespread fame of David's son. Requesting that the "son of David" heal him may also suggest that the blind man sensed the approach of the kingdom of God (after all, this was the essence of Jesus' proclamation) and assumed that healings and other blessings were more readily at hand (cf. 4Q521, where the coming of God's Messiah will occasion healing, even resurrection from the dead).

There is no evidence in early sources that anyone challenged Jesus' Davidic descent. In later rabbinic polemic, Jesus is said to have been fathered by a Roman soldier (*t. Hullin* 2.23); but this is little more than slander in response to Christian claims of Jesus' miraculous conception. Bartimaeus' acclamation of Jesus as "son of David" and the later shouts of the crowd, "blessed is the kingdom of our father David that is coming" (11:10), offer important early evidence that Jesus was known by his contemporaries to have belonged to the house of David.

Mark 11:1–11

Jesus' entry into Jerusalem and the manner in which his disciples and other onlookers greet him recall other royal entries, such as the entry of Alexander the Great (Josephus, *Ant.* 11.325–39) or Simon, brother of Judas Maccabeus, who enters Jerusalem and is met by crowds "with praise and palm branches, and with harps and cymbals and stringed instruments and with hymns and songs" (1 Macc 13:49–51).

The shouts of the crowd, which allude to Ps 118:26 ("Blessed is he who comes in the name of the Lord"), is consistent with the imagery of Jesus mounted on the royal mule, much as Solomon did shortly before the death of his father David (1 Kgs 1:32–40). The crowd interpretively adds to Pslm 118 the words: "Blessed is the kingdom of our father David that is coming!" (Mark 11:10). The addition of the name David reflects the Aramaic paraphrase of Pslm 118, in which the story of David's selection as king is woven into the celebrative Pslm. Although Jesus is not directly called "son of David" in the entrance narrative, the allusion to "the kingdom of our father David that is coming," shortly after Bartimaeus' appeal to Jesus as "son of David," suggests that this identity is very much in mind.

Mark 12:35–37

It is perhaps best to understand 12:35–37 as a fragment of a controversy or scholastic dialogue similar to the others found in Mark 12. This passage is essentially in its proper context and setting: that is, in the context of debate between Jesus and the religious authorities in the Jerusalem temple precincts. Although we cannot ascertain why or how the opening challenging question was lost (Gagg), it is clear that the point of issue concerned messianism and how this related to Davidic tradition (Chilton; Schneider 1972).

Jesus' question implies that there is no scriptural basis for calling the Messiah the "son of David." On the face of it, this is a curious position to adopt. While it is true that nowhere in the Scriptures of Israel is the Messiah so identified, Jeremiah promises a "branch" that will be raised up to "David" (Jer 23:5; 33:15). Here progeny is clearly envisioned. Jeremiah's prophetic hope is probably based on Isa 11:1: "There shall come forth a shoot from the stump of Jesse, and a branch shall grow out of his roots." In Zechariah, as we have seen, "Branch" becomes a messianic epithet (cf. Zech 3:8; 6:12). In view of prophecies such as these, the scribal habit of referring to the Messiah as "son of David" seems reasonable (for rabbinic examples, see *b. 'Erub.* 43a; *Yoma* 10a; *Sukk.* 52a ["Messiah, son of David"]; 52b; *Meg.* 17b; *Hagiga* 16a; *Yebam.* 62a; *Ketub.* 112b; *Soṭah* 48b; *Sanh.* 38a; etc.; and in the midrash, see *Gen Rab.* 97 [on Gen 49:10]; *Exod. Rab.* 25.12 [on Exod 16:29]; *Num. Rab.* 14.1 [on Num 7:48]), even if not specifically attested in Scripture. So what is Jesus' point?

"David himself" bears witness against the sufficiency of the scribes' messianic epithet. This testimony is, moreover, prophetic, which is the import of the modifier "in the Holy Spirit." The tradition of David's being inspired and prophetic reaches back to ancient Scriptures themselves and is augmented in later literature. For example, according to 2 Sam 23:2, the Holy Spirit speaks by the tongue of David. This idea is attested in early Christian literature (e.g. Acts 4:25 "it is you who said by the Holy Spirit through our ancestor David, your servant"). This claim can be made matter-of-factly; there appears to be no controversy. Accordingly, any statement that David makes regarding the Messiah would be understood as representing the divine perspective.

Jesus reminds his opponents that in Ps 110:1 David calls the Messiah "lord." If David recognizes his messianic descendent as lord, in what sense then can the Messiah be David's "son"? The point of the question rests in the assumption that to be "son" of someone is to be in some sense subordinate or even inferior. Is the Messiah inferior to David? In other words, is it true that the Messiah will only be a junior David? Jesus disputes this assumption on the basis of Ps 110:1 ("The Lord said to my lord, 'Sit at my right hand'"). Jesus understands this to mean: "The Lord (God) said to my (David's) lord (the Messiah)." Thus, David the famous king recognizes the Messiah as his "lord"; so in what sense is the Messiah nothing more than David's son? Evidently in no sense at all. (On the linguistic aspects of the appeal to Ps 110:1, see Fitzmyer.)

Jesus has not denied the physical Davidic descent of the Messiah (which would not be possible, in light of texts like Isa 9:2–7; 11:1–9; Jer 23:5–6; 33:14–18; Ezek 34:23–24; 37:24). It is the scriptural legitimacy of referring to the Messiah as "son of David" that Jesus questions. There is no scriptural evidence for this manner of speaking (which in rabbinic literature becomes commonplace). In Scripture there is the anticipation that the Messiah will be recognized as *God's* son, not David's son. One should recall Ps 2:2, 7, where it is said of the "Lord's Messiah" (v. 2), "You are My Son, today I have begotten you" (v. 7), as well as 2 Sam 7:14a, where God promises David, "I will be his father, and he shall be my son." The latter passage is cited in a messianic sense in later literature, as reviewed above.

Mark 15:1–41

The Roman soldiers mocked Jesus as "king of the Jews" (Mark 15:16–20). The mockery included being clothed in purple, a crown of thorns, the salute "Hail," a reed placed in his hand as a scepter, men kneeling before him, and being spat upon, which may have signified kissing. In short, Jesus was mocked as a king. The mockery finds an approximate parallel in Philo (*Flaccus* 36–39), who tells of a simple-minded man who is tricked out in royal apparel, in order to mock Agrippa I, Israel's king in 41–44 CE. The nature of the mockery of Jesus, as well as the *titulus* placed on or beside his cross, which stated "The King of the Jews" (Mark 15:26), lends important support to the supposition that Jesus was recognized by his followers as a royal, Davidic Messiah.

Gospel of Matthew

The Gospel of Luke follows Mark, with some minor editing. But the number of passages in which Jesus is called "son of David" multiplies in the Gospel of Matthew.

Matthew identifies Jesus as "Messiah (or Christ), the son of David" in his incipit (Matt 1:1). The Evangelist identifies him as a descendent of David in the genealogy (Matt 1:2–16) and then refers to Joseph, husband of Mary, as "Joseph, son of David" (Matt 1:20), thus underscoring Jesus' Davidic descent.

Burger (170) correctly observes that in the gospel tradition, especially in Matthew, the epithet "son of David" almost always appears in contexts of healing or exorcism (cf. Matt 9:27–31; 12:22–24; 15:21–28; 20:29–34; 21:1–11, 14–16). In the context of exorcism, in which Jesus is accused of being in league with Satan (Mark 3:20–22), the crowd is amazed and asks, "Can this be the son of David?" (Matt 12:23). This part of the story is Matthean,

evidently presupposing the link between David and his son with healing and exorcism (Charlesworth; Duling). Another remarkable episode in Matthew is in the context of the Temple in Jerusalem. There the "blind and the lame came to him ... and he cured them" (Matt 21:14), whereupon people cry out: "Hosanna to the Son of David" (v. 15), recalling the entry into Jerusalem and thus reinforcing Jesus' Davidic identity.

The epithet "son of David" is admittedly very important in Matthew, but it probably does not constitute the highest title in the Evangelist's Christology (*pace* Burger). After all, the Evangelist Matthew does carry over Mark 12:37 (= Matt 22:45), which implies that the epithet "son of David" is not adequate for the Messiah. The implication is that the Messiah, who is of course the son of David, is the Son of God.

CRAIG A. EVANS

Further reading

Burger, C. *Jesus als Davidssohn: Eine traditionsgeschichtliche Untersuchung*, FRLANT 98, Göttingen: Vandenhoeck & Ruprecht, 1970.

Charlesworth, J. H. "Solomon and Jesus: The Son of David in Ante-Markan Traditions (Mark 10:47)," in L. B. Elder, D. L. Barr, and E. S. Malbon (eds) *Biblical and Humane: A Festschrift for John F. Priest*, Homage 20, Atlanta, GA: Scholars Press, 1996, pp. 125–51.

Chilton, B. "Jesus *ben David*: Reflections on the Davidssohnfrage," in C. A. Evans and S. E. Porter (eds) *The Historical Jesus: A Sheffield Reader*, Sheffield: Sheffield Academic Press, 1995, pp. 192–215.

Duling, D. C. "Solomon, Exorcism, and the Son of David," *HTR* 68 (1975) 235–52.

Dunn, J. D. G. "Messianic Ideas and their Influence on the Jesus of History," in J. H. Charlesworth (ed.) *The Messiah: Developments in Earliest Judaism and Christianity*, Minneapolis, MN: Fortress Press, 1992, pp. 365–81.

Fitzmyer, J. A. "The Son of David Tradition and Matt 22:41–46 and Parallels," in *Essays on the Semitic Background of the New Testament*, London: Chapman, 1971, pp. 113–26.

Gagg, R. P. "Jesus und die Davidssohnfrage: Zur exegese von Markus 12,35–37," *TZ* 7 (1951) 18–30.

Johnson, S. E. "The David-Royal Motif in the Gospels," *JBL* 87 (1968) 136–50.

Jonge, M. de. "Jesus, Son of David and Son of God," in *Jewish Eschatology, Early Christian Christology and the Testaments of the Twelve Patriarchs*, NovTSup 63, Leiden: Brill, 1991, pp. 135–44.

Lohse, E. "Huios Dauid," *TDNT* 8 (1972) 478–88.

Pomykala, K. E. *The Davidic Dynasty Tradition in Early Judaism: Its History and Significance for Messianism*, SBLEJL 7, Atlanta, GA: Scholars Press, 1995.

Schneider, G. "Zur Vorgeschichte des christologischen Prädikats 'Sohn Davids'," *TTZ* 80 (1971) 247–53.

—— "Der Davidssohnfrage (Mark 12,35–37)," *Bib* 53 (1972) 65–90.

SON OF GOD

In Christian thought the term 'son of God' has become inextricably linked with Jesus, and more or less from the beginning. For Christians Jesus is *the* Son of God, pre-eminently and without compare. In the early development of Christian understanding of the relation between God and Jesus, 'Logos (Word)' proved to be the most helpful defining term. But the third and fourth century controversies (with Gnostics and Arians) crystallized that relationship in the contrast of the Nicene creed, 'begotten not made', and in terms of God as Father to Jesus as Son. In an encyclopedia focused on the historical Jesus, however, it is important to inquire behind this technical Christian usage and to appreciate how the imagery of 'son of God' would have been understood at the time of Jesus.

'Son of God' at the time of Jesus

The term 'son' denotes primarily a male child produced by procreation. But from as far back as we can trace, the phrase quickly expands in usage to include a male person who has been creatively influenced by an older figure, or who has been the beneficiary or heir of some formative conditions or events. Still today, teachers will sometimes refer to their pupils as their 'children'; a successful PhD candidate refers to his teacher as his 'Doctor-father'. 'Sons of the soil', or 'sons of the revolution' or some such phrase, indicates the circumstances or forces which have shaped the character of the persons referred to. Such usage was already established in the Semitic idiom whereby the family or hereditary relationship of son to father ('son of') was extended to denote a variety of relations, including professional groups (e.g. 'sons of Korah', 'sons of Asaph', 'sons of Aaron') or even those who shared particular characteristics (e.g. the valiant = 'sons of strength', 'sons of Belial, 'sons of light') (Haag). In early Christian literature, for example, Jesus refers to 'sons of the bridal chamber' (Mark 2.19), 'sons of the kingdom' (Matt 8.12), 'sons of this age' and 'sons of light' (Luke 16.8), Peter refers to Mark as 'my son' (1 Pet 5.13), and Justin refers to 'the sons of the prophets' (*Dialogue* 86.6).

'Son of God' has only rarely and in legend been used literally, of one created by the physical union of a god and goddess or mortal female. For example, Apollo, the god who more than any other represented the values of Greek civilization, was the son of Zeus and Leto; and the hero of heroes, Heracles, was the son of Zeus and Alcmene. But as

with the wider phrase 'son of', so the specific usage, 'son of god', extended much more widely. *Oriental rulers*, especially Egyptian, were thus designated, the Ptolemies in particular laying claim to the title 'son of Helios' from the fourth century BCE onwards. And at the time of Jesus 'son of God' was already widely in use in reference to *Augustus* (*Divi filius*). Similarly, as Origen notes in his response to Celsus (*Cels.* 1.37), there was a natural impulse to attribute the gifts of wisdom or power beyond the average, like those of *Plato or Pythagoras*, to their having been divinely born (from Apollo). And particularly among the Stoics it was an accepted thought that Zeus was the father of *all men*, since all shared the divine reason (Epictetus e.g. 1.13.3). In the speech attributed to Paul in Acts 17.28, the Greek philosopher Aratus (third century BCE) is quoted to the same effect: 'For we are indeed his [the creator god's] offspring' (*Phaenomena* 5).

The Judaism of Jesus' day was also well accustomed to using the phrase 'son of God' in a broader way. *Angels or heavenly beings* were regarded as 'sons of God', as being not simply created by the one God, but also as members of the heavenly council under Yahweh the supreme God (Gen 6:2, 4; Deut 32:8; Job 1:6–12; 2:1–6; 38:7; Pss 29:1; 89:6; Dan 3:25). As with the surrounding nations, *Israel's king* could be called, though infrequently, God's 'son', as notably in the influential passages 2 Sam 7:14, and Pss 2:7 and 89:26–27. More typical was the thought of *Israel or Israelites* as God's son(s): 'Israel is my first-born son' (Exod 4:22; Jer 31:9; Hos 11:1; see also e.g. Deut 14:1; Isa 43:6; Hos 1:10). Quite common was the thought that God's discipline is like that of a father disciplining his son (Deut 8:5; 2 Sam 7:14; Prov 3:11–12; Wis 11:10).

In Second Temple Judaism these uses of 'son of God' were extended. In *1 Enoch* angels are called 'sons of heaven' and 'sons of God of heaven' (13:8; 106:5). The Alexandrian Jewish philosopher, Philo, in his unique blend of Stoic and Jewish thought, calls God 'the supreme Father of gods and men' (*Spec.* 2:165; *Opif.* 84) and does not hesitate to call both the *cosmos* God's son (*Immut.* 31–32; *Spec.* 1:96) and the *Logos* 'God's first-born' (*Conf.* 146; *Som.* 1:215). Not only is Israel as a nation called 'son of God' (Wis 9:7; 18:13; *Jub.* 1:24–25; *Pss. Sol.* 17:30), but also *individual Israelites*, specifically the righteous man (Wis 2:13, 16, 18; 5:5; Eccl 4:10; 51:10; *Pss. Sol.* 13:8), the Maccabean martyrs ('children of heaven' – 2 Macc 7:34), or those who do what is good and pleasing to nature (Philo, *Conf.* 145–47; *Spec.* 1:318). In the

Hellenistic Jewish romance, *Joseph and Asenath*, Joseph is called 'the son of God' by the Egyptian Asenath because of his great beauty (6:2–6; 13:10; 21:3).

Of special interest for historical Jesus studies are two other usages which came to light in the second half of the twentieth century. One is the use of the term with reference to two Jewish charismatics (Vermes). According to rabbinic tradition, Honi, the 'circle-drawer' (first century BCE), prayed to God 'like a son of the house' and his relationship of intimate sonship with God ensured the success of his petitions (*m. Taan.* 3:8). And a heavenly voice was said to have addressed Hanina ben Dosa (from the generation following Jesus) as 'my son' (*b. Taan.* 24b). The other is the evidence from the Dead Sea Scrolls that God's expected emissary (messiah) could be spoken of as God's 'son', thereby refuting an earlier view that 'son of God' was not a 'messianic title' in Second Temple Judaism. In particular, 1QSa (= 1Q28b) 2.11–12 speaks of God 'begetting the Messiah'; and 4QFlor (= 4Q174) 1.10–12 interprets 2 Sam 7:12–14 as referring to the Davidic messiah ('the Branch of David').

Early Christian usage in reference to Jesus

By common assent the earliest extant Christian writings are those of the apostle Paul. He was converted to the movement he had been persecuting within two or at most three years of the crucifixion of Jesus and wrote most of his letters in the 50s, that is, less than thirty years after Jesus. So any material quoted by Paul as Christian tradition is likely to take us back to the first few years of what was to become 'Christianity'.

The most significant of such traditional material here is the passage Paul quotes at the beginning of his letter to Rome, probably to reassure the Roman believers of his 'good faith'. The quasi-creedal statement affirms Jesus' descent from the seed of David and his 'appointment' as 'Son of God in power as from the resurrection of the dead' (Rom 1:3–4). This is sometimes described, anachronistically, as an 'adoptionist' statement; it would only rightly be so described if it was denying some earlier affirmation of Christ's pre-existent sonship. But Paul himself clearly saw the complete formula as referring to God's 'Son' (1:3). So talk of Jesus having been 'appointed Son of God' as from his resurrection should be seen simply as a reflection of the impact made by the conviction that Jesus had been raised from the dead and exalted to God's right hand (Ps 110:1). The same is probably true of the quotations of Ps 2:7 ('You are my son, today I have begotten you') in reference to Jesus' resurrection in Acts 13:33 and Heb 5:5.

Paul himself referred to Jesus as God's 'Son' relatively infrequently (only seventeen occurrences in the Pauline letters; contrast 'Christ' and 'Lord'). Distinctive of his usage, however, is an association between Jesus as God's Son and his death on the cross (Rom 5:10; 8:3; Gal 2:20; 4:4–5). Central to Paul's appreciation of Jesus' death was the thought that God had not spared his son, his only son (Rom 8:32, in echo of Abraham's sacrifice of Isaac – Gen 22:16). No doubt it was with this thought in the forefront of his mind that Paul saw his commission as to proclaim Jesus as God's Son 'among the Gentiles' (Gal 1:16). And the impact of the resurrection of Jesus as the beginning of the end (eschatological) events is likewise reflected in Paul's recollection of the Thessalonians who 'turned to God from idols ... to wait for his Son from heaven' (1 Thess 1:9–10). Most regard the phrase 'God sent his Son' (Rom 8:3; Gal 4:4) as referring to God sending his pre-existent Son from heaven (cf. Wis 9:10), although the motif of 'God sending' is much more frequently used of prophets (e.g. Judg 6:8; Jer 1:7; Ezek 2:3; Mic 6:4; Obad 1; Hag 1:12; Mal 3:1), as in the parable of the vineyard let out to tenant farmers (Mark 12:1–9).

The Gospels make significant play of the term 'Son of God' in relation to Jesus. Mark, the earliest Gospel, suspends his whole account between the heavenly intimation at Jesus' baptism, 'You are my Son, the Beloved; with you I am well pleased' (Mark 1:11), and the centurion's confession in 15.39, 'Truly this man was God's Son.' The narrative is punctuated with such affirmations (3:11; 5:7; 9:7; 12:6; 13:32; 14:61–62). But the climax, a confession of the crucified Christ as God's Son (15.39), underlines the same emphasis as in Paul: that it was precisely as God's Son that Jesus died.

Matthew strengthens Mark's emphases in several ways. He identifies Jesus with Israel as God's son (2:15; 4:3, 6). He adds appropriate confessions of Jesus as Son of God in 14:33 and 16:16 (cf. 27:40, 43). And the whole Father/Son imagery is greatly extended (God as Father in Mark 3; Matt 44). Most striking is the saying he shares with Luke 10:22: 'All things have been handed over to me by my Father; and no one knows the Son except the Father, and no one knows the Father except the Son and anyone to whom the Son chooses to reveal him' (Matt 11:27).

Luke's main contribution to the theme is the way he highlights Jesus' divine sonship in the birth narrative, which he also shares to some extent with

Matthew. The key emphasis for Luke is that Jesus is 'the Son of the Most High', 'the Son of God' (1:32, 35), because the Holy Spirit 'came upon' Mary and the power of the Most High 'overshadowed' her (1:35). This is the nearest the early Christian tradition comes to the legends of the Olympian gods begetting children of mortal women, but in contrast to such tales the restraint and reverence of the gospel narratives is striking.

In John's Gospel the motif of Father/Son in relation to Jesus is expanded far beyond the precedent of Matthew. Typically Johannine is the elaboration of the sending motif of Mark 12:6 and Gal 4:4/Rom 8:3: the Johannine Jesus speaks regularly of God as 'him who sent me' (4:34; 5:24, 30, 37; 6:38–39, 44; etc.). Here the thought is explicitly of Jesus having been 'sent (from heaven) into the world' (3:17; 10:36; 17:18). Likewise elaborated is the exclusive intimacy between Father and Son asserted in Matt 11:27/Luke 10:22: for example, the Son is worthy of the same honour as the Father (5:23); 'I and the Father are one' (10:30); 'I am in the Father and the Father is in me ... the Father who dwells in me does his works' (14:10). Most striking is the climax to the prologue: 'No one has ever seen God; the only begotten God [or Son?] who is in the bosom of the Father, he has made him known' (1:18).

The only other NT author worthy of mention here is Hebrews, who refers to Jesus as God's Son regularly, particularly through the first seven chapters. Heb 4:14 implies that 'Jesus is the Son of God' was a basic confession common to the author and his readers. As with John the note of pre-existent sonship is clear: 'in these last days God has spoken to us by a Son ... through whom also he created the world' (1:2). Jesus as Son is in view when the Psalmist says, 'Your throne, O God, is for ever and ever' (1:8). In contrast to Moses, Jesus was as a son of the house (3:6). Jesus' sonship, like Melchizedek's priesthood, is eternal (7:3). At the same time, Hebrews does not hesitate to apply to Jesus the paradigm of parental chastisement as the means by which a son learns discipline: 'Although he was a Son, he learned obedience through what he suffered; and having been made perfect' (5:8; 7:28; 12:5–7).

The theme of Jesus as God's Son in the NT thus has several striking features: it grows and expands through the later writings; the decisive moment in Jesus 'becoming' as Son is pushed further back over the same literature – from resurrection, to baptism, to birth, to eternity; and the importance of Jesus suffering as God's Son is maintained throughout.

The historical Jesus as Son of God

An inquiry into Jesus' own perception as to his status before God runs into almost insuperable obstacles. Not only are there the thick layers of Christian faith in Jesus as God's Son, a faith which stretches back to the earliest days of Christianity, not to mention the Christian conception of what divine sonship means in the case of Jesus. But there is also the a priori impossibility of penetrating into the mind of a historical individual who left no written record, let alone one who was quite exceptional – indeed, on Christian presuppositions, wholly unique.

What we do have, however, are two major factors in our favour. One is the much better sense we now have of what 'son of God/god' must have conveyed to the contemporaries of Jesus. The other is the *impact* which Jesus evidently made on his disciples. We have no documents written by Jesus, of course, but we do have the impression he left, not by ink and pen, but by the impact of his person, actions and teaching on those who responded to his call and message. That response is present to us in greater or lesser measure in the gospels, which were clearly intended to convey that impression to those who never met or heard Jesus in person. Of course, there is considerable dispute as to how much that impression has been diluted or reinforced or transformed by the developing faith in and reflection about Jesus of the period covered by the NT documents. But the fact is that the first three gospels convey a remarkably coherent and consistent impression of the Jesus who called men into discipleship. And while the narrative is certainly told from the perspective of Christian faith (as 'gospels', climaxing in the passion and resurrection of Jesus), the content of individual episodes and teaching retain the character of Jesus' pre-Easter and Galilean mission to a remarkable degree (Dunn 2003). So twenty-first-century readers can be as confident as with many other historical characters, and more so than most, that they are in direct touch with the way Jesus interacted with those who became his disciples and the impact he made on them.

This becomes all the more important if we follow recent attempts to redefine 'personal identity'. Traditionally identity has been understood in terms of some inner 'essence' or character which comes to expression in speech and action, and which therefore can be read off in some degree from that speech and action. But recent work suggests that a better way of understanding identity is in terms of a person's interaction with other persons

(Meeks); the person becomes who he/she is by responding to and interacting with others – initially parents and other siblings, then friends, schoolmates, neighbours, etc. In that case, the identity of Jesus as God's s/Son is not best conceived in terms of inner essence/substance, or even solely in terms of Jesus' relation to God, but rather (or at least also) in terms of the interaction he had with and the impact he had on others, his disciples in particular. In which case, it also follows that the response of Jesus' disciples to Jesus is not something which has to be stripped away in order to gain sight of an entity ('Jesus' sonship') unaffected by human perception. Rather, the impact made by Jesus and the resulting impression of Jesus left on his disciples is an integral part of what might constitute or determine Jesus as 'Son of God'.

The Abba prayer

The classic expression of this is the Christian prayer addressed to God as 'Abba! Father!'. Paul cites the prayer twice (Rom 8:15; Gal 4:6). Several features should not escape notice. The fact that Paul could take it for granted that this was a prayer known to and used by the Christians in Rome (which he had never visited) assuredly indicates that the prayer was in wide use in the churches of the Mediterranean area – otherwise he could not have made that assumption. Noteworthy also is the retention of the Aramaic term 'Abba' ('father'). This must mean that the prayer was inherited from the original Aramaic-speaking disciples. Moreover, the prayer must have been distinctive of the Christians, otherwise, if it was in general use among Jews, or even among some Jews, Paul could hardly have regarded it as proof that the Christians (distinctively) had received the Spirit (Rom 8:15).

Most striking of all is the inference that those who utter this prayer of sonship thereby demonstrate their share in Christ's sonship – 'The Spirit itself (thereby) bears witness with our spirit that we are children of God, and if children, also heirs, heirs of God and heirs together with Christ' (Rom 8:16–17; similarly Gal 4:6–7). The obvious conclusion to be drawn is that the prayer was itself part of the impact left by Jesus on his disciples. They prayed the prayer because he had so prayed, or even because he had taught them so to pray. And they continued to pray the prayer because it reflected the very relationship with God which Jesus expressed in the prayer. Not only so, but praying Jesus' own prayer evidently brought them a deeper sense of their own relationship with God,

as a relationship which mirrored Jesus' relationship during his mission. That was evidently a very powerful impression Jesus left on his disciples.

Such inferences are borne out, though not as strongly as we might have expected, in the traditions about Jesus retold in the gospels. All five strata (the four gospels, and the Q/sayings source used by Matthew and Luke) agree that Jesus consistently addressed God as 'Father' in his prayers (Jeremias). Indeed, the only prayer recalled of Jesus when he did not begin by addressing God as 'Father' was the prayer of his crucifixion agony, quoting Ps 22:2: 'My God, my God, why have you forsaken me?' (Mark 15:34).

There are three very striking instances of Jesus' prayer to God as 'Father'.

1 Matt 11:25–26/Luke 10:21: 'At that time Jesus said, "I thank you, Father, Lord of heaven and earth, because you have hidden these things from the wise and the intelligent and have revealed them to infants; yes, Father, for such was your gracious will"'. Behind the Greek vocative, 'Father', it is fair to deduce lies the Aramaic 'Abba'. The thought of wisdom revealed to innocents is familiar in Jewish wisdom writings. But it is hardly likely that the early Christians would have expressed their own sense of illumination as a prayer of Jesus, or that they would have designated him as an 'infant' of their own accord. In contrast, it is just the sort of prayer that would have made the impression on the disciples that they should follow Jesus' own lead in so praying.
2 'The Lord's prayer' is explicitly attributed to the direct personal teaching of Jesus (Matt 6:9–13/Luke 11:1–4). The Lukan version is generally regarded as earlier in form: 'Father, hallowed be your name ... ' (Luke 11:2). Here again, almost certainly, underlying the Greek vocative 'Father' lies the Aramaic 'Abba'. There is no good reason to doubt that Jesus did teach this prayer, not least because it confirms the inferences drawn from Rom 8:15–17/Gal 4:6–7: Jesus was indeed remembered as teaching his disciples so to pray.
3 Only one Gospel episode portrays Jesus as actually using the term 'Abba' in his prayer. That is when Jesus is recalled as praying in the garden of Gethsemane: 'Abba, Father, all things are possible to you. Let this cup pass from me' (Mark 14:36). The very honest, unmartyr-like and hardly hagiographical

portrayal of Jesus, 'greatly distressed and troubled' (14:33) and asking to be exempted from the coming trial, implies a further occasion when the anguish and prayer of Jesus burnt themselves deep into the memory of those who had been closest to him; the recollection is echoed in Heb 5:7–8.

However we read these passages it is difficult to escape the impression that Jesus' prayer to God as 'Abba, Father' left a lasting impression on his disciples. And not simply as a prayer, but as an expression of sonship, or of a sense of sonship (as clearly indicated in Rom 8:15–17). The impression left on Jesus' disciples was that he prayed to God as a son, and with the family intimacy that 'Abba' expresses. Whatever Jesus may or may not have said on the subject, this was a significant aspect of the impact made by Jesus on his disciples. The impact he left was an integral part of his identity as God's son. Paul certainly attests that the first Christians believed they shared Jesus' sonship; like him they experienced a relationship with God as sons. But it was *Jesus'* sonship that they shared; they had to be conformed to his sonship 'in order that he should be firstborn among many brothers' (Rom 8:29). It would be perverse to argue conversely, that the Christian belief in Jesus as God's Son derived solely from their own sense of sonship.

Did Jesus claim to be God's son?

Whether Jesus actually taught his disciples that he was God's son is one of the most contested issues in historical Jesus scholarship. In terms of that scholarship and the methodology involved, it is virtually impossible to achieve a large-scale consensus on the point – far less so than in the case just presented regarding the 'Abba prayer'. This is simply because there is clear evidence that the thought of Jesus as Son of God became more insistent and more confidently part of the gospel tradition with the later gospels. When the statistics (referred to earlier) for reference to God as 'Father' in the words of Jesus are reformulated into a sequence with Mark and the Q material earliest, then the material distinctive of Luke and of Matthew, and finally John, the trend is clearly indicated – Mark 3; Q 4; special Luke 4; special Matt 31; John 100 (Jeremias). Moreover, the fuller motif of Jesus as God's Son is very clearly expressive of what can only be regarded as developed Christian reflection regarding Jesus: the pre-existent Son ('the only-begotten God') is clearly the divine

Logos who was 'with God' and 'was God' from the beginning and before creation (John 1:1, 18); the divine(ly sent) Son can even echo in self-reference the identifying formula of Israel's God ('I am who I am' – Exod 3:14) when he makes claims like, 'Before Abraham was, I am' (John 8:58). Where the Jesus as 'Son of God' motif has so clearly been elaborated, it will always be an open question whether an unelaborated strand can be identified, that is unelaborated by the fresh insight and revelation which the Easter experience and its aftermath brought to the first Christians.

The problem is indicated by the two passages where Jesus is attested as speaking of himself as 'the s/Son' in the earlier versions of the gospel tradition.

1 Matt 11:27/Luke 10:22 (quoted above) is the closest parallel in the Synoptic Gospels to the developed Johannine Son-theology. As such, of course, it indicates that John's Son-theology was not John's own creation but expresses in full measure a feature already present in the earlier forms of the Jesus tradition (the Q material). But it also raises the question whether the theological reflection so fully expressed in John was already well under way even at that earlier stage. What particularly smacks of developed theology is talk of Jesus as 'the Son', with the unavoidable implication that he is the only one to be so called. Of course, it can be argued that whatever Jesus had said was more likely to be in terms of father–son imagery (familiar in the Jewish thought of God's disciplining Israel or individuals as a father disciplines his son), without necessarily exclusive connotations (as in John 10:15). It can further be argued that such remembered language and imagery used by Jesus lent itself, without being forced, to the more exclusive formulation of subsequent Christian theology. The trouble with such an argument is that it cuts away the very feature – the exclusiveness of the mutual knowledge of Father and Son ('no one knows the Son except the Father, and no one knows the Father except the Son') – which is the very point of the saying (at least in its present form).

2 Mark 13:32 – 'About that day or hour no one knows, neither the angels in heaven, nor the Son, but only the Father' (also Matt 24:36). Here the methodological impasse is similar. On the one hand it can be argued that the early Christians were unlikely to attribute

ignorance to Jesus (the Son) of their own accord. On the other, it is easily imaginable that a saying of Jesus lacking 'nor the Son' was given more force in transmission and re-use by inserting just that phrase, to underline just how unknown the day and hour of the expected denouement or consummation was; if even Jesus did not know during his mission, how much less could they (or their questioners) expect a clear answer on the issue? Here again, it is that talk of Jesus as 'the Son', already redolent of the subsequent talk of Jesus as 'the only-begotten Son', which makes it more difficult to envisage Jesus himself so speaking. The problem, in other words, is circular: to envisage Jesus as saying something like this, it would be necessary to assume that he was indeed 'the Son of God'; but in terms of historical scholarship, the only basis for that assumption is just such a saying. As such, the argument is open to the charge of *petitio principii*, begging the question.

There is one other reference in the Synoptic Tradition which holds out more hopeful prospects. This is the parable of the dishonest tenant farmers (Mark 12:1–9, also Matt 21:33–41, Luke 20:9–16 and *Gospel of Thomas* 65). In this case there need not be so many historical scholarly inhibitions in tracing the parable back to Jesus himself, since it is quite credible to envisage Jesus speaking of his own mission as some sort of climax to the history of God's sending prophets to express his claim on Israel. There are other indications that he did so: for example, in the implication from Luke 6.20/ (Matt 5:3–4) and Matt 11:5/Luke 7:22 that Jesus understood his mission in terms of Isa 61:1–2 (explicitly in Luke 4:18–21). What is particularly interesting is that the contrast between the servants (sent initially by the owner of the vineyard) and the owner's son (sent last of all) makes sense entirely in terms of the narrative drama of the parable itself. Comparison of the four different versions of the parable certainly indicates that the parable was probably elaborated in subsequent retellings in Christian circles (e.g. 'my *beloved* son', 'threw him out of the vineyard'). But the *Gospel of Thomas* may have preserved a less elaborated version, where the Son-theology and its implications are not developed. In which case, we may have further evidence strengthening the implications of Jesus' Abba prayer, that Jesus on occasion was remembered as speaking in a way that expressed a sense of sonship to God as Father.

Does the issue depend on whether such evidence exists?

For belief that Jesus of Nazareth was (already) the Son of God, it is not necessary, of course, to find evidence that he thought or spoke of himself in these terms. Jesus was who he was whether or not he knew it or spoke of it in so many words preserved for us. This, we might infer, is the point of the birth narratives. At the heart of the two birth narratives (Matt 1–2; Luke 1–2) is the double conviction that Jesus was both son of David and Son of God – the same confession attested for very early days in Rom 1:3–4, but now clearly asserted that he was so from the beginning; there never was a time when Jesus was not God's Son. As we saw earlier, Luke's version brings out the point with some emphasis. The problem for Christian theology is that such an affirmation may seem to be more in the eye of the beholder – a status attributed to Jesus – rather than claimed (or lived out) by Jesus himself. And Christian theology is bound to be sensitive about key theological claims about Jesus which cannot claim to have any rootage in Jesus' own mission and teaching. Hence, of course, the whole 'historical Jesus' enterprise.

In this case, however, it is possible to conclude, on the Historical critical grounds hitherto employed in historical Jesus research, that insofar as Jesus' prayer habit expressed how he saw his relation to God, he prayed in intimate family terms ('Abba') to God as Father, and that he was remembered as at least occasionally speaking of his mission in similar father–son terms.

JAMES D. G. DUNN

Further reading

Bosslooper, T. *The Virgin Birth*, Philadelphia, PA: Westminster, 1962.

Brown, R. E. *The Birth of the Messiah: A Commentary on the Infancy Narratives in the Gospels of Matthew and Luke*, New York: Doubleday, 1977, 1993.

Dodd, C. H. *Historical Tradition in the Fourth Gospel*, Cambridge: Cambridge University Press, 1963.

Dunn, James. *Christology in the Making: A New Testament Inquiry into the Origins of the Doctrine of the Incarnation*, London: SCM Press, 1989²; Grand Rapids, MI: Eerdmans, 1996, ch. 2.

—— *Jesus Remembered*, Grand Rapids, MI: Eerdmans, (2003): 708–24.

Fitzmyer, J. A. "Abba and Jesus' Relation to God," in R. Gantoy (ed.) *A Cause de l'Évangile*, J. Dupont Festschrift, Paris: Cerf, 1980, pp. 15–38.

Haag, H. *"ben," TDOT* 2 (1977) 147–59.

Hahn, F. *The Titles of Jesus in Christology*, London: Lutterworth, 1969.

Hengel, M. *The Son of God: The Origin of Christology and the History of Jewish-Hellenistic Religion*, London: SCM Press, 1976.

Jeremias, J. *The Prayers of Jesus*, London: SCM Press, 1966.

—— *New Testament Theology 1. The Proclamation of Jesus*, London: SCM Press, 1971.

Jonge, M. de. *God's Final Envoy: Early Christology and Jesus' Own View of His Mission*, Grand Rapids, MI: Eerdmans, 1998.

Martitz, W. v. and E. Schweizer. *"huios," TDNT* 8 (1972) 334–92.

Meeks, W. A. *Christ is the Question*, Louisville, KY: Westminster John Knox, 2006.

O'Collins, G. *Christology: A Biblical, Historical and Systematic Study of Jesus*, Oxford: Oxford University Press, 1995.

Schnackenburg, R. *Jesus in the Gospels: A Biblical Theology*, Louisville, KY: Westminster John Knox, 1995.

Vermes, G. *Jesus the Jew*, London: Collins, 1973, ch. 8.

Witherington, B. *The Christology of Jesus*, Minneapolis, MN: Fortress Press, 1990.

SON OF MAN

In the canonical gospel tradition, Jesus' most common self-designation is "son of man," or, more literally, "the son of the man." The meaning of this phrase is as ambiguous in Greek or Aramaic as it is in English. What is meant by the phrase "son of man"? What is its derivation? Theories about the meaning and origin of the phrase include: it was Jesus' own self-designation used as a title; it was Jesus' own self-designation, but not meant as a title; and it was a title that derived from the preaching of the early church.

Use of the phrase "son of man" in the gospels

The phrase "son of man" is found in every layer of the canonical Jesus tradition. In Mark it is used fourteen times (Mark 2:10, 28; 8:31, 38, 9:9, 12, 31; 10:33, 45; 13:26; 14:21ab, 41, 62.). In material peculiar to Matthew, it is found seven times (Matt 10:23; 13:37, 41; 16:28; 24:30; 25:31; 26:2). It occurs seven times in material peculiar to Luke (Luke 17:22, 30; 18:8; 19:10; 21:26; 22:48; 24:7). In passages of the common tradition of Matthew and Luke, which scholars designate as "Q," it is found ten times (Matt 8:20//Luke 9:58; Matt 11:19//Luke 7:34; Matt 12:32//Luke 12:10; Matt 12:40//Luke 11:30; Matt 24:27//Luke 17:24; Matt 24:37b+39b//Luke 17:26; Matt 24:44//Luke 12:40; Matt 19:28; Luke 6:22; 12:18). It is also found thirteen times in John (John 1:51; 3:13–14; 5:27 [without articles] 6:27; 53, 62; 8:28; 9:35; 12.23, 34a; 13:31).

In the gospels, the phrase is used by Jesus alone, with one partial exception. In John 12:34, the crowd quotes Jesus, saying, "We have heard from the law that the Messiah remains forever. How can you say that the Son of Man must be lifted up? Who is this Son of Man?" (NRSV). Outside the gospel tradition, "son of man" is found only once, in Acts 7:56, when Stephen views the exalted Christ standing at God's right hand and states, "I see the heavens opened and the Son of Man standing at the right hand of God" (NRSV). The references to "one like a son of man" in Rev 1:13; 14:14 are quotations from Dan 7:13, and cannot be linked directly to Jesus' usage. These instances may, however, reflect some indirect influence, if Jesus identified himself with the "one like a son of man" of Dan 7:13. The phrase "son of man" in Heb 2:6 is a quotation of Ps 8:4 and lacks articles, unlike the predominate usage in the gospel tradition.

Antecedents of "son of man" in Hebrew Bible and Jewish literature

Not only is the phrase "the son of man" used only by Jesus in the gospel tradition, it is also obscure in Greek. The Greek "*ho huios tou anthrōpou*" is a direct translation either from the one of two Aramaic phrases (*bar nasha* or *bar enasha*), or from the Hebrew *ben adam*. The Hebrew *ben adam* is found in Ezekiel some ninety times, but not as a self-designation. Rather, in Ezekiel it is God who addresses the prophet as *ben adam*, or "son of man," an indication of the prophet's human weakness, which stands in contrast to divine glory (see Ezek 2:1). A further problem arises in seeing Ezekiel's use of *ben adam* as the inspiration for the usage since the LXX does not translate the phrase as *ho huios tou anthrōpou*, but as *huios anthrōpou*.

In addition to Ezekiel's usage of the phrase *ben adam*, or "son of man," in Dan 7:13 the reader encounters the peculiar figure of the "one like a son of man" (*cebar enosh*). This individual is a figure, who "comes with the clouds" of heaven and approaches the Ancient of Days. It is to this figure that dominion, honor and glory are given, as well as an eternal kingdom. Is it possible that Jesus' usage of the phrase, *huios tou anthrōpou*, or "son of man," derives from this figure?

Besides Dan 7:13, the figure of an exalted human being or "son of man" is found in *4 Ezra* 13 and *1 Enoch*. In *4 Ezra* 13, the seer has a vision of a heavenly human arising out of the sea (13:1–13). This vision is interpreted in 13:20–57 in terms of God's "son" or the messiah. While this passage can provide a direct link to the imagery of the "human being" and a messiah, this conclusion may be misleading. First, *4 Ezra* was not written until the 90s CE, and postdates most of the gospels.

Second, the description of the figure of the "human being" may also be in contrast to the Christian designation of Jesus as "son of man." Finally, while the figure in *4 Ezra* is a "human being," he is not described as a "son of man."

A closer analogy may be founding *1 Enoch* 48:2; 62:9 and 71:14, with the description of a heavenly figure of a "son of man" who participates in God's judgment. This figure is closely associated with, if not identified with, the figure of the "elect one" of *1 Enoch* 49 and 61. This latter figure is described as "full of glory," and as "the one who will judge all things" (*1 En.* 49:4). Is it possible that traditions found in 1 En are applied to Jesus in his description of himself as "son of man"?

Preliminary observations about the "son of man" in the gospel tradition

Since the phrase "son of man" is used exclusively by Jesus in the gospel tradition and Jesus is never addressed by others or prayed to within the Church as "son of man," it is natural that in the precritical period exegetes assumed that all the uses of the phrase were derived from Jesus himself. In the early church's conflict with Gnosticism, the phrase "son of man" was understood a defense of the doctrine of incarnation (see Tertullian *Against Marcion* 4.10 and Justin Martyr in *Dialog with Trypho* 76 and 100). Similarly, Ignatius in *Eph.* 20.2 notes that Jesus is both Son of Man and Son of God, i.e. the incarnate son of God.

Despite the statistics, however, we cannot assume that all the instances where Jesus calls himself "son of man" are authentic. Textual evidence of Luke 9:56 indicates that the words "for the son of man came not to destroy but to save human lives," are a later addition, missing in the best manuscripts. Likewise, the phrase "son of man" in Matt 18:10 is a secondary addition. The occurrence of the figure of the son of man in Matt 13:37 in the explanation of the parable of the weeds in the field is also considered to be likely secondary, since most scholars understand the explanation of the parable to derive from the preaching of the early church and not from Jesus. Finally, usage of the phrase "son of man" in the Gospel of John appears to demonstrate the Johannine community's reflections upon the term, as John 5:27 makes especially evident when it states that judgment is handed over to the son because "he is the son of man."

Thus, while the phrase "son of man" is used at all levels of the gospel tradition as Jesus' self-designation, scholars do not assume that every instance is an authentic saying of Jesus. Rather, they attempt to isolate the ways in which the phrase is used to determine which usage(s) most likely derive from Jesus himself. In the Synoptic Tradition, the term "son of man" is used in three different ways. On the one hand, it is used eschatologically, referring to the son of man as a coming judge (see Mark 8:38//Matt 10:30//Luke 12:8; Matt 12:40//Luke 11:30; Matt 24:27//Luke 17:26; Matt 24:44//Luke 12:40). "Son of man" is also used to describe Jesus' life of humble service to God (see Matt 8:20//Luke 9:58). Finally, "son of man" is used in the context of predictions of Jesus' passion, death and resurrection (see Mark 8:31; 9:31; 10:33–34).

While the phrase is found in eschatological contexts, in descriptions of Jesus' life of service, and in passion predictions, scholars do not agree that Jesus utilized the term in all of these settings (contra Hooker in 1967). Rather, many have argued that Jesus only used the phrase in one of these three contexts. The other usages derive from the meditation of and exegetical work by the early church. Still other scholars contend that Jesus never used the phrase at all, and that all of the instances of "son of man" in the gospels derive from the preaching of the early church.

"Son of man" as Jesus' own usage derived from Dan 7:13 and *1 Enoch*

Because it is incontestable that a figure of "one like a son of man" is found in apocalyptic texts, such as Dan 7:13 and in *1 Enoch*, it is understandable that some scholars have concluded that Jesus' references to the "son of man" are best understood in terms of early Jewish apocalypticism. Indeed, some, such as Bultmann (English translation 1968) and Tödt (1965), have argued that Jesus only used the phrase "son of man" in an apocalyptic context (see Mark 8:38; Matt 10:32//Luke 12:8; Matt 12:40//Luke 11:30; Matt 24:27//Luke 17:26; Matt 24:44//Luke 12:40). In these statements, Jesus referred to the apocalyptic son of man who would be responsible for final judgment.

Jesus' references to this mysterious figure, however, are not necessarily references to himself. For example, Mark 8:38 quotes Jesus saying, "Who is ashamed of me in this adulterous and sinful generation, the son of man will be ashamed of that person." Bultmann and Tödt both assumed that here Jesus was speaking of a second figure, the heavenly, pre-existent "son of man," to whom God has entrusted final judgment. They interpreted a similar statement found in Matt 10:32//Luke 12:8 in the same way. In Matt 10:32, however, the phrase "son of man" was replaced by a first-person reference, implying Jesus is the agent of eschatological judgment. Yet Tödt understood Matt 10:32 as a reflection of Matthew's own editing, and thought Luke 12:8 represented the more authentic tradition, where the reference to a heavenly son of man is a figure other than Jesus (pp. 55–60).

Likewise, in Matt 24:27//Luke 17:24, "for just as the lighting goes out from the east and shines to the west, so it will be in the coming of the son of man," the son of man is not Jesus, but a heavenly figure that will act as judge. Similarly, the son of man who comes suddenly as judge in Matt 24:44// Luke 12:40 is, again, not Jesus, but a pre-existent heavenly figure.

Yet not all scholars who have linked Dan 7:13 and *1 Enoch* 37–71 to Jesus' use of the phrase "son of man" have understood it as referring to a pre-existent heavenly figure. T. W. Manson (1950) asserted that when Jesus employed the phrase "son of man," he creatively combined concepts. First, Jesus was certainly aware that the "son of man" was a figure derived from Dan 7:13, as Mark 14:62 makes evident. Second, the imagery of Dan 7:13 is of a communal figure, so that when Jesus referred to the "son of man" as having authority to forgive sins in Mark 2:10, or as "lord of the Sabbath" in Mark. 2:27–28, it is the community, embodied in Jesus, that was able to forgive sin or decided what was appropriate Sabbath behavior. Third, Jesus redefined the concept of son of man. For Jesus' contemporaries, this figure was a powerful heavenly figure, who would establish justice and political power. Jesus transformed the meaning of the phrase by combining the eschatological son of man with that of the servant of the Lord of the servant songs of Isaiah (see Mark 10:45). In Jesus' ministry, the phrase was, thus, redefined in light of Jesus' own life of service and sacrifice.

E. Schweizer in 1960 and 1963 adopted a similar view to Manson's. Jesus adopted the phrase "son of man" as a self-identification pointing to his life of service and sacrifice. An example is seen in Mark 8:31, which Schweizer understood as undoubtedly deriving from Jesus himself. Jesus used the term, however, not because it was well understood, but because it was not yet a title. As such, he could invest it with new meaning.

Another view was that of E. Lemcio (2005), who has understood Jesus' use of "son of man" from a different perspective. Working from the Greek text of Daniel as preserved in the translations of the LXX and Theodotion, he noted the presence of a human figure not only in Dan 7, but also in Dan 8:14 and 10:11, 19. In Dan 8:14,

Daniel has undergone a period of fasting and has a heavenly vision, where he himself is addressed by the angel as "son of man." In 10:11, 19 the figure of a human being is a "pitiable human." Likewise, in Dan 7:13, in the interpretation of Dan 7:23–27, the community of the faithful was vindicated only after it had gone through suffering at the hands of the fourth beast (7:23–25). Only at the completion of the persecution was the community vindicated. Thus, the figure of the "son of man" in Daniel, therefore, was less a triumphant figure and more a representation of humanity in weakness dependent upon God. It is this meaning that Jesus employs when using the phrase "son of man."

Finally, C. C. Caragounis (1986) also interpreted Jesus' teaching in terms of Dan 7:13. The figure of the "son of man" in Dan 7, later reinterpreted by *1 Enoch* and *4 Ezra*, was employed by Jesus for a specific reason. Jesus used the term to redefine the messianic mission. Whether referring to himself as the earthly, humble son of man, or as the coming apocalyptic judge, or referring to his Passion and death, when Jesus used the phrase "son of man," he meant the same thing. Jesus pointed to himself as the one who proclaimed God's kingdom and its triumph over evil powers. Caragounis, therefore, understood that Jesus viewed all aspects of his mission, including preaching, healing and miracles, as the point where God decisively acted in defeating the hidden forces of darkness. To express what this mission meant, Jesus needed to find a new self-identifier, and for that reason utilized the phrase "son of man."

"Son of man" as Jesus' non-titular self-identification

Although the view that Jesus derived the phrase "son of man" from the apocalyptic texts of Daniel and *1 Enoch* enjoyed significant popularity in nineteenth- and early to mid twentieth-century scholarship, not all scholars were satisfied with this conclusion. In the first place, the status of *1 Enoch* is uncertain. The only section of *1 Enoch* not found at Qumran is the so-called "parables" of Enoch, *1 En.* 36–71. This section of *1 Enoch* is precisely where the figure of the "son of man" is found. Thus, it is questionable whether *1 En.* 36–71 represents an influence upon Jesus, or an independent tradition unrelated to the gospel tradition.

Instead of an apocalyptic "son of man," a number of scholars have pointed out that a proper understanding of Jesus' usage must reflect the idiomatic features of Palestinian Aramaic. Thus, conclusions such as those of Lemcio's are immediately considered suspect for Jesus' use of the phrase. Any interpretation based on the LXX would only explain how a Christian community speaking Greek and using the LXX as scripture would understand the meaning of "son of man." For these scholars, a proper solution must answer two important questions. First, how did Jesus use the Aramaic phrase "son of man" (*bar enasha,* or *bar nasha*) in the context of first-century Palestine? Second, what possible meaning could the phrase have had in that original setting?

One of the most vigorous proponents for understanding "son of man" in the context of its Aramaic original *bar enasha* or *bar nasha* has been G. Vermes (1973). Vermes concluded that the phrase "son of man" as used in the gospels could not derive from Dan 7:9–14. First, the description of the figure of one "like a son of man" is stylistically characteristic of dream language, in the same way that the beasts are described as "like" a lion, or a leopard or a bear. The figure "like a son of man" in Dan 7:13, therefore, is a corporate entity in the same way the beasts of Dan 7:1–8 are. It is a symbolic representation of the eschatological victory of the "saints of the Most High."

Second, in rabbinic exegesis a messianic interpretation of Dan 7:9–14 is rare. Even when the passage was understood as prophesying the coming of a Davidic messiah enthroned beside God (Dan 7:9), the "one like a son of man" in Dan 7:13 did not figure in the discussion (see *b. Hag.* 14a; *b. San.* 38b; 98a). Similarly there is no evidence that the rabbis ever understood the passage as describing the humiliation and later exaltation of a messianic figure. Furthermore, the figure of the "one like a son of man" is never understood as a pre-existent heavenly figure.

If the evidence is sparse that the apocalyptic "son of man" of Dan 7:13 influenced Jesus' usage, Vermes considered it practically nonexistent for the theory that Jesus understood himself in terms of the "son of man" in *1 Enoch.* The "son of man" of *1 Enoch* is not a pre-existent figure revealed in the last age. In *1 En.* 71:14 he is specifically identified with Enoch himself. The "son of man" certainly is present with God in judgment, but unlike the "son of man" in Matt 25:31–46, he never speaks in *1 Enoch.* The "son of man" in *1 Enoch.* also does not refer to a humiliated, then exalted figure. Vermes concludes, therefore, that the phrase, "son of man" was not an apocalyptic figure in Judaism, for such a figure never existed except in the minds of theologians in nineteenth-century German universities. Nor is the phrase "son of man" a title. Its origins must lie elsewhere.

If "son of man" is not used as a title, what was its meaning? Vermes answered that it could only be understood properly in terms of the Aramaic underlying the Greek "*ho huios tou anthrōpou.*" Vermes translated the phrase back into the Aramaic as either "*bar enasha,*" or "*bar nasha.*" In the context of the historical Jesus, the phrase can mean only one thing: it is a circumlocution for the first-person singular, or "I." Thus in Mark 2:1, Jesus is stating that "on earth I have the authority to forgive sins." Likewise, in Mark 2:28, Jesus is saying that "I am lord of the Sabbath."

Another scholar who asserts that the meaning "son of man" in the gospel tradition must be found in Aramaic idiom is M. Casey (1979). In contrast to Vermes, Casey understood the idiom as referring to human beings in general, rather than simply the circumlocution for the term "I." Thus, in Matt 11:19//Luke 7:34, "the son of man came eating and drinking," the meaning would be "a person came eating and drinking." In this case, the reader can assume that it referred to Jesus. The meaning is less clear in Mark 2:10 and 2:28, for in both of these cases the meaning is only generic. The "son of man" here refers to the role of humans in general, either as lords of the Sabbath, or in forgiveness of sins on earth.

B. Lindars in 1983 also concluded that the meaning of "son of man" in the gospel tradition must be explained by Aramaic usage. Only those sayings where the phrase could be translated back to the Aramaic idiom as circumlocutions for the first person singular are authentic sayings of Jesus. Lindars concluded that only six of the son of man sayings, Matt 8:20//Luke 9:58; Matt 11:16–19//Luke 7:31–35; Matt 12:32//Luke 12:10; Luke 11:30; Matt 9:6//Mark 2:10–11; Luke 5:24; Matt 10:32–33//Luke 12:8–9 can confidently be traced to Jesus himself. In none of the other references to the "son of man" in the gospels is the usage is consistent with idiomatic Aramaic.

The work of these and other scholars has contributed greatly to the understanding of how Jesus utilized the term "son of man." It can no longer be simply assumed that the "son of man" in the gospels is an apocalyptic title. Indeed, Levistad concluded in 1972 that we can no longer assume that an apocalyptic son of man figure existed in Judaism in the first century. Thus, when Jesus employs the phrase "son of man" it cannot be anything other than a circumlocution for "I," or a reference to humanity in general. It was never a title in Jesus' usage. Titular usage of the phrase is the product of the early church. Likewise, it is in the preaching of the later church that connection is made between Jesus' non-titular usage of the "son of man" and the figure of Dan 7:13.

It is also a positive development to understand the "son of man" figure of *1 En.* 36–71 as representing not as a source for the "son of man" of the gospel tradition, but an independent exegetical tradition based upon Dan 7:13. Yet, even if *1 En.* 36–71 in its written form does represent a post-70 CE tradition, it cannot for this reason be excluded from our evaluation of the significance of the "son of man" figure in the first century in general. Neither can it be excluded from our study of the background of the use of the phrase "son of man" by the historical Jesus. Rather, *1 En.* 36–71 may reflect a first-century Palestinian Jewish exegetical tradition in which Dan 7:13 played an important role. If this conclusion is correct, then it may also be assumed that Dan 7:13 was a source of reflection both for Jesus' audience and Jesus himself.

In addition, it has not been universally agreed that *bar enasha* was a circumlocution for "I." While the hypothesis is plausible on a superficial level, some have found the argument unconvincing. Fitzmyer (1979), for example, has pointed to the lack of evidence for *bar enasha* being utilized in an idiomatic manner before 70 CE. Indeed, the evidence indicates we cannot conclude that *bar enasha* would be commonly understood as a circumlocution. Thus, the support for the hypothesis is far weaker than its proponents would suppose.

Also, the hypothesis *bar enasha* can only be a circumlocution for the first person singular posits a false alternative: that Jesus either used the phrase "son of man" as a circumlocution for the first-person singular, or he utilized it as a title derived from Dan 7:13 and *1 En.* A more satisfying conclusion is that when Jesus referred to himself as the "son of man" he was making both a circumlocutory self-reference and an allusion to the obscure figure of Dan 7:13. It is true that early Judaism did not understand the "one like a son of man" in an exclusively messianic sense. It is also true that the rabbis did not understand the figure of Dan 7:13 as a suffering Messiah who is later exalted by God. Yet it is entirely possible that Jesus himself did make these connections. Thus, with Dunn (2002), we can conclude that is very plausible that Jesus utilized the phrase *bar enasha* both as a self-reference and an allusion to the obscure figure of Dan 7:13. In this way, Jesus looked forward to final vindication from God despite human rejection.

"Son of man" as a title of the early church

Finally, other scholars have proposed that Jesus' use of the phrase "son of man" is, ultimately, irrelevant, since Jesus himself did not use it. Rather, the origin of the phrase is to be found in the preaching of the early church, which was later imposed on the lips of Jesus. In an important essay (English translation 1969) E. Käsemann, reexamined Mark 8:38 and other texts considered likely examples of Jesus' use of the phrase "son of man." He concluded that there is nothing distinctive of Jesus' preaching in these verses. Instead, what we encounter is an example of a "sentence of holy law" typical of early Christian preaching. Thus, "son of man" sayings had their origin not in the life of Jesus, but in the preaching of the Greek-speaking Hellenistic Christian community.

N. Perrin (1967) has been particularly adamant that the phrase "son of man" cannot derive from the historical Jesus. Perrin pointed to the fact that the phrase is not found in Judaism for a messianic figure. Nor is it found elsewhere in the New Testament writings as a designation for Jesus. Thus, the designation of Jesus as "son of man" is the product not of Jesus' own usage, but the exegesis of the church, placed on the lips of Jesus by a later generation.

M. Goulder (2002) proposed a solution to the source of the phrase "son of man." According to Goulder, the phrase derived both from the figure of Dan 7:13 and from the church's exegesis of Ps 8. An example of this exegesis is found in Heb 2:6. Thus, meditation on the meaning of Jesus as the one "made a little lower than the angels" was combined with Dan 7:13. The result is that Jesus was understood to be the humiliated and exalted "son of man."

Of all the proposed solutions, the hypothesis that the phrase "son of man" was never used by Jesus but derived from the exegesis of the Church is probably the least satisfactory. Neither Käsemann, Perrin nor Goulder offered convincing explanations as to why the Church: designated Jesus as the "son of man" based upon exegesis of Dan 7:13 and Ps 8; placed this phrase almost exclusively upon the lips of Jesus; and never used it as a title of Jesus, such as the title Lord (*Kyrios*). Perrin's conclusions were the least helpful. Perrin himself noted that the litmus test for authenticity of a saying of Jesus is the criterion of dissimilarity; that is, only those sayings that have no precedent in Judaism, and are not found in the preaching of the later church can, with confidence, be ascribed to the historical Jesus. If any phrase meets the criterion of dissimilarity, with the exception of Acts 7:56, it is "son of man."

In addition to the criterion of dissimilarity, Jesus' use of the phrase "son of man" also meets the criterion of multiple attestation; that is, a saying or phrase that is found in multiple levels of gospel tradition is likely to derive from the historical

Jesus. As we have seen above, the phrase "son of man" is found in every layer of gospel tradition. Jesus uses it in Mark, in Q, in material peculiar to Matthew, in material peculiar to Luke and in John. If Jesus never used the phrase, what impacted different Christian communities so strongly that "son of man" is found in all these layers of tradition? Also, why is "son of man" only used by Jesus and only as a self-designation?

Finally, Jesus' use of the phrase "son of man" is also consistent with the criterion of coherence, that a teaching or usage of Jesus had such an impact upon later hearers that they preserved it in the way Jesus used it. Again, the remarkable feature about the phrase, "son of man" is that it is Jesus' own self-designation. Jesus' disciples never referred to Jesus in this way. Nor did Jesus' opponents use it. Nor was Jesus designated as "son of man" in the epistolary literature. It remained Jesus' own peculiar self-identifier. Thus, on the basis of three major criteria for authenticity, we can confidently assert that Jesus did, in fact, utilize the phrase "son of man" as his own unique self-reference.

Conclusion

Any discussion of the phrase "son of man" must take into account the following facts. First, aside from Acts 7:56, the phrase is not used outside the gospels in the NT as a designation of Jesus. Even in Acts, it is not a designation of Jesus' earthly life, but in his status at the right hand of God. In all traditions, Mark, Q, Matthew, Luke, and John, the phrase is Jesus' own self-designation. On the grounds of dissimilarity, multiple attestation, and coherence, we can assert that the phrase was utilized by Jesus. Other NT writers did not employ the phrase "son of man" as a title of Jesus. There are no NT prayers addressed to the "son of man." Likewise, in the NT the phrase "son of man" is not utilized to indicate Jesus' pre-existent status. Rather, when the Church wanted to refer to the pre-existent and exalted Lord it employed the term *Kyrios*, Lord.

Yet these observations do not mean that we can conclude with precritical writers that every time the phrase is encountered we find an authentic saying of Jesus. The textual evidence of the addition to Luke 7:56 alone indicates that the phrase could be and was placed on Jesus' lips by later writers. Thus, any understanding of Jesus' own use of the phrase must be pursued with the utmost rigor.

Finally, we cannot assume that when Jesus referred to himself as "son of man" he was employing a well-known phrase. One likely reason why Jesus chose "son of man" as a self-designation

was because the language was obscure. Jesus' usage recalled both the visionary figure of Dan 7:13, who was "like a son of man" with an idiomatic reference to a human being (see Theissen and Mertz 1998). By referring to himself in this opaque manner, Jesus utilized the phrase to define his message and mission on his own terms. Thus, while not every instance of the phrase "son of man" as found in the gospels necessarily represents an authentic saying of Jesus, an authentic memory is preserved: that "son of man" is Jesus own self-designation, and that the phrase provides us with insight into his own understanding of his mission and message.

RUSSELL MORTON

Further reading

Borsch, F. H. *The Son of Man in Myth and History*, Philadelphia, PA: Westminster Press, 1967.
—— "Further Reflections on the 'Son of Man': The Origins and Development of the Title," in James H. Charlesworth (ed.) *The Messiah: Developments in Earliest Judaism and Christianity*, Minneapolis, MN: Fortress Press, 1992, pp. 130–44.
Bultmann, Rudolf. *History of the Synoptic Tradition*, revised edition, New York: Harper & Row, 1968.
Burkett, Delbert. *The Son of Man in the Gospel of John*, JSNTSup Series 56, Sheffield: JSOT Press, 1991.
—— *The Son of Man Debate: A History and Evaluation*. SNTSMS 107, Cambridge: Cambridge University Press, 1999.
Caragounis, Chrys C. *The Son of Man: Vision and Interpretation*, WUNT 38, Tübingen: Mohr Siebeck, 1986.
Casey, Maurice. *Son of Man: The Interpretation of the Influence of Daniel 7*, London: SPCK, 1979.
—— "Method in Our Madness, and Madness in Our Methods: Some Approaches to the Son of Man Problem in Recent Scholarship," *JSNT* 42 (1991) 17–43.
—— "Aramaic Idiom and the Son of Man Problem: A Response to Owen and Shepherd," *JSNT* 25 (2002) 3–32.
Chilton, Bruce. "(The) Son of (the) Man and Jesus," in Bruce Chilton and Craig A. Evans (eds) *Authenticating the Words of Jesus*, Boston, MA and Leiden: Brill, 2002, pp. 259–88.
Colpe, Carsten. "*Ho Huios tou Anthrōpou*," in Gerhard Kittel (ed.) *Theological Dictionary of the New Testament*, trans. Geoffrey W. Bromiley, Grand Rapids, MI: Eerdmans, 1972, Vol. 7, pp. 400–77.
Dalman, Gustaf. *The Words of Jesus: Considered in the Light of Post-Biblical Jewish Writings and the Aramaic Language*, Edinburgh: T. & T. Clark, 1902.
Danove, Paul. "The Rhetoric of the Characterization of Jesus as the Son of Man," *Biblica* 84 (2003) 16–34.
Donahue, John R. "Recent Studies on the Origin of the 'Son of Man' in the Gospels," *CBQ* 48 (1986) 484–98.
Dunn, James D. G. *Jesus Remembered*, Grand Rapids, MI: Eerdmans, 2002.
Fitzmyer, Joseph A. "The New Testament Title 'Son of Man,' Philologically Considered," in *A Wandering Aramean: Collected Aramaic Essays*, Missoula, MT: Scholars Press, 1979, pp. 143–60.

Goulder, Michael. "Pslm 8 and the Son of Man," *NTS* 48 (2002) 18–29.

Hahn, Ferdinand. *The Titles of Jesus in Christology: Their History in Early Christianity*, New York: World Publishing, 1969.

Hare, Douglas A. *The Son of Man Tradition*, Minneapolis, MN: Fortress Press, 1990.

Higgins, A. J. B. *Jesus and the Son of Man*, Philadelphia, PA: Fortress Press, 1964.

—— *The Son of Man in the Teaching of Jesus*, SNTSMS 39, Cambridge: Cambridge University Press, 1980.

Hooker, Morna. *The Son of Man in Mark: A Study of the Background of the Term "Son of Man" and its Use in St Mark's Gospel*, Montreal: McGill University Press, 1967.

Käsemann, Ernst. "Sentences of Holy Law in the New Testament," in *New Testament Questions of Today*, Philadelphia, PA: Fortress Press, 1969, pp. 66–81.

Kim, Seyoon. *The Son of Man as the Son of God*, Grand Rapids, MI: Eerdmans, 1983.

Lemcio, Eugene E. "'Son of Man,' 'Pitiable Man,' 'Rejected Man': Equivalent Expressions in the Old Greek of Daniel," *TynBul* 56 (2005) 43–60.

Levistad, Ragnar. "Exit the Apocalyptic Son of Man," *NTS* 18 (1972) 243–67.

Lindars, Barnabas. *Jesus Son of Man: A Fresh Examination of the Son of Man Sayings in the Gospels in the Light of Recent Research*, Grand Rapids, MI: Eerdmans, 1983.

Luz, Ulrich. "The Son of Man in Matthew: Heavenly Judge or Human Christ," in *Studies in Matthew*, Grand Rapids, MI: Eerdmans, 2005, pp. 97–112.

Manson, T. W. "The Son of Man in Daniel, Enoch and the Gospels," *BJRL*, 32 (1950) 171–93.

Moule, C. F. D. *The Origin of Christology*, Cambridge: Cambridge University Press, 1977.

Olson, Daniel C. "Enoch and the Son of Man in the Epilogue of the Parables," *JSP* 18 (1998) 27–38.

Perrin, Norman. *Rediscovering the Teachings of Jesus*, New Testament Library, London: SCM Press, 1967.

Schweizer, Eduard. "The Son of Man," *JBL* 79 (1960) 119–29.
—— "The Son of Man Again," *NTS* 9 (1963) 256–61.

Theissen, Gerd and Annette Merz. *The Historical Jesus: A Comprehensive Guide*, Minneapolis, MN: Fortress Press, 1998.

Tödt, H. E. *The Son of Man in the Synoptic Tradition*, New Testament Library, London: SCM Press, 1965.

Vermes, Geza. *Jesus the Jew: A Historian's Reading of the Gospels*, Philadelphia, PA: Fortress Press, 1973.

Vielhauer, P. "Gottesreich und Menschensohn in der Verkündigun Jesu," in W. Schneemelcher (ed.) *Festschrift für Günther Dehn*, Neukirchen: Neukirchen Verlag, 1957, pp. 51–79.

Yarbro Collins, Adela. "The Influence of Daniel on the New Testament," in John J. Collins (ed.) *Daniel: A Commentary on the Book of Daniel*, Hermeneia, Minneapolis, MA: Fortress Press, 1993, pp. 90–123.

SOURCE CRITICISM

Definition and focus

Source criticism is the investigation of the source materials used by the author of a given text. New Testament source criticism focuses primarily on the gospels, three of which are given the label "Synoptic" (*syn*: together, *optic*: seen) because they can be viewed together in a "synopsis" of the gospels. These three are Matthew, Mark and Luke and they distinguish themselves from John in having substantial parallels with one another in both wording and order. The parallels are so extensive that they point to some kind of literary relationship between the three.

The Synoptic Problem is the study of the similarities and differences of the Synoptic Gospels in an attempt to explain their literary relationship with one another. In order to understand the theories that offer solutions to the Synoptic Problem, it is important first to understand the nature of the problem.

Synoptic data

Most of the material in the Synoptic Gospels falls into one of four basic categories. Although there is also material that blurs these neat distinctions, these categories are helpful ways of seeing the major contours of the Synoptic data that are in need of explanation. Triple tradition is material common to all three Synoptic Gospels (e.g. Parable of the Sower, Mark 4:1–9 and par.; much of the Passion Narrative, Mark 14–15 and par.). This is the largest category of material, and incorporates a lot of Mark's Gospel. Double tradition is material common to Matthew and Luke not found in Mark (e.g. the Lord's Prayer, Matt 6:9–13 and par.; the Beatitudes, Matt 5:3–10 and par.). It consists of roughly 200 verses of material, largely but not entirely made up of sayings material. Special Matthew (also known as M or Matthean *Sondergut*) is material found only in Matthew (e.g. Parable of the Sheep and Goats, Matt 25:31–46). Special Luke (also known as L or Lucan *Sondergut*) is material found only in Luke (e.g. Parable of the Good Samaritan, Luke 10:25–37).

Mark has very little special material. Nearly everything in his Gospel is also found in Matthew, or Luke, or both. This relates to the most striking fact of all, that Mark is usually the middle term among the Synoptics. This means that in the triple-tradition material, there are substantial agreements in wording and order between Matthew, Mark and Luke, between Mark and Luke and between Mark and Matthew. Agreements between Matthew and Luke against Mark are not as substantial. All solutions to the Synoptic Problem begin by attempting to explain how Mark is the middle term.

Priority of Mark

There are a variety of possible explanations for Mark as middle term, but the major explanation in recent literature is the Priority of Mark, the theory that Mark is the first gospel and that it was used by both Matthew and Luke. Thus, sometimes Matthew copies from Mark, sometimes Luke copies from Mark and sometimes both copy from Mark. Most scholars think that this explanation is preferable to the idea that Mark was the third gospel and that it used Matthew and Luke (the Griesbach Hypothesis, or Two-Gospel Hypothesis) (Farmer; Peabody).

There are several arguments in favour of Markan Priority, some of which are inevitably formulated as arguments against the Griesbach Hypothesis.

Markan omission of congenial material

If Mark used Matthew and Luke, then he often omitted material we might have expected him to include, e.g. the Lord's Prayer (Matt 6:9–13//Luke 11:1–4), which might have fitted well at Mark 11:20–25.

Markan addition of elements uncongenial to Matthew and Luke

There are only a few passages of material unique to Mark (including Mark 7:33–36, Healing of a Deaf Mute; Mark 8:22–26, Blind Man of Bethsaida; Mark 14:51–52, Man Running Away Naked). It is generally thought more likely that these are verses that Matthew and Luke both omitted (e.g. because of the physical nature of the healings, or the hint that Jesus' power was limited) than that they are the few passages that Mark added. A more consistent picture of Mark's editorial activity emerges on the assumption of Markan Priority.

Harder readings

Mark often has readings that would be difficult to explain as secondary to Matthew and Luke, but are more straightforward to explain as Matthew's and Luke's modifications of Mark, for example:

Mark 10:17–18: As he was setting out on a journey, a man ran up and knelt before him, and asked him, "Good Teacher, what must I do to inherit eternal life?" Jesus said to him, "Why do you call me good? No one is good but God alone." (Contrast Matt 19:16–17.)

Mark 6:5–6: And He could do no miracle there except that He laid His hands on a few sick people and healed them. And He wondered at their unbelief. (Contrast Matt 13:58.)

Dates of the gospels

A key moment in early Jewish and Christian history is the Fall of Jerusalem in 70 CE. Matthew and Luke appear to be more specific in allusions to this event than is Mark:

Matt 22:7: The king was angry, and he sent his troops and destroyed those murderers and burned their city.

Matt 23:37–39//Luke 13:34–35: Behold your house is forsaken.

Luke 20:20–24: and Jerusalem will be trodden down by the Gentiles.

Editorial fatigue

There are several examples of Matthew and Luke making characteristic changes to Mark in the earlier part of a pericope, but failing to sustain these changes throughout, and gradually lapsing into the wording of their source. The lapse creates a minor contradiction, and the phenomenon is labelled editorial fatigue. In the story of the death of John the Baptist (Mark 6:14–29//Matt 14:1–12), for example, Matthew correctly calls Herod *tetrarch* (14:1), only to lapse into calling him the less accurate "king" later in the story (14:9), apparently reproducing Mark (6:26) who has called him "king" throughout. Similarly, Luke re-sets the scene for the Feeding of the Five Thousand (Mark 6:30–44//Luke 9:10–17) in "a city called Bethsaida" (Luke 9:10), only to lapse into the Markan wording later, "We are here in a deserted place" (Luke 9:12, cf. Mark 6:35).

The two-source theory

If Matthew and Luke were both dependent on Mark, this raises the additional question about how the double-tradition material is to be explained. The majority view is that Matthew and Luke were using Mark independently, which necessitates the view that the double-tradition material is explained by the existence of an hypothetical source, named Q (for *Quelle*, German "source"). Markan Priority and Q are the two elements that make up the Two-Source Theory.

Arguments for the existence of Q are thus primarily arguments in favour of the independence of

Matthew and Luke, and they are usually expressed as arguments against Luke's use of Matthew, which is the dominant alternative (Streeter; Stein; Tuckett; Kloppenborg). The four primary arguments are as follows, with the first two the most important.

Luke's order

Luke's order of the double tradition is inexplicable on the assumption that he was working with Matthew. Luke has disrupted Matthew's fine order, including Matthew's neat ordering of the double tradition into five big blocks. In particular, if Luke used Matthew, he has ruined the literary masterpiece of the Sermon on the Mount (Matt 5–7).

Alternating primitivity

Sometimes Matthew, sometimes Luke appears to have the more primitive version of a given double-tradition saying. This is inexplicable on the assumption that Luke knew Matthew. Key examples include the Lord's Prayer (Matt 6:9–13//Luke 11:2–4) and the Beatitude on the Poor (Matt 5:3// Luke 6:20).

Luke's ignorance of Matthew's additions to Mark

Luke appears to be ignorant of Matthew's modifications of Mark in triple-tradition material, something that is inexplicable if Luke knew Matthew. For example, Luke has no parallel to Matt 12:5–7 (in the Cornfield on the Sabbath); 14:28–31 (Peter walks on water); 16:7–9 (Jesus commends Peter).

Luke's ignorance of M

Luke is apparently ignorant of the M material (Special Matthew). He would have included material like Matthew's Birth Narrative (Matt 1–2), and especially the Magi (Matt 2:1–12) if he had known of it.

The Farrer Theory

The Farrer Theory agrees with the Priority of Mark but argues that Luke also knew Matthew, thus dispensing with Q (Goulder; Sanders and Davies; Goodacre 2001, 2002).

Those who adopt this theory argue that there is evidence of direct contact between Matthew and Luke, including a number of Minor Agreements between Matthew and Luke against Mark (e.g. Matt 26:67–68//Mark 14:65//Luke 22:64 'Who is it

who smote you?'). They also note that there are some pericopae where Matthew, and not Mark, is the middle term, and explain these as places where Luke prefers Matthew to Mark in triple tradition. The Farrer Theory counters the arguments for Q in the following ways.

Luke's order

The preference for Matthew's order is simply a value judgement. Luke had his own narrative strategy and attempted to create a plausible biographical narrative in which the sayings did not go on for as long as they do in Matthew. Luke's tendency to abbreviate long discourses in his sources is already evident from his use of Mark. For example, Luke halves the length of Mark 4 (Parables) in Luke 8.

Alternating primitivity

Arguments for Luke's secondary nature are often overlooked. For example, Luke 6:20 ("Blessed are the poor ... ") makes sense as Luke's redaction of Matt 5:3 ("Blessed are the poor in spirit ... ") because it is characteristic of his writing in general, which champions the poor and engages in eschatological reversal. Further, one should not confuse literary priority with age of traditions – Luke may have had access to parallel oral traditions of material that he also found in his literary sources Mark and Matthew, for example the Lord's Supper in Mark and the Lord's Prayer in Matthew.

Luke's ignorance of Matthew's additions to Mark

Q sceptics argue that Luke shows considerable knowledge of Matthew's additions to Mark, but these places (Luke 3–4, John the Baptist and Temptation; Luke 11:14–26, Beelzebub Controversy; Luke 13:18–19, Mustard Seed) are called "Mark-Q overlap" and thus get overlooked by those making this argument. Moreover, the examples given by Q theorists are problematic. Luke omits Peter's walking on the water, for example, because he omits the whole of that pericope from Mark.

Luke's lack of M

It is unsurprising that Luke lacks M material since if he had included it, it would be labelled Q material. There are good reasons for thinking Luke omitted particular pieces of M like Matt 2:1–12 because of his dislike of magi and sorcerers (Acts 8:9–13; 8:18–24; 13:6–12; 19:19).

M and L

However one explains the triple-tradition and double-tradition material in the Synoptics, the question of the origins of the Special Matthew and Special Luke material remains. M and L used to be thought of as distinct, written sources behind this material (Streeter), but this view is now less common and most scholars are more inclined to talk about the sources for this material as a variety of written and oral traditions. Scholars differ on the extent to which the evangelists themselves invented Special Matthew and Special Luke.

Source criticism of John

Source criticism of the Gospel of John is inevitably a more speculative business than source criticism of the Synoptic Gospels because of the lack of verbatim agreement between the Synoptics and John. Scholarship is evenly divided on the question of whether John was familiar with one or more of the Synoptics, though all are agreed that he was at least familiar with some Synoptic-type traditions (e.g. John tells of the Feeding of the 5,000 and the Walking on the Water in John 6 and there are several parallels between the Synoptics and John in the Passion Narrative, John 18–20).

Whether or not John was familiar with the Synoptics, there are other questions about his source materials. In particular, some have argued that John is dependent on a "Signs Source" for the first half of his Gospel, whereby John worked from a written text that narrated several of Jesus' miracles.

Source criticism and the historical Jesus

It is a consensus that source criticism is an essential component of studying the historical Jesus. The Synoptic Gospels are almost universally held to be more valuable sources of historical information on Jesus than John and the most valuable Synoptic sources are often held to be Mark and "Q". Virtually all Historical Jesus scholars accept the Priority of Mark, but it receives different degrees of emphasis. E. P. Sanders avoids too wooden an adherence to Markan Priority in Jesus research, noting, for example, that Matthew's versions of triple-tradition material sometimes appear to be more primitive than their Markan parallels. Sanders is also sceptical of the existence of Q and his *Jesus and Judaism* makes no appeal to Q whatsoever. N. T. Wright also makes no appeal to Q, though he differentiates himself from Sanders in abandoning tradition-history, source criticism and

redaction criticism altogether in his work on Jesus. By contrast, Q plays a key role in the work of the Jesus Seminar, in particular the work of John Dominic Crossan, for whom Q, along with the *Gospel of Thomas*, provides an especially early witness to Jesus tradition. Q remains important in German Historical Jesus research and plays an important role, for example, in Gerd Theissen's work.

MARK GOODACRE

Further reading

Carlson, Stephen. *The Synoptic Problem*, online; available at www.hypotyposeis.org/synoptic-problem (1996–).

Farmer, William R. *The Synoptic Problem: A Critical Analysis*, New York: Macmillan, 1964; second edition Dilsboro, NC: Western North Carolina Press, 1976.

Goodacre, Mark. *The Synoptic Problem: A Way Through the Maze*, London and New York: T. & T. Clark, 2001.

—— *The Case Against Q: Studies in Markan Priority and the Synoptic Problem*, Harrisburg, PA: Trinity Press International, 2002.

Goulder, Michael. *Luke: A New Paradigm*, JSNTSup, 20; Sheffield: Sheffield Academic Press, 1989.

Kloppenborg Verbin, J. *Excavating Q: The History and Setting of the Sayings Gospel*, Minneapolis, MN: Fortress Press; Edinburgh: T. & T. Clark, 2000.

New Testament Gateway. *Synoptic Problem and Q*, online; available at http://ntgateway.com/synoptic (1998–).

Peabody, David B., with Lamar Cope and Allan J. McNicol (eds) *One Gospel from Two: Mark's Use of Matthew and Luke*, Harrisburg, PA: Trinity Press International, 2003.

Sanders, E. P. and M. Davies. *Studying the Synoptic Gospels*, London: SCM Press; Philadelphia, PA: Trinity Press International, 1989.

Stein, Robert H. *The Synoptic Problem: An Introduction*. Grand Rapids, MI: Eerdmans, 1987.

Streeter, B. H. *The Four Gospels: A Study of Origins*, London: Macmillan, 1924.

Tuckett, Christopher. *Q and the History of Early Christianity: Studies on Q*, Edinburgh: T. & T. Clark, 1996.

SOURCES, EXTRA-NEW TESTAMENTAL

Our knowledge of the historical Jesus comes predominantly from early Christian writings. But a few ancient Roman and Jewish writings also deal with the historical Jesus, usually in polemical contexts that must be taken into account when weighing their value.

Jesus in classical writings

Pliny the Younger

Gaius Plinius Caecilius Secundus (*c.* 61–*c.* 113) published ten books of letters. Letter 96 of Book 10, dated at 112, deals with Christians and mentions

Christ. Pliny gives the emperor Trajan a report of how he has been conducting trials of suspected Christians:

> I decided to dismiss any who denied that they are or ever have been Christians when they repeated after me a formula invoking the gods and made offerings of wine and incense to your image, which I had ordered to be brought with the images of the gods into court for this reason, and when they reviled Christ. I understand that no one who is really a Christian can be made to do these things.
>
> ... They all venerated your image and the images of the gods as the others did, and reviled Christ. They also maintained that the sum total of their guilt or error was no more than the following. They had met regularly before dawn on a determined day, and sung antiphonally a hymn to Christ as if to a god.

Murray Harris, following Maurice Goguel, has argued that this last sentence contains a reference to the historical Jesus, implied in "as if" (*quasi*). This is possible, but in the opinion of most not likely; even if Harris is correct, Pliny furnishes only the barest witness to the historical Jesus.

Suetonius

The Roman writer Gaius Suetonius Tranquillus (c. 70–c. 140) published his *Lives of the Caesars* around 120. In *The Deified Claudius* chapter, Suetonius writes tersely in section 25.4, "He [Claudius] expelled the Jews from Rome, since they were always making disturbances because of the instigator Chrestus."

The overwhelming majority of scholarship holds "Chrestus" to be the original reading. Suetonius identifies "Chrestus," most probably a mistake for "Christ," as an instigator against public order. He seems to place him in Rome during the reign of Claudius. What likely happened was that preaching of Jesus as the Christ stirred up trouble among Jews in Rome during the 40s, leading to some violence. Although Suetonius tries to refer to what we call the "historical Jesus," that he goes so far astray is an indication of how otherwise well-informed Romans could misunderstand Jesus.

Tacitus

Our main Roman source on the historical Jesus, and much more accurate than Suetonius, is taken from the *Annals* of the Roman historian Cornelius Tacitus, dating from around 116. Chapters 38 through 45 of *Annals* describe the great fire in Rome and its aftermath in the year 64. Tacitus first lists the official acts, done according to Roman religion and custom, to cope with the aftermath of the fire.

> To put down the rumor [that he ordered the fire], Nero substituted as culprits and punished in the most unusual ways those hated for their shameful acts, whom the crowd called "Christians." The founder of this name, Christ, had been executed in the reign of Tiberius by the procurator Pontius Pilate. Suppressed for a time, the deadly superstition erupted again not only in Judea, the origin of this evil, but also in the city [Rome], where all things horrible and shameful from everywhere come together and become popular.
>
> (*Ann.* 15:44)

What Tacitus explicitly says about Christ is confined to 15.44.3: "The founder of this name, Christ, had been executed in the reign of Tiberius by the procurator Pontius Pilate." His most likely source of information about Christ is his own dealing with Christians, directly or indirectly; it is possible that he corroborated this with a Roman historical record. In his sparse but accurate detail, Tacitus gives the strongest evidence outside the New Testament for the death of Jesus. His brief mention of Christ may fairly be claimed to corroborate some key elements of the New Testament account: Christ, the founder of the movement named after him, was executed for crime against Rome by Pontius Pilate.

Celsus

About 175, Celsus wrote an attack on Christianity entitled *True Teaching* (*Alēthēs Logos*), the earliest known comprehensive polemical writing against Christianity. *True Teaching* perished, but not before a large amount was incorporated into Origen's vigorous response, *Against Celsus* (*c.* 250).

Celsus discounts or disparages Jesus' ancestry, conception, birth, childhood, ministry, death, resurrection, and continuing influence. In 1.28, he relates the background of Jesus. The words that likely derive from Celsus are italicized (following H. Chadwick).

> [Celsus] portrays the Jew having a conversation with Jesus himself, refuting him on many charges. First, *he fabricated the story of his birth from a virgin*; and he reproaches him because *he came from a Jewish village and from a poor country woman who made her living by spinning*. He says that *she was driven out by her husband, who was a carpenter by trade, when she was convicted of adultery*. Then he says that *after she had been driven out by her husband and while she was wandering disgracefully, she secretly bore Jesus*. He says that *because (Jesus) was poor he hired himself out*

as a laborer in Egypt, and there learned certain magical
powers which the Egyptians are proud to have. He
returned full of pride in these powers, and gave himself
the title of God.

(Cels. 1.28)

Later, Celsus expands on the charge of illegitimacy: "*The mother of Jesus* is described as being *turned out by the carpenter who was engaged to her, because she had been convicted of adultery and had a child by a soldier named Panthera*" (Cels. 1.32).

These charges of illegitimacy are the earliest datable statement of the Jewish charge that Jesus was conceived as the result of adultery, and that his true father was a Roman soldier named Panthera. Most interpreters hold that this name was used by some Jews because of its similarity to *parthenos*, "virgin." If this is the case, it would mean that this is a Jewish reaction to the Christian doctrine of the virgin birth, which probably did not become a leading Christian theme until near the end of the first century. Celsus presents his source for this Jewish polemic about Jesus as a Jewish contemporary. Modern scholarship agrees with Origen's criticism that this was a literary device that Celsus employed to give a unity to information he likely culled from diverse Jewish traditions.

Among pagan authors Celsus is unique in relaying both Jewish and Greco-Roman objections to Christianity. His witness to Jewish tradition is especially valuable.

Jesus in Jewish sources

Rabbinic literature

To search the rabbinic literature for historical information about the first or second centuries is a difficult task. The rabbis wrote primarily to maintain the people in the Torah, not to discuss the past. In particular, the Talmud seldom mentions historical events from the Second Temple period, and those events mentioned are often garbled and unreliable. When we study this literature for its references to Jesus, additional difficulties arise. Christianity was a heretical movement to the rabbis who wrote down their traditions. Jesus was a heretical teacher of whom they seem to have spoken infrequently, perhaps from lack of interest or sheer disdain.

Modern scholars correctly discount most putative "code" references to Jesus in the Talmud, especially "a certain one," "Balaam," and "Ben Stada." "A certain one" is so intentionally vague in itself as to refer to almost anyone. The associations of Balaam and Ben Stada with Jesus come from layers of the Talmud developed much later than the second century, so their value for understanding Tannaitic polemic against the historical Jesus is nil. However, one proposed code name, Ben (son of) Pantera, is reasonably identified with Jesus. In the Talmud, this name occurs in conjunction with Ben Stada in *b. Shabbat* 104b:

> It is taught that Rabbi Eliezer said to the Wise, "Did not Ben Stada bring spells from Egypt in a cut in his flesh?" They said to him, "He was a fool, and they do not bring evidence from a fool." Ben Stada is Ben Pantera. Rabbi Hisda [d. 309] said, "The husband was Stada, the lover was Pantera." The husband was [actually] Pappos ben Judah, the mother was Stada. The mother was Miriam, the dresser of women's hair. As we say in Pumbeditha, "She has been false to [*satath da*] her husband."

(*b. Šabb.* 104b)

This passage reflects confusion over the identity of Stada: Mary's husband, or Mary herself? It settles on the latter, using a pun to illustrate the point: she is called "Stada" because she has been false to (*satath da*) her husband. While the passage is clearer about Pantera as Mary's extramarital lover, it offers no description of him. In fact, this tradition of Jesus as Ben Pantera is so slim and difficult here that, were it not for external corroboration, this passage's reference to Jesus probably would be given up for inauthentic.

As previously noted, we have independent testimony from Celsus around 180 that Jews were telling stories about Mary's conception of Jesus by a Roman soldier named Pantera. While this name remains somewhat enigmatic, Pantera likely derives from a polemical reaction to the second-century Christian proclamation of Jesus' virgin (Gk. *parthenos*) birth. Such a punning attack on Jesus' origins would be entirely natural for the rabbis. Far from being born of a virgin, they argued, Jesus was illegitimately born from Mary's adultery with Pantera. Thus, he should have no religious authority. This is a certain mention of Jesus by pseudonym in the Talmud. This more certain code name may have provided a model by which other names such as Ben Stada and Balaam were later treated as code names and identified with Jesus.

We have one passage in the Talmud on the trial and death of Jesus believed to come from pre-third century rabbinic tradition:

> It was taught: On the day before the Passover they hanged Jesus [Yeshu]. A herald went before him for forty days [proclaiming], "He will be stoned, because he practiced magic and enticed Israel to go astray. Let anyone who knows anything in his favor come forward

and plead for him." But nothing was found in his favor, and they hanged him on the day before the Passover.

(b. Sanh. 43a)

This short narrative is the only surviving rabbinic treatment of the death of Jesus. It centers on a legal practice (mentioned only here in the Talmud) of sending a herald out to announce charges against a person accused of a capital crime and to solicit witnesses for his defense. It is universally agreed that the Jesus (Yeshu) here is Jesus of Nazareth. The contrast between this presentation of a lengthy, public procedure and the canonical gospels' portrayal of the speed and secrecy of Jesus' trial before the Sanhedrin could hardly be more pronounced.

The charge against Jesus is that by magic (probably a reference to his miracles) he enticed Israel to go astray from the one true God to the worship of other gods. These are technical Jewish religious charges not at all connected here with Roman rule, and b. Sanh. 43a envisions the Sanhedrin itself carrying out this whole process from trial to execution. "They" at the beginning and end refers in context to the Sanhedrin. The "stoning" referred to by the herald is the prescribed biblical punishment. But the rabbis knew somehow that Jesus was crucified, not actually stoned, and so the passage refers at its beginning and end to "hanging," a Hebrew–Aramaic approximation of crucifixion. This passage is extraordinary: a Jewish writing in which Jews, not Romans, execute Jesus on solely Jewish charges after a solely Jewish trial. On the whole, this short narrative seems to be an inner-Jewish explanation and justification of how one famous criminal, Jesus of Nazareth, was put to death, and implicitly a warning to stay away from his movement.

Josephus

The most reliable witness to Jesus in any Jewish source remains that passage in Flavius Josephus's *Ant.* traditionally known as the *Testimonium Flavianum.* The present text reads,

Around this time lived Jesus, a wise man, if indeed it is right to call him a man. For he was a worker of amazing deeds and was a teacher of people who accept the truth with pleasure. He won over both many Jews and Greeks. He was the Messiah. Pilate, when he heard him accused by the leading men among us, condemned him to the cross, [but] those who had first loved him did not cease. For on the third day he appeared to them alive again, because the divine prophets had prophesied these and myriad other things about him. To this day the tribe of Christians named after him has not disappeared.

Few scholars today accept this passage as fully authentic, pointing out that its view of Jesus must be the result of later Christian interpolations. A few scholars reject the entire passage as a Christian interpolation into *Antiquities*, arguing that most of the early Christian apologists do not seem to have knowledge of it. The majority of scholars today prefer a middle position between accepting the entire passage as authentic or rejecting the entire passage as inauthentic. Perhaps the most tenable argument from those preferring something of a middle position is a reconstruction of the passage that presents Jesus from a neutral perspective. If those parts of the passage believed to be Christian interpolations are expunged from the *Testimonium Flavianum*, a neutral witness to Jesus results:

Around this time lived Jesus, a wise man. For he was a worker of amazing deeds and was a teacher of people who gladly accept the truth. He won over both many Jews and many Greeks. Pilate, when he heard him accused by the leading men among us, condemned him to the cross, [but] those who had first loved him did not cease [doing so]. To this day the tribe of Christians named after him has not disappeared.

(Meier p. 161)

This reconstruction makes good sense of the pattern of ancient Christian witnesses to the *Testimonium Flavianum*. That Origen, in 250, gives no indication that he knew of the passage while Eusebius several decades later does know of it (*Hist. eccl.* 1.1.7–8) fits the hypothesis that interpolation occurred, perhaps in the years between Origen and Eusebius. If this neutral passage was known to earlier apologists, they would not have been inclined to cite it, because it provided no real testimonium.

What is the source of Josephus's information? If a reconstructed *Testimonium Flavianum*, such as presented above, is reasonably true to the original, then there is little or no evidence that Josephus drew upon first- or second-century Christian writings as his source. Probably he gained his knowledge of Christianity from living in Palestine. He supplemented it in Rome, as his words, "to this day" may imply. Whether Josephus acquired his data by direct encounter with Christians, indirect information from others about their movement, or some combination of both, we cannot say.

ROBERT E. VAN VOORST

Further reading

Bruce, F. F. *Jesus and Christian Origins Outside the New Testament*, London: Hodder & Stoughton, 1974.

Chadwick, Henry. *Origen: Contra Celsum*, Cambridge: Cambridge University Press, 1980.

Harris, Murray. "References to Jesus in Classical Authors," in David Wenham (ed.) *Jesus Traditions Outside the Gospels*, Sheffield: Sheffield University Press, 1982, pp. 275–324.

Meier, John P. *A Marginal Jew: Rethinking the Historical Jesus*, Vol. 1, New York: Doubleday, 1991.

Twelftree, Graham. "Jesus in Jewish Traditions," in David Wenham (ed.) *Jesus Traditions Outside the Gospels*, Sheffield: Sheffield University Press, 1982, pp. 290–325.

Van Voorst, Robert E. *Jesus Outside the New Testament: An Introduction to the Ancient Evidence*, Grand Rapids, MI and Cambridge: Eerdmans, 2000.

Vermes, Geza. "The Jesus-Notice of Josephus Re-examined," *JJS* 38 (1987) 1–10.

STOICISM AND CYNICISM

There is no question that similarities exist between early Christian ethics and the doctrines of certain Hellenistic philosophers. These similarities might be explained by a shared intellectual milieu, i.e. a "philosophical koinē," or by genealogical influence in either direction. In the New Testament the similarities are especially striking in the writings of Paul. In certain second-century Fathers the engagement with Hellenistic philosophy is explicit and systematic. This article, however, will focus primarily on comparisons between the Jesus tradition and the Hellenistic schools of Stoicism and especially Cynicism for their potential yield in illuminating the study of the historical Jesus.

Stoicism: origins, history, and relation to the historical Jesus

The etymological and historical roots of Stoicism are found in a portico (*stoa*) of ancient Athens. In 313 BCE Zeno of Citium came to Athens and subsequently organized a school in the *Stoa Poikilē* (Painted Portico). Zeno divided his philosophical system into logic, physics, and ethics, although some of his students stressed one division to the near exclusion of the others and thereby developed Stoicism in directions that were later regarded as unorthodox. Cleanthes, the immediate successor to Zeno and head of the school from 263 to 232, was perhaps best known for the religious tenor he gave to Stoicism. His "Hymn to Zeus" is a celebrated expression of the piety that accompanied the philosophy. Chrysippus, who led the school from 232 to 207, was credited in antiquity with restoring the true doctrines of Stoicism and giving them their definitive expression. The fragmentary state of the writings of all the early Stoics makes a comparison of Zeno and Chrysippus impossible, and thus prevents an evaluation of this claim.

Chief among the Middle Stoics were Panaetius (*c.* 185–109 BCE) and his student Posidonius (*c.* 135–51 BCE). The former revised Stoicism by rejecting its doctrine of a periodic universal conflagration (*ekpyrōsis*), softening its rigid intellectualism, and relativizing the absolutism of its ethics, i.e. the idea that virtue was the possession of the perfect sage, not the pursuit of ordinary persons. Posidonius founded a school in Rhodes which became an important center for the continued revision and elaboration of Stoicism, particularly in its relationship to the sciences. Posidonius was a remarkable polymath, authoring works not only on philosophy but on astronomy, botany, geography, history, zoology, and other subjects. His work was a massive attempt to synthesize philosophy with all other domains of human knowledge. It is a considerable loss that his writings are known to us only by title or scattered quotations.

Late Stoicism is represented in the first and second centuries CE by such figures as Seneca, Musonius Rufus, Epictetus, and Marcus Aurelius. Substantial writings from each of these philosophers are extant and constitute a wealth of data for Roman Stoicism. The broad appeal of Stoicism during this time is seen in the social spectrum of its advocates: slaves and clients (Epictetus, Cornutus), political advisors (Seneca, Arius Didymus), and a Roman emperor (Marcus Aurelius). During this era abstract philosophical discussion retreats into the background, as ethical and practical concerns move to the fore, a development begun by Panaetius.

The fundamental principle of Stoic ethics was living according to reason (*logos*), a goal that is equated with living according to nature. To do this is to achieve virtue. All incidental conditions in life – health, sickness, wealth, poverty, fame, hardship – were inessential to the pursuit of virtue. These were indifferent matters (*adiaphora*), things which in themselves neither contributed to nor detracted from virtuous living. Such things were outside the moral sphere, hence neither good nor evil. Indifference toward the *adiaphora* is what gives Stoicism its popular image of impassivity, self-discipline, and aloofness from pleasure or pain. Most Stoics acknowledged, however, that *adiaphora* could be divided into the "preferred" (health, wealth, etc.) and the "rejected" (their opposites). The former, though not essential to happiness or virtue, had obvious practical benefits.

The emphasis on reason was accompanied by the disparagement of the passions, since these were irrational responses to one's environment. The sage was not driven by the passions but was guided by reason and virtue. But to insist that the truly wise and virtuous person always made right judgments, as the early Stoics did, was to relegate virtue to an unrealized ideal. Stoics who operated with this strict definition were caught in the awkward position of regarding all people, including themselves, as fools. Roman Stoicism moderated this view by allowing for the pursuit of virtue by imperfect persons, those who were making progress toward the ideal.

Stoicism's role as a background element and/or influence in the study of the historical Jesus has been modest. Van der Horst (1974; 1975; 1981) and Lightfoot (270–333, see esp. 283–87) have collected parallels between Stoic authors and the New Testament. These range from lexical and stylistic parallels to matters of theology and ethics. Among the more noteworthy similarities are the following: both Jesus (Matt 5:48) and Musonius Rufus (*Discourse* 17) call people to imitate divine virtues; both appeal to the birds of the air as examples of creatures who are adequately fed (Matt 6:25–26; *Disc.* 15), although Jesus makes explicit the fact of divine provision; both appeal to the manifold yield of the earth's harvest (Luke 8:8; *Discourse* 11); both Jesus and Seneca locate evil in human intention, not just action (Matt 5:21–28; *Ep.* 57); both speak hyperbolically of bodily mutilation to rid oneself of evil (Matt 5:29; *Ep.* 51.13); both condemn ostentatious piety (Matt 6:16–18; *Ep.* 5.1–2); both condemn a judgmental attitude (Matt 7:1–5; *Vit. beat.* 27); both espouse versions of the Golden Rule (Matt 7:12; *Ben.* 2.1); and both Jesus and Epictetus use crucifixion as a symbol of the suffering that befalls the just (Mark 8:34; *Disc.* 2.2.20).

Since the careers of the Roman Stoics fall later than that of Jesus, chronology makes impossible that which geography, culture, and language make unlikely, namely, direct borrowing of Roman Stoic thought by Jesus. The reverse influence is likewise improbable. The rare occasions in which the Roman Stoics seem to refer to Christians are more disapproving than sympathetic (Epictetus, *Disc.* 4.7.6; Marcus Aurelius, *Meditations* 11.3). The similarities listed above are aspects of a broad Hellenistic ethic in which Stoic philosophy and Jewish wisdom share. Stoicism's similarity to early Christianity is seen in Paul even more than in the gospels. The centers of Stoicism had always been in the western half of the Mediterranean world: Athens, Rome, Rhodes, Nicopolis. It is not clear that Stoicism made formal inroads into first-century Palestine beyond those values that already enjoyed broad currency in the Hellenistic world. Paul's writings likely bear more resemblances to Stoicism because of his travels in the Diaspora, including

some of its intellectual centers. Later Christian writers such as Clement of Alexandria (*c.* 150–215), Tertullian (*c.* 160–240), and Origen (*c.* 185–254) show explicit engagement with Stoic authors and ideas (see Long 235–36; Malherbe 1992: 267–70; and Colish). Even Rudolf Bultmann, who was a pioneer in pointing out their similarities, observed that Stoicism and Christianity ultimately held up two different moral ideals: the Stoic sage characterized by self-sufficiency and imperturbability, and the Christian motivated by love of God and neighbor (Colish 370).

Cynicism: origins, history, and relation to the historical Jesus

The seed of Cynicism lies in the circle of Socrates, specifically his student Antisthenes, who adopted the austere, self-sufficient lifestyle of his teacher. Some ancient writers thus treated Antisthenes as the founder of Cynicism (e.g. Diogenes Laertius 6.2), but more commonly the movement's origins are associated with Diogenes of Sinope, who in the fourth century BCE developed a distinctive philosophy that was practical as opposed to theoretical, in accord with nature rather than law or convention, and characterized by an embrace of poverty, itinerancy, asceticism, anti-intellectualism, and shamelessness. The latter charge in particular gave rise to the name Cynic, which derives from *kynikos*, "dog-like," based on the fact that Diogenes, like a dog, engaged in natural functions (sexual, excretory, etc.) publicly and without shame.

For Diogenes "life according to nature" required a minimalist existence. His possessions were limited to a cloak, a staff, and a purse for food. He sustained himself by begging and living off the land. He endured all manner of hardships, but refused to be hampered by conventions or public sensitivities. Civilized life, education, culture, and society's distinctions were rejected in favor of the freedom and self-sufficiency of the natural life. Despite this affirmation of independence, Diogenes did engage and exhort others and tried to win converts by outrageous actions. Plato aptly described him as "a mad Socrates" (Diogenes Laertius 6.54).

By its nature Cynicism never rose to the level of a formal school. Since Diogenes himself discovered and modeled the ideal life, elaboration of the philosophy was scarcely needed. There were, however, disciples exhibiting varying degrees of commitment. Crates of Thebes (*c.* 365–285) was perhaps the best known. He adopted the life of poverty, independence, and shamelessness that Diogenes had advocated, but was more lenient toward others and gained admiration through his humanitarianism and mediation of disputes. One of Crates' students, Zeno of Citium, provides a link between Cynicism and Stoicism, and the latter can be seen as a version of the former, plus a theoretical foundation and minus its extremes.

Cynicism waned in the first and second centuries BCE but flourished again during the Roman Empire. Wandering Cynic philosophers would probably not have been a rare sight in the larger cities of the empire (e.g. Alexandria) from the late first century CE on. Indeed, a point of agreement in the contested history of Cynicism is that the movement was primarily urban.

The influence of Cynics consisted in the impartation of ethical guidance more so than the recruitment of disciples. Cynicism is thus more appropriately understood as a way of life than as a recognized body of distinctive teachings (Tuckett 351–53). The practical guidance dispensed by Cynic philosophers included exhortations to an austere lifestyle, the endurance of hardships, the rejection of convention, and the practice of self-sufficiency and bold, free speech.

Some scholars of Christian origins have compared Cynic ideas with aspects of the Gospel tradition, including the proclamation and practices of Jesus' early followers and, by implication, the historical Jesus himself. (The thesis has been most thoroughly developed by F. Gerald Downing, but also by others. See Downing 1988; 1992; Mack 1988: 67–74, 179–92; 1993: 114–21; Crossan 1991: 80–88, 338–41; 1994: 114–22, 198; and Vaage 17–39, 66–86). These comparisons include similarities between the genre of the Q material and collections of Cynic sayings, the attire of the early Christian missionaries vis-à-vis that of itinerant Cynics, and most significantly, alleged parallels in the content of specific sayings.

It has been questioned, however, whether the literary similarities between Q and Cynic lives would have been sufficient for the genre of the former to evoke the latter (Tuckett 359–63). Moreover, all historical and literary analyses of the genre of Q are limited by the conjectural nature of the putative document.

The matter of the philosopher's attire is adduced as one of the most striking points of correspondence. The Cynics were widely identified by their accoutrements: a beggar's bag, a staff, and a heavy cloak (Diogenes Laertius 6.13). Scholars who argue for the similarity between Cynics and early Christians note that in Jesus' instructions to his followers as he prepares to send them out, a staff and bag are mentioned (Mark 6:8–10; Matt 10:10;

Luke 9:3; 10:4). But with the exception of the staff in Mark 6:8, this equipment is *forbidden* for the followers of Jesus. The significance of this fact is disputed. On the one hand, if the gospel passages consciously allude to Cynic attire, it may be by way of contrast, i.e. to distinguish Christian missionaries from Cynics. On the other hand, such an allusion would be evidence for early Christian awareness of Cynic practices, perhaps including Jesus' own awareness, if the saying is authentic.

Many comparisons of sayings have been adduced, and while the significance of these comparisons varies, some undeniably have merit (see the thorough catalogue in Downing 1988: 9–149, 175–86; and the critique in Witherington 1994: 127–41). Jesus' command to love one's enemies (Matt 5:44; Luke 6:27, 35) finds a rough parallel in Epictetus's description of Cynics as those who, when flogged, must love those who abuse them as a father or brother (*Disc.* 3.22.54). The Cynic correlation of happiness and poverty is superficially similar to Jesus' beatitude for the poor (Matt 5:3; Luke 6:20), although the Cynic perspective lacks Jesus' emphasis on eschatological reversal. For the Cynic, poverty *constituted* freedom and happiness; Cynics were ascetic for the sake of asceticism. Christian missionaries were called to surrender their security for the sake of God's Reign. Epictetus occasionally speaks of the Cynic's kingdom (*Disc.* 3.22.63, 76, 80), but it is instructive that outside of early Christian literature the precise expression "kingdom of God" is found only in Jewish writings (e.g. Wis 10:10; Philo *Spec. Laws* 4.164; see *TDNT* 1.574–76). Finally, as in the case of Stoicism, Jesus' appeal to God's provision for the birds of the air (Matt 6:25–26; Luke 12:22–24) finds a parallel in Dio Chrysostom's injunction to consider how the beasts and birds live more trouble-free lives than human beings *because* they own no property (*Oration* 10.16). The causal clause, however, reflects a kind of Cynic reasoning not found in Jesus' saying. Regarding these parallels and others, scholars have raised questions about the degree of similarity, the religious assumptions behind the sayings, and their motives and aims. (In addition to those already cited, see Betz; Horsley; Boyd; Eddy; Wright 66–74; and Meier 90–91).

Any allegation of direct dependence of the Jesus tradition on Cynicism must face fundamental questions about the plausibility of Cynic influence in first-century Palestine. As noted above, Cynicism declined in the two centuries prior to the Common Era. Its revival seems to be dated to the middle of the first century. The first Cynic figure who appears after the decline is Demetrius, who was exiled from Rome by Nero in 66 CE. We know of a few Cynics associated with Gadara in Syria, but none in the period of 150 BCE to 100 CE. Explicit evidence for Cynic philosophers in the early first century, particularly in Galilee, is lacking (Betz 471–72; Tuckett 355–58; Meier 90; Eddy 463–67).

As in the case of Stoicism, contacts between Cynics and early Christians are more frequent and certainly more explicit in the patristic era (Dudley 172–75, 202–7; Betz 460–62). Peregrinus (d. 165 CE), a pagan convert to Christianity, was imprisoned for his faith but later apostatized and became a Cynic. The second-century ascetic sect known as the Encratites may have been influenced by Cynic ideas. Hippolytus calls them "more Cynic than Christian" (*Haer.* 8.20.1). Maximus the Cynic, who combined the philosophy with Nicene Christianity and nearly became a bishop, was praised by Gregory Nazianzen. As Christian asceticism emerged, Diogenes was sometimes viewed favorably (although selectively) as a pagan exemplar. In all these instances, the resurgence of Cynicism and the geographical spread of Christianity facilitated an explicit engagement between them that is much less evident in the time of Jesus and his earliest followers. Ultimately, the effort to cast Jesus as a Cynic-like sage relies heavily on similarities that might easily have developed independently, while running the risk of downplaying Jesus' essential Jewishness (Wright 66–74). Although Hellenistic philosophy provides a number of rough parallels to gospel traditions, the source of Jesus' teachings, ethos, and self-understanding is more fruitfully to be sought in Judaism.

N. CLAYTON CROY

Further reading

Betz, Hans-Dieter. "Jesus and the Cynics: Survey and Analysis of a Hypothesis," *JR* 74 (1994) 453–75.

Boyd, Gregory A. *Cynic Sage or Son of God? Recovering the Real Jesus in an Age of Revisionist Replies,* Wheaton, IL: Victor Books, 1995.

Colish, Marcia L. "Stoicism and the New Testament: An Essay in Historiography," in W. Haase and H. Temporini (eds) *ANRW,* Part 2, *Principat,* 26:1, New York: de Gruyter, Berlin, 1992, pp. 334–79.

Crossan, John Dominic. *The Historical Jesus: The Life of a Mediterranean Jewish Peasant,* San Francisco, CA: HarperSanFrancisco, 1991.

—— *Jesus: A Revolutionary Biography,* San Francisco, CA: HarperSanFrancisco, 1994.

Downing, F. Gerald. *Christ and the Cynics: Jesus and Other Radical Preachers in First Century Tradition,* Sheffield: JSOT Press, 1988.

—— *Cynics and Christian Origins,* Edinburgh: T. & T. Clark, 1992.

Dudley, Donald R. *A History of Cynicism: From Diogenes to the 6th Century AD,* second edition, London: Bristol Classical Press, 1998.

Eddy, Paul Rhodes. "Jesus as Diogenes? Reflections on the Cynic Jesus Thesis," *JBL* 115 (1996) 449–69.

Horsley, Richard A. "Jesus, Itinerant Cynic or Israelite Prophet," in James H. Charlesworth and Walter P. Weaver (eds) *Images of Jesus Today,* Valley Forge, PA: Trinity Press International, 1994, pp. 68–97.

Lightfoot, J. B. *Saint Paul's Epistle to the Philippians,* London: Macmillan, 1913.

Long, A. A. *Hellenistic Philosophy: Stoics, Epicureans, Sceptics,* second edition, Berkeley, CA: University of California Press, 1986.

Mack, Burton L. *A Myth of Innocence: Mark and Christian Origins,* Philadelphia, PA: Fortress Press, 1988.

—— *The Lost Gospel: The Book of Q and Christian Origins,* San Francisco, CA: HarperSanFrancisco, 1993.

Malherbe, Abraham J. *The Cynic Epistles: A Study Edition,* Atlanta, GA: Scholars Press, 1977.

—— "Hellenistic Moralists and the New Testament," in W. Haase and H. Temporini (eds) *ANRW,* Part 2, *Principat,* 26:1, New York: de Gruyter, Berlin, 1992, pp. 267–333.

Meier, John P. *A Marginal Jew. Volume 3: Companions and Competitors,* New York: Doubleday, 2001.

Seeley, David. "Jesus and the Cynics Revisited," *JBL* 116 (1997) 704–12.

Tuckett, C. M. "A Cynic Q?," *Biblica* 70 (1989) 349–76.

Vaage, Leif E. *Galilean Upstarts: Jesus' First Followers According to Q,* Valley Forge, PA: Trinity Press International, 1994.

Van der Horst, P. W. "Musonius Rufus and the New Testament," *NovT* 16 (1974) 306–15.

—— "Hierocles the Stoic and the New Testament," *NovT* 17 (1975) 156–60.

—— "Cornutus and the New Testament," *NovT* 23 (1981) 165–72.

Witherington, Ben, III. *Jesus the Sage: The Pilgrimage of Wisdom,* Minneapolis, MN: Fortress Press, 1994.

Wright, N. T. *Jesus and the Victory of God,* Minneapolis, MN: Fortress Press, 1996.

STRAUSS, DAVID FRIEDRICH

David Friedrich Strauss (1808–74) was a German theologian who greatly influenced "the quest of the historical Jesus" by providing his own interpretation of the life of Jesus and by thrusting Christology to the forefront of theological deliberations. A native of Ludwigsburg, Germany, Strauss began his seminary education in 1821 at Blaubeuren studying under F. C. Baur. Later in 1825 he enrolled at the Tübingen *Stift* where he was influenced by the works of Friedrich Schleiermacher and especially Georg Hegel. Consequently, Strauss can be grouped together with a cluster of nineteenth-century philosophers and theologians who hoped to reinterpret ancient, pre-critical Christian teachings for a modern world in the wake of the Enlightenment.

In 1832, after he had completed his formal training, he was hired as a private tutor at the

Tübingen seminary. Strauss's indelible mark on biblical and theological studies, though, was most profoundly felt beginning in 1835–36 when he published *Life of Jesus: Critically Examined*. Others had previously questioned traditional Christian doctrines, but Strauss questioned the ground upon which those doctrines were built. Following Hegel's philosophical distinctions between "form" and "idea" in religion, Strauss ultimately argued that the stories about Jesus in the gospels could best be described as myths or traditions that corresponded to the "form" of Christianity, whereas the theological thrust of the mythical stories corresponded to the true "idea" of Christianity.

Rather than follow the rationalists who thought they could discern a historical kernel beneath layers of embellished tradition, Strauss argued that these mythical stories originated after Jesus' death. The early Christians were not attempting to mislead anyone. Instead, they were merely communicating in the language and concepts of their ancient culture while illustrating their conviction that the historical person, Jesus, was in fact the Messiah as prophesied in the Old Testament. As a result, Strauss believed all supernatural elements, like Christ's supernatural birth, miracles, and resurrection, were attributed to Jesus by the early Christians while articulating their belief that he was the messiah.

Consequently, Strauss began his *Life of Jesus* by dismantling the notion that the true value of the gospels was in providing a historical picture of Jesus of Nazareth. In order to accomplish this task, Strauss methodically pointed out the numerous contradictions and inconsistencies among the four canonical gospels. While others had previously pointed to a few discrepancies, Strauss was the first to survey the gospels systematically from beginning to end. Moreover, Strauss drew particular attention to the discrepancies between the Synoptic Gospels and John, which Strauss thought was written considerably later and therefore even more influenced by early Christian doctrine. In the end, Strauss's readers were left with a pervasive skepticism about the historical accuracy of all four gospels.

Second, Strauss aimed to construct a new interpretation of the gospels that would preserve their importance for modern readers living in the age of the Enlightenment. As Strauss himself put it, he hoped "to re-establish dogmatically that which has been destroyed critically" (Strauss 1998: 3.396). From Strauss's perspective, the essence of Christianity stands apart from historical questions about

Jesus. As a result, he proposed reading the gospels in an ahistorical, mythical fashion in the hope of discovering the "truth" about Jesus. Despite the cultural assumptions of antiquity that are present within the narratives, the stories nonetheless illustrate important religious truths.

Not surprisingly, Strauss's *Life of Jesus* was met by strong resistance. Because of public reaction, Strauss was released from his duties at the university shortly after this two-volume work was published. In response to the intense criticism, Strauss attempted to soften his previous comments on the gospel of John in the third edition of his *Life of Jesus* (1838–39). This less controversial approach contributed to his appointment as the chair of Dogmatics at Zurich in 1839, but the offer was quickly rescinded in response to public pressure. Notably, when the fourth and final edition of *Life of Jesus* was published in 1840, Strauss returned to his more pessimistic stance on the historical value of John's gospel.

In 1840–41 Strauss went on to write another controversial book on the development of Christianity when he published *Die christliche Glaubenslehre*. This two-volume work sought to trace the evolution of Christian theology from its earliest days. Afterward, however, Strauss turned to the writing of biographies and to a career in politics including service in the Stuttgart parliament from 1840 to 1848.

Eventually, however, Strauss returned to his theological roots when in 1857 he wrote about the life of Ulrich von Hutten, the humanist, and in 1862 he sketched the life and work of Hermann Samuel Reimarus. In particular, Strauss believed Reimarus's *Apology*, despite its weaknesses, helped to lend credence to Strauss's mythical view of the miracles and other supernatural elements in the gospels. Thereafter, Strauss directly engaged the topics he had previously set aside. For instance, he published a popularized version of *Life of Jesus* entitled *Life of Jesus for the German People* in 1864. Next in 1865 he wrote *The Christ of Faith and the Jesus of History*, in which he challenged Schleiermacher's desire to combine those two concepts. Finally, in 1872 he published *The Old Faith and the New*. In this piece, Strauss overtly advocated scientific materialism over against orthodox Christianity.

It is difficult to overestimate the impact that Strauss's "myth theory" exerted upon subsequent generations of biblical scholars and Christian theologians. Strauss was the first scholar to question systematically the historicity of the gospels, to devalue the gospel of John in general, and to publish a notable work that experienced a wide readership among the German people. Furthermore, once the historicity of the gospels had been questioned, Strauss and all subsequent theologians were forced to reassess how they discussed Christology as well as the historical Jesus. Notably, in 1910 when Albert Schweitzer summarized previous scholarship on the life of Jesus in *The Quest of the Historical Jesus*, Schweitzer praised Strauss highly, comparing him to a modern-day prophet. In Schweitzer's opinion, Strauss straightforwardly spoke truth and then suffered the consequences.

ANDREW ARTERBURY

Further reading

Baird, William. *History of New Testament Research, 1: From Deism to Tübingen*, Minneapolis, MN: Fortress Press, 1992.

Cromwell, Richard S. *David Friedrich Strauss and His Place in Modern Thought*, Fair Lawn, NJ: R. E. Burdick, 1974.

Harris, Horton. *David Friedrich Strauss and His Theology*, Cambridge: Cambridge University Press, 1973.

Kümmel, Werner Georg. *The New Testament: The History of the Investigation of Its Problems*, Nashville, TN: Abingdon, 1972.

Lawler, Edwina G. *David Friedrich Strauss and His Critics: The Life of Jesus Debate in Early Nineteenth-Century German Journals*, New York: Lang, 1986.

Morgan, Robert C. "David Friedrich Strauss," in Donald K. McKim (ed.) *Historical Handbook of Major Biblical Interpreters*, Downers Grove, IL: InterVarsity Press, 1998, pp. 364–68.

Schweitzer, Albert. *The Quest of the Historical Jesus: A Critical Study of Its Progress from Reimarus to Wrede*, New York: Macmillan, 1968.

Strauss, David Friedrich. *The Christ of Faith and the Jesus of History*, Philadelphia, PA: Fortress Press, 1977.

—— *The Old Faith and the New*, trans. Mathilde Blind, with an introduction and notes by G. A. Wells, Amherst, NY: Prometheus, 1997.

—— *The Life of Jesus: Critically Examined*, 3 vols, trans. George Eliot, Bristol: Thoemmes, 1998.

SUFFERING, MARTYRDOM

Towards the end of his public ministry, when opposition to him has hardened to the point of irreversibility, Jesus spells out the consequences of the rejection of him and his message. Among other things, he explains that he will be unjustly executed and his followers persecuted and even martyred. Jesus' view that the application of divine retributive justice can be suspended for a time is also found in the Old Testament and in Second-Temple Judaism.

In Daniel, "those who understand" are warned that some of their number will fall by the sword, be burned, captured or plundered (Dan 11:33–35).

Only the group will be vindicated at the appointed time; the individual is at the mercy of the larger historical designs of God. Nonetheless, God will vindicate the martyred righteous, raising them to everlasting life (Dan 12:2–3).

The notion that the righteous in Israel suffer because God inscrutably suspends the application of retributive justice occurs in Second-Temple texts, especially those composed in the contexts of the Antiochan persecution and the Jewish war with Rome. The righteous suffer at the hands of the wicked and are sometimes martyred; the application of retributive justice is postponed until the eschatological future, at which time the righteous will be vindicated (see *1 En.* 91–105; *Jub.* 23:14–31; *2 En.* 50:3–4; 51:3–5; *4 Ezra* 5:1–13; 6:20–24; 8:57–58; 8:63–9:13; 13:14–20; *2 Bar.* 70).

A constant in Qumran sectarian texts is the belief that the community alone will be the beneficiaries of God's "visitation." In the present, the members of the community may suffer at the hands of their opponents, because God, for undisclosed reasons, has suspended the application of retributive justice. Accordingly, throughout the historical period represented by these texts, the situation of the community as a marginalized and persecuted minority within the larger Jewish population is always seen as temporary. At the appointed time, God will intervene in history on behalf of his righteous ones, and bring about an eschatological reversal (see 4Q171; 1QS; 1QpHab; 1QH^a; 1QM; 4QInstruction). In addition, the experience of rejection and persecution by the Teacher of Righteousness, the founder of the Qumran community, is a partial historical parallel to that of Jesus (1QH^a 10[2].11–12, 14–15, 32–33; 1QpHab).

Jesus sees his own rejection by his generation as anticipated in the rejection and mistreatment of the prophets. Israel has consistently persecuted and killed those whom God has sent to the nation (see Matt 5:12||Luke 6:23; Matt 23:29–31||Luke 11:47–48; Matt 23:37 = Luke 13:34). In light of the salvation-historical tragedy of his rejection and impending death, Jesus prepares his disciples for the hostility that they also will encounter from unbelieving Jews and Gentiles. His followers must face the same opposition. Even though God suspends the application of retributive justice, nevertheless there will be an eschatological vindication.

There are two sayings of Jesus that presuppose that his followers will experience persecution and even martyrdom for his sake. These should be placed historically in the context of later hostility to Jesus and the eventual rejection of him and his message. Matthew and Luke have a saying in which Jesus affirms that, in order to be his follower, a person must bear his own cross (Luke 14:26 = Matt 10:37). Jesus means that to be his follower a person must be willing to suffer persecution and martyrdom for his sake and that of the kingdom of God. Jesus also teaches that the one who loses his life for his sake will gain it (Luke 17:33 = Matt 10:39). He means that the one who is martyred for his sake will find eternal life in the kingdom of God in its future fulfillment, at the time of the resurrection. This is part of the eschatological reversal, which extends to those who have died unjustly because of the suspension of retributive justice. Similarly, Jesus informs his disciples James and John that if they want a share in the future glory of the kingdom, they must be prepared to suffer in the present, because the kingdom of God and its messenger have been rejected (Mark 10:35–40 = Matt 20:20–23). In the context of his rejection, Jesus explains that he has not come to bring peace to the earth but division (Luke 12:51–52 = Matt 10:34–35; see *Gos. Thom.* 16). In other words, people will be divided on account of him. The minority of Jews who accept him and his message will find themselves in conflict with the majority. In contrast to the conditions that prevailed at the time when he sent them out to announce the dawning of the kingdom of God, Jesus tells his disciples just before his arrest that conditions have changed drastically, so that they must now be prepared for opposition (Luke 22:35–36).

Jesus explains to his disciples that they will face resistance from Jewish and gentile authorities (Mark 13:9–13 = Matt 24:9–14 = Luke 21:12–19). There are several sayings in which Jesus warns his disciples that they will suffer on account of their identification with him at the hands of official governing bodies (Matt 10:17–18; Matt 10:19–20 = Luke 12:11–12; Matt 10:21–22 = Mark 13:12–13). He tells his disciples that they must share the fate of their teacher and master (Matt 10:24–25). These warnings belong in the historical context of Jesus' rejection and impending death and possibly even in a post-resurrection context.

Jesus promises that rewards will be given to those who have sacrificed for him; this will take place in "the age to come," at which time there will be a reversal of social status: "The last will be first and the first will be last" (Mark 10:28–31 = Matt 19:27–30 = Luke 18:29–30). Since "the age to come" is synonymous with the kingdom of God, this reversal is part of the new social order of the kingdom of God in its eschatological realization. An important reason for the suffering of Jesus'

followers is the temporary suspension of the application of retributive justice. Likewise Jesus also pronounces blessed those who experience persecution in the present because of their identification with him. They are blessed because they will have eschatological reward (Matt 5:11–12||Luke 6:22–23).

In his Upper Room Discourse in the Gospel of John, Jesus prepares his disciples for the persecution and suffering that they will soon undergo (John 15:18–21; 16:1–4, 33). He explains that, if it hates him, the world will also hate them. The reason that the world persecutes Jesus and his disciples is that it does not know the Father. Jesus expects, however, that there will be an eschatological reversal.

BARRY D. SMITH

Further reading

Dumke, James A. "The Suffering of the Righteous in Jewish Apocryphal Literature," dissertation, Duke University, 1980.

Lohse, Eduard. *Märtyrer und Gottesknecht. Untersuchungen zur urchristlichen Verkündigung vom Sühnetod Jesu Christi*, FRLANT 64, second edition, Göttingen: Vandenhoeck & Ruprecht, 1963.

Meyer, Ben F. *The Aims of Jesus*, London: SCM Press, 1979.

Nickelsburg, George W. E. *Resurrection, Immortality, and Eternal Life in Intertestamental Judaism*, HTS 26, Cambridge, MA: Harvard University Press, 1972.

SYNAGOGUE

The synagogue as an institution is well known in the New Testament and in Flavius Josephus. It also figures in one inscription from ancient Judaea, the famous Theodotos Inscription dating to some decades before 70 CE.

"Synagogue" in the New Testament

The synagogue is presupposed as a developed institution in the Gospels and in Acts. The word appears in both sources at least fifty-three times, sometimes meaning a gathering and sometimes meaning a building, though the second meaning has been debated in recent scholarship. These texts mention the institutional functions of the Palestinian synagogue, such as assemblies for the reading or declamation of Torah, for teaching, for sermons, for communal prayer, for a law court, for a community center, and perhaps for communal meals. The synagogue as an institution resembles the collegium or free, voluntary association in the Roman world.

Luke 4:16–30 gives us Torah reading and reading from the Prophets as synagogue practice. Jesus "stood up to read," so the congregation was seated. It also suggests that the proper posture for Torah reading in public is standing. Furthermore, a scroll of Isaiah was handed to him, which suggests that there were scrolls present, that there was someone in charge of the scrolls, and that there may have been already a cycle of readings from the Bible that was followed even at Nazareth. We read that Jesus handled the scroll himself, reading and holding the scroll in his hands (though Luke does not tell us whether this was standard practice) and handed it back to the *attendant*, which suggests that this synagogue office was already developed. When Jesus sat back down (v. 20), all "fixed their eyes on him," which has been interpreted to mean that the home town crowd expected him to deliver a sermon.

Luke reports in Acts 15:21 that James the brother of Jesus declared, "For Moses from ancient generations has in every city those who preach him, since he is read in the synagogues every Sabbath." This apparently refers to Torah reading and sermons.

Luke also reports in Acts 13:14–16 there was a reading from the Law and the Prophets followed by a sermon. Since the narrative is set in Antioch of Pisidia, the practice may not match exactly that of Judaea. When the (seated) congregation in Antioch had heard the reading from the Torah and the Prophets, the Archisynagogos (Head of the Synagogue) sent word to ask the visitors – even though they were strangers – to address them: that is, to deliver a homily, called a "word of exhortation" in verse 15. The "Head of a Synagogue" (Archisynagogos) in that verse is surely a well-placed or high-ranking official in the synagogue. "Archon" ("Leader") means a community leader, but not generally a synagogue official in the New Testament.

We have hints that teaching and instruction were a normal and expected practice in the synagogue, because the congregations accepted it when Jesus taught in their synagogues (Matt 4:23, 9:35, 13:54; Mark 1:21, 6:2; Luke 4:15; Luke 6:6, 13:10; John 6:59, 18:20). Paul also spoke in synagogues in the Diaspora, sometimes "boldly," as Luke reports many times in Acts. It is interesting that different verbs of speaking in these verses suggest more than preaching, since Paul "reasoned" (dialogued?) with them (Acts 17:2, 17, 18:4, 19) as well as "proclaimed" (Acts 17:13). The "teaching of the commandments" appears in the Theodotos Inscription.

That prayer was a feature of the synagogue is suggested by the name of the building in the Diaspora: the *proseuché* or "House of Prayer" (see below). Exactly what constituted communal prayer in the synagogue is a matter of intense debate in scholarship. The New Testament, Philo Judaeus of Alexandria (first century CE), and the Theodotos Inscription do not mention synagogue prayer, but Josephus speaks of meeting in the synagogue of Tiberias and being "engaged in the duties of the [fast] day and ... our prayers" in *Life* 295 (see below). There are many prayer texts in the Dead Sea Scrolls.

It appears that the synagogue functioned as a village or town law court in some of the sayings of Jesus. In Matt 10:17–18 and Mark 13:9 Jesus warns his followers that they will be handed over to councils and will be flogged "in their synagogues." Luke 21:12 says, "They will hand you over to synagogues and prisons." These sayings fit well with Paul's own confession in Acts 22:19 in front of the barracks in Jerusalem: "Lord, here of all places they know that I imprisoned those who believed in you or beat them in the synagogues." This suggest that the aforementioned council may have met in the synagogue to try offenders, that sentences were meted out in the synagogue, and that more serious cases could be referred to higher authorities (Luke 21:12, "kings and governors"). This would be a judicial function of the synagogue.

The gospel texts that mention Jesus' healing in synagogues suggest that healing and miracles are not to be excluded from that venue except on the Sabbath. The Second Temple contained a Chamber of Lepers, which is explained in later tradition as a chamber of ritual baths for lepers who had already been orally declared clean by priestly inspection (Lev 14; *m. Neg.* 14). Healings associated with temples were ordinary in Roman and Greek paganism.

The synagogue in Flavius Josephus

Josephus knows of a very large and splendid synagogue in Tiberias, which he calls a *Proseuché* or "House of Prayer," which was the normal word in Egypt and the most common name in the rest of the Diaspora. It has been suggested that this building had been built by Herod Antipas or perhaps during the reign of Herod Agrippa I. Both these rulers were known for the connections with the Diaspora. Josephus relates that his enemies met in this synagogue on a Sabbath and debated whether to fight the Romans in open revolt (*Life* 276–79). No service is described, but the meeting suggests that at the very least the synagogue of Tiberias functioned sometimes as a community center. In their third meeting in the Proseuché, proclaimed a fast day, Josephus reports that they first attended to their prayers. This suggests that there were prescribed prayers for a fast day in a synagogue or a Proseuché.

Josephus also speaks of instruction of children, which some scholars locate in the synagogue. In *Against Apion* 2.204 he explains that the Law ordains instruction of children "in both the laws and deeds of their forefathers" so that they can imitate these deeds and know their own laws. Roman readers would recognize this as teaching the children virtue, and instruction is also understood as a public duty in the Roman Empire.

The evidence of the Theodotos Inscription and Imperial decrees in Josephus

The Theodotos Inscription was found in Jerusalem in 1914 and records the refounding of a synagogue by a certain Theodotos, hence the name.

> Theodotos, son of Vettenos, priest and Archisynagogos, son of an Archisynagogos, grandson of an Archisynagogos, constructed the synagogue for the reading of the Law and for the teaching of the commandments, and the hostel and the rooms and the water systems, for lodging those from abroad who need [them], which his fathers founded and the elders and Simonides.

The first function of the synagogue is "reading of the Law." (See above.) The second function is "teaching of the commandments," which some believe refers to teaching children. The hostel and the rooms are evidently for foreign pilgrims, so hospitality was an important function of the synagogue.

The "water systems" are often interpreted as ritual baths. There is no law that requires ritual bathing before synagogue attendance, but the two are often found together anyway.

It is possible that there were communal meals also, as Josephus reports a decree of Julius Caesar allowing Jews alone to "assemble and feast in accordance with their native customs and deliberations" (*Ant.* 14.214–16). Furthermore Caesar Augustus condemns those "stealing their holy books, or their sacred money, whether it be out of the synagogue or public school" (*Ant.* 16.164). The word translated "public school" also means a "dining hall." If so, communal meals were recognized and expressly allowed by Julius Caesar and Augustus Caesar.

Archaeology

The Theodotos Inscription informs us that there was a first-century synagogue in Jerusalem, but as

yet no foundations have been found. Luke lists several Jerusalem synagogues in Acts 8:8–9: "Some of those from the Synagogue of the Freedmen and of the Cyreneans and of the Alexandrians, and of those from Cilicia and Asia ... " Scholars debate whether there were five synagogues or only one in these verses. The gospels seem to assume that there were synagogues everywhere in Galilee, though only the Capernaum and Nazareth synagogues are named.

The putative first-century CE synagogue at Capernaum has been excavated beneath the great white limestone synagogue so well known to visitors since 1916. The black basalt building beneath the late synagogue is 80 x 60.7 ft (24.4 x 18.5 m) on the interior. It includes walls 4–4.3 ft (1.2–1.3 m) wide, which suggests a public building. There is evidence for two rows of columns on the interior and a paved floor. There were carved moldings beneath the roofline.

Another synagogue of similar size was found at Gamla. The interior dimensions of the prayer hall were 69.6 x 55.1 ft (21.2 x 16.8 m) with benches around four sides. Four rows of columns define a central, rectangular and unpaved space. The only decoration is meanders on the capitals in low relief and two incised palm branches on two lintels. A niche in the southwest corner may have held an ark. An elaborate atrium conducts the public into the prayer hall. South of the synagogue in the next block of houses there stood a ritual bath in antiquity. It is disconnected from the synagogue, but convenient for those who may desire it.

At the village of Qiryat Sefer north of Jerusalem archaeologists unearthed a small, nearly square synagogue building only 27.6 x 27.6 ft (8.4 x 8.4 m) with walls only 1.6 ft (0.5 m) thick. Two rows of square columns and pilasters defined a rectangular space between the columns. This space was further defined by two ranks of benches on four sides. Entry was through the facade's double doors.

Northwest of Jerusalem was found a synagogue assigned to the ancient city of Modi'in. This one is relatively small, only 34.8 x 26.2 ft (10.6 x 8 m) with walls about 3 ft (1 m) thick. The interior space was defined by two rows of four (square) columns. It is unclear as yet whether benches stood all around.

Probably the best-known first-century CE synagogue was found at Masada. It measures 40.4 x 34.4 ft (12.3 x 10.5 m) on the interior with walls 2.6 ft (0.80 m) thick and with three ranks of plastered benches around the walls. It was built into the defense wall at the top. A small room stands in the far right corner where fragments of Deuteronomy and Ezekiel were found, testifying to the importance of reading from the Law and Prophets. Five columns form a rectangular space in the center.

Another well-known first-century synagogue is that of Herod's fortress of Herodion (Herodium). This 49.7 x 34.8 ft (15.15 x 10.6 m) building features four columns defining the central space and three ranks of benches on three walls. It was converted during the First Revolt from a triclinium or dining hall built in Herod's day. Just outside the front door stood a stepped pool generally interpreted as a ritual bath.

The smallest synagogue found so far was found in Herodian Jericho. The interior dimensions of the central hall measure only 21.2 x 15.4 ft (6.45 x 4.68 m), not counting the protrusion of the added dining room. Four rows of square columns all around define the central rectangle of space. There is no published date for the addition of the dining room, but its presence tends to support the contention that communal meals were part of the synagogue as an institution. There is one bench all around, which is built in line with the columns. A niche for a possible ark was found in the northeast corner. An attached apartment on the west may have housed a synagogue official, and two pools on the north side of the prayer hall were evidently a ritual bath and its filling pool.

Scholars generally believe that there was no single pattern that the ancients followed when building these synagogues. They were instead influenced by local building traditions. There is also a marked absence of decorative elements or Jewish art except in the case of Gamla, though this may change with more discoveries. On the other hand, there is one constant pattern of nesting architectural elements. All the floor plans are rectangular, though one is almost square (Qiryat Sefer). The builders nested benches inside the walls around two, three, or all four walls. They nested a walkway all around inside the benches. Next they nested a rectangle of columns inside the walkway. Finally the builders nested a central space inside the columns, presumably for declamation of the Torah and other formal speaking occasions. The result is cumbersome for vision, but good for audition. In other words, these buildings identified as early synagogues were not for spectacles, for visual performances, but for speaking and hearing.

Since these buildings do not contain inscriptions identifying them as synagogues, they can only be identified as such because later, highly decorated buildings of more or less the same plan are identified as synagogues in donors' inscriptions.

The overall effect was a building that resembled the Roman basilica more than any other contemporary structure. The width of six out of seven of these buildings ranges from 70 to 80 percent of the length, wider than a basilica according to Vitruvius (*On Architecture* V.1.4), but a proportion encountered in the eastern empire. These seven buildings can also be linked to the Second Temple, mainly to the courts and the great basilica usually reconstructed on the south side of the Temple Mount, though this linkage is still controversial in scholarly circles.

The temple courts were where the Torah was read aloud to the people. The open temple courts also allowed discussions of daily life and other matters. The courts were roofed from wall to the line of columns. Jesus "sat" on the Temple Mount to teach the people, so we infer benches against the walls (Matt 26:55; Mark. 12:41). For example, contemporary temples from southern Syria and Nabataea have benches along the inner walls. Also the ideal temple in the *Temple Scroll* has "seats" for the priests inside the courtyard in the inner colonnade. The basilica was already available in Judaea as a part of Roman culture. The basilica seems to combine architectural elements of the colonnaded porch.

This is a small sample of seven buildings, compared to the about fifty synagogues of all periods that have been excavated in Galilee, Samaria, and Judaea. Yet the geographical distribution of these few, architecturally similar structures from the Golan Heights to the Judaean desert argues that synagogues did not appear solely because of local interests, but because of the interests of the people as a whole, who saw to it that they were sufficiently constant in plan to answer to the requirements of the emerging, more or less standard elements of declamation of Torah, studying and teaching, sermons, communal prayer, a law court, a community center, healing, and perhaps communal meals.

JAMES F. STRANGE

Further reading

Binder, Donald. *Into the Temple Courts: The Place of the Synagogues in the Second Temple Period*, Atlanta, GA: Society of Biblical Literature, 1999.

Chiat, Marilyn Joyce Segal. *Handbook of Synagogue Architecture*, Chico, CA: Scholars Press, 1982.

Kee, Howard Clark and Lynn H. Cohick (eds) *Evolution of the Synagogue: Problems and Progress*, Harrisburg, PA: Trinity Press International, 1999.

Levine, Lee I. *The Ancient Synagogue: The First Thousand Years*, New Haven, CT and London: Yale University Press, 2000.

Richardson, Peter. "Early Synagogues as *Collegia* in the Diaspora and Palestine," in J. S. Kloppenborg and S. G.

Wilson (eds) *Voluntary Associations in the Graeco-Roman World*, London: Routledge, 1996, pp. 90–109.

Strange, James F. "The Synagogue as Metaphor," in A. J. Avery-Peck and J. Neusner (eds) *Judaism in Late Antiquity: Part Three, Where We Stand: Issues and Debates in Ancient Judaism. Vol. Four, The Special Problem of the Synagogue*, Leiden, Boston, MA and Cologne: Brill, 2001, pp. 93–120.

—— "Archaeology and Ancient Synagogues up to about 200 CE," in A. J. Avery-Peck, D. Harrington, and J. Neusner (eds) *When Christianity and Judaism Began: Essays in Memory of Anthony J. Saldarini*, Boston, MA and Leiden: Brill, 2004, pp. 483–508.

Urman, Dan and Paul Flesher (eds) *Ancient Synagogues: Historical Analysis and Archaeological Discovery*, Leiden, New York, and Cologne: Brill, 1995.

T

TARGUMS

The Aramaic translations of Hebrew Scripture are known as Targums. They shed important light on biblical interpretation in Jewish circles in late antiquity and as such are part of a very important interpretive method that developed in late antiquity, in which Scripture was translated, paraphrased, and rewritten. At many points Jesus' appeal to Scripture indicates familiarity with interpretive tradition coherent with the Targums.

Origin of Targums

How early Hebrew Scripture was translated into Aramaic is unknown. Most of the extant Targums are products of the Rabbinic Period, dating from the fourth to tenth centuries AD (see York). However, the discovery of at least one Targum at Qumran (i.e. 11QtgJob) and possibly three others (i.e. 6Q19 [Genesis], 4QtgLeviticus, 4QtgJob) demonstrates that some Targums existed in the first century BC, perhaps even earlier. The impulse to translate Hebrew Scripture into Greek (i.e. the Septuagint, or LXX) for one Jewish constituency, which began in the third century BC, may have coincided with a similar impulse to render Scripture into Aramaic for another constituency.

The Aramaic translation became known as *targum* (pl. *targumim*), a Hebrew and Aramaic word that means "translation." There are extant Targums of every book of Scripture, with the exceptions of Ezra, Nehemiah, and Daniel. These books may not have been translated into Aramaic because parts of them were already in Aramaic.

The Targums originated in the synagogue and perhaps also in the rabbinical academies as homiletical and interpretive paraphrases of the passage of Hebrew Scripture that was to be read (such as the *haftarah*). Following the Babylonian and Persian exile (*c*. 600–500 BC), many of the Jewish people came to speak Aramaic with greater ease than the cognate Hebrew, the language of Scripture. Therefore, it became useful to translate Hebrew Scripture into Aramaic (cf. Neh 8, where Ezra the scribe translates Hebrew Scripture into Aramaic; cf. *b. Meg.* 3a). The translator was called the *meturgeman* ("translator"). He recited his translation after the reading of the Hebrew passage.

Classifications of Targums

Targums fall into three basic classifications: Targums to the Pentateuch, Targums to the Prophets, Targums to the Writings (or Hagiographa). These Targums exemplify individual characteristics and should be studied accordingly.

Targums to the Pentateuch

The major extant Targums to the Pentateuch include the traditional Onqelos (see Sperber, vol. 1), the much later *Pseudo-Jonathan* (see Clarke), the *Fragment Targum* (see Klein 1980), and the recently discovered *Neophyti* (or *Neofiti*; see Díez Macho). Of these, the last is considered to reflect the oldest language and interpretive tradition. The so-called *Fragment Targum* is in reality a Targum made up of selected readings. Its name is a misnomer; it would have been better to call it the *Excerpt Targum*. There are many Targum fragments in the vast collection of materials recovered from the genizot of synagogues in Cairo (see Klein 1986).

Targums to the Prophets

At one time it was commonplace to refer to Targum Jonathan to the Prophets, as if the whole corpus reflected a single school or tradition. Recent study has made it clear that the Prophets should be studied individually, for each reveals a character of its own (in the Aramaic Bible series, see the introductory essays by Chilton, on Isaiah; Hayward, on Jeremiah; Levey, on Ezekiel; and Cathcart and Saldarini, on the Twelve). Chilton (1982) has concluded that the exegetical framework of the *Isaiah Targum* took shape between the two great Jewish wars for liberation (i.e. from AD 70 to 132). There are indications that the other Prophets Targums took shape in this approximate period.

Targums to the Writings

The Targums to the Writings are individualistic; indeed, there are two Targums to Esther. These Targums are quite midrashic and often accommodate large insertions of interpretive or homiletical material (e.g. *Tg. Ruth* 1:1, which contains a homily concerning ten great famines in Israel's history). The most difficult of these Targums are those to Job and the Psalms, for there is no fixed text for either. Also puzzling is the relationship of the Targum to the Proverbs and the Syriac version of this book.

Character of Targums

The Targums are sometimes literal in their translation, but more often they are paraphrastic and interpretive. Targums are part of the phenomenon sometimes called "rewritten Bible," though not identical to it. Rewritten Bible, as seen, for example, in *Jubilees* or Pseudo-Philo's *Biblical Antiquities*, freely omits, rearranges, and radically alters the biblical text. In comparison, Targums are more conservative, following the text. Concern to update the text, answer questions raised by the text, even correct the text, is seen in the Targums.

Jesus and Targumic tradition

At several points Jesus' utterances and scriptural interpretation cohere with targumic tradition, especially as seen in the extant *Isaiah Targum*.

According to Mark 4:12, Jesus paraphrased Isa 6:9–10 to explain in part why some did not comprehend or respond supportively to his teaching: "in order that seeing they should see and not perceive, and hearing they should hear and not understand, lest they should turn [i.e. repent] and it be forgiven them." Only the *Isaiah Targum* reads "forgive"; the Hebrew (MT and 1QIsaᵃ) and the LXX read "heal." (The Peshitta also reads "forgive," either because it has followed the Targum or because it has been influenced by the version found in Mark.) It might be added that not only is there dictional coherence, there may be thematic coherence as well. According to the Targum, the prophet is to speak the word of obduracy to those *who* do not hear and do not see. In other words, the word of obduracy is directed only to the obdurate. In the Markan context Jesus' word is directed to "outsiders." This application approximates the idea of the Targum. Jesus' quotation, therefore, appears to have been influenced by an Aramaic reading heard in the synagogue of his day (see Chilton 1984: 90–98).

According to Matt 26:52, Jesus rebuked Peter for his rash act of striking the high priest's servant: "All who take a sword on the sword will be destroyed" (only in Matthew). Chilton suspects (1984: 98–101) that Jesus has alluded to the Aramaic version of Isa 50:11: "Behold, all you kindling a fire, *grasping a sword*, go, fall in the fire you kindled and *on the sword* you grasped. This is yours from my word: you shall return to your *destruction*" (with the distinctive elements of the Targum emphasized). The Greek words of Jesus' saying ("take a sword," "on the sword," "destroyed") cohere with the distinctive elements of the Targum.

When Jesus warns his followers to beware of being cast into "Gehenna" (Mark 9:47), he quotes part of Isa 66:24: "where 'their worm does not die and the fire is not quenched'" (Mark 9:48). The Hebrew version of Isaiah says nothing about Gehenna, but the Targum does: "for their *breaths* will not die and their fire shall not be quenched, and *the wicked* shall be *judged in Gehenna*" (with the distinctive elements of the Targum emphasized). Again, Jesus' use of this verse from Isaiah may very well reveal a familiarity with the Aramaic tradition that is now preserved in the *Isaiah Targum* (see Chilton 1984: 101–7). Moreover, Jesus' warning that the one who hates his brother is liable to be cast into the "Gehenna of fire" (Matt 5:22; 18:9) may also echo targumic diction: "a fire *of Gehenna* not fanned will consume him" (*Tg. Job* 20:26, with the distinctive element emphasized; cf. *Tg. Neof.* Gen 15:17).

Jesus' metaphorical saying about new wine bursting old wineskins (Mark 2:22 par.) coheres with Job 32:19: "My heart is like wine that has no vent; like new wineskins, it is ready to burst." The *Job Targum* parallels it even more closely: "My belly is like *new* wine" (*Tg.* Job 32:19, with the distinctive element of the Targum emphasized).

In Luke 16:9 Jesus tells his disciples to "make friends of the mammon of injustice [*or* dishonesty]." Although the Aramaic word *mamôna'* occurs in the talmuds, especially the Palestinian version, the expression "mammon of injustice/dishonesty" coheres with the targumic description of bribery as "mammon of falsehood/deceit" (cf. *Tg.* 1 Sam 12:3; *Tg.* Hos 5:11; *Tg.* Isa 5:23; 33:15; *Tg.* Job 27:8). The targumic expression, especially since it often has to do with political corruption or economic oppression, appears to offer a closer parallel than the Qumranic expressions "wealth of violence" (1QS 10:19) or "wealth of evil" (CD 6:15). Not only are the respective concerns different, Qumran used the word *hôn*, not *mamôna'*. The appearance of *mamôna'* in 11QtgJob 11:8 (at MT Job 27:17) proves, moreover, that the word was utilized in the targumic tradition in the first century (see Chilton 1984: 117–23).

In Matt 6:19–20 Jesus admonishes his disciples:

> Do not lay up for yourselves treasures on earth, where moth and rust consume and where thieves break in and steal, but lay up for yourselves treasures in heaven, where neither moth nor rust consumes and where thieves do not break in and steal.

The promises of future reward cohere with *Tg. Neof.* Gen 15:1: "the reward of your good works is prepared for you before Me in the world to come." We find in Luke 11:27–28:

> As he said this, a woman in the crowd raised her voice and said to him, "Blessed is the womb that bore you, and the breasts that you sucked!" But he said, "Blessed rather are those who hear the word of God and keep it!"

We find in *Neof.*, *Ps.-J.* Gen 49:25: "Blessed are the breasts that you sucked and the womb that bore you." A nearly identical form of this saying appears in *Gen. Rab.* 98.20 (on Gen 49:25), but this later midrash may in fact be dependent upon the Targum. The woman's utterance may well reflect targumic tradition.

Luke 10:25–28 provides an instance of exegetical coherence. When an expert in the Mosaic law answered his own question, "What should I do to inherit eternal life?" (Luke 10:25), by reciting the "double commandment" (Luke 10:27; cf. Deut 6:5; Lev 19:18), Jesus is said to have replied, "Do this and you will live" (Luke 10:28). These words constitute a paraphrase of Lev 18:5 "doing them the man will live." But Leviticus 18 has nothing to do with eternal life, so why would appeal to it give reassurance to the man who had asked the question about eternal life? Leviticus 18 concerns long life and prosperity in the promised land, as a reward for obeying the laws of the covenant. Jesus' understanding of Lev 18:5 reflects targumic exegesis. According to Onqelos: "You shall therefore keep my statutes and my ordinances, by doing which a person shall live through them *in eternal life*; I am the LORD." According to *Pseudo-Jonathan*: "You shall therefore keep my statutes and my ordinances, by doing which a person shall live *in eternal life, and his portion shall be with the righteous*; I am the LORD" (cf. Evans 1997).

Jesus' confident expectation of being raised up "*on* the third day" or "*after* three days" appears to be based on Hos 6:2 in the Aramaic. According to Mark 8:31, "And he began to teach them that the Son of man must suffer many things, and be rejected by the elders and the chief priests and the scribes, and be killed, and *after* three days rise again" (cf. Mark 9:31; 10:34). According to Luke 18:33, "they will scourge him and kill him, and *on* the third day he will rise" (cf. Luke 24:7). The *after* and *on* prepositional phrases in the New Testament tradition probably reflect the synonymous parallel prepositional phrases of Hos 6:2. The Hebrew reads: "*After* (*min*) two days he will revive us [lit. "make alive"]; *on* (*be*) the third day he will raise us up, that we may live before him"; the LXX reads: "*After* two days he will heal us; *on* the third day we shall be raised up and shall live before him"; but the Aramaic: "*on the day of resurrection from the dead* he will raise us up and we shall live before him." The explicit reference in the Aramaic version to resurrection strongly suggests that Jesus' allusive usage of this text reflects the Aramaic, more so than either the Hebrew or Greek (cf. Evans 1999).

Jesus bases his parable of the Wicked Vineyard Tenants (Mark 12:1–11) upon Isaiah's Song of the Vineyard (Isa 5:1–7). When the parable is finished, the chief priests perceive that he has told the parable against them (Mark 12:12). Although Jesus has clearly drawn upon Isaiah's song for the imagery of his parable, it is not clear that he has drawn upon its message. According to the Hebrew and Greek versions of Isaiah, the people of Judah as a whole are guilty of fruitlessness, and it is they who are in danger of judgment. But according to Jesus' parable it is the religious leaders, not the people, who are guilty and in danger of judgment. From the *Isaiah Targum* we are able to explain this apparent discrepancy. According to it God did not build a *tower* (as in the MT and LXX), but his *sanctuary* in the midst of his people. He did not provide a *wine vat* (as in the MT and LXX), but his *altar to atone for their sins*. But despite these benefits the people did not produce *good deeds* (instead of the MT's "grapes"); they produced *evil deeds*. Therefore God will remove his *Shekinah* and will break down their *sanctuaries* (i.e. temple and synagogues). The *Isaiah Targum* has narrowed the focus from the people of Judah to the temple establishment (as is also attested in 4Q500). It is therefore quite probable that Jesus' usage of Isa 5:1–7, which was directed against the temple establishment, presupposed the interpretation that is now reflected in the *Isaiah Targum* (see Chilton 1984: 111–14).

CRAIG A. EVANS

Further reading

Aramaic texts

Clarke, E. G. *Targum Pseudo-Jonathan of the Pentateuch: Text and Concordance*, Hoboken, NJ: KTAV, 1984.
Diez Macho, A. (ed.) *Neophyti 1: Targum Palestinense*, 6 vols, Madrid: Consejo Superior de Investigaciones Científicas, 1968–78.
Klein, M. L. *The Fragment-Targums of the Pentateuch: According to their Extant Sources*. Volume I: *Texts, Indices, and Introductory Essays*, AnBib 76, Rome: Pontifical Biblical Institute Press, 1980.
—— *Genizah Manuscripts of Palestinian Targum to the Pentateuch*, 2 vols, Cincinnati, OH: Hebrew Union College Press, 1986.
Sperber, A. *The Bible in Aramaic Based on Old Manuscripts and Printed Texts*, 5 vols, Leiden: Brill, 1959–73.

English translations

Grelot, P. *What Are the Targums? Selected Texts*, Collegeville, PA: Liturgical Press, 1992.
McNamara, M. J., M. Maher, and E. G. Clarke (eds) *The Aramaic Bible*, Wilmington, DE: Michael Glazier, 1987–89; Collegeville, PA: Liturgical Press, 1990–.

Studies

Beattie, D. R. G. and M. J. McNamara (eds) *The Aramaic Bible: Targums in their Historical Context*, JSOTSup 166, Sheffield: JSOT Press, 1994.
Bowker, J. *The Targums and Rabbinic Literature*, Cambridge: Cambridge University Press, 1969.
Cathcart, K. J. and M. Maher (eds) *Targumic and Cognate Studies: Essays in Honour of Martin McNamara*, JSOTSup 230, Sheffield: Sheffield Academic Press, 1996.
Chilton, B. D. *The Glory of Israel: The Theology and Provenience of the Isaiah Targum*, JSOTSup 23, Sheffield: JSOT Press, 1982.
—— *A Galilean Rabbi and His Bible: Jesus' Use of the Interpreted Scripture of His Time*, GNS 8, Wilmington, DE: Glazier, 1984.

—— "From Aramaic Paraphrase to Greek Testament," in C. A. Evans (ed.) *From Prophecy to Testament: The Function of the Old Testament in the New*, Peabody, MA: Hendrickson, 2004, pp. 23–43.
Churgin, P. *Targum Jonathan to the Prophets*, Yale Oriental Series 14, New Haven, CT: Yale University Press, 1927.
Evans, C. A. "'Do This and You Will Live': Targumic Coherence in Luke 10:25–28," in B. Chilton and C. A. Evans, *Jesus in Context: Temple, Purity, and Restoration*, AGJU 39, Leiden: Brill, 1997, pp. 377–93.
—— "Did Jesus Predict His Death and Resurrection?," in S. E. Porter (ed.) *Resurrection*, JSNTSup 186, Sheffield: Sheffield Academic Press, 1999, pp. 82–97.
—— "The Aramaic Pslter and the New Testament," in C. A. Evans (ed.) *From Prophecy to Testament: The Function of the Old Testament in the New*, Peabody, MA: Hendrickson, 2004, pp. 44–91.
Forestell, J. T. *Targumic Traditions and the New Testament*, SBL Aramaic Studies 4, Missoula, MT: Scholars Press, 1979.
Levey, S. H. *The Messiah: An Aramaic Interpretation. The Messianic Exegesis of the Targum*, MHUC 2, Cincinnati, OH: Hebrew Union College Press, 1974.
McNamara, M. J. *Targum and Testament: Aramaic Paraphrases of the Hebrew Bible: A Light on the New Testament*, Shannon: Irish University Press; Grand Rapids, MI: Eerdmans, 1972.
—— *The New Testament and the Palestinian Targum to the Pentateuch*, AnBib 27A, second edition, Rome: Pontifical Biblical Institute, 1978.
York, A. D. "The Dating of Targumic Literature," *JSJ* 5 (1974) 49–62.

TAX, TAX COLLECTORS

In antiquity, nations collected taxes to pay for governmental operations, the infrastructure of the city-state, and its military and police services. States could not have existed had there been no ability to tax the citizens, and from classical times and well before the Greeks, Egyptians, and Romans collected taxes from the people they ruled, others also collected taxes. Because officials held public office in the Greek city-states only temporarily (often just a year), it was not possible or practical to have consistency in collecting taxes so governmental leaders contracted with tax farmers to collect the taxes from their citizens.

In Old Testament times, taxes were imposed on citizens to maintain the royal household, its guards and soldiers, and public projects (1 Sam 8:15–17; 2 Kgs 12:4–8). Taxes were also collected to satisfy occupying foreign powers (2 Kgs 15:17–20; 23:35). Solomon collected tolls and customs from those who passed through the land or brought their goods to the land (1 Kgs 10:15), as did Jehoshaphat (2 Chr 17:5, 11). Another form of taxation often employed in antiquity was forced labor to work on public projects and to support the military of an occupying force (Exod 1:11; Josh 16:10; cf. Matt 5:41).

The most common taxes in New Testament times included the personal poll or head tax (*tributum capitis*) that was determined by a census. This tax is referred to in Luke 2:1–2 (see Acts 5:37). The land tax was also central to taking care of the needs of the state, namely taxes on land and what it produced called the *tributum soli* (and sometimes the *tributum agri*) levied on land, houses, slaves, and ships. Taxes were also imposed on the transportation of goods.

Besides these taxes imposed by the Roman government, there were other taxes imposed on the Jews in their homeland, namely the temple tax of one half-shekel a year (roughly two days of a laborer's pay) and the tithe of the produce of the land given to the priests. The temple tax was initiated to maintain the tabernacle and its cult and subsequently the Temple and its many activities (Neh 10:32–33; 2 Chr 24:6; Matt 17:24–25). It was initially a third-shekel, but was later increased to a half-shekel, the price for each person for atonement (Exod 30:11–16). Because the Jews had used the temple tax in their war against the Romans (AD 66–70), Vespasian added a compulsory temple tax on Jews that was sent to the Temple of Jupiter in Rome (Josephus, *J.W.* 6.335) and also imposed a head tax of two *drachmas* (or *denarii*) on all Jews in the empire after the fall of Jerusalem (Josephus, *J.W.* 7.218).

In NT times, Rome imposed taxes on all conquered or subjugated peoples to support their troops, the building and maintenance of roads, and other public building projects throughout the empire (Matt 22:17–22; Luke 2:2). One of the reasons for the rise in the shipping industry in antiquity was the high cost of tolls and customs over land at various places throughout the empire. The tolls paid in one district did not always cover the same tax in the next.

The primary persons responsible for collecting taxes among the Greek city-states and the Roman Republic were called "publicans" (Latin = *publicani*) because they were engaged in public business, and generally came from the *societas publicanorum*, those mostly from the equestrian rank. These wealthy individuals and the groups they represented paid the taxes levied by the state and then were given authority to collect that much plus their expenses and profit. Various wealthy groups helped these publicans pay the taxes in advance to Rome or guaranteed payment by putting their own estates up as security. These publicans, known as "tax farmers" (Gk. = *telonai*, singular = *telones*), employed various groups locally to collect taxes, including priests. Tax farmers made lucrative gains

from this activity and competition for getting the bid for these services was considerable. Tax contracts often went to those who offered the most to the government (Josephus, *Ant.* 12.177). After making a successful bid, tax farmers normally had thirty days to get guarantors to help them pay the amount of the tax required by the government. They, in turn, extracted not only enough to pay the government tax, but also enough to cover their own expenses and considerable profit.

This system of collection was often dominated by greed and heavy taxes were common. There were generally three different groups of collectors, namely tax farmers (publicans), supervisory tax collectors (Luke 19:2), and those who worked for them in collecting taxes from the people at tollbooths in commercial centers (Mark 2:13–17; 3:12–13; Matt 17:24–25). On the coast, these tollbooths were located at Gaza, Ascalon, Joppa, and Caesarea and inland they were at Jerusalem, Jericho, and Capernaum. Both Augustus (Octavian) and Tiberius restricted the use of tax farmers in favor of *direct* taxation (*tributa*) by local authorities (client kings or provincial governors) because of the many abuses that had been connected with collections. *Direct* taxes were not levied on Roman citizens, but on conquered peoples.

In Judea, under the direction of the Roman procurator, the collection of taxes was assigned to the Sanhedrin. As an imperial province, Judea did not pay its taxes to the *aerarium populi Romani*, as did most others, but directly to the imperial treasury, the *fiscus* (see Mark 12:14–17). The two major direct taxes included the head tax (*tributum capitis*) levied on men from age 14 to 65 and women 12–65, and the land tax (*tributum agri*). Besides this, there was an indirect tax (*vectigalia*, also referred to as the *portium* or *portoria*) on all purchases and leases in Jerusalem (Josephus *Ant.* 17.205; 18.90). Those who collected the taxes were generally local natives and not necessarily Roman citizens. Tax collectors were not able to use force to extract delinquent taxes, but Roman officials had that authority and they used it.

One of the serious problems with taxation in antiquity, of course, was the graft of those responsible for collecting more taxes than was prescribed by law (Luke 3:12–13; Matt 18:17). This is why they were considered among the worst of sinners along with murderers and robbers (Matt 9:10–11). Holy people avoided contact with them.

By the end of the first century, the amounts to be collected were often posted at the various collection or tollbooths in the commercial centers in the country to help prevent abuses, but even then the rates of taxation were not always known at the local level. Tax collectors generally were the only ones with adequate knowledge of the tax statutes and they were not known for their integrity and honesty (Cicero, *Quint. fratr.* 1.1.35). Some tax collectors had no rates that could be checked and they did not post the official rates of taxation (*b. Ned.* 28a; *b. BQ* 113a). There are many examples of abuse of taxation in antiquity and also resistance to it, but there is little information in the Bible on how taxes were collected. Generally a census was taken to provide information for a head tax. It was not uncommon for persons to hide when census takers for tax purposes came to their village to avoid paying the head tax (*b. Sanh.* 25b–26a). The amount of taxation in Palestine is difficult to determine in the first century, but Tacitus mentions a request for a reduction in taxes because the provinces of Syria and Judaea were "exhausted by their burdens" and "were pressing for a diminution of the tribute" (*Ann.* 2.42).

Rebellion against foreign taxation was frequent since it often came on top of other taxes imposed to care for the temple and other governmental projects in the land (Acts 5:37). Because tax collectors often worked for foreign powers and taxed excessively, they were generally looked upon as evil and were despised and classified among the worst sinners in Roman and Hellenistic literature (Cicero, *Off.* 15–51; Diogenes Cynicus, *Ep.* 36.2; Lucan, *Pseudolog.* 30; Dio Chrysostom, *Orat.* 14.14).

Negative language about the *telonai* is also found in Jewish and Christian literature as well. Early rabbinic traditions compare tax collectors with sinners, robbers, and murderers (*m. Tohar.* 7.6; *m. B. Kam.* 10.2; *m. Ned.* 3.4) and they are among despised trades that no observant Jew should pursue (*b. Sanh.* 25b). Jesus told a story about how a Pharisee contrasted himself with sinners, extortionists, and even tax collectors (Luke 18:11). In the NT, tax collectors are regularly equated with sinners and immoral people because they collected more that was due (Luke 3:12–13) and were known for their fraud (Mark 2:15; Matt 9:10; 11:19; 21:31; Luke 7:34, 15:2). Pharisees, who considered themselves righteous, contrasted their piety with the evil deeds of the tax collectors and other known sinners (Luke 18:11).

Jesus was severely criticized by the Pharisees for being a friend to tax collectors and sinners (Matt 11:19), but he occasionally associated with them (Mark 2:15; Matt 9:11; Luke 5:30; Luke 15:1). His concern for the lost sinner (Luke 15:11–32) and his association with tax collectors (Mark 2:15) shows,

however, that Jesus believed that the worst of sinners, even tax collectors, could receive God's love and grace and forgiveness (Luke 19:1–10; Luke 18:14). Jesus may have been influenced in this regard by a Jewish parable about a certain Ma'jan, a tax collector, who did a single good deed in his life when he invited the poor to a banquet when the city counselors did not come (*y. Sanh.* 6.23c; cf. Luke 14:15–24). It is especially interesting that he invited a tax collector (Levi) into his group of disciples (Mark 2:14).

Jesus commanded his disciples to obey the tax laws (Luke 20:22), including payment of the temple tax (Matt 17:24–25). Like Jesus, the Apostle Paul also admonished his readers to respect the authorities and pay their taxes (Rom 13:6–7).

LEE MARTIN MCDONALD

Further reading

Baden, E. *Publicans and Sinners: Private Enterprise in the Service of the Roman Republic*, Oxford: Oxford University Press, 1972.

Donahue, John R. "Tax Collector," *ABD* 6 (1992) 337–38.

Freyne, Sean P. *Galilee from Alexander the Great to Hadrian 323 BCE to 135 CE*, Wilmington, DE and Notre Dame, IN: Notre Dame University Press, 1980.

Michael, Otto. "τελώνης," *TDNT* 8 (1972) 88–105.

Neusner, Jacob. "Tax Collectors," and "Taxes," in J. Neusner (ed.) *Dictionary of Judaism in the Biblical Period*, London, Toronto and Mexico City: Simon & Schuster and Prentice Hall, 1996, Vol. 2, pp. 618–19.

Perkins, Pheme. "Taxes in the New Testament," *JRE* 12 (1984) 182–200.

Schmidt, T. E. "Taxes," in J. B. Green, S. McKnight, and I. H. Marshall (eds) *Dictionary of Jesus and the Gospels*, Downers Grove, IL: InterVarsity Press, 1992, pp. 804–7.

Snell, Daniel C. "Taxes and Taxation," *ABD* 6 (1992) 638–40.

Stambaugh, John E. and David L. Balch. *The New Testament in Its Social Environment*, LEC, Philadelphia, PA: Westminster Press, 1986.

TAYLOR, VINCENT

During the 1920s and 1930s the quest of the historical Jesus was subsumed under the impetus of a new critical methodology, namely, form-criticism, which was adapted from an approach to Old Testament narrative pioneered by Hermann Gunkel to the units of the Synoptic Gospel tradition. By the application of form-critical method, scholars sought to uncover the setting in life, or *Sitz im Leben*, of the various units of the synoptic tradition properly classified. Vincent Taylor (1887–1968) was among the first to mediate the seminal form-critical New Testament German scholarship to English-speaking audiences and to make his own distinctive contribution to the scholarly debate that focused on the relationship between the form and content of the units of gospel tradition, the experience of the early church and the life and ministry of Jesus.

Vincent Taylor was a Methodist clergyman. From 1930 until his retirement in 1953 he taught New Testament at Wesley College, Headingley, Leeds (UK), serving as Principal from 1936. His scholarly interest in the historicity of the Jesus tradition can be traced to his University of London PhD thesis which was published in 1920 as *The Historical Evidence for the Virgin Birth*. Although his published work was wide-ranging, he did pay much attention to the Synoptic Gospels, with special attention to the proto-Luke hypothesis advanced by B. H. Streeter in 1921 and which Taylor championed from the early 1920s, and biblical facets of the doctrine of the atonement. Taylor also wrote a commentary on the Greek text of Mark's Gospel (Macmillan, 1952, 1966), his *magnum opus* of 700 closely printed pages.

Of Taylor's books which bear most on the question of the historical Jesus, *The Formation of the Gospel Tradition* (1933, 1935) and *The Life and Ministry of Jesus* (1954) are the most significant. The former remains a major study of form-criticism and the Synoptic Gospel tradition in dialogue with the German scholars beginning with Martin Dibelius, whose *Die Formgeschichte des Evangeliums* ("The Form History of the Gospel") appeared in 1919. But it is the work of Rudolf Bultmann and his *Die Geschichte der synoptischen Tradition* (1921, 1931) ("The History of the Synoptic Tradition") that most attracts Taylor's scrutiny.

Taylor is appreciative of form-criticism as an interpretative tool for classifying the various forms of the gospel units, such as pronouncement stories (corresponding to Bultmann's "apophthegms" and Dibelius' "paradigms"), sayings, parables and miracle stories, and elucidating the hand of the Evangelists in shaping these to the narrative thrust of each of the Synoptic Gospels. More importantly, form-critical method helps the New Testament interpreter understand something of the life situation of the early communities which has determined the preservation of the units and hence the shaping of the Gospels (Taylor 1935: 20).

However, Taylor is unerringly critical of scholars who are sceptical that units of gospel tradition can provide historical knowledge of the life and ministry of Jesus. Bultmann argued that the gospel units arose out in the early communities. The units are the product of imagination to answer apologetic, catechetical and life needs such that Jesus is made to address communal concerns with an authoritative word (1935: 14). Taylor, by contrast, argues that the communities naturally retold those stories and remembered those sayings of Jesus which had the most immediate relevance to their life. This view had been already expressed in *The Gospels* (1930) where he argues that, far from being creations of the communities, it is much more reasonable to locate the origins of Gospel narratives in the story of Jesus, "in sound historical fact". The experiences of the early believers, Taylor continues, "must have supplied the impulse to repeat stories of Jesus and to cite his words" (1930: 17). He also contends for the influence of the disciples of Jesus as eye-witnesses in the formation of the gospel tradition. It was they who mediated the stories about and the sayings of Jesus to the earliest communities (1935: 41–42). In an article entitled "Is it Possible to Write a Life of Christ? Some Aspects of the Modern Problem" published in volume 53 of *Expository Times* (1941–42), Taylor repeats his objections to form-criticism that is sceptical of arriving at reliable historical knowledge about Jesus. Agreeing with the French scholar Lagrange, he contends that a "crowd" (i.e. the early communities) does not create anything. Rather, the early communities had "masters": that is, disciples and eye-witnesses who were custodians of the tradition about Jesus and ensured the trustworthiness of its transmission. Taylor is quite prepared to accept the historicity of the healing stories and classifies the raising of the widow of Nain's son and Jairus' daughter as healings. However, the raising of Lazarus and the feeding of the 5,000 present quite a different challenge. These and the several nature miracles suggest the work of a docetic Christ that threatens to eclipse the humanity of Jesus so clearly portrayed in the Synoptic Gospels. The historian may resort to rationalizations in attempting to account for such miracles, and will accept, Taylor writes in his *Expository Times* article, that units of gospel tradition have suffered "historical perversions and distortions" (63). He admits that there is difficulty in weaving together the various gospel narratives to present an ordered and coherent account of the life of Jesus even if the relative order of the major events and turning points, such as the Baptism, the Confession of Peter at Caesarea Philippi and the Transfiguration, can be plotted. The case for the historicity of the Virgin Birth, Taylor contends, is not proven. While the Virgin Birth tradition is only attested in the New Testament in Matthew and the final form of Luke – 1:34–35 is a late Lukan interpolation – it appears not to be known in the other New Testament sources, such as Mark, Q and Paul, or be required for confession of the divinity of Christ. The tradition of the empty tomb will likewise present a difficulty to the historian, even if he or she believes that Jesus appeared objectively to the disciples after his death.

Nevertheless Taylor is persuaded that the gospel tradition is in the main a highly trustworthy source for the historical Jesus. Taylor argues that Mark preserves a plethora of vivid details that can only testify to the antiquity of the tradition he is using (1966: 135–39), though few scholars would agree with this conclusion. A continuous Passion narrative appeared at an early stage in the formation of the tradition to account for the death of Jesus, a fact widely acknowledged by form-critics. The Evangelists are restrained in their witness to Jesus. Embellishment and legendary accretion are comparatively rare in the New Testament Gospels; a factor that is thrown into sharp relief when contrasted with the corpus of apocryphal gospels. The canonical gospel sources at times provide double and triple attestation for the work and words of Jesus. The apologetic, doctrinal and catechetical interests of the early church can be readily detected in the gospel units in a way that shows that these concerns have not obscured the original import of the tradition in the life and ministry of Jesus.

Recent scholarship has taken advantage of new discoveries (such as the Nag Hammadi corpus and more especially the *Gospel of Thomas*) and a fresh appreciation of the apocryphal gospels and papyrus gospel fragments that were available to scholars (such as Taylor) in the first half of the twentieth century. Thus contemporary scholars have posed a diverse array of early sources for the historical Jesus that extends beyond the canonical gospels. These sources radically affect the portraits of Jesus that might be drawn. However, much of Taylor's defence of the integrity and essential historicity of the New Testament Gospel tradition still carries weight among many scholars today.

MARK HARDING

Further reading

Evans, Owen E. (comp.) "A list of the published writings of Vincent Taylor," in Vincent Taylor, *New Testament Essays*, London: Epworth, 1970, pp. 141–46.
Taylor, Vincent. *The Historical Evidence for the Virgin Birth*, Oxford: Clarendon, 1920.
—— *The Gospels: A Short Introduction*, London: Epworth, 1930.
—— *The Formation of the Gospel Tradition*, second edition, London: Macmillan, 1935 [1933].
—— "Is it Possible to Write a Life of Christ? Some Aspects of the Modern Problem," *ExpTim* 53 (1941–42) 60–65.
—— *The Gospel According to St Mark*, London: Macmillan, 1966 [1952], pp. 130–49.
—— *The Life and Ministry of Jesus*, London: Macmillan, 1955.

TEACHER, TEACHING FORMS, AND STYLES

The title "teacher"

Flavius Josephus

The general impression that Jesus made on his contemporaries was that of a miracle worker and teacher. This is shown by the substantially genuine testimony of the Jewish historian writing one generation after the events. Josephus characterized Jesus as "a wise man (*sophos anēr*), a worker of paradoxical deeds, and a teacher (διδάσκαλος, *didaskalos*)" (*Ant.* 18:63). The same impression is given by several summaries in the Synoptic Gospels (Mark 2:13; 4:1; Matt 7:28–29; Luke 5:3, etc.). One of the most frequent words to describe the activity of Jesus in the gospels is "teach" (διδάσκειν).

The gospels

In all four canonical gospels Jesus is addressed as "teacher" with the vocative *didaskale* (διδάσκαλε). The parallelism in Matt 23:8, "You are not to be called *rabbi* (ραββί), for you have one teacher (*didaskalos*)," shows that this vocative translates the Hebrew/Aramaic address *rabbi* (רבי), which originally meant "my Great One." The equation is explicitly made in John 1:38: "'Rabbi', which translated means 'teacher'" (cf. also John 20:16; *CIJ* 2:1266, 1268–69). In the first century this appellation was not yet a fixed title reserved for an academically trained or an officially ordained scribe. Thus it is anachronistic to assume that Jesus must have been a follower of a teacher or that as a rabbi he would have been required to marry. This is not to deny that in NT times the address *rabbi* was mainly used as an actual reverential form of address for a person who acted as a teacher.

Mark and John's description of Jesus as "teacher" shows little evidence of later redaction. In both gospels *didaskale* is used by Jesus' followers (Mark 4:38; 9:38; 10:35; 13:1; John 1:38; 20:16) and in Mark also by outsiders (Mark 9:17; 10:17,20; 12:14,19,32). Disciples use the term *rabbi* (Mark 9:5; 11:21; 14:45; John 1:38,49; 4:31; 9:2; 11:8), as do outsiders in John (John 3:2; 6:25). The more exalted-sounding *rabbuni* (ραββουνί), from Aramaic *ribbon*, is used by an outsider (Mark 10:51) and by a female follower (John 20:16). Luke omits the term *rabbi* completely, since it would have been meaningless to his non-Jewish readers. In Luke, Jesus is never addressed as *didaskale* by disciples but many times by outsiders (Luke 7:40; 9:38; 10:25; 11:45; 12:13, etc.). The disciples' preferred form of address for Jesus is *epistata* (ἐπίστατα) from *epistatēs* (ἐπιστάτης), a more general term for a supervisor of some sort (Luke 5:5; 8:24,45; 9:33,49; 17:13). Luke thus makes clear that Jesus appeared as a teacher, but had an even higher authority for his disciples. In Matthew, too, *didaskale* is never used as a form of address by the disciples, though sometimes by outsiders (Matt 8:19; 12:38; 19:16; 22:16,24,36). It is a deliberate exception when Judas, the betrayer, twice makes use of the appellation *rabbi* (Matt 26:25,49). There are two Matthean parallels to Markan passages that use *rabbi*. In one of these Matthew omits the title (Matt 21:20) and in the other prefers κύριε/*kyrie* (Matt 17:4). The later term is also used twice where the Markan parallels have *didaskale* (Matt 8:25; 17:15).

The change to the more exalted *kyrie* in Matthew is probably deliberate, but one cannot completely exclude the possibility of interference from special written or oral sources. According to John 13:13–14, Jesus was addressed by the disciples as "the Lord and the teacher" (*ho kyrios kai ho didaskalos*). Indeed, "Teacher and Lord" (*rabbi wemari*) was a regular form of address for a respected teacher (*b. Ket.* 103b; *b. B.Q.* 73b). The titles "Lord" and "teacher" could have been interchangeable, since in contemporary Aramaic *rabbi/ribbon* was roughly equivalent to "lord" (cf. 4QEnᵃ 13:13; 4QEnᵇ 12:17; etc.). Thus the gospels may well reflect pre-Easter usage of the title "Lord" in spite of the fact that it was later used in conjunction with the worship of Jesus (cf. 1. Cor 16:22). It is possible that Matt 23:10, "You are not to be called instructors, for you have one instructor (καθηγητής/*kathēgētēs*)", was directed against Essene teachers (cf. *CD* 20:1). In that case the underlying Semitic term would have been *moreh* (מורה). The Semitic equivalent behind the absolute "the teacher" (ὁ διδάσκαλος with definite article) could also have been *ha-moreh* (cf. Mark 14:14). Once Jesus is spoken of as a "true teacher" (Mark 12:14; Matt 22:16; Luke 20:21), in some way resembling the Essene "Teacher of Righteousness" (*moreh ha-tsedeq*).

The title's function

The use of *rabbi/rabbuni* in three of the canonical gospels is pre-Rabbinic and conforms to the situation in the pre-Jamnia era before 90 AD. In the NT outside the gospels Jesus is never called "teacher." This title resurfaces in the Apostolic Fathers (Ignatius, *Eph.* 15:1; *Magn.* 9:1) and then becomes more prominent as a honorary designation with the Apologists (Justin Martyr, *Apol.* 1:19,21,32). The epigraphical evidence for *rabbi* outside Palestine is extremely meager, and only in one later Christian source do we find some corrupted forms of the Semitic term (*PBerol.* 11710). Thus the linguistic usage of the gospels points back to a historical fact: Jesus was addressed as "teacher" because he acted as a teacher in some ways.

Teaching authority

Teacher

Born into a pious Jewish family, Jesus was first educated at home (cf. Matt 11:27; Luke 10:22 with *3 En.* 45:2) and then probably in the elementary school of Nazareth's synagogue (cf. Luke 4:20 with *m. Shab.* 1:3–4), learning to read and to write (Luke 4:16–17; Pseudo-John 8:6,8). In the synagogues of his hometown and of other Galilean towns he would have heard the readings from the Torah and the Prophets and memorized large portions of the OT. For fluent recitation the Sabbath lectures had to be learnt by heart (cf. *Tanh. Jithro* 90a). The deep scriptural knowledge of carpenters, the profession of both Joseph and Jesus (Mark 6:3; Matt 13:55), was proverbial (*y. Rosh HaSh.* 1 [57b]). In many synagogues scrolls were available for study (cf. Acts 17:10–11; *b. Qidd.* 66a). There were also Torah scrolls in private use (1 Macc 1:56–57). In Galilean cities like Sepphoris, Giscala or Tiberias and, of course, in Jerusalem, Jesus was able to hear famous scribes (cf. Luke 2:46–47). Jesus was accepted as a partner in discussions by at least some scribes (Mark 12:18–34). Even they addressed him as "teacher" (Mark 12:19,32), as did many people in the crowds.

Prophet

Although Jesus praised John the Baptist as the greatest of the prophets (Matt 11:7–14), Jesus was neither his disciple nor the pupil of any other teacher. Jesus never referred to the authority of any scribe. The impression he made on his hearers was "that he taught them not as the scribes but as one having authority" (Mark 1:22) – that is with prophetic authority. Indeed, many viewed Jesus as an eschatological prophet (Mark 8:28; Matt 21:46; Luke 24:19, etc.), and he readily accepted this role

(Mark 6:4; Luke 13:33). Already in the OT prophets one can find apocalyptic and wisdom elements side by side. The same is true for the Dead Sea Scrolls. Thus there is no need to deny one or the other of these elements in the preaching of Jesus. He was neither simply an apocalyptic prophet nor simply a wisdom teacher in the tradition of the Cynics. Even in OT times the roles of teacher and prophet were not mutually exclusive (Isa 8:16; 28:9; Sir 24:32–33).

Messiah

Since Jesus was convinced that he had to fulfill the role of the "Servant of the Lord" (Mark 10:45; cf. 1:11) he initially made no public messianic claims (cf. Isa 42:2; 49:2). But Jesus linked the beginning of the "kingdom of God" to his person in such a way (Matt 12:28; Luke 11:20) that many hoped or even believed that he was the promised Messiah (Mark 10:47; 11:9–10). After the so-called "Galilean crisis" when his call to repentance was refused by the majority (cf. Matt 11:21–24; Luke 10:13–15), Jesus revealed his Messiahship to his inner circle of disciples (Mark 8:27–33). During his interrogation by the high priest Caiaphas, Jesus publicly confessed to being the Messiah and the coming "Son of Man" (Mark 14:60–64; cf. Dan 7:13; Ps 110:1). This explains why he was sentenced to death by the Roman prefect Pontius Pilate as the "King of the Jews" (Mark 15:26).

Various Jewish groups expected that the Messiah would teach with divine wisdom. This expectation is found for the priestly Messiah in the Essene scrolls from Qumran (CD 6:11; 4Qflor 1:11; 4Q541, etc.), for the Davidic Messiah in the probably Pharisaic *Psalms of Solomon* (*Pss. Sol.* 17:42–43; 18:4–9), in the relatively old Targum to Isaiah (to 53:5,11) and in rabbinic writings (*Midr. Ps. 21* [90a] etc.), for both Messiahs in the *Testaments of the Twelve Patriarchs* (*T. Jud.* [A] 21:1–4; *T. Levi* 18:2–6). Even the Messiah-like prophet of the Samaritans was expected to be a perfect teacher (*Memar Marqa* 4:12; John 4:25). Jesus himself made clear that his words were invested with an authority different from that of any other Jewish teacher. The words he spoke were revealed to him by his heavenly father (Matt 11:25–26; Luke 10:21) and full of divine wisdom (Matt 12:42; 23:37–39; Luke 11:31; 13:34–35). They will remain after heaven and earth pass away (Mark 13:31) and will serve as a criterion in God's last judgment (Mark 8:38; Matt 7:26–29; Luke 6:47–49; 9:26). Not only the Johannine speeches, but also the Synoptic sayings tradition is characterized by an emphatic "I."

J. Neusner notes a marked difference between Jesus and other contemporary Jewish teachers in this regard: "No rabbi ... prophesied as an independent authority. None left a category of 'I'-sayings, for none had the prestige to do so" (*Development of a Legend*, 1970: 190).

Teaching settings

Synagogue teaching

Even very skeptical scholars do not doubt that Jesus taught in synagogues (cf. Mark 1:21; 6:2; Luke 4:15; John 6:59, etc.). One characteristic form of teaching in that context was the exposition of the Sabbatical lectures from the Torah and the Prophets. Luke 4:16–28 is the most comprehensive and accurate description of a synagogue service we have from the first century, but the sermon given by Jesus on Is. 61:1–2 is clearly stylized and composed of three originally independent units (Luke 4:23, 24, 25–27). We may have some traces of exegetical patterns used by Jesus elsewhere. Luke 10:25–37 (the scribe's question, the citation of the Shema Israel from Deut 6:5, and the parable of the Good Samaritan) resembles the form of a yelammedenu-midrash and Mark 12:1–11 (the parable of the Wicked Husbandmen and the concluding citation from Ps 118:22–23) that of a proem-homily. The synagogues provided opportunity to study and to discuss the scriptures during the week (cf. Acts 17:10–11). Even anti-Jewish critics like Seneca (*De superstitione* [Augustine, *Civ.* 6:11]) and Juvenal (*Sat.* 14:100–3) recognized that the religious knowledge of Jews was considerably greater than that of other inhabitants of the Roman Empire.

Scribal debates

The gospels report many debates with scribes, some of whom were Pharisees (Mark 2:16–17; 7:5; Luke 7:36–50, etc.) or Sadducees (Mark 12:18–27), whereas others apparently did not belong to any religious party (cf. Mark 2:6; 3:22; 12:13–34, etc.). These debates ("*Streitgespräche*") are clearly presented in a stylized manner, generally comprising the situation, the question or reproach of the disputants, and Jesus' answer. Nevertheless, one can observe some typical argumentation techniques used by Jesus, such as answering by a counter-question, which were characteristic in such debates.

Proclamation to the masses

The contemporary Jewish teachers normally taught a chosen circle of pupils in fixed locations.

Jesus also preached outdoors at heavily populated locations like the north-western shore of the Sea of Galilee, which lies on a main route from the eastern Diaspora to Jerusalem (cf. Mark 4:1; 6:30–44; Luke 6:17–19; Josephus, *Ant.* 17:26). Like the prophetic teacher John the Baptist, Jesus tried to reach as many people as possible with his call to repentance, and thus he was at times an itinerant teacher (Mark 1:14–15, 38–39). Because he addressed large crowds in open spaces, Jesus resembled a revolutionary Zealot preacher in the minds of some (cf. John 6:15). Although Jesus distanced himself from such expectations (Mark 12:13–17; Matt 13:24–30), he, again like John the Baptist, was feared by the Galilean tetrarch Antipas as a potential rebel leader (cf. Mark 6:14–29; Luke 13:31–33). The proclamation to the masses posed a special challenge to make the essence of Jesus' teaching understandable and memorizable (see later).

Instruction of sedentary sympathizers

Not all of those believing in the preaching of Jesus followed him on his wanderings. His sedentary sympathizers were expected to host the itinerant Jesus and his disciples (cf. Mark 6:10; Matt 10:41–42). A section of the Lukan special tradition may give us a glimpse of the special instruction for such sympathizers. While Jesus was in the house of Lazarus he praised Lazarus' sister Mary because she was "sitting at his feet" like the pupil of a Torah teacher (cf. Acts 22:3; *m. Ab.* 1.4) and listening carefully to his words (Luke 10:38–42; cf. John 11:1–2; 12:1–8). It is not impossible that some notes of Jesus' teachings were taken in these circles even before Easter. The use of wax-tablets as notebooks was rather widespread (cf. Luke 1:63). A Qumran text (4Q Halachic Letter), probably written by the "Teacher of Righteousness" and copied as many as six times (4Q394–99), shows in what high esteem the words of the founder of a specific religious group were held.

Instruction of disciples

The relationship of Jesus and his disciples is expressed by the Greek term *akolouthein* (δευτε). As the parallel expression *erchesthai opisō* (δεῦτε ὀπίσω) shows (Mark 1:17–20) *akolouthein* goes back to the Hebrew *halakh 'aharej* (הלכו אחרי) "to go after" a teacher (cf. *CD* 4:19; 19:31–32). But the relationship of the disciples to Jesus was different from the proto-rabbis and their pupils. Jesus' disciples did not choose him as teacher (cf. *m. Ab.* 1:6;), but were called by him (Mark 1:16–20; Luke 9:57–62;

John 15:16). Normally, the pupil of a proto-rabbi would choose another teacher after a certain amount of time because no one teacher could embody all the wisdom of the Torah (*b. A.Z.* 19a). For Jesus' disciples he was "the only teacher" (Matt 23:8–10), and they understood their call to follow him to be temporally unlimited (Mark 3:14), extending even to the point of death (Mark 8:34). This total personal commitment points back to Jesus' messianic authority that transcended the authority of every other teacher (cf. *b. Ber.* 63b). The closest parallel is the call of Elisha by the prophet Elijah (1 Kgs 19:19–21). Nevertheless, the close followers of Jesus were referred to not only by outsiders but by Jesus himself by the common designation "disciples" (Matt 10:24–25; Luke 6:40, etc.). The Hebrew/Aramaic words *talmid/talmida'* (תלמיד / תלמידא) stand behind the Greek term *mathētēs* (μαθητής), and all three expressions mean "one who learns." They imply that the closest followers of Jesus were to learn from his words and example. In the NT the terms *akolouthein* and *mathētai* are mainly limited to the gospels and stress the special historical relationship between the earthly Jesus and his first followers.

Because they followed Jesus incessantly, the disciples were witnesses of all his words and deeds. They would have memorized the carefully formulated teaching summaries and parables of Jesus in preparation for being sent out as preachers of repentance to the people of Galilee (Mark 1:17; 3:14). The disciples acted as the "messengers" (*apostoloi* [ἀπόστολοι] from Hebrew/Aramaic *shelihim/shelihajja'* שליח / שלוח) of Jesus (cf. Matt 10:16; Luke 10:3), and their preaching must have taken place in the same content as his teaching (cf. Matt 10:7; Luke 10:9). In this pre-Easter mission context a logion creates a chain of tradition from the revelation of God to Jesus and then through him to the disciples: "Whoever listens to you, listens to me; and whoever rejects you, rejects me. But whoever rejects me, rejects him who sent me" (Luke 10:16). Preparation for the sending (probably more than one) of the disciples involved a special instruction (cf. Luke 12:3) that is already reflected in the Pauline letters (1 Cor 9:16). For the Galilean listeners the disciples themselves became teachers (cf. Matt 5:19).

After the "Galilean crisis" Jesus withdrew to the circle of twelve disciples (cf. John 6:66–70) who would be witnesses against the people of God in the Last Judgment (Matt 19:28; Luke 22:30). Like the prophet Isaiah, who "sealed the teaching among his disciples" after his preaching was rejected (Isa 8:16), Jesus gave these disciples special instruction (Mark 9:30–32; 10:32–34), the subject of which was his claim to be the messianic "Son of Man" (Mark 8:27–30), his future suffering (Mark 8:31) and expiatory death (Mark 10:45; 14:17–25), and the troubles that will precede God's final judgment and the restoration of the world (Mark 13). In this way "the mystery of the kingdom of God" was revealed to the disciples (Mark 4:11–12; cf. Matt 11:25–27; Luke 10:21–22). Since they were both eye-witnesses and ear-witnesses, the remaining Eleven became a living bridge between the pre-Easter teaching of Jesus and the developing Jesus tradition after Easter (cf. Luke 1:1–4; Acts 1:21–26; 2:42; 6:2–4; 1. Cor 15:1–11; John 15:27).

Teaching forms

Languages of instruction

In Galilee Jesus taught mainly in the colloquial language Aramaic. The gospels even preserve some words and sentences in Aramaic (Mark 3:17; 5:41, etc.). Some writings among the Dead Sea Scrolls confirm the assumption that Hebrew was not only the sacred language of the OT, but also the language spoken in some circles of Judea. This dialect represented an intermediate stage of development between biblical and Mishnaic Hebrew. It is possible that Jesus used this Middle Hebrew when he taught in Judean and/or scholarly contexts. Indeed, we meet some Hebrew expressions in scribal debates (Mark 7:11; Matt 10:25). Even in Galilee many knew Greek, as indicated by the Greek names of some of the disciples of Jesus (Andreas, Philippos), and in Jerusalem there were Greek-speaking synagogues (Acts 6:9). So it is possible that Jesus sometimes taught in Greek (cf. John 12:20–22). The early Jerusalem community was bilingual from the beginning (Acts 6:1). Greco-Palestinians like John Mark played an important role in the transmission and translation of the Jesus tradition (cf. Acts 12:12; 13:5; Papias [Eusebius, *Hist. eccl.* 3:39:15]).

Teaching summaries

Within the Synoptic tradition of the sayings of Jesus one can distinguish about 250 independent units. About 80 percent of the words of Jesus are short (comprising an average of four stanzas) and composed in one kind of *parallelismus membrorum* or another (see below). These short units are very dense teaching summaries. Jesus could start with this sort of summary as a proposition to be explained in a longer speech. Or a speech might end with a summary of its essential content.

Against the background of ancient rhetorical habits it is also possible that Jesus repeated such summaries throughout a longer speech (cf. Mark 7:1–15). He could have drawn attention to them by raising his voice (Luke 8:8; 10:21) or using introductory formulas. Many times Jesus invited his hearers to "listen" (*akouein* [ἀκούειν])" (Mark 4:3; 7:14; Matt 11:15; Luke 14:35, etc.). The corresponding Hebrew expression *shema'* (שמע) serves in certain contexts to call attention to a teaching that should be memorized (Deut 6:4; Prov 1:8; Sir 16:24, etc.). The non-responsorical use of "Amen" is not merely characteristic of but actually unique to Jesus. When used to introduce a saying of Jesus, the word "Amen" serves as a pointer to the revelatory character of his teaching (cf. Matt 11,25–27; Luke 10: 21–22; 2 Cor 1:19–20).

Parables

Although they make up only 20 percent of the independent units, the longer sayings of Jesus comprise about 56 percent of the extent of the Synoptic logia. These longer units are almost entirely parabolic. Apparently most of them were not spontaneous creations, but were constructed consciously and with great care, as the presence of a strophic structure and sometimes even parallelisms reveals. In the gospels the Greek word *parabolē* (παραβολή) like its Hebrew equivalent *mashal* (משל) covers a wide range of forms from a simple illustration or comparison to an elaborate allegory. Some of these parables of Jesus have a simple didactic purpose. Like the teaching summaries, they are short, and the illustrative material is very understandable to the listeners (e.g. Matt 7:3–5). Other parables include exaggerated or unreal elements making them enigmatic in some way. Not in all cases is this due to allegorizing tendencies in the communities after Easter. Some of the parables touch on the "mystery of the kingdom of God" (Mark 4:10–12) and are apocalyptic revelations rather than simple didactic illustrations. Some metaphors like God as a king (Matt 22:2) or the prophets as servants (Mark 12:1–5) were already conventionalized in Judaism. The non-literal sense of other expressions could be detected through the context Jesus gave them (cf. Mark 2:18–19) or by a comparison with Jesus' situation (cf. Luke 15:1–10). According to Matthew, Jesus "put parables before them (*parabolēn parethēken autois* [παραβολήν παρέθηκεν αὐτοῖς])" (Matt 13:24,31), apparently with the intention that the listeners should memorize them and meditate on them (cf. Exod 19:7; 21:1: Deut 4:8; 1 Tim 1:18; 2 Tim 2:2).

Parabolic acts

Like the OT prophets Jesus also taught through parabolic acts ranging from pure illustrations to mysterious announcements. To show the disciples their total dependence on God and his kingdom "he put a child in their midst" (Matt 18:1–4). Jesus exposed the de facto loyalty of his critical inquirers to the emperor by making them show him a Roman denarius (Mark 12:13–17). Healing a paralytic demonstrated his "authority to forgive sins" (Mark 2:1–12). Healing on the Sabbath revealed him to be "lord even of the Sabbath" (Mark 2:28). Driving sellers of sacrificial animals out of the Temple pointed to the end of sacrificial worship (John 2:13–22). Riding into Jerusalem on a donkey was a tacit claim to be the "humble" Messiah-king of Zech 9:9 (Matt 21:1–9; John 11:12–16).

Personal example

Jewish teachers taught not only by words, but also through their example (Prov 23:26; *m. Suk.* 3:9). Friends and foes alike took it for granted that Jesus' disciples patterned their lives according to the example of their master (cf. Mark 2:15–16; 2:18; 15:1–2, etc.). Indeed, Jesus took responsibility for them (Matt 12:1–8). Some of his words presuppose that the disciples should learn from his example (Mark 10:42–45; Matt 11:28–30). Like Jesus, the disciples left their homes and professions and led the lives of impoverished vagabonds (Mark 10:28). Above all, Jesus expected that the disciples would follow him despite defamation (Matt 10:24–25) and persecution (Mark 8:34–38).

Teaching styles

Short and vivid

It was an insight of the ancient Jewish schools that brevity helps the memory (*b. Pes.* 3b; *b. Hul.* 63b). A rhetorically trained Christian writer like Justin Martyr remarked that the sayings of Jesus were characteristically "short and concise" (*Apol.* 1:14:5). A great help for memorizing was the use of pictures, comparisons, metaphors, proverbs, and riddles. Jesus impressed his teachings on the minds of the listeners through overstatement (Mark 9:43–47; Matt 5:38–42, etc.), hyperbole (Mark 10:24–25; Matt 23:23–24, etc.), paradoxes (Mark 4:22; Luke 14:11, etc.), wit (Matt 6:25–34; Luke 12:22–32), irony (Mark 7:9; Luke 7:35, etc.), contrasts (Mark 4:30–32; Matt 7:24–27), antitheses (Matt 5:21–48), and symbolic numbers (Matt 18:22; Luke 16:28). If one goes back to the Aramaic or Hebrew form of

the words of Jesus one can detect various kinds of wordplay like paronomasia, double entendre, or the deliberate alteration of words. Jesus used logical devices like argument from the greater to the lesser, reduction to the absurd, and conclusions from analogy or the contrary. All these techniques are known from ancient Jewish-Hellenistic rhetoric, but their frequent use in the sayings of Jesus is remarkable. Whereas the Rabbis preferred a participial style in their teaching, Jesus, like the OT prophets, made his preaching very personal through the direct address of his listeners, the use of many imperatives, and the typical question "Who among you . . . ?" (Matt 7:9; Luke 11:11–13, etc.).

Poetical techniques

The most common technique in Hebrew/Jewish poetry is *parallelismus membrorum*, the technique by which one sentence is paralleled by another through the use of a similar thought and, quite often, through the repetition of words as well. This repetitive character of *parallelismus membrorum* facilitates memorization. Jesus used all sorts of parallelism: synonymous (Matt 7:7–8; Like 6:27–28, etc.), antithetical (Mark 8:35; Luke 16:10, etc.), synthetic (Matt 23:5–10; Luke 12:49–51, etc.), step or climactic (Mark 5:7; Matt 10:40, etc.) and chiastic parallelism (Mark 8:35; Matt 23:12, etc.). Other poetic techniques like alliteration, assonance, or end-rhyme can only be detected by retroversion into a Semitic language. Sometimes, however, a certain rhythmic character of the teaching summaries is still detectable in translation. Apparently Jesus varied the use of rhythm according to the character of his sayings. Central propositions were emphasized through the use of short rhythms with two stresses. Rhythms with three stresses that were already common in the OT psalms and wisdom literature occur quite often. Four stresses seem to be characteristic of sayings intended for the instruction of disciples. A mix of three and two stresses was used in laments for the dead (*qinah*). This meter allowed Jesus to express strong emotions in statements such as exhortations, warnings or threats, as well as beatitudes and promises. It should be noted that, unlike Greek poetry, rhythm was not used in a strict or slavish way in OT and Jewish poetry.

Memorizable form

Ancient education laid great stress on the memory (Quintilian, *Inst.* 1:3:1) and this was especially true in contemporary Judaism (Philo, *Legat.*

210; Josephus, *C. Ap.* 2:178; cf. 1QS 1:6–7). The stylistic devices and poetical techniques used by Jesus were not just ornamental. They also served a mnemonic purpose. The form of the teaching summaries of Jesus made them especially easy to memorize. Through their characteristic form it is possible to detect Synoptic-like teaching summaries even at the center of some Johannine speech compositions (John 3:3; 5:19–20; 6:51, etc.). M. Black wrote:

> Jesus did not commit anything to writing, but by His use of poetic form and language He ensured that his sayings would not be forgotten. The impression they make in Aramaic is of carefully premeditated and studied deliverances.
>
> (185)

RAINER RIESNER

Further reading

Bauckham, R. *Jesus and the Eyewitnesses: The Gospels as Eyewitness Testimony*, Grand Rapids, MI and Cambridge: Eerdmans, 2006.

Baum, A. D. "Bildhaftigkeit als Gedächtnishilfe in der synoptischen Tradition," *TBei* (2004) 4–16.

Binder, D. D. *Into the Temple Courts: The Place of the Synagogue in the Second Temple Period*, Atlanta, GA: SBL, 1999.

Black, M. *An Aramaic Approach to the Gospels and Acts*, third edition, Oxford: Clarendon, 1967.

Bock, D. L. "The Words of Jesus in the Gospels: Live, Jive, or Memorex?," in M. J. Wilkins and J. P. Moreland (eds), *Jesus Under Fire*, Grand Rapids, MI: Zondervan, 1995, pp. 73–101.

Byrskog, S. *Jesus the Only Teacher: Didactic Authority and Transmission in Ancient Israel, Ancient Judaism and the Matthean Community*, Stockholm: Almqvist & Wiksell, 1994.

Daube, D. "Responsibilities of Master and Disciples in the Gospels," *NTS* 19 (1972/73) 1–15.

Deines, R. *Die Gerechtigkeit der Tora im Reich des Messias*, Tübingen: Mohr Siebeck, 2004.

Dillon, J. T. "The Effectiveness of Jesus as Teacher," *LV* 36 (1981) 135–62.

Dunn, J. *Jesus Remembered*, Grand Rapids, MI and Cambridge: Eerdmans, 2003.

Ego, B. and H. Merkel (eds) *Religiöses Lernen in der biblischen, frühjüdischen und frühchristlichen Überlieferung*, Tübingen: Mohr Siebeck, 2005.

Ellis, E. E. *Prophecy and Hermeneutic in Early Christianity*, Grand Rapids, MI: Eerdmans, 1978.

Evans, C. A. *Jesus*, Grand Rapids, MI: Baker, 1992.

Gehring, R. W. *House Church and Mission*, Peabody, MA: Hendrickson, 2004.

Gerhardsson, B. *Memory and Manuscript and Tradition and Transmission in Early Christianity*, Grand Rapids, MI: Eerdmans, 1998.

Grassi, J. A. *Teaching the Way: Jesus, the Early Church and Today*, Washington, DC: University of America Press, 1982.

Hengel, M. *The Charismatic Leader and His Followers*, New York: Crossroad, 1981.

Hezser, C. *Jewish Literacy in Roman Palestine*, Tübingen: Mohr Siebeck, 2001.

Jaffee, M. S. *Torah in the Mouth. Writing and Oral Tradition in Palestinian Judaism 200 BCE–400 CE*, Oxford: Oxford University Press, 2001.

Jeremias, J. *New Testament Theology*, trans. J. Bowden, London: SCM, 1971.

Kalmin, R. *The Sage in Jewish Society of Late Antiquity*, London and New York, Routledge, 1999.

Kealy, J. P. *Jesus the Teacher*, Denville, NJ: Dimensions Books, 1978.

Kennedy, G. A. *New Testament Interpretation through Rhetorical Criticism*, Chapel Hill, NC: University of North Carolina, 1984.

Levine, L. I. *The Ancient Synagogue*, New Haven, CT and London: Yale University Press, 2000.

Lund, J. A. "The Languages of Jesus," *Mishkan* 17/18 (1992/93) 139–55.

Millard, A. R. *Reading and Writing in the Time of Jesus*, Sheffield: Sheffield Academic Press, 2000.

Morgenstern, J. "Jesus the Teacher," in *Some Significant Antecedents of Christianity*, Leiden: Brill, 1966, pp. 1–7.

Mussies, G. "Jesus' idiolect," *TD* 26 (1978) 254–58.

Perkins, P. *Jesus as Teacher*, Cambridge: Cambridge University Press, 1990.

Rengstorf, K. H. "διδάσκω κτλ.," *TDNT* 2 (1965) 135–65.

Riesner, R. "Jesus as Preacher and Teacher," in H. Wansbrough (ed) *Jesus and the Oral Gospel Tradition*, Sheffield: Sheffield Academic Press, 1991, 185–210.

Rüger, H. P. "Das Problem der Sprache Jesu," *ZNW* 59 (1968) 111–22.

Schürmann, H. *Jesus: Gestalt und Geheimnis*, Paderborn: Bonifatius, 1994.

Stanton, G. *The Gospels and Jesus*, second edition, Oxford: Oxford University Press, 2002.

Stein, R. H. *The Method and Message of Jesus' Teachings*, second edition, Louisville, KY: Westminster/John Knox, 1994.

Theissen, G. and A. Merz. *The Historical Jesus: A Comprehensive Guide*, trans. J. Bowden, London: SCM Press, 1998.

Vincent, J. J. "Did Jesus Teach His Disciples to Learn by Heart?," *TU* 88 (1964) 105–18.

Wegenast, K. and D. Fürst. "Teach," *NIDNTT* 3 (1992) 759–81.

Wilkins, M. J. *Discipleship in the Ancient World and Matthew's Gospel*, Grand Rapids, MI: Eerdmans, 1995.

Winton, A. P. *The Proverbs of Jesus: Issues of History and Rhetoric*, Sheffield: Sheffield Academic Press, 1990.

Witherington, B. *Jesus the Sage*, Minneapolis, MN: Fortress Press, 1994.

TEMPLE

Archaeology and architectural design

The Herodian temple

The Temple at the time of Jesus is frequently referred to as the Second Temple, i.e. the one succeeding Solomon's temple (destroyed 587 BCE), built after the return from the Babylonian exile under Zerubbabel's leadership (520–515 BCE).

However, King Herod the Great (37–4 BCE) set off such a grand expansion and redesign of the Temple from approximately 20 BCE onwards that it is appropriate to label the temple of the first century CE more distinctively as Herodian.

Our written sources for the Herodian temple are, first of all, Josephus's two accounts (*Jewish War* 5.184–237 and *Jewish Antiquitates* 15.380–425), and the Mishnah tractate *Middot,* as well as a number of further references in the works of Josephus, the New Testament and the rabbinic literature. The information from these sources is supplemented by the discoveries made in archaeological investigations among which the survey by Charles Warren (1867–70) and the excavations carried out on a grand scale after 1967 south and west of the Temple Mount (today a Moslem holy site called Haram ash-Sharif) are the most important.

The Temple proper remained the innermost part of the huge Herodian complex, with the same division on an east–west axis into three parts as in the preceding temples, viz., the Porch, the Sanctuary, and the Holy of Holies. However, the area with courts and porticoes surrounding the temple building was expanded by Herod's architects to twice its previous size. The location of this Herodian platform is still clearly recognizable. Actually, it is identical with the present Haram ash-Sharif, as is particularly evidenced by the massive retaining walls on the southern and western sides of the platform. These walls are built in courses of huge stones with drafted margins and smooth raised central bosses. In building the enormous artificial esplanade topographical obstacles had to be overcome; to the north and west earth was moved, rock was cut and valleys were filled in; in the south-eastern section, where the incline of the mountain is very steep, a vaulted substructure was constructed to alleviate the pressure on the exterior enclosure. There are some slight variations in the literature regarding the dimensions of the Temple Mount; the measurements given by K. and L. Ritmeyer (27) are 1,590 ft on the west, 1,035 ft on the north, 1,536 ft on the east and 912 ft on the south. The major work of constructing the vast platform and of raising the porticoes and buildings upon it was finished after ten years, by 10 BCE. However, partly due to some major damage, (caused by fire, for instance) there was continuous renovation work almost until the outbreak of the Jewish war in 66 CE (see John 2:20). The most serious threat to the Herodian temple during its existence was the intent of the emperor Caligula to set up a statue with his effigy there, only avoided by the cautious policy of procrastination of the governor Petronius and the death of Caligula in 41 CE. In 70 CE the temple was finally destroyed when Roman troops captured Jerusalem after months of siege.

The inner part

Fundamental to the structure and functions of the Herodian temple was the division between its inner and outer parts. A stone screen marked the crucial dividing line. On it Greek and Latin inscriptions were installed forbidding Gentiles from entering any further, on penalty of death. Behind this screen a flight of steps led upwards to the plateau on which, from east to west, the three inner courts – the Courts of the Women, the Israelites, and the Priests respectively – and the temple building were situated, surrounded by a solid wall. Despite some dissenting voices (especially Kaufman 2004), the location of the temple building of both the Herodian complex and its predecessors is most likely more or less identical with the present Dome of the Rock. The rock, above which the Umayyads, the first Moslem rulers in Jerusalem, built this marvelous edifice marking the highest point on the Temple Mount, was the site either of the Holy of Holies or of the sacrificial altar in the Court of the Priests in front of the temple building.

The outer court and porticoes

All around the blocked-off inner part the much bigger outer court, frequently called the Court of the Gentiles because non-Jews were permitted access to it, was located. This court was surrounded on three sides by porticoes, about 30 ft high. On the fourth, southern side there was an immense basilica-like hall, labeled by Josephus the Royal Portico because of its beauty and grandeur; "it was a structure more noteworthy than any under the sun" (*Ant.* 15.412). Josephus mentions four gates in the western wall, facing the central part of the city, all of which have been archaeologically confirmed and today carry the names of their respective discoverers (Robinson, Barclay, Wilson, and Warren). In the southern wall there were two gates, called the Huldah gates, the name given to the southern gates in *Middot* 1.3. From these gates, which apparently served as the principal entrance and exit for regular temple visitors, underground passageways led toward the outer court. The passageway of the western Huldah gate is preserved beneath today's al-Aqsa Mosque. The high retaining walls, consisting of enormous stone courses, together with the huge columns, high ceilings and elaborately decorated stone domes in this passageway, give today's observer a breathtaking impression of the architectural and artistic magnificence of Herod's expanded temple complex. The magnitude and beauty of the Herodian temple is reflected in the New Testament (see Mark 13:1) and commemorated in the Talmudic saying: "Whoever has not seen Herod's building has not seen a beautiful building in his life" (*Bava Batra* 4a, cf. *Sukkah* 51b).

The expansion and renewal of the Temple in Jerusalem was the most ambitious of all the building projects undertaken by Herod the Great. On the one hand, he sought legitimacy from his Jewish subjects in bestowing unprecedented glories upon their temple and, hence, their God. On the other hand, however, this grandiose enterprise likely had even more to do with Herod's own glory. A central aspect of Hellenistic ruler ideology was the undertaking of various construction and building projects to the benefit of both their own people and foreign cities. Josephus tells about many such philanthropic undertakings of Herod, far beyond the borders of his kingdom, but none was comparable to the operations at the Temple Mount in Jerusalem. Herod seems to have followed the architectural model that was currently regarded as the most appropriate one for a project at such a grand scale. This Hellenistic model for monumental cultic and cultural centers called for a platform surrounded by porticoes on all sides (i.e. a *quadriporticus*), of which preferably one would be a basilica-like hall. A temple stood in the center of the platform or, sometimes, off to one side. The model is labeled the *Caesareum*, presumably because it originated with buildings in Alexandria and Antioch initiated by Julius Caesar in 48 and 47 BCE respectively, and archaeologically it is known from excavations in the north African city of Cyrene. As is obvious, for example from Philo's description of the *Caesareum* in Alexandria in his day (see *On the Embassy to Gaius* 150f.), the surrounding porticoes were richly decorated with votive gifts and spoils, and a wide range of religious and cultural activities were performed there.

An additional architectural aspect of the Herodian *quadriporticus* complex was its function as *agora* (Greek) or *forum* (Latin), in other words the counterpart to the central public square in Hellenistic and Roman cities. Like a Roman basilica, adjoining the *forum*, the Royal Portico apparently served important communal and in particular commercial functions in relation to the *agora* or *forum*. This role of the Royal Portico is further corroborated by the fact that it was directly connected by a monumental staircase with Jerusalem's central market street, running alongside the western retaining wall, as can be learnt from the archaeological evidence in this area.

The Herodian temple as institution

The most permanent aspects of the Israelite and Jewish temples in Jerusalem throughout the ages were the belief that it was the dwelling place of the God of Israel, respectively of his name or *Shekhinah*, and the conviction that legitimate sacrifices were to be offered in this one sanctuary only. As a result of this exclusive status the temple in Jerusalem was recognized by almost all Jews, wherever they lived, as the unrivalled religious and communal center of their people. A number of vital functions and services were organized to let the temple operate in accordance with these commitments.

Priests

Due to the centrality of the sacrificial cult the operation of the Temple was completely dependent on the service of its priestly personnel. In the first century a number of priestly aristocratic families residing in Jerusalem controlled all the principal offices. The most prominent position was that of the high priest (Gk: *archiereus*) who was in charge of all activities relating to the Temple and who officiated on all major occasions, in particular on the Day of Atonement. The longest presiding high priest in the Herodian temple was Caiaphas (18–36/37 CE), who according to the gospels interrogated Jesus after his arrest and had him delivered to the Roman prefect Pontius Pilate. Both Josephus and the New Testament use the plural of the term for "high priest" to designate the whole group of leading office holders, *archiereis* (e.g. Mark 11:18, 27 par.), usually rendered as "chief priests." The vast majority of priests lived outside Jerusalem, however, and were divided into twenty-four courses, each of which served for one week twice a year (see Luke 1:5–23).

Sacrifices

The priests conducted the sacrificial service in the Temple daily. First, they offered the sacrifices prescribed for all of Israel as a community. The sacrificial cult was understood as the indispensable means for effecting holiness and atonement without which the Jewish people could not continue to exist as God's people. Second, the priests assisted individuals in offering obliged sacrifices, for example mothers after childbirth (see Luke 2:22–24) or lepers on the conclusion of their infirmity (see Mark 1:44 par.).

Pilgrims and links between the Diaspora and the Temple

For the three annual pilgrimage festivals, Passover, Weeks (Pentecost) and Tabernacles, tens of thousands of Jews traveled to Jerusalem, from the neighboring regions as well as from the distant Diaspora. Both the notes in Luke 2:41, 44 about a seemingly large group of travelers from Galilee to Jerusalem on the annual occasion of Passover and the repeated journeys of Jesus to different festivals in Jerusalem recounted in John (2:13; 5:1; 7:10; 12:12) are evidence of frequent participation of Galilean Jews in the pilgrim festivals. Many naturally combined their presence in Jerusalem as pilgrims with offering sacrifices to which they were obliged for some specific reason, or they provided on this occasion some voluntary offerings and gifts. A conspicuous effect of the exclusivity of the Jerusalem temple was that it drew more distant pilgrims, who had to take the inconveniences and dangers of a long journey upon themselves, than any other sanctuary in the Roman Empire. The gathering in Jerusalem constituted an experience of unity among the Jews of the Diaspora which was unique to any people, as is reflected in the descriptions of the pilgrimage given by the contemporary Jewish authors Philo and Josephus. The loyalty of Jews to their temple was generally known and respected throughout the Diaspora. This found its clearest expression in the contribution of the half-shekel temple tax *per capita* from Jews everywhere (see Matt 17:24–27) and in a number of decrees from imperial and local authorities which recognized this Jewish practice and offered protection for the transport of huge sums of collected taxes to Jerusalem. The temple tax financed the maintenance of the Temple and the purchase of animals for the daily offerings. Hence, by paying the tax even those who never or only most infrequently could visit the Temple had a share in the sacrifices offered on behalf of the people of Israel.

Other religious functions

Though distinctly inferior to the priests, the Levites were also part of the temple personnel (see Luke 10:31f.), being in charge of security and music during cultic ceremonies. Whereas the sacrificial activity was located in the Court of the Priests, with the individuals making offerings present in the adjacent Court of the Israelites and attending from there, non-sacrificial religious ceremonies and rituals, for example reading from the Scriptures on festivals, probably took place in the Court of the Women. This court is also likely the scene for individual prayer as presupposed in the parable about the Pharisee and the publican in Luke 18:10–14. The outer court and in particular the porticoes, giving shade from the burning sun in summer and protecting against rain and winds in winter, were the arena for religious teaching and debate, as amply illustrated in the gospels (cf. John 7:14; 28; 10:22f.; Mark 11:27–13:2 par.; 14:49 par.). However, despite all these functions and activities the temple did not make synagogues as sites for non-sacrificial worship and Torah study superfluous.

Fiscal functions

It was a common practice in the ancient world to deposit both personal and public funds in the temples. The Temple in Jerusalem was no exception in this regard; private monies were deposited there (see 2 Macc 3:10–12), as were the huge temple tax contributions to be spent for running the whole temple apparatus. Hence, among the different functionaries in the Temple the treasurers held particularly important posts. They administered the funds and were responsible for supplies of wood, flour, wine, oil, and animals needed for offerings. The wealth of the Temple, recollected by the Roman historian Tacitus (*Hist.* 5.8.1), was obviously a permanent temptation to secular rulers looking to easily acquire financial means; for instance, Pontius Pilate caused considerable dissatisfaction when he used money from the temple treasury for the construction of an aqueduct to Jerusalem.

Temple market

Temple visitors who wanted to offer sacrifices could buy the inanimate offering ingredients as well as doves on the market in the Royal Portico. Sacrificial animals, sheep and cattle, had to be purchased at other markets in or around the city. Due to the monopoly position of Tyrian silver shekels for the temple tax and other transactions in the temple, there were also money-changers present in the Royal Portico, offering their services to far-traveling pilgrims arriving in the holy city with foreign currencies (see Mark 11:15).

Agora and Caesareum

The outer court with its surrounding porticoes served further communal and cultural functions corresponding to its role as Jerusalem's *agora*; it was the main arena for public meetings of all kinds. However, any activities or decorations which might have violated the strict Jewish regulations against idolatry and images were prevented. The display in the porticoes of Nabataean and barbarian spoils captured by Herod in his wars was, however, tolerable.

JOSTEIN ÅDNA

Further reading

Ådna, J. *Jerusalemer Tempel und Tempelmarkt im 1. Jahrhundert n.Chr*, Wiesbaden: Harrassowitz, 1999.

Bahat, D. "The Herodian Temple," in W. Horbury, W. D. Davies, and J. Sturdy (eds) *The Cambridge History of Judaism* Vol. 3: *The Early Roman Period*, Cambridge: Cambridge University Press, 1999, pp. 38–58.

Geva, H. "The Temple Mount and its Environs," in E. Stern, A. Lewinson-Gilboa, and J. Aviram (eds) *The New Encyclopedia of Archaeological Excavations in the Holy Land*, Vol. 2, Jerusalem: The Israel Exploration Society and Carta, 1993, pp. 736–44.

Goodman, M. "The Temple in First Century CE Judaism," in John Day (ed.) *Temple and Worship in Biblical Israel*. London: T. & T. Clark, 2005, pp. 459–68.

Jacobson, D. M. "Herod's Roman Temple," *BAR* 28:2 (2002) 18–27, 60–61.

Kaufman, A. S. *The Temple Mount: Where Is The Holy of Holies?*, Jerusalem: Har Yéra'eh Press, 2004.

Levine, L. I. *Jerusalem: Portrait of the City in the Second Temple Period (538 BCE–70 CE)*, Philadelphia, PA: Jewish Publication Society, 2002, pp. 219–60.

Mazar, B. *The Mountain of the Lord*, Garden City, NY: Doubleday, 1975.

Mazar, E. *The Complete Guide to the Temple Mount Excavations*, Jerusalem: Shoham Academic Research and Publication, 2002.

Reid, D. G. "Sacrifice and Temple Service," in C. A. Evans and S. E. Porter (eds) *Dictionary of New Testament Background*, Downers Grove, IL, and Leicester: Inter-Varsity Press, 2000, pp. 1036–50.

Ritmeyer, K. and Ritmeyer, L. "Reconstructing Herod's Temple Mount in Jerusalem," *BAR* 15.6 (1989) 23–42.

Ritmeyer, L. "Locating the Original Temple Mount," *BAR* 18.2 (1992) 24–45, 64–65.

Safrai, S. "The Temple," in S. Safrai and M. Stern (eds) *The Jewish People in the First Century: Historical Geography, Political History, Social, Cultural and Religious Life and Institutions*, CRINT I, Vol. 2, Assen/Maastricht: van Gorcum; Philadelphia, PA: Fortress Press, 1976; repr. 1987, pp. 865–907.

Sanders, E. P. *Judaism: Practice and Belief 63 BCE–66 CE*, London: SCM Press; Philadelphia, PA: Trinity Press International, 1992, pp. 47–53, 54–69, 70–169, 305–14.

Schürer, E. *The History of the Jewish People in the Age of Jesus Christ (175 BC–AD 135)*, Vol. II, Edinburgh: T. & T. Clark, 1979, pp. 227–313.

TEMPLE ACTION OF JESUS

The temple demonstration is one of the most remarkable actions of Jesus in the gospel tradition. It is characterized by sudden, dramatic action, provocative teaching, and (by this point in the wider context of the Markan narrative) a not unexpected reference to deadly plotting on the part of Jesus' enemies. Jesus enters the temple precincts and "began to drive out those who were selling and buying in the temple." Further, he does not permit people to carry vessels through the precincts, and finally, he appeals to various prophetic scriptures that speak of the Temple. The narrative is marked by succinctness and action, and functions as a turning-point in the Markan narrative: Jesus has entered Jerusalem on a positive, promising note, but now with this action (and what prompted it is not made clear) an escalating series of accusations and charges begins to unfold.

The historicity of the temple action

The historicity of the tradition has been much debated. Some commentators have raised serious questions about how Jesus alone could have done what is depicted in Mark 11:15b–17. Some think perhaps the story developed from a saying in which Jesus criticized the Temple. Others speak about the impossibility of this story as a historical event. Questions are raised about the immensity of the task, the presence of hundreds of animals, merchants, temple officials, temple police, Roman authorities, as well as those loyal to the Temple who are present to change their money, buy animals, and offer sacrifice. These people would not have stood by and allowed Jesus to carry on as Mark describes. So go the arguments against historicity.

Recent research in the historical Jesus has by and large come to accept the historicity of the temple demonstration. Sanders (161–76, with notes on 363–69) regards the event as of vital importance for understanding Jesus' self-understanding and what triggered the events of his Passion. B. F. Meyer (168–70) finds the event "solidly probable." G. Theissen (1976: 146–48) finds Jesus' attitude toward the Temple entirely plausible. Other scholars have shown how the temple demonstration coheres with the destruction–rebuilding saying in Mark 14:58 (a point also underscored by E. P. Sanders; see also N. T. Wright 334–35, 418–28).

Much of the skepticism expressed by German commentators grows out of a misunderstanding of the nature and extent of Jesus' actions in the temple precincts. His actions were a *demonstration*, not a *takeover* of the temple precincts. At the earliest stage of the tradition, which in this instance is surely rooted in the actions and sayings of Jesus himself, the emphasis probably fell as much on the words as on the deeds. Jesus' allusions to Isaiah and Jeremiah would have been as provocative and offensive in the minds of the ruling priests as the actions themselves. But with the presence of many supportive pilgrims (presumably mostly from Galilee) there was an understandable reluctance to escalate the situation by taking immediate and public action against Jesus. As Sanders (69–70, 75) has plausibly suggested, Jesus' actions were symbolic and quite limited. He could not and did not bring temple traffic to a standstill. Most people in the precincts (whose dimensions are enormous – approximately 450 m north to south and 300 m east to west) that day would not have even noticed him. His words and actions would eventually have been passed on to anxious temple authorities.

Support for the historicity of the temple action lies in Josephus and the Gospel of John. According to Josephus (*Ant.* 18.63–64), Jesus was handed over to Pontius Pilate by "the first men among us." Elsewhere in Josephus these "first men" are ruling priests (*Ant.* 11.140–41; 18.121; cf. Luke 19:47; Acts 25:2; 28:17). Why would Jerusalem's ruling priests hand over Jesus to the Roman governor? The most probable answer is that he had said and done things within the temple precincts (the ruling priests' domain of authority) that they found offensive and dangerous. The juridical process depicted in the Gospel of Mark is, moreover, consistent with Josephus's account of Ananias the peasant prophet who proclaimed the doom of the city and the Temple. Josephus tells us that this man was seized, beaten, and handed over by the "leading citizens" and "rulers" to the Roman governor (*J.W.* 6.300–9).

Support for the historicity of the temple action is also seen in the Gospel of John, whose version appears to be independent of Synoptic sources: At Passover time, Jesus comes to Jerusalem with his disciples (John 2:13, 17 = Mark 11:1, 15); he enters the Temple (John 2:14 = Mark 11:11, 15); he drives out merchants and money-changers (John 2:15 = Mark 11:15); and he rebukes the priestly authorities for turning the Temple into a place of business (John 2:16 = Mark 11:17). Scripture citations appear in both accounts (John 2:17 = Mark 11:17). Following the temple demonstration, Jesus is asked about his authority (John 2:18–22 = Mark 11:27–33). In John 2:18, Jesus is asked: "What sign do you show us that you do these things?" In Mark 11:28 Jesus is asked by scribes, ruling priests: "By what authority do you do these things?" and "Who has given to you this authority, that you dare to do these things?" Once stripped of their respective redactional and contextual differences, the

accounts in Mark and John are remarkable similar. Independently of one another, they provide a common three-part cluster: (a) Jesus enters the temple precincts and demonstrates against some aspect or aspects of trade; (b) he speaks out against temple polity, appealing to scripture; and (c) temple authorities challenge Jesus, wanting to know by what right he "does these things."

The principal reason that E. P. Sanders (66–67, 364 n. 1) rejects the authenticity of Mark 11:16–17 is that he doubts Jesus' demonstration was a prophetic protest against corruption. It is at this point that Sanders's thesis is vulnerable, for there is ample evidence that Jesus' contemporaries were critical of the Jewish high priesthood and regarded it in various ways as corrupt. We find such evidence in some of the Dead Sea Scrolls, where the Jerusalem high priest is dubbed the "Wicked Priest" (1QpHab 1:13; 8:9; 9:9; 11:4), who has robbed the poor (1QpHab 8:12; 9:5; 10:1; 12:10), has amassed wealth (1QpHab 8:8–12; 9:4–5), and has defiled the "Sanctuary of God" (1QpHab 12:8–9). The *Testament of Moses* condemns the ruling priests:

> They consume the goods of the (poor), saying their acts are according to justice, (while in fact they are simply) exterminators, deceitfully seeking to conceal themselves so that they will not be known as completely godless because of their criminal deeds (committed) all the day long, saying, "We shall have feasts, even luxurious winings and dinings. Indeed, we shall behave ourselves as princes." They, with hand and mind, touch impure things, yet their mouths will speak enormous things, and they will even say, "Do not touch me, lest you pollute me in the position I occupy."
>
> (7:6–10)

While the pesher on Habakkuk dates from 100 BCE, and so originally targeted Hasmonean priests, the *Testament of Moses* was probably composed some time around 30 CE. Other first-century sources criticize the ruling priests and call into question temple polity. Josephus tells of high priestly bribery (*Ant.* 20.213; *Life* 195–96) and violence (*Ant.* 20.179–81, 207), and *2 Baruch* has the priests confess, in the wake of the Temple's destruction, that they have been "false stewards" (10:18). The scene is fictional, of course, but it expresses the view of the author at the end of the first century. Such an expression could scarcely have impressed readers unless many Jews did in fact view the pre-70 high priesthood as corrupt. Later rabbinic sources are very critical of the first-century ruling priests (see Evans 1989: 531–34).

There is also significant evidence in the dominical tradition to indicate that Jesus also was critical of the temple establishment. The parable of the Wicked Vineyard Tenants (Mark 12:1–9) threatens the priestly aristocracy with the loss of their position and power. The abuses of power and privilege described in the parable of the Faithless Servant (Matt 24:45–51 = Luke 12:42–46) probably reflect how the ruling aristocracy was perceived in the minds of Palestinian peasants. Jesus' pronouncement on the half-shekel temple tax (Matt 17:24–27) may have been a repudiation of the temple establishment and its political and economic policies. Jesus' comment regarding the poor widow and the others who were contributing to the Temple's coffers (Mark 12:41–44) was probably a lament – not a word of commendation – and an implicit criticism of the economic oppressiveness and inequity of the temple establishment. The condemnation of the "scribes" who "devour widows' houses" (Mark 12:38–40) is probably in reference to efforts to collect gifts for the temple. In Jesus' lament for Jerusalem (Matt 23:37–38 = Luke 13:34–35) there are significant parallels to Jeremiah, the prophet who had severely criticized Jerusalem's first temple (Jer 7:14, 34; 12:7; 22:5; 26:9), whose criticism Jesus may have had in mind when he took action in Jerusalem's second temple (Jer 7:11 in Mark 11:17). Various other details during Passion Week cohere with the criticisms of the priestly aristocracy. The priests demand to know by what authority Jesus acted the way he did (Mark 11:27–33). The ruling priests cannot arrest Jesus immediately because of their fear of the multitude (Mark 12:12). Jesus is arrested by "servants of the ruling priests" who are armed with "clubs" (Mark 14:43–50).

In view of such evidence there really are no compelling grounds for rejecting the authenticity of v. 17: "Is it not written, 'My house shall be called a house of prayer for all the nations'? But you have made it a den of robbers." This is the kind of critical statement that would account for the antagonism that arose between Jesus and the priestly aristocracy. Moreover, one wonders why early Christians, having been rejected by Israel's religious establishment, would invent a dominical saying in which the *Temple*, as opposed to the *church*, is recognized as the place of prayer for Gentiles. The allusion to Isa 56:7 is consistent with Jesus' restorative hopes for Israel. Moreover, the conflation of elements from Isaiah and Jeremiah (i.e. 7:11) is characteristic of Jesus, not the early church, which tended to quote scripture verbatim and often with an introductory formula (on the historicity of the temple cleansing, see Chilton 91–111).

On the historical level it is very probable that Jesus' action in the Temple was the principal element that triggered the events that led to his death. One is reminded of another Jesus, one son of Ananias, who some thirty years after the death of Jesus of Nazareth also appealed to Jeremiah 7 in his pronouncement of woe upon the Temple and the city of Jerusalem (Josephus, *J.W.* 6.300–309). The leading citizens of Jerusalem, by which is meant the temple authorities and their allies, took strong exception to this man's gloomy prophecies. The juridical procedure that involved the son of Ananias closely paralleled that which earlier had overtaken Jesus of Nazareth: Jewish authorities interrogate and beat both men; both men are then handed over to the Roman governor; the Roman governor interrogates and beats both men and then decides whether to release or execute them.

Meaning of the temple action

The meaning of the temple action is to be discovered primarily in the prophetic scriptures to which Jesus made allusion. Jesus' criticisms of the temple establishment cannot be adequately probed and understood apart from careful consideration of Isa 56:7 and Jer 7:11. The importance of these texts is seen in their respective literary contexts. The first one, from Isaiah 56, describes an eschatological scenario in which the nations of the world come to Jerusalem to worship and pray to God. Part of the oracle announces:

> And the foreigners who join themselves to the Lord, to minister to him, to love the name of the Lord ... these I will bring to my holy mountain, and make them joyful in my house of prayer; their burnt offerings and their sacrifices will be accepted on my altar; for my house shall be called a house of prayer for all peoples.
>
> (vv. 6–7)

The second passage, from Jeremiah 7, warns that the presence of the Temple in the city is no guarantee that Jerusalem is safe from the Babylonian menace. Israel's sin will result in judgment and the very Temple in which the religious authorities have placed their trust will itself be destroyed. Portions of the passage read:

> Stand in the gate of the Lord's house, and proclaim there this word, and say Hear the word of the Lord, all you men of Judah who enter these gates to worship the Lord ... Amend your ways and your doings, and I will let you dwell in this place ... Has this house, which is called by my name, become a den of robbers in your eyes?
>
> (vv. 2–3, 11)

The appeal to Isaiah 56, which echoes Solomon's prayer of dedication for the first temple (cf. 1 Kgs

8:41–43), suggests that Jesus' indictment against the temple establishment was not simply prophetic but was inspired in part by a Solomonic understanding of the purpose of the temple. Jesus entered the temple precincts and acted with messianic authority. He alluded to prophetic traditions, which themselves had earlier alluded to Solomon's famous prayer of dedication. The prophetic tradition may have regarded the ruling priests of the first temple as failing to live up to the requirements of the implied temple covenant between God and Israel. Failing to dispense justice, the ruling priesthood is now in danger of destruction (cf. Isa 5:1–7, on which Jesus bases his parable of the Wicked Vineyard Tenants in Mark 12:1–9). Similarly, Jesus has invoked the same prophetic tradition and does so not simply as the prophet of the Eschaton, but as God's messianic agent that calls for a corrupt temple establishment to repent.

CRAIG A. EVANS

Further reading

Ådna, J. *Jesu Stellung zum Tempel: Die Tempelaktion und das Tempelwort als Ausdruck seiner messianischen Sendung*, Wissenschaftliche Untersuchungen zum Neuen Testament 2/119, Tübingen: Mohr Siebeck, 2000.

Barrett, C. K. "The House of Prayer and the Den of Thieves," in E. E. Ellis and E. Grässer (eds) *Jesus und Paulus*, Göttingen: Vandenhoeck & Ruprecht, 1975, pp. 13–20.

Bauckham, R. J. "Jesus' Demonstration in the Temple," in B. Lindars (ed.) *Law and Religion*, Cambridge: James Clarke, 1988, pp. 72–89.

Chilton, B. D. *The Temple of Jesus: His Sacrificial Program Within a Cultural History of Sacrifice*, University Park, PA: Penn State Press, 1992.

Culpepper, R. A. "Mark 11:15–19," *Interpretation* 34 (1980) 176–81.

Eppstein, V. "The Historicity of the Gospel Account of the Cleansing of the Temple," *Zeitschrift für die neutestamentliche Wissenschaft* 55 (1964) 42–58.

Evans, C. A. "Jesus' Action in the Temple and Evidence of Corruption in the First-Century Temple," in D. J. Lull (ed.) *Society of Biblical Literature 1989 Seminar Papers*, SBLSP 28, Atlanta, GA: Scholars Press, 1989, pp. 522–39.

—— "Jesus and the 'Cave of Robbers': Toward a Jewish Context for the Temple Action," *BBR* 3 (1993) 93–110.

—— "From 'House of Prayer' to 'Cave of Robbers': Jesus' Prophetic Criticism of the Temple Establishment," in C. A. Evans and S. Talmon (eds) *The Quest for Context and Meaning: Studies in Intertextuality in Honor of James A. Sanders*, BibInt 28, Leiden: Brill, 1997, pp. 417–42.

Manson, T. W. "The Cleansing of the Temple," *BJRL* 33 (1950–51) 271–82.

Meyer, B. F. *The Aims of Jesus*, London: SCM Press, 1979.

Sanders, E. P. *Jesus and Judaism*, London: SCM Press; Philadelphia, PA: Fortress Press, 1985.

Stein, R. H. "The Cleansing of the Temple in Mark (11:15–19)," in *Gospels and Tradition: Studies on Redaction Criticism of the Synoptic Gospels*, Grand Rapids, MI: Baker, 1991, pp. 121–33.

Theissen, G. "Die Tempelweissagung Jesu," *TZ* 32 (1976) 144–58.

Trocmé, E. "L'Expulsion des marchands du Temple," *NTS* 15 (1968) 1–22.

Watty, W. W. "Jesus and the Temple: Cleansing or Cursing?," *ExpTim* 93 (1981–82) 235–39.

Winkle, R. E. "The Jeremiah Model for Jesus in the Temple," *AUSS* 24 (1986) 155–62.

Wright, N. T. *Jesus and the Victory of God*, Christian Origins and the Question of God 2, London: SPCK; Minneapolis, MN: Fortress Press, 1996.

TEMPTATION OF JESUS

The wilderness temptation story in the canonical gospels

The account of Jesus' temptation in the wilderness appears in Mark 1:12–13 and in a more expanded and developed version is found in Luke 4:1–13/ Matt 4:1–11. It is generally held that the Lucan and Matthean editions stem from a common source known as Q. There is an additional version of the story in the *Gospel of the Hebrews* (cf. Origen, *Comm. Jo.* 2:12; *Hom. Jer.* 15:4; Jerome, *Comm. Mich.* 7:6; *Comm. Isa.* 40.19; *Comm. Ezechk.* 16.13) but this is probably secondary and dependent upon the canonical gospels. In all three gospels, the temptation episode is placed after Jesus' baptism and subsequent to the commencement of his public ministry. This contrasts with the *Gospel of Philip* (74.29–31) where Jesus emerges from his baptism laughing scornfully at the world.

Mark's account begins with his stylistic trait "and immediately" (*kai euthys*), creating a sharp transition away from the baptismal story into the temptation episode. The Spirit that came upon Jesus at his baptism is reported to have "expelled" or "drove" (*ekballō*) him into the wilderness, the wilderness being a place of prayer (Luke 5:16), where Israel was tested (Ps 78:17–20) and where God would begin a new covenant with Israel (Hos 2:14–23). The short narrative recounts how Jesus spent forty days in the desert while "being tempted by Satan". This comports with the view that the wilderness was the haunt of demons (Isa 13:21 [LXX]; *1 En.* 10:4–5; *4 Macc.* 18:8; Tob 8:3; *2 Bar.* 10:8). The figure of "forty days" evokes images of Israel and their forty years in the wilderness (Deut 8:2), Moses at Sinai (Exod 34:28), and the prophet Elijah at Mt Horeb (1 Kgs 19:8). The exact character and nature of the temptations are never elaborated.

One has to look to elsewhere in Mark for signs of Satanic (Mark 3:23, 26; 4:15; 8:33) and demonic (Mark 1:21–28, 39; 3:11; 5:1–20; 7:24–29; 9:14–29) activity. Mark adds that Jesus was "with the wild beasts". The significance of the beasts could be: (1) Jesus faced substantive danger in the wilderness as bears and lions were known to reside in the Judean countryside; (2) it foreshadows a time when the earth will again experience an Edenic tranquillity between humans and animals (Gen 1:26–28; Isa 11:6–9; 32:14–20; 65:25; Hos 2:18; Job 5:22–23; *Sib. Or.* 3:793; *2 Bar.* 73:6; cf. Justin, *Dial. Tryph.* 103); (3) the imagery depicts Jesus as the second Adam who is sovereign over the animal kingdom; (4) the mention of beasts is perhaps made for the sake of comforting Mark's persecuted community in Rome where exposure to wild beasts was a real possibility in the aftermath of the Neronian persecution (Tacitus, *Ann.* 15.44; Ignatius, *Romans* 4–5). Mark indicates that Jesus experienced the dangers of wild beasts after his baptism and so sets forth a pattern of discipleship and perseverance. The additional phrase "angels began ministering to him" indicates that divine assistance is given to Jesus in this time of testing, much as it was given to Elijah. It may also echo a tradition that Adam and Eve were ministered to by angels (*Adam and Eve* 4.1–2; *b. Sanh.* 59b). Mark has orchestrated the complex to show the opposition between Satan and the wild beasts on the one hand, and against Jesus and the angels on the other. The outcome of the conflict is never unambiguously stated, but it seems implied that Jesus prevailed and this victory enabled him to carry out his ministry of exorcisms (Mark 3:23–27; cf. Luke 10:18; John 12:31; 16:11). A Christian interpolation in the *Testaments of the Twelve Patriarchs* captures the thrust of Mark's temptation story: "The devil will flee from you; wild beasts will be afraid of you, and the angels will stand by you" (*T. Naph.* 8:4; *T. Benj.* 5:2; cf. *T. Iss.* 7.7).

The introduction to the story by Matthew and Luke are probably revisions of Mark's material since they both describe the Spirit's agency in taking Jesus into the wilderness in less abrupt terms (Luke 4:1; Matt 4:1). Unlike Mark, Luke uses the designation "Devil" (*diabolos*) instead of Mark's "Satan" (*satanas*), whereas Matthew uses both titles. Luke prefers the word "led" (*agō, anagō*), whereas Matthew utilizes "took alongside" (*paralambanō*) to describe how the Devil directed Jesus to different locations for the temptations.

Matthew's edition adds that Jesus was "fasting" (like Moses, Exod 24:18; 34:28) in the wilderness and specifies the duration as forty days "and forty nights" (cf. Deut 9:9; Exod 34:28). There is a progression in the Matthean temptations from lower to higher localities (wilderness – temple – mountain). In the first temptation the Devil is described as the "Tempter" (Matt 4:3; cf. 1 Cor 7:5; 1 Thess 3:5; Rev 2:10) and Jesus' reply is a more extended quote of Deut 8:3 including the words "but every words" that proceeds from the mouth of God". Matthew uses the designation the "Holy city" in contrast to Luke. In the third temptation, the Devil leads Jesus up a "very high mountain" (cf. Moses in Deut 3:27; 9:9; 34:1–4) and shows Jesus the kingdoms "of the world". Matthew also follows Mark's ending by noting that "suddenly angels came and waited on him" which is absent from Luke. In the context of the gospel, Jesus emerges as a New Moses (cf. Matt 2:13, 16, 20–21) and the true Israel (cf. Matt 2:15 = Hos 11:1).

Luke emphasizes that it was the "Holy" Spirit that led Jesus into the wilderness in order to link back to the baptismal account where Jesus received the Holy Spirit, and to show that Jesus is empowered by the Spirit for his test of filial obedience. Luke also specifies that the Devil offers Jesus "all authority and glory" and locates the Temple in "Jerusalem". At the end of the temptation, the Devil departs until "an opportune time", implying that further testing would follow (Luke 4:13). In Luke's perspective Jesus' entire ministry is viewed as a form of temptation (Luke 22:28). It is in the Passion that Luke identifies the intense time of temptation and the ultimate test of Jesus' obedience to the Father (Luke 22:42).

The primary purpose behind the temptation stories is to highlight the faithfulness of Jesus as the Son of God to his messianic mission. As such, Jesus is portrayed as the triumphant sequel to the failures of Adam and Israel in temptation.

The wilderness temptation story in Q

There are far too many agreements between Matthew and Luke against Mark to think of the story as an enlargement of the Markan account. Therefore, the Matthean and Lucan temptation narratives are correctly attributed to Q. The suggested origin and function of the Q temptation narratives varies from a haggadic midrash on Deuteronomy 6–8 (Gerhardsson), to a mythological elaboration of Mark 1:12–13 (Sanders 117) and other proposed settings in a Q community or among Jewish Christians (e.g. Schiavo; Taylor).

Luke and Matthew disagree as to the order of the second and third temptations. It seems more likely that the temptations would climax with the offer from the Devil "worship me" which concludes

Matthew's temptations. The two Son of God temptations naturally lend themselves as linking together. Luke's version climaxes with the third temptation in the Jerusalem temple, and given Luke's theological interest in Jerusalem and the temple, such a placement is probably redactional (cf. Luke 9:51; 19:28; 24:53; Acts 1:4, 8). All this suggests that Matthew's ordering is more original.

The three temptations (cf. "three nets" of Belial in CD 4.15–19) recall elements of the Exodus where Israel disobeyed God: wilderness (Exod 16:35), hunger (Exod 16:2–8), testing God (Exod 17:1–3), and idolatry (Exod 32). The first temptation (Matt 4:3–4; Luke 4:3–4) calls on Jesus to turn stones into bread. The Devil proposes that hunger is unbecoming Jesus' status as God's Son. The temptation evokes the story of the miraculous provision of manna in the wilderness for Israel (Exod 16:13–21). The challenge is for Jesus to use a manna-like miracle to set forth his messianic status (cf. John 6:1–50) or for Jesus to assert his independence from God by performing a miracle for his own benefit. Jesus' reply "a person shall not live on bread alone" (Deut 8:3) shows that Jesus refuses to grumble against God as the Israelites did (Deut 2:7; Neh 9:21; Ps 78:18–22), and underscores his trust in God to sustain him. In the second temptation (Matt 4:5–7; Luke 4:9–12), the Devil quotes Ps 91:11–12 and invites Jesus to throw himself off the pinnacle of the Temple. The Devil never denies Jesus' sonship, but tries to exploit this fact so as to tempt Jesus to use his powers independent of God's eschatological purpose. The temptation is countered by Jesus' citation of Deut 6:16 and a refusal to test God's faithfulness. The third temptation (Matt 4:8–10; Luke 4:5–8) could be of a quasi-political nature with Jesus urged to seize the messianic kingdom without going by way of the cross. Ps 2:8 promises the messianic son that he will inherit the nations and rule over them. In this temptation the Devil attempts to offer what God offers and constitutes an attempt to replace God as Jesus' patron. The seduction to "worship" the Devil recalls the idolatry of Israel in the wilderness with the golden calf incident (Exod 32:4–8; Deut 9:16; Neh 9:18), and idolatry was frequently associated with demon worship (Ps 106:37–38; 1 Cor 10:20–21; Rev 9:20; *1 En.* 99:7). Jesus retorts with Scripture (Deut 6:13) that God alone is to be worshipped, exactly what Israel failed to do in the wilderness.

Authenticity

There are several reasons why the wilderness temptation narratives may well be authentic.

1 The fact that Jesus had a "wilderness" experience is multiply attested in Mark (1:12–13) and Q (Matt 4:1–11/Luke 4:1–13).

2 The story also corresponds with at least three other reliable traditions about Jesus. First, Jesus is reported as going out into desert places for times of respite and prayer (Mark 1:35, 45; 6:32; Luke 5:16; 6:12; John 6:15; 11:54). Second, the tradition probably relates to the enigmatic saying in Luke 10:18 ("I saw Satan fall like lightning from heaven") which comprises a visionary account from Jesus where he intimates Satan's downfall (on fasting as a prelude to visions Dan 10:3; *4 Ezra* 5:20; *2 Bar.* 20:5–6). Luke 10:18 does not refer to a vision from Jesus' baptism, or to the future fall of Satan (cf. Rom 16:20; John 12:31; Rev 20:1–3), but signifies a prior victory that Jesus believed he had achieved over Satan, a victory that was being replicated in the itinerant ministry of his followers. The logion interlocks comfortably with the temptation story as the occasion for the vision. Indeed, the notion that Jesus had engaged and was still engaging Satan in eschatological combat seems presupposed in sayings such as Luke 11:20 and Mark 3:23–27 (see Evans). Third, the temptation story correlates with the general portrait of Jesus as both periodically ascetic and an apocalyptic visionary.

3 The scriptural traditions of Moses and Elijah fasting for forty days (Exod 34:28; Deut 9:9, 18; 1 Kgs 19:8) shape the temptation narratives in their current form, but they may also have motivated Jesus' withdrawal into the wilderness as a pattern for his prophetic vocation.

4 In regard to historical plausibility, other individuals and groups of the same period were known to have retreated to the wilderness in search of a revelation from God including John the Baptist (Mark 1:4–8; Luke 3:1–19/Matt 3:1–12); Bannus (Josephus, *Life* 11–12), Paul (Gal 1:12, 17), and the Qumran sectarians (1QS 8:14; 9:19–20 = Isa 40:3).

5 A *Religionsgeschichte* perspective opens up new possibilities for understanding the temptation narratives, as they may reflect a religo-cultural phenomenon whereby Holy men (such as Buddha and Zarathustra) are meant to experience acute periods of temptation.

There appears to be reasonable evidence that the temptation story does have a kernel of authentic tradition (Murphy-O'Connor; Allison). Perhaps Jesus communicated such visionary experiences to his disciples in a teaching context pertaining to temptations and the coming *peirazmos* or eschatological testing that was approaching (Twelftree 822–23). The authenticity of the story would also would account for other traditions including Mark 3:27, Luke 10:18, Jesus' belief in the presence of the kingdom, and the call for a return to pre-Edenic conditions, e.g. Mark 10:2–9 (Davies and Allison: 1.357).

Jesus and temptation

It is probable that Jesus faced temptation/testing on a variety of fronts. The Pharisees purportedly tested Jesus by seeking a sign from him (Mark 8:11–12; Luke 11:16, 29–32/Matt 12:38–42). He is tested again about payment of taxes (Mark 12:13–17). Jesus is depicted in the Synoptic Gospels as engaged in prayerful struggle against temptation in the garden of Gethsemane (Mark 14:38; Luke 22:46; Matt 26:41). Even Jesus' disciples provide a tacit seduction to renege his messianic mission (Mark 8:33). The temptations in the wilderness may also disclose something of Jesus' self-understanding. The sojourn into the wilderness may represent a deliberate attempt to emulate the Mosaic and prophetic patterns of ministry. The wilderness was a place of new beginnings, the place where God had previously called Israel to be his own people, so it was the appropriate place to begin the formation of a new Israel setting out on a new exodus (cf. Josephus; *J.W.* 2:261–62; 7:438; Hos 2:14–18). Furthermore, the temptation story might signify that Jesus understood his primary battle not with the Jewish leaders or Rome, but principally against the supernatural evil embodied by the adversary, Satan.

MICHAEL F. BIRD

Further reading

Allison, Dale C., Jr. "Behind the temptations of Jesus: Q 4:1–13 and Mark 1:12–13," in Craig A. Evans and Bruce D. Chilton (eds) *Authenticating the Activities of Jesus*, Leiden: Brill, 1999, pp. 195–213.

Davies, W. D. and Dale C. Allison, Jr. *Saint Matthew*, 3 vols, ICC, Edinburgh: T. & T. Clark, 1988–97.

Dormandy, Richard. "Jesus' temptations in Mark's Gospel: Mark 1:12–13," *ExpTim* 114.6 (2003) 183–87.

Edwards, James R. "The Baptism of Jesus in the Gospel of Mark," *JETS* 34 (1991) 43–57.

Evans, Craig A. "Defeating Satan and Liberating Israel: Jesus and Daniel's Visions," *JSHJ* 1 (2003) 161–70.

Gerhardsson, Birger. *The Testing of God's Son (Matt 4.1–11 and Par.): An Analysis of an Early Christian Midrash*, Lund: Gleerup, 1966.

Gibson, Jeffrey B. *The Temptations of Jesus in Early Christianity*, JSNTSup 112, Sheffield: Sheffield Academic Press, 1995.

Kammler, Hans Christian. "Sohn Gottes und Kreuz: die Versuchungsgeschichte Matt 4:1-11 im Kontext des Matthäusevangeliums," *ZTK* 100 (2003) 163–86.

Murphy-O'Connor, Jerome. "Triumph over *Temptation*: The Historical Core Behind the Testing of Jesus," *BRev* 15 (1999) 34–43, 48–49.

Sanders, E. P. *The Historical Figure of Jesus*, London: Penguin, 1993.

Schiavo, Luigi. "The temptation of Jesus: the eschatological battle and the new ethic of the first followers of Jesus in Q," *JSNT* 25 (2002) 141–64.

Taylor, Nicholas H. "The temptation of Jesus on the mountain: a Palestinian Christian polemic against Agrippa I," *JSNT* 83 (2001) 27–49.

Twelftree, Graham. "Temptation of Jesus," in Joel B. Green, Scot McKnight, and I. Howard Marshall (eds) *Dictionary of Jesus and the Gospels*, Downers Grove, IL: InterVarsity Press, 1992, pp. 821–27.

TEXTUAL CRITICISM AND OLDEST GOSPEL MANUSCRIPTS

Textual criticism – as it is usually understood in New Testament studies in terms of establishing the earliest text of a given writing (see Metzger, *Text*, 207–19) – has been relatively neglected in studies of the historical Jesus. The major reason for this is that, for at least the last hundred years, various forms of the Aramaic (and Semitic) hypothesis have been ascendant. The Aramaic (or Semitic) hypothesis occurs in a number of different forms, but often includes the supposition that Jesus spoke Aramaic and that the words of Jesus found in the gospels have been rendered into Greek from Aramaic. Some have even gone further and posited that the gospels in whole or in part are a translation from an original Aramaic Vorlage (e.g. Eberhard Nestle, C. F. Burney, Charles Torrey, among others). Since the words in the gospels, at least in terms of the words of Jesus, are not authentic but a translation (so the theory goes), there is less reason to be rigorous in a traditional application of textual criticism. As a result, apart from the kinds of required text-critical comments that a given variant might warrant, there are very few scholars who address the issue of textual variants in the Jesus tradition, and apparently no large-scale systematic and complete treatment of such issues.

One of the few scholars to be concerned with matters of textual criticism was Norman Perrin. In his work on Jesus' language of the kingdom, he shows concern to establish the text that he is going to analyze. Only recently has textual criticism been re-introduced as a major critical concern in historical Jesus studies. There are several reasons for consideration of textual criticism when studying the historical Jesus. One is that it has been a neglected area, despite the fact that study of the historical Jesus is meant to be a discipline grounded in particular texts. Another is that there is increased discussion of whether the Aramaic hypothesis is adequate in and of itself as a basis for all the study of the words of Jesus. There is the recognition that Jesus may have spoken other languages, such as Greek (and possibly Hebrew), and criteria need to be developed to assess alternative hypotheses adequately, beginning with the actual documents themselves and their specific wording. A third is that, even if one is primarily concerned with the language of Jesus, this language is embedded within a Greek narrative. A full appreciation of the relation of the words of Jesus to the surrounding Greek narrative requires that one study the text of both components (see Porter, 2000: esp. 89–99).

Principles of textual criticism regarding the Jesus tradition

In two recent articles, criteria for systematic text-critical analysis of the words and activities of Jesus have been put forward (see Porter and O'Donnell, 1998a and 1998b). The issue of the limitations of using the standard Nestle–Aland text of the New Testament both as the base text and as the source of variants will not be addressed here, but would need to be addressed at such a time as a complete systematic study of text-critical issues regarding the words and activities of Jesus were to be developed.

Concerning the words of Jesus, Porter and O'Donnell (1998b: 106–10) defined a number of different types of variant. The attempt is to formulate a means for analysis of variants in the actual words of Jesus as recorded, as opposed to a study of Jesus that is confined to the concepts associated with him as mediated through translated text. These types of variant include:

addition/insertion – when one or more manuscripts add or insert a word or more to the base text;

subtraction/omission – when one or more manuscripts subtract or omit a word or more from the base text;

lexical differentiation/replacement – when a different lexical item(s) is substituted in the base text;

morphological alteration – when the morphology of a word in the base text is changed, such as aspect, mood, voice, case or number;

syntactical word order variation – when the order of words or phrases has been changed in the variant text from the base text;

syntactical other variation – when there is a complex of changes, often including the ordering of syntactical elements, as well as possibly other grammatical changes.

Preliminary findings are that roughly 20 percent of the words of Jesus in any of the gospels (the data are preliminary and confined to Matt 1–16, all of Mark, and Luke 1–11:17) have textual variants (Luke is slightly higher at 23 percent). In terms of the categories of textual variant, addition/insertion is consistently the highest and syntactical word order the lowest across the gospels (there are only a few isolated instances of syntactical other variation). The other three types of variant were somewhere in between for all of the gospels. This pattern is perhaps to be expected, as the tendency seems to be for later scribes to clarify by expansion. It is perhaps not surprising that none of the papyri are cited among the fifteen most frequently cited manuscripts, as they are for the most part fragmentary (the most frequently cited manuscripts tend to be codexes). However, one of the papyri, P75, occurs with one of the highest ratios of supporting the base text as opposed to the variant reading (a ratio of 4:1, comparable to codex 892, more than Sinaiticus at 3:1, but behind Vaticanus at 6:1).

Concerning the activities of Jesus, Porter and O'Donnell (1998a: 123–25) propose a similar set of criteria for evaluation. However, the issue is immediately complicated by the fact that it is difficult to define what constitutes an activity of Jesus. Hence, the criteria are less systematically developed or rigorously applied across the corpus of the gospels, although the same definitions of variants are used as with the words of Jesus. Instead, concerning the activities of Jesus, different types of actions or levels of activity are posited. These actions focus upon the verbal forms used in the Greek, as the verbs grammaticalize the processes in which Jesus and others engage. These actions include:

direct action (level 1) – where Jesus is the grammatical subject, and actor or agent of a process;

indirect action (level 2) – where (1) Jesus, though the grammatical subject, is the recipient of an action that is performed by an explicit or unstated agent (often involving a passive voice form of the verb), or (2) Jesus is the grammatical object of the verb, and the recipient of the action;

concomitant action (level 3) – where Jesus, though the grammatical subject (either agent or recipient), is not directly involved in the action but is involved in supportive actions to the major action;

discursive action (level 4) – where temporal, locative or other discourse indicators are given (deixis).

Examples of each of these types of action involve textual variants in the Gospels. So far, study has been confined to Mark's Gospel, where the types of variants span the range. The differentiation of types of variants and the levels of action provide a much more precise means of speaking of variants in the activities of Jesus. These variants raise particular questions regarding synoptic parallels, and merit further exploration.

Manuscripts for consideration

One of the preliminary conclusions reached regarding the words of Jesus was that the evidence from early manuscripts, including especially the papyri, was very limited (see Porter and O'Donnell, 1998b: 114–16). According to the criteria of Nestle–Aland, the textual base of Mark's Gospel should consist of: three papyri, P45, P84 and P88, and the four major codex manuscripts, Sinaiticus, Vaticanus, Bezae and Washington/Freerianus. An analysis of the variants classified by their differing types indicates that there is significant variance within the manuscripts noted above, even though the number is fairly limited. The words of Jesus as presented in the Nestle–Aland text appear to be an eclectic text that draws from the range of manuscripts, rather than a single manuscript. Nevertheless, there are a number of patterns. The major one is that P45 and Vaticanus seem to be the basis of the words of Jesus in Mark's Gospel. However, even these two manuscripts, along with Sinaiticus, are rejected in favor of other manuscripts in a number of places. Only a systematic study of all of the manuscripts available, over the extent of the entire corpus, promises to clarify this situation, and perhaps with it to bring more explicit criteria to the basis for text-critical decisions regarding issues surrounding study of the historical Jesus.

The early manuscripts of the New Testament must be paid special attention in this regard. There were a number of changes that took place in the fourth century that provide a useful cutting-off point for what constitutes an early manuscript. An early manuscript is one that precedes the major codexes, Sinaiticus and Vaticanus. There have been a number of papyri that have been recently published that should be included in this discussion. Of the early manuscripts, a number of them contain

portions of Matthew's Gospel (P1, P38, P45, P53, P64, P67, P70, P77/103, P86, P101, P102, P104, P110, 0171) and John's Gospel (P5, P22, P28, P39, P45, P52, P66, P75, P80, P90, P95, P106, P107, P108, P109, 0162), but only one early papyrus contains any of Mark's Gospel (P45), and only six contain portions of Luke's Gospel (P4, P45, P69, P75, P111, 0171). In the light of this, the following (approximately) thirty-two manuscripts need to be taken into consideration in future text-critical work on the gospels (I do not include P.Antin. 2.54, as it is clearly an amulet and has not been given a Gregory–Aland number). (See Comfort and Barrett, *Text*, for texts and descriptions followed here; Aland and Aland, *Text*, and Metzger, *Text*, whose information on the manuscripts is also used.)

P1 – This third-century fragment contains Matthew 1:1–9, 12, 14–20. This manuscript does not contain any words of Jesus but it does contain part of the Matthean genealogy. The text is Alexandrian.

P4 – (see P64 and P67) – This controversial manuscript, perhaps to be linked with P64 and P67 (and dated to before *c.* 200), contains portions of Luke's Gospel (1:58–59; 1:62–2:1, 6–7; 3:8–4:2, 29–32, 34–35; 5:3–8; 5:30–36:16). There are several sections that contain words of Jesus. This manuscript is quite similar to P75 and Vaticanus (see Comfort and Barrett, *Text*, 43).

P5 – This third-century fragment contains John 1:23–31, 33–40; 16:14–30; 20:11–17, 19–20, 22–25. The manuscript contains several sections with words of Jesus. It tends to reflect Sinaiticus, and hence is described as Western.

P22 – This third-century fragment contains John 15:25–16:2, 21–32, and is mostly words of Jesus. The text is mixed, with similarities to Sinaiticus and Bezae.

P28 – This third-century fragment contains John 6:8–12, 17–22, and contains a couple of verses of the words of Jesus. The text tends to agree with P75.

P35 – This probably third-century fragment contains Matt 25:12–15, 20–23, all words of Jesus. This text reflects Vaticanus.

P39 – This third-century fragment contains John 8:14–22, with about half being words of Jesus. This text agrees entirely with Vaticanus and almost completely with P75.

P45 – This major early third-century manuscript contains portions of all four gospels (and Acts), and is the only early manuscript to contain Mark's Gospel. It contains numerous passages with the words of Jesus. The textual tradition reflected is complicated. According to Comfort and Barrett

(*Text*, 162), Matthew, Luke and John reflect a mix of Alexandrian and Western features, while Mark is closest to the so-called Caesarean tradition as found in codex Washington/Freerianus and families 1 and 13.

P52 – This early second-century fragment contains John 18:31–33, 37–38, and contains a few words of Jesus. Though small, the text seems to be Alexandrian.

P53 – This small third-century manuscript contains Matt 26:29–40 (a second leaf contains text from Acts). There are some verses with words of Jesus. This text does not seem to conform to any particular textual tradition.

P64 – This controversial fragmentary manuscript, perhaps to be linked with P4 and P67 (and dated to before *c.* 200), contains portions of Matthew Gospel (26:7–8, 10, 14–15, 22–23, 31–33). There are several small sections that contain words of Jesus. This manuscript shows similarities to Alexandrinus (see Comfort and Barrett, *Text*, 45).

P66 – This major manuscript is probably dated to no later than *c.* 200. It contains major portions of John's Gospel, including major portions of Jesus' words. The textual tradition of this manuscript is very complex. It seems to be a mixed text (with some proto-Alexandrian tendencies; see Metzger, *Text*, 216) that has been subjected to several types of correction.

P67 – This controversial fragmentary manuscript, perhaps to be linked with P4 and P64 (and dated to before *c.* 200), contains portions of Matthew's Gospel (3:9, 15; 5:20–22, 25–28). This manuscript contains mostly words of Jesus. It shows similarities to Alexandrinus (see Comfort and Barrett, *Text*, 45).

P69 – This third-century fragment contains Luke 22:40, 45–48, 58–61 (it appears not to have vv. 43–44, along with Sinaiticus in the original hand, Vaticanus, codexes Borgianus and Washington/Freerianus). It contains some words of Jesus. The text is mixed, with some Western tendencies.

P70 – This third-century manuscript contains a number of passages from Matthew's Gospel (2:13–16; 2:22–23:1; 11:26–27; 12:4–5; 24:3–6, 12–15). There are a number of passages with words of Jesus. This text seems to follow the Alexandrian tradition.

P75 – This significant late second- or early third-century manuscript contains portions of twelve chapters in Luke and major parts of the first fifteen chapters of John's Gospel. This manuscript is proto-Alexandrian (Metzger, *Text*, 216).

P77/P103 – This second- or third-century fragment contains Matt 13:55–56; 14:3–5; 23:30–39. Only the last section contains words of Jesus. The text is proto-Alexandrian.

P80 – This fragment contains John 3:34 (the fact that it contains *hermeneia* and commentary below indicates it perhaps should not be classified as a New Testament manuscript; see Porter, "Use"). This passage is entirely words of Jesus, but its textual type is indeterminate.

P86 – This manuscript from *c.* 300 or early fourth century contains Matthew 5:13–16, 22–25, and is entirely words of Jesus. The text is in agreement with Sinaiticus and Vaticanus.

P90 – This late second-century manuscript contains John 18:36–19:7, and contains two verses with words of Jesus. The text is similar to that of P66.

P95 – This third-century fragment contains John 5:26–29, 36–38, all with words of Jesus. The text has Alexandrian tendencies, but its fragmentary nature makes determination difficult.

P101 – This third-century fragment contains Matthew 3:10–12; 3:16–4:3, and contains no words of Jesus. This manuscript is proto-Alexandrian, and more similar to Sinaiticus than Vaticanus (Comfort and Barrett, *Text*, 637).

P102 – This manuscript dated to *c.* 300 contains Matthew 4:11–12, 22–23, and contains no words of Jesus. The textual type is indeterminate.

P103 (see P77)

P104 – This second-century fragment (possibly early in the century, and hence one of the earliest manuscripts) contains Matthew 21:34–37, 43, 45 (?) (but not apparently v. 44, being the earliest witness to exclusion of it). The manuscript consists of all but one verse of the words of Jesus. The text agrees with Vaticanus and is Alexandrian.

P106 – This third-century manuscript contains John 1:29–35, 40–46. There are two verses that contain the words of Jesus. The text is similar to that found in P66, P75, Sinaiticus and Vaticanus, and hence Alexandrian.

P107 – This third-century manuscript (it could be as early as *c.* 200) contains John 17:1–2, 11. Most of it is words of Jesus. Its text is similar to that of codex Washington/Freerianus.

P108 – This fragment from *c.* 200 contains John 17:23–24; 18:1–5. It contains some words of Jesus. It is similar to Sinaiticus.

P109 – This second-century fragment contains John 21:18–20, 23–25. This fragment contains a few words of Jesus. The textual character is indeterminate.

P110 – This late third-century fragment contains Matthew 10:13–15, 25–27. The entire fragment is words of Jesus. Comfort and Barrett (*Text*, 657) label this an independent text.

P111 – This early third-century fragment contains Luke 17:11–13, 22–23. There are words of

Jesus in the second section. This manuscript seems to be in agreement with P75.

0162 – This parchment from c. 300 contains John 2:11–22. It contains several verses with words of Jesus. The text is similar to that in P66, P75 and Vaticanus.

0171 – This parchment from c. 300 contains Matthew 10:17–23, 25–32 and Luke 22:44–50, 52–56, 61, 63–64. The Matthean section is entirely words of Jesus and the Lukan portion also contains some words of Jesus. This appears to be an early form of the Western text.

Conclusion

Much more work needs to be done to take into account textual variants among the earliest manuscripts that depict the words and activities of Jesus. There are two issues to consider. The first is developing an appropriate method to perform such textual criticism. The method above has been suggested as a way forward. The second concerns the manuscripts themselves, where due consideration to the earliest manuscripts must be given. General trends are that the Synoptic Gospels will be informed mostly by the Alexandrian tradition although with some Western and other readings, while a mixed text with Western tendencies will need to be taken into strong consideration along with the Alexandrian for the Gospel of John. However, in so far as specific manuscripts are concerned, P45, P66 and P75 are the largest, and must be given their full weight in text-critical analysis.

STANLEY E. PORTER

Further reading

Aland, K. and B. Aland. *The Text of the New Testament*, Grand Rapids, MI: Eerdmans, 1989.
Comfort, P. W. and D. P. Barrett. *The Text of the Earliest New Testament Greek Manuscripts*, Wheaton, IL: Tyndale, 2001.
Metzger, B. M. *The Text of the New Testament*, New York: Oxford University Press, 1968.
Perrin, N. *Jesus and the Language of the Kingdom: Symbol and Metaphor in New Testament Interpretation*, London: SCM Press, 1976.
Porter, S. E. *The Criteria for Authenticity in Historical-Jesus Research: Previous Discussion and New Proposals*, Sheffield: Sheffield Academic Press, 2000.
—— "The Use of *Hermeneia* and Johannine Manuscripts," in H. Harrauer and B. Palme (eds) *Akten des 23. Internationalen Kongresses für Papyrologie, Wien, 22.–28. Juli 2001*, Vienna: Österreichische Nationalbibliothek, in press.
Porter, S. E. and M. B. O'Donnell. "The Implications of Textual Variants for Authenticating the Activities of Jesus," in B. Chilton and C. A. Evans (eds) *Authenticating the Activities of Jesus*, Leiden: Brill, 1998a, pp. 121–51.
—— "The Implications of Textual Variants for Authenticating the Words of Jesus," in B. Chilton and C. A. Evans (eds) *Authenticating the Words of Jesus*, Leiden: Brill, 1998b, pp. 97–133.

THEISSEN, GERD

Gerd Theissen was Professor of New Testament at Heidelberg University and one of the first to introduce the sociology of religion into the interpretation of the New Testament. His groundbreaking study was published in German in 1977 and translated into English in 1978 under the title *Sociology of Early Palestinian Christianity* in America and *The First Followers of Jesus: A Sociological Analysis of Early Christianity* in the UK. He attempts to transcend the subjectivity of the liberal "lives of Jesus" tradition without abandoning the historical quest, by focussing on the community of Jesus as a renewal movement in a period of social and economic crisis in Palestine rather than on Jesus himself. Nevertheless, since continuity between Jesus and the Jesus movement can be assumed, he does envisage that his study will also afford insights concerning Jesus. Theissen's sociological analysis builds on the study of the origin of Syrian asceticism by Georg Kretschmar (1964) and on Martin Hengel's *The Charismatic Leader and his Followers* (published in German in 1968). He is deeply influenced also by Max Weber (1864–1920) and his model of the emergence of "charismatic" leaders in times of social crisis as alternatives to "traditional" and "legal-rational" models of leadership.

On this basis, Theissen analyses three interactive social roles: Jesus as the homeless charismatic Son of Man and "the Bearer of Revelation"; the group of "wandering charismatics" who follow him, whose lifestyle is characterised by homelessness, lack of family, possessions and protection, and by radical social norms free from law; and settled local communities of sympathisers who support them financially since they are tied down by family, possessions, property and neighbours and are thus not free with regard to the law. After the death of Jesus, the wandering charismatics continue the radical life of poverty and charismatic ministry of the founder, moving between a growing network of local communities who support them financially and look to them for leadership and authority. The transition from Palestinian to Hellenistic communities sees a new form of leadership emerge in the settled local communities which wrests control from the wandering charismatics, after a period of conflict, and creates the institutional church in which the charismatics and their radical ethical norms are driven to the periphery but never extinguished completely in the life of the Church.

Theissen's methodology first analyses contemporary "pre-scientific material" to delineate the social environment, second draws inferences from biblical texts and third makes comparative analogies from other movements, especially within Judaism. However, what he set out as an analogy between the ethical radicalism of Jesus' first disciples and wandering Cynic philosophers has been taken further in many modern reconstructions which see Jesus himself as a Cynic wisdom teacher (e.g. Downing 1988; Mack 1997; Crossan 1991; for a critique see Betz 1994). Theissen himself later critiques "the disguising of Jesus as an innocuous itinerant philosopher and country poet" (*The Shadow of the Galilean* 1987: 141), seeing him rather as a wonder-working prophet in the tradition of ancient Israel.

Theissen is fundamentally concerned with the positive and negative functions of religion in society in a time of social crisis. He finds evidence of social disintegration at the time of Jesus in abandonment of the land and proliferation of robbers and beggars. This evokes renewal movements in Israel: the escapism of the Qumran community, the aggression of the Zealots, and supportive prophetic movements. The social function of the Jesus movement is to provide an outlet for the simmering aggression brought on by Roman rule through compensatory love, transference to supernatural figures, substitution through eschatological judgment and the reversal or internalisation of aggression. This "made room for the new vision of love and reconciliation at whose centre stood the new commandment to love one's enemy" (1978: 110). The Jesus movement simultaneously demands a stricter fulfilment of the ethical requirements of the Torah and relaxes these norms on the basis of human need, producing a new kind of ethical radicalism for social renewal.

Theissen's model of "wandering charismatics" has proved influential but has also been strongly challenged, especially in terms of his sociological model (e.g. Horsley 1989; Draper 1998).

While many scholars have minimised or rejected miracles in studies of the Jesus of history as later embroidery or as misunderstandings of natural phenomena, Theissen has insisted on the centrality of miracles in the Jesus movement, especially exorcism and healing. In *Miracle Stories of the Early Christian Tradition* (1983), he situates his study within form critical methodology, but utilises the insights of studies of folk tradition by Vladimir Propp (1968) and Claude Lévi-Strauss (1967) and

others. He defines the *Sitz im Leben* of the miracle form in terms of structural functionalist sociology. Miracle stories in the Jesus tradition are "symbolic actions of human subjectivity in which a revelation of the holy is given shape and 'empirical' reality transcended" (1983: 35). In this way, the intolerable experience of actual poverty and distress in first-century Palestine is given a different meaning, human limitations and boundaries are overcome. Miracle stories deny that negative human experience is final and, through their mediation of the holy, represent an obligation to transform unjust social situations.

One of Theissen's most interesting attempts to reconstruct the Jesus movement is in his narrative *The Shadow of the Galilean*, in which Jesus himself is never seen except as a dead figure in the distance, hanging on the cross. Instead, he emerges as a multi-faceted and ambivalent reflection of the experiences of others, reconstructed from contemporary sources and the gospels. The narrative is interspersed with letters between Theissen and a fictional professor discussing the implications and problems of the enterprise. His narrative approach is designed to overcome the pretence of objective historical research and facilitate "our own exodus out of an immaturity for which we ourselves are responsible: the 'Enlightenment'" (1987: 153).

Although his earlier writings studiously avoid a direct focus on Jesus, except through the Jesus movement, *The Historical Jesus: A Comprehensive Guide* (1998), co-authored with Annette Merz, approaches the historical study of Jesus directly, summarising his previous research.

JONATHAN A. DRAPER

Further reading

Betz, Hans Dieter. "Jesus and the Cynics: Survey and Analysis of a Hypothesis," *JR* 74 (1994) 453–76.
Crossan, John Dominic. *The Historical Jesus: The Life of a Mediterranean Jewish Peasant*, San Francisco, CA: Harper, 1991.
Downing, F. G. *Christ and the Cynics*, Sheffield: JSOT, 1988.
Draper, Jonathan A. "Weber, Theissen, and 'Wandering Charismatics' in the *Didache*," *JECS* 6:4 (1998) 541–76.
Hengel, Martin. *The Charismatic Leader and his Followers*, Edinburgh: T. & T. Clark, 1996.
Horsley, Richard A. *Sociology and the Jesus Movement*, New York: Crossroad, 1989.
Kretschmar, Georg. "Ein Beitrag zur Frage nach dem Ursprung frühchristlicher Askese," *Zeitung für Theologie und Kirche* 61 (1964) 27–67.
Lévi-Strauss, Claude. *The Structural Study of Myth and Totemism*, London: Tavistock Press, 1967.
Mack, Burton L. "Q and a Cynic-Like Jesus," in William E. Arnal and Michel Desjardins (eds) *Whose Historical Jesus?* Waterloo: Wilfrid Laurier Press, 1997, pp. 25–36.

Propp, V. *Morphology of the Folktale*, Austin, TX: American Folklore Society Publications, 1968.

Theissen, Gerd. *Sociology of Early Palestinian Christianity*, trans. J. Bowden, Philadelphia, PA: Fortress Press, 1978 or *The First Followers of Jesus: A Sociological Analysis of Early Christianity*, London: SCM Press, 1978.

—— *Miracle Stories of the Early Christian Tradition*, trans. F. McDonagh, Edinburgh: T. & T. Clark, 1983.

—— *The Shadow of the Galilean*, trans. J. Bowden, London: SCM Press, 1987.

Theissen, Gerd and Annette Merz. *The Historical Jesus: A Comprehensive Guide*, trans. J. Bowden, London: SCM Press, 1998.

Weber, Max. *Economy and Society*, Berkeley, CA: University of California Press, 1978.

TITHING AND PAYING TAXES

Although it has been suggested that "a tithe" could stand for any hieratic tax (Baumgarten 251), this entry outlines the usual distinction between tithes and the temple tax. The latter can then be reviewed together with other types of taxes. Further, the entry will distinguish tithes from, for example, first fruits or firstlings, which will not be included in the discussion.

Tithing

Giving tithes (Hebr., Gk. "one tenth") is a form of religious observance decreed by the Torah. In early Judaism, the Torah was usually understood to require two different yearly tithes (cf. Lev 27:30–33; Num 18.21–32; Deut 14:22–26): a tenth part of farming products and herd given to the Levites, who in turn tithed to the priests, and a tithe to be consumed by the tither in Jerusalem. Additionally, Deut 14:28–29 was sometimes understood to ordain a third tithe, one that should be given for the poor every third year (so e.g. *Ant.* 4:240). The fact that the gospels mention tithes on only two occasions should not lead us to regard tithes as being of lesser importance among the various modes of serving God in early Judaism. According to the Torah, tithes ultimately belonged to God. Tithing also carried important associations to Jerusalem, its temple and the temple cult, as well as to a compassionate way of life (cf. esp. the third tithe). Hence, tithing is often presented as a central ingredient of piety and loyalty (Neh 10:39–40; Sir 35:1–11; Tob 1:6; Jdt 11:9–13; see even *Jub.* 13:25–27; 11QT 43:2–17). There are also reasons to believe that paying the tithes did not remain a mere ideal (see *Spec.* 1:152; *Vita* 63).

Jesus' woe to the Pharisees in Matt 23.23/Luke 11.42 has sometimes been seen as an utterance against the particular Pharisaic tithing halakhah (Pharisees probably gave tithes even of herbs, which was not required by the Torah), sometimes as a criticism of a meticulous observance of minutiae in general. However, Jesus does not here nor anywhere else present a better or more appropriate way of giving tithes. Nor does he in the woe seek to sort the various commands of the Torah according to their importance (the Matthean "weightier things of the law" is generally seen as a later amendment; similarly, the ending statement in v. 23d/42d is often deemed secondary). The interpretation of the woe should above all consider that in common early Jewish thinking the tithes did have a bearing on the virtues listed in the woe: justice (Matt and Luke), love of God (Luke), faith (Matt), and even mercy (Matt). These can all be perceived as lying behind the Torah's arguments for the various tithes. Thus, Jesus is questioning the relevance of the tithes as such, rather than just some particular form of giving them or their importance in relation to other things. In Jesus' view, giving tithes does not lead to the expected results: that is, to the accomplishment of the listed virtues. Strictly speaking, Jesus does not oppose the practice of tithing as if recommending one ought to give it up. Instead, he is simply uninterested in the practice because it fails to serve a purpose.

This understanding also fits the mention of tithes in the parable of the Pharisee and the tax collector in Luke 18.10–14 (cf. *Ant.* 4.242–43; Deut 26). There is in the parable no direct objection to the practice of tithing. Still, the parable ending reveals that tithing (among other things) does not lead to the hoped-for result. In fact, even someone who collects taxes and pays to a pagan overlord can have it better.

Paying taxes

At the time of Jesus, Jews in Palestine were paying two kinds of taxes: a yearly half-shekel tax for the Temple and some largely indefinable payments for the Roman power. Obviously, the temple tax was seen as a religious duty serving the Jews' own purposes and the Roman levies attested to the state of oppression of the Jewish people. The Roman taxes had to be paid but this did not prevent Jews from detesting them. The question posed to Jesus in Mark 12:13–17 is thus a trap leading to the quandary of either openly opposing the Roman taxation or openly approving it. Choosing the former alternative would raise the suspicions of political authorities; the latter again would cause the ordinary Jews to wonder where Jesus' loyalties lie. In order to avoid – or even to realize – the looming difficulties, Jesus would need to resort to the kind of consideration that the questioners emphatically seek to rule out in v. 14. However, Jesus does coin an answer that corresponds to the wit of the questioners (cf. Mark 11:30–33): "Give to Caesar the things that are Caesar's, and to God the things that are God's."

The expositions of Jesus' reply range from treating it as mere irony to seeing it as lending support to the idea of two parallel kingdoms (or regimes), political and religious (cf. Rom 13). The reply has also been explained both as being against a refusal to pay the Romans (let Caesar have his) and for it (everything belongs to God; cf. Luke 23:2). These and many other difficulties of interpretation that surface tell about the inherent ambiguity of Jesus' reply. Indeed, the story as a whole – as a wit vs wit scene – clearly advises against making too much of Jesus' answer. It is understandable that with its evasive import the answer does not really mean to say anything definite. This would suggest that the Roman taxation was not a question of great relevance to Jesus.

Surprisingly, perhaps, a similar picture emerges when inquiring into Jesus' view of the temple tax. Resting on a historical reminiscence, Matt 17:24–27 reveals Jesus as rather indifferent to the issue: the sons are in fact free but pragmatic reasons suffice to give the payment. In Mark 11:15 Jesus is said to have overturned the tables of the money changers in the outer temple court. The temple tax had to be paid with Tyrian currency and caused therefore the need to change money. Whatever this separate instance means in the contexts of Jesus' temple action and view of the temple, it can be seen to fit both the message of Matt 17:24–27 and the suggested upshot of the saying about the Roman taxation.

TOM HOLMÉN

Further reading

Baumgarten, J. M. "On the Non-Literal Use of ma'aser/dekate," *JBL* 103 (1984) 245–51.
Evans, C. A. "The Pharisee and the Publican: Luke 18.9–14 and Deuteronomy 26," in C. A. Evans and W. R. Stegner (eds) *The Gospels and the Scriptures of Israel*, Sheffield: Sheffield Academic Press, 1994, pp. 342–55.
Holmén, T. *Jesus and Jewish Covenant Thinking*, Brill: Leiden, 2001.
Liver, J. "The Half-Shekel Offering in Biblical and Post-biblical Literature," *HTR* 56 (1963) 173–98.
Newport, K. G. C. *The Sources and* Sitz im Leben *of Matthew 23*. Sheffield: Sheffield Academic Press, 1995.
Sanders, E. P. *Jewish Law from Jesus to the Mishnah*, London: SCM Press, 1990.
Stevens, M. E. *Temples, Tithes, and Taxes*, Peabody, MA: Hendrickson, 2006.
Tuckett, C. M. "Q, the Law and Judaism," in B. Lindars (ed.) *Law and Religion: Essays on the Place of the Law in Israel and Early Christianity*, Cambridge: James Clarke, 1988, pp. 90–101.
Vischer, L. *Tithing in the Early Church*, Philadelphia, PA: Fortress Press, 1966.

TOMB OF JESUS?

In March 1980 construction workers in East Talpiot (equidistant between Jerusalem and Bethlehem) inadvertently exposed a Jewish burial crypt from late antiquity. Work was halted and archaeologists Yosef Gat and Amos Kloner, with the assistance of Shimon Gibson, representing the Department of Antiquities and Museums (now the Israel Antiquities Authority), were permitted a few days (28 March–4 April 1980) to excavate the tomb and collect ossuaries and human skeletal remains. (In the following months apartments were built over the tomb and a second, unexcavated tomb.) Gat published a brief report of the find in the Hebrew language *Hadashot Arkheologiyot* (Gat). A more detailed study (in English) was published by Amos Kloner fifteen years later (Kloner). The detailed study was delayed due to the death of lead archaeologist Gat. Concise descriptions, with facsimiles of the inscriptions and black-and-white photographs of the ossuaries, are found in Rahmani's catalogue (1994: nos 701–9).

The stone blocking the tomb's entrance was not found, presumably having been removed in antiquity. The tomb had been disturbed, with ossuaries broken and human skeletal remains scattered on the floor. Two ossuary lids and a few early Roman (or Herodian) pot sherds were also found on the floor amidst debris and soil fill measuring about 0.5 m in depth. Ten ossuaries were recovered, six with inscriptions. Two of the inscribed ossuaries are ornamented. Three of the uninscribed ossuaries are ornamented. One ossuary, the tenth, is neither inscribed nor ornamented. This tenth ossuary is not listed in Rahmani's catalog, but it is described in Kloner's report (21). The ten ossuaries are catalogued and numbered by the Israel Antiquities Authority as 80.500–580.509, inclusive.

Because of the vandalism and looting of the tomb it was not possible to determine the exact number of humans originally interred. Kloner estimates thirty-five persons, with at least seventeen skeletons in the ossuaries. It is further estimated that the tomb contained the remains of an extended family, perhaps representing four generations. Six of ten ossuaries inscribed and five of ten ornamented represent ratios significantly above averages.

The inscribed names are as follows:

Yeshua'(?), bar Yehoseph [Aramaic]
Jesus(?), son of Joseph
Mariamenou e Mara [Greek]
(Ossuary) of Mariamne (also called) Mara
Mariah [Hebrew or Aramaic]
Maria
Mattia [Aramaic or Hebrew]
Matthew
Yehudah, bar Yeshua' [Aramaic]
Judah, son of Jesus
Yosah [Aramaic or Hebrew]
Josah

The reading "Jesus, son of Joseph" is problematic. The first name, "Jesus," is barely decipherable and appears to have been written over another name. The reading "Jesus" is supported by the appearance of this name on another ossuary (i.e. "Judah, son of Jesus"). The reading "of Mariamne (also called) Mara" is also difficult, with variations suggested. It should also be noted that "Mara" is sometimes a shortened form of "Martha."

In a BBC documentary aired in 1996 the possibility was explored that the East Talpiot tomb was the tomb of the family of Jesus of Nazareth. However, virtually no archaeologist or scholar adopted this proposal. In a documentary aired in 2007, accompanied by a book (see Jacobovici and Pellegrino 2007), this identification has again been proposed. It is suggested that *Yeshua'* (or Jesus) refers to Jesus of Nazareth, *Mariamenou e Mara* refers to Mary Magdalene, *Mariah* refers to Mary the mother of Jesus, *Mattia* refers to Matthew, perhaps a relative of Mary the mother of Jesus, *Yosah* (throughout the documentary pronounced as *Yosey*) refers to Jesus' brother Yoses, and *Yehudah* (or Judah, who is not explicitly mentioned in the New Testament) may be the "disciple whom Jesus loved," mentioned a few times in the Gospel of John.

The documentary also suggests that the James Ossuary, which is of uncertain provenance, originally came from the East Talpiot tomb (i.e. it is the tenth, "missing" ossuary). The James Ossuary bears an interesting inscription, which reads: "James, son of Joseph, brother of Jesus." If the James Ossuary is identified as the "missing" tenth ossuary of the East Talpiot tomb, then the statistical chances that it is indeed the family tomb of Jesus are increased.

The documentary argues that the pointed gable (or chevron) and circle (or rosette) sculpted over the entrance to the tomb is an early Jewish-Christian symbol. This novel suggestion gains support, we are told, because it may be present on at least one ossuary from Dominus Flevit (on the Mount of Olives), an ossuary that may have contained the remains of an early Jewish Christian. The documentary argues further, on the basis of the *Acts of Philip* and other dubious sources, that Mariamne is none other than Mary Magdalene and that "Mara" is not a *name* but a *title of honor* perhaps meaning "Master," as in the sense of "Mariamne the Master."

Finally, DNA samples taken from the "Jesus, son of Joseph" and "Mariamne (also called) Mara" Ossuaries show that Jesus and Mariamne were not related by blood and therefore, according to the documentary, were probably married. Thus it is proposed that Jesus of Nazareth and Mariamne, understood to be Mary Magdalene, were married and had at least one child, the person identified as "Judah, son of Jesus."

The problems with this startling hypothesis are legion, the errors egregious.

The pointed gable and rosette pattern has nothing to do with Christianity. In fact, this pattern predates Jesus and the Christian movement by many years. It is found on Hasmonean coins and on coins struck by the tetrarch Philip, son of Herod the Great, well before the activities of Jesus and the emergence of his movement. The gable and rosette pattern is also found in Jewish funerary and synagogue art, usually symbolizing the temple or the ark of the covenant. The pattern is seen on several ossuaries that we have no reason to think are Christian (see Rahmani nos 282, 294, 392, 408, 893). In short, the pointed gable over the rosette is a pre-Christian Jewish symbol that referred to the temple, not a Jewish Christian symbol.

The suggestion that the "Mary Magdalene" ossuary inscription should read "Mariamne the Master" is very doubtful. Some epigraphers think the Greek inscription actually reads "Mariamne and Mara" (i.e. *Mariamne kai Mara*). This interpretation is supported by similar, even identical forms in Greek papyri (e.g. P.Oslo 2.47; P.Oxy. 2.399; 4.745; P.Columbia 18a; and, from Palestine, 5/6Hev 12; 5/6Hev 16; and XHev/Seiyal 63 and 69). And in fact, there is another ossuary in which the names "Martha and Mary" are inscribed (at Dominus Flevit), thus attesting an example where the names of two women are given.

The documentary suggests that *Mariah* (written in Hebrew letters), evidently a "Latinized" form of Miriam, is quite rare and thus supports identification with Mary the mother of Jesus. This is not convincing, however, for *Mariah* (written in

Hebrew letters) is found on ossuaries from Mount Scopus (Rahmani no. 26), Mount of Olives (no. 27), Jericho (no. 55), in Jerusalem (e.g. nos 48, 49, 53, 56–58), and elsewhere (nos 33–36, 41). Moreover, the name *Maria* (written in Greek letters) occurs in Josephus (*J.W.* 6.201) and on ossuaries (nos 25, 28, 46). There is nothing about this name – written in Hebrew or in Greek – that compels us to think of Mary the mother of Jesus.

The suggestion that the James Ossuary, whose inscription reads "James, son of Joseph, brother of Jesus," is the tenth "missing" ossuary from the Talpiot tomb is not convincing. Amos Kloner, who excavated the tomb, rejects the suggestion. Not only was the James Ossuary in circulation years before the Talpiot tomb was accidentally discovered, its dimensions do not correspond with the dimensions of the tenth Talpiot ossuary.

There are also problems with the interpretations of the other names found in the Talpiot tomb. We know of no one in the family of Jesus by the name of "Mattia" (or Matthew). Appeals to cognate names that appear in Luke's genealogy of Jesus are not convincing.

Furthermore, the name יוסה should be pronounced *Yosah*, as Professor Tal Ilan in fact does in the documentary. This form of the name probably does not represent the Hebrew equivalent of the Greek Ἰωσῆς (*Yoses*), which is said to be the name of Jesus' brother (in Mark 6:3). We should expect the Hebrew equivalent to be spelled יוסי (*Yosey*). The documentary's discussion of this name is very misleading.

The Talpiot tomb also mentions a "Judah, son of Jesus." The documentary suggests this Judah is the son of Jesus and his wife Mary Magdalene. This whole line of interpretation is highly problematic.

There is no credible evidence anywhere at any time that suggests that Jesus had a wife and children. Had he a wife, this would not have been an embarrassment or something that needed to be kept secret. A wife of Jesus would have been a celebrated figure; children would have occupied honored places in the church. But there is no hint of this. Even the second-century Gnostic Gospels of Mary and of Philip do not support the claim some make that Jesus and Mary Magdalene were married or were lovers.

This important point seems not to have registered with the filmmakers. The inscription "Judah, son of Jesus" in fact argues against the identification of the Talpiot tomb as the tomb of Jesus and his family. Whoever this Jesus was, he had a son named Judah; Jesus of Nazareth had no children and he had no wife.

The evidence as a whole, when carefully studied in proper context, argues strongly against the hypothesis that the Talpiot tomb is the tomb of Jesus and his family.

CRAIG A. EVANS

Further reading

Bauckham, R. *Gospel Women: Studies of the Named Women in the Gospels*, Grand Rapids, MI: Eerdmans, 2002.

Evans, C. A. *Jesus and the Ossuaries: What Jewish Burial Practices Reveal about the Beginning of Christianity*, Waco, TX: Baylor University Press, 2003.

Gat, Y. "East Talpiot," *Hadashot Arkheologiyot* [= *Archaeological News*] 76 (1981) 24–25.

Ilan, T. *Lexicon of Jewish Names in Late Antiquity. Part I: Palestine 330 BCE 200 CE*, TSAJ 91, Tübingen: Mohr Siebeck, 2002.

Jacobovici, S. and C. Pellegrino. *The Jesus Family Tomb: The Discovery, the Investigation, and the Evidence that Could Change History*, San Francisco, CA: HarperCollins, 2007.

Kloner, A. "A Tomb with Inscribed Ossuaries in East Talpiyot, Jerusalem," with sketches by S. Gibson, *Atiqot* 29 (1996) 15–22.

Rahmani, L. Y. *A Catalogue of Jewish Ossuaries in the Collections of the State of Israel*, Jerusalem: Israel Antiquities Authority, 1994.

TRADITION CRITICISM

In search of a definition

The term "tradition criticism," translated somewhat awkwardly into English from the German *Traditionsgeschichte*, is a term that is difficult to define, due to the linking of the words *tradition* and *geschichte*. The latter word is usually rendered "history," as in the significance or meaning of history, so this term could be broadly conceived as "the meaning of the history-of-traditions." Thus perhaps more properly understood as "tradition history," TC concerns itself primarily with identifying the pre-literary forms that were used during the oral phrase of Scripture transmission. Moreover, TC attempts to distinguish between what is sometimes called authentic (genuinely preserved) versus inauthentic (creatively shaped for its context) traditions, examining, among other things, the *Sitz im Leben* ("setting in the life") of the document. This is especially pertinent as one examines the teachings of Jesus recorded in the gospels. TC might be considered the methodological "bridge" between determining what actually occurred and how those events were later preserved in texts.

Scholars are unanimous that the stories of Israel, Jesus and the early church were initially transmitted orally (B. Gerhardsson and those of the so-called Scandinavian School also add that oral transmission coexists with literary forms). Scripture attests to traditions being passed down from generation to generation (see Deut 6:7–10 and Judg 2:10, which note a negative consequence when traditions are *not* passed down). Further, the Apostle Paul duly notes, "I commend you because you remember me in everything and maintain the traditions just as I handed them on to you" (1 Cor 11:2). So traditions were an inevitable phenomenon in Judaism and Christianity (see also A. N. Wilder [1895–1993], who argues that an understanding of "rhetoric" has the advantage of including both oral and written discourse).

The use of oral tradition and the preservation of literary tales have been widely attested in other cultures by Albert Bates Lord (1912–91), *The Singer of Tales*; Jan Vansina, *Oral Tradition: A Study of Historical Methodology*; and Walter J. Ong, SJ (1912–2003), *Orality and Literacy*. Oral and written traditions are therefore central in the life of any community.

So, TC seeks to determine which forms preceded the written texts (i.e. pre-literary stage). In other words, what were the available oral forms used to remember and preserve sacred texts and tradition?

TC is also closely related to the following criticisms: *Form* (what oral forms were available for transmission of tradition), *Redaction* (how an editor/redactor changed a written text) and *Source* (which sources were available and how they were used/incorporated by an author). Some may consider TC as a subset of these criticisms.

A nagging question that remains for TC is: Were the forms that were used in the transmission relatively stable and consistent? Moreover, how much flexibility was acceptable in the forms during their transmissions? Scholars continue to debate this topic to the present day, since the answer to this question determines the level of reliability that one attributes to the text.

Old Testament tradition criticism

In OT studies, TC originated with H. Gunkel (1862–1932), G. von Rad (1901–71), M. Noth (1902–68) of Germany, S. Mowinckel (1884–1965) of Norway, and I. Engnell (1907–64) of Sweden. Engnell notes the following general characteristics of TC: (1) it rigorously analyses the text by comparing and contrasting it with different traditions and literary units; (2) this analysis must be accompanied

by the synthesis – the ability to interpret smaller units in relationship to the larger context; (3) one must also evaluate the scope and significance of oral tradition; (4) one must also question the reliability (i.e. the stability) of the oral tradition; and (5) one must evaluate the role of confidence in the tradition. Engnell observes,

> within Judaism, the tradition which was inherited was passed on according to very conservative principles ... Furthermore, the recitation of Old Testament passages as liturgical texts in the synagogue to a large extent relied on memorization, and had the character of oral recitation, not of reading.
>
> (p. 9)

Thus, the "passing on of tradition" is an essential dimension in Judaism. Attested within Scripture, Jews preserved traditions utilizing two basic modes: by remembering and writing. The Pentateuch, especially Deuteronomy, emphasizes the mode of "remembering" (Hebr. *zākar*). "Remember the days of old, consider the years long past; ask your father, and he will inform you; your elders, and they will tell you" (Deut 32:7).

"To remember" implies an inward recollection of events coupled with external responses, by retelling the events/stories with the purpose of persevering these events/stories in written texts for posterity.

There are also many exhortations to write things down (Hebr. *kātab*) for future generations (see Exod 17:14). Here the inference is to preserve religious traditions via written documents, hence creating a collective sacred religious tradition. Douglas A. Knight and others have demonstrated that Judaism was a religion of "tradition" – a religion of inextricably connected oral and written traditions.

New Testament tradition criticism

Gospels

It is evident that the gospel writers grappled with the role of tradition. In Mark 7:3–13 (and parallels) the noun "tradition" (Gk. *paradōsis*) is used to demonstrate the core teaching of the elders – the traditions that the disciples of Jesus did not follow. Here "tradition" is couched in a polemical context, yet it unequivocally demonstrates the continued use and importance of tradition in Judaism. The "traditions of the elders" (Mark 7:3) refers not only to oral traditions but also to written ones, as exemplified by the Jewish practices of the day (e.g. halakah).

One could argue that the seeds for TC were planted in 1919 by the publication of two books:

K. L. Schmidt's *Der Rahmen der Geschichte Jesu* and M. Dibelius's *Die Formgeschichte des Evangeliums*. Yet the most influential work for Gospel criticism is R. Bultmann's (1884–1976) groundbreaking *The History of the Synoptic Tradition* (1921, English Translation 1963). Bultmann held that early believers transmitted the Jesus tradition in multiple forms, which they regarded with ample flexibility – namely, the early church significantly shaped the teachings of Jesus to oblige a predetermined theological agenda. "In the Synoptic Gospels the literary form as such did not achieve a life of its own. These works are completely subordinate to Christian faith and worship" (1963: 374). Contrary positions are offered by V. Taylor's *The Formation of the Gospel Tradition* (1960), which suggests that FC is not the only way to interpret the gospel narratives. "Form-Criticism is a key to some of the doors which hide the Gospel tradition in its formative period: for other doors we require other keys; and for some we have no keys at all" (p. 21).

Perhaps the most influential, yet initially silenced, critic of FC is B. Gerhardsson, in his watershed work *Memory and Manuscript*, who observes that although there was inevitably some shaping to the tradition, the forms were essentially stable since they were linked to a sacred tradition – that is, the disciples of Rabbis had "fixed" forms from which to remember, preserve and transmit traditions (e.g. memorization, didactic and poetic devices, repetition, recitation and other methods; Gerhardsson's teacher Harald Riesenfled at Uppsala in a 1959 seminal article, "The Gospel Tradition and Its Beginning," tilled the ground for Gerhardsson's later work).

How then does one begin to determine whether a saying/text/tradition is authentic? There are at least three standard criteria (some scholars suggest more; however, these are the agreed-upon ones): (1) Criterion of Dissimilarity; (2) Criterion of Coherence; and (3) Criterion of Multiple Attestation (I will briefly use Norman Perrin's [1920–76] classic *Rediscovering the Teaching of Jesus* to define each criterion).

The first criterion is dissimilarity ("distinctiveness"):

> the earliest form of a saying we can reach may be regarded as authentic if it can be shown to be dissimilar to characteristic emphases both of ancient Judaism and of the early church, and this will particularly be the case where Christian tradition oriented towards Judaism can be shown to have modified the saying from its original emphasis.
>
> (39)

Simply, there would be no reason for the early church to "create" this saying of Jesus. Examples include: the literary formula "but I say" (Gk. *egō de legō*) in the Sermon on the Mount (Matt 5:22, 28, 32, 34, 39, 44) and the Sabbath sayings in Mark 2:27–28 (e.g. "the Sabbath was made for humankind").

The second criterion is coherence ("consistency"): "material from the earliest strata of the tradition may be accepted as authentic if it can be shown to cohere with material established as authentic by means of the criterion of dissimilarity" (p. 43). Obviously, this criterion is heavily dependent on the presupposition of the first criterion and is probably the most subjective. Examples would include: Jesus' association with the tax collectors and sinners (Matt 9:10–11; Mark 2:15–16; Luke 5:30; 7:34), his exorcisms (Matt 8:31; Mark 1:32; Luke 4:41 among others), and the antagonism Jesus provoked with the scribes and Pharisees (see Matt 22:18 among others).

The third and final criterion is multiple attestation ("cross-section method"): "This is a proposal to accept as authentic material which is attested in all, or most, of the sources which can be discerned behind the synoptic gospels" (p. 45). These sources include *Q* (= sayings source; scholars are at odds as to whether Q is primarily oral, written or both. It is still debated as a "hypothetical" source), the canonical Gospel of Mark (if one assumes Markan priority), Special Matthean material (referred to as "M") and Special Lukan material (referred to as "L"). For a balanced critique of form criticism and the criteria of authenticity, see M. D. Hooker, "On Using the Wrong Tool," *Theology* 75 (1972): 570–81. A notable example of this final criterion is the kingdom of God (heaven) motif in Jesus' teaching which is situated in multiple testimonies (Mark, Q, Special M, Special L and John) and is included in various literary genres (e.g. parable, beatitude, prayer, aphorism and miracle story).

It is important to realize that when a text meets a standard of criteria, it adds to the confidence of its authenticity. On the other hand, one must also realize that if a text fails to meet a specific criterion, one should not immediately assume its inauthenticity. As noted by Hooker,

> It is the duty of every scholar, in considering every saying, to give a reasonable account of all the evidence; for he [she] is not entitled to assume, simply in the absence of contrary evidence, either that a saying is genuine or that it is not.
>
> (p. 580)

Luke–Acts

Luke's prologue (Luke 1:1–4) demonstrates that he relied on traditions (written and oral) to compose his Gospel and sequel (see Acts 1:1–5). Luke's *modus operandi* is his intention (1) to acknowledge that many others (Matthew? Mark? John? the writer of Q?) have also undertaken to set down an orderly account of the events; (2) to utilize traditions (Gr. *paradōsis*) that were handed on to him; (3) to investigate everything carefully; and finally (4) to write an orderly account of events. Essentially, Luke's historical methodology clearly reinforces for the Gospel narrative and early church the twin emphases of oral and written traditions.

Gerhardsson also purports the existence of a *collegium* in Jerusalem, centered on the preservation of "the word of the Lord" (Gk. *ho logos tou kyrios*) – a technical phrase in Acts, which implies the teachings of Jesus and the early church – both in oral and written forms. After the Apostle Paul's encounter with the sons of Sceva, Luke writes: "So *the word of the Lord* grew mightily and prevailed" (Acts 19:20). The Twelve (another technical term for the author, see Luke 9:1; 18:31) would be, according to Gerhardsson, bearers and preservers of "the word of the Lord."

Epistles/letters

It is perhaps even more apparent that the early Christian movement, spearheaded by the Apostle Paul, was concerned about persevering and passing on traditions. "For I received from the Lord what I also handed on to you, that the Lord Jesus on the night when he was betrayed took a loaf of bread" (1 Cor 11:23). Here Paul's practice of receiving and then "handing on" (Gk. *paradōsis*) implies a formal process already in place from Judaism. In the disputed letter 2 Thessalonians, the author also affirms the existence of tradition and its function in the faith community: "Now we command you, beloved, in the name of our Lord Jesus Christ, to keep away from believers who are living in idleness and not according to the tradition that they received from us" (2 Thess 3:6).

Contributions of tradition criticism

With any prescribed methodology, one must jointly understand both the purpose and limitation of the methodology. This caveat is especially apropos with regards to TC. Nevertheless, TC has provided the field of biblical studies with a number of important contributions.

First, and perhaps the most obvious one, TC acknowledges that Scripture was initially transmitted orally – that is, there was a pre-literate stage. Second, and related to the first, one must examine the various written forms found in Scripture to begin understand the sacred traditions. During this investigation, one will be introduced to a significant aspect of literary criticism: the idea of genres (see K. L. Sparks and C. A. Evans). Third, one must accept and grapple with the creative dynamics of what C. Blomberg calls "a flexible transmission with fixed limits" as it pertains to the congruency between oral and written processes. How much latitude did the preservers of oral tradition have once it became a written document? Moreover, how can one determine historical veracity of the final written documents? Is there an ineffable chasm between oral and written traditions? These are ongoing questions for the interpreter. Finally, TC works in tandem with the other critical methodologies to assist the interpreter in (re)discovering the historical Israelites and the historical Jesus.

JOSEPH B. MODICA

Further reading

Blomberg, C. L. *The Historical Reliability of the Gospels*, Downers Grove, IL: InterVarsity Press, 1987.

Bultmann, R. *The History of the Synoptic Tradition*, trans. J. Marsh, revised edition, Peabody, MA: Hendrickson, 1963.

Byrskog, S. *Story as History, History as Story: The Gospel Tradition in the Context of Ancient Oral History*, Boston, MA: Brill, 2002.

Catchpole, D. R. "Tradition History," in I. Howard Marshall (ed.) *New Testament Interpretation*, Grand Rapids, MI: Eerdmans, 1977; reprint 1983, pp. 165–80.

Davids, P. H. "Tradition Criticism," in J. B. Green and S. McKnight (eds) *Dictionary of Jesus and the Gospels*, Downers Grove, IL: InterVarsity Press, 1992, pp. 831–34.

Engnell, I. *A Rigid Scrutiny*, trans. J. T. Willis, Nashville, TN: Vanderbilt University Press, 1969.

Evans, C. A. *Ancient Texts for New Testament Studies: A Guide to the Background Literature*, Peabody, MA: Hendrickson, 2005.

Gerhardsson, B. *Memory and Manuscript: Oral Tradition and Written Transmission in Rabbinic Judaism and Early Christianity (with Tradition and Transmission in Early Christianity)*, Grand Rapids, MI: Eerdmans, 1998 [1961, 1964].

—— *The Reliability of the Gospel Tradition*, Peabody, MA: Hendrickson, 2001.

Gunkel, H. *The Legends of Genesis: The Biblical Saga and History*, trans. W. H. Carruth, New York: Schocken Books, reprint 1964 [1901].

Hengel, M. "Eye-witness Memory and the Writing of the Gospels," in Markus Bockmuehl and Donald A. Hagner (eds) *The Written Gospel*, New York: Cambridge University Press, 2005, pp. 70–96.

Hooker, M. D. "On Using the Wrong Tool," *Theology* 75 (1972) 570–81.

Kelber, W. H. *The Oral and the Written Gospel: The Hermeneutics of Speaking and Writing in the Synoptic Tradition, Mark, Paul and Q*, Bloomington, IN: Indiana University Press, 1997 [1983].

Knight, D. A. *Rediscovering the Traditions of Israel*, Atlanta: Society of Biblical Literature, 1973.

—— "Tradition History," in David Noel Freedman (ed.) *ABD*, Vol 6, New York: Doubleday, 1992, pp. 633–38.

Lord. A. B. *The Singer of Tales*, second edition, Cambridge, MA: Harvard University Press, 2000 [1960].

Mowinckel, S. *Prophecy and Tradition*, Oslo: ANVAO, 1946.

Noth, M. *A History of Pentateuchal Traditions*, Englewood Cliffs: Prentice-Hall, 1972 [original German 1948].

Ong, W. J., SJ. *Orality and Literacy*, second edition, New York: Routledge, 2002 [1982].

Perrin, N. *Rediscovering the Teachings of Jesus*, New York: Harper & Row, 1976.

Sanders, J. A. *Torah and Canon*, Eugene, OR: Wipf and Stock, 1999 [Fortress Press, 1972].

Sparks, K. L. *Ancient Texts for the Study of the Hebrew Bible: A Guide to the Background Literature*, Peabody, MA: Hendrickson, 2005.

Vansina, J. *Oral Tradition: A Study in Historical Methodology*, trans. H. M. Wright, Aldine, TX: Transaction, 2005.

Wilder, A. N. *Early Christian Rhetoric: The Language of the Gospel*, Peabody, MA: Hendrickson, reprint, 1964.

TRANSFIGURATION OF JESUS

All three Synoptic Gospels (Matt 17:1–8; Mark 9:2–10; Luke 9:28–36) feature an account of Jesus taking his disciples Peter, James, and John up a mountain, where they witness his transfiguration into a being of brilliant light (Mark: "his clothes brighter than any fuller could make them"; Matthew: his face shining "like the sun"; Luke: "the appearance of his face changed"), and his being joined in this dazzling state by Moses and Elijah. Neither Matthew nor Mark explicitly discloses the topic of Jesus' discussion with the two heavenly visitors, but Luke tells us that they discussed Jesus' upcoming death ("exodus") in Jerusalem. In response to the disciples' fear, a heavenly voice from the cloud announces, "This is my son, the Beloved [Matthew adds "with whom I am well pleased"]. Listen to him!" Upon seeing this sight, Peter proposes that they (the three disciples) might build three booths on the mountain, one for Jesus, one for Moses, and one for Elijah, a suggestion that Jesus ignores. According to Mark and Matthew, after he leads the three disciples down the mountain, Jesus commands them to tell no one what they have witnessed, while Luke relates simply that they told no one what they had seen. After this meeting on the mountain, Jesus seems more determined (and perhaps more spiritually

prepared) for the difficult days ahead, and there is an unmistakable connection between the Transfiguration and the Passion narrative. (In Luke the connection is explicit, and one of Mark's Passion predictions ensues on the departure from the mountain.) Matthew calls the whole encounter a "vision" (17:9), but Mark's and Luke's failure to use that term in this context need not signal a difference of understanding.

The Transfiguration's place in the gospels and geography

The Transfiguration is undoubtedly the most otherworldly pericope in the gospels. In many ways, it smacks of something we might expect to find in a more mystical apocryphal writing, and it is not surprising that some older (esp. German) scholarship sought its influences among the Homeric Demeter hymns, Hermetic writings, etc. Yet the Transfiguration's placement within the gospel narrative is hardly artificial – it fits with what precedes and what follows in such a way that we can scarcely doubt that it had circulated within a framework shared by other stories in the gospels. There are, to be sure, some things suggesting that its precise placement may have been motivated by a felt need to resignify the predictions of Jesus' soon return (see below), but the account as a whole does not look like a stray bit of tradition. There has been some debate over whether certain allusions to the Transfiguration in 2 Pet 1:16–18 are dependent on the Synoptic Gospels, and it is possible that these could affect our understanding of the Transfiguration's pre-gospel career. (See Miller 1996.)

The mountain on which the Transfiguration takes place has traditionally been identified as Mt Tabor (a site connected with sacred activity in Ps 89:13; Jer 46:18, and Hos 5:1). A number of scholars have suggested that Mt Hermon might actually be in view, principally because the preceding episode within the gospels takes place in nearby Caesarea Philippi, and because Mt Hermon is more likely than Mt Tabor to be described as "high" (Matt 17:1; Mark 9:2). Numerous locales have actually been suggested down through the years. (See Manns.)

Meanings and background associations

Scholars have proposed a number of background associations as interpretive contexts for the Transfiguration. By far the most widely subscribed of these associations is the account of God's appearing to Moses in Exodus 24 and 34, two

653

passages widely held to resonate with the Transfiguration in several details. Both Exodus and the Transfiguration: (1) contain references to a passage of six days (Luke has "eight" instead of "six"); (2) refer to three associates accompanying the main figure; (3) take place on top of a mountain; (4) involve the transfiguration of the protagonist's appearance; (5) include the figure of Moses; and feature (6) a cloud and (7) a heavenly voice. In spite of the impressive number of parallel features, the case for the Transfiguration having been modeled on the Exodus theophany is not watertight, as most of these points of contact are generic features of theophanies, and those that are not ([1], [2], and [5]) appear less parallel when examined more closely (see Poirier).

Another association that may inform the Transfiguration is the widespread messianic tradition about Moses and Elijah (see Basser; Poirier). It should be borne in mind that the association of Jesus with Moses and Elijah is also found in Revelation 11, perhaps showing another side of Jesus' association with Moses and Elijah in some shared eschatological task. (The early Christian reading of Revelation 11 as pairing Elijah with Enoch is almost certainly wrong, and many first-century Jews held that Moses, like Elijah, had not died but rather had been taken to heaven directly.)

What is the point (assuming there is one) of the appearance of Moses and Elijah? For some, this question is answered more specifically in terms of why *those* two figures and not two others, and the answer has often been merely that Moses and Elijah had both ascended to heaven without dying. (Elijah's not dying is told in the Bible, while Moses' not dying is found in Jewish tradition.) This consideration connects with a further possibility: Moses and Elijah were popularly expected to return, as the endtime prophet (see Deut 18:15, 18) and the priestly messiah respectively. It should be noted, however, that not every scholar identifies Elijah with the priestly messiah.

There are at least two more important interpretative contexts, one of which sees in Moses and Elijah symbols of the Law and Prophets (Thrall; but cf. Carlston: 237). The fact that this position is less capable of explaining the reappearance of Elijah and Moses in Revelation 11 may be a besetting consideration, but scholars have not been in a habit of bringing the Revelation passage to bear on the interpretation of the Transfiguration. Another interpretative context is intratextual within the gospel narrative: it lies in the narrative link between the voice on the mountain and the voice at Jesus' baptism, both of which announce

the same thing. The connection between the Transfiguration and the baptism in the Jordan becomes somewhat stronger if we assume, for the baptism, a detail found in early Jewish Christian tradition: that a bright light shone in the Jordan when Jesus was baptized. Working strictly with the Synoptic Gospels, we have less to go on, but the fact that the divine voice says the same thing on both occasions, and that the message, in both instances, is aimed at showing Jesus' messianic identity to a privileged disciple (e.g. John the Baptist) or set of disciples (Peter, James, and John), is significant in itself. Whether a literary interconnection is intended, or the connection is merely one of borrowing without any intention of creating a live interconnection, is not really clear.

Luke's reference to Jesus' "exodus"

Each of the three Transfiguration accounts differs from the others in a few details. Scholars are not agreed on the significance (if any) of these differences, although some of them are of great interest. Most of these details have received their share of explanations. For example, while the passage of "six days" that introduces Matthew's and Mark's accounts is most commonly linked with the mention of six days in Exod 24:16, several other associations have been suggested (see Carlston 236), and it is also possible that the number has little meaning, so that any guess at a significant parallel is an over-interpretation. (As Trocmé suggested, "six days" may be "a meaningless phrase left over from some indication in the tradition" [230 n. 3].)

Perhaps the most intriguing difference among the three gospel accounts is that of Luke's reference to Jesus, Moses, and Elijah discussing the "exodus" that Jesus "must accomplish in Jerusalem" (9:3). Luke's reference to Jesus' "exodus" has often been linked with the Lukan theme of the "way" (*hodos*). While it fits well within that context, it might also be that Luke is providing a narrative hook for Peter's otherwise inexplicable bid to make booths for Jesus, Moses, and Elijah. (A widespread failure to explain Peter's words has usually written them off as bathetic amazement.) Perhaps Luke, who lacks Mark's temporal markers for a so-called "Passion week," envisions Jesus entering the holy city just in time for the feast of Tabernacles (in the fall), in which case Peter's suggestion to build booths at a different site than Jerusalem would appear to be a last-ditch effort to deter Jesus from going to Jerusalem, where he presumably planned to celebrate Tabernacles (see Turner 3.81; cf. the palms of the Triumphal Entry, which are most easily explained as paraphernalia of the feast of Tabernacles). (Attempts by the disciples to deter Jesus from going to Jerusalem is a Lukan theme.) In that case, the discussion about Jesus' "accomplishing an exodus in Jerusalem" could have been misunderstood by Peter as a reference to celebrating the exodus-themed feast in Jerusalem. The merits of this way of reading Luke should be considered separately from whether it explains the tradition as a whole, but it has the additional advantage of explaining a detail that otherwise has never been satisfactorily explained (viz. Peter's suggestion about the booths). It is also possible, although perhaps less likely, that Luke's reference to an exodus was brought on by the words of the heavenly voice, announcing Jesus as God's son, thus possibly (to Luke's mind) evoking the reference to Israel as God's son in Exodus 4. For some reason, Luke places the Transfiguration at night.

A misplaced resurrection account?

One popular form-critical explanation for the Transfiguration has been that it is a "misplaced resurrection account" (Carlston; but see Stein), an idea widely credited to Josef Blinzler. This view, which is less popular now than in the heyday of form criticism, is based on the view that a more primitive understanding of Jesus' resurrection did not differentiate it from his exaltation. According to this position, the Transfiguration is an early tradition. It should also be noted that, in the *Apocalypse of Peter*, the Transfiguration is presented as an ascension account.

Disagreeing with the "misplaced resurrection account" scenario does not commit us, however, to accepting that the Transfiguration was always placed within its present context, or that it was not touched by the redactional program either of Mark or of a preceding (oral or written) stage. As noted above, this "vision" (as Matthew calls it) of the glorified Christ immediately follows Jesus' promise that some of those present would not die before they saw the kingdom of God arrive with power (Mark 9:1). If this saying of Jesus had become as widespread as most scholars assume, it undoubtedly would have become more and more problematic as time went on, especially as the generation of promise began to pass away without any sign of Jesus' return. At some point, the dominant feeling must have become that the promise would not be fulfilled in the way generally expected, and Christians may have sought (as a matter of damage control) an alternative understanding of the promise. Viewed in that light, the Transfiguration may have

been intended, in the mind of Mark or his predecessor, as a clever resignification of Jesus' promise that some would remain to see the Son of Man coming on the clouds. In other words, the Transfiguration became an account of disciples seeing the Lord return in glory.

The Transfiguration and the historical Jesus

What relevance has the Transfiguration account for Historical Jesus studies? For many, anything so otherworldly cannot be historical, and the account must be explained either as a heightening of tendencies latent within a more authentic report or as a wholecloth invention. For others, experiences of this sort represent real religious experiences – or substantial literary refittings of real experiences – for which the question of whether "real" refers to objective or subjective categories is often conveniently ducked. The most that can be said, perhaps, is that the tradition appears to be early (as is widely attested). To a large degree, the possibility of a historical kernel reduces to the secularity or non-secularity of the criteria by which it is judged, and there may be no getting around that. It should be said, in that connection, that the question of how early the Transfiguration achieved a form approximating what we find in the gospels is dependent upon the point at which messianic understandings of Jesus entered the gospel tradition. While that question is answered in different ways by different scholars, an increasing openness to the historical Jesus' conceiving of his own mission in messianic terms suggests that the Transfiguration could be one of the older parts of the tradition. Given the nature of the material, a more positive evaluation is probably not possible.

JOHN C. POIRIER

Further reading

Basser, Herbert W. "The Jewish Roots of the Transfiguration," *BRev* 14:3 (1998) 30–35.
Carlstons, C. E. "Transfiguration and Resurrection," *JBL* 80 (1961) 233–4.
Chilton, Bruce D. "The Transfiguration: Dominical Assurance and Apostolic Vision," *NTS* 27 (1980) 115–24.
Manns, Frédéric. "Mount Tabor," in James H. Charlesworth (ed.) *Jesus and Archaeology*, Grand Rapids, MI: Eerdmans, 2006, pp. 167–77.
Miller, Robert J. "Is There Independent Attestation for the Transfiguration in 2 Peter?," *NTS* 42:4 (1996) 620–45.
Moses, A. D. A. *Matthew's Transfiguration Story and Jewish–Christian Controversy*, Sheffield: Sheffield Academic Press, 1996.
Poirier, John C. "Jewish and Christian Tradition in the Transfiguration," *RB* 111:4 (2004) 516–30.

Stein, Robert H. "Is the Transfiguration (Mark 9 2–8) a Misplaced Resurrection Account?," *JBL* 95:1 (1976) 79–96.

Thrall, Margaret E. "Elijah and Moses in Mark's Account of the Transfiguration," *NTS* 16 (1970) 305–17.

Trocmé, Etienne. *The Formation of the Gospel According to Mark*, London: SPCK, 1975.

Turner, C. H. "Commentary on the Gospel of Mark," in Charles Gore, Henry Leighton Goudge, and Alfred Guillaume (eds) *A New Commentary on Holy Scripture, Including the Apocrypha*, 3 vols, New York: Macmillan, 1929, Vol. 3, pp. 42–124.

TRIAL OF JESUS

The passages that present some form of trial or examination of Jesus include: an inquiry made by Annas (John 18:13–24); the examination before the Jewish leadership (Matt 26:57–68; Mark 14:53–65; Luke 22:54–71); Jesus before Pilate (Matt 27:11–14; Mark 15:2–5; Luke 23:2–5; John 18:29–38); Jesus before Herod (Luke 23:6–12, 13–16); Pilate's decision (Matt 27:24–26; Mark 15:15; Luke 23:24–25; John 19:16). There is no trial scene in the *Gospel of Thomas* as it lacks any discussion of Passion events. The likelihood of other extra-biblical gospels giving us anything historical about these events is small.

Four preliminary issues

In looking initially at this material, four issues are important: (1) working backwards gets us to the Roman involvement; (2) the need to distinguish between a trial and various types of examinations where no decisive verdict was given; (3) the nature of potential witnesses who could have been sources for the various proceedings; and (4) the chronology of this sequence.

The very fact that Jesus was crucified tells us Rome was involved. The crucifixion is multiply attested. Not only do the gospels attest to it, but so does the teaching of other major NT writers (Paul, Peter, author of the Hebrews, and John). In addition, the non-Christian testimony from Josephus (*Ant.* 18.63–64) alludes to this event, noting that both Jewish leaders and Pilate had a role. Tacitus, *Annals* 15.44 also says that a figure called "Christ" was executed under Pilate. Only Rome could authorize crucifixion (*J.W.* 2.117; *Ant.* 18.2; John 19:10), although this claim as stated in John 18:31–32 has been challenged by Winter and Lietzmann. This position has been refuted by the work of Strobel. So Rome's involvement in Jesus' death stands on historically solid ground.

A second important question is how to view any potential Jewish involvement. The term "trial" is often associated with the various Jewish examinations, but if one means an examination that leads to a verdict that exacts a penalty, then these meetings with the Jewish leadership were not trials. Four options exist here (Theissen/Merz): (1) a Sanhedrin trial was historical (Blinzler; Strobel); (2) it is unhistorical and an invention of the early church (Lietzmann); (3) an interrogation by the Sanhedrin was recast as a trail later (Gnilka); and (4) several processes were fused into a trial (R. E. Brown).

The issue is important because there has been much discussion about the irregularity of these procedures in light of the Mishnaic types of considerations (*m. Sanh.* 4.1; 7.5; 11:2; *Besah* 5.2). These texts require a trial during the day, not on a sabbath or feast day, with no judgment on the day of the examination, blasphemy only involving the use of the divine name, and no gathering at the home of the high priest. Again this discussion was pointedly raised by Lietzmann. Of all the points, the one most often challenged is the possibility of an evening examination at this celebratory time of the year. Strobel brought forward evidence that shows that such rules were not kept in special circumstances where one is dealing with a potential deceiver (a *mesith*, one who leads an individual astray into idolatry, or *maddiach*, one who leads a whole community astray; *m. Sanh.* 11.3–4; *t. Sanh.* 7.11; 10:11). Theissen and Merz question this approach, suggesting that Jesus was not leading the nation astray to other gods and idolatry, but this objection depends on how the claims of Jesus are evaluated from a Jewish point of view.

Two special circumstances may well have pushed for such a special examination: (1) the fact that Pilate was readily available only for a short time; and (2) the fact that it might have been viewed as risky to hold on to Jesus for any length of time. Betz has noted that the role of Jewish courts in provincial contexts was that they were often responsible for the investigation of a case (*cognitio*) as well as the preparation of an accusation (*accusatio*). He concludes his observations saying,

> That is why the nocturnal hearing of Jesus, carried through by a commission of the Sanhedrin under the High Priest (Mark 14:53–65), and the morning session of the Sanhedrin (Mark 15:1) should not be treated as unhistorical creations of the Christian church; these events fit the legal situation of the Roman province of that time.

That such a meeting with the Jewish leadership is likely historical is based on several factors: (1) the tension Jesus' ministry raised as it relates to questions tied to Judaism (Sabbath conflict, purity issues, the temple act, claims about forgiveness, Jesus' association with sinners); (2) Jesus did not represent a military threat to anyone so as to naturally raise Roman concern; (3) Jesus' ability to disturb the peace was an issue that was triggered by his challenge of Jewish institutions, like the temple; (4) the corroborative testimony of Josephus indicates that in a Jewish setting there was recognition of a role by the Jewish leadership; and (5) Jewish charges of Jesus being a sorcerer, multiply attested in Mark and Q, as well as in later Jewish materials (Stanton) suggest the ancient presence of a polemic against Jesus. More debated is whether this meeting involved only a few key leaders (Sloyan) or many of the Jewish leaders at that time (Betz). Of the four views cited above for Jewish involvement, views 1 (Sanhedrin examination) or 4 (several processes fused) are the most likely options.

As to the issue of sources for this event, several possibilities exist. It is important to remember that a thirty-year-long debate existed in Jerusalem between the family of Annas and key figures of the church such as Jesus and James. Annas II was responsible for James' death in *c.* 62 CE (*Ant.* 20.197–203). This Jewish family supplied a run of high priests from 6 to 62 CE. There would have been public debate and awareness of what took place and why in Jerusalem. The fact that charges about issues like the law or Jesus' powerful work are noted on each side indicates that the grapevine we have access to in this debate is a good one. Beyond this, the existence of figures like Joseph of Arimathea or the access Paul had previously to the Jewish leadership in his role as a persecutor of the church means that there were people who would have known the reasons for Jewish concern and action against Jesus. These factors suggest that there is good reason to believe that Jesus had an examination by the Jewish leadership, who sought to gather evidence to take Jesus to Pilate (representing Rome) as one who was a risk to the public peace. So at the very least, this would mean that Jesus was examined by the Jewish leadership and by Rome, claims we can argue have corroborative evidence.

The final preliminary issue involves chronology. Many read the synoptics and John as possessing an irreconcilable difference in the timing of these trials. John appears to have Jesus crucified on the day of Passover (John 13:1; 18:28; 19:14), while the Synoptics appear to have the Last Supper on Passover with the crucifixion on the following day (Mark 14:12, 14, 16; Luke 22:15).

Many interpreters simply see this difference as an error in one set of the accounts (Brown having

presented the options). However, various explanations have been supplied for this difference:

1 Some appeal to a distinct one-day calendar difference at work between the synoptics and John, whether a Galilean (one day earlier) versus Judean difference, a Pharisaic (one day earlier) versus Sadducean difference, a solar versus lunar calendar difference, or a combination of the two (Jaubert; Hoehner). The practicality of getting all the lambs slain is said to be a factor in this difference. The issue here is whether Jerusalem would have sanctioned two distinct calendars in the first century.
2 Either the synoptics (Brown, McKnight) or John (Morris, Moo) have made a symbolic move in light of the fact that the entire season is considered a part of the Passover.
3 Others argue that it is wrong to see the reference to the preparation of the Passover in John as a reference to the day before the Passover meal. Rather, the expression for John applies to any day running from the day before Passover through the period of Unleavened Bread on the premise that the entire feast could share either name and that purity was required throughout this period (2 Chr 35:7–9, where all meals during this time are called *pesah*; Carson; also, the care of the priests in not entering a gentile house during this time, where impurity might be contracted, versus staying in the courtyard reflects a view like *m. Oholoth* 18.7, 10). Of these options, either the second or third is possible with, perhaps, the third being slightly more likely.

A preliminary holding of Jesus

Following Jesus' arrest it is not surprising that there would be a "holding" period for Jesus as things got organized to examine him. This is noted briefly in John 18:12–24. The likely locale would be the home of Annas and Caiaphas, which would be private and secure. A preliminary attempt to get Jesus to speak meets with his response that he has taught openly. Nothing much comes from this scene. Its almost sidebar feel suggests the scene could well be plausible. John 18:24 notes that Jesus is then passed on to Caiaphas. This leads us into the major examination by the Jewish leadership.

The examination by the Jewish leadership

The examination before the Jewish leadership appears to have extended from the evening into the early morning. It proceeded in two stages: (1) the attempt to see if a charge could be gathered around the Temple incident with its seeming implication of reform or destruction of the temple without consent of the leadership; and (2) the examination of Jesus' self-understanding. The goal of the examination was to determine whether a charge related to some form of sedition could be brought before Pilate. In terms of historical credibility, there is a pattern in the sequence of arrest, appearances before the Jewish leadership and Pilate, Peter's denials, crucifixion and empty tomb that is so deeply imbedded in all versions of these events that this basic outline appears to be historically credible.

The attempt to see whether a charge could be connected to the temple appears only in Mark 14:53–56 and Matt 26:59–63a. It fits the cultural backdrop for the examination to begin here. Jesus' act in the Temple was public and would have been controversial. The act coheres with remarks in John 2:19 about Jesus rebuilding a destroyed temple. Mark 14:58 has a similar remark that parallels other Markan texts (13:2; 15:29; 11:17–18). The act also coheres with the idea that the Eschaton would bring a cleansing and restoration of Jerusalem (Tob 14:5–7; *Pss. Sol.* 17–18). The charge is dismissed on two basic grounds. First, the testimony is called false, because the witnesses are not able to agree (Mark 14:59). Matthew strengthens this to say the council sought such testimony (Matt 26:59). So, this effort goes nowhere. Apparently the leadership had a sense that this charge would not be convincing to Pilate. The gospels are circumspect enough to note that they sensed this. The key here may be the attribution of these witnesses that Jesus claimed he would destroy the Temple. The remark as it is tied to Jesus in the tradition appears to be that the Temple will be destroyed by someone other than Jesus. In remarks about the temple's or Jerusalem's fate that do go back to Jesus, it appears Jesus anticipates a judgment on the nation for covenant unfaithfulness (Luke 13:34–35; 19:41–44; Mark 13:2 and parallels; Dodd). The fact that this charge became a dead end meant that it was not related in Luke's account of this scene. John skips this interrogation completely, probably because it was well known in the Church's oral tradition.

By far the most important portion of this account is the examination by the high priest and Jesus' response (Mark 14:60–65). Mark juxtaposes this scene with Peter's denials (14:66–72). The most common objection to the historicity of this scene is the juxtaposition of christological titles (Messiah,

Son, Son of Man) and texts (Ps 110:1; Dan 7:13–14) in Jesus' reply (Theissen/Merz).

Some question whether the transition from temple charge to a question about being Messiah is a natural one. They argue that the transition is too abrupt and the topics are too unrelated. However, the work of Betz and the association of renewal of Jerusalem with the end show that the sequence is a natural one, especially given the range of claims associated with Jesus that are made upon his entry into the city. The high priest's question about Jesus being the Son of the Blessed has the ring of respect for God about it that fits such a solemn setting about such grave issues. The "Blessed" is an indirect reference to God rooted in language that ties God to acts of blessing. It is not a common expression in Judaism or in Christianity, so it does not have the feel of being a created title by Mark (Bock contra Sloyan; *m. Ber.* 7.3; *1 En.* 77:2; 4Q209). Jesus' reply in Mark keeps the tone of respect by speaking of the right hand of power (*1 En.* 62:7; numerous texts in *Mekilta* where the power exercised at the Exodus is the point: *Mek-Beshallah* 2 [26a] on Exod 14:2; *Mek-Amalek* 1 on Exod 17:3 [54b]; *Mek-Amalek* 4 [59b] on Exod 18:19; *Mek-Bahodesh* 9 [71a] on Exod 20:18; *Sifre* Num:112; *ARN*). Such exceptional usage is against a Markan creation, especially when Mark is comfortable referring to the "Son of God" (Mark 1:1; 3;11; 5:7; 15:37; Bock).

The most crucial element within this scene is Jesus' reply. Two basic views exist about Jesus' reply. First, this reply was placed on Jesus' lips as a christological summary of the confession of the early church (Perrin, who Sloyan mostly follows here). In this reading, Jesus is the model of how one responds to persecution for the communities to which the gospels are written. Second, this is a faithful summary of what Jesus said (Bock). The most discussed part of the reply is the juxtaposition of Ps 110:1 with Dan 7:13–14, given that all the synoptics appear to affirm the association with the Christ, in at least a qualified manner. Mark has an unqualified "yes" open the reply, while Matthew and Luke speak in terms of "you have said so," an idiomatic response that means, "Yes, but not entirely in the sense in which it has been asked." This is not a complete rejection of the category, but more a qualification on it. The remainder of the response makes that qualification clear, so that the force of the three synoptics is in agreement as to the thrust of Jesus' response. It is hard to understand how the term "Christ" became so completely attached to Jesus in the early church, if he in fact absolutely rejected the title.

Since it is this portion of the scene that is the most crucial, it is important to walk through the issues of historicity pro and con a step at a time. Against the scriptural connection going back to Jesus are two key arguments: (1) the christological reflection here looks advanced, even post-Easter; (2) Jesus did not normally link such texts together in such a midrashic manner.

However, these objections are not as strong as they initially seem. On (1): the key to Jesus' reply is his reference to the Son of Man, while the priest's messianic question is basically what the temple action was likely to have suggested, especially if the concern is to consider a political charge to raise with Pilate. The availability of Son of Man speculation to Jesus (Collins, Horbury; 11QMel 2.18; *Ezekiel the Tragedian* 76; *1 En.* 46:2–4; 48:2; 62:5–14; 63:11; 69:27–29; 70:1, 14–17; *4 Ezra* 13) and Jesus' exclusive use of this title speak to its likely role as a self-reference by Jesus. The multiple attestation that belongs to the apocalyptic Son of Man sayings also speaks for its availability versus being a creation in a gospel that is aimed at a predominantly Greek audience (Mark [Mark 8;38 par.; Mark 13:26 par.; Mark 14:62 par.], Q [Matt 24:27 Luke 17:24; 24:37 Luke 17:26; 24:39 Luke 17:30], M [Matt 10:23; 13:41; 24;44; 25:31], L [Luke 17:22]). On (2): there is evidence that Jesus did link texts together in a midrashic style (Mark 7:6–10 = Matt 15:4–9; Matt 22:33–39 like Mark 12:29–31). More important is a point Raymond Brown makes with emphasis in his work about Jesus' death: "The perception that OT passages were interpreted to give a christological insight does not date the process." He goes on to add:

> Hidden behind the attribution to the early church is often the assumption that Jesus had no christology even by way of reading the Scriptures to discern in what anticipated way he fitted into God's plan. Can one really think that credible?

The issue of who Jesus was is just as live an issue in the 30s as it was in the 60s. There is nothing in these objections that requires a church creation and several factors argue against it.

What would have been Jesus' point in such a qualified reply? Jesus answers somewhat affirmatively to the messianic query of the high priest but then adds to it to make it clear that the question really misses the point. Jesus does not merely affirm the query; he goes beyond it. The remark about the Son of Man, whether it was heard as a reception into heaven or a return to earth to rule (and that is debated), affirms a divine vindication of Jesus that assumes (1) a session by God's side

and (2) the right to judge one day. In other words, Jesus may be on trial now, but one day he would be vindicated so that rejecting him meant being a defendant before God and his chosen representative. To a leadership that did not accept that Jesus was a candidate for such vindication, this claim was blasphemous. For them blasphemy would have included making oneself too close to God (Josephus, *Ant.* 6.183; 10. 233, 242; Philo, *Dreams* 2.130–31; *Decalogue* 13–14.61–64). In claiming to be their future judge one day, he may well have also tripped over Exod 22:27. Luke's failure to mention blasphemy at this point of the examination means little, as he tells his story for an audience that only needed to understand that what Jesus said led him to Pilate. Neither is there a need to have pronounced the divine name to get to such a verdict, although this has been argued by Gundry. This view is possible, but by itself it cannot explain the reaction of the leadership, since the divine name would have come in the context of the citing of Scripture. Other contextually noted elements, namely the extent of Jesus' claim of vindication, triggered the negative reaction to Jesus' response.

In sum, this event has a stronger claim to authenticity than suggestions that Mark or the early church created the scene. With some form of a regal claim for divine vindication into heaven, Jesus ironically supplies the testimony that led to his being taken on to Pilate so that Rome could now make the decisive judgment.

One final point needs to be made about this scene. It is often suggested that the Evangelists are more interested in their contemporary theology than they are in history. The details of this text, however, suggest that one need not choose between such options as competing alternatives.

The trial of Pilate

That some type of meeting took place involving Jesus and Pilate is one of the most solid facts we have about Jesus. It is one of the few events that appears in all four gospels (Mark 15:1–5b; Matt 27:2, 11–14; Luke 23:1–5; John 18:28–38). Such an examination is historically solid because only Rome could crucify. The evidence from the *titulus* that said Jesus was a King of the Jews makes it likely that Jesus was executed by Rome for sedition. This charge is too embarrassing for Christians to have invented it (Bond, Bammel, Theissen/Merz). Trials of non-citizens in the provinces for this period involved a process called *cognitio extra ordinem* or "criminal jurisdiction outside the list" (Sherwin-White). This process gave the governor great flexibility in how a case was handled. Theissen/Merz argue that the likely charge was that Jesus was a *crimen lasae maiestatis populi romani*, or a detriment to the reputation of the Roman people (Tacitus, *Ann.* 2.50; 3.38; Suetonius, *Tib.* 58), if he was not simply charged as a *perduello* or a major public enemy.

Beyond the almost universal recognition that Jesus was crucified by Rome for some form of sedition, debate exists about what we can know about this scene. Luke 23:2 has a threefold charge: (1) Jesus perverts our nation; (2) he said one should not pay taxes to Caesar; (3) he says that he is Christ, a king. This is probably intended to be a summary of what was raised against Jesus by the leadership as opposed to being seen as the formal opening of the examination. The first charge suggests that Jesus is a public agitator, the second that he defies Rome, and the third that he claims to be a competing ruler. Since Pilate is charged with keeping the peace, collecting taxes, and protecting Caesar's interests, all three charges would touch on his responsibilities. Of the charges, Luke 20:25 shows the second charge to be false. However, the subsequent questioning shows that only the claim to be king concerns Pilate. Mark 15:3 simply says that they charged him with many things. The question about whether he was the King of the Jews is the central concern in all the accounts. This concern is clearly one that would have led to the type of charge that appeared on the *titulus*.

In all the accounts there is nothing substantive that is brought up with respect to such charges, although the suggestion of "perverting" the nation is that Jesus' claims about Jewish law and practices is part of what the leadership found disturbing. However, this would be of little relevance to Pilate. Only a kingship claim would matter to him. However, Jesus had no army and did not behave as did previous threats to Rome. Josephus details these figures in *Ant.* 17.271–78 and speaks of Judas, Simon, and Athronges. So it is likely that Pilate initially would not sense much of a threat from Jesus.

Examination by Herod Antipas (Luke 23:6–12)

That Jesus met with Herod Antipas is noted only by Luke among the four gospels. Interestingly, his involvement does appear in other sources in an intensified manner from the portrait in Luke (*Gospel of Peter* 1.1–2.4, where Herod urges his execution; *Acts of Thomas* 32, where the serpent is said to have kindled the reaction of Herod and Caiaphas to lie before Pilate). Herod's role is alluded to by Justin Martyr (*Apology* 1.40 where Justin alludes to Acts 4:27, which also notes a role for Herod in Jesus' death; *Dialogue* 103, where he notes Pilate sent him to Herod as a compliment) and Ignatius, *Smyrneans* 1.2 (which says Jesus was nailed to the cross under Pilate and Herod). Potential sources for such an examination also exist (Joanna or Chuza, Luke 8:3 or Manaen, Acts 13:1). The roots in an early tradition seem likely (Brown, who also sees Lucan elaboration in this material). Nothing much came of this visit. Luke portrays Herod as indifferent to the main issue involving Jesus in a manner dissimilar to the portrait from the later Christian sources where he shares the responsibility for Jesus' death. After this short scene, Herod sends Jesus back to Pilate.

Barabbas and sentencing by Pilate

Another much discussed detail involving Pilate is the choice to release Barabbas instead of Jesus (Mark 15:6–15; Matt 27:15–23; Luke 23:17–23). In particular, we have no corroboration of the annual offer of amnesty to the Jews. It is hard to know what to make of this lack of corroboration, for although Josephus gives us a great deal of detail about Judea in this period, and controversial aspects of Pilate's rule, he only speaks once about Jesus. However, we do have some accounts of occasional grants of such amnesty in other provinces (Papyrus Florentinus 61 speaks of a release of a prisoner in Egypt in about 85 CE; Albinus in Judea also is noted as making such a release in 64 CE: *Ant.* 20.215). Many opt for a contemporaneous release for Barabbas that was turned into a choice made by the people (Brown; Theissen/Merz; Bond), but it is not clear why this should be a better rationale for the detail than the way the gospels relate the event. The figure of Barabbas does seem well embedded in the early tradition, while Pilate appears to be willing to allow the popular voice to speak in a particularly delicate situation. This action stands in contrast to Pilate's previous insensitivity that had brought him trouble (Strobel). This seeking of popular opinion is not unprecedented (*Ant.* 13.288–96, Hyrcanus with Eleazar; *J.W.* 1.654–55, where people pass judgment on those who pulled down the Roman symbol of the eagle and hacked it to pieces; Bond, but while expressing uncertainty as to the detail's historical value). This entire portrait shows Pilate as a skilled politician negotiating his way through controversial ground.

What is one to make of the portrait of Pilate being so sensitive to Jewish concerns and the people, given the portrait of him in other materials as rather a boorish figure? The circumstances behind Pilate's rule up to this point may help us work through this question.

Pilate probably became more sensitive to Jewish concerns after three key incidents where his insensitivity caused him to receive an official rebuke. First there is the remark in Josephus *J. W.* 2.169–77 and *Ant.* 18.55–62 that Pilate set up standards with images of Caesar in Jerusalem, having placed them there during one evening. Such images would be an offense to the Jewish view that there should be no divine images. On top of this in the same accounts, Josephus notes that Pilate used sacred temple money to extend an aqueduct. This action caused the Jews to gather in protest and surround the tribunal of Pilate. It is important to note that Josephus narrates these two events before moving on to discuss Jesus and Pilate in *Ant* 18.63–64. This suggests that these two events likely preceded the death of Jesus that 18.63–64 discuss. A third incident follows. Philo's *Embassy to Gaius* 299–305 relates the account of the offensive setting up of gilded Roman shields in Herod's palace in Jerusalem. A desire to annoy the Jews is stated as Pilate's motive for setting up the shields, which probably contained a reference to the divine Augustus, if the decoration followed the common pattern in referencing Tiberius. This statement would offend the Jews and their view that there is only one God (Bond). To impose such a declaration in their holy city would have added to the offense. That these shields were later removed to the temple of Augustus in Caesarea makes such a reference likely. This final incident so exasperated Tiberius that according to Philo he wrote Pilate a letter rebuking him.

Now it is very probable that the first two incidents predate the crucifixion, while the third incident Philo relates may or may not do so. This is because the date of Jesus' crucifixion is variously placed at 30 to 33 CE, with 30 CE being the most common choice, while 33 CE is the next most accepted candidate. There are good reasons to prefer the 33 CE date, for if Pilate had recently been rebuked by the emperor then his care to send Jesus to Herod and to seek a popular resolution of this internal Jewish dispute makes sense (Hoehner). However, even if one places the crucifixion in 30 CE, such a move in such a sensitive situation given what Pilate had already provoked in Judea would be the step of a leader who may well have learned some lessons from his previous experiences with the reaction of the populace.

Summary

The examinations of Jesus leading to his execution involved a complex set of social and political interrelationships that were a part of Judea in the 30s. The Jewish leadership viewed Jesus as a threat to the stability of their faith and the region. They believed this because of the popular following he was developing and the consistent tendency he had to operate in an independent manner with respect to the law and the sacred space in Jerusalem. This led them to formulate a political charge they could take to Pilate, suggesting that Jesus was a seditious figure who represented an independent claim to kingship detached from any Roman recognition. Although Pilate seems not to have seen Jesus initially as such a threat, since he had no force that could threaten Rome and gave no evidence of raising an army, the circumstances around his arrest and the clamor that emerged made it clear to Pilate that he had no choice but to act. Given his responsibility to defend the interests of Caesar, Pilate could not risk the responsibility of allowing someone making regal claims to forward their work under his watch. So in the end, Pilate gave the decisive order to have Jesus crucified. In doing so, Pilate saw himself as doing his job as procurator, just as the Jewish leadership in pursuing the matter originally saw themselves as exercising their role of oversight over the Jewish faith. Thus, it was for different reasons that these two groups became involved in what led to the examination and official sentencing of Jesus. The result, Jesus' crucifixion and all that followed it, is one of the most widely debated and significant events of world history.

DARRELL L. BOCK

Further reading

Bammel, Ernst. "The Trial before Pilate," in Ernst Bammel and C. F. D. Moule (eds) *Jesus and the Politics of His Day*, Cambridge: Cambridge University Press, 1984.

Betz, Otto. "Probleme des Prozesses Jesu," in H. Temporini and W. Hasse (eds) *Aufstieg und Niedergang der Römanischen Welt*, Vol. II, 25.1, Berlin: de Gruyter, 1982, pp. 565–647.

Blinzler, Josef. *Der Prozess Jesu*, fourth edition, Regensberg: Verlag Friedrich Pustet, 1969.

Bock, Darrell. *Blasphemy and Exaltation in Judaism and the Final Examination of Jesus*, WUNT II/106, Tübingen: Mohr/Siebeck, 1998.

—— *Blasphemy and Exaltation in Judaism: The Charge against Jesus in Mark 14:53–65*, Grand Rapids, MI: Baker, 2000.

Bond, Helen K. *Pontius Pilate in History and Interpretation*, SNTSMS 100, Cambridge: Cambridge University Press, 1998.

Brown, Raymond, E. *The Death of the Messiah*, 2 vols, Anchor Bible Reference Library, New York: Doubleday, 1994.

Carson, D. A. *The Gospel According to John*, Pillar New Testament Commentary, Grand Rapids, MI: Eerdmans, 1991.

Collins, John. *The Scepter and the Star: The Messiahs of the Dead Sea Scrolls and Other Ancient Literature*, Anchor Bible Reference Commentary, New York: Doubleday, 1995.

Dodd, C. H., "The Fall of Jerusalem and the 'Abomination of Desolation'," *JRS* 37 (1947) 47–54.

Gnilka, Joachim. "Der Prozeß Jesu nach den Berichten des Markus and Matthäus: mit einer Rekonstruktion des historischen Verlaufs," in Karl Kertelge (ed.) *Der Prozeß gegen Jesus: Historische Rückfrage und Theologische Deutung*, Questiones Disputatae Vol. 112, Freiburg: Herder, 1988, pp. 11–40.

Gundry, R. H. "Jesus' Blasphemy according to Mark 14:61b–64 and *Mishnah Sanhedrin 7:5*," in *The Old Is Better: New Testament Essays in Support of Traditional Interpretations*, WUNT 178, Tübingen: Mohr Siebeck, 2005.

Hoehner, Harold W. *Chronological Aspects of Christ*, Grand Rapids, MI: Zondervan, 1977.

Horbury, William. *Jewish Messianism and the Cult of Christ*, London: SCM Press, 1998.

Jaubert, A. "Jésus et le Calendrier de Qumrân," *NTS* 7 (1960–61) 1–30. Lietzmann, Hans. "Der Prozeß Jesu," *SPAW* 14 (1931) 313–22.

Lietzmann, H., "Der Prozeß Jesu," *SPAW* 14 (1931) 313–22.

McKnight, Scot. *Jesus and His Death: Historiography, the Historical Jesus, and Atonement Theory*, Waco, TX: Baylor University Press, 2005.

Moo, Douglas J. *The Old Testament in the Gospel Passion Narratives*, Sheffield: Almond Press, 1983.

Morris, L., *The Gospel according to Matthew*, Grand Rapids, MI: Eerdmans; Leicester: Apollos, 1992.

Perrin, Norman. "Mark XIV.62: The End Product of a Christian Pesher?" *NTS* 12 (1965–66) 150–55.

Sherwin-White, A. N. *Roman Society and Roman Law in the New Testament*, Oxford: Clarendon, 1963.

Sloyan, G. S. *Jesus on Trial: A Study of the Gospels*, second edition, Minneapolis, MN: Fortress Press, 2006.

Stanton, Graham. "Jesus of Nazareth: A Magician and a False Prophet who Deceived God's People?" in Joel B. Green and Max Turner (eds) *Jesus of Nazareth Lord and Christ: Essays on the Historical Jesus and New Testament Christology*, Grand Rapids, MI: Eerdmans, 1994.

Strobel, August. *Die Stunde der Wahrheit*, WUNT 21, Tübingen: J. C. B. Mohr (Paul Siebeck), 1980.

Theissen, Gerd and Annette Merz. *The Historical Jesus: A Comprehensive Guide*, Minneapolis, MN: Fortress Press, 1998.

Winter, Paul. *On the Trial of Jesus*, second edition, revised T. A. Burkill and G. Vermes, Studia Judaica, Vol. 1, Berlin: de Gruyter, 1974.

TRIBES OF ISRAEL

Whether the word 'tribe' is the most helpful rendition of the Hebrew (*šēbeṭ/maṭṭeh*) and Greek (*phulē*) remains disputed, with one scholar suggesting 'clan' as a more consistent translation (Mojola). For example, in Judg 20:12 the word *sēbeṭ* is used to denote a subdivision *within* the tribe of Benjamin. Translation problems thus remain unresolved. Whatever rendition is adopted it also needs to be remembered that 'tribe' doesn't simply indicate an origin of descent to a particular nomadic group. The tribal divisions were based on matters more involved than simple genealogy (especially after the Monarchy). Furthermore, the history of each of the tribes of Israel and their relation to one another in the OT is complex (cf. the classic treatment by Noth).

The beginning of the scriptural story traces the origin of the twelve tribes to the descendants of Jacob in Gen 29–35, but the rest of the narrative is not always consistent as to the number (varying from eleven to thirteen) nor the names of the tribes. This is usually due to the occasional displacement of Simeon or Levi and the addition of Ephraim and Manasseh. Nevertheless, the final form of the Hebrew Scriptures paints a clear picture of twelve tribes of patriarchal origin (cf. Gen 49:28; Exod 24:4) and symbolic significance. For example, they all surrounded the tabernacle (Num 2) and the high-priestly breastplate was inscribed with the names of all twelve tribes (Exod 28:21).

As shall be seen, important for Historical Jesus scholarship is that in the Assyrian exile (722 BCE) the ten northern tribes (or nine-and-a-half tribes in some texts of the second Temple period – cf. 2 Bar.) were scattered throughout the gentile nations (cf. 1 Kgs 11:29–37; 2 Kgs 15–17; Josephus, *Ant.* 11:133). This generated a widespread prophetic tradition in the literature of Second Temple Judaism, and not just in apocalyptic literature, concerning the return of the 'scattered' or lost ten tribes to the Holy Land (cf. Deut 30:3–5; Isa 11:10–16; 49:6; 54:7; 63:17; Jer 23:3–8; 29:14; 31:8–10; 32:37; Ezek 11:17; 28:25; 34:13–16; 37:15–25; 39:27–28; 47:13; Tob 13; Sir 36:1–22; Bar 2:34; 4:37; 5:5; 2 Macc 2:18; *Pss. Sol.* 8:28; 11:2–4; 17:26, 28, 44; *4 Ezra* 13:39–49, etc.).

The Samaritans claimed to be descendants of the two tribes of Joseph, Ephraim and Manasseh (cf., e.g., Josephus, *Ant.* 11:341), but most Jews did not consider this claim legitimate (cf. Luke 17:18; Josephus, *Ant.* 9.291). In the first century, descendants of the 'scattered' tribes were known to be living in the eastern diaspora (Josephus, *Ant.* 11.133; *2 Bar.* 77:2; *T. Mos.* 4:9).

In the gospels, the existence and significance of the twelve tribes, including knowledge of descendants of the scattered northern tribes, is taken for granted (Matt 4:13; 19:28; Luke 2:36; 22:30. Cf. also Acts 26:7; Jas 1:1; Rev 21:12). To these matters we now turn.

Individual tribes mentioned in the gospels

In first-century Judaism, and in the gospels, it was not uncommon to name certain individuals according to the alleged tribe of their ancestry. This was done by explicitly stating the name of a tribe (e.g. Luke 2:36 'Anna ... of the tribe of Asher') or by tracing a genealogical lineage (as in Matthew's genealogy and the association of Jesus with the tribe of Judah – cf. 1:2–3). Asher was considered the 'most blessed' of the tribes and was apportioned much wealth and a desirable coastal region (cf. Deut 33:24). However, the narrative of Judg 5:17 informs us that their pleasant coastal possession made them complacent when called for war. They were scattered in the Assyrian exile. It is not entirely clear, but it may be of significance that Anna, in a context that speaks of the hope for the 'consolation of Israel' and the 'redemption of Jerusalem' (Luke 2:25, 38) is associated with a 'scattered' northern tribe. That Jesus was of the tribe of Judah is probably to be understood in light of the promise of royalty associated with this tribe (Gen 49:10).

Matt 4:13 also evidences that, under the influence of the prophecy in Isa 9:1–2, geographical areas could be described according to traditional tribal divisions – further evidence that the tribes of Israel were part of first-century Jewish self-consciousness. Matthew mentions the territory of Zebulun (cf. Gen 49:13; Deut 33:18; Josh 19:10–16) and Naphtali (Gen 49:21; Deut 33:23; Josh 19:32–39; 20:7).

The twelve tribes of Israel in the gospels

The phrase 'tribes of Israel' only appears twice in the gospels. Matt 19:28 informs us that those who followed Jesus will 'sit on twelve thrones, judging the twelve tribes of Israel'. Luke 22:30 likewise speaks of those who 'sit on thrones judging the twelve tribes of Israel'. Most, though not all, consider the underlying tradition part of 'Q'. Probably most accept the authenticity of this important Jesus tradition, especially in light of the 'criterion of embarrassment', for it is difficult to explain why the early church would invent a tradition that would give a throne to Judas, one of the Twelve, who was later to betray Jesus.

These verses, especially in light of their probable authenticity and the focus on Jesus and the restoration of Israel in the 'third Quest', have raised much scholarly interest. There is debate concerning the meaning of the word for 'judge' in these verses. Is it referring to the Semitic notion of 'rule' (e.g. Evans) or rather to the (in most arguments, punitive) judgment of the tribes of Israel (e.g. Dunn)? If the latter, Jesus meant to say that the tribes of Israel will not be reconstituted but rather judged. A related debate concerns the issue of whether the twelve disciples are the remnant of Israel, i.e. that they are themselves the fulfilment of Israel's eschatological hopes for the tribes (M. Elliott, S. Bryan), or whether Jesus chose them that they (notionally) represent, embody or symbolize the restoration of the twelve tribes (e.g. E. P. Sanders, J. P. Meier, D. Allison, N. T. Wright). Related to this, Witherington argues that the twelve disciples were not meant to *be* Israel, but rather to *free* them, while Wright, on the other hand, speaks of the twelve disciples as themselves the return-from-exile people. B. Pitre argues that notion of 'return from exile' in Jesus's teaching makes sense in light of the lost ten tribes after the Assyrian exile, and the prophetic tradition expecting their return to the Holy Land. This would mean that Jesus, in choosing twelve disciples, was prophetically indicating that the regathering of all tribes, including those scattered, was at hand. Ultimately, there is no consensus as to the relation between the twelve disciples and the twelve tribes, nor the fate of the tribes of Israel in Jesus's teaching.

CHRIS TILLING

Further reading

Allison, Dale C. *Jesus of Nazareth: Millenarian Prophet*, Minneapolis, MN: Fortress Press, 1998.
Bauckham, Richard. "The Restoration of Israel in Luke–Acts," in James M. Scott (ed.) *Restoration: Old Testament, Jewish and Christian Perspectives*, Leiden: Brill, 2001, pp. 435–87.
Bryan, Steven M. *Jesus and Israel's Traditions of Judgement and Restoration*, SNTSMS, Cambridge: Cambridge University Press, 2002.
Elliott, Mark Adam. *The Survivors of Israel: A Reconsideration of the Theology of Pre-Christian Judaism*, Grand Rapids, MI: Eerdmans, 2000.
Evans, Craig A. "The Twelve Thrones of Israel. Scripture and Politics in Luke 22:24–30," in Bruce Chilton and Craig A. Evans, *Jesus in Context: Temple, Purity, and Restoration*, Brill: 1997, pp. 455–79.
Meier, John P. "Jesus, the Twelve, and the Restoration of Israel," in James M. Scott (ed.) *Restoration: Old Testament, Jewish, and Christian Perspectives*, Köln: Brill, 2001, pp. 365–404.
Mojola, Aloo O. "The 'Tribes' of Israel? A Bible Translator's Dilemma," *JSOT* 81 (1998) 15–29.
Noth, Martin. *Das System der zwölf Stämme Israels*, Stuttgart: W. Kohlhammer, 1930.
Pitre, Brant. *Jesus, the Tribulation, and the End of the Exile: Restoration Eschatology and the Origin of the Atonement*, Tübingen: Mohr Siebeck, 2005.
Sanders, E. P. *Jesus and Judaism*, London: SCM Press, 1985.

Whybray, R. N. "Tribes of Israel," in Bruce M. Metzger (ed.) *The Oxford Companion to the Bible*, New York: Oxford University Press, 1993, pp. 778–79.

Witherington, B. *The Christology of Jesus*, Minneapolis, MN: Fortress Press, 1990.

Wright, N. T. *Jesus and the Victory of God*, London: SPCK, 1996.

TYPOLOGY

Typology is the strategy for discerning the correspondence, pattern, shape or structural affinity between two of God's acts. These divine acts involve God's work through persons, events, and institutions. The words "type" and "antitype" are used to express the relationship between the two events. "Type" comes from the Greek word *tupos* meaning "example" or "model." In a typological interpretation "type" is used to refer to an original historical act that serves as a model for a later, corresponding act ("antitype"). The original may stand in a positive, synthetic relationship to the later event or in a negative, antithetic relationship. An example of a synthetic typology would be the reference to Jesus as "the lamb of God who takes away the sin of the world" (e.g. John 1:29). The imagery of the lamb comes from the Passover event (Exod 12; 1 Cor 5:7), adjusted perhaps by prophetic reference to the servant of the Lord (Isa 53:4–7). The point in this typology is the way that Jesus is similar to the Passover lamb even if his sacrifice is understood to be universal in scope. An example of an antithetical typology would be Paul's reference to Jesus as a second Adam (Rom 5). While Adam and Jesus share a certain likeness as the heads of the first and new creations respectively, Paul's point is their dissimilarity, not their similarity. Through the first Adam sin and death come to all people; through the second Adam righteousness and life are available to all. Both synthetic and antithetic typologies illumine the contemporary act of redemption by correlating it with a known event from the past.

Several theological assumptions drive typology. First, typology assumes that history is the arena of God's saving activity. In any typological scheme the historicity of persons, events and institutions is taken for granted and essential. When Paul refers to Adam as a type of Jesus, it was necessary that Adam had been a person in history and not some mythic figure. The historicity of the type and antitype distinguishes typological from allegorical readings. Second, typology presumes that God is faithful to his promises and that his work in history is constant. This does not mean, of course, that there are no new acts of God; what it does

mean is that a new act can be understood best in reference to God's earlier acts. So typology emphasizes the unity of God's actions in history; as such it is employed theologically as a strategy to underscore the unity between the testaments as a witness to God's acts. Third, typology is based upon a linear view of history in which events intensify or escalate as God's plan moves toward its ultimate goal (*eschaton*). In NT parlance, the new redemptive event may be said to "fulfill" the prophet's word even if the prophecy had an earlier fulfillment (e.g. Matt 1:23; cf. Isa 7). For example, the redemption associated with the Passover lamb involved a particular people at a particular time (Exodus 12) whereas the redemption associated with Jesus as "the lamb of God" intensifies and universalizes the hope.

Typology is evident in Jewish and Christian circles during and after the Second Temple period. The use of typology found in the NT is consistent with and likely derived from hermeneutical practices within the Hebrew Bible.

Hebrew Bible

The writers, editors and compilers of the Hebrew Bible employed typology to recall God's past faithfulness and to anticipate new acts of redemption. Creation and exodus themes are common. In Isa 65:17–25, for example, the prophet describes God's promise to create a new heaven and a new earth that stands in continuity with and yet eclipses the first creation. God's work to repair the world effectively makes it new again, reverses the curse, and returns it to its paradisiacal form. In this way God's earlier covenant promises to his people can be realized: long life in the land, prosperity, peace, God's permanent presence with his people.

Because of its significance in Israelite history, the exodus becomes the "type" for new hopes for redemption as Israel is enslaved by and in exile in hostile nations. So, e.g., in Isa 11:16 the prophet foresees a day when the Lord will make a highway out of Assyria for the remnant just as he brought Israel up from the land of Egypt (cf. Isa 40:3–5; 43:16–24; 49:8–13). Similarly, in Mic 7:14–20 the prophet envisages a new act of redemption that will be like earlier times when Israel came out of Egypt. But not all new exodus imagery is future-oriented. Within the stories of Israel's past typological correspondence is also evident. So, e.g., the Lord promises Joshua that he will be with him as he had been with Moses (Jos 1–5), thus fulfilling the earlier, divine promises. Joshua becomes a new

Moses, parting the Jordan and reinitiating the Passover. These later acts of redemption take on a new meaning precisely because of their associations with the older types.

Another typology involves the expectation of a "new covenant." Jeremiah prophesies that God will make a new covenant with Israel in the future (31:31–34; cf. Ezek 36:22–32). Because of its reference to coming out of Egypt, this is a variation on the new exodus theme. But the new covenant typology is primarily antithetical, for the oracle points out all the ways in which the new covenant will not be like the old.

Jesus and the New Testament

New Testament authors make extensive use of typology in order to express their understanding of the transcendent significance of Jesus and his work of salvation. To be successful, typologies depend on the competence of the audience. While any typology can be lost on some hearers – assuming that the NT Gospels were initially read aloud – the ideal audience will perceive the correspondence between type and antitype. Some of the typologies listed below, though certainly not all, derive from Jesus' own teaching and use of scripture. Others are expansions or reflections on his significance by later theologians. Scholars disagree on the methods used to distinguish between dominical and non-dominical sayings. As we have seen with the Hebrew Bible, creation, exodus, and covenant typologies dominate (Ellis 2001: 105–6).

New covenant

In the words of institution (Mark 14:24; Matt 26:28; Luke 22:20) Jesus is said to appropriate the "new covenant" prophesied by Jeremiah (31:31–34) and link it with the pouring out of his blood. His crucifixion is understood to establish the new covenant, symbolized by the cup of wine from the Passover celebration. The new covenant inaugurated by Jesus is thereby linked with both the Passover as a perpetual remembrance of the exodus and the new covenant of Jeremiah.

Son of God

For many reasons the NT employs the title "Son of God" in reference to Jesus. The interest here is the typological association expressed in fulfillment language: "out of Egypt I called my Son" (Matt 2:15; quoting Hos 11:1). Clearly, this is an example of exodus typology that links the flight and return

of Joseph, Mary and Jesus from Egypt with Israel's exodus. In the type (Hos 11:1), "my Son" refers to Israel. Effectively, the Evangelist's use of the quotation constitutes Jesus as a new Israel. This means that Jesus takes up Israel's role in relation to God's work in the world. But the typology itself has antithetical elements because Jesus is not only like Israel, he is also unlike Israel. Whereas Hosea's Israel ("my son") abandoned and disappointed God (Hos 11:1–7), Matthew's Jesus obeys and is well-pleasing to God as the Son (e.g. Matt 3:17).

Son of David

The title "Son of David" is associated with Jesus in a variety of settings (e.g. Matt 1:1, 6; Mark 11:9–10 and par.; Mark 12:35–37 and par., cf. Rom 1:3–4) and has typological overtones. The titular use is almost certainly derived from 2 Sam 7:12–16, commonly understood as God's covenant with David. Within the narrative of 2 Samuel, the "son of David" refers to Solomon, but already by the time of the Chronicler (1 Chr 17:11–14) the promise has taken on broader, messianic significance. In Matthew's genealogy, for instance, Jesus' messianic status as "the Son of David" is demonstrated by tracing his lineage through the royal line (Matt 1:1, 6, 17). Further, the Evangelist employs gematria to structure Jesus' genealogy around the number fourteen (14), which is the number associated with David's name (Matt 1:17). Although these construals are not dominical, they may depend on Jesus' self-understanding (cf. Mark 12:35–37 and par.). By referring to Jesus as "the Son of David," it became possible to associate him with God's promise of an everlasting kingdom. The title "Son of David" becomes an explicit claim to Jesus' messiahship.

Son of Man

Jesus' favorite self-designation appears to have been "Son of Man." Since other NT writers do not use it, it is almost certainly a dominical expression. According to the intracanonical gospels, Jesus employs it in a variety of settings. Interpreters have debated its meaning, and to date there is no scholarly consensus. One prominent theory, however, relates the expression "Son of Man" with Dan 7:12–14. In this text Daniel sees a vision in which "one like a son of man" comes on the clouds before the Ancient of Days and receives an eternal, universal kingdom. In the vision's interpretation Daniel identifies the son of man with the saints of the Most High (Dan 7:18, 22), taken as a reference to Israel. If this is the background, the expression

"Son of Man" used by Jesus connects him with Israel's eschatological task of ruling the nations. Pslm 8 may also have played a role in the christological formulation "Son of Man." With its celebration of creation and Adam's dominion over it, Pslm 8 supplied the early Jesus movement with a variation on the creation typology.

Servant of the Lord

The gospels never explicitly designate Jesus "the Servant of the Lord" (cf. Acts 3:13, 26), but a Servant typology appears beneath the surface of the narratives. The designation derives from prophetic oracles recorded in Isaiah (42, 49, 50, esp. 53). In the prophetic stream, the Servant is identified with Israel (e.g. 49:3) so its christological appropriation links Jesus with the covenant people. NT writers and perhaps even Jesus himself understood the vocation of the Servant as "fulfilled" in his actions. Jesus' teachings and healings are said to fulfill the prophet's message in proclaiming justice and bringing hope to the nations (Matt 12:17–21; quoting Isa 42:1–4; cf. Matt 8:16–17). His coming arrest and trial fulfill the oracle that the Servant must be counted among the transgressors (Luke 22:37; quoting Isa 53:12). It is particularly in the details of his passion that allusive use is made of Isaiah 53, where suffering for others is the primary vocation of God's Servant (see, e.g., Mark 10:45). If Jesus understood himself to be the Servant of the Lord, fulfilling Israel's destiny, then these oracles may well have directed his mission.

Prophet-like-Moses

According to Deut 18:15–18, God will raise up a prophet-like-Moses to lead the covenant people. Apparently, this expectation was current in the Second Temple period and assisted in the formulation and expansion of certain christological claims. While this language is more explicit in Acts (e.g. Acts 3:22; quoting Deut 18:15–20; cf. Acts 7:37), echoes of this hope can be heard in a variety of settings in the gospels. In the transfiguration, e. g., the heavenly voice declares: "this is My beloved Son, listen to him!" (Mark 9:7 and par.). The command to listen recalls God's directive to his people when the eschatological prophet arrives. In Matthew's Gospel, a Moses typology is clearly at work. First, the slaughter in Bethlehem and Jesus' escape is reminiscent of a similar carnage in Egypt under the Pharaoh's cruel policies (cf. Matt 1–2; Exod 1–2). Second, as we saw above in regard to Hos 11:1, the return of Joseph and his family from

Egypt to the land of promise has resonance with Moses and the exodus. Third, Jesus' success during the wilderness temptations stands in typological antithesis to Israel's failures in the wilderness under Moses' leadership. Fourth, Jesus ascends the mountain and writes his teachings on the hearts of his disciples in ways similar and yet dissimilar to Moses' ascent of Mt Sinai. In these and other ways, the portrayal of Jesus as the eschatological prophet-like-Moses provides an important clue to the early Christians' assessment of his significance.

Of course, Jesus' work is linked with prophets other than Moses. For example, in announcing the fulfillment of God's jubilee promises, Jesus associates his mission with Elijah's and Elisha's work among non-Jews (Luke 4:1–30; 1 Kgs 17–18; 2 Kgs 5). Since rumors around Jesus relate him to prophets (Matt 16:13–20), it is likely that the earliest appraisals of his significance among "the people of the land" regard his prophetic role. If, as the gospels portray, Jesus anticipated his death, then he did so in solidarity with prophets before him (e.g. Matt 23:37).

"Something greater"

The phrase "something greater" characterizes three sayings in Matthew 12. Each has typological import. In Matt 12:6 Jesus justifies his disciples' harvesting of grain on the Sabbath by appealing to David's example (1 Sam 21:1–7) and the weekly violation of the Sabbath by priests performing their duties. The declaration "something greater than the temple is here" (Matt 12:6) likely refers to Jesus himself and by extension the community he establishes. By appealing to the deeds of David and the priests, Jesus associates his activities with royal and priestly actions. It is impossible to overestimate the significance of the Jerusalem Temple. However, because of corruption the Temple and its leadership had already fallen out of favor with many Jews. The constitution of the community of Jesus as a temple "not made with hands" (Mark 14:58) is a typological move already made by the people of Qumran who left the Temple because of corruption and withdrew to the wilderness to establish a new temple and new covenant people.

In Matt 12:38–41 Jesus responds to the Pharisees' demand for a sign by promising "the sign of Jonah" and concludes by saying "something greater than Jonah is here." For Matthew Jonah becomes a type of Jesus in two ways: (1) Jonah's near-death experience in the belly of the fish three days and three nights corresponds to "the Son of Man"'s death and burial for three days in the heart of the earth (Jonah 1–2); (2) Jonah's success in turning Nineveh back to God (Jonah 3–4) corresponds to the success Jesus has in preaching to Israel and the nations. The competent audience will also pick up on the antithetical elements in the typology. Jonah's recalcitrance stands in opposition to Jesus' faithful obedience.

In Matt 12:42 Jesus commends the Queen of the South for traveling far to learn Solomon's wisdom and simultaneously condemns those who refuse to acknowledge God's wisdom. He concludes by declaring "something greater than Solomon is here." Typologically speaking, Jesus corresponds to Solomon (who is also a son of David); both are purveyors of wisdom. But later generations of Christians expand the association by identifying Jesus with divine wisdom (*sophia*; e.g. 1 Cor 1:24, 30).

With each of these sayings the phrase "something greater" depicts an escalation which is already evident in the work of Jesus.

The serpent in the wilderness

According to John 3:14–15, Jesus said: "And just as Moses lifted up the serpent in the wilderness, in the same way the Son of Man must be lifted up so all who believe in him may have eternal life." The type recalls the healing of many Israelites afflicted by venomous snakes in the wilderness. Following God's instructions, Moses fashioned a serpent and lifted it up on a standard so that anyone who looked at it would have life (Num 21:4–9). The antitype refers to the lifting up of the Son of Man, i.e. the crucifixion, and its universalized result: all who believe have eternal life.

The stone

At the end of the parable of the wicked tenants (Mark 12:1–9 and par.) Jesus applies Ps 118:22–23 to the situation he faced, i.e. the growing opposition and final rejection (crucifixion) by the powers-that-be in Jerusalem. As it stands in the synoptics, Jesus re-plots the story implicit in the passage to foreshadow his crucifixion (rejected stone) and resurrection (rejected stone made cornerstone). If, as some have concluded, the rejected stone referred originally to Israel, this passage is another example of an Israel–Jesus typology. Jesus' rejection is typified in Israel's defeat at the hands of its enemies. His vindication is anticipated as "the Lord's doing." Stone passages are found elsewhere in the NT in reference to Jesus and the church (e.g. Acts 4:11; Rom 9:33; 1 Pet 2:1–8). Some "stone" passages may

have even taken on messianic implications (e.g. Isa 8:14; 28:16; cf. Rom 9:30–33).

"The twelve"

While Jesus had a sizeable company of disciples (e.g. seventy or seventy-two in Luke 10:1), including men and women (e.g. Luke 8:1–3), the NT Gospels indicate that he established a special group known as "the Twelve" (Mark 3:13–19 and par.). Apparently, "the Twelve" had unique access to Jesus and served to extend his mission in the world by preaching and healing (e.g. Mark 3:14; Matt 10:1–42). Jesus' election comprises a prophetic act that effectively establishes a new people of God, the antitype to the twelve tribes of Israel. As the foundation of a new people of God, "the Twelve" come out of Israel and yet have eschatological significance in judging the people of God (Matt 19:28).

Conclusion

The NT's use of the OT is central to how early Christians did theology. Typology is the primary method used to read and appropriate Scripture. As we have seen, most typological readings emphasize the transcendent significance of Jesus and by extension his community as a new Israel.

DAVID B. CAPES

Further reading

Baker, D. L. *Two Testaments, One Bible*, revised edition, Downers Grove, IL: InterVarsity Press, 1991.

Daube, David. *The Exodus Pattern in the Bible*, London: Faber & Faber, 1963.

Ellis, E. Earle. *The Old Testament in Early Christianity: Canon and Interpretation in Light of Modern Research*, WUNT 54, Tübingen: J. C. B. Mohr (Paul Siebeck), 1991.

—— *History and Interpretation in New Testament Perspective*, SBL Biblical Interpretation Series Volume 54, Atlanta, GA: Society of Biblical Literature, 2001.

Evans, Craig. "Typology," in Joel B. Green and Scot McKnight (eds) *Dictionary of Jesus and the Gospels*, Downers Grove, IL: InterVarsity Press, 1992.

Fishbane, Michael. *Biblical Interpretation in Ancient Israel*, Oxford: Clarendon Press, 1985.

France, R. T. *Jesus and the Old Testament: His Application of Old Testament Passages to Himself and His Mission*, Grand Rapids, MI: Baker, 1971.

Goppelt, Leonhard. *Typos: The Typological Interpretation of the Old Testament in the New*, trans. D. H. Madvig, Grand Rapids, MI: Eerdmans, 1982.

McKnight, Scot. "Jesus and Prophetic Actions," *BBR* 10 (2000) 197–232.

V

VERMES, GEZA

Geza Vermes was born in 1924 in Hungary in a Jewish family that converted to Roman Catholicism. Studied in Budapest and Louvain; ordained 1950; wrote a doctoral dissertation on the historical framework of the Dead Sea Scrolls (1953). Left the priesthood and the Catholic Church in 1957. In 1965 he became a reader, later professor, of Jewish Studies at the University of Oxford. Gradually he became more immersed in the Jewish society, and in 1970 he became a member of the Liberal Jewish Synagogue of London.

Vermes's name is closely linked with his popular English translation of the Dead Sea Scrolls (first published in 1962), the rewriting and re-editing of Emil Schürer's classical work, *The History of the Jewish People in the Age of Jesus Christ* (1973–87), and his trilogy on Jesus the Jew (Vermes 1973, 1983 and 1993).

Jesus, the Galilean holy man

Vermes's main contribution to the study of the historical Jesus is probably his revival of the theory that Jesus has to be understood as a *hasid*, a Galilean holy man, clearly distinguished from the rabbi. A *hasid* was, according to Vermes, a pious and charismatic Jew who worked miracles. Typical representatives for the *hasidim* are Hanina ben Dosa and Honi the Circle-drawer. Honi, active in the first century BCE, was famous for his powerful prayer in time of drought (cf. *m. Ta'an.* 3.8; Joseph, *Ant* 14.22–24), while Hanina ben Dosa,

active in the first century CE, is described as a pious man with power to enact healings through prayer (cf. *b. Ber.* 34b). These figures, in the tradition from Elijah and Elisha, represent a charismatic Judaism typical for the rural Galilee, distinguished from the Pharisaic Judaism of Judea.

Vermes has been criticized for not taking into account all relevant material on the *hasidim*; if he had done so the difference between them and Jesus would be more conspicuous (cf. Freyne; Martola). In any case there are marked differences: Unlike Honi and Hanina Jesus did not pray for miracles, and he spoke and acted in his own name (cf. Evans 213–43). Further, it is difficult to uphold charismatic Judaism as a specifically Galilean phenomenon; only Hanina may be placed in Galilee. More generally, the notion of Galilee isolated from Judea and from Pharisaic influence has been seriously questioned (cf., e.g., Deines 145–53; 278 ff.). Besides, there was no sharp and clear distinction between Rabbis and holy men. The validity of Vermes's theory has also been questioned because it is based, at least partly, on late rabbinical material (Meier 581–88).

The son of man

Another issue to which Vermes has made a noteworthy contribution is the interpretation of the expression "Son of man," frequently found in the gospels. In Aramaic (the language spoken by Jesus), the phrase essentially means "human being," and often serves as an indefinite pronoun. According to Vermes the phrase was also used as a circumlocution by which the speaker referred to himself, in contexts implying awe, reserve or modesty; in Aramaic the expression was never used as a title. The authentic occurrences of the expression in the gospels must be interpreted similarly. Passages that directly (Mark 13:26; 14:62) or indirectly refer to Dan 7:13 – a text that in the course of time acquired a definite messianic association – are not genuine, but reflect a secondary interpretation of the phrase "the son of man" in the early church.

Though Vermes's interpretation has been accepted by many scholars, others have contested parts of it. First, the Aramaic idiom "Son of man" is clearly generic; the phrase is self-referential only because the speaker is included in the class of human beings (cf. Jer 1971: 257–76). Besides, the evidence for the circumlocution for "I" is much later than the first century and some of the supposed evidence is not relevant (cf. Fitzmyer). Second, Jesus' use of the phrase cannot be fully understood in light of the Aramaic idiom. Jesus on the whole referred to "*the* son of man" (with the definite article), which in all likelihood is meant to call to mind a particular son of man, i.e. the one known from Daniel 7. There are good reasons to believe that this usage originated by Jesus himself since there are no evidence of a Son of Man Christology in the early church (cf. Moule 10–22).

Vermes's methodological approach

Vermes's approach to the study of Jesus is programmatically seen in the subtitle of his first book on Jesus: "A Historian's Reading of the Gospels." He claims to do his research without any ulterior motive; he is just searching for "the historical truth" (1983/2003: 1). It is, however, axiomatic for Vermes that the "real" Jesus was not like the Christ of the Church (1973: 17; cf. 1993: 214). The material, e.g. concerning Jesus' resurrection and *parousia* (second coming), has to be attributed to the "creative imagination" of nascent Christianity (1983/2003: 23). Basically Vermes seems to utilize the criterion of dissimilarity in his evaluation of the gospel material: If a teaching has no parallel in Judaism or in the primitive church, it most probably originates in Jesus. His expressed reservations about the criterion (1983/2003: 20) are, however, only manifest in relation to ancient Judaism. By and large the features in Jesus' life and teaching that have a parallel in other Jewish sources are regarded as authentic. Jesus is depicted as a pious Jew who taught and did nothing that was contrary to the Law. Possible evidence of the contrary (e.g. Mark 7:15) is dismissed as inauthentic. Since Jesus

is interpreted by the categories of first-century Palestinian Judaism, there is little room for the possibility that Jesus could have had a unique self-understanding (cf. Hagner 1984: 257, 263). Jesus was "second to none in profundity of insight and grandeur of character" (1973: 224); nevertheless he fits well into the category of the Galilean holy man.

The Christological question

According to Vermes Jesus did not think that he was the Messiah. This was, however, the conviction of his followers. "By the end of the first century Christianity had lost sight of the real Jesus and of the original meaning of his message. Paul, John, and their churches replaced him by the other-worldly Christ of faith" (2000: 263). This change was, according to Vermes, due to a change in cultural perspective: from the Semitic, Palestinian, Jewish setting to the Greek-speaking pagan Mediterranean world.

Objections can, and have been, raised against this description of the development of Christology (cf. Knights). First, despite Vermes's conviction to the contrary (cf. 1983/2003: 24), it is difficult to uphold such a strong dichotomy between Jewish and Hellenistic culture. Besides, Vermes seems to neglect the indisputable Jewishness of both Paul and John, a feature emphasized in recent research. Besides, one has to take seriously the evidence for a "high" christology already in Paul's letters, even in earlier material utilized by Paul. To suggest, as Vermes does (2000: 78–79), that, e.g., the Christological hymn in Philippians 2:5–11 is inserted in the letter by a later editor, is highly speculative and – of course – without any support in the manuscript tradition.

Vermes is a profiled scholar whose views will continue to be debated in future research. His most lasting influence on New Testament scholarship is undoubtedly his contribution to today's common opinion that Jesus was a Jew and has to be interpreted within the frames of first-century Judaism.

REIDAR HVALVIK

Further reading

Deines, R. *Jüdische Steingefässe und pharisäische Frömmigkeit*, WUNT 2:52, Tübingen: Mohr-Siebeck, 1993.
Evans, C. A. *Jesus and His Contemporaries: Comparative Studies*, Leiden: Brill, 1995.
Fitzmyer, J. A. "Another View of the 'Son of Man' Debate," *JSNT* 4 (1979) 58–68.
Freyne, S. "The Charismatic," in J. J. Collins and G. W. E. Nickelsburg (eds) *Ideal Figures in Ancient Judaism:*

Profiles and Paradigms, SBLSCS 12, Chico, CA: Scholars Press, 1980, pp. 223–58.

Hagner, D. A. *The Jewish Reclamation of Jesus: An Analysis and Critique of the Modern Jewish Study of Jesus*, Grand Rapids, MI: Zondervan, 1984.

Hubbard, B. J. "Geza Vermes's Contribution to Historical Jesus Studies: An Assessment," *SBLSP* 24, 1985, pp. 29–44.

Jeremias, J. *New Testament Theology. Volume One: The Proclamation of Jesus*, London: SCM Press, 1971.

Knights, C. "Jesus' Changing Faces: A Response to Geza Vermes," *The Expository Times* 113. 6 (2002) 203–5.

Martola, N. "Jesus – the Jew," in J. Neusner (ed.) *Approaches to Ancient Judaism*. New Series 7, Atlanta, GA: Scholars Press, 1995, pp. 189–201.

Meier, J. P. *A Marginal Jew: Rethinking the Historical Jesus. Volume Two: Mentor, Message, and Miracles*, New York: Doubleday, 1994.

Moule, C. F. D. *The Origin of Christology*, Cambridge: Cambridge University Press, 1977.

Vermes, G. *The Dead Sea Scrolls in English*, Harmondsworth: Penguin, 1962.

—— "The Use of *bar nash/bar nasha* in Jewish Aramaic," in M. Black (ed.) *An Aramaic Approach to the Gospels and Acts*, third edition, Oxford: Clarendon, 1967, pp. 310–28.

—— *Jesus the Jew: A Historian's Reading of the Gospels*, London: Collins, 1973.

—— *Post-biblical Jewish Studies*, Leiden: Brill, 1975.

—— "The Gospels without Christology," in A. E. Harvey (ed.) *God Incarnate: Story and Belief*, London: SPCK, 1981, pp. 55–68.

—— *Jesus and the World of Judaism*, London: SCM Press, 1983; republished as *Jesus in His Jewish Context*; Minneapolis, MN: Fortress, 2003.

—— *The Religion of Jesus the Jew*, London: SCM Press, 1993.

—— *Providential Accidents: An Autobiography*, London: SCM Press, 1998.

—— *The Changing Faces of Jesus*, London: Allen Lane, 2000.

—— *The Authentic Gospel of Jesus*, London: Allen Lane, 2003.

—— *The Complete Dead Sea Scrolls in English*, revised edition, New York: Penguin, 2004.

—— *Scrolls, Scriptures, and Early Christianity*, London: T. & T. Clark International, 2005.

—— *The Passion*, London: Penguin, 2005.

VIOLENCE

Violence is physical force employed for the purpose of hurting and humiliating another person. In his personal ethical teaching, Jesus rejects the use of violence, even the biblical *jus talionis*, the principle of an eye for an eye and a tooth for a tooth (Exod 21:23–25; Lev 24:19–20; Deut 19:21). Matthew and Luke preserve two different collections of sayings that give expression to Jesus' teaching on non-retaliation (Matt 5:38–42; Luke 6:27–30). In the Sermon on the Mount, Jesus says "not to resist an evil person" (Matt 5:39) and in Luke's Sermon on the Plain he explains symbolically that "If someone strikes you on one cheek, turn to him the other

also" (Luke 6:29). Probably Jesus believes that the *jus talionis* set out in the Torah, though a means of controlling vengeance, is not actually God's true will, which is that no revenge should be taken at all. Jesus' summary of the Law by means of the ethical principle of reciprocity precludes the use of violence against another, since no one wants to be the recipient of violence (Matt 7:12; Luke 6:31).

Jesus teaches that a person should love his or her enemies (Matt 5:44–45; Luke 6:27–28, 35b). He says that his hearers have heard that they should love their neighbors and hate their enemies. The former refers to Lev 19:18, where the Israelites are commanded to love their fellow Israelites; the latter, however, is not found in the Torah, but seems to have arisen as the correlation to Lev 19:18: if one is to love one's neighbor, one should also hate one's enemy, which assumes that one's enemy is also God's enemy. The Essenes hold that its members have a religious duty to hate those who oppose their community and God, who are known as the sons of darkness or the men of the pit (1QS 1.9–11; 9.21–22; see Ps 139:21–22). By contrast, Jesus teaches that the correlation of hating one's enemies does not follow from the commandment to love one's neighbor; rather, one should also love one's enemies (see parallels in Prov 25:21–22; Sir 28:6–7; *Jos. Asen.* 28:14; see 23:9; *T. Jos.* 18). He believes that God's will is to love even those who intend to do one harm. In loving one's enemies, a person is being like God, who gives his blessings to all without discrimination: "He causes his sun to rise on the evil and the good, and sends rain on the righteous and the unrighteous" (Matt 5:45). Not hating others obviously would remove all grounds for inflicting violence on another person. Jesus also teaches that inflicting violence inevitably leads to suffering violence: "All who take the sword die by the sword" (Matt 26:52).

Absent from Jesus' teaching is any notion that Jews have a duty to use violence in the cause of their religion. The example of the biblical hero Phineas, whom the Maccabeans emulate in their use of violence against Law-breaking Jews and gentile oppressors, does not occur among Jesus' sayings (see 1 Macc 2:26–27). Clearly, Jesus' Zealot contemporaries see it as their religious obligation to use violence against those they judge to be enemies of God. The so-called sicarii, for example, take it upon themselves to assassinate in public high-ranking Jews whom they consider to be collaborators with the Romans and therefore traitors (*Ant.* 20.186; *J.W.* 2.254–57). The author of *Pss. Sol.* 17 expects the Messiah, no doubt with the assistance of the righteous under his leadership, to purge Jerusalem of Jewish sinners and Gentiles (17:3, 22–25, 35), and in *Sib. Or.* 3.55–65 the appearance of the kingdom of God will mean the destruction of the Romans (see *T. Mos.* 10:1–12). Likewise, the *War Scroll* foresees a seven-year eschatological war of the sons of light against the sons of darkness and the Kittim (Romans). But no such teaching about the kingdom of God is found in the canonical gospels. In fact, because of his openness to Law-breaking Jews, Jesus is known as friend of tax-collectors and sinners (Matt 11:19 = Luke 7:34), and his occasional encounters with non-Jews are positive (Mark 7:24–30 = Matt 15:21–28; Luke 7:1–10 = Matt 8:5–13; John 4:43–54). Jesus' directive that "Whoever forces you to go one mile, go with him two" is distinctly anti-Zealot and anti-revolutionary, since he is referring to being pressed into service and forced to carry messages or equipment for the benefit of the occupying Romans (Matt 5:41).

Jesus does use the language of violence when speaking about the conflict of the kingdom of God with Satan's kingdom. There are two different versions of a saying about the plundering of the strong man, both of which make the same point: in order to subdue a strong man and then plunder his home one must be stronger than he is (Mark 3:27 = Matt 12:29; Luke 11:21–22; see *Gos. Thom.* 35). Jesus is speaking metaphorically, for the strong man is Satan and the house is his kingdom or sphere of influence. He is claiming that there has come one who is stronger than Satan and is in the process of attacking and plundering his kingdom, which is an oblique reference to his exorcisms.

There are a few passages that are said to provide evidence that Jesus advocates the use of violence in the cause of religion. Jesus' saying that he has not come to bring peace to the earth but division or a sword is said to imply this (Luke 12:51; Matt 10:34). But Jesus is not saying that his goal is violent revolution, but that Jews will be divided on account of him. Jesus also drives the money changers and sellers of sacrificial animals from the Temple, but there is no evidence that he inflicted violence on anyone in the process (Mark 11:15–19 = Matt 21:12–17 = Luke 19:45–48; John 2:13–22). Finally, after his last Passover Jesus tells his disciples that their situation will now be different from the time when he sent them out to preach the kingdom of God. In this context he instructs them, "If you do not have a sword, sell your cloak and buy one" (Luke 22:36). Probably Jesus' point made symbolically is that the disciples will be in danger after his arrest. It is safe to say that he does not intend for his disciples to procure swords and attack those who oppose them (see Luke 22:49–51). At most Jesus intends that being armed will function as a deterrent to being attacked.

BARRY D. SMITH

Further reading

Brandon, S. G. F. *Jesus and the Zealots. A Study of the Political Factor in Primitive Christianity*, Manchester: Manchester University Press, 1967.

Hengel, M. *Victory over Violence: Jesus and the Revolutionists*, Philadelphia, PA: Fortress, 1973.

—— *Was Jesus a Revolutionist?*, Philadelphia, PA: Fortress, 1971.

Horsley, R. A. *Jesus and the Spiral of Violence. Popular Jewish Resistance in Roman Palestine*, Philadelphia, PA: Fortress, 1993.

Lampe, G. W. H. "The Two Swords (Luke 22:35–38)," in E. Bammel and C. F. D. Moule (eds) *Jesus and the Politics of his Day*, Cambridge: Cambridge University Press, 1984.

Meyer, B. F. *The Aims of Jesus*, London: SCM Press, 1979.

Piper, J. *"Love Your Enemies"*, Cambridge and New York: Cambridge University Press, 1979.

Yoder, J. H. *The Politics of Jesus*, Grand Rapids, MI: Eerdmans, 1972.

VISIONS

References to Jesus' visionary experience are not numerous, yet their significance should not be underestimated. The accounts of the baptism in the Synoptic Gospels (Matt 3:16–17; Mark 1:10; Luke 3:21–22; in John the baptism account is presented as a vision of John the Baptist, not Jesus, cf. John 1:32), and the transfiguration (Matt 17:1–8; Mark 9:2–7; Luke 9: 28–36) are key moments in the synoptic narratives. Apart from these, which are attested in all three Synoptic Gospels, Luke records a vision of Jesus in which Satan is seen 'falling like lightning from heaven' (Luke 10:18) which has its parallels in John 12:31 and Revelation 12:9.

The visionary background in the Bible and ancient Judaism

Visions have a central role in biblical religion, the call-visions of Isaiah (Isa 6) and Ezekiel (Ezek 1) being the most obvious examples. Visions are central to the apocalypses ascribed to heroes of the Jewish past, such as Enoch (*1 Enoch* 14), Abraham (*Apocalypse of Abraham*) and Levi (*Testament of Levi* 2). Recent study has shown that the world of early Christianity was one in which dreams and visions and their interpretation were all a crucial part of religious culture. The New Testament evidence indicates that visions and dreams were a significant part of early Christian experience and were perhaps one of the most important driving forces in early Christian religious development. Because visionary practice may have formed a significant part of the religion of various groups within the Second Temple period, not least the early Christians, caution was expressed in emerging rabbinic Judaism. Thus, in the *m. Ḥag.* 2:1 brief reference is made to exposition of the first chapters of Genesis and Ezekiel and the visionary potential of the latter. It seems probable that esoteric traditions associated with Ezek 1 and similar passages were inherited by some of the early Tannaim from this apocalyptic milieu. These traditions (as in apocalyptic) had both an exegetical and a 'practical' (i.e. visionary–mystical) aspect. Ecstatic–mystical and esoteric–exegetical traditions were being developed in circles associated with some rabbinic teachers during the first century CE. Perhaps in the light of evidence from 2 Cor 12:2 we might surmise that Gamaliel, Paul's teacher, was familiar with these traditions. By the early second century the esoteric tradition seems to have been known to and practised by leading Rabbis such as Akiba. We know Paul was influenced by apocalyptic ascent ideas, and he emphasises the importance of this visionary element as the basis of his practice (Gal 1:12 and 1:16 cf. Acts 22:17). Perhaps he should be linked with those other significant figures who became marginal to rabbinic Judaism or a focus of hostility: Eliezer ben Hyrcanus, Eleazar ben Arak and Elisha ben Abuyah. After all, his apocalyptic outlook enabled him to act on his eschatological convictions, so that his apocalypse of Jesus Christ became the basis for his practice of admitting Gentiles to the messianic age without the Law of Moses. The threat posed by apocalyptic may be discerned elsewhere (and indeed could have contributed to the development of Christology in early Christianity). It may be that the controversy about two centres of divine power with roots deep within the apocalyptic tradition may lie behind the stories of Elisha ben Abuyah's confrontation with the archangel Metatron, when he was led through his visionary experience to believe that there were two gods in heaven, a major betrayal of Jewish monotheism (Segal).

Jesus and visions

In discussions of the historical Jesus the baptism and transfiguration have very little part to play, except at the margins of scholarship. In the gospels, just as Ezekiel had glimpsed the fiery manifestation of the divine glory by a river in Babylon rather than in the Jerusalem Temple, that which angels had longed to look upon appears in humble surroundings (Luke 10.23, cf. 1 Pet 1.11). The Markan version of the baptism has connections with Ezekiel, the 'open heaven' (Ezek 1:1) though the content of the vision has little close link with other biblical texts even if the voice from heaven echoes Isa 42:1 and Ps 2:9. In the Synoptic Gospels the story functions as a typical prophetic commissioning experience analogous to Isa 6 and Ezek 1, though with the major difference that the commission is not to be a prophet so much as revealing the identity of Jesus as divinely appointed son. The 'high' Christology in this passage has led to suspicion of its authenticity. Nevertheless one should not exclude too quickly the possibility that the basis of such an account may reflect the kind of visionary encounter, which is typical in Jewish apocalypticism and may have been part of mystical practice in Second Temple Judaism. The importance of the baptism of John as a context for Jesus' own prophetic vocation is suggested by the account of the debate about Jesus' authority (Matt 21:23–7; Mark 11:27–33; Luke 20:2–8).

Similarly, the transfiguration has affinities with Ezekiel. Indeed, the passage with which it has the closest affinities is Rev 1:213 ff. and three similar theophanic passages in *Apoc. Ab.* 110 and *Joseph and Aseneth* 14. Its role in the gospels as we have them is relatively clear: it functions as a further validation of the calling of Jesus in which an inner circle of chosen disciples is let into the mystery of Jesus' person and calling. This pattern of esotericism is familiar to us from the early rabbinic tradition where the secrets of divinity and creation (*ma'aseh merkabah* and *ma'aseh bereshith*) are reserved for those qualified to receive and understand them. Few discussions of the historical Jesus include any significant discussion of the transfiguration, but its high christological content in its present form should not lead to immediate suspicion that participation in such mystical experiences of heavenly transformation is necessarily to be excluded as part of the basis of reconstructing the Jesus of history. While nothing is said about ascent into the heavens in this passage, or for that matter the transformation of the disciples into angelic existence, the participation of the life of heaven on earth is something which is central to aspects of the communal experience described in the Dead Sea Scrolls (e.g. 1QH 3:20, etc.).

The brief description of Jesus' sight of Satan failing like lightning from heaven suggests the report of a vision which Jesus had which is regarded as the basis for the kinds of exorcistic ministry booth Jesus engages in, and his disciples as well. The form of the saying is peculiar. The imperfect tense suggests perhaps a past experience and perhaps one which Jesus was wont to see on a number of occasions. The content of the saying has affinities with both John 12:31 and Rev 12:7, and like the baptism story is very much tied up with the heart of Jesus' activity.

Throughout the history of Christianity visionary experience has been a key motor of change and challenge. In this respect, the New Testament is no exception, and the Jesus tradition especially. We can understand Jesus' prophetic vocation and the kind of authority which differs from 'the scribes' (Mark 1:22) if we allow the possibility that the brief but centrally important visionary accounts represent a key way into the understanding of Jesus' role and sense of his identity.

CHRISTOPHER ROWLAND

Further reading

Ashton, J. *The Religion of Paul the Apostle*, New Haven, CT: Yale University Press 2000.

Chilton, B. *Rabbi Jesus: An Intimate Biography*, New York: Doubleday, 2000.

Collins, J. J. *The Encyclopaedia of Apocalypticism*, Vol. 1, New York: Continuum 2000.

Flannery-Dailey, F. *Dreamers, Scribes, and Priests. Jewish Dreams in the Hellenistic and Roman Eras*, JSJSup 90, Leiden: Brill, 2004.

Rowland, C. *The Open Heaven: A Study of Apocalyptic in Judaism and Early Christianity*, London: SPCK, 1982.

—— "A Man Clothed in White Linen: A Study in the Development of Jewish Angelology," *JSNT* 24 (1985) 99–110.

—— *Christian Origins: An Account of the Setting and Character of the Most Important Messianic Sect of Judaism*, revised edition, London: SPCK, 2002.

Segal, A. *Paul the Convert: The Apostolate and Apostasy of Saul the Pharisee*, New Haven, CT: Yale University Press 1990.

Smith, M. *Clement of Alexandria and a Secret Gospel of Mark*, Cambridge, MA: Harvard, 1973.

WEISS, JOHANNES

Johannes Weiss (1863–1914) was the son of the NT scholar Bernhard Weiss and the son-in-law of the eminent liberal systematic theological Albrecht Ritschl. After theological studies in Marburg, Berlin, and Göttingen and after advanced studies in the areas of NT theology and the history of the NT canon, Weiss received in 1888 the *venia legendi* to teach "the exegesis of the New Testament" from the University of Göttingen. Weiss first teaches in Göttingen (1888 to 1895); he is awarded the title of doctor of theology in 1895. In 1895 he is appointed *ordentlicher Professor* by the University of Marburg (successor of E. Kühl), where he teaches from 1895 to 1908. In Marburg he is co-founder of the Nationalsozialer Verein, a political party of non-conservative Christian social democrats. He accepts the responsibility for reviewing new publications on the Synoptic Gospels in the *Theologische Rundschau* (established in 1897). In the spring of 1908 Weiss accepts a call to the University of Heidelberg (successor of A. Deissmann), where he teaches from 1908 to 1914. In spring 1911 Weiss is able to travel to Palestine. He dies of cancer in 1914 at the age of fifty-one.

Weiss' programmatic work *Jesus' Proclamation of the kingdom of God* was published during his tenure at Göttingen. Weiss presented an exegetical investigation of Jesus' preaching of the kingdom of God, which he explained in eschatological terms. This sixty-seven-page study shaped exegetical and theological discussion for years to come (see further below). In a footnote in a book review Weiss voices his frustration that colleagues quote his work on Jesus' proclamation only when they criticize him, while generally ignoring him (*ThR* 2, 1899: 150 n. 1). In the second edition, Weiss omitted the discussion of the consequences of his interpretation of Jesus for systematic theology. The eschatological approach to Jesus' proclamation is evident in Weiss' commentary on Luke (1892).

During his tenure at Marburg, Weiss edits a popular two-volume commentary on the NT (1907), writing the introduction and the commentaries on the Synoptic Gospels, the introduction to the Pauline epistles and the commentary on the Revelation of John. He publishes lectures on concept of the kingdom of God and its significance for theology (1901) and on Christian freedom in Pauline theology (1902). In a major study on the Gospel of Mark (1903), Weiss attempts to clarify details of the two-source hypothesis in terms of a synthesis of suggestions by C. Holsten, C. Weizsäcker and his father, B. Weiss. He argues for the existence of pre-literary material that the author has incorporated in his work: Mark is a compiler of traditions of the early Christian communities rather than an independent author. A short volume on the Revelation of John presents observations on literary forms and on *religionsgeschichtliche* parallels (1904).

In the six years at Heidelberg, Weiss publishes lectures on the task of NT theology (1908) and on the historicity of Jesus (1910), several short studies on Jesus Christ and the beginnings of Christian dogmatic theology (1909), on the relationship between Paul and Jesus (1909), on Jesus in the faith of the early church (1910), and on the historicity of Jesus of Nazareth (1910), as well as a synopsis of the Synoptic Gospels (1913). Major publications are a commentary on First Corinthians in Meyer's *Kritisch-Exegetischer Kommentar* (1910) and the first three books on the history of early Christianity in the first century (1914; vols 4 and 5 were published 1917).

Weiss was one of the early pioneers of the form-critical method (Schmithals). His lecture on the task of NT theology (1908) outlined the program of the *formgeschichtliche* method whose application he probed in essays on individual pericope which appeared mostly in *ZNW* (note also Weiss 1912). His studies on the Synoptic Gospels and on "Pauline problems" (published in *Theologische Studien und Kritiken*, 1895) secure Weiss a place in the first generation of the History of Religions School (Lüdemann, Lannert). It should be noted that, contrary to W. Bousset and others, Weiss understands early Christianity not on the basis of parallels in syncretistic Hellenistic traditions but in terms of an eschatological messianic movement which must be understood in the context of the prophetic Jewish religion (Wesseling).

Weiss' place in the study of the historical Jesus is tied up with Albert Schweitzer's assertion that Weiss must be credited for asking the third "either/or" question in the quest of the historical Jesus in an appropriately one-sided manner, i.e. whether Jesus' proclamation should be understood as being either eschatological or non-eschatological. Schweitzer credits Weiss with the rediscovery of the apocalyptic character of Jesus' proclamation and describes his study of 1892 as a landmark work of "historical theology." A "consistent" eschatological interpretation of Jesus' proclamation of the kingdom of God means that Jesus did *not* expect God's kingdom to break into the present: it arrives in the *future*.

Weiss summarizes the exegetical results of his study of Jesus' preaching of the kingdom of God as follows (1892: 61–62):

1 The basis of Jesus' proclamation is the feeling that the messianic era is imminent ("*ganz nahe bevorsteht*").
2 Jesus expects the arrival of the kingdom of God as one indivisible reality in the immediate future; he teaches his disciples to pray for the coming of the kingdom.
3 The kingdom will be brought about by God alone, not by human beings, who are expected to wait for the arrival of the kingdom of God by practicing a "new righteousness."

4 In moments of specific prophetic insight Jesus perceives that the greatest obstacle for the arrival of the kingdom of God – the kingdom of Satan – has already been overcome; it is in these moments that he speaks with bold faith of the presence of the kingdom of God.
5 Jesus' statements about the presence of the kingdom of God must be understood in the context of Jesus' religious sentiments; they must not be evaluated in terms of conclusions that replace Jesus' faith (in God and in God's kingdom) with an implied faith *in* Jesus. Modern notions of a gradual development of the kingdom of God that begins in the present, or of various stages of God's kingdom (concerns of systematic theology and of Christian ethics) must not be confused with Jesus' wholly eschatological understanding of the kingdom of God. In later publications Weiss suggests that the "application" of Jesus' proclamation of the kingdom of God in the church today should focus on the concepts of being God's children (*Gotteskindschaft*) and of discipleship (*Nachfolge*).

ECKHARD J. SCHNABEL

Further reading

Bultmann, Rudolf. "Johannes Weiß zum Gedächtnis," *TBl* 18 (1939) 242–46.
Burkitt, Crawford. "Johannes Weiss in memoriam," *HThR* 8 (1915) 291–97.
Holland, David Larrimore. "History, Theology and the kingdom of God: A Contribution of Johannes Weiß," *BR* 13 (1968) 54–66.
Lannert, Berthold. *Die Wiederentdeckung der neutestamentlichen Eschatologie durch Johannes Weiss*, TANZ 2, Tübingen: Francke, 1989.
—— "Weiß, Johannes," *TRE*, 35 (2003) 523–26.
Lüdemann, Gerd. "Die Religionsgeschichtliche Schule," in B. Moeller (ed.) *Theologie in Göttingen*, Göttingen: Vandenhoeck & Ruprecht, 1987, pp. 325–61.
Prümm, Karl. "Johannes Weiss als Darsteller und religionsgeschichtlicher Erklärer der paulinischen Botschaft. Ein Beitrag zur Vorgeschichte der Entmythologisierung," *Biblica* 40 (1959) 815–36.
Regner, Friedemann. "Johannes Weiß: 'Die Predigt vom Reiche Gottes'. Gegen eine theologiegeschichtliche fable convenue," *ZKG* 84 (1973) 82–92.
Schäfer, Rolf. "Das Reich Gottes bei Albrecht Ritschl und Johannes Weiß," *ZThK* 61 (1964) 68–88.
Schmithals, Walter. "Johannes Weiß als Wegbereiter der Formgeschichte," in C. Breytenbach (ed.) *Paulus, die Evangelien, und das Urchristentum. Beiträge von und zu Walter Schmithals*, AGAJU 54, Leiden: Brill, 2004, pp. 328–54.
Schuster, Hermann. "Die konsequente Eschatologie in der Interpretation des Neuen Testaments, kritisch betrachtet," *ZNW* 47 (1956) 1–25.

Schweitzer, Albert. *Von Reimarus zu Wrede: Eine Geschichte der Leben-Jesu-Forschung*, Tübingen: Mohr, 1906; second and augmented edition: *Geschichte der Leben-Jesu-Forschung*, 1913; ET: *The Quest of the Historical Jesus*, first complete edition by John Bowden, Minneapolis, MN: Fortress, 2001.

Weiss, Johannes. *Der Barnabasbrief kritisch untersucht*, Berlin: Wilhelm Hertz, 1888.

—— *Die Evangelien des Markus und Lukas*, KEK 2, ed. Bernhard and Johannes Weiß, Göttingen: Vandenhoeck & Ruprecht, 1892.

—— *Die Predigt Jesu vom Reiche Gottes*, Göttingen: Vandenhoeck & Ruprecht, 1892; second edition 1900; ET: *Jesus' Proclamation of the kingdom of God*, Philadelphia, PA: Fortress, 1971.

—— *Das älteste Evangelium. Ein Beitrag zum Verständnis des Markus-Evangeliums und der ältesten evangelischen Überlieferung*, Göttingen: Vandenhoeck und Ruprecht, 1903.

—— *Die Offenbarung des Johannes. Ein Beitrag zur Literatur-und Religionsgeschichte*, FRLANT 3, Göttingen: Vandenhoeck & Ruprecht, 1904.

—— "Die drei älteren Evangelien," in J. Weiß (ed.) *Die Schriften des Neuen Testaments neu übersetzt und für die Gegenwart erklärt. Erster Band*, Göttingen: Vandenhoeck & Ruprecht, 1907, pp. 28–484.

—— "Die Offenbarung des Johannes," in J. Weiß (ed.) *Die Schriften des Neuen Testaments neu übersetzt und für die Gegenwart erklärt. Zweiter Band*, Göttingen: Vandenhoeck & Ruprecht, 1907, pp. 597–684.

—— *Die Aufgaben der neutestamentlichen Wissenschaft in der Gegenwart*, Göttingen: Vandenhoeck & Ruprecht, 1908.

—— *Christus. Die Anfänge des Dogmas*, Tübingen: Mohr, 1909; ET: *Christ. The Beginnings of Dogma*. London: P. Green, 1911.

—— *Paulus und Jesus*, Berlin: Reuther & Reichard, 1909; ET: *Paul and Jesus*, London; New York: Harper, 1985.

—— *Der erste Korintherbrief*, KEK 5, Göttingen: Vandenhoeck & Ruprecht, 1910.

—— *Jesus von Nazareth. Mythus oder Geschichte?* Tübingen: Mohr, 1910.

—— "Literaturgeschichte, Christliche, I A. Literaturgeschichte des Neuen Testaments," *RGG* 3 (1912) 2175–215.

—— *Das Urchristentum. 1. Teil, 1.-3. Buch*, Göttingen: Vandenhoeck & Ruprecht, 1914; *Das Urchristentum*, edited and augmented by Rudolf Knopf, Göttingen: Vandenhoeck & Ruprecht, 1917; ET: *Earliest Christianity: A History of the Period AD 30-150*, New York: Harper, 1959.

Wesseling, Klaus-Günther. "Weiss, Johannes," *Biographisch-Bibliographisches Kirchenlexikon* 13 (1998) 659-66, online; available at www.bautz.de/bbkl.

WILDER, AMOS N.

Amos Niven Wilder (1895–1993) was born in Calais, Maine, and was educated at various institutions including Oberlin College (1913–15), Mansfield College (1921–23), and Yale Divinity School, where he received his PhD in 1933. He was ordained as a Congregational minister in 1926 and, after a number of pastoral and teaching positions,

came to Harvard University in 1954 as New Testament Scholar, serving as Hollis Professor of Divinity from 1956 to 1963. As a practicing poet, literary critic, and New Testament scholar, Wilder had a far-reaching and enduring impact on literary and narrative approaches to the New Testament. Perhaps the most influential of his numerous publications was *Early Christian Rhetoric*, a work which pioneered discussion of the formal literary and aesthetic qualities of the New Testament, and promoted a departure from the prevailing historical-critical methodology. In particular, Wilder's focus on the aesthetic and metaphorical qualities of biblical language exerted a profound influence on the study of the parables of Jesus, as well as on the literary tropes characteristic of apocalyptic and eschatological literature.

The constitutive power of language

Wilder helped to expose the limitations of the historical-critical tradition in biblical scholarship by drawing attention to the place of imagination and symbolism within the corpus of biblical literature. Especially significant for the development of New Testament literary criticism was Wilder's emphasis on the power of metaphorical language. As a poet, he was able to recognize the creative power of parabolic and apocalyptic discourses when viewed as symbolic language. Because words were a constitutive feature of human existence, they were used to construct human identity and the worlds which humans inhabited. Not only did language symbolically establish humans within these worlds, it also influenced how humans understood themselves *qua* humans. While there were naturally profound discontinuities between the world views of ancient and modern humans, Wilder nevertheless maintained that some degree of continuity existed in the way humans appropriated and made sense of the events in their cultural, social, and historical worlds. The overriding similarities in human nature and experience made it possible for moderns via the act of historical imagination to enter into the late Jewish and Early Christian frame of mind.

The parables of Jesus

While Wilder was fully cognizant of the advances made in parable research by New Testament scholars, he nevertheless believed their efforts to be hobbled by Jülicher's influential dictum that a parable should have only one point, an approach that fundamentally misunderstood and neglected the metaphorical qualities to be found in the parables. Wilder maintained that a metaphor was not simply a referent pointing to something beyond itself, but also a sign or an image which invited the reader's participation. Wilder posited a basic distinction between parables that functioned as example stories, such as The Good Samaritan (Luke 10:30–35) and The Rich Fool (Luke 12:16–20), and those that served as revelatory narratives, such as The Lost Sheep (Luke 15:4). This distinction between "parables that exemplify" and "parables that reveal" was fundamental. Example stories were designed to impart a moral application to their recipients, while revelatory narratives were calculated to invade the hearer (or reader) and elicit a revelatory jolt. For Wilder, parables had the effect not simply of imparting transcendental ideas and instruction but of inflaming the imagination, and of provoking shock and transformation in their recipients.

Wilder also drew attention to the realism of the parables. In the parable of the shepherd (Luke 15), for instance, the reference was to an actual, concrete shepherd, not to a symbolic shepherd meant to represent God in his role as shepherd of Israel. The aspect of realism was designed to evoke the actual details of the auditors' everyday lives. But much more than that, the listeners were also forced to make judgments about matters pertaining to their lives. Sitting on the fence was not an option. The stories compelled humans to view things as they really were in their stark actuality. Parables stimulated aural awareness – "let those who have ears to hear, hear" – and obliged the listener to consider seriously the personal challenges embedded in the stories. Jesus' speech, of necessity, had the force not merely of delivering instruction and ideas, but of firing the imagination of the hearers. His vision of reality required expression in the mode of evocative and mind-teasing language that ordinary discourse simply could not capture. Wilder was clear that the interpretation of parables must go beyond the ideational, theological, moral, or historical concerns.

Apocalyptic eschatology

Wilder's perception of the depth and power of eschatological symbolism drew heavily on Albert Schweitzer's *Quest of the Historical Jesus* and was refracted through his own experience of the disruption, horror, and ultimate hope of war in which he served as a corporal in the US Army's 17th Field Artillery during World War 1. In *Armageddon Revisited*, he addressed the larger questions of meaning and human existence that were raised by his participation in the Armageddon that was the First World War. In contrast to Bultmann's program of demythologizing, which translated the ancient mythological language of apocalyptic into modern existentialist categories, Wilder employed the concept of symbolics. The ancient metaphorical language of apocalyptic was not removed from human experience but was mythopoetic in character and therefore provided justifiable visual depictions of the world and dramatization of human existence. Eschatology was a form of myth that represented the unknown in the future and not a type of myth that represented the unknown in the past. Wilder was unhappy with the disparagement of apocalyptic associated with such terms as dualistic, pessimistic, esoteric, deterministic, ahistorical, escapist, fantastic, and compensatory because they did not take into account the social-psychological dimension of apocalyptic eschatology and the whole domain of cultural dynamics. In *Apocalyptic Rhetorics*, he wrote that

> there are veiled powers that live our lives; there are arcane transactions beneath the surface of experience that make fate for us; there are buried hierophanies and scenarios which are still potent in our orientation to existence. All this is the domain of apocalyptic encounter and utterance.
>
> (153)

In the ancient world, widespread personal, social, religious, and political crises threatened the foundations that had for long provided stability. Disorientation was the outcome as the traditional structures eroded and crumbled with humans consequently exposed to the dynamics of naked existence. In the crucible of crisis, competing myths, in the form of visions and auditions, arose. Jesus' symbolics shared with early Jewish and Christian eschatology the impulse to provide a vision of history in its entirety, to transform the given world, and to embrace it in its transformed state. Symbolic imagination directly addressed the crisis of human existence and assigned meaning and hope to it in terms of the wider cosmic drama. Jesus' vision of the calamity of human existence had to do with the crisis of recreation, not with the catastrophic end of all things.

DIETMAR NEUFELD

Further reading

Beardslee, William A. "Amos Niven Wilder: Poet and Scholar," *Semeia* 12 (1978) 1–14.
Breech, James (ed.) *Jesus's Parables and the War of Myths. Essays on Imagination in the Scripture*, Philadelphia, PA: Fortress Press, 1982.

Bultmann, Rudolf. *History and Eschatology. The Presence of Eternity,* Edinburgh: Edinburgh University Press, 1975.

Crossan, John Dominic. *A Fragile Craft. The Work of Amos Niven Wilder,* SBL Biblical Scholarship in North America 3, Chico, CA: Scholars Press, 1981.

Dewey, Arthur J. "Bibliography and Vita of Amos Niven Wilder," *Semeia* 13 (1978) 263–87.

Perrin, Norman. *Jesus and the Language of the Kingdom. Symbol and Metaphor in New Testament Interpretation,* Philadelphia, PA: Fortress Press, 1976.

Robinson, James M. and John B. Cobb (eds) *The New Hermeneutic,* New York: Harper & Row, 1964.

Schweitzer, Albert. *The Quest of the Historical Jesus: A Critical Study of its Progress from Reimarus to Wrede,* London: A. & C. Black, 1954.

Wilder, Amos Niven. "The Eschatology of Jesus in Recent Criticism and Interpretation," *JR* 28:3 (1948) 177–87.

—— *Eschatology and Ethics in the Teaching of Jesus,* revised edition, New York: Harper, 1950.

—— *Otherworldliness and the New Testament,* first edition, New York: Harper, 1954.

—— *Kerygma, Eschatology, and Social Ethics,* Philadelphia, PA: Fortress Press, 1966.

—— *Early Christian Rhetoric: The Language of the Gospel,* Cambridge, MA: Harvard University Press, 1971 [1964].

—— "The Rhetoric of Ancient and Modern Apocalyptic," *Int* 25 (1971) 436–53.

—— "Telling from Depth to Depth," *Semeia* 2 (1974) 134–51.

—— *Theopoetic: Theology and the Religious Imagination,* Philadelphia, PA: Fortress Press, 1976.

—— "Apocalyptic Rhetorics," in James Breech (ed.) *Jesus's Parables and the War of Myths. Essays on Imagination in the Scripture,* Philadelphia, PA: Fortress Press, 1982, pp. 153–68.

—— *The Bible and the Literary Critic,* Minneapolis, MN: Fortress, 1991.

—— *Armageddon Revisited: A World War I Journal,* New Haven, CT: Yale University Press, 1994.

WISDOM

Wisdom was a well-established literary genre by the time of Jesus. Its antecedents were in Egypt and the Ancient Near East. It was well represented in the Hebrew Bible in the books of Proverbs, Job, Ecclesiastes, and Song of Solomon, and was a motif in some of the Psalms. During the Second Temple period of Judaism, wisdom literature was produced both in Palestine (Ben Sirach) and in Egypt (Wisdom of Solomon). It has even been proposed that apocalyptic thought had its origins not in the prophetic heritage of Israel, but in its wisdom tradition (von Rad 1962–65: 2.307). Wisdom is also found in Greco-Roman society, represented by several philosophical groups, including the Sophists (whose name means "wise"), the Cynics, and, likely after the time of Jesus, by Gnosis. It should not be surprising, therefore, to find wisdom motifs are found in several layers of the Jesus tradition, most particularly the parables.

Wisdom in Israel

Since wisdom spans a number of works both in the Hebrew Bible and in the Second Temple period of Judaism, it is best understood as a general concept, covering a broad spectrum of thought. Wisdom generally refers to observations from life. Thus, it need not require divine inspiration. Nor does wisdom necessarily derive from Israel. Proverbs 31, for example, represents advice given to Lemuel, King of Massa, by his mother. Yet one must not make too much of the non-Israelite character of this chapter since its acrostic form indicates that the work was composed in Hebrew (Murphy 240). When wisdom interprets experience, it takes on the form of advice on the conduct of daily life. One collection of this sub-genre is found in Prov 10:1–22:16. Examples include:

> The Lord does not let the righteous go hungry,
> But he thwarts the craving of the wicked
> A slack hand causes poverty,
> But the Hand of the diligent makes rich.
> (Prov 10:3–4, NRSV)

And:

> A soft answer turns away wrath,
> But a harsh word stirs up anger.
> (Prov 15:1, NRSV)

In the NT, the Epistle of James, especially Jas 3:1–12 on the taming of the tongue, provides some of the clearest examples of this type of wisdom teaching outside the gospel tradition.

On the other hand, it would be incorrect to assume that Israelite wisdom was utterly, for lack of a better term, "secular." In Prov 1–9, we encounter wisdom's divine origins. Wisdom is personified as the virtuous woman (Prov 8:1–21). Proverbs 8:22–36 represents lady wisdom as God's hypostasis, who assisted in creation. The hypostatic feature of wisdom is also found in Wis. 1–5. In Ben Sirach, all wisdom comes from God (Sir 1:1–10) and is described in hypostatic terms (Sir 24:1–22) as well. It is communicated, however, through the law (Sir 24:23–34), and is accessible through study (Sir 39:1–11).

From Proverbs and Ben Sirach, one could conclude that wisdom leads to proper behavior, guaranteeing the good life. Life, however, is not so simple, as both Ecclesiastes and Job note. Job struggles with the wisdom theology of just retribution in light of his own circumstances, as well as the comfort of his friends. Ultimately, Job receives a revelation from God (Job 38–41). In the end Job's only appropriate response is repentance (Job 42:1–6). Yet Job's conundrum is never answered.

Likewise, the Preacher of Ecclesiastes explores the seeming meaninglessness of life, exemplified by the fact that death is the ultimate reward for both the righteous and the wicked (Eccl 3:16–22). The law of retribution does not work (Witherington 1994: 63). Instead of the law of just rewards and punishments, the author of Ecclesiastes posits that one can only accept fate as divinely ordained destiny (Eccl 3:1–15). Thus, the Preacher can be understood to teach a fatalism, similar to that common in the Greco-Roman world (see Hengel 1.120–21). Such determinism also finds a home in Jewish apocalypticism, and prepares for the combination of wisdom with eschatology. Likewise, the observation of Eccl 5:10–20 on the dangers of the riches prepares for Jesus' warning recorded in Matt 6:19–21//Luke 12:33–34; Matt 6:25–34/Luke 12:22–32, pointing to the futility of wealth.

Wisdom in the teaching of Jesus

In 1921 Bultmann identified wisdom elements in various strata of the gospel tradition (Bultmann 69–108). While he did not think all of these layers originated from the historical Jesus, it certainly is probable that the memory of Jesus as a wise man influenced the way a number of Jesus' followers remembered his teachings. This witness was preserved not only in the canonical gospels, but also in the *Gospel of Thomas* and in Josephus (*Ant.* 18.3.3). While the passage from *Antiquities* has been heavily edited by later Christians, it is likely that his description of Jesus as a "wise man" who did wondrous deeds derives from Josephus himself (see Meier 59–69).

The wisdom teachings of Jesus are concentrated in the Sayings source known as "Q" and include numerous genres, such as parables, aphorisms and sayings. The question arises, however: what manner of wisdom teacher was Jesus? Does his teaching belong to the traditions of the Hebrew Bible and Second Temple Judaism, or is it dependent upon Greco-Roman precedents? It is indisputable that there are elements of the Jesus tradition that reflect his Jewish background. For example, Jesus' advice on table etiquette in Luke 14:7–11 is so similar to traditional Jewish wisdom (Prov 25:6–7; Sir 3:17–18) that Bultmann thought it amazing that such a statement was ever applied to Jesus (Bultmann 1968: 104).

Wisdom tradition is present in parabolic form as well. In the parable of the Rich Fool (Luke 12:13–21), we encounter what appears to be a midrash, or interpretive story, on Ps 14:1//53:1 (LXX 13:1//52:1), which states that the "Fool has said in his heart there is no God." In the parable, the rich man responds to an abundant harvest not by using the surplus to aid the needs of others, but by tearing down his barns and building structures adequate for the increased produce. He then plans to retire at ease. God's response to the man is to reply "Fool, in this night your soul (or life) is demanded back from you. And the things you prepared, for what are they?" (Luke 12:20, my translation). The term for "fool" in both Ps 13:1//52:1 (LXX) and Luke 12:20 is *aphrōn*, which, like the Hebrew word it translates, *nabal*, does not mean intellectually foolish, but refers to a person who is ethically obtuse and does not recognize the claims of God upon one's life. The same Greek word is also used some sixty times to translate the term most commonly employed for "fool" in Proverbs, Ecclesiastes, and Sirach, *kasīl* (Bertram 225). Thus, the rich fool is one who hoards his wealth at the expense of the poor, an attitude condemned in both the wisdom tradition (Prov 17:5) and the prophetic writings of Amos, Micah, and Isaiah.

While it is certain that a number of sayings attributed to Jesus have precedents in the wisdom tradition of Israel, one feature of that heritage is conspicuously absent from the gospel Sayings source. One looks in vain for examples of wisdom as observations on how to live the good life. Instead, the Q tradition contains numerous examples of Jesus' teaching on the danger of riches (see Matt 6:19–21//Luke 12:33–34; Mark. 10:17–22// Matt 19:16–22; Luke 18:18–23). Likewise, both Luke (6:20) and the *Gospel of Thomas* (*Gos. Thom.* 54) record the first beatitude as "Blessed are the poor, because yours is the kingdom of God." While there are statements in the biblical wisdom texts on the need to care for the poor (see Prov 14:31; 17:5) or the desire to avoid both riches and poverty (see Prov 30:8), nowhere is poverty blessed. The closest one comes is the warning that riches do not profit in the day of wrath (see Prov 11:4). Yet in itself wealth is neutral, if it comes without sin (see Sir 13:24).

Even more striking are Jesus' statements about family. In Mark 6:33–35//Matt 49–51//Luke 8:20/–21, Jesus redefines family in terms of those who "do the will of God." Luke 14:26 goes further, stating that if someone does not "hate one's own father and mother brothers and sisters, and even one's own life, that person cannot be my disciple." This saying not only violates the Fifth Commandment on honoring parents (Exod 20:12), but also would call on disciples to adopt the role of the rebellious son, whose punishment was death (Deut 21:18–21). Thus, some scholars have understood the origin of Jesus' wisdom teaching as having derived not from the precedents of the OT and Second Temple Jewish wisdom, but from the Greco-Roman environment. One example commonly cited is that of wandering philosophers, such as the Cynics.

The Cynics also rejected familial relationships, as well as the norms of Greco-culture itself. In light of Jesus' teachings on wealth and family, it is natural to see an analogy between Jesus' teaching and that of the Cynics (Crossan 71–88, 421–22). Furthermore, Jesus' instructions on the occasion of the commission of his disciples (Mark 6:7–13// Matt 10:1–16//Luke 9:1–6; 10:1–16) call upon them to adopt a lifestyle that is strikingly similar to that of Cynic preachers, as a comparison with Epictetus' statements in *Diss.* 3.22.46–48 (Theissen 1978: 14–15; 1992: 44). The presence of Hellenistic influence in Galilee, including in Sepphoris and Gadara, may also lend credence to the possibility that Jesus appropriated Cynic teaching for his own movement. Gadara in particular is important, for this is "where two significant named Cynics, two famous sons, had originated . . . and where another, Oenomaus, would emerge" (Downing 200).

Another possibility is that Jesus' wisdom represents a Hellenistic-Jewish tradition, represented by Philo of Alexandria, in which Wisdom, or Sophia, is a hypostasis of God. According to this hypothesis, the Q tradition originally portrayed Jesus as a preacher of Sophia. Jesus is a messenger of the Sophia-God, who mourns the murder of her messengers (Luke 13:34), and embodied the sentiments of Galilean peasants against the governing Jewish authorities in Jerusalem (Schüssler Fiorenza 142). In this reconstruction, Jesus was a representative of divine wisdom, the Sophia. Like his precursors, Jesus was persecuted and executed in the course of his mission as a representative of the Sophia (Schüssler Fiorenza 142). Since it cannot be proved that women were not originally a part of the community that produced the Q document, it can be assumed that they were, and that their original interests were submerged under androcentric language of later male editors (Schüssler Fiorenza 29). It is the role of later exegesis to excavate the layers of accumulated tradition to recover Jesus' liberating message as a servant of the Divine Wisdom, the Sophia-God.

While both of these reconstructions are intriguing, neither is ultimately convincing. While there are analogies between Jesus and the Cynics, the presence of analogies does not constitute dependence (Dunn 85). Moreover, Cynic preachers were associated with Hellenistic cities. It is in the cities that their message was heard and from which they gained their support. Jesus' teaching, on the other hand, reflected the life of rural Palestine (see Mark 4:1–32; 12:1–12; Luke 12:13–21). The worlds of Jesus and the Cynics are very different.

The portrayal of a Jesus as a preacher of the Sophia-God is, likewise, unconvincing. While the differences between so-called Hellenistic Judaism of the Diaspora and Palestinian Judaism have been overdrawn, one feature common to all first-century Judaism was its commitment to the monotheism of Deut 6:4, "Hear, O Israel, the Lord our God the Lord is One." While Philo employs the language of the logos and of wisdom (*sophia*) to communicate Judaism's distinctive features within the context of a hostile Greco-Roman environment, he does not compromise basic Jewish monotheism. To say that wisdom is a hypostasis of God is very different than proclaiming a wisdom God. It is even more unlikely that a first-century Jewish prophet living in the patriarchal environment of Palestine would gain a significant audience by proclaiming the Sophia-God.

These portrayals do not consider an important feature in Jesus' wisdom message: its co-ordination with the proclamation of the kingdom of God (Mark 1:15). Unless one is willing to discount the entire gospel tradition of Jesus' proclamation of the kingdom of God in all its forms, parables, aphorisms, and eschatological preaching, as later accretions originating in the life of the later church (see Borg; Mack), it must be concluded that: "It is clear that Jesus was not simply kicking against convention or rebelling against the social order . . . He evidently saw in his ministry, in his own deeds and words, an expression of God's final will for his people Israel" (Dunn 91). Jesus' directions to his disciples in Mt 10; Mark 6, Luke 9 and 10 may, then, be understood in the context of adoption of the role of Elijah, who would precede the God's coming anointed one (see Matt 10:23). Jesus, then, proclaims a wisdom, but it is a wisdom with an eschatological element, at home in the environment of Palestinian Judaism, and also attested in apocalyptic writings and apocalyptic sects, such as the Essenes.

Wisdom applied to Jesus

Yet Jesus was not only a proclaimer of wisdom. He came to be understood as the incarnation of wisdom itself. In John 1:1–11, Jesus is described in Philonic terms as the incarnate *logos*, or word. This term means more than the English translation "Word," and includes such ideas as "reason" or "essence." It was employed in Stoicism, and adopted by Philo as an expression of God's hypostatic self-expression (Kleinknecht 84–90). In the Johannine prologue, this hypostatic expression of God now finds its ultimate expression in Jesus himself. Jesus is also understood as the expression of God's wisdom as early as Paul in 1 Cor 1:24. Jesus also bears God's stamp and nature (*hypostasis*) in Heb 1:3. While these titles can naturally be understood as the later church's glorification of the resurrected Jesus, it is likely that this connection was based upon Jesus' own teaching as the final arbiter of God's wisdom in the context of his message on God's impending kingdom.

Conclusion

From our analysis, we may observe that a significant feature of Jesus' teaching fits within the general category of wisdom. This association may have contributed to Jesus himself being identified within strands of the tradition, such as John 1:1–18, as wisdom itself. Yet if Jesus is a teacher of wisdom, it is a wisdom characterized by the traditions of Israel. There is no need to locate Jesus' teachings in the strata of Greco-Roman Cynic teaching. Jesus' wisdom is well grounded in the biblical tradition and the concerns of Second Temple Judaism. In contrast to the urban orientation of the Cynics, Jesus' teachings reflect the observations from the daily life of rural Palestine, confirming the likelihood that, like most pious Jews, Jesus likely avoided Hellenistic cities of the Galilee, such as Sepphoris (Dunn 85).

RUSSELL MORTON

Further reading

Barré, Michael L. *Wisdom, You are My Sister: Studies in Honor of Roland E. Murphy, O. Carm., on the Occasion of his Eightieth Birthday*, Catholic Biblical Association Monograph Series, Washington, DC: Catholic Biblical Association, 1997.

Bertram, Georg. "φρήν, κτλ.," in Gerhard Friedrich (ed.) *Theological Dictionary of the New Testament*, Vol. 9, trans. Geoffrey W. Bromiley, Grand Rapids, MI: Eerdmans, 1974, pp. 220–35.

Blenkinsopp, Joseph. *Wisdom and Law in the Old Testament: The Ordering of Life in Israel and Early Judaism*, revised edition, Oxford Bible Series, Oxford; New York: Oxford University Press, 1995.

Borg, Marcus. *Jesus A New Vision: Spirit, Culture and the Life of Discipleship*, San Francisco, CA: Harper & Row, 1988.

Bultmann, Rudolf. *The History of the Synoptic Tradition*, revised edition, trans. John Marsh, New York: Harper & Row, 1968.

Clifford, Richard J. *The Wisdom Literature*, Interpreting Biblical Texts, Nashville, TN: Abingdon, 1998.

Crossan, John Dominic. *The Historical Jesus: The Life of a Mediterranean Jewish Peasant*, San Francisco, CA: Harper & Row, 1991.

Day, John, Robert P. Gordon, and H. G. M. Williamson (eds) *Wisdom in Ancient Israel*, Cambridge: Cambridge University Press, 1995.

Downing, F. Gerald. "The Jewish Cynic Jesus," in Michael Labahn and Andreas Schmidt (eds) *Jesus Mark and Q: The Teaching of Jesus and Its Earliest Records*, JSNTSup 214, Sheffield: Sheffield Academic Press, 2001, pp. 184–214.

Dunn, James D. G. "Jesus: Teacher of Wisdom or Wisdom Incarnate," in Stephen C. Barton (ed.) *Where Shall Wisdom Be Found? Wisdom in the Bible, the Church and the Contemporary World*, Edinburgh: T. & T. Clark, 1999, pp. 75–92.

Hengel, Martin. *Judaism and Hellenism: Studies in Their Encounter in Palestine During the Early Hellenistic Period*, 2 vols, trans. John Bowden, Philadelphia, PA: Fortress Press, 1974.

Kleinknecht, Hermann Martin. "λέγω, κτλ.," in Gerhard Kittel (ed.) *Theological Dictionary of the New Testament*, Vol. 4, trans. Geoffrey W. Bromiley, Grand Rapids, MI: Eerdmans, 1967, pp. 69–91.

Mack, Burton. *A Myth of Innocence: Mark and Christian Origins*, Philadelphia, PA: Fortress Press, 1988.

Meier, John Paul. *A Marginal Jew: Rethinking the Historical Jesus*. Vol. 1. *The Roots of the Problem and the Person*, ABRL, New York: Doubleday, 1991.

Murphy, Roland E. *Proverbs*, WBC 22, Nashville, TN: Thomas Nelson, 1998.

Rad, Gerhard von. *Old Testament Theology*, 2 vols, trans. D. M. G. Stalker, New York: Harper & Row, 1962–65.

—— *Wisdom in Israel*, Nashville, TN: Abingdon, 1972.

Schüssler Fiorenza, Elisabeth. *Jesus: Miriam's Child, Sophia's Prophet: Critical Issues in Feminist Christology*, New York: Continuum, 1994.

Theissen, Gerd. *The Sociology of Early Palestinian Christianity*, trans. John Bowden, Philadelphia, PA: Fortress Press, 1978.

—— "The Wandering Radicals: Light Shed by the Sociology of Literature on the Early Transmission of Jesus Sayings," in *Social Reality and the Early Christians: Theology, Ethics and the World of the New Testament*, trans. Margaret Koh, Minneapolis, MN: Fortress Press, 1992, pp. 33–59.

Theissen, Gerd and Annette Merz. *The Historical Jesus: A Comprehensive Guide*, trans. John Bowden, Minneapolis, MN: Fortress Press, 1998.

Torjesen, Karen. "Wisdom Christology, and Women Prophets," in Marvin Meyer and Charles Hughes (eds) *Jesus Then and Now: Images of Jesus in History and Christology*, Harrisburg, PA: Trinity Press International, 2001, pp. 184–200.

Winton, Alan P. *The Proverbs of Jesus: Issues of History and Rhetoric*, JSNTSup 35, Sheffield: Sheffield Academic Press, 1990.

Witherington, Ben. *Jesus the Sage: The Pilgrimage of Wisdom*, Minneapolis, MN: Fortress Press, 1994.

WREDE, WILLIAM

William Wrede (1859–1906) was born in a small town called Bücken, near Hanover. He studied theology in Leipzig where he became acquainted with the young Adolf (von) Harnack and was later influenced by Albrecht Ritschl in Göttingen. After teaching in a private school and being a seminarian in the theological elite institute of Loccum, Wrede became inspector at the Theologisches Stift at Göttingen from 1884 to 1886. His friendship with Albert Eichhorn helped introduce him to historical study and method. During his studies in Göttingen he was influenced by and took part in the *Religionsgeschichtliche Schule* (= "History of Religion School [of thought]") that tried to understand the New Testament and its writings in their religious historical context. In 1891 he finished his habilitation, *Untersuchungen zum Ersten Klemensbrief* (= "Investigations in the First Letter of Clement") (Göttingen: Vandenhoeck & Ruprecht, 1891). In 1892 he became *extraordinarius*, and in 1895 he became a full professor in Breslau where, at forty-six years old, he died in 1906 after a long illness. His collected studies (now re-edited by Zager) show his wide-ranging interest with important and much discussed contributions to discussions on Paul and the Gospel of John.

Although his famous study on the messianic secret dealt with Mark, the initial question led to a basic problem of the quest for Jesus: Did Jesus consider himself Messiah and in fact lay claim to be this figure (1901: V)? For apparent contradictions within the Markan text that could not be explained away by psychological interpretation, the answer was no:

> Konnte unsere Anschauung nur entstehen, wenn man von einem offenen messianischen Anspruche Jesu nichts wusste, so scheinen wir in ihr *ein positives geschichtliches Zeugnis dafür zu haben, dass sich Jesus thatsächlich nicht für den Messias ausgegeben hat.*

> [= If our view could only arise where nothing is known of an open messianic claim on Jesus' part, then we would seem to have in it a *positive historical testimony for the idea that Jesus actually did not give himself out as Messiah.*]

(1901: 229)

Wrede established this position in very careful detail but the overall presentation of a negative assessment is mostly evident. If Jesus had considered himself as Messiah, a concept of messianic secret could not have come into being. In a paper from 1904 on "Jesus als Davidssohn" we find analogous ideas: the Davidic origin of Jesus was not a historical datum but rather a theological construct (for Wrede's doubt on the authenticity that Jesus considered himself as the Son of Man, see Wrede's letter to Lietzmann from 25 June 1896 [2004: 42]).

In a letter to Adolf von Harnack, dating from 2 January 1905, Wrede stated that he was ready to change his mind regarding a messianic appeal in Jesus' self-understanding ("Ich bin geneigter als früher zu glauben, daß Jesus selbst sich als zum Messias ausersehen betrachtet hat" [= "I am more inclined than previously to think that Jesus had considered himself to be the Messiah"]; 2004: 81). These lines, however, did not contain any statement about the use of christological titles. Wrede only discerned directly and in contrast to his addressee, Harnack, that he did not believe that Jesus considered himself as Son of God.

Furthermore, Wrede repeated his basic assumption that there was a change of understanding between the religion of Jesus and that of early Christianity that later developed – an interesting aspect when compared to the teaching of Jesus, for changes may have been brought up, for example, by the Easter visions. Although these formulations resembled an implicit Christology, Wrede tried to approach the problem differently. In a lecture in 1894, he assumed a kind of proleptic Christology (1907: 101–8), contrasting the traditional politically oriented expectation of a messiah, which had no affinity to the un-political preaching of Jesus, to his eschatology that awaited the future kingdom, which also brought up the Messiah. Jesus knew that he would become the future Messiah (1907: 101). The approach of Wrede's *Messiasgeheimnis* (= "messianic secret") consequently highlighted the productive and creative part of the community transmitting the Jesus tradition that reached a formerly unknown kind of skepticism (cf. Strecker 1979: 341).

That was the framework for his epochal work on the messianic secret in Mark. Here, he understood the concept of the messianic secret, including the misunderstanding of the disciples and the esoteric teaching of Jesus in parables as a pre-Markan hermeneutical tool to solve the problem how a Christian author could present a tradition of Jesus which was not messianic and guided by faith after Easter, and still believe he was the expected Messiah. The author of the Gospel of Mark elaborated the tool further to write a story of Jesus as Messiah using older tradition.

Although Wrede's book originated before the explicit approach of redaction criticism (*Redaktionsgeschichte*), it was an important forerunner of that method (Merk 381). Owing to his critique of the historical reliability of the gospel texts, Wrede claimed that the concept and theology of the gospel writers have to become subject of New Testament exegesis (1901: 2). This concept already outlined the task of redaction critical methods.

Regarding the messianic secret, Wrede in his monograph showed how the different Gospel writers changed the motif with reference to their theological concept to present the life of Jesus. His insights in the creative formation of the early Christian Jesus tradition also fostered the form-historical investigation of the Jesus tradition (Van Oyen 45).

Although Wrede did not write a monograph on Jesus or any life of Jesus, he contributed important ideas to this topic. His programmatic, challenging and much disputed essay *Über Aufgabe und Methode der sogenannten Neutestamentlichen Theologie* (English translation "The Tasks and Methods of 'New Testament Theology'") should be mentioned as it draws a critical balance of New Testament research during his life. In this essay, New Testament theology is defined as an enterprise to ask for the historical distance of ideas, their connection and their effects (1907: 50); he pleads for a constructive method based on well-argued principles (1907: 51f) criticizing older approaches using a dogmatic method asking for the so-called *Lehrbegriff* (= "teaching concept"). An aim of this historical-constructive method was to replace the older New Testament theology with a concept of history of Early Christian Religion and Theology to find answers from the "historical situation" of the different writings (1907: 54). In recent studies Heikki Räisänen and Gerd Theissen actualize Wrede's methodological program. In the same essay, Wrede asked for a critical reconstruction of the life of Jesus as part of analyzing New Testament theology. Pointing out that the authentic voice of Jesus was not accessible, he claimed that the only access to Jesus was reading his reception by the early community that influenced the tradition with their later conceptions (1907: 62–63).

Although Wrede was not able to realize all his scholarly plans because of his early death, we can find several ideas that reappear in the scholarly work of others, especially his ideas on the messianic secret, which is still part of controversial discussions (Blevins 1981). Above all, his insightful idea that study of New Testament theology had to start with a reconstruction of the teaching of Jesus retains a surprising currency.

MICHAEL LABAHN

Further reading

Blevins, James L. *The Messianic Secret in Markan Research 1901–1976*, Washington, DC: University Press of America, 1981.
Evang, Martin. *Rudolf Bultmann in seiner Frühzeit*, BHTh 74, Tübingen: Mohr Siebeck, 1988, pp. 243–48.

Lüdemann, Gerd and Martin Schröder. *Die Religionsgeschichtliche Schule. Eine Dokumentation*, Göttingen: Vandenhoeck & Ruprecht, 1987.
Merk, Otto. "Redaktionsgeschichte II. Neues Testament," *TRE* 28 (1997) 378–84.
Rollmann, Hans. "The Historical Methodology of William Wrede," PhD dissertation, McMaster University, 1980.
—— "From Baur to Wrede: The Quest for a Historical Method," *SR* 17 (1988) 443–54.
—— "William Wrede, Albert Eichhorn, and the 'Old Quest' of the Historical Jesus," in David J. Hawkin and Tom Robinson (eds) *Self-Definition and Self-Discovery in Early Christianity*, Studies in the Bible and Early Christianity 26, Lewiston, NY: Mellen, 1990, pp. 79–99.
—— "Wrede, William," in Donald K. McKim (ed.) *Major Biblical Interpreters*, Downers Grove, IL: InterVarsity Press, 1998, pp. 394–98.
—— "Wrede, Friedrich Georg Eduard William," *DBI* 2 (1999) 659–61.
Schreiber, Johannes. "Wellhausen und Wrede: eine methodische Differenz," *ZNW* 80 (1989) 24–41.
Strecker, Georg. "William Wrede," in *Eschaton und Historie. Aufsätze*, Göttingen: Vandenhoeck & Ruprecht, 1979, pp. 335–59.
Van Oyen, Geert. *De Studie van de Marcusredactie in de Twintigste Eeuw*, SNTA 18, Leuven: Peeters, 1993, pp. 27–46.
Wesseling, Klaus-Gunther. "Wrede, William," *Biographisch-Bibliographisches Kirchenlexikon* XIV, Nordhausen: Verlag Traugott Bautz, 1998, cols 98–102.
Wrede, William. *Das Messiasgeheimnis in den Evangelien. Zugleich ein Beitrag zum Verständnis des Markusevangeliums*, Göttingen: Vandenhoeck & Ruprecht, 1901; fourth edition 1997; ET: *The Messianic Secret*, Library of Theological Translations, Cambridge: James Clarke, 1971.
—— *Über Aufgabe und Methode der sogenannten Neutestamentlichen Theologie*, Göttingen: Vandenhoeck & Ruprecht, 1907; ET: "The Tasks and Methods of 'New Testament Theology'," in Robert Morgan (ed.) *The Nature of New Testament Theology. The Contribution of William Wrede and Adolf Schlatter*, SBT 2:25, London: SCM Press, 1973, pp. 68–116, 182–93.
—— *Gesammelte theologische Studien*, 2 vols, ed. and introduced by Werner Zager, ThST 14, Waltrop: Spenner, 2002, pp. 84–126 ("Die Predigt Jesu vom Reiche Gottes" [paper delivered in 1894]); 147–77 ("Jesus als Davidssohn" [paper delivered in 1904]).
—— "Unveröffentlichte Briefe William Wredes zur Problematisierung des messianischen Selbstverständnisses Jesu," in Werner Zager (ed.) *Liberale Exegese des Neuen Testaments: David Friedrich Strauß, William Wrede, Albert Schweitzer, Rudolf Bultmann*, Neukirchen-Vluyn: Neukirchener Verlag, 2004, pp. 25–89.
Zager, Werner. "Wrede, William," *TRE* 36 (2004) 337–43.

WRIGHT, N. T.

Nicholas Thomas Wright (1948–) was born in Morpeth, Northumberland, England. He received the BA (1971), MA (1975), and DPhil (1981) degrees from Oxford University. He has held a series of significant posts, both academic and ecclesiastical. From 1975 to 1978 Wright was

Junior Research Fellow at Merton College, Oxford; from 1978 to 1981 he was Fellow and Chaplain at Downing College, Cambridge, as well as College Tutor in Theology. From 1981 to 1986 he was Assistant Professor at McGill University in Montreal, Canada. Wright returned to Oxford where from 1986 to 1993 he served as University Lecturer in New Testament and as Fellow, Tutor, and Chaplain of Worcester College. From 1994 to 1999 he was Dean of Lichfield, then from 2000 to 2003 Canon of Westminster, and from 2003 to the present he has served as the Bishop of Durham.

Wright is a prolific author, having produced more than fifty volumes. Some of his books are quite learned; however, many are written for non-specialists, including his multi-volume *New Testament Commentary "For Everyone."* His ambitious publishing program includes major works in the historical Jesus and in the apostle Paul. Wright is a recognized authority in both subjects.

His major works on Jesus include *The New Testament and the People of God* (1992), the first volume in a projected six-volume series under the heading "Christian Origins and the Question of God"; *Who Was Jesus?* (1992); *Jesus and the Victory of God* (1996), the second volume in the aforementioned series; *The Challenge of Jesus* (1999); *The Contemporary Quest for Jesus* (2002); and *The Resurrection of the Son of God* (2003), the third volume in the "Christian Origins" series.

Life and teaching of Jesus

In the lengthy *Jesus and the Victory of God* Wright examines the "consistent skepticism" of William Wrede's *Das Geheimnis in den Evangelien* (1901) and the "consistent eschatology" of Albert Schweitzer's *Von Reimarus zu Wrede* (1906). Wright follows the lead of Schweitzer, but interprets his eschatology very differently at important points. The Jesus of Wright never despaired and made no desperate attempt to force the hand of God.

Wright concludes that Jesus lived and ministered in a thoroughly Jewish context. Jesus was no Cynic (as in John Dominic Crossan's very problematical reconstruction). Jesus' message and his challenge to the religious elites of his day were steeped in Israel's sacred traditions of Torah, temple, sacred land, and Abrahamic descent. Accordingly, Jesus is best understood as a Jewish prophet, both in his words and in his deeds. Jesus' prophetic vision called for justice, not for violence. Jesus called for change, not for the end of the world.

Jesus' prophetic stance presupposed an Israel still in exile, notwithstanding the existence of a fractured state and a functioning cultus. Aspects of his interpretation have drawn sharp criticism from some (e.g. Casey 1998), but they also have been vigorously defended by others (see the essays in Newman 1999).

Wright argues that Jesus believed Israel's exile would come to end through his ministry, through himself acting as the Lord's anointed, empowered with the Spirit. Jesus' own life and experience fulfilled all that Israel herself was destined to be. Through his obedience and suffering, and through the ongoing ministry of his disciples, Israel (and the world) would be redeemed. All that Jesus said and did, including his dramatic actions and statements in the temple precincts and at the Last Supper, should be interpreted in this light.

Resurrection of Jesus

Originally Wright had intended to conclude *Jesus and the Victory of God* with a treatment of the resurrection of Jesus. The immensity of this work (running to more than 700 pages) made that impossible. So Wright produced a separate volume, also quite lengthy (some 800 pages), entitled *The Resurrection of the Son of God*.

Wright begins with an assessment of Paul's understanding of the resurrection, which is then broadened to include resurrection ideas elsewhere in the New Testament, the Apostolic Fathers, early Christian apocrypha, early apologists (e.g. Justin Martyr, Athenagoras), early theologians (e.g. Tertullian, Irenaeus, Origen), and early Syrian and Gnostic sources. Tellingly, it is not until one reaches the last of these sources that ideas of a spiritual, non-corporeal resurrection begin to surface. Wright concludes that the conviction that Jesus was raised bodily reaches back to the very beginning of the Easter announcement.

Wright then critically examines the resurrection accounts of the four New Testament Gospels, finding in them several indications of early, historically reliable tradition. He argues that the exalted terms by which Jesus' earliest followers regarded their Master are hard to explain if there had been no resurrection. After all, many charismatic Jewish teachers and revolutionaries met violent deaths, yet their followings almost in every case came to an end, and in no case did their followers begin proclaiming their leaders as divine or as "Lord."

Wright is also impressed with the role played by the women. Given their relatively low status, especially in legal matters, it is hard to see the gospels' resurrection narratives as the products of imagination and fiction. If the New Testament Gospel stories were fiction, we should expect accounts like the one we find in the *Gospel of Peter*, in which the witnesses are men, and hostile witnesses at that.

Wright also draws attention to the fact that Jews who believed in resurrection believed in a *general* resurrection, not the resurrection of an *individual*. In fact, there was no particular idea about resurrection and Messiah. Accordingly, the belief that Jesus was Israel's Messiah would not in itself prompt the expectation that the executed Jesus was to rise from the dead. Had Jesus not been raised, it is much more likely that Jesus' death would have ended his movement. There would have been no proclamation of resurrection, and there would have been no proclamation of Jesus as Messiah, Son of God, and Lord. In Jewish minds, the death and non-resurrection of Jesus would have resulted in obscurity, not in exaltation. Indeed, even the proclamation of the resurrection of Jesus failed to persuade some Jewish thinkers (e.g. Trypho, in Justin Martyr's *Dialogue*) that Jesus was Messiah. Resurrected or not, the shame of the crucifixion disqualified Jesus from such an exalted office.

Wright's work on the resurrection of Jesus has also attracted considerable popular and scholarly attention. One issue of the *Journal for the Study of the Historical Jesus* (2005) and a book (2006) containing a dialogue between Wright and Crossan, along with several responses, have appeared, in which Wright's views are assessed (see Allison 2005; and the essays in Stewart 2006).

Wright is still actively engaged in research, writing, and lecturing. His series "Christian Origins and the Question of God" is about half complete. His work on Paul, which is also substantial, contributes to the historical Jesus, especially touching issues of Jesus' self-understanding and resurrection. A complete assessment of Wright's work is not yet possible.

CRAIG A. EVANS

Further reading

Allison, D. C., Jr. "Explaining the Resurrection: Conflicting Convictions," *Journal for the Study of the Historical Jesus* 3 (2005) 117–33.

Borg, M. J. and N. T. Wright. *The Meaning of Jesus: Two Visions*, San Francisco, CA: HarperCollins, 1999.

Bryan, D. J. "The Jewish Background to The Resurrection of the Son of God by N. T. Wright," *Journal for the Study of the Historical Jesus* 3 (2005) 155–69.

Casey, M. "Where Wright is Wrong: A Critical Review of N. T. Wright's Jesus and the Victory of God," *JSNT* 69 (1998) 95–103.

Crossley, L. G. "Against the Historical Plausibility of the Empty Tomb Story and the Bodily Resurrection of Jesus: A Response to N. T. Wright," *Journal for the Study of the Historical Jesus* 3 (2005) 171–86.

Goulder, M. "Jesus' Resurrection and Christian Origins: A Response to N. T. Wright," *Journal for the Study of the Historical Jesus* 3 (2005) 187–95.

Hurtado, I. W. "Jesus' Resurrection in the Early Christian Texts: An Engagement with N. T. Wright," *Journal for the Study of the Historical Jesus* 3 (2005) 197–208.

Marsh, C. "Theological History? N. T. Wright's Jesus and the Victory of God," *JSNT* 69 (1998) 77–94.

Newman, C. C. (ed.) *Jesus and the Restoration of Israel: A Critical Assessment of N. T. Wright's Jesus and the Victory of God*, Downers Grove, IL: InterVarsity Press, 1999.

—— "Resurrection and Re-embodiment: N. T. Wright's Resurrection of the Son of God," *ExpTim* 116 (2005) 228–33.

Stewart, R. B. (ed.) *The Resurrection of Jesus: John Dominic Crossan and N. T. Wright in Dialogue*, Minneapolis: Fortress, 2006.

Wright, N. T. *The New Testament and the People of God*, Christian Origins and the Question of God 1, London: SPCK; Minneapolis, MN: Fortress Press, 1992.

—— *Jesus and the Victory of God*, Christian Origins and the Question of God 2, London: SPCK; Minneapolis, MN: Fortress Press, 1996.

—— *The Challenge of Jesus: Rediscovering Who Jesus Was and Is*, Downers Grove, IL: InterVarsity Press, 1999.

—— *The Resurrection of the Son of God*, Christian Origins and the Question of God 3, Minneapolis, MN: Fortress Press, 2003.

—— "Resurrecting Old Arguments: Responding to Four Essays," *Journal for the Study of the Historical Jesus* 3 (2005) 209–31.

Index

References are to page and column: the left-hand column on a page is 'a' and the right-hand column 'b'. Hence a reference such as 593b–4a indicates that the information concerned may be found on pages 593 column b and 594 column a. References in emboldened type indicate a major treatment of a topic.

INDEX

INDEX

Artaxerxes I 336b
Artaxerxes II 287b
Artemis 121a, 224a
artos 203b
as 119b, 120b
Ascalon: taxation tollbooths 621b
ascension **41b–2b**, 62b, 178b–9a, 221a, 473b
Ascension of Isaiah: apocalyptic in 11b
Asclepius: cult, inscriptions (Epidaurus) 301b
'asham 570b
Asher: tribe 663a
Ashkelon 120b, 271b
Asia Minor: Jewish Diaspora 156a
assarion 120b
Astarte 36b
Astronomical Book (*1 Enoch*) 18b
Aśvaghosa: *Buddhacarita* 79b
Athens: inscription referring to Herod the Great 299b
Athrongaeus (shepherd) 525b
atonement 111b: Jesus' death 202b; Last Supper 390a, 391a, 391b; and the ransom saying 489a–b, 490b, 491a; sacrificial system 388a; Taylor's interest in 623a; theology in the passion predictions 445b
Atonement, Day of *see* Day of Atonement
Atrahasis Epic 343b
Attalus (crucified Christian martyr) 145b
Augustesians: inscriptions 301a
Augustine of Hippo 4b–5a, 249a, 256a
Augustus (Roman emperor) 68a, 522a, 523a, 524a, 525b; allows communal meals in synagogues 614a; arrival in Syria and the accession of Herod the Great 115b; authority 170a; census associated with Quirinius 114b; cult 269b; dedicatory inscriptions 301a–b; divine birth 73b, 587b; finances daily whole burnt offering in the Temple 527a; honored by Herod the Great at Caesarea Philippi 88b; imposition of the *Pax Romana* 450b; possibly arranges marriage between Herod Antipas and the daughter of Aretas IV 277b; and the powers of the Sanhedrin 544b; receives Herod the Great after his defeat at Pharsalus 522a; taxation system 621b; transfers control of Strato's Tower to the Roman province of Palestine 87a
Aune, David E. 233b, 384a, 467b, 507b
authenticity: criteria 26a, **43a–51a, 53a–4a**
authenticity analyses: and authenticity criteria **45b–54a**
authenticity indexes 45b
authors: intentions 374a
authorship: in relation to John 237b
Autocratoris 269b–70a
autopsy 286b
Avi-Yonah, Michael: on Galilee's roads 515a
Avigad, Nahman: on the Jerusalem pottery industry 518a
Azariah, Prayer of 16b, 388a–b
Azazel 151b–2a
Azekah 39a
El-'Aziriyeh *see* Bethany

Baal 152a, 343b–4a, 375a
Baal-Shamim 36b
Baalshamim temple (Seeia, Auranitis): Herodian inscription 299b
Baba ben Buta 396b
babies: abandoned babies taken into slavery 577b
Babli *see* Babylonian Talmud
Babylon: Jewish Diaspora 156a
Babylonia 486b: Rabbinic academies 486b–7a

Babylonian captivity: influence on resurrection concept in Judaism 499b; possible references to in Matthew's genealogy 211a
Babylonian Talmud 413a, 487a; on burial practices 33a; livestock farming in Judea 518b; mention of Chorazin 97a; and miracle working 337a; sees Jesus as a magician 384a; *Shabbat* 31a, 69a, *see also* Talmud
Bagatti, Bellarmino 93a
Bahrdt, Karl F. 417a
Bailey, Kenneth 174a
Baillet, Maurice 140a, 141a
Baird, William 290b
Bakhtin, Mikhail 254a
Balaam 6b, 604a–b
Balabanski, Victoria 440a
Balas, Alexander 142a
Balla, P. 96b
Balsam 40b
Bammel, Ernst 659b
Banias *see* Caesarea Philippi
Bannus (prophetic sage) 339a, 339b, 639b
baptism 574a; allegorical interpretations 5a; Great Commission 162a; initiation rite, and confession of Jesus' lordship 377b; John the Baptist baptismal practices 339a, 339b, 340a–b; as judgment 443b; Peter's understanding 573a–4a; as prefiguration of resurrection 503b; and repentance 498a, *see also* Jesus' baptism
Bar'am (Upper Galilee): cultic figurines 36b
bar enasha 593b, 596a, 596b, 597a
Bar Kochba revolt 119b, 252a, 398a–b, 485b
Bar Koziba 398b
bar nasha 593b, 596a, 596b
Bar-Jesus (sorcerer) 190a, 383a
Barabbas 523a, 660b
baraita 413b
Bardy, Gustav 26b, 362a
Barkay, Gabriel 433b
Barlaam; and Josaphat 80a
Barnabas: disciples in 405b 406a
Barr, J. 30b
barrenness/childlessness 94a
Barrett, C. K. 236a, 490a, 642b, 643b
Barth, Karl 208a, 274b, 351a
Barthelemy, D. 135b, 136b
Barthes, Roland 372a
Bartimaeus: healing 582b–3a, **583b–5a**
Baruch 15b, 17a, 17b
basileia 354b
basilicas: synagogues' similarity to 615b
Batanea 218a
Bathyra: sons of 396b
Bauckham, Richard 206b, 235a
Baur, Ferdinand Christian 289a, 289b, 351a, 552a, 552b, 609b
beasts: significance in the temptations 638a
beatitudes **58b–61b, 562a–4a**, 566a; and the Dead Sea Scrolls 134b; and discipleship 161a; in Greek and Hebrew **58b**; and the poor 204a, 680b; righteousness in 511b–12a; and woes 125a, 126b
Beck, Johann Tobias 351a
Beelzebul 7a, 76a, 152a, 190a, 191b
Beersheba (north): cultic figurines 36b
begging 197b–8a, 321a
Bekennende Kirche (Confessing Church) 77a
Bel and the Dragon 16b, 129a
Belial 152a

690

Beliar 7a; sons of 247a–b
belief: and faith 194a, **194b–5a**
believers: experience of the Holy Spirit **292a–3a**
Beloved Disciple 237a–b, 316b
Belshazzar: blasphemy of 75b
ben adam 593b
Ben Azzai: on the encompassing principle of the Torah 483a
Ben Pantera: Talmudic 'code reference' to Jesus 604b
Ben Sira 15b, 16a, 17a; beatitudes 60b; influence on Jesus 20a–1a; references to scriptural divisions 430b–1a; on righteousness and sin 510a; on the Samaritans 540a; on scribes 554b, 555a; skepticism about the afterlife 275b
Ben Stada: Talmudic 'code reference' to Jesus 604a–b
Benedictus (Song of Zechariah) 72a, 513a, 537b, 538a
Benghazi (Libya)(Berenice, Cyrenaica): synagogue inscriptions 301a
Benoit, P.: excavations of Herod's palace (Jerusalem) 461a
Berenice: inscription 299b
Berenice (Agrippa II's consort and half-sister) 89a, 288a
Berenice (Cyrenaica)(Benghazi; Libya): synagogue inscriptions 301a
Berger, Klaus 99a
Bernas, Casimir 396a
Bersabe (possibly Kefar Hananya, Galilee) 514b
Beth Ha-kerem Valley (Lower Galilee): cultic figurines 36b
Beth Horon 515b, 519b
Beth Luban (al-Lubban)(Judea)(vineyard) 517a
Beth Rimma (Bet Rimma)(Judea)(vineyard) 517a
Beth Shean *see* Scythopolis (Beth Shean/Tell Iztaba)
Beth She'arim (rabbinical centre) 398a, 485a
Bethabara **62b**
Bethany **62a–b**, 221a
Bethany beyond the Jordan 62b, 217b–18a
Bethesda: sheep pool 221b
Bethlehem (in Galilee) 33b–4a, 63a, 220b
Bethlehem (in Judea) **63a–b**, 72b, 74a, **220b–1a**; star of Bethlehem 114b–15a
Bethphage **62b–3a**, 221a–b
Bethsaida **64a–7a**, 91b; geographical location **219b–20a**; hometown of the disciples 571b–2a; Jewish immigration 90b; judgment 350a; woes against 125a, 125b, 213b
betrothals 169a
Betz, Hans Dieter: 'divine man' Christology in the Gospels 166a; language criticism 363b; on Q and the Sermon on the Mount 282b; on the sermons on the Mount and Plain 564a–b
Betz, Otto: criticisms of 'divine man' hypothesis 166b–7a; on Jewish involvement in Jesus' trial 656b, 657a, 658b
Bezae: textual criticism 642a
Bible: historical meaning 352a, *see also* individual books of the Bible
Biblical Archaeology Review 433a
biblical studies: and social scientific criticism 579a
Bieler, Ludwig 165a, 167b
Billerbeck 77b
Binding of Isaac 368a, 388a
binyan 'ab mikkatub 'ehad ('constructing a father [i.e. principal rule] from one [passage]') 414b
binyan 'ab mishshene ketubim ('constructing a father [i.e. principal rule] from two writings [or passages]') 414b
biographical apophthegms 101a; Bultmann's views 81b, 99a, 206a
biography **68a–71a**, 550a; accounts of Jesus **70a–1a**; ancient biography **68a–70a**; genre in Luke–Acts 288a–b; and the Gospels 70a–1a, **232b–3a**, **233b–5b**, **306b–7a**, 507b; Mark as **253a–4a**

bioi 68a, 70a, 74b, 471b, 507b
Bir Karazeh spring (Chorazin) 97b
Bird, Michael F. 213b
Birkeland, H. 362b
birth narratives: Jesus' divine sonship 592b
bit Hilani 65a
Black, Matthew 29b; *Aramaic Approach to the Gospels* 27b, 30a; on conception of wrongdoing in the Lord's Prayer 346b; on Jesus' use of Aramaic 26b; on Jesus' use of poetical forms 630a; language criticism 361b, 362a, 362b
Blackburn, Barry 167a–b
blasphemy: against the Holy Spirit 247a–b, 292a, 292b; and Jesus **76a–b**; in Judaism **75a–b**
Blass, Friedrich 361b
'Blessed': title applied to God 658b
blessings *see* beatitudes
Blinzler, Josef 655a, 656b
Blomberg, Craig L. 236b–7a, 438a, 652b
blood: as atonement for life 388a; sacrificial blood used as fertiliser 519a
'blood of the covenant' 366a
boats: Galilee Boat **558a–9b**
Bock, Darrell L. 99a–b, 658b
Boethusians: and Sadducees 536b
Bond, Helen K. 659b, 660b, 661a
Bonhoeffer, Dietrich 565b
'Book of the Watchers' (*1 Enoch*) 18b, 275b
Booths *see* Tabernacles, Feast of
Borg, Marcus J. 335a, 566a; on Christianity and Buddhism 90a; lack of mention of the 'divine man' hypothesis 168a; views about Jesus 13b, 477a
Borgianus: textual criticism 643a
Bornkamm, Günther **76b–8b**, 352a, 520b, 542b; *Jesus* 476a; on Matthew 233a, 257a, 259a; on miracles 419a; redaction criticism 308a, 308b, 493b
Bosch, David: on the church's Gentile mission 213b
Bosporan Kingdom (Black Sea); manumission inscriptions 301a
Bostra: papyri 301a
boule 270a
Bousset, Wilhelm 542b
Brahmanical Hinduism 79a
'the Branch' 583b, 585b
Branch of David (Dead Sea Scrolls) 104b
bread: 'daily bread' 464a; symbolism 204a
brigandage: Judea 519b
British Archaeology Report: Judean roads 515a
British Mandatory Government: excavations of Gerasa 223b
British School of Archaeology in Jerusalem: excavations of Gerasa 223b
Brown, R. L. 233b
Brown, Raymond E.: on Barabbas' release 660b; on christological use of Old Testament 659a; on discipleship in John 162b; Herod Antipas' involvement in Jesus' trial 660b; on Jewish involvement in Jesus' trial 656b, 657a–b
Bryan, Steven: on Wright's use of sources 254b
Buddha: and Jesus **79a–b**
Buddhism **79a–80a**
Bultmann, Rudolf **80b–1a**, **83a–b**, 308a, 352b, 542b, 549a; on apophthegms 98b, 100a–1a; authenticity criteria 43a; Bornkamm's teaching contrasted with 76b, 77a, 78a; collection of pagan miracle stories 166b; comparisons with Dibelius's views of form criticism 158a, 158b; contrast between Christianity and Stoicism; criticisms of Kähler 351a; Dahl's criticisms of 127b–8a;

INDEX

INDEX

INDEX

Made in the USA
Las Vegas, NV
12 September 2021